in Kashmir and between India and China in the north are disputed.

ENCYCLOPEDIA OF ASIAN HISTORY

ENCYCLOPEDIA OF ASIAN HISTORY

Prepared under the auspices of
The Asia Society

Ainslie T. Embree
EDITOR IN CHIEF

Volume 1

Charles Scribner's Sons
New York
Collier Macmillan Publishers
London

Charles Scribner's Sons
Macmillan Publishing Company
866 Third Avenue, New York, N.Y. 10022

Collier Macmillan Canada, Inc.

Library of Congress Catalog Card Number: 87–9891

Library of Congress Cataloging-in-Publication Data

Encyclopedia of Asian History

Includes bibliographies and index
1. Asia—History—Dictionaries I. Embree, Ainslie Thomas
DS31.E53 1988 950 87-9891
ISBN 0–684–18619–5 (set)
ISBN 0–684–18898–8 (v. 1)

Acknowledgments of permissions to reproduce photographs are gratefully made in a special listing in volume 4.

Printed in the United States of America

printing number

2 3 4 5 6 7 8 9 10

The editors
and
the staff of the Asia Society
respectfully dedicate this work
to
Datus C. Smith, Jr.

Editorial preparation of the encyclopedia has been
made possible by generous grants to the Asia
Society from the following organizations:

The National Endowment for the Humanities
The Surdna Foundation
The Rockefeller Foundation
The Exxon Educational Foundation
The Lee Foundation of Singapore
The Kechik Foundation of Kuala Lumpur

EDITORIAL AND PRODUCTION STAFF

PUBLISHER
Charles E. Smith

PROJECT EDITOR
Mark D. Cummings

ASSOCIATE PROJECT EDITOR
Jeffrey P. Edelstein

EDITORIAL STAFF
W. Cunningham Bissell, *illustrations editor*
Constantina Bailly, *copyeditor*
Rita M. Campon, *copyeditor*
David Sassian, *copyeditor*
John Wehba, *copyeditor*
Michael Scott Cooper, *proofreader*
Loretta Denner, *proofreader*
Ellen Dreyer, *proofreader*
Anthony Emmerick, *proofreader*
Candice L. Gianetti, *proofreader*
Julia Palmore, *proofreader*
Eugene K. Waering, *proofreader*
Kate Altgeld Seid, *editorial assistant*
Margaret A. Smith, *editorial assistant*

PRODUCTION STAFF
Morton I. Rosenberg, *production manager*
Ann Marie Fernandez, *production assistant*
Rhea Plecha, *production assistant*

INDEXERS
Charles Klamkin
Marian Klamkin

BOOK AND CASE DESIGNER
J. Paul Kirouac, A Good Thing, Inc., New York

CARTOGRAPHERS
Carta, Jerusalem

CONTENTS

PREFACE

"The history of the world travels from East to West," Hegel, the great German philosopher, declared in 1830; "in Asia is the beginning of the history of the world." Hegel was expressing his own peculiar understanding that history was the struggle for freedom, an experience that culminated in the history of western Europe, but he maintains again and again that there can be no understanding of the present without a knowledge of what Asia means, and has meant, to mankind.

One cannot argue that this vision of the importance of Asia to world history was widely recognized in the West, but knowledge of all the great civilizations of Asia did in fact increase enormously in the nineteenth and twentieth centuries in both Europe and the United States. Work on the languages, literatures, religions, and history of Asia engaged the attention of scholars in Western universities, with the result that this new learning greatly influenced scholarship in Asia itself. This was true in both China and Japan, but it was particularly so in India, where Western interpretations of its civilization transformed the way Indians understood their own past. On the other hand, while this great expansion of knowledge of Asian civilizations was taking place in the West, remarkably little of it was finding its way into the consciousness of the educated public. Hegel's idea of world history, in which Asia would have a creative role, was replaced by a definition of world history, as endless textbooks bear witness, that centered on western Europe and, to some extent, on North America. This *Encyclopedia of Asian History* is an attempt to bring some of that modern scholarly knowledge produced in North America, Europe, and Asia to a wider audience in an accessible form.

The period from 1600 to 1900 is often referred to as the "Age of European Dominance," a time when most of the world, directly or indirectly, came under European control. With the end of World War II that dominance, which had already begun to recede after World War I, came to an end. In Asia, the end of this long period of European control of the world economic and political system took divergent forms. In the Indian subcontinent, power was transferred by the imperial rulers to indigenous elites that maintained many of the political and social structures created in the nineteenth century. China, by way of contrast, experienced a vast social and political revolution, as did Iran at a later period, although in a very different fashion. Japan emerged from defeat to claim a commanding role in a world economic system that had been long dominated by the industrialized West, while the countries of Southeast Asia, some of which had been wrested from their former European rulers by Japan, created new social and political forms. The present and the future of the region is as complex as its past, but it seems likely that the twenty-first century will be, if not the "Age of Asian Dominance," at least one in which the balance of power will have shifted dramatically. The *Encyclopedia* was prepared not only because of this sense of the importance of Asia for the future, but also because it expresses the conviction of its sponsor, the Asia Society, and its editors and contributors that the history of the many countries and civilizations of the vast continent of Asia are of transcendent intellectual and cultural importance for the world.

The use of the words *history* and *Asia* raises at once the question of what we mean by the two terms. Each of the editors would doubtless have his own definition of history, but we are all professional historians, as are the majority of the contributors, so a short, if evasive, answer is that we include under the rubric of history those aspects of the human story that find a primary place in our teaching and writing. In this usage, history is the interaction of the political, social, intellectual, and economic movements that produce civilizations in all their rich and bewildering complexity. Such interaction takes place at particular times and places, and centers on events and human actors. This means that in this encyclopedia we give less attention to art, religion, and literature, although all of the Asian cultures exhibit these forms of human creativity in great profusion and depth, simply because we are focusing on history in its dictionary sense of a chronological record of past events along with an interpretation of their meaning and significance. Thus, while the articles on Buddhism inevitably touch upon its metaphysics and doctrines, their main emphasis is on its enormously important role in the transmission of cultures and ideas and on its frequently significant political role. Emphasis on history also means that we have not produced a gazetteer of geographical features or of towns and cities of Asia; places appear as entries because they have had some significant role in historical developments.

Asia, as our article on the word points out, is the name used for the great continental landmass since very ancient times by Western writers. The geographical area we have defined as Asia includes Iran and Central Asia; the Indian subcontinent, or South Asia, as it is now usually known; Southeast Asia, which comprises the great sweep of islands of the Indonesian archipelago and the Philippines as well as the mainland countries of Burma, Thailand, Laos, Kampuchea, Vietnam, and Malaysia; and East Asia, which includes China, Korea, and Japan. Modern geographers generally include in their definition of Asia all of the Arabian peninsula and the countries of the Middle East such as Syria, Israel, Iraq, and Turkey, as well as the areas in the Soviet Union east of the Ural Mountains, but these areas, with the exception of Central Asia, have been excluded. Their inclusion would have necessitated so much coverage of non-Asian history as to have defeated our purpose of concentrating on the historical experience of the Asian heartland. Proper attention is given, however, to the role of the Turkic peoples in many areas of Asia. Iran is included not only for its own sake but also because of the importance of its culture to the cultures of Afghanistan, India, and Pakistan and for its many links with China.

None of the editors would argue that there is an "Asian" civilization in the same way that there is a European civilization, but while insisting on the immense cultural variety of the Asian subcontinent, we nonetheless argue that throughout history there have been interactions between the different cultural regions. The influence of China on the culture and history of Japan is an obvious example, as is the meeting in Southeast Asia of influences from the Chinese, Indian, and Islamic worlds. The pervasive influence of Buddhism is another example, while in the modern period the intrusion of the West has provided new linkages between all the regions of Asia.

It is important that users of the *Encyclopedia* remember the purpose the Asia Society had in mind when it sponsored its publication. The *Encyclopedia* was meant to make available the highest level of contemporary scholarship on Asia to a nonspecialist audience. For that reason, while we chose authors primarily because they were authorities on the topics on which we asked them to prepare articles, we specified that the articles should be written in such a way that the information would be readily available to a person who is not a specialist in the field. This decision presented us with the difficult problem of transliterating words from the many Asian languages. *Kṛṣṇa* and *Śiva,* for example, are the conventional ways that scholars transliterate the names of two great Hindu gods, but we have preferred to use the forms *Krishna* and *Shiva,* which are more familiar to the English reader who is not a specialist. Languages that use the Arabic script posed special difficulties, since three of the languages—Arabic, Persian, and Urdu—often spell the same word in slightly different forms. We asked our writers to provide what they considered to be the correct scholarly transliteration, and then the editors attempted to give a measure of internal consistency by using forms that were free of the diacritical marks that are necessary for exact transliteration. In general, the system we have adopted is in conformity with that used in scholarly works on modern history, if not those on religion and literature.

Chinese words posed special problems, since most English books have long used what is known as the Wade-Giles system of transliteration. Since 1958, however, the Chinese government has promoted a new system, known as *pinyin,* which is now being widely adopted in the West. We decided, therefore, to use *pinyin* in our entries, although "blind" entries are given in the Wade-Giles system when the words are well known in this form. Thus, the article on the capital of China will be found under *Beijing,* but there is an entry under *Peking* that directs the reader to the main article. We have included in the back matter a table that makes it possible to move from the Wade-Giles to the *pinyin* system.

Contributors have added to the usefulness of their entries by supplying bibliographies, even for quite short articles. Because of our intended audience, we asked that they confine their listings to English works that were likely to be accessible to readers. Journal articles are cited mainly when there exist no books of equal value.

ACKNOWLEDGMENTS

The Asia Society received a generous grant from the National Endowment for the Humanities that made it possible for this project to be initiated. The Society received further grants from the Surdna Foundation, the Rockefeller Foundation, the Exxon Educational Foundation, the Lee Foundation of Singapore, and the Kechik Foundation of Kuala Lumpur. In an enterprise of this kind there are many individuals who deserve our thanks, but the one who is most deserving is Datus C. Smith, Jr., whose vision, knowledge, and effort made this work possible. The editors and the Asia Society take great pleasure in dedicating the *Encyclopedia of Asian History* to him. We are also grateful to Lionel Landry, former executive vice president of the Asia Society, for his constructive role in the formulation of the project, and to our many contributors, most of whom are our friends and colleagues. Five assistants who worked with us at various times—Dawn Welfare, Ann Hiemstra, Christina Files, Dorothy Grant, and Alison Dalton—get special thanks from all of us. In the early stages of the work Marshall de Bruhl, then of Scribners, gave us much-needed guidance and support. In the final editing, we were fortunate in having the services of Mark D. Cummings of Macmillan Publishing Company, who labored with great skill to turn our vast manuscript into a usable work. As editor in chief, I have the very pleasant right to thank the editors whose efforts have brought this project to fruition—professors Richard Bulliet, Edward Farmer, Marius Jansen, David Lelyveld, David Wyatt, and Dean Robin Lewis.

Ainslie T. Embree
February 1987

ENCYCLOPEDIA OF ASIAN HISTORY

A

ABAHAI. *See* Huang Taiji.

ABANGAN, literally, "brown (or red) ones," Javanese term used to describe those Javanese who are only nominally committed to Islam, the dominant religion of Indonesia. They are generally unconcerned about the formal ritual obligations of Islam (reciting five daily prayers, keeping a month-long fast, giving alms, etc.) and are culturally committed to pre-Islamic Javanese art forms, such as *wayang* (shadow theater), and to mystical religious ideas. In the early twentieth century the Dutch amalgamation of peasant villages often placed strict Muslims *(santri)* and nominal Muslims *(abangan)* under a single administration. Social tensions between the two populations were heightened by the *santri* community's pressures for religious orthodoxy. These tensions were exploited by Indonesian nationalists, who embraced the *abangan* as a counterbalance to Islamic political pretensions. Sukarno (1901–1970), the first president of Indonesia (1949–1967), was particularly adept as a spokesman for the *abangan* community. The Indonesian Communist Party (PKI), rather than emphasizing the theoretical doctrines of Marx and Lenin, drew most of its membership from among the Javanese *abangan* community by promising a return to a great pre-Dutch and pre-Islamic egalitarian age.

[*See also* Java *and* Santri.]

Clifford Geertz, *Religion of Java* (1960).

KENNETH R. HALL

ABBAS I (1571–1629), known as "Abbas the Great," shah of Safavid Persia. His reign (1588–1629) is one of the longest and most celebrated in Persian history.

Born on 27 January 1571, the third son of Sultan Muhammad Shah, Abbas was placed on the throne in 1588 by a rebellious Turkmen tribal chief. His accession came at a critical moment in the history of the Safavid dynasty. The two principal enemies of the Safavid state, the Ottoman Turks and the Uzbeks, had occupied important areas of territory in the west and east of Persia, respectively. Before he could move against either, Abbas had to restore the authority of the central government. This had been dangerously weakened, and the internal security of the country impaired, by the intertribal factionalism of the Turkmen chiefs (known as Kizilbash, "red heads," because of their distinctive red headgear) who constituted the backbone of the Safavid army. In order to gain time to deal with the domestic problems, Abbas signed a peace treaty in 1589–1590 with the Ottomans in which he ceded to them those regions that they had occupied during his father's weak rule. Ten years elapsed before Abbas was ready to take the offensive against the Ottomans and Uzbeks. During that period, he reorganized the army and made major changes in the administrative system.

Prior to the accession of Abbas I, the Kizilbash tribes had held a privileged position in the state. As a military elite, they had constituted the greater part of the armed forces. They had dominated the administrative system because they held many of the most important offices of state. As provincial governors they had controlled most of the revenue of the state and had remitted only a small portion to the central treasury. In return, they had supplied the shah on request with an agreed-upon number of fully armed and equipped troops. Essentially cavalry, the Kizilbash troops were heavily armed with bow, lance, sword, dagger, and battle-ax. Their fierce tribal loyalty had engendered a fighting spirit that had earned the respect even of the formidable Ottoman Janissaries.

Abbas's principal innovations in regard to the reorganization of the army were the creation of a standing army and the establishment of regiments equipped with muskets and of a corps of artillerymen. Although the English gentleman-adventurers Sir Anthony and Sir Robert Sherley were not responsible (as they themselves claimed) for the introduction of firearms into Persia, Sir Robert did assist the shah with the reorganization of the army and the training of the men in the use of artillery. The new corps of musketeers *(tufangchis)*, for the most part mounted, was recruited mainly from the Persian peasantry. The artillerymen *(tupchis)*, however, and the cavalry corps, which formed part of the new standing army and included the royal bodyguard *(mulaziman)*, were composed of Armenians, Georgians, and Circassians.

These ethnic groups had first been brought to Persia by Shah Tahmasp (1524–1576), mainly as prisoners taken in the course of his Caucasus campaigns, although some Georgian nobles had voluntarily entered Safavid service. Known as the shah's *ghulams* ("slaves"), these Caucasian elements were obliged to adopt Islam and were then trained for service in the army or in some branch of the royal household. The influence of these new ethnic elements rapidly increased as individual *ghulams* rose to high military and administrative posts. This trend was encouraged by Abbas, who felt he could rely on the loyalty of these men, since they had no tribal affiliations. Abbas further reduced the influence of the Kizilbash chiefs by breaking up the tribal fiefs and transferring groups of Kizilbash to other parts of the country. The problem of how to pay the new standing army was solved by removing many of the state provinces *(mamalik)* from the jurisdiction of the Kizilbash chiefs and constituting them as crown provinces *(khassa)*, administered by intendants appointed by the shah who farmed the taxes and remitted them to the royal treasury. Because the royal intendants (unlike the Kizilbash chiefs) had no vested interest in the provinces under their jurisdiction, the economic prosperity of the crown provinces declined.

In 1598 Abbas took the offensive against the Uzbeks, and a great victory at Herat restored the province of Khurasan to Persia after ten years of Uzbek occupation. Between 1602 and 1605 Abbas inflicted a series of major defeats on the Ottomans and recovered the province of Azerbaijan and areas of the southern Caucasus that had been overrun by the Ottomans. Abbas concluded a peace treaty with the Ottomans, this time on favorable terms, at Sarab in 1617–1618. In the Persian Gulf, Bahrein was annexed to the Safavid state in 1601–1602, and in 1620 Abbas cooperated with the English to expel the Portuguese from their base at Hormuz, a key strategic position at the mouth of the gulf; it had been in Portuguese hands for more than a century.

Abbas I is as celebrated for his devotion to the arts of peace as for his skill in the arts of war. A pragmatist in all things, Abbas eschewed the religious bigotry of the times and fostered a climate of tolerance that encouraged Jewish and Armenian merchants to develop Persia's domestic and international trade, respectively, and enabled Catholic religious orders to operate in Isfahan and other cities without hindrance. Convinced that a policy of state capitalism was necessary to enable Persian merchants to compete with foreign business interests, Abbas developed the Persian carpet and textile industries to a degree far exceeding previous levels. Silk production was made a royal monopoly, and silk was exported to Europe in large quantities. Persian ambassadors, on being sent on a mission, were expected to take with them bales of silk for sale and to remit the proceeds to the royal coffers. In the realm of the fine arts, the arts of the book, including calligraphy, the illumination and illustration of manuscripts, and bookbinding, reached new heights under royal patronage, as did the ceramic arts.

Innumerable stone bridges still stand today as testimony to Abbas's zeal in improving the road system, as do the ruins of numerous caravansaries along the main trade routes; in Safavid times, these caravansaries provided the traveler with overnight shelter. But the greatest material monument to Abbas is the city of Isfahan, to which he transferred his capital from Qazvin in 1598. As an exercise in town planning, it has rarely been surpassed, and the new city, adorned with broad, tree-lined boulevards, a majestic central square, and superb mosques and theological colleges, justified the jingle composed by a contemporary poet: "Isfahan nisf-i jahan," "Isfahan is half the world."

Abbas I, although far ahead of his age in his lack of religious bigotry and in his concern for the common people, reflected the mores of his times in his relationships with members of his own family. The experiences of his youth, when he had been a pawn in the hands of ambitious tribal chiefs and had survived an order for his execution issued by his uncle only through a quirk of fate, had left him morbidly suspicious of plots against himself. As a result, of the three sons of Abbas I who reached adulthood two were blinded and one was put to death on his orders. Thus, at his death on 19 January 1629, Abbas had no son capable of succeeding him.

[*See also* Isfahan; Kizilbash; *and* Safavid Dynasty.]

Eskandar Beg Monshi, *History of Shah ʿAbbas the Great,* translated by Roger M. Savory (1978). Roger M. Savory, *Iran under the Safavids* (1980). Anthony Welch, *Shah ʿAbbas and the Arts of Isfahan* (1973).

ROGER M. SAVORY

ABBASID DYNASTY. The Abbasids were an important dynasty of caliphs based in Iraq from 749/750 to 1258; after the Mongol sack of Baghdad in 1258 the dynasty was maintained at least nominally by the Mamluk sultans of Egypt from 1261 to 1517. The Abbasids took their name from al-Abbas, born Abd al-Muttalib, one of the uncles of the prophet Muhammad.

The early history of the family is obscure. Despite his close kinship to Muhammad, Abbas was a relatively late convert to Islam and was most likely not as socially prestigious as later Abbasid historiography made him out to be. According to the traditional sources, the Abbasids shared the conviction, out of which Shi'ite Islam later developed, that the family of the prophet Muhammad (which the Abbasids interpreted to include the whole clan of Hashim) was entitled to a special status in the Muslim community. The family, the *ahl al-bait,* supposedly inherited from Muhammad a number of financial, social, religious, and political privileges that had been usurped from them and that they endeavored to recover. The most important and most controversial of these was that the legitimate political and spiritual authority of the caliphate/imamate belonged to a charismatic leader (known as al-Rida) from the *ahl al-bait.*

During the Umayyad period (661–750), a number of sectarian or factional movements supporting the right of one or another of Muhammad's kinsmen to rule as his true successor appeared. The Abbasid family, living in exile in the village of Humaima near the Dead Sea, reportedly gained control (c. 716) of one of these sects, known as the Hashimiyya after their original leader (a distant relative of the Abbasids), and managed to transform it into an active and successful conspiratorial, revolutionary organization. Presumably directed from Humaima by the Abbasid family, one branch of the movement operated out of Kufa (a center of vaguely proto-Shi'ite agitation) and another had its headquarters in Merv, the provincial capital of Khurasan.

The mission in Khurasan was composed of an inner circle of twelve chiefs *(nuqaba)* and numerous propagandists *(du'at)* who fanned out through the province encouraging whatever antigovernment sentiment they encountered, most often without explicitly stating their own objectives. In this way the conspirators built up a large base of support, including armed followers, in the province.

By 747 the authority of the Umayyad dynasty was collapsing everywhere; in Khurasan the new leader of the clandestine movement, Abu Muslim, involved the Abbasid organization in a general revolt against the last Umayyad governor of Khurasan. After a few months of intrigue and combat, Abu Muslim succeeded in seizing control of the government in Khurasan, eliminating potential rivals, and raising an army that rapidly marched across the Iranian provinces into Iraq and crushed the remaining Umayyad forces. Under circumstances that are anything but clear, the clique of officers commanding the Khurasani forces then hailed as the new caliph a member of the Abbasid family who had been in hiding in Kufa. The reign of this caliph, Abu al-Abbas, known as al-Saffah (r. 749–754), was rather weak and insecure. It was his brother and successor, Abu Ja'far al-Mansur (r. 754–775), who managed to provide the dynasty with a solid foundation by disciplining the revolutionary forces, eliminating several too-powerful leaders of the Abbasid movement (including Abu Muslim), suppressing a variety of anti-Abbasid revolts, perfecting propaganda to legitimize Abbasid claims to the caliphate, creating the great capital city of Baghdad, and developing a centralized imperial administration.

The significance of this Abbasid "revolution" is a matter of considerable controversy. In some ways there was not a dramatic break with the policies of the earlier Umayyad caliphs (for many of whom Mansur expressed admiration); as far as the Abbasids were concerned, the key difference was probably that their dynasty had a religious legitimacy and right to rule that the Umayyads (and by extension other rivals) lacked. However, the advent of Abbasid rule did coincide, deliberately or not, with a number of fundamental changes. These included the displacement of Arab tribesmen as the mainstay of the military forces, the "persianization" of the government in both the norms of statecraft and the numbers of Iranians holding government offices, and a shift in the focus of state concerns away from the Mediterranean and toward the east, hence the placement of the new capital in Iraq. In addition, urbanization and long-distance trade became more important, often to the detriment of the agricultural economy, and a more pronounced emphasis was placed on the Islamic nature of the society; in fact, it was primarily under the Abbasids that Muslim arts, sciences, literature, law, and theology acquired their classical forms.

The heyday of the Abbasid caliphate lasted less than a century. Mansur's efforts to build a cohesive empire with a strongly centralized bureaucratic and military administration were continued by al-Mahdi (r. 775–785), al-Hadi (r. 785–786), and to a lesser degree Harun al-Rashid (r. 786–809). For reasons that are still not satisfactorily explained, this was a losing battle. Abbasid authority was never well established in Spain or North Africa. A survivor of the massacre of the Umayyad family escaped to Spain and resurrected the Umayyad caliphate there (756–1031); Ibadi Kharijite rebels in Algeria founded the Rustamid principality (777–909); an Alid adventurer set up the Idrisid dynasty in Morocco (789–926); and a Khurasani general sent to govern the province of Africa (roughly equivalent to Tunisia) founded, with the tacit approval of the Barmakid vizier, the autonomous Aghlabid state (800–909). Even in the eastern part of the Abbasid empire, many areas were only nominally under Abbasid rule, and in others efforts to establish the control of the central government provoked much resistance and resentment. Misgovernment in the vitally important province of Khurasan led to revolts that forced Harun to dismiss his governor (807) and to go to the province in person to try to restore order.

Harun appears to have recognized that in order to survive the dynasty would need to begin some decentralization of the government. He arranged to have the provincial administration divided among his sons, although only one would inherit the office of caliph. The scheme was unworkable, and after Harun's death a civil war broke out between the new caliph al-Amin (r. 809–813), backed by the central government establishment, and his brother al-Ma'mun, supported by the Khurasani military elite. Amin was defeated and executed, and Ma'mun, despite persistent opposition in Baghdad, became the new caliph (r. 813–833). His caliphate was clearly a transitional period in Abbasid history. He considered, and then abandoned, the ideas of moving the capital to Khurasan and of turning over the caliphate to an Alid Shi'ite imam. Ma'mun generally acquiesced to the diminution of the political authority of the caliphate and actually facilitated the rise of provincial dynasties (the Tahirids in Khurasan), presumably in the belief that it was better to have the provinces governed by local powers that derived legitimacy from the caliphate and would reciprocate by recognizing the nominal suzerainty of the Abbasid caliphs. On the other hand, Ma'mun seems to have attempted to bolster the spiritual authority of the Abbasid caliphate by intervening in religious controversies and attempting to enforce Mu'tazilite theology. He also patronized learning; the cultural vitality of his reign was unmatched by any other Abbasid caliph.

The caliph al-Mu'tasim (r. 833–842) attempted to reverse the process of Abbasid political decline by building up a military force of mostly Turkish slave soldiers and by consolidating Abbasid rule in previously neglected provinces such as Azerbaijan. The slave troops proved impossible to control and soon came to dominate their Abbasid masters. As a result, the Abbasid caliphs after Mu'tasim were, almost without exception, weak or powerless nonentities whose authority, when it existed at all, seldom extended beyond Iraq or even the city of Baghdad. As a result, the focus of Islamic history during this period shifted away from the Abbasid caliphate to the provincial dynasties.

The Shi'ite Fatimid dynasty that came to power in Egypt and North Africa (909) openly challenged Abbasid title to the caliphate. From 945 to 1055, the Abbasid caliphs were under the control of the Buyid *amirs;* from 1055 to the late twelfth century they were under the "protection" of the Seljuk sultans. Under such circumstances, the survival of the dynasty was chiefly due to its usefulness as a propaganda weapon against the Fatimids, its relative harmlessness, and perhaps the success of its founders in establishing the theocratic legitimacy of the Abbasid caliphate. When Seljuk power collapsed, the caliph al-Nasir (r. 1180–1225) tried to revive the political authority of the dynasty, but this came to nothing. The Mongol leader Hulegu was unimpressed by the supposed sanctity of the Abbasid caliphate and had al-Musta'sim executed (1258). The Abbasid shadow caliphate preserved by the Egyptian Mamluks was of minimal importance or significance, except perhaps as testimony to Muslim reluctance to let the caliphate, however dissipated, expire completely.

[*See also* Buyid Dynasty; Khurasan; Seljuk Dynasty; Tahirid Dynasty; *and* Umayyad Dynasty.]

Nabia Abbott, *Two Queens of Baghdad* (1946). E. Daniel, *The Political and Social History of Khurasan under Abbasid Rule* (1979). Hugh Kennedy, *The Early*

Abbasid Caliphate (1981). J. Lassner, *The Shaping of Abbasid Rule* (1980). Farouq Omar, *The 'Abbāsid Caliphate* (1969). David Waines, "The Third Century Internal Crisis of the Abbasids," *Journal of the Economic and Social History of the Orient* 20 (1977): 282–306.

E. L. DANIEL

ABBAS MIRZA (1789–1833), the Qajar crown prince under Fath Ali Shah (r. 1798–1834) and viceroy of the all-important province of Azerbaijan from 1799 to 1833. Almost a partner to his father's throne, his sincere efforts to create a modern army *(nizam jadid)* and an efficient administration did not prevent his disastrous defeats in two rounds of Russo-Persian wars (1804–1813 and 1826–1828) and the loss of Caucasian provinces to Russian expansionism. An advocate of modernization and European reforms, his provincial seat Tabriz grew to become Iran's chief trade center. After 1831 he extended his control over eastern Iran, but his devastating campaigns failed to secure Herat. He predeceased his father, but Anglo-Russian guarantees made monarchy hereditary in his line.

[*See also* Qajar Dynasty.]

H. Busse, "'Abbās Mīrzā," in *Encyclopaedia Iranica* (1982–). P. M. Sykes, *A History of Persia* (1930).

ABBAS AMANAT

ABDALIS, a group of Pakhtun clans inhabiting the area between Kandahar and Herat, first mentioned in history in 1589, when the Safavid shah appointed Sado as their chief, entrusting him with the safe passage of long-distance trade from India.

The Abdalis remained in the Safavid orbit until 1717, when they declared themselves independent in Herat. Defeated by Nadir Shah Afshar in 1732, they were incorporated into his army and moved to Kandahar. Upon Nadir's death in 1747 they founded the Afghan state, changing their name to Durrani.

[*See also* Durranis *and* Nadir.]

ASHRAF GHANI

ABD AL-RAHMAN (1844–1901), the last ruler of Afghanistan to have died peacefully while still in power. His reign (1880–1901), however, was far from peaceful. He overcame his challengers in four civil wars and weathered one hundred rebellions.

His character was molded by experiences of both power and exile. The only son of Dost Mohammed's eldest son, he was appointed subgovernor of the Tashkurgan District in northern Afghanistan at the age of thirteen. Upon the death of his grandfather, he actively took part in a five-year war of succession, twice winning the throne for his father and an uncle before being defeated by yet another uncle, Sher Ali. Forced into eleven years of exile in the Asiatic colonies of Russia, he returned when a British invasion ended Sher Ali's reign. He took over the throne in July 1880, having won Britain's recognition in return for agreeing to British control over Afghanistan's foreign relations.

Once in power, he pursued a rigorous policy of centralization. He imposed taxation, conscription, and adjudication on the defeated clans and aristocrats. He incorporated the religious establishment within the machinery of the state, ending many of its privileges. He spent the bulk of his enhanced revenues on an army that he continuously kept in the field, forcefully carrying out his policies.

Abd al-Rahman was able to concentrate on consolidating his rule at home because of Britain's and Russia's desire to avoid direct confrontation with each other. Afghanistan became a buffer state between the two empires; they imposed its present boundaries. Playing on their rivalry, Abd al-Rahman refused to allow European railways, which were touching on his eastern, southern, and northern borders, to expand within Afghanistan, and he resisted British attempts to station European representatives in the country. Toward the end of his reign, he felt secure enough to inform the viceroy of India that treaty obligations did not allow British representatives even to comment on his internal affairs.

He died in October 1901, and his son and heir apparent, Habibullah (r. 1901–1919), succeeded him uncontested.

[*See also* Afghanistan.]

Ashraf Ghani, "Islam and State-Building in a Tribal Society: Afghanistan 1880–1901," *Modern Asian Studies* 12.2 (1978): 269–284. Hasan Kakar, *Afghanistan: A Study in Internal Development, 1880–1896* (1971) and *Government and Society in Afghanistan* (1979).

ASHRAF GHANI

ABDUL JALIL RIAYAT SYAH (d. 1721), *bendahara* (chief minister) of the Malay state of Johor (1697–1699), became sultan in 1699 after the murder of Sultan Mahmud. His right to the Johor throne was challenged in Perak, Palembang, and in some quarters of Johor itself—notably among the Orang Laut—because he was not a direct descendant of the Melaka (Malacca) sultans and therefore did not carry the magical "white blood" of Paramesvara, the founder and first ruler of Melaka. These initial problems were overcome by the energetic rule of his two brothers, but despite efforts to establish Abdul Jalil's *daulat* (magical right to rule), mounting difficulties led to a rebellion in 1718 in which Abdul Jalil was deposed. He was murdered in Pahang in 1721. With the help of immigrant Bugis warriors, his son Sulaiman regained the throne in 1722, but Johor remained fragmented, split between Raja Kecil in Siak, the Bugis, and the original Malay forces.

[*See also* Bugis; Kecil; Mahmud Riayat Syah III; *and* Tun Mahmud.]

Leonard Y. Andaya, *The Kingdom of Johor 1641–1728* (1975). Dianne Lewis, "The Last Malay Raja Muda of Johor," *Journal of Southeast Asian Studies* 13.2 (1982): 221–235.

DIANNE LEWIS

ABDULLAH, MUHAMMAD (1905–1982). One of the most complex political figures of modern India, Shaikh Abdullah spent much of his life in office or in prison, under house arrest or residing outside his province in Kashmir. Born into a family of shawl merchants, he was educated at Islamia College in Lahore and Aligarh Muslim University, where he earned a master of science degree in physics in 1930. The following year he began his political career and was arrested for the first time. While he campaigned to oust the Hindu maharaja of Kashmir, he did not support an accession to Pakistan and was a signatory of the Indian constitution. Although once arrested on suspicion of having dealings with Pakistan, he was also believed to support a completely independent Kashmir. Both Muslim and non-Muslim Kashmiris revered him and called him the Lion of Kashmir. At his death he was serving as chief minister of Jammu and Kashmir.

[*See also* Kashmir.]

P. N. Bazaz, *History of the Struggle for Freedom in Kashmir* (1976).

GREGORY C. KOZLOWSKI

ABDULLAH BIN ABDUL KADIR (1797–1854), considered the father of modern Malay literature. Of Tamil and Arab descent, Abdullah translated and taught Malay in the service of the British. While working in Melaka (Malacca) and Singapore, Abdullah was influenced by British government officials (including Sir Thomas Stamford Raffles) and missionary employers.

Although they often follow the conventions of traditional Malay, Abdullah's writings are marked by a realistic and individualistic prose style and articulate a view of the world greatly influenced by contemporary European notions of the self and of government. His best-known writings are the *Voyage of Abdullah,* which describes his journey up the east coast of the Malay Peninsula, and his autobiography, *The Story of Abdullah,* a valuable account of events and personalities up to 1846. Abdullah died on a pilgrimage to Mecca.

A. H. Hill, ed., *The Hikayat Abdullah* (1970).

A. C. MILNER

ABDUL MUIS (1890–1959), writer, editor, political activist, and influential figure among the early Indonesian nationalist intelligentsia. Strongly opposed to communism and a leader of the Muslim party Sarekat Islam, Muis was elected in 1920 to the Volksraad, one of Holland's modest concessions to Indonesian nationalism. In 1922 he was arrested for labor agitation and confined to Java. His political influence then waned, but he later wrote several novels and translated *Tom Sawyer* and *Don Quixote* into Indonesian. Muis's best-remembered book is *Salah Asuhan (Wrong Upbringing),* his 1928 tragedy about the failure of a racially mixed marriage and the painful social and intellectual dilemmas confronting Western-educated Indonesians coming of age in a modern colonial society.

Deliar Noer, *The Modernist Muslim Movement in Indonesia, 1900–1942* (1973). A. Teeuw, *Modern Indonesian Literature* (1967).

JAMES R. RUSH

ABDUL RAHMAN, also known as Raja Jumaat and as Si Komeng, sultan of Johor (Lingga) from 1812 to 1830, younger of the two sons of Sultan Mahmud III of Johor and Riau. In 1819, the English recognized Abdul Rahman's elder brother, Hussein, as sultan of Johor and Singapore. The existence of two "rival" sultans symbolized the effective breakup of the old Johor/Riau state into what became British and Dutch spheres and, ultimately, the states of Malaysia, Singapore, and Indonesia.

Abdul Rahman was proclaimed sultan on the death of Mahmud by the Bugis Yamtuan Muda Raja

Jaafar. Since he maintained a residence on the island of Lingga, Abdul Rahman became known as the sultan of Lingga after 1819. The famous Malaysian chronicle the *Tufhat al-Nafis* credits him with a reputation for piety and claims that he did much to make Riau and Lingga centers of Islamic study.

[*See also* Hussein, Sultan of Johor and Singapore; Mahmud Riayat Syah III; Johor; Riau; *and* Lingga.]

Raja Ali Haji, *Tufhat al-Nafis (The Precious Gift)*, translated by Virginia Matheson and Barbara W. Andaya (1981).

CARL A. TROCKI

ABDUL RAHMAN ALHAJ. Born 8 February 1903 to a Thai mother and the sultan Abdul Hamid of Kedah, Tunku (Prince) Abdul Rahman Alhaj, also known as Bapa Merdeka ("father of independence"), led the struggle to secure Malaya's independence from Britain in 1957 and served as the first prime minister of independent Malaya (1957–1963) and then of Malaysia (1963–1970). The eclectic nature of Abdul Rahman's education—in Thai-, Malay-, and English-language schools, later at Cambridge University (where he earned a BA in 1928), and finally, after World War II, at the Inner Temple in London—and his natural ebullience combined to give him an abiding tolerance of other cultures.

Abdul Rahman began his public career in 1931 as an administrative officer in the Kedah state government and continued in this role throughout the Japanese occupation of the area. Toward the end of the occupation, he participated in the formation of an incipient nationalist political party called Saberkas, or Unity, but later withdrew his support because of the group's demand for immediate postwar independence, which Abdul Rahman thought impracticable, and because of its confrontational, socialist rhetoric. His nationalism was further boosted by the ill-conceived British proposals for a Malayan Union, which led him, as a leader of the newly formed United Malays National Organization (UMNO), to campaign actively and successfully for their rejection. Abdul Rahman's rise to primacy within UMNO—he was elected its president in 1951—was partly a consequence of the exit of Dato Onn bin Ja'afar, who left to form the multiracial Independence of Malaya Party. Abdul Rahman opposed Ja'afar's move, believing that Malaya would best be served at this stage of its development by permitting each ethnic community to organize according to its own needs; only then, he argued, would the resultant Malay, Chinese, and Indian parties reconcile their differences and form a multiethnic coalition. Setting the stage for a system of politics that still persists, Abdul Rahman inspired the Selangor branches of UMNO and the Malayan Chinese Association to announce in January 1952 that the two would contest the Kuala Lumpur municipal election in coalition. This political merger, first called the Alliance Party and then, after embracing other parties much later, the National Front, has ruled the country ever since.

In May 1961 Abdul Rahman broached the concept of merging Malaya, Singapore, Brunei, North Borneo, and Sarawak into a single political federation. At first the idea aroused vociferous opposition in Singapore and in the Borneo territories, but with British backing Abdul Rahman was able to preside over the birth of the new country—less Brunei—in 1963, earning him yet another triumphant honorific: Bapa Malaysia ("father of Malaysia"), a title marred only by the acrimonious departure of Singapore two years later.

In May 1969, following an election in which the Chinese had increased their political strength, riots broke out in Kuala Lumpur between the Chinese and the Malays. These disturbances led directly to Abdul Rahman's resignation in 1970. Although Abdul Rahman initially claimed that the Communists had backed them, the riots had been brought about by Malay frustrations over lack of economic benefits and by the quantum increase in non-Malay political power that seemed to be implied by the 1969 election results. Militant young Malay ultranationalists, who believed Abdul Rahman and his government had been overly tardy in promoting Malay interests, campaigned remorselessly for Abdul Rahman's resignation. Although he remained prime minister for another fifteen months, Abdul Rahman's power effectively ended with the declaration of a national emergency in May 1969. Since his resignation Abdul Rahman has remained active, both as secretary general of the International Islamic Secretariat and, more typically, as an entertaining newspaper columnist—part moralist, part gadfly, and part elder statesman.

Abdul Rahman represents the best of his generation. As the father of his country's independence, he successfully spanned the transition from colonial rule to the important first years of independence. He was the right man at the right time, a pragmatic democrat who distilled the heady brew of independence into values of ethnic tolerance and democracy that are still idealized, if not always pursued. That he was able to preside over such momentous change for so long a period with only one eruption of major violence—in a country where ethnic differences pervade all political, social, and economic life—secures Abdul Rahman's place in history.

[*See also* Malaysia; Malayan Union; United Malays National Organization; Onn bin Ja'afar, Dato; Independence of Malaya Party; Malayan Chinese Association; *and* Alliance Party.]

Gordon P. Means, *Malaysian Politics* (2d ed., 1976). Harry Miller, *Prince and Premier* (1959). K. J. Ratnam, *Communalism and the Political Process in Malaya* (1965).

STANLEY BEDLINGTON

ABDUL RAZAK (1922–1976), second prime minister of Malaysia (1970–1976). The son of a major chief, Abdul Razak was born in Pahang and educated locally at a Malay-language school, then at the exclusive Malay College in Kuala Kangsar. In 1939 Abdul Razak joined the Malayan Administrative Service, and after serving with distinction with the British-sponsored resistance forces during World War II, he read law in England. During his studies in England he became active in Malayan student politics and was a loyal supporter of Abdul Rahman, under whose aegis he would later prosper. Returning to Malaya, Razak joined the United Malays National Organization (UMNO) while it was still in its infancy and was made head of UMNO Youth in 1950 and deputy president in 1951. He was appointed deputy prime minister under Abdul Rahman after independence in 1957 and succeeded to the premiership and UMNO presidency when Abdul Rahman resigned in September 1970. Abdul Razak died in 1976 from leukemia, a disease he had carefully kept hidden from public attention.

Several important achievements illuminate the career of this quiet, able, and honest man. In 1956, for example, his Committee on Education produced guidelines (known as the Razak Plan) that integrated Malaya's various ethnic groups under a single educational system designed to promote a common Malayan awareness without sacrificing ethnic identity. After becoming prime minister following the devastating riots between Malays and Chinese in May 1969, Abdul Razak was able to return stability to the land. At the same time he reintroduced democracy—despite reports of its death—following the National Operations Council interregnum of 1969–1970 by persuading a number of former opposition groups to join the ruling coalition. He helped control simmering Malay dissatisfaction by implementing the Second Malaysia Plan, a new economic program designed to restructure society and correct the economic disparity between Malays and Chinese. Finally, he was the architect of a new foreign policy that recognized the People's Republic of China, promoted Southeast Asia as a "zone of peace, freedom, and neutrality," and supported regionalism within the ambit of the Association of Southeast Asian Nations.

[*See also* Malaysia; Abdul Rahman Alhaj; United Malays National Organization; *and* Alliance Party.]

William Shaw, *Tun Razak: His Life and Times* (1976).

STANLEY BEDLINGTON

ABU BAKAR (1835–1895), generally credited as being the founder of the modern Malay state of Johor. Eldest son of Temenggong Ibrahim, Abu Bakar was raised in the kampong, or village, of Teluk Belanga in Singapore. The first English-educated Malay prince, he succeeded his father in 1862 and continued his policy of populating Johor with Chinese pepper and gambier planters and creating a formal administration along British lines. He maintained intimate relations with the British in Singapore and gained entry into European aristocratic circles after being presented to Queen Victoria in 1866. He was affiliated with British advances in the peninsular states during the 1860s and 1870s and recognized as sultan of the State and Territory of Johor in 1885.

[*See also* Johor; Singapore; Ibrahim; *and* Temenggong.]

Carl A. Trocki, *Prince of Pirates: The Temenggongs and the Development of Johor and Singapore, 1784–1885* (1979).

CARL A. TROCKI

ABU'L FAZL (1551–1602), adviser and historiographer of the Mughal emperor Akbar. Abu'l Fazl rose from being the son of a persecuted religious preacher to a high position in court, gaining the personal confidence of Akbar. Although Abu'l Fazl died as a lone ambushed soldier, his principal contribution was an official history of Akbar's reign until 1601. The work, *Akbarnama*, originally comprised three volumes, two of narrative history and the third a detailed gazetteer of information of the empire, the *'Ain-i Akbari*. The *Akbarnama* was the point of departure in medieval Indian historiography. Unlike its predecessors, this was a well-researched work and not an impressionistic narrative of events. Its argument was a mix of the notion of the semidivinity of Akbar's personality and a secular projection of events. Abu'l Fazl's treatment of history was essentially teleological; he began his narrative with Adam and showed history moving toward its fulfillment in Akbar's reign. The language of the *Akbarnama* is highly ornate Persian.

[*See also* Akbar.]

Harbans Mukhia, *Historians and Historiography during the Reign of Akbar* (1976). HARBANS MUKHIA

ACEH, historic port and kingdom of North Sumatra. Tomé Pires was the first writer to mention "the kingdom of Acheh and Lambry" in his *Suma Oriental* (1512–1515), indicating that together the two seaports formed one political unit. Lamri, located on the strategic corner of North Sumatra, owed allegiance to the Buddhist kingdom of Srivijaya, also on Sumatra, but in the thirteenth century North Sumatran kingdoms began to go over to Islam. In the fifteenth century the expansion of Pedir forced the rulers of Lamri to move into the Aceh Valley and establish a new sultanate at Bandar Aceh. Aceh leapt into prominence under the "pirate-king" Ali Mughayat Syah (c. 1514–1530), who seized the opportunity created by the Portuguese capture of Melaka (Malacca) in 1511. Having acquired sufficient European arms, he thwarted the Portuguese attempt to gain a foothold in Pasai (1521) and conquered North Sumatra. Gujarati merchants, pulling out of Melaka, rallied to Aceh, which grew into a powerful maritime kingdom ready to challenge the Portuguese and defy the authority of Johor over the Malays. Sultan Alauddin Riayat Syah al-Kahar (1537–1571) secured military and technical assistance from Turkey and continued the fight against the Portuguese and Johor. With Gujarati collaboration, the Acehnese built up a profitable pepper trade, making Aceh the biggest emporium for pepper and Indian cloth in western Indonesia.

The drive for islamization came from Aceh, which replaced Melaka as the headquarters of Indonesian Islam. Aceh reached its zenith under Sultan Iskandar Muda (r. 1607–1636), expanding its borders into Sumatra and Malaya. But the sultan's policy of centralizing all foreign trade in Kutaraja (Banda Atjeh) was not entirely successful. He also failed to attain his twin aims of destroying Portuguese Melaka and establishing Acehnese hegemony over the Malay states. Nonetheless Iskandar Muda's time is looked upon as a golden age in which the cosmopolitan city of Aceh attracted worldwide notice as a major Asian port. The king ruled with a strong hand: the Orang Kayas were subdued, and the *uleebalangs* (local nobility), who held *mukims* (districts) in feudal tenure, were held in check. The court's reputation was enhanced by the presence of such famous Malay writers as Hamzah Fansuri and Syamsuddin of Pasai, whose mystical ideas were later criticized by Nuruddin ar-Raniri and Abdurrauf of Singkil. For Muslims, Aceh was a center of learning as well as the eastern gateway to Mecca.

After the Dutch conquest of Melaka (1641), Aceh declined rapidly. The *uleebalangs* reasserted their power, favoring female rule (1641–1699) to restrict royal authority. Moreover, the Dutch encouraged Minangkabau chiefs on the west coast of Sumatra to free themselves from Acehnese control. Finally, despite Asian competition, the tin and pepper trade eventually fell into Dutch hands. By the eighteenth century Aceh's power had reached an all-time low. Establishment of a British base at Penang (1786) and the founding of Singapore (1819) revived trade in the Straits region, and a boom in the pepper trade attracted British, French, and American traders to North Sumatra. Aceh became a bone of contention in imperialist power rivalry. For a time its independence was guaranteed by the Anglo-Dutch Treaty of 1824. In 1871, however, the British allowed the Dutch a free hand in Aceh to guard against French intervention. The Dutch invasion of Aceh began in 1873, fiercely opposed by the sultanate, the *uleebalangs,* and the *ulamas.* After winning over the *uleebalangs* to their side, however, the Dutch won the Aceh War in 1903. Guerrilla resistance, which the *ulamas* called a "holy war," continued until 1912.

The Japanese occupation of Indonesia in 1942 gave the *ulamas* (now organized as the All-Aceh Association of Ulama, or PUSA) a chance to strengthen their position toward the *uleebalangs.* After the Japanese surrender in 1945, the Dutch did not dare to return to Aceh, and the *ulamas* were able to carry out a social revolution by killing and imprisoning leading *uleebalangs.* This was a victory for the Islamic forces, which gave Aceh a coherent leadership and political stability in the crucial years of the Indonesian Revolution. In postindependence Indonesia Aceh fitted easily into the framework of an anti-Dutch Muslim republic. Yet its autonomous spirit found expression in Daud Beureu'eh's involvement with Darul Islam and the open rebellion of 1953–1959. In 1959 Aceh was given the status of a special district (Daerah Istimewa). Although fully integrated in Indonesia's New Order after the fall of Sukarno, Aceh continues to prove its distinctiveness by remaining a bastion of the oppositionist Islamic forces.

[*See also* Srivijaya; Iskandar Muda; Anglo-Dutch Treaty; *and* Daud Beureu'eh, Muhammad.]

C. Snouck Hurgronje, *The Achenese,* 2 vols., translated by A. W. S. O'Sullivan (1906). Anthony Reid, *The Contest for North Sumatra: Atjeh, the Netherlands and Britain, 1858–1898* (1969) and *The Blood of the People: Revolution and the Traditional Role in Northern Sumatra* (1979). P. Voorhoeve and Th. W. Juynboll, "Atjeh," in *The Encyclopedia of Islam* (new ed., 1960–).

ARUN DASGUPTA

ACHAEMENID DYNASTY. The Achaemenids, the first of the three great pre-Islamic Iranian dynasties, were a Persian princely clan whose eponymous ancestor, Achaemenes (eighth century BCE), probably lived before the migrations of the Persians to Persis from northwestern Iran.

Cyrus II ("the Great"; r. 559–530 BCE) began nearly a century of uninterrupted Persian expansion, extending his rule over the Elamites from Anshan and overthrowing Astyages in 550. Herodotus's account of that event is a folkloric legend later applied to Ardashir I's triumph over the Parthian Ardavan V. Cyrus invaded Anatolia and conquered the Lydian empire of Croesus in 547; in 539 he seized Babylon, where he had won support against the ruler, Nabonidus, by championing the cult of the god Marduk, whose clergy extolled Cyrus in the name of the god as a righteous and beneficent ruler.

Cyrus released the Jews from the Babylonian exile to rebuild the Temple in Jerusalem, and in Second Isaiah he is praised as messiah, shepherd, and righteous man. These terms may derive from the *Gathas,* where Zoroaster (Zarathushtra), the *vastrya* ("shepherd") and *ashavan* ("righteous one"), proclaims the coming of the future Saoshyant ("savior"). It has been suggested that the Median Magi, the Zoroastrian priesthood, influenced the religious conceptions of the Jews, for the Zoroastrian beliefs in God the Creator, heaven and hell, resurrection, and final judgment appear in Judaism for the first time in postexilic texts. Mary Boyce regards Zoroastrianism as the state religion of the Achaemenids and as the principal faith of the Iranians, despite incidents of unorthodox practice such as human sacrifice and cremation recorded by Herodotus. Ehsan Yarshater justly concludes that, while there may be no firm resolution of the issue, more problems are raised by assuming that the Achaemenids were not Zoroastrians than by accepting that they were.

Persia under Darius I. Cyrus died fighting the nomadic Massagetae in the east; he was buried at his capital, Pasargadae, in Pars (Fars), in a stepped, pitched-roof tomb based upon an Anatolian prototype but adapted to the requirements of Zoroastrian purity laws. He was succeeded by his son, Cambyses (r. 530–522), who conquered Egypt and is praised in the hieroglyphic inscriptions of that country for his correct and pious conduct; the account of his "madness" by Herodotus does not accord with these native, contemporary records and is probably based upon the subsequent hostile propaganda of Darius, who belonged to another branch of the Achaemenid line and was, presumably, eager to impugn the reputation of a predecessor whose brother he had overthrown. It appears that Cambyses' throne was seized by his brother Bardya (Greek, Smerdis) while the former was fighting in Ethiopia. Cambyses set out for Persia when he heard the news, but died en route.

Bardya was deposed and slain by Darius I (r. 522–486) and six confederates of noble lineage whose families were later second to the king in the empire. The twenty-three satrapies, or provinces, of the Persian empire immediately rose in revolt under various local leaders; Darius suppressed them, commemorating his triumph with a bas-relief and an inscription in Old Persian, Elamite, and Akkadian on the rock of Behistun (Old Persian, **Bagistana;* Greek, *bagistanon oros,* "place [mountain] of the gods") on the Babylon-Ecbatana (Hamadan) road. In the relief, which is based upon a nearby Elamite prototype, Darius is shown treading upon one captive rebel chieftain and facing a shackled chain of others. In the inscription, of which an Aramaic version on parchment was circulated throughout the empire, Darius claims that the usurper was not Bardya, but a Magus named Gaumata who had masqueraded as the brother of Cambyses; Herodotus repeats this story, which would absolve Darius of the charge of violating the sanctity of the Achaemenid line.

Darius, then, is famed as Dara(b) in later Iranian tradition, while the memory of Cyrus and his line was lost. (The folkloric legend of Cyrus's accession, however, is applied to the first Sasanid king, Ardashir, and A. Shahpur Shahbazi has suggested that Cyrus was confused with Hystaspes, the father of Darius, in Persian tradition.) Darius and his successors built a new capital, Parsa (Greek, Persepolis), near Pasargadae. The city was the royal autumn

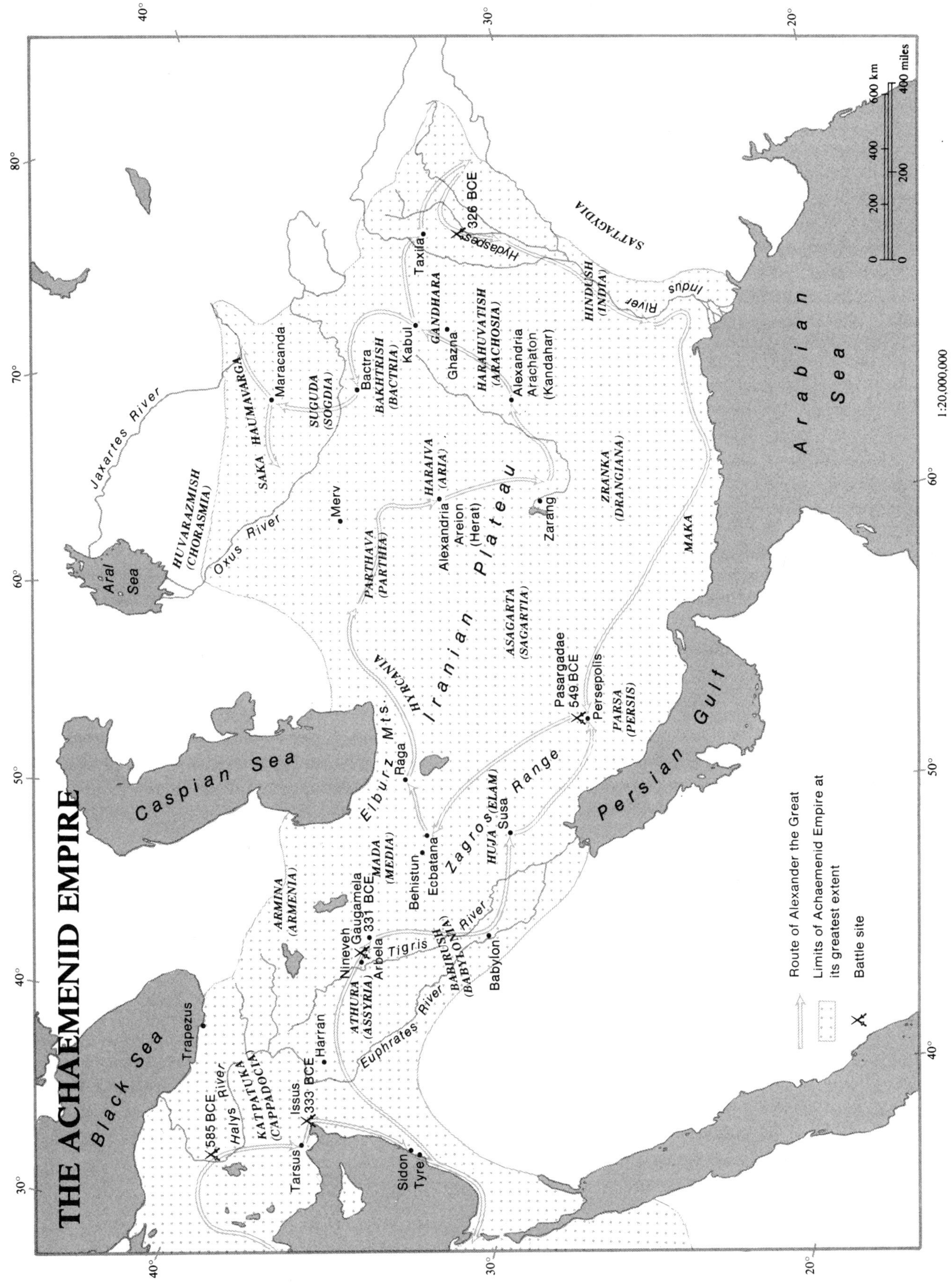
THE ACHAEMENID EMPIRE
Black Sea
Caspian Sea
Aral Sea
Persian Gulf
Arabian Sea
Trapezus
Halys River
585 BCE
KATPATUKA (CAPPADOCIA)
Tarsus
Issus 333 BCE
Sidon
Tyre
Harran
Euphrates River
ATHURA (ASSYRIA)
Nineveh
Gaugamela 331 BCE
Arbela
Tigris River
BABIRUSH (BABYLONIA)
Babylon
ARMINA (ARMENIA)
MADA (MEDIA)
Behistun
Ecbatana
Zagros Range
HUJA (ELAM)
Susa
Elburz Mts.
Raga
HYRCANIA
Iranian Plateau
Pasargadae 549 BCE
Persepolis
PARSA (PERSIS)
ASAGARTA (SAGARTIA)
PARTHAVA (PARTHIA)
Merv
HUVARAZMISH (CHORASMIA)
Oxus River
Jaxartes River
SAKA HAUMAVARGA
Maracanda
SUGUDA (SOGDIA)
Bactra
BAKHTRISH (BACTRIA)
HARAIVA (ARIA)
Alexandria Areion (Herat)
Zarang
ZRANKA (DRANGIANA)
MAKA
Kabul
Ghazna
GANDHARA
HARAHUVATISH (ARACHOSIA)
Alexandria Arachaton (Kandahar)
Taxila
Hydaspes
326 BCE
SATTAGYDIA
HINDUSH (INDIA)
Indus River
Route of Alexander the Great
Limits of Achaemenid Empire at its greatest extent
Battle site
0 200 400 600 km
0 200 400 miles
1:20,000,000
40°
30°
20°
80°
70°
60°
50°
40°
30°

residence; Susa to the west was the center of administration, and Babylon and Ecbatana served as the winter and summer capitals. The feast of Mithrakana (Pahlavi, Mihragan) was celebrated at Persepolis with gift-bearing delegations of the empire's peoples, who are shown in a processional relief before the *apadana,* the royal colonnaded palace. The subject nations appear again in the relief above Darius's rock-cut tomb in the nearby cliff face of Naqsh-i Rustam: there, they uphold the great throne upon which Darius stands facing a fire altar; above him hovers the winged figure that has been variously identified as the divine glory given to kings (Avestan, *khvarenah;* Pahlavi, *khwarna*), the king's spirit (Avestan, *fravashi*), or the supreme God, Ahura Mazda. It was the last, Darius declares, who bore him aid against rebels, and by whose will he became king.

Greek and Hebrew writers admired the rule of law in Persia. Administration was efficient and highly centralized, with fixed tribute exacted from each satrapy. The royal road from Sardis to Susa ensured rapid passage for messengers and officials. Records were kept and correspondence was transmitted in so-called Chancellery Aramaic: the Aramaic-speaking scribe would write in that language a letter dictated in Persian, occasionally transcribing a name or technical term in Aramaic script; the letter upon receipt in Sogdiana might then be read aloud in Sogdian to an official by another Aramaic-speaking scribe. This practice gave rise to the heterographic writing systems of many Middle Iranian dialects, and scripts derived from Aramaic were generally preferred to the Greek alphabet (with the notable exception of Bactria); perhaps this facilitated the adoption of a similar Semitic script, Arabic, centuries later in the Iranian East.

Xerxes and the Greeks. Xerxes (r. 486–465) inherited his father's empire. Toward the end of Darius I's reign, Babylon had risen in rebellion and was devastated by the Persians. Demonstrating a sternness evident in his own harsh repression of revolts in Babylon and Egypt, Xerxes now styled himself "King of the Persians and the Medes," later adding the title "King of Babylon" that his predecessors had placed at the head of Babylonian documents. In an inscription at Persepolis, Xerxes boasts of having destroyed a place of worship of the *daivas* ("demons"), referring perhaps to Iranian pagans, and of instituting the worship of Ahura Mazda there "with proper rites"; he calls upon his subjects to obey the law, that they may be happy in life and be remembered as righteous after death. These acts of militant piety, coupled with a concern for the afterlife, foreshadow the policies of the Sasanid high priest Kartir, except that Xerxes did not, apparently, persecute the cults of non-Iranians; rather, he ordered Babylonian and Greek subjects to solemnize their rites.

In 480, Xerxes flung the vast resources of the empire into the invasion of Greece that Darius had begun. Interrupted by the latter's death and ill-starred by defeat at Marathon in 490, the invasion failed again, with the Athenian sea victory at Salamis. Heroic resistance to the Persians by the Spartan force at Thermopylae was seen by the Greeks as a symbol of the superiority of free men to the hordes of an opulent oriental tyranny. Although from the Persian point of view Greek victories were of comparatively minor importance, and Persia was to interfere in mainland Greek affairs for a century to come, Salamis proved the limits of real Persian power and served as a watershed of Greek, particularly Athenian, national consciousness, producing the extraordinary golden age of fifth-century Greek arts and letters. Aeschylus, who fought at both Marathon and Salamis, produced at Athens his tragedy *The Persians,* enshrining as heroic epic—perhaps for the first time in Greek history—an event in the lives of author and spectators.

Greek prejudices have colored somewhat the Western understanding of the Persians. Although Greece was a slave society, it is still contrasted with Iran as somehow "free," while the Persian word *bandaka,* literally "one who is bound," applied to all subjects of the King of Kings, is mistranslated as "slave." *Bandaka* has, rather, the sense of a party to a sacred covenant, in this case with the ruler, who was himself "bound" to Ahura Mazda. (The Zoroastrians to this day call the act of prayer *bandagi,* "binding [in service].") Similarly, Xerxes' flogging of the Hellespont is condemned as insane hubris; rather, it might have been the ritual act of a pious Zoroastrian chastising the salt sea, made bitter by the Evil Spirit, for the wanton destruction of the Persian bridge (the Greeks, too, personified the waters and occasionally fought them, notably Achilles at the Skamandros).

In 465 Xerxes was assassinated and his throne usurped by a younger son, Artaxerxes I (r. 465–424), in whose reign are found the first references in Greek to Zoroaster; his death was followed by another struggle for the succession: Darius II reigned until 404, and his son Cyrus the Younger in his unsuccessful internecine war with Artaxerxes II Mnemon (r. 404–359) engaged the assistance of Greek mercenaries under Xenophon, whose *Anabasis* records their flight over the mountains of Armenia to Trapezus (Trebizond) on the Black Sea.

Alexander's Invasion. Philip of Macedon unified the Greek states under his rule following the Battle of Chaeronea in 338; a Macedonian invasion of Persian-held Asia Minor, long restive, sparked a rebellion in Egypt, and Philip's son, Alexander, routed the armies of the last Achaemenid, Darius III (r. 336–330), on the Granicus and then at Arbela in 331. The last generations of Achaemenid rule had been marked by corruption and a crippling tax burden, but the invader, generally called *gizistag* ("the accursed") in later Middle Persian texts, caused unprecedented destruction. Persepolis was burned after a drunken orgy, and Alexander's armies massacred Zoroastrian priests, the living repositories of the orally transmitted lore of the Avesta; a Sogdian text calls Alexander "the Magi-killer."

The Macedonian quickly adopted many of the trappings of Persian royalty, such as the practice of *proskynesis* ("prostration") before the king, to which Arrian says many Greeks objected; he also tried, through marriages to Iranian princesses and the abduction and training of Iranian boys, to create a Greco-Persian world civilization. These plans died with him in 323; with the division of the Macedonian conquests under the generals, Seleucus ruled Iran as an appanage held by garrison settlements. Greek art and language had little appeal for the Iranians, and Greek religion none at all; with the liberation of the country by the Parthian Arsacids in the middle of the third century, many of the institutions and usages of the Achaemenids were restored.

[*See also* Alexander III; Artaxerxes II; Behistun; Cyrus II; Darius I; Darius III; Elamites; Hamadan; Khwarna; Medes; Parthians; Pasargadae; Persepolis; Xerxes; *and* Zoroastrianism.]

H. Bengtson, ed., *The Greeks and the Persians from the Sixth to the Fourth Centuries* (1965). Mary Boyce, *A History of Zoroastrianism* (1982). J. M. Cook, *The Persian Empire* (1983). R. G. Kent, *Old Persian* (2d ed., 1982). A. T. Olmstead, *History of the Persian Empire* (1959). E. Porada, "Achaemenid Art, Monumental and Minute," in *Highlights of Persian Art,* edited by Richard Ettinghausen and Ehsan Yarshater (1979). M. Smith, "II Isaiah and the Persians," *Journal of the American Oriental Society* 83 (1963).

JAMES R. RUSSELL

ADAMS, WILLIAM (1564–1620), English ship's pilot aboard the Dutch vessel *de Liefde,* out of Rotterdam in 1598, who was blown ashore at Usuki, in the province of Bungo in eastern Kyushu, Japan, with the survivors of his crew on 19 April 1600; he thus became the first Englishman in Japan. William Adams arrived at a critical moment in Japanese history, six months before the Battle of Sekigahara, at which Tokugawa Ieyasu's victory laid the military foundations for a shogunal dynasty that would last until 1868.

Some Portuguese denounced Adams and his crew as pirates, but they managed to survive their capture. Within the month Adams was brought before Ieyasu at Osaka and questioned about European political affairs, navigational techniques, geography, religion, and many other topics. Ieyasu recognized Adams as a man of talent and valued English and Dutch Protestantism as an alternative to the evangelical, Counter-Reformation Catholicism of the Portuguese. He took Adams on as an adviser on trade and foreign relations. At Adams's urging Ieyasu granted the London-based East India Company trading privileges in Japan. Adams received from Ieyasu a small fief of 250 *koku* (a measure of value in terms of rice equivalence) at Hemi, on the Miura Peninsula; from his fief and his profession he came to be called Miura Anjin ("Miura the pilot").

Little is known of Adams beyond a half-dozen surviving letters and a few entries in the diaries of other Englishmen who later came to Japan. Yet it is clear that he worked to promote English trading opportunities in Japan, including the establishment of the English trading factory at Hirado in northwestern Kyushu, which flourished between 1613 and 1622. He constructed two ships for Ieyasu (Adams had apprenticed with an English shipbuilder named Nicholas Diggins), and on at least three occasions he was licensed by Ieyasu for trading voyages to Southeast Asia. Adams left a wife and daughter in his native Gillingham, Kent, England, but also married in Japan, where he had two children. He seems to have lost influence after Ieyasu's death in 1616 and died at Hirado on 6 May 1620, never having returned to England.

[*See also* Hirado.]

Richard Cocks, *Diary Kept by the Head of the English Factory in Japan, The Diary of Richard Cocks, 1615–1622,* 3 vols. (1978–1980). Philip G. Rogers, *The First Englishman in Japan: The Story of Will Adams* (1956). Thomas Rundall, ed., *Memorials of the Empire of Japon in the XVI and XVII Centuries* (1850).

RONALD P. TOBY

ADAT, Arabic term that refers to the body of traditional, often unwritten Islamic law, including customs and codes, as distinct from revealed prescription. In the major Islamic areas of Southeast Asia (Malaysia, Indonesia, South Thailand, and the southern Philippines), *adat* has been much elaborated and has become widely used to resolve legal issues. In this instance, a simple social usage has become a "customary law" or "*adat* law" or "*adat* with legal consequences."

The shift into a technically legal definition took place in the late nineteenth century in British Malaya, British Borneo, and the Netherlands East Indies. The laws for the populations of these areas are prescribed in the forms developed by the respective colonial regimes and administered and applied in the colonial legal bureaucracies.

On the English law side (Malaya, Borneo), *adat* was an exception to the general law for the population. It was confined to matters of property, inheritance, and, in one area of Malaya (Negri Sembilan), to constitutional matters. Within these limits, it was seen as overriding *shari'a.*

In the Netherlands East Indies, on the other hand, *adat* was taken as the basic law for the indigenous populations, which made up the majority of the population. Hence it determined all aspects of life, including land rights and transactions, obligations, law of persons, and family law, including inheritance, civil wrongs, and legal writing. Islam, the religion of the majority of the populations governed by *adat,* had no application unless allowed by custom. *Adat* now means "law" in both Malaysia and Indonesia and dictates the content of statutes, judicial decisions, and textbooks. It is sometimes seen as in conflict with Islamic prescription and sometimes as an amalgam of, or compromise with, Islamic tenets. However, whatever the particular case, *adat* is now part of the national and state laws of Malaysia and Indonesia.

Adat can now be defined as "prescriptions, reformulated in English and Dutch law, derived from Malaysian and Indonesian cultures and now part of the laws of Malaysia and Indonesia." Its relation with Islamic prescription is culturally variable and determined by the organs of state. Sociologically speaking, compromise between the theoretically opposed systems of *adat* and Islam is the norm.

[*See also* Malaysia *and* Indonesia, Republic of.]

B. ter Haar, *Adat Law in Indonesia,* translated by G. Hass and M. Hordyk (1948). M. B. Hooker, *Adat Laws in Modern Malaya* (1972).

M. B. HOOKER

ADIVASIS, original inhabitants of India, identified as tribes in India's constitution, numbering 52 million (1981), or 7.76 percent of the Indian population. They are situated in the hilly and forested tracts along the Himalayas and international borders in the north northeast, in middle and South India, and in the islands. With the exception of Jammu and Kashmir, the Punjab, Haryana, and the union territories of Chandigarh, Delhi, and Pondicherry, tribal peoples are found throughout India.

Tribes form the majority community in six states and union territories, namely Meghalaya, Nagaland, Mizoram, Arunachal Pradesh, Lakshadweep, and Dadra and Nagar Haveli. According to the 1961 census, tribals form about 10 percent of the population in 169 of India's 334 districts; they are an absolute majority in 28 and a sizable community, with their population varying from 30 to 49 percent, in 44 districts. They are the dominant community in the great belt of tribal territories lying across middle India and extending up to the northeast.

The tribes are heterogeneous, differing in language, culture, and physical features. There are about 250 "major" tribes, most of whom have taken to settled agriculture; however, 72 of these tribes are grouped as "primitive communities" and are isolated, preliterate, and preagricultural. There are several other tribes with whom no contact has been made. Tribals have captured political power in the states where they dominate, and have emerged as an influential political force elsewhere.

There are five major tribal regions in India, with a wide range of variation in population density, level and pace of change and development, and social formation. The northeast, where tribal communities form the majority, has remained, for historical and ecological reasons, relatively free from the influences that have eroded tribal identity elsewhere. Tribal institutions there are relatively intact, and the tribal population, despite small-scale influx of nontribals from the plains, is in control of its resources and the apparatus of political power. The region has also witnessed the rise of movements centered on the issue of identity.

Tribal middle India, stretching from Gujarat to West Bengal across Madhya Pradesh and the upper regions of Andhra Pradesh, has been the theater of probably the most radical changes in the tribal society, changes that gathered momentum during the colonial period and have intensified in the postindependence phase. The middle region accounts for the largest number of tribes emerging as agrarian communities. Large-scale immigration of nontribals in search of land and employment, the commercial exploitation of the area's forest and mineral resources, and the rise of industrial centers and towns have disrupted tribal patterns and have caused many tribals to lose their land and to join the working force in agriculture and industry.

The southern pockets that comprise the Nilgiris, together with the hilly regions of Tamil Nadu, are the homeland of probably the smallest tribal communities on the mainland. The majority of these tribals are laborers working in agriculture or on plantations. However, there are also, among the Toda, Badga, and Kurchians, a few affluent groups who have profited from the introduction of a cash economy and education.

The northwestern Himalayas, one of the most sparsely populated and resource-scarce regions of India, have tribal pockets in Himachal Pradesh and Uttar Pradesh. Cessation of border trade with Tibet has upset the traditional economy of these tribals, who are now switching over to farming and allied activities.

The Andaman and Nicobar Islands have two groups of tribes, the Onge, Jarwa, Sentinelese, and Great Andamanese, who are among the most isolated and primitive tribes in India, with an almost stagnant level of population, and the Nicobarese, who have a flourishing economy and a growing population, mainly owing to their trade in coconuts. In the Laccadive, Minicoy, and Amindivi Islands, tribals form the majority of the population.

The development process since the mid 1960s reflects perception of (1) the deleterious impact on tribal communities of environmental disturbance of tribal regions; (2) the increasing incidence of exploitation of tribal peoples, their loss of land, and their indebtedness; and (3) diversities of tribal situations that require an area-specific approach to planning and development. Today there are 181 integrated tribal development projects (ITDP) responsible for the needs of tribal-project areas. Their reports are compiled into the subplan that is a part of the plan prepared by the state. The interests of dispersed tribals are considered under the Marginal Area Development Agencies (MADA). Together, the ITDP and MADA projects cover 75 percent of the total tribal population and have resulted in an increased flow of funds into tribal areas. In the Sixth Five-Year Plan, about 50,000 million rupees have been invested to develop tribal infrastructure and to raise tribals above the poverty line. A plethora of legislation has been enacted to prevent alienation of tribal lands, to regulate moneylending, and to abolish the practice of bonded labor. [*See* Five-Year Plans.]

Nevertheless, although a great deal of progress has been made in the field of tribal development since the 1930s, progress most dramatically illustrated by the rise of the tribal population, as against the threat of its extinction, and by the spread of education and social benefits, more remains to be done in many, if not all, regions, to bring them up to the level of more advanced communities.

[*See also* Andaman and Nicobar Islands; Arunachal Pradesh; Assam; Gondwana; Manipur; Meghalaya; Nagaland; Nilgiri Hills; Santal; *and* Todas.]

N. K. Bose, *Some Indian Tribes* (1977). Stephen Fuchs, *The Aboriginal Tribes of India* (1973). Christoph von Fürer-Haimendorf, *Tribes of India: The Struggle for Survival* (1982). K. S. Singh, ed., *The Tribal Situation in India* (1972).

K. S. SINGH

AFGHANI, JAMAL AL-DIN AL- (1839–1897), a leading activist and pan-Islamist who inspired a variety of individuals and movements in the Muslim world. Many biographical accounts are incorrect, and sufficient material for a correct account became available only with the 1963 cataloguing of his papers, left in Tehran when he was expelled from there in 1891. These and other primary sources disprove his claim to have been born and raised in Afghanistan (probably adopted mainly to give him a Sunni provenance), and show that he was born near Hamadan and educated in Iran and the Shi'ite shrine cities of Ottoman Iraq. Educated in rationalist philosophy, taught more in Iran than elsewhere in the Muslim world, Afghani was also influenced by the philosophically oriented and innovative Shaikhi school of Shi'ism. In about 1857 he went to India, where he seems to have learned his lifelong hatred of British imperialism. After a trip, probably via Mecca and Iraq, he went to Afghanistan and entered the counsels of the Afghan *amir,* advising him to fight the British. When his patron was defeated by Amir Shir Ali, the latter expelled Afghani, who was forgotten in Afghanistan until a 1916 newspaper article praised him. Afghani went briefly to India and Cairo, and then to Istanbul, where he became a friend of the head of the Dar al-Fonun, the new university. In 1870 Afghani gave a lecture at the university. He compared philosophy to prophecy and implied that prophecy was a craft, thus giving the Ottoman *ulama* (religious scholars), already hostile to the secular university, an excuse to attack the university and bring on Afghani's expulsion.

Afghani stayed then in Cairo from 1871 to 1879; there he did his most fruitful work. He was given a stipend by the Egyptian government to teach young Egyptians. Among his disciples was the later great Muslim reformer Muhammad Abduh. From 1875 on Afghani entered politics by (1) leading an Arab Masonic lodge, which he tried to use to achieve the abdication of Isma'il in favor of his son Taufiq, (2) promoting the formation of political newspapers by his disciples, and (3) giving effective mass orations, directed especially against Westerners in Egypt. When Taufiq took power with Franco-British aid in 1879 and Afghani continued to attack the British, he was exiled to India in August 1879.

In India, Afghani went to the Muslim principality of Hyderabad, where he published several Persian articles and his one treatise, known as the *Refutation of the Materialists,* which was aimed mainly at the pro-British Sir Sayyid Ahmad Khan and his school. After detention by the British in Calcutta, Afghani left for Paris, stopping in London. In London and Paris he wrote articles against the British occupation of Egypt, and also wrote the irreligious French "Answer to Renan." He got Abduh to join him in Paris, where they published the reformist and anti-British paper, *Al-urwa al-wuthqa* in 1884. Now Afghani first expressed the pan-Islamic views most often associated with him; until then he had spoken rather in terms of regional nationalisms.

In 1886 Afghani sailed to the Iranian port of Bushehr, where his books and papers had been sent from Egypt. He planned to go to Russia, where the Slavophile editor M. N. Katkov had invited him, but the Iranian minister of press invited him to Tehran. Jamal al-Din stayed with the wealthy Amin al-Zarb. His antiforeign talk evidently disturbed the shah, who asked Amin al-Zarb to take Afghani with him to Russia, which he did. There he made futile attempts to convince Russia to fight Britain. Afghani overtook the shah's party in Munich in 1889, and after a brief return to Russia he came back to Iran, where the prime minister refused to see him. Afghani then began to encourage secret organization and leaflets against the government, and forestalled expulsion by taking sanctuary at a shrine. In January 1891 he was expelled from Iran after a leaflet attacked the government for its concessions to foreigners. Afghani went to Iraq, and when the Tobacco Rebellion broke out in Iran, a *mujtahid* expelled from Shiraz visited Afghani, who wrote a letter against the shah and the concession to the leading *mujtahid,* Mirza Hasan Shirazi, who was important in the concession's cancellation.

In 1891 and 1892 Afghani spent months speaking and writing in England with Malkom Khan. In 1892 Afghani was invited to be the guest of the Ottoman Sultan Abdulhamid in Istanbul. There he worked with a group of Iranians and Shi'ites to get Shi'ites to recognize Abdulhamid's claim to be caliph of all Muslims. In 1896 Afghani's disciple, Mirza Riza Kirmani, visited Afghani, who inspired him to kill Nasir al-Din Shah on 1 May 1896. Iran's futile efforts to extradite Afghani ended with Afghani's death in 1897. His cancer of the jaw is well attested, and the stories that the sultan poisoned him are similar to the many myths (some self-created) that surround his life. As a believer in reform and as a pioneer in various forms of political activism and agitation in many countries, Afghani had an important influence that continues in the Muslim world today.

[*See also* Malkom Khan; Qajar, Nasir al-Din; *and* Tobacco Rebellion.]

Nikki Keddie, *An Islamic Response to Imperialism: Political and Religious Writings of Sayyid Jamal ad-Din "al-Afghani"* (1968) and *Sayyid Jamal ad-Din "al-Afghani"* (1972).

NIKKI KEDDIE

AFGHANISTAN is bounded on the north by the Soviet Union, on the northeast by the People's Republic of China, on the east and south by Pakistan, and on the west by Iran. Its present shape was determined in the last quarter of the nineteenth century through negotiations between the Russian and British empires. Of these imperially drawn boundaries, however, only the border with Pakistan, which splits the Pakhtun ethnic group between the two states, has been disputed by Afghan regimes.

The Hindu Kush chain of mountains, which divides the country into a northern third and a southern two-thirds, is the dominant geographical feature of the land. The lateral stretch of the range is about 600 miles; its average north–south measurement is about 150 miles, and its highest peaks in central Afghanistan rise to between twenty and twenty-five thousand feet. The Hindu Kush mountain system can be divided into six zones: the Wakhan Corridor-Pamir Knot (the "roof of the world"), Badakhshan, the central mountains, the eastern mountains, the northern mountains and foothills, and the southern mountains and foothills. The remaining part of the country, which consists of the deserts and plains surrounding the Hindu Kush, can be divided into the following five zones: the Turkestan plains, the Herat-Farah lowlands, the Sistan Basin-Helmand Valley, the western stony deserts, and the southwestern sandy deserts. [*See also* Hindu Kush.]

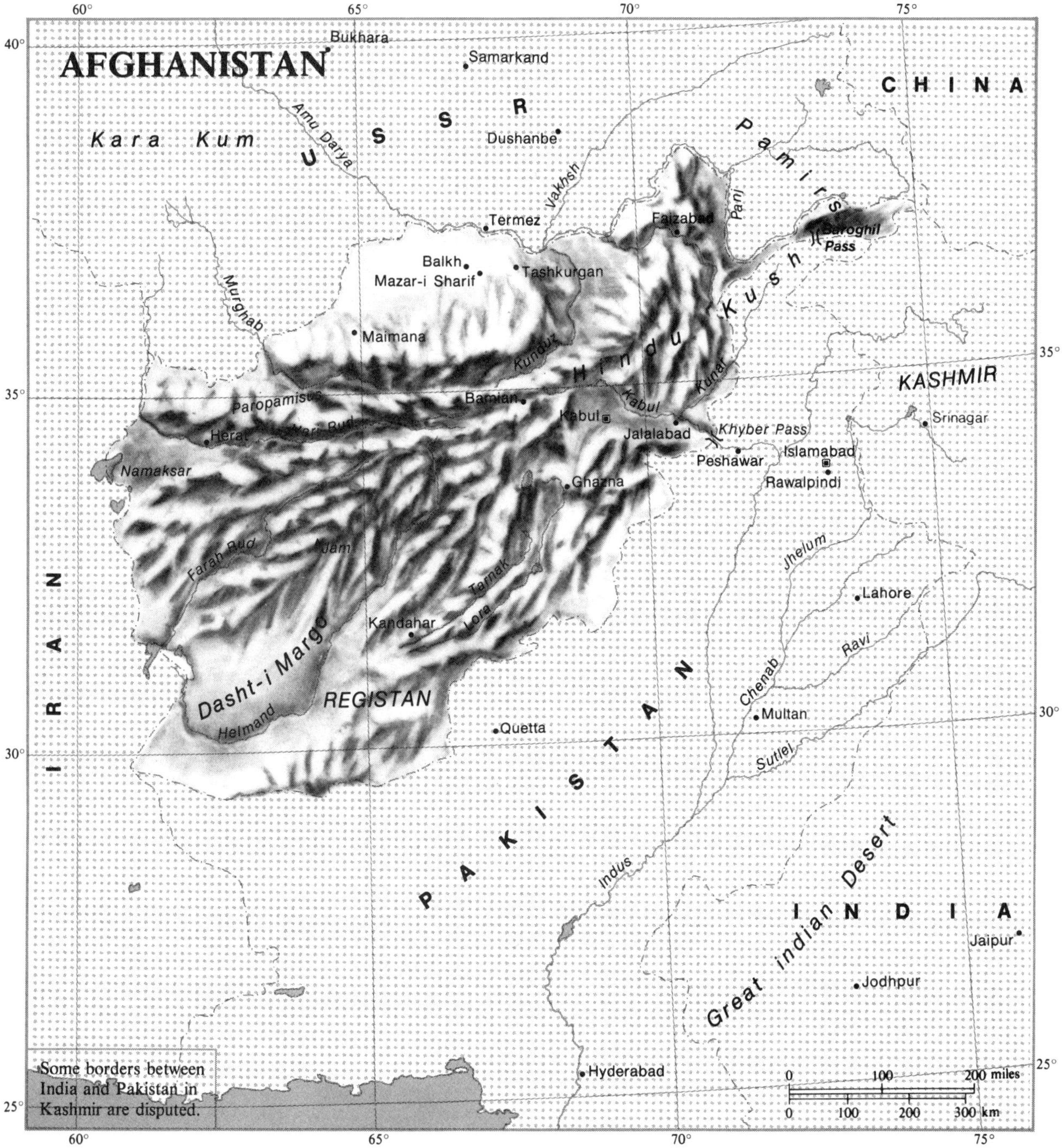

Climatically, however, five zones, crosscutting the above eleven zones, can be distinguished. These are as follows:

1. *Desert.* Amounting to one-fifth of the total area of the country, the desert zone is mostly situated below three thousand feet, covering the plains in the south, southwest, west, north, and east.
2. *Steppe or desert with vegetation.* The steppe encompasses the plains near the foothills. This zone is generally located between three and five thou sand feet. It includes regions of warm or hot and humid climate in the eastern, southern, western, and northern regions.
3. *Subhumid climate or cool steppe.* This zone encompasses most of the pastureland and grassland of the country. It is found in scattered fashion in the eastern and southern regions but is more concentrated in the northern region.

4. *Humid climate.* Coinciding with the forested areas of the country, this zone is found in small concentrations in all regions of the country.
5. *Very cold climate.* This zone, which covers all the areas above ten thousand feet, is divided into a lower part fit for polar vegetation and an upper part too cold for any vegetation.

The total area of Afghanistan is 245,000 square miles, of which only about 12 percent is cultivated annually. It is shortage of water, not land, that accounts for the small percentage of the cultivated area. Annual precipitation in most areas is either too little or too irregular to make rainfall agriculture practical. Irrigation, therefore, is the dominant form of agriculture, although rainfall agriculture is an important supplementary activity. Water from springs, wells, underground channels *(karez),* and rivers, with the latter clearly the most important source, is tapped for irrigation. This dependence on irrigation has, in turn, a determining impact on the pattern and size of settlements, which are characteristically concentrated in regional nodes engulfed by large areas of general dispersion.

The location of the rivers, their pattern of flow and discharge, and the technological means available for harnessing the water have, therefore, been important factors in the distribution of the population in this predominantly agricultural country. The Amu Darya (Oxus) in the north, the Hari Rud in the north and northwest, the Helmand-Arghandab in the south and southwest, and the Kabul in the east are the four major river systems of the country. All except the Kabul, which joins the Indus, are inland rivers. In addition to the main systems, the Panjshir, Logar, Laghman, and Kunar are major perennial rivers in the east. The Surkhab, Kunduz, Kokcha, and Band-i Amir are perennial tributaries in the north.

None of the river systems connects the northern third of the country with its southern two-thirds, and, even when potentially navigable, none in the last three centuries has been important as a communications link, for transport of goods or people, between different regions. Transport, before the introduction of motor vehicles and paved roads in the twentieth century, was by animals, the camel being the long-distance carrier. The camel was a fairly effective means of transport in the weight-efficient long-distance luxury trade passing through Afghanistan, but the movement of bulk agricultural produce between different regions was still quite difficult. Consequently, until the 1960s, when the trend toward the formation of a national market in agriculture was accelerated, the existence of distinctive regional economies was an important feature of the land.

Regional economies greatly enhanced regional identities. Thirty-two languages belonging to four linguistic families are spoken in Afghanistan; thus, language has been a major element in the self-conceptualization of Afghan ethnic groups. The most important of these groups are the Pakhtuns, who speak Pakhtu and who since 1747 have been the dominant political and, probably, numerical element in the country; Tajiks, who speak Persian; Hazaras, who speak a dialect of Persian; and Uzbeks and Turkmens, who speak Turkic languages. Central Afghanistan has been predominantly populated by Hazaras, and the majority of the Turkic groups have lived in the northern region. Until the 1880s, Pakhtuns were largely absent from the northern and central regions. Even during the current century, the majority of Pakhtuns have lived in the eastern, southern, and northwestern areas. Tajiks have formed the major segment of the population in the northeast and northwest, as well as in the capital city of Kabul, its surrounding valleys, and a number of other urban centers.

Not surprisingly, some regions have been named after the major groups inhabiting them. The central region is still known as Hazarajat, after the Hazaras. Until the 1960s, part of the northern area was known as Turkestan and another part as Katagan, after a major Uzbek clan. The name *Afghanistan* itself referred at first to a geographically far more restricted area. From the fourteenth century until the founding of the Afghan state in 1747, the name represented the area occupied by the Pakhtuns who inhabited the valleys of the Sulaiman mountain range, or what is presently the North-West Frontier Province of Pakistan and eastern and southern Afghanistan. As late as the reign of King Habibullah (1901–1919), the official title of the Afghan monarch was "Ruler of the God-Granted Kingdom of Afghanistan, Turkestan, and Their Dependencies." It was in the reign of King Amanullah (1919–1929) that the term *Afghanistan* was officially used to refer to the whole country. [*See also* Pakhtun; Hazaras; *and* Hazarajat.]

For millennia the present territory of Afghanistan has been the arena of major political events, the archaeological and historical details of which still have to be pieced together. Its history from 1747 on can be usefully divided into the following five periods:

1. *1747–1818.* In 1747, the Durrani Pakhtuns chose Ahmadshah (r. 1747–1773) as their king in Kandahar. He quickly carved out an empire, but rivalry between Pakhtun monarchs and aristocrats coupled with changed international conditions brought about its breakdown.

2. *1818–1880.* The collapse of the empire unleashed a period of clannish warlordism that finally resulted in the unification of the present territory of Afghanistan under a Pakhtun ruler in 1863. Twice (in 1839–1842 and 1878–1880) British forces invaded Afghanistan but, failing to defeat popular resistance, were forced to withdraw.

3. *1880–1929.* Britain gained control of Afghanistan's foreign relations and retained it until 1919. Abd al-Rahman (r. 1880–1901), whom they recognized as ruler, used the respite from foreign conflict to pursue a systematic policy of centralization, subordinating all hitherto autonomous groups to the state. These gains were consolidated during the reign of his son. His grandson, Amanullah, was able to wrest political independence from a war-weary Britain. Amanullah's internal policies, however, gave rise to popular opposition, and he was ousted by an armed rebellion in 1929. [*See also* Abd al-Rahman *and* Amanullah.]

4. *1929–1978.* A new Pakhtun dynasty emerged in the wake of the 1929 civil war. The ruling family, realizing the financial weakness of the state, followed a gradual policy of centralization. It first entered an alliance with the merchant class, allowing it to embark on a coherent economic course. In the 1950s, as substantial foreign aid became available, the royal family did without the merchant class but failed to evolve a viable political and economic program. Mohammed Daud Beureu'eh, prime minister from 1953 to 1963, overthrew his cousin, Mohammed Zahir Shah (r. 1933–1973) in 1973 and declared Afghanistan a republic. In April 1978 Daud was in turn overthrown in a bloody coup by the leftist Khalq party. Thus, the Durrani Pakhtun hegemony established in 1747 came to an end. [*See also* Daud Beureu'eh, Mohammed; *and* Zahir, Mohammed.]

5. *From 1978.* The policies and rhetoric of the leaders of the Khalq brought them into collision with all sectors of Afghan society. The leaders' resort to brutal repression fanned the armed opposition and disenchanted their Soviet allies, who invaded Afghanistan in December 1979 and replaced their erstwhile friends with more pliant local subordinates. [*See also* Khalq.] Afghan resistance to Soviet occupation has been both intense and general. Soviet pacification efforts have resulted in the death of thousands, the flight of millions, and immense destruction of the country's infrastructure.

[*See also* Iran; Pakistan; Badakhshan; Herat; Kabul; Durranis; *and* Percham.]

H. Amin and G. B. Schilz, *A Geography of Afghanistan* (1974). Louis Dupree, *Afghanistan* (1980). Monstuart Elphinstone, *An Account of the Kingdom of Caubul,* 2 vols. (1839). N. J. Hanifi, *Annotated Bibliography of Afghanistan* (1982). M. N. Shahrani and E. Canfield, eds., *Revolutions and Rebellions in Afghanistan* (1984).

ASHRAF GHANI

AFSHARID DYNASTY, an Iranian dynasty (1736–1796) founded by Nadir Shah. Nadir's empire at its zenith included the whole of Iran and Afghanistan, with vassals in Iraq, Central Asia, and northern India. After his death, the rule of his successors was soon confined to the city of Mashhad and the metropolitan province of Khurasan.

Nadir's last years were punctuated by rebellions throughout his empire. His nephew Ali Quli Khan, sent to quell a revolt in Sistan, joined the rebels and was already marching on Mashhad when Nadir was assassinated in June 1747. He was proclaimed king under the regnal name Adil Shah ("the just king"). Having secured Nadir's fortress of Kalat, he massacred all his uncle's male issue, preserving only Shahrukh, a teenage grandson by a daughter of the last Safavid monarch, as a hedge against a pro-Safavid coup. Adil sent his younger brother Ibrahim to govern western Iran from the old Safavid capital of Isfahan; he himself remained in Mashhad. Most of Nadir's tribal levies, however, were now returning home, especially to the hinterland of Isfahan. Ibrahim used these reinforcements in a bid for power and defeated Adil Shah's forces near Zanjan in June 1748. He was proclaimed shah at Tabriz in December, but meanwhile Shahrukh had been raised to the throne in Mashhad by a junta of Kurd and other tribal chiefs. In the spring of 1749 Ibrahim's army evaporated on the advance of Shahrukh's forces; he was taken to Mashhad (together with Adil, whom he had already blinded) and executed.

Mir Sayyid Muhammad—like Shahrukh a grandson of the last Safavid shah and an influential figure as warden of the shrine mosque at Mashhad—now became the figurehead of a popular insurrection orchestrated by yet another military faction. Shahrukh Shah was deposed (and later blinded), and in January 1750 the *sayyid* was crowned Shah Sulayman II of the Safavid dynasty. He soon alienated his patrons by disbursing Nadir's waning treasury to parasitical relatives; within three months he had been deposed and blinded. Shahrukh was reinstalled, *faute de mieux,* and ruled nominally for a further forty-five years.

By this time Iran's political center of gravity had shifted to Isfahan and Shiraz, under Karim Khan Zand. Afghanistan and Mughal India were ruled by Ahmad Shah Durrani, who had escaped with his Afghan contingent from the debacle of Nadir's assassination to be elected first shah of Afghanistan. Afsharid Khurasan remained an impoverished buffer zone between these states, ravaged by continuing power struggles between tribal chieftains and Shahrukh's sons Nasr Allah Mirza and Nadir Mirza, and invaded three times by Ahmad Shah. The booty Nadir had brought from India was long dissipated, and Shahrukh's sons resorted to stripping the shrine of ornaments to pay their fickle forces. Although Mashhad retained its prestige as a Shi'ite shrine, chronic anarchy reduced commercial and pilgrim traffic and plunged Khurasan into an economic depression that lasted well into the nineteenth century. In 1796 Aqa Muhammad Qajar, having secured western Iran, stormed Mashhad and tortured Shahrukh to death to reveal the remnants of the fabled Afsharid jewels.

[*See also* Durranis; Nadir; Safavid Dynasty; Zand Dynasty; *and* Zand, Karim Khan.]

Laurence Lockhart, *Nadir Shah* (1938), pp. 259–265. John R. Perry, *Karim Khan Zand* (1979), pp. 1–10.

John R. Perry

AFZAL KHAN, seventeenth-century general in the service of the sultan of Bijapur. Afzal was sent with an army of ten thousand men to suppress Shivaji, the rebel leader who would later found the independent Maratha Hindu kingdom. The Muslim general's campaign was marked by religious intolerance: he destroyed Hindu shrines, particularly one dedicated to Amba Bhavani, tutelary guardian of Shivaji's family. The campaign stalled when Shivaji retreated to his fortress, Pratapgarh. A meeting between the two was eventually negotiated for 10 November 1659. At this meeting Afzal Khan tried either to stab or strangle Shivaji, who, using a concealed weapon called tiger claws, ripped open Afzal Khan's belly, killing him. The Bijapur army was then ambushed and routed by Shivaji's Maratha troops.

[*See also* Karnataka; Maharashtra; *and* Shivaji.]

A. R. Kulkarni

AGENCY HOUSE SYSTEM, a major form of Western commercial organization particularly prominent in Malaya during the late nineteenth and twentieth centuries, although the system also has a long history in India. The prime functions of the agency houses in Malaya were to organize the raising of capital for rubber plantation companies and to provide commercial management of estates. By considerably reducing the risks of investment in colonial territory, the agency houses ensured a major flow of metropolitan capital into colonial enterprises, most notably the rubber industry in Malaya. The most prominent Malayan agency houses included Harrisons and Crosfield; Guthrie; Edward Boustead; and Sime, Darby. These firms had commonly evolved from mercantile houses established earlier in the nineteenth century, and to varying degrees they retained their interests in trading into the later period.

G. C. Allen and Audrey G. Donnithorne, *Western Enterprise in Indonesia and Malaya* (1954). J. H. Drabble and P. J. Drake, "The British Agency Houses in Malaysia: Survival in a Changing World," *Journal of Southeast Asian Studies* 12 (1981): 297–328.

Ian Brown

AGE OF CONSENT ACT. The Age of Consent Act, enacted in India in 1891, made unlawful the consummation of a marriage in which the wife was less than twelve years old. The issue had been hotly debated by Indian intellectuals and reformers through the 1880s. Opponents to reform objected to government interference in religious and social questions; Bal Gangadhar Tilak argued that change must emanate from within a society. Also at issue was whether Indians should emulate Western standards and whether they should use Western—or Indian—institutions for change. The debate was important in that it helped both to polarize the Indian elite and to politicize it.

[*See also* Hindu Renaissance *and* Tilak, Bal Gangadhar.]

Charles H. Heimsath, *Indian Nationalism and Hindu Social Reform* (1964). Stanley A. Wolpert, *Tilak and Gokhale: Revolution and Reform in the Making of Modern India* (1962).

Usha Sanyal

AGHA KHAN (or Aga Khan), a Persian noble title, granted in 1818 to the modern Isma'ili imams of the Nizari line by Fath Ali Shah, ruler of Iran.

The first of the imams to receive this designation was Hasan Ali Shah Mahallati (1800–1881). Especially favored by Iranian royalty, he was raised to a prominent political position, which included the governorship of Kerman province, before subsequent shifts of policy and court intrigue forced him into revolt in 1838. As an outlaw he finally chose exile and, while crossing into India, provided valued service to the British then attempting the conquest of Afghanistan. He settled in Bombay among an already extensive community of his own followers. The result of a legal challenge to his religious authority before the High Court of Bombay in 1866 brought a sweeping vindication under British law of his total, personal control over all property belonging to his Isma'ili sect, thus confirming a source of substantial long-term wealth for himself and his successors in the imamate.

A son, Ali Shah, ruled briefly as Agha Khan II, followed upon his death in 1885 by his own son, Sultan Muhammad Shah (1877–1957), who assumed the imamate at the age of seven. As Agha Khan III, Muhammad Shah enjoyed an unusually long and prosperous reign, which featured a decided turn away from a strictly Muslim and Oriental culture toward integration into European society. Educated in both traditions, the third Agha Khan, urbane and affluent, became an important fixture of post–World War I high society. He was a noted breeder of racehorses and a president of the League of Nations (1937). Four marriages produced two sons, Aly Khan and Sadr al-Din Khan. After Sultan Muhammad Shah's death in 1957, the imamate passed, by his own choice of successor, to his grandson Karim al-Hussain Shah (b. 1936).

[*See also* Imam *and* Isma'ili.]

Agha Khan, *Memoirs* (1954). P. Hardy, *Muslims of British India* (1972). PAUL E. WALKER

AGLIPAY Y LABAYAN, GREGORIO (1860–1940), first supreme bishop of the Philippine Independent Church (PIC), born in Batac, Ilocos Norte. He graduated from the Universidad de Santo Tomas and the Vigan Seminary and was ordained to the priesthood in 1889. During the Philippine Revolution, he served as military vicar-general of Filipino forces and ecclesiastical governor of Nueva Segovia, and during the Philippine-American War he led guerrilla resistance in his home province. Accepting the leadership of the schismatic PIC in 1902, he headed its hierarchy for the rest of his life. In this office he espoused the causes of a rationalist theology and a fully Filipino clergy, and he became a public figure who evoked memories of the Filipino struggle for religious and political independence. An ardent nationalist and defender of dissidents and the dispossessed, he ran unsuccessfully for the commonwealth presidency in 1935 with a communist vice-presidential candidate. He is honored as a patriotic hero, religious leader, and friend of the common man.

[*See also* Philippine Independent Church; Philippine Revolution; *and* Philippine-American War.]

WILLIAM HENRY SCOTT

AGRA, city on the Yamuna River in Uttar Pradesh, India. Agra likely was controlled by Rajputs until Sikander Lodi established his capital there in 1505. Babur, the first Mughal, maintained Agra as his capital, embellishing it with planned gardens and baths. Humayun shifted his capital to Delhi, but in 1558 Akbar reestablished Agra as the imperial city, naming it Akbarabad. In 1565 he commenced a red sandstone fort, although the work was interrupted by the construction of Fatehpur Sikri, which temporarily served as Akbar's capital. Toward the end of Akbar's reign, Lahore replaced Agra as the capital; however, Agra, the primary seat of the Mughal Agra Province, remained a major city. Under Jahangir's reign and much of Shah Jahan's, Agra again was the Mughal capital.

European visitors compared Agra to London and Paris in size; they were struck by Agra's beauty, enhanced by structures such as the Taj Mahal, I'timad ud-Daulah's tomb, and numerous mansions. In 1648 Shah Jahan moved the capital to Shahjahanabad, diminishing Agra's political and cultural significance. In the late eighteenth century Agra was occupied by Jats and Marathas until the British annexed it in 1803, establishing it as headquarters of Agra Presidency; later it was incorporated into the North-Western Province. Today Agra is a flourishing center of commerce, higher education, railways, and tourism.

[*See also* Akbar; Babur; Delhi; Fatehpur Sikri; Humayun; I'timad ud-Daulah; Jahangir; Jats; Lodi Dynasty; Mughal Empire; Rajput; Red Fort; Shah Jahan; Nur Jahan; *and* Taj Mahal.]

François Bernier, *Travels in the Mogul Empire, 1656–1668* (reprint, 1916). R. Nath, *Agra and its Monumental Glory* (1977). CATHERINE B. ASHER

AGRICULTURAL PRODUCERS' COOPERATIVES, collective farming units in China and Vietnam roughly equivalent to the *kolkhoz* of the Soviet

Union. The Agricultural Producers' Cooperative (APC) is distinguished from the state farm by the fact that an APC is officially owned by its members and by the fact that once investment funds and obligatory deliveries to the state have been subtracted from the crop the remainder belongs to the members.

The APCs were introduced in two stages. In the lower-stage (semisocialist) APC, a group of families in the same village pooled their land, draft animals, and major tools. They worked the land collectively. They kept records, measured in "work points," of the labor done by each family each day. At the end of the year, the crop was divided among the member households. The division depended partly on how much labor each household had done, and partly on how much land and capital each household had contributed.

In the higher-stage (fully socialist) cooperative, the income of each household no longer depended on the amount of land and capital it had contributed but only on the number of work points it had earned. The higher-stage APC was also in most cases larger, often incorporating three or more lower-stage APCs, but the difference in size was not fundamental to the distinction between the two types of organization.

APCs were created very rapidly in China, mostly in 1955 and 1956. Two percent of peasant households were in APCs in 1954; 97 percent were in APCs, most of them fully socialist, in 1957. In North Vietnam, most of the peasants were gathered into lower-stage APCs between 1958 and 1960, but the transition to higher-stage APCs was very gradual. In China the APCs were absorbed into the communes in 1958. In North Vietnam, they are still the predominant form of agricultural organization. Some APCs were being established in South Vietnam by the end of 1975.

[*See also* Agriculture, Collectivization of.]

Franz Schurman, *Ideology and Organization in Communist China* (1968). Edwin E. Moise

AGRICULTURE. Agriculture evolved first in Asia, well before its origins elsewhere, and Asia remains the home of more than two-thirds of the world's farmers. South Asia and China, each with about one billion people, are still predominantly agricultural, with about three-quarters of their populations engaged in farming; the same is true of most of Southeast Asia and southwest Asia. Only Japan and the city-states of Hong Kong and Singapore have as yet industrialized to a Western level. As a result, their farm population has dwindled to less than 5 percent of the total, although Korea and Taiwan are moving rapidly in the same direction.

Two main areas seem most likely as cradles of agriculture, both located in the upland edges of major river valleys where people gradually evolved from hunting and gathering to purposeful cultivation of the most desirable species, planting seeds or rooting cuttings in tended fields. The evidence is clearest for southwest Asia—on the flanks of the Zagros Mountains in western Iran, Kurdistan in northern Iraq, southern Anatolia, and Palestine, where wild ancestors of wheat and barley occurred as steppe grasses. Agriculture may also have begun independently, and just as early, in the upland fringes of one or more of the great river valleys of Southeast Asia, where archaeological work is more recent and much spottier and where the tropical climate is less conducive to preservation of organic evidence. The transition to agriculture everywhere was a long one, probably taking place over several millennia and beginning in these two areas perhaps by about 10,000 BCE. Stone sickles dating from approximately that time have been found at several southwest Asian sites bearing an unmistakable sheen that could have come only from their use in cutting wild grasses or gathering their seeds or grain heads. Stone querns and mortars from the same period indicate that the grain was milled and that it helped support a population beginning to grow beyond what earlier Neolithic cultures could sustain. By about 8000 BCE storage pits for grain begin to appear, and by 7000 einkorn and emmer wheats, barley, and peas are identifiable as domesticated. Sheep and goats were also domesticated by the same time, as were cattle and swine within another millennium. There is a reasonably clear record of this gradual evolution at a number of sites, including Jericho in southern Palestine, Cayon and Catal Huyuk in southern Anatolia, Jarmo in northern Iran, and Hassuna and Ali Kosh in western Iran, among many others.

By about 4000 BCE or slightly earlier agricultural techniques were far enough advanced in this area, and populations numerous enough, to permit an expansion into the different environment of the Tigris-Euphrates lowland. Somewhat later that expansion continued into the Indus Valley in what is now Pakistan, with a model transmitted via early agricultural settlements in eastern Iran and Afghanistan that antedate the beginnings of Indus Valley farming but that were later than those farther west. The river flood plains were potentially very productive, especially given their fertile alluvial soil, but massive problems of flooding and drainage had first to be solved and the techniques of irrigation mastered; lower Mesopotamia and the Indus Valley were largely rainless, the rivers being fed by remote rains and snowmelt from their mountain source areas and hence subject to seasonal flooding. Soon after 4000 BCE villages grew into small cities in the lower Tigris-Euphrates, including Jemdet Nasr, Nippur, Ur, Erech, and Eridu, all supported largely by irrigated farming—now employing bronze tools—and supplemented by a wide-ranging trade.

Perhaps through the medium of trade, irrigated agriculture was diffused to eastern Iran and Afghanistan soon after 4000 BCE and was fully developed at sites such as Sistan (also a trade hub) by at least 3500. Sistan and other eastern Iranian settlements were in turn directly in contact with Afghanistan, Baluchistan, and the fringes of the Indus Valley. By or before 3000 BCE irrigated agriculture was well established in the Indus Valley, first at late Neolithic village sites, such as Amri and Kot Diji along the lower Indus, and shortly thereafter at major city sites, the best known of which are Mohenjo-Daro on the lower Indus and Harappa and Kalibangan on Indus tributaries farther up but still on lowland flood plains. Radiocarbon dating, still the best means of estimating chronology, continues to provide ambiguous results, so that we cannot be certain of these dates. Some estimates put the beginnings of these urban-centered farming cultures well before 3000, others several centuries later, but by at least 2500 they were fully formed and the cities themselves surprisingly large and well planned, suggesting a large surplus and an evolution that must have taken place over several preceding centuries. A longish period of development is also suggested by the impressively wide spread of the Indus agrarian-based culture, with similar sites scattered quite thickly over the whole of the lowland area and extending east as far as Delhi and south as far as Bombay by 2500 or soon after. [*See* Indus Valley Civilization.]

The main Indus crop was also wheat, domesticated in two varieties and probably derived from southwest Asia; two varieties of barley, probably of similar origin, were also grown, as were peas, lentils, dates, melons, and cotton, the last almost certainly domesticated first by the Indus people and probably native to the subcontinent. Sugarcane and black pepper, also probably native, occur somewhat later as domesticates. Domesticated cattle (the traditional Indian humpbacked species), sheep, and goats were also important elements from the beginning of the Indus civilization. Rice was absent until quite late, until almost the eve of the apparent collapse of the civilization by or soon after 2000. The reason for this collapse may have been the progressive siltation of the irrigation works and of salinization of the fields after centuries of irrigation in an arid climate, during which time there was insufficient rainfall to flush away minerals left on the surface by evaporating irrigation water; there is clear evidence of fields abandoned for such reasons. Rice was almost certainly native to Southeast Asia, as a swamp plant around the shores of the Bay of Bengal or in the valleys of the great southeastern rivers, but its diffusion westward was presumably slowed by the arid conditions of the intervening areas as well as by the lack of close contact. There was also a wide zone of nonagricultural cultures in most of central India and much of Southeast Asia.

It is probably the accident of the few sites excavated so far in Southeast Asia that suggests a clustering of early agriculture in northern and central Thailand and northern Vietnam. Subsequent work may fill out the pattern suggested of agricultural beginnings in the upland fringes of river valleys, with perhaps also sites on or near the coast where gathering and early cultivation could be supplemented by fishing and by collecting from fixed shellfish beds. It is eminently plausible that gathering cultures could have begun the transition to planted and tended fields in this area of unbroken growing season, where several tropical root and tree crops as well as rice were native in wild forms. It is probable that early developments centered on root crops, easily cultivated in this tropical climate by vegetative reproduction (roots, stolons, cuttings) from plentiful wild material. Taro and yams are still grown this way in Southeast Asia and offer plentiful output for minimal labor. But there is as yet no hard evidence, let alone reliable dating. It is probable that rice was also first domesticated somewhere in this area, but here too the evidence is elusive.

By about 8000 BCE a late Neolithic culture called Hoabinhian (from the type site near Hanoi) had evolved, the stone tools and other remains of which suggest a move from strict gathering to at least protoagriculture, with fixed settlements, some of which depended also on shellfish. There are severe dating problems, associated with the ambiguities of radiocarbon techniques, at the best-known sites, such as Spirit Cave, Ban Chiang, and Non Nok Tha (all in

Thailand), however, with estimates ranging from 4500 to as late as 2000 BCE. Although these cultures had a reasonably well-developed bronze metallurgy, there is still disagreement over whether the few identifiable food remains, including rice, which is present in the earliest layers, represent cultivated or wild forms. Remains of chickens and pigs and the presence at Ban Chiang of a large cemetery do suggest agriculture to support so large and technically advanced a population, but specific proof is still lacking. Tropical and semitropical conditions extend well into what is now southern and central China, and there too one may expect to find similar or related early developments.

Other evidence suggests that, as in China, millet may have been the first cereal actually cultivated in Southeast Asia. Rice could be gathered wild, but millet was introduced from northwest China or from central Asia and hence could be grown only on a tended basis. Originally a steppe grass, it too was better suited to the uplands or to elevated sites than to the flood plains, and it was apparently not until about 1000 BCE, with irrigation, flood control, and the rise of rice as the dominant crop, that farmers began to occupy and increasingly to concentrate in the lower river valleys and deltas in both Southeast Asia and China. Wild rice may originally have invaded taro plantations as a weed and been domesticated from such a basis. Like rice, taro is a hydrophytic plant that was probably domesticated first in upland savanna zones in the seasonally dry Southeast Asian tropics, where shallow depressions fill with water each rainy season.

For the origins of agriculture in China there are similar dating problems. It is clear that the dominant and perhaps only important early domesticate at least in North China was millet, probably native there and domesticated in two varieties by at least 4500 BCE, perhaps by 5000. Dependence on millet, with other evidence, strongly suggests independent development, at least in the North, rather than diffusion from southwest or Southeast Asia. Banpo, near modern Xi'an, the major early northern site, was well established as a large agricultural village by at least 4000 BCE. Domesticated rice, almost certainly diffused from the South, appeared relatively late in the North, as did wheat and barley, both diffused from southwest Asia. Agricultural sites in the lower Yangtze River valley may well be earlier; these include Hemudu (near Hangzhou) and Qingliangang (eastern Jiangsu), both dated variously between 5500 and 4500 BCE. Evidence of a probably domesticated form of rice as well as domesticated pigs and water buffalo occur in both sites. In the North, the Banpo people had sheep, goats, and pigs, but buffalo and rice probably did not spread widely to the North until late Shang times (c. 1200 BCE). Until perhaps as late as the Han (c. 200 BCE) South China belonged culturally as it does environmentally more with Southeast Asia than with North China. The first form of rice domesticated was the *indica* variety, like the wild ancestor *(Oryza perennis)* a swampy plant adapted to warm climates. The *japonica* variety, better suited to colder temperatures and shorter growing seasons, was developed later and has been since at least Han times the dominant form in China, Korea, and Japan. Excavated sites in South China are too scarce to demonstrate early developments in domesticated root crops on a par with sites in Thailand or Vietnam or to attest to the domestication of rice before about 4000 BCE, although both facts seem likely.

By late Shang times wheat and barley had joined the northern crop complex and the political center of Chinese civilization was firmly established in a northern locus. Banpo and most other early northern sites are in the loess uplands well away from the main valley of the Yellow River. In China too it was only after the rise of water controls that the major farming centers moved onto river valleys and deltas, in the North beginning about 2000 BCE but not acquiring full momentum for another millennium, by which time wheat had replaced the earlier dominance of millet and was supplemented by barley and rice. Chinese agriculture has been consistently dominated by cereal cultivation and the role of animals has always been small. Population pressure put a premium on calorie yields per hectare, hence root crops were not a viable option for most of the country until the introduction, by the Spanish in the sixteenth century, of the potato from the New World. The Spanish also introduced maize and tobacco. Animals were used for essential draft purposes or flourished as scavengers (pigs, chickens, ducks) who could subsist on leavings and required neither pastures nor fodder. India has always maintained a large bovine population, as well as large numbers of sheep and goats, and milk and milk products have remained important parts of the diet. Korea and Japan, with population pressures similar to China's, have followed the Chinese pattern, while Southeast Asia has continued heavier dependence on roots, tubers, and tropical tree crops (jackfruit, coconuts, other fruits) and has maintained a larger place for animals, mainly pigs and chickens, supplemented near the more populous coast by marine products. Japan also departs from the Chinese model in its consistently heavy dependence on marine supplements to the diet, as does Korea; in both countries the great bulk of the population has always lived close to the sea.

Agriculture, first in the form of millet, diffused from North China into Korea probably by about 2000 BCE, although some radiocarbon dates suggest millet cultivation by the Chulmun culture in the Han River valley (near Seoul) as early as 5000. Rice entered later, almost certainly via North China, possibly aided by the flow of refugees from the fall of the Shang (c. 1100 BCE); *japonica* may have been developed by selection in Korea to adapt to a still colder climate. In any case, only *japonica* was then transmitted to Japan, via Korea. The earliest finds of rice in Japan are dated about 300 BCE, and Japanese agriculture seems to have begun abruptly at about this time out of the previous hunter-gatherer culture.

As populations increased on their newly productive agricultural bases, farming expanded into new areas, including the Ganges River valley, which seems to have remained largely forested until after the fall of the Indus civilization. By about 500 BCE cultivation and population had increased to the point where the Ganges valley had become the chief agricultural and demographic center of the subcontinent, as it still is. In ensuing centuries agriculture spread into the more accessible and productive parts of central and South India, including the east and west coastal plains. Although there had been some islands of very early agriculture in parts of the South, populations were now much larger and techniques more advanced. The same general process took place in China, accelerating with the conquest, by the Han dynasty, of most of the South in the first century BCE, as river valleys leading south from the Yangtze and then the gentler uplands of the South were cleared and farmed by the advancing wave of Chinese settlement, displacing the earlier preagricultural inhabitants. In Korea and Japan farming remained limited by the steep mountains that cover most of both countries, but rising population totals increasingly pushed cultivation onto all lowland areas and onto gentler slopes, where irrigated rice predominated and wheat and barley were cultivated as dry-field and winter crops. The original core area of Japanese culture was the lowland plain at the head of the Inland Sea. Northern Honshu remained alien and probably outside the agricultural pale until quite late, but by the tenth century CE Japanese settlement based on rice began to expand farther northward, completing the full occupation of Hokkaido only by the twentieth century.

In Southeast Asia most of the area remains lightly used even now. Shifting cultivators who clear a small patch by burning and girdling the trees raise a variety of crops there for two or three years, until the low-fertility tropical soil is exhausted and the patch invaded by weeds. They then move on to repeat the process elsewhere as part of a cycle that may return to the same patch only once in a decade or two. In the deltas and river valleys, and on the volcanic island of Java, fertile soils and dense populations are accompanied by a far more intensive system that concentrates on irrigated rice. In west coastal Malaysia, parts of Sumatra, much of Java, and small areas elsewhere a newer form, the plantation system, has grown up since the late nineteenth century. The system allows the cultivation of a range of commercial crops for export: rubber, palm oil, coconuts, sugar, tea, kapok and other fibers, tobacco, spices, and other crops where the Asian tropics have a comparative advantage. Plantations generally avoid the fertile and crowded rice areas; tree or bush crops do not require good soil but need good drainage, such as is provided on slopes. Such crops can also be profitably grown in areas with good commercial access. Sugar and tobacco grow in areas of rich volcanic soil, such as on Java and parts of Luzon.

The modern history of agriculture in South Asia and China is a story of increasing population pressure and consequent expansion of cultivated land into increasingly marginal areas, including steeper slopes (which require terracing for rice growing) and steppe regions with periodically inadequate rainfall. Especially in hilly or mountainous areas this has meant massive deforestation, with its attendant erosion, siltation, and flooding. There is now little land left for further expansion that would repay the effort and cost; production increases must come from more intensive methods and the use of modern technology to raise per hectare and per worker yields from existing farmland. Southeast Asia needs the same infusions into its relatively low-yield agricultural system. Japan, and to a large extent Taiwan and Korea, have shown that new, higher-yielding strains of all major crops, heavy fertilization, pesticides, and increased irrigation can double or even triple yields, as has happened in Japan (and the West) over the past fifty years. By the 1960s this combination of new intensiveness, using specially developed high-yield varieties plus fertilizer and water, was labeled the "Green Revolution." It has spread differentially in blocks of suitable areas in most Asian countries and has already about doubled total output (for example, in India and in China), with another doubling potentially possible as its components are spread more widely and applied more completely.

Those components are expensive, however, and the process is necessarily slow and spotty. Fertilizers, irrigation equipment, pesticides, and research also need a large and efficient industrial base if they are to be available in adequate amounts at bearable cost. East Asian agriculture in particular has long been noted for its intensiveness and high yields. The introduction of potatoes, maize, and, later, peanuts raised output still further and made use of land not suitable for rice cultivation. Technological advances in the West (and Japan) have overtaken this achievement only recently, but meanwhile Asian populations have doubled or tripled. Virtually all cultivated land is extremely crowded and there is also a new and rapidly growing urban sector to be fed. The need for new technology in agriculture, as in the Green Revolution formula, is urgent. In terms of social equity it is also urgent that the benefits of increased production be shared more widely. In many areas those regions and farmers who have local advantages and the capital to pay for new inputs have done very well out of the Green Revolution, while others have gained little and may even have retrogressed in a relative sense. Such imbalances may not be completely correctable, but especially for Asia, where most people outside Japan are still farmers, it is important that the revolutionary changes now taking place in agriculture redound at least to some degree to the benefit of all. The major battle—against famine and for the achievement of food self-sufficiency despite continued population growth—appears now to have been won, although in some countries, notably China, the margin is still precarious. It remains to win the bigger battle—against poverty—by revolutionizing all phases of agriculture and providing enhanced well-being for that great majority of Asians still engaged in it.

[*See also* Irrigation; Economic Development; *and* Land Tenure and Reform.]

R. Barker and R. Sinha, eds., *The Chinese Agricultural Economy* (1982). Kwang-chih Chang, *The Archaeology of Ancient China* (3d ed., 1977). B. H. Farmer, ed., *Green Revolution?* (1977). Karl Hutterer, "The Natural and Cultural History of Southeast Asian Agriculture," *Anthropos* 78 (1983). David N. Keightley, ed., *The Origins of Chinese Civilization* (1983). J. W. Mellor, *The New Economics of Growth: A Strategy for India and the Developing World* (1976). S. M. Nelson, ed., "The Origins of Rice Agriculture in Korea: A Symposium," *Journal of Asian Studies* 41 (May 1982): 511–548. Dwight Perkins, *Agricultural Development in China, 1368–1968* (1969). G. L. Possehl, ed., *Ancient Cities of the Indus* (1979). C. A. Reed, ed., *Origins of Agriculture* (1977).

RHOADS MURPHEY

AGRICULTURE, COLLECTIVIZATION OF.

[*This article treats the agricultural policies of the People's Republic of China. For a discussion of land ownership in other countries, see* Land Tenure and Reform.]

The Chinese Communist Party (CCP) made limited experiments with the collectivization of agriculture even before it came to power in 1949, but the shift from private to collective farming was undertaken mostly in the mid-1950s. Since that time, the forms and degree of collectivization have continued to vary.

The one-family farm was the basis of agriculture in early modern China. Peasant practices of mutual assistance and labor exchange provided a certain limited foundation for collective agriculture, but in their traditional forms they had not seriously compromised the independence of the households involved in them. Until the early 1950s the CCP for the most part accepted the family farm. (Li Lisan, the early Communist leader, showed some interest in rapid collectivization, but this policy was discarded when Li fell from power in 1930.) The Party treated socialist agriculture as a long-range goal, but its land reform efforts were directed in the short run to improving the system of private family farms.

The first step toward collective agriculture was the mutual-aid team, in which a small number of families (usually fewer than ten) joined together to help one another work their farms. The purpose was to ensure that enough labor, tools, and draft animals were available to handle crucial tasks on the fields of all the team members. Each family retained ownership of its own fields, and the crops grown on those fields basically belonged to that family. Payments were made to balance accounts if one family had done more labor on the fields of others than others had done on that family's fields.

The CCP began to develop mutual-aid teams during World War II, both because such teams could boost agricultural production and because they were a step toward the ideological goal of socialism. Their number, however, remained small. The movement developed far more broadly in the early 1950s, during and immediately after land reform. By late 1952 about 40 percent of all peasant households were in mutual-aid teams.

During this period a small number of peasants were starting to move to the next stage of collectivization, the semisocialist Agricultural Producers' Cooperative (APC). The income of a member family did not come from the crops of the particular fields that family had contributed, as had been the case in the mutual-aid team. Instead, the peasants collectively worked all the fields of the cooperative. Records were kept, usually measured in daily "work points," of the amount of labor done by each family. At the end of a season or a year, after taxes and funds for investment had been subtracted from the crop, the remainder was divided among the members of the cooperative. The division depended not only on the number of work points earned, but also on the amount of land and the number of tools and draft animals contributed by each family. In the semisocialist APC, therefore, the relationship between a family's income and its individual landholdings was partially preserved. The family still retained nominal ownership of its land. In the early years the semisocialist APC contained an average of fifteen to twenty households. By 1956, however, the average had increased to about fifty households.

The next stage was the fully socialist APC, sometimes called a collective. In it the division of crops depended only on work points; the amounts of land and capital contributed by each family were no longer taken into account, and the land was legally the property of the cooperative. In 1956, the first year in which really large numbers of collectives were created, each collective averaged about 150 households.

The CCP had originally planned a very slow transition to collective agriculture. When some leaders decided that the movement was progressing too fast, in 1953 and again in 1955, tens of thousands of cooperatives were disbanded. Mao Zedong was quite bitter about this; he felt that the course of socialist development was being blocked, and indeed reversed, for no good reason. Despite the reluctance of some other leaders, Mao succeeded in launching a "high tide" of collectivization in the autumn of 1955. Once begun, this campaign moved to completion much faster than even Mao had initially proposed. By the end of 1956 the transition to cooperatives and indeed to fully socialist cooperatives was almost complete in the ethnically Han areas of China.

When the high tide began, the CCP had envisaged the cooperatives as organizations of the poor and middle peasants. It did not want the former landlords and rich peasants, with their superior education and commercial skills, to have an opportunity to take over the new organizations. The Party therefore ordered that no landlords or rich peasants be allowed to join a cooperative for several years after it was founded. Early in 1956, however, the Party relaxed this policy.

The creation of cooperatives was carried out without the sort of bloodshed that had accompanied land reform a few years earlier, or that had accompanied the collectivization of agriculture in the Soviet Union. Although there was some opposition to the cooperatives from peasants who did not believe that their income as members of cooperatives would match what they had as individual farmers, very few were so adamantly set against cooperatives that massive force was required to obtain their acquiescence.

In August 1958 first Mao Zedong and then the Politburo as a whole endorsed the "people's commune" as a new organizational form for the countryside. Within a few months the cooperatives of China had been amalgamated into communes. In the early years both the size and the nomenclature of the subdivisions within a commune varied substantially. In most, the principal internal unit was the production brigade, which often corresponded to a former fully socialist cooperative. Each brigade included several production teams.

The extent of collectivism continued to fluctuate over time after the creation of the communes. Several factors contributed to this variance:

1. *The survival of the household economy.* Individual households were in most periods allowed "private plots." These were not legally the property of the household, but the household could grow what it wished on the private plots, and the produce belonged entirely to the household. Many households also kept private livestock and sometimes trees. Some peasants also engaged in nonagricultural sidelines.

2. *The level of accounting in regard to work points.* If the level was the brigade, then at the end of each year the net production of the brigade was divided by the total number of work points earned in the brigade to determine the value of a work point. Any two households in the brigade that had done the same amount of work would get the same amount of income from the brigade. On the other hand, if the unit of accounting was the team, then the value of a work point was likely to vary substantially between teams in a single brigade. Some

of the variations would come from such factors as soil quality and location, but a significant part of the variation would derive from the quality of the work done by the members of different teams.

3. *The extent of free distribution and unpaid labor.* The former refers to the more or less equal distribution of commodities and services among the population, without regard to how much work each person had done. The latter indicates the work people were expected to perform as an obligation to society without receiving any remuneration. These practices represented a very extreme version of equal sharing, popularly known as "eating out of a big pot."

The high tide of 1955 to 1956 represented a massive move toward collectivization. In the autumn of 1958 the Great Leap Forward brought a much more extreme drive for collectivism and egalitarianism, later described as the "communist wind." Food, and in some cases clothing and other commodities as well, were distributed free to commune members. At the same time peasants were expected to do significant amounts of labor for which they received no work points. The level of accounting in regard to work points was in many areas actually the commune. Private plots were abolished.

This extreme egalitarianism combined with economic errors of other sorts, and very bad weather, to produce severe crop failures from 1959 to 1961. In response to the crisis, the level of collectivism was lowered substantially; private plots were restored, large communes were split into smaller ones, and the level of accounting within the communes shifted downward. Some collectively owned land was contracted out to individual households for cultivation. Collectivism was reemphasized later in the 1960s, but not to the levels of 1958 and 1959.

Thereafter, beginning in about 1978, the level of collectivism was again reduced very dramatically. In many areas, as much as 15 percent of the land was devoted to private plots. Beyond this, much land was assigned to peasants on contract under the responsibility system. This is different from private plots, in that the contracts the peasants must sign under the responsibility system involve their handing over a substantial portion of their crops. Under some (not all) versions of the responsibility system, however, the peasants have relative autonomy in the use of their land, as long as they make their contracted payments. In the most extreme cases, found especially in mountainous and thinly settled areas where collective operation had been very difficult, the post-1978 reforms have amounted to a de facto abolition of collective agriculture.

[*See also* Agricultural Producers' Cooperatives; People's Communes; Great Leap Forward; *and* Responsibility System.]

William Hinton, *Shenfan* (1983). Roderick MacFarquhar, *The Origins of the Cultural Revolution,* 2 vols. (1974–1983). Franz Schurmann, *Ideology and Organization in Communist China* (1968). Vivienne Shue, *Peasant China in Transition* (1980). EDWIN E. MOISE

AGUINALDO, EMILIO (1869–1964), foremost leader of the Philippine Revolution from 1897 until his capture in 1901. Born in Cavite to Carlos Aguinaldo and Trinidad Famy, he enrolled at the Colegio de San Juan de Letran but was unable to finish his studies. In 1895 the Spanish government appointed him *capitan municipal* of Kawit; he also joined the Katipunan, a separatist society planning an armed resistance against Spain. A few days after the outbreak of the revolution, Aguinaldo became a hero overnight because of his successful assault on the Spanish garrison, distinguishing himself as the undisputed leader of Cavite. He was elected president of the revolutionary government created at the Tejeros Convention in March 1897. As such, he was faced with disunity and the inevitable struggle for power within the revolution. As president, Aguinaldo superseded Andres Bonifacio, founder of the Katipunan, who was executed for supposedly antirevolutionary activities. [*See* Katipunan.]

A spirited campaign against the rebels drove Aguinaldo to Bulacan, where he set up the Biaknabato Republic on 1 November with himself as president. When the revolution developed into a military stalemate, both sides agreed to a truce. This resulted in the exile of Aguinaldo and his staff to Hong Kong. The Americans tried to get his cooperation when the Spanish-American War broke out. He himself had hoped that the Americans would help the Filipinos obtain their independence from Spain.

Aguinaldo and his companions returned to Cavite on 19 May 1898 aboard the American ship *McCulloch.* On 25 May he set up a dictatorial government; on 12 June he proclaimed the country's independence. On 23 June he established a revolutionary government. This in turn was succeeded by the first Philippine Republic, which Aguinaldo established on 23 January 1899 in Malolos, Bulacan, amid increasing tension between Filipino and American forces in and around Manila. On the night of 4 February hostilities broke out. Aguinaldo declared war against the Americans.

In a few months American military superiority and disunity of the Filipino leaders forced Aguinaldo to retreat from one provisional capital of the republic to another. He disbanded the regular army and ordered guerrilla warfare against the Americans. His leadership of the guerrilla resistance lasted until his capture on 23 March 1901 in Palanan, Isabela. On 1 April 1901, he swore allegiance to the United States. His capture was a great blow to the resistance movement against the Americans, as one Filipino leader after another surrendered.

He returned to Cavite, where he spent a relatively quiet life. In 1935 he was persuaded to run against Manuel L. Quezon for the presidency of the commonwealth government, but Quezon trounced him severely in the polls. Aguinaldo's subsequent public appearances consisted of gracing celebrations commemorating the Philippine Revolution. He died of a heart attack at the age of ninety-five.

[*See also* Philippine Revolution *and* Malolos Republic.]

Teodoro A. Agoncillo, *The Revolt of the Masses: The Story of the Bonifacio and Katipunan* (1956) and *Malolos: The Crisis of the Republic* (1960).

MILAGROS C. GUERRERO

AGUNG, sultan of Mataram (r. 1613–1646), considered the greatest ruler of the Mataram dynasty of Java. Sultan Agung (called "the greatest sultan," a posthumous appellation) succeeded his grandfather Senapati Ingalaga (reigned c. 1584–1601) and father, Seda ing Krapyak (reigned c. 1601–1613), who had laid the foundations for hegemony in the Javanese-speaking heartlands of Central and East Java. Agung completed the conquest of this area by defeating a coalition led by the great city of Surabaya, which itself fell to Agung in 1625. This war caused much death and devastation.

Agung then turned to deal with the Dutch East India Company (VOC), which had established its headquarters in Batavia (now Jakarta) in West Java in 1619. In 1628 and 1629 Agung's armies besieged the VOC post but failed to take it. Minor hostilities between Mataram and the VOC continued for several years, but neither Agung nor any other Javanese king ever again attacked Batavia.

Batavia's defeat of Agung encouraged some of his vassals to reassert their independence, but Agung responded by brutally crushing these attempts. Some of these were led by religious figures; about 1636 Agung therefore destroyed the most important center of religious opposition to him, a shrine located at Giri, the holy grave site of one of the putative walis (apostles) of Islam, near Surabaya. From 1636 to 1640 Agung conquered the Eastern Salient of Java, which had previously been under Balinese rule. Finally Agung's conquests came to an end, and the last years of his reign saw peace.

Agung was a brilliant general, a ruthless and brutal king. Yet he paid attention to the legitimation of his rule, seeking consensus, constructing a new court, and taking the title of sultan in 1641. Javanese tradition also remembers him as a pious Muslim.

[*See also* Dutch East India Company *and* Mataram.]

Theodore G. Pigeaud and H. J. de Graaf, *Islamic States in Java 1550–1700* (1976). M. C. Ricklefs, *A History of Modern Indonesia* (1981). M. C. RICKLEFS

AGUS SALIM, HAJI (1884–1954), Indonesian political leader, born in Kota Gadang, West Sumatra. Before becoming prominent in the Sarekat Islam (PSII), an Indonesian nationalist party, he was employed at the Dutch consulate in Jeddah. He joined the Sarekat Islam in 1915 and represented it in the Volksraad ("people's council") from 1921 to 1924. During his Sarekat Islam years, Agus Salim was editor of such periodicals as *Bataviaasch Nieuwsblad, Neratja, Fadjar Asia,* and *Moestika* and was active in the labor movement. In 1937 he was expelled from the party when, dissatisfied with its policy of noncooperation with the Dutch, he founded the Barisan Panjedar PSII ("movement to make the PSII conscious"). In 1945 he helped draft the Jakarta Charter. From 1946 to 1949 he served as the vice-minister and later as the minister of foreign affairs.

[*See also* Sarekat Islam; Volksraad; *and* Barisan Sosialis.]

C. VAN DIJK

AHALYA BAI (1725?–1795), widowed daughter-in-law of Malhar Rao Holkar, the Maratha founder of the Indore ruling family. After his death in 1766, she ruled the Holkar state in southwest Malwa for nearly three decades. John Malcolm *(A Memoir of Central India,* 1824) described her success in the internal administration of her domains as "altogether wonderful" and observed that "she certainly appears, within her limited sphere, to have been one of the purest and most exemplary rulers that ever existed." Her subjects enjoyed peace and increasing prosperity, and her name is honored in Indore to the present time. Following the two-year reign of her successor, a period of chaos and confusion ensued, lasting until the imposition of British power in 1818. [*See also* Indore.] DORANNE JACOBSON

AHL-I HADIS (Wahhabis). Much controversy was generated among Indian Muslims in the late nineteenth century over the applicability of the term *Wahhabi* to the followers of Sir Sayyid Ahmad Khan. [*See* Ahmad Khan, Sir Sayyid.] The term was earlier used derisively for the followers of the fundamentalist Arabian reformer Muhammad bin Abdul Wahhab (1703–1792), some of whose puritanical actions after the occupation of Mecca and Medina had created misgivings in the Muslim world. In India, some Hanafi Muslims denounced Sayyid Ahmad's followers as *ghair muqallid* ("nonconformist") and for considering British India a *daru'l harb* ("abode of war"), while many British officers considered them potential rebels. Both these groups posited a link between the Arabian and Indian reform movements and therefore dubbed the Indian reformists Wahhabis. They did so with the ulterior motives of sharpening sectarian differences and governmental suspicion against Sayyid Ahmad's adherents. The latter defended themselves on both counts, rather apologetically. More justifiably, they argued that *Wahhabi* was a misnomer and had become a term of religio-political abuse. They called themselves Muwahhidin ("unitarians") and later, Ahl-i Hadis ("people of tradition"). They petitioned the government to be called Ahl-i Hadis, not Wahhabis. The change was adopted in official usage in 1886, but in common parlance the term *Wahhabi* continued.

[*See also* Islam.]

Qeyamuddin Ahmad, *The Wahhabi Movement in India* (1966). W. W. Hunter, *The Indian Musalmans* (1871).

QEYAMUDDIN AHMAD

AHMAD, AHMUADZAM SHAH (c. 1836–1917), first sultan of Pahang (1882–1914), then a province of old Johor. A strong and resourceful leader, Ahmad possessed the "softness of voice" and refined manners that the Malay appear to value in their leaders. In 1863, after a six-year civil war, he became *bendahara* (chief minister) of Pahang and sought to consolidate the independence of Pahang from Johor; in 1882 he assumed the title of sultan and established a court on the old Johor model. He reluctantly accepted a British resident (a so-called adviser) in 1888 and supported him, with little enthusiasm, in the revolt that followed (1891–1895). When convinced of British determination, however, he adapted ably to the colonial presence.

[*See also* Bendahara; Johor; Pahang; *and* Pahang War.]

W. Linehan, "A History of Pahang," *Journal of the Malaysian Branch of the Royal Asiatic Society* 14 (1936): 1–256. A. C. Milner, *Kerajaan: Malay Political Culture on the Eve of Colonial Rule* (1982). A. C. MILNER

AHMADABAD (Ahmedabad), principal city (1981 population 2,515,195) of Gujarat, India. Guided by the Sufi saint Shaikh Kattu Ganj-Baksh, Sultan Ahmad Shah founded the city in 1411 as a new capital. He and his descendants, especially his grandson Mahmud Begara, sponsored an Indo-Saracenic architecture of great beauty, with significance for architectural development throughout India. [*See also* Architecture: South Asian Architecture.]

A crosslands linking India's west coast with the interior, Ahmadabad attracted Jain and Vaishnavite Hindu merchants, often organized into guilds *(mahajans),* who gave direction to the city under the independent Sultanate of Gujarat (1411–1572); Mughal rule (1572–1758); joint Mughal-Maratha administration (1758–1818); and thereafter British rule. Long famous for handmade cotton and silk cloth often interwoven with filaments of precious metals, after the mid-nineteenth century Ahmadabad became India's second largest center of industrialized textile production after Bombay, through the investments of local businessmen.

From 1915 to 1930 Mohandas Gandhi made Ahmadabad his headquarters, helped found the powerful Ahmadabad Textile Labour Association, inspired a nationalist political cadre directed by Sardar Patel, and promoted associations for social reform. In 1960 Ahmadabad became the temporary capital of Gujarat state until 1970, when the new city of Gandhinagar was built seventeen miles away. Since 1969 the rapidly expanding city of Ahmadabad has experienced some of India's most severe urban riots.

[*See also* Gujarat; Gandhi, Mohandas Karamchand; Patel, Sardar Vallabhbhai; *and* Khadi.]

Kenneth L. Gillion, *Ahmedabad: A Study in Indian Urban History* (1968). M. F. Lokhandwala, trans., *A Persian History of Gujarat* (1965). Howard Spodek, *Ahmedabad: Life of a City in India (A Film Guide)* (1983).

HOWARD SPODEK

AHMADIYYA. Founded by Ghulam Ahmad of Qadiyan (1839–1908) in the Punjab, India, this sect created a religious dilemma for Muslims in South Asia. At first, even the "orthodox" considered Ghulam Ahmad's preaching an appropriate response to missionizing by Christians and Arya Samajis in the Punjab. After he claimed to be the messiah *(masih)*, the expected one *(mahdi)*, Jesus, and an incarnation of Krishna, however, most Muslims decided that the movement was heretical. Riots against Ahmadis occurred in Lahore in 1953. Later, at the urging of their Saudi financial patrons, the government of Pakistan declared them a "religious minority" and revoked its previous classification of them as Muslims. Despite that, Ahmadis remain some of Islam's most effective missionaries, especially in Europe and East Africa.

[*See also* Islam *and* Arya Samaj.]

A. Ahmad, *An Intellectual History of Islam in India* (1969). W. C. Smith, *Islam in Modern History* (1957).

GREGORY C. KOZLOWSKI

AHMAD KHAN, SIR SAYYID (1817–1898), educational, political, and religious reformer and the major formulator of the modern concept of communal identity among Muslims of India in the latter half of the nineteenth century. As founder of the Muhammadan Anglo-Oriental College at Aligarh and leader of the Aligarh movement, he atttempted to bring about a synthesis between the culture of the Mughal empire and the institutions of British rule.

Son of an official of the Mughal court, by then a protectorate of the British East India Company, Sayyid Ahmad was raised in the religious and cultural style of the Mughal literati and scholastic tradition associated with Shah Wali Ullah. In defiance of the wishes of his elders he took service as a subordinate official of the British regime in 1836 and spent the next forty years of his life posted in a series of small North Indian towns. At the same time he was editor of one of the first Urdu newspapers and author of religious and historical works. During the 1857 Revolt he remained a staunch supporter of British rule, but afterwards published a sharp critique of British policies and attitudes. [*See also* Mutiny, Indian.]

During the 1860s Sayyid Ahmad became an active public leader, journalist, and orator, as well as the founder of a series of schools and associations—all aimed at reconciling British and Indian ideologies and institutions. He established a Scientific Society in 1864, which moved to Aligarh the following year, dedicated to translating European historical and scientific works into Urdu and publishing older works of Indian and Islamic scholarship.

Following a trip to England in 1869/1870 Sayyid Ahmad determined to establish an autonomous Indian Muslim educational system, which would prepare a new intellectual leadership grounded in Western knowledge as well as in a reformed Islam. Although his religious liberalism inspired intense opposition, the Muhammadan Anglo-Oriental College, Aligarh, founded in 1875, became a center and symbol of a new concept of communal unity for Indian Muslims.

In 1887 "Sir Syed," as he came to be known, led a movement of opposition to the Indian National Congress, arguing that its program was inconsistent with the nature of Indian society and the interests of Muslims. After his death these opinions were deemed a charter for separatist Muslim politics, although Sayyid Ahmad represented more the imperial ideologies of the Mughals and British than the religious nationalism of the movement to create the state of Pakistan.

[*See also* Hali, Altaf Husain; Indian National Congress; *and* All-India Muslim League.]

David Lelyveld, *Aligarh's First Generation: Muslim Solidarity in British India* (1978). Christian W. Troll, *Sayyid Ahmad Khan: A Reinterpretation of Muslim Theology* (1978).

DAVID LELYVELD

AHMADNAGAR, a fort and city in the northwestern Deccan Plateau of peninsular India. It was named after its founder, Malik Ahmad, a governor of the Bahmani dynasty who carved out the independent Nizam Shahi sultanate in the late fifteenth century when the Bahmani kingdom was disintegrating. This kingdom ruled over much of the Marathi-speaking, or northwestern, Deccan from 1460 to 1600. In the latter date pressure exerted by the Mughal emperor Akbar resulted in the dynasty's near extinction, despite a valiant defense by its dowager queen, Chand Bibi; and although the able *vazir* Malik Ambar rescued the kingdom for a while longer, it was finally extinguished by Mughal arms in 1633.

[*See also* Bahmani Dynasty *and* Deccan.]

H. K. Sherwani and P. M. Joshi, eds., *History of Medieval Deccan (1295–1724)* (1974). Radhey Shyam, *The Kingdom of Ahmadnagar* (1966).

RICHARD M. EATON

AHMAD SHAH ABDALI. *See* Durannis.

AHMAD SHAHI DYNASTY, independent sultanate of Gujarat, India, established in 1396. It is named aftter its second ruler, who did much to consolidate the new state as well as the position of Islam in Gujarat. The later Ahmad Shahis were in frequent conflict with Portuguese, Mughal, and other powers until Gujarat finally was incorporated into the Mughal empire in 1593. Vigorous patrons of architecture, the Ahmad Shahis established several new capital cities; Ahmadabad, the first and most famous, today remains a thriving commercial center.

[*See also* Ahmadabad; Gujarat; *and* Architecture: South Asian Architecture.]

CATHERINE B. ASHER

AHMAD SHAH QAJAR. *See* Qajar, Ahmad Shah.

AHOM. The name *Ahom* refers to a group of lowland Assamese people residing in northeastern India, who until 1931 were formally recognized as a separate subcaste in the Indian census. The number of people who may at present claim Ahom descent is probably between 400,000 and 500,000. Most live in the upper parts of the Brahmaputra Valley in the Assamese districts of Sibsagar and Dibrugarh.

At the beginning of the thirteenth century the ancestors of the Ahom migrated from the Hukong Valley (located at the upper reaches of the Chindwin River, in present-day Burma) across the Patkai Range to a location in the upper Brahmaputra Valley. At the time of their migration they called themselves Tai people. They spoke a Tai language and it appears almost certain that they had already adopted a script, after the model of Mon or early Burmese writing. Non-Tai peoples called them Ahom, a term related to the Old Burmese Rham and tangentially to words such as Shan and Siam.

According to their own chronicles *(buranjis)* the Ahom arrived in 1228 in the Brahmaputra Valley, under the leadership of Sue Ka Pha, where they subdued the indigenous Morans and Borahis. Until the beginning of the sixteenth century the Ahom kingdom remained relatively obscure in the region's history with the Ahoms occupying the rather isolated area south of the Brahmaputra and east of the Dikho River. Further west in the valley the Koch, Kachari, and Jaintia kingdoms had absorbed more of the traditions of the old Kamarupa civilization. It was not until the long reign of Sue Hung Mueng (1497–1539) that the Ahom realm was greatly expanded, chiefly by incursions into Chutiya and Kachari territory. This expansion coincided with a growing influence of Brahmanism and Vaishnavism in Ahom society. During the sixteenth century Ahom power had grown to such an extent that it began to rival that of the Koch. In 1563 the Koch seemed to have decisively won supremacy when they took the Ahom capital and exacted tribute. Not long afterward, however, the Ahom reasserted independence.

The seventeenth century was the most dramatic in Ahom political history. The kingdom expanded to encompass most of the Brahmaputra Valley. It is during this century that the name *Ahom* (in indigenous literature *Acama* or *Asama*) was first used to denote the whole region—hence the present-day name *Assam*. During the second half of the seventeenth century the Ahom rulers boldly encroached upon territory that had traditionally been under Muslim control, and as a result the redoutable Mir Jumla marched deep into Ahom country. In 1662 Mir Jumla took Garhgaon, the Ahom capital, and the Ahom had to sue for peace. Five years later the Ahom refused to continue sending tribute and a new war broke out. Eventually the Ahom succeeded in throwing off Muslim domination. [*See* Mir Jumla.]

The eighteenth century was characterized by factionalism in the court, increasing dissent, and eventually, during the latter half of the century, a series of full-scale rebellions. The inability of the Ahom rulers to restore unity precipitated the Burmese invasion from 1819 to 1824, which in its turn led to the consolidation of British rule and the eclipse of Ahom leadership. During the days of great power the Ahom had adopted the indigenous lingua franca and Hindu religion. Tai-Ahom language and culture were gradually superseded and only in a few isolated Ahom villages are Tai customs still practiced. Through the efforts of indigenous organizations such as the Tai Historical and Cultural Society of Assam, a knowledge of some aspects of the Ahom past is preserved.

[*See also* Assam; Tai Peoples; *and* Burma.]

BAAS TERWIEL

AHRAR PARTY. A Muslim political party, the All-India Majlis-i Ahrar-i Islam was founded at Amritsar in 1931. Active primarily in the Punjab and

United Province districts near Delhi, its membership included former Khilafatists and ex-Congressites. Lacking a consistent intellectual approach, the Ahrar's history is a catalogue of the causes it supported. After 1940 the movement split, with one group under Habibur Rahman and Maulana Hussain Ahmad Madni rejoining the Congress, and a second, under Afzul Haq, supporting the Muslim League.

[*See also* Indian National Congress; Khilafat Movement; All-India Muslim League; Punjab; *and* Uttar Pradesh.]

Peter Hardy, *The Muslims of British India* (1972). Wilfred Cantwell Smith, *Modern Islam in India* (1946).

GREGORY C. KOZLOWSKI

AHURA MAZDA ("lord wisdom"), later called Ohrmazd, is the name of the monotheistic deity in Zoroastrianism. Ahura Mazda was conceived by Zoroaster as being totally good and the creator of all else that is good. Through Spenta Mainyu, the "holy spirit," he evoked six Holy Immortals called Amesha Spentas. Each Amesha Spenta is connected with a part of creation. The Amesha Spentas and their creations are Vohu Manah, or "good mind" (cattle); Asha, or "truth" (fire); Armaiti, or "devotion" (earth); Khshathra, or "power" (metal); Haurvatat, or "health" (water); Ameretat, or "life" (plants).

Pitted against Ahura Mazda is Angra Mainyu, the "hostile spirit," later called Ahriman. Fundamentally, he represents falsehood; he attacks the creation of Ahura Mazda, although in the end Ahura Mazda will destroy him. Because of the existence of Angra Mainyu, Zoroastrianism may be called a theological monotheism with dualist ethical overtones.

[*See also* Zoroastrianism.]

Mary Boyce, *A History of Zoroastrianism* (1975), vol. 1.

LUCIANNE C. BULLIET

AIDIT, DIPA NUSANTARA (1923–1965), Indonesian Communist leader and Marxist theorist. Aidit joined the illegal Indonesian Communist Party (Partai Komunis Indonesia, or PKI) in 1943 and was among the youth leaders selected by the Japanese for political training. At independence (1945) he was active in the nationalist youth movement in Jakarta and rose in the party hierarchy, becoming a member of the PKI Central Committee (1947) and a full member of the Politburo (1948). After the Madiun Affair he fled to China and Vietnam but returned in mid-1950, becoming Party secretary in January 1951.

Aidit argued that Indonesia's national revolution had not been won and that Indonesia, though nominally independent, remained a semicolonial, semifeudal society. He maintained, however, that just as the superstructure reflected the base, so the Indonesian state reflected both "antipeople" and "propeople" elements of Indonesian society. He did not advocate the violent overthrow of the state, therefore, but rather an expansion of the propeople aspect over the antipeople aspect. To achieve this he gave the PKI a high public profile and emphasized the inculcation of Marxist values into all levels of society, especially through mass action and mass organization. His analysis led the PKI to participate in the parliamentary system up to 1957 and to support Sukarno's program of Guided Democracy. Aidit himself became minister without portfolio in 1961.

He stressed the need for a united national front of workers, peasants, petty bourgeoisie, and national bourgeoisie under proletarian leadership in order to bring about a people's democratic government, but he has been accused of identifying the front's components on the basis of political orientation rather than class. He stayed largely aloof from the Sino-Soviet split and insisted on the sole right of Marxists working within Indonesia to decide correct communist practice there.

After the Gestapu coup in October 1965, Aidit went underground in Central Java but was captured and shot the following month.

[*See also* Indonesia, Republic of; Partai Komunis Indonesia; Madiun; Sukarno; *and* Gestapu.]

Dipa Nusantara Aidit, *Indonesian Society and the Indonesian Revolution* (1958) and *The Indonesian Revolution and the Immediate Tasks of the Communist Party of Indonesia* (1965). Donald Hindley, *The Communist Party of Indonesia, 1951–1963* (1965). Rex Mortimer, *Indonesian Communism under Sukarno* (1974).

ROBERT B. CRIBB

AINU, the indigenous people of northern Japan and much of the Okhotsk Sea basin. The Ainu now live only on the island of Hokkaido, with the exception of a few hundred residents of Sakhalin Island. The Ainu of northeastern Honshu, Kamchatka, and the Amur basin have died out, and those of Sakhalin and the Kurile Islands were mostly relocated to Hokkaido by the Japanese government. Although there are about 24,000 people in Hokkaido who identify themselves as Ainu, all but about 200 of them are of mixed ancestry. The Ainu population now is about the same as in 1804, the first year a survey was conducted, but it is higher than the figure of 17,000 given in 1902. The assimilation of the Ainu into the Japanese population is the product of both Japanese governmental policies dating from the Tokugawa period and efforts of the Ainu themselves, who see assimilation as a survival strategy in an aggressively homogeneous Japanese society. In recent years, however, attempts have been made to preserve traditional Ainu language and culture.

The Ainu people's origins are unclear. Their relatively light skin and abundance of body hair have led to speculation that they may ultimately be derived from a Caucasoid people, but there is little conclusive evidence. What connection, if any, the Ainu may have had with the Emishi, Ezo, or other northern peoples mentioned in early Japanese writings is still a matter of debate. There is little doubt, however, that the ancestors of the Ainu did live in northeastern Honshu, as the abundance of Ainu place names there attests.

The Ainu language is not, as far as can be definitely ascertained, related to the languages spoken by neighboring peoples, including Japanese. The few native speakers of Ainu are dying out rapidly. Of the three major dialect groups (Hokkaido, Sakhalin, and Kurile), only the former two survive. The dialects are mutually unintelligible. Ainu has no written language, but there is a rich folklore, of which the epic poetry *(yukar)* is best known.

The Ainu religion was animistic and centered on the belief that spiritual forces *(kamuy)* control the visible universe. Traditional Ainu society was based on fishing, hunting, and gathering. The people lived in small groups, called *kotan,* of a few households each. Although regional federations of Ainu existed in pre-Meiji times, there was never anything like an Ainu state. That lack of organization made the Ainu vulnerable to the encroachments of the Japanese, who first began to occupy southern Hokkaido during the twelfth century. The Ainu employ a bilineal descent system, in which males trace descent through patrilineages and females through matrilineages.

John Batchelor, *Ainu Life and Lore* (reprint, 1971). M. Inez Hilger, *Together with the Ainu* (1971). Shin'ichirō Takakura, "The Ainu of Northern Japan: A Study in Conquest and Acculturation," *Transactions of the Philosophical Society of Philadelphia* 50.4 (1960).

David L. Howell

AIRLANGGA, Javanese monarch (r. 1016–1045), son of a Javanese princess whose grandmother Sindok (929–947) had married the Balinese prince Dharmadayana and ruled over central and eastern Java. When the Sumatra-based Srivijaya maritime empire raided his father-in-law's Javanese court in 1006, Airlangga escaped with his faithful servant Narottama and took refuge among a community of hermits at Wonogiri. In 1016 he left his hiding place to claim his father's authority over a small portion of eastern Java and Bali. When the South Indian Cholas shattered Srivijaya's hegemony in their 1024–1025 raid in the Melaka (Malacca) Strait region, Airlangga began to restructure a network of alliances among regionally based Javanese elites.

Airlangga's reign set the standard for monarchs in Java. He is celebrated in Javanese history for having reunified central and eastern Java, although historians believe that his direct administrative control was limited to the Brantas River basin. A semiautonomous, regionally based elite continued to hold the real power in Java, but Airlangga is believed to have begun a shift of administrative authority away from these regions to his court.

One source of Airlangga's power was his development of the Brantas River delta. Airlangga supervised the construction of a water-management network that brought the annual flooding in the delta under control. This made cultivation of the Brantas River delta possible, and new settlements of peasants began to emerge. Furthermore, the project provided a deep-water harbor in the Surabaya region that attracted international shipping. The Brantas River delta's surplus rice became an important export commodity that was exchanged for spices from the eastern Indonesian archipelago.

Airlangga's reign also had an important impact on Javanese culture. He modified the style of Javanese statecraft by emphasizing localized Javanese culture rather than patronizing unadulterated Indian cultural forms, as had been the case during the previous era of central Java sovereignty. The result was a syncretic artistic and literary tradition that became the model for future Javanese cultural development. The most famous literary accomplishment of Airlangga's reign, composed in Airlangga's honor by the court poet Mpu Kanwa, was the *Arjunavivaha (The Marriage of Arjuna),* an allegorical representation of Airlangga's own life based on the *Mahabharata*'s story of the ascetic Arjuna. Airlangga himself claimed to be an incarnation of Vishnu, Arjuna's charioteer in the *Mahabharata* epic, and his tomb at Belahan contained a portrait statue depicting him as Vishnu riding on the man-eagle Garuda. His various inscriptions record his patronage of both Vishnu and Shiva, as well as of a Tantric Mahayana Buddhist cult that incorporated local spirit and ancestor worship into a secret sect to which only the highest elite of the realm belonged.

Four years before his death in 1049, Airlangga retired from the throne to become an ascetic and divided his kingdom between his two sons. One ruled the region west of the Brantas River, which became known as Kediri; the second was bestowed with the eastern region, known as Janggala, which was the base from which the later Singosari-based monarchs reunited central and eastern Java in the thirteenth century.

[*See also* Java; Srivijaya; *and* Singosari.]

Kenneth R. Hall, *Maritime Trade and State Development in Early Southeast Asia* (1985). Claire Holt, *Art in Indonesia: Continuity and Change* (1965).

KENNETH R. HALL

AIZAWA INCIDENT, the assassination, in 1935, of Nagata Tetsuzan, a high-ranking officer in the Japanese army, that precipitated the February Twenty-sixth Incident of the following year.The incident was the climax of a feud between two factions in the Japanese army that competed for power. One of these, the Kōdōha (Imperial Way faction), was connected with General Araki Sadao and was supported by radical young officers. This faction suffered a serious blow when Araki was forced to resign in January 1934. The other faction, nicknamed Tōseiha (Control faction), led by Major General Nagata Tetsuzan and others, assumed control and tried to phase out the members of the former faction from positions of power.

In July 1935 the Kōdōha suffered another blow when Araki's closest friend, General Mazaki Jinzaburō, was dismissed from his post as inspector general of military education. Lieutenant Colonel Aizawa Saburō, a member of the Kōdōha, protested the dismissal to Nagata Tetsuzan, director of the Military Affairs Bureau in the Ministry of the Army. In retaliation Aizawa was transferred to Taiwan.

On 12 August 1935 Aizawa walked into Nagata's office and killed him with his sword. He later claimed that he was merely performing his duty of killing a traitor. Aizawa's public court martial, which opened in January 1936, stirred much excitement in the ranks of the army.

Apprehensive about the repercussions, the army ordered the transfer of the Tokyo-based First Division to Manchuria. This order triggered the February Twenty-sixth Incident, in which young officers seized the center of Tokyo for four days and assassinated prominent political and military figures.

After the rebellion was suppressed a second, secret court martial sentenced Aizawa to death. He was executed on 3 July 1936.

[*See also* February Twenty-sixth Incident.]

Hugh Byas, *Government by Assassination* (1943). Ben-Ami Shillony, *Revolt in Japan* (1973). Richard Storry, *The Double Patriots* (1957).

BEN-AMI SHILLONY

AIZAWA YASUSHI (1781–1863), a prominent Japanese Confucian scholar and educator of the Later Mito school, which arose in the last half of the Tokugawa period. Aizawa Yasushi was born to a lower-ranking samurai family in Mito domain, studied under Fujita Yūkoku, and assumed research and teaching posts in the domain's Historiographical Institute in the first two decades of the nineteenth century. He was tutor to Tokugawa Nariaki, who wielded power in Mito from 1829 to 1860, and counseled the *bakufu* on foreign policy during the 1840s and 50s. Aizawa was a domain administrator in the 1830s and was a member of the Mito reform faction led by Nariaki. In 1831 Aizawa was named head of the Historiographical Institute, and in 1841 he became head of the Mito domain school, the Kōdōkan. By this time he was receiving an annual stipend of 350 *koku* (measures of rice), and in the 1850s, 450 *koku*. Thus he attained upper-class samurai status, becoming a case of upward social mobility in a supposedly "fixed" social system due to his superior scholastic abilities and participation in reform politics.

Aizawa wrote his most famous and important work, *New Theses,* in 1825. In it he advocated "revering the emperor and expelling the barbarians," maintaining the *bakufu's* policy of "national isolation," and utilizing the imperial court in Kyoto to reinforce the *bakufu's* political authority. By the 1860s, however, he had abandoned many of his former ideas and was arguing for foreign trade and diplomatic intercourse. Even so, he continued to support the *bakufu* against those who sought to overthrow it and return power to the imperial court.

[*See also* Fujita Yūkoku; Tokugawa Nariaki; *and* Tokugawa Period.]

H. D. Harootunian, *Toward Restoration* (1970).

BOB TADASHI WAKABAYASHI

AIZU, a feudal domain of Tokugawa-era Japan. For most of its existence, Aizu (located in what is now Fukushima Prefecture) would not have been considered one of Tokugawa Japan's more noteworthy daimyo domains. It attracted national attention on just two occasions, each time through the activities of its daimyo. The first of these was Hoshina Masayuki (1611–1672), half brother to the third Tokugawa shogun. In 1651, on his brother's death, Masayuki was to become shogunal guardian and hence *de facto* ruler of Japan. The second was Matsudaira Katamori (1835–1893). Like other members of the *kōbu-gattai* faction, whose advocates favored a union of civil and military authority, Katamori took advantage of the political turmoil of the 1860s to embark upon a career in national politics. For a time he was remarkably successful. He served as "protector" of Kyoto from 1862 to 1867 and cooperated with Satsuma in the defeat of Chōshū insurgents in 1864. Such success, however, was short-lived. By the autumn of 1868, branded an enemy of the court, he was obliged to surrender his castle in Aizu to a besieging army of thirty thousand men. Katamori spent the remainder of his life in comfortable obscurity, but his domain and his vassals were not so fortunate. The domain was effectively abolished, and his vassals were condemned to extremes of poverty and hardship.

HAROLD BOLITHO

AJANTA, located in Maharashtra, India, is noted for more than thirty rock-cut Hinayana and Mahayana Buddhist temples and monasteries of the mid-second century BCE to the late fifth century CE. Hinayana excavations (mid-second to first century BCE) included astylar residence halls and two worship halls (caves 9 and 10), where pillars mark apsidal processional paths around monolithic stupas. Mahayana excavations began around 475 and ended by 500, patronized by and dedicated to feudatories of the Vakatakas and Asmakas, mentioned in inscriptions in caves 16, 17, and 26. Two apsidal, vaulted worship halls, lit by arched facade windows, house monolithic stupas: in cave 19 a standing Buddha is carved on the stupa; in cave 26 the image is seated. In the elaborately pillared residence halls, colossal, seated, "teaching-attitude" *(dharmacakramudra)* Buddha images were carved in rear-wall shrines. Painting (best preserved in caves 1, 2, 16,

FIGURE 1. *Veranda of Rock-cut Temple, Ajanta.*

and 17) originally covered most surfaces with Jataka (birth-story) scenes, Buddha images, and decorative motifs.

[*See also* Painting: South Asian Painting.]

J. Fergusson and J. Burgess, *Cave Temples of India* (1880). G. Yazdani, *Ajanta,* 4 vols. (1931–1955).

GERI HOCKFIELD MALANDRA

AJIVIKA SECT, prominent school of nonorthodox wandering ascetics *(shramanas)* established in the Ganges basin during the time of Shakyamuni Buddha. The teachings of the founder, Gosala Maskariputra, combined atheism, belief in fully determined fate *(niyati),* and a severe ascetic ideal that prescribed complete nudity. Although an Ajivika community existed in India until at least 1300, none of their texts has survived.

A. L. Basham, *History and Doctrines of the Ajivikas* (1951).

TODD THORNTON LEWIS

AJMER. Although archaeological evidence exists for much earlier occupation of this Rajasthani city, local legend identifies a Chauhan Rajput prince, Aja, as its founder. The etymology for the place was Aja's name joined with the Sanskrit word for mountain, *meru.* The city has been fought over by the Delhi sultans, the Rajputs, the Mughals, the Marathas, and the British. Since the thirteenth century the city has been famous for the tomb of Shaikh Muinuddin Chishti (d. 1236). The emperors Akbar and Jahangir showed special respect for this saint, made frequent pilgrimages to his tomb, and showered wealth on his descendants. Their patronage helped to make the town one of the most popular shrine centers in India, attracting devotees from as far away as Afghanistan and Bengal.

[*See also* Rajasthan.]

Rajasthan District Gazetteers (1966).

GREGORY C. KOZLOWSKI

AKALI DAL, Indian political party founded to promote Sikh interests in 1920. Initially formed to assist in retoring control of *gurdwaras* (Sikh temples) to the Sikh community, it assumed the role of a full-fledged political party in 1937. Following independence in 1947 it campaigned for Punjabi Suba (statehood for Punjabi-speaking people), eventually succeeding in 1966. During the same period it had contested control of the Punjab with Congress, significantly aided by its firm hold on the *gurdwaras.* Previously dominated by urban Sikhs, the Akali Dal now draws its principal support from rural landowners of the Jat caste.

[*See also* Sikhism; Punjab; *and* Jats.]

Baldev Raj Nayar, *Minority Politics in the Punjab* (1966). Dalip Singh, *Dynamics of Punjab Politics* (1981).

W. H. MCLEOD

AKBAR (1542–1605), the third Mughal emperor, ruled a major part of India from 1556 to 1605. Born to royal parents constantly in flight, Akbar inherited his father Humayun's throne when he was fourteen. His fifty-year reign marked major breaks in several spheres. Although he inherited a small territory, Akbar expanded it into a vast empire comprising all of North India, eastern Afghanistan, western and much of eastern India, and the northern and middle parts of the peninsula.

Akbar put this empire on an administrative footing that was to sustain it until the mid-eighteenth century. The basic institution of this administrative structure was the *mansabdari* system. Akbar integrated leaders of the indigenous ruling class, the Rajputs, into the imperial framework. In the preceding three centuries Rajputs and the imperial rulers at Delhi had been at loggerheads, neither side gaining a decisive victory over the other. Akbar resolved the conflict with generous treatment of those who submitted to his authority and ruthless treatment of the few who did not. Akbar had inherited a nobility almost equally divided between Mughals and Persians. Over the next quarter century he gradually altered this composition by inducting at the highest echelon diverse elements such as Afghans, Indian Muslims, and Hindus so that by 1580 every group had been reduced to a small minority in no position to dominate over others or the emperor. In this context Akbar's political and religious philosophy of mutual tolerance ("peace with all") found ready acceptance. The diverse yet well-balanced elements in the nobility, along with the efficient administrative apparatus, also gave successive Mughal emperors a much greater degree of centralized power than any other dynasty in Indian history.

Akbar also perfected a mechanism of revenue administration that was to last until the end of the empire. After several experiments, the "Ten-Year Settlement" was formulated. Land was divided into four categories according to the period for which it lay uncultivated, the ideal being uninterrupted cultivation. Differential rates of revenue were imposed on these categories with an increase in the rate as land moved from a lower to a higher category. Average yields of each field over the preceding ten years were assessed, as were average prices of crops in neighboring markets over the same period. Revenue was fixed at between one-fourth and one-half of the gross produce, depending on the region and the crop; this share was then converted into market prices. If revenue was collected in kind, this was also converted into cash through sale. Rates were subject to revision. This tax system was essentially regressive, for it imposed the same rates on all cultivators without respect to their resources.

Several Jesuit missionaries visited Akbar's court in the hope of converting him to Christianity. Akbar sought to harmonize different religious tenets, however, in the *din-i Ilahi* ("religion of God"). Akbar's long reign is as remarkable for intellectual and cultural achievements as it is for political and administrative innovation. Although he was illiterate, Akbar took keen interest in history writing, translation of Hindu scriptures into Persian, painting, and architecture. New schools were established in each of these areas mainly by blending Indian and Persian culture.

[*See also* Mughal Empire; Delhi; Agra; Humayun; Mansabdari System; *and* Din-i Ilahi.]

Bamber Gascoigne, *The Great Moghuls* (1971). I. A. Khan, "The Nobility under Akbar and the Development of His Religious Policy," *Journal of the Royal Asiatic Society* (1968): 29–36. HARBANS MUKHIA

AKECHI MITSUHIDE (d. 1582), a powerful daimyo (feudal lord) of the late Sengoku period of Japanese history, remembered for assassinating Oda Nobunaga in 1582. Born of humble and obscure origins, Akechi Mitsuhide fought in the service of Asakura Yoshikage and then in 1568 pledged his loyalty to Oda Nobunaga. He rose to great prominence within the Oda vassal band and served as Nobunaga's political agent in Kyoto in the early 1570s, representing his lord's interests to the emperor and aristocrats. He accumulated a long list of battlefield exploits: victories in Wakasa and Echizen in 1570; at Sakamoto in Omi the next year; in Yamato and Mino in 1573; in Kii and Tamba, Settsu, and Tamba again in the late 1570s, when he was granted all of Tamba in fief, a holding nearly equal to that of Nobunaga's other leading generals, Toyotomi Hideyoshi in Harima and Shibata Katsuie in Echizen.

In 1582, however, Mitsuhide killed the lord he had served so well. In the spring of that year Nobunaga stopped at the Honnōji in Kyoto for several days while preparing to lead troops into western Japan, where his general Hideyoshi had become bogged down in fighting against the Mōri family. Mitsuhide entered Kyoto at dawn on 21 June and immediately attacked Nobunaga at the Honnōji. Consumed in the fire that destroyed the temple, Nobunaga's body was never recovered. When Hideyoshi received the news, he immediately returned by forced march to Kyoto, where he took revenge on Mitsuhide, displaying his severed head in the ashes of Honnōji temple.

Several explanations have been advanced to account for Mitsuhide's actions. Some historians have seen him as the quintessential Sengoku warrior, caught up in the vortex of intrigue and betrayal that so characterized the age; others portray Mitsuhide as paranoid, harboring a bitterness against Nobunaga for alleged past criticisms and fearful that Nobunaga was about to demote him. There exists no conclusive evidence to promote one explanation over the others, but it is hard to ignore the role of pure ambition. Mitsuhide was close to the center of power, and a successful move against Nobunaga would have thrust him fully into the ranks of those who might aspire to national hegemony.

[*See also* Oda Nobunaga *and* Sengoku Period.]

JAMES L. MCCLAIN

AKHBARI, a school of Shi'ite jurisprudence that stresses narrow and literal reliance on the traditions *(akhbar)* of the prophet Muhammad and the twelve imams as a source of legal ordinances *(ahkam)* equal in authority to the Qur'an itself. A traditionalist current of jurisprudence existed in the lifetimes of the imams themselves, but it was not until the twelfth century that the position of the traditionalists crystallized and the designation *Akhbari* is first encountered. The Akhbaris remained generally subordinate to their Usuli rivals until Mulla Muhammad Amin Astarabadi (d. 1624) gave luster to their doctrine and caused it to predominate in Shi'ite circles—both in Iran and the Arab lands—during most of the seventeenth and eighteenth centuries. The Akhbaris' supremacy was brought to an end largely by the efforts of the great Usuli scholar, Agha Muhammad Baqir Bihbahani; their defeat enabled the scholars of Shi'ite Islam to be more than sifters of tradition and to assume a directive role in society. After Bihbahani, the Akhbari school survived only in Shi'ite communities in Khuzistan and on the eastern shore of the Persian Gulf.

[*See also* Bihbahani, Muhammad Baqir *and* Usuli.]

Etan Kohlberg, "Akbārīya," in *Encyclopaedia Iranica* (1982–). HAMID ALGAR

AKIHITO (b. 1933), crown prince of Japan, the eldest son of Emperor Hirohito and Empress Nagako. Akihito's first title was Prince Tsugu. During the Pacific War he was evacuated to the mountain resort of Karuizawa. After the war, while at the Gakushūin High School, he studied English with an American tutor, Elizabeth G. Vining, who had a strong influence on his education. In 1952, at the ceremony of his coming of age, he was designated crown prince. He then attended Gakushūin University, where he majored in political science.

Brought up in the postwar liberal era, Akihito symbolizes the democratization of the imperial house. This was highlighted on 10 April 1959, when he married a commoner, Shōda Michiko, the daughter of a businessman. They have three children: Prince Hiro (Naruhito, b. 1960), Prince Aya (Fumihito, b. 1965), and Princess Nori (Sayako, b. 1969). He has often gone abroad with his wife on state visits. (In 1975, while on a visit to Okinawa, he narrowly escaped death when a molotov cocktail was thrown at him.) Because of his father's unusually long reign, Akihito has been crown prince longer than any of his predecessors.

[*See also* Hirohito.]

Elizabeth G. Vining, *Windows for the Crown Prince* (1952). BEN-AMI SHILLONY

AKKOYUNLU, a federation of Turkmen tribes that arose in eastern Anatolia in the late fourteenth century and at their height, around 1470, controlled much of Persia. The Akkoyunlu, or "White Sheep," were led by the Bayandur clan of the Ghuzz (Oghuz), which had been living in the area for some time but did not achieve prominence until after the breakup of the Ilkhanid empire in 1336. The Akkoyunlu are usually regarded as a Sunni dynasty, although they had close links with the Shi'ite Safavid family.

The dynasty was founded by Kara Usman in the Diyarbakir area. His rule was guaranteed by Timur after he participated in Timur's defeat of the Ottoman Bayazid I at Ankara in 1402. Kara Usman ruled for thirty-two years and transformed the Akkoyunlu from a tribal clan of little significance to a large principality impinging on the domains of its neighbors, the Karakoyunlu, or "Black Sheep" Turkmens, as well as the major powers of the day, the Ottomans, the Mamluks, and the Timurids.

Uzun Hasan (r. 1457–1478), the grandson of Kara Usman, was the most outstanding Akkoyunlu leader. He transformed them into a major Islamic power, extending from Anatolia to Khurasan, Fars, Kerman, and the Persian Gulf. He defeated his chief rival and leader of the Karakoyunlu, Jahanshah, in 1467, ending that dynasty, and Abu Sa'id the Timurid in 1469.

Uzun Hasan was active in international diplomacy, allying with Venice against the Ottomans, his enemy in the west. The Akkoyunlu had longstanding marriage ties with the Byzantine kings at Trebizond; there were also marriage ties to the Safavids. Uzun Hasan was decisively defeated by the Ottomans at Bashkent in 1473. His son and successor, Ya'qub (r. 1478–1490), promoted high Islamic culture and carried on an ostentatious court life at his capital, Tabriz, but the fortunes of the dynasty never recovered.

The succession crises typical of Turkish dynasties sapped the strength of the Akkoyunlu and facilitated the Safavid rise to power. The last ruler, Sultan Murad, was defeated by the Kizilbash supporters of Shah Ismail and relinquished Azerbaijan to the Safavids in 1501. Sultan Murad did, however, manage to hold on to some land in Iraq and Diyarbakir until 1508. While the power of the Safavids, like that of the Akkoyunlu, was based at first on Turkic tribesmen, and continuity between the two dynasties was ensured by the Tajik bureaucracy, the Safavids were able to unify Iran in a way the Akkoyunlu could not.

[*See also* Karakoyunlu; Kizilbash; Safavid Dynasty; Tabriz; *and* Uzun Hasan.]

Michel M. Mazzaoui, *The Origins of the Ṣafawids: Šīʿism, Ṣūfism, and the Ġulāt* (1972). John E. Woods, *The Aqquyunlu: Clan, Confederation, Empire* (1976).

LAWRENCE POTTER

AKŌ GISHI, better known as the Forty-Seven Loyal Retainers, a group of samurai retainers whose famous vendetta in 1702 is celebrated in Japanese puppet plays, theater, and television. Most accounts, in the interests of dramatic appeal, ignore or distort the historical facts and significance of this incident.

In the spring of 1701 Lord Asano of the Akō domain attacked and wounded (but failed to kill), Lord Kira inside the shogunal palace. Primary sources do not disclose his true motives; we know for sure only that he bore Kira a grudge for some insult. On that very day, and in a dictatorial fashion, Shogun Tsunayoshi ordered Asano to commit ritual suicide, confiscated his domain, and terminated his family line. But Tsunayoshi allowed Kira, who had fled his attacker, to go unpunished. In the eyes of Asano's old-fashioned samurai retainers, the verdict was unfair: "In a feud, both parties are to blame." Their code of honor demanded that Kira's cowardice be punished. (In 1627 the *bakufu* had punished the fleeing party in a similar case.) Moreover, their lord had been publicly humiliated as a samurai for having failed to kill Kira. They suggested that the *bakufu* reconsider its verdict, punish Kira, and thus eliminate their lord's disgrace, a disgrace they considered their own. Only when the *bakufu* failed to respond did they take the law into their own hands by attacking Kira's mansion and beheading him in the winter of 1702. After some debate, the *bakufu* allowed them all to commit ritual suicide.

The retainers acted out of a sense of samurai pride and asserted an old privilege of private redress of grievances. Such ideas could no longer be tolerated by the shogunate. The retainers fell victim to the demands of a new peaceful age: public law and order.

Donald Keene, trans., *Chūshingura* (1971).

BOB TADASHI WAKABAYASHI

AKSAI CHIN, ill-defined, high, barren plateau (with elevations from around 14,000 feet to more than 19,000 feet), between the Kunlun Mountains to the northeast and the Karakoram Range to the southwest. China regards the Aksai Chin (White Stone Desert) as part of its Xinjiang Uighur Autonomous Region, while India treats it as part of the administrative district of Ladakh in the state of Jammu and Kashmir. The legitimacy of India's claim to this area is also disputed by Pakistan. Sketchily surveyed by several British exploration parties, beginning with that of W. H. Johnson in 1865, the area was also crossed by a Chinese military mission under Li Yuanping between 1891 and 1892. Chinese troops entered the area in 1950 and 1951 and in 1956 to 1957 they built a road across it linking Tibet with its major settlements in western Xinjiang. Skirmishes with Indian patrols ensued and in 1962 there were large-scale hostilities at the close of which China was in possession of more than 10,000 square miles claimed by India.

[*See also* Kashmir.]

Frederick Drew, *The Jummoo and Kashmir Territories: A Geographical Account* (1875). Margaret W. Fisher, Leo E. Rose, and Robert A. Huttenback, *Himalayan Battleground: Sino-Indian Rivalry in Ladakh* (1963). Neville G. A. Maxwell, *India's China War* (1970).

JOSEPH E. SCHWARTZBERG

AKUSŌ. The two Sino-Japanese characters making up the word *akusō* mean "evil monk." *Aku* has the meaning of "powerful," as well as "evil." The term came into widespread use in Japanese diaries, chronicles, and other documents of the late Heian period (794–1185). The slackening authority of the imperial court during this period gave greater license to powerful Buddhist monasteries and at the same time presented them with the problem of regulating themselves and protecting their communities and landholdings. While most monks and nuns probably observed the rules of monastic life and kept the peace, many did not.

The term *akusō* was frequently directed at the unruly warrior monks of Kōfukuji and the great monasteries of Nara or the mountain centers of Hieizan, Kōyasan, and Hakusan. These communities feuded amongst themselves, challenged the authority of the court government, and resisted the emerging power of local warrior chieftains.

The Tale of the Heike (Heike monogatari), which depicts the warfare between the Heike and Genji warrior bands in the late twelfth century, presents such an *akusō* from Enryakuji: "Now there was a certain notorious priest from the West Precinct called Kaijō-bō Ajari. He was a huge fellow who stood seven *shaku* high. He wore armor laced loosely with black, iron studded leather, and extremely long thighpieces." (*The Tale of the Heike,* translated by Hiroshi Kitagawa and Bruce Tsuchida, 1975).

Akusō made up the bands of *sōhei,* or monk-soldiers, that plagued medieval society until they were brought to heel by Oda Nobunaga and Toyotomi Hideyoshi in the sixteenth century.

MARTIN COLLCUTT

ALAMUT, a rocky promontory high in the Elburz mountains northeast of Qazvin, chosen by the Isma'ili leader and chief propagandist Hasani Sabbah as the place for his fortress headquarters commencing about 1090. In time Alamut became the political and intellectual center of a loose network of similar outposts that together formed the territory ruled by his successors. They claimed themselves to be imams of the Fatimid line descended via Nizar from al-Mustansir, caliph in Cairo (1036–1094), and in turn from the prophet Muhammad through his daughter Fatima. Their followers were notorious for the selective use of assassination against opponents. Among their many enemies, only the Mongols succeeded in actually attacking their remotest mountain redoubts. Alamut itself was finally sacked and destroyed in 1256 by the armies of Hulegu as part of his victorious march across Iran toward Baghdad.

PAUL E. WALKER

ALAUNGHPAYA (1714–1760), the charismatic founder and first ruler (1752–1760) of Burma's Konbaung dynasty. A local official in the Mokhsobo area of Upper Burma, U Aung Zeiya, as he was originally known, was one of the first local leaders to take advantage of the power vacuum created when forces of the delta kingdom of Pegu swept away the remains of the moribund Toungoo state in 1751–1752. He systematically co-opted or defeated his Burman rivals, organized the growing population under his control into service groups, and cleared the last of the southern forces from Upper Burma in May 1754. By mid-1753 he had already been crowned king and appointed his eldest son crown prince. The execution of the captive Toungoo ruler by Pegu authorities led to a Burman revolt in Prome in 1754 and brought central Burma over to Alaunghpaya. Carrying the war to the delta in 1755, he sacked the enemy capital of Pegu in 1757 and established permanent Burman hegemony over the entire Irrawaddy River basin.

His success was based on his leadership qualities, his open appeals to Burman chauvinism, and his careful formation and augmentation of his administrative and military base. His domain emerged from five years of intensive warfare—which had been preceded by decades of poor administration and disorder—with an orderly administration, a relatively settled population base, and a strong military system. Alaunghpaya thus bequeathed to his successors a strong legacy of material power.

Turning next to the security of his frontiers, Alaunghpaya reasserted the historical Burmese dominance over the upper Irrawaddy Valley and the highlands west of the Salween River in 1758, and in 1759 he launched a campaign for the comprehensive subjugation of the Tai states east of the Salween. After some initial successes, the campaign failed as it reached the walls of the Thai capital of Ayudhya. Alaunghpaya died of disease on 11 May 1760 during the retreat. He was succeeded by the crown prince, who became Naungdawgyi (r. 1760–1763).

[*See also* Konbaung Dynasty; Pegu; Toungoo Dynasties; Prome; *and* Ayudhya.]

Victor B. Lieberman, *Burmese Administrative Cycles: Anarchy and Conquest, c. 1580–1760* (1984).

WILLIAM J. KOENIG

ALAUNGSITHU, also known as Aloncansu, enjoyed the longest reign (1113–1169) of the kings of Pagan in Burma. Grandson of King Kyanzittha, Alaungsithu established, made permanent, and consolidated what became known as the classical Burmese tradition. The stability and longevity of Alaungsithu's reign were partly responsible for this accomplishment, but it was also the result of Kyanzittha's synthesis of a variety of cultures, which simply made the right political, economic, and social conditions come to fruition.

Alaungsithu is known in Burmese history as the "king long lived," the one who reached the tree under which the Buddha sat, the one who journeyed throughout Burma as well as to Sri Lanka and parts of Southeast Asia, and the one whose public-works program was extensive. Yet there is evidence of rebellion during his reign, most notably by one of his sons, and there is suggestion of his arrogance. Nineteenth-century historians admonished him for his pride and record a rather unbecoming death for a monarch of his stature: he was suffocated by one of his sons, who is known in Burmese history—for this and other reasons—as probably the most cruel of all Pagan monarchs. Alaungsithu saved, among others, his grand Thatbyinnyu and the delicate Pahtothamya temples, which were thought to have been more austere in style and decoration, thereby suggesting a return to the purity of the past.

[*See also* Pagan.]

Michael Aung-Thwin, *The Origins of the Classical Burmese State: An Institutional History of the Kingdom of Pagan* (1985). G. H. Luce, *Old Burma—Early Pagan*

(1969–1970). Pe Maung Tin and G. H. Luce, trans., *The Glass Palace Chronicle of the Kings of Burma* (reprint, 1960).

MICHAEL AUNG-THWIN

ALBUQUERQUE, AFFONSO DE (1459?–1515), great naval commander who went to India in 1503. He became governor of the Portuguese possessions in India in 1509 and determined that to gain commercial supremacy over the Indian Ocean, and thereby provide revenue adequate to maintain a Portuguese dominance, it was necessary to seize and control the crucial points of Asian trade. In 1510 he captured Goa, from which he developed control over the west-coast Indian trade. Albuquerque's capture of Melaka (Malacca) in 1511 with a fighting force of some twelve hundred men and seventeen or eighteen ships gave the Portuguese dominance over this chief distribution center for the Southeast Asian spice trade, although it soon became evident that holding Melaka did not give the Portuguese control over the Asian trade that had been centered there. This victory also fulfilled an obligation delegated to the Portuguese by the pope. Melaka was considered the Southeast Asian center of Islam and its conquest was seen as necessary to prevent the diffusion of Islam in Indonesia. Albuquerque failed to take Aden in 1513 but captured Hormuz in 1515. He died in a ship off Goa in the same year. Albuquerque's policy of erecting forts and establishing Portuguese authority over native rulers rather than concentrating on trade has been held to be one of the primary causes for the subsequent failure of the Portuguese Asian enterprise.

[See also Goa *and* Melaka.]

KENNETH R. HALL

ALCALDE MAYOR. In the seventeenth century, when the Spanish Philippines were divided into twelve provinces called *alcaldías*, an *alcalde mayor*, or provincial governor, held royal authority in each province. His primary responsibility was to enforce directives from Manila and to hear appeal cases that had been judged by the *gobernadorcillo* at the municipal level. Since the *alcalde*'s salary was only three hundred pesos a year, graft was commonplace. In the nineteenth century the major duties of the *alcalde mayor* were publishing decrees from Manila, insuring that food supplies were adequate, overseeing upkeep of highways and roads, granting licenses for public performances, seeing that elections for municipal offices were honest, and collecting taxes. In 1886 the post of *alcalde mayor* was done away with and replaced by a civil governor whose major task was economic administration.

[*See also* Philippines.]

NICHOLAS P. CUSHNER

ALEXANDER III of Macedon (356–323 BCE), son of Philip II and Olympias, claimed descent from Herakles and Achilles. He was brought up as crown prince, steeped in Greek myth and Homer, and for three years tutored by Aristotle. In 338 he played a decisive part in the battle of Chaeronea, which led to Philip's organization of Greece under his supremacy, but he fell into disgrace after Philip divorced Olympias and remarried. In 336, shortly after launching his long-prepared Hellenic crusade against Persia, Philip was assassinated and Alexander, probably involved in the plot, was proclaimed king. He eliminated possible rivals, enforced his recognition by all as Philip's successor, and in the spring of 334 resumed the invasion of Asia, with ceremonies alluding to the Trojan War.

Defeating the ill-organized satrapal forces of Asia Minor at the Granicus River, Alexander quickly occupied Sardes and proclaimed the "liberation" of the Greek cities of Asia. Ignoring a counterattack by the Persian fleet, he marched along the coast of Asia Minor, with an excursion to Gordium to untie the "knot of Midas" (the "Gordian knot") as an omen for the rule of Asia. (He cut it with his sword.) At Issus in the autumn of 333 he defeated the Persian army led by Darius III and captured his harem and treasure, while Darius escaped eastward. After a long and difficult siege he destroyed Tyre, then organized the Levant and occupied Egypt, where he founded Alexandria. He visited the oracle of Ammon in Libya, where he was proclaimed the god's son and promised victory and probably deification.

In 331 Alexander marched east and at Gaugamela (near modern Arbil) decisively defeated Darius in a hard-fought battle. Darius fled to Ecbatana (Hamadan), giving up Babylon, Susa, and Persepolis, with their treasures, to the conqueror. At Persepolis Alexander spent four months (February–May 330?), with short campaigns to subdue the interior and occupy Pasargadae, perhaps waiting for the outcome of a Spartan-led rising against him in Greece. Before leaving Persepolis he destroyed the royal buildings, impressing Greece with vengeance for Xerxes' invasion. At Ecbatana, after hearing that the Greek rising had been defeated, Alexander proclaimed the end of the Hellenic crusade and set out to pursue Darius, who had again fled eastward.

Alexander did not catch Darius alive. The king had been killed, probably to prevent his doing homage to Alexander, by eastern Iranian nobles accompanying him, one of whom now assumed the tiara to continue resistance. (He was later captured and executed.) Darius received royal burial and his family was treated with special distinction.

After taking over Mazandaran, Alexander turned east and advanced as far as Mashhad, but turned off the route to Merv and marched south, via Herat to Sistan and up the Helmand Valley to Kandahar. Near Ghazna he crossed the mountains in winter, despite severe suffering, then rested his army at Begram, where he founded a satrapy capital. Crossing the Hindu Kush, he occupied Bactra (Balkh), and in Bactria and Sogdiana (across the Amu Darya) he fought bitter campaigns against guerrillas. In 327 he married Roxana, the daughter of a chieftain, after defeating her father, who then became a loyal ally and helped Alexander to pacify the country.

This marriage marks the climax of a long transformation. The slogan of the Hellenic crusade begun by Philip had been politically useful in convincing some of the Greeks of its necessity and had been emotionally satisfying to Alexander in his identification with his heroic ancestors. Yet in his policies he always showed the cool opportunism of his father. The Achaemenid administrative system was simply taken over. The Greeks, nominally free, were closely supervised, and to barbarians Alexander proclaimed himself a "liberator" whenever appropriate, as in Lydia and Caria. In Egypt he was depicted, although never crowned, as pharaoh. In Babylonia, long a center of intermingling of native and Iranian, he honored the god Marduk and installed an Iranian with local family connections as satrap. Henceforth he began to act as "Great King," generously rewarding Iranians who collaborated with him and severely punishing those who resisted. He needed to attract the Iranian aristocracy, for peace and for the administration of the countries he intended to conquer.

Alexander's decision to destroy Persepolis was politically disastrous. Proclaiming the end of the Hellenic crusade was the best he could do (although still not enough) to compensate. Darius's death deprived him of the hope of formal recognition of his "legitimacy" and left him plainly a barbarian invader. Yet he also had to minimize offense to his Macedonian subjects. Henceforth he wore a carefully modified version of Achaemenid dress and began to surround himself with a full Persian court, separate from the simple Macedonian establishment kept up for Europeans. Yet eastern Iran continued to resist fiercely, while Macedonians and Greeks complained at having to serve a new "Great King." Near Sistan, Alexander struck the first blow against them. Aided by loyal friends, he had Philotas, commander of the Macedonian cavalry and outspoken opponent of accommodation with the Iranians, seized in a coup d'état; Alexander accused him of treason before the army and gained their approval for his execution.

Philotas's father, Parmenio, Alexander's second-in-command, had at one time dominated the army. After playing a major part in Alexander's victories, he had been left at Ecbatana as commander of the army of western Iran. Alexander now ordered his assassination. The only potential leadership for Macedonian opposition was thus removed. But tension remained. At Maracanda (Samarkand), Alexander killed his old comrade Clitus after a drunken altercation. The army, showing its unquestioning loyalty, posthumously condemned Clitus of treason. But Alexander's attempt to make prostration before him compulsory in salutation failed, and he was forced to exempt Greeks and Macedonians from the duty.

He now organized Bactria and Sogdiana as his northeastern bastion, drafting Greek mercenaries into colonies there, and then invaded India to claim the remainder of the kingdom once ruled by Darius I. The advance across the Punjab was successful, but he was stopped by his soldiers' refusal to cross the Beas River. This was beyond all old Achaemenid boundaries, and they saw no sign that Alexander would ever stop. For the first time, Alexander had to give in. He never forgave those whom he held responsible.

Turning south, Alexander led the army through months of hard fighting to the mouth of the Indus, regaining its full allegiance when he received an almost fatal wound. Determined Indian resistance was countered by extermination. After setting up four satrapies, on the lines of the earlier Achaemenid ones, in the conquered territory, Alexander ordered the fleet to sail along the coast, sent part of the army back by an easier route, then led the rest, with all the camp followers, back through Makran, partly in order to outdo the feats of legendary heroes. Most of the camp followers and many soldiers perished in the desert. One consequence of this disaster was a purge among his satraps and commanders on his return. But when Alexander reached Susa in 324 he arranged an extravagant victory celebration, distributing gifts and prizes. He and eighty of his commanders now married Iranian noblewomen—a grandiose solution to the irreducible antagonisms between Europeans and Iranians: within a generation, when he expected still to be king, a mixed aristocracy could govern the empire. Fittingly, he now showed himself eager to be worshiped as a god by the Greeks.

At Opis, the next stop, the Macedonian army mutinied against his favor for Orientals, but this time Alexander had them at his mercy. He simply told them to go home if they wished to. They had to accept his terms, and a feast of general reconciliation ended with prayers for joint rule by Macedonians and Persians. He now rewarded and discharged ten thousand Macedonians, keeping their children by native women to form the nucleus of a future "royal" army with no national roots. That autumn, at Ecbatana, Alexander's only friend, Hephaestion, died; Alexander never recovered from the blow. Ammon was asked permission to have Hephaestion worshiped as a god, but he refused; the sacred fires dedicated to him as a god were extinguished all over Iran. A few months later, at Babylon, Alexander died of illness aggravated by heavy drinking.

Alexander left and perhaps wanted no successor. His sole aim had been conquest for personal glory. His empire, bound up with his person, soon disintegrated. But in the countries through which he had passed like an angel of destruction his name remained, to become a legend of supernatural greatness or evil.

[*See also* Achaemenid Dynasty; Greeks; Arachosia; Aria; Bactria; Pasargadae; Persepolis; Sogdiana; Darius III; Seleucus I; *and* Xerxes.]

Arrian, *The Campaigns of Alexander,* translated by A. de Selincourt (1971). Quintus Curtius Rufus, *The History of Alexander,* translated by J. Yardley (1984). D. W. Engels, *Alexander the Great and the Logistics of the Macedonian Army* (1978). Plutarch, *The Age of Alexander,* translated by Ian Scott-Kilvert (1973). U. Wilcken, *Alexander the Great,* translated by G. C. Richards, edited by E. N. Borza (1967). Ernst Badian

ALI, SULTAN OF JOHOR (r. 1855–1877), eldest son of Sultan Hussein of Singapore and Johor (d. 1835) and last of his line to hold a royal title. His claim to the office of sultan of Johor was not recognized until 1855, by which time the Temenggongs had assumed solid control of the government there and brought in Chinese settlers. In 1855 he signed a controversial treaty with Temenggong Ibrahim and Governor W. J. Butterworth of Singapore in which he was recognized as his father's successor, but by which he also recognized the Temenggong as "the sole and absolute sovereign of Johor." He retained control over only the small territory between the Kessang and Muar rivers (approximately 260 square miles), but even this was absorbed into Johor after his death.

[*See also* Johor; Hussein, Sultan of Johor and Singapore; Ibrahim; *and* Abu Bakar.]

John Cameron, *Our Tropical Possessions in Malayan India* (reprint, 1965). Carl A. Trocki

ALI AL-RIDA (c. 765–818; Persian, Reza), Abu Hasan ibn Musa ibn Ja'far al-Sadiq, eighth imam of the Ithna Ashari (Twelver) line, born in Medina. He was summoned from a quiet, scholarly life by the reigning Abbasid caliph al-Ma'mun to accept appointment as heir apparent, with the title al-Rida, while the caliph was in Merv, locked in a determined struggle to preserve his own power. Ali al-Rida, as the head of the house of Ali and, therefore, leader of the Shi'ites, could bring a vast claim of potential support for the cause of whoever made an alliance with him. The caliph brought him to Transoxiana and replaced the black insignias of the ruling Abbasids with those of Alid green. This strange episode ended soon, however, when Ali al-Rida died while traveling with Ma'mun from Merv back to Baghdad. Shi'ites, doubting the honesty of the caliph's motives in the first place, believe that he had had Ali al-Rida poisoned. Ali al-Rida was interred at Tus by Ma'mun in a mausoleum already containing the remains of Ma'mun's father Harun al-Rashid, the Abbasid caliph of *Arabian Nights* fame. The spot soon grew in significance because of the presence there of the Alid imam; its name was changed to Mashhad (lit., "shrine" or "sanctuary"). It became one of the most important centers for Shi'ite pilgrimage and is now at the center of Iran's third-largest, to which it gives its name.

[*See also* Mashhad.]

Paul E. Walker

ALI BROTHERS. Shaukat Ali (1873–1938) and Mohamed Ali (1878–1931) were among the leading Indian Muslim political activists of their generation. They both attended Aligarh College and gained renown in the Union debating society. Mohamed studied at Oxford but failed to gain entrance to the Indian Civil Service. Both brothers entered government service, Shaukat in the Opium Department and Mohamed in the princely state of Baroda. Both took an active interest in the affairs of their alma mater and its alumni association. Shaukat's first nationwide exposure came during his fundraising tours for Aligarh College in 1911. Mohamed wrote frequent articles championing the university and Muslim involvement in national politics. In 1911 he started his famous English weekly, *Comrade,* and a year later an Urdu journal, *Hamdard.*

The Ali brothers became firm opponents of British rule under the combined shock of the Balkan wars, British refusal of university status to Aligarh College in 1912, and the Kanpur Mosque incident in 1913. They were interned for four years during World War I for their pro-Turkish activities. Released in 1919, they led the Khilafat movement and were imprisoned again in 1921. Following their release, Mohamed served as president of the Indian National Congress in 1923 and briefly revived *Comrade* and *Hamdard.* Mohamed died in London during the first Round Table Conference and, as he wished not to return to an India that was unfree, was buried in Jerusalem.

[*See also* Khilafat Movement; Indian National Congress *and* Mohamed Ali.]

Mohamed Ali, *My Life: A Fragment,* edited by Afzal Iqbal (1942). Mushirul Hasan, *Mohamed Ali: Ideology and Politics* (1981). Afzal Iqbal, *The Life and Times of Mohamed Ali* (1974). GAIL MINAULT

ALIGARH MOVEMENT. *See* Ahmad Khan, Sir Sayyid.

ALIMIN PRAWIRODIRDJO (1897–1964), Indonesian Marxist and architect of the 1926–1927 Indonesian Communist Party (Partai Komunis Indonesia, or PKI) uprisings. He stressed the need to coordinate revolution in Indonesia with international conditions; he was returning from Moscow, where he had requested authorization for the risings, when they broke out. On his return to Indonesia in 1946 after twenty-two years in exile, including a period in Yan'an with Mao Zedong, he argued in favor of postponing social revolution until Western recognition of Indonesian independence had been secured. He later resisted the policies of Aidit, arguing that the PKI had become opportunist and insufficiently class-conscious. He left the Party in 1956.

[*See also* Indonesia, Republic of; Partai Komunis Indonesia; *and* Aidit, Dipa Nusantara.]

Alimin, *Analysis* (1947). Ruth T. McVey, *The Rise of Indonesian Communism* (1965). ROBERT B. CRIBB

ALI SASTROAMIDJOJO (1903–1975), Indonesian nationalist politician. As a student in the Netherlands, Ali was arrested in 1927 for his activities in the nationalist Perhimpunan Indonesia Association. In Indonesia he was active in successive radical nationalist organizations, Partai Nasional Indonesia (PNI), Partindo, and Gerindo. He became a leader of the postwar PNI and headed two cabinets (July 1953–July 1955, March 1956–March 1957). One of the architects of Indonesia's participation in the nonaligned movement, he hosted the Asian-African conference in Bandung in 1955. Under Sukarno's Guided Democracy he led the dominant left wing of the PNI but was removed from leadership in 1966.

[*See also* Partai Nasional Indonesia *and* Gerindo.]

J. Eliseo Rocamora, *Nationalism in Search of Ideology: The Indonesian Nationalist Party, 1946–1965* (1975). Ali Sastroamidjojo, *Milestones on My Journey* (1979).

ROBERT B. CRIBB

ALIVARDI KHAN (1678?–1756), title of Mirza Muhammad Ali, third-generation Mughal *mansabdar.* Backing a loser in the succession wars, he left the court for service under Shuja-ad-din Muhammad Khan in 1720, helped him become nawab of Bengal (July 1727), and was rewarded with the deputy governorship of Bihar in 1733. From this power base he siezed Bengal himself in 1740 and ruled ably, despite devastating Maratha invasions of 1742 to 1751, until his death at Murshidabad on 10 April 1756.

[*See also* Mughal Empire; Mansabdari System; Bengal; *and* Marathas.]

Kalikinkar Datta, *Alivardi and His Times* (1963).

FRITZ LEHMANN

ALLAHABAD, Indian city in Uttar Pradesh, located at the confluence of the Ganges and Yamuna rivers; its population is 650,000. Its position on the sacred rivers made the town a major center of Hindu pilgrimage while its strategic and commercial importance caused the Mughals and, after 1765, the British to create a military stronghold there. Allahabad's status as a district headquarters and small commercial town was enhanced after its savage reoccupation by British troops during the 1857 rebellion (mutiny), when it became the capital of the North-Western Provinces and Oudh (Awadh; later United Provinces). In 1866 it became the seat of the provincial High Court; the creation of Allahabad University in 1887 made it the most important educational center in the region. The legal and commercial communities of Allahabad were active in nationalist and social reform activities after 1888. Madan Mohan Malaviya represented the Hindu nationalist strand, while the Nehrus, Tej Bahadur Sapru and Purshottam Das Tandon were major figures in the secular, populist tradition. Allahabad politicians remained "moderate" between 1905 and 1910, but from 1916 a growing radicalism impelled them into the Awadh countryside, where they forged links with peasant protest. After 1920, with the transfer of the provincial capital to Lucknow, Allahabad, which had little industry, declined in importance.

C. A. Bayly, *The Local Roots of Indian Politics: Allahabad, 1880–1920* (1975). H. R. Nevill, *District Gazetteers of the United Provinces of Agra and Oudh,* vol. 23, *Allahabad* (1911). C. A. Bayly

ALLEN, HORACE NEWTON (1858–1932), physician, diplomat, and first resident Protestant missionary in Korea. Allen first went to China as a Presbyterian missionary (1883) but transferred to Korea, arriving 20 September 1884. Although mission activity was prohibited by Korean law, Allen was permitted to stay as physician to the American legation. In the December 1884 coup d'état he saved the life of Prince Min Yong-ik, nephew of the queen, and was allowed to open a hospital, the first legally permitted Christian institution and first Western medical center in Korea. Shortly thereafter Allen was given honorary noble rank as court physician. In 1886, with fellow missionaries Heron and Underwood, he started a medical school.

Allen's brief career as a missionary pioneer in Korea (1884–1890) included a two-year leave of absence as adviser at the Korean legation in Washington, D.C. (1887–1890). On his return to Korea he left the mission and accepted an appointment as American legation secretary (1890–1897) and American minister (1897–1905), but he always retained his missionary interest and sympathies.

It was as a diplomat that Allen made his enduring mark on Korean history. He used his close contacts with royalty to promote American business interests with vigor and played a significant role in the country's modernization. He contributed to the introduction of Korea's first streetcars and railroad, the first city water system and electrical city lighting, and modern mines (the giant Oriental Consolidated Mining Company, which prospered until World War II).

In international affairs, Allen was as fiercely protective of Korean independence as of American diplomatic and business interests. The triumph of Japan in the Russo-Japanese War left him depressed by Korean governmental weakness, angry at President Roosevelt's approval of a Japanese protectorate, and unhappily convinced of the inevitability of Japanese rule. He was recalled to America in 1905 and practiced medicine in Ohio.

Horace N. Allen, *A Chronological Index* (1901). F. H. Harrington, *God, Mammon and the Japanese: Dr. Horace N. Allen and Korean-American Relations, 1884–1905* (1944; 2d ed., 1961). Samuel Hugh Moffett

ALLIANCE PARTY, the nucleus of a coalition that has ruled Malaya, and later Malaysia, ever since its independence in 1957. The coalition was born in January 1952 out of a decision by the Selangor branches of the United Malays National Organization (UMNO) and the Malayan Chinese Association (MCA) to contest the Kuala Lumpur municipal election. Its electoral success inaugurated a pattern of political representation that by and large still obtains: a ruling coalition is formed by a group of political parties, each carefully preserving its Malay, Chinese, Indian, or other ethnic identity but able to reconcile competing demands within an alliance of shared interests.

Historically, the Alliance was founded on two basic premises. First, the moderate Malay and Chinese elites needed to prove to the British that they could work in harmony and that early independence was possible. Second, the UMNO—the leading power in the coalition then as well as now—felt that politics pursued by individual parties open to all ethnic groups would result in direct ethnic confrontation and conflict. UMNO wanted to demonstrate that Alliance-style politics was preferable to the multiracial party path advocated by the Independence of Malaya Party in 1951. UMNO and MCA leaders also agreed—for the first few years after independence, at least—that Malays would exercise political power while the Chinese would continue their economic preeminence. The Malayan Indian Congress joined the Alliance almost three years later. Although it has never played a decisive role in Alliance policymaking, from time to time it has arbitrated differences between its two senior partners.

The serious riots that broke out between the Malays and the Chinese in May 1969, after an ethnically divisive election campaign, compelled Alliance leaders to reappraise their previous assumptions. They decided to place the greatest emphasis on the maintenance of ethnic harmony and public security by giving Malays a larger slice of the economic cake—even at the expense of non-Malays—and by expanding the Alliance to include a number of opposition parties. In 1972 the old Alliance Party officially came to an end. Its leadership, influence, and philosophy have since been continued under the banner of the National Front.

[*See also* United Malays National Organization; Malayan Chinese Association; Independence of Malaya Party; *and* Malaysia.]

Stanley S. Bedlington, *Malaysia and Singapore: The Building of New States* (1978). Gordon P. Means, *Malaysian Politics* (2d ed., 1976). K. J. Ratnam, *Communalism and the Political Process in Malaya* (1965).

STANLEY BEDLINGTON

ALL-INDIA MUSLIM LEAGUE. On 1 October 1906 a delegation claiming to represent the views of the Muslim community of the Indian subcontinent met the viceroy in Simla and asked for separate representation of their community in all levels of government—district boards, municipalities, and legislative councils. Characterized as a "command performance" in several historical accounts, the Simla deputation was a catalyst to the formation of the All-India Muslim League. Founded in Dhaka (Dacca) on 30 December 1906, the league emerged as a powerful political force in the early 1940s and led the demand for a separate Muslim homeland under the leadership of Bombay lawyer-politician Mohammad Ali Jinnah. [*See* Jinnah, Mohammad Ali.]

The Muslim League gained ascendancy after years of political inactivity. Dominated by the landed gentry and the government servants of the United Provinces whose interests were inextricably linked with the Raj, the league in its early years did little beyond meeting during Christmas week and passing a few pious resolutions. Shibli Numani, an eminent *alim* of Nadvat al-Ulama, a Muslim religious seminary in Lucknow, assailed its leaders for their inactivity and their politics of subservience. In a series of articles published in 1913 he pressed for substantial changes in the social composition as well as the political orientation of the Muslim League, and called for a concerted Hindu-Muslim endeavor to achieve common political objectives.

Shibli's argument struck a favorable chord among the Muslim intelligentsia of northern India, who were already uneasy over the Balkan wars, the annulment of Bengal's partition in 1911, and the rejection of the Aligarh Muslim University proposal. Led by Mohamed Ali, an Aligarh graduate and editor of the influential English weekly, *Comrade,* a number of groups among Muslims favored a course, unforeseen by their political mentor, Sir Sayyid Ahmad Khan, of abandoning the politics of conciliation in favor of agitational methods and working out their political destiny in unison with the rest of the Indian people, including those associated with the Indian National Congress. [*See* Ali Brothers; Ahmad Khan, Sir Sayyid; *and* Indian National Congress.]

An important change, pressed by the more advanced political group, was the transfer of the Muslim League headquarters from Aligarh to Lucknow in March 1910. The organization at Aligarh was an adjunct of the college and was controlled by those who learned their lesson of loyalty at the feet of Sayyid Ahmad Khan. But with the initiative passing into the hands of the politically advanced Lucknow-based politicians, the Muslim League began to reflect the radical temper of many of its followers, especially the "younger men," the standard-bearers of "new ideals," "new forces," and "new light." This is evident from another vital decision adopted in March 1913: the incorporation of a clause on "the attainment under the aegis of the British Crown of a *system of self-government suited to India*" in the Muslim League constitution (emphasis added).

These developments paved the way for an alliance between the Indian National Congress and the Muslim League that culminated in the Lucknow Pact of December 1916, the high watermark of Hindu-Muslim unity. The decline of some Muslim League stalwarts was its other consequence. The Isma'ili leader, Agha Khan, who presided over the league's destiny from 1906 to 1913, resigned on 3 November 1913. Sweeping changes were also made at Aligarh College, once regarded as the most loyal of institutions. British writer E. M. Forster sensed the drift of things on his visit to Aligarh in October 1912: "The Mohammedans had an air of desperation," he wrote, "which may be habitual, but was impressive." [*See also* Forster, Edward Morgan.]

After the initial burst of activity, especially in the aftermath of the Lucknow Pact, the Muslim League lost its initiative to the Khilafat committees that organized the massive protest against the dismemberment of the Turkish empire. [*See* Khilafat Movement.] The league remained inactive throughout the 1920s and the early 1930s. It was split into different factions, with Jinnah and the Punjabi politician Mohammad Shafi arrayed against each other into rival camps. It had to contend with the All-India Muslim Conference, a group founded in 1929 in the wake of the controversy generated by the (Jawaharlal) Nehru Committee Report, published in August 1928. In the two Muslim-majority provinces it had to contend with the unionists in the Punjab and the Proja Krishak Party in Bengal. The provincial leagues were equally ineffective; the branch in the Bombay presidency, the home of Jinnah, had only 71 members in 1928.

Jinnah's endeavors in 1925 and 1926 to infuse some life into the organization were poorly rewarded: the total league membership rose from 1,093 in 1922 to a mere 1,330 in 1927. When Muhammad Iqbal presented his historic address in 1930 demanding the establishment of a Muslim state in northwest India, the meeting at Allahabad did not even have its quorum of 75 members. [*See* Iqbal, Sir Muhammad.]

Jinnah made another attempt to revive the Muslim League soon after his return to India from London, but he did not meet with immediate success. In the crucial 1937 elections the Muslim League won only 104 out of the total 489 Muslim seats. This was hardly an impressive show for a party claiming sole representation of the Muslim community. In the Punjab the unionists swept the board; in Bengal, Jinnah and the Muslim League had to accept a coalition led by Fazlul Huq, who did not acknowledge their writ; and in the North-West Frontier Province, where almost the entire population was Muslim, was the worst humiliation of all, a Congress ministry. [*See* Fazlul Huq, Abul Kasem]. In the Muslim-minority provinces, where the league did best, the Congress did much better than anyone had expected, and did not need the league's help to form stable ministries. The way in which the Muslim vote split lent some credence to the Congress line that it was a secular party, ready and able to speak for Muslims, many of whom had entered its camp.

A new phase in the history of the Muslim League began with Jinnah's renewed efforts to resuscitate the organization. Soon after the 1937 elections he recognized the importance of extending the social base of the Muslim League, refurbishing its image, and reorganizing its loosely knit structure. Consequently, the old provincial and district branches were reconstituted, the membership fee was reduced from one rupee to two annas, and the Muslim League Council was enlarged from 300 to 465 members. The thrust of the new orientation was toward accommodating various interest groups, extending the social base of the Muslim League, and turning it into an active, viable party with a clear-cut ideological platform, which was enunciated in the Pakistan Resolution and adopted by the Muslim League in March 1940. The onetime "ambassador of Hindu-Muslim unity" was now the chief protagonist of the two-nation theory that formed the basis for the Muslim League's demand for a separate Muslim homeland.

Jinnah's efforts to popularize the league were duly rewarded. It is said that 100,000 new members were recruited in the months immediately after the Lucknow session in 1937. In 1944 the league officially claimed a membership of some 2,000,000. The most convincing testimony of its strength, however, came from the 1945–1946 elections, wherein the league polled about 4.5 million, or 75 percent, of the Muslim votes; it won 460 out of the 533 Muslim seats in the central and provincial elections. This phenomenal electoral success paved the way for the creation of Pakistan in August 1947. [*See* Pakistan.]

Historians have attributed the league's success to the charisma, drive, and organizing ability of Jinnah, the shortsightedness of the Indian National Congress in excluding the league representatives from the provincial governments in 1937, the alleged persecutions that the Muslims suffered during the Congress ministries in 1937–1939, and, above all, to the appeal of the two-nation theory to important sections of the Muslim community: the landlords of the Punjab and the United Provinces, the pirs of Sind, the *ulama* of the Barelwi school and a section of the influential seminary at Deoband, and the Muslim intelligentsia at Aligarh Muslim University. These groups were in the forefront of the massive mobilization campaign, launched soon after the adoption of the Pakistan Resolution in March 1940.

After independence the Muslim League ceased to be an effective political force in Pakistan. Jinnah's chief lieutenants, Liaqat Ali Khan and Choudhry Khaliquzzaman, failed to keep the party together, which was now split into numerous factions. [*See* Liaqat Ali Khan.] The political fortunes of the league were eclipsed in most provinces, particularly in Bengal, where it was defeated in the 1954 elections and was never able to stage a comeback. In India, the Muslim League survives in the state of Kerala, where it has had an uneasy political existence. Efforts to revive it in northern India have not met with success.

[*See also* Partition of India.]

Mushirul Hasan, *Nationalism and Communal Politics in India, 1916–1928* (1979). Ayesha Jalal, *The Sole Spokesman: Jinnah, the Muslim League, and the Demand for Pakistan* (1985). Francis Robinson, *Separatism Among Indian Muslims: The Politics of the United Provinces' Muslims 1860–1923* (1974). Khalid bin Sayeed, *Pakistan: The Formative Phase, 1857–1948* (1960). S. R. Wasti, *Lord Minto and the Indian Nationalist Movement 1905–1910* (1964).

MUSHIRUL HASAN

ALMEIDA, LOURENCO DE (d. 1508). Son of the first viceroy of Portuguese possessions in India, Almeida led the Portuguese fleet against the Moors off the Maldives. A fierce storm drove his fleet off course and led to the chance discovery of Ceylon in 1505. He negotiated a treaty with Dharma Parakramabahu IX, whereby the Sinhalese king agreed to pay an annual tribute of cinnamon in return for Portuguese protection of Sinhalese ports. Almeida died in battle off Chaul (in western India) in 1508.

[*See also* Muslims in Sri Lanka *and* Portuguese: Portuguese in Sri Lanka.]

S. Gnana Prakasar, *A History of the Catholic Church in Ceylon* (1924).

PATRICK ROCHE

ALTAIC LANGUAGES. A group of languages that developed in North Asia, the Altaic languages include Mongolian, Manchu-Tunguz, and Chuvash-Turkic. Some scholars classify Korean as an Altaic language, and a tiny minority argue that Japanese is part of the group as well. Numerous loanwords and borrowings are found among the diverse Altaic languages.

The Altaic languages share certain common characteristics. They all have long vowels (e.g., ō, ā) and vowel harmony—that is, a word can only contain either back vowels or front vowels. They are also agglutinative, which simply means that it is through the addition of suffixes to the basic stems that new words are formed and that inflections and possession are indicated; prepositional forms are denoted in the same way. For example, the Mongolian word *ger* ("house") becomes *gerte* ("in the house") or *gerēs* ("from the house"). The parts of speech are not as distinct as in English, although nouns and verbs are sharply distinguished.

Quite a number of languages and dialects are found in each of the Altaic language groupings. The Mongolian languages may be divided into the Western Mongolian languages, including Buriat and Oirat, and the Eastern Mongolian languages, including the Khalkha and Chakhar dialects. The earliest Mongolian script, which was developed at Genghis Khan's direction, was based upon the Uighur Turkic script. In 1269 the Tibetan Buddhist Phags-pa introduced a new, more accurate script, and in 1648 the Mongolian Buddhist Jaya Pandita produced an Oirat script, but neither superseded the original. With growing Russian influence in the twentieth century, however, the Cyrillic script has become the standard except in Inner Mongolia.

The Manchu-Tunguz languages include Jurchen, Manchu, Goldi, and Evenki, some of which are still spoken as far away as Siberia. The Chuvash-Turkic languages include Chuvash (spoken in the Chuvash Soviet Socialist Republic), Volga and Danube Bulgarian, and Chagatai, Kipchak, and other Turkic dialects. In the twentieth century, Cyrillic has replaced the traditional scripts for the Chuvash-Turkic languages found in the USSR.

The affinities in vocabulary and structure have given rise to the so-called Altaic theory. Proponents of this theory assert the existence of a proto-Altaic language from which all the Altaic languages developed. Other scholars argue that the languages developed independently, but proximity led to loans of words and structure.

[*See also* Turkic Languages.]

Karl H. Menges, *The Turkic Languages and Peoples* (1968). Nicholas Poppe, *Introduction to Altaic Linguistics* (1965). Nicholas Poppe and John R. Krueger, *The Mongolian Monuments in hP'ags-pa Script* (1957).

MORRIS ROSSABI

ALTAI MOUNTAINS. The Altai, located at the conjunction of the USSR, China, and Mongolia, are mostly middle-elevation mountains (5,000 to 8,000 feet), reaching 15,159 feet at Tabun-Bogdo in Mongolia. Continental climate assures cold winters and warm summers, and the rainfall ranges from 40 to 80 inches in the northwest to less than 5 inches in the Gobi to the southeast. The Altai of the Kazakh republic of the USSR are particularly important for lead and zinc mines and are sources of tin, copper, tungsten, mercury, gold, and silver as well.

MICHAEL BONINE

ALTAN KHAN (1507–1583), Mongol prince who sought to unify the various Mongol peoples under his leadership. Fearing that such a confederation might pose a threat to its territory, the emperors of the Chinese Ming dynasty (1368–1644) consequently tried to prevent efforts at Mongol unity and to limit relations with Altan Khan. Early in his career, Altan Khan, who needed and desired Chinese products, was repeatedly denied trade by the Ming court. These rejections almost inevitably led to Mongol raids across the Great Wall on Chinese frontier towns to obtain the goods they could not secure by peaceful means. The Ming court finally relented in 1551 and permitted the establishment of markets along the border for trade between Altan Khan's people and Chinese merchants. When Altan Khan attempted shortly thereafter to purchase grain at these fairs, the Ming rulers hastily disbanded the markets.

Relations between the Ming and Altan Khan remained hostile until 1571. A reconciliation was effected in that year because of self-interest: the Ming court was concerned that many Chinese had defected to Altan Khan and had provided him with the technological, military, and administrative skills not only to raid but also to rule Chinese territory; for his own part, the Mongol ruler wished to defuse tensions with the Chinese in order to concentrate on establishing internal unity. Under the terms of the peace agreement negotiated in 1571 the border markets were reopened. Altan Khan was allowed to send an annual tribute of five hundred horses, for which he was rewarded with Chinese goods, and the title Shunyi Wang (Obedient and Righteous Prince) was conferred on the Mongol leader. In turn, Altan Khan pledged to reduce the number of Chinese in his service. Tensions between the Mongols and the Chinese subsided and their borderlands were peaceful for more than half a century.

Meanwhile, Altan Khan persisted in his efforts to unify the Mongol peoples using religion as the means of achieving his goal. In 1578 he invited the leader of the Yellow Hat sect of Tibetan Buddhism to Mongol lands. This Tibetan lama, who himself faced opposition from the Red Hat sect in Tibet, accepted the invitation, hoping for Mongol support against his religious enemies. Altan Khan granted the Tibetan Buddhist the title Dalai Lama (Oceanic or Universal Lama), while the lama asserted that the Mongol ruler was a reincarnation of Kublai Khan. Converted to Buddhism in this way, Altan Khan ordered the translation of Buddhist sutras into Mongol, built monasteries and temples, and patronized Buddhist sculptors and artists. Within a century most Mongols had converted to Buddhism, but Altan Khan's vision of a politically centralized and unified Mongol state was not realized.

[*See also* Ming Dynasty.]

L. Carrington Goodrich and Chaoying Fang, eds., *Dictionary of Ming Biography, 1364–1644* (1976). Dmitrii Pokotilov, *History of the Eastern Mongols during the Ming Dynasty from 1368 to 1631,* translated by Rudolph Lowenthal (1947–1949). Henry Serruys, "Four Documents Relating to the Sino-Mongol Peace of 1570–1571," *Monumenta Serica* 19 (1960): 1–66. MORRIS ROSSABI

ALVARS. *See* Dravidian Languages and Literatures.

AMAKUSA, an island group off the western coast of Kyushu, Japan, a major center of Christian missionizing during the sixteenth and seventeenth centuries and the scene of a major rebellion in 1637–1638.

In 1556, when Luis de Almeida began preaching under the protection of local lords, Amakusa became a center of Jesuit missionary activity. It was the home of the Jesuit *collegium* in Japan from 1592 to 1598, and from 1590 to 1614 it was the site of a Jesuit printing press that published twenty-nine titles in Japanese, including works of theology, literature, and grammar. The press was closed in 1614, when the *bakufu* (shogunal government) expelled the last missionaries from Japan.

After the Battle of Sekigahara in 1600, the new *bakufu* ruler, Tokugawa Ieyasu, placed Amakusa under the rule of the Terasawa clan, lords of Karatsu. Against a background of the increasing persecution of Christianity in the early seventeenth century, the peasant population of Amakusa reacted to rebellion on the nearby Shimabara Peninsula by rebelling in like manner. The Shimabara Rebellion (1637–1638), as the uprising on the peninsula and on Amakusa is known, was touched off by widespread poverty and starvation and excessive taxation, but it was widely perceived as a Christian rebellion. The local daimyo in Shimabara was unable to supress the revolt, and it took shogunal armies nearly two months to put it down. After the rebellion the islands were administered by shogunal deputies as a fisc *(tenryō)* of the *bakufu*. The rebellion confirmed the *bakufu* in its anti-Christian policies, and it is widely believed to have provoked the expulsion of the Portuguese from Japan in 1639, the last step in the establishment of policies of "seclusion" *(sakoku).*

In most of Japan, the *bakufu* was successful in exterminating Christianity, but in Amakusa the surviving believers went underground, preserving their Christian beliefs in highly syncretized form until the modern period. With the end of the proscription of Christianity in 1873, the Amakusa Christians reestablished contact with Rome, but they retain their distinctive syncretic beliefs and practices.

[*See also* Shimabara.]

C. R. Boxer, *The Christian Century in Japan, 1549–1650* (1951). George Elison, *Deus Destroyed: The Image of Christianity in Early Modern Japan* (1973). Ivan Morris, *The Nobility of Failure: Tragic Heroes in the History of Japan* (1976). RONALD P. TOBY

AMANGKURAT I, emperor of Mataram (r. 1646–1677), son and successor of Sultan Agung (1613–1646) and the quintessential Javanese tyrant. He attempted to centralize the administration and finances of the Mataram empire for his benefit but in doing so offended regional interests and deep-rooted Javanese political traditions of consultation, consensus, and the dispersal of economic, political, and military power. One of his main administrative techniques was to murder his opponents. This tyranny precipitated the greatest rebellion of seventeenth-century Java, led by Trunajaya, which broke out in 1674 and culminated in the conquest of the court in 1677. Amangkurat I died while fleeing the capital.

[*See also* Mataram *and* Trunajaya.]

Theodore G. Pigeaud, *Islamic States in Java, 1500–1700* (1976). M. C. RICKLEFS

AMANULLAH (1892–1960), king of Afganistan from 1919 to 1929. During his reign he gained Afghanistan's political independence from Great Britain and launched an ambitious program of modernization, opposition to which cost him his throne.

When his father, King Habibullah (r. 1901–1919), was assassinated in Jelalabad, Amanullah was governor of Kabul. He convinced the army and the power elite to prefer his claim to that of his uncle and elder brothers. In May 1919 he launched a *jihad* (holy war) against Great Britain; although the one-month war was militarily inconclusive, diplomatic negotiations brought about the end of British control over Afghanistan's foreign relations. The Soviet leader V. I. Lenin welcomed Amanullah's anticolonial stand, extended diplomatic recognition, and offered material assistance and a treaty. The Soviet policy of repression in Muslim Central Asia, however, quickly led to friction between the two states. Amanullah soon sought relations with countries that did not seem to have territorial designs on the area; he established ties with France, Germany, Italy, Japan, and Turkey, although he failed to initiate official relations with the United States.

Advised by Ottoman-educated Afghans and impressed by Turkey's example, Amanullah embarked on his own scheme of development. First, he gave the country its first constitution and three times convened the Loya Jirga (Grand Assembly), composed of various segments of the power elite, to ratify his important decisions. Second, he systematized the administrative divisions of the country into a territorial hierarchy of subdistricts, districts, and provinces. The centrally appointed administrators at each level were assisted by a locally elected consultative body. Third, he replaced tax farming with directly collected taxes in cash. Fourth, he tolerated a free press, entrusted the intelligentsia with responsible positions in the government, and spent a major portion of the revenue of the state on the expansion of education.

Amanullah neglected his army, however, and failed to forge a national consensus. In 1924 he overcame a rural rebellion but was unable to withstand a series of revolts in 1929. He was forced into exile in Italy, where he died on 26 April 1960.

[*See also* Afghanistan.]

L. Adamec, *Afghanistan 1900–1923: A Diplomatic History* (1967). Leon Poullada, *Reform and Rebellion in Afghanistan 1919–29: King Amanullah's Failure to Transform a Tribal Society* (1973). ASHRAF GHANI

AMARAPURA, central Burma, Burmese capital from 1782 to 1823 and from 1837 to 1858. Bodawhpaya (r. 1782–1819) ordered construction of a new capital in 1782 because Ava, then the capital, was considered inauspicious as a result of the various coups and bloodletting that had taken place there that year. On 12 May 1783, the entire court and populace were shifted to Amarapura (Pali, "city of immortals"). The palace and its environs were destroyed by fire in 1810 but rebuilt by 1812. Bagyidaw (r. 1819–1837) moved the capital back to Ava in 1823 after another major fire. Tharrawaddy (r. 1837–1846) reestablished Amarapura as the capital in 1837, and it remained so until the building of Mandalay by Mindon (r. 1853–1878) in 1857.

[*See also* Bodawhpaya; Ava; Bagyidaw; Tharrawaddy; *and* Mindon.]

William J. Koenig

AMARAVATI (ancient Dhanyakataka), Buddhist site of the third century BCE to the twelfth century CE, located on the Krishna River in Andhra Pradesh, east India. The main stupa, erected in the third century BCE by the emperor Ashoka, was significantly enlarged in the second and third centuries of the common era. It consisted of a dome resting on a drum,with rectangular platforms *(ayaka)* projecting in the direction of the four cardinal points, each platform culminating in a group of five pillars *(aryaka)*. The stupa was surrounded by a circular passage and lined by a carved balustrade. Stone slabs, carved with narrative scenes of the Jatakas and the life of the historical Buddha, covered the stupa and railing; the outer side of the latter, dating from around 150 CE, illustrates the best sculpture of this period. Sculpture of Vajrayana deities and inscriptions of the seventh to twelfth century indicate continued activity of later sects at the site.

D. Barrett, *Sculptures from Amarāvatī in the British Museum* (1954). James Burgess, *The Buddhist Stupas of Amaravati and Jaggayyapeta* (1887).

Geri Hockfield Malandra

AMATERASU ŌMIKAMI ("great heaven-illuminating deity"), the sun deity central to Shinto mythology, identified as progenetrix of Japan's imperial family. The *Kojiki* (712) describes the goddess' difficulties with her younger brother Susano-o no Mikoto, as a result of which she hid herself in a cave, bringing darkness on the world. Lured out by the other divinities, she resumed her benevolent leadership and sent her grandson Ninigi no Mikoto to pacify the Japanese islands with the imperial regalia—the mirror, sword, and curved jewel *(magatama)*. His great-grandson became the first emperor, Jimmu.

The Ise Shrine is sacred to Amaterasu and the imperial family, and in time it became the object of great pilgrimages. The feminine, shamanistic, and solar attributes of Amaterasu have affected Japanese attitudes toward the ruling house. In addition, most Japanese popular religions relate in some way to Amaterasu and sun worship.

[*See also* Ise *and* Shinto.]

Marius B. Jansen

AMBEDKAR, BHIMRAO RAMJI (1891–1956), lawyer, statesman, author, reformer, educator, law minister in India's first cabinet, and chairman of the drafting committee of the Indian constitution, known affectionately as Babasaheb in his capacity as the revered spokesman for India's Untouchables. Ambedkar was born in the cantonment town of Mhow, where his father, who had left the traditional duties of his Untouchable *mahar* caste, was an army school headmaster. In 1901 the family moved to Bombay to educate the youngest and brightest of fourteen children; Ambedkar graduated from Elphinstone College and with the help of non-brahman princes, chiefly the *gaikwad* of Baroda, secured a Ph.D. from Columbia University in New York and a D.Sc. from the University of London as well as passing the bar from Gray's Inn. When he returned permanently to Bombay in 1923 he was the second member of his large caste to secure a college degree and one of the most highly educated men in Bombay Province.

Ambedkar worked to reform, invigorate, and unify Untouchables through his newspapers and widespread Depressed Classes Conferences. He also worked for political rights and economic opportunity as a member of the Bombay Legislative Assembly and through testimony to the Southborough and Simon Commissions and the Starte Committee. Selected as a delegate to the Round Table Conferences of 1930–1932, he pleaded for separate electorates for Untouchables as a minority, a position that brought him into conflict with Mohandas K. Gandhi. Their "Poona Pact" of 1932 achieved the compromise of reserved seats in legislatures for "scheduled" (Untouchable) castes that still obtains. Ambedkar founded the Independent Labour Party (1936), the Scheduled Castes Federation (1942), and the Republican party (1956), but although he succeeded in politicizing many Untouchables and creating special governmental privileges for them, his parties did not achieve effective political power.

Ambedkar's educational and religious concerns have had far-reaching effect. The People's Education Society, established in 1945, and other Ambedkar-inspired groups now run complexes of colleges in Bombay, Aurangabad, Mahad, and Nagpur. The stress on education has produced an important Dalit ("downtrodden") literary movement in Marathi. A recent agitation to rename Marathwada University in Aurangabad after Dr. Ambedkar, however, brought about violence against scheduled castes and Buddhists.

After a series of unsuccessful temple *satyagrahas*

in the early days of his movement, Ambedkar announced in 1935 that he "would not die a Hindu." Twenty years later, two months before his death, Ambedkar converted to Buddhism at a mass meeting in Nagpur. Over four million subsequent conversions have resulted in a revival of Buddhism in India.

[*See also* Untouchability *and* Caste.]

Dhananjay Keer, *Dr. Ambedkar: Life and Mission* (3d ed., 1971). W. N. Kuber, *B. R. Ambedkar* (1978). Vasant Moon, ed., *Dr. Babasaheb Ambedkar: Writings and Speeches*, multivolume series (1979–). Eleanor Zelliot, "Gandhi and Ambedkar—A Study in Leadership," in *The Untouchables in Contemporary India*, edited by J. Michael Mahar (1972).

ELEANOR ZELLIOT

AMBOINA MASSACRE, the execution by Dutch authorities in 1623 of ten English merchants of the British East India Company and ten Javanese "co-conspirators." They had been charged with conspiracy to seize the local Dutch fortress by the governor of Amboina Island (in the Malay Archipelago), a member of the Dutch East India Company. The execution is often cited in colonial histories as an illustration of either British or Dutch treachery: the Dutch call it the Amboina "conspiracy," while the English point out that the merchants were trading under the protection of the governor of Amboina. Nonetheless the Amboina episode was part of a process in the early seventeenth century through which the Dutch gained an upper hand over their British competitors, who withdrew to India shortly after the affair, as well as over the eastern Indonesian indigenous states and their populations—the primary victims of the company's violent seizure of the spice trade.

[*See also* East India Company; Dutch East India Company; *and* Spice Trade.]

JAMES R. RUSH

AMIDISM. Devotion to the Buddha Amida (Sanskrit, Amitabha; Chinese, Amituofo) and belief that through Amida's compassion the deceased can be reborn in his Western Paradise, or Pure Land, has been a powerful current in Mahayana Buddhism throughout Asia. In Japan, in particular, Amida has attracted the deepest devotion of all the Buddhas in the Mahayana pantheon. The power of Amidism lies in the promise it offers to ordinary men and women, as well as to monks and nuns, that access to the Pure Land is open to them through an "easy path" of religious practice. All that is required is faith in Amida expressed in the invocation of the Buddha's name known as the *nembutsu:* "Namu Amida Butsu" ("Praise to the Buddha Amida"). Amidism also gave rise to a rich devotional literature and art depicting the delights to be found by the faithful in Amida's paradise and the pains of the hells to which sinners could expect to be consigned.

The title *Amida* derives from the Sanskrit names *Amitabha,* meaning "infinite light," and *Amitayus,* meaning "eternal life." The principal teachings relating to Amida and his Pure Land are found in the *Pure Land Sutra,* or *Sukhavativyuha.* The longer and older version of this sutra, incorporating Hinayana notions of *karma* and individual striving for salvation, stresses the attainment of rebirth in the Pure Land through the performance of meritorious deeds and faith in Amitabha. The shorter version, which was more widely used in China and Japan, teaches that the only requirement for salvation is faith in Amida.

The origins of the cult of Amida are ancient and obscure. Amitabha is hardly mentioned in the earliest Buddhist scriptures. When he does appear he is a very minor figure. He only begins to emerge as one of the Buddhas of the Mahayana pantheon around the first century CE, when he is identified as a Buddha of longevity and infinite light presiding over a "Western Paradise." The early cult may have blended Indian and West Asian notions. Ahura Mazda, a divinity of light in the Iranian Avesta is also enthroned in a "Western Paradise." The idea of Amida as a compassionate saving divinity, one who is frequently depicted as the central figure of a trinity, may also have owed something to Greek or early Christian influences.

The cult of Amida was further developed in China. During the third and early fourth centuries monks like Que Gongce (died c. 274), Weishidu, and Zhi Dun all expressed devotion to Amituofo and vowed to be reborn in his paradise. These figures sought to integrate Amidist ideas with indigenous Daoist notions of longevity and the (Daoist) Western Paradise, presided over by the Queen Mother of the West.

Huiyuan (334–417), a disciple of Daoan and head of the monastic community at Lu Shan, is credited with the founding of the Pure Land school, as it later came to be called. Like Daoan, Huiyuan was a master of the Prajnaparamita sutras and of meditation. He taught that access to the glories of Amituofo's paradise could be attained through meditation. Huiyuan is sometimes said to have founded a group consisting of monks and laypeople devoted to Amituofo and known as the White Lotus Society. Whether Huiyuan actually founded such a group and whether this group of scholars and recluses actively spread Pure Land teaching is open to question. There is no doubt, however, that he and his followers meditated on Amituofo and made vows to be reborn in the Western Paradise. He thus served as an inspiration and a model and came to be regarded as the first Pure Land patriarch in China. Tanluan (476–542), Daochuo (562–645), and Shandao (613–681) were also active in spreading Amidist devotion. In his *Essays on the Western Paradise (Anluoji)*, for instance, Daochuo argued that in an age of decline of the Buddha's teaching, invocation (*nianfo*) of the Buddha Amitabha's name was the surest way to assure rebirth in the Pure Land. Shandao also stressed the efficacy of the *nianfo*. As a result of the activities of these influential monks and their followers, Amidist devotion took root in China both as a school of Buddhism and as a current of popular devotionalism that persisted through the purges of Buddhism during the Tang dynasty.

Amidism came to Japan early. It is recorded that the *Sukhavativyuha* was publicly recited there in 640. A Pure Land school was slower to develop. For several centuries Amidism was known mostly to monks and nuns within the scholarly framework of Nara Buddhism and then within Tendai and Shingon Buddhism as part of an esoteric practice of contemplation on the virtues of the various Buddhas. The practices of praying for the dead, invoking Amida through the *nembutsu* (the Japanese pronunciation of the Chinese term *nianfo*), and circumambulating while concentrating on Amida *(jōgyō zanmai)* were also common.

In the mid-Heian period, Amidist devotion began to attract members of the court nobility. The vivid descriptions of Amida's Western Paradise and of the Buddhist hells provided by Genshin (942–1017) in his *Essentials of Salvation (Ōjōyōshū)* helped to spread Pure Land devotion among monks and laypeople and inspired in their minds visions of bliss and terror. Genshin argued that mere repetition of the *nembutsu* was sufficient for rebirth *(ōjō)*. Nobles built special halls and temples, such as the Byōdōin at Uji, in which to enshrine Amida. Moreover, the strong belief that in the year 1052 Japan would enter the third and final age of devotion of the Buddha's teaching (the era known as *mappō*) strengthened the tendency to stress dependence on the "other power,"or saving compassion *(tariki)* of Amida. The teachings of Ryōnin (1072–1132), Yōkan (1032–1111), and Chingai (1091–1152) further spread Pure Land devotion among the Heian aristocracy, while the wandering mendicant Kōya (903–972) began to carry the promise of rebirth to the common people.

However, it was only with Hōnen (1133–1212), the founder of the Pure Land school, or Jōdoshū; his disciple Shinran (1173–1262), founder of the True Pure Land school, or Jōdo Shinshū; Rennyo (1415–1499), eighth-generation patriarch of Jōdo Shinshū; and the medicant Ippen (1239–1289), founder of the Timely school, or Jishū, that Amidism established its independence of the older schools. The various Amidist schools established by these medieval pioneers came to constitute the most vigorous and popular current in Japanese Buddhism. There are today in Japan more than thirteen million Jōdo Shinshū followers, some three million Jōdoshū devotees, and forty thousand Jishū members.

[*See also* Tendai, Shingon, Pure Land, Hōnen, Shinran, *and* Rennyo.]

Wm. Theodore deBary, ed., *The Buddhist Tradition in India, China, and Japan* (1969). H. Byron Earhart, *Japanese Religion: Unity and Diversity* (1974). Joseph M. Kitagawa, *Religion in Japanese History* (1966).

MARTIN COLLCUTT

AMIN, HAFIZOLLAH (1928–1979), briefly president of Afghanistan. Amin was born in 1928 in Paghman. After studying education in Afghanistan he received an M.A. from Teachers' College at Columbia University (1956–1958). Between 1963 and 1965 he spent two additional years at Columbia but returned to Afghanistan before receiving his Ph.D. According to Amin, it was in the United States that he gained his "political consciousness." In 1965 he joined the People's Democratic Party of Afghanistan and was sympathetic to the Khalqi faction. He was elected for a four-year term to the Afghan parliament in 1969.

Amin's principal function in the party was to recruit and organize sympathizers in the armed forces. Because of this role, after the April 1978 coup the official press called Amin the "commander of the revolution." Between April 1978 and September 1979, while Noor Mohammed Taraki was the country's president, Amin was generally regarded as the regime's strongman. Internal difficulties led to a power struggle within the party, which led in turn to Amin's election as president in September 1979. In December 1979, however, Amin was overthrown and killed by the Soviets.

ZALMAY KHALILZAD

AMIR ALI (1849–1928), Indian lawyer-jurist, politician, and "liberal" Muslim thinker. A member of a family formerly in service to the nawabs of Awadh, Amir Ali attended British-sponsored schools in Calcutta and was called to the bar from London's Inner Temple. A successful barrister in Calcutta, he became a justice of that city's High Court. In 1908 he became the first non-Briton to sit as a "Law Lord" of the Privy Council. Active in the Muslim League, Amir Ali's move to England gave him some influence in government circles. His books, most important of which was *The Spirit of Islam,* were written for European readers. An admirer of British "Progressive" thinkers, he emphasized the role of Islam in inspiring human development. Ali argued that a reworking of the faith along "rational" lines would ensure Islam its rightful place in the vanguard of human evolution.

[*See also* Awadh *and* All-India Muslim League.]

Amir Ali, *Memoirs and Other Writings,* edited by S. R. Wasti (1968). P. Hardy, *Muslims of British India* (1972).

GREGORY C. KOZLOWSKI

AMIR KABIR (1807–1851), Mirza Taqi Khan Farahani (Amir Nizam), Iranian prime minister and reformer of the Qajar period. Son of a minister's cook, he was first employed in the administration of the crown prince in Tabriz. He rose to prominence as the head of the Iranian mission to the Erzurum Conference (1843–1846). Upon accession to the throne, Nasir al-Din Shah (r. 1848–1896) appointed him to premiership with broad executive power. He embarked on a comprehensive program of reforms, which included administrative, military, and financial reorganizations; new agricultural and industrial projects; reduction of the trade deficit; and the foundation of the first technical college. His authoritative centralization policies brought the defeat of the Babi resistance (1848–1850). His brief term of office came to an end when he lost control over the shah and the administration and was executed. Perhaps the most prominent of nineteenth-century reformers, his idealized image served as a model for future generations.

[*See also* Qajar, Nasir al-Din.]

Robert Watson, *A History of Persia from the Beginning of the Nineteenth Century to the Year 1858* (1866).

ABBAS AMANAT

AMIR KHUSRAU (1253–1325), the most celebrated Persian poet of India. Khusrau was a versatile genius, accomplished not only as a poet but also as an artist, humorist, soldier, historian, naturalist, linguist, mystic, and inventor of musical tones. A Lachin Turk by descent, he had an Indian taste and temperament. He was the court poet of seven Delhi sultans, for whom he produced most of his works; he also composed five historical idylls (1299–1302) as a rejoinder to the *Khamsa* of the Persian poet Nizami. His *Ijaz-i Khusravi* (1319) contains letters and documents that he drafted to be used as models for specific occasions. Khusrau's lyrical poetry has depth of emotion, rhythmic beauty, and artistic perfection. A disciple of Shaikh Nizam ud-Din Auliya, he had strong mystic leanings. He lies buried near his master's cenotaph in Delhi. Deep humanism, profound faith in the higher values of mysticism, and patriotic fervor characterize his poetry.

[*See also* Delhi Sultanate *and* Nizam ud-Din Auliya.]

Mohammed Habib, *Hazrat Amir Khusrau of Delhi* (1927). Mohammad Wahid Mirza, *The Life and Works of Amir Khusrau* (1935).

KHALIQ AHMAD NIZAMI

AMIR SJARIFUDDIN (1907–1948), Indonesian political leader. Born in Medan, Sumatra, Amir received a Western-language education, graduating from the faculty of law in Jakarta in 1933. In the closing years of Dutch rule he was a leader of the nationalist organizations Partindo and Gerindo, and in 1940 he became a member of the Department of Economic Affairs. In 1944 he was arrested and sentenced to death for organizing and heading an underground movement to overthrow the Japanese government, but thanks to the intercession of President Sukarno and Vice President Hatta the sentence was commuted. Amir then served in Premier Sjahrir's cabinet as the minister of defense and information (1945–1947) and founded what eventually became the Indonesian Socialist Party. On 3 July 1947 he became premier as well as defense minister. He headed the Indonesian delegation in the negotiations with the Dutch that led to the controversial Renville Agreement of January 1948. Discredited by his role in this unpopular agreement, Amir was compelled to resign. Joining radical opposition to the Sukarno-Hatta government, he became involved in the Madiun Affair of 18 September 1948 and was arrested and executed by the Indonesian army in December of that year.

[*See also* Indonesia, Republic of; Gerindo; Partai Sosialis Indonesia; *and* Madiun.]

AUDREY R. KAHIN

AMOY. *See* Xiamen.

AMRITSAR, city in Punjab, India, near the Pakistan border, with a population of about 600,000 (in 1981); an important religious, commercial, industrial center. It was founded by Ramdas, the fourth guru of the Sikh religion, in 1577. According to Sikh tradition, the sacred scripture, the *Granth Sahib,* was compiled here by the fifth guru, Arjun, in 1603–1604 and placed in a shrine, known as the Hari Mandir, or temple of God, in the middle of a vast tank. Because it is covered with gold leaf, the Hari Mandir became known to Europeans as the Golden Temple. The temple acquired special sanctity because of its connection with the gurus and the scriptures.

While Lahore was the capital of the Sikh kingdom founded by Ranjit Singh, it was at Amritsar that he signed the treaty with the East India Company in 1806 acknowledging his sovereignty over the territories west of the Sutlej River and British sovereignty over the areas of the Punjab to the east. It was also here that a treaty was signed in 1846 marking the defeat of the Sikhs by the British.

After the annexation of the Punjab by the British in 1849, Amritsar took on new importance because it was at the center of the railways and highways linking the northwest to the rest of India. The establishment of light industry, such as weaving and tanning, and the development of a prosperous agricultural economy based on wheat and cotton led to rapid growth in the population by the end of the century. With the growth of nationalism the Golden Temple and its precincts also acquired a new role, becoming the center for political activity as Sikh leaders asserted the special place of the Sikh community in the Punjab.

Amritsar was the scene of two great tragedies that helped to shape Indian history in the twentieth century. One was the Jallianwala Bagh Massacre of 1919, in which the British army opened fire on a crowd attending a nationalist protest meeting, killing at least four hundred and wounding many hundreds more. This action caused widespread revulsion toward the British throughout India. The second event occurred after a group of militant Sikhs, led by Jarnail Singh Bhindranwale, a fiery young religious leader, seized the Golden Temple and used it as a base for armed attacks against the

FIGURE 1. *The Golden Temple, Amritsar.*

government of Indira Gandhi, which the group regarded as pursuing anti-Sikh policies. On 6 June 1984 the Indian army invaded the temple, killing Bhindranwale and hundreds of his followers and damaging the temple buildings. The anger that this event aroused in the Sikh community led directly to the assassination of Prime Minister Gandhi and, in turn, to the revenge killing of hundreds of Sikhs in Delhi and elsewhere.

[*See also* Jallianwala Bagh Massacre; Punjab; Singh, Ranjit; *and* Sikhism.]

MARK JUERGENSMEYER

AMU DARYA. *See* Oxus River.

AMUR RIVER, called Heilongjiang (Black Dragon River) in Chinese. The Amur River begins at the confluence of the Argun and Shilka rivers; flowing east and southeast, it forms part of the border between China and the Soviet Union until it reaches the northeastern tip of Heilongjiang Province. From there it turns sharply northward, flowing through the Soviet Union into the subarctic waters of the Strait of Tatary.

The Amur River region has been the site of Sino-Soviet conflict since the seventeenth century, when the Treaty of Nerchinsk (1689) established the border between Siberia and Manchuria. In the nineteenth century the Russian seizure of lands north of the Amur and east of the Ussuri was ratified in unequal treaties, which have been the source of territorial disputes between the USSR and China in the twentieth century.

JOHN A. RAPP

ANAHITA. Aredvi Sura Anahita, a Zoroastrian goddess whose name means "the moist, mighty, undefiled one," appears to be an amalgam of two deities: an Indo-Iranian river goddess called Sarasvati in Sanskrit, and an alien goddess, possibly the Assyro-Babylonian Ishtar, a goddess of love, war, and fertility.

Zoroaster did not recognize a water deity; Anahita is first mentioned in the inscriptions of the Achaemenid king Artaxerxes II (405–359 BCE). She appears to have been the patron deity of the Sasanid dynasty, and her cult extended to Asia Minor and Armenia.

In the Avestan hymn to Anahita she is represented as the personification of a river or spring. Because of her connection with water she is worshiped as a goddess of fertility, but she also bestows riches and brings victory in battle.

[*See also* Artaxerxes II *and* Zoroastrianism.]

Mary Boyce, *A History of Zoroastrianism* (1975), vol. 1. H. Lommel, "Anahita-Sarasvati," in *Asiatica: Festschrift Friedrich Weller* (1954), pp. 405–413.

LUCIANNE C. BULLIET

ANALECTS. *See* Lunyu.

ANANDA MAHIDOL (1925–1946), King Rama VIII of Thailand, was born 30 September 1925 in Heidelberg, Germany, son of Prince Mahidol Adulyadej and grandson of King Chulalongkorn. After the death of his father in 1933, Ananda left for Switzerland with his mother, brother, and sister to continue his studies. Ananda succeeded his uncle, King Prajadhipok, who abdicated in 1935, but since Ananda was a minor, Chaophraya Yommarat (Pan Sukhum) and Prince Athitthipapha were appointed regents. Ananda remained in neutral Switzerland throughout World War II, and he returned to Siam on 5 December 1945. On 9 July 1946, four days before his scheduled departure to complete his studies in Europe, Ananda was found dead of a mysterious gunshot wound. He was never officially crowned. His death put a blemish on the premiership of Pridi Phanomyong, who eventually had to resign.

[*See also* Thailand *and* Pridi Phanomyong.]

THAK CHALOEMTIARANA

ANARCHISM. A tradition that existed in both ancient and modern China, anarchism can be viewed as both a philosophical idea and a political movement, to follow the distinction of historian George Woodcock.

Philosophical Anarchism. As the pure idea of a society without government, anarchism in China perhaps has origins in the writings of the early Daoists of the Spring and Autumn (722–481 BCE) and Warring States (403–221 BCE) periods. The philosopher Yang Zhu (440–c. 350 BCE) is said to have advocated an extreme individualism, in which there was no need for government. Laozi, traditionally thought to be the author of the *Daode jing (The Way and Its Power),* which was written between the seventh and third century BCE, called for sages to rule by *wuwei,* or doing nothing that is not spontaneous, and specifically denounced both the Confucian concept of government by moral virtue and the Legalist concept of government by rewards and punishments. In the *Daode jing,* moreover, the very underpinnings of the state, including law, war, taxation, and education, are condemned as unnatural and disastrously counterproductive, in that they introduce artificial constraints or impinge on natural forces. The thinker Zhuangzi (c. 360–290 BCE) extended the anarchistic tendencies in Daoism by equating the rise of sages who were trying to order the world with the rise of great brigands and thieves. The ideal society for both Laozi and Zhuangzi was a small, self-sufficient community, with few inhabitants and simple technology, in which no individual or group dominated another.

Some scholars, nevertheless, while admitting that the Daoist political critique called for an extremely limited government, deny that Laozi or Zhuangzi were philosophical anarchists, since both framed their writings as advice to the ruler on how best to govern. If one follows Joseph Needham, however, and treats their ideal rulers as the leaders of chiefs of China's "prefeudal collectivist society," the possibility exists that the early Daoists were harking back to a dimly remembered primitive communal past and thus were early advocates of stateless communism. [See also Daoism; Laozi; *and* Zhuangzi.]

The anarchist potential of philosophical Daoism was most fully realized during the Wei–Jin era (220–420 CE) of the Period of Disunion (220–589). After the coup of the Sima family against the Wei rulers and their founding of the Western Jin dynasty (265–317), disillusioned scholars and poets, using the language of the prevailing *qingtan* revival of Daoism, celebrated *ziran* (the spontaneous or natural) as a superior way of life, free from convention and requiring refusal to serve in government. The poet Ruan Ji (210–263) and the obscure thinker Bao Jingyan (fl. about 300) both condemned government as unnatural and harmful, equating it with the domination of the strong and wealthy over the weak and poor, thus linking government with the protection of private property seized by theft. Both claimed that in the distant past, society was well ordered and peaceful, without any government at all. The poet Tao Qian (365–427) showed much influence from this anarchistic interpretation of Daoism in his famous poem *Taohua yuanji (Peach Blossom Spring),* an allegory in which a fisherman accidentally discovers a long-lost idyllic community flourishing without government. [*See also* Qingtan.] Nevertheless, only scattered individuals in later epochs, such as the Buddhist-influenced thinker Wu Nengzi of the late Tang dynasty (618–907), echoed the Daoist depiction of an ideal stateless society. In the popular Chinese consciousness Daoism was more often equated with passive acquiescence to the natural order of things rather than with opposition to government.

The Modern Anarchist Movement. It is perhaps because of the traditional equation of Daoism with a passive acceptance of fate that when the Western anarchist movement reached China in the early twentieth century, Daoism was seen as only one more indication of China's weakness and backwardness in the face of the Western onslaught and thus was seldom referred to for inspiration. This anarchist movement, which was part of the larger socialist movement of the late nineteenth and early twentieth centuries, first entered China through the students who were sent to Europe and Japan at the turn of the century. In Tokyo, a group of Chinese students who followed the Japanese anarchist Kōtoku Shūsui (1871–1911) founded an anarchist study group and the influential journal *Tianyi bao (Heavenly Justice)* in 1907. Their brand of anarchism was inspired by the antimodern, primitivist communism of Leo Tolstoy (1828–1910), and at times it drew on the Chinese utopian tradition, both Daoist and Confucian. Simultaneous with the activities of the Chinese anarchists in Japan, a group of students in Paris began publishing the journal *Xin shiji (New Century),* which was heavily influenced by the ideas of Peter Kropotkin (1842–1921), who called for full anarchist communism based on scientific application of the evolutionary principle of mutual aid.

Although after the 1911 Revolution many of the returning students joined the Guomindang (Kuomintang, or Nationalist Party) and drifted toward right-wing politics, the anarchist movement nevertheless did flourish for a while among intellectual circles in the large urban centers. The greatest anarchist leader of this period was Shifu (1884–1915), who dropped his family name, Liu, to demonstrate his refusal to participate in any corrupt institutions aiding domination of or by the state. Shifu formed a series of societies to study and practice anarchist morality, most notably the Huimingshe (Cockcrow Society), and propagated anarchist ideas in the journal *Minsheng (People's Voice).* Shifu had been an exponent of "propaganda by deed," that is, political assassination and bombings, to the point of losing a hand in a bomb explosion. By 1912, after serving nearly two years in prison, however, he had converted to a more peaceful interpretation of anarchism, although he still called for a social revolution.

Shifu's activities provided much of the inspiration for anarchist activity in China until the late 1920s and early 1930s, although many scholars date the beginning of the demise of the anarchist movement with his death from tuberculosis in 1915.

Anarchists did achieve some success among the working class in the larger cities, and from Shifu's death until the founding of the Chinese Communist Party (CCP) in 1921, anarchism was perhaps the leading socialist movement among the Chinese avant-garde intellectuals and radical trade union organizers. After 1917, however, and the introduction of the model of the Bolshevik Revolution to China as a more successful mode of nationalistic, scientific socialism, anarchism gradually faded into oblivion. Anarchist intellectuals did, however, carry out vigorous debates with the Communists throughout the 1920s, starting with the exchanges between the anarchist Ou Shengpai and the Marxist Chen Duxiu in 1921 and continuing between 1924 and 1925, when the anarchists condemned the Guomindang's policy of cooperation with the Soviets and attacked the totalitarian direction of the Bolshevik Revolution. Perhaps the last Chinese anarchist of note was the novelist Li Feigan (b. 1904), more famous under his pseudonym, Ba Jin, formed from the names of the two most influential Western anarchists, Bakunin and Kropotkin. Ba Jin's works continued to contain anarchist characters and ideas well into the 1940s. [*See also* Ba Jin.]

Although eventually totally eclipsed by Marxism-Leninism, Chinese anarchism nevertheless had a long-lasting impact on Chinese socialism. In their iconoclasm and attempt to borrow the most modern, radical, and scientific ideas from the West while preserving the advantages of China's cultural heritage, the anarchists were the precursors of Maoism. Indeed, Mao Zedong (1893–1976) himself was an anarchist for a short period in his youth. One could perhaps speculate that at least unconsciously, the anarchist critique of Marxism survived in the antibureaucratic strands of his thought that surfaced in the Cultural Revolution. Nevertheless, it is perhaps the Marxist critique of anarchism for its failure to sustain the socialist revolution in the face of well-organized and entrenched opposition that had the most influence on Mao's thought and on the course of the Chinese revolution. In retrospect, however, considering the recent official revelation of the despotism and oppression of the Cultural Revolution, perhaps the early-twentieth-century Chinese anarchist opposition to Marxism still has lasting value.

[*See also* Marxism and Socialism: Marxism in China.]

Étienne Balazs, "Nihilistic Revolt or Mystical Escapism: Currents of Thought in China during the Third Century A.D.," in *Chinese Civilization and Bureaucracy: Variations on a Theme,* edited by Arthur F. Wright and translated by H. M. Wright (1967). Martin Bernal, "The Triumph of Anarchism over Marxism, 1906–1907," in *China in Revolution: The First Phase, 1900–1913,* edited by Mary C. Wright (1968). Arif Dirlik and Edward S. Krebs, "Socialism and Anarchism in Early Republican China," *Modern China* 7.2 (April 1981): 117–151. Internationalist (pseudonym), *The Origins of the Anarchist Movement in China* (1968). Joseph Needham, *Science and Civilisation in China,* vol. 2, *History of Scientific Thought* (1956). Robert A. Scalapino and George T. Yu, *The Chinese Anarchist Movement* (1961). George Woodcock, *Anarchism: A History of Libertarian Ideas and Movements* (1962).

JOHN A. RAPP

ANAUKHPETLUN (r. 1606–1628), a principal architect of the precolonial Burmese state. Although unable to fulfill his original ambition of reconstituting the far-flung First Toungoo empire, he conquered the southern sector of the Irrawaddy River basin, as well as an extensive Shan region east of the Salween River, between 1607 and 1626. With minor alterations, the area of Burmese suzerainty at the time of his death was preserved until the British conquest. In addition to reoccupying the coast from his Upper Burma base, Anaukhpetlun was also responsible for commercial initiatives and for experimental reforms in provincial administration.

[*See also* Toungoo Dynasties.]

G. E. Harvey, *A History of Burma from the Earliest Times* (1925; reprint, 1967). Maung Htin Aung, *A History of Burma* (1967).

VICTOR B. LIEBERMAN

ANAWRAHTA (Aniruddha), traditionally considered the founder of the Pagan dynasty of Burma, although he was in fact preceded by several centuries of able monarchs. He reigned from 1044 to 1077.

Under Anawrahta, the civilization of Pagan underwent major transformations. Anawrahta was most noted for his military and administrative abilities: he secured the vulnerable northern frontier by building several dozen forts; he repaired old irrigation works and built new ones to feed his growing population; and he asserted his authority over the lower Burma port cities, thereby providing his growing kingdom with much-needed skilled labor, the more sophisticated Mon culture, and commercial revenues. Thanks to Anawrahta's economic and cultural reforms, the small kingdom of Pagan, essentially an inland, agrarian, and simple peasant-military society, grew into a large urban center. Myriad temples and other religious edifices were built on its plains, and its political, administrative, cultural, and military presence subsequently extended over most of the Irrawaddy River valley, from Bhamo on the China border to Mergui on the Gulf of Martaban.

Anawrahta's reputation went beyond Burma's borders to Sri Lanka, where his kingdom was recognized as a bastion of Theravada Buddhism against the might and power of the Hindu Cholas, then threatening both Sri Lanka and coastal Southeast Asia. He was said to have provided money and supplies to the beleaguered Vijayabahu I of Sri Lanka. Anawrahta's patronage of a certain temple (Shwezigon) in Pagan made its style the most popular form until today.

Anawrahta instituted the kind of leadership that began the highly important process of transforming Burmese society, thereby allowing his successors to institutionalize changes into permanent traditions. Along with Kyanzittha and several other monarchs, Anawrahta goes down in Burma's history as one of its most effective leaders.

[*See also* Pagan.]

G. E. Harvey, *A History of Burma, from the Earliest Times* (1925; reprint, 1967). G. H. Luce, *Old Burma—Early Pagan* (1969).

MICHAEL AUNG-THWIN

AN CHAE-HONG (1891–1965?), a leader of the Korean nationalist movement, journalist, moderate right-wing politician, and civil administrator of the South Korean Interim Government.

Born into a rich rural family in Kyŏnggi Province in central Korea, An received both a traditional and modern education. He graduated from Waseda University, Tokyo, in 1914. In 1919 he was imprisoned for three years for his covert activities in support of the Korean Provisional Government established in Shanghai in the wake of Japan's 1910 annexation of Korea. Upon release, An became the chief editorial writer and eventually the president of the Korean-language daily newspaper *Chosŏn ilbo;* he wrote 1,550 editorials and commentaries, many of which had distinctly nationalistic overtones and some of which caused the Japanese colonial officials to suspend the paper and imprison the author. An was also active in the Sin'ganhoe, a nationalist organization of intellectuals, and in the Chosŏn'ŏ Hakhoe, an organization devoted to the study of the Korean language. If these activities helped establish An as a widely acknowledged nationalist, they also landed him in prison nine times; his prison terms totaled more than seven years.

An played a prominent role as a moderate right-wing politician after Korea's liberation in 1945. He occupied such positions as vice-chairman of the Kŏnjun (Preparatory Committee for the Founding of the Nation) and president of the Kungmindang (Nationalist Party) and unsuccessfully endeavored to build a political coalition between those on Korea's political right and left. He was appointed civil administrator by the American occupation authorities in 1947 to head the Korean components of the US military government in South Korea. In 1950 he ran successfully for a seat in the National Assembly of the fledgling Republic of Korea.

An was captured and taken to North Korea in 1950. In 1956 the North Korean government identified him as a ranking member of a consultative council for promoting peaceful reunification of Korea. He was reported to have died in P'yŏngyang in March 1965.

Gregory Henderson, *Korea: The Politics of the Vortex* (1968). Joungwon Alexander Kim, *Divided Korea: The Politics of Development, 1945–1972* (1975).

HAN-KYO KIM

AN CH'ANG-HO (1878–1938), moderate nationalist, educator, and key member of the Korean Provisional Government during the period of Japanese rule. An also was the founder of the Hŭngsadan, a fraternity of nationalist intellectuals.

Born near P'yŏngyang in P'yŏng'an Province, An attended a missionary school in Seoul and became a Christian in the mid-1890s. He was an enthusiastic participant in the activities of the Independence Club, especially in his own home district, where he also set up a coeducational school for local youths. In search of further education for himself, An went to the United States in 1902 but spent most of his time organizing the nascent Korean community in the San Francisco area. On his return to Korea in 1906, he plunged into a flurry of activities, organizing the patriotic secret society Sinminhoe, the Taesŏng School in P'yŏngyang, and the academic youth society Ch'ŏngnyŏn Hag'uhoe, among others.

When Japan annexed Korea in 1910, An went on a self-imposed exile to America, where he created the central office of the Kungminhoe (National Association) and founded, in 1913, the Hŭngsadan, an organization that came to include many Western-educated future leaders of Korea. In the years after 1919, as the Korean Provisional Government (KPG) was being organized in Shanghai, An played a key role as a peacemaker among contending factions and personalities, although he himself considered an exile government to be premature. An's formal positions in the KPG included minister of home affairs, acting premier, and director of the labor bureau. Disillusioned by the lack of unity and effectiveness of the KPG, An advocated a gradualist strategy for national salvation that emphasized education and moral uplift. He nevertheless joined Kim Ku and others in establishing the Han'guk Tongnipdang (Korean Independence Party) in 1928 and was captured by the Japanese shortly after a Korean, on Kim's order, had set off a bomb at a Japanese victory parade in Shanghai in 1932. Brought back to Korea, An spent the remainder of his life in prison.

[*See also* Korea, Japanese Government-General of; Independence Party and Club; *and* Kim Ku.]

Chong-Sik Lee, *The Politics of Korean Nationalism* (1963).

HAN-KYO KIM

AN CHUNG-GŬN (1879–1910) a leader of Korea's armed struggle to block the impending Japanese annexation of the country. An is principally known as the assassin of the Meiji statesman who was the first resident-general of Korea (1905–1909), Itō Hirobumi. An killed Itō and wounded several other Japanese officials on the train station plaform in Harbin, Manchuria, on 26 October 1909. He was arrested immediately and executed in March 1910.

An was born in Hwanghae Province and schooled in Chinese studies. At the Ch'ŏnju School, French Catholic priests introduced An to Western studies. After graduation he became a successful coal merchant. When the Japanese established their protectorate over the country in 1905, however, An sold his business to establish the Tonŭi School and participate in the patriotic education movement.

By the end of 1907, however, An had gone into exile in Manchuria and then Vladivostok. It was there that he joined with other exiles in the armed struggle against the Japanese. He held leadership positions in several guerrilla bands *(ŭibyŏng)* in 1908; in 1909 he established his own force with Yi Pŏm-jun and Ch'oe Kae-hyŏng called the Ŭiyŏng-gun.

In 1909 a meeting between former Resident-General Itō and Russian Finance Minister Kokovtsev in Harbin provided An with an opportunity to make a dramatic strike against the Japanese. According to his diary, An believed that the impending talks were a prelude to formal annexation, and he devised a plot to kill Itō. An disguised himself as a Japanese in a crowd of well-wishers on the station platform in Harbin, and he shot Itō at close range after the official party stepped off the train.

An's diary provides a chronicle of guerrilla activity in the period between 1905 and 1910. His *Treatise on Peace in the Far East,* written while in prison, illustrates the political fervor of Korean patriots during this period.

[*See also* Itō Hirobumi *and* Korea, Japanese Government-General of.]

MICHAEL ROBINSON

ANCIENT TEXT SCHOOL. *See* Guwen.

ANDAMAN AND NICOBAR ISLANDS, a union territory of the Republic of India, located in the Bay of Bengal. The Andaman group consists of 204 islands and the Nicobars include twelve inhabited and seven uninhabited islands. In the mid-eighteenth century the British established a penal colony on the Andaman Islands. The islands were occupied by the Japanese from 1942 to 1945; in 1948 the Andamans became part of the independent Republic of India. In the 1950s they were populated with people displaced from East Pakistan (now Bangladesh), evacuees from Burma, and Indian emigrants from Guyana.

WILLIAM F. FISHER

ANDA Y SALAZAR, SIMON DE (1709–1776), interim governor-general of the Philippines (October 1762–March 1764) during the British occupation of Manila and Cavite; governor-general from July 1770 to October 1776. Anda y Salazar was born in Subijana, Alava, Spain, on 28 October 1709 and studied philosophy and law at the University of Alcalá. In July 1761 he was appointed to the advisory board to the governor-general of Manila. He was designated lieutenant governor and *visitador general* in September 1762, with a mission to rally the support of Filipinos against the British. In October of that year Anda y Salazar proclaimed himself acting governor-general with a temporary capital in Bacolor, Pampanga. He accepted the return of Manila from the British in April 1764 and was reappointed governor-general of the Philippines in 1770. Anda's second term as governor-general took place during a turbulent period of Philippine history, and he was concerned mainly with the partial liquidation of Jesuit temporalities after the expulsion of the order in 1768. He was also involved in the religious controversy that pitted Archbishop Santa Justa against the friar-curates on the issues of diocesan visitation and secularization of parishes. His administration, despite some attempts at economic and military reform and commercial innovations, was hardly a success because of the controversies he generated and his abrasive personality. He died of dropsy in Cavite on 30 October 1776.

[*See also* Philippines.]

BERNARDITA REYES CHURCHILL

ANDHRA PRADESH, the largest state in South India. Its forty-three million people (1971) live in an area of 171,000 square miles. Although 88 percent of the state's population speak Telugu, and 86 percent are Hindu, the twin cities of Hyderabad-Secunderabad contain large numbers of Urdu-speakers and Muslims. Christian communities are scattered throughout the state, and substantial populations of tribals live in the northern districts.

The state's eastern border follows the Bay of Bengal for six hundred miles. Two great rivers, the Krishna and the Godavari, flow from dry plateaus in the west to wide deltas on the east coast. The large irrigation works at the heads of these deltas were built in the nineteenth century and have yielded coastal Andhra a permanent prosperity.

Telugu-speakers are the second-largest linguistic group in India, and most live in Andhra Pradesh. Until 1953, when the linguistic state of Andhra was formed, most Telugus lived in the multilingual Madras state. In 1956 the Telengana region of Hyderabad state joined the Andhra state to form Andhra Pradesh, with Hyderabad city as its capital.

Historically, the state had been divided into three regions, each with separate political, economic, and cultural interests. Coastal Andhra came under East India Company administration in the last part of the eighteenth century as a result of Britain's defeat of France and its ally, the *nizam* of Hyderabad. Called the Northern Circars by the British, this region developed a lively cultural life in the late nineteenth century. Education for girls, widow remarriages, vernacular literary movements, heterodox religions, and political conferences flourished.

The second region, Rayalaseema, came under British control in the first decade of the nineteenth century; the British called this the Ceded Districts. Rayalaseema was a dry, arid land that was administered, like coastal Andhra, directly from Madras city. [*See* Madras.] Madras developed as the political, legal, educational, and transportation center for these two regions, while Hyderabad city remained the center of Telengana, the third Telugu-speaking region. The only movement that persisted in both British India and Hyderabad state was the vernacular literary movement, which established libraries and published historical and scientific works in Telugu.

The political movement to establish an Andhra state began in the early twentieth century with annual conferences, fervent appeals to the British whenever constitutional change appeared imminent, and frequent lecture tours. The Andhra movement remained subordinate to the nationalist struggle against the British, but, after 1947, the economic and political benefits of an Andhra state outweighed any advantages to regional leaders of staying in Madras state. The delay in creating an Andhra state occurred because the Indian government, especially Jawaharlal Nehru, was reluctant to encourage separatist forces. After the Congress lost electoral support in 1952 in Andhra and Gandhian action against the government led to riots and instability, Nehru conceded. The Andhra state was established in 1953.

A large minority in Hyderabad state wanted the Telengana region to form a separate state after 1948, but the demands grew for "Vishalandhra," a state including all Telugu-speakers. Eventually an agreement on the new state's finances, civil service staffing, development projects, and political representation from Telangana persuaded that region's leaders to form Andhra Pradesh. The new state's leaders have continued to focus public attention on these matters whenever the cry of economic disadvantage is heard in a region. The ensuing crises have led the central government to impose President's Rule on the state several times since its inception.

[*See also* Hyderabad; Telangana Movement; *and* Dravidian Languages and Literatures.]

John G. Leonard, "Politics and Social Change in South India: A Study of the Andhra Movement," *Journal of Commonwealth Political Studies* 5.1 (1967): 60–77. K. V. Narayana Rao, *The Emergence of Andhra Pradesh* (1973). R. P. Rao, *History of Modern Andhra* (1978).

JOHN G. LEONARD

ANDŌ SHŌEKI (1703?–1762?), Japanese thinker of the Tokugawa period who was critical of the existing social order. Little is known for certain about Andō Shōeki's life. He was born in Akita, lived as a physician in Hachinohe in northeastern Japan from 1744 to 1758, moved to the village of Niida in present-day Akita Prefecture in 1758, and died there four years later. He was a prominent physician in Hachinohe: the domain called upon his services occasionally, and among his disciples were samurai, domain physicians, Shinto priests, and merchants.

Shōeki's thought contained the most thoroughgoing repudiation of Tokugawa institutional arrangements and ideological forms to be found in the Edo period. Against the existing hereditarily determined, hierarchic social order, he posited "the world of nature," where there was no distinction of rulers and ruled and all people were of equal status in "directly cultivating" the soil. Reminiscent of Chinese Daoist thinkers, he held that this primitive, utopian anarchy had been man's original state of being, but that deceitful "sages" had invented concepts such as "benevolent government" that allowed powerful, nonproducing members of society to justify dominating and exploiting the toiling agrarian producers. BOB TADASHI WAKABAYASHI

AN DUONG VUONG, founder of the Viet kingdom of Au Lac (c. 210–179 BCE). His actual name was Thuc Phan; thus the period of his reign was sometimes called the Thuc dynasty. An Duong Vuong was probably a historical figure, distantly related to the former ruling clan of Shu in Sichuan, who ruled a small territory between the Red River delta and the Chinese states to the north. He led an army, possibly composed of Au Viet refugees from Qin attacks, against the Lac Viet state of Van Lang, overthrew the last Hung Vuong ("Hung King"), and established the kingdom of Au Lac. A vast new capital was built at Co Loa by his orders. He supposedly committed suicide after Au Lac was absorbed by Nanyue sometime after 180 BCE.

[*See also* Au Lac; Thuc Dynasty; Lac Viet; Van Lang; Hung Vuong; *and* Co Loa.]

Keith W. Taylor, *The Birth of Vietnam* (1983).

JAMES M. COYLE

ANG CHAN (c. 1500–1567), king of Cambodia (r. 1516–1567). After a period as a refugee in the Thai capital of Ayudhya, Ang Chan returned to Cambodia, was victorious in a civil war, and established a new capital at Lovek (1527). During his long reign, he fought several wars against the Thai, restored some of the temples at Angkor, and opened trading relations with European powers recently arrived in Southeast Asia. As the last powerful Cambodian king between the Angkorean era and the present, Ang Chan is honored by Cambodian legends and memorialized in historical texts.

[*See also* Angkor.]

David P. Chandler, *A History of Cambodia* (1983).

DAVID P. CHANDLER

ANG CHAN (1791–1835), king of Cambodia (r. 1797–1835). He succeeded his father, King Ang Eng, as a small boy and was closely supervised by Thai advisers. When he assumed the throne in 1806, he tried to weaken his dependency on Thailand by forging an alliance with Vietnam. Chan's attempts to play his neighbors against one another foreshadowed the tactics of his great-grandnephew, Norodom Sihanouk, vis-à-vis the great powers more than a century later. During Ang Chan's reign, Cambodia was battered by invasions from Thailand and Vietnam and all but disappeared as an independent state.

[*See also* Cambodia *and* Norodom Sihanouk.]

David P. Chandler, *A History of Cambodia* (1983).

DAVID P. CHANDLER

ANG DUANG (1796–1860), king of Cambodia (r. 1848–1860), succeeding his niece, Ang Mei (r. 1835–1847). Duang was the youngest brother of King Ang Chan (r. 1797–1835). Following a Vietnamese invasion in 1811, Duang fled with two other brothers to Bangkok, where he sought the protection of the court. In 1835, following Chan's death and a Thai defeat inside Cambodia at the hands of the Vietnamese, the Thai placed Duang in charge of a formerly Cambodian province, Siem Reap, which had been in their hands since 1794. Three years later, in an obscure incident that probably involved a Vietnamese offer to Duang of the Cambodian throne, he was arrested by the Thai, taken to Bangkok, and forced to swear allegiance to King Rama III. In 1841, he was allowed to return to Cambodia, accompanying a powerful military expedition against the Vietnamese to both Cambodia and Vietnam. As the Thai-Vietnamese War sputtered along inside Cambodia in the 1840s, Duang struggled to enlist support among Cambodia's decimated elite. When the Vietnamese withdrew in 1847, the Thai placed him on the throne, and he settled in the former Cambodian capital of Udong. Although he was always supervised closely by Thai, Duang is treated respectfully by most Cambodian historians, who see him as the founder of a modern, independent nation. He was an accomplished poet, a fervent Buddhist, and, as kings of the period went, a well-liked monarch. Toward the end of his reign, he successfully led Cambodian forces against Cham rebels and also sought to lessen Thai political influence by secretly appealing for French support; the Thai court snuffed out this initiative, but it was revived by Duang's son Norodom in 1863, ushering in the French protectorate.

[*See also* Cambodia; Ang Chan; *and* Siem Reap.]

David P. Chandler, *A History of Cambodia* (1983).

David P. Chandler

ANG ENG (c. 1774–1797), king of Cambodia (r. 1794–1797), founder of the dynasty that ruled the country from 1794 to 1970. Eng spent much of his boyhood as a refugee in Thailand, protected by the Thai king. He was crowned king of Cambodia in Bangkok in 1794 and allowed back to his country under close Thai supervision. At that time, the Thai assumed control over two Cambodian provinces, Battambang and Siem Reap, which were returned to Cambodia in 1907. Eng's reign was uneventful, but because it came after a prolonged period in which there was no king, he is revered in Cambodian chronicle histories.

David P. Chandler, *A History of Cambodia* (1983).

David P. Chandler

ANGKATAN PEMUDA INSAF (Organization of Youth for Justice) was the youth branch of the Malay Nationalist Party. Formed in 1946, it was led by Ahmad Boestaman and the more radical Malay nationalists and was openly anticolonial as well as contemptuous of the traditional Malay elite. Many of its members had collaborated with the Japanese during the occupation of Malaya. Although some of its adherents were attracted to the Malayan Communist Party (MCP), it was never a front organization for the Communists. It was proscribed by the British in July 1947, but in January 1948 an attempt was made to revive it through the founding of the Pemuda Radikal Melayu (Malay Radical Youth), which joined the All Malaya Council of Joint Action in opposing the federation agreement. It was dissolved upon the outbreak of the MCP revolt in June 1948.

[*See also* Malayan Nationalist Party; Malay Communist Party, *and* Malaya, Federation of.]

John Funston, *Malay Politics in Malaysia* (1980). Gordon P. Means, *Malaysian Politics* (1976).

Rajeswary Ampalavanar

ANGKOR. Conventionally dated 802–1432, the kingdom of Angkor, in what is now Cambodia, united the Khmer, or Cambodian, people. At its height it controlled, to some degree, the territories of present-day Vietnam, Laos, and Thailand, as well as Burma and the Malay Peninsula.

Angkor's culture was strongly influenced by Indian concepts, which were adapted to local religious and social institutions. Sanskrit was used in the imperial courts, and several Hindu and Buddhist shrines were built, especially in the area southeast of modern Siem Reap, site of Angkor's successive capitals. This area, thick with ruins, is what is usually meant by Angkor. The word *Angkor* (Khmer, *nokor;* Sanskrit, *nagara,* "city") designates either the capital city or the kingdom ruled from it, although the kingdom had no precise frontiers containing and defining it.

Angkor was established in a fertile area north of the Great Lake (Tonle Sap). It was linked by trade routes with neighboring settlements and benefited from the lake's fish and water supply, regularly replenished by seasonal backflows from the Mekong River. As the Khmer population expanded, areas north of the lake were successively colonized. Many rulers constructed enormous reservoirs using corvée (unpaid labor); the major ones were the Indratataka ("Indra's lake,") built by Indravarman I, the Eastern Baray, and the Western Baray, although these no longer hold water. Aerial photography reveals the presence of a complex network of canals that linked these reservoirs with the moats of major cities and shrines.

It is generally supposed that Khmer agriculture depended upon irrigation from these waterworks, although some earlier assumptions about the economic importance of water-management techniques have recently been questioned. The responsibility of inaugurating hydraulic works fell to Angkor rulers. An inscription about Indravarman I reads, "From the time when he received the royal power, he made this promise: 'In five days from today, I shall begin to dig.' "

"Floating rice," a quick-growing rice from Champa that can grow in three meters of water, appears to have been used in Angkor. Khmer agriculture may have had as many as three harvests a year, which may have aided the empire's great population growth and imperial expansion.

Angkor's social organization cannot be reconstructed in great detail. It is generally agreed that the Indian caste system was not adopted, although some of its terminology was used. Hindu priests were called brahmans, and aristocrats claiming royal ancestry were called *kshatriyas,* but these were not hereditarily distinct groups; a single family could have members in both. Rulers did not own all of the land, but they taxed everything produced on it, and they manipulated the noble families by granting or redistributing revenue entitlements in the districts. A number of noble families, many descended from autonomous princely houses from Zhenla times, owned large estates. It has often been assumed that there was no dominant class of free landholders but that society was controlled by a lordly elite and supported by a great mass of slaves; Claude Jacques, however, has questioned this assumption, arguing that the ordinary freemen may have been more important, and slavery less important, than the inscriptions initially suggest.

There was indeed a substantial servile class, and many of its members were descended from non-Khmer mountain tribes, who were attached by birth to particular pieces of land and who could be bought or sold. Many worked for the great temples, some in capacities that suggest that though they may have been slaves in a sense, they had important ritual functions and their slavery was an honor. However, Zhou Daguan, a thirteenth-century Chinese source, attests the existence of a large class of slaves who were despised and lowly.

Angkor's many temple complexes—some Buddhist, most Hindu—were important socially, economically, and probably politically and religiously. They were endowed with buildings, land, slaves, and goods by rulers or great families who wished to obtain merit; in some circumstances, donors could give part of the value of their land and slaves to a religious foundation and avoid taxes on the property. The temples were staffed by priests or sometimes by eminent teachers from the families that endowed the complexes.

It is clear that the temples were important centers of social and economic interaction. Inscriptions show, for example, that when new land was colonized, the rights over the tract were often granted by the ruler to a priestly family, and new settlements would grow around the temples founded on the land through lavish endowments of slaves and other property.

The remains of Angkor are largely religious structures. Some of these monuments are tower shrines or groups of such towers on platforms, dedicated as acts of piety to royal ancestors, who are symbolically identified with particular patron gods and goddesses. Stone buildings were reserved for the gods. Many are temple-tombs built for the cults of particular gods by kings whose remains were interred beneath the central cult icons, embodying the association or identification of the kings with their patron gods. These shrines are huge pyramidal monuments representing Mount Meru, the home of the gods and center of the universe in Hindu mythology. Ambitious rulers with sufficient time and resources sought immortality by building such shrines, each the symbolic center of the kingdom, with the capital city reorganized around it. The patron deity was usually Shiva, but the most famous shrine complex, Angkor Wat, was dedicated to Vishnu, and the Bayon of Jayavarman VII was dedicated to the Buddhist bodhisattva Avalokiteshvara. Dominated by towering piles such as these, Angkor gradually assumed the aspect of a necropolis.

Knowledge of the chronology of Angkor depends a great deal upon information contained in Khmer inscriptions that were intended as permanent records of endowments to religious foundations. Inscriptional details of endowments by a ruler or dignitary were often prefaced with a Sanskrit verse telling about the family history of the donor, albeit with stylized poetic exaggeration. Later Cambodian sources do not help much, and otherwise only a few Chinese references to Angkor supply historical source material. Our knowledge is therefore skewed in the direction of religious foundations and royal activities.

Before the foundation of Angkor, there were at least two and probably several Khmer principalities, known to the Chinese as Zhenla. Java appears to have claimed suzerainty over the area until a Khmer prince, who named himself Jayavarman II (r. 802–850), emerged as paramount ruler; in the year 802 he established a cult, the *devaraja* ("god-king"), whose celebration was designed to commemorate the new unity of the Khmer people and their independence from Java. Jayavarman ruled from a series of capitals. The last, which remained the center of Angkor's power throughout most of the ninth century, was Hariharalaya (present-day Poules), several miles southeast of where most later capitals were situated. It is now thought unlikely that Jayavarman fully controlled the whole of the Khmer territory; evidence from the period and afterward suggests that the regional noble families continued to exercise much autonomy.

Jayavarman's successor, Indravarman I (877–889), ruled from Hariharalaya and built the Indratataka reservoir (877), the Preah Ko (Sacred Cow) monument (877), and the Bakong royal cult shrine (881). Yasovarman I (r. 889–900) was the first to set up his capital at the Angkor site; his city, Yasodharapura, was centered on the Bakheng cult shrine, a pyramid on a hill. He built the East Baray and claimed an empire extending as far as lower Laos and the Gulf of Siam.

In the tenth century, Jayavarman IV (928–942) and his son and successor moved the capital north to Koh Ker, but Rajendravarman II (944–968) moved it back to Angkor proper and in 952 founded the East Mebon shrine on an island in the center of the East Baray. He also waged war against the Cham. Suryavarman I (1002–1050) became the undisputed ruler of Angkor after he defeated two other claimants to the throne; in 1011 all the major dignitaries of the land swore an oath of allegiance to him. His empire absorbed the Mon territory to the west and also extended northward. Buddhism was patronized during his reign.

In the twelfth century, Suryavarman II (1113–1150) reunified the country after a series of civil wars. He engaged in campaigns against Cham, Vietnamese, and Mon enemies and founded the most famous royal cult shrine of all, Angkor Wat.

A later ruler, Jayavarman VII (1181–c. 1218), had to fight his way to power after Angkor had fallen to Cham conquest. He defeated Champa (and succeeded for a while in keeping a nominee on the Cham throne) and claimed an empire extending far afield. His new capital city, Angkor Thom, was centered on the Bayon Buddhist shrine, and he was responsible for an enormously ambitious program of public works, including shrines, rest houses, and hospitals.

Curiously, perhaps, the era of temple building and Sanskrit inscriptions came to an end soon after the reign of Jayavarman VII. Late in the thirteenth century, the Chinese visitor Zhou Daguan reported recent exhausting wars against Siamese forces and attested to the presence of Theravada Buddhist monks. In the fourteenth century Angkor had repeated conflicts with the Siamese. The history of the end of the Angkor kingdom is obscure, but a new series of Khmer rulers, farther south at Phnom Penh, appears from 1432. They replaced Angkor's extravagant ceremonies with a more subdued style of court culture, used Pali instead of Sanskrit, and patronized the less ritual-oriented Theravada school of Buddhism.

There is no agreement on what caused the decline and fall of Angkor. Explanations include the fatal extravagance of Jayavarman VII; the rise of Theravada Buddhism, which militated against the autocratic hierarchical social order; the collapse of the overcomplex irrigation system; the onslaught of disease carried by malarial mosquitoes; the southward shift of the focus of economic activity in the fourteenth century (with enhanced sea trade encouraging the rise of centers near the coast); and of course Siamese attacks. By the time Angkor fell, though, there was an interbred Siamese-Khmer elite, so that at the court level there was no straightforward ethnic opposition.

The old center of Angkor became an outer, rural area, and in later centuries the stone monuments were hardly used. Details of the history of Angkor were forgotten or inaccurately remembered. Thus, although the ruins were not totally lost to the jungle, or unknown to earlier Western visitors, there was an air of exciting rediscovery when archaeological and epigraphic work was initiated by the French late in the nineteenth century. In the twentieth century, the shrines and their inscriptions and statuary have been maintained and in many cases restored. Together they have become one of the most spectacular archaeological complexes in Asia.

[*See also* Cambodia; Khmer; Indianization; Cham; Jayavarman VII; Angkor Wat; Devaraja; Suryavarman I; Suryavarman II; Champa; Zhenla; Angkor Thom *and the map accompanying* Sukhothai.]

Lawrence P. Briggs, *The Ancient Khmer Empire* (1951). David P. Chandler, *A History of Cambodia* (1983). G. Coedès, *Angkor: An Introduction,* edited and translated by Emily Floyd Gardiner (1963), and *The Indianized States of Southeast Asia,* translated by Susan B. Cowing (1968). Bernard P. Groslier and Jacques Arthaud, *Angkor: Art and Civilization* (1966). W. J. Van Liere, "Traditional Water Management in the Lower Mekong Basin," *World Archaeology* 11 (1980): 265–280. IAN W. MABBETT

ANGKOR THOM, the capital city built by Jayavarman VII (r. 1181–c. 1218) at Angkor, Cambodia. About 3.3 kilometers square, it was built symmetrically around its ritual center, the Bayon, a Mahayana Buddhist shrine. A wall seven to eight meters high surrounded the city and was encircled, in turn, by a moat about one hundred meters wide;

at five different points across the moat there were causeways leading to gateways. These gateways, as well as the towers of Bayon, were ringed by four massive sculpted faces, shown in relief, of the city's patron deity, the bodhisattva Avalokiteshvara. From here, five avenues, one of which formed the entrance to the royal palace, led the way to the sanctuary of the temple. The design of the whole city embodied a Hindu myth of creation, thereby serving to glorify the ruler.

[*See also* Jayavarman VII *and* Angkor.]

G. Coedès, *The Indianized States of Southeast Asia*, translated by Susan B. Cowing (1968). Bernard P. Groslier and Jacques Arthaud, *Angkor: Art and Civilization* (1966).

IAN W. MABBETT

ANGKOR WAT, best known of the monuments of Angkor, Cambodia. Built by Suryavarman II (r. 1113–c. 1150), it is one of the largest temple-tombs created by a succession of Khmer rulers as symbolic religious centers of the kingdom and of the whole universe. Their remains were interred in the central shrines, thus uniting them with the patron deities to whom the monuments were dedicated.

Angkor Wat is a modern name; a wat is a Buddhist temple or monastery, but Suryavarman's shrine was Hindu, essentially Vaishnavite. The plan of the complex is rectangular, oriented to the cardinal points, and surrounded by a moat 180 meters wide; the overall dimensions are about 1,550 by 1,800 meters. The main approach was from the west, over a causeway and through two terraced courtyards, framed by galleries and ascending to the central part of the pyramidal monument, on which stood five towers. The largest, the *sanctum sanctorum,* was in the middle; the others surrounded it at the intermediate compass points.

These towers partly symbolized Mount Meru, the mountain of the gods located at the center of the universe, and its four buttress mountains. But they were only one part of an elaborate cosmographic and astronomical symbolism that governed the design and measurements of every part of the monument's structure.

The walls of the outer gallery were decorated with bas-reliefs more than 2 meters high and extending in long sections, in all a total of more than 1,600 meters. Of considerable historical and artistic interest, they depict the kings giving orders and a march or progression of soldiers, as well as mythological scenes from Hindu epics and texts. Angkor Wat is one of the largest and most impressive of the ancient Cambodian monuments.

FIGURE 1. *Angkor Wat.* Dating from the early twelfth century, the temple at Angkor is one of the finest examples of Khmer architecture.

[*See also* Angkor; Suryavarman II; *and* Architecture: Southeast Asian Architecture.]

Lawrence P. Briggs, *The Ancient Khmer Empire* (1951). G. Coedès, *The Indianized States of Southeast Asia,* translated by Susan B. Cowing (1968). B. P. Groslier, *Angkor: Art and Civilization* (1966). Eleanor Moron, "Configuration of Time and Space at Angkor Wat," in *Studies in Indo-Asian Art and Culture,* vol. 5 (1977), pp. 217–267.

Ian W. Mabbett

ANGLO-BURMESE WARS, three wars fought in 1823–1826, 1851–1852, and 1885. The Burmese were defeated each time. The first war was concluded by the Treaty of Yandabo and resulted in the loss of the coastal provinces of Tenasserim and Arakan. The Burmese refused to sign a treaty to terminate the second war formally but acknowledged the loss of Pegu province, which included the lower reaches and the mouth of the Irrawaddy River. The third war lasted two weeks and resulted in Burma's ultimate loss of sovereignty and the deposition of King Thibaw, the last of the Konbaung-dynasty monarchs.

The results of the wars are easier to identify than their causes. Depending on the nationality and politics of the writer, the wars were aggressive, defensive, nationalist, or products of imperialism or xenophobia. There is little consensus other than that they occurred and the Burmese lost.

The origins of the first war lay in the final expansion of the Burmese empire, under King Bagyidaw, into areas that were perceived to be neutral buffer zones or the spheres of influence of the British East India Company, headquartered in Calcutta. The Burmese expanded into Arakan, Assam, Manipur, and Cachar. The British were reluctant to engage the Burmese, primarily because British aspirations focused on the Indian subcontinent rather than on Southeast Asia, which they called Further India. Bagyidaw's advisers—General Mahabandula and Queen Mai Nu and her brother, the Salin Myosa—urged confrontation. A series of border incidents involving sporadic murders, robberies, kidnappings, disruption of trade, and clashes with British forces led the British to take the Burmese threat seriously. Of the three wars, the first can be seen as a defensive response by the British. The English military was under the command of Major General Sir Archibald Campbell; Mahabandula commanded the Burmese until his death in battle in April 1825. It was one of the first wars in which the British employed steam-powered gunboats.

Manpower losses caused by battle and disease, rising costs of the war, and the length of the conflict exceeded British expectations. As British martial involvement increased, Governor-General Lord Amherst sought territorial gains to justify the expedition. The Treaty of Yandabo concluded the war and provided for a British representative at the Burmese capital, but in response to Burmese harassment, this diplomat was withdrawn in 1839. Thereafter only tenuous contact was maintained between kings Tharrawaddy and Pagan Min and the expatriate British in the port of Rangoon and the British establishment in Moulmein.

During the 1840s British merchants in Rangoon and Moulmein, such as May Flower Crisp, and American Baptist missionaries Adoniram Judson and Eugenio Kincaid continually urged the British to intervene in behalf of free trade and Christianity. When Commodore George Robert Lambert arrived in Burma in 1851 to investigate, he quickly became convinced of the righteousness of the lobbyists' claims, and the second war began. This time British ground forces were commanded by General Godwin, who had also fought in the first war. King Pagan never appeared to have control of the Burmese forces; his commander was General Bandula, son of Mahabandula.

Rangoon was lost quickly, and military losses led to desertion. A coup resulted in the displacement of Pagan by Mindon. Although Mindon avoided signing a humiliating treaty to terminate the war, he acknowledged the loss of Pegu. Burma was now landlocked, with only the Irrawaddy River as its path to the outside world. King Mindon tried desperately and repeatedly to break the British stranglehold by opening diplomatic relations with other European countries as a counterpoise to British power. He was not very successful at these ventures, for the British used their influence in European capitals to dissuade or neutralize Burmese advances.

The first war lasted over two years; the second war, one year; and the third war, two weeks. This collapsing time scale aptly demonstrates the increasing technological and organizational gap between the British and the Burmese that occurred during the course of the nineteenth century.

The third war, in 1885, was a result of growing competition and internationalization of Indochina and occurred at the same time as the scramble for Africa. As the French staked their claims in Annam (northern Vietnam), Cochinchina (southern Vietnam), Laos, and Cambodia, the British feared French expansion into Siam (Thailand) and Upper

Burma. Credence was given to these fears by rumors about railroad, postal, mint, ruby, and river concessions and loans. Moreover, the Burmese military had Italian military advisers, and the Burmese had interfered with British acquisition of teak timber. British humanitarian concern was also piqued by the actions of King Thibaw, who sought to stabilize his monarchy by murdering about seventy of his siblings. In 1879 the British had withdrawn their diplomatic agent, in part over the "footwear controversy," which resulted when the British resisted the Burmese request that they remove their shoes when acting as envoys.

Although the Burmese were quickly defeated, a guerrilla movement, whose members were referred to as dacoits (gang robbers) by the British and nationalists by the Burmese, persisted for several years.

[*See also* Burma; Yandabo, Treaty of; Thibaw; Bagyidaw; Mahabandula; Lambert, George Robert; Pagan Min; *and* Mindon.]

Charles Lee Keeton, *King Thibaw and the Ecological Rape of Burma* (1974). Laurence Kitzan, "Lord Amherst and the Declaration of War on Burma, 1824," *Journal of Asian History* 9 (1975):101–127. Maung Htin Aung, *The Stricken Peacock: Anglo-Burmese Relations, 1752–1948* (1965). Oliver B. Pollak, *Empires in Collision: Anglo-Burmese Relations in the Mid-Nineteenth Century* (1979). A. T. Q. Stewart, *The Pagoda War: Lord Dufferin and the Fall of the Kingdom of Ava, 1885–6* (1972).

OLIVER B. POLLAK

ANGLO-DUTCH TREATY, agreement, signed on 17 March 1824, that defined British and Dutch spheres of influence in the Melaka (Malacca) Straits. Dutch Melaka was transferred to the British, and the Dutch agreed not to make any treaties or settlements on the "peninsula of Melaka." The British made similar undertakings for all places south of Singapore as well as for the island of Sumatra, surrendering Benkulen. The treaty had a crucial effect on the Johor empire, whose territories spanned the straits. In the past the sea had been the lifeblood of the empire, but from 1824 it became a boundary.

[*See also* Melaka; Singapore; Sumatra; *and* Johor.]

Harry Marks, *First Conquest for Singapore, 1819–1824* (1959).

DIANNE LEWIS

ANGLO-INDIANS, persons of mixed European and Indian blood. During the nineteenth century the term *Anglo-Indian* was used to refer to an English person who resided in India. People of mixed European and Indian parentage were known as Eurasians, East Asians, half-castes, or, less frequently, mustees. In 1883 protest over the Ilbert Bill brought Europeans and people of mixed European and Indian blood together in the European and Anglo-Indian Defense Association. In the discussions that brought this organization into existence the term *Anglo-Indian* was chosen as the most appropriate name for people of mixed European and Indian backgrounds. The British government officially sanctioned the use of this term in 1911. In 1949 Anglo-Indians received constitutional status as a minority group.

[*See also* Ilbert Bill.]

V. R. Gaikwad, *The Anglo-Indians* (1967). Henry Yule and A. C. Burnell, "Eurasian," in *Hobson-Jobson* (1903; reprint, 1968).

JUDITH E. WALSH

ANGLO-JAPANESE ALLIANCE. Signed on 30 January 1902, the Anglo-Japanese Alliance brought together Great Britain, one of the world's great powers at the time, and Japan, a nation that was just emerging into a significant role in world affairs. The alliance was of particular significance to Japan because it was accepted on a footing of equality by a great power.

The alliance revolved around the positions of the two countries in China and Korea. While the signatories of the treaty of alliance recognized the independence of China and Korea and disavowed any aggressive intentions toward them, they mutually agreed that the special interests of Great Britain related principally to China, and those of Japan to both China and Korea, especially the latter.

The terms of the alliance further provided that: (1) each power could take measures to defend their interests; (2) strict neutrality would be maintained by one if the other became involved in war with a third power over China or Korea; and (3) one would become the fighting ally of the other if its enemy were joined by another power.

On balance the treaty favored Japan, which gained a powerful ally and recognition of its increasing influence over Korea. The benefit to Great Britain was that it gained a useful ally in Asia.

The alliance was a significant development in the diplomatic power struggle among the Western powers and Japan over the development and defense of political, economic, and strategic positions in China and Korea. In this struggle, the alliance particularly strengthened Japan's hand with respect to imperial Russia, with which it was to go to war in 1904.

On 12 August 1905, just three weeks before the Treaty of Portsmouth that ended the Russo-Japanese War, the alliance was strengthened. The most significant changes were the inclusion of India in the area covered and Great Britain's specific recognition of Japan's special interests in Korea. The two countries also strengthened their commitments to go to war against a common enemy. Russia remained the unstated objective of the renewal; Japan feared a war of revenge and Britain considered Russia a threat to India's northern frontier.

The alliance was renewed for ten years and slightly modified in 1911, but by the end of World War I it had outlived its usefulness, as Korea had become a Japanese colony in 1910 and Russia and Germany had been eliminated from the power struggle in Asia. The United States had become increasingly concerned about the alliance as tensions between the US and Japan escalated over China; the possibility that Great Britain would be either neutral or a Japanese ally in the event of an American-Japanese conflict was particularly disquieting.

The result was the conclusion of the Four Power Pact (Britain, Japan, the US, and France) as a part of the Washington settlement of 1922. This pact replaced the Anglo-Japanese alliance.

Alfred L. P. Dennis, *The Anglo-Japanese Alliance* (1923). Ian H. Nish, *The Anglo-Japanese Alliance* (1966) and *Alliance in Decline* (1972). JOHN M. MAKI

ANHUI, province of east central China, between Jiangsu and Zhejiang to its east and Henan and Hubei to its west; capital, Hefei. Its area is approximately 130,000 square kilometers, and in 1980 its population was estimated at 48,900,000, of which 6,630,000 is urban.

In the Spring and Autumn period (722–481 BCE), the area constituted the kingdom of Wan (a name still used to designate the region south of the Yangtze River). This was soon taken over by the states of Wu and Chu. After the founding of the Qin empire (221–207 BCE), the region was repeatedly subdivided. The modern province (along with Jiangsu) was created in 1662, when Ming-dynasty Nan Zhili was divided in two. The name Anhui, meaning "peaceful and honorable," was composed from the first Chinese characters in the names of two of its cities, Anqing (the province's first capital) and Huizhou (home of many wealthy merchant families).

Traversed by two of China's largest rivers, the Huai and the Yangtze, Anhui is best known for its agriculture and commerce. The drier area north of the Huai is part of the North China Plain and was already an important wheat and grain producer in the third to second century BCE. The hillier parts to the south, where a warmer and wetter climate prevails, has been an important rice producer since the Tang dynasty (618–907). From as early as the time of the Southern Song (1127–1279) and well into the early Qing (1644–1911), a lucrative trade in tea and timber flourished to the advantage of the Huizhou merchants. In addition, calligraphy paper, writing brushes, ink and inkstones, lacquerware, and bamboo were traded as far as Hangzhou and often overseas as well, making Huizhou's merchants among the wealthiest in the empire.

In the nineteenth century, rapid population growth reduced productivity, and severe disruptions caused by the Taiping Rebellion further aggravated the downward economic trend. Periodic flooding also hampered development in modern times. The most catastrophic instance was in 1938, when retreating Nationalist armies destroyed the Yellow River dikes in order to impede Japanese pursuit. However, the ensuing floodwaters killed thousands of Chinese peasants and destroyed countless acres of farmland in three provinces, including northern Anhui.

Since the 1950s new irrigation and water control projects have greatly reduced flooding and restored productivity. Industry has also significantly expanded. Today, the largest cities include the capital, Hefei (pop. 770,000), noted for cotton textiles, food-processing, and machine tools; two transportation hubs, Bengbu and Wuhu (400,000 each); Huainan (350,000), a producer of coal since 1929; and Maanshan, supplier of nearly half of China's iron and steel. Tongling (400,000) has one of China's oldest copper mines, founded in the Tang period. Among Anhui's scenic mountain resorts, Huangshan is by far the most famous, having been much celebrated by generations of poets and landscape painters. ROLAND L. HIGGINS

ANHUI CLIQUE. *See* Warlord Cliques.

ANIRAN, a Middle Persian designation meaning "non-Iran" (non-Aryan), or the people not under Sasanid rule. The word first occurs in the early inscriptions of Shapur I (240–272). It is uncertain whether the term was used in Parthian times, although the idea of an Iranian or Aryan world probably did exist, and Strabo (XI, 508) uses the word *Anariakai,* "non-Aryans." RICHARD N. FRYE

ANIRUDDHA. *See* Anawrahta.

AN LUSHAN (705–757), foreign commander of Chinese armies and leader of a rebellion (753–757) from which the Tang dynasty never recovered. Part Turkic, part Sogdian by birth, An was raised in the modern Liaoning region northeast of the Great Wall. His meteoric rise in the Tang military ranks was aided by Chief Minister Li Linfu's policy of appointing non-Chinese as frontier commanders because he believed that they would not participate in factional politics. Eventually, as concurrent military governor *(jiedushi)* of three northeastern regions, An came to control a huge military force and to have powerful dynastic ambitions. On periodic trips to the capital he disarmed the court by carefully calculated displays of unsophisticated manners; the emperor Xuanzong (r. 712–756) fell under his spell, as did his paramour, Yang Guifei. But Yang Guifei's cousin Yang Guozhong, who succeeded Li Linfu as chief minister in 752, attempted to block An's political ambitions.

Late in 755 An rebelled, seized the eastern capital, Luoyang, and in 756 declared himself emperor of the Great Yan Dynasty. In the middle of the following year, An's armies forced the emperor, Yang Guifei, and Yang Guozhong all to flee Chang'an for safe haven in Sichuan. On the way, both Yangs were put to death for their roles in the Tang debacle. This was the high point of An's rebellion. Eye and skin disorders soon maddened him into committing acts of personal cruelty, and he quickly lost the support of his followers. Early in 757 he was killed by his second son, who was himself soon driven from Luoyang by loyalist forces. In 759 this son was killed by Shi Siming, a former confederate of his father's, who continued the rebellion until 763. The effect of the An Lushan Rebellion was so devastating that the Tang lost much of its empire and never again regained control over all its provinces.

[*See also* Tang Dynasty.]

Howard S. Levy, trans., *Biography of An Lu-shan* (1960). Edwin G. Pulleyblank, *The Background of the Rebellion of An Lu-shan* (1955) and "The An Lu-shan Rebellion and the Origins of Chronic Militarism in Late T'ang China," in *Essays on T'ang Society,* edited by John Curtis Perry and Bardwell L. Smith (1976).

HOWARD J. WECHSLER

ANNADURAI, C. N. (1908–1969), leader of the Dravida Munnetra Kazhagam (Dravidian Progressive Association; DMK) from the founding of the party in 1949 until his death, and one of the most popular political leaders in postindependence South Indian history. Born into a poor, lower-caste family, Annadurai was nevertheless able to gain recognition as a gifted orator, poet, and Tamil playwright. As the general secretary of the DMK he led the party in advocating social reform, opposing Hindi as the official language of India, and propagating Tamil nationalism. In 1967, when the DMK assumed control of the government of Tamil Nadu, Annadurai became chief minister—a position he held until his death.

[*See also* Dravidian Movement.]

Marguerite Ross Barnett, *The Politics of Cultural Nationalism in South India* (1976). Robert L. Hardgrave, Jr., *The Dravidian Movement* (1965).

MARGUERITE ROSS BARNETT

ANNAM (Chinese, "pacified south"), the official name by which the country of the Viet was known to the Chinese between 679 and 1804. The Protectorate of Annam *(An-nam do ho phu)* was one of four similar protectorates established by the Chinese Tang dynasty on the fringes of its empire. After 1164 the Viet ruler was customarily recognized by the Chinese emperor as An-nam Quoc Vuong ("king of the country of Annam"), except when China was ruled by the Ming dynasty.

The name was revived by France in 1884 when it created the Kingdom of Annam (after 1887, the Protectorate of Annam) in the central region of modern Vietnam, between Thanh Hoa in the north and Xuan Loc in the south. This usage continued until 1949. The term *Annam* has frequently been misused to denote Vietnam in its entirety.

[*See also* Vietnam.]

Thomas Hodgkin, *Vietnam: The Revolutionary Path* (1981). Keith W. Taylor, *The Birth of Vietnam* (1983).

JAMES M. COYLE

ANQUETIL-DUPERRON, A. H. (1731–1805), French orientalist and founder of Avestan studies. Anquetil set out for India at age twenty-two to obtain manuscripts of the Avesta and instruction from Parsi priests. His translation, *Zend-Avesta, ouvrage de Zoroastre* (1771), was denounced as a hoax by the young (later Sir) William Jones. Although Anquetil devoted several memoirs to establishing its authenticity, he was vindicated only by later scholarship. His Latin translation of fifty Upanishads (1801–1802) aroused much interest, yet was immediately outdated insofar as it derived from a Persian translation at a time when British scholars were making knowledge of Sanskrit the new standard for research on Indian culture.

[*See also* Avesta; Jones, Sir William; *and* Upanishads.]

Jean-Luc Kieffer, *Anquetil-Duperron* (1983).

ROSANE ROCHER

ANSARI (1004–1089), Abu Isma'il Abd Allah ibn Muhammad Herawi, commentator on the Qur'an, polemist, preacher, and mystic of eleventh-century Herat. Born in Herat to an ascetic father, he attended school in his hometown at the age of four. At the age of nine he was already taking down dictations from eminent traditionists of Herat; later he traveled to Nishapur and Bistam in Khurasan to study with masters there. He made two unfinished trips to Mecca, during one of which he met the well-known mystics Shaikh Abu Sa'id Abu al-Khair and Qassab Amuli, but it was the illiterate mystic Abu al-Hasan Kharaqani who left a decisive influence on his spiritual life. Upon returning to Herat, Ansari founded his own circle of disciples, first teaching only *hadith* (sayings of the Prophet) and then giving his own commentaries on the Qur'an. A Hanbali zealot showing little or no tolerance for Ash'arites and theologians, Ansari often resorted to violence. On one occasion a philosopher-theologian was severely beaten by Ansari's followers, who also burned his residence. Ansari's uncompromising attitude brought him banishment from Herat on at least four occasions, but each time he was able to return in triumph.

In 1082 Ansari was honored by the caliph, who sent him a robe of honor and called him Shaikh al-Islam. Ansari went blind toward the end of his life and died in 1089. He is buried at Gazargah in Herat. He led the life of an ascetic and had an indisputable knowledge of the Qur'anic sciences, particularly *hadith*. His works, considered among the finest specimens in Persian, include *Tabaqat al-Sufiyya,* a Persian translation of a similar work by al-Sulami, with a good deal of additional material.

E. G. Browne, *Literary History of Persia* (1928), vol. 2, pp. 269–270.

MANOUCHEHR KASHEFF

ANSHAN, industrial city in Liaoning Province in southern Manchuria (northeast China), population 1,210,000 (1982). Its iron and steel industry was first established by the Japanese in 1917, dismantled by the Soviets after their occupation of Manchuria in 1945, and reconstructed under the People's Republic of China. Since 1949 Anshan has become the largest center of the iron and steel industry in China, although its dominance has declined since the heyday of the First Five-Year Plan (1953–1958).

JOHN A. RAPP

AN SHIGAO, Parthian monk among the earliest known missionaries to China; responsible for the first systematic translations of Buddhist scriptures into Chinese. Of royal lineage, An renounced his throne to enter monastic life. In the year 148 he reached the Han capital, Luoyang, where he presided over a thriving center of preaching and translation for twenty years. The number of titles attributed to An ranges from 35 to 176; however, of the 19 that are extant only 4 can be reliably attributed to the patriarch. His translations are mainly of works treating the *dhyana* practices of meditation, concentration, and breath control.

[*See also* Buddhism: Buddhism in China.]

Kenneth Ch'en, *Buddhism in China: A Historical Survey* (1964). E. Zürcher, *The Buddhist Conquest of China* (rev. ed., 1972).

M. LAVONNE MARUBBIO

ANTI-COMMUNIST CAMPAIGNS. *See* Communist-Extermination Campaigns.

ANTI-FASCIST PEOPLE'S FREEDOM LEAGUE. Normally known by its initials, AFPFL (or, in Burmese, Pa Hsa Pa Lat), the Anti-Fascist People's Freedom League was the major legal political organization in Burma from the time of its formation in March 1945 until its final split in 1958. Initially a coalition of the Burma Communist Party, the People's Party Revolution group, and Burmese army leaders, the AFPFL sought to expel the Japanese during World War II and then to regain Burma's independence from Britain. From 1945 through 1947 the AFPFL, led by Chairman Aung San and General Secretary Than Tun, provided the major opposition to the British. However, the league began to disintegrate in 1946 over policy disagreements between its communist and noncommunist factions and, following the expulsion of the communist parties, became more narrowly based. But as the British changed their policies toward Burma, the AFPFL was included in the Governor's Executive Council (cabinet). When Burma regained independence on 4 January 1948, the league controlled the government.

Never tightly organized, the AFPFL had little ideological coherence and a poorly articulated organizational base. Although successful in returning to power in elections in 1952 and 1956, it never gained the support of half the voters. Presided over by Prime Minister Nu, the league was split by rival factions of Socialists and conservative interests, which made it difficult to form stable governments. Corruption spread, and in 1956 clashes of interest among the leaders threatened its coherence. In 1958, conflicts became so severe that the league and the government split, opening the way for the military "caretaker government" of 1958–1960. The AFPFL name continued to be used by the Socialist faction, but the party failed to win the election of 1960. The AFPFL never returned to power and was banned by the Revolutionary Council in 1964.

[*See also* Burma; People's Party of Burma; Aung San; Than Tun, Thakin; *and* Nu, U.]

Maung Maung, *Burma's Constitution* (1961). Hugh Tinker, *The Union of Burma* (1967). Frank N. Trager, *Burma: From Kingdom to Republic* (1966).

ROBERT H. TAYLOR

ANTIOCHUS III (d. 187 BCE), Seleucid ruler, probably the first king to be called "the Great." Succeeding to the throne in 223, he overcame rebellion in Iran and briefly seized Syria from Ptolemy IV, but was defeated at Raphia in 217. After eliminating opposition in Asia Minor and making peace with Attalus I of Pergamum, he marched through the eastern satrapies as far as Bactria and Gandhara (212–205), receiving homage from their rulers, who had seceded from the kingdom and whom he now installed as his vassals. After the death of Ptolemy IV, he next conquered Syria and much of Asia Minor and crossed to Europe, where the Romans had just defeated Philip V of Macedon and set themselves up as champions of Greek freedom. After prolonged negotiations and cold war with them he invaded Greece in 192 but was defeated by them in two battles and, in a humiliating peace, was forced to give up Asia Minor as well as his elephants and fleet and to pay a crushing indemnity in 188. He was killed trying to seize a temple treasure near Susa, and his restoration of Seleucid suzerainty over the east, much admired by contemporaries, proved ephemeral.

[*See also* Seleucid Dynasty.]

E. Badian, *Studies in Greek and Roman History* (1964), pp. 112–139.

ERNST BADIAN

ANTIOCHUS VII SIDETES (d. 129 BCE), Seleucid ruler who succeeded to the throne in 139, defeated a pretender, and reasserted Seleucid suzerainty over the Jews. He drove the Parthians out of Mesopotamia and Media, refused an offer of peace, and, trying to rival Antiochus III, had himself called "the Great." But he proved unable to control his army and died in battle in Media in 129. He was the last Seleucid to challenge Parthian rule beyond the Euphrates and to claim suzerainty over the Jews.

[*See also* Seleucid Dynasty.]

ERNST BADIAN

ANTI-SEPARATION LEAGUE, a political coalition formed in July 1932 by Burmese politicians but funded by Indian businesses to oppose the separation of Burma from India as proposed by the British government. In the November 1932 elections the league won forty-two of the eighty seats contested. While most Burmese nationalists at this time opposed the large Indian role in Burma's economic life, they suspected that the British wished to separate Burma from India in order to retard the possibility of Burmese self-government. These fears were encouraged by Indian financial interests, which felt that the separation would limit their opportunities in the province. Despite the election results, the league's leaders remained ambivalent on the separation issue and accepted with relief the ultimate British decision to establish an autonomous Burma government.

John F. Cady, *A History of Modern Burma* (1958).

ROBERT H. TAYLOR

ANU, also known as Anuvong or Anuruttharat, king of the Lao principality of Vientiane (1804–1827). His military resistance to Siamese domination brought an end to his kingdom.

One of numerous sons of King Siribunyasan, Anu was among the members of the royal family taken captive by Siamese armies when they invaded Vientiane in 1778. He appears to have remained in Bangkok during the last years of his father's reign and that of his brother Nanthasen (r. 1781–1795). When the Bangkok court deposed Nanthasen, accusing him of plotting to end Siam's domination, it installed his younger brother Inthavong (r. 1795–1804) as vassal king of Vientiane and appointed Anu as his *uparat,* or deputy ruler and heir presumptive. In the ensuing decade, Anu regularly led Vientiane troops in assisting Siamese armies in their wars with Burma and distinguished himself as a commander. His apparent loyalty to Siam bore fruit when, on the death of Inthavong in 1804, Anu was named vassal king of Vientiane.

During the early years of his reign, Anu concentrated on strengthening his weakened country. He expanded and beautified his capital, consolidated the provincial administration, and firmed diplomatic relations with newly reunited Vietnam (1802). At the same time, he chafed under the rough blanket of Siamese suzerainty, resented the division of Laos into three mutually hostile principalities (Luang Prabang, Champassak, and Vientiane), and dreamed of the reunification of the Lao in a revived Lan Sang kingdom. Chronic disorder and instability in Champassak gave him his opportunity. Unable to find strong and reliable leadership from within the Champassak ruling family, King Rama II of Siam in 1819 appointed Anu's son, Prince Yo, to rule Champassak. Within months, Anu began plans to challenge Siam's suzerainty. He instructed Yo to fortify his territory in the south and made friendly overtures to King Mangthaturat of Luang Prabang, intending thereby to neutralize this northern rival. Anu's resolve must have been strengthened during a visit of several months to Bangkok in 1825 for the cremation of King Rama II, in which he saw the Bangkok court's irresolution in the face of new threats from Britain in Burma and on the Malay Peninsula. Anu felt his grievances did not receive the consideration an ally of his stature deserved, and he resented the greater favors bestowed upon Mangthaturat of Luang Prabang. He returned to Vientiane, mobilized his troops, and bade for support from Luang Prabang and Vietnam.

In January 1827 his armies marched out from Vientiane and Champassak. They took Nakhon Ratchasima (Khorat) by a ruse—claiming to be marching to assist Siam in resisting a British attack—and advanced to Saraburi before the Bangkok court responded. Siam responded in force and by May had taken Champassak and Vientiane. Anu fled, but on the Siamese army's withdrawal he returned with Lao and Vietnamese troops to Vientiane. This time the Siamese responded ferociously: they leveled Vientiane, captured Anu, and sent him back to captivity in Bangkok where, after several days' public display in an iron cage, he died early in 1829. Soon Siamese forces systematically removed tens of thousands of the population of central Laos for resettlement in what is now northeastern Thailand. With Anu's "rebellion" and the Siamese reaction to it died all hopes of a strong and united Laos for many decades to come.

[*See also* Burney, Henry; Bodindecha Sing Singhaseni; Champassak; Lan Sang; Luang Prabang; Siribunyasan; *and* Vientiane.]

Walter F. Vella, *Siam under Rama III* (1957). David K. Wyatt, "Siam and Laos 1767–1827," *Journal of Southeast Asian History* 4 (1963). DAVID K. WYATT

ANURADHAPURA, the principal town and later the capital city of the Sinhalese kingdom from the second century BCE to the end of the tenth century CE. In Ptolemy's map of the first century CE it appears as Anurogrammum Regium, the capital of the island.

In time Anuradhapura became one of the great cities of the ancient world, its landscape dominated by large manmade irrigation lakes (called tanks) and channels, elegant public buildings, monasteries, and parks, and its skyline dominated by *dagobas,* or stupas, that were comparable in size to the pyramids of Egypt. The Mahavihara monastery there, established by Devanampiya Tissa (c. 247–207 BCE), was the historic center of Theravada Buddhism in Sri Lanka. [*See also* Devanampiya Tissa.] Also in his time, a branch of the sacred Bodhi Tree *(Ficus religiosa)* under which the Buddha attained enlightenment was planted at Anuradhapura. It still survives—the oldest historical tree in the world—and is the object of veneration.

When the capital of the Sinhalese kingdom was shifted to Polonnaruva, Anuradhapura declined in importance. [*See* Polonnaruva.] In British times it was "rediscovered" by Ralph Backhouse, the collector of Mannar, in 1817, covered by impenetrable forests and rendered practically uninhabitable by malaria. Its importance increased with the creation of the North Central Province in 1871, of which it became the administrative center. Restoration of its principal monuments began in the late nineteenth century, and continued rapidly thereafter, especially with the passage of the Anuradhapura Preservation Ordinance of 1942. It is now a bustling town with a sound agricultural base, and it is also a major center for tourists and Buddhist pilgrims.

[*See also* Sri Lanka.]

K. M. de Silva, *A History of Sri Lanka* (1981). W. Geiger, *Culture of Ceylon in Medieval Times,* edited by H. Bechert (1960). K. M. DE SILVA

ANUVONG. *See* Anu.

ANYANG, small town in northern Henan Province, China; best known as the location of a group of early civilization sites. These sites, first discovered in 1899 and subsequently excavated in 1928, are associated with the last capital of the Shang (or Yin) dynasty (1766?–1122 BCE). Traditionally the Shang was considered the second Chinese dynasty, following the legendary Xia (2205?–1766? BCE). The Anyang excavations provided the first evidence to document the existence of the Shang and its development as a highly advanced Bronze Age civilization.

The remains of palace foundations, tombs, and temples unearthed at Anyang, along with magnificent bronze ceremonial vessels and thousands of oracle bones, have provided important clues about Shang society. Bronze metallurgy represented the key to Anyang's social stratification, since the use of bronzes was reserved exclusively for weapons and ritual vessels of the Shang aristocracy.

Paul Wheatley points to Anyang's importance as an urbanized administrative and ceremonial center surrounded by smaller dependent villages. K. C. Chang concludes that the Anyang sites, while fairly self-sufficient in subsistence and domestic activities, formed a tightly organized unit for administrative, religious, and ceremonial purposes.

After the fall of the Shang dynasty, the environs of Anyang were left in obscurity until the twentieth-century excavations, which continue to provide archaeological data about this earliest site of Chinese civilization.

[*See also* Shang Dynasty.]

K. C. Chang, *The Archaeology of Ancient China* (2d rev. ed., 1977) and *Shang Civilization* (1980). Ping-ti Ho, *The Cradle of the East: An Inquiry into the Indigenous Origins of Techniques and Ideas of Neolithic and Early Historic China, 5000–1000 B.C.* (1976). David N. Keightley, *Sources of Shang History: The Oracle Bone Description of Bronze Age China* (1978). Paul Wheatley, *The Pivot of the Four Quarters* (1971).

ANITA M. ANDREW

AOKI SHŪZŌ (1844–1914), Japanese diplomat who played a major role in Japan's efforts to revise the "unequal treaties." The son of a Chōshū village doctor, Aoki was adopted by the domain medical schoolmaster, Aoki Kenzō. For further study of medicine he was sent to Prussia, where he began to study law instead. In 1874 Aoki was appointed minister to Germany. In 1889 he became foreign minister in the first cabinet of Yamagata Aritomo and in this position attempted to revise the treaties with the Western powers. The Ōtsu Incident of 1891, in which an antiforeign zealot attacked the Russian crown prince (later Nicholas II), forced him to resign.

In 1892 Aoki was named minister to Germany again. Serving concurrently as minister to Great Britain, he contributed to the conclusion of the 1894 Anglo-Japanese Treaty of Commerce and Navigation, which signaled the end of the unequal treaties. Recalled in 1898 for making an excessive concession in negotiating a new treaty with Germany, Aoki nevertheless became foreign minister in the second cabinet of Yamagata Aritomo, and in 1906 he was appointed as the first ambassador to Washington. He was recalled once again for initiating negotiations with the Roosevelt administration without instructions from Tokyo. Married to a German baron's daughter, Aoki was known throughout his career for his pro-German stance. He was instrumental in the introduction of the German constitutional system to Japan. Aoki died less than a year before Japan entered World War I against Germany. His autobiography, *Aoki Shūzō jiden,* was published in 1970. SHUMPEI OKAMOTO

APRIL FIFTH MOVEMENT, demonstrations in Tiananmen Square, Beijing, on 5 April 1976, in memory of Zhou Enlai, and the dissident movement growing out of that incident. Following limited official memorials for Zhou Enlai, who had died in January 1976, thousands of individuals brought wreaths to Tiananmen Square in a spontaneous outpouring of respect and affection for the departed premier. To prevent such demonstrations, which were understood to imply a criticism of Mao Zedong, the Party Center declared the period of mourning over and forbade any further expressions of mourning.

Beginning first in Nanjing and then in other cities, public resentment burst forth in late March, at the time of the Qingming Festival, a traditional time for paying respects to departed ancestors. In Beijing, wreaths bearing poems, many of which contained disguised attacks on Mao's closest associates, were massed at the Monument to the People's Heroes in Tiananmen Square. Before dawn on 5 April the authorities cleared the wreaths from the square and arrested demonstrators who resisted, provoking a violent conflict later in the day in which more than one hundred were killed and thousands were arrested. On 7 April the Politburo of the Chinese Communist Party, acting on orders from Chairman Mao, stripped Zhou's chosen successor, Deng Xiaoping, of all his offices and condemned the Tiananmen demonstrations as counterrevolutionary. Following Mao's death on 9 September 1976, the political tide shifted. Mao's closest associates—now termed the Gang of Four—were arrested, and eventually the demonstrations of 5 April were declared to have been revolutionary in character.

In 1978 and 1979, as Deng Xiaoping regained power, Party control of public expression was briefly relaxed, leading to an intense period of public debate led by young people who had grown up since liberation. Some referred to their activities as the April Fifth Movement (Siwu Yundong), stressing a kinship with the patriotic and intellectual struggles of the May Fourth Movement (Wusi Yundong) of 1919. So-called Democracy Walls were designated in city centers where big-character posters could be displayed and public debates could take place. The tone of the movement was strongly critical of Mao Zedong and the Cultural Revolution. A self-proclaimed human rights movement developed and a number of unofficial journals such as *April Fifth Forum (Siwu luntan)* and *Exploration (Tansuo)* were published by irreverent activists, the best known of whom was Wei Jingsheng. In March 1979, Wei was arrested and the movement was suppressed, presumably because criticism of the Gang of Four had served its purpose and those in power had no desire to be subjected to uncontrolled scrutiny.

[*See also* Democracy Wall; Deng Xiaoping; Gang of Four; *and* Wei Jingsheng.]

Roger Garside, *Coming Alive: China after Mao* (1981). Jonathan D. Spence, *The Gate of Heavenly Peace* (1981).

EDWARD L. FARMER

APRIL NINETEENTH STUDENT REVOLUTION. In the eight days from 18 to 26 April 1960, massive demonstrations of students and activists in Seoul and other cities in South Korea brought the nearly twelve years of rule by President Syngman Rhee (Yi Sŭng-man) to an unexpected end. Rhee's government was replaced by a more open and responsive regime and, after free elections, there were eight months of democratic rule. Although democracy was then overthrown in a military coup, the memory of this extraordinarily explosive, spontaneous event remains a goad to students, a portent to authoritarian government, and an impetus toward responsive rule among citizens.

Korea's students of 1960 were enraged by corruption, repression, lack of development, and the gap between the democratic ideals fostered by a fading octogenarian president and his grasping, corrupt Liberal Party. Students viewed themselves as the people's conscience, a role exercised for more than four hundred years, often through demonstration, in Korea's moralistic society whose centralism discouraged other group criticism. Although it was not masterminded by the political opposition, the revolt responded to hopes for change engendered by the rise of a two-party system. The opposition Democratic Party had been effective enough to capture the vice presidency in 1956 and to win more than one-third of the Assembly seats, including most of those from urban areas, two years later.

The unrest centered on the presidential elections of 15 March 1960. President Rhee had aged beyond his capacity to control the country, and his running mate as vice president, Yi Ki-pung, hardly moved without help. The Liberal Party reacted to this adversity with extensive plans for election fraud. Already on 28 February several hundred students had clashed with police over being marshaled into classrooms away from an opposition campaign rally in Taegu. On election day in Masan on the south coast, demonstrations against fraudulent elections resulted in several killed, wounded, and missing. One missing boy was found on 11 April with a police tear-gas shell in his skull. The people of Masan then went out of control; police stations were stormed and policemen were beaten by mothers and students. As news of this trickled through censorship to Seoul, three thousand students of Korea University rallied before Seoul's National Assembly building and were attacked with chains and clubs by Liberal Party thugs as they returned home.

The next morning, 19 April, the students of the elite Seoul National University stormed into the streets, followed by tens of thousands of students from almost every university and many primary and secondary schools, demanding new and fair elections. As they pressed against the barricades to the presidential mansion amid tear gas, the police lost their nerve and fired rounds of bullets at the unarmed demonstrators. In the electric atmosphere, the demonstration instantly became a revolt. Street youths joined the ranks, waving towels dipped in the blood of the dead from commandeered jeeps and trucks; police stations and vehicles, government newspapers, and an information center were burned. Rifles crackled through Seoul as, finally, the army was called in and martial law declared. Some 140 were killed and more than 1,000 wounded. Although public support was chiefly tacit (unlike in Masan), it was evident, with some adults joining in. Demonstrations also spread to other major cities. Sporadic trouble continued under the presence of troops, which maintained neutrality. On 25 April, with the implicit acquiescence of martial law authorities, about one hundred demonstrating professors demanded Rhee's resignation. In their wake, the houses of the vice president–elect and others deemed hostile to democracy were plundered.

Increasingly terroristic demonstrations on 26 April, pressure from the American embassy, which had publicly noted "justified grievances," and the urging of some officials close to Rhee brought the president's resignation and, two days later, the suicides of Yi Ki-pung, his wife, and their two sons. The students then policed the streets and maintained order as the president retired to his private house and, after a few days, left for Hawaii. The Liberal Party, which a week before had seemed so entrenched and ubiquitous, collapsed without its leader. An interim administration under former minister Ho Chong smoothly took over the old governmental apparatus, and democracy was returned by a strong vote in free elections in July, with Prime Minister Chang Myŏn leading the new government.

The collapse of the Rhee regime, neither expected nor planned by the students, seemed a revolution at the time. The students, however, had no will to hold power or alter structures. The police lost ground but the essential governmental system endured with only a limited short-term influence on it exerted by the students; revolt, not revolution had been wrought.

Many of the achievements and intentions of the April Nineteenth Revolution failed to survive. Democracy, liberalization, freedom of the press, and freedom of expression have once again been eclipsed by authoritarian rule. Student protest endures and is watched with a respect born of April 1960. In a far more complex society, however, with the military now in power, it is questionable if a repetition of 1960 is likely or even possible. Yet the movement and its startling success shortened Korea's political fuses and altered its politics. Korean elections, although far from perfect, have never since descended to the level of fraud the students fought. The 1960 revolt still lies behind the determinations of later years to forge more responsive politics and government.

[*See also* Rhee, Syngman; Chang Myŏn; *and* Korea, Republic of.]

Sungjoo Han, *The Failure of Democracy in South Korea* (1974). Quee-Young Kim, *The Fall of Syngman Rhee,* Korea Research Monograph, no. 7 (1983).

GREGORY HENDERSON

AQASI, MIRZA (1783–1849), chief minister to Muhammad Qajar Shah, ruler of Iran, from June 1835 to September 1848. His tenure in office was marked by encouragement of the shah's Sufi proclivities, which led to the total alienation of the *ulama* (clerics); maladministration of state finances; and a series of foreign policy disasters, including the definitive loss of Herat and the granting to Russia of a seafaring monopoly on the Caspian Sea. He is nonetheless affectionately remembered for his witticisms and for eccentric enterprises, such as the shoeing of camels by analogy with horses.

HAMID ALGAR

AQQOYUNLU. *See* Akkoyunlu.

AQUINO, BENIGNO (1932–1983), chief opposition leader during the era of martial law under Philippine President Ferdinand E. Marcos.

Few political leaders in Philippine history could match the career of Benigno Aquino, Jr., who was assassinated on 21 August 1983 after returning from exile in the United States. Starting out as a war correspondent at seventeen, he became mayor at twenty-three, governor at twenty-nine, and senator at thirty-five. He was known as "the wonder boy of Philippine politics." If the 1973 election had not been preempted by President Marcos's declaration of martial law, Aquino, it was generally believed, would have become the next Filipino president.

Ninoy, as he was popularly called, came from a political family. His grandfather was a general in the Philippine Revolution who defied the Spanish, and later American, colonial authorities. His father was a well-known representative, senator, cabinet secretary, and Philippine independence negotiator in the 1920s and 1930s. In addition to his elective posts, Ninoy was technical adviser to several Philippine presidents. One of his famous achievements—accomplished while he was a twenty-one-year-old journalist—was securing the surrender of Huk leader Luis Taruc, which ended the rebellion that had threatened the republic in the early postwar period.

As Marcos's chief rival, Aquino was arrested in 1972, when Marcos declared martial law, and spent the next eight years in prison. He was sentenced to die by a military court on charges of murder and subversion in November 1977. In 1980, however, he was allowed to undergo heart surgery in America. After three years of exile, he decided to return to the Philippines. Aquino was assassinated in August 1983, moments after arriving in Manila from the United States. His assassination was attributed to the Communist Party by the government, but his family and various groups were certain he was killed by the military. According to a Marcos-appointed commission that investigated the assassination, several close Marcos allies in the military were responsible. But as a result of pressure from Marcos, all the defendants were acquitted when tried. When Corazon Aquino became president, the Supreme Court declared a mistrial, and another investigation was initiated.

Aquino's last written statement summarizes the ideals he stood for: "I have returned on my free will to join the ranks of those struggling to restore our rights and freedoms through nonviolence. I seek no confrontation. I only pray and will strive for a genuine national reconciliation founded on justice."

[*See also* Philippines; Marcos, Ferdinand E.; Huk; Taruc, Luis; *and* Aquino, Corazon Cojuangco.]

Belinda A. Aquino, "Political Violence in the Philippines: Aftermath of the Aquino Assassination," *Southeast Asian Affairs* (1984). John Bresnan, *Crisis in the Philippines: The Marcos Era and Beyond* (1986). Nick Joaquin, *The Aquinos of Tarlac* (1983). Ken Kashiwahara, "Aquino's Final Journey," *The New York Times Magazine*, October 16, 1983, pp. 41–43, 61. Spencer A. Sherman, "A Conversation with Benigno Aquino," *Mother Jones* (January 1984): 13–22, 45. BELINDA A. AQUINO

AQUINO, CORAZON COJUANGCO (b. 1933), president of the Philippines since February 1986. She was born in the province of Tarlac and completed her freshman year of high school in Manila. In 1946 she and her family moved to the United States, and she completed her high-school studies at the Notre Dame Convent in New York. She graduated from Mount Saint Vincent College in New York in 1953 and married Benigno "Ninoy" Aquino, then a young journalist and law student in Manila, the following year. Until 1972, Corazon Aquino was a homemaker raising five children while her husband rose from mayor to governor and finally senator.

Cory Aquino's political involvement began when her husband was imprisoned by his political archrival, President Ferdinand Marcos, in 1972. During the eight years he spent in prison, she served as his liaison with the political opposition to Marcos. In 1980, when Marcos released Ninoy Aquino from prison in order that he might undergo heart surgery in the United States, the family moved to Newton, Massachusetts.

After her husband's assassination upon his return from exile in August of 1983, Cory Aquino came back to the Philippines. When Marcos announced presidential elections in November 1985, support for Corazon Aquino as the opposition candidate grew vigorously. Amid intense political negotiations that threatened to split the opposition wide apart, Aquino ran for president, choosing political rival Salvador Laurel as her running mate.

Seeing Aquino as the embodiment of her husband's dream to restore democracy to the country and as a person of impeccable integrity, Filipinos supported her campaign with an enthusiasm never before witnessed in their country's political history. With only two months of campaigning, she claimed victory on 9 February 1986 on the basis of favorable election returns and called on Marcos to concede defeat. The four-day "people power" revolution began on 22 February as Filipinos poured into the streets to support Marcos defectors Defense Minister Juan Enrile and General Fidel Ramos and ultimately brought Aquino to power. Aquino and Marcos were both sworn in as president on 25 February, but that same evening, Marcos left Malacanang Palace for the United States, and Corazon Aquino became the seventh president of the Philippine Republic.

Cory Aquino survived several coup attempts during her first year as president. Since 2 February 1987 her government has operated under a newly enacted constitution that gives her a six-year term as president. President Aquino faces many crises, including a growing armed insurgency movement and the need for formidable economic reform measures. Her broadly based political support is separate from any close association with a particular party. A widely held belief among Filipinos is that Cory Aquino was brought to power by the occurrence of a miracle, and her popular following is likely to endure.

[*See also* Philippines; Aquino, Benigno; Marcos, Ferdinand E.; Nacionalista Party; *and* New People's Army.]

John Bresnan, *Crisis in the Philippines: The Marcos Era and Beyond* (1986). Robert Shaplen, "A Reporter at Large: From Marcos to Aquino," *The New Yorker,* August 25, 1986 (pp. 33–73) and September 1, 1986 (pp. 36–64).
DAVID R. CLAUSSENIUS

ARABS have been present in Iran and, to a lesser extent, in Central Asia since antiquity. Numerous Iranian rulers relied on Arab vassals to provide buffer states on their western borders or encouraged the settlement of Arab tribesmen in frontier areas as a counterbalance to other troublesome tribal groups. The heyday of Arab political and cultural influence in Iran and Central Asia, however, was undoubtedly the early Islamic period (seventh to ninth century CE).

The first major incursion of Arab Muslim warriors onto the Iranian Plateau began in 641/642. After the decisive battle of Nihavand (probably in 642), the Arab armies quickly moved across southern Iran to Sistan, north into Azerbaijan and the Caucasus, and east to the important province of Khurasan. After the capitulation of the Khurasani provincial capital, Merv, in about 656, this first wave of conquests subsided, and the Arabs were primarily engaged in consolidating their positions. A second wave of expansion took place under the Umayyad dynasty, which carried the Arabs beyond the Oxus deep into Central Asia. The climax of this phenomenal expansion came in the early Abbasid period, when the governors of Khurasan and their generals conquered most of the surviving principalities of Transoxiana and decisively defeated the Chinese forces in the region that had been assisting them. After the defeat of the Chinese at the battle of Talas (also known as Taraz) in 751, the formerly strong influence of Buddhism and Chinese civilization collapsed completely, to be permanently replaced by Arabo-Iranian and Islamic cultural dominance.

The question of where and how many Arabs actually settled in Iran and Central Asia following these conquests is still a complex and controversial one. Small garrisons of Arab troops were certainly scattered throughout the region. Various private Arab colonists are also known to have seized estates in western Iran and elsewhere. The Arab sources report large-scale official settlements of Arab warriors and their families in eastern Iran, notably the settlement of some fifty thousand Kufan and Basran families in Khurasan in 671. Whatever their number, there can be no doubt that these Arabs left a permanent imprint on Iran and Central Asia through the establishment of Islam as the dominant religion and the influence of their language and culture. Yet by the tenth century they themselves had virtually disappeared as a distinct ethnic community in these conquered regions.

In modern times, the Arab presence has been much more limited, except in the predominantly Arab areas of southwestern Iran (Khuzistan, sometimes appropriately called Arabistan) and along the littoral of the Persian Gulf. Some isolated communities that consider themselves ethnically Arab still survive in Afghanistan and Soviet Central Asia; although they often trace their origins back to the early Arab colonists, their presence is probably explained as the result of forced migration and resettlement by more recent Iranian rulers.

[*See also* Islam *and* Umayyad Dynasty.]

Thomas Barfield, *The Central Asian Arabs of Afghanistan* (1981). Richard N. Frye, *The Golden Age of Persia: The Arabs in the East* (1975). H. A. R. Gibb, *The Arab Conquests in Central Asia* (1923; reprint, 1970). Julius Wellhausen, *The Arab Kingdom and Its Fall,* translated by Margaret Weir (1927).
E. L. DANIEL

ARACHOSIA, the Greek name for the province of the Achaemenid empire called Harahuvati in Old Persian inscriptions. The name is taken from the river now called Arghandab, which runs through the principal city of Kandahar in Afghanistan. The river was called Sarasvati by neighboring Indians who, however, used the name for other rivers as well. With India to the east, the Hindu Kush mountain range to the north, Sistan to the west, and Baluchistan to the south, Arachosia experienced conquest from all sides throughout its history. The Greek name continued into Islamic times as al-Rukhkhaj.

Wilhelm Barthold, *An Historical Geography of Iran* (1984), p. 73.
RICHARD N. FRYE

ARAKAN, premodern Burmese state situated along the northeastern coast of the Bay of Bengal. Arakanese history has been determined by its geographical boundaries, the Arakan Yoma and the Bay of Bengal; its land and sea routes with Burma proper and India; and its agricultural base, limited to the narrow deltaic plains along the major rivers, which necessitated central control of water to maintain surplus production.

Greek, Roman, and Sanskrit sources from the first centuries of our era tell of the emergence of coastal trading centers engaged in the export of forest products of the hill tribes. This led to the growth of power of local chiefs, remembered in later inscriptions as ancestral monarchs.

The first known city, Dinnyawadi, built in about the mid-fifth century by a king of the Candra dynasty, controlled the fertile Kaladan Valley. Facing the sea and external trade routes, it dominated the hill–coast trade. Like the Pyu city of Halin, it was circular in plan, with the palace in the center. Northeast of the palace stands the Mahamuni shrine, center of the royal cult. The sculptures and inscriptions of Dinnyawadi attest to a Buddhism with strong Mahayana influences and to a contact with the art of North India. Later chronicles assert that the Mahamuni was the site to which Gautama Buddha himself flew and where he converted the king and miraculously caused an image of himself to be cast. As the royal paladin, the Mahamuni image has always been closely connected with the fortunes of the country, which dissipated after the image was taken to Amarapura following the Burmese conquest.

The capital moved south to Vesali at the beginning of the sixth century, possibly in response to the threat of kingdoms emerging in southeast Bengal following the disintegration of the Gupta empire. Similar in plan to Dinnyawadi, the palace was the center of a complex irrigation system. Archaeological remains show close contact with the Calukyas and the Pallavas of South India and the Mahayana centers of Nalanda and Mainamati in the north, as well as with the Pyu across the Arakan Yoma. While Theravada Buddhism dominated, there is evidence of Shaivite and Vaishnavite cults. The circa 729 Anandacandra inscription portrays an indianized court culture, with political and religious structures more akin to contemporary states to the east. By the ninth century, the country was threatened by the kingdoms of Burma proper: the Chin, whose raids resulted in the settlement of Kuki-Chin speakers along the length of the Yoma; the Pyu, who took advantage of weak governments at Vesali to attack the north and south; and the Mon, who are said in the chronicles to have occupied the south. Burmans began infiltrating over the Yoma in the early ninth century and eventually gained control of the lowlands.

By the mid-eleventh century, the external economy was weakened by the Chola raids, and control of the Kaladan Valley was threatened by raids from hill tribes and Pala expansion into eastern Bengal. The capital was moved east to the Lemro Valley, where a series of small cities—Pyinsa, Parein, Hkrit, and Launggret—were dominated by central Burma for the next three hundred years. While independence was regained following the fall of Pagan, raids from Bengal, the Burmans, and the Mon dominated the thirteenth and fourteenth centuries.

Arakanese fortunes changed with the foundation of the city of Mrohaung (Mrauk-U) in 1433. Commanding both the Kaladan and Lemro rivers, Mrohaung became a prosperous port. Its successive kings, while Buddhist, used Muslim designations as well as their own names and maintained control of Chittagong for much of the fifteenth to seventeenth century. Most powerful was Minbin (1531–1553), who with Portuguese mercenary assistance built a complex moat-defense system capable of flooding invaders; fortress pagodas; and a fleet armed with cannons. A raid on the Toungoo capital of Pegu brought an immense booty of slaves and treasure to Arakan, which for a short time then extended its influence to Martaban through de Brito, its governor at Syriam. In the seventeenth century Arakan was noted as a supplier of slaves and rice to Batavia, and it became involved in the Mughal succession by granting asylum to Shah Shujah, son of the Emperor Shah Jahan.

With the rise of Mughal power in Bengal and the decline of Portuguese power, Arakan lost its Bengal territories, and with the strengthening of the Burmese kings, its lands diminished until it was finally overthrown in 1784. So discouraged were the Arakanese that many welcomed the first Anglo-Burmese War as a chance to regain their country, and only today, when Arakan is a state of the Socialist Republic of the Union of Burma, are compromises being reached.

[*See also* Burma; Pyu; Chin; Mon; Pagan; Toungoo Dynasties; Pegu; Anglo-Burmese Wars; *and* Indianization.]

Pamela Gutman

ARAKI SADAO (1877–1966), Japanese general and aggressive nationalist. During his military career Araki developed a reputation as a Russian specialist.

As army minister (1931–1936) he called for the spiritual reinvigoration of the Japanese army in order to face what he and others of the Imperial Way faction within the army saw as an impending crisis with the Soviet Union, toward which he was bitterly antagonistic. During this period Araki became the idol of the younger army officers who were dedicated to radical reform, and he took a sympathetic view toward the February Twenty-sixth Incident (1936), an abortive rebellion by radical officers. As a result, Araki was forced to retire from active duty. He was appointed minister of education in 1938 and worked to promote militaristic education in Japan. After Japan's defeat in 1945 he was tried by the Allies as a war criminal and sentenced to life imprisonment (1948), but he was released and pardoned in 1955 because of illness.

[*See also* February Twenty-sixth Incident *and* Aizawa Incident.]

Ben-Ami Shillony, *The Young Officers and the February 1936 Rebellion* (1973). Richard Storry, *The Double Patriots: A Study of Japanese Nationalism* (1957).

MARK R. PEATTIE

ARAL SEA, the ancient Oxianus Lacus, with an area of 25,659 square miles, is the fourth largest inland sea in the world. Located in the Turan Lowland between the Kizil Kum to the east and the Ustyurt Plateau on the west, the sea straddles the Kazakh and Uzbek republics of the USSR. The Amu Darya (Oxus) and Syr Darya (Jaxartes) rivers originating in the Hindu Kush, Pamir, and Tian Shan ranges are the source of water. MICHAEL BONINE

ARCHITECTURE

CHINESE ARCHITECTURE

Chinese architecture is distinctive in its dedication to the use of wood as the primary building material for even the most important structures. The overall plan, the relation of structure to site, is an equally distinctive element of Chinese architecture, although it is one that is not immediately apparent.

The discovery of an extensive prehistoric site at Banpo, inhabited as early as 5000 BCE during the Yangshao phase of the Neolithic era, demonstrates the concern for plan and illustrates standard building techniques. Located in a suburb of modern Xi'an in Shaanxi Province, the oval-shaped village extended over thirty thousand square meters oriented on a north-south axis. Houses, either oblong, round, or square in plan, were clearly separated from an adjacent cemetery by a moatlike ditch that provided a rudimentary demarcation of the village from the surrounding area. The houses were constructed directly on the ground or were semisubterranean. Walls fashioned from saplings were covered over with wattle and daub made from the fine local soil (loess), which gave them a durable surface that in some instances was tinted rose pink. The finished product, with a thatched roof partially supported by internal posts, a plastered floor, a central hearth, and an open entrance, had a spacious interior measuring several meters across and provided a pleasant and functional living space. In some instances, communal longhouses gave a central focus to the village complex. [*See also* Yangshao Culture.]

The evidence from the excavated sites dating from the Shang dynasty (1766–1122 BCE) confirms the practice of separating burial grounds from ritual, administrative, or habitation centers. The plan of the ritual center at Anyang (in Henan Province) indicates that the location of structures according to their function and a general north-south orientation represents an abstract concept, some ideal plan rather than a random grouping of buildings. The long rectangular "palace" buildings found at Anyang had a wooden superstructure with some filling material for the walls and internal columns, beams, and rafters to support the thatched roof. The foundation of pounded earth was raised to provide an impressive platform. Durable materials like stone were used only in a secondary way, as a base for the columns or foundations, but not for the walls themselves.

By the end of the Bronze Age this building tradition was well established. Tile was used as roofing material and the size of individual buildings and the scope of city plans increased. The vaulting of the partially excavated tomb of Qin Shihuangdi (r. 221–210 BCE) demonstrates the knowledge of the arch, yet this form seems not to have been employed above ground except in the construction of bridges and monumental gates. Rather, it was the elaboration of post-and-lintel architecture through the use of a nonrigid system of construction and the employment of brackets or cantilever systems that made possible the erection of the magnificent buildings described in the poetry of the period. These multistoried structures achieved a size that far surpassed that dictated by the natural size of trees or the inherent characteristics of wood.

Although little can be known of the actual houses or manors of the period there is a rich fund of secondary evidence, primarily from tombs, that gives some idea of their appearance. The traditional pit tomb of the Shang and Zhou dynasties was replaced by vertical shaft burials during the Western and Eastern Han dynasties. Early Han tombs were constructed of hollow tiles; the later ones were made of solid bricks, and later yet, of stone. Some were carved in cliffs. All present a kind of house plan with inner and outer chamber flanked by side corridors with grave offerings. Often, there are vaulting, gabled "roofs," and even interior pictorial designs that illustrate contemporary houses or estates. These are essentially underground replicas of the homes of the period.

The marking of the tomb site with a prominent mound was another innovation of this period, one that was maintained throughout the later dynasties. The tombs of the Tang royal family (outside Xi'an) or those of the Ming monarchs (near Beijing) illustrate the classic type. A *pailou,* or large commemorative archway, set in what is now open countryside, serves as an introduction to the Ming tomb complex (see figure 1). The tomb area proper is walled off and marked by broad avenues that served as "spirit ways." Individual tombs are also walled off and contain ritual halls and gardens that lead to the burial mound. A memorial stele, erected in front of the mound, records the accomplishments of the deceased. Entering the tomb, one proceeds down a long ramp to the burial chamber, which contains a stone house, as though the tomb were an alternative, spiritual, living space.

The capital cities of the Western and Eastern Han dynasties (in Chang'an and Luoyang, respectively) were large. Bounded by walls and gates oriented on the points of the compass, they had broad thoroughfares that established the natural flow of traffic and also defined the subdivision of the city's wards, marked districts, or administrative centers. Palace compounds, also walled off within the town, and various administrative centers occupied a large portion of the city space. Beyond the walls, large parks provided a royal hunting preserve set with pavilions and an artificial lake. The imperial academies as well as the chief ritual edifices, the Hall of Ritual, the Hall of Spirits, and the Hall of Learning, were also beyond the walls. The latter had a peculiar plan: The structure itself was set on a raised circular platform within a square area surrounded by a wall and (ideally) a moat. The configuration, discussed in the ancient literature, is meant to suggest cosmological notions regarding the circular canopy of heaven and the square of the earth (see figure 2).

The mounds that crowned the tombs of ancient rulers, like those that appear above the graves of the Ming emperors erected centuries later, also introduce a landscape element within the architectural compound, which was intentionally isolated from nature by the prominent walls and towers enclosing it. Bizarre rocks, carefully placed groupings of

FIGURE 2. *Tiantan.* The circular construction of the Temple of Heaven in Beijing reflects the continuation of the architectural style of Han-dynasty ritual edifices.

FIGURE 1. *Pailou.* The entrance to the Yonghegong, a Tibetan Buddhist temple, in Beijing.

plants, and winding streams and pathways occur often within the more formal precincts of palatial residences. The palace compound provided ideal order on the corporate, societal level; the garden satisfied the uniquely personal need to sense a universal order of a different sort.

The Imperial City in Beijing, built centuries after the Han, is the most perfect extant example of this ideal. Everything is laid out in an exact order that suggests that this earthly bureaucratic edifice was but the parallel for some less mudane spiritual order. The walls, which were once the most prominent feature of this city (only recently removed to improve traffic flow), provided the framework for a basic grid, oriented on a north-south axis, which gave a sense of unity and design to the disposition of the buildings contained within their perimeters. The orderly progression of gates and courtyards modulates the space within, bringing one from the most public to the most private enclosures in a rhythmic manner. The official halls are of immense size, set on raised foundations of richly carved white marble, brightly painted, and have gleaming yellow roof tiles. In various courtyards in the residential quarters within the Forbidden City, gardens provide an unexpected note of quiet and informality. All of the features found in the Forbidden City, begun in the fourteenth century, were apparent in the capital cities of the Han dynasty constructed one thousand years earlier (see figure 3).

The conservative nature of the Chinese architectural tradition is not the result of any lack of exposure to influence from foreign sources. The introduction of Buddhism posed a potential challenge of the highest order. The sanctuaries carved from the living rock at pilgrimage sites like Dunhuang or Yungang are adaptations of Indian types. Yet much of the architectural detail, including the painted depiction of buildings occurring in the murals that decorate these shrines, is typically Chinese. The classic Buddhist (or Daoist) temple of later centuries is not radically different in appearance from contemporaneous civil structures. The integrity of the Chinese architectural tradition was so powerful that by the eighth century the architectural styles of China, including the important element of the orientation of site, served as a model for the greater part of East Asia.

The future of that tradition is uncertain. Although the government of the People's Republic of China is undertaking an extensive study and renovation of traditional Chinese monuments, it is doubtful that

FIGURE 3. *Palace of Heavenly Purity, Forbidden City.* The first hall in the back portion of the Forbidden City, this palace, known in Chinese as the Qianqinggong, was used as an imperial residence during the Ming and early Qing periods and then as an audience hall where foreign envoys were received. Its form is typical of the buildings within the imperial compound, with their distinctive roofs and massive pillars.

the well-conceived and brilliantly executed schemes that served for centuries of imperial rule could function as effectively in a modern society. Significantly, the contemporary building programs are of a Western, utilitarian style. In the cities at least, the traditional Chinese house, with courtyard and walled enclosure, has given way to the ferroconcrete, multiunit apartment block.

Andrew Boyd, *Chinese Architecture and Town Planning* (1962). Ssu-ch'eng Liang, *A Pictorial History of Chinese Architecture* (1984). Laurence Sickman and Alexander Soper, *The Art and Architecture of China* (1968). Zhongshu Wang, *Han Civilization,* translated by K. C. Chang (1982). William Willetts, *Chinese Art,* 2 vols. (1958).

ROBERT POOR

SOUTH ASIAN ARCHITECTURE

The architecture of South Asia covers a period of more than five thousand years and includes monuments dedicated to several faiths, including Hinduism, Buddhism, and Islam. It also includes secular monuments such as palaces, forts, and civic buildings that arose under Muslim and British rule and more recently in independent India.

The tradition of constructing monuments in a perishable material reaches back into the third millennium BCE, when the cities of the Indus Valley civilization were built of sun-dried bricks, with wood, thatch, and bamboo used in the smaller settlements. Stone was not a medium in common use, even after the prosperous and extensive Maurya empire was established in the fourth century BCE. [*See* Indus Valley Civilization.]

The first century BCE saw a metamorphosis in building methods, and stone was brought into use on a large scale as the medium of construction. This innovation is seen first in the Buddhist stupas, hemispherical earthen mounds containing relics of the Buddha, which thus far had been faced with brick; these were now faced with slabs of stone and surrounded by stone railings and gateways. [*See* Stupa.] The Buddhists also constructed rock monasteries by excavating into the face of a mountain. Each rock monastery consisted of one or more chapels for worship *(chaityas)* and several residential halls *(viharas)* for the monks. Wooden additions made to these rock-cut structures, including curved wooden ribs inserted into the vaulted ceilings of the *chaityas,* testify to the long tradition of woodworking in India. [*See* Ajanta *and* Ellora.]

It was only five hundred years later that the Hindus began using stone, and stone temples began to be built all over the country. Early temples were of modest proportions and consisted merely of a small shrine to house the image of the deity with a spire added above, and a hall in front for worshipers. Increasing familiarity with the medium of stone made temple builders more ambitious, and the size

FIGURE 1. *Vishvanath Temple, Khajuraho.* An example of Hindu stone temple architecture.

of such structures increased sharply until in both North and South India we find temple towers reaching up to a height of two hundred feet. Indian temples are divided into northern and southern styles, largely on the basis of the type of temple spire, the northern being crowned with a fluted melon-shaped cushion known as an *amalaka*, and the southern with a rounded *stupi*. Such temples as the Lingaraj in Orissa and the Great Temple at Tanjore are covered with exquisite sculptured images of gods, goddesses, and semidivine beings as well as with exuberant decorative details; in South Asia it is impossible to discuss architecture without taking into account the masses of sculptural decoration with which the architecture is overlaid. [*See* Orissa *and* Mahabalipuram.]

Stone temples were raised to impressive heights without the use of cementing mortar, the large blocks of stone being laid dry and kept in position mainly by their weight and balance; occasionally dowels and interlocking flanges were used along with iron clamps. Inclined planes of earth as much as four miles long were built to transport the heavy blocks up to their great heights. The stone temples were usually commissioned by royalty, but these same rulers continued to build their palaces in brick and wood. However splendid a palace, the monarch was content to treat it as a relatively ephemeral structure; only an abode of the gods was worthy of permanent survival and could thus be constructed in the lasting medium of stone.

With the coming of Islam, stone was used both for religious structures—mosques and tombs—and for secular monuments—forts and palaces. From the thirteenth century, the skyline of northern India took on a new look, with temple towers being superseded by white bulbous domes. Islamic builders introduced the true arch, which became a standard architectural feature, and they also brought with them a cementing agent in the form of mortar. Islamic architecture in India, in contrast to other Islamic areas, is almost entirely in stone, since Indian masons had for centuries built in stone and were able to handle the medium with great confidence. Large fortified capitals were erected with impressive public buildings and luxurious palaces, while spacious mosques for worship, open to light and air, sprang up in every town. Garden tombs, of which the most famous is the Taj Mahal, were built by every monarch. Because Islam forbids the representation of the human form in sculpture, the builders decorated their walls with an inlay of glazed tiles, marble, and semiprecious stones in geometric or floral designs, or in the form of calligraphic borders.

FIGURE 2. *Taj Mahal, Agra.* Built between 1631 and 1653 by Shah Jahan (r. 1627–1658) as a tomb for his wife, the Taj Mahal is an enduring legacy of the Mughal architectural style.

FIGURE 3. *High Court, Bangalore.* Example of the architectural style used by the British during the period of imperial rule.

Elaborate latticework was also an Islamic speciality. [*See* Taj Mahal *and* Tilework.]

With British rule in India to another distinct phase in the architecture of South Asia began. Imposing monuments such as the Victoria Memorial Hall in Calcutta or the Victoria Terminus railway station in Bombay drew upon the Gothic style with its profusion of ornament, its vaulted roofs, and its pointed arches. Combining with this several Venetian and other European details, and incorporating Islamic domes and kiosks, the British produced a hybrid style that was termed Indo-Saracenic. The last and most grandiose of imperial monuments was the capital of New Delhi and its centerpiece, the Viceroy's Palace, designed by Edwin Lutyens. This magnificent stone palace, which incorporates several styles and defies classification, reveals Lutyens's strong belief in the classical tradition as well as the influence of the Buddhist stupa, which is clearly evident in its central dome. [*See* Lutyens, Sir Edwin *and* Delhi.]

FIGURE 4. *High Court, Chandigarh.* Built by Le Corbusier between 1952 and 1956.

The most significant phase of postindependence architecture in South Asia is Le Corbusier's city of Chandigarh, the capital of the states of Punjab and Haryana. [*See* Chandigarh.] His pupil B. V. Doshi continued to build in Le Corbusier's style, and his handiwork may be seen primarily in the city of Ahmadabad. [*See* Ahmadabad.]

The architects of ancient South Asia, whether building Buddhist or Hindu monuments or even the Islamic Taj Mahal, have remained anonymous figures. Among the complex reasons for this is the fact that South Asian monuments were regarded as joint projects in which several guilds of craftsmen, all specialists in their own spheres, gave of their finest effort. In such a context, individual names were considered unnecessary and perhaps even irrelevant.

Percy Brown, *Indian Architecture,* 2 vols. (1956).

VIDYA DEHEJIA

SOUTHEAST ASIAN ARCHITECTURE

The study of Southeast Asian architecture is essentially the documentation of religious developments in the region. Historical examples of secular architecture are scarce because domestic structures

FIGURE 1. *Stone Temple.* Prambanan, Java, ninth century. This structure shows the influence of Indian architectural style on Southeast Asia.

are normally built of perishable materials and rarely survive longer than a few generations. Religious and secular architecture display varying degrees of foreign influence, primarily from India and China, although Islam has had an impact in recent centuries.

Small-scale architectural models provide important details about early house forms. For instance, a model of a two-story thatch-roof pile dwelling from the top of a bronze ritual drum cast by the Dian culture of South China's Yunnan Province (second century BCE) is of a type still found among the Batak and Minangkabau peoples of Sumatra. The presence of this form of dwelling in both China and Sumatra suggests that historically it was probably much more widely distributed than at present. Terra-cotta house models intended as tomb furniture and dating from the first through the fifth century have been found in northern Vietnam; these two-story tile-roof buildings face onto a courtyard, following Han Chinese practice.

Malay chieftains throughout Southeast Asia, many of whom converted to Islam, built extensive and often elaborate royal compounds in wood and other plant materials. Contemporary travel accounts and indigenous literature, particularly from the sixteenth century onward, provide tantalizing descriptions of these vanished legendary enclaves.

Religious architecture in Southeast Asia is equally diverse. For example, the multiple-story *pasada* of Sri Lanka was copied in northern Thailand, where there is also a replica of the famous Mahabodhi temple at Bodh Gaya. Burmese architecture follows southern and northeastern Indian models as well. Early temples take the form of either a long hall preceded by a vestibule or a cell surrounded by a passageway. During the Pagan period the cell was greatly elaborated upon, ultimately resulting in the cruciform Ananda temple. Likewise, early Javanese temples are small chambers with a single entrance, but by the thirteenth century the sanctuaries were much enlarged. In addition, the exteriors are characterized by heavy carvings, and the buildings have a diamond profile. A similar style of temple was adopted in Bali.

Much of mainland Southeast Asian architecture aspired to the Khmer temple-mountain ideal, the key ingredient of which is the *prasat,* or "tower." Early Khmer temples are simple structures placed on a raised platform; later, multiple levels are added, and these are accompanied by groups of towers and surrounded by long hallways, such as can be seen at Angkor Wat. Cham architects copied the Khmer sanctuary but built it in brick rather than stone. Thai

FIGURE 2. *Phimai, near Nakhon Ratchasima.* Khmer, eleventh century(?). Especially prominent is the *prasat* (tower).

temple-towers, called *prang*, are also similar to the Khmer *prasat* but may have originated independently.

The elegant bell-shaped Buddhist stupa of Sri Lanka was influential throughout Southeast Asia. In Burma the earliest stupas are conical or cylindrical, but by the eighth century the Burmese had adapted the Sri Lankan type of stupa and transformed it into a multifaceted structure with a prominent finial. In Thailand, the bell-shaped stupa is the major form found in early history; during later periods, however, more elaborate forms were preferred, such as the "flowing vase" and "lotus bud" types common to northern Thailand and Laos. An outstanding example of the elaborate form is the Borobudur stupa in Java, a monumental cosmic diagram that captures Buddhist philosophy in stone.

Mention should also be made of European colonial architecture, of palaces and forts constructed by local rulers, and of places of worship erected by faithful immigrants wanting to preserve their own religious heritage. All these forms contribute to Southeast Asia's architectural richness and diversity.

FIGURE 3. *Shwedagon Stupa, Rangoon, Burma.* One of Burma's most famous monuments, Shwedagon typifies the bell-shaped stupa construction style that is derived from Sri Lankan architecture.

Jeannine Auboyer et al., *Oriental Art: A Handbook of Styles and Forms* (1980). A. J. Bernet Kempers, *Ancient Indonesian Art* (1959). Mario Bussagli, *Oriental Architecture* (1974). Bernard P. Groslier, *The Art of Indochina* (1962). ROBERT S. WICKS

ARCOT, a fort and city west of Madras, India. After the Mughal emperor Aurangzeb conquered the surrounding area in 1698, he appointed a governor (nawab) for the region. In 1712 Sa'adat-ullah took the title "Nawab of the Carnatic" and chose Arcot as his capital.

Because of its proximity to both French and British bases and because its hinterland was comparatively rich, the fortress of Arcot became the focus of conflict between the European powers as well as the sultans of Mysore and assorted Maratha chiefs. Robert Clive made his reputation as a military leader there in 1751 when he took the fort with a small force and successfully defended it against a much larger army. The British annexed the area in 1801.

[*See also* Aurangzeb *and* Clive, Sir Robert.]

H. H. Dodwell et al., *The Cambridge History of India,* vol. 5 (1968). V. Smith et al., *The Oxford History of British India* (1967). GREGORY C. KOZLOWSKI

ARDASHIR I (r. 227–245), son of Papak king of Fars (Persis). Ardashir overthrew the Arsacids and founded the Sasanid empire of Iran. His family supervised the temple of the Zoroastrian goddess Anahita at Istakhr. Succeeding his elder brother, Shapur, to the throne around 220, he built a palace at his capital of Gor (Firuzabad, called Ardashir-Khwarra, "fortune of Ardashir"), which controlled central Fars. Expanding into Kerman and Khuzistan, and joined by the rulers of Adiabene and Kirkuk, he defeated and killed his Arsacid master, Ardavan V, in the battle of Hormizdagan, the location of which is uncertain, in about 224 or 227. He then occupied or conquered the rest of Arsacid territory, destroyed the fire temples of local rulers, and confiscated their endowments.

Arsacid coins issued at Seleuceia in 228/229 indicate either the survival of a local regime or a brief restoration attempt there. Joint resistance by the Arsacid rulers, Khosrov of Armenia and Vehsadjan of the Kushans, led him to conquer the Kushans and incorporate Bactria, Gandhara, and Baluchistan into the Sasanid empire. He also conquered Mesene, killing its last local dynast, and the east Arabian coast. In 230 he besieged Nisibis and invaded Roman Mesopotamia, Syria, Cappadocia, and Armenia, either to restore the extent of the ancient Persian empire, according to contemporary Romans, or to occupy those regions the Romans had used to invade Iran. By 232 his westward expansion had been halted by Alexander Severus, but in 238 he took Nisibis and Carrhae. He commemorated these achievements in several relief carvings in Fars.

Ardashir's accession favored the establishment of Zoroastrianism. He remained priest of Anahita; adopted the divine symbols of Ahura Mazda, Anahita, Verethraghna, and Mithra for his crown; and received his temporal power from Ahura Mazda. His own royal fire, kindled in 227, marked the official start of his reign and was depicted on the reverse of his coins.

Ardashir began to centralize power, although several local kings survived the fall of the Arsacids in Abrenag, Abarshahr, Sakastan, Kerman, Adiabene, and Iberia at first and attended his court, as did members of the locally powerful Suren, Karen, Varaz, and Andigan clans. But Ardashir made members of his own family subkings of Mesene and the Kushan territory, and then in Kerman and Merv. In 240 he had his son, Shapur, crowned coruler. Royal cities were founded at strategic points as military and administrative centers to control conquered territory and secure communications. These cities and their crown districts were governed by royal deputies and were founded in Fars, Khuzistan, Bahrein, Iraq, Kerman, Sistan, and eastern Khurasan.

[*See also* Parthians; Sasanid Dynasty; Shapur I; *and* Zoroastrianism.]

Ehsan Yarshater, ed., *The Seleucid, Parthian and Sasanian Periods* (1983), vol. 3 of the *Cambridge History of Iran.*

MICHAEL G. MORONY

ARIA, or Areia, the Greek and Latin name of a province of the Achaemenid empire called Haraiva in Old Persian, situated on both sides of the river today called Hari Rud, with its principal city, Herat, in Afghanistan. The boundaries of Aria varied and seem to have been larger in Seleucid and Parthian times than earlier. Confusion between this name and the name of the land of the Aryans (Ariane) by some classical authors during the Parthian period, however, was ended by the time of the Sasanids in the third to seventh century, when Harev (Middle Persian) and Iran were clearly distinguished.

[*See also* Herat.]

Richard N. Frye, *The Heritage of Persia* (1976).

RICHARD N. FRYE

ARMENIANS IN SOUTH ASIA. From an early date Armenians were energetic traders in South Asian ports. They enjoyed special privileges at the court of the Mughal emperor Akbar, and their contacts with India multiplied after 1605 when Shah Abbas I of Persia transferred thousands of Armenians from Old Julfa to the Isfahan suburb of New Julfa. From there, Armenian merchant magnates *(khojas)* extended their commercial network westward into Europe, northward into Russia, and eastward into India, Ceylon, Burma, Java, Manila, and beyond. Most of the Armenians in South Asia were centered in Agra, Calcutta, Surat, Dhaka, Madras, and Bombay, where they developed extensive shipping interests and acted as brokers, interpreters, and agents for European companies. In 1688 the East India Company signed an agreement with the "Armenian nation," granting Armenian merchants special privileges in return for Armenians carrying their own trade from India and Persia, and thence to Europe, via England. During the seventeenth and eighteenth centuries many Armenian churches were built; they can still be seen in South Asian cities, among them Dhaka, Calcutta, and Madras.

Contact with the British had a significant impact on Armenian thought. The social and political concerns of the European Enlightenment gave a distinctly secular orientation to Armenian writing in India. With the establishment of a press in 1771, Calcutta and Madras became centers of a lively literary and educational activity. Among the most influential propagators of the new ideas during the eighteenth century were Shahamir Shahamirean, Movses Baghramean, and Harutiun Shmavorean. The first Armenian periodical, *Azdarar* (*The Monitor*), appeared in Madras in 1794. The seeds of a socially and politically oriented ideology that were contained in the writings of these Armenians became germane to Armenian liberation activities during the nineteenth century. A particularly revealing portrait of Armenian life and thought in eighteenth-century India is the autobiography of Joseph Emin (1726–1809), *The Life and Adventures of Joseph Emin, an Armenian, written in English by himself,* printed in London in 1792.

Armenian communities in South Asia experienced a decline in the nineteenth century; after World War II the majority of their members emigrated to Australia and New Zealand.

B. C. Colless, "The Traders of the Pearl: The Mercantile Activities of Persian and Armenian Christians in South-East Asia," in *Abr-Nahrain* 9 (1969–1970), 10 (1970), 11 (1971), 13 (1972–1973), 15 (1974–1975), 18 (1978–1979). Mesrovb Jacob Seth, *Armenians in India, from the Earliest Times to the Present Day* (1937).

LORETTA TOPALIAN NASSAR

ARROW WAR, China's war with Britain and France (1856–1860), which resulted in the Treaties of Tianjin (1858) and the Conventions of Beijing (1860). This war had the general effect of opening the whole Chinese empire to Western contact, and led to the Self-Strengthening Movement. In the West this episode is known as the Arrow War or the Second China War, which led to the second treaty settlement of 1858 to 1860. In China it is generally referred to as the War with Britain and France and, after 1949, the Second Opium War.

After the Treaty of Nanjing (1842), the people of Guangzhou (Canton) became increasingly antiforeign and refused to admit the British into the city. The British not only insisted on entering Guangzhou, but also actively sought treaty revision because of their desire to expand trade in China, their demand for resident ministers in Beijing, and their intention to reduce customs dues. Yet the Chinese avoided negotiations after Qiying was replaced in 1848 by two xenophobic officials in Guangzhou: Governor-general Xu Guangjin and Governor Ye Mingchen. The new emperor, Xianfeng, was also opposed to Western contact.

Convinced that the treaty system would deteriorate in China if not reaffirmed and extended, Britain finally found a *casus belli* in 1856, when Ye refused to give Consul Harry Parks redress for an insult to a British flag lowered by Chinese police from a Chinese-owned vessel registered with the British authorities of Hong Kong—the lorcha *Arrow*. The French government, capitalizing on the murder of a missionary, decided on a joint expedition with Britain. The Anglo-French expedition nominally originated in these rather small incidents, in which the rights of the matter were certainly debatable. Nevertheless the clear-cut underlying issue was whether the Chinese or Western mode of Sino-foreign relations was to prevail.

The Anglo-French forces, led by Lord Elgin and Baron Gros, seized Guangzhou in December 1857 and Tianjin four months later. In June 1858 the Treaties of Tianjin were concluded, containing the following provisions: (1) the establishment of permanent Western legations at Beijing; (2) the opening of ten new ports, including four on the Yangtze River; (3) the permission of foreign travel in all parts of China; (4) the imposition of inland transit dues *(likin)* for foreign imports not to exceed 2.5 percent ad valorem; (5) the payment of an indemnity of six million taels; and (6) the guarantee of freedom of movement throughout China for missionaries.

When the British and French ministers arrived off Tianjin a year later to go to Beijing in order to exchange treaty ratifications, a controversy over the passage to Beijing touched off skirmishes. Elgin and Gros were forced to retreat but returned again in 1860 with stronger forces, occupied Beijing, and burned the Summer Palace. In October they signed the Conventions of Beijing with Prince Gong, the emperor having fled to Manchuria. The new conventions confirmed the treaties of 1858 and included further concessions from China: the indemnity was increased to sixteen million taels; Tianjin was opened to foreign trade; Britain was to acquire the Kowloon Peninsula; and France secured the right for Catholic missionaries to own properties in interior China. Shocked by the Western seizure of Beijing, some Chinese officials initiated the Self-strengthening Movement through adoption of Western diplomatic practices and military and technological devices.

[*See also* Qing Dynasty.]

David Bonner-Smith and E. W. R. Lumby, *The Second China War: 1856–1860* (1954). Douglas Hurd, *The Arrow War: An Anglo-Chinese Confusion, 1856–1860* (1967). Frederic Wakeman, Jr., *Strangers at the Gate: Social Disorder in South China, 1839–1861* (1966). J. Y. Wong, *Yeh Ming-ch'en: Viceroy of Liang Kuang, 1852–8* (1976).

YEN-P'ING HAO

ARSACID DYNASTY. *See* Parthians.

ARTAXERXES II (r. 404–358 BCE), Persian king of the Achaemenid dynasty, surnamed Mnemon (Greek, "mindful"). His younger but abler and more ambitious brother, Cyrus ("the Younger"), marched with thirteen thousand Greek mercenaries toward Babylon; only his death in the Battle of Cunaxa (September 401) and the generalship of Tissaphernes, Persia's ablest commander, saved the king.

His long reign saw Egypt in rebellion, Sparta invading Asia Minor, and the royal palace breeding intrigues. Although he succeeded in dividing the Greeks and imposing his will on them through the Treaty of Antalcidas (in 386), his own son Darius conspired against him and was executed. The old king died soon afterward. His religious policy of supporting the Magi and favoring the setting up of statues—especially those of Anahita/Artemis—won him a sanctified name.

[*See also* Achaemenid Dynasty.]

J. M. Cook, *Persian Empire* (1981). A. T. Olmstead, *History of the Persian Empire* (1948).

A. SHAHPUR SHAHBAZI

ARTAXERXES III (r. 358–338 BCE), Persian king of the Achaemenid dynasty. He succeeded Artaxerxes II, but unlike him he was brutal, vigorous, politically farsighted, and resolute. Artaxerxes III murdered many of his kin, reconquered Egypt, put down a revolt of the satraps, and reunited and reorganized the empire. He judiciously pursued a divide-and-conquer policy toward the Greeks and checked their ambitions. He also keenly recognized the rising Macedonian threat and in consequence planned military actions that aided Philip's Greek adversaries. His assassination by a court eunuch deprived Iran of a leader who was militarily able and politically experienced precisely when Alexander's invasion made such qualities absolutely indispensable. He was entombed in a rock-cut sepulcher next to Persepolis. Of all successors of Darius I, he was nearest to his diplomatic style.

[*See also* Achaemenid Dynasty.]

J. M. Cook, *Persian Empire* (1981). A. T. Olmstead, *History of the Persian Empire* (1948).

A. SHAHPUR SHAHBAZI

ARTHASHASTRA. *See* Kautilya.

ARUNACHAL PRADESH, a union territory of the Republic of India, constituted from what was formerly known as the Northeast Frontier Agency (NEFA) in January 1972. It lies in the northeast of the subcontinent and shares borders with China and Tibet in the north, Bhutan in the west, and Burma and Assam in the east and south. It is made up of the six districts of Kameng, Lohit, Siang, Subansiri, and Tirap. The area is populated predominantly by Tibeto-Burman-speaking hill tribes, the most important of which are the Dafla, Apatani, and Mishmi. The early history of the area is unknown, there being almost no archaeological record and few useful references to it in the Indian texts. The Mughals made little effort to penetrate it. In the early 1960s, confrontation with China increased the Indian government's awareness of its strategic importance. New roads and airstrips were built linking the chief centers with the plains, and the area was rapidly brought into contact with the modern world.

THEODORE RICCARDI, JR.

ARYANS, a group of tribes speaking Indo-European-related languages, presumably from Central Asia, who occupied the land from Iran to northwest India in the second millennium BCE. One tribe penetrated as far as northern Mesopotamia, where they ruled the Hurrite state of Mitanni in the middle of the second millennium BCE. The subgroup called Indo-Aryans probably occupied all these territories until the invasion of the subgroup called Iranians displaced and absorbed the Indo-Aryans in Iran, beginning about 1400 BCE.

The Indo-Aryans of India have left a major body of writings, as have the Eastern Iranians. That of the Indians is the *Rig Veda,* a collection of hymns, the oldest of which may go back to the eighteenth century BCE. The Eastern Iranians left the Avesta, the sacred book of the Zoroastrians.

The Aryans, who called themselves Arya, Airya, and Ariya in Sanskrit, Avestan, and Old Persian, respectively, maintained a consciousness of their tribal roots even after they had settled down in Iran and India. In an Old Persian inscription from western Iran, Darius the Great (c. 549–485 BCE) calls himself a member of an "Aryan" tribe. And the phrase with which the composers of the Avesta designated their land—*airyana vaejah,* or "the home of the Aryans"—has the same meaning as the modern term *Iran.*

[*See also* Vedas *and* Zoroastrianism.]

T. Burrow, "The Proto-Indoaryans," *Journal of the Royal Asiatic Society* (1973): 123–140.

LUCIANNE C. BULLIET

ARYA SAMAJ, Hindu reform movement. Swami Dayananda Saraswati established the first successful Arya Samaj in Bombay on 10 April 1875 as a vehicle for his vision of a revived and reformed Hinduism.

The first substantive growth of the Arya Samaj resulted from Dayananda's tour of the Punjab from 19 April 1877 to 11 July 1878. The Lahore Arya Samaj was established on 24 July 1877; new principles and bylaws were composed and the movement quickly spread.

Following Dayananda's death in 1883, Arya Samajes in the Punjab, Uttar Pradesh, and Rajasthan sought to found a school in his honor. The Dayananda Anglo-Vedic High School opened in Lahore on 1 June 1886. It soon gained students and community support. By 1889 college classes were added. Differences arose within the movement during the educational campaign. Two opposing interpretations of Dayananda and his message coalesced into a militant, deeply religious group and a more moderate wing that saw Dayananda as a reformer rather than an inspired sage. When the Samaj split in 1893 the moderates retained control over the schools and the militants controlled a majority of the local Arya Samajes as well as the representative body for the Punjab, the Arya Pratinidhi Sabha. Moderate Aryas concentrated their attention on developing a system of schools and on famine and orphan relief. The militants focused on proselytization, women's education, and the creation of a purely Hindu school. This became the Gurukula Kangri, founded in 1902. The militants used *shuddhi* as a ritual of purification and reconversion. [*See* Shuddhi.]

The Arya Samaj grew rapidly from a base of 39,952 in 1891 to 990,233 in 1931, the last year they were counted in the Indian census. The 1941 *Arya Directory* listed over 2,000 individual Samajes, 178 schools, 10 colleges, and 33 educational institutions called *gurukulas*. Provincial representative organizations were founded in Uttar Pradesh (1886), Rajasthan (1888), Bengal and Bihar (1889), Madhya Pradesh (1889), and Bombay (1902). The growth of the Samaj led to the creation of an overall representative body, the Sarvadeshik Arya Pratinidhi Sabha. Similar Sabhas were organized outside of the subcontinent, in British East Africa (1922), South Africa (1927), Fiji (1928), Mauritius (1930), and Dutch Guyana (1937). Expansion also continued inside British India with a separate Pratinidhi Sabha organized for Bihar in 1930 and for the state of Hyderabad in 1935.

The twentieth century saw the Samaj involved in defense of the Hindu community. In 1921 it sent missionaries to Kerala to reconvert Hindus lost to Islam during the Moplah (Mappila) uprising. In 1923 the Samaj led in the creation of the Bharatiya Shuddhi Sabha and in the campaign to reconvert the Malkana Rajputs from Islam to Hinduism. In 1925 it held a centenary celebration in honor of Dayananda's birth. The success of this meeting led to the holding of a *mahasammelan* ("great meeting"). Before 1947 the Aryas conducted four *mahasammelans:* Delhi (1927), Bareilly (1931), Ajmer (1933), and Delhi again in 1944. The Samaj also entered into communal conflict with a *satyagraha* against the ruler of Hyderabad in 1939 and another with the Sind government in 1946. [*See* Satyagraha.] The partition of British India caused a major upheaval in the Samaj, but after reorganizing themselves the Aryas became once more an important religious and political force in northwestern India as they entered into further struggles in defense of Hindi and the Hindu community.

[*See also* Dayananda Saraswati *and* Mappilas.]

W. Eric Gustafson and Kenneth W. Jones, eds., *Sources on Punjab History* (1975). Kenneth W. Jones, *Arya Dharm: Hindu Consciousness in Nineteenth-Century Punjab* (1976) and "The Arya Samaj in British India 1875–1947," in *Religion in Modern India*, edited by Robert D. Baird (1981), pp. 27–54. Lala Lajpat Rai, *The Arya Samaj* (1915).

KENNETH W. JONES

ARYAVARTA, "land of the Aryans," the central region in a fivefold division of India, covering much of the Ganges plain. Aryavarta is first described in the *Dharmasutras* and in Manu's *Dharmashastra* (where it is equated with Madhyadesha) to have extended from the terminus of the Sarasvati River in the west to Prayaga in the east to the Himalayas in the north to the Vindhyas in the south. Later it became synonymous with a larger, generalized Indo-Aryan cultura area.

[*See also* Hindustan.]

B. C. Law, *Historical Geography of Ancient India* (reprint, 1976).

GERI HOCKFIELD MALANDRA

ASAF UD-DAULAH (1750–1797), fourth nawab, or ruler, of the North Indian state of Awadh (Oudh) from 1775 until his death. A weak sovereign but an active patron of arts and letters, he reigned during the turbulent period of political decentralization following Mughal decline, when the East India Company was becoming increasingly able to manipulate his regime's finances and policies.

[*See also* Awadh.]

RICHARD B. BARNETT

ASAHI SHIMBUN, one of Japan's leading daily newspapers during the modern period. Founded in 1879 by Kimura Noburu, the Osaka-based *Asahi shimbun* was purchased two years later by Murayama Ryūhei and Ueno Riichi. The newspaper initially appealed to a mass urban audience with frequent entertainment features. In 1888 the owners bought Tokyo's *Mezamashi shimbun,* which became the *Tōkyō asahi shimbun* (the original was renamed the *Ōsaka asahi shimbun*). The two dailies gradually shifted to a full news format with national and international coverage. Together they achieved the largest circulation in pre–World War II Japan.

The *Asahi* was known for its liberal, democratic positions. After 1905 the company attracted several young reporters who advocated responsible cabinets and expanded suffrage. In 1918 the *Ōsaka asahi* incurred the wrath of officials when it opposed the government's Siberian expedition and called for the resignation of the cabinet of Prime Minister Terauchi Masatake. The newspaper escaped suppression only after executives announced a new policy of self-censorship and Murayama and four others resigned. Despite these concessions, the two papers, particularly the *Ōsaka asahi*, played a pivotal role in the democratic movement of the 1920s, championing universal suffrage and labor reform. In the 1930s the *Asahi* courted rising nationalism, enthusiastically endorsing the Japanese army's occupation of Manchuria. Editors remained critical of the military's interference in politics, however, prompting young army officers to vandalize company headquarters during the insurrection of 26 February 1936. In 1940 the Tokyo and Osaka dailies consolidated themselves into the *Asahi shimbun* under government pressure. In 1980 the *Asahi shimbun* enjoyed a readership of 7.5 million, making it the largest of Japan's five national dailies.

[*See also* Journalism: Journalism in Japan.]

Richard H. Mitchell, *Censorship in Imperial Japan* (1983). SHELDON M. GARON

ASH'ARI, a school of theology in Islam named after Abu al-Hasan al-Ash'ari (d. 936), whose teachings together with those of his principal disciples laid the basis for a doctrine that sought to occupy a middle ground between the rationalism of the Mu'tazilis and the traditionalist views of the Hanbalis. Against the Mu'tazilis, whose views al-Ash'ari himself had once espoused, the Ash'ari school insisted, among other things, on the following: (1) the reality of God's eternal attributes, (2) the createdness of the Qur'an, (3) the absolute sovereignty of God over human actions, and (4) the reality of the beatific vision. While thus accepting the substance of traditionalist doctrine, Ash'aris, however, insisted on the legitimacy of reason as a tool for the defense of the truths of revelation. Since the Ash'ari position was rejected by both Mu'tazilis and Hanbalis, what early Ash'aris had hoped would form the basis for a reconciliation of the two polar positions ended by becoming a third school of thought. Although the position represented by al-Ash'ari and his early defenders underwent some degree of modification in the subsequent period, repudiation of Mu'tazili doctrine, attachment to tradition, and insistence on the value of reason as an apologetic device remained characteristic features of Ash'ari thought during the medieval period. Among the leading Ash'aris of the period are al-Baqillani (d. 1013), al-Juwaini (d. 1086), and al-Ghazali (d. 1111).

From Baghdad, the main center of the early school, Ash'arism found its way to the major centers of the Near East, especially Khurasan, where it became a major intellectual force. Although Ash'arism is not to be equated with the Shafi'i school of law, it found its greatest acceptance in areas where Shafi'i law was the dominant legal influence. Whether Ash'arism ever achieved the status of orthodoxy, as I. Goldziher and others have argued, remains a disputed point among historians of medieval Islam.

[*See also* Ghazali, al-; Hanbali; *and* Mu'tazili.]

William Montgomery Watt, *Islamic Philosophy and Theology* (1962). MERLIN SWARTZ

ASHIGARU, soldiers who were "agile, nimble, and quick of foot," first emerged as highly specialized warriors in Japan during the medieval period. Most conventional battles of that time were fought on plains and hillsides between mounted samurai armed with swords and spears. When fighting moved into city areas, however, such mounted fighters could not be successfully deployed, and commanders turned to the *ashigaru,* who were trained to set fire to urban streets and residential areas, divert water supplies away from enemy strongholds, and otherwise harass the opponent with guerrilla-like tactics.

The term *ashigaru* first appears in medieval warrior tales such as the *Heike monogatari,* indicating that they may have seen action as early as the Gempei wars of 1180 to 1185. Their numbers increased during the medieval period, and the *ashigaru* became infamous for their actions in Kyoto during the bitter fighting of the Ōnin War of 1467 to 1477, when they were commonly condemned for their "evil acts" of looting, arson, and changing sides at the drop of a copper coin.

From the late fifteenth to the sixteenth century, battles fought between mounted warriors gradually gave way to larger-scale engagements between massed formations of infantry armed with muskets, especially after the Battle of Nagashino in 1575. To fill these new, mass ranks, many daimyo began to recruit from the lower stratum of the peasant population and started to refer to these recruits as *ashigaru,* thus redefining the term to mean infantry, or general foot soldier.

In the early modern period, the term was applied to the lowest-ranking subdivisions within the *bushi* (warrior) class, men who were organized into units of archers, lancers, musketeers, and so forth for military purposes, and who served as personal attendants, messengers, or minor police officials in times of peace. Following the Meiji Restoration in 1868, the *ashigaru* were designated as *sotsuzoku,* and then were reclassified as *shizoku* after the abolition of domains.

[*See also* Ōnin War *and* Nagashino, Battle of.]

James L. McClain

ASHIKAGA PERIOD. *See* Muromachi Period.

ASHIKAGA TAKAUJI (1305–1358), Japanese ruler, the first of the Ashikaga shoguns and the founder of the Muromachi *bakufu.* The leader of a powerful warrior family in eastern Japan, Takauji began his rise to power as a vassal of the Hōjō regents, who dominated the Kamakura *bakufu.* In 1333 he was dispatched by the Hōjō to western Japan to put down a revolt against the *bakufu* led by Emperor Go-Daigo. Takauji joined Go-Daigo, called on other eastern warrior bands to revolt against the Hōjō, and attacked the *bakufu's* deputy in Kyoto. Although Takauji was granted court titles by the victorious Go-Daigo, he was not permitted to play a leading role in Go-Daigo's short-lived imperial restoration government and was angered when Go-Daigo did not grant him the title of shogun. [*See* Kemmu Restoration.]

In 1336 Takauji revolted and forced Go-Daigo to relinquish his throne to an emperor of the northern line of the imperial family. Go-Daigo fled to Yoshino, where he set up a rival government, known as the Southern Court. Until the breach was healed in 1392 the political life of Japan was wracked by warfare between the rival courts and their warrior backers. [*See* Nambokuchō *and* Yoshino Line.]

In firm control of Kyoto, Takauji ordered the compilation of a warrior code, the *Kemmu shikimoku,* secured for himself the title of shogun in 1338, and established his shogunate, or *bakufu,* in the Muromachi district of Kyoto. Takauji's later years were troubled by rivalry with his brother Tadayoshi, whom he ordered poisoned in 1352, and by the sporadic warfare between the rival courts.

Although he was a ruthless and ambitious warrior, Takauji was also a poet of some ability, a devotee of Pure Land, or Amidist, Buddhism, and a patron of the Zen monk Musō Soseki, for whom he built the Tenryūji monastery as a memorial to placate the troubled spirit of Go-Daigo.

[*See also* Go-Daigo *and* Muromachi Period.]

H. Paul Varley, *Imperial Restoration in Medieval Japan* (1971). H. Paul Varley, trans., *A Chronicle of Gods and Sovereigns: Jinnō shōtōki of Kitabatake Chikafusa* (1980).

Martin Collcutt

ASHIKAGA YOSHIMASA (1436–1490), Japanese ruler, the eighth Ashikaga shogun. Yoshimasa was the son of Ashikaga Yoshinori, the sixth Ashikaga shogun, who was assassinated in 1441 by a rebellious vassal. If Yoshimitsu and Yoshinori headed the Muromachi *bakufu* at its zenith, Yoshimasa presided over a declining institution, and by his own weakness he contributed to its further deterioration. Like Yoshimitsu, Yoshimasa was a cultivated ruler and patron of the arts. Unlike Yoshimitsu, however, his cultural activities were less the expression or enhancement of his political authority than they were a means of escape from the heavier responsibilities of shogunal office.

Yoshimasa was appointed shogun in 1449. He held the office until 1473, when he abdicated in favor of his son Yoshihisa, took Buddhist orders, and retired to a retreat in Higashiyama, the Eastern Hills of Kyoto. The *bakufu* in the mid-fifteenth century was beset by serious political and economic problems and needed strong leadership. The assassination of Yoshinori by one of his vassals had dealt a severe blow to the political authority of the shoguns. Moreover, lacking extensive direct domain, the *bakufu* economy was always under strain. Taxes on merchants and guilds and the sporadic proceeds from the China trade added something to the shogunal treasury but did not offset the fundamental financial weakness of the *bakufu*. Shogunal efforts to raise funds by imposing regional levies merely provoked outbursts of violence by peasants and samurai, many of whom already complained of the exactions of moneylenders.

The weakness of the *bakufu* encouraged the territorial ambitions of powerful provincial warriors, especially the *shugo* (constables, military governors). Yoshimasa lacked the military power and the will to restrain these ambitions. His frequent debt moratorium laws, *tokusei*, created commercial confusion without appeasing aggrieved peasants and samurai. Efforts to engage more actively in the taxable trade with China were more than counterbalanced by his outlay for building construction, pilgrimages, and works of art. With little aptitude for, or interest in, administration, Yoshimasa allowed himself to be dominated by his wife, Hino Tomiko, and her family. He seriously weakened the *bakufu* by allowing a dispute over the shogunal succession to broaden into a full-scale war. Lacking an heir, Yoshimasa first designated his younger brother as his successor. In the following year, when Tomiko gave birth to a son, he reversed himself and made the child his heir. The ensuing succession squabble quickly enbroiled rival courtiers, as well as many *shugo* led by the rival Yamana and Hosokawa families. This dispute brought destruction to Kyoto and widened into the Ōnin War (1466–1477), the prelude to a century of provincial warfare and decentralization in Japan.

Although Yoshimasa was inept as a political leader, he was an informed and enthusiastic patron of the arts. The temple-retreat of Jishōji, more commonly known as the Ginkakuji ("temple of the silver pavilion"), that he built for himself in the Eastern Hills of Kyoto became the focus, in the midst of warfare, of the cultural epoch known as Higashiyama culture. Like the Jishōji itself, this cultural surge reflected Yoshimasa's interests in Zen and Pure Land Buddhism. His reign saw developments over a broad cultural spectrum, including domestic architecture, garden design, flower arrangement, *nō* and *kyōgen,* the tea ceremony, ink painting, and linked verse. This epoch gave final shape to what has come to be known as the classical Japanese aesthetic, with its strands of *yūgen,* "mysteriousness," *sabi,* "withered" or "faded," and *wabi,* "deliberate restraint." Among the artists patronized by Yoshimasa who contributed to this cultural flowering were the painters Sesshū Tōyō (1420–1506), Oguri Sōtan (d. 1486), and Kanō Masanobu (1454–1530); the *nō* actors Komparu Zenchiku (1405–1468) and Kanze Kojirō (1435–1516); the poet, painter, and architect Nōami (1397–1471); the garden designer Zen'ami (1393-?); the tea master Murata Jukō (1422–1502); and the renga poet Sōgi (1421–1502).

[*See also* Ōnin War *and* Muromachi Period.]

H. Paul Varley, *The Onin War* (1967) and *Japanese Culture* (1973).

MARTIN COLLCUTT

ASHIKAGA YOSHIMITSU (1358–1408), Japanese ruler, the third of the Ashikaga shoguns. Yoshimitsu played a major role in the consolidation of the Muromachi *bakufu,* which reached its apogee under his forceful leadership. He was also at the center of the cultural renaissance known as *Kitayama bunka,* or "the culture of the northern hills."

Son of Yoshiakira, the second Ashikaga shogun, and grandson of Takauji, the founder of the *bakufu,* Yoshimitsu was appointed shogun in 1368 while still a child. For the first decade of his reign he was guided by a warrior deputy, the *kanrei* Hosokawa Yoriyuki. As he gained experience and maturity, however, Yoshimitsu quickly imposed his own will on the warrior and courtier elites of his day, became a lavish patron of the arts, and encouraged the reestablishment of close diplomatic and commercial relations with China.

Of the Ashikaga shoguns, Yoshimitsu was the most effective in enforcing his authority over the warrior order headed by the coalition of provincial warrior constables, the *shugo,* that sustained the Muromachi *bakufu.* He did this by force—putting down revolts by *shugo* like the Toki, Yamana, and Ouchi who challenged his power—and by the grandiose demonstration of his political and cultural hegemony over the country. To increase his political authority, Yoshimitsu sought influence over the court nobility by consorting with members of the imperial family and having himself promoted to high rank and office within the imperial court. Early in his reign he built a magnificent shogunal palace, the Hana no Gosho ("palace of flowers") close to the imperial palace. There he entertained emperors, nobles, monks, and warriors. His settlement in 1392 of the war between the Northern and Southern Courts enhanced his authority over the court. [*See* Nambokuchō.] He came to hold the junior first rank in the court hierarchy and the office of "great minister of state," *daijō daijin,* and had dreams of marrying his offspring into the imperial line.

In his later years Yoshimitsu transferred the shogunal title to his son and took Buddhist orders. He thus added a transcendent spiritual aura to his political and military authority, but without relinquishing any of his political control.

Throughout his life he was a generous patron of Buddhism and the arts. His retreat in the northern hills of Kyoto, the Kinkakuji ("golden pavilion"), became a cultural symbol for his age. Through his patronage of the actors Kan'ami and Zeami he helped raise the early *nō* drama to new heights of dramatic intensity; he also led the way in the collecting of Chinese objects and the appreciation of Chinese culture. Eager to resume diplomatic and commercial ties with China, he used the subordinate tributary title Nihon Kokuō ("king of Japan"), for which he was sharply criticized, and sent an embassy to China in 1401. Yoshimitsu's patronage of the disciples of Musō Soseki raised Rinzai Zen to leadership in the religious world of late fourteenth-century Kyoto.

[*See also* Muromachi Period.]

H. Paul Varley, *Imperial Restoration in Medieval Japan* (1971) and "Ashikage Yoshimitsu and the World of Kitayama: Social Change and Shogunal Patronage in Early Muromachi Japan," in *Japan in the Muromachi Age*, edited by John W. Hall and Toyoda Takeshi (1977).

MARTIN COLLCUTT

ASHIO COPPER MINE, a highly productive copper mine usually associated with Japan's first modern pollution incident. Located in Tochigi Prefecture, the Ashio copper mine dates to the early seventeenth century, when copper was first discovered along the Watarase River approximately seventy-five miles northwest of Tokyo. The mine was extensively developed during the Tokugawa period (1600–1868) and Ashio copper was regularly exported to China and Europe through the Nagasaki trade.

By the time of the Meiji Restoration the Ashio mine was thought to have been exhausted. In 1877, however, the mine came under the control of Furukawa Ichibei, one of the entrepreneurial geniuses of the Meiji period, who was later known as the "Copper King" of East Asia. Under Furukawa's supervision Ashio underwent a rapid transformation. Using the latest technology, including hydroelectric power, the Bessemer smelting process, and new methods for deep tunneling, Ashio was transformed into a major mining complex. By 1890 it ranked with Anaconda, Calumet-Hecla, and Rio Tinto as one of the world's leading copper producers. Production statistics jumped from 29 tons in 1876 to 4,287 tons in 1891. By the beginning of the twentieth century Ashio accounted for 40 percent of Japan's total copper output, and copper represented Japan's third most important export commodity.

Ashio's successful modernization was carried out at considerable ecological and social cost. Preoccupied with increases in production, the mine overlooked the effects of growth on the environment. Rapid expansion destroyed the watershed in the Watarase Valley and resulted in flooding. Moreover, flood waters coursed through the mine's carelessly discarded wastes. By the time these floods moved downstream, as they did in 1888, 1892, and 1896, and entered the northern Kantō Plain through the Watarase and Tone rivers, they were heavily laden with sulphuric acid, copper wastes, and other pollutants that turned the rich farmland of this region into a virtual desert. The 1896 flood inundated more than thirteen thousand homes and immediate flood damage alone was estimated at ¥14 million.

What resulted was a national protest movement that included farmers from Gumma, Tochigi, Saitama, and Ibaragi prefectures; urban social reform groups that included Christians, Christian-Socialists, Socialists, women's organizations, and university students; and members of Parliament, such as Tanaka Shōzō, creating what can be described as Japan's first modern "citizen's movement." After a series of direct confrontations, the government finally pressured Furukawa to clean up. While antipollution measures brought Ashio's pollution to a level where it became acceptable for most of the farming population living along the banks of the Watarase and Tone rivers during the Meiji–Taishō periods, such pollution continued. In fact, the "one-hundred-year pollution war," as it is often known, was not settled until 1974, when the mine and farmers accepted an arbitration settlement worked out by the government and the mine was closed.

What the Ashio copper mine represented were the two faces of Japanese modernization—a high degree of industrial success, but at considerable social and environmental cost. The controversy surrounding Ashio, therefore, foreshadowed similar issues that were to confront Japan again with the industrial boom that followed World War II.

F. G. NOTEHELFER

ASHOKA, king of Magadha and third emperor of the Maurya dynasty, ruled over all but the southern tip of the Indian peninsula from about 272 to about 232 BCE. His grandfather, Chandragupta, had established the empire, and his father, Bindusara, had governed it from about 300 to about 272 BCE. It is Ashoka, however, who is remembered as the greatest monarch of his line and as one of the most remarkable rulers in the history of India.

The two major sources of information about Ashoka are his own edicts, which he had inscribed on rocks and stone pillars throughout his realm, and the many Buddhist legends that recount his conversion to and support of Buddhism.

The edicts of Ashoka constitute one of the oldest epigraphical records in Indian history. They present a remarkable picture of a sovereign who was obviously in control of his empire yet also very much involved with the well-being of his subjects.

Ashoka's main concern was the propagation of *dharma,* a word that has many connotations in the Indian context. In the edicts it seems to imply a polity of active social concern, religious tolerance, ecological awareness, observance of common ethical precepts, and the renunciation of war. It may also have been an ideology designed to help unify the empire. In the name of *dharma,* Ashoka regretted the suffering caused by his conquests of new territories, most notably in the land of the Kalingas. He provided for communications to be developed, for resthouses to be built, and trees to be planted along roads; he established medical facilities for beasts and men, ordered an end to the killing of most animals in the royal kitchens, enjoined religious tolerance and respect for parents, priests, and ascetics, and commissioned "officers of righteousness" *(dharmamahamatra)* to propagate his policies. He sent representatives to foreign nations and personally went on tours of his realm, and he offered moral advice to his subjects and made donations to Buddhist sects and even to rival religious groups such as the Ajivikas.

There is much debate among scholars whether or not Ashoka himself was actually converted to Buddhism, and whether or not his *dharma* should be understood in specifically Buddhist terms. Hints in some of the edicts suggest that it should, but the overall evidence from the inscriptions remains ambiguous.

The Pali and Sanskrit legends about Ashoka, however, unambiguously maintain that he became a Buddhist. They recount his early impetuous days as a violently inclined monarch known as "Ashoka the Fierce" (Chandashoka), who stole the throne away from his older brother, the rightful heir. They then feature his conversion to Buddhism by a young monk, after which he came to be called "Ashoka the Righteous" (Dharmashoka).

FIGURE 1. *Capital of an Ashokan Pillar.* The pillar at Sarnath is one of the many examples of monuments erected by Ashoka. Inscribed on such pillars were edicts designed to promote the concept of *dharma* and the achievements of Ashoka's reign.

As "Dharmashoka," his greatest legendary act was the division and redistribution of the bodily relics of the Buddha, over which he is reputed to have had eighty-four thousand stupas (reliquary mounds) built throughout his realm. He is also credited with establishing the basic Buddhist pilgrimage sites in India, and with providing for the needs of the Buddhist community so beneficently that he became a paradigm of piety for Buddhist monarchs throughout history. In the Pali legends, he is further portrayed as an upholder of the orthodox Theravada tradition, purging heterodox monks from the community and sponsoring a great council of elders at Pataliputra [*See* Pataliputra.] He is said to have sent missionaries to various lands, including his own son Mahendra and daughter Sanghamitra—both of whom, it is said, he sent to Sri Lanka. Other traditions attributed to him, either directly or indirectly, are the establishment of Buddhism in Kashmir, Nepal, Khotan, and Southeast Asia.

[*See also* Buddhism: An Overview; Mahendra;

Maurya Empire; *and* Sri Lanka. *For the extent of Ashoka's empire, see map 2 accompanying* India.]

B. G. Gokhale, *Asoka Maurya* (1966). Radhakumud Mookerji, *Asoka* (1928; reprint, 1972). N. A. Nikam and Richard McKeon, eds. and trans., *The Edicts of Asoka* (1958). Vincent A. Smith, *Asoka the Buddhist Emperor of India* (1909; reprint, 1964). John S. Strong, *The Legend of King Asoka* (1983).

JOHN S. STRONG

ASHURA, the tenth day of Muharram, the first month of the Islamic lunar calendar, regarded as possessing a certain holiness by Muslims. The fast, therefore, is recommended for this day in Sunni piety. In the Shi'ite world, however, it is a day on which Husain ibn Ali, the grandson of the Prophet, together with his family and friends, fell fighting against the Umayyads in Karbala in 680. It is therefore the great Islamic day of mourning, celebrated by visitations to the shrines (sg., *mashhad*) of the imams, especially Husain's shrine at Karbala, and by *ta'ziya* recitations. Consequently, Ashura, with Husain and his family at its center, has had a remarkable history of folklore, literature, art, and religious piety of the Shi'ite community. Ashura continues to live and grow in this community, reflecting its experiences of failure and expressing its hopes and aspirations for an Islamic order.

[*See also* Husain ibn Ali *and* Mashhad.]

Mahmoud Ayoub, *Redemptive Suffering in Islam: A Study of the Devotional Aspects of ʿĀshūrāʾ in Twelver Shīʿism* (1979). S. H. M. Jafri, *The Origins and Early Development of Shīʿa Islam* (1981).

ABDELAZIZ SACHEDINA

ASIA is the largest of the seven continents into which modern geographers divide the world, with an area of approximately seventeen million square miles. While Europe and Asia form a continuous landmass, sometimes referred to as Eurasia, it is generally accepted that the boundary between them is the eastern edge of the Ural Mountains. The line runs along the northern shore of the Caspian Sea and the Caucasus Mountains to the Black Sea, and then along the coast of Asia Minor, up to the Isthmus of Suez and south along the western and southern shores of the Arabian Peninsula. It includes the Indian subcontinent and the lands bordering the eastern shores of the Bay of Bengal to the tip of the Malay Peninsula, as well as the great sweep of islands bordering on the Indian Ocean and the Pacific: Sri Lanka, the Indonesian archipelago, the Philippines, Taiwan, and Japan. On the mainland, it includes Indochina and the vast expanses of China as well as the areas of the Soviet Union to the east of the Urals, stretching to the Pacific Ocean, with the Arctic Ocean in the north. For reasons noted in the preface, the Arabian Peninsula, the Levant, Turkey, and the parts of the USSR in Asia, with the exception of its Central Asian republics, will not be treated here.

The word *Asia,* and its application to much of the region we now know by that name, came from the ancient Greeks, but some scholars have traced it to pre-Greek sources in the second millennium BCE from a word that the Hittites used for Anatolia, or modern Turkey. It was applied to this region in the Homeric epics. By the fifth century BCE, however, the Greeks had begun to think of the known world, the *oikoumene,* as divided into three parts, to which they gave the names Europe, Asia, and Africa (or Libya). It was Alexander's ambition to unite these three continents under one political supremacy that led to his expedition to the banks of the Indus in India. This division of the world into three continents was accepted by Roman historians and geographers and it passed into Western intellectual history.

Writers on Asia have used a number of different systems of subdividing it into regions to make its cultural and historical developments more understandable. Geographers have noted, for example, five fairly well marked physical divisions in mainland Asia. One of these is the group of plateaus that make up Inner Asia, covering about a fifth of the whole continent. These lands, sparsely populated, with extremes of heat and cold and unfertile soils, are bordered on the south by the great mountain range of the Himalayas, which culminate in the northwest in the tangle of mountains and plateaus known as the Pamirs. From the Pamirs, a second group of plateaus stretch westward into Afghanistan, Iran, and Turkey. North and east of the plateaus and mountains of Inner Asia is the lowland area of Siberia, in the Soviet Union. A fourth, and historically very important, region is made up of the great river plains of the Huang He (Yellow River) of North China, the Yangtze of Central China, and the Si Jiang of South China. These areas have been the heartlands of Chinese political and cultural life. Beyond these mainland divisions are a great circle of islands, including Indonesia, the Philippines, and Japan. Finally, there is the very distinctive and well-defined unit that formerly was referred to as the

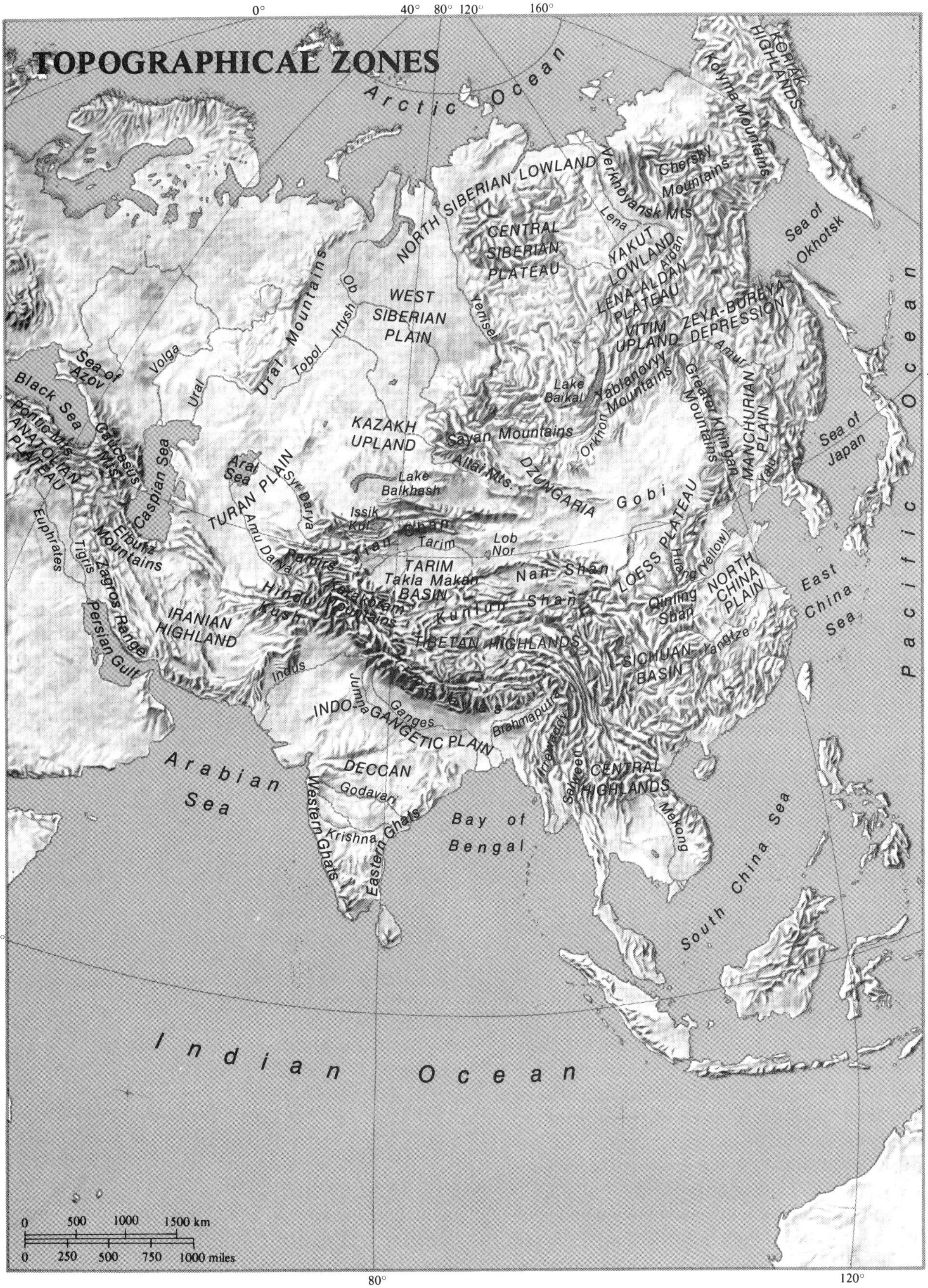
TOPOGRAPHICAL ZONES
Arctic Ocean
NORTH SIBERIAN LOWLAND
CENTRAL SIBERIAN PLATEAU
Verkhoyansk Mts.
Chersky Mountains
Kolyma Mountains
KORIAK HIGHLANDS
Lena
YAKUT LOWLAND
Aldan
LENA-ALDAN PLATEAU
VITIM UPLAND
ZEYA-BUREYA DEPRESSION
Sea of Okhotsk
Pacific Ocean
Ural Mountains
Ob
Irtysh
Tobol
WEST SIBERIAN PLAIN
Yenisei
Volga
Ural
Sea of Azov
Black Sea
Pontic Mts.
ANATOLIAN PLATEAU
Caucasus Mts.
Caspian Sea
Lake Baikal
Yablonovyy Mountains
Amur
Greater Khingan Mountains
MANCHURIAN PLAIN
Orkhon
Sea of Japan
KAZAKH UPLAND
Sayan Mountains
Altai Mts.
DZUNGARIA
Gobi
Aral Sea
TURAN PLAIN
Syr Darya
Lake Balkhash
Issik Kul
Tian Shan
Tarim
Lob Nor
Amu Darya
Pamirs
TARIM
Takla Makan
BASIN
Nan Shan
LOESS PLATEAU
Huang (Yellow)
NORTH CHINA PLAIN
Yalu
Qinling Shan
East China Sea
Euphrates
Tigris
Elburz Mountains
Zagros Range
Hindu Kush
Karakoram Mountains
Kunlun Shan
IRANIAN HIGHLAND
TIBETAN HIGHLANDS
SICHUAN BASIN
Yangtze
Persian Gulf
Indus
Jumna
Ganges
INDO-GANGETIC PLAIN
Brahmaputra
Irrawaddy
Salween
CENTRAL HIGHLANDS
Mekong
Arabian Sea
DECCAN
Godavari
Western Ghats
Krishna
Eastern Ghats
Bay of Bengal
South China Sea
Indian Ocean
0 500 1000 1500 km
0 250 500 750 1000 miles
0° 40° 80° 120° 160°

Indian subcontinent. Sri Lanka is usually regarded as part of the subcontinent, although physically separated by a narrow strait.

Political historians tend to make a somewhat different division of Asia, based more on historical and cultural factors than on geography. Western Asia, or Southwest Asia, as some prefer to call it, includes the countries of the Arabian Peninsula, Turkey, Iraq, and Iran. Afghanistan is sometimes included in this group, sometimes in South Asia. The cultural and political life of these countries has been deeply colored by the dominance of Islam. With the exception of Iran, their links with the rest of Asia have not been very strong or continuous. South Asia is basically the Indian subcontinent, now made up of India, Pakistan, Bangladesh, Bhutan, Nepal, Sri Lanka, and the Maldive Islands.

The pervasive influence of indigenous Indian culture, especially in such religious expressions as Buddhism and Hinduism, is very strong throughout the area, as are the legacies of the intrusions by Islamic and Western civilizations. Southeast Asia is the term generally applied to the mainland countries with independent histories and cultures along the Bay of Bengal and the South China Sea, including Burma, Thailand, Malaysia, Cambodia, Laos, and Vietnam, and the neighboring island countries of Indonesia, the Philippines, and Singapore. The historical experiences, the languages, the religions, and the economies of these countries are extraordinarily diverse, with very complex relationships to Indian and Chinese cultures as well as to their own indigenous traditions, but nonetheless they constitute an intelligible unit for study and analysis. China, Korea, and Japan are usually grouped together as East Asia, but Japan and Korea, for purposes of academic study, are often referred to as Northeast Asia.

While a great variety of cultures and civilizations have been found in Asia throughout the ages, those that had their origins in China, India, and the Islamic regions of western Asia have had the most pervasive impact. All the great religions of the world—Hinduism, Buddhism, Zoroastrianism, Daoism, Judaism, Christianity, Islam, Sikhism—originated in Asia, and, with the exception of Christianity, the bulk of their adherents are found in Asia. Three of these, Buddhism, Christianity, and Islam, were great missionary movements, carrying not only their characteristic religious ideas but also many other aspects of civilization throughout the world. From ancient times, Asia has also been the home of great empires, with China having the most enduring of the great imperial centers. India, while not having such long-lasting political structures as China, has had an equally long record of continuous civilization, reaching back at least to the great urban civilization of the Indus Valley. Out of Central Asia have came great nomadic empires, such as those of Ghengis Khan, which transformed the areas included in their sway. All of this means that there is not one "Asian" civilization but rather numerous civilizations that have developed in very different ways because of the accidents of history and geography. Such unity as Asia possesses comes partly from the fact that Western scholars and writers since ancient times have imposed a concept of "Asia" upon the whole area, despite the heterogeneity of its geography, history, and culture. This is evident, for example, in the adjective *Asiatic,* often used in a pejorative sense. Asia is thus in some sense a Western construct, one not found before modern times in the intellectual usage of the area itself; nonetheless, there are common elements recognizable in many parts of Asia, despite the diversity of cultures there. Many of these commonalities are the result of the widespread influence of Buddhism; others are the result of intra-Asian trade; others of deliberate cultural borrowings, as in the case of Japan from China; some are the result of migrations of peoples; and some of actual territorial conquest. Tibet is an example where all these forces were at work.

Asia has the largest population of all the continents, estimated at about 2.8 billion, with the two largest countries in the world, China and India, accounting for nearly three-quarters of this. Two other countries, Japan and Indonesia, each have more than one hundred million people, with two more, Pakistan and Bangladesh, each having nearly as many. The majority of the people live in rural areas, but of the eight largest cities in the world, six (Shanghai, Calcutta, Seoul, Tokyo, Bombay, and Beijing) are in Asia.

George B. Cressey, *Asia's Lands and Peoples: A Geography of One-Third of the Earth and Two-Thirds of Its People* (1968). Harold R. Isaacs, *Images of Asia: American Views of China and India* (1972). Joseph M. Kitagawa, *Religions of the East* (1968). K. M. Panikkar, *Asian and Western Dominance: A Survey of the Vasco da Gama Epoch of Asian History, 1498–1945* (1953). Dudley Stamp, *Asia: A Regional and Economic Geography* (1967).

AINSLIE T. EMBREE

ASIAN-AFRICAN CONFERENCE OF 1955.

See Bandung Conference.

ASIATIC SOCIETY OF BENGAL, founded in Calcutta in 1784, was the first and most enduring creation of British orientalism in India. William Jones instituted the Asiatic Society "for inquiring into the history, civil and natural, the antiquities, arts, sciences, and literature, of Asia" (inaugural discourse). It was the model for the Royal Asiatic Society of Great Britain and Ireland (founded in 1823 by a former president of the Calcutta Society, H. T. Colebrooke) and other Asiatic societies in India, Europe, and America. Its first organ, the *Asiatic Researches* (1788–1839), set standards for oriental research. After the Anglicists' victory over the Orientalists in 1835, which meant that government money went to the support of English, the Society rescued the publication of oriental works from which government support was withdrawn. This led the way for the Bibliotheca Indica series, begun in 1847. The Society spearheaded the collection and description of oriental manuscripts, coins, and antiquities. Its early membership constitutes a Who Was Who of British orientalism in Bengal. Jones's inaugural discourse considered the possibility of admitting "learned natives," yet Indian members were first inducted in 1829. The Society still pursues the goals of its founder in encompassing all aspects of the humanities and of the social and natural sciences.

[*See also* Jones, Sir William.]

Sibadas Chaudhuri, *Index to the Publications of the Asiatic Society 1788–1953* (1956); *First Supplement 1954–1968* (1971). *Centenary Review of the Asiatic Society of Bengal from 1784 to 1883* (1885). *150th Jubilee of the Royal Asiatic Society of Bengal (1784–1934) and the Bicentenary of Sir William Jones (1746–1946)* (1946).

ROSANE ROCHER

ASSAM, one of the twenty-two states of the Indian Union, located in the extreme northeast of India. Assam is bounded on the north by Bhutan and Arunachal Pradesh (formerly N.E.F.A.); to the east by Arunachal Pradesh, Nagaland, and Manipur; to the south by Mizoram and Meghalaya; and to the west by Bangladesh and Tripura. Except for a narrow corridor running through the foothills of the Himalayas that connects the state with West Bengal, Assam is almost entirely isolated from India by Bangladesh.

Assam comprises an area of 78,523 square miles divided into three principal geographical regions: the Brahmaputra Valley in the north; the Barak Plain in the south, and the Mikir and Cachar Hills that divide the two regions. Assamese-speaking Hindus represent a majority of the state's population of nearly 20 million, and indigenous Tibeto-Burman tribal groups make up another 16 percent of that total. More than 40 percent of Assam's population is thought to be of migrant origin, however, with Bengali-speaking Hindus and Muslims representing the largest minorities, followed by Nepalis and caste and tribal populations from neighboring regions of India.

The early history of Assam is obscure, although there are numerous references in the *Mahabharata,* the Puranas, and the Tantras to a great kingdom known as Kamarupa that encompassed the Brahmaputra Valley, Bhutan, and eastern Bengal. The legendary king Narakasura, whose son Bhagadatta distinguished himself in the Mahabharata war, ruled Kamarupa from his capital at Pragjyotishpura, the site of a famous temple dedicated to the Tantric goddess Kamakhya, near modern Gauhati. The first reliable description of the kingdom is provided by the Chinese pilgrim Xuanzang, who in 640 CE attended the court of Bhaskaravarman, an ally of the great Gupta monarch Harsha and a patron of Hinduism. Stone and copperplate inscriptions dating from the seventh to the twelfth century indicate a succession of Hindu dynasties, but it is unclear to what extent the indigenous population of Kamarupa had embraced Hinduism beyond the royal patronage of brahmans.

On the eve of the Ahom invasion in the early thirteenth century, any semblance of a centralized kingship in the region had collapsed into a fragmented system of tribal polities and loose confederacies of petty Hindu rajas, called *bhuyan.* The Ahom, a Shan tribe from which the name Assam is derived, crossed the Patkoi Mountains from Burma in 1228 and by the sixteenth century had absorbed the Chutiya and Kachari kingdoms of the upper Brahmaputra, subdued the neighboring hill tribes, and integrated the *bhuyans* into the administrative apparatus of their feudalistic state. During the latter part of the sixteenth and much of the seventeenth centuries the Ahom repulsed a succession of Mughal invasions of their territory from Bengal as they moved to annex the eastern portion of the powerful Koch kingdom (1682) and to consolidate their rule over the entire Brahmaputra Valley. The kingdom of the Ahom reached its height under Rudra Singh (r. 1696–1714), the renowned military strategist and patron of the *buranji,* or Ahom chronicles, who established an extensive trade with Tibet and built the great cities of Nowgong and Rangpur.

During the latter half of the sixteenth century the revered *gossain* (teacher, saint) and Assamese culture hero Shankara Deva inspired a popular Vaishnavite movement that sought to reform the esoteric practices of Tantric Hinduism and to limit the prerogatives of the brahmans attached to the Ahom court. The Ahom came to sponsor an extensive network of Vaishnavite monasteries, whose monks played an important role in the reclamation of wastelands for wet-rice cultivation throughout the Brahmaputra Valley. Because of its repudiation of caste privilege, Shankara Deva's Vaishnavism appealed to the broad tribal base on which the Ahom had erected their state. From 1769, disaffected tribals under the leadership of the Moamaria Gossain took part in a series of uprisings against Ahom rule that devastated upper Assam. At the request of king Gaurinath Singh (r. 1778–1795), the governor-general of British India dispatched a mission to Rangpur, the Ahom capital, which restored peace to the kingdom. Civil strife persisted, however, and in 1817 the Burmese took advantage of dissensions within the Ahom nobility and overran the Brahmaputra Valley. Fearing incursions on their own territory, the British drove the Burmese from the Brahmaputra Valley and, under the conditions of the treaty of Yandabo concluded with the Burmese in 1826, annexed the Ahom kingdom. In 1838, all of northeast India became part of the Bengal Presidency.

Rapid steps were then undertaken to develop the region for agricultural and commercial revenues. The British dismantled the Ahom ruling structure, made Bengali the official language, and staffed administrative and professional positions with educated Bengali Hindus. Coal, limestone, and iron mines were opened and the government offered incentives to European entrepreneurs to start plantations for the production of rubber, chinchona (from which quinine is derived), hemp, jute, and, most importantly, tea. Because the native population of Assam was ill disposed to plantation labor, the British were forced to develop an extensive system of contract labor that recruited impoverished tribals from southern Bihar. By the turn of the century more than one-half million of these "coolies" were employed on 700 plantations producing 145 million pounds of tea annually. [*See* Tea in India and Sri Lanka.]

Early in the nineteenth century the government of India made vast tracts of land available to predominantly Muslim farmers from the provinces of eastern Bengal for settlement and cultivation. Nepalis were employed as dairy herders and similarly encouraged to colonize new lands. The subsequent migration of Indian traders, merchants, and small-scale industrialists, such as Marwaris and Sikhs, stimulated capital development in Assam and strengthened its ties to India. This enormous influx of migrants—Assam has been the fastest-growing region of the subcontinent throughout the twentieth century—transformed the ethnic composition of the state and gradually diminished the political and economic prerogatives of the native Assamese. As a result, ethnicity and migration have become prominent issues in Assamese politics. [*See also* Marwaris.]

Following Indian independence in 1947 the Assamese won control of their state parliament and launched a campaign to reassert the preeminence of Assamese culture in the region and improve employment opportunities for native Assamese. However, the Indian government's partitioning of former Assamese territories into the tribal states of Nagaland, Mizoram, and Meghalaya over the next twenty years was seen by Assamese leaders as a deliberate division of their constituency. Following the Pakistan civil war in 1971, nearly two million Bengali Muslim refugees migrated to Assam. Their settlement and their support of Indira Gandhi's Congress government further aggravated Assamese fears of Bengali cultural domination and central government ambitions to undermine Assamese regional autonomy. Since the 1970s, persistent disputes between the government and a number of Assamese political factions over the rights of these immigrants to citizenship and suffrage have led to some of India's worst communal violence since Partition.

[*See also* Adivasis; Nagaland; Meghalaya; Burma; Tantra; Vaishnavism; *and* Ahom.]

S. K. Bhuyan, *The Assamese Buranjis* (1933). A. Cantlie, *The Assamese* (1984). E. Gait, *The History of Assam* (1933). A. Guha, "The Medieval Economy of Assam," in *The Cambridge Economic History of India,* edited by T. Raychaudhuri and I. Habib (1983). M. Weiner, *The Sons of the Soil* (1978) and "The Political Economy of Assam's Anti-Immigrant Movement," *Population and Development Review* 9.2 (1983). RICHARD ENGLISH

ASSOCIATION OF SOUTHEAST ASIAN NATIONS (ASEAN), organization established by Indonesia, Malaysia, the Philippines, Singapore, and Thailand on 8 August 1967 in Bangkok, Thailand, to maintain the internal stability of each of its members. Its sixth member, Brunei, joined in January 1984 after gaining independence from Great Britain.

At the time of the organization's inception, the

primary threat to each nation was believed to be domestic upheaval, rather than external intervention. Because economic problems were seen as the cause of domestic unrest, the association sought to increase the security of its members by encouraging economic cooperation and development. The possibility of military cooperation was rejected, for the organizers believed that it might lead to external security threats.

ASEAN's initial efforts at cooperation were ineffective owing to conflicts between the economic advantages and the political costs of cooperation for each state. The Communist victories in Vietnam and Cambodia (Kampuchea) in 1975, however, revived the perception of a threat to internal stability and spurred efforts to increase economic cooperation. These renewed efforts achieved only partial success until the Vietnamese invasion and occupation of Cambodia from 25 December 1978 to 20 January 1979. This invasion, as well as subsequent violations of the Thai border, made direct, external challenges to stability appear more serious than internal threats. ASEAN responded by evolving into an organization capable of effectively protecting its members' political interests through diplomatic activities. Ironically, this greater political effectiveness was achieved at the cost of reducing the objective of economic cooperation and development to a subsidiary position within the association. Still, the organization's recent political orientation is consistent with its original, primary purpose of maintaining the internal stability of member states.

Kim Khanh Huynh and Hans Indorf, "Southeast Asia 1981: Two Currents Running," *in Southeast Asian Affairs 1982* (1982). Arnfinn Jorgensen-Dahl, "ASEAN 1967–1976: Development or Stagnation?" *Pacific Community* 4 (July 1976): 519–535. Chong Yah Lim, "ASEAN's Internal Advances and External Unity," *Asia Pacific Community* 6 (Fall 1979):31–43. Laurence D. Stifel, "ASEAN Cooperation and Economic Growth in S. E. Asia," *Asia Pacific Community* 4 (Spring/Early Summer 1979):113–146.

WILLIAM A. KINSEL

ASTROLOGY AND ASTRONOMY, ISLAMIC. The disciplines that were known in Islamic medieval times as astrology (*ilm al-nujum,* more precisely *ilm ahkam al-nujum,* or simply *ilm al-ahkam*) and astronomy (*ilm al-falak,* or *ilm al-hai'a*) were part of the general scientific culture of the time and were not confined to the Asian side of the vast Islamic cultural domain that stretched at one time as far west as southern Spain. In theory, both disciplines derived from their Hellenistic antecedents; they were based on such classical texts as the *Tetrabiblos* and the *Almagest* of Claudius Ptolemy (fl. 150 CE), the *Carmen astrologicum* of Dorotheus of Sidon (first century CE), and the *Anthology* of Vettius Valens (c. 150 CE)—known in Pahlavi as Visidhak and arabized as Bizidhaj.

All of these texts were available during Islamic times in Arabic translations, some as early as the first part of the ninth century. Although it is still doubtful whether the Arabic translations of the *Tetrabiblos,* for example, were done directly from the Greek, or through Syriac, it is quite certain that the remaining two texts of Dorotheus and Valens reached Arabic through Pahlavi; they thus mark an interest in practical astrological lore at least in the Persian part of Asia well before the advent of Islam. A similar interest in astronomical texts can also be documented from references by later authors to such texts as the *Zij-i shah.*

During Islamic times, and during the early period, there must have been a widespread interest in astrological practice, as the office of court astrologer was brought into being and can probably be dated to the late eighth or early ninth century. Soon after that, however, astrological dogma came in direct conflict with religious dogma, mainly because of problems connected with the eternity of the world, free will and predestination, and the immortality of the soul. All this led to a lively debate that began with elementary dogmatic refutations of astrology and progressed to very detailed defenses of it. As a result of this debate, philosophers, mathematicians, and even astronomers finally gave in and identified themselves as opponents of astrology per se. As a by-product, astronomy could then be defined as a discipline independent of astrology, and the first attempts at such a distinction are found in the works of Biruni (d. about 1050). By the fourteenth century the case against astrology was won, and the most elaborate refutation of its tenets was put forth by the Hanbali theologian Ibn Qayyim al-Jauziyya of Damascus in his famous work *Miftah dar al-sa'ada.*

Astronomy, on the other hand, was first introduced to the Islamic cultural sphere from Pahlavi and Indian sources. The recovery of fragments of the *Zij-i shah* and the *Sindhind* (the *Siddhanta* of Brahmagupta) leaves no doubt as to the importance of the Persian and Indian traditions to the early Muslim astronomers. As soon as the Greek tradition, as represented by the *Almagest,* became dominant, however, the Indian and Pahlavi sources were forgotten and rapidly gave way to new astronomical texts written under the inspiration of the Greek works.

FIGURE 1. *Astrolabe.* Made for Sultan Umar around 1296 to 1297, this Yemenite brass astrolabe (diameter 15.5 cm.) is typical of the instruments used by medieval Islamic astronomers. Although the astrolabe is not an Islamic invention, Muslim scholars were responsible for calculating the angle of the ecliptic, measuring the size of the earth, and calculating the precession of the equinoxes.

In the early period several commentaries, abridgments, and introductory texts used the *Almagest* as their object of study. By the ninth century, however, original works began to be composed with the object of double-checking the results of the *Almagest.* In these texts the values for precision, solar apogee, and ecliptic declination that were obtained by observation were considerably closer to the true values than the ones given by Ptolemy.

The next generation of original astronomical work went a step further in investigating the theoretical foundations of the *Almagest.* The results reached then, expressed as "doubts" about the Ptolemaic masterpiece, created a wide-ranging impact on all further research. After the doubts of Ibn al-Haitham (d. 1038) and the objections of Jabir Ibn Aflah (d. about 1175), for example, a new group of astronomers took upon themselves the task of reformulating the Ptolemaic mathematical models preserved in the *Almagest* and the *Planetary Hypothesis,* in order to "cleanse" these models of the inconsistencies that were so heavily criticized in those "doubts" works. Bitruji of Spain (fl. 1200), Tusi of Persia (d. 1274), Urdi (d. 1266) and Ibn al-Shatir (d. 1375) of Damascus are all associated with original proposals to reformulate Ptolemaic astronomy. The works of Tusi, Urdi, and Ibn al-Shatir are currently being studied for their possible impact on the works of medieval European astronomy in general and those of Copernicus in particular.

[*See also* Biruni, al-.]

Noel M. Swerdlow and Otto Neugebauer, *Mathematical Astronomy in Copernicus's De Revolutionibus* (1984).
GEORGE SALIBA

ASUKA, the name given to a region of ancient Japan that corresponds roughly to the basin of the Asuka River in the southern corner of the Yamato Plain. Although the *Nihon shoki (Chronicles of Japan)* attests to imperial palace sites occurring in Asuka as early as the fifth century, it was in the seventh century that Asuka became the center of Japanese culture. Except for three brief periods when it was temporarily moved to other areas, the palace was located on different sites within Asuka from 592, when Empress Suiko's palace was established at Toyura (near present-day Amagashi Hill), to 710, when the capital was moved to its first permanent location, in Nara. During the Asuka period the palace was rebuilt on a new site following the decease of an emperor, in order to avoid the pollution of death. The final palace site in Asuka was the Fujiwara capital, constructed by Empress Jitō in the 690s on the plain between the "three hills of Yamato": Kagu, Miminashi, and Unebi. It was in the Fujiwara capital, often considered Japan's first city, that Kakinomoto no Hitomaro composed Japan's first great classical poetry, under Jitō's patronage. The *Man'yōshū* poetry anthology is filled with references to the geographical features of Asuka. [*See also* Man'yōshū.] IAN HIDEO LEVY

ATISHA (Sri Dipamkara Jnana; 982–1054), Bengali prince, Buddhist scholar-monk, author, and translator of 115 texts in the Tibetan Tanjur (the commentarial section of the Tibetan Buddhist canon). Wooed from North Indian *viharas* at the age of sixty, Atisha arrived at Thoding monastery in western Tibet in 1042; at this monastery he composed the famous *Lamp for the Path (Bodhipathapradipa),* and began thirteen years of monastic reform, restoring celibacy and preaching correct

Tantric practice. He is regarded as the initiator of the "second propagation" of Mahayana Buddhism in Tibet after its earlier persecution and 150-year decline. His disciples founded the Kadampa monastic order, the parent tradition of Tsong Khapa's Gelugpa order, to which Dalai Lamas belong. Atisha died at Narthang in central Tibet, where his shrine is preserved.

[*See also* Gelugpa.]

Alaka Chattopadhyaya, *Atīśa and Tibet* (1967). Richard Sherburne, trans., *A Lamp for the Path and Commentary* (1983). RICHARD SHERBURNE

AU CO, in Viet legend, the fairy who was abducted by Lac Long Quan; she subsequently bore him one hundred sons from an egglike sac. The bravest of these sons became the first Hung Vuong (ruler) of Van Lang. After the birth, Lac Long Quan took fifty sons and returned to his home in the sea, leaving the remaining fifty with Au Co on top of Tan Vien Mountain. This legend may refer to the separation of the Viet of the delta from the Muong people of the uplands or possibly to bilateral inheritance.

[*See also* Lac Long Quan; Hung Vuong; Van Lang; Tan Vien Mountain; *and* Muong.]

Keith W. Taylor, *The Birth of Vietnam* (1983).

JAMES M. COYLE

AUDIENCIA, highest court of appeal for criminal and civil cases in the Spanish colonies. The Philippines was initially under the jurisdiction of the Audiencia of Mexico, but on 5 May 1583 Philip II ordered the formation of the Audiencia of Manila. Except for the six years from 1589–1595, the Audiencia existed throughout the Spanish period and had extensive authority in governmental matters. Between 1565 and 1898, for example, it ruled eight times when there was no governor-general. Until 1861 the Audiencia served as an advisory body to the governor-general. Although it was especially enjoined to look after the welfare of the *indios,* the personal integrity of its members was not high, and there were many instances of miscarriage of justice.

Onofre D. Corpuz, *The Bureaucracy in the Philippines* (1957). Charles H. Cunningham, *The Audiencia in the Spanish Colonies, As Illustrated by the Audiencia of Manila* (1919). *Documents on the Audiencia of Manila,* in *The Philippine Islands,* edited by Emma Blair and James Robertson (1903-1909), vols. 5–7 and 9–11.

BERNARDITA REYES CHURCHILL

AUGUST REVOLUTION, a successful uprising launched by the Communist-led Viet Minh (League for the Independence of Vietnam) against the Japanese occupation regime in Vietnam in 1945. The revolt combined small-scale military attacks in rural areas with a popular uprising in the major cities. Meeting little resistance from Japanese forces in the north, the Viet Minh set up a Democratic Republic of Vietnam in Hanoi in early September. In the south (Cochinchina), however, Viet Minh representatives were forced to share power with rival nationalist groups in a so-called Committee of the South. In October, the committee and its supporters were driven from Saigon by returning French expeditionary forces.

[*See also* Vietnam; Viet Minh; *and* Vietnam, Democratic Republic of.]

Archimedes Patti, *Why Viet Nam? Prelude to America's Albatross* (1980). WILLIAM J. DUIKER

AU LAC, a short-lived (c. 210–180 BCE) Viet kingdom located in the northern Red River delta and its surrounding hills. The kingdom was founded by the semilegendary An Duong Vuong, who defeated the last of the Hung kings of Van Lang, changed the name of the country to Au Lac, and built a new capital at Co Loa (about twenty kilometers north of modern Hanoi). Au Lac appears to have originated in the disturbances surrounding the unification of China by Qin Shihuangdi. This may have led the Xi Ou (Tay Au) to extend their influence over their southeastern neighbors, the Lac Viet, a closely related people.

The fusion of the Au and Lac Viet peoples and their efforts to maintain Viet autonomy in the face of Chinese attempts at control are the most significant legacy of Au Lac. Sometime after 180 BCE Au Lac accepted the nominal suzerainty of Nam Viet (Nan Yue). Local authority, however, remained in Viet hands.

[*See also* An Duong Vuong; Hung Vuong; Van Lang; Co Loa; Lac Viet; *and* Nam Viet.]

Keith W. Taylor, *The Birth of Vietnam* (1983).

JAMES M. COYLE

AUNG SAN (1915–1947), the preeminent leader of the Burmese independent movement during and after World War II. Aung San was in the center of Burma's nationalist politics from 1936, the year he led a national student strike. Before the war he was secretary-general of both the Dobama Asiayon, a popular nationalist organization, and the first Communist cell. In 1940, seeking aid against the British from the Chinese Communist Party, he went to Amoy, where he met Japanese agents who offered to train and arm a Burmese nationalist force. Accepting their offer, he returned to Rangoon and gathered twenty-nine others as the nucleus of an anti-British army. After training on Hainan Island, they formed the Burma Independence Army in Bangkok and under Aung San's command entered Burma with the invading Japanese in January 1942.

Aung San became minister of defense and commander of the re-formed Burma Defense Army in August 1942 but grew disillusioned with the Japanese. He took a leading role in the underground Anti-Fascist Organization in cooperation with the Communist and People's Revolution movements and publicly turned his troops against the Japanese on 27 March 1945. From then until his assassination in 1947 he was a leading figure in the Anti-Fascist People's Freedom League (AFPFL), which was trying to regain Burma's independence from Britain. After signing the Kandy Agreement, which incorporated his forces into the British Burma Army, Aung San resigned from the military and became president of the AFPFL. He was able to supplant the Communist leaders of the league, thanks to his popularity and their mistakes, and to dominate the organization. In 1946 he became, in effect, prime minister of Burma in the Governor's Executive Council, and in January 1947 he traveled to England where he negotiated the Aung San–Attlee Agreement, which guaranteed Burma's independence in one year. His assassination by a political rival made him a martyr, and Aung San is now Burma's major national hero.

[*See also* Burma; Dobama Asiayon; Burma Defense Army; *and* Anti-Fascist People's Freedom League.]

Aung San, *Burma's Challenge* (1974). Maung Maung, ed., *Aung San of Burma* (1962). Josef Silverstein, ed., *The Political Legacy of Aung San* (1972).

ROBERT H. TAYLOR

AURANGZEB (1618–1707), Mughal emperor, son of Shah Jahan and his principal wife, Mumtaz Mahal. Muhammad Aurangzeb assumed the imperial title of Muhyiuddin Muhammad Alamgir in 1659. His first responsible assignment under his father as emperor came with his appointment to the viceroyalty of the Deccan (1636–1644). He was subsequently governor of Gujarat (1645–1647) and of Multan (1648–1652). He led two expeditions against Kandahar (1649 and 1652), but was unsuccessful. In 1652 he was reappointed viceroy of the Deccan. He reorganized the revenue administration of the Deccan with the assistance of Murshid Quli Khan and led successful expeditions against Golconda (1656) and Bijapur (1657). He seized the opportunity offered by a sudden illness of Shah Jahan to unite with his younger brother Murad Bakhsh and overthrow the imperial forces at Dharmatpur (April 1658). This was followed by his great victory against Crown Prince Dara Shikoh near Samogar, close to Agra (May 1658). The civil war continued for some time, but the ultimate result was that Shah Jahan (d. 1666) became his prisoner; Dara Shikoh was captured and executed (August 1659); his other elder brother Shuja driven to exile and death in Araccan (1660–1661); and Murad Bakhsh imprisoned (1658) and executed (1661).

Aurangzeb formally crowned himself emperor in June 1659. He began his reign by organizing a vigorous campaign in the Deccan against Bijapur and the Marathas under Shaista Khan (1660–1661) and against Cooch Bihar and Assam under Mir Jumla (1661–1663). These campaigns were not as successful as expected; and in the Deccan the Mughals received a great setback when Shivaji overran Shaista Khan's camp at Pune in 1663 and plundered Surat in 1664. A large army under Jai Singh forced Shivaji to accept the treaty of Purandhar (1665), but the subsequent campaign against Bijapur proved a failure (1665–1666). This lack of success was compounded by Shivaji's flight from Agra (1666) and his renewal of war with a second sack of Surat (1670). This period was also one of considerable agrarian distress, marked by scarcities and high prices, which continued till 1670. Aurangzeb issued two important *farmans* containing detailed regulations to protect peasants against excessive revenue demand and to encourage them to extend cultivation. Whether these had any practical effect is debatable. The agrarian "crisis" might have been one factor behind uprisings such as those of the Jats in 1669 and the Satnamis in 1672. The Afghan tribes revolted from 1672 to 1675, necessitating Aurangzeb's own stay at Hasan Abdal from 1674 to 1675.

These difficulties probably explain Aurangzeb's recourse to a more orthodox religious policy than his predecessors' as a possible means of gathering firmer Muslim support. He doubled customs duties on non-Muslims (1665), sanctioned temple destruction (1669), and imposed the poll tax *(jizya)* on non-Muslims (1679). These measures were not without qualifications. Many great ancient temples were allowed to stand; many areas, and the Rajputs and Hindu officers, were exempted from the *jizya*. The Rajput and Maratha component in the nobility was not directly affected by the new policy. The Rajput revolt of 1679 to 1681 involved the Marwar and Mewar principalities, and the latter returned to its allegiance in 1681. But the revolt was complicated when Aurangzeb's son Akbar joined it (1681). As the revolt died out Akbar fled to Shambhuji in Maharashta, and this compelled Aurangzeb in 1682 to march to the Deccan, never to return to the North.

Aurangzeb initiated vigorous campaigns against the Deccan powers. Bijapur was annexed in 1686, and Golconda in 1687. Shambhuji was captured and executed in 1689. A four-year campaign (1691–1695) by Asad Khan and Zulfiqar Khan resulted in the occupation of all of South India, with the exception of Kerala. But Maratha power was revived in its homeland, and Aurangzeb's armies proved unable to contain the Maratha *sardars* (chiefs). Aurangzeb himself besieged and took fort after fort while large parts of the Deccan were sacked by the Marathas. During a great famine in the Deccan from 1702 to 1704 more than two million people perished, according to a contemporary estimate. Aurangzeb was compelled to open the ranks of the Mughal nobility so as to win over opponents, and this brought about a crisis in *jagirs,* which was also a reflection of the financial strains caused by war on the Mughal administration. In spite of revolts such as those of the Jats and Sikhs, North India by and large remained peaceful.

Aurangzeb died in February 1707, and lies buried in a simple grave at Khuldabad, near Aurangabad. Unlike his three predecessors, Aurangzeb was not a great builder nor a great patron of the arts. His interests lay elsewhere; he patronized the compilation of a great collection of rules of Muslim law, the *Fatawa-i Alamgiri,* and liberalized awards of land grants to theologians. He was not, however, a blind fanatic, and tried to maintain the administrative machinery of the empire in as efficient a shape as he had found it. He had few personal vices, and remained dedicated to his work until his death. His death was followed by a war of succession among his sons Mu'azzam (Bahadur Shah), Azam, and Kam Bakhsh; and although Mu'azzam was successful (1709), the empire was badly shaken by the war. Aurangzeb's failure to resolve the Maratha question also left alive a threat to the empire that would only grow with time.

[*See also* Mughal Empire; Shah Jahan; Akbar; Marathas; Islam; Rajput; Jats; *and* Sikhism.]

M. Athar Ali, *Mughal Nobility under Aurangzeb* (1966). Jadunath Sarkar, *History of Aurangzib,* 5 vols. (1912, 1916, 1930).

M. Athar Ali

AUSTROASIATIC LANGUAGES. The Austroasiatic language family comprises some 150 languages spoken by approximately 75 million people in East India, Burma, Thailand, Malaysia, Laos, Cambodia, Vietnam, and South China. Two Austroasiatic languages serve as national languages: Vietnamese in the Democratic Republic of Vietnam and Khmer in Cambodia (Kampuchea). All others are spoken by minority or upland groups, most of whom also speak the regional or national language of their country. The detailed subgrouping of Austroasiatic languages has yet to be fully worked out, but based on current research, lexicostatistical evidence, and typological characteristics, the family can be divided into groups and subgroups. (See table 1.)

Typologically, Austroasiatic languages form a rough continuum from the inflectional Munda languages of East India (influenced perhaps by contact with the morphologically complex Indian languages) to the monosyllabic and tonal Viet-Muong languages (influenced by two thousand years of contact with the Chinese languages). The great majority of Austroasiatic languages between the western and eastern extremes tend to be characterized by words of one or two syllables; the use of derivational affixes (prefixes or infixes); lack of tones (with the exception of certain two-tone systems); complex vowel systems, frequently on two "registers"; and subject-verb-object word order.

Three Austroasiatic languages have a long literary tradition. The writing systems of Mon and Khmer are derived from the southern Indian script in which Sanskrit was written; Mon inscriptions in Burma date from the sixth century and Khmer inscriptions from the seventh. Vietnamese was first written in the thirteenth century in modified Chinese characters; in the seventeenth century Jesuit missionaries devised the romanization in which it is written today. The great majority of Austroasiatic languages, when written at all, are written either in the script of the country in which they are located or in roman alphabets devised fairly recently by missionaries or linguists.

The age of the family is not known, but its wide geographical distribution, its typological diversity, and the age of its extant inscriptions indicate that Austroasiatic is one of the oldest linguistic stocks in

TABLE 1. *Austroasiatic Language Groups*

Language Group				
Group	Subgroup	Locale	No. of Speakers	Primary Languages/Peoples
Munda		East India	8,000,000	Mundari; Santali; Kharia
Khasi		Assam; India	200,000	Standard Khasi; Lyngngam; War
Nicobarese		Nicobar Islands	7,000	Car; Nancowry; Great Nicobar
Aslian		Malay Peninsula	40,000	Jahai; Semai; Mah Meri
Mon-Khmer			[10,000,000]	
	Monic	Burma; Thailand	500,000	Mon; Nyah Kur
	Khmer	Kampuchea; Vietnam; Thailand	6,000,000	Khmer
	Bahnaric	Vietnam; Laos; Kampuchea	600,000	Bahnar; Stieng; Loven
	Katuic	Vietnam; Kampuchea; Laos Thailand	300,000	Katu; Kuy; Bru
	Palaungic	Burma; Thailand	1,000,000	Palaung; Wa; Lawa
	Khmuic	Laos; Thailand	5,000	Khmu; Thin; Mlabri
	Pearic	Kampuchea; Thailand	5,000	Pear; Chong; Samre
Viet-Muong			[50,000,000]	
	Vietnamese	Vietnam	50,000,000	Northern, Southern, and Central Dialects
	Muong	Vietnam	250,000	Muong; May; Arem

Southeast Asia. The term *Austroasiatic* was first coined by Wilhelm Schmidt, who in 1907 proposed the affiliation of the Mon-Khmer, Munda, Khasi, Aslian, Nicobarese, and Chamic languages of Vietnam. This original formulation, with the exception of the Chamic languages, which have since been shown to be Austronesian, and with the inclusion of the Viet-Muong languages, is generally accepted today, although not without controversy. The inclusion of the Munda languages was disputed, but the work of Heinz-Jürgen Pinnow and Norman H. Zide showed conclusively that Munda belongs in the Austroasiatic family; the work of H. L. Shorto on Palaungic and of Gérard Diffloth on Aslian clarified the relationships of those groups. It is the inclusion of Vietnamese that has been most controversial; the relationship of Vietnamese to Mon-Khmer in a Mon-Annam family was proposed as early as 1852, but in 1912 Henri Maspéro argued that a tonal language such as Vietnamese could not be related to the nontonal Mon-Khmer languages and suggested instead that Vietnamese was related to the Tai languages. In 1953 André-Georges Haudricourt proposed a plausible hypothesis for the development of Vietnamese tones from an earlier nontonal stage and argued for the inclusion of Vietnamese in Austroasiatic, a position supported by most specialists today.

The wider affiliation of Austroasiatic in Asia is unresolved, with several scholars supporting Schmidt's hypothesis of a relationship between Austroasiatic and Austronesian (or Malayo-Polynesian) in an Austric superstock and others adhering to Paul K. Benedict's hypothesis of a relationship between Austronesian and the Tai languages in an Austro-Thai stock with an Austroasiatic substratum.

[*See also* Austronesian Languages.]

Paul K. Benedict, *Austro-Thai: Language and Culture, with a Glossary of Roots* (1975). Gérard Diffloth, "Austro-Asiatic languages," in *Encyclopaedia Britannica* (15th ed., 1974) 2:480–484. Philip N. Jenner, Laurence C. Thompson, and Stanley Starosta, eds., *Austroasiatic Studies,* parts 1 and 2 (1976). H. L. Shorto, Judith M. Jacob, and E. H. S. Simmonds, eds., *Bibliographies of Mon-Khmer and Tai Linguistics* (1963). Norman H. Zide, ed., *Studies in Comparative Austroasiatic Linguistics* (1966).

FRANKLIN E. HUFFMAN

AUSTRONESIAN LANGUAGES. The Austronesian (AN) languages, formerly called the Malayo-Polynesian languages, are a large group of some five to seven hundred languages spoken throughout much of the island areas of the Pacific, stretching from Sumatra across to Easter Island and Hawaii on the east and from Taiwan in the north to the Philippines and Indonesia. In Maluku (the Moluccas) and eastward past Papua New Guinea and as far as the Solomon Islands, both AN and non-AN (i.e., Papuan) languages are found, and no AN languages are native to Australia. In addition, AN languages are found on mainland Southeast Asia in the mountain areas of Vietnam, among the Cham of Cambodia and Vietnam, and in the Malay Peninsula south of the Isthmus of Kra and on its west coast and the adjoining the Mergui Archipelago of Burma. An AN language, Malagasy, is also spoken in Madagascar, brought there from Indonesia in the first millennium CE.

These languages are thought to derive from a single protolanguage, now called Proto-AN. Their tremendous spread and the great typological differences among them point to a long period of development from Proto-AN times, but it is difficult to say where Proto-AN had its homeland. It was once thought that the AN languages originated somewhere on the Asian mainland, but since the current languages of the mainland are all closely related to each other and also close to some of the languages on the islands, it is likely that they were brought there from the islands. Proto-AN names for many items can be reconstructed by making a comparison of languages from the entire range of the AN field. These names show that Proto-AN was spoken in a tropical area near the sea by a people whose lives were bound to the sea. We can reconstruct the names for numerous tropical plants, words associated with the sea or seashore, and nomenclature connected with seafaring. The reconstruction of these terms, however, is by no means a matter of final proof; we still do not know which forms are actually inherited from Proto-AN, which spread by borrowing, and what these terms actually meant in Proto-AN.

The determination of subgroups for the AN languages is not unequivocal, for language contacts, language shifts, spread of areal features, and migrations have provided contradictory evidence. Because all of the AN languages except those of Taiwan made important innovations in their phonology and morphology, some scholars suggest that the Formosan languages make up their own subgroup. However, subsequent contact with neighboring AN languages in the Philippines has led to typological similarities and shared vocabulary, thus obscuring the deep and ancient split between Formosan languages and the others. Within the non-Formosan subgroup, all of the languages from east of Papua New Guinea, as well as some of the AN languages within Papua New Guinea itself, show a series of common innovations that have led scholars to conclude that these languages form an eastern subgroup, termed Oceanic. Furthermore, some scholars have proposed that several languages of western New Guinea, Maluku (including Halmahera), and the Lesser Sundas form a subgroup similar to Oceanic and that all of the other AN languages of Indonesia, the Philippines, and the mainland are in a subgroup similar to the other two.

When it comes to further subgrouping, language contacts, spread, and shifts make the picture even more obscure. On the basis of shared innovations in phonology in the western group, we know that the languages of the Philippines and northern Sulawesi (Celebes) and some of the languages of Sabah and Sarawak form a subgroup, although there are a few languages in the region that do not belong in the subgroup (and two of the subgroup, Chamorro and Palauan, are spoken in Micronesia). In western Oceania there is a tremendous diversity of languages, probably caused by thousands of migrations and conquests, by adoption of new languages, and by other kinds of language contact (a process that continues today). Thus the Polynesian languages, including outlying Polynesian languages in Micronesia, are in a subgroup, but not all by themselves, for some languages from Melanesia are also grouped with them.

Attempts have been made to relate the AN languages to other families on mainland Southeast Asia and even to languages in South America. None of these attempts, however, have been serious or systematic, and no outside congenitors of the Austronesian languages have been found. Apparently, in typology and structure AN languages are unlike anything found elsewhere. The languages of Taiwan and the Philippines, which are thought to be the most conservative and are characterized by an elaborate and complex morphology but a rather simple phonology, are unlike any of the non-AN languages of mainland Southeast Asia, where typically we find complex phonology and a simple morphology.

The vast majority of the AN languages are poorly documented, and many remain unwritten and unrecorded. A few, however, are important languages, and three—Cham, Malay, and Javanese—were the languages of important Southeast Asian empires and are used in inscriptions dating back more than a millennium. Cham, the language of Champa, appears in numerous inscriptions dating from the beginning of the fifth century CE (constituting the oldest text in any AN language). After the decline of Champa, however, Cham was spoken by only a minority. Inscriptions in Javanese, the language of the Hindu and Buddhist kingdoms of Central Java and of the later Javanese kingdoms, date from the ninth century. The Majapahit period in the thirteenth century marks the beginning of a literary efflorescence that lasted for six centuries and produced a succession of masterworks that make Javanese literature one of the world's greatest. [*See also* Majapahit.] Javanese was also important as a court language throughout western Indonesia. In the seventeenth and eighteenth centuries, for example, it was used by the courts of Palembang and strongly influenced the languages used in courts from Sumatra east to Lombok. Today—although it is spoken by some fifty million people and ranks among the largest languages of the world in terms of numbers—Javanese, like Cham, has declined to the status of an ethnic language.

Only Malay has survived in its role as a language of political importance. The language of Srivijaya, Malay was used in the empire's most important epigraphic monuments, dating from the end of the seventh century. Only a few ancient Malay inscriptions have been found, and the language is not well attested until the sixteenth century, which produced several manuscripts that have survived to the present and reveal the presence of a rich literature in Malay during the period. There is good evidence that Malay was the lingua franca throughout insular Southeast Asia: Malay loanwords of demonstrable antiquity are found in insular languages, and early documents, explorers' accounts, and the existence of an isolated archaic Malay dialect on Bacan Island, off Ternate (Maluku), point to the use of Malay as a language of the spice trade.

Its history as a second language has enabled Malay to maintain its political importance today. Malay has been adopted as a national language by Indonesia, where it is called Indonesian (Bahasa Indonesia), and by Malaysia and Brunei, where it is called Malaysian (Bahasa Malaysia). Buttressed by a tradition of bilingualism, the population of Indonesia was able to use Indonesian as an official language immediately upon the fall of the Dutch colonial government, and thus Malay has become the one AN language of international importance.

Other AN languages spoken in former colonial territories have become national languages. In the Philippines, Tagalog, renamed Filipino, has been made the national language and is rapidly becoming known as a second language in non-Tagalog regions of the islands. [*See also* Tagalog.] In the Malagasy Republic, the Merina dialect of Malagasy has been designated the national language, and in Fiji the Bauan dialect has been made an official national language. Other areas of Oceania also adopted their local language as the national one when they achieved independence.

The AN languages supply much information to the historian. They are the key to the interpretation of inscriptions and other documents providing historical evidence; moreover, their loanwords from each other serve as important evidence of movements of populations and contacts among different groups, as well as the nature of the contact. A study of Malay and closely related languages and of their spread, area of settlement, and influences on other languages is likely to yield substantial information that we can use to re-create our picture of Southeast Asia prior to the coming of the Europeans.

Isidore Dyen, *A Lexicostatistical Classification of the Austronesian Languages* (1963). C. F. Voegelin and F. M. Voegelin, "Languages of the World: Indo-Pacific Fascicles," in *Anthropological Linguistics* 6.4 (1964).

JOHN U. WOLFF

AUTUMN HARVEST UPRISING. *See* Mao Zedong.

AVA, founded in 1365, served as the capital of Upper Burma for over four hundred years and was the name by which Asians and Europeans frequently referred to the Burmese kingdom itself well into the nineteenth century.

Located on the great bend of the Irrawaddy River, Ava enjoyed three geographical advantages. Its riverine position facilitated trade and communications with both the middle Irrawaddy and the upper Sittang Valley and also afforded reliable access to the manpower and rice of Upper Burma's chief granaries, especially the well-watered district of Kyaukse. At the same time, its proximity to upland areas containing Tai-speaking Shan allowed Ava to supplement Burman military levies. Ava's chief weakness—a disadvantage of which its rulers were keenly aware—was its excessive distance from the ports of Lower Burma.

As early as the late thirteenth century the attractions of Ava's location encouraged a shift in the political center of gravity from the old Burman capital of Pagan to the region of the great bend in the Irrawaddy. Ava itself was founded by the prince Thadominbya following the eclipse of earlier towns in the general vicinity. During its first 250 years, Ava enjoyed a fluctuating authority only over Upper Burma and some of the more accessible Shan principalities. The southern sector of the Irrawaddy basin, including the ports, constituted an independent kingdom, with which Ava engaged in a long and fruitless series of wars. Following severe disorders in the south, however, the entire Irrawaddy basin, together with an extensive Tai-speaking upland perimeter, was joined under Ava's suzerainty between 1597 and 1626. Through novel administrative and economic institutions, a new line of Ava kings secured control over both the labor of the north and the revenues of the ports, and the empire enjoyed a long period of comparative stability. Although southern rebels sacked the city in 1752, the north reasserted its hegemony, and Ava again served as capital of Burma from 1764–1783 and 1822–1837.

"Golden Ava, the dwelling of kings" was described in Burmese and European accounts as divided into two sectors: an outer city containing common residences and markets and an inner city containing administrative buildings and the palace (which was laid out according to traditional cosmic-magical principles.) The intramural population in 1826 was said to be under fifty thousand, although suburbs contained perhaps six times that number of people.

[*See also* Burma; Upper Burma; Toungoo Dynasties; Konbaung Dynasty; Pagan; *and the map accompanying* Ayudhya.]

John Crawford, *Journal of an Embassy . . . to the Court of Ava* (1835). G. E. Harvey, *A History of Burma from the Earliest Times* (1925; reprint, 1967). Maung Htin Aung, *A History of Burma* (1967).

VICTOR B. LIEBERMAN

AVADH. *See* Awadh.

AVESTA (probably "fundamental or authoritative speech"), the sacred scriptures of Zoroastrianism, containing texts in Avestan, an eastern Old Iranian language whose earliest dialect is closely akin to Vedic Sanskrit. The earliest stratum comprises the *Gathas* ("hymns") of the prophet Zoroaster (Zarathushtra) himself, composed around 1500 BCE, and the older portions of the *Yasna*, a liturgical text of seventy-two chapters recited in the daily ceremony of the pounding of the sacred *haoma* plant. The *Yasna* contains the Zoroastrian creed and the four oldest prayers of the religion, of which the *Ahuna Vairya* is regarded as the most potent *manthra* (divine word).

Hymns to individual divinities of the Zoroastrian pantheon, the *Yashts*, are composed in a later dialect, although many of the sacred beings invoked, the *yazatas*, are Indo-Iranian, and the contents of some of the hymns predate Zoroaster. The *Visperad* and *Afrinagan* are litanies recited at ceremonies in honor of the spirits of the righteous; the *Sih Rozag* and the *Gahs* specify prayers for the thirty days of the month and the five watches of the day, respectively; and the *Nirangistan* and *Aogemadaeca* contain ritual prescriptions. The *Hadhokht Nask*, of which only three chapters survive, describes the judgment of the soul after death; the *Videvdat* is a compendium of law and ethics. The *Niyayishn* comprises five short litanies to the sun, moon, fire, water, and the *yazata* Mithra.

The Avesta was transmitted orally and memorized; the spoken *manthra* was believed to possess greater power than the written word. A few written copies of Avestan works are referred to in the Parthian period and earlier, but these have been lost; there were three redactions of the sacred text under the Sasanids. The script in which Avestan is written was invented around the fourth century CE. The final redaction into twenty-one *Nasks* (divisions), corresponding to the twenty-one words of the *Ahuna Vairya,* was made under Khusrau Anushirvan. The Avestan scripture was accompanied by its *Zand,* an interlinear translation and commentary into vernacular (Middle) Iranian languages; only parts of the *Zand* in Pahlavi, or Middle Persian, survive. The *Denkard* provides a summary of the *Nasks,* treating those that deal with legal matters in the greatest detail, but most of the canon has been lost, and the extant texts mentioned above represent only a small part of the Sasanid Avesta.

In the Pahlavi books, the Avesta (*Abastag ud Zand,* "Avesta and Zand"), is divided into three parts: *gasanig* (relating to the *Gathas*), the most spiritually sublime and difficult texts, to be studied and explicated only by a few priests of proven wisdom; *hadamansrig* (relating to that accompanying the *manthra*), spiritual teachings of greater accessibility; and *dadig* (legal), precepts by which the simple or unenlightened were to be governed. Despite their wealth of scripture, and because of their strong oral tradition, the Zoroastrians were on occasion denied the rights of *ahl al-kitab* ("people of the book") when it suited the Muslim invaders of Iran. European study of the text of the Avesta began in the late eighteenth century with the researches of the French scholar Anquetil-Duperron among the Parsis of India. Until then, knowledge of the religion of ancient Iran had been limited to references in classical and Muslim works. There is still no unanimity among scholars, however, on the meaning of the archaic and complex *Gathas,* and widely varying translations continue to be published.

[*See also* Bundahishn; Denkard; Videvdat; *and* Zoroastrianism.]

J. Darmesteter and L. H. Mills, trans., *The Zend-Avesta* (1974). K. F. Geldner, ed., *Avesta: Sacred Books of the Parsis,* 3 vols. (1896; reprint, 1982). Ilya Gershevitch, "Old Iranian Literature," in *Handbuch der Orientalistik,* edited by Bertold Spuler, pt. 1, vol. 4, sec. 2, chap. 1 (1968), pp. 1–30.

JAMES R. RUSSELL

AVESTAN, the Old Iranian language in which the "scripture" of the Zoroastrians, collectively called the Avesta, is preserved. The extant Avesta can be divided on linguistic criteria into two parts. Although those texts in Gathic Avestan are invariably older in their date of composition than those in Younger Avestan, some of the latter, particularly the *Yashts,* contain ancient material that clearly predates even the prophet Zoroaster (Avestan, Zarathushtra). The most important Gathic Avestan texts are the *Gathas* (*Yasna* 28 to 34, 43 to 51, and 53), seventeen verse sermons that are the only part of the extant Avesta that can be unequivocally attributed to the prophet Zoroaster.

The most characteristic feature of the Avestan textual tradition is oral preservation and transmission. Only during the late Sasanid period (sixth and seventh centuries) were the Avestan texts committed to writing, in an alphabetic script derived from the late Sasanid heterographic script used for Pahlavi (literary Middle Persian). That this original "Sasanid Avesta" was more copious than what has survived until modern times is clear from the summary of nineteen of the twenty-one *Nasks,* or sections, of the "Sasanid Avesta" preserved as chapter eight of the Zoroastrian Pahlavi *Denkard* in the ninth century.

[*See also* Avesta; Denkard; *and* Pahlavi.]

Mary Boyce, *Zoroastrians: Their Religious Beliefs and Practices* (1979). Ilya Gershevitch, "Old Iranian Literature," in *Handbuch der Orientalistik,* edited by B. Spuler, part 1, vol. 4, *Iranistik: Literatur* (1968), pp. 1–30.

DAVID A. UTZ

AVICENNA. *See* Ibn Sina.

AWADH, major historical region in North India since classical times. A riverine plain defined by the Yamuna River to the southwest, the Himalayas to the north, the Gandak River to the east, and Varanasi (Banaras) to the southeast, Awadh was named for the city of Ayodhya, the birthplace of Rama, near modern Faizabad. This important tract was named Oudh by the British, who annexed it in two stages in 1801 and 1856.

Owing mainly to geographical and linguistic features (with variations, Hindi is spoken by all its inhabitants, who are 87 percent Hindu and 11 percent Muslim) Awadh was an administrative unit in all pre-Muslim empires: it is called Kosala in the *Ramayana.* Rulers of the Delhi sultanate and the Mughal empire retained it as a unit, with the brief exception of the Sharqi sultanate of Jaunpur in the fourteenth century. Awadh did not become historically significant until the eighteenth century, when regional political systems were breaking away from the declining Mughal empire. From Faizabad and, after 1776, Lucknow a ruling dynasty of nawabs presided over periods of expansion, consolidation, political experimentation, cultural investment, and confrontation with the rising power of the British East India Company in Bengal, managing in an era of considerable upheaval to preserve cultural, economic, and much political autonomy for twenty million people during six generations of rule.

There were several noteworthy developments during the Nawabi period (1722–1856) besides the achievement of maintaining, with frequent hired support from the British, Awadh's political independence. Commodity production and markets were protected from the encroachments of the East India Company's monopolies. A new capital was built at Lucknow, using an eclectic set of architectural styles; by 1800 it presented an admirable array of mosques, palaces, inns, gardens, ceremonial buildings, and gateways, designed on refined and elaborate Mughal patterns. Urdu and Persian belles lettres, late Mughal painting, light classical music (especially *khyal*), biography, history, lexicography, Islamic studies both Shi'ite and Sunni, and India's first indigenous theater all were heavily sponsored, encouraged, and appreciated. [*See also* Lucknow.]

After 1801 Awadh was reduced by annexation to less than half of its former size. Surrounded by British territory, its ruler and court were exempted from the need for defensive readiness; the payment of the subsidy to the British also ended. In this protected, isolated situation, its educated and ruling elites suffered increasing ennui and demoralization. Political and cultural forms arose that sterner British proconsuls took as proof of enough effeteness and decadence to justify annexing the rest, and the resulting unrest was a major cause of the 1857 Revolt

(Mutiny) one year later. Awadh's political and military importance had been eclipsed; its more lasting achievements lay in the realms of social awareness, literary conservation, and religious reform in the second half of the century.

Richard B. Barnett, *North India between Empires: Awadh, the Mughals, and the British, 1720–1801* (1980). Ralph Russell and Khurshidul Islam, *Three Mughal Poets: Mir, Sauda, Mir Hasan* (1968). Abdul Halim Sharar, *Guzishta Lakhnau,* edited and translated by E. S. Harcourt and Fakhir Hussain as *Lucknow: The Last Phase of an Oriental Culture* (1975). RICHARD B. BARNETT

AWAMI LEAGUE (originally Awami Muslim League), Pakistani political party founded in June 1949 by Hussain Shahid Suhrawardy as a vehicle for his political ambitions and as a party that could present an alternative program to the ruling Muslim League. Suhrawardy opposed the exclusiveness of the Muslim League (hence the early dropping of the word "Muslim" from the title of the Awami League). Designed to be a national party, it had its greatest strength in East Pakistan and very little in the west. Key Bengalis associated with Suhrawardy were Sheikh Mujibur Rahman, his de facto successor in 1963, and Maulana Abdul Hamid Khan Bhashani, a leftist agrarian leader who left the party in 1957.

The program of the Awami League was moderate in economics but, especially under Mujib, supported a high level of autonomy for the provinces and parity in administrative, economic, and developmental matters between the eastern and western portions of the country. These ideas were embodied in the six-point program announced by Mujib in 1966. On this platform the Awami League won a majority in the Pakistan National Assembly in 1970 but was denied the opportunity to take the reins of government. The party was the spearhead of the civil war of 1971 leading to Bangladeshi independence. The postindependence program emphasized democracy, secularism, socialism, and nationalism, but before the assassination of Mujib in August 1975, the rule of the Awami League had become authoritarian. The party has not since governed in Bangladesh, but remains politically important. In the 1979 parliamentary election it won about 10 percent of the seats. There have been several changes of leadership culminating in the selection of Mujib's daughter, Hasina Wajid, as the current leader. The party favors a parliamentary system with a socialist and secular society and economy.

[*See also* Bangladesh; Pakistan; Mujibur Rahman, Sheikh; *and* Suhrawardy, Hussain Shahid.]

Moudud Ahmad, *Bangladesh: Constitutional Quest for Autonomy* (1979). Craig Baxter, *Bangladesh: A New Nation in an Old Setting* (1984). Muhammad Abdul Wadud Bhuiyan, *The Emergence of Bangladesh and the Role of the Awami League* (1982). CRAIG BAXTER

AYATOLLAH, a term meaning "the supreme sign of God." The full title, *ayatollah al-uzma,* was given during the Qajar period of Iranian history (eighteenth or nineteenth century CE) to the Twelver (Ithna Ashari) Shi'ite jurist *(mujtahid)* who is regarded as the most learned in the matters of the *shari'a* and whose righteousness *(adala)* and piety are well established.

The title is given to any Shi'ite jurist who is able to make independent judgments on the basis of principles laid down in Shi'ite Ja'fari jurisprudence. Such a jurist is designated as *marja-i taqlid,* a competent juridical authority who is followed in the matters of the *shari'a*. In order to facilitate the following of the Shi'ites, the ayatollah publishes a *risalat al-amaliyya* (treatise on practical religious guidance) expounding his legal rulings (sg., *fatwa*), which is accessible to his followers throughout the world. Although any jurist's advice can be sought in the *shari'a,* according to later consensus among the Twelver Shi'ite scholars it is obligatory to seek the guidance of the one who is acknowledged as the most learned *(a'lam)* and supreme *(al-uzma)*. In the absence of any well-defined hierarchy among the jurists, the position of the ayatollah is based on the level of his learning, usually determined through his students.

In South Asia the use of the title *ayatollah* for the learned jurists is more recent than in the Iranian context; among the Arabic-speaking Shi'ites the title *imam* is more commonly used for the *marja-i taqlid.* Indirectly, behind the authority of an acknowledged ayatollah is the authority of the infallible imam of the Shi'a.

[*See also* Imam; Ithna Ashari; Ja'fari; Mujtahid; Mulla; *and* Shari'a.]

Roy Mottahedeh, *The Mantle of the Prophet* (1985).

ABDELAZIZ SACHEDINA

AYODHYA, in Faizabad district, eastern Uttar Pradesh, India, on the Sarayu River, was the capital of the Ikshvaku dynasty's Kosala kingdom (sixth century BCE), and also a center of the Gupta domain (third to fifth centuries CE). The legendary capital of Rama, hero of the *Ramayana* epic, Ayodhya is today a pan-Indian pilgrimage site for Vaishnavite Hindus. [*See also* Rama *and* Ramayana.]

USHA SANYAL

AYUB KHAN, MOHAMMAD (1907–1974), Pakistani military and political leader; president of Pakistan from 1958 to 1969. Ayub Khan grew up in a village in the Hazara district of northwest Pakistan. His father was a noncommissioned officer in the British Indian Army. After his early education in local schools and two years at a university, Ayub Khan was admitted to the Royal Military College in Sandhurst, England. He received his commission in the British Indian Army in 1928. While serving in the 14th Punjab Regiment during World War II, Ayub Khan saw action in Burma against the Japanese forces. In 1947, when the British colony of India was partitioned into the two states of India and Pakistan, Ayub Khan joined the Pakistan Army. He was posted General Officer Commanding in East Pakistan in 1948 and 1949. In 1951 he was appointed full general and commander in chief of the Pakistan Army.

As commander in chief Ayub Khan played a key role in negotiating Pakistan's entry into a number of military alliances sponsored by the United States. His opportunity to take over the presidency of Pakistan came in 1958 when President Iskander Mirza abrogated the constitution and imposed martial law in Pakistan. On 28 October 1958 Ayub Khan dismissed Mirza and proclaimed himself president.

General (later Field Marshal) Ayub Khan's rule is best remembered for the inconclusive 1965 border war with India over Kashmir, the "Basic Democracy," and the "Great Decade." "Basic Democracy" was represented by the constitution of 1962, which instituted indirect elections in Pakistan and gave the president extraordinary powers. The "Great Decade" was the official characterization of development plans executed during the ten years of the Ayub regime, providing special incentives for private enterprise and foreign investment. Ironically, just as the official celebrations of the Great Decade got underway a mass revolt broke out against the economic and political policies of the regime. Ayub Khan resigned in 1969, leaving the country once more under martial law.

[*See also* Pakistan.]

Herbert Feldman, *From Crisis to Crisis: Pakistan, 1962–1969* (1972). Mohammad Ayub Khan, *Friends Not Masters: A Political Autobiography* (1967).

HASSAN N. GARDEZI

AYUDHYA (also Ayutthaya), classical kingdom of old Siam (1351–1767).

Ayudhya arose in the heart of the great Central Plain of what is now Thailand, surrounded by thou-

FIGURE 1. *Ayudhya.*

sands of square miles of level land and well watered by the Chaophraya River system.

By the fourteenth century, Cambodian Angkor's control over the region, long exerted by the neighboring Khmer kingdom of Lopburi, had weakened. Substantial numbers of Tai speakers, moving into the region from the north and northeast, had joined the resident Mon minority in professing Theravada Buddhism and aspiring to political and cultural autonomy. Their cause was taken up by an obscure adventurer, Prince U Thong, who was related to the ruling houses of both Tai Suphanburi and Lopburi, as well as to immigrant Chinese trading communities. On 4 March 1351, U Thong established a new, independent capital and kingdom at Ayudhya, located on a spacious island in the Chaophraya River some ninety kilometers from the sea at the farthest point on the river to which seagoing vessels could sail. The early strength of the kingdom was founded on the combination of old Lopburi/Angkor bureaucratic expertise; Tai labor, agricultural production, and military skills; and a heavy involvement in international trade, which made Ayudhya both a wealthy and a cosmopolitan city.

During its first century, Ayudhya's rulers alternated between two disparate policies. One, associated with the Lopburi faction and with kings Ramathibodi I (U Thong), Ramesuan, and Ramaracha, defined Ayudhya's role in terms of challenging and succeeding to Angkor's old hegemony. The other, associated with the Suphanburi faction and with kings Borommaracha I, Intharacha, and Borommaracha II, wanted to establish Ayudhya's leadership over the Tai peoples of the interior and saw Sukhothai as Ayudhya's rival. The alternate pursuit of both policies led to the kingdom's military expansion and growing dominance in the central portions of the Indochinese peninsula. Following the final collapse of Angkor at Ayudhya's hands in 1431 and the elimination of Sukhothai in 1438, Ayudhya grew from a local to a regional power in Southeast Asia. Although King Borommatrailokanat (r. 1448–1488) was successful in strengthening the state bureaucracy, neither he nor his successors were ever able to bring the Tai of the north—the kingdom of Lan Na—into Ayudhya. In the mid-sixteenth century, when the monarchs of Lan Sang (Laos), Lan Na, and Burma all joined King Chakkraphat (r. 1548–1569) in aspiring to imperial expansion, major warfare ensued, and after a decade of warfare the Burmese sacked Ayudhya in August 1569.

Ayudhya was not fully reconstituted until the last decade of the sixteenth century, when it was ruled by King Naresuan the Great (r. 1590–1605). Under a variety of names (e.g., Yodia), but especially as Siam, the kingdom attracted European shipping and trade, and during the reign of King Narai (r. 1656–1688) it was the scene of an abortive French attempt at colonial aggrandizement, ended by an internal "revolution" that evicted French troops. Although by then it had been largely abandoned by Western traders, Ayudhya continued to expand its Asian trade during the next century, mainly by supplying rice to China. Economic development strengthened

TABLE 1. *Kings of Ayudhya*

King	Reign Dates
1. Ramathibodi I (U Thong)	1351–1369
2. Ramesuan	1369–1370
3. Borommaracha I	1370–1388
4. Thong Chan	1388
5. Ramesuan (2d reign)	1388–1395
6. Ramaracha	1395–1409
7. Intharacha	1409–1424
8. Borommaracha II	1424–1448
9. Borommatrailokanat	1448–1488
10. Borommaracha III/Intharacha II	1488–1491
11. Ramathibodi II	1491–1529
12. Borommaracha IV	1529–1533
13. Ratsada	1533–1534
14. Chairacha	1534–1547
15. Yot Fa	1547–1548
16. Khun Worawongsa	1548
17. Chakkraphat	1548–1569
18. Mahin	1569
19. Mahathammaracha	1569–1590
20. Naresuan the Great	1590–1605
21. Ekathotsarot	1605–1610/11
22. Si Saowaphak (?)	1610–1611?
23. Song Tham	1610/11–1628
24. Chettha	1628–1629
25. Athittayawong	1629
26. Prasat Thong	1629–1656
27. Chai	1656
28. Suthammaracha	1656
29. Narai the Great	1656–1688
30. Phra Phetracha	1688–1703
31. Sua	1703–1709
32. Phumintharacha (Thai Sa)	1709–1733
33. Borommakot	1733–1758
34. Uthumphon	1758
35. Suriyamarin	1758–1767

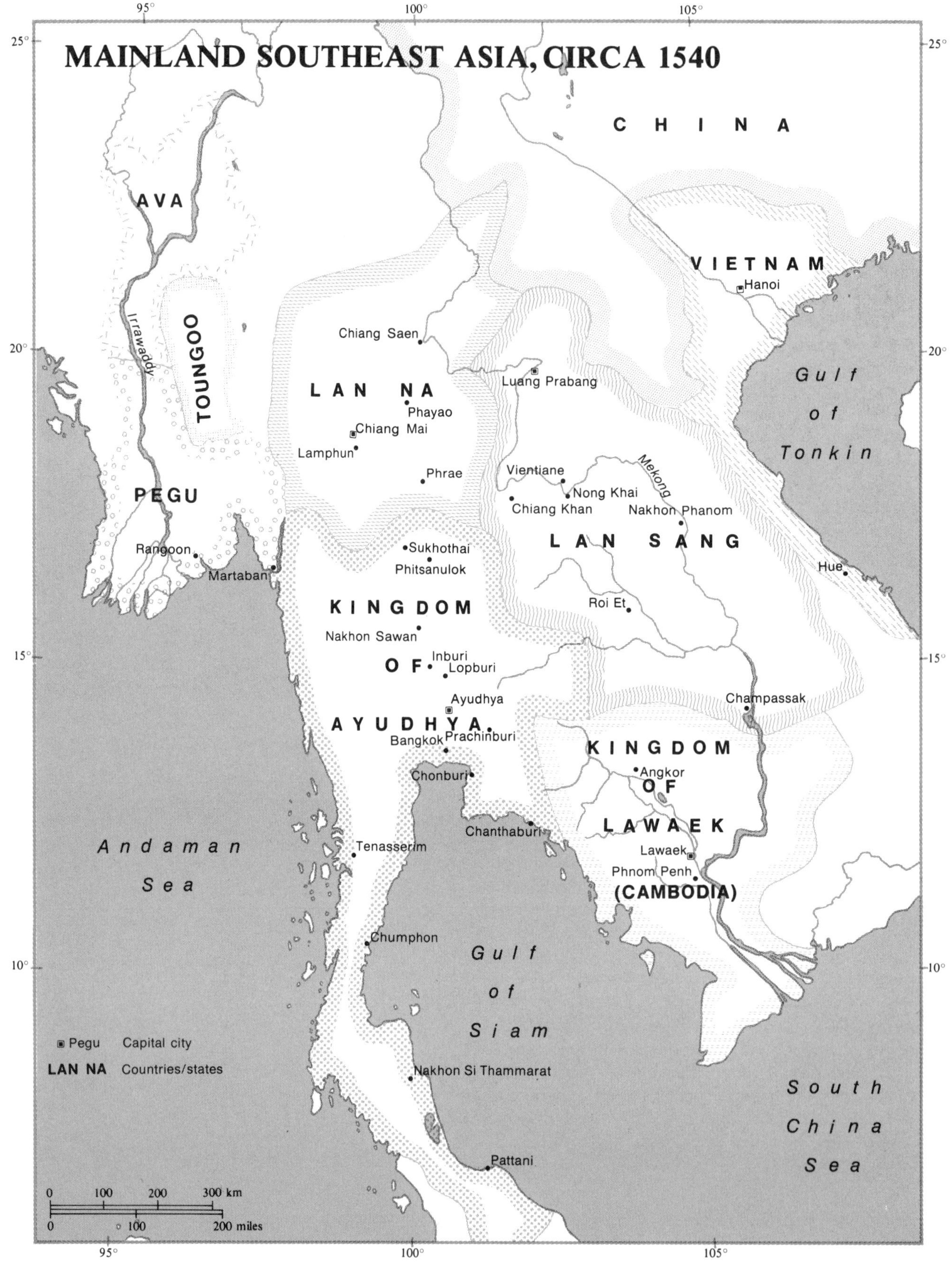
MAINLAND SOUTHEAST ASIA, CIRCA 1540
95°
100°
105°
25°
20°
15°
10°
CHINA
AVA
TOUNGOO
Irrawaddy
PEGU
Rangoon
Martaban
VIETNAM
Hanoi
Gulf of Tonkin
Chiang Saen
LAN NA
Phayao
Chiang Mai
Lamphun
Phrae
Luang Prabang
Vientiane
Nong Khai
Chiang Khan
Mekong
Nakhon Phanom
LAN SANG
Hue
Sukhothai
Phitsanulok
KINGDOM OF AYUDHYA
Nakhon Sawan
Inburi
Lopburi
Ayudhya
Prachinburi
Bangkok
Chonburi
Roi Et
Champassak
KINGDOM OF LAWAEK (CAMBODIA)
Angkor
Lawaek
Phnom Penh
Chanthaburi
Andaman Sea
Tenasserim
Chumphon
Gulf of Siam
Nakhon Si Thammarat
Pattani
South China Sea
Pegu Capital city
LAN NA Countries/states
0 100 200 300 km
0 100 200 miles

1:10,000,000

individuals and groups but undermined the administration, and the state was too weak to withstand the final Burmese attacks in the 1760s that ended in the sack of the capital in April 1767. Although Siam soon would revive, the Bangkok monarchy would prove to be very different from that of classical Ayudhya.

The Ayudhya state was based primarily on its control of workers in a region where land was plentiful but the population sparse. Although in theory kings controlled the labor of every person, in practice they depended on a pyramid of finely graded relations of lords to vassals, superiors to inferiors, and masters to servants, which stretched from the capital to the countryside. Ultimately these were personal, rather than formal and institutional, relationships, despite persistent royal attempts to the contrary. Because they were personal, and thus dependent upon the qualities of the individuals involved, the relationships were fragile.

Throughout most of its history, Ayudhya controlled what is now central Thailand, the southern quarter of the northeast, and the northern half of the Malay Peninsula.

[*See also* Angkor; Borommakot; Borommaracha I; Borommatrailokanat; Chakkraphat; Ekathotsarot; Kalahom; Lan Na; Lan Sang; Lopburi; Mahathammaracha; Mahatthai; Narai; Naresuan; Phaulkon, Constantine; Phetracha; Phrakhlang; Prasat Thong; Ramathibodi I; Ramesuan; Sakdi Na; Song Tham; *and* Sukhothai.]

H. G. Quatrich Wales, *Ancient Siamese Government and Administration* (1934; reprint, 1965). Akin Rabibhadana, *The Organization of Thai Society in the Early Bangkok Period* (1969). W. A. R. Wood, *A History of Siam* (1926). David K. Wyatt, *Thailand: A Short History* (1984).

DAVID K. WYATT

AYUTTHAYA. *See* Ayudhya.

AZAD, ABUL KALAM (1883–1958), Indian journalist, politician, and religious thinker. Educated along traditional lines in India, Azad toured centers of Muslim learning in the Arab world from 1907 to 1909. Emerging as a nationalist critic of the Raj, he also repudiated the Aligarh movement and Muslim separatism. Not easily classified as a thinker, his writings stressed the *Qur'an* as the highest authority in matters of faith. On *shari'a,* he advised scholars to consolidate the opinions of previous generations of thinkers in order to establish a core of fundamental doctrines. Such notions indicate Azad's agreement with traditional religious thought. At the same time, his stress on the importance of evolutionary adaptation to environment resembled the "naturalism" of Sayyid Ahmad Khan and the "vitalism" of Muhammad Iqbal. He also showed interest in Hindu and Buddhist doctrines and accepted religious pluralism. Although it is certainly acceptable in "orthodox" terms, traditionalist scholars have either criticized or ignored Azad's work. His influence was primarily political. A close associate of Gandhi, he became the most prominent Muslim in the Congress Party and first minister of education in independent India.

[*See also* Ahmad Khan, Sir Sayyid; Iqbal, Sir Muhammad; Gandhi, Mohandas Karamchand; *and* Indian National Congress.]

A. Ahmad, *Islamic Modernism in India and Pakistan* (1967). A. K. Azad, *India Wins Freedom* (1959).

GREGORY C. KOZLOWSKI

AZERBAIJAN. Today the Azerbaijani region is divided between two political units. The Iranian province, of which the capital is Tabriz, lies along the southwest littoral of the Caspian Sea; Azerbaijan SSR, of which the capital is Baku, has been one of the constituent republics of the Soviet Union since 1936. It is situated in the eastern portion of Transcaucasia.

The region owes its name to the Median satrap Atropates, who ruled after Alexander's invasion in 239 BCE. The Arab conquest of Azerbaijan took place during the years 639–641. Large migrations of Ghuzz tribes in the eleventh century rendered the area Turcophone (Azeri Turkish). An important commercial zone for the Ilkhanids, Azerbaijan served as a base for empire-building in the Iranian plateau for successive Turkmen dynasties in the post-Timurid era. During the long years of Safavid-Ottoman hostilities it was frequently invaded, and at the demise of the Safavids it was the subject of tsarist pretensions. Under the terms of the Russo-Qajar treaty of Turkomanchay (1828), the border was set at the Aras River. In the twentieth century Iranian Azerbaijan has been occupied by tsarist Russia (1908–1917), Turkey (1917–1921), and the USSR (1941–1946).

Wilhelm Barthold, *An Historical Geography of Iran* (1984), pp. 214–229. Vladimir Minorsky, "Ādharbaydjān," *The Encyclopaedia of Islam* (new ed., 1960–).

ARIEL SALZMANN

B

BABAD, Javanese word meaning "chronicle" as well as "to clear [the forest]," suggesting a link between chronicle writing and the foundation of states. All Javanese chronicles were written during the Islamic period, and all surviving manuscripts date from the eighteenth century or after. The origin of the genre is obscure, but chronicle writing almost certainly developed indigenously; it does not appear to have been inspired by Arabic historical traditions. With a few exceptions from the nineteenth and twentieth centuries, Javanese *babads* are all in verse.

Babads contain two classes of material. The first can be described as long legendary sections, often beginning with the story of Adam, followed by accounts of Hindu deities and of the mythical figures who are said to be the first beings to live in Java. These legends are full of gods, goddesses, spirits, demons, and chivalric heroes and often concern kingdoms that existed in the pre-Islamic period. As reconstructed from more reliable sources, however, the history of these kingdoms bears little relation to that given in the mythologized *babad* accounts. Nonetheless these mythological passages are often useful to historians for the light they shed upon contemporary ideas.

The second class of *babad* concerns historical events (i.e., those in the seventeenth century and afterward). Chronicles from this class normally center on a particular monarch, kingdom, hero, or sequence of events. They have been used successfully by historians in conjunction with other forms of evidence, but as is the case with any historical evidence, due regard must be given to social and cultural context and to the purposes for which they were written.

The two classes of material are combined in texts called *Babad tanah Jawi (Chronicles of the Land of Java)*, which begin with the story of Adam and extend into the eighteenth century. Several variant versions are known. *Babad* is also used for "chronicle" in Balinese.

H. J. de Graaf, "Later Javanese Sources and Historiography," in Soedjatmoko et al., eds., *An Introduction to Indonesian Historiography* (1965). Th. G. Th. Pigeaud, *Literature of Java*, vol. 1, (1967). M. C. Ricklefs, "Javanese Sources in the Writing of Modern Javanese History," in *Southeast Asian History and Historiography*, edited by C. D. Cowan and O. W. Wolters (1976).

M. C. Ricklefs

BABAK (d. 838), leader of one of the more famous of several anti-Abbasid insurrections in the Iranian provinces and the reputed head of an antinomian sect called the Khurramiyya. Probably alarmed by increasing Arab-Muslim colonization and attempts to centralize the administration, Babak led the indigenous mountain peasants and nomads in the area around Badhdh (northwest Azerbaijan) to revolt around 816 and successfully resisted government forces until the rebellion was crushed by the general Afshin in a series of campaigns (835–837). Babak attempted to flee to Byzantine territory but was betrayed by an Armenian prince, taken captive to Samarra, and executed in January 838. The revolt is extensively documented in the Muslim sources but so inconsistently and unconvincingly that its significance, especially in its sectarian aspects, is still obscure.

Edwin Wright, "Bābak of Badhdh and al-Afshīn during the Years 816–841 A.D.," *The Muslim World* 38 (1948).

E. L. Daniel

BABI, a nineteenth-century messianic movement led by a young merchant from Shiraz, Mirza Ali Muhammad (1819–1850), known as the Bab, who radically transformed Shaikhi ideas into a concrete program of action for the establishment of a new religion in Iran. Its history has received scant attention from scholars of modern Iran. Muslim sources available in Persian and Arabic are generally hostile, while distortions and selective omissions abound in accounts written after the Bab's death by followers of the rival contenders for his succession, the Azalis (followers of Mirza Yahya Nuri Subh-i Azal) and the Baha'is (followers of Azal's older half-brother Mirza Husain Ali Nuri Baha Allah). While Babi/Azali accounts insist on the Bab's legitimate claims to prophethood, Baha'i sources refer to him merely as the herald, or precursor, of Baha Allah.

The few scholars who have worked on the early history of Babism, A. Gobineau, E. G. Browne, and A. L. Nicolas (before he revised his views), generally accepted the account of Lisan al-Mulk Sipihr. The official Qajar chronicler maintained that Mirza Ali Muhammad had opportunistically first declared himself to be the successor of the Shaikhi leader Kazim Rashti, then the Bab ("gate") to the imam's teachings, then the expected imam himself, before finally proclaiming a new prophetic revelation. The Bab's early writings suggest the adoption of the cautious policy of issuing gradual proclamations.

It was while in prison in Maku in 1847–1848 that the Bab's views took a more definite shape, written down in what the Babis came to consider as the new holy book, the Bayan. He abrogated the Qur'an and all prior revealed books, annulled all Muslim and Shi'ite centers of pilgrimage, and substituted Shiraz for Mecca as a holy center. The message appealed to religious reformists, the political revolutionists, and the nationalists who rejected Islam as the "religion of the Arabs." Unlike the Shaikhis, the Babis resorted to militant means to achieve their goal: the destruction of the traditional Iranian Shi'ite sociopolitical order and the announcing of the dawn of a new religious era. Short-lived but bloody insurrections erupting in Mazandaran (October 1848–May 1849) and in Zanjan, Yazd, and Nairiz in 1850 met with defeat and merciless massacre at the hands of government troops. A number of Babi leaders lost their lives on the battlefield, others were subsequently executed, and the Bab was finally sentenced to death in July 1850.

The movement went underground but continued through its subversive means to undermine the established order. Dispute over succession to the Bab split the community. The smaller group of Azalis chose to remain faithful to the original Babi doctrine and keep up the spirit of revolt against both the secular and the religious establishment in Iran, while the majority followed Baha Allah, who in 1866 publicly proclaimed a new dispensation.

[*See also* Baha'i; Shaikhi; *and* Shiraz.]

M. Balyuzi, *The Bab* (1973). M. Bayat, *Mysticism and Dissent: Socioreligious Thought in Qajar Iran* (1982). E. G. Browne, trans., *Tarikh-i Jadid or New History of Mirza Ali Muhammad the Bab* (1893). M. Momen, ed., *The Babi and Baha'i Religions, 1844–1944: Some Contemporary Western Accounts* (1981). MANGOL BAYAT

BABUR (1483–1530), first Mughal ruler of India (1526–1530). Babur belonged to Central Asian royalty claiming descent from Genghis Khan and Timur. From childhood Babur became involved in internecine conflicts. In his twelfth year he succeeded his father to the throne of Ferghana, which lay, in his words, "at the limit of settled habitation." Successes and failures rapidly followed one another until early in the sixteenth century he had to move to Afghanistan and from there to India.

In 1526 he fought a major battle at a field near Panipat, a township close to Delhi. North India was at this time under the rule of an Afghan dynasty, the Lodis. Babur was helped by dissension within the ruling family and by his superior war strategy. He introduced India to the use of mobile field guns in battle, although muskets had been used earlier. He had learned the use of guns from an Ottoman master and often defeated numerically superior enemies. In the less than four years that he ruled India he conquered large parts of the north and made a few experiments in administration. A man of refined tastes, Babur was himself a major literary figure in his native Turki.

[*See also* Mughal Empire; Panipat, Battles of; Lodi Dynasty; *and* Delhi.]

Bamber Gascoigne, *The Great Mughals* (1971). R. P. Tripathi, *Rise and Fall of the Mughal Empire* (1976). L. F. Rushbrook Williams, *An Empire Builder of the Sixteenth Century* (1918). HARBANS MUKHIA

BACH DANG, BATTLES OF (939 and 1288), famous for the Vietnamese use of tides to trap enemy fleets with man-made underwater barriers in the Bach Dang River, an estuary on the water route between China and northern Vietnam. In the first battle, which took place around January 939, Ngo Quyen annihilated an invading fleet commanded by Liu Hongcao, son of Liu Gong, ruler of the Southern Han dynasty at Canton. The Vietnamese remember this battle as the beginning of their independence from Chinese imperial rule. In the second battle, in April 1288, Tran Hung Dao annihilated a fleet commanded by the Mongol General Umar as it attempted to withdraw from Vietnam back to China. This was the last major battle of the Mongol-Viet Wars.

Keith W. Taylor, *The Birth of Vietnam* (1983).

KEITH W. TAYLOR

BACH VIET (Chinese, Bai Yue, or "hundred Yue"), a general term for the presumably numerous principalities formed by Yue leaders after the conquest of Yue by Qin in 333 BCE. There is historical evidence for four Yue states: Nanyue, centered on Canton; Minyue in Fujian; and Eastern and Western Ou in Zhejiang and Guangxi, respectively. The Western Ou probably formed the major element of the forces of An Duong Vuong when he overthrew the last of the Lac Viet kings of Van Lang (c. 210 BCE) and founded the kingdom of Au Lac. Viet legend holds that the Hundred Viet were the descendants of Lac Long Quan and Au Co.

[*See also* An Duong Vuong; Lac Viet; Van Lang; Au Lac; Lac Long Quan; *and* Au Co.]

Keith W. Taylor, *The Birth of Vietnam* (1983).

JAMES M. COYLE

BAC SON UPRISING, a revolt led by the Indochinese Communist Party against French rule in the fall of 1940. The uprising broke out when Japanese troops stationed in South China crossed the border to emphasize Japanese demands for economic and military privileges in French Indochina. In the chaotic situation that ensued, local party leaders led minority tribesmen in a rebellion against colonial authority. Although the uprising was quelled by the French, the surviving rebels were organized in guerrilla bands that continued their operations in the border area and eventually became part of the Vietnamese National Salvation Army.

[*See also* Vietnam.]

John T. McAlister, Jr., *Vietnam: The Origins of Revolution* (1971). Chu Van Tan, *Reminiscences on the Army for National Salvation* (1974). WILLIAM J. DUIKER

BACTRIA, in antiquity the land north and south of the upper Oxus River, present-day Tajikistan and northern Afghanistan. Some authors throughout history, however, limited the term *Bactria* to the area south of the Oxus. The larger area, extending from the Hissar mountain range in the north to the Hindu Kush in the south, probably took its name from the river Bakhtri, on which was the principal city of the same name, later called Bahl, and in Islamic times Balkh.

The earliest mention of Bactria is in the Old Persian inscription of Darius as one of the lands that supported him in his bid for power. This satrapy, or province, was the eastern bastion of the Achaemenid empire, as it later was under Alexander and his successors. Heavily colonized by the Seleucids, Apollodorus (in Strabo XV, 686) called it a land of a thousand cities. Bactria was undoubtedly an important center of the Kushan empire, both religious (Iranian Buddhist) and artistic. Probably in the fourth century Bactria came under Sasanid rule, as we infer from the coins of governors, but in the following century the Hephthalites ruled it until around 558, when the Sasanids again exercised sway over the area.

Under the Arabs Bactria again became a center of their rule in the east, and it continued to flourish under various Islamic dynasties until the Mongol capture of Balkh in 1221. Thereafter the area lost its importance.

[*See also* Balkh.]

RICHARD N. FRYE

BADAKHSHAN, the mountainous area of modern Afghanistan south of the Oxus and drained by the Kokcha, Panj, and Wakhan rivers. The name appears first in the works of the early Islamic geographers and Chinese sources of the same period. The name also appears as *Balakhshan* and perhaps means the land of a gem similar to a ruby. Several Iranian Pamir languages are spoken in Badakhshan, evidence of the isolation of its many valleys throughout history. Never a populous area, Badakhshan was ruled by local chiefs, although it was nominally part of states to the west or north. RICHARD N. FRYE

BADAUNI, ABDUL QADIR (1540–1596), courtier of Emperor Akbar of India. An orthodox Muslim theologian who helped Akbar challenge the dominance of other Muslim theologians, Badauni later became a bitter critic of Akbar's religious eclecticism. When Abu'l Fazl was commissioned to write an official history of Akbar's reign reflecting religious liberalism, Badauni set out to write the three-volume *Muntakhab-ut Tawarikh* to counterbalance it. Realizing that the venture could prove dangerous, he kept the work secret during his lifetime.

[*See also* Akbar; Abu'l Fazl; *and* Mughal Empire.]

Harbans Mukhia, *Historians and Historiography during the Reign of Akbar* (1976). HARBANS MUKHIA

BADGHIS, a district in northwestern Afghanistan and the Turkmenistan border area of the Soviet Union, bounded by the Hari Rud and Murghab rivers. Badghis is noted for its fine pastures, fertile land, and pistachio trees. In the past it was favored by nomadic tribes and was an important source of food and animals for Herat under the Timurids. Badghis was often devastated by conquering armies; today it is home to numerous archaeological remains. The principal ethnic groups living there at present are Jamshidis and Hazaras, and, on the Soviet side of the border, Turkmens.

[*See also* Hazaras.]

Guy Le Strange, *The Lands of the Eastern Caliphate* (1905). LAWRENCE POTTER

BAGYIDAW (1783–1846), seventh ruler of Burma's Konbaung dynasty (r. 1819–1837). His father was the eldest son of Bodawhpaya (1782–1819) and was made crown prince in 1782. Appointed crown prince on his father's death in 1808, Bagyidaw played an increasingly greater role in government as his grandfather aged. Together they were able to contain the serious threat posed by Bagyidaw's uncles the Prome and Toungoo princes. On Bodawhpaya's death in 1819, Bagyidaw ascended to the throne without armed conflict and executed his two uncles.

He was nevertheless an inexperienced and weak ruler, strongly influenced by his chief queen, Mei Nu, formerly a low-born concubine, and her brother, whom Bagyidaw named prince of Salin. Bagyidaw's policies accelerated the political and economic decline begun during the sovereignty of his predecessor.

From the beginning Bagyidaw's reign was weakened by long-standing tensions with the British East India Company, which culminated in the First Anglo-Burmese War of 1824–1826. Burma's defeat brought the cession of Arakan, Assam, and Tenasserim, a large monetary indemnity, and a British residency. The war also adversely affected Bagyidaw's already weak administration, which imposed heavy taxes to pay the indemnity, and spurred Mon and Karen rebellions in Lower Burma. Disorder and banditry increased, particularly after 1831 when Bagyidaw, already severely affected by the humiliation of defeat, began to experience periods of derangement.

Bagyidaw's younger brother, the Tharrawaddy prince, was appointed nominal head of a commission of regency. Tharrawaddy's conflicts with the chief queen, however, led Bagyidaw to relinquish the throne to his brother. Bagyidaw remained in the palace until his death by natural causes on 10 October 1846.

[*See also* Konbaung Dynasty; East India Company; Anglo-Burmese Wars; *and* Tharrawaddy.]

W. R. Desai, *History of the British Residency in Burma, 1826–1840* (1939). WILLIAM J. KOENIG

BAHA'I, religion founded by Mirza Husain Ali Nuri (1817–1892), known as Baha Allah. The Baha'is view the Bab, Mirza Ali Muhammad Shirazi, founder of the Babi faith, as a herald, or forerunner, whose chief task was to announce the advent of Baha Allah's dispensation. Following the Bab's death in 1850, disputes over succession, in addition to the extremist tendencies of some individuals, severely split the Babi community. Although there seems to be no doubt that Mirza Ali Muhammad had indeed appointed Mirza Yahya Nuri Subh-i Azal to succeed him, Baha Allah rapidly eclipsed his younger half-brother and assumed de facto leadership. In 1863 he reportedly declared himself to a few disciples to be "he whom God shall make manifest," and in 1866 he publicly proclaimed the new dispensation, which was accepted by the majority of the Babis.

As the "Prophet of the Age" Baha Allah drastically revised older Babi directives, aiming at transforming the new religion into a universal one, transcending national and cultural peculiarities, and expanding it beyond the Iranian borders. He abrogated or changed earlier doctrines, discarding elements of mystic-philosophical speculative thought, and divorced the new faith more completely from Islamic traditions. He exalted humanitarianism over patriotism, forbade the use of arms, even for holy causes, and commanded his followers to avoid political involvement, thus eliminating the militant spirit that had characterized original Babism. His successor, Abd al-Baha (1844–1921), also known as Abbas Effendi and Shoghi Effendi, further accentuated universal, apolitical characteristics and undertook Western-inspired innovations, especially in education and matters pertaining to the legal status of women.

Baha'is in Iran, like their Babi predecessors, suffered persecution at the hands of the religious, and at times governmental, authorities. They have been consistently denied the legal status as a recognized religious minority enjoyed by the Jews, Christians, and Zoroastrians. Under the secular regime of the Pahlavis the Baha'is were granted a certain measure of individual freedom and safety, despite occasional outbursts of blatant discrimination and isolated cases of individual persecution. Since the establishment of the Islamic Republic in 1979, however, the Baha'i community has suffered the loss of all its rights.

[*See also* Babi.]

H. M. Balyuzi, *Edward Granville Browne and the Baha'i Faith* (1970). E. G. Browne, *Materials for the Study of the Babi Religion* (1918). Shoghi Effendi, ed. and trans., *The Dawnbreakers: Nabil's Narrative of the Early Days of the Baha'i Revelation* (1932). M. Momen, ed., *The Babi and Baha'i Religions 1844–1944: Some Contemporary Western Accounts* (1981). MANGOL BAYAT

BAHMANI DYNASTY, line of Indo-Turkish kings who ruled over the Deccan Plateau of peninsular India between 1347 and 1526. Named after its first sultan, Ala ud-Din Bahman Shah, the dynasty was founded by settlers and soldiers who had colonized the northern Deccan plateau following the invasions of the area by the sultan of Delhi, Ala ud-Din Khalji, in the early fourteenth century. Its sultans based their capitals first at Gulbarga and later at Bidar, and deliberately recruited administrators and soldiers from the Middle East. Factional rivalry between these newcomers and descendants of original settlers doomed the kingdom to civil strife, however, and it disintegrated into five independent sultanates in the late fifteenth century.

[*See also* Deccan Sultanates.]

H. K. Sherwani, *The Bahmanis of the Deccan* (1953). H. K. Sherwani and P. M. Joshi, eds., *History of Medieval Deccan (1295–1724)* (1974). RICHARD M. EATON

BAHRAM GUR (r. 420–438 CE), Sasanid ruler Bahram V; son of Yazdigird I. Raised at Hira by the client Arab king al-Mundhir, who taught him to ride, hunt, and fight, Bahram was famous for his physical strength and enjoyment of hunting, drinking, music, and women. His epithet *Gur* ("the wild ass") refers to his reputation for hunting onagers. At his father's death the nobles enthroned a descendant of Ardashir I called Khusrau, so Bahram marched on Ctesiphon with an Arab army and took the throne. He drove the Hephthalites back into the east and founded Marv-i Rud to secure the frontier. He inherited the services of Mihrshapur, chief of the Magi, and Mihrnarseh, the *wuzurg framadar,* from his father's reign. Their continued persecution of Christians provoked a brief war with the Romans in 421. The treaty of 421 provided religious toleration for Christians in Iran and Magians under Roman rule and provided Roman contributions to defend the Caucasus. In 428 Bahram Gur replaced the Arsacid ruler of Armenia with a Persian *marzban* supported by the Armenian nobles but opposed by the clergy.

[*See also* Huns *and* Sasanid Dynasty.]

Ehsan Yarshater, ed., *The Seleucid, Parthian and Sasanian Periods* (1983), vol. 3 of the *Cambridge History of Iran.* MICHAEL G. MORONY

BAI CHONGXI (1893–1966), leader of the Guangxi clique during the Republican period (1911–1949) in China. Bai's career began in the Guangxi provincial military and is linked with another Guangxi officer, Li Zongren. The connection with the Nationalists started in 1923 when Bai Chongxi provided military help to Sun Yat-sen. Guangxi forces became a major element in the Northern Expedition (1926–1928). Bai personally led several important actions, including the massacre of Communists at Shanghai in April 1927.

After successfully completing the Northern Expedition the Guangxi clique came under pressure to disband part of their forces. They rebelled in 1929 and in 1931 linked up with Guangdong provincial dissidents. By reconciling with Chiang Kai-shek, Bai Chongxi and Li Zongren received Chiang's permission to entrench themselves further in Guangxi. Bai had a reputation as a military strategist and played a leading role in the disastrous Nationalist campaign against Japan of 1939 to 1940, his last important battlefield assignment. He continued to serve in central military posts, including minister of defense. When Nationalist control of the mainland crumbled, Bai joined Chiang Kai-shek on Taiwan, where he lived as a figurehead from the pre-1949 era who loyally continued to support the Nationalists.

[*See also* Chiang Kai-shek; China, Republic of; Guangxi Clique; Guomindang; *and* Li Zongren.]

"P'ai Ch'ung-hsi," in *Biographical Dictionary of Republican China,* edited by Howard Boorman (1967–1971), vol. 3, pp. 51–56. DAVID D. BUCK

BAI JUYI (Bo Juyi; 772–846), Chinese poet and official; his poems were highly influential in Japan. Bai followed a typical official career, on a relatively high level owing in part to his literary abilities: appointments in the capital (808–810, 820–822, 826–829) alternated with provincial postings, some of which were banishments (815–819) and some desirable (governor of Hangzhou, 822–824, and of Suzhou, 825–826). He then obtained a sinecure post at Luoyang (829) until his retirement (841).

Bai's poems, simple and many of them apparently singable, were widely known even among nonliterati. Especially popular were "Song of Everlasting Sorrow" and "Pipa Song." His friendship with Yuan Zhen (779–831) became famous through their exchanges of poems. For a Tang-dynasty poet, Bai's life is unusually fully documented, so he is of great importance to Chinese literary history. He met the ideal of being both poet and official and is an example of a poet who was influenced by Buddhism and who followed Chinese poetry's original purpose (remonstrating on behalf of the people, chiefly 808–810). Nonetheless, Chinese critical opinion has never placed Bai among the first rank of poets.

The situation is quite different in Japan, where he is known as Haku Rakuten. Bai's great influence is part of the complex subject of Chinese influence on Japanese literature, both the literature written in Japanese and that written in Chinese. His collected works, *Hakushi monjū,* had reached Japan at least by 838, and until the Gozan era (late thirteenth century), poetry by Bai and from the late Six Dynasties was considered the epitome of Chinese literature. Especially during the Heian period, for example in *Genji monogatari* and in the *waka* poems, the influence of Bai is marked. Attitudes to Bai changed as the response to and knowledge of Chinese literature became more complicated, but lines from Bai's poetry remain widely known and quoted even today.

Eugene Feifel, *Po Chü-i as a Censor: His Memorials Presented to Hsien-tsung during the Years 808–810* (1961). Arthur Waley, *The Life and Times of Po Chü-i, 772–846 A.D.* (1949).
SHAN CHOU

BAIQARA, HUSAIN (1438–1506), more fully Mirza Sultan Husain ibn Mansur ibn Baiqara ibn Umar Shaikh, known as Sultan Husain Baiqara. A great-great-grandson of Timur, he ruled a greatly reduced Timurid empire, consisting mainly of the province of Khurasan, from 1469 until his death in 1506.

Born into the service of various family members, Husain Baiqara emerged from the internecine struggles that had plagued the Timurid realm since the 1450s as master of Herat in 1469. During his relatively stable, nearly forty-year reign, Herat became not so much the political as the cultural capital of the entire eastern Islamic world. Although ethnically a Turk and a member of the Timurid hereditary military elite, Husain Baiqara proved to be one of the greatest patrons of medieval Persian Islamic culture. A cultivated and worldly man, a poet in Chagatai Turkish who used the pen name Husaini, Husain Baiqara managed to assemble at his court the finest talents of his day. Among these were the poets Jami and Bina'i, the painters Bihzad and Shah Muzaffar, the calligrapher Sultan Ali Mashhadi, the historians Mirkhvand and Khvandamir, and numerous singers, musicians, and dancers. Many were personally supervised and patronized by his foster brother, courtier, and confidant, Mir Ali Shir Neva'i, the outstanding Chagatai Turkish poet in whose works the Chagatai language assumed its classical form.

It was on account of this exceptional cultural and artistic activity that the period of Husain Baiqara's rule has often been dubbed a Timurid Renaissance. Pressure from the nomadic Uzbeks, however, brought about the demise of the Timurid house in Khurasan. In 1507 Herat was captured from Husain Baiqara's sons and successors, Muzaffar Husain Mirza and Badi al-Zaman Mirza, by Muhammad Shaibani Khan, but the prestigious Timurid cultural tradition epitomized by the achievements of Husain Baiqara's court lived on at the courts of the Timurids' political successors—the Uzbeks and the Safavids.

[*See also* Bihzad; Chagatai Literature; Herat; Jami; *and* Neva'i.]

Wilhelm Barthold, *Four Studies on the History of Central Asia*, vol. 3 (1962). René Grousset, *The Empire of the Steppes,* translated by Naomi Walford (1970). G. Hambly, ed., *Central Asia* (1969). J. Rypka, *History of Iranian Literature* (1968).
MARIA E. SUBTELNY

BA JIN (b. 1904), pseudonym (from *Ba*kunin and Kropot*kin*) of Li Feigan, Chinese novelist. From his youth, Ba Jin was active in the Chinese anarchist movement. Interested in conveying a vision of possibilities rather than in technique, he wrote rapidly. Between 1927 and 1947 he published eighteen novels and numerous volumes of short stories, essays, travelogues, and translations (chiefly Turgenev and Kropotkin). His best-known novel, *Family* (1931), closely reflects his own youthful break with tradition. Under the People's Republic, he was attacked in 1957 and 1958. In his collected works (1958–1961), he deleted references to anarchism and altered novel endings. He wrote in 1977 of his treatment during the Cultural Revolution.

[*See also* Anarchism *and* May Fourth Movement.]

Olga Lang, *Pa Chin and His Writings: Chinese Youth between the Two Revolutions* (1967). Nathan K. Mao, *Pa Chin* (1978). Pa Chin (Ba Jin), *The Family,* translated by Sidney Shapiro (1972).

SHAN CHOU

BAKER, GEORGE, first Englishman to visit, in 1755, the early Konbaung dynasty capital of Mokhsobo in northern Burma. The British East India Company sent Baker to negotiate a treaty with Alaunghpaya, the first Konbaung ruler (r. 1752–1760), in the hope that the Burmese would recognize the company's settlement on Negrais Island, at the mouth of the Bassein River. Although he was interested in obtaining arms for his final campaign against the rival kingdom of Pegu in the Burmese Delta, Alaunghpaya offered the British only trading privileges at Rangoon and Bassein and the prospect of further negotiations. After a ten-day stay in Mokhsobo, Baker wrote the first Western eyewitness account of Alaunghpaya and his capital, subsequently published in Dalrymple's *Oriental Repertory.*

[*See also* Konbaung Dynasty; East India Company; *and* Pegu.]

Alexander Dalrymple, *Oriental Repertory* (1808). D. G. E. Hall, *Europe and Burma* (1945).

WILLIAM J. KOENIG

BAKHTIAR, SHAHPUR (b. 1916), prime minister of Iran from December 1978 to February 1979, educated in Paris, son of an important khan of the Bakhtiari tribe. He was active in the National Front and, along with his colleague Karim Sanjabi, remained a vocal critic of the shah, as their open letter to him in June 1977 demonstrated. He broke with his National Front colleagues in December 1978 when he agreed to the shah's request to form a coalition government if the shah would depart the country. Bakhtiar remained prime minister until 11 February 1979, when he resigned and fled Iran for Paris, where he was active in émigré politics in the 1980s.

[*See also* Pahlavi, Mohammed Reza.]

JERROLD D. GREEN

BAKSAR, BATTLE OF. Fought near the junction of the Ganges and Karamnasa rivers on 23 October 1764, the Battle of Baksar was "perhaps the most important battle the British ever fought in South Asia" (Barnett, p. 64). It was there that the British commander Hector Munro won a decisive victory over Shuja ud-Daula, nawab of Awadh, and his allies Mir Qasim of Bengal and Mughal emperor Shah Alam.

[*See also* Awadh; Bengal; East India Company; Mir Qasim; *and* Mughal Empire.]

Richard B. Barnett, *North India between Empires: Awadh, the Mughals and the British 1720–1801* (1980). A. L. Srivastava, "Battle of Buxar," in *Comprehensive History of India,* edited by A. C. Banerjee and D. K. Ghosh (1978), vol. 9.

FRITZ LEHMANN

BAKUFU (lit., "tent government"), the central administrative structure utilized by the military class to rule Japan during the period 1192 to 1868. The *bakufu* coexisted with the powerless imperial regime based in Kyoto. There were three *bakufu:* the Kamakura *bakufu* (1192–1333), the Muromachi (or Ashikaga) *bakufu* (1338–1573), and the Tokugawa *bakufu* (1603–1868).

The term *bakufu* is the Japanese pronunciation for the Chinese *mufu,* which referred to the headquarters of a general in the field. In Japan *bakufu* was initially used to refer either to the residence of the commander of the Inner Palace Guard or to the commander himself. When Minamoto Yoritomo (1147–1199) was appointed to that position in 1190, his residence was called the *bakufu,* and after he became shogun in 1192, the term was applied to the military government he established at Kamakura in east-central Japan.

At the head of the *bakufu* stood the shogun. The term *shogun* derived from the ancient title *sei-i tai shōgun* ("barbarian-subduing generalissimo"), which was originally bestowed on government officials engaged in military campaigns. Legitimation took the form of a formal appointment by the emperor, who entrusted the shogun with the responsibility for national security and domestic peace and tranquillity.

In his capacity as principal administrator, the shogun presided over a feudal administrative structure that governed the shogunal family's own domains and its direct vassals, as well as exercising some modicum of control over the domains of the shogun's principal vassals (the daimyo) and the territory under the control of Shinto and Buddhist religious establishments. The ability of the shogun to fulfill these responsibilities varied greatly; the great majority were ineffectual leaders whose personal qualities and lack of interest in the pragmatic aspects of administration quickly transformed them into figureheads who were adroitly manipulated by their adviser officials within the *bakufu.*

Beneath the shogun as national hegemon was an administrative apparatus that was as sophisticated as any premodern bureaucracy in terms of structural development and differentiation of function. The long centuries of military hegemony reveal a process of institutional evolution that transformed the *bakufu* from the rather simple structure of the Kamakura period into the much more elaborate and sophisticated apparatus of the Tokugawa *bakufu,* with its advisory councils (Senior and Junior councils), Supreme Court, Inspectorate-General, Finance Commission, Superintendancy of Temples and Shrines, and so forth.

The *bakufu* administrative apparatus was located in the confines of shogunal headquarters in the national military capital (Kamakura for the Minamoto *bakufu,* Kyoto for the Ashikaga *bakufu,* and Edo [modern Tokyo] for the Tokugawa *bakufu*). The exceptions were those officials whose duties demanded residence in another part of the country (such as at Nagasaki, Osaka, or Kyoto). Offices were assigned in terms of size and location, in accordance with the importance of the functions and responsibilities of each administrative component.

Participation in the administrative responsibilities of the *bakufu* was restricted to the warrior class, which constituted the elite stratum in a social system that had become highly stratified by Tokugawa times. Status and rank distinctions within the warrior class, as well as relationship to the shogunal family, were important criteria in determining the level and nature of the bureaucratic posts held. In the mature Tokugawa *bakufu,* for example, the important positions of senior councillor (*rōjū*) were reserved for *fudai* daimyo, senior vassals whose loyalty to the Tokugawa was unquestioned. Although most *bakufu* officials had no "formal" training, they obtained the knowledge necessary to discharge their duties by prior service elsewhere in the shogunal bureaucracy or as administrators of daimyo domains.

Despite the long period of military rule, none of the three *bakufu* solved certain structural and functional problems. In addition to the question of ineffective shogunal leadership and the delegation of power to *bakufu* officials, the *bakufu* suffered from (1) a high degree of structural rigidity that rendered it incapable of the flexibility needed to deal with emergency situations, despite sporadic reform efforts (such as the Kyōhō and Kansei reforms of the Tokugawa period); (2) a highly restrictive recruitment process that saw offices allotted on the basis of status and rank, not ability; (3) occasional inability (especially true during the Muromachi *bakufu*) to control shogunal vassals whose wealth and military power frequently tipped the fragile balance of power in their direction; and (4) an archaic and irrational economic system that continued to deny the reality of an emerging national economy.

[*See also* Shogun.]

Harold Bolitho, *Treasures among Men: The Fudai Daimyo in Tokugawa Japan* (1974). Kenneth Grossberg, *Japan's Renaissance: The Politics of the Muromachi Bakufu* (1981). Jeffrey Mass, *Warrior Government in Early Medieval Japan* (1974). Herman Ooms, *Charismatic Bureaucrat: A Political Biography of Matsudaira Sadanobu* (1975). Conrad Totman, *Politics in the Tokugawa Bakufu, 1600–1843* (1967). RONALD J. DICENZO

BALAMBANGAN, small island off northern Borneo, situated on the western edge of the so-called Sulu Zone and bound by the islands of Palawan and Mindanao on the north, Borneo and Sulawesi (Celebes) on the south, and centered on Jolo, home of the sultanate of Sulu. Alexander Dalrymple was responsible for the establishment, in 1773, of Balambangan as a trading station for the British East India Company, which found itself facing the possibility of bankruptcy owing to the continued flow of silver into China in exchange for tea. The British turned to the Sulu Zone's forests, seas, and coastlines as a source of the needed trade goods for the Canton tea market. In exchange for sea and forest products, the Taosug of Sulu received opium, munitions, and piece goods from Balambangan. A decisive event in the history of Sulu occurred in 1775 when the Taosug sacked the Balambangan settlement and carried away an enormous cache of munitions, allowing Sulu to gradually reduce the influence of neighboring sultanates. The downfall of the Balambangan settlement marked a turning point in the rise of Sulu as the major maritime state in the eastern part of insular Southeast Asia.

[*See also* Jolo *and* Sulu.]

Howard Fry, *Alexander Dalrymple and the Expansion of British Trade* (1970). James Francis Warren, *The Sulu*

A presidential commission of inquiry created by the victorious United National Party government found Mrs. Bandaranaike guilty of "abuse of power," and she was expelled from Parliament in October 1980. A highly controversial move, her forced removal from politics opened up a leadership struggle within the SLFP, which has had a debilitating effect on its standing. Mrs. Bandaranaike, however, remains one of the most popular politicians in Sri Lanka.

[*See also* Bandaranaike, Solomon West Ridgeway Dias; Sri Lanka Freedom Party; *and* Sri Lanka.]

VIJAYA SAMARAWEERA

BANDARANAIKE, SOLOMON WEST RIDGEWAY DIAS (1899–1959), prime minister of Ceylon (present-day Sri Lanka) from 1956 to 1959. Entering national politics in the mid-1920s, Bandaranaike unhesitatingly embraced the multifactioned workings of the nationalist movement. His founding of the Sinhala Maha Sabha (SMS) in 1937 reflected his concern with widening his personal support among the groups that were to provide him with a powerful base, the Sinhalese and Buddhist intelligentsia. He brought the SMS within the United National Party (UNP) and became the minister of health and local government in D. S. Senanayake's United National Party government of 1947.

Although Bandaranaike saw himself as Senanayake's successor, with other contenders around him there was no assurance that the party leadership would become his. He resigned from the cabinet and the UNP in June 1951 and founded the Sri Lanka Freedom Party, which was to be the vehicle for his accession to power. Bandaranaike consciously molded his party's image in centrist terms, as one that would appeal to those not specifically attracted to the UNP on the right or the Marxists on the left. The new party failed to make an impact on the electorate in 1952, but its—and Bandaranaike's—fortunes were to change dramatically at the 1956 polls.

The mid-1950s saw remarkable stirrings among the Sinhalese Buddhists, who found powerful expression in the cause for linguistic nationalism. Bandaranaike effectively mobilized and channeled this populism through the Mahajana Eksath Peramuna (People's United Front), which he formed by bringing together the Sri Lanka Freedom Party, Sinhalese Buddhist interest groups, and a political organization that leaned toward the left. The coalition won a sweeping victory in 1956. Sinhalese Buddhist populism was triumphant, but the realization of its agenda proved to be no easy task for Bandaranaike in the pluralist setting. Soon after coming into power he redeemed a major promise by supporting legislation making Sinhalese the official language of the country. The measure evoked the hostility of the Tamils, and pressure exerted by extremists within his own party prevented Bandaranaike from pursuing the compromises that were necessary to resolve the grievances of the minority.

Bandaranaike's problems were compounded by the tension and conflicts that arose between the conservative members of his government and those who leaned toward the left. The sure grasp of leadership and charisma that he displayed in bringing about what is often described as the 1956 Revolution deserted Bandaranaike within two years of his triumph in the face of divergent and unresolved forces, both within and without his own party. Bandaranaike sought and achieved greater visibility for Ceylon through his role in the nonalignment movement, but his successes in foreign policy were not matched domestically. Bandaranaike eventually fell victim to a plot hatched by some of his leading supporters. His assassination on 26 September 1959 did not mark the end of Bandaranaike's impact upon Ceylonese politics: the hagiography that quickly emerged was an assurance that the Bandaranaike name would continue to influence the course of national politics.

[*See also* United National Party *and* Sri Lanka.]

W. Howard Wriggins, *Ceylon: Dilemmas of a New Nation* (1960).

VIJAYA SAMARAWEERA

BANDE MATARAM ("I Salute Thee, Mother"), famous Indian nationalist song written by Bankim Chandra Chatterji. It appeared in his novel *Anandamath* in 1882. The song equated the mother goddess Kali with the motherland of India. It first reached popularity as both song and slogan during the protest over the partition of Bengal in 1905 and subsequently remained a popular nationalist song.

[*See also* Chatterji, Bankim Chandra.]

S. K. Bose, *Bankim Chandra Chatterji* (1974). Haridas Mukherjee and Uma Mukherjee, *'Bande Mataram' and Indian Nationalism (1906–1908)* (1957).

JUDITH E. WALSH

BANDUNG CONFERENCE, held in Bandung, Indonesia, from 18 to 25 April 1955 and attended by representatives from twenty-nine Asian and African countries; among the most notable representatives were China's Zhou Enlai, India's Nehru, Egypt's Nasser, Indonesia's Sukarno, and Burma's

U Nu. The conference reflected the desire of many newly independent nations to play a larger role in international affairs, as well as their fear of dangerous worldwide consequences that could result from the growing tension between China and the United States. The conference's final declaration, though general in character, condemned the evils of "colonialism in all its manifestations" and emphasized the interdependence of freedom and peace. It also contained implicit criticism of both the Soviet Union and the United States.

George McT. Kahin, *The Asian-African Conference* (1956). Carlos P. Romulo, *The Meaning of Bandung* (1956). AUDREY R. KAHIN

BANEPA, hamlet lying about twenty-four kilometers east of the Kathmandu Valley in Nepal. Banepa is one of the seven important Newar historical settlements in that area, the six others being Panauti, Khadpu, Chaukot, Dhulikhel, Nala, and Sanga. It probably grew mainly as a trading outpost of Nepal en route to Tibet, hence perhaps its Newari name Bhotha (Tibet). It was a stronghold of a feudatory Rama family in the time of Jayasthitimalla (r. 1382–1395), and exchanged embassies with China's Ming rulers. Benepa enjoyed an independent existence in the fifteenth century but was soon annexed by Bhaktapur.

[*See also* Nepal *and* Newar.]

Luciano Petech, *Mediaeval History of Nepal* (1958). Mary Slusser, *Nepal Mandala: A Cultural Study of the Kathmandu Valley* (1982). PRAYAG RAJ SHARMA

BANERJEA, SURENDRANATH (1848–1925), leading moderate in the Indian National Congress. Although his admission to the Indian Civil Service in 1871 ended in dismissal, after 1875 Banerjea established himself in India as an educator, publisher, orator, and nationalist leader. Imprisoned twice by the British for nationalist activities, Banerjea was president of the Indian National Congress in 1895 and 1902. Following a disagreement with the extremist faction, he and other moderates left the Congress in 1918 and formed the National Liberal Federation of India. He won election to the Bengal Legislative Council in 1919 and in 1921 was knighted by the British government. Two years later he lost his government position to Chittaranjan Das's extremist faction, a loss that prompted his retirement from public life.

[*See also* Indian National Congress.]

Daniel Argov, *Moderates and Extremists in the Indian Nationalist Movement, 1883–1920* (1967). Surendranath Banerjea, *A Nation in the Making* (1925; reprint, 1963). S. K. Bose, *Surendranath Banerjea* (1968).

JUDITH E. WALSH

BANGKOK (also known as Krung Thep), largest city (1980 population, 4,711,000) and capital of Thailand.

A small fishing village that was given a fort to cover the river passage to Ayudhya in the seventeenth century, Bangkok leapt to prominence after the fall of Ayudhya in 1767, when King Taksin moved the capital to Thonburi, directly across the

FIGURE 1. *Wat Arun (Temple of Dawn), Bangkok.* The temple was built when King Taksin moved the capital from Ayudhya to the Bangkok area in 1767.

river. In 1782 King Rama I made Bangkok his capital.

For more than two centuries, Bangkok has been at the center of almost all aspects of Thai life. As Siam's chief port it received such heavy Chinese immigration that by 1900 it was predominantly a Chinese city. Bustling with commerce, it was the outlet for Siam's rice and teak exports and the port of entry for all the imports needed by a rapidly developing state. As the centralized bureaucracy mushroomed under the reign of King Chulalongkorn (1868–1910), the Thai qualities of the city were reasserted, and it became an aggressive center of modernization by means of bureaucracy. Still forty times more populous than Thailand's next largest city, Bangkok remains Thailand's administrative, economic, manufacturing, tourist, religious, and educational center, and it has sprawled to encompass much land belonging to neighboring provinces.

[*See also* Thailand; Taksin; *and* Chakri Dynasty.]

G. W. Skinner, *Chinese Society in Thailand* (1957). Alec Waugh, *Bangkok: The Story of a City* (1970). David K. Wyatt, *Thailand: A Short History* (1984).

DAVID K. WYATT

BANGLADESH, republic in South Asia. It became an independent state on 16 December 1971, following a civil war in East Pakistan. It was on that date that Pakistani forces surrendered to the Indian army, which had entered the conflict on the side of the Bangladeshi liberation forces. Prior to that date and after the independence of Pakistan on 14 August 1947, the area had been a province of Pakistan known first as East Bengal (1947–1955) and later as East Pakistan (1955–1971). Bangladesh approximates the Bengali-speaking portion of the former British Indian province of East Bengal and Assam (1905–1911).

Most of the area of Bangladesh (about 55,600 square miles) is made up of the flat deltaic regions of the mouths of the Ganges and Brahmaputra rivers. It contains alluvial, fertile soil interspersed with numerous waterways. Many of these are navigable by small boats and form an important means of transport. The Meghna River, rising in the southern slopes of the Assam hills, joins the other two river systems. There are few hilly areas, these mainly in the Chittagong hill tracts bordering India and Burma in the southeast, and along the northeastern border with India. Only in the southeast, along the Karnaphuli River, is a site, now developed, suitable for hydroelectric power. Chittagong harbor serves as the principal seaport, with a second port at Chalna anchorage near Khulna in the southwest.

The population of Bangladesh was estimated in mid-1983 to be 95.5 million. The growth rate was estimated at 2.3 percent, giving an expected population in 2000 of 141 million. The population density is more than 1,700 per square mile.

The people of Bangladesh are a mixture of several groups, the dominant being Bengalis, a branch of the Indo-Aryans who migrated to the subcontinent in the second millennium BCE. Little is known about the population preceding the Aryans, but it was probably Dravidian and relatively small in number. There is also a Mongoloid admixture, especially in the east. Tribal populations live in the Chittagong hill tracts and in the Sylhet and Mymensingh regions.

Bengali, an Indo-Iranian language, is spoken by almost all of the people. Tribal languages are used but most speakers also speak Bengali. Urdu, also an Indo-Iranian language, is used by less than 1 percent of the population, a group that migrated from Bihar to Bangladesh at the time of the partition of India in 1947; many have gone to Pakistan since 1971.

About 85 percent of the population is Muslim; most of the remainder is Hindu, with small numbers of Christians and Buddhists. Nearly all of the Muslims are Sunni; there are few Shi'ites of either the Ithna Ashari or Isma'ili sects. The majority of the Hindus are of the scheduled castes.

History. Little is known about the history of the area before about 300 BCE, when it is known to have formed the eastern extremity of the Maurya empire. During that period much of the population converted to Buddhism. The Gupta empire of the fourth and fifth centuries CE exacted tribute from Bengal, and between the decline of the Guptas and the rise of the emperor Harsha in the seventh century there was a kingdom based at Samtata (in present Chandpur District). Bengal became the center of an important force in India under the Pala dynasty (c. 750–1150), although during the period of greatest strength its capital was at Monghyr in Bihar. The Palas were Buddhists and encouraged that religion. This was reversed when the Senas overthrew the Palas and restored Brahmanic Hinduism. In 1202 the last major Sena ruler was expelled from his capital, Nadia, and effective control of the area passed to the Muslims. [*See* Pala Dynasty *and* Sena Dynasty.]

Bengal had a loose association with the sultanate of Delhi before becoming completely independent in 1341. The Muslim rulers of Bengal asserted their

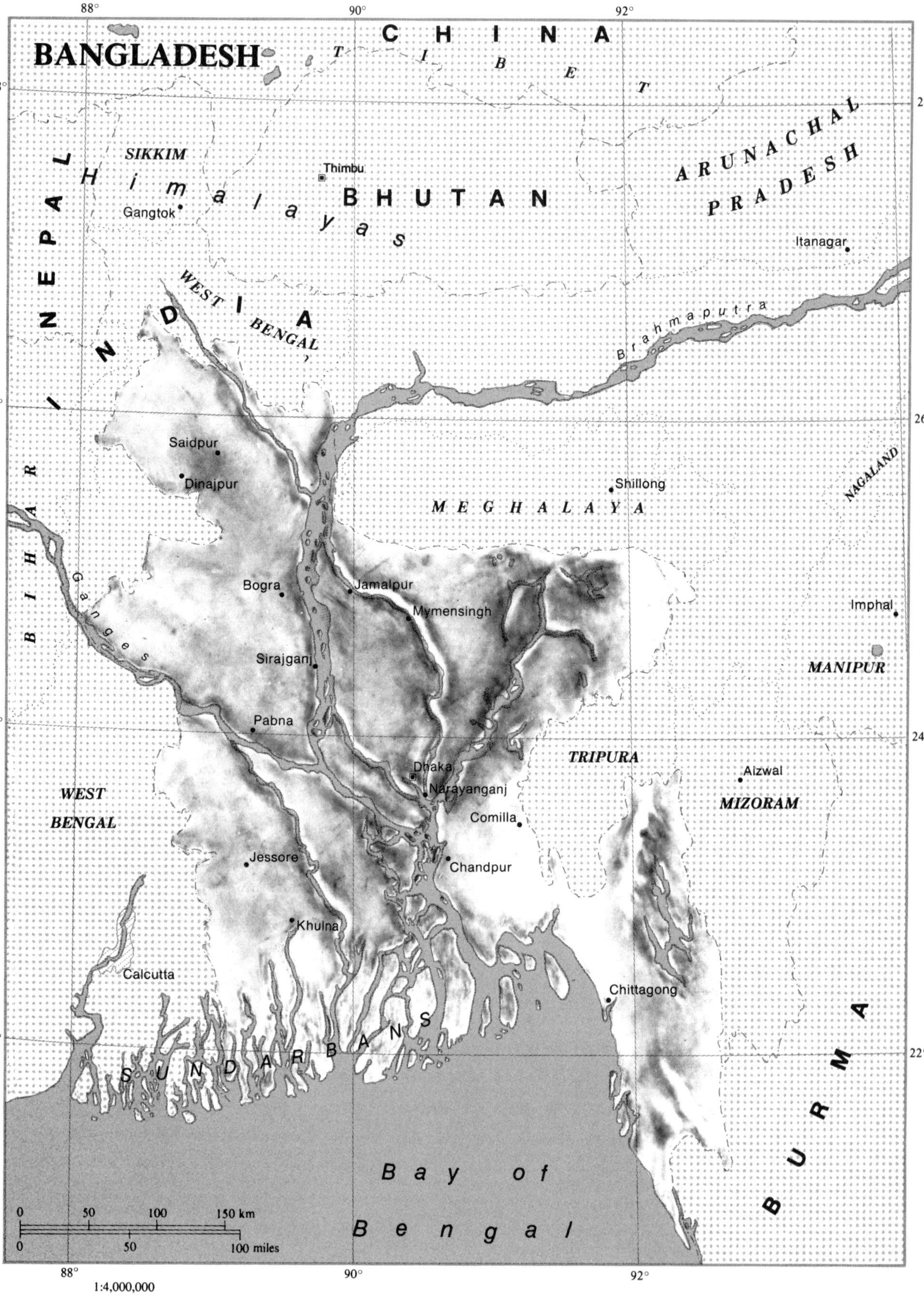
BANGLADESH
CHINA
TIBET
SIKKIM
Thimbu
Gangtok
Himalayas
BHUTAN
ARUNACHAL PRADESH
Itanagar
NEPAL
INDIA
WEST BENGAL
Brahmaputra
Saidpur
Dinajpur
Shillong
MEGHALAYA
NAGALAND
BIHAR
Ganges
Bogra
Jamalpur
Mymensingh
Imphal
MANIPUR
Sirajganj
Pabna
TRIPURA
Dhaka
Aizwal
Narayanganj
WEST BENGAL
MIZORAM
Comilla
Jessore
Chandpur
Khulna
Calcutta
Chittagong
SUNDARBANS
BURMA
Bay of Bengal
0 50 100 150 km
0 50 100 miles
88°
90°
92°
28°
26°
24°
22°
1:4,000,000

independence despite challenges until 1541, when the region was taken by Afghans. Dhaka was the capital during much of this period and continued to be so after the city was captured by forces of the Mughal emperor Akbar in 1576. The capital was moved to Murshidabad in 1704. The Mughal governors in Murshidabad became virtually independent rulers following the death of Aurangzeb in 1707. [*See* Akbar *and* Aurangzeb.]

In 1517 the Portuguese established a settlement at Chittagong, presaging the eventual control of the area by Europeans. The Dutch arrived in 1602 and the British in 1650, founding Calcutta in 1686. The British assured their full and permanent (until 1947) control of Bengal when Sir Robert Clive defeated the forces of the nawab of Bengal, Siraj ud-Daula, at Plassey (Pilasi) in January 1757. [*See* Portuguese: Portuguese in India; Dutch East India Company; *and* East India Company.]

The new city of Calcutta became the premier city of British India, eclipsing both Dhaka and Murshidabad in Bengal. [*See* Calcutta.] The area now comprising Bangladesh became very much a hinterland of the commercial and later industrial activities of Calcutta, supplying labor and raw materials (notably jute) to these enterprises. The Permanent Settlement (1793) during the first administration of Lord Charles Cornwallis worked greatly to the disadvantage of the Muslim peasants of eastern Bengal. [*See* Cornwallis, Charles.] The step transformed tax farmers into owners of the land (*zamindars*). Almost all of these were Hindus. Most of the few Muslims were non-Bengalis who had entered Bengal in the service of the Mughals. Eastern Bengal was little affected by the Sepoy Mutiny of 1857, as few Muslims were members of the Bengal army. The concept of "martial races" that developed after the mutiny, however, all but precluded later Bengali Muslim recruitment into the army and contributed to the great disparity between East and West Pakistanis in the Pakistan army. Muslim Bengalis were also very few in number in the civil services of India. [*See* Mutiny, Indian.]

Bengal was partitioned in 1905 and the seat of the province of East Bengal and Assam was Dhaka. Muslims were favorable to the creation of the new province as it was one with a Muslim majority. Strong objections by Hindus were met, however, in 1911 by the revocation of the Bengal partition and the creation of a new province of Bengal, one excluding Assam, Bihar, and Orissa. In 1906 the Muslim League was founded in Dhaka under the leadership of Nawab Salimullah of Dhaka.

Under the 1919 Government of India Act several Muslims were prominent in the Bengal government, including Abul Kasem Fazlul Huq, who in 1937, under the new constitutional act of 1935, became the first premier. Fazlul Huq headed the ministry in coalitions first with the Muslim League and then with non-Congress Hindus until 1943. He was followed by Khwaja Nazimuddin of the Muslim League and, after the 1946 election, by Husain Shahid Suhrawardy, then also of the Muslim League. In that election, seen as a referendum on Pakistan, Bengali Muslims voted 82 percent in favor of the Muslim League, the highest vote of any Muslim-majority province in India.

In 1947, the area became the province of East Bengal within Pakistan. A number of issues quickly divided the peoples of the two wings of Pakistan. Language was the most important of these, as Bengalis demanded equal status with Urdu for their mother tongue. Rioting in February 1952 left several dead but achieved the objective of linguistic equality. Other forms of parity were more difficult, such as in the civil and military services and especially in economic development. The Bengalis accepted parity in the Pakistan legislature but with the understanding that parity would be achieved in other areas.

When these goals were not reached, autonomist sentiment grew in East Pakistan (as the province was renamed in 1955). The Muslim League was heavily defeated in the 1954 provincial elections by a United Front, which included the Awami League of Suhrawardy and the Krishak Sramik Party of Fazlul Huq and made autonomy the foundation of its political manifesto. [*See* Awami League.] The military regime (1958–1962) and the controlled civilian government (1962–1969) of Muhammad Ayub Khan (president, 1958–1969) did nothing to lessen Bengali grievances. [*See* Ayub Khan, Mohammad.] These were addressed by the "six points" of Suhrawardy's successor, Sheikh Mujibur Rahman, in 1966. [*See* Mujibur Rahman, Sheikh.] The program formed the basis of the Awami League's election campaign in 1970; the Awami League won 160 of 162 national seats in East Pakistan, a number that was also a majority of the seats in all of Pakistan. Negotiations for the convening of an assembly to write a new constitution for Pakistan broke down. In March 1971 the Pakistan army began action against Bengalis, who now made independence their goal. After the entry of India into the civil war Bangladesh won independence with the surrender of the Pakistan army at Dhaka on 16 December 1971.

Bangladesh became a parliamentary democracy under the 1972 constitution, with Mujibur Rahman as prime minister. Economic problems, the difficulties of reconstruction, the collapse of law and order, and growing opposition led to the establishment of a civilian authoritarian single-party regime under Mujib in 1974 and 1975. Mujib was assassinated 14 August 1975 by dissident military officers. A short-lived regime was displaced following a series of rebellions in November 1975. The eventual leader of the new martial law government, General Ziaur Rahman, became president in April 1977 and was elected to the office in June 1978. He was assassinated 30 May 1981, and was succeeded by a civilian, Abdus Sattar. Sattar was ousted by the military led by General Husain Muhammad Ershad on 24 March 1982.

Administrative and Social Conditions. The 1972 constitution has been amended to create a modified presidential system, although martial law has been in effect since 1982. The constitution calls for a single-house parliament; a cabinet headed by a prime minister, appointed by the president but also responsible to the parliament; an independent judiciary; and a wide range of basic rights of the people. The last can be curtailed in periods of emergency or martial law.

Local government is headed both by elected officials and by appointed administrators. There are 64 districts; these are divided into 495 subdistricts *(upazillas),* which are the basic units of development. Some administration is based on a smaller unit, the union council, of which there are 4,472. In urban areas, councils and appointed administrators share in governing.

Under martial law political party activity is restricted but not banned. The Awami League was the governing party under Mujib and the principal opposition under Ziaur Rahman. The latter had a party formed to support him, the Bangladesh Nationalist Party. Both oppose the Ershad regime; a new party, the People's Party (JANODAL), gives its support to Ershad.

It is estimated that more than 70 percent of Bangladeshis live in conditions that are below the local poverty level. In 1982 the average Bangladeshi received 1,922 calories per day, or 83 percent of the recognized minimum requirement. Moreover, the bulk of this is in carbohydrates and there is a severe deficiency of protein in the diet. Health services are below standard, with one physician to 7,810 people; this condition exists especially in the urban areas (which in 1983 contained about 17 percent of the total population).

The labor force, severely underemployed, is largely agricultural (74 percent in 1981), with services accounting for 15 percent and industry 11 percent. However, the distribution of the gross national product in 1983 showed agriculture as contributing only 47 percent, services 40 percent, and industry 13 percent. The yearly per capita income in 1983 was US $130.

Economy. Rice is the most important crop; its production has increased considerably since the mid-1970s (to about 15 million tons in 1982/1983) but still falls short of the requirements. Jute is the principal cash and export crop, but production and exports have dropped as the fiber faces competition from synthetic materials. Tea is also exported. [*See also* Jute.]

The loss of West Pakistani capital and entrepreneurship and the doctrinaire insistence on state ownership by the Mujib regime hurt the industrial sector after independence, but there has been some recovery as the Ziaur Rahman and Ershad governments have encouraged both domestic and foreign private investment. The balance of trade showed a deficit of $713 million in 1983. Food accounted for 26 percent of imported goods.

Bangladesh received $568 million of gross capital inflow in 1983 and repaid $80 million of prior debt for a net inflow of $488 million. Debt service in the same year was 1.3 percent of the gross national product and 14.7 percent of exports.

The transport system remains primitive. Key to the system are the inland waterways that crisscross the country. Rail facilities are minimal and roads are also underdeveloped. Telecommunications have been improved with international satellite and microwave links.

[*See also* Dhaka; Bangladesh Nationalist Party; Bengal; *and* Pakistan.]

Kamruddin Ahmad, *A Socio-Political History of Bengal* (1975). Sufia Ahmad, *Muslim Community in Bengal, 1884–1912* (1974). Craig Baxter, *Bangladesh, a New Nation in an Old Setting* (1984). Just Faaland and J. R. Parkinson, *Bangladesh: Test Case of Development* (1976). Talukdar Maniruzzaman, *The Bangladesh Revolution and Its Aftermath* (1980). Humaira Momen, *Muslim Politics in Bengal* (1972). Charles Peter O'Donnell, *Bangladesh: Biography of a Muslim Nation* (1984). Shila Sen, *Muslim Politics in Bengal, 1937–1947* (1976).

CRAIG BAXTER

BANGLADESH NATIONALIST PARTY, political grouping created as a vehicle for the associates of President Ziaur Rahman in 1978. Zia had been elected president in June 1978 as the candidate of JANODAL (an acronym for the Bengali equivalent of "People's Party"). JANODAL and portions of the conservative Muslim League, the leftist National Awami Party (formerly led by Maulana Abdul Hamid Khan Bhashani), and several other smaller parties joined together to support Zia's nineteen-point development program. Justice Abdus Sattar, who succeeded Zia as president of the nation in 1981, was the titular leader of the party. It won 207 of the 300 directly elected seats in the parliamentary poll in February 1979. Since Zia's assassination in May 1981 and the coup that ousted Sattar in March 1982, the party has been led by Zia's widow, Begum Khalida Zia. It remains an important political force.

[*See also* Bangladesh *and* Rahman, Ziaur.]

Talukder Maniruzzaman, *The Bangladesh Revolution and Its Aftermath* (1980). CRAIG BAXTER

BANI SADR, ABU AL-HASAN (b. 1933), first president (1980–1981) of the Islamic Republic of Iran, but before and after that a political exile in France. Born in the western Iranian city of Hamadan to Ayatollah Hajj Sayyid Nasrollah Bani Sadr, a religious scholar of some standing, he formed his political ambitions early, predicting at the age of seventeen, it is said, that he would be the first president of post-shah Iran. He began studies of theology and economics at Tehran University and was at the head of a student delegation that met Prime Minister Amini in 1962. The following year, however, he was imprisoned for four months after participating in demonstrations; on his release he left for France to continue his studies. He concentrated on economics and sociology, studying these under the guidance of the Marxist scholar Paul Vieille. He also helped in organizing Iranian students in Paris hostile to the shah's regime. In early 1972 Bani Sadr had his first contact with Ayatollah Khomeini when he traveled to Najaf, Khomeini's place of exile, in order to attend the funeral of his father (the elder Bani Sadr had died in Beirut, and the body was brought to Najaf for burial). Thereafter Bani Sadr intensified his political activity, and he began to write a number of works on Islamic politics and economics.

In November 1978 Khomeini himself arrived in Paris, and Bani Sadr became a highly visible member of his entourage. Returning to Iran with Khomeini in February 1979, Bani Sadr was appointed to the Council of the Islamic Revolution. In July he was given the post of acting minister of economy and finance, and on 5 November, after the occupation of the United States embassy by Islamic militants and the resignation of the Bazargan government, he was appointed acting minister of foreign affairs. He soon extricated himself from the latter post and concentrated on preparations for the presidential elections due the following January. As a result of his intensive campaigning—as well as to disarray in the Islamic Republican Party—he received 10.7 million out of the 14.3 million votes cast on 25 January and was sworn in as first president of the Islamic Republic on 4 February 1980.

The size of Bani Sadr's victory was deceptive, however, and in the Majles, elected in two stages, that first met in May 1980 he had no organized support. Friction soon arose between him and a majority of its members, especially those associated with the Islamic Republican Party. Three persons he proposed to the Majles as candidates for prime minister were successively turned down, and in August he was obliged to accept the premiership of Mohammed Ali Rejai. One month later, Iraq attacked Iran, but the war served only to widen the gap between Bani Sadr and his opponents. In November, by denouncing the Islamic Republican Party in a series of speeches, he defied the orders of Khomeini that all parties should observe a political truce. In March 1981, when Bani Sadr ordered his personal guards to arrest hecklers at a meeting at Tehran University, he had reached a point of no return. The efforts of a conciliation committee were fruitless, and events moved swiftly to their denouement. On 10 June, Khomeini dismissed Bani Sadr from his post of commander in chief, and ten days later the Majles proclaimed him "politically incompetent," thus removing him from the presidency. Bani Sadr then went into hiding, and on 28 July he fled to Paris in the company of Mas'ud Rajavi, leader of the Mujahidin-i Khalq, to set up a "National Council of Resistance" and a government-in-exile. But these were ineffectual charades, for the Islamic Republic was able to surmount the crisis that occurred after many of its leading figures were assassinated by Rajavi's men. By contrast, the "National Council of Resistance" foundered when Rajavi had a friendly meeting in Paris with Iraqi officials and Bani Sadr found it politic, in April 1984, to distance himself from him.

Bani Sadr may be characterized as a man of acute ambition who fundamentally misread the climate of his homeland. His following was never firm and he was unequipped to compete with the charisma of the religious leadership.

[*See also* Bazargan, Mehdi; Hostage Crisis; *and* Khomeini, Ruhollah Musavi.]

S. Zabih, *Iran since the Revolution* (1983). S. Bakhash, *The Reign of the Ayatollahs* (1984).
HAMID ALGAR

BANNERS, Manchu military and social organization established by Nurhaci after 1601. Troops were organized into companies of three hundred men, and each company was enrolled into larger organizations known as banners (Manchu, *gusa;* Chinese, *qi*). At first there were four, distinguished by yellow, white, blue, and red banners. In 1615 Nurhaci doubled their number, creating banners identified by the same colors but with colored borders.

The banners became the basic administrative units of Manchu social, political, economic, and military organization and included civilians, serfs, slaves, and family members as well as soldiers. Banner organization crossed tribal lines, and banners were commanded by appointed officers. Under Abahai (Huang Taiji), Nurhaci's successor, Mongol and Chinese banners were established, comprising the Mongol and Chinese allies of the Manchus.

The fundamental organizational unit within the banner was the company. After the Manchu conquest of China in 1644, garrison companies were stationed in major cities and strategic places. Household companies were attached to the households of the emperor and the imperial clan. External companies supplied combat troops. When the banner forces proved ineffective against the rebellions and foreign incursions of the nineteenth century, the Qing government came to rely more and more on militias and local armies organized by provincial officials.

[*See also* Huang Taiji; Nurhaci; *and* Qing Dynasty.]

Lawrence Kessler, *K'ang-hsi and the Consolidation of Ch'ing Rule, 1661–1686* (1976). Franz Michael, *The Origin of Manchu Rule in China* (1942).
ROBERT ENTENMANN

BANTEN (commonly called Bantam in European sources), city located at the western end of the north coast of Java. Around 1524 it was founded as an Islamic trading and military base by forces led, according to semilegendary Javanese accounts, by Sunan Gunungjati, one of the nine *walis* ("apostles") of Javanese Islam. Throughout its history, Banten has been a devoutly Islamic area. In the mid-sixteenth century it conquered the pepper-producing Lampung district of South Sumatra; thereafter Banten became one of the main pepper ports of the Indonesian archipelago, attracting large numbers of Asian and European traders.

Hostilities broke out between Banten and the Dutch East India Company (VOC) even before the Dutch conquered Banten's vassal Jayakerta (Jakarta) in 1619 and renamed it Batavia, an acquisition that brought about still more fighting.

Under Sultan Ageng (or Sultan Tirtayasa, r. 1651–1683), Banten enjoyed something of a golden age. But dynastic conflict, combined with an ill-timed decision to renew warfare with the VOC in 1680, offered an opportunity for the VOC to intervene in 1682, resulting in VOC dominance of the state. Despite a rebellion against the VOC-based royal house in 1750, by 1751 the Dutch had restored their influence, though with some difficulty.

In the course of the nineteenth century Banten's agriculture was heavily exploited by means of the cultivation system (Kultuurstelsel) and by subsequent economic arrangements that were found throughout Java. Various social tensions resulted, which led in part to a peasants' revolt in Banten in 1888. In the early twentieth century the Indonesian Communist Party (PKI) maintained a staunchly Islamic style in Banten, which was one of the three main centers of the PKI uprising of November 1926. Subsequently, Bantenese were active in the Indonesian Revolution of 1945–1949. They have continued their strong commitment to the Islamic faith.

[*See also* Java; Pepper; Dutch East India Company; Batavia; Kultuurstelsel; Partai Komunis Indonesia; *and* Indonesian Revolution.]

Sartono Kartodirdjo, *The Peasants' Revolt of Banten in 1888* (1966). Th. G. Th. Pigeaud and H. J. de Graaf, *Islamic States in Java 1500–1700* (1976). M. C. Ricklefs, *A History of Modern Indonesia c. 1300 to the Present* (1981).
M. C. RICKLEFS

BAO DAI (b. 1914), last emperor (1926–1945) of the Nguyen dynasty in Vietnam. After 1932 he was permitted to exercise limited powers under the French colonial regime, but in August 1945 he was compelled to abdicate by representatives of the new Democratic Republic of Vietnam. Four years later he became chief of state in the French-dominated Associated State of Vietnam. Chief of state in South Vietnam after the Geneva Conference, he was defeated in a plebiscite by Prime Minister Ngo Dinh Diem in 1955 and retired from politics.

[*See also* Nguyen Dynasty; Vietnam, Democratic Republic of; *and* Ngo Dinh Diem.]

Joseph Buttinger, *Vietnam: A Dragon Embattled* (1967). Ellen J. Hammer, *The Struggle for Indochina, 1940–1955* (1955).

William J. Duiker

BAOJIA SYSTEM. The *baojia,* or "watch group," system represented the most sophisticated form of subbureaucratic social control in late imperial China (fourteenth to nineteenth century). Precedents date back to the Qin dynasty (221–206 BCE), but the modern use of this control apparatus was developed during the Song dynasty (960–1279) under the stewardship of the controversial reformer Wang Anshi (1021–1086). Wang's system was organized on the basis of numbers of households: ten households constituted a *bao,* and ten *bao* formed a *jia.* Each division chose a chief who bore the responsibility for those under his jurisdiction. Each household was required to contribute manpower to its division's militia. The system also encouraged mutual surveillance and responsibility from its membership to ensure local peace. The *baojia* relied on the disciplinary power of kinship groups and public opinion to keep order in the rural community. The peak of *baojia* effectiveness was reached during the Qianlong period (1736–1796) of the Qing dynasty (1644–1911). The chief innovation of this period was the "door sign" *(menpai)* that was hung outside each household containing information about the number of adult males residing within, including their names and occupations.

The *baojia* system was intended as a means to minimize the contact of the local community and the "official" government bureaucracy while at the same time providing an internal mechanism of social control. The program encountered difficulties in enforcement during the late Qing and could not fulfill the state's great expectations for control. However, it did function well enough to be continued in a modified form well into the twentieth century.

T'ung-tsu Ch'u, *Local Government in China under the Ch'ing* (1962). Kung-chuan Hsiao, *Rural China: Imperial Control in the Nineteenth Century* (1960). Frederick Wakeman, Jr., and Carolyn Grant, eds., *Conflict and Control in Late Imperial China* (1975). John R. Watt, *The District Magistrate in Late Imperial China* (1972).

Anita M. Andrew

BAOTOU, Chinese city located astride the upper reaches of the Yellow River and the largest industrial center in Inner Mongolia. In 1983 its population numbered 1,051,000. Prior to the twentieth century this area was largely rich, undeveloped grasslands used as pasture by deer and antelope from the nearby Daqing Mountains. From this use comes its Mongol name, Baoketu, or Deer Park. Baotou is located in a portion of Mongolia that has been controlled by numerous nomadic peoples including the Huns, the Xiongnu, the Tuoba, the Khitan, the Jurchen, and the Mongols. It has also served as an important hub on the Mongolian caravan routes.

C. R. Bawden, *The Modern History of Mongolia* (1968). Owen Lattimore, *Inner Asian Frontiers of China* (1951).

Sally Hart

BA PE (b. 1883), Burmese nationalist politician. Ba Pe was deeply involved in Burma's politics during the first half of the twentieth century. He was a founder of the Young Men's Buddhist Association (1906), the *Sun (Thuriya)* newspaper (1911), the General Council of Burmese Associations (1920), and the People's Party (1925); he was also a member of two delegations to London in 1919 and 1920 that demanded constitutional reforms for Burma. He took part in the India Round Table Conference in 1931 and was also minister for Forests and Home Affairs during the 1930s. When the British returned to Burma in 1945, Ba Pe became a leading member of the Anti-Fascist People's Freedom League and served on the Governor's Executive Council. Retiring from politics in 1947, he continued as a spokesman for business interests and was confined for high treason between 1954 and 1958.

[*See also* Anti-Fascist People's Freedom League *and* People's Party of Burma.]

John F. Cady, *A History of Modern Burma* (1958).

Robert H. Taylor

BA PHNOM, a small hill in Prei Veng Province, southeastern Cambodia, and an important cult center. It was a significant religious site, typical of those associated with cults of mountain divinities widespread in Southeast Asia, until well into the twentieth century. In the 1870s it is known to have been a scene of human sacrifice. It may have been important in ancient times as well; G. Coedès proposed that the kingdom known as Funan was centered on Ba Phnom, but this has been disputed.

[*See also* Funan.]

David P. Chandler, *A History of Cambodia* (1983). Paul Wheatley, "The Mount of the Immortals: A Note on Tamil Cultural Influence in Fifth Century Indo-China," *Oriens Extremus,* 21 (1974): 97–109.

Ian W. Mabbett

BARANGAY, a pre-Spanish Philippine word for a community of families under a local chieftain, or *datu*. Suggesting a maritime origin (a *balangay*, or *barangay*, is a kind of sailing ship), it was applied by the Spaniards to the administrative subdivision of a municipality *(pueblo)*. It consisted of a group of families (usually numbering between thirty and one hundred) whose tribute payments and labor services were the responsibility of a hereditary (later appointed) head, the *cabeza de barangay*, who was the lowest official of the Spanish colonial bureaucracy.

From 1900 on, the *barangay* increasingly became a territorial unit and was eventually replaced in official usage by the term *barrio* ("village"). *Barrios* developed around *poblaciones*, small, rural towns founded by the Spaniards, and eventually were further divided into *sitios*, or "hamlets."

During the reorganization of local government in 1973, the term *barangay* was revived. Today it designates an officially recognized administrative institution, resembling an assembly or council, of a village or of an urban or suburban district of a municipality or city under an elected official, the *kapitan ng barangay*.

[*See also* Barrio *and* Principalia.]

MICHAEL CULLINANE

BARANI, ZIA UD-DIN (c. 1285–1357), distinguished Indo-Muslim historian whose *Tarikh-i Firoz Shahi* was an important source of information for and about the Delhi sultans. Barani had been a courtier of Muhammad bin Tughluq (r. 1325–1351) and was known for his brilliant conversation. He fell on difficult times when Firoz Shah Tughluq (r. 1351–1388) came to the throne. Barani's extant works include the above-mentioned *Tarikh*, which contains advice and accounts concerning the sultans from Balban (r. 1266–1286) to the early years of Firoz Shah; the *Fatawa-i-Jahandari*, containing his recommendations on the political theory of the Delhi sultanate; the *Na't-i Muhammadi*, on the life of the Prophet; and the *Akhbar-i Barmakiyyan*, his Persian translation of an Arabic account of the Barmakids. Barani had a rare historical perception of character and is unique in his analysis of men and movements, although he has been criticized for the extreme subjectivity of his views.

[*See also* Delhi Sultanate *and* Tughluq Dynasty.]

P. Hardy, *Historians of Medieval India: Studies in Indo-Muslim Historical Writing* (1960), pp. 20–39. Khaliq Ahmad Nizami, *On History and Historians of Medieval India* (1983), pp. 124–140.

KHALIQ AHMAD NIZAMI

BARISAN SOSIALIS (Socialist Front), founded in Singapore in July 1961 by thirteen procommunist People's Action Party (PAP) assemblymen who had broken away from PAP because they had failed to win its ideological soul. Although it initially attracted grass-roots Chinese support, the Barisan declined rapidly after many of its leaders were detained indefinitely. In 1965 it suffered its greatest defeat: it failed to deter the electorate from endorsing the merger proposals. Thereafter the party became divided over whether to take the parliamentary road to power. It boycotted the 1968 election in favor of so-called street democracy, contested the 1972 election unsuccessfully, and today is virtually moribund.

[*See also* Singapore *and* People's Action Party.]

T. J. Bellows, *The PAP of Singapore: Emergence of a Dominant Party System* (1970). STANLEY BEDLINGTON

BARODA, one of the three leading Maratha states along with Gwalior and Indore. This Indian princely state began with the appointment of Damaji Rao Gaekwar as the deputy commander of the Maratha army. The Gaekwars pushed the Mughal forces from Gujarat and moved their capital to Baroda in 1766. The state first entered treaty relations with the British East India Company in 1772 and consolidated a client-patron relationship with the British in several subsequent treaties. [*See also* Marathas.]

Under the able leadership of Maharaja Sayaji Rao III (r. 1881–1939), an adopted heir, the state became known for its progressive policies. These included a legislative council (1903), universal primary education (1906), and state support for commercial development, including an extensive railway system. Baroda was integrated into Bombay state of independent India in 1950 and became part of Gujarat state in 1960.

[*See also* Gujarat *and* Princely States.]

Ian Copland, *The British Raj and the Indian Princes: Paramountcy in Western India, 1857–1930* (1982). Stanley Rice, *Life of Sayaji Rao III, Maharaja of Baroda* (1931). BARBARA N. RAMUSACK

BARRIO, Spanish word used in the Philippines to mean "place of settlement" or "village." The *barrio* became a territorial subunit of the municipality *(pueblo)* but did not possess administrative function. By the nineteenth century, most *barrios* had fairly well defined boundaries and were often subdivided into smaller hamlets *(sitios)*. Eventually, the *barrio* became unofficially merged with the local administrative unit, the *barangay,* and eventually the two terms were used interchangeably.

After 1900, *barrio* became the term adopted for the lowest unit in Philippine local government, headed by a *capitán de barrio* (or *kapitan ng baryo*). The term *barrio* continued in official usage until 1973, when it was replaced by *barangay.*

[*See also* Barangay.]

Michael Cullinane

BASCO Y VARGAS, JOSE DE, governor-general of the Philippines (1778–1787). During his nine-year rule of the Philippines, Jose Basco y Vargas Valderrama y Rivera encouraged widespread development of agriculture, commerce, and industry. Trade restrictions were lifted, tobacco was cultivated seriously, the Royal Philippine Company began operations, and the Economic Society of Manila was founded. Basco y Vargas was a true Bourbon reformer, a product of the eighteenth-century revolution in Spain.

Soon after his arrival in the Philippines, Basco published his "General Economic Development Plan," designed to stimulate private enterprise so that it would exploit the country's natural resources. Incentives were offered for agriculture, mining, and silk production, and instructions were circulated concerning the latest methods of cotton and silk raising and silk production. Basco called for a radical change in the home government's attitude toward the Philippines' economic life and proposed a system of trade that would allow only Philippine-produced goods to be exported to Spain from Asia. His efforts toward development prepared the way for the agricultural and commercial progress of the nineteenth century.

[*See also* Philippines *and* Spain and the Philippines.]

Nicholas P. Cushner

BA SWE (b. 1915), prominent Burmese nationalist politician. Ba Swe was a leader of the All-Burma Students Union in the late 1930s and was arrested by the British for leading a peasants' march on Rangoon. He was a founder of the People's Revolution Party in 1940 and an official in the government of Dr. Ba Maw (1942–1945). After his arrest by the Japanese in 1945 for involvement in the Anti-Fascist Organization, he became a leader of the Anti-Fascist People's Freedom League (AFPFL) and first president of the Burma Socialist Party. Strongly anti-Communist and a key trade union figure, he served in many cabinets during the 1950s and was prime minister in 1956–1957. After the split of the AFPFL in 1958, he was a leader of the so-called Stable faction but lost political influence following the elections in 1960.

[*See also* Anti-Fascist People's Freedom League *and* Ba Maw.]

Frank N. Trager, *Burma: From Kingdom to Republic* (1966).

Robert H. Taylor

BATAK, Indonesian people whose original homeland was in the uplands of the present province of North Sumatra. The Batak can be regarded as a single people, incorporating several ethnic and linguistic subgroups. The largest of these, the Toba Batak, inhabited mountain valleys near Lake Toba. North of them were the Pakpak (Dairi), Karo, and Simalungun and south were the Angkola and Mandailing Batak—all of whom speak Batak dialects, some mutually unintelligible. The patrilineal kinship system is dominant among all Batak groups, and all observe as custom the *marga,* or exogamous patrilineal clan. Traditionally, the village has been the major governing territorial unit of the Toba, but some other Batak groups (notably the Karo) have had larger administrative units, often village confederations ruled by rajas.

The Batak uplands were generally isolated until the mid-nineteenth century, when Protestant missionaries, the Dutch government, and the lowland plantation agriculture encroached on them simultaneously. Most Karo and Simalungun were administratively incorporated into the East Coast Residency, while the others were included in Tapanuli. About half the Toba became Christians, as did numbers of Simalungun and other North Tapanuli Bataks. The southern Angkola and Mandailing are largely Muslim, having been converted by the Paderi in the early 1800s. Many other Batak retained their traditional religions. (The 1930 census recorded 345,408 Muslims, 299,856 Christians, and 512,327 "pagans" among the Batak.)

Before 1940, members of ruling lineages held most of the positions of prestige, but their legitimacy was largely repudiated by peasants during the independence revolution (1945–1950), which saw widespread violence among Batak of both Tapanuli and East Sumatra. In its aftermath there were massive migrations, particularly of Toba, to the former plantation lands of East Sumatra.

[*See also* Indonesia, Republic of.]

Clark E. Cunningham, *The Postwar Migration of the Toba-Bataks to East Sumatra* (1958). J. Keuning, *The Toba Batak, Formerly and Now*, translated by Claire Holt (1958). R. S. and R. D. Kipp, eds., *Beyond Samosir* (1983). R. W. Liddle, *Ethnicity, Party, and National Integration: An Indonesian Case Study* (1970).

AUDREY R. KAHIN

BATAVIA. *See* Jakarta.

BATTAMBANG, city in northwestern Cambodia, seat of Battambang Province. It has a population estimated (1980) at 50,000. Located at the western end of the Great Lake (Tonle Sap), Battambang Province has long been the most productive agricultural region of Cambodia, partly because of irrigation works and land-tenure patterns introduced during the era of Thai control (1794–1907). The Thai regained control of the region from 1941 to 1946. A Communist-led rebellion against Prince Norodom Sihanouk broke out in rural Battambang in 1967. The city was forcibly evacuated by Pol Pot in 1975 but regained its importance after 1979 under the Vietnamese-backed regime of Heng Samrin.

[*See also* Cambodia.]

DAVID P. CHANDLER

BAYINNAUNG (r. 1551–1581), Burma's most celebrated warrior-king and one of the most successful monarchs in the history of Southeast Asia. Contemporary Europeans claimed, perhaps with some exaggeration, that within East Asia his military strength was second only to that of the Chinese emperor.

Bayinnaung ruled the First Toungoo empire, centered on Pegu, in Lower Burma, which had been founded by his brother-in-law Tabinshweihti. Like Tabinshweihti, Bayinnaung was determined to seize the profit of the expanding maritime trade by forcing rival coastal states, most notably Siam, into a position of vassalage. Bayinnaung also shared Tabinshweihti's esteem for Portuguese firearms. But whereas his predecessor had attempted to extend Lower Burma's authority directly along the Southeast Asian littoral, Bayinnaung recognized the necessity of first subduing Upper Burma and the interior Tai-speaking areas. This Bayinnaung accomplished with breathtaking rapidity between 1554 and 1558, thanks to both lavish use of firearms and tactical concentrations of superior manpower. In a wider sense it has been suggested that growing commercial exchanges between the ports of Lower Burma and interior supply centers helped pave the way to political unification. The campaigns of 1554–1558 were of decisive importance, for they ended over 260 years of fragmentation within the Irrawaddy River basin and inaugurated an era of permanent lowland control over the nearer Tai states. At the same time, these conquests afforded Bayinnaung indispensable demographic and strategic advantages for his Siamese ventures. Between 1563 and 1569 Siam, together with its peninsular ports, fell under Lower Burma's control.

Military success, however, was not accompanied by the creation of administrative mechanisms by which the domain could be securely integrated. As it expanded, the First Toungoo empire became an ever more loosely controlled assemblage of principalities, held in orbit by personal ties to the high king and by the threat of chastisement. Siam and other outlying states successfully asserted their independence on Bayinnaung's death.

[*See also* Burma; Nandabayin; Tabinshweihti; Toungoo Dynasties; *and* Thailand.]

G. E. Harvey, *A History of Burma from the Earliest Times* (1925; reprint, 1967). Victor B. Lieberman, *Burmese Administrative Cycles: Anarchy and Conquest, c. 1580–1760* (1984). Maung Htin Aung, *A History of Burma* (1967).

VICTOR B. LIEBERMAN

BAZARGAN, MEHDI (b. 1905), prime minister of Iran in 1979. As a young man, Bazargan studied engineering in Paris, and although he maintained a strong commitment to Islam, he attempted to ally it with technological progress. He returned to Iran in 1936 and remained active in Islamic causes, while also becoming closely involved with Mohammed Mossadegh and the National Front.

Under Mossadegh, Bazargan managed Iranian oil policy and later founded the Freedom of Iran movement. As a consistent critic of the shah, he became heavily involved in the Islamic Revolution. In 1977 he founded the Iranian Committee for the Defense of Liberty and Human Rights. He was later arrested for his political activities but was soon released. Late in 1978 Bazargan flew to Paris to meet with Ayatollah Khomeini and to negotiate a policy of opposition to the government of the shah. On 11 February 1979, after Khomeini's return to Iran and the subsequent revolution Bazargan was named prime minister. Soon afterward he referred to his role in the new government as "like that of a knife without a blade," and in mid-November 1979 he resigned. At present Bazargan lives in Tehran, where he is a member of the Majles (parliament).

[*See also* Khomeini, Ruhollah Musavi.]

Oriana Fallaci, "Everybody Wants to Be Boss," *The New York Times Magazine,* 28 October 1979. Jerrold D. Green, *Revolution in Iran: The Politics of Countermobilization* (1982).

JERROLD D. GREEN

BE, also known as *tomo,* the predominant form of economic organization in Japan from about 450 CE until the early eighth century. A *be* consisted of peasants or craftsmen who delivered tribute such as cloth, weapons, labor, fish, or grain to the Yamato court or one of the various aristocratic groups known as *uji.* Sometimes translated as "guild," the term *be* is actually Korean in origin, and many *be* were comprised of skilled Korean artisans who fled the wars on the continent.

Be were of two types: those belonging to the court and those serving *uji.* Every *be* was overseen by a bureaucrat known as a *tomo no miyatsuko.* The tie between a *tomo no miyatsuko* and a *be* was hereditary. Some of the more common *uji-be* pairs included the Ōtomo *uji,* who oversaw the palace guards known as the *yugei* ("quiver bearers"), and the Mononobe *uji,* who managed a *be* of warriors also called *mononobe.* In addition, certain *be* were established in the sixth century to supply the needs of the Yamato king and his family. These *be* were called *koshiro* and *nashiro* and might be named after an office (*oshisakabe,* or the queen's *be*) or an individual (*Anahobe,* or King Anaho's *be*). *Be* called *tabe* also worked the king's land. Little is known of the *uji*-administered *be,* but a few examples include the *Sogabe* (affiliated with the Soga) and the *Nakatomibe* (with the Nakatomi).

In 645 the Taika Coup took place, and the court, led by Prince Naka (later Emperor Tenji, r. 668–671), declared its intention to do away with the *be* and substitute head taxes, after the Chinese model. Emperor Tenji first attempted to place restrictions on the *be* held by aristocratic *uji* in 664. Later, Emperor Temmu announced the abolition of all such *be* in 675. The effectiveness of both pronouncements is difficult to judge; *be* of highly specialized craftsmen *(shinabe)* continued to serve the Nara court throughout the eighth century.

[*See also* Uji.]

Cornelius Kiley, "State and Dynasty in Archaic Yamato," *Journal of Asian Studies* 33 (November 1973): 25–49. George Sansom, *A History of Japan to 1334* (1958).

WAYNE FARRIS

BEHISTUN, the cliff in Iran on the main road from Kermanshah to Hamadan, 39 kilometers east of the former, where Darius the Achaemenid king carved his inscription about his rise to power in 520 BCE. The name is derived from *Bagastana,* "place of the god," and at present is called Bisutun. Presumably, Behistun is where Darius killed the ruler Gaumata, his first opponent, and thus established his claim to the Achaemenid throne. The long inscription in Elamite, Akkadian, and Old Persian provided the key to the decipherment, in the first half of the nineteenth century, of these languages written in cuneiform characters. As an important Persian historical source, the inscription also is a counterpart to information in Herodotus about the accession of Darius. In the Sasanid period a palace existed here, but in Islamic times it was only a village.

RICHARD N. FRYE

BEIJING, the capital of the People's Republic of China, previously served as the capital and principal residence of the emperors of the Ming (1368–1644) and Qing (1644–1911) dynasties. A capital city has stood on the site of modern Beijing since 938, when the Khitan Liao emperor Taizong (r. 927–947) built his southern capital on the ruins of the Tang dynasty (618–907) prefectural city of Youzhou, which lay in what corresponds to the southwest quadrant of the present city. The succeeding Jurchen Jin dynasty (1115–1234) destroyed the Liao city and between 1150 and 1152 rebuilt a larger capital on the same site. After 1190 the Jin emperors regularly summered at a palace complex to the north of their capital, on a site to the northwest of the present Forbidden City. This region had been a marsh; under the Liao and Jin the marsh was drained into a lake, and earth from the excavation was used to build an artificial mountain in the lake. The Jin summer palaces were built on this mountain and around the lake. These buildings were later incorporated into the capital city of the succeeding Mongolian Yuan dynasty (1279–1368), which built its southern capital around the Jin summer palaces.

In 1215 the Jin capital was beseiged by the Mongols, and by 1216 it had been sacked, burned, and razed. Virtually nothing remained where the city once stood. In 1264 the Mongol emperor Kublai (r. 1260–1294) decided to rebuild the walls of the Jin city and to designate it as the site of his southern capital. His principal architect persuaded him to renovate the Jin summer palaces first and to build his capital around them, however, for in this way he would have a place to reside while his imperial palace was under construction. Work on the city wall of the Yuan capital began in 1267, work on the audience halls began in 1272, and in 1274 the emperor held his first audience in this new capital, called Dadu, the "great capital."

The Yuan city and palaces were built on the model of the Jin capital, which had in turn been loosely modeled on the Northern Song (960–1126) capital. The city was oriented on a north–south axis and enclosed by a rectangular tamped earth wall. In the southern part of this enclosure lay the Yuan imperial palace. This palace was larger in scale than the Ming and Qing palaces. It comprised two palace complexes of almost equal size, which were situated on the east and west sides of the lake. The palaces on the west housed the empress dowager, the imperial consorts, and for a short time the heir apparent, while the walled palace city on the east contained the residence of the emperor and empress and the audience halls. The entire complex was then surrounded by the wall of the imperial city. Although almost nothing of the Yuan palaces remains, it is clear from written records that the city was grander and more elaborate than the Ming and Qing capitals.

Marco Polo arrived in the Yuan southern capital, which he called Cambaluc (from the Mongolian *khanbaliq* or "city of the ruler"), in 1275 and was very impressed by its scale and beauty. The palace of the emperor was, according to his description, "the greatest and most wonderful that ever was seen." Marco Polo arrived in Dadu while construction was still underway, for the city walls were finished only in 1292, and the walls around the imperial palaces only in 1296. Construction on the palaces continued into the 1340s. In fact, the Mongol emperors stopped using felt tent palaces in the imperial city only in 1352, fifteen years before the end of the Yuan dynasty.

The water supply and water transport to the city were greatly improved during the Yuan dynasty. Water from the hills to the north and west was channeled southwest into the city to ensure that there would be a sufficient supply for the moats; this water was also used to irrigate lands to the north and west. In 1293 a canal was dredged from the east of the city to the northern terminus of the transport canal at Tongzhou; this eliminated the need to carry grain overland for about fifteen miles. After these large irrigation and construction projects were finished, the city was far more accessible and could support a larger population than before. Such improvements made it possible for the third emperor of the succeeding Ming dynasty to establish it as his northern capital (which is what Beijing literally means) in 1403.

The armies of the succeeding Ming dynasty entered Dadu in 1368. Zhu Yuanzhang (r. 1368–1398), the founder of the Ming dynasty, rose to power in the Yangtze delta, and he consequently established his capital there. During his reign the city was made a prefectural seat and served as the principal garrison on the northern frontier. First of all, the city was reduced in size. The northern wall of the Ming city was rebuilt to the south of the Yuan city's northern wall, and the northern third of the Yuan city was abandoned. The city walls now formed a square. Some of the Yuan palaces were dismantled to provide building materials for the first Ming capitals at Nanjing and Fengyang. The remaining palaces became the seat of Zhu Di, the prince of Yan, who subsequently became the Yongle emperor (r. 1402–1424).

When the founder of the Ming dynasty died in 1398, he was succeeded by his grandson. Late in 1398 this young man's advisers launched a campaign to strip his uncles (such imperial princes as Zhu Di) of their military powers, a policy that led to civil war. In 1402, after several years of fighting, the prince of Yan's armies entered Nanjing in triumph. During the last days of the war the palace compound in Nanjing had burned down. It made little difference, however, because the prince of Yan (who was now the Yongle emperor) never intended to reside in Nanjing. He had lived in Beijing since 1380; his base of power was in the north, and he intended to locate his capital there. Since he could not totally abandon his father's capital at Nanjing, early in 1403 he decided to have two capitals: Beijing in the North and Nanjing in the South.

Work on the walls and palaces of the northern capital began in 1406 and continued without interruption until the death of the prince of Yan in 1424. It is difficult to imagine the monumental scale of this undertaking. In the course of this building project, almost 200,000 artisans and as many as one million people were conscripted to carry out the work. The work force was made up from convicts, military conscripts, and common people sent in rotation to work in Beijing. Modern scholars have estimated that more than 20 million bricks were required to pave the palace courtyards and more than 80 million to face the city walls and gate towers (in all about 1.93 million tons of brick). The largest blocks of stone used in the imperial causeways leading to audience halls and palaces weighed as much as 300 tons and were dragged overland from a quarry about 25 miles southwest of Beijing. (In the 1590s, when one of the palaces was being rebuilt, it took more than 20,000 conscripted laborers twenty-eight days to haul just one 180-ton block to Beijing.)

The Ming capital also comprised three walled cities. The outer walls enclosed the capital proper; within these walls, another set of walls enclosed the imperial city; and within the imperial city, another set of walls enclosed the palace city, which in Ming and Qing times was referred to as the Forbidden City. The Forbidden City, which covered about 250 acres, contained the audience halls and residential palaces of the emperor, the empress, and other members of the imperial family. The imperial city, which covered an area about six times larger than the Forbidden City, contained the offices of the eunuch bureaucracy that ran the palace, warehouses, workshops, stables, and pleasure palaces. The western portion of the imperial city, which was known in Ming times as the "west park," served as a place of retreat for the emperors. During both the Ming and Qing dynasties building went on almost without interruption in the west park, and over the course of five centuries it was covered with palaces, verandas, belvederes, pavilions, temples, walkways, and gardens (see figure 1).

There were two main differences between the Yuan and Ming cities. First, in 1419 the Yongle emperor ordered the southern wall of the capital moved farther south, because he felt the approach to the palace was not majestic enough. A new enclosed passage, the imperial causeway, was then built from the southern gate of the imperial city to the main gate in the southern city wall. Second, the main palaces in Beijing were modeled on the palaces in Nanjing and built in groups of three, whereas the Yuan palaces were built in groups of two, with a covered passage linking an audience palace and a residential palace.

The Yongle emperor first used Beijing as a base for his campaigns into the Mongolian steppe. During the first decade of his reign a large standing army was quartered around the city, and much of the revenue and grain delivered to Beijing went to support it. He was at first content to have two capitals, for Beijing was under construction and was not yet

FIGURE 1. *Summer Palace.* Now converted to a public park, the Summer Palace was formerly reserved for the exclusive use of the imperial family.

ready to house the imperial court. In 1416, during a trip to Nanjing, however, he made it clear that he intended to designate Beijing as the principal capital of the empire. This policy met with widespread opposition, for moving the court to the North raised many logistical problems, and officials from the South were loathe to make the move. The emperor insisted, however, and late in 1420 he ordered that henceforth Beijing would be the capital of the empire and the seat of the imperial court.

In May 1421, less than six months later, a great fire destroyed the principal audience halls in the Forbidden City, which had just been completed. Arson cannot be ruled out: there was still widespread opposition to a capital in the North. After the Yongle emperor died in 1424, his successor began to refer to Beijing as his temporary residence, and there was again discussion about returning the court to Nanjing. Nothing ever came of this; although Beijing was referred to as a temporary imperial residence between 1425 and 1441, construction on walls, gate towers, moats, and bridges continued. In 1440 work began again on the palaces that had burned down in 1421, and when they were finished in 1441, Beijing was once again designated the capital of the Ming empire.

Other parts of the Forbidden City were destroyed by fire later in the Ming dynasty. In 1514 the entire residential compound burned down. The Zhengde emperor (r. 1506–1521), who staged mock battles in the palace, had stored gunpowder in the courtyards. The gunpowder accidentally exploded, and the palaces caught on fire. The rebuilding took seven years. In 1557 the audience palaces and the main gate to the Forbidden City were destroyed in a fire that began during a storm; in this instance the rebuilding took five years. Finally, in 1596 the residential palaces were again damaged by fire. The records of this rebuilding provide the only detailed accounts of the expense of Ming palace construction: the palaces were rebuilt in two years at a cost of 730,000 ounces of silver.

Most of the other major construction projects undertaken during the Ming dynasty were carried out under the Jiajing emperor (r. 1522–1566). In 1530 he ordered that a new altar to Heaven (Tiantan) be built slightly to the south of the altar then in use (see figure 2). He also built other altars: to the earth in the north, to the moon in the west, and to the sun in the east. In 1553 he had an earthen wall built around the southern suburbs of the city, for in 1550 the Mongol prince Altan (1507–1582) had raided Beijing and had looted and burned the suburbs. Since it was possible that he might raid again, the

FIGURE 2. *Tiantan.* Located on the southern compass point of the layout of Beijing, the Tiantan (Temple of Heaven) is noted for its circular form atop a square base, symbolizing Heaven and earth, respectively. The temple served as an imperial altar where rites were performed to seek good harvests and to atone for the sins of the people.

emperor approved a plan to protect the southern suburb, which was the wealthiest and most populous area outside the city (and the site of the new Tiantan), with an earthen wall. Henceforth, the old city was called the northern city and the area enclosed by the new wall the southern city. The walls of the northern city ran 4 miles from east to west and 3.5 miles north to south; the walls of the southern city ran 5 miles from east to west and 1.75 miles from north to south.

In 1644 the armies of the succeeding Qing dynasty entered Beijing. Four years later the Chinese populace in the northern city was relocated in the southern city, and the northern city was then populated by Manchus. For this reason the northern city was subsequently referred to as the Tartar or Manchu city and the southern city as the Chinese city.

The Qing emperors simply took over the Ming capital. The Manchus inherited a well-supplied, well-fortified metropolis that rivaled in splendor the greatest cities of South China. Although such cities as Constantinople may have equaled it in size at some points in the seventeenth century, from about 1450 until 1800 (when it was eclipsed by London), Beijing was the largest city in the world. It was, as many seventeenth- and eighteenth-century European travelers and diplomats attested, far larger and grander than any European capital. The city reached its heyday under the Qing during the reign of the Qianlong emperor (r. 1736–1795). For more than half a century this emperor renovated, rebuilt, repaired, or restored almost everything in the city: construction projects and public works were constantly underway.

European armies first entered Beijing in 1860 to force the Qing court to ratify the treaty that had ended the Opium Wars and thereby to gain the right to trade and reside in China on terms suitable to their governments. Unable to take the imperial city, French and British forces sacked and looted the summer palaces to the northwest instead. In 1900, when the armies of several Western powers and Japan arrived to suppress the Boxer Uprising, the Forbidden City was occupied and looted. During this uprising the principal offices of the civil administration, which were located just south of the imperial city, were destroyed by fire. The entire area was subsequently made the Legation Quarter under the treaty of 1900. The first extensive photographic survey of the imperial palaces, prepared at this time for the Japanese imperial household, shows the buildings and courtyards in a state of general disrepair.

From 1912 until 1928 Beijing was the capital of the new Republican government, although in fact the city successively fell under the control of a number of warlords. In 1928, after the Nationalist armies of Chiang Kai-shek had defeated the last of these warlords, Nanjing (where Chiang's armies were headquartered) became the capital of the Republic of China. Beijing was then known as Beiping ("northern peace") and served as the principal Nationalist garrison in North China. Between 1937 and 1945 the city was occupied by the Japanese; from 1945 until 1949 it reverted to the Nationalist government. In 1949 the Communist armies of Mao Zedong entered the city, and since October 1949 Beijing has been the capital of the People's Republic of China.

Since the establishment of the People's Republic Beijing has developed as an administrative and industrial center. Its population exceeds 9 million (1982). The old city walls have been torn down to be replaced by broad avenues and a subway line. Apartment houses have been constructed in large numbers. The old imperial palace is now a public park and museum complex. The ceremonial center of China has been moved to the great square just south of the old imperial city (see figure 3). The square is framed by the Gate of Heavenly Peace

FIGURE 3. *Tiananmen Square.* Facing the Forbidden City, Tiananmen is the world's largest public square. Built after the establishment of the People's Republic in 1949, it has been the site of official parades and demonstrations as well as popular protests.

(Tiananmen) on the north, the Great Hall of the People on the west, historical museums on the east, and a remaining city gate on the south. Parades move across the northern end of the square along Chang'an Boulevard, which runs east to west. In the center of the square stands the Monument to the People's Heroes. The southern end of the square is occupied by the Mao Zedong Memorial Hall, containing the body of the founding leader of the People's Republic of China.

[*See also* Ming Dynasty *and* Qing Dynasty.]

L. C. Arlington and W. M. Lewisohn, *In Search of Old Peking* (1935). Edward L. Farmer, *Early Ming Government: The Evolution of Dual Capitals* (1976). James Geiss, *Peking under the Ming, 1368–1644* (1979). Osvald Sirén, *The Walls and Gates of Peking* (1924) and *The Imperial Palaces of Peking,* 3 vols. (1926). William G. Skinner, ed., *The City in Late Imperial China* (1977). Nancy Schatzman Steinhardt, "The Plan of Khubilai Khan's Imperial City," *Artibus Asiae* 44 (1983): 137–158.

JAMES GEISS

BELL TRADE ACT, enacted by the US Congress in April 1946 and implemented by an executive agreement between presidents Harry Truman and Manuel Roxas on 4 July 1946. Although presumably designed to meet the needs of the Philippine economy in the difficult transition period following the grant of independence, the Bell Trade Act effectively maintained the islands' economic dependence on US capital and markets. According to its terms, Philippine exports received preferential treatment in return for restrictions on Philippine currency management and export controls and "national treatment" for American businessmen, granting them the same rights as Philippine nationals to exploit natural resources and to own and operate public utilities. A Trade Agreement Revision Act of 1956 partly removed these restrictions on Philippine sovereignty.

[*See also* Philippines; Roxas, Manuel; *and* Jones Act.]

Sung Yong Kim, *United States-Philippine Relations, 1946–1956* (1968). George E. Taylor, *The Philippines and the United States: Problems in Partnership* (1964).

RICHARD E. WELCH, JR.

BENARES. *See* Varanasi.

BENCOOLEN. *See* Bengkulu.

BENDAHARA, Melakan/Malay court title, now archaic. Generally the *bendahara* was considered the prime minister and was ranked second in the hierarchy, after the sultan. *The Code of Malacca* describes the *bendahara* as "he who rules the peasantry, the army and those dependent on the state. His sway extends over all the islands and it is he who is the King's lawgiver." The exact status of the office varied over time. In 1512 it was held by the sultan's younger brother, Mutahir, who was also the heir apparent. At other times (e.g., 1699) it was held by the most important lineage chief. In the early nineteenth century the last *bendahara,* under the Johor/Riau sultanate, was actually a territorial chief who ruled Pahang. His descendants were recognized as sultans of Pahang in 1890.

[*See also* Johor; Pahang; *and* Abdul Jalil Riayat Syah.]

T. J. Newbold, *British Settlements in the Straits of Malacca* (1971).

CARL A. TROCKI

BENGAL, the region in South Asia where the Bengali language is spoken, that is, the Republic of Bangladesh and the state of West Bengal in India. Bengali is also the main language spoken in Tripura and Kuch Bihar in the Indian union.

Historical Overview. Traces of a pre-Aryan culture, including remains of urban sites, have been discovered in Bengal. The region was definitely outside the Vedic culture zone, but Bengal's aryanization had made considerable progress by the days of the Maurya empire. By the fourth century CE the greater part of Bengal had been absorbed in the pan-Indian empire of the Guptas. The kingdom of Samatata in eastern Bengal, a vassal state under Samudragupta, was also conquered at a later date and the region remained a part of the Gupta empire until its downfall. The region was again briefly united under one rule by Sasanka, the celebrated enemy of Harshavardhana of Kanauj, but his kingdom was destroyed by 650 and a century of anarchy followed, which ended with the rise of the Pala dynasty. The Palas suffered a temporary breakdown in the late tenth century, independent dynasties ruled in southern and eastern Bengal, and the territory was invaded by the Chandellas and Kalachuris. In 1021 Rajendra Chola conquered eastern Bengal, but only briefly. In the mid-tenth century there was a revival in Pala fortunes under Mahipala, famed for his patronage of Buddhism. But on his death, there were fresh invasions, by the Chalukyas of Karnataka and the Orissan kings, while an independent dynasty ruled in east Bengal. The Palas were overthrown a second time, by Divvoka, a leader of Kaivartas, a peasant caste. The latter's son, Bhima, was overthrown by Ramapala, who recovered northern and western Bengal and fought a war with Kulottunga, the Chola king. By the middle of the twelfth century the Palas were finally supplanted by the Senas, Brahma-Kshatriyas from Karnataka who were already established as feudatories in Bengal. The Senas did not suppress all local dynasts but their territories did extend to Kalinga and Kamarupa. It was from their third ruler, Lakshmanasena, that Ikhtiyaruddin Muhammad bin Bakhtiyar Khalji, a general of the new Turkish rulers of Delhi, wrested western Bengal in a surprise attack on Nadiya, the capital city (c. 1201). The Sena power survived in eastern Bengal for quite some time but by the end of the thirteenth century that area was also absorbed into the Turko-Afghan empire. [*See also* Pala Dynasty *and* Sena Dynasty.]

Buddhism and Hinduism. The Chinese pilgrim Faxian found Bengal a prosperous region under the Guptas with an extensive sea trade centered on the seaport of Tamralipti, mentioned earlier by Ptolemy and in the *Periplus of the Erythrian Sea.* Bengal also had a flourishing overland commerce with distant parts of the subcontinent. Faxian and his later compatriot Xuanzang also mention numerous Buddhist *viharas* in Bengal, despite the allegation that Sasanka was an enemy of Buddhism. The *viharas* flourished under the Palas as great centers of Buddhist learning. The remains of Somapuri Vihara, in Rajshahi (Bangladesh) surpass in scale those of Nalanda. The Vajrayana and Sahajayana forms of Buddhism, with their strong affinities with Tantra, developed in this period. Savants from the *viharas* of Bengal, of whom the most famous was Dipankara Srijnana, played an important role in spreading these new Buddhist cults to Tibet and other parts of the world.

Local cultures with distinct scripts and languages began to develop in India around this time, and Bengal under the Palas was a part of this pattern. The earliest surviving specimens of the Bengali language are the *charyapadas,* lyrics written by poets who were masters of the Sahaja cult. Buddhism appears to have lost state patronage in the post-Pala period. Both the Senas and Varmanas, local dynasts of eastern Bengal, were staunch supporters of orthodox Brahmanism. Sanskrit court poetry flourished under their patronage: the most famous of Lakshmanasena's court poets, Jayadeva, composed the *Gitagovinda,* celebrating the loves of Radha and Krishna, a work that was later accepted as a devotional text throughout India. Tradition attributes to King Vallalasena orthodox reforms in the caste system and the introduction of Kulinism in Bengal. [*See* Kulinism.] King Adisura of the Sura dynasty, local rulers in west Bengal in the last phase of Pala rule, is credited with having brought the first brahmans to Lower Bengal, from Kanauj in northern India. There are hardly any traces of Buddhism among the elite in Bengal under the Turko-Afghan rulers. Brahmanical supremacy had evidently been established even before the conquest.

Muslim Rule. The sultans of Delhi rarely exercised effective control over Bengal. Under Balban's descendants the province became virtually independent, and the Tughluq attempt to reassert control by setting up three administrative units had only brief success. A succession of independent dynasties ruled Bengal, the Turkish Ilyas Shahis, from 1345 to 1486, with a long break in the fifteenth century when a Hindu feudatory, Ganes, and his sons held sway; the Arab Husain Shahis, from 1493; and thereafter the Afghan Surs and Karranis, from whom Akbar finally wrested the control over Bengal in 1575–1576. Even the Abyssinian slaves imported by the Ilyas Shahis ruled for a few years. Besides the usual story of palace intrigues and continual struggles for the throne, the period was marked by wars with neighboring kingdoms including Nepal, Orissa, Assam, the Sharqi kingdom of Jaunpur, and the Lodi sultans of Delhi. Some of the sultans in the Ilyas Shahi and Husain Shahi dynasties were great builders and patrons of literature. Ghiyas ud-Din of the former dynasty corresponded with the great Persian poet Hafiz and exchanged embassies with the emperor of China. Husain Shah, who overthrew the last of the Abyssinian slave-kings and was chosen to rule Bengal by his peers, is remembered in folk tradition as a wise and just king. [*See* Husain Shahi Dynasty.]

The most significant fact in the history of these times is of course the advent of Islam. Afghan and Turkish migrants no doubt constituted the initial core of the Muslim community in Bengal. But the mass converts in northern and eastern Bengal certainly came from the underprivileged sections of the local population. *Pirs,* a ubiquitous term applied to holy men, pioneer settlers, soldiers, and mythical personages, and later to those who presented the Islamic traditions in Bengali and in a highly bengalicized garb, were instrumental in the growth of the community as a major element in local society. Popular Islam in Bengal was syncretic in outlook. This syncretism was reflected in the sultans' commissioning of translations from the Sanskrit epics into Bengali and the construction of mosques based on local architectural styles. Bengali language and literature developed as distinctive phenomena now for the first time. Within the Hindu fold, the movement initiated by Chaitanya in the sixteenth century, with its emphasis on ecstatic devotion to Krishna, emerged as a major force. [*See* Chaitanya.] Orthodox traditions were powerfully reaffirmed in the writings of Raghunandana, and Bengal came to be recognized as a major center of the Nyaya school of Hindu philosophy.

The Mughal conquest of Bengal, first attempted by Babur himself, but eventually stabilized by Akbar in 1576, never quite lost its character of foreign rule. The local chieftains, both Hindu and Afghan, long resisted the authority of the Mughals and it was only in the reign of Jahangir that all such resistance was finally crushed. Under Aurangzeb, the governor Mir Jumla set forth from Bengal on an abortive campaign to conquer Assam. His successor Shayesta Khan tried to end the depredations of the Magh or Arakanese pirates and their Portuguese allies by annexing Chittagong, but their slave raids on the coastal areas continued well into the eighteenth century. The Mughals were no patrons of local culture, yet some of the best works of Bengali literature, such as the *mangala kavyas,* or ballads celebrating the exploits of local deities, and the Vaishnavite biographical literature were produced under their rule. Partly as a result of the activities of the Dutch and English East India companies, but due more so to Mughal centralization, Bengal's export trade in textiles and other commodities flourished. In the last years of Aurangzeb's reign the administration and the army of the empire were sustained entirely by the revenue sent from the *subah* of Bengal. By that time, however, the eastern province, which included Orissa, was de facto independent under the *subadar* Murshid Quli Khan, who transferred the capital from Dhaka to Murshidabad. In 1740 his grandson lost the throne to Alivardi Khan, the deputy governor of Bihar, who had to cope with the Maratha incursions leading to the loss of Orissa. It was Alivardi's grandson and successor Siraj ud-Daulah who became engaged in conflict with the English East India Company. Following his defeat by Sir Robert Clive in the Battle of Plassey in 1757, Bengal passed under de facto British rule. [*See also* Siraj ud-Daulah; Fort William; Clive, Sir Robert; *and* East India Company.]

Modern European trade with Bengal was initiated by the Portuguese in the sixteenth century. In the seventeenth century the Dutch and the English East India companies and later the French and the Danes opened trade, exporting cotton and raw silk from Bengal and importing chiefly bullion. The English company eventually triumphed in this competition, a fact signalized by the grant of special trading privileges in 1717. Abuse of these privileges started the conflict that led to the conspiracy against Siraj ud-Daulah initiated by Clive. The new nawab, Mir Ja'far, was Clive's puppet. The English triumph was soon rounded off with victories over the French and the Dutch. Their de facto power was reinforced when the Mughal emperor granted them *diwani,* or the right to collect revenue, a power formally assumed in 1765. [*See* Mir Ja'far.]

The company's territories in the region were now organized as the Bengal Presidency, and following the disastrous famine of 1770—which attracted the attention of the home authorities toward the extreme abuses of power by the company's servants the Indian possessions, including Bengal—they were brought under effective parliamentary control. The misadministration and plunder were ended by the days of the governor-generalship of Lord Charles Cornwallis, from 1786 to 1793. Cornwallis introduced *inter alia* the permanent settlement of land, which conferred proprietary right, subject to regular payment of revenue, on a class of erstwhile revenue collectors. [*See* Cornwallis, Charles *and* Governor-General of India.]

Modern Movements. The company's middlemen and its functionaries constituted a new landed class who required a knowledge of English. The new Western-educated middle class led by the pioneer Rammohan Roy began agitations for social and religious reform. Assisted by the British philanthropist David Hare, they established the first institution of Western higher education, the Hindu College, in 1817. A bitter controversy developed over the governmental measure abolishing widow-burning, which Roy and many others supported. He started a Vedantic society, open to all monotheists, which developed into the Brahmo Samaj. Ishwarchandra Vidyasagar, a Sanskrit scholar, initiated a campaign for the legalization of widow remarriage that was eventually approved by the government. There was also an outburst of literary creativity. The poet Michael Madhusudan Dutt, the novelist Bankimchandra Chattopadhyay, and later the poet Rabindranath Tagore were products of this literary renaissance. An awareness of political rights and aspirations, a national consciousness consistent with loyalty to British rule was a part of this awakening. Its manifestations, however, included specific criticisms of British rule, especially in the numerous journals and political associations, such as the British India Association. The resentment was exacerbated by Anglo-Indian racial attitudes, especially over issues of equality in the eyes of law. Surendranath Banerjea emerged as the acknowledged leader of this new tendency, which became a part of the pan-Indian nationalism when the Indian National Congress was established in 1885. [*See also* Roy, Rammohan; Brahmo Samaj; Vidyasagar, Isvarchandra; Dutt, Michael Madhusudan; Tagore, Rabindranath; Banerjea, Surendranath; Anglo-Indians; *and* Indian National Congress.]

By the mid-nineteenth century Muslims constituted nearly half the population of Bengal; in northern and eastern Bengal they were the majority. But most were underprivileged peasants. Hindus dominated the spheres of education, jobs, professions, and land ownership. With the growth of nationalist sentiment among the Hindus and the increasing criticism of the government, there was a tilt in governmental policy in favor of the Muslims that helped in the growth of a Muslim middle class. Muslims also constituted the majority of the population by 1911. Fundamentalist reform movements such as the Ahl-i Hadis preached against the popular folk practices of Bengal Muslims as un-Islamic, and in the face of this challenge the traditionalists felt the need to emphasize an exclusive Muslim identity, underlining the differences with the Hindus [*See* Ahl-i Hadis.] Partly to take advantage of this growing exclusiveness and the Muslim elite's competition with the Hindus, partly for administrative reasons, the government decided in 1905 to partition the unwieldy province of Bengal, Bihar, and Orissa, dividing the two parts of Bengal and creating a Muslim-majority province of East Bengal and Assam. This led to a mass agitation by nationalist leaders. The protest against partition was initially supported by a section of the Muslims, but Muslim leaders eventually decided to support partition. The partition also triggered off a movement of revolutionary terror that aimed ultimately at independence through a violent struggle. The partition was annulled in 1911 with the creation of the province of a united Bengal, separate from Bihar and Orissa. The politicized Bengal Muslims felt cheated. In the 1920s the Muslims participated in the noncooperation Khilafat movement on a large scale, and the charismatic leader Chittaranjan Das forged a Hindu-Muslim entente, but it collapsed soon after his death in 1925. [*See also* Khilafat Movement *and* Das, Chittaranjan.]

When provincial autonomy was introduced in 1937 the predominantly Muslim Krishak Praja Party led by Abul Kasem Fazlul Huq emerged as the single largest party in the legislature, but by 1945 the Muslim League, committed to the establishment of Pakistan, had the support of the majority of Muslims. When Mohammad Ali Jinnah gave the call for a Direct Action Day to be observed on 16 August 1946, a Muslim League ministry under H. S. Suhrawardy was in power. The riots on that day led to extensive massacres in Calcutta but finally opened the way to Pakistan and the partition of Bengal. A section of both the Indian National Congress and the Muslim League proposed the creation of a united sovereign Bengal, but the idea was rejected by Lord Mountbatten and the Congress High Command. It was eventually decided that East and part of North Bengal would go to Pakistan and the rest of the province to the Indian union. The former, along with the Bengali-speaking Sylhet district of Assam, constituted East Pakistan. [*See also* Pakistan.]

The state of West Bengal in India, after a succession of Congress ministries and a period of uneasy shifts in power between the Congress and leftist parties, has been for some years under a leftist united front government dominated by the (Marxist) Communist Party.

[*See also* Calcutta; Bangladesh; *and* Communism: Communist Parties in South Asia.]

Rafiuddin Ahmad, *The Bengal Muslims, 1871–1906* (1981). Marcus F. Franda, *Radical Politics in West Bengal* (1971). Leonard A. Gordon, *Bengal: The Nationalist Movement* (1974). *The History of Bengal,* vol. 1, *The Hindu Period,* edited by R. C. Majumdar (1943); vol. 2, *The Muslim Period,* edited by J. N. Sarkar (1948); vol. 3, *1757–1905,* edited by N. K. Sinha (1967). David Kopf, *The Brahmo Samaj* (1979). Ratnalekha Ray, *Change in Bengal Agrarian Society* (1979). T. Raychaudhuri, *Bengal under Akbar and Jahangir* (1969).

TAPAN RAYCHAUDHURI

BENGKULU, settlement on Sumatra's southwest coast. Bengkulu was the British East India Company's major foothold in the Indonesian archipelago from 1685, when the Dutch forced the British out of Banten, until 1824. Through Fort Marlborough (built in 1714), the company tried to monopolize West Sumatran pepper, but, away from major trading routes, the enterprise was never very profitable. In 1760 the British named Bengkulu capital of their West Sumatran presidency. Sir Thomas Stamford Raffles, who was governor from 1818 to 1824, tried to establish a more liberal administration and encouraged cultivation of spices including nutmeg, cloves, and cassia. Bengkulu was ceded to the Dutch in 1824 under the Anglo-Dutch Treaty, but they did not move to subdue the region, which became a center of piracy, until 1868. It languished as a backwater, never reemerging as a major trading center. It was Sukarno's place of exile from 1938 to 1942 and became capital of the newly reconstituted province of Bengkulu in 1967.

[*See also* East India Company; Banten; Anglo-Dutch Treaty; Pepper; *and* Raffles, Sir Thomas Stamford.]

John S. Bastin, *The British in West Sumatra (1685–1825)* (1965). M. A. Jaspan, "Bencoolen (Bengkulu) 136 Years after the Ending of the British Settlement," *Sumatra Research Bulletin* 4 (October 1974): 19–30. J. Kathirithamby-Wells, *The British West Sumatran Presidency (1760–85)* (1977). AUDREY R. KAHIN

BENKEI (known also as Musashibō Benkei, d. 1189), Buddhist monk and warrior of medieval Japan. More a legendary than a historical figure, Benkei is remembered for his huge physical size and fighting prowess and for his steadfast loyalty to one of the great samurai heroes of the age, Minamoto Yoshitsune (1159–1189). Although mentioned briefly in the historical records, Benkei is brought to life primarily in the fourteenth-century literary work *Gikeiki (Chronicle of Yoshitsune)*. This work comprises fanciful tales about the youth and last years of Minamoto Yoshitsune, who led the armies of the Minamoto to victory over the Taira in the Gempei War of 1180 to 1185, a struggle that ushered in the medieval age. After the war, Yoshitsune had a falling out with his more powerful brother, Yoritomo (1147–1199), who founded Japan's first warrior government, the Kamakura shogunate (1185–1333). Forced to flee into the provinces, Yoshitsune and a small band of followers that included the redoubtable Benkei were finally tracked down and killed. In the legends surrounding this flight, which have been notably recreated in *nō* and *kabuki* drama, Benkei emerges as a peerless model of the faithful follower. PAUL VARLEY

BENTAN ISLAND, located about thirty miles southeast of Singapore in the Republic of Indonesia, is the largest island in the Riau Archipelago and forms the eastern side of the Strait of Riau. The island is mentioned in the *Sejarah Melayu* as the home of the sea peoples, or Orang Laut, who brought Sri Tri Buana to Melaka and recognized him as king. It served as the capital of the Johor empire on several occasions between the sixteenth and nineteenth century. In the eighteenth century, its capital, Tanjungpinang, was a major entrepôt serving the India-China trade. Bentan was surpassed as a trading site in the nineteenth century because of the popularity of Singapore, but it remained a gambier planting center and a Dutch administrative center until the twentieth century.

[*See also* Johor; Orang Laut; Bugis; *and* Gambier].

CARL A. TROCKI

BENTINCK, WILLIAM CAVENDISH (Lord Bentinck; 1774–1839), governor of Madras (1803–1807) and of Bengal (1823–1833), and first governor-general of India (1833–1835). The second son of the duke of Portland, Bentinck began his career in the army. He was high-principled and a sound administrator and is acknowledged as one of the most important of all India's British rulers. Blame for the Vellore Mutiny (1806) blighted his early career, but he was vindicated by his achievements as governor-general. A visionary who combined Utilitarian, Evangelical, and Liberal convictions, Bentinck devoted himself to causes of social reform and national unity (independent nationhood), whether in Britain, Italy, or India. He believed in Indian nationality, striving to create it or to strengthen it wherever possible. As head of the Indian empire, he did all he could to abolish social evils, prevent abuses, restore finances, reorganize judicial and revenue systems, and further the education and employment of able Indians in places occupied by Europeans. A liberal spirit, based on a conviction that the interests of the people of India should come first, pervaded his administration.

John Rosselli, *Lord William Bentinck* (1974).

ROBERT E. FRYKENBERG

BERNIER, FRANÇOIS (1620–1688), French physician, considered to be the most learned and perceptive of the large number of European travelers who visited India during the seventeenth century. Bernier traveled throughout India between 1658 and 1667. In his book, *Travels in the Mogul Empire,* first published in French in 1670, he commented on conditions and events at all levels of Mughal society and sought to explain these in terms of basic differences between Mughal and European society.

François Bernier, *Travels in the Mogul Empire, A.D. 1656–1668,* translated by A. Constable (1968).

HARBANS MUKHIA

BESANT, ANNIE (1847–1933), English theosophist and Indian public speaker and political leader. Besant became president of the Theosophical Society in 1907; in 1916 she founded the Home Rule League, an organization dedicated to the cause of Indian self-government. At the end of that year she was elected president of the 1917 session of the Indian National Congress, but in 1918, after disagreements with the Congress leadership over the Montagu-Chelmsford reforms, Besant abruptly withdrew from political activity. She remained president of the Theosophical Society until her death.

[*See also* Home Rule League; Indian National Congress; *and* Montagu-Chelmsford Reforms.]

Arthur H. Nethercot, *The First Five Lives of Annie Besant* (1960) and *The Last Four Lives of Annie Besant* (1963). Gertrude Leavenworth Williams, *The Passionate Pilgrim* (1931).

JUDITH E. WALSH

BETHUNE, NORMAN (b. 1890 in Ontario, Canada; d. 1939 in China), social activist and physician. Son of a Presbyterian minister father and a missionary mother, Norman Bethune was early dedicated to the social gospel. Although he was a pioneer in the medical sciences and in organizing mobile operating units, he is known most for his involvements as a Canadian communist in the major social revolutions of the twentieth century.

As a surgeon, Bethune worked for the republicans in the Spanish Civil War and for Mao Zedong's guerrilla troops in China. After just a year and a half of working in medical facilities in Communist-controlled areas, he died of blood poisoning. His death resulted in Mao Zedong's famous eulogy, "In Memory of Norman Bethune." During the ten years of the Cultural Revolution, this two-page memorial was read daily throughout China. In it, Norman Bethune was depicted as an example of "absolute selflessness" and a model for the "spirit of internationalism" and the "spirit of communism." Bethune was buried near Beijing, and his name is memorialized in the Bethune Peace Hospital and Medical School network in China.

Ted Allen and Sydney Gordon, *The Scalpel, the Sword: The Story of Dr. Norman Bethune* (1952; rev. ed., 1973); Mao Tse-tung (Mao Zedong), "In Memory of Norman Bethune; December 21, 1939," in *Selected Works of Mao Tse-tung,* vol. 2 (1965), pp. 337–338.

RICHARD C. KAGAN

BHABHA, HOMI JEHANGIR (1909–1966), Indian nuclear physicist. Bhabha was an eminent Parsi related to the Tata family. As chairman of the Indian Atomic Energy Commission and founder of the research center at Trombay, he pioneered India's nuclear research effort. He was India's representative to the United Nations and other international bodies, and in 1954 received the Padma Bhushan, one of the highest awards for national service granted by the Government of India. [*See also* Tata Family.]

USHA SANYAL

BHAGAVAD GITA, one of the most revered texts of the Hindu tradition. Its title has usually been interpreted to mean "Song of the Lord," but this translation is misleading. It is not a lyric poem, but a spiritual dialogue in Sanskrit verse between the god Krishna and the warrior Arjuna. It is embedded within the sixth book of the great Indian epic the *Mahabharata,* and belongs to that layer of the epic that took form during the first centuries of the common era. Its setting is the battlefield of Kurukshetra, as the war is about to begin. Krishna is the incarnation of infinite power who, in Hindu belief, periodically descends to earth to accomplish the restoration of order in times of chaos. He serves as adviser and charioteer to Arjuna, the mightest warrior in the epic. Arjuna's nerve fails in the face of doing battle against his relations. The *Gita* includes a series of arguments on why Arjuna must overcome his uncertainty and fear of the battle. A doctrine of duty and order *(dharma)* is developed in terms of reciprocal cosmic and human activity *(karma).* Arjuna's objections to killing his relatives are personal and social; Krishna's answer has cosmic dimensions. The warrior's religiously ordained duty is crucial to universal order, even though it involves killing and violence.

The *Gita*'s doctrine of disciplined action *(karma yoga)* is based on absence of personal involvement. When the puzzled Arjuna asks, "Why then do you compel me to kill?" Krishna answers that all action done as sacrifice to him is conducive to order and freedom if it is done without regard for ends but only because it is correct in itself. On the one hand, he advocates a life of action and moral duty according to the traditional rules of society; on the other, transcendence of empirical experience in the search for wisdom and freedom.

The dialectic of renunciation and disciplined action that is central to the *Gita* has inspired centuries of Indian philosophers and practical men of wisdom, as well as Western thinkers such as Ralph Waldo Emerson, Henry David Thoreau, and T. S. Eliot. Notable among Indian interpretations are those of the Vedanta philosophers Shankara (eighth century) and Ramanuja (eleventh century), as well as modern political leaders such as B. G. Tilak and M. K. Gandhi. The varied interpretations they have attached to the text reflect its intentionally multifaceted message. It is not a systematic presentation of an argument, but a speculative, mystical teaching in which Krishna is the object of an intense devotional love *(bhakti)*.

[*See also* Hinduism; Mahabharata; Krishna; Vedanta; Bhakti; Shankara; Ramanuja; Tilak, Bal Gangadhar; *and* Gandhi, Mohandas Karamchand.]

J. A. B. van Buitenen, trans., *The Bhagavadgita in the Mahabharata* (1981). Barbara Stoler Miller, trans., *The Bhagavadgita: Krishna's Counsel in Time of War* (1985). R. C. Zaehner, trans., *The Bhagavad-Gita, With Commentary Based on Original Sources* (1969).

BARBARA STOLER MILLER

BHAKTAPUR, district as well as capital town in what is now Nepal, annexed by Gorkha in 1769. Its cultural center, the town, is relatively undisturbed by modern encroachments even now, thus enabling it to preserve some archaic features of a typical medieval South Asian town. It grew from an agrohamlet in the fifth to eighth century, when it was called Khripung (the Newar name *Khopa* probably derives from it), to a well-planned walled city and a political center of note in medieval times. The town displays some outstanding examples of Newar woodwork and pagodas, as well as an impressive palace square.

[*See also* Gurkhas *and* Newar.]

Niels Gutschow and Bernhard Kölver, *Ordered Space: Concepts and Functions in a Town of Nepal* (1975). A. Haaland, *Bhaktapur: A Town Changing Process Influenced by Bhaktapur Development Project* (1982).

PRAYAG RAJ SHARMA

BHAKTI. The Sanskrit noun *bhakti* is derived from the verb *bhaj,* meaning broadly "to share, to possess," and occupies a semantic field that embraces the notions of "belonging," "being loyal," even "liking." References to *bhakti* by the grammarian Panini reveal this range of meanings in the fourth century BCE and suggest that even in that early period the word's most important usage was in the domain of religion: Panini speaks of "*bhakti* to Vasudeva" (i.e., Krishna). *Bhakti,* which comes to mean "devotion" or "love" in later literature, is one of the central concepts of Hinduism. It describes that side of Indian religion in which the personal engagement of a devotee with a personally conceived divinity is understood to be the core of the religious life.

Unlike other concepts through which Hindus understand their religion, *bhakti* is recognized as having an important historical dimension. It is widely acknowledged that Tamil culture played an early and critical role in establishing the sense of *bhakti* as an all-encompassing emotional reality. In the *Padma Purana* this sort of *bhakti* is personified as a woman who was born in South India and wandered northward through the western provinces, aging all the while, until she arrived in the Braj region, where she experienced a sudden rejuvenation. The process being described—the so-called *bhakti* movement in Indian religion—spanned the millennium from the sixth to the sixteenth century, and genuine continuities can be found throughout the period that are in force even today. These include the singing of devotional songs composed in vernacular languages by poets who have attained the status of saints; a sense of the mutual companionship of many of these poet-saints; a tendency to consider both sexes and all strata of society as potential devotees; and above all a cultivation of personal experience as against external or ritual punctiliousness. Collectively, these traits present a formidable contrast to the ritually oriented Vedic traditions preserved by the brahman caste. [*See also* Vedas *and* Brahman.]

Early Bhakti. The ancient roots of Vedic practice are easy to establish, since the relevant texts have been preserved. Equally ancient *bhakti* texts do not exist, but it would be a mistake to conclude that the emphases of *bhakti* religion are on that account more recent in their origins. When non-Vedic religion does begin to leave its traces—in early Buddhist and Jain texts—much of it sounds like *bhakti.* In these texts one hears of such characteristic *bhakti* practices as the enthusiastic offering of flowers and perfumes; the love of music, singing, and dancing; and the veneration of particularly sanctified places. The divinities who are the objects of such worship change over time, from the spirits and snakes *(yakshas* and *yakshis, nagas* and *nagis)* whose images dominate the earliest Hindu sculptures to the most recent additions to the Hindu pantheon (Santoshi Ma, for example, the goddess whose worship became widespread only after she was the subject of a popular film), but the practices by means of which they are worshiped remain recognizably the same. These endure as hallmarks of the *bhakti* tradition.

These practices make their appearance in the *Bhagavad Gita* (between the second century BCE and the second century CE[?]) as a kind of lowest common denominator upon which a higher theology of *bhakti* is elaborated. Krishna, whose divine utterances to his mortal charioteer Arjuna make up the great bulk of the *Gita,* says that he accepts what by implication are the simplest offerings—"a leaf, a flower, a fruit, or water"—if they are presented to him in a spirit of *bhakti* (*Bhagavad Gita,* "Bhaktya" 9.26). Just what Krishna means by *bhakti* has been a matter of debate. Some scholars have found evidences in the *Gita* of an emotionalism associated with later *bhakti;* but others, such as Friedhelm Hardy, have argued that the author of the *Gita* was referring to a form of fixed mental concentration when he spoke of *bhakti.* It is this "intellectual" dimension, to use Hardy's term, that makes it so appropriate for the *Gita* to speak of *bhakti* as a kind of yoga, and several commentators have concluded that of the three yogas recommended in the *Gita*—*jnana* ("insight"), *karma* ("action"), and *bhakti*—the last is the most fundamental. Yoga is conducive to detachment from the world, and in the *Gita* Arjuna is encouraged to withdraw from his immediate attachments to family and teachers so that he may attain the inner concentration requisite for equanimity in waging life's battles. Arjuna's *bhakti*—his devotion to Krishna—provides the intermediary step: it is a form of attachment to the divine that makes detachment from the world possible.

***Bhakti* in South India.** Considerable distance separates the *bhakti* of the *Bhagavad Gita* from that found in the writings of the earliest Tamil singer-saints, who were to determine much of the subsequent history of *bhakti,* even to the present day. In the compositions of the Alvars and Nayanars, groups of South Indian poets who sang of Krishna and Shiva, respectively, precisely the opposite tone from that of the *Gita* is adopted. For the Tamil poets, *bhakti* is "hot" rather than "cool": the poet Manikkavacakar says that Shiva melts him with his irresistible fire. Here *bhakti* is basic, even alimentary, rather than cerebral: Nammalvar announces that Vishnu has eaten him whole, and marvels on occasion that he has done the same in return. And here the root meaning of *bhakti* attains new overtones as devotion verges on possession in the extreme sense of the word. Vaishnavites and Shaivites alike report that *bhakti* can be a form of madness, in which one is no longer in control of oneself. Furthermore, because this experience of possession is shared, it creates new communities of those possessed—entities based on ties that are quite distinct from traditional caste, occupational, and geographic affiliations.

Our first detailed knowledge of such institutions comes from the South. Although such early northern sects as the Bhagavatas and Pashupatas—Vaishnavite and Shaivite groups, respectively—may have had similar institutional identities, our information concerning them is too meager to know this with certainty. In the South, by contrast, we can see a clear process of institutional development, according to which the Alvars came to be revered as the foreparents of the Sri Vaishnava community, and the Nayanars as the source of inspiration for adherents to the Shaiva Siddhanta theological system. The leadership of the Sri Vaishnava fold came to be firmly the province of brahmans, while Shaiva Siddhanta leadership was exercised primarily by Vellalas. Both groups controlled networks of temples, and both enjoyed the patronage of several South Indian dynasties. [*See* Vellala.]

On both the Vaishnavite and Shaivite sides, such institutionalization was accompanied by some determined hagiographical work. Not only were the poems of the twelve Alvars and the sixty-three Nayanars collected, but the lives of the saints themselves were given canonical form. The poetic *Prabandham* of Nathamuni (tenth century[?]) and the hagiographical *Arayirappati Guruparamparaprapavam* of Pinpalakiya Perumal Jiyar (thirteenth century) and *Divyasuricaritam* of Garudavahana (sixteenth century[?]) fulfilled this function for the Sri Vaishnavas, of whom Nathamuni himself was the founding teacher *(acharya).* For Shaivas, Nampi Antar Nampi (eleventh century) performed a similar task by arranging the hymns of the Nayanars in what was to become the Shaivite canon *(Tirumurai).* It was completed when an additional collection, the hagiographical *Periya Puranam* of Cekkilar, was added to it in the twelfth century.

Although the Vaishnavite and Shaivite *bhakti* institutions of the Tamil country were firmly managed by the powerful brahman and Vellala castes, who administered initiation and perpetuated the traditions *(sampradayas)* of doctrine and teachings to which they were heir, the poet-saints to whom they looked for inspiration were neither exclusively upper-caste nor exclusively male. Among the Alvars, for instance, Tirumankai was a member of the lowly ranked thief caste, Tiruppan was an Untouchable, and Antal, perhaps the most popular of the Alvars, was a woman. Furthermore, accounts of the lives of these saints specifically underline the point that their *bhakti* had the power to vault them ahead of members of the "purer" castes in the eyes of Vishnu.

***Bhakti* in Western India.** This counterstructural thrust in the *bhakti* heritage took on new force as the *bhakti* movement spread toward the northwest. Like the Alvars and Nayanars, the Virashaiva saints of Karnataka (twelfth century) included outcastes and women, and at least initially their fundamental institutions were defined in counterstructural terms as well. The Virashaivas questioned the close association between sacred locale and intense devotion that had been one of the fundamental emphases of Tamil *bhakti.* Rather than pondering the mystery of a God who could encompass all yet become manifest in particular temples, the Virashaivas insisted that the only true temples are those inside human beings. In consequence, a set of institutions centering on temples and their priests was abjured.

In the course of time the Virashaiva teaching centers *(mathas)* and the ascetics who gathered there came to assume many of the functions of a temple, but elements of the stringent Virashaiva message continued to set the community apart. In the hagiographical accounts that grew up around the Virashaiva saints (e.g., *Shunyasampadane,* fifteenth century), one finds an emphasis on the transcendent value of work, which is foreign to earlier Tamil teaching. This assessment of ordinary labor as an expression of *bhakti* has led to comparisons between the Virashaivas and European Protestants on the part of Max Weber and subsequent scholars persuaded of the cogency of Weber's thesis concerning the Protestant ethic.

In contrast to the Virashaivas, the poet-saints of Maharashtra, the most significant of whom were Vaishnavite rather than Shaivite, have come to be associated by means of a literary and festival tradition focused on a particular sacred site, the temple of Vithoba (Vishnu) at Pandharpur. Again the saints represent a variety of social stations—from Jhaneshvar and Eknath (thirteenth and sixteenth centuries), both brahmans, to Namdev, a lowly tailor, and Chokhamela, an outcaste Mahar (both fourteenth century)—and all levels of society have always participated in the semiannual pilgrimage to Pandharpur. As is typical in the *bhakti* movement, however, the full message is not pure egalitarianism but rather an inner freedom to serve God that calls into question the ultimate validity of all caste conceits. Hence the legacy of caste continues to make itself felt in many expressions of *bhakti.* Various castes travel together to Pandharpur, but rules of caste commensality are honored; until recently Untouchable pilgrims were denied entrance to the temple that is the goal of the journey. [*See also* Maharashtra.]

***Bhakti* in North India.** The poems attributed to the *bhakti* saints of North India contain a number of references to their predecessors in western India—particularly to Namdev and to Narasi Mehta of Gujarat—and a less obvious but equally significant debt is owed to their southern forebears. A number of motifs that occur in the popular descriptions of Krishna's childhood by Sur Das (sixteenth century)—the child's insistence on having the moon as his toy, for example—are to be found nowhere in Sanskrit literature but appear eight centuries earlier in the Tamil poems of Periyalvar. Evidently, a vernacular network of transmission connected the *bhakti* saints of various regions.

Customarily it is said that more formal lines of initiation and community affiliation tied together many *bhakti* figures from different regions. The fifteenth-century weaver Kabir, for instance, has been depicted since the seventeenth century as an initiate of Ramananda, who in turn is understood to have belonged to the Sri Vaishnava Sampradaya. But a close examination of the legend leads one to doubt its veracity, as does the fact that Kabir nowhere mentions Ramananda in his poetry. Similarly dubious are several of the bonds that are claimed to exist between the more recent *sampradayas* of North India and their South Indian predecessors—the connection between the followers of Vallabha (sixteenth century) and those of Vishnusvami (twelfth to thirteenth century[?]), for example. [*See also* Kabir.]

The thematic and stylistic similarities that draw together *bhakti* poetry from all parts of India cannot be gainsaid, however, nor can one overlook the common patterns that emerge in the lives of the saints, whatever their provenance, or the fact that they are everywhere found together in hagiographical anthologies. In every region, too, *bhakti* literature contains songs that express a visual fascination with God and songs that bemoan the deity's absence and invisibility. And almost everywhere one finds poems extolling the glories of particular places that have been touched by God.

The North and West, furthermore, characteristically distinguish between poets who adopt a *saguna* ("with qualities") approach, accepting that God is to be worshiped by means of images, and poets who reject this in favor of a *nirguna* approach, the effort to worship God "without qualities." The latter group, which includes Kabir and Nanak, are typically called Sants ("good people") in the North, and owe a debt to the followers of Gorakhnath that is shared by some of the saints of Maharashtra. The various *bhakti* institutions of North India divide along the *saguna*/*nirguna* line far more neatly than do the poets themselves, with communities such as the Gaudiya (or Chaitanya) Sampradaya and Vallabha Sampradaya serving as examples of the former, and the Dadu Panth and Kabir Panth as examples of the latter. The Sikh community too, which claims the sixteenth-century *bhakti* poet Nanak as its founder, falls in the latter camp. [*See also* Nanak.]

As one might expect, the institutions of *bhakti* are subject to continuous change. Not only does the *bhakti* movement itself honor individual inspiration, but the Hindu tradition as a whole places considerable store in the sort of learning that can only be transmitted from person to person, from teacher to pupil. Hence doctrine is often a relatively weak guarantor of institutional identity and new waves of the *bhakti* movement are constantly being emitted. These may be excited by the appearance of an inspired teacher or a newly popular divinity, a disagreement in a *sampradaya* about proper lines of succession, or by the gathering in urban settings of groups that possess formerly independent traditions. To this extent *bhakti* embraces not only a single, overarching current—the *bhakti* movement as a whole—but a series of more or less parallel streams, such as the *panths* and *sampradayas,* all in a sea of ever-shifting, interdependent eddies and vortices that catch up individual believers in various aspects of their devotional lives.

[*See also* Bhagavad Gita. *For further discussion of* bhakti *within broader contexts, see* Hinduism; Dravidian Languages and Literatures; Indo-Aryan Languages and Literatures; Shaivism; *and* Vaishnavism.]

Friedhelm Hardy, *Viraha-Bhakti: The Early History of Kṛṣṇa Devotion in South India* (1983). John Stratton Hawley, *Sūr Dās: Poet, Singer, Saint* (1984). Norvin Hein, "Hinduism," in *A Reader's Guide to the Great Religions,* edited by Charles Adams (1977), pp. 126–140. Linda Hess and Shukdev Singh, *The Bījak of Kabir* (1983). V. Raghavan, *The Great Integrators* (1966). A. K. Ramanujan, *Speaking of Śiva* (1973). R. D. Ranade, *Mysticism in India* (1933; reprint, 1983). Eleanor Zelliot, "The Medieval Bhakti Movement in History," in *Hinduism: New Essays in the History of Religions,* edited by Bardwell Smith (1976), pp. 143–168.

JOHN STRATTON HAWLEY

BHARATI, SUBRAMANYA (1882–1921), Tamil poet. Born into a brahman family in Ettiapuram, his precocity led him to the court of the raja of Ettiapuram, where court pandits conferred on him the title *bharati* in recognition of his brilliant forensic exploits. Influenced by the nationalist movement and especially by Bal Gangadhar Tilak and Sister Nivedita, eclectic in his interests and pursuits, Bharati was a distinguished philosopher, teacher, essayist, social reformer, journalist, recluse, and freedom fighter, and the doyen of modern Tamil poets. He died in poverty in Madras on 12 September 1921.

[*See also* Tilak, Bal Gangadhar.]

S. Vijaya Bharati, *Subramanya Bharati: Personality and Poetry* (1975). Kuldip Roy, *Subramanya Bharati* (1974).

PATRICK ROCHE

BHAVAVARMAN, a sixth-century ruler of a Khmer kingdom located on the middle Mekong and known to the Chinese as Zhenla. He is known from Chinese sources and from two Sanskrit inscriptions. Descended from the royalty of Funan, he became ruler of Zhenla by marrying a Khmer princess. He and his cousin Chitrasena successfully attacked Funan, and Bhavavarman established Zhenla as a preeminent power in the Indochinese region. It is known that he reigned during the 590s. Funan continued to exist as a vassal state with reduced territory until it finally disappeared about 627.

[*See also* Zhenla *and* Funan.]

Lawrence P. Briggs, *The Ancient Khmer Empire* (1951). G. Coedès, *The Indianized States of Southeast Asia,* translated by Susan B. Cowing (1968). IAN W. MABBETT

BHAVE, VINOBA (1895–1982), spiritual heir of Mohandas Gandhi and, together with Jayaprakash Narayan, cofounder and leader of the Sarvodaya movement. Bhave walked 45,000 miles barefoot around India after 1951, preaching nonviolence, collecting land from the wealthy, and redistributing it as *bhoodan* ("land-gift") to the poor. Supporters saw Bhave's self-sacrifice, peaceful nonviolence, and redistribution of land (amounting to almost the size of Israel) as solutions to India's problems, but detractors pointed out that most *bhoodan* land was nonproductive and uneconomic, and criticized Bhave for taking a vow of silence rather than speaking out against violations of human rights and civil liberties during the period of Emergency rule.

[*See also* Narayan, Jayaprakash; Gandhi, Mohandas Karamchand; *and* Emergency in India, The.]

T. K. Oommen, *Charisma, Stability and Change: An Analysis of Bhoodan-Gramdan Movement in India* (1972). Sachchidananda et al., *Sarvodaya and Development: Multi-Disciplinary Perspectives from Musahari* (1976).

MARCUS FRANDA

BHOPAL, city in Madhya Pradesh, India. Dost Mohammad, an Afghan adventurer who arrived in India in 1709, founded Bhopal, which would emerge as the largest Muslim princely state in central India. By the 1790s, however, the state was severely threatened by Maratha armies. In 1817, on the eve of the Pindari war, Bhopal entered an alliance with the British East India Company which guaranteed its existence. From 1859 to 1926 three women ruled, as female succession was permitted under Muslim law in the absence of male heirs. In 1926 Sultan Jahan Begum abdicated in favor of her third son, Hamidullah. Both of these rulers were active in princely politics, especially the Chamber of Princes, and in Muslim politics, particularly the Muslim College at Aligarh.

In 1931 Bhopal had an area of 6,902 square miles, a population of 729,955, and an average annual revenue of 6,210,000 rupees. In 1949 the state became a chief commissioner's province and in 1956 it was amalgamated into Madhya Pradesh, whose capital is at Bhopal city.

After it became the capital, Bhopal city underwent very rapid development, becoming a center for heavy industry, with a population of about 673,300 in 1981. One of the most important of the new industries was a large plant operated by a subsidiary of Union Carbide, an American corporation, for the manufacture of chemicals. The worst industrial disaster in history occurred at the plant in 1984, when a malfunction in the storage tanks caused the release of highly toxic fumes that killed thousands and injured unknown numbers of people in the areas near the plant. Charges that the disaster was the result of poor plant design and careless maintenance on the part of Union Carbide were countered by accusations from Union Carbide that it was the result of sabotage by disgruntled workers. Lawsuits against Union Carbide were instituted by the Government of India on behalf of the victims, but the complexity of the legal issues made a settlement difficult.

[*See also* Princely States; Marathas; *and* Madhya Pradesh.]

Sultan Jahan Begam, Nawab of Bhopal, *An Account of My Life*, 3 vols., translated by C. H. Payne and Abdus Samad Khan (1910–1927). Ward Morehouse and Arun Subramanian, *The Bhopal Tragedy* (1986).

BARBARA N. RAMUSACK

BHUBANESWAR (Sanskrit, Bhuvaneshvara), capital of Orissa State, India, originally a temple city dedicated to the Hindu god Shiva, the "lord" *(ishvara)* of the "world" *(bhuvana)*. It has some five hundred temples—at one time several thousand—that were constructed between the eighth and twelfth centuries. Among the earliest is the Parasurameshvara Temple (c. 750 CE), the classic form of a North Indian temple; its main sanctum is surmounted by a five-storied curvilinear tower and crowned with a large *amalaka* (ribbed disk). In the Mukteshvara Temple (c. 950), erected through the patronage of the Somavamshi king Yayati I, the ribbed tower was elongated and the porch was covered with a multistaged roof. The Lingaraja Temple (c. 1040), constructed in the final years of Somavamshi rule, was even taller than its predecessors and became the main sanctuary of the city. Enclosed in a walled courtyard, this temple complex includes a separate entrance hall, a dining house, and a hall for sacred performances. Additional temples to Shiva and other Hindu deities were built or renovated after 1100, in the early years of the Ganga period. For Shaivites and Vaishnavites Bhubaneswar remains a pilgrimage center of great sanctity.

[*See also* Orissa.]

Rajendralala Mitra, *The Antiquities of Orissa* (1875–1880; reprint, 1961). K. C. Panigrahi, *Archaeological Remains at Bhubaneswar* (1961).

GERI HOCKFIELD MALANDRA

BHUMIBOL ADULYADEJ, rules Thailand (Siam) as King Rama IX. Born 5 December 1927 in Cambridge, Massachusetts, Bhumibol was the son of Prince Mahidol of Songkhla and the grandson of King Chulalongkorn. Prince Mahidol, who died when Bhumibol was only a year old, was studying public health and medicine at Harvard University when his son was born. Five years after Mahidol's death, Bhumibol, his sister, and his brother Ananda (later Rama VIII) left Thailand to study in Switzerland.

Throughout World War II, the family continued to live in Switzerland, returning briefly to Thailand in early December 1945. Tragically, four days before he was to leave for Switzerland to complete his studies, the young Ananda died in his chambers of a mysterious gunshot wound. Bhumibol became king but did not remain in Thailand to witness the ensuing political turmoil; he and the rest of the family returned to Switzerland. To prepare for his future responsibilities, Bhumibol switched from scientific studies to law and political science at the University of Lausanne. As monarch, Bhumibol is still keen on agricultural research (the palace operates an experimental farm in Bangkok), hydraulic engineering, the practical application of artificial rain, and the manufacture of synthetic fuels.

In 1950, Bhumibol interrupted his studies and returned to Thailand to marry M.R.W. Sirikit Kitiyakorn. On 5 May of that year he was crowned Rama IX. The king has a son and three daughters, two of whom, Crown Prince Vajiralongkorn and Crown Princess Maha Chakri Sirindhorn, have been designated heirs apparent to the throne.

As a constitutional monarch, Bhumibol symbolizes the unity of the Thai nation. His long reign has allowed him to develop an important role for the monarchy. His status and prestige were greatly enhanced during the regime of Prime Minister Sarit Thanarat (1958–1963), during which a symbiotic relationship between king and the military regime was institutionalized. Since that time, the throne has exercised direct and indirect legitimizing prerogatives during times of political crisis and instability. Members of the royal family are active in charitable organizations and cultural groups. They have become active patrons of the conservative and nationalistic village scout movement, which played pivotal roles in political events of the late 1970s.

Following the ouster of the government of Thanom Kittikachorn in October 1973 and the ensuing political polarization, the royal family became more involved in the machinations of faction politics in Thailand. In fact, the conservative Thanin Kraiwichien government, formed after the army coup of 6 October 1976, has the tacit support of the throne. The most recent coup, the Young Turks' coup of 1 April 1981, illustrated the importance of monarchical support: the young army officers gave up their attempt to overthrow the government by force when the queen made public her support of the incumbent Prem government. Although Bhumibol himself is still respected and revered by his subjects, open criticism and ridicule have been leveled at some members of the royal family.

[*See also* Thailand; Ananda Mahidol; Sarit Thanarat; *and* Thanom Kittikachorn.]

Thak Chaloemtiarana, *Thailand* (1979). John Girling, *Thailand* (1981). Chaianan Samudvanija, *The Thai Young Turks* (1982). THAK CHALOEMTIARANA

BHUTAN, an independent kingdom situated north of the Bengal-Assam plain in the eastern Himalayas. With an area of 18,000 square miles, this rugged, mountainous country borders Sikkim and Tibet's Chumbi Valley on the west, and the Indian state of Arunachal Pradesh on the east. The crest of the Himalayan range demarcates the country's northern border with Chinese-occupied Tibet.

Bhutan's population is made up largely of Bhotias who migrated from Tibet's eastern Khams province as early as the ninth century CE. A number of indigenous Tibeto-Burman ethnic groups such as the Monpa and Sherdukpen of eastern Bhutan make up a significant proportion of the population. In the nineteenth century the British encouraged Nepalese Hindus to settle and cultivate the *duars,* Bhutan's alluvial lowland river valleys. These people now represent nearly 30 percent of the total Nepalese population.

The early history of the country is obscure, but by the twelfth century rival Buddhist sects from Tibet had extended their influence over central Bhutan through alliances with regional chieftains. Buddhist monasticism provided the foundation and administrative framework for the eventual unification of the country under the first *dharmaraja* (spiritual ruler) during the latter half of the sixteenth century. The administration of government was entrusted to a number of provincial lords, called *penlop* and *dzongpen,* who governed from monastic fortresses called *dzong.* Each derived revenues from the Indo-Tibetan trade carried on through his province and from land taxes levied on cultivators inhabiting the *duars* under his jurisdiction. Provincial governors formed a council from which they elected a *deb raja* who oversaw the secular administration and foreign affairs of the state, in conjunction with the overriding spiritual authority of the *dharma raja* and his reincarnate successors. Perennial competition among the governors over succession to the office of *deb raja,* access to power and influence at court, and control of state revenues underlay the regional conflict that characterized much of Bhutan's history through the nineteenth century.

British interests in Bhutan developed after the East India Company's annexation of Assam in 1826. The desire to control the trade and agricultural revenues of the fertile lowlands bordering Assam prompted the British to annex much of Bhutan's *duar* region between 1841 and 1865. [*See* East India Company.] Despite the compensation provided by the British in the form of an annual subsidy, the cession of the *duars* dealt a disastrous blow to the Bhutanese economy and exacerbated the country's civil strife. Weary of Bhutan's chronic instability and anxious to create a secure buffer between its northern territories and Tibet, the British government took steps to establish a durable, centralized rule. In 1907 Ugyen Wangchuk, the *penlop* of Tongsa Province who had assisted the 1904 British mission to Lhasa under Sir Francis Younghusband, was established as the first hereditary maharaja of Bhutan. The Anglo-Bhutanese Treaty of 1910 placed all of Bhutan's foreign relations under the supervision of the Government of India, supervision that has been retained by the Republic of India since 1949.

Jigme Dorje Wangchuk, grandson of Bhutan's first maharaja, succeeded to the throne in 1952 and introduced steps to speed the country's economic and political modernization. These included the encouragement of foreign (chiefly Indian) investment in small-scale industry and agriculture, and the creation of a national assembly of popularly elected representatives to advise the king on constitutional matters. On his death in 1972, Jigme Dorje was succeeded by his seventeen-year-old son Jigme Singye Wangchuk. Bhutan became a member of the United Nations in 1971 and of the Nonaligned Movement in 1973.

[*See also* Wangchuk, Jigme Dorje; Wangchuk, Jigme Singye; Wangchuk, Ugyen; Tibet; Sikkim; *and the map accompanying* Nepal: History of Nepal.]

M. Aris, *Bhutan* (1983). P. Karan, *Bhutan: A Physical and Cultural Geography* (1967). B. Miller, *Lamas and Laymen* (1958). R. Rahul, *Modern Bhutan* (1971). L. Rose, *The Politics of Bhutan* (1977).

RICHARD ENGLISH

BHUTTO, ZULFIQAR ALI (1928–1979), prime minister of Pakistan (1971–1979). Bhutto was born into a family of landlords living in the Larkana district of the Sindh province of Pakistan. He received a bachelor's degree from the University of California, Berkeley, in 1950 and later received a master's degree in jurisprudence from Oxford University.

After teaching international law for a year at Southampton University, Bhutto returned to Pakistan in 1953 and opened a law practice. In 1958 he joined President Ayub Khan's cabinet, and in 1963 he became foreign minister. In that capacity he strengthened Pakistan's ties with China and other countries in Asia and Africa. [*See* Ayub Khan, Mohammad.]

Following the1965 Indo-Pakistan war, Bhutto denounced Ayub's pro-US policies and left his cabinet. In 1967 he organized the Pakistan People's Party (PPP), with a socialist manifesto that became a rallying ground for the mass movement against Ayub's regime. Ayub resigned in 1969, entrusting the government to General Yahya Khan, who reimposed martial law and promised to hold elections on the basis of universal suffrage. These elections were held in 1970, giving a majority of National Assembly seats to the Awami League, an exclusively East Pakistan–based party. The refusal of Yahya Khan's regime to accept this outcome precipitated the secession of East Pakistan in 1971. [*See* Bangladesh *and* Yahya Khan, Agha Muhammad.]

Thereafter Bhutto, whose party had won a majority of National Assembly seats from West Pakistan, took over as head of state. A new constitution was passed in 1973, allowing for elections to be held in 1977; these resulted in another victory for Bhutto's party. The remaining parties disputed the validity of this result and started street agitation demanding new elections. In the midst of this agitation General Zia-ul Haq staged his coup and removed Bhutto from the office of prime minister. [*See* Zia-ul Haq, Mohammad.] In September 1977 Bhutto was arrested, charged with conspiracy in a murder case, and condemned to death. He was executed on 4 April 1979 by the Zia regime, sparking fierce public protests.

[*See also* Pakistan.]

Zulfiqar Ali Bhutto, *The Great Tragedy* (1971). S. J. Burki, *Pakistan under Bhutto, 1971–77* (1980). Charles Moritz, ed., *Current Biography, 1972* (1973).

HASSAN N. GARDEZI

BIHAR, a state of the Republic of India. It consists of two geographic regions: the Ganges Plain and the Chota Nagpur Plateau. The Ganges Plain is divided into a northern part (with the Videha and Vaishali regions) and southern part (the Magadha region).

These areas witnessed significant political, religious, and cultural developments in the ancient period. Videha became a notable center of Brahmanical religion and learning in the eighth and seventh centuries BCE. At Vaishali, the Vajjis or the Licchavis established the world's first republican government (c. 725–484 BCE). Magadha was the base of a large, well-organized empire under the Mauryas (321–185 BCE) and the Guptas (319–510 CE). Gautama Buddha attained enlightenment at Bodh Gaya in Magadha, and Vardhamana Mahavira founded Jainism there. [*See* Buddhism *and* Jainism.] The earliest Buddhist councils were held in ancient Bihar to decide doctrinal and organizational matters. Ashoka (r. 268–231 BCE) organized Buddhist missionary activities from his famous capital, Pataliputra (modern Patna). The greatest center of Buddhist learning was established (c. 425 CE) at nearby Nalanda. The Pala dynasty (c. 775–1200 CE) revived centralized rule, and there developed a distinct school of stone and bronze sculpture and manuscript painting.

The Turkish Muslims (who would establish the Delhi sultanate in 1206) conquered Magadha in 1197 and gave it a new name—Bihar—derived from *vihara* (Buddhist monastery), many of which they found dotting the area. Bihar proved congenial to the growth of pantheistic Sufism, and Makhdum Sharuf ud-Din (1263–1381) is one of its major figures. Sher Shah (r. 1540–1545) experimented with revenue reforms in, and founded a Pathan empire from his *jagir* at Sasaram. He founded a new city—Patna—on the site of the ancient Pataliputra, which henceforth remained the capital. Akbar (1556–1605) restored Mughal rule and constituted Bihar in 1582 as a *suba* (province) of the Mughal empire with boundaries nearly similar to the modern ones. Chota Nagpur (Jharkhand), inhabited by Adivasis (original inhabitants), witnessed new tribal settlements and state formation. [*See* Adivasis.] Economically, Bihar was an important commercial and industrial center noted for its saltpeter, textiles, and indigo. [*See* Indigo.] Guru Gobind Singh, born in Patna in 1666, transformed Sikhism from a passive religion into a forceful sociopolitical body. [*See* Sikhism.]

In the mid-1750s Bihar became drawn into the whirlpool of Bengal politics, ultimately falling under East India Company rule in 1765. [*See* Bengal.] Consolidation of British supremacy, anti-British risings and movements of varying backgrounds and durations, including the Ahl-i Hadis movement against Western rule and culture (1820s–1880s), and the revolt of 1857 characterize its subsequent history. [*See* Ahl-i Hadis.] It became a "subprovince" in the sprawling, populous Bengal Presidency and suffered political and administrative neglect. Economic development was uneven, with mining overshadowing manufacturing activity. Growth of Western education and political consciousness fostered demand for Bihar's separation from the presidency, which was achieved in 1911. Nationalist India was stirred by Mohandas Gandhi's (1869–1948) experiment in *satyagraha* (passive resistance) at Champaran in 1917. [*See* Gandhi, Mohandas Karamchand *and* Satyagraha.]

Postindependence Bihar is the second most populous Indian state (area, 173,876 square kilometers; population, 69,914,734, 1981 census) with rich mineral resources in Chota Nagpur. Industrial progress has been achieved in key sectors—heavy engineering (Ranchi), steel (Bokaro), thermal power and a refinery (Barauni)—but agriculture dominates the economy. Literacy (26.20 percent, 1971 census) is below the national average, which is 34.45 percent. Hindi is the main language; Maithili, Magadhi, Bhojpuri, and Urdu are spoken as well. In tribal areas Mundari, Kurukh, and Malto are spoken.

[*See also* Bokaro; Patna; Pataliputra; Nalanda; Maurya Empire; Gupta Empire; *and* Licchavi Dynasty.]

Enayat Ahmad, *Bihar: A Physical, Economic and Regional Geography* (1965). R. R. Diwakar, ed., *Bihar through the Ages* (1959). John Houlton, *Bihar, the Heart of India* (1949). B. P. Sinha, K. K. Datta, and S. H. Askari, eds., *Comprehensive History of Bihar,* vols. 1–3 (1976–1984).

QEYAMUDDIN AHMAD

BIHBAHANI, ABD ALLAH (1840–1910), Iranian religious scholar and one of the main leaders of the Constitutional Revolution. In 1891, alone among prominent clericals of Tehran, he opposed the celebrated tobacco boycott, thereby gratifying the prime minister of the day and the British legation. In the following decade he gradually assumed a more patriotic stance, however, denouncing the extravagance of the court and its subordination to Russia. In November 1905 he concluded an alliance with Sayyid Muhammad Tabataba'i, a respected and enlightened religious leader, to seek fundamental changes in the government; this alliance is commonly regarded as the origin of the Constitutional Revolution. Bihbahani played a leading role in all the events of the movement, himself entering the Majles that resulted from it. He was assassinated on 16 July 1910 by four men linked to a secularist group in the Majles (parliament).

[*See also* Constitutional Revolution; Tabataba'i, Muhammad; *and* Qajar Dynasty.]

Hamid Algar, "'Abdallāh Behbahānī," in *Encyclopaedia Iranica* (1982).

HAMID ALGAR

BIHBAHANI, MUHAMMAD BAQIR (1704/1706–1792/1793), Iranian religious scholar who decisively vindicated the Usuli position in Shi'ite jurisprudence and secured for it the dominance it has ever since enjoyed in Iran. Born in Isfahan, he was taken as a child by his father—a pupil of Muhammad Baqir Majlisi—to Karbala in Iraq, which was to be his home for the rest of his life. After completing his studies in Karbala, Bihbahani first intended to return to Iran, but he decided to stay behind to combat the rival Akhbari school of jurisprudence. A vigorous debater and prolific writer, he attained the goal he had set himself and uprooted the Akhbaris from Karbala and other centers of Shi'ite learning. The numerous pupils he trained returned to Iran in the early nineteenth century to inaugurate a tradition of assertive religious leadership that has continued down to the present.

[*See also* Akhbari *and* Usuli.]

Hamid Algar, *Religion and State in Iran, 1785–1906* (1969).

HAMID ALGAR

BIHZAD (d. 1537), more fully Ustadh Kamal al-Din Bihzad, the most famous of Persian miniature painters, born in Herat (in present-day northwest Afghanistan) sometime between 1450 and 1460. His artistic activity began around 1480 at the Timurid court of Sultan Husain Baiqara, where his first patron was Ali Shir Neva'i. Bihzad's name is synonymous with the Timurid style of painting (sometimes called the Herat school), which reached its high point under his direction in the second half of the fifteenth century. Bihzad's work represented the consummation of a new style of painting, characterized by refinement of composition, lifelike representation, a heightened sense of pictorial drama, and perfection of color technique. After the conquest of Herat by the Safavids in 1510, Bihzad entered the service of the Safavid Shah Isma'il in Tabriz, where he was appointed head of the royal library and artists' ateliers in 1522. Not only did he exert a great influence on the development of the Safavid style of painting, but, through his numerous pupils, the Timurid style was carried to Bukhara, where Timurid artistic traditions were preserved until the late sixteenth century under the patronage of the Shaibanid Uzbeks, as well as to the Mughal courts of India.

[*See also* Baiqara, Husain; Herat; Neva'i; Painting: Iranian and Central Asian Painting; *and* Tabriz.]

R. Ettinghausen, "Bihzad," in *The Encyclopaedia of Islam* (new ed., 1960–). F. R. Martin, *The Miniature Painting and Painters of Persia, India and Turkey, from the 8th to the 18th Century* (1912).

MARIA E. SUBTELNY

BIJAPUR, city and district in the northern part of the state of Karnataka, in the western Deccan Plateau of peninsular India. First mentioned in 1074 as Vijayapura ("city of victory"), the city served as a provincial capital of the Chalukya dynasty of Hindu kings. Around 1318 it fell under Muslim rule, governed as a local administrative unit first of the Delhi sultanate and from 1347 of the Bahmani kingdom. In 1490 a Turkish governor, Yusuf Adil Khan, declared his independence and established an independent dynasty that ruled over the western Deccan Plateau until 1686, when the kingdom was absorbed into the Mughal empire. It was during this dynasty's rule that Bijapur, then a city of more than five hundred thousand, attained its height as a center of Indo-Muslim culture.

[*See also* Karnataka *and* Chalukya Dynasties.]

H. Cousens, *Bijapur and its Architectural Remains* (1916). Richard M. Eaton, *Sufis of Bijapur, 1300–1700* (1978).

RICHARD M. EATON

BIKANER, city in Rajasthan, India, formerly a princely state founded in 1465 by Rao Bikaji, a Rathor Rajput and second son of the founder of Jodhpur. In 1570 Rao Kalyanmal became a *mansabdar,* or high-ranking officer, of the Mughal empire, to obtain assistance against attacks from Jodhpur and his own rebellious nobles. Again in 1818 Surat Singhji entered treaty relations with the British to obtain protection both from disruptive nobles and from raiding Pindaris. Bikaner achieved international renown because of the activities of Maharaja Ganga Singh (r. 1898–1942). He was the representative of Indian princes at the Versailles Peace Conference, the chancellor of the Chamber of Princes for several terms, and a political confidant and host to British viceroys and royalty. In 1949 Bikaner joined the Greater Rajasthan Union of independent India.

[*See also* Rajasthan *and* Princely States.]

K. M. Panikkar, *His Highness the Maharaja of Bikaner: A Biography* (1937). Karni Singh, *The Relations of the House of Bikaner with the Central Powers, 1465–1949* (1974).
BARBARA N. RAMUSACK

BIMBISARA (c. 544–493 BCE), scion of the Indian Haryanka line, ruler of Magadha from its capital at Girivraja (Rajagriha). Bimbisara was a patron of the Buddha and possibly of the founder of Jainism, Mahavira. With conquests, peaceful acquisitions through matrimonial alliances, and diplomatic relations with distant states he began the expansion of Magadha that, in the Maurya period, was ultimately destined to embrace nearly the whole of India.

[*See also* Maurya Empire; Magadha; Buddhism; *and* Jainism.]

R. C. Majumdar, ed., *The Age of Imperial Unity* (1968).
A. K. NARAIN

BINH DINH VUONG. *See* Le Loi.

BINH XUYEN, underworld movement in Vietnam between 1945 and 1955. Led by Le Van Vien, known as Bay Vien, the Binh Xuyen was a powerful force in the Saigon-Cholon underworld. Collaborating in turn with the Japanese, Viet Minh, and French, they increased their influence in the post–Japanese occupation period. Breaking with the Communists in 1947, the Binh Xuyen enjoyed official protection while gaining control of Saigon's gambling and vice operations and even its police. After 1954, they formed a shaky alliance with the Cao Dai and Hoa Hao against the Ngo Dinh Diem government but were defeated in bloody fighting during April and May 1955.

[*See also* Vietnam; Cao Dai; Hoa Hao; *and* Ngo Dinh Diem.]

Dennis Duncanson, *Government and Revolution in Vietnam* (1968). Bernard Fall, "The Political-Religious Sects of Vietnam," *Public Affairs* 28 (September 1955): 235–253.
BRUCE M. LOCKHART

BINTAN ISLAND. *See* Bentan Island.

BIRBAL (1528–1586). A brahman in the service of a petty ruler, Birbal joined the emperor Akbar's court and became his confidant. He influenced Akbar toward religious liberalism and was the only Hindu noble to join Akbar's syncretic religion, *din-i Ilahi*. He participated in several military and diplomatic missions, none very spectacular, and died trying to quell an Afghan tribe in the northwest. Akbar bestowed on him the titles Kavi Rai (poet laureate) and Raja Birbal ("prince of heroic strength") and had built for him an elegant stone house at Fatehpur Sikri. Folktales portraying Raja Birbal as court jester are later fabrications.

[*See also* Akbar; Din-i Ilahi; *and* Fatehpur Sikri.]

Parameshwar Prasad Sinha, *Raja Birbal* (1980).
HARBANS MUKHIA

BIRCH, JAMES W. W. (1826–1875), first British resident in Perak, Malaysia. In 1846, after having spent some time in the royal navy, Birch joined the colonial service in Sri Lanka. In 1870 he became colonial secretary of the Straits Settlements, and in 1871, as part of a more aggressive British policy toward the Malay States, he was sent to extract a promise of good conduct from the sultan of Selangor. The Pangkor Engagement of January 1874 confirmed Abdullah as sultan of Perak and inaugurated the British "residential system." In November, Birch, after an unsuccessful mission to persuade ex-sultan Ismail to accept the provisions of the new system, arrived at Bandar Bahru (Perak River) as resident. Neither his temperament nor his experience fitted him for the tasks of establishing the succession and reforming the administration in the context of the ambiguous treaty and fluid political situation. Unfamiliar with Malay and appalled by customs of debt slavery and revenue collection, Birch antagonized Sultan Abdullah and most chiefs. He was assassinated on 2 November 1875 while posting proclamations announcing the direct administration of Perak by the British. Although the ensuing uprising was swiftly suppressed, the fate of Birch warned the British against high-handedness and ignorance in their dealings with Malays.

[*See also* Perak *and* Pangkor Engagement.]

P. L. Burns, ed., *The Journals of J. W. W. Birch* (1976).
A. J. STOCKWELL

BIRENDRA (b. 1945), tenth in the line of Nepal's Shah kings. Birendra succeeded to the throne on the death of his father Mahendra in 1972. The Western-educated Birendra oversaw a liberalization of Mahendra's autocratic "*panchayat* democracy" under the prime ministry of Tulsi Giri (1975–1977). Reports of high-level government corruption and misrule, and the arrest of the exiled opposition leader B. P. Koirala, however, fueled growing popular unrest and demands for political reform. In response to widespread and violent political demonstrations in the spring of 1979, Birendra called for a national referendum on the restoration of political parties. The existing *panchayat* system was favored by a narrow margin, but the king initiated reforms to allow greater public participation in the selection of regional and national legislators. Birendra has continued to uphold Nepal's commitment to the Nonaligned Movement, and, on his coronation in 1975, he announced his determination to make Nepal an international "zone of peace."

[*See also* Giri, Tulsi; Koirala, Bishweshwor Prasad; Mahendra; *and* Nepal: History of Nepal.]

L. R. Baral, *Nepal's Politics of Referendum* (1983).

RICHARD ENGLISH

BIRLA FAMILY, leaders of commerce and industry in Rajasthan, India. The Birla family's ancestral home is in Pilani, in the Shekhavati region of Rajasthan. Seth (later Raja) Baldevdas Birla (1860–1902), a Maheshwari Marwari by caste, migrated to Calcutta in the 1890s and established himself as a broker and trader. During the early twentieth century, Baldevdas's sons expanded the business into areas not previously open to Indians—jute mills, cotton, coal, and paper—with such success that since independence, the Birlas have been among India's leading industrialists. Ghanshyamdas Birla (1894–1983), Baldevdas's second son, contributed generously to Mohandas Gandhi's nationalist campaigns and created extensive educational and research institutions in Pilani and elsewhere in India.

[*See also* Marwaris.]

G. D. Birla, *In the Shadow of the Mahatma: A Personal Memoir* (1953). Thomas A. Timberg, *The Marwaris: From Traders to Industrialists* (1978). USHA SANYAL

BIRUNI, AL- (973–c. 1050), more fully Abu Raihan Muhammad ibn Ahmad al-Biruni, astronomer, mathematician, chronologist, astrologer, mathematical geographer, pharmacologist, historian, and eclectic writer on various scientific subjects. He was born in the district of Khwarazm, now in the USSR, and may have died in the city of Ghazna, in modern Afghanistan.

All of what we know of Biruni's life derives from circumstantial evidence from his own writings and two rather sketchy medieval biographies. After having served at various courts of the Khwarazmshahs he was taken (probably forcibly) by Mahmud of Ghazna, sometime around 1017, to accompany him on his campaigns in India as his personal astrologer. Those campaigns lasted for about thirteen years, and his services were later on passed to Mahmud's son Mas'ud, and from him to his own son Maudud. Those events seem to confirm Biruni's attachment to the Ghaznavid house until about the year 1049, when Maudud died. After that we are in total darkness as to the whereabouts of Biruni.

Although Biruni seems to have made a living of astrology, he wrote very little about it. Of more than 140 books that are known to have been written by Biruni only one is a substantial text on the subject, amounting to about 330 folios; the others are devoted to various disciplines, mainly astronomy and mathematics, and include pharmacology, mineralogy, history, literature, religion, and philosophy.

His most famous works that are available to the English reader are *The Chronology of Ancient Nations,* in which he treats the eras, traditions, and histories of the various religious and ethnic groups known in medieval Islam; *The Determination of Coordinates of Cities,* the most extensive treatise on mathematical geography written in medieval times; *Elements of Astrology,* already mentioned; his book known as the *India,* a sourcebook for the social, intellectual, and cultural life of medieval India; and his *Pharmacology,* a detailed compilation of sources on drugs known in antiquity and medieval times. Unfortunately, the most important astronomical work of Biruni, *Al-qanun al-Mas'udi,* is still untranslated, and the printed Arabic text amounts to some 1,500 pages. Similarly, Biruni's extensive work on mineralogy awaits full translation and study.

In spite of the prolific output of Biruni, medieval biographers devoted to him only a few lines, and the European Latin translators of Arabic works did not show any interest in his works. One wonders why he was treated with such disregard when his contemporaries such as Ibn Sina and Ibn al-Haitham received much more than their share of attention. The answer to that must be sought in the kind of writings Biruni was engaged in, and in his reputation among his contemporaries. For although Biruni was supposed to have been writing in the medieval tradition of natural philosophy, his biographers seem to think that "he was not especially gifted in philosophical matters."

[*See also* Ibn Sina *and* Mahmud of Ghazna.]

D. J. Boilot, "Bīrūnī," in *The Encyclopaedia of Islam* (new ed., 1960–). GEORGE SALIBA

BLACK FLAGS, a bandit organization that operated in northern Vietnam during the last half of the nineteenth century. Created from remnants of Taiping rebel groups that operated in South China during the 1860s, the Black Flags moved across the border into French Indochina and, under the leadership of the Chinese pirate Liu Yongfu (Vietnamese, Luu Vinh Phuc), preyed on farm villages in Tonkin. During the 1870s and 1880s, the Black Flags fought against the French, killing the famous French adventurer Francis Garnier in a skirmish near Hanoi in 1873. After the French conquest of Tonkin, the organization was disbanded and Liu Yongfu retired to China.

[*See also* Vietnam *and* Garnier, Francis.]

Henry McAleavy, *Black Flags in Vietnam* (1968).

WILLIAM J. DUIKER

BLACK HOLE, room in old Fort William, Calcutta, where British prisoners were kept after an attack on the fort by Siraj ud-Daulah in June 1756. British reports claimed that the small room (eighteen feet by fourteen feet ten inches) held 146 prisoners, of whom 123 died by suffocation. More recent accounts suggest that it held at most only 64 prisoners, of whom 43 died.

[*See also* Siraj ud-Daulah *and* Fort William.]

Brijen K. Gupta, *Sirajuddaullah and the East India Company, 1756–1757* (1962). LYNN ZASTOUPIL

BLUE MUTINY. In 1859 peasants in Lower Bengal refused to grow indigo for European planters, claiming it was unprofitable. Violence erupted between planters and cultivators. Magistrates jailed peasants who broke indigo contracts, and by 1860 some peasants were refusing to pay land rents. A government commission reported in 1860 that the payments made to cultivators for the indigo crop were too low. In Calcutta, Dinabandhu Mitra's play *Nil Darpan (The Mirror of Indigo)*, critical of the planters, circulated among sympathetic Indians, missionaries, and government officials. After 1861 indigo production continued in Bengal, but usually at higher rates of payment to the peasant cultivators.

[*See also* Indigo.]

Jogesh Chandra Bagal, *Peasant Revolution in Bengal* (1953). Blair Kling, *The Blue Mutiny* (1966).

JUDITH E. WALSH

BODAWHPAYA (1744–1819), sixth ruler (r. 1782–1819) of Burma's Konbaung dynasty. Fourth son of Alaunghpaya (r. 1752–1760), Maung Yaik seized the throne on 11 February 1782 from his nephew Maung Maung, eldest son of Naungdawgyi (r. 1760–1763), who seven days earlier had deposed another nephew, Singu (r. 1776–1782).

Bodawhpaya's domestic and foreign policies were failures and brought about a long decline in the health of the Konbaung state. In 1783 and 1802, in an unsuccessful attempt to end the embezzlement of crown lands, services, and revenues, Bodawhpaya issued reams of edicts and ordered kingdom-wide cadastral, revenue, and population surveys.

To retrieve the Burmese position in the east, which had been forfeited by Singu, Bodawhpaya pursued a sporadic and unsuccessful war with Thailand, at large costs in manpower, from 1784 to 1811. In 1784, he made the chaotic kingdom of Arakan a directly ruled province. From 1790 to 1802, he imposed heavy taxes and levies to raise money for the construction of the huge Mingun Pagoda and the Meikhtila tank and canal system. The long-term effect of the wars and construction projects, coupled with a great famine from about 1805 to 1812, was to significantly disturb Burma's social and economic organization, as can be seen from the widespread banditry and insurrections common until 1814.

By 1794 Burmese rule in Arakan produced unrest and insurrections, involving tense and occasionally armed confrontations with the neighboring British East India Company. The company's attempts between 1795 and 1812 to establish political and commercial relations were fruitless; Bodawhpaya was profoundly suspicious of its motives and perceived complicity in Arakanese dissidence, particularly in the Chin Pyan rebellion of 1811–1815.

Lacking serious opposition from uncles or brothers, Bodawhpaya's position was generally secure. In 1808, his eldest son, the crown prince, died, and he named his grandson as heir apparent. Bodawhpaya's two next eldest sons, the Prome and Toungoo princes, opposed this move, and each made long-range plans to contest the succession. Bodawhpaya's skillful management of the conflict and his grandson's superior resources secured the throne. After Bodawhpaya's death on 5 June 1819, Bagyidaw (1819–1837) was able to succeed his grandfather without armed conflict.

[*See also* Konbaung Dynasty; Alaunghpaya; Singu; Arakan; *and* East India Company.]

WILLIAM J. KOENIG

BODINDECHA SING SINGHASENI (1777–1848), Thai military leader and administrator. The son of Chaophraya Aphairacha (Pin), Sing entered royal service as a page *(mahatlek)*, rising rapidly to become head of the Mahatthai, the military division of the government, in 1827. At that time he held the title *phraya rachasuphawadi*, which was later changed to *chaophraya bodindecha*. Sing led Thai troops in campaigns against Vientiane in 1827–1828, against Vietnam in 1833–1834, and against the Vietnamese in Kampuchea (Cambodia) in 1840–1842 and 1845–1847. He succeeded in strengthening Thai administrative authority in the Khorat Plateau, the Mekong Valley, and western Cambodia, thereby adding to the kingdom's wealth and influence.

CONSTANCE M. WILSON

BOEDI OETOMO. *See* Budi Utomo.

BOHRAS (Bohoras), members of a Shi'ite Muslim sect of predominantly Indian ethnic origin, ultimately derived religiously from colonies of Arab missionaries and merchants sent first from Fatimid Egypt (tenth to twelfth century) and later from Yemen. Although a few Bohras have become Sunni, most are followers of the Tayyibi Isma'ili Da'i Mutlaq, whose headquarters are in Bombay and Surat. The main branches of this group are the Da'udis, the Sulaymanis, and some smaller offshoots, such as the Aliyyas and Nagoshias. Total membership in all Bohra communities is most probably less than half a million. [*See also* Islam.]

PAUL E. WALKER

BOKARO, a major industrial city in Bihar, where one of India's two Soviet-built steel plants is located (the other is at Bhilai, in Madhya Pradesh). Negotiations surrounding the Bokaro steel plant became a major issue in the early 1960s when US president John F. Kennedy originally agreed to build the plant but backed down when it could not be built in the private sector. The Soviet-built plant, which is in the public sector, does not operate to capacity and has been troubled by bureaucratic difficulties, thus becoming a symbol of failure for critics of Indo-Soviet relations.

Marcus Franda, "India and the Soviets," in *American Universities Field Staff Reports* 19 (1975): 1–11.

MARCUS FRANDA

BOKHARA. *See* Bukhara.

BOLAN PASS, southernmost of the major passes linking Inner Asia with the Indus Plain. The pass runs about fifty-five miles through the Central Brahui Range of Baluchistan Province, Pakistan, from Kolpur in the northwest to Rindli in the southeast; its elevations range from about 750 to 5,900 feet and can be traversed by highway and broad-gauge railway from Sibi to Quetta. The scene of many battles, the pass was negotiated by the British in the first and second Afghan Wars (1839 and 1878) and was transferred by the khan of Kalat to the British in 1888.

The Imperial Gazetteer of India (1908).

JOSEPH E. SCHWARTZBERG

BOMBAY. One of the largest cities in India and the largest port on its western coast, Bombay is an industrial and cultural center and the administrative capital of Maharashtra. Bombay's name probably derived from a local goddess, Mumba Devi. Other theories assign it to the Portuguese *Bom Bahia* ("good bay") or the Muslim *mubarak* ("lucky"). In Marathi, the regional language, Bombay is known as Mumbai, a usage adopted by the state government but not by the Indian government.

Initially a cluster of seven islands that were joined by reclamation mainly during the nineteenth century, Bombay is also linked with adjacent Salsette Island to the north to form the contiguous territory of Greater Bombay. In 1971 work began on a twin city on the mainland; it is called New Bombay and will eventually have a population of two million.

Inhabited since prehistoric times, the area was ruled by early Indian dynasties from Central India. Of the surviving Buddhist and Hindu cave temples, the most noteworthy are those dedicated to the god Shiva in the eighth-century caves on Elephanta Island in the harbor.

In 1534 the Bombay islands were ceded to the

Portuguese, who established a trading post facing the Arabian Sea at Mahim. They were given to Charles II of England in 1661 as part of his dowry when he married Catherine of Portugal; he assigned them to the East India Company in 1668. In 1687 the company moved its headquarters on the western coast from Surat to Bombay, which became the capital of the Presidency of Bombay. On independence in 1947 the city continued as capital of Bombay State and later of Maharashtra, after the state was split into Gujarat and Maharashtra in 1960.

The company established a trading post, a fort, and docks on the southern tip of the islands facing the harbor. Threats from European and Indian enemies led to the development during the eighteenth century of a walled town to protect the cosmopolitan population. As dock facilities expanded Bombay developed both an entrepôt role for coastal and overseas trade and, beginning in the 1750s, a major shipbuilding industry under a Parsi master shipbuilder from Gujarat. Despite the efforts of early governors, particularly Gerald Aungier (1669–1677), growth was slow and sporadic; in 1661 the population was estimated at 10,000 and in 1780 at 100,000. Nor did Bombay produce the profits expected by company directors in London; toward the end of the century they seriously discussed reducing its status.

Bombay prospered in the nineteenth century. It ruled Gujarat by 1808 and Maharashtra by 1818. As the company trade monopoly broke, Indian merchants accumulated wealth. The first cotton mill went into production in 1856; by 1890, sixty-nine mills made Bombay a significant Indian-owned textile center. Though shipbuilding disappeared with the sailing ship, dock facilities became crucial after the Suez Canal opened.

In 1803 a great fire in the walled town led to a planned settlement slightly to the north. By the 1860s the walls were no longer useful and were pulled down when Governor Bartle Frere gave the city its characteristic Indo-Gothic public buildings. Population increased (to 821,764 in 1891) and slums worsened. Some slums were cleared and roads widened by the Improvement Trust after an epidemic of the plague at the end of the nineteenth century. By then Bombay was a modern city with water, sewerage, electricity, gas, and transport.

Twentieth-century developments were promoted by a largely Indian-elected Municipal Corporation, by the Port Trust, and by the state government. Active nationalist and trade union movements emerged. Bombay hosted the first Indian National Congress in 1885 and supported Mohandas Gandhi's campaigns from 1919 with money and personnel.

FIGURE 1. *Victoria Terminus.* This imposing structure is a legacy of the period when Bombay served as a center of British power in India.

After independence, the population grew by about 1,000,000 to 2,329,020 in 1951 and has continued to expand, straining amenities. The official population of Bombay City in 1981 was 3,258,117. The obsolescent textile industry is being replaced by new industries. The city remains preeminent within the Indian republic because of its finance, banking, trade, commerce, industry, culture, and harbor base.

[*See also* East India Company; Portuguese: Portuguese in India; *and* Maharashtra.]

S. M. Edwardes, *The Rise of Bombay* (1902). *Gazetteer of Bombay City and Island,* 3 vols. (1909; reprint, 1977). N. Harris, *Economic Development, Cities and Planning: The Case of Bombay* (1978). James Masselos, *Towards Nationalism* (1974). M. D. Morris, *The Emergence of an Industrial Labour Force in India: A Study of the Bombay Cotton Mills, 1854–1947* (1965). G. Tindall, *City of Gold: The Biography of Bombay* (1982).

JIM MASSELOS

BOMBAY-BURMAH TRADING CORPORATION (BBTC), a major British-owned timber and trading firm that evolved from an earlier company formed in 1862. The BBTC operated in Burma until its nationalization in 1948. In 1862 King Mindon gave the firm timber-extraction rights in the district of Pyinmana. When the king's council *(hluttaw)* imposed a fine of 23 lakhs of rupees in August 1885 for the illegal export of logs, the BBTC appealed to the British government in Rangoon and London for assistance. Burmese were pressed to reduce the fine, but before a final settlement could be reached, the British presented an ultimatum with a deadline on this and other issues that the Burmese were unable to meet. The result was a war that culminated in the annexation of Upper Burma and the deposition of Mindon's successor, King Thibaw. The BBTC thus earned a reputation in Burmese nationalist history not only as an exploitative, foreign capitalist firm but also as a major culprit in Burma's loss of independence. The firm's timber and other trading activities extended for many years beyond Burma to other regions of Southeast Asia.

[*See also* Burma; Mindon; Anglo-Burmese Wars; *and* Thibaw.]

John F. Cady, *A History of Modern Burma* (1958).

ROBERT H. TAYLOR

BONE-RANK SYSTEM. *See* Korea, Class Structure in *and* Silla.

BONIFACIO, ANDRES (1863–1897), political organizer who founded the secret society called Katipunan, which was to initiate the Philippine Revolution. Although he was born in Manila to a relatively humble family and had only limited formal education, Bonifacio was an original member of the middle-class Liga Filipina in 1892. After Jose Rizal's exile, however, Bonifacio proceeded to found the Katipunan, which was committed to revolution, within the framework of the Liga. He was familiar with the writings of the Propaganda movement and diligently made copies of Rizal's letters (later seized by the police). He was also an assiduous reader of works on the French Revolution and kindred subjects, which nurtured in him and his associates enthusiasm for the revolution they planned.

During its first years the Katipunan was a small, Masonic-type secret society, confined mostly to Manila. It began to expand in 1895, particularly in Cavite, where two councils—Magdiwang and Magdalo—divided the province. The betrayal of the Katipunan in Manila precipitated the uprising on 31 August 1896. Bonifacio's forces were repeatedly defeated, and he retired into the hills. The Caviteños, however, were successful in driving the Spaniards out of the province, particularly under the leadership of Emilio Aguinaldo. But friction arose between the two councils, and Bonifacio was invited to come to Cavite to mediate.

In Cavite, Bonifacio immediately sided with the Magdiwang, thus alienating the Magdalo, which had been the most successful militarily under Aguinaldo. Not realizing that the revolution had now developed beyond the confines of the Katipunan, Bonifacio agreed only reluctantly to electing a revolutionary government. When the elections were held, Bonifacio not only lost the presidency to Aguinaldo; his election to the modest post of minister of interior was also challenged, on the grounds of his little education. Stung by the challenge, Bonifacio, in his capacity as *supremo* of the Katipunan, declared the elections null and void. Soon, however, he found that regionalism was the real force working against him, as most Magdiwang supported the new government. Thwarted in his attempts to persuade two of Aguinaldo's generals to mount a coup d'état, Bonifacio resolved to leave Cavite for other provinces that recognized him.

Aguinaldo's men captured his party, killing one brother and wounding Bonifacio. In a farce of a trial, he and his other brother were condemned to death. Although Aguinaldo commuted the sentence, he later claimed to have been persuaded by his leaders that the execution had to be carried out for the sake of the revolution. To what extent Aguinaldo's assent was meant to save the republic or to remove a rival is still debated.

Teodoro Agoncillo's portrayal of Bonifacio as the leader of a proletarian revolution has been countered by the middle-class composition of the Katipunan, as has the image of a "people's war." Reynaldo Ileto has seen Bonifacio as the articulator of peasant perceptions of change, which are derived from the religious epic of the *Pasyon* (the life and death of Jesus), rather than as a fundamentally secular leader formed by the Propaganda movement. Those who concede that Bonifacio spoke the "Pasyon language" of the masses still point to his antireligious attitudes (emphasized by his opponents in Cavite) as part of the reason for his downfall in Cavite, where the revolution was promoted by many Filipino clergy as a holy war.

[*See also* Katipunan; Philippine Revolution; Liga Filipina; Rizal, Jose Mercado; Propaganda Movement; *and* Aguinaldo, Emilio.]

Teodoro A. Agoncillo, *The Revolt of the Masses* (1956). Reynaldo C. Ileto, *Pasyon and Revolution* (1979). Carlos Quirino, ed., *The Trial of Andres Bonifacio*, translated by Virginia Palma-Bonifacio (1963). Epifanio de los Santos, *The Revolutionists* (1973). John N. Schumacher, "Recent Perspectives on the Revolution," *Philippine Studies* 30 (1982): 445–492. JOHN N. SCHUMACHER, S.J.

BORNEO. *See* Kalimantan.

BOROBUDUR, Buddhist monument representing the highest expression of the artistic genius of early Java. It is an immense stupa in the form of stone terraces covering the upper part of a natural hill, on the flattened top of which stands the central stupa. It is 150 feet tall; a walk of the entire distance from the galleries to the summit covers more than three miles. The walls of the galleries are decorated with 1,500 pictorial relief panels of the Buddha's teachings and 1,212 ornamental panels that illustrate Mahayana Buddhist texts. There are also 400 statues of the Buddha. The base has a series of reliefs depicting the effects of good and evil in daily life, but these are largely covered by a broad casement of stonework.

The stupa as a whole forms an impressive and convincing textbook of the teachings of the Nalanda school of Buddhism. The sculpture is in the classical style of Gupta India, but the reliefs are not Indian but Javanese; local artists adopted Indian models to conform with Javanese traditions. Shaped like a mandala, a mythical model of the universe, the Borobudur combines the symbols of the circle (heaven), the square (earth), and of a stupa (the Buddha). The pilgrim's walk leads around the temple nine times before reaching the top. At each level the pilgrim is swallowed symbolically by a *kala* monster, and then given new life. The movement from richly decorated terraces full of reliefs, Buddhas, and other ornaments to circular terraces devoid of all decorations symbolizes the pilgrim's progress from the material attachments of this world to the spacious simplicity of nirvana, one's release from the endless chain of rebirth.

J. G. de Casparis infers from a 842 inscription that the full name of the Borobudur was "the mountain of accumulation of virtue on the ten stages of the bodhisattva" and that this was a proclamation of the legitimacy of the Sailendra monarchs, who

FIGURE 1. *Buddha, Borobudur.* Sculpted from lava stone in the late eighth century, this figure is derived from Gupta prototypes. In the background are several of the small perforated stupas that surround the Great Stupa.

then held authority over Central Java. He argues that the Borobudur and its subordinate temples, the Candi Mendut and Candi Pawon, must be interpreted as a whole and analyzed as representing a synthesis of Mahayana Buddhism and local ancestor worship. Candi Mendut, the "temple of the bamboo grove," represented the first stage in one's preparation for the path leading to buddhahood; the nine bodhisattvas sculpted on its outside represented the realization of the Sailendra monarch that he followed a line of ancestors who had attained enlightenment. The theme of Candi Pawon was a royal cremation that represented the last stage of worldy attachment and gave entrance to the supermundane stages in the progress of the bodhisattva to buddhahood, which are represented in the Borobudur itself. Casparis believes that nine Sailendra princes each had his place on the path leading to buddhahood, which was depicted on the covered lower terraces of the Borobudur. The princes were followed by the founder of the Sailendra dynasty, the "lord of the mountain," who had achieved the final level of existence before obtaining buddhahood. The lord of the mountain's path beyond his predecessors was represented by the movement from the lower terraces and culminated in the pinnacle of the stupa at the top.

[*See also* Java; Sailendra; *and* Architecture: Southeast Asian Architecture.]

Luis Gómez and Hiram W. Woodward, Jr., eds., *Borobudur: History and Significance of a Buddhist Monument* (1981). Claire Holt, *Art in Indonesia: Continuities and Change* (1967). F. H. van Naerssen and R. C. de Iongh, *The Economic and Administrative History of Early Indonesia* (1977). KENNETH R. HALL

BORODIN, MICHAEL (Mikhail Markovich Grusenberg; 1884–1951), most prominent Russian adviser in China during the civil war of 1923–1927; prime mover for the forces of national revolution that established the nationalist Republic of China in 1927. Trusted by Lenin, Borodin was dispatched to China in 1923 to strengthen the flagging Guomindang (Kuomintang, KMT, or Nationalist Party). In his short tenure he managed to rejuvenate the Guomindang through internal reforms, mass campaigns, and a united front strategy with the Chinese Communist Party (CCP). Borodin worked with the Chinese Communists to strengthen their position for ultimate takeover of the Chinese Revolution. The failure of this policy resulted in his secret flight from China in 1927.

Michael Borodin was born on 9 July 1884 in the Vitebsk province of the Russian Pale, an area in which the tsars required Jewish subjects to live. Named Mikhail Markovich Grusenberg, he later adopted many non-Jewish aliases, the most famous being Michael Borodin. He first attended a local Jewish school, then an evening Russian school in Riga. There he participated in Jewish worker movements and at the age of nineteen became active in the Bolshevik faction of the Riga Russian Social Democratic Labor Party. In 1904 Borodin traveled from Riga to Switzerland, where he met Russian émigrés, including Lenin, and where he became an active revolutionary. When the 1905 Revolution failed, Borodin went into forced exile in England and the United States. He became a courier of money and information for the continuing revolutionary movement.

While in America he attended Valparaiso University in Indiana, where he met his future wife. To make money to support his wife and infant son, he taught English to foreigners at Chicago's Hull House. Later he opened his own school. During his stay in Chicago from 1909 until 1918 Borodin became an active socialist and learned in intimate detail the hardships of the working class. His loyalties, however, remained with the Russian revolutionary movement.

In 1918, with the success of the Russian Revolution, Borodin returned to the Soviet Union. He became a translator for Lenin, wrote a book on conditions in Great Britain, and was sent to Mexico, where he formed the Mexican Communist Party.

According to his son, Borodin's assignment to China came as a "total surprise." He was most likely chosen because he was a Russian, knew English, had superior organizing skills, and was able to get along with people. Borodin represented three Soviet authorities: the Soviet government, the executive committee of the Communist International, and the Russian Communist Party. He was charged with a threefold task: (1) to form a Soviet-Guomindang alliance that would drive the imperialists out of China, (2) to persuade Sun Yat-sen to reorganize the KMT to create a centralized party with an anti-imperialist platform and a radical social program, and (3) to harness the Chinese Communists to the KMT's national revolution through a united front strategy, which would prepare them to take over and lead a social revolution. In sum, Borodin was ordered to accomplish the contradictory tasks of constructing a stable KMT-Soviet alliance and front against imperialism, while planning to implement a subsequent Communist takeover.

Borodin arrived in China in September 1923. His first two years, until the death of Sun Yat-sen in early 1925, were filled with success. He drafted the KMT constitution of 1924 (in English) and reorganized the party into a tight structure, based on democratic centralism in the image of the Russian Communist Party. He elevated Sun Yat-sen to a position of unquestioned authority within the party. To protect Sun and provide the Soviet Union with a reliable ally, he built an army at Whampoa. Locally, he promoted a mass mobilization of peasants and workers under the Chinese Communist leadership. Sun's death and the subsequent assassination of Liao Zhongkai severed Borodin's close personal relationships with the KMT. Now on his own, Borodin engaged in disputes with three antagonists: the KMT, the CCP, and the Soviet Union.

In positioning himself as Sun's heir to power, Chiang Kai-shek combined his military base at Whampoa, where he had been commandant, with the strong anticommunist KMT leaders. In successive purges of the Communists in 1926 and 1927, he destroyed Borodin's domestic support. Borodin unsuccessfully joined a KMT opposition group in Wuhan but that front collapsed, leaving him a fugitive. In 1927 he made his way secretly in a caravan of camel trucks across the Chinese frontier to the Soviet Union. The Chinese Communists had been wary of Borodin. Some balked at Borodin's leadership, blaming him for the failures of 1926 and 1927.

Unwilling to admit the defeat of his agent, Stalin at first ordered Borodin to stay with the KMT and at nearly the same time ordered Communist-led uprisings. The result was the near destruction of the Chinese Communist Party. Upon his return to Moscow, Borodin was accused of losing the Chinese Revolution. After two years of interrogation he was given minor jobs and in 1932 was made editor of an English-language paper, the *Moscow Daily News*.

In 1949, a victim of Stalin's anti-Semitism and embarrassment over Mao's successful revolution, Borodin was arrested and dispatched to Yakutsk, one of the harshest Siberian prison camps, where he died in 1951. His death was not reported until 1953.

[*See also* Comintern; Guomindang; Northern Expedition; *and* Sun Yat-sen.]

Lydia Holubnychy, *Michael Borodin and the Chinese Revolution, 1923–1925* (1979). Dan N. Jacobs, *Borodin* (1981).

RICHARD C. KAGAN

BOROMMAKOT, king of Ayudhya (r. 1733–1758), remembered as the last great king of Siam, for the peace and prosperity of his reign were not regained for generations.

As Prince Phon, Borommakot was the designated heir of his elder brother, King Thai Sa (r. 1709–1733), but had to battle his nephews to gain the throne. He balanced royal and noble power in his administration and diminished the manpower resources of competing princes. His reign is best known for his assistance in restoring Buddhism in Sri Lanka (Ceylon), to which the king sent monastic missions in the 1750s.

The king's name, which means "golden urn," comes from the cremation urn in which his remains lay in state on his death. His regnal name was Song Tham (II) or Borommathammikarat.

[*See also* Ayudhya.]

W. A. R. Wood, *A History of Siam* (1926). David K. Wyatt, *Thailand: A Short History* (1984).

DAVID K. WYATT

BOROMMARACHA I, king of Ayudhya (r. 1370–1388), also known as Phangua, established and led an important early political faction in Siam. He was the maternal uncle of King Ramathibodi I (r. 1351–1369). Borommaracha contributed military leadership, as well as the manpower he controlled in the western provinces from his base at Suphanburi, to the new kingdom. When Ramathibodi's young son Ramesuan ascended the throne, Borommaracha seized power. His foreign policy focused on gaining leadership over the Thai peoples of the interior and was not in competition with Cambodian Angkor. His main achievement was his contribution to the growth of Ayudhya's centralized power.

[*See also* Ayudhya *and* Ramathibodi I.]

Charnvit Kasetsiri, *The Rise of Ayudhya* (1976). David K. Wyatt, *Thailand: A Short History* (1984).

DAVID K. WYATT

BOROMMATRAILOKANAT (1448–1488), king of Ayudhya (r. 1431–1488), also known as Trailok; legislative architect of Siam's premodern government. He was the son and designated heir of King Borommaracha II (r. 1424–1448) and in his youth served briefly as the titular ruler of conquered Angkor and Sukhothai before succeeding peacefully to his father's throne.

A century after its foundation, Ayudhya was in an expansionistic phase. It had incorporated vast territories at the expense of Cambodia and Sukhothai during Trailok's father's reign and had attempted to subdue the kingdom of Lan Na in the north. Trailok is credited with fashioning the laws that defined Ayudhya's state administration and the social and political hierarchy. Together, the law of the civil hierarchy and the law of the military and provincial hierarchies assigned a numerical rank *(sakdi na)* to everyone in the kingdom, specifying exactly their relative statuses and grouping them into functional or territorial units for administrative and military purposes. Presumably working on the basis of existing government units, the administration was divided into civil and military divisions, the Mahatthai and Kalahom, respectively. Under the Mahatthai were ministries of the capital, the palace, agriculture or lands, and the treasury (Phrakhlang), each with numerous subdivisions, including provincial units, while in parallel fashion four great generals were under the Kalahom. The functions of each unit were specified, and everyone in the kingdom was permanently attached to a department *(krom)* for compulsory labor service. Although considerably elaborated later, Trailok's laws were to serve as the foundation of Siamese bureaucracy for the next four hundred years.

For much of his reign, Trailok was engaged in constant warfare against King Tilok of Lan Na—the subject of the great contemporary poem "Yuan phai." To pursue the war, Trailok ruled from Phitsanulok from 1463, leaving his son Borommaracha III, or Intharacha II, to rule in Ayudhya and succeed him in 1488.

[*See also* Ayudhya; Sukhothai; Lan Na; Sakdi Na; Mahatthai; Kalahom; Phrakhlang; *and* Tilokaracha.]

A. B. Griswold and Prasert na Nagara, "A Fifteenth-Century Siamese Historical Poem," in *Southeast Asian History and Historiography,* edited by C. D. Cowan and O. W. Wolters (1976). Charnvit Kasetsiri, *The Rise of Ayudhya* (1976). H. G. Quaritch Wales, *Ancient Siamese Government and Administration* (1965). W. A. R. Wood, *A History of Siam* (1926). David K. Wyatt, *Thailand: A Short History* (1984).

DAVID K. WYATT

BOSCH, JOHANNES VAN DEN (1780–1844), Dutch colonial official. Bosch was a respected military officer in Java and in Europe (1799–1819) before he turned his energies to a humanitarian scheme for settling urban poor on open lands in the eastern Netherlands (1818–1827). In 1815 and 1818 he published his views on colonies and political economy, which were contrary to the prevailing liberal attitudes. In 1827 he was sent to the Dutch West Indies and Suriname to reform finances and administration. Appointed governor-general of the East Indies upon his return (1828), he was asked to formulate a plan for making Java profitable. His proposal was the Kultuurstelsel, or cultivation system, which he introduced into Java (1830–1833) and guided to success as minister of colonies (1834–1839).

[*See also* Kultuurstelsel.]

ROBERT VAN NIEL

BOSE, SUBHAS CHANDRA (1897–1945), an important Indian nationalist who went on to lead the Indian National Army and form the provisional government of Azad Hind during World War II; he was popularly called Netaji ("revered leader"). Born a Bengali Kayasth, Bose was raised in Cuttack, and attended Presidency College, Calcutta. Expelled for complicity in beating a professor, Bose was allowed to enter Scottish Churches College a year later. He graduated, and, urged by his father, he went to England in 1919 and took the Indian Civil Service examination. Surprising all, Bose placed fourth in the examination, but then resigned and returned to India to enter the nationalist movement.

Bose found his political guru in Chittaranjan Das and was given important posts including chief executive officer of the Calcutta Corporation in 1924. [*See* Das, Chittaranjan.] A few months later, Bose was imprisoned and from 1925 to 1927 held in Mandalay Prison. In ill health, he was released, whereupon he returned to politics. For a brief time he was the president of the Bengal Provincial Congress Committee. In 1928 he became a general secretary of the Indian National Congress and a widely popular leader of the younger leftists. He pressed Mohandas Gandhi to move more quickly and forcefully for complete independence.

Bose spent a good deal of the years 1933 to 1937 in Europe recovering his health. While in Europe he wrote *The Indian Struggle,* an account of Indian politics from 1920 to 1934, and *An Indian Pilgrim,* a brief, insightful autobiography. He also did propaganda work for Indian nationalism and visited many countries.

In 1938 Bose became president of the Indian National Congress with Gandhi's blessing. The next year he decided to run again, against Gandhi's wishes. He defeated Gandhi's candidate, P. Sitaramayya, but then was moved to resign his presidency after a controversy about the selection of the Working Committee. Bose formed the Forward Bloc, a pressure group working for more direct action against the Raj. [*See* Gandhi, Mohandas Karamchand.]

Imprisoned again in 1940, Bose fasted, was released, and on 16 January 1941, slipped out of his house, reached the frontier, and walked into Afghanistan. Receiving Italian and German help, he traveled to Berlin, where he set up the Free India Center and the Indian Legion, a small fighting force. In 1943 Bose reached Southeast Asia and, with Japanese aid, reconstituted the Indian National Army (INA) and set up the Provisional Government of Azad Hind. After the INA and Japanese were beaten in Burma, Bose fled and was killed in a plane crash in Taiwan in August 1945, although controversy surrounds his death.

Sisir K. Bose, Alexander Werth, and S. A. Ayer, eds., *A Beacon across Asia* (1973). Subhas Chandra Bose, *The Indian Struggle 1920–1942* (1964) and *Netaji: Collected Works,* edited by Sisir K. Bose, vol. 1 (1980). Leonard A. Gordon, *Bengal: The Nationalist Movement 1876–1940* (1974).

LEONARD A. GORDON

BOUN OUM (1911–1980), prince of the Laotian kingdom of Champassak and prime minister of Laos (1949–1950; 1960). Born at Bassac, Boun Oum was the son of Prince Ratsadanay, head of the former royal family of Champassak and governor of Champassak Province. A former vassal state of Siam, Champassak straddles the Mekong River at the southern extremity of what became the French colony of Laos. Boun Oum entered the colonial administration in 1934 and gained great authority in southern Laos. A man of simple courage, personal force, and princely charm, he played an outstanding part in the Franco-Lao resistance to the Japanese in 1945. After the Japanese surrender he welcomed the returning French and resisted the Lao Issara, in whom he saw the threat of Vietnamese domination.

Under the new constitution of Laos, in 1947 Boun Oum merged his ancestral royal rights into the sovereignty of Laos and in recognition was created inspector-general of the kingdom for life, with precedence after the king and crown prince. Boun Oum was prime minister in 1949–1950 and again in December 1960. He was the popular figurehead of the southern-based right-wing faction that drove out the government formed under Prince Souvannaphouma after the Neutralist coup d'état of August 1960. The ensuing civil war was ended briefly in June 1962 by agreement between princes Boun Oum, Souvannaphouma, and Souphanouvong on a national government and by the Geneva Agreement of 1962 on the neutrality of Laos. Boun Oum then retired from politics. When Laos was taken over by the Communists in 1975, he was undergoing medical treatment in France, where he died.

[*See also* Champassak; Lao Issara; Souvannaphouma; Souphanouvong; *and* Laos.]

A. J. Dommen, *Conflict in Laos* (1971).

HUGH TOYE

BOWRING, SIR JOHN (1792–1872), British author, editor, and statesman. Bowring served as governor of Hong Kong from 1854 to 1859 and during this period was also appointed Great Britain's envoy to several other Asian countries, including Thailand. In 1855 he visited Bangkok, where he successfully negotiated a Treaty of Friendship and Commerce with the Thai court. The treaty opened Thailand to foreign trade and provided for extraterritorial privileges, the exchange of consuls, and the limitation of customs duties. The expansion of trade, which followed this and similar treaties with other Western nations, encouraged the development of commercial agriculture and the export of Thai products.

Bowring published his journal of the 1855 visit and treaty negotiations in his book *The Kingdom and People of Siam.* After the success of this book, he wrote a second, a compilation of information about the Philippine Islands, which he visited in 1858.

Sir John Bowring, *The Kingdom and People of Siam; with a Narrative of the Mission to that Country in 1855* (1857; reprint, 1969) and *A Visit to the Philippine Islands* (1859).

CONSTANCE M. WILSON

BOXER REBELLION. *See* Yihetuan.

BRAHMAN (Sanskrit, *brahmana*), the highest of the four traditional *varnas,* or broad delineations of caste, in Hinduism. The term originally meant "one possessed of *brahman,*" a mysterious magical force of potency, and it referred to specially trained priests endowed with such magical potency. By the end of the Rig Vedic period (c. sixth century BCE), the term was used for all members of the priestly group, whether family priests, kings' advisers, or teachers of the Vedas (or of other branches of learning). By the same time, the brahmans had come to be regarded as the uppermost of the four classes or castes, celebrated in *Rig Veda* 10.90 as the mouth of the primeval man, responsible for maintaining the natural cosmic order by accurately performing the sacrifice.

Brahmans now have numerous regionally, and even locally, distinct endogamous caste groups, the number of which has varied with time, which exhibit wide-ranging cultural and organizational diversity. The brahmans of the North and the South differ widely from each other in language and customs and are traditionally divided into two classifications: the northern five groups (the *pancha gaura*) generally reside north of the Vindhya Mountains and are the Kanyakubja, Sarasvata, Gauda, Maithila, and Utkala. The southern five divisions (the *pancha dravida*), are the Maharashtra, Gurjara, Karnataka, Telanga, and Dravida. Writing by brahmans about brahmans has been an integral part of Indian social history from ancient times and has often been intended to justify and maintain the high social status and priveleges of the brahman caste. Modern critics have maintained that the classical brahman writers did not recognize differences between ideal and practice and that they freely colored interpretation of the society and history with their own bias. This criticism applies retrospectively to the *Laws of Manu* and in modern times to popular accounts written to further the cause of "brahman history."

The ancient brahmans not only wrote much but for centuries shaped and dominated Indian social life. It would be historically naive, however, to assume that brahmans in ancient and medieval Hindu kingdoms enjoyed either undisputed or uniform power and dominance. Although they constrained rulers as state priests, they were also challenged as brahman rulers. Indeed, their fortunes changed with particular rulers and emperors. For example, Sikandar (1393–1416), the sixth sultan of Kashmir, persecuted the brahmans and destroyed their temples, forcing them to flee or to die if they refused to convert to Islam. Zain-ul Abidin (1420–1467), the eighth sultan of Kashmir, recalled the exiled brahmans, repealed taxes, and even allowed new temples to be built. [*See* Kashmir.] Under such circumstances, brahman ritual orthodoxy acquired a dual role. It signaled to Muslim rulers a cultural tenacity and rigidity, and to regional Hindu rulers and local householders, a social retreat for protection and support.

In democratic India the brahman stands at the center of increasing religious, political, and economic conflicts and controversies, his historically favored position challenged as never before.

[*See also* Chitpavan Brahmans; Caste; Vedas; Hinduism; Kshatriya; Vaishya; *and* Shudra.]

Louis Dumont, *Homo Hierarchicus, an Essay on the Caste System* (1980). J. H. Hutton, *Caste in India* (1963). Eugene F. Irschick, *Politics and Social Conflict in South India* (1969). R. S. Khare, *The Changing Brahmans* (1970). T. N. Madan, *Family and Kinship: A Study of the Pandits of Rural Kashmir* (1965).

RAVINDRA S. KHARE

BRAHMO SAMAJ, loosely translated as "Society for the Worship of the One True God," established in Calcutta by Debendranath Tagore in 1843, partly to arrest Christian conversions among the Bengali intelligentsia and partly to institutionalize Rammohan Roy's ideology of Hindu Reformation. Although it underwent two major schisms in 1866 and 1878, the Brahmo Samaj remained until 1930 the most creative and articulate movement of radical intelligentsia under British colonialism, dedicated to reshaping the Hindu tradition and laying the intellectual foundations of Hindu modernism.

The Brahmo legacy of Hindu modernism, or the reinterpretation and purification of the Hindu tradition according to contemporary needs and conditions inspired by intracivilizational encounters with the West, represented a series of sociocultural innovations that directly challenged the ideas, values, and practices of Hindu orthodoxy. Rammohan Roy (1772–1833), founder of the Calcutta Unitarian Committee in 1823 and of the Brahmo Sabha in 1828, sought to historicize the pre-Muslim Hindu past, using the building blocks of British Orientalist scholarship, and in so doing he rediscovered a golden age in Vedic India. It was Rajnarain Bose (1826–1899) who promoted the idea of using a defined scriptural source as the holy book of the Hindus—whether the Vedas, Upanishads, or *Bhagavad Gita.* To Keshub Chandra Sen (1838–1884) we owe the earliest attempt to translate Brahmo modernism into such popular Hindu sectarian movements as Shaktism and Vaishnavism, as part of a larger campaign of indigenous modernization. From 1879 until his death, Sen also endeavored to endow Hindu rituals with deeper religious significance as he strived to formulate guiding principles for his New Dispensation. The new philosophic-aesthetic reinterpretation of Hindu festival images was largely accomplished by Rabindranath Tagore (1861–1941).

Efforts to reform Hindu society kept pace with efforts to reform Hindu religion. In 1850 Debendranath Tagore (1817–1905) was the first Brahmo to codify the Brahmo Dharma, or "this-worldly Hindu ethic," as a functional equivalent to the Protestant ethic of the West. The redefinition of Hindu *dharma* (religious code) as social service and the reevaluation of the Upanishadic ethic as the basis of an egalitarian ideology of salvation for India, often attributed to Vivekananda and the Ramakrishna Mission, was an established goal of the Brahmo missionary program as early as the 1860s. The struggle to emancipate Hindu women from an oppressive system was for over a century waged almost exclusively as a crusade by dozens of radical Brahmos. The earliest legal recognition of widow and intercaste marriage was enacted in 1872 as the Brahmo Marriage Act, which also prohibited child marriage, polygamy, and a number of other such practices.

After 1878 the more progressive Sadharan Brahmos pioneered educational reform for Hindu women by extending the equality of education to women in their own families and supporting the principle of equal professional opportunities for them. We may add to this list another series of Brahmo firsts in establishing night schools for workers and peasants (1870), cheap vernacular newspapers for the masses (1871), savings banks for workers (1872), and missions to improve the lot of the depressed castes and Untouchables (1906).

Although the Brahmo Samaj was largely a manifestation of the Bengal Renaissance, Brahmoism did spread to other colonial metropolises throughout South Asia and won converts among non-Bengali urban elites in quest of a new Hindu identity in the modern world. The Brahmo phenomenon reached its peak on the eve of World War I, when 232 branches of the Samaj were reportedly active from Bombay to Singapore and from Lahore to Colombo. On the other hand, Brahmoism per se never appealed to the Hindu masses but remained an intellectual guide to a reformed Hindu style of life and faith. Nevertheless, the Brahmo legacy of Hindu modernism, in modified forms, was transmitted to the ever-widening ranks of the Hindu middle classes by more popular associations such as the Arya Samaj and the Ramakrishna Mission.

[*See also* Hindu Renaissance; Roy, Rammohan; Sen, Keshub Chandra; Vivekananda; *and* Ramakrishna.]

David Kopf, *The Brahmo Samaj and the Shaping of the Modern Indian Mind* (1979). Protap Chandra Mozoomdar, *The Life and Teachings of Keshub Chandra Sen* (1887). Hemchandra Sarkar, *The Religion of the Brahmo Samaj* (3d ed., 1931). Sivanath Sastri, *History of the Brahmo Samaj,* 2 vols. (1911). DAVID KOPF

BRAHUI, a tribally organized people of diverse origins whose homeland is the present Kalat District in Pakistan. Brahuis are Sunni Muslims; the extended family is a cultural ideal, with a preference for marriage within the patrilineal clan. The Brahui language is related to the Dravidian tongues of South India, and its presence in Southwest Asia is something of a linguistic mystery.

The Brahui habitat is divided among the two mountainous areas of Sarawan and Jhalawan and the lowland Kachhi Plain. Historically, sheep and goat pastoralism was widely practiced, and families lived in small nomadic camps. Under British paramountcy in the nineteenth and early twentieth centuries, cultivation expanded and many nomads settled in transhumant villages, where they planted grains and vegetables, migrating with their animals to the lowlands in winter. Recently, there has been substantial investment in irrigation accompanied by full sedentarization.

The Brahui were politically unified in a chiefdom headed by the Ahmadzai dynasty from around 1666 to Pakistan independence in 1947. The khanate controlled the nontribal cultivators of Kachhi, exacting tribute. Political centralization was weakly developed, each tribal chief in effect a petty khan within his own territory. With the postindependence rise of Baluch nationalism, ethnic distinctions between Brahui and neighboring Baluch, never sharply defined, have become even more fluid, and many tribesmen who support local autonomy now claim Baluch identity.

[*See also* Baluchistan.]

Nina Swidler, "The Development of the Kalat Khanate," in *Perspectives on Nomadism,* edited by William Irons and Neville Dyson-Hudson (1972), pp. 115–121; "The Political Context of Brahui Sedentarization," *Ethnology* 12 (1973): 299–314. Warren W. Swidler, "Adaptive Processes Regulating Nomad-Sedentary Interaction in the Middle East," in *The Desert and the Sown,* edited by Cynthia Nelson (1973), pp. 23–41. NINA SWIDLER

BRONZE AGE IN CHINA. The full span of the Bronze Age occurred within the era that traditional Chinese histories called the Sandai, meaning the

Three Dynasties: the Xia (2205–1760 BCE), the Shang (1766–1122 BCE), and the Zhou (1122–256 BCE). This collective dynastic period conforms to the level of state societies in the system proposed by social evolutionists and to the developmental stage of a slave society in the Marxian schema adopted in the People's Republic of China. The term *Bronze Age* is itself a developmental one first proposed in the nineteenth century by the Danish antiquarian Christian Thomsen in an attempt to classify cultures according to the materials used to make their tools. However, it is not tools but ritual implements that are the premier objects of this period of Chinese history. In the Bronze Age, the possession of the metal signified both secular and spiritual power, a power that was further symbolized by the deposition of ceremonial weapons and ritual vessels in the graves of the rulers whose tombs are the chief source of evidence for this ancient period of Chinese history.

The question of the ultimate origin of the use of metal in China remains unresolved, although recent archaeological discoveries in the area of the Yellow River flood plain in North China have pushed back the date of known bronze casting to the earlier part of the second millennium BCE. At the site of Erlitou (modern Yanshi) in Henan Province the practice of casting bronze objects in piece molds is documented by the discovery of a small number of bronze objects, including some vessels for serving wine. This site is in the region that was traditionaly called the homeland of the first of the Three Dynasties, the Xia. These vessels are datable to the period 1781–1534 BCE, well within the lower limits of the Xia dynasty or the opening years of the Shang dynasty, which succeeded the Xia in this area.

The extreme thinness of some of the vessels from Erlitou (in one case only a millimeter thick) and the design features of these and other early vessels suggest the possible imitation of sheet metal prototypes. This possibility has led to speculation concerning the existence of a smithy tradition of working metal and raises questions about the existence of a "copper age" culture that made the transition from the use of stone artifacts to that of objects cast in an alloy of copper and tin (bronze), preceding the era of the Erlitou phase. All of these arguments center on the origins of the Bronze Age in China. Whereas the very existence of the Xia was a matter of debate only a generation ago and the origins of bronze casting were assumed to be in some source outside of China, today the question of stimulus diffusion or direct influence from other cultures on China is proposed with less authority and confidence than ever before. Irrespective of the dynastic date of the Erlitou phase or the existence of a sheet metal tradition preceding the period when objects were commonly cast, the recent archaeological discoveries have prompted a strong challenge of all diffusionist ideas. Instead, a growing body of opinion now favors the idea of the independent origin of metal acquisition and use in ancient China.

The apparent complexity of the shape of many bronzes, the general lack of duplicates, and especially the extraordinary quality of Chinese bronze work led early critics to assume the use of the lost-wax method of casting, but this is not the case. Piece-mold casting was the preferred, if not exclusive, method used throughout most of the Bronze Age. To achieve complicated shapes it was necessary to devise a technique of prefabrication. Thus, legs, handles, and other protruding members were cast first and then the body was cast onto them. This technique permits the casting of surprisingly complex objects of extraordinary size, some vessels weighing hundreds of pounds.

The motif that is the hallmark of dynastic Shang art, the *taotie* design, suggests some kind of creature but does not describe any real species. The meaning of the *taotie* remains elusive. Containers for ritual food offerings, the vessels were sacred utensils and it is only logical to assume that the decoration on them symbolized the political, social, and religious forces that governed the society. The terse inscriptions that appear on the bronzes and the more extensive specimens of oracular texts inscribed on bones and shells do not settle the question. The schematic design became ever more forceful and expressive as the dynasty progressed, reaching its most complete form at the site of the last of the many dynastic capitals of the period, Anyang. It is not surprising that the *taotie* motif, which appeared on almost every object of importance made in the Shang dynasty, disappeared within a generation or so following the conquest of the Shang people by their western neighbors the Zhou, whose early capital was in the city called Hao (near modern Xi'an) in the Wei River valley.

Although the full character of predynastic Zhou art has yet to be ascertained, it is clear that it is not the *taotie* but birdlike forms or other kinds of animals often seen in concert with purely ornamental devices, including spikes and vertical ribs, that better represent the new fashion in the first century of Zhou rule. Within another generation the emphasis was on ornamental patterns that reveal little interest

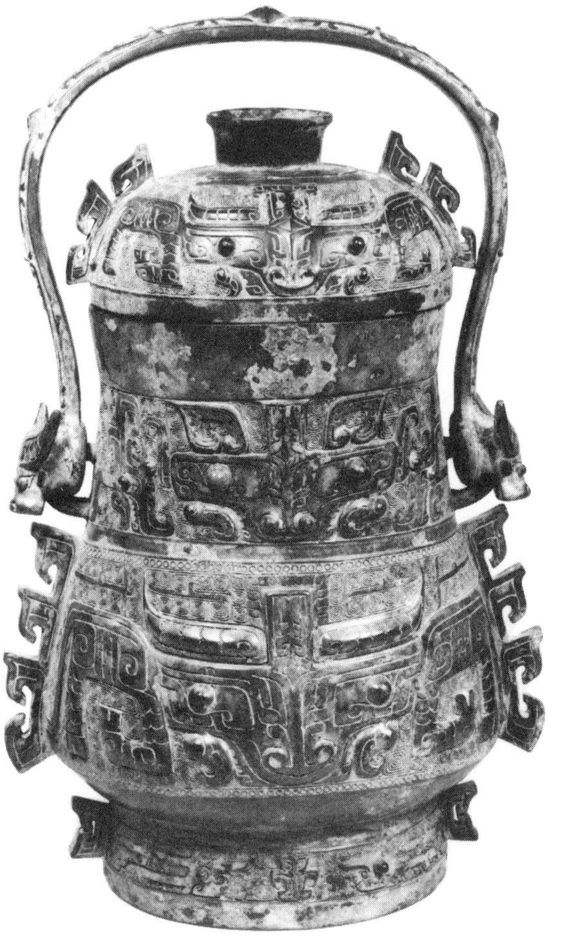

FIGURE 1. *Yu (Ritual Wine Vessel).* Early Western Zhou period (c. eleventh century BCE). Bronze, with bovine and *taotie* decoration, the body and cover both inscribed *Fu Ding Xi* ("Father Ding Sacrificial Buffalo"). Height 37.8 cm., diameter 22.2 cm.

in the depiction of a coherent zoomorphic motif. Concurrently, certain kinds of wine vessels long popular in the Shang period were abandoned and new ones introduced. Although the general practice of using bronze primarily for the manufacture of ritual implements was maintained during the Zhou dynasty, the more general distribution of bronze technology over the ever-expanding area of the Zhou cultural sphere led to a greater diversification of regional styles than had occurred in the preceding dynasty. In addition, the inscriptions of the period are more extensive and informative as historic documents.

The range in size, weight, and complexity of shape and ornament found in Zhou bronzes often exceeds the standard set in the Shang dynasty. The level of technical excellence is evident throughout the Zhou cultural sphere, not only in the western capital at Luoyang but in the other important cities that came into being as provincial centers developed into nearly autonomous states. The rapid growth of technology is further demonstrated by the introduction of a new but related industry, the production of cast iron.

The transition from the casting of bronze to the casting of iron requires the redesign of the basic firing equipment to generate the greater heat needed to melt the ore and cast the material. The change occurred swiftly in China, where there is ample evidence of the mass production of iron by 500 BCE. However, the use of iron did not revolutionize the use of metal in general. While iron was more suitable for utilitarian objects such as agricultural tools, bronze was still the favored material for casting ritual implements that were artistically attractive as well. Some of the most accomplished and beautiful bronzes ever cast were made in the latter years of the Zhou dynasty.

[*See also* Shang Dynasty *and* Zhou Period.]

Noel Barnard, *Bronze Casting and Bronze Alloys in Ancient China* (1961). K. C. Chang, *The Archaeology of Ancient China* (3d rev. ed., 1977). Wen Fong, ed., *The Great Bronze Age of China: An Exhibition from the People's Republic of China* (1980). Ping-ti Ho, *The Cradle of the East: An Inquiry into the Indigenous Origins of Techniques and Ideas of Neolithic and Early Historic China, 5000–1000 B.C.* (1975). David N. Keightley, ed., *The Origins of Chinese Civilization* (1983). Jessica Rawson, *Ancient China: Art and Archaeology* (1980).

ROBERT POOR

BROOKE, SIR CHARLES (1829–1917), second White Raja of Sarawak. Brooke joined the service of his uncle, Raja James Brooke, at the age of twenty-three, serving mostly in Iban districts of Sarawak. In 1863 he assumed control of the government, and in 1868 he became raja, ruling until his death. During his half-century as raja, Brooke molded Sarawak through personal rule, serving as an austere but mostly benevolent autocrat. During these years Chinese immigration increased, gambier and rubber planting developed, interior peoples were incorporated (sometimes forcibly) into the Raj, and the state expanded to its present boundaries. Brooke sought to protect Sarawak peoples from foreign investors and land alienation, earning him a somewhat undeserved reputation as an archconservative.

[*See also* Sarawak; Iban; *and* Brooke, Sir James.]

Robert M. Pringle, *Rajahs and Rebels: The Ibans of Sarawak under Brooke Rule, 1841–1941* (1967). Steven Runciman, *The White Rajahs: A History of Sarawak from 1841 to 1946* (1960). CRAIG A. LOCKARD

BROOKE, SIR CHARLES VYNER, (1874–1963), third and last White Raja of Sarawak. The Cambridge-educated Vyner Brooke served in various Sarawak administrative posts before succeeding his father, Charles, as raja in 1917. Vyner proved less dedicated and ambitious than his father but more personable, bureaucratic, and development oriented. During the 1930s Vyner took less interest in Sarawak affairs, leaving the administration chiefly to European civil servants. His marriage to Sylvia Brett produced three daughters but no male heir. During the Japanese occupation he lived in Australia. In 1946, tired of politics, disillusioned with his heir (nephew Anthony Brooke), and lacking the will and resources to rebuild the Raj, he ceded Sarawak to Britain as a colony and retired to Britain.

[*See also* Raja Muda; Brooke, Sir Charles; *and* Sarawak.]

R. H. W. Reece, *The Name of Brooke: The End of White Rajah Rule in Sarawak* (1982). Steven Runciman, *The White Rajahs: A History of Sarawak From 1841 to 1946* (1960). CRAIG A. LOCKARD

BROOKE, SIR JAMES (1803–1867), first White Raja of Sarawak and a major British imperialist of the nineteenth century. Born in India, Brooke was wounded in the first Anglo-Burmese War. In 1838 Brooke sailed to Southeast Asia on a boat he had purchased with a generous inheritance. In 1839 he visited Sarawak, then engulfed in rebellion by local Malay chiefs against Brunei rule. After more travel Brooke returned to Kuching in 1840 and helped suppress the rebellion in exchange for appointment as Kuching-based governor (raja) by the sultan of Brunei. In 1841, at age thirty-eight, Brooke became white ruler of the then-small district of what is now southwestern Sarawak, heralding a new form of imperial, quasi-colonial activity.

Brooke moved quickly to consolidate his control, importing a small European administrative staff and incorporating the defeated Malay chiefs into the government. The idealistic raja issued new laws designed to attract Malayo-Muslim or Chinese settlers and modify some local practices. Brooke claimed, and probably believed, that his government would protect the local population from outside oppression and inaugurate an era of British-inspired political liberalism tempered by Bornean realities. But his critics were quick to point out that he also made himself the undisputed, Borneo-style local ruler, increasingly free of Brunei control. It is also debatable whether northwestern Borneo needed the "law and order" he claimed to provide or whether he had any legal right to extend his control into the traditionally autonomous interior. Brooke served concurrently as governor of Labuan and British consul to Borneo until dismissed from these posts in 1849.

As raja, Brooke generated many changes. The Raj welcomed Chinese immigrants on the assumption that they would facilitate commerce and economic growth. Although he opposed heavy foreign investment and Western-owned plantation agriculture, Brooke allowed one British company to develop mining and planting schemes for the financially perilous state. A small Anglican missionary effort labored among the Dayak and Chinese. Brooke participated in British naval attacks upon what Europeans viewed as Malayo-Muslim "pirates" operating along the northwest Borneo coast. These antipiracy struggles also served to annex territory from the increasingly weak and embattled Brunei sultanate. By 1860 Brooke's domain extended as far northeast as the Mukah district. In 1850 the raja traveled to Bangkok to conclude a commercial treaty between Britain and the Siamese.

While Brooke could claim considerable local support from Malays, Dayak, and Kuching Chinese, not all Sarawak inhabitants welcomed the new order. Brooke faced chronic opposition and crises throughout his rule. The antipiracy campaigns and bloody military expeditions against Iban resistance generated considerable criticism in the Straits Settlements and Britain. Furthermore, Brooke remained antagonistic to the long-autonomous Chinese gold-mining settlements upriver at Bau, resulting in the Chinese Rebellion of 1857. The rebels occupied Kuching, forcing the raja to flee temporarily. Although his forces later routed the Chinese, Brooke lost considerable prestige. All of these internal problems, combined with the legal difficulties resulting from British criticism, left Brooke tired, disillusioned, and increasingly in debt. Nor was Britain immediately willing to recognize his status as a British citizen serving as the autocratic ruler of an independent Asian polity. In 1864, however, Britain finally legitimized Brooke by recognizing Sarawak as an independent state under British protection. The bachelor raja quarreled with and disinherited his nephew and apparent successor, Brooke Brooke.

In 1863 Brooke returned permanently to England, leaving the state in the hands of his nephew and new heir, Charles Brooke. But it was James Brooke who had founded a ruling dynasty that would endure for one hundred years and had created a coherent and unique state out of a complex mosaic of peoples and political jurisdictions, in the process redefining the possibilities of imperial British influence.

[*See also* Sarawak; Anglo-Burmese Wars; Labuan; Dayak; Iban; Brooke, Sir Charles; *and* Brooke, Sir Charles Vyner.]

Emily Hahn, *James Brooke of Sarawak* (1953). Robert Pringle, *Rajahs and Rebels: The Ibans of Sarawak under Brooke Rule, 1841–1941* (1967). Steven Runciman, *The White Rajahs: A History of Sarawak From 1841–1946* (1960). Nicholas Tarling, *The Burthen, the Risk and the Glory: A Biography of Sir James Brooke* (1982).

CRAIG A. LOCKARD

BROWNRIGG, SIR ROBERT (1759–1833), governor of Ceylon from 1811 to 1820. Brownrigg completed the conquest of the island by invading the Kandyan kingdom in 1815, negotiating the Kandyan Convention with chieftains, and suppressing a rebellion in 1817–1818. The Kandyan Convention contained extensive guarantees of the privileges of the chiefs and of Kandyan laws and customs, including protection of the Buddhist religion. The Kandyan provinces were administered separately until the 1830s, but the Kandyan Convention was largely ignored.

[*See also* Kandy *and* Sri Lanka.]

H. A. J. Hulugalle, *British Governors of Ceylon* (1963).

PATRICK PEEBLES

BRUNEI. Present-day Brunei is a remnant of an ancient kingdom strategically centered on Brunei Bay in northwest Borneo (whose name is apparently a hispanicized version of *Brunei*). The kingdom of Brunei was probably at its apogee when the Magellan expedition visited it in 1521. The expedition's chronicler, Antonio Pigafetta, left a glowing description of Brunei's old capital, now known as Kota Batu ("stone fortress"). Kota Batu's ruins are the most substantial on Borneo. At the time of Pigafetta's visit, Brunei possessed hegemony as far north as Manila and south to some uncertain point in Borneo. The Brunei tradition that Bruneis conquered all of coastal Borneo can be corroborated for two-thirds of the circumference of the island.

Brunei's first recorded event occurred in 977 when it sent an envoy to China. Contacts between Brunei and China persisted off and on for centuries but culminated in the early fifteenth century when two Brunei rulers, father and son, visited the Chinese capital and were given unusually lavish treatment. The father died in China; his tomb still stands near Nanjing. Brunei's state visits to China terminated a period of Brunei vassalage to the Javanese kingdom of Majapahit.

Before the coming of Islam, a process that began in Brunei in the 1400s or earlier, Brunei's religion and culture were at least partly Hindu-Buddhist. Many Hindu-Buddhist elements persist in titles and ceremonies to the present day. But by the time Pigafetta described Brunei, its ruler had already become a Muslim, and in the sixteenth century Brunei proselytized vigorously in the southern Philippines.

In the 1570s Spanish forces in the Philippines launched two attacks on Brunei. After initial success the Spaniards withdrew from Borneo, but Brunei hegemony and maritime affairs to the north were much reduced. The southern Philippine kingdom of Suli, at times a Brunei rival but its vassal when the Spaniards attacked, rose to absorb much of what Brunei lost. The armada of sea nomads that once served Brunei switched allegiance to Sulu by the seventeenth century; late in the century Brunei lost control of part of northern Borneo when Sulu intervened in a dynastic dispute in Brunei.

In the eighteenth century Brunei sought a British connection by granting concessions on offshore islands. The British connection took a fateful turn in the nineteenth century after Singapore's founding. Parties predominantly linked to Great Britain partitioned Brunei until 1906, when the irregularly bounded remainder of Brunei became a protected state with a British resident.

Oil production after 1929 made the state economically viable. World War II saw Brunei temporarily reunited with its former Bornean territories under Japan. Since the end of the war, steadily rising petroleum sales have brought the country great prosperity.

Brunei received internal independence in 1959, followed shortly by popular elections. The People's Party, which had swept virtually all elected offices, rebelled in 1962 but was crushed by Britain. The sultan's hand had been greatly strengthened throughout the protected period; after the rebellion any plans for democratization first faltered and then died. In 1984 Brunei received full independence as a monarchy.

[*See also* Majapahit; Islamization of Southeast Asia; Sulu; Sarawak; *and the map accompanying* Malaysia.]

D. E. Brown, *Brunei: The Structure and History of a Bornean Malay Sultanate* (1970). Robert Nicholl, ed., *European Sources for the History of the Sultanate of Brunei in the Sixteenth Century* (1975). Nicholas Tarling, *Britain, the Brookes, and Brunei* (1971).

DONALD E. BROWN

BUCK, PEARL (1892–1973), American novelist; popular and prolific writer on China. Almost singlehandedly, Pearl Sydenstricker Buck changed the American image of the Chinese peasantry from a faceless heathen rabble to one of noble yeoman farmers heroically struggling to overcome poverty and ignorance. Although she wrote or edited more than eighty books, the basis of her reputation (and Pulitzer and Nobel prizes for literature) was the novel *The Good Earth* (1931), which sold more than four million copies in her lifetime and reached millions more as a feature film. Buck used material derived from the years she spent in China as the daughter and wife of missionaries. During the 1930s and 1940s she lived and worked mostly in the United States, editing the popular monthly *Asia* with her second husband, Richard J. Walsh, and later establishing the Pearl Buck Foundation, which focused on the welfare of abandoned children of mixed Asian-American parentage.

STEPHEN R. MACKINNON

BUDDHISM. [*This entry consists of an overview, which treats Buddhism's origins in India and its doctrines, and two surveys of the religion's development in specific countries,* Buddhism in China *and* Buddhism in Korea. *For a discussion of Buddhism in Tibet, see* Lamaism *and* Gelugpa. *For Buddhism in Japan, see the following articles on individual Buddhist sects:* Amidism; Pure Land; Shingon; Shinshū; Tendai; *and* Zen.]

AN OVERVIEW

A major world religion, Buddhism has flourished at one time or another in most of the cultural and geographical areas of Asia. In the period of its greatest geographical extent, from roughly the seventh to the ninth century of the common era, Buddhism played a major religious and cultural role in India, Sri Lanka, Tibet and the Himalayas, Central Asia, Mongolia, China, Korea, Japan, and Southeast Asia, including parts of what is now Indonesia. Even today, after centuries during which its institutional power gradually waned in many of these areas, Buddhism continues to be an important religious and political force in such places as Sri Lanka, parts of mainland Southeast Asia, Korea, and Japan. The success of modern European ideologies in Asia, particularly but not exclusively communism, has greatly attenuated the formal influence of the *sangha* (as the Buddhist religious community is known) in Tibet, Mongolia, China, North Korea, Vietnam, Cambodia, and Laos, but even in these areas, the influence of Buddhism persists on both popular and elite levels. Significantly, Buddhism had all but disappeared from the land of its origin, India, by the fourteenth century, but has enjoyed a modest renaissance in modern times.

Origins. Buddhism began with the enlightenment (religious awakening) of an Indian prince, Siddhartha, heir to the throne of the Shakya clan, in approximately 528 BCE. At the age of twenty-nine Sid-

FIGURE 1. *Mahabodi Temple, Bodh Gaya, Bihar.* The temple is build on the site where, according to Buddhist tradition, the Buddha attained enlightenment.

dhartha made a serious break with his native culture, society, and religion, leaving his father, wife, and newborn son, and renouncing his throne, his duty to his subjects, indeed, his very identity as a man in the world. For six years he courted death as a severe ascetic. At the age of thirty-five he then abandoned asceticism and took food, bathed, sat in meditation under a tree at Gaya in the center of India, and at dawn after a night of trance attained what he himself called "unexcelled perfect enlightenment." From that time he called himself a "Buddha," an "Enlightened One," and after pausing for a few weeks began his mission of teaching the whole world the way to end all suffering.

He saved his first teaching for the five ascetics who had been his companions. He taught them the Four Noble Truths (perhaps more accurately translated "Four Holy Facts"): that all unenlightened life is suffering; that suffering originates from misknowledge; that there is freedom from suffering; and that there is a path to that freedom. The path has eight branches: authentic view, intention, speech, livelihood, effort, mindfulness, terminal action, and concentration. The ascetics began to experience insight and attain that freedom right then and there, and he accepted them in his community, exhorting them to spread the teaching to all beings everywhere.

The Buddha did not demand belief in a faith, nor did he command a code of action, as does a prophet invested with a religious mission by a revelation from a god. He sought instead to generate understanding by teaching, himself providing an example of the possibility and fruits of such insight. And he himself invested his followers with the ethical, religious, and philosophical mission of spreading his teaching and its method of practice. He claimed he had discovered a "Dharma (teaching, truth) like an elixir; deep, peaceful, luminous, uncomplex, and uncreated."

He offered his growing body of followers "refuge" in Three Jewels: the Jewel of the Buddha (himself or any other Buddha); the Jewel of the Absolute Truth, the Dharma; and the Jewel of the Community, the *sangha,* the new society of enlightened men and women helping each other on the way to freedom. He set forth a clear ethical code, the "tenfold path of good and evil evolution," that prohibits killing, stealing, adultery, lying, slandering, abuse, frivolity, greed, malice, and false ideologies, and enjoins saving lives, giving gifts, and so on.

What was the essence of this Dharma he had discovered anew? "Deep," it was no mere rule of duty. "Peaceful," it was a state of being, not a mere idea or law. "Luminous," it was real, a source of light and no mere abstraction. "Uncomplex," it was not a mere doctrine. "Uncreated," it could only be the transcendent Absolute itself, the realm of nirvana, freedom, reality, truth. *Dharma* already had important meanings in the Buddha's culture, all relating to notions of "pattern maintenance," "duty," "law," even "religion" in its sense of a symbol system that holds a culture together. Siddhartha had already broken all his "dharmas" in those senses, leaving family, country, gods, and his royal identity. The new Dharma was actually totally opposite, holding one *out* of the world of suffering, holding one in freedom. He transvalued the term, in line with the philosophical rebellion widespread in his time, to mean a transcendental Absolute, an ultimate reality that held supreme value. This transcendent real was the "Realm of Freedom," whose gates he proclaimed open to all, low caste or high, woman or man, Indian or foreigner, human or god or demon or animal or any living being. He was careful not to claim that he could merely install them in that Dharma. He could only teach and show the way. They had to understand and act according to that understanding. His most important title was Teacher.

The Buddha taught for forty-five years, until his death, or *parinirvana* (complete enlightenment), in about 461 BCE. He taught many different types of teachings to many different types of people. He was widely accepted as an enlightened teacher, but he and his community never achieved complete harmony with his culture. His main message was that misknowledge caused all suffering. Misknowledge is not just passive ignorance but is the misperception of self and things as having intrinsic reality or fixed identity. This misperception leads to exaggerated emotions, such as lust, hate, pride, and jealousy. These lead to evil actions, which in turn cause suffering in human life and eventually rebirth in hellish states of woe. Thus, the Buddha announced that all persons were "selfless," lacking fixed self or intrinsic identity. A brahman was not rigidly a brahman, a king not fixedly a king, and so forth. This teaching was a challenge to culture, religious belief, social stratification, sexual subordination, even racial and species superiority. It is easy to see why his teaching never catered to ordinary egotism, individual, cultural, or national, and so always maintained an educative tension with its social habitat.

On the other hand, because of the rapid expansion of Indian civilization in those times, his movement became quite widespread, achieving pan-Indian popularity by the time of Emperor Ashoka in the third century BCE. The Buddha's teaching was catholic, hence useful to help members of a new empire transcend old antagonistic identities. It was also rationalistic, not requiring any special belief system. The Buddha invented the new institutional form that would come to be known as monasticism, a central mediating institution that later became of enormous value to ruler and ruled alike. Buddhist monasteries served as churches and temples for members of castes previously excluded from the Vedic rites. They served as religious sanctuaries for the world-weary of all classes, a place for the individual to cultivate his or her own highest potential. They were schools, hotels and hospitals, old age homes, libraries, museums, banks, and perhaps discreet mental asylums. The monastic institutions were a major asset of Buddhism as it expanded throughout Asia.

Development in South Asia. After the Buddha's death, the community held a great council of monks to assemble a canon of his discourses (Sutra), laws (Vinaya), and systematic philosophies (Abhidharma). These "Three Collections" constituted the "textual Dharma," with a corresponding "practical Dharma" consisting of the "Three Exceptional Educations": ethics *(sila),* meditation *(samadhi),* and scientific wisdom *(prajna).* These categories provided a framework for Buddhism's complex ethical, religious, and scientific and philosophical traditions.

Schisms among the monks began to occur almost immediately, and soon there were eighteen orders *(nikayas)* of monastic Buddhists, the most important groupings of which were the Sthaviravada and the Mahasamghika. These orders differed little in points of doctrine, disagreeing most strongly about matters of disciplinary law. The Sthaviravada orders eventually took roots in Sri Lanka, and eventually became the Theravada Buddhism that spread throughout Southeast Asia.

After the time of Ashoka, in whose pillar edicts the Buddhist community is simply "the community," the monastic leaders, especially in the Mahasamghika orders, became more and more concerned with lay society. [*See* Ashoka.] These monks eventually developed a new vehicle of teaching, "discovering" a new set of discourses allegedly given by the Buddha and kept hidden away for four centuries. The scholar-saint Nagarjuna (c. 150–250) was important in the beginning of this movement and in its philosophical elaboration. [*See* Nagarjuna.] This movement called itself the Universal Vehicle (Mahayana), referring to the coexisting monastic Buddhism as the Individual Vehicle (Hinayana). In the Mahayana the Buddha emerged with a dazzling set of divine qualities, and a host of angelic messiah figures, the bodhisattvas, or "heroes of enlightenment," emerged as saviors of the world. This messianic form of Buddhism spread through Central Asia to China from the second century CE, where it achieved what has been called a cultural "conquest" over the next four centuries. From the sixth and seventh centuries it spread directly from India to Tibet, Cambodia, and Indonesia, and from China to Korea, Japan, and Vietnam. Finally, the Tibetans spread it throughout the Mongol nations, from the twelfth century on, although Buddhism is attested in some Mongol areas centuries earlier.

The final flourishing of Buddhism in India from the fifth to the tenth century saw the emergence of the apocalyptic Buddhism of the Tantric Vehicle, also termed Mantric or Diamond Vehicle. As the monastic Buddhist archetype was the monk or nun, and the messianic Buddhist archetype was the bodhisattva savior hero or heroine, the apocalyptic Buddhist archetype was the great adept *(mahasiddha)*, an extraordinary figure of total nonconformity—mystic, ecstatic, manifesting an apocalyptic fruition of immediate enlightenment in the midst of all dichotomies. Although avowedly these adepts were socially marginal types, like the age-old Indian *sadhus*, they had an enormous impact on the literature of the times, being great poets in the vernacular languages, especially those of eastern India. They also figured importantly in the overseas missions, counting among their number such figures as Bodhidharma, who allegedly went to Sri Lanka and China to start Chan; Amoghavajra; Padmasambhava, who "tamed" Tibet; and Kūkai, who was seminal in the transmission to Japan. Their charismatic power and unconventional, direct method of turning their audiences' minds toward selflessness and enlightenment enabled them to deal with tribal peoples and peoples of non-Indian cultures. Within India, they sought out those of low caste or outcaste status, those who were illiterate and ignored by Hindu and urban and monastic Buddhist alike. These adepts and their apocalyptic Buddhism were looked upon by Western missionary scholars and proper medieval Hindus as degenerate manifestations of Indian Buddhism. The bulk of the enormous literature of the Tantras was translated into Tibetan; only a few texts were translated into Chinese. Therefore, the philosophical, poetical, and religious achievements of the adepts is only now becoming known to scholars, enabling them to reevaluate the adepts' great development of depth psychology.

Development in East Asia. From the second to the sixth century, Buddhism spread inexorably throughout Chinese civilization. Much has been made of the fact that China was in a state of disorder after the collapse of the Han dynasty (202 BCE–220 CE), provoking world-weary Chinese to turn to the otherworldly Buddhist teaching, but this view is simplistic. In fact, there were many long-lasting, well-ordered kingdoms during the centuries following the collapse of the Han. It is only their unification in a central empire that was lacking. Buddhism could never have conquered an entire culture unless it reinforced a number of trends already present and at the same time satisfied pressing new needs. On the popular level, Buddhism offered devotionalistic transcendentalism through the cult of the Buddha Amitabha, the scriptures of which opened up a vision of a Pure Land that had already proved immensely satisfying to the Indian and Central Asian popular imagination. Amitabha was a cosmic emperor, more majestic than any human "son of Heaven," and immediately concerned with the welfare and salvation of every individual, no matter how lowly. Buddhist monasticism offered an alternative social realm into which unhappy men and women could escape from the daily struggle for material existence, turning themselves to spiritual pursuits; as in India, the monasteries performed numerous social functions in addition to the religious one. For the elite classes, Buddhist philosophies immeasurably enriched the Daoistic stream of metaphysical transcendentalism with great numbers of new ideas along with a sophisticated contemplative psychology. The Indian lay sage Vimalakirti became popular with intellectuals already fond of the Daoist sages Laozi and Zhuangzi. Finally, for the rulers, Buddhism offered a new source of legitimacy and charisma: legitimacy as "Dharma protector," a role intelligible to both Chinese and non-Chinese peoples involved in forming new polities, and charisma backed by the ritual blessings of the monastic community, who began to serve a popular ritual role filling social needs unsatisfied by Confucian scholar-bureaucrats or Daoist priests or recluses.

Initially, various important scriptures, such as the *Pure Land,* the *Lotus,* the *Samdhinirmocana,* the *Vimalakirti,* and others commanded their own followings, and translators and scholars gave their own versions of contemplative and intellectual teachings. Only with the formation of the Sui and Tang dynasties of the sixth and seventh centuries did the Chinese indigenize Buddhism and create truly Chinese Buddhist schools. The four most important schools were the Pure Land (Qingtu), the Heavenly Platform (Tiantai), the Garland (Huayan), and the Contemplation (Chan). This last tradition was based on no scripture formally, although practically it relied upon the Transcendent Wisdom scriptures, such as the *Diamond Cutter* and the *Heart Scripture.*

These schools flourished until the first of the great persecutions in 845. By this time, Buddhism had become so popular and such an economic drain on the state that the emperors from time to time would be moved by Confucian critics to confiscate *sangha* lands, defrock its clergy, and otherwise curtail the power of its institutions. After persecutions became more regular in late Tang and Song (tenth to thirteenth century), the iconoclastic Chan school, its monasteries further from the cities and the reach of kings and officials, became the bastion of Chinese Buddhist culture. At the same time, the Neo-Confucian movement finally incorporated Buddhist metaphysics and contemplative techniques into a revived national ideology, much as medieval Hinduism incorporated much of Buddhist thought, adapted to the Indian national identity.

Buddhism began to spread to Korea, Japan, and Vietnam from the sixth century, bringing with it elements of Confucianism and Chinese civilization by then entangled with Indian ideas, practices, and texts. In Japan Buddhism flourished as a court-sponsored religion during the Nara period (710–784) and began to develop a strong tradition of independent monasticism during the Heian period (794–1185), owing to the powerful missions of Saichō (767–822), founder of the Tendai monastery on Mount Hiei, and Kūkai (774–835), founder of the Shingon monastery on Mount Kōya. With the rise of the Kamakura shogunate (1185–1333) and the decrease of court sponsorship, more grass-roots movements generated a powerful renaissance of Buddhism. The major figures were Hōnen (1133–1212) and Shinran (1173–1262) of the Pure Land (Jōdo) school, Eisai (1141–1215) and Dōgen (1200–1253) of the Zen school, and Nichiren (1222–1282), who took the *Lotus Sutra* school out of the Mount Hiei Tendai monasteries to form a popular movement. Buddhism maintained a stable presence in Japan into the modern period, when the Meiji government moved consciously to weaken it in favor of the nationalistic State Shinto. [*The figures mentioned above are the subject of independent entries.*]

Development in Inner Asia. The final flourishing of Indian Buddhism, from about 500 to 1000, spread very little beyond India, where it was eventually destroyed. Tibet, Cambodia, and Indonesia received transmissions of late Tantric Buddhism, and of these, only Tibet preserved any significant amount of the literature of that era. The translated Tibetan canons, the Kanjur and the Tanjur, are the major repositories of the esoteric scriptures and treatises, as well as of a vast number of philosophical treatises never translated into Chinese. Tibet also preserved the monastic educational traditions of Nalanda and Vikramashila, the great Indian monastic universities. [*See* Nalanda.] After many centuries of a slow "taming" process, Buddhism and its monasticism prospered in Inner Asia, Tibet being the only Buddhist nation ever to produce a monastic government, a political administration staffed by monk-bureaucrats and led by lama hierarchs. The Tibetan lamas worked as missionaries among the Mongols, eventually converting all the Mongol nations to Tibetan Buddhism. The Mongol Yuan, Chinese Ming, and Manchu Qing dynasties all became involved with Tibetan Buddhism and its Tantric aspects, partly owing to the personal interest of a number of rulers and members of their families, and partly out of a wish to maintain legitimacy in the eyes of the powerful warrior nations of Inner Asia.

Buddhism in Modern Times. As Buddhism is rationalistic in tendency, emphasizing the cultivation of reason and advocating individual wisdom as the means of liberation, its advocates have tended to argue for its fundamental compatibility with modernity, with its nontheistic and scientific attitudes. Thus, Asian Buddhist leaders tended to ambivalence about Marxist movements, finding the egalitarian, ethical ideals of socialism appealing from the point of view of Buddhist ethics. Just like Eastern Christianity in Russia, however, Buddhism has been devastated by Asian communism during the last sixty years, officially losing its vast numbers of adherents among the Mongols, Chinese, North Koreans, Vietnamese, Laotians, Khmer, and Tibetans, losing tens of thousands of monasteries and temples and millions of acres of land. In noncommunist countries of Asia, it has lost many more followers to secular modernity. Thailand, Burma, and Sri Lanka may be its only remaining official bastions. On the other hand, there have been a number of revival movements of Buddhism in Japan (Reiyūkai, Risshō Kōsekai, Sōka Gakkai), in Indonesia, and in India (Ambedkar movement). The Tibetan presence in India and Nepal has stimulated strong revival of Himalayan Buddhism in a broad belt from Ladakh to the Monpa regions of Arunachal Pradesh. And, perhaps most important for the future of Buddhism among Asia's younger generations, Buddhist movements in Europe, Australia, and North America have taken firm root and are showing strong expansion.

Kenneth Chen, *Buddhism in China* (1964). Heinrich Dumoulin and John C. Maraldo, eds., *Buddhism in the Modern World* (1976). Mircea Eliade, ed., *The Encyclopedia of Religion* (1987), s.v. "Buddhism," vol. 2, pp. 334–439. Charles Eliot, *Japanese Buddhism* (1935). Lal Mani Joshi, *Studies in the Buddhist Culture of India* (1977). Walpola Rahula, *What the Buddha Taught* (1967). Melford Spiro, *Buddhism and Society* (1971). D. T. Suzuki, *Zen and Japanese Culture* (1959). Stanley J. Tambiah, *World Conqueror, World Renouncer* (1976). A. K. Warder, *Indian Buddhism* (1970). Holmes Welch, *The Practice of Chinese Buddhism* (1967) and *Buddhism under Mao* (1972).

ROBERT A. F. THURMAN

BUDDHISM IN CHINA

Numerous legends relate to the introduction of Buddhism into China; none has much basis in fact. Presumably this Indian religion, with many Central Asian accretions, was brought in by non-Chinese merchants and travelers who followed the Silk Road leading to Dunhuang, a major oasis on the northwestern border of China, and from there to the plains of northern China. The time was probably from the mid-first century BCE to the first century CE, during the flourishing of the Han dynasty (206 BCE–220 CE). Initially this new religion had few Chinese converts; a foreign religion, it served a foreign community. Evidence exists that places a group of Buddhist believers in Pengcheng, the capital of the kingdom of Chu, north of the Huai River, around 65 CE, and in Luoyang around 100 CE. About this time the first Buddhist scripture in Chinese, the *Sutra in Forty-two Sections,* made its appearance. Allegedly a translation from Sanskrit, it consists chiefly of Hinayana-like sayings ascribed to the Buddha. The work, however, may well be a Chinese compilation.

By the late second century the Buddhist church had established itself in Luoyang, and a center for the translation of texts had been set up. The Parthian missionary An Shigao, who arrived in 148, was the first to organize a team for the systematic translation of Buddhist works. Texts translated dealt chiefly with yogic meditation practices and detailed explanations of the numerical categories descriptive of the teachings that were so common to Indian Buddhism. Most of these translations consisted of subjects that appealed to current Daoist interest in breathing techniques and mental exercises. Native Chinese gradually came to be attracted to this new religion, at first as lay believers, although precise details are wanting because of the lack of historical documentation. Buddhism in this early period may have been viewed as a new method of Daoist practice or a new school of Daoism; the search for immortality may well have been equated with the Buddhist nirvana. [*See also* An Shigao.]

Early Buddhism. The Han empire that had once extended into Central Asia began to disintegrate in the mid-second century as rival factions struggled for control against an ineffectual government and provincial warlords began to assert their independence. In 220 the Han dynasty collapsed, followed in the North by a succession of short-lived dynasties. Of these, the Wu (222–280) was of particular significance, as it set out to colonize and sinicize the "barbarian" areas south of the Yangtze River. North China had always been the center of Chinese civilization and the South was at that time a lightly populated, undeveloped region. Several Indian and Scythian Buddhist missionaries settled in the Wu capital at Jianye (modern Nanjing) and devoted themselves to translation activities. Meanwhile, in northern China the Wei (220–265) had been superseded by the Western Jin (265–317), which made its capital at Luoyang. The Jin maintained relatively close contact with the Buddhist nations of Central Asia, and missionary and translation activities flourished in the larger cities. After about 300, however, unrest and warfare disrupted the interchange between China and Central Asia. By this time Buddhism had been accepted by the leading families, had to a certain extent penetrated to areas south of the lower Yangtze, and had been adopted by the Xiongnu rulers, who were in the process of consolidating their hold on North China.

Translation activities during the Western Jin centered at Chang'an under the supervision of the great Indo-Scythian translator Dharmaraksha (Chinese, Fahu; 230–308). Born in Dunhuang of a substantial merchant family, he received a thorough Chinese classical education to supplement his superior knowledge of Buddhist literature. Traveling extensively in Central Asia, he collected texts and produced translations, and on his return to Chang'an, together with Chinese and foreign collaborators, he turned out over 150 translations. The school that he established is said to have attracted thousands of disciples. Among his translations were early renditions of such works as the *Lotus Sutra* and *Vimalakirti Sutra* and other Mahayana scriptures. The renderings were literal and often difficult to follow and made no attempt to achieve literary elegance.

The end of the third and the early fourth century witnessed a distinct shift in the audience that Buddhism attracted. There was a distinct penetration of the Buddhist teachings into the elite society of the gentry. At this time the gentry were immersed in the *xuanxue* ("dark learning") of the Neo-Daoists, and Buddhist philosophical concepts of *prajna* ("wisdom") and *shunyata* ("emptiness") had an immediate appeal. In addition, the turmoil of the times made the monasteries a haven for those who enjoyed the contemplative life or sought to escape from the hardships of the world. Buddhism was gradually gaining a following and support among the cultured elite.

Northern and Southern Buddhism. The early fourth century saw the consolidation of the various Xiongnu tribes in the North under the leadership of Liu Yuan and the complete rout of the native Chinese. Luoyang fell in 311 and Chang'an, captured first in 311, fell again in 316. A large portion of the population of these cities fled to the South, to the area of the lower Yangtze in what had been the state of Wu. With a capital at Jiankang (formerly Jianye), the state known as Eastern Jin (317–420) was established, controlled in part by the northern refugees and in part by the elite families of the South. A constant struggle for control among these families marked this period; the weak Eastern Jin court played an inconsequential role. The older families that had long lived in the Yangtze Valley area tended to be conservative in nature, defenders of a Confucian orthodoxy that no longer held much attraction for the northern refugees. The elite of the Eastern Jin were much inclined toward Neo-Daoist speculations on the nature of the universe, speculations that found a congeniality with the prevalent Buddhist teachings. Many of the texts of the Prajna school had by this time been translated, and their emphasis on emptiness and the attainment of wisdom through the realization of emptiness was compatible with many Neo-Daoist ideals. Buddhism was for a time spoken of in Neo-Daoist terms and vocabulary. Gradually the richness of the Buddhist teaching proved overwhelming in its diversity, and although still at times expressed in Daoist terminology, it began to attract converts in greater numbers. [*See also* Jin Dynasty.]

Representative of the Buddhist monks of this period was Zhi Dun (314–366), a descendant of a family long associated with Buddhism. A scholar-priest of eloquence and wit, he was equally conversant with Buddhism and Neo-Daoism and was instrumental in systematizing Buddhism and presenting it in a new and attractive light.

Whereas in South China the Eastern Jin managed to maintain a fairly peaceful existence, North China, from which the gentry had been driven, was the scene of constant warfare among non-Chinese tribes, mostly Xiongnu and Tibetan, who were seeking to control the area. During the fourth and fifth centuries a succession of short-lived dynasties engaged in a constant struggle for power. In order to advance their teachings, Buddhist missionaries found it expedient to associate themselves with the ruling houses. They advised the princes and performed such services as predicting the future and displaying various acts of magic. Among these adepts was the famed Fotudeng, a Central Asian monk, who was so proficient at magical arts and prayers for rain and successful predictions in regard to military matters that he served as a close adviser to the ruler. [*See also* Fotudeng.]

During this period the capital of these northern non-Chinese kingdoms remained at Chang'an. It was here that the celebrated foreign monk Kumarajiva (c. 344–413) developed his center for the translation of Buddhist texts during the late fourth century. Born in Kucha, he traveled to Kashmir and Kashgar, studying Hinayana texts and Indian literary works, as well as the Mahayana sutras. Seeking to go to Chang'an, he was held in captivity in Kucha for some seventeen years by a local warlord. During this time he learned Chinese and eventually reached Chang'an in 401. Kumarajiva was accorded royal patronage and, assembling a group of more than one thousand monks, set out to undertake the translation or retranslation of a large body of Mahayana *sutras.* Older translations were compared and doctrinal problems analyzed. Kumarajiva did not translate directly, often abbreviating texts to emphasize the essential meanings and making textual alterations where he felt it would make ideas more intelligible to the reader. Much of the material translated by Kumarajiva was written in graceful Chinese, with a distinct literary appeal; this has accounted for the continued popularity of his translations in the following centuries. Among the works translated were the *Lotus Sutra,* the *Vimalakirti Sutra,* the 25,000-line *Perfection of Wisdom Sutra,* and the enormous hundred-volume *Dazhidu lun (Treatise on the Great Perfection of Wisdom).* Kumarajiva devoted particular efforts to revision of the Daoist terminology that had been used in earlier translations and had tended to obscure the essential Buddhist teachings. Kumarajiva must be regarded as one of the most important figures in this early period of Chinese Buddhism, one whose lucid translations contributed greatly to the intellectual developments in later Chinese Buddhism. [*See also* Kumarajiva.]

One further figure of this period requires particular mention: the monk Huiyuan (344–416). Born into a literati family, in his youth he studied both the Confucian and the Daoist classics before turning to Mahayana studies. A disciple of the famous northern master Daoan (312–385), he eventually moved south to the mountain known as Lushan in present-day Jiangxi, which he found so attractive that he stayed there for the rest of his life. His renown brought him a large number of students, both monks and laymen, who formed a community celebrated for the strictness of its religious discipline. Huiyuan, much of whose writing remains, was an ardent defender of the monastic community and did much to help spread the new translations that were being produced under Kumarajiva's direction in the North. Huiyuan emphasized *dhyana* meditation practices, also associated more closely with Northern Buddhism, and is revered as one of the founders of Pure Land Buddhism in China. In 402 he brought together a group of about 120 disciples who all vowed to be reborn in Amitabha Buddha's Western Paradise. It is doubtful, however, if this was anything other than an early isolated expression of devotion to this particular Buddha; it can scarcely be described as the start of a Pure Land movement in China.

In 420 the Eastern Jin dynasty in the South was deposed by what came to be known as the (Liu) Song dynasty, which in turn was followed by a succession of short-lived dynasties in which Buddhist and Neo-Daoist schools both flourished. In the North the non-Chinese Northern Wei dynasty (386–535) gained temporary control, and was followed by two ephemeral dynasties. This period (420–589), lasting until the ultimate unification of China by the Sui in 589, is known as the period of the Northern and Southern Dynasties.

In the South the emphasis on literary and philosophical approaches to Buddhism continued. The aristocratic elite flocked to Buddhism, *sutra* translations were revised and polished, and commentaries were written. Emperor Wu (r. 502–557) of the Liang became a staunch believer in Buddhism. Not only did he build temples and support the *sangha,* personally lecture on Buddhist texts, and follow many of the rules incumbent on monks, he also decreed that Daoist temples be abolished (517) and required their priests to return to lay life. Buddhism spread rapidly throughout the South, gaining a strong support among the populace in general, while strengthening its hold among the gentry.

In the North the Chinese who had been unable to flee to the South were obliged to serve a succession of alien rulers, each more violent than the one before. Danger and insecurity were ever present; Buddhism, non-Chinese by origin yet universal in its accommodation to all, whether Chinese or alien, ruler or peasant, had a particular appeal to these alien rulers. They came to support Buddhism, adopt monks as advisors, erect elaborate temples, and support great artistic endeavors such as the cave statuary at Yungang. By this time Buddhism had achieved enthusiastic acceptance among the alien and native populations, both elite and peasant.

Buddhism was, however, not universally accepted during this period. Twice, under the Northern Wei and Northern Zhou dynasties, persecutions of Buddhism took place, the first from 446 to 452 and the second from 574 to 578. Occasioned chiefly by economic conditions and with the instigation of Daoist and Confucian rivals who were able to influence the emperors, temples were destroyed, their wealth confiscated, and monks and nuns returned to lay life. Each of these persections was followed by a relaxation of the ordinances against Buddhism. In the long run the great translation projects, the gradual sinicization of the alien conquerors, and the extirpation of Daoist influences, led to a gradual acceptance of Buddhism at all levels of society. [*See also* Datong; Longmen; Northern Wei Dynasty; Six Dynasties; *and* Southern and Northern Dynasties.]

Sui and Tang Dynasties. In 581 Yang Jian, an officer in the Northern Zhou army, was able to gain control of the country by a series of fortuitous circumstances and to establish the Sui dynasty. By 589 he had conquered the Chen dynasty in the South and for the first time in almost three hundred years China was again unified. The Sui, like the succeeding Tang dynasty, recognized Buddhism as the official religion yet made concerted efforts to keep it under control. At the same time, the Sui acknowledged Daoism and paid respect to its deities and made a conscious effort to restore Confucianism by using it as a basis for the examination system. The Sui emperor Yang indulged in extravagant palace construction and engaged in unsuccessful military expeditions, however, bringing about a revolt and his assassination in 618. The Tang dynasty (618–907), which succeeded the short-lived Sui, has been described as the most glorious era in Chinese history. In its early years the Tang controlled a vast empire that extended into Central Asia. Poetry, art, and literature flourished, and the capital cities of Luoyang and Chang'an were cosmopolitan metropolises rivaling any in the world. [*See also* Luoyang *and* Chang'an.]

Both of these dynasties witnessed the growth of sectarian Buddhism. Until that time a bewildering variety of teachings had been promulgated and priests concentrated on specific scriptures or practiced particular techniques, but few organized groups that could be described as schools of Buddhism can be identified. As Buddhism became further removed from its Indian and Central Asian origins it began to take on a Chinese coloration and to acquire forms far removed from Indian Buddhism. One school, the Sanjiejiao, or Three Stages school, attained great popularity during the Sui dynasty. It based its teaching on scriptural reference to three periods of Buddhism: the era when "true" Buddhism was preached, the era when "simulated" Buddhism was propagated, and a degenerate age when no Buddha would appear in the world. The length of time ascribed to each period varies with the scripture, but it was widely believed that China had by this time entered the degenerate period. Xinxing (540–594), the leader of this school, held that the only means to salvation was to practice austerities and to maintain monastic discipline. The sect emphasized almsgiving and to this end established in a temple in Chang'an an "Inexhaustible Treasury," to which the faithful contributed vast sums to be used to build temples and to help the ill and destitute. The school emphasized the degeneracy of the times, holding that no government was worthy of respect or allegiance. This view was naturally opposed by the Sui and Tang rulers; the school was severely condemned and in 713 the wealth of the Inexhaustible Treasury was confiscated. The Three Stages school did not survive the Tang dynasty and, unlike other schools, its teachings were not exported to Japan, although the concept of a degenerate age was to play a major role in Japanese religious history some five hundred years later.

Of major significance, at least during the Sui dynasty, was the Tiantai school. Its founder, Zhiyi (538–597), had studied under a northern monk, Huisi (515–577), a meditation specialist who had moved to the South. Zhiyi was renowned as a teacher and established his own school at Mount Tiantai in present-day Zhejiang Province. His writings, as recorded by his disciples, demonstrate a genius for organization and analysis. Addressing the enormous body of translated Buddhist literature, he analyzed it under a system of five periods (the alleged sequence in which the Buddha taught various doctrines) and eight teachings. Ranking the various teachings in order of excellence, he placed the *Lotus Sutra* first, together with the Tiantai teachings derived from this text. Zhiyi formulated a great number of doctrinal analyses that had a significant impact on later Buddhism. His major teachings are found in the *Mohe zhiguan (Great Concentration and Insight)*. Because the Sui dynasty had supported Zhiyi, the Tang took a negative attitude toward his school, and Tiantai had little influence in China after Zhiyi's death. In fact, the texts of the school were dispersed in the late Tang and had to be retrieved from Korea and Japan when a later attempt to revive the teaching was made.

Perhaps the most intricate and intellectually attractive school of Buddhism was Huayan, called in English the Flower Garland school, which based its teachings on the abstruse *Avatamsaka Sutra*. Fazang (643–712), although not the traditional founder of the school, was the first to organize its doctrines. The leaders of the school enjoyed imperial patronage during the Tang and its teachings had a significant influence on other schools of Buddhism.

The Faxiang, or Dharma-Characteristic, school flourished briefly during the Tang. It centered on the famous Xuanzang (596–664), whose sixteen-year pilgrimage to India and Central Asia is celebrated in Chinese history and literature. Returning in 645, he was accorded a tumultuous welcome by the imperial court and furnished with extensive patronage. He devoted himself to the translation of the many *sutras* he had brought back with him. His teachings were abstract and obscure and never acquired an extensive following. [*See also* Xuanzang.]

Also of significance during the Tang, if only for a brief period, were a group of teachers of Esoteric Buddhism (Chinese, Zhenyan). Although this form of Buddhism can scarcely be described as a school in China, several of its teachers, visitors from India, were greatly revered by the Tang ruling house. Under the name of Shingon Buddhism, the Esoteric teachings were taken to Japan by the famous Kūkai (774–835), where they dominated the Buddhism of the Heian period and still continue as a major school of Buddhism. [*See also* Zhenyan; Shingon; *and* Kūkai.]

Pure Land Buddhism, with its faith in Amitabha Buddha and his Western Paradise, has from early times captured the interest of large segments of the Chinese population. The teaching held that all who had faith in this Buddha and relied upon his vow to postpone his entrance into buddhahood until all sentient beings are saved, would be reborn in the Western Paradise. The school emphasized the recitation of the Buddha's name *(nianfo)* as a means to bring about this rebirth. Throughout Chinese history a number of Pure Land practitioners have gained prominence; however, it is scarcely possible to speak of a developed Pure Land school of Buddhism.

Chan (Japanese, Zen) Buddhism developed also in the Sui–Tang period and became the most important and most enduring of all Chinese schools of Buddhism. Chan emphasizes enlightenment, the awakening to the Buddha nature with which all sentient beings are endowed (a concept held in common with most schools of Mahayana Buddhism), achieved through a process of intensive meditation under the guidance of a teacher. Tradition has it that Chan was introduced to China by an Indian monk Bodhidharma, who is honored as the twenty-eighth patriarch, descended in a direct line from the historical Buddha. Bodhidharma was followed by a succession of Chinese patriarchs leading up to Huineng (638–713), the sixth patriarch, to whom all present-day Chan in both China and Japan traces its ancestry.

The name of Dunhuang, an oasis in Gansu Province on the northwestern border of China, figures prominently in Buddhist history from early times. Dunhuang was an important city on the trade route from Central Asia, controlled at times by China, but more frequently by non-Chinese tribes. It was the site of a huge complex of cave temples carved into the cliffs near the city. In 1900 a walled-up cave was discovered, revealing thousands of documents, many of them Buddhist, that had been hidden away to protect them from invading barbarians. The cave was sealed in the early eleventh century and when opened was found to contain materials dating between 406 and 966. These documents are a major source for information on the history, literature, art, religion, and language of this period. Many figures of whom only passing mention is made elsewhere in Buddhist literature emerge as significant leaders whose importance was lost to later chroniclers. This is especially true of Chan Buddhism. [*See also* Dunhuang.]

The early Tang emperors had supported Buddhism to a certain extent, but were largely Daoist sympathizers. Their support of Buddhism was in many ways a means to control it. It was not until the incapacity of the third emperor in 660 enabled the remarkable Empress Wu to gain control and herself become ruler in 690 that the Tang court accorded elaborate patronage to Buddhism. [*See also* Wu Zhao.] Empress Wu welcomed Fazang, the Huayan master, supported several of the Tantric Buddhist adepts, and paid homage to the Chan monk Shenxiu (606?–706), the leader of what came to be known as Northern Chan. Chan practitioners, specialists in meditation, had begun to form communities in the mid-seventh century and by the beginning of the eighth century had spread throughout China. Seeking to establish themselves as a legitimate school of Buddhism, they created a lineage traceable to the historical Buddha. The Northern Chan school, headed by the followers of Shenxiu dominated the first decades of the eighth century. Then in 732 a priest by the name of Shenhui (672–762) launched an attack on what he called the Northern Chan school, claiming that the school of his own teacher Huineng, which he called the Southern school, was the legitimate teaching of Chan. Huineng, he claimed, was the true sixth Chan patriarch, not Shenxiu of the Northern school. So persuasive was Shenhui that by the start of the ninth century Huineng and the schools descended from him came to be accepted as the legitimate Chan lineage. Shenhui himself and his own particular school, however, virtually disappeared from the pages of traditional Chan history.

By the mid-eighth century the Tang dynasty was gradually weakening and the central government was losing control of vast areas of the country. The An Lushan Rebellion of 755 to 763 shattered the effectiveness of the dynasty as the capital cities were lost to rebel forces. The government was eventually able to suppress the rebellion, but the power of the Tang was lost and foreign invasion sapped the strength of the country. Buddhism appeared to be gaining more and more power, and it began to be blamed for some of the ills from which the country was suffering. Finally, from 842 to 845, a suppression of Buddhism was put into effect by the Emperor Wu. Vast temple holdings were confiscated, numerous temples destroyed, and much of the clergy was returned to lay life. This persecution of Buddhism, together with the revival of Confucianism in the Song period, brought to an end the dominance of Buddhism in government circles. The Buddhism of the capital cities was destroyed; the Chan schools and other forms of Buddhism that had received imperial support were virtually eliminated. The Tang court, however, did not have effective control of the country as a whole. Local warlords dominated the outlying areas and gave their support to the Chan that flourished in their domains. It was here that Chan persisted and developed. The new Chan leaders in Jiangxi and Hunan professed a rural, rustic, popular Chan that sought lay support. The recorded sayings of its masters were written in an unpretentious, colloquial style. The individual, the patriarch or Chan master, came to be esteemed; emphasis was on personal enlightenment to be achieved as a result of intensive meditation practice. [*See also* Sui Dynasty *and* Tang Dynasty.]

The Later Period. In the Five Dynasties period (907–960) Chan spread throughout China, developing large temple complexes organized under strict monastic regulations. Chan divided into various schools and houses, some of which lasted only briefly; others, the Linji and Caodong, flourish today in Japan as the Rinzai and Sōtō schools.

Buddhism during the Song period (960–1279) is usually described as suffering a decline. The Song government, pressed for funds, sold monks' certificates and in other ways debased the status of the religion. Printing was developed during the Song and had a major impact on the whole of Chinese culture. Buddhist works, particularly of the Chan school, were produced in abundance, lending a literary quality to what was originally a nonliterary method of teaching. Printing also made possible the publication of a large number of Neo-Confucian works that were basically hostile to Buddhism. Neo-Confucianism was adopted as the basis of government and of moral and ethical education. The civil service system was expanded and all examinations for those who sought appointment in the imperial bureaucracy required a thorough knowledge of the Confucian classics. During this period Chan retained its importance, particularly in the circles of literati, and many Chan monks were closely connected with high-ranking government officials. Chan itself was changing as it became more and more literary in character. The use of the *gong'an* (Japanese, *kōan*), Chan stories that became meditation topics, developed in the Song. When the Song was threatened by the Mongol invasions, many of its priests fled to Japan to become teachers there, although Japanese monks continued to come to China for instruction. In 1279 the Song surrendered to the Mongol invaders and China was once again under the control of an alien dynasty, the Yuan (1279–1368).

The Mongol conquerors possessed an uncomplicated folk religion and were also followers of Lamaism, a form of Buddhism related to the Esoteric

Buddhism of the Tang. [*See also* Lamaism.] The Yuan were sympathetic to existing Buddhist institutions and Chan temples continued to thrive. Japanese monks continued to come to study Chan, particularly under the prominent master Zhongfen Minben (1263–1323), who taught a form of Buddhism that combined Pure Land teachings with Chan. Chan–Pure Land association can be traced to the Tang dynasty, but by the advent of the Ming dynasty (1368–1644) Chan and Pure Land came to be taught together and the strict *gong'an* Chan of the Song period was abandoned. Buddhism moved more and more into the realm of popular religion and a tendency to merge Buddhist and Daoist pantheons emerged. Lay Buddhism, centering on Pure Land practices, increased significantly. Buddhism, mostly popular, but with a modicum of concern for the more abstruse teachings, continued to exist after the Ming, but it came to occupy an increasingly insignificant position in the intellectual scene as a whole.

[*See also* Zhenyan *and* Daoism.]

Kenneth Ch'en, *Buddhism in China* (1964). Arthur Wright, *Buddhism in Chinese History* (1959). Philip Yampolsky, *The Platform Sutra of the Sixth Patriarch* (1967). Erik Zürcher, *The Buddhist Conquest of China* (1959).

PHILIP YAMPOLSKY

BUDDHISM IN KOREA

Buddhism was introduced into Korea from China during the Three Kingdoms period. In 372 CE King Fu Jian of the Former Qin dynasty is said to have sent an envoy, the monk Sundo (Chinese, Shundao), to the Koguryŏ court of King Sosurim (r. 371–384) with gifts of scriptures and images. He was followed in 384 by the Serindian monk Maranant'a (*Kumaranandin), who arrived in the kingdom of Paekche from the court of the Eastern Jin dynasty. From these new bastions in Korea, Buddhism and the rudiments of Chinese civilization were subsequently introduced into Japan, laying the foundations for the rich Buddhist culture of the Asuka and Nara periods. Finally, in 529, the kingdom of Silla also officially embraced the Buddhist faith and, after its conquest of the entire Korean peninsula in 668, Buddhism became the official state religion of the new Unified Silla dynasty.

Several features of the Buddhism of this earliest period of its tenure on the peninsula remain characteristic of the religion in later times as well. First, the steadily increasing influence in Korea of Chinese civilization during the Three Kingdoms period eventually led to the eclipse of more primitive cultural associations with the tribes of the Central Asian steppes. This resulted in Chinese domination of trends within the Buddhist tradition from its very inception in Korea, and virtually all Korean Buddhist teachings and schools had their Chinese counterparts. Second, this captivation with things Chinese allowed the Koreans to form one of East Asia's most ecumenical traditions, which was able to see the value in contrasting approaches to Buddhist ideology and practice. Syncretism became the watchword of Korean Buddhism and inspired the writings of all its greatest philosophers. Finally, until the Yi dynasty (1392–1910) Buddhism also had close associations with the ruling powers on the peninsula, and Buddhist ecclesiastics wielded immense political and economic influence. Both government and religion profited from their symbiotic relationship—Buddhist monks entreating the Buddhas and bodhisattvas through ritual observances to ensure the security of the kingdom, the courts taking an active role in the dissemination of the religion throughout their domains. Indeed, many of the signal accomplishments of the Korean tradition, such as carving the woodblocks of the Korean Buddhist canon (the Koryŏ Tripitaka), were initiated as means of ensuring national security.

The success of the Silla kingdom in unifying the peninsula ushered in an era of prosperity for the religion that was unparalleled in its history. Buddhist scholasticism in particular profited from the munificent support of the Silla court and a variety of doctrinal schools appeared, led by a number of important figures whose achievements in Buddhist exegetics loom large in any accounting of East Asian Buddhism. According to tradition, five main scholastic schools of Buddhism were prominent during the Unified Silla period: the Kyeyul-chong, which was concerned with Buddhist monastic discipline (Vinaya); the Yŏlban-chong, whose doctrine focused on the *Mahaparinirvana Sutra;* the Wŏnyung-chong, or the Flower Garland (Chinese, Huayan; Korean, Hwaŏm) school; the Pŏpsŏng-chong, a syncretic school with prominent Hwaŏm tendencies; and the Pŏpsang-chong, based on the mere-consciousness *(vijnanavada)* teachings of Yogacara.

Ŭisang (625–702) was the founder of the Wŏnyung-chong. He was a student of Zhiyan (602–668), who is regarded as the second patriarch of the Huayan school in China, and a colleague of Fazang (643–712), one of the most important scholiasts of the Chinese tradition and the effective systematizer of Huayan doctrine. Ŭisang's major work, *Hwaŏm ilsŭng pŏpkye-to (Diagram of the Dharma-Realm According to the One-Vehicle of Huayan)*, explores the relationship between the absolute and phenomenal realms that is so vital to Huayan philosophy. Through his efforts, Hwaŏm philosophy became one of the mainstays of Korean Buddhist thought and exerted tremendous influence over all later developments within the church.

The Pŏpsŏng-chong was a uniquely Korean school of philosophy that had no precise counterpart in China. Its founder was Wŏnhyo (617–686), perhaps the greatest Korean philosopher of any persuasion. Wŏnhyo authored more than 240 works, of which some 20 are still extant. Most of his writings display a strong concern with establishing the connections between different texts and schools of thought, rather than with promoting the viewpoint of any particular sect. This was commonly achieved by demonstrating that most of the distinctive doctrinal features of the disparate elements of the Buddhist tradition could be collapsed into a single, unifying ideal: the one mind. Wŏnhyo's synopses of the ideological perspectives of major Buddhist sects also sought to promote fraternal harmony rather than sectarian conflict, so as eventually to yield an all-inclusive vision of Buddhist philosophy. His syncretic thought would inspire all future generations of Buddhist thinkers in Korea. Despite his daunting intellectual achievements, however, Wŏnhyo did not neglect to administer to the needs of the common people, and he brought directly to them a popular form of Buddhism that would be of immediate application to their workaday lives.

It was also during the Unified Silla period that Sŏn (Chinese, Chan; Japanese, Zen) was introduced to Korea. An obscure monk, Pŏmnang (fl. 632–646), a Korean who studied under the fourth patriarch of the school, Daoxin (580–651), is said to have first brought the teachings of that tradition to the peninsula, and a later teacher in his succession, Chisŏn Tohŏn (824–882), eventually founded the Hŭiyang-san school, the oldest Sŏn lineage in Korea. During the eighth and ninth centuries eight other sites were established by other Korean Sŏn pilgrims, forming what came to be called the Nine Mountains school of Sŏn (Kusan Sŏnmun). Because the introduction of Sŏn coincided with the zenith of Buddhist scholasticism in Korea, however, its new message encountered much resistance from entrenched elements within the Korean ecclesia and the modicum of popularity the Nine Mountains school was able to gain during the Silla period gradually waned.

It was the Koryŏ dynasty (918–1392), which supplanted Unified Silla, that marked the ascendency of Sŏn in Korean Buddhism. The mature school of Korean Sŏn is called the Chogye-chong, and its effective founder was Chinul (1158–1210), a charismatic figure whose vision of the unity of Sŏn and the scholastic teachings restored the vitality of the enervated mid-Koryŏ tradition. Chinul developed an approach to Buddhism in which the theoretical aids of the scholastic doctrine of Hwaŏm were used to support the development of Sŏn meditative techniques, particularly the investigation of the "primary topic" (Korean, *hwadu;* Chinese, *huatou*). While there are similarities between various aspects of Korean Sŏn thought and practice and those found in the Zen sects of other countries, the Korean school founded by Chinul was an autonomous development that evolved independently of its Chinese and Japanese counterparts. Chinul's systematization of Sŏn soteriological techniques, as well his amalgamation of Hwaŏm philosophy with Sŏn practice, constitute two of the most distinctively Korean contributions to Buddhist thought, and are both indicative of the orientation of the later Korean tradition.

Chinul's disciple, Chin'gak Hyesim (1178–1234), contributed to the rapid crystallization of Korean Sŏn practice around the *hwadu* technique. In addition, his examinations of the similarities between the teachings of Buddhism, Confucianism, and Daoism, which paralleled those of Chinese philosophers of the Song dynasty, widened the Korean Buddhist syncretic outlook so that it could embrace other religions as well. T'aego Pou (1301–1382) worked to merge the remnants of the earlier Nine Mountains lineages into an ecumenical Chogye school, and grafted onto it the Chinese Linji (Japanese, Rinzai; Korean, Imje) lineage, which he had introduced from Yuan China. His contemporary, Naong Hyekŭn (1320–1376), one of the "three great masters" *(sam daejosa)* of the late-Koryŏ church, was also instrumental in establishing "investigation of the *hwadu*" *(kanhwa-sŏn)* as the principal practice of the tradition.

With the advent of the Yi dynasty, the fortunes of Korean Buddhism began to wane. While they were consolidating their rule, the first Yi sovereigns continued to sponsor construction projects, maigre offerings to monks, and Buddhist ritual observances. The dynastic founder, Yi Sŏng-gye (T'aejo; r. 1392–1398), even appointed the renowned monk Muhak Chajo (1327–1405) as a royal master *(wangsa)*, following Koryŏ precedents. Throughout his reign, however, Confucian officials had remonstrated for a stricter selection process for monks, express limits on the numbers of monasteries and sects, and reorganization of the ecclesiastical system so as to provide more centralized control. With the ascension of T'aejo's fifth son, T'aejong (r. 1400–1418), to the throne as the third ruler of the dynasty, long-festering antagonism toward Buddhism on the part of the Confucian officialdom eventually resulted in a severe proscription of the religion that would persist until the modern era. A move to reduce the number of allowable sects finally culminated in the 1424 proclamation of King Sejong (r. 1418–1450) that merged the Chogye, Ch'ont'ae (Chinese, Tiantai; Japanese, Tendai), and Vinaya schools into the Sŏn ("meditation") school, and all the remaining scholastic sects into the Kyo ("doctrine") school. Monastery paddy lands and forest properties were appropriated by the state, and temple serfs were enlisted into the army. Large numbers of monks were forcibly returned to lay life, new regulations were promulgated concerning the issuance of monks' ordination certificates, and the highest ecclesiastical ranks of national master *(kuksa)* and royal master were abolished. No Buddhist temples were allowed within the environs of the capital or major cities, and strict restrictions were placed on intermonastery pilgrimages. Given these exigencies, there was a marked decline in the quantity and quality of scholarly work.

During this dire period, it is perhaps Sŏsan Hyujŏng (1520–1604) to whom most credit is due for sustaining the creative drives of Korean Buddhism. Hyujŏng looked back to Chinul for his inspiration, and made great efforts to show the common purposes of the Sŏn and Kyo schools in his *Sŏn'ga kugam (Guide to the Sŏn School)*. Similar guides to Confucianism and Daoism were also intended to ease tensions between Buddhism and its rival religions. Despite the best efforts of Hyujŏng and his successors, however, Buddhism remained isolated from the mainstream of Korean intellectual life.

The end of the Yi saw another resurgence of Sŏn practice in Korea, principally brought about by the eminent meditation master Kyŏnghŏ (1857–1912) and his numerous disciples. Such monks enabled Korean Buddhism to maintain its own distinct traditions and practices, despite new pressures during the Japanese occupation period (1910–1945). With independence, Korean Buddhism was split between a faction of married monks (T'aego-chong), which had flourished under Japanese patronage and which catered especially to the lay population in the cities, and a sect of celibate monks (Chogye-chong), who sought to restore the original scholastic and meditative foci of the tradition. After many years of conflict, the Chogye-chong eventually prevailed, and today remains the dominant school of Buddhism in Korea. At the present time, the Korean church is flourishing and remains one of the most vibrant schools of Mahayana, and particularly Chan, Buddhism to be found anywhere in Asia.

[*See also* Koryŏ Tripitaka *and* Pulguk Temple.]

Robert E. Buswell, Jr., trans., *The Korean Approach to Zen: The Collected Works of Chinul* (1983). J. H. Kamstra, *Encounter or Syncretism: The Initial Growth of Japanese Buddhism* (1967), part 3, pp. 142–223. Hee-sung Keel, *Chinul: Founder of the Korean Son Tradition* (1984). Peter H. Lee, trans., *Lives of Eminent Korean Monks: The Haedong Kosŭng Chŏn*, Harvard Yenching Institute Studies, no. 25 (1969). Steve Odin, *Process Metaphysics and Hua-yen Buddhism: A Critical Study of Cumulative Penetration vs. Interpenetration* (1982). Sung-bae Park, *Buddhist Faith and Sudden Enlightenment* (1983).

ROBERT E. BUSWELL, JR.

BUDI UTOMO, or Boedi Oetomo, cultural organization that contributed to the national awakening of Indonesia early in the twentieth century.

Inspired by a visit of Dr. Wahidin Soedirohoesodo (1857–1917), students of the medical school at Weltvreden formed Budi Utomo ("beautiful endeavor") in May 1908. It attempted to promote Javanese interests through modern education in both Western languages and science and in traditional Javanese culture, implicitly rejecting any Islamic way to modernization. At its peak in 1910 the organization had ten thousand members but waned thereafter because it was seen as too exclusively the organization of the lower ranks of the traditional Javanese aristocracy *(priyayi)*. It contributed to the building of Indonesian national sentiment that grew to a flood in the following decade.

[*See also* Sarekat Islam *and* Priyayi.]

Akira Nagazumi, *The Dawn of Indonesian Nationalism: The Early Years of the Budi Utomo, 1908–1919* (1972).

DAVID K. WYATT

BUENCAMINO, FELIPE (1848–1929), member of a well-to-do *principalia* family of Bulacan, Philippines, and of the government of the new republic. Buencamino studied in Manila (LL.B., Santo Tomas, 1876), and, after holding high posts in the Spanish colonial bureaucracy and fighting for Spain in the 1896 rebellion, he joined the revolutionary government in mid-1898. Through his association with

Emilio Aguinaldo, he rose to secretary of foreign affairs in the new republic. After his capture and release by the Americans (mid-1900), he helped to found the Federal Party and was named to the Civil Service Board of the central government. By 1904 he had withdrawn from public office and settled in the Manila district of Tondo, where his independent spirit led him into a range of political, social, and religious activities.

[*See also* Philippines; Philippine Revolution; *and* Aguinaldo, Emilio.]

MICHAEL CULLINANE

BUGIS. The Bugis, or Buginese, are the largest of four ethnic groups inhabiting South Sulawesi (Celebes). By the seventeenth century they had been converted to Islam. In the last third of that century, a stream of Bugis refugees began appearing in various parts of Southeast Asia, and the migration continued well into the eighteenth century, providing a constant infusion of new blood for the settlements made by the original Bugis groups and enabling them to retain strong cultural ties with their previous homelands. The exodus followed the defeat of the Makassarese kingdom of Goa by the Dutch and their Buginese allies in 1667 and 1669. Leonard Y. Andaya argues that a new oppressive overlord system, introduced by the ruler of Bone, Arung Palakka, and enforced by his Dutch allies, forced the Bugis to leave their homelands.

Skilled soldiers, merchants, and seamen, the Bugis had a significant impact on Southeast Asia, particularly on the relatively underpopulated Malay world. Bugis settlements were made in Borneo, Sumatra, and the Malay Peninsula, and Buginese groups seized power in Johor and attained powerful positions in other states. In the mid-eighteenth century they founded their own state of Selangor, encompassing rich tin fields in the Malay Peninsula that had been previously subject to Johor. Their pattern of widely spread yet interconnected settlement allowed the Bugis to dominate intra-archipelago trade by the late eighteenth century, making first Riau and then Singapore the center of their operations. They were employed widely as mercenaries, especially by the Dutch, who nevertheless feared them as "pirates and smugglers." The British, however, tended to admire Bugis industry and enterprise. The Bugis are also notable for their chronicles, which celebrate the deeds of their ancestors and are more factual in style than is normally the case in this genre of Southeast Asian literature.

[*See also* Makassar; Goa; Riau; Daeng Parani; Raja Muda; Selangor; *and* Johor.]

Leonard Y. Andaya, *The Kingdom of Johor* (1975) and *The Heritage of Arung Palakka: A History of South Sulewesi (Celebes) in the 17th Century* (1981). Virginia Matheson and Barbara Watson Andaya, trans., *The Precious Gift (Tuhfat al-Nafis)* (1982).

DIANNE LEWIS

BUKHARA, a city and oasis in the southern part of the Uzbek SSR, dependent on irrigation from the Zeravshan River (a tributary of the Amu Darya) and also a commercial and artisan center, long noted for its bazaars and its production of rugs. The city is perhaps more famous still as a long-established center of Islamic learning based at its numerous religious colleges *(madrasas)*. Al-Bukhari (810–870), who compiled the most comprehensive and authoritative collection of the prophet Muhammad's sayings and traditions *(hadith)*, was a native of this city.

The western empire of the Turk (known in Chinese sources as Tujue) gained control of Bukhara by the mid-sixth century but succumbed to the Arab conquest in the eighth century. Under the Iranian Samanids (tenth century) Bukhara became the seat of a great kingdom and the center of a Persian literary renaissance. At the end of the century, Bukhara fell to the Karakhanids, who ruled until the early thirteenth century. A succession of Turkic dynastic clans from the Chagatai khanate to the Uzbek Shaibanids ruled the area for most of the succeeding period (apart from a brief interlude in the 1740s when Nadir Shah, himself an Afshar Turk, made a bid to incorporate it into his nascent empire centered at Kandahar) until the Russian takeover in 1866. Somewhat overshadowed politically and commercially by Samarkand, approximately 250 kilometers to the east and linked with it by the Zeravshan, Bukhara has traditionally retained its distinction as a center of learning and of libraries. Although for many centuries the major east–west trade route from China to the Levant, via Kashgar and Samarkand, passed through Bukhara and helped to nourish its prosperity, like other cities of Central Asia it is mainly a monument to past glories. Still, there has been rapid commercial, industrial, urban, and irrigated agricultural growth under Soviet control.

[*See also* Samanid Dynasty.]

Wilhelm Barthold, *Turkestan down to the Mongol Invasion* (2d ed., 1958).

RHOADS MURPHEY, JR.

BUKHARA, KHANATE OF, a Central Asian state in existence from the sixteenth century until 1920. The name *Bukhara,* more properly used for its capital, was given as a matter of convenience in European sources; in indigenous works the khanate was known either by the name of the ruling dynasty, by the name of its main region, Mawarannahr (i.e., Transoxiana), or by the literary name *Turan.* At the beginning of the sixteenth century the nomadic Uzbeks under Shaibani Khan conquered the two Timurid states of Central Asia and Khurasan. The resulting Shaibanid state included Transoxiana, Balkh and Badakhshan (provinces to the south of the Amu Darya), Ferghana, Tashkent, Turkestan, and sometimes parts of Khurasan occupied during the wars with Safavid Iran.

The Shaibanid state was divided into appanages between all male members (sultans) of the dynasty, who would designate the supreme ruler (khan), the oldest member of the clan. The seat of the khan was first Samarkand, the capital of the Timurids, but some of the khans preferred to remain in their former appanages. Thus, Bukhara became the seat of the khan for the first time under Ubaid Allah Khan (r. 1533–1539). During the internal feuds of the middle of the sixteenth century, one of the Shaibanid sultans, Abd Allah, took possession of Bukhara in 1557; there, in 1561, he proclaimed his father Iskandar as the supreme khan of the Uzbeks. Thereafter, Bukhara remained the Transoxianian capital of the Uzbek khanate and of later dynasties.

The nomadic Uzbeks who conquered the country seized the pastures and some of the best-irrigated lands on the plains, pushing both the old sedentary and the pre-Uzbek nomadic population out toward the mountainous areas in the eastern parts of the khanate. In many places, however, the old Tajik rural population remained, interspersed with the Uzbeks. The sedentarization of the Uzbeks by the nineteenth century was accompanied by the turkization of the Tajiks, especially in the countryside on the plains. But the population of the main urban centers, such as Bukhara and Samarkand, remained predominantly Tajik: Tajik was the language of literature and chancery in the khanate until the end of its existence. The term *Uzbek* was applied to both the descendants of the nomadic conquerors and the later newcomers, while the term *Tajik* was applied to both Iranian- and Turkic-speaking sedentary nontribal people. (In Ferghana, Khwarazm, and Tashkent the term *Sart,* instead of *Tajik,* was used in this latter sense.) Until the nineteenth century, the Uzbek nobility formed the ruling elite in the khanate, as military commanders, court officials, and provincial governors; civil and especially financial affairs remained in the hands of the Tajik bureaucracy.

Abd Allah Khan ibn Iskandar (first ruled in the name of his father; khan from 1583 to 1598) united the khanate and abolished the system of appanages in the course of long wars with the other members of the Shaibanid dynasty. During his reign, Khurasan and Khwarazm were conquered and the khan's military campaigns were extended as far as the central parts of the Kazakh steppes in the north and Kashgar in the east. The strengthening of the central government was accompanied by new economic measures: the construction of irrigation canals and numerous public buildings, the improvement of roads, and monetary reforms that contributed to the development of commerce.

The period of political expansion and economic prosperity of the khanate was short-lived. Soon after the death of Abd Allah Khan the Shaibanid dynasty died out, to be replaced by the Janid (or Ashtarkhanid) dynasty, another branch of the descendants of Jochi, whose founder was related through marriage to Abd Allah Khan. The Janids, as outsiders for the Uzbeks, depended more than the Shaibanids on the support of the tribal chiefs; thus the power of the latter greatly increased during the seventeenth century. The Janid state was divided between the khan sitting in Bukhara and his heir (brother or son), often also bearing the title khan, who ruled the provinces to the south of the Amu Darya, with his capital in Balkh. The ruler of Balkh was sometimes independent from Bukhara, and they were at odds with one another and often at war.

The first half of the seventeenth century, especially the reign of Imam-Quli Khan (1611–1642), was a period of relative political and economic stability for the Janids. Although they could not regain Khurasan, finally lost to Iran by the beginning of the seventeenth century, and although Khwarazm again became independent, the Janids were able to maintain their possessions against the attacks of the Kazakhs and Dzungars in the north and the Mughals in the south. However, already in the second half of the seventeenth century the signs of decline were obvious. Continuing sedentarization of the Uzbeks negatively affected the military prowess of the tribal troops of the khanate, and from the 1650s on Bukhara suffered from the recurrent raids of the Uzbeks of Khwarazm. The central government was unable to check the growing local particularism and tribal feuds. By the end of the seventeenth century the khanate lost Ferghana and Badakhshan. An attempt by Khan Ubaid Allah II (r. 1702–1711) to suppress the tribal nobility and restore some degree of centralization failed, after which the khanate disintegrated into a number of tribal principalities. From 1723 to 1729 the country suffered from devastations caused by the Kazakhs, who, fleeing from the Dzungars, invaded the Zeravshan Valley. In 1740 the khanate was conquered by Nadir Shah, the ruler of Iran. The Janid khan Abu al-Fayz retained his throne, becoming Nadir's vassal.

After the death of Nadir Shah in 1747, the chief of the Uzbek Manghit tribe, Muhammad Rahim Biy Ataliq, overcame his rivals from other tribes with the support of the urban population, consolidated his rule in the khanate, and was proclaimed khan in 1756. His successor, however, ruled in the name of puppet khans of Janid origin. The third Manghit ruler, Shah Murad (r. 1785–1800), finally deposed the Janids and acceded to the throne himself. He did not assume the title of khan, preferring the title *amir,* as did the subsequent Manghit rulers. The khanate was smaller under the Manghits than under their predecessors: it lost important provinces to the south of Amu Darya and in the Syr Darya basin, and Merv, conquered by Shah Murad in 1785–1789, was lost in 1823. For half a century the *amirs* were unable to subdue the small principality of Shahrisabz (about fifty miles south of Samarkand), ruled by the chieftains of the Uzbek tribe of Keneges, hostile to the Manghits. Another small principality, Ura-Tube, between Bukhara and Khokand, was a bone of contention between the two khanates, but mostly remained independent.

Under the Manghits, the administration of the country was more centralized. Uzbek tribal nobility finally lost its power under Amir Nasr Allah (r. 1827–1860), who killed many of the members of the aristocratic clans and created a small standing army, including some artillery. The khanate became a despotic monarchy in which the *amir* enjoyed almost unlimited authority and ruled through a ramified bureaucratic apparatus. The country was divided into more than twenty provinces, each administered by an appointed governor to whom all authority in the province was delegated. The first minister *(qoshbegi)* was always a Persian slave or a descendant of slaves; this status ensured his personal loyalty to the *amir.*

Besides frequent diplomatic exchanges with its Central Asian neighbors, the khanate of Bukhara perennially maintained limited relations with other states of the Islamic world: Iran, the Ottoman empire, the Mughal empire, and Afghanistan. Relations with Europe were practically nonexistent, and the country did not experience any Western influence before the Russian conquest. Diplomatic and commercial relations with Russia began in the second half of the sixteenth century and grew steadily in importance. Peaceful relations were undisturbed until the early 1860s, even when Russia began its military offensive against Khokand. A conflict started in 1865, shortly after the Russian conquest of Tashkent. The army of Bukhara was utterly defeated in three battles, and on 18 June 1868 Amir Muzaffar al-Din (r. 1860–1885) signed a peace treaty with the Russian governor-general of Turkestan, A. P. von Kaufman. Samarkand and its province were annexed by Russia and the country was opened to the Russian merchants. The *amir* retained his throne as a vassal of Russia and made up for his territorial losses by establishing, with Russian help, control over mountainous regions in the upper Zeravshan Valley in 1870 and by annexing the principalities of the western Pamir in 1895. The sovereignty of the khanate was not formally limited, but it became a de facto protectorate, especially after the crossing of its territory by the Central Asian Railroad (1887) and the subsequent inclusion of the khanate in Russia's customs frontier (1895).

Officially, the last two *amirs* were treated by the Russian government as independent rulers, maintaining close relations with the imperial court in Saint Petersburg. The Russians did not interfere in the internal affairs of the khanate, and the Russian conquest had but a superficial effect on the life of the country. A reform movement developed after 1905, but it met with strong opposition from the conservative Islamic clergy and was suppressed by the *amir.* At the end of August 1920 the last *amir,* Sayid Alim Khan, was overthrown as a result of the invasion of the khanate by Soviet troops, and on 6 October 1920 the khanate was abolished and proclaimed the Bukharan People's Soviet Republic.

[*See also* Bukhara; Shaibanid Dynasty; Kazakhs; Khokand, Khanate of; *and* Khwarazm.]

Wilhelm Barthold, "A Short History of Turkistan," in *Four Studies on the History of Central Asia,* translated by V. and T. Minorsky (1956–1962), vol. 1, pp. 64–68. Wilhelm Barthold and Richard N. Frye, "Bukhara," in *The Encyclopaedia of Islam* (new ed., 1960–). S. Becker, *Russia's Protectorates in Central Asia: Bukhara and Khiva, 1865–1924* (1968). M. Holdsworth, *Turkestan in the Nineteenth Century: A Brief History of the Khanates of Bukhara, Kokand and Khiva* (1959).

YURI BREGEL

BUKHAR-KHUDA, the title of the rulers of Bukhara in Sasanid and early Islamic times (probably the arabicized form of the Sogdian original). The *bukhar-khudas* were descended from an old, rich, and powerful family of *dihqans* who, according to Narshakhi, had made most of the common people their peasants and servants. The consort of the *bukhar-khuda* was known as the khatun; a regency headed by her was in power in Bukhara when the Arab Muslims arrived there. In Sasanid times, the *bukhar-khudas* enjoyed the status of autonomous frontier princes; they preserved this prestige in early Islamic times by paying tribute to the caliphs and becoming nominal Muslims. The last of the *bukhar-khudas* in this sense was stripped of the title to his estates by the Samanid *amir* Isma'il (r. 892–907) in an effort to centralize the government. He continued to receive an annual payment from the state until his death in 913 or 914. His descendants remained in villages near Bukhara for some time thereafter.

[*See also* Bukhara *and* Dihqan.]

Narshakhi, *The History of Bukhara,* translated by Richard Frye (1954). E. L. DANIEL

BUMIPUTRA, also known as Bumiputera, are the Malays, the aborigines in peninsular Malaysia, and the indigenous people in Sarawak and Sabah who qualify for special help in overcoming their economic disadvantages under Malaysia's New Economic Policy (NEP). The term *Bumiputra*, which literally means "sons [princes] of the soil," became current in Malaysia from 1969 onward. The policy of aiding the Bumiputra is an extension of Article 153 of the Malaysian constitution, which discusses the "special position" of the Malays as opposed to the Malaysian Chinese and Indians. The Bumiputra benefit in such areas as ownership of assets, employment, and education.

[*See also* Malaysia.]

Barbara W. Andaya and Leonard Y. Andaya, *A History of Malaysia* (1982). R. S. MILNE

BUNDAHISHN *(Book of Creation),* also called *Zand-agahih* (*Knowledge of the Commentary,* i.e., upon the Avesta), the first Pahlavi text studied in Europe. It exists in two recensions, the shorter "Indian" and the "Greater," or "Iranian." The first chapters deal with the creation of the world by Ohrmazd, the Wise Lord, and the invasion and pollution of it by the Evil Spirit, Ahriman. Other chapters describe the ensuing battle between good and evil, predict the resurrection of the dead and the triumph of Ohrmazd, and enumerate the categories of creation and the generations of the legendary heroes of ancient Iran; the text is thus a Zoroastrian *Genesis,* with primary emphasis on the cosmic and ethical dualism of the faith. Much of the *Bundahishn* echoes Avestan syntax and thus reflects ancient teachings, despite the late date of its compilation.

[*See also* Avesta *and* Avestan.]

B. T. Anklesaria, *Zand-Ākāsīh, Iranian or Greater Bundahisn* (1956). E. W. West, trans., *Pahlavi Texts* (1974). R. C. Zaehner, *The Teachings of the Magi* (1976).

JAMES R. RUSSELL

BUNDI, an Indian princely state, reputed to have been founded in 1342 by Rai Deva, a member of the Hara branch of the Chauhan clan of Rajputs. First known as Haraoti, or "land of Hara [Krishna]," Bundi was located in the rugged Chambal River valley. In 1579 Kotah state was separated from Bundi to provide a patrimony for Madho Singh, a favorite younger son. Bundi entered relations with Akbar and the Mughal empire in 1569 and with the British in 1818. Bundi was most noted for its physical and cultural isolation and a distinctive school of Rajput miniature painting. In 1931 it had an area of 2,220 square miles, a population of 216,722, and an average annual revenue of 1,320,000 rupees. In 1948 Bundi joined the Rajasthan Union, which was merged into an expanded Rajasthan state of independent India.

[*See also* Princely States *and* Rajasthan.]

William G. Archer, *Indian Painting in Bundi and Kotah* (1959). James Tod, *Annals and Antiquities of Rajasthan Or, the Central and Western Rajpoot States of India,* vol. 2 (1832; reprint, 1971). BARBARA N. RAMUSACK

BUNGA MAS, gold and silver presented by "vassal" rulers to their suzerains in premodern Southeast Asia. In a political world in which states were regarded as inherently unequal, weaker rulers regularly presented valuable gifts as tokens of submission to more powerful rulers. In the Malay and Thai regions, such gifts often took the form of ornamental trees or flowers, fashioned of gold and silver, whence comes their Malay name, *bunga mas,* "golden flowers." The sultans of Kedah, Kelantan, and Terengganu presented the *bunga mas* every three years to the king of Siam. Examples of *bunga mas* are housed in the National Museum of Thailand.

DAVID K. WYATT

BUNNAG FAMILY, political and economic leaders in Siam from the early seventeenth century to the late nineteenth century.

The Bunnag family is descended from a pair of Persian-speaking brothers who arrived in Ayudhya from the Persian Gulf in 1602. The elder, Sheikh Ahmad, married a Siamese woman and entered the service of the Phrakhlang (a ministry of civil government), dealing with Muslim traders from the west. Soon he headed that ministry, and later he became prime minister. His son and grandson continued in that position until 1685, and throughout the century the family played an important role in court politics. Throughout the eighteenth century they retained control of units of the Phrakhlang and Kalahom (the military department and organ of provincial government) and included several *chaophraya* (ministers) in their ranks.

The nineteenth-century role of the family was secured by a fortuitous kin relationship: King Rama I's chief queen, mother of Rama II, was the sister of the mother of Chaophraya Mahasena (Bunnag, from whom comes the family name), who was the *kalahom* under Rama I. His son, Chaophraya Phrakhlang (Dit Bunnag), concurrently controlled both the Kalahom and the Phrakhlang through most of Rama III's reign and helped bring Prince Mongkut to the throne in 1851. Dit's son, Somdet Chaophraya Sisuriyawong (Chuang Bunnag), was the dominant figure in Siam from 1851 until his death in 1883, and various of his sons and nephews rose to ministerial rank in the early twentieth century.

Regularly at the center of power for three hundred years, the family's leading members seem consistently to have been politically astute, alert to the importance of the economic dimensions of power, and well informed of events and conditions in the world outside Siam. Throughout the nineteenth century they could be counted among the kingdom's few "progressives," favoring conciliatory relations with the West.

[*See also* Ayudhya; Bangkok; Kalahom; Sisuriyawong; Thiphakorawong; Chulalongkorn; Mongkut; *and* Phra Nang Klao.]

David K. Wyatt, "Family Politics in Nineteenth-Century Thailand," *Journal of Southeast Asian History* 9.2 (1968), and *Thailand: A Short History* (1984). John O'Kane, trans., *The Ship of Sulaiman* (1972).

DAVID K. WYATT

BUNRAKU, Japanese puppet drama, also known as *jōruri*. *Bunraku* originated, along with *kabuki*, in the late sixteenth century as casual entertainment performed in the dry bed of the Kamo River in Kyoto. *Bunraku* soon became associated with the mercantile city of Osaka. Puppets were used as early as the eleventh century to act out stories, but *bunraku* proper begins not long after the 1570s, when the *samisen* was imported from the Ryūkyū Islands. Although early *bunraku* was performed outdoors, it had moved into theaters by the seventeenth century. The components of a *bunraku* performance are the puppets, each of which is usually operated by three men; the chanter, who narrates and recites the characters' dialogue; and the *samisen* accompanist, whose music provides cues for the puppet operators. The puppets appear on a stage with sets

FIGURE 1. *Bunraku Puppets and Operators.*

within which the operators work. The two minor operators of a puppet (who are charged with manipulating its left hand and its feet) are dressed in black, with black hoods over their faces, but the principal operator wears traditional dress, usually blue or gray, and is not hooded. The chanter and accompanist sit on a raised dais to the right of the stage.

A puppet consists basically of a carved wooden head, a wig, hands, and a frame to carry the clothing. Often the head is equipped with devices to make the mouth, eyes, and eyebrows move, and wrists and fingers are also jointed. Since puppet heads are made to suggest types (for example, a sweet young woman, a good-hearted middle-aged man, an evil general, or a jealous concubine) rather than individuals, a given puppet character will often change heads between acts, to show a change in personality.

Before the 1680s, puppet plays were essentially stories presented by a reciter and mimed by puppets. *Bunraku* chanting was transformed into a polished art through the efforts of Uji Kaganojō (1635–1711), a chanter who incorporated into *bunraku* some of the language, themes, and musical symbols employed in the *nō* theater. The early plays succeeded mainly by depicting gory scenes or superhuman feats that could not be performed by human actors. Bunraku was revolutionized in the late seventeenth century by the playwright Chikamatsu Monzaemon (1653–1725), whose plays about ordinary men and women trapped by circumstance changed much of the *bunraku* repertoire. Throughout the eighteenth century, *bunraku* was the most popular entertainment for all classes of society, eclipsing *kabuki*. It entered into decline thereafter, however, and survives now with the help of government support.

[*See also* Chikamatsu Monzaemon; Kabuki; *and* Nō.]

Donald Keene, trans., *Major Plays of Chikamatsu* (1961). Donald Keene, *Bunraku: The Art of the Japanese Puppet Theatre* (1965; rev. ed., 1973) and *World within Walls* (1976).

AILEEN GATTEN

BURAKUMIN, also known as *buraku*, a class of people within Japanese society who are the object of both conscious and unconscious discrimination on the basis of social and religious beliefs that have their origins in early Japanese history. The *buraku* population of Japan is commonly estimated to be approximately two million people, but the exact size of the population is difficult to determine because of the lack of physical or racial attributes or exact criteria for determination or definition.

Those discriminated against have been given a variety of names throughout Japanese history, but the terms that have historically been most common are *eta* and *hinin*. The name *eta*, which literally means "great filth," was apparently given to members of early Japanese society who were in some manner forced into contact with objects considered to be unclean. Buddhist beliefs, reinforced by popular superstition, made contact with death or disease a source of such defilement. Most explanations for the origin of the *eta* class include discussion of contact with dead bodies, either human or animal. The earliest use of the term *eta* is in the *Chiribukuro*, a work written sometime during the late thirteenth century, although it is known that the class existed centuries before this time. The term and status became clearly designated during the seventeenth century. The term *hinin*, which means "nonperson," was applied during the Tokugawa period (1600–1868) to people who held occupations distinct from those of the *eta* but who were nonetheless subject to the same type of discrimination. *Eta* have been traditionally associated with leather manufacture, while *hinin*, whose status was inherited, were beggars or those engaged in dishonorable forms of entertainment.

The Meiji government legally designated the *eta* and *hinin* members of the commoner class on 28 August 1871, but distinctions and discrimination remained in the popular consciousness despite this legislation. A movement organized by the *burakumin* during the 1920s known as the Suiheisha, or Movement for the Leveling of Society, was likewise unable to erase popular prejudices. Following World War II the *buraku* organized the Buraku Kaihō Dōmei (Buraku Liberation League) to bring the problems of the *burakumin* to the attention of society once again, but subtle forms of discrimination remain to the present day. Although greater numbers of *buraku* have traditionally lived in the Kyoto-Osaka area, and in western Japan in general, there are few areas in Japan that are not in some way influenced by this unfortunate legacy of a distant past.

George De Vos and Hiroshi Wagatsuma, *Japan's Invisible Race: Caste in Culture and Personality* (1966). Nagahara Keiji, "The Medieval Origins of the *Eta-Hinin*," *Journal of Japanese Studies* 5 (Summer 1979): 385–403.

THOMAS R. SCHALOW

BUREAUCRACY IN CHINA. One of the most distinctive features of the Chinese imperial system of the period 206 BCE–1911 CE was its vast bureaucracy. The formation of a state system of government was an integral part of the establishment of a universal empire. It enabled the ruler to divide his realm into a hierarchy of administrative units at the central, intermediate, and regional levels of society. Staffing such an apparatus was an elite pool of educated men who managed the administration of government for the many emperors of Chinese history. This basic structure of Chinese bureaucracy endured with modifications for two millennia and has caused China to be characterized as a "permanently bureaucratic society" (Balazs, 1964). Significant institutional changes occurred during most of the major Chinese dynasties: the Han (206 BCE–220 CE), Tang (618–907), Song (960–1279), Ming (1368–1644), and Qing (1644–1911). Such changes affected the relationship of the emperor to his bureaucracy, the development of the organs of imperial government, and the operation of the personnel system during each period.

Imperial Power and the Bureaucracy. The Han dynasty set the precedent for the institution of bureaucracy that all subsequent dynasties would follow. The ruling system that developed at this time was organized as a strict political and social hierarchy. Han bureaucratic order had a pyramidal configuration, with the emperor at the top, followed by a central ruling triumvirate of general administration, military, and censorial agencies. This administrative structure was reproduced at intermediate and regional levels as well; during the Han there were thirteen circuits, one hundred commanderies, and twelve hundred counties.

The highest-ranking officials of the Han bureaucracy were the chief councillor, the grand marshal, and the chief censor. The chief councillor served as a type of prime minister and also presided over a number of central government agencies such as the nine chief ministers (attending to the administration of the imperial household) and the thirteen department heads (in charge of routine fiscal, judicial, and military administration). Important policy issues were decided by a consultative committee consisting of the emperor and the top echelon of his bureaucracy, thus providing a forum for the exchange of ideas.

During the years of the Former Han dynasty (206 BCE–8 CE) the office of chief councillor enjoyed great prestige. This status did not last long, however, owing to the ascendancy of the "inner court," the emperor's personal attendants and members of the imperial family. By the beginning of the Latter Han (25–220), the power of the office of chief councillor had been superseded by the above group and the position had fallen in status to little more than an honorary one. As a result, the Han bureaucratic apparatus was seriously weakened.

It was not until the Tang dynasty that a new balance between the contending constituencies of the "inner court" and the regular bureaucracy emerged. The traditional Han structure of government was modified in the Tang to include a general military staff, a more complex Censorate apparatus, and a general administration agency comprising the Department of State Affairs, the Secretariat, and the Chancellery (all of which had originally been part of the "inner court" network of the Former Han). Beneath this stratum of government were the intermediate- and regional-level agencies represented by 20 supervising circuits, 358 prefectures (replacing the commanderies of the Han), and 1,573 counties.

The Tang founder, Taizong (r. 626–649), had sanctioned the formation of a Council of State during his reign that was reminiscent of the Former Han's consultative committee in its function as the bureaucratic agency most responsible for deciding major policy issues. In addition, those officials who participated in the Council of State were able to check the power of early Tang emperors. An important institutional innovation of the Tang general administration was the formation of the Department of State Affairs, which, although taking the same name as its Han predecessor, served as a new apparatus within the bureaucracy. Here was the functional arm of Tang administration; government directives were carried out through a subordinate group of six ministries: Personnel, Revenue, Rites, War, Justice, and Public Works. The Six Ministries retained their functional importance in the Chinese bureaucratic system and were a part of all dynastic administrations to follow.

It was during the reign of the first Song emperor, Taizu (r. 960–976), that the imperial institution first experienced a dramatic change of style. The position of the emperor was now elevated above and isolated from his highest administrative officers. The transition from an age of aristocratic domination to an age of autocracy was well under way by the time of the Northern Song (960–1127). The clearest indication of the change in the imperial self-perception may be seen in the treatment of the chief bureaucratic officers at court. The relatively informal interaction between an emperor and his chief advisers in earlier periods had been replaced in the Song with an entirely different style of rule. The Song emperor no longer viewed himself as "first among equals"; he now emphasized his preeminent position in the bureaucratic hierarchy.

Despite the newfound autocratic style of the early Song emperors, the bureaucracy continued to function effectively. The bureaucratic institutions of the Northern Song followed much of the Tang's structure and function in fashioning its own framework of government. The chief bureaucratic organs of this period included the Bureau of Military Affairs; the Censorate, with a separate Bureau of Remonstrance; and the Council of State, which housed the Department of State Affairs and its Six Ministries, the Secretariat, and the Chancellery. Beneath this level of bureaucracy the administrative apparatus was considerably more fragmented as the early Song emperors sought to eliminate intermediate agencies and attempted to extend government control directly to the prefectures and counties. This trend was somewhat reduced by the Southern Song (1127–1279), when the system threatened to become too unwieldy. There was also a resurgence in the executive power of the officials of the Council of State when a number of weak emperors ascended the throne during the Southern Song.

The Ming dynasty, founded by Zhu Yuanzhang (posthumously, Ming Taizu; r. 1368–1398), represented the peak of autocratic government. However, the development of the quintessential autocratic state was not realized until twelve years after the Ming founding. During the first years of the dynasty a delicate balance had been maintained between the inner court and the bureaucracy by means of the Chief Councillors of the Left and Right. Beneath this layer were the top-echelon agencies inherited from the Mongol Yuan dynasty (1279–1368): the Chief Military Commission, Chief Surveillance Office, and Central Secretariat (which extended bureaucratic control to a network of 13 provinces, 159 prefectures, 240 subprefectures, and 1,140 counties).

The entire structure of Ming government would change in 1380. Taizu suspected one of his chief councillors of plotting a rebellion against the state. In an unprecedented measure, he not only executed the official, his relatives, and his associates in a bloody purge but also eliminated the Central Secretariat, the Chief Military Commission, and the post of chief councillor. The Ming central government after 1380 was intentionally fragmented so that only the emperor would be able to exercise bureaucratic power. However, Ming Taizu eventually formed a personal staff of eunuchs and other palace functionaries in the inner court to supervise his reorganized government.

The development of Ming autocracy may be traced to a number of factors. Certainly, the worldview of the Neo-Confucian state orthodoxy (synthesized by Zhu Xi in the twelfth century) would supply legitimacy for Taizu's autocracy. The emperor was considered the instrument of social justice and therefore was thought to be perfectly justified in strengthening his rule at the center. Taizu also was influenced by a group of fiscal reformers in Jinhua Prefecture (in modern Zhejiang Province) that the would-be emperor had encountered during his drive for territory at the end of the Yuan. These scholar-bureaucrats advocated a centralist approach in economic reform and political control that the Ming founder found very attractive. He capitalized on their frustrations with the Yuan court and eagerly recruited them between 1358 and 1359 to serve as the backbone of his new bureaucracy.

The Qing dynasty, led by the conquering Manchus, continued to use the Ming's basic structure of bureaucracy and much of its autocratic style. As alien rulers, however, they also brought their own traditions to bear on the nature of their government institutions. They ruled China by means of a dyarchy, an administrative system that entailed a dual staffing of all offices, using Chinese officials for expertise and Manchu officials for political reliability.

Personnel Recruitment and the Development of a Chinese Civil Service. The development of the central government's ruling apparatus necessitated the creation of a pool of "managers" to administer the realm in the name of the emperor. From the Han dynasty to the beginning of Song times, the criteria for choosing such government officials were at least in theory based on "merit" rather than one's status by birth. However, "merit" seemed to be determined and dominated by the landed aristocracy. Therefore, the early imperial bureaucracy (Han–mid-Tang) was quite aristocratic in character. From the time of Han Wudi (r. 141–87 BCE), the dominant system of bureaucratic recruitment was based on a recommendation system. Yet recommendation alone did not automatically guarantee one an official position; all candidates for office were also required to submit to a written or oral examination to test their worthiness for office.

The Han also ranked all officials in an elaborate grading system. Salaries were figured in piculs of grain (equivalent to 133 pounds) granted annually.

Each official was also evaluated every third year by his superiors to determine his fitness to continue in the bureaucratic service. In addition, there was a prohibition against an official's serving in his home region, a "rule of avoidance" that attempted to limit the opportunity for corruption.

The Sui dynasty (581–618) first established the precedent for a universal civil service recruitment system based on examination success. The Confucian canon (the texts and commentaries associated with the philosopher Kongzi, or Confucius) became the educational foundation for these examinations. The civil service examination system was further perfected during the Tang dynasty, when the old landed aristocracy began to be replaced by a bureaucracy of merit, demonstrated by success in the examination system.

The process of regularizing the examination system was completed by the Song dynasty. Thereafter, scholar-bureaucrats were chosen for state service in a series of open, competitive written examinations demonstrating a mastery of the Confucian canon, history, and literary skills. By 1145 the scope of the examinations had been narrowed to account for current trends in the state orthodoxy. In addition, such examinations were now offered on a triennial schedule. The number of prospective candidates also increased at this time owing to the great advancement of printing techniques and the availability of materials for education, thus producing a widening of the social base of the examination system.

The Ming dynasty introduced a standard three-tiered examination system as part of its bureaucrat recruitment process. The first level of examination was held within the county. Successful candidates were awarded the "flowering talent" *(xiucai)* degree and thus qualified for "gentry" status, whereby they were permitted to wear certain types of official insignia and were exempted from the labor service obligations required of all adult males. However, candidates were subject to reexamination every three years to maintain their status. A second level of examination was then held at the provincial capital every three years. These examinations were much more competitive and thus had fewer successful candidates. However, those who did distinguish themselves received the "recommended man" *(zhuren)* degree and were accredited as permanent members of officialdom. The third level of the examination process was held at the imperial capital in Beijing, also on a triennial schedule. Few candidates ever reached this stage of competition. The ones who were successful at this level were part of the educated elite and received the "presented scholar" *(jinshi)* degree. The final test of talent was conducted in the imperial palace before the emperor and was used to rank the new "presented scholars" in order of excellence for purposes of appointment.

The Ming examination system described above was finally regularized after 1384, sixteen years after the Ming founding. This was largely the result of Ming Taizu's distrust of officialdom. A quota system regulating the number of degrees awarded from each province was introduced in order to prevent any one region from dominating the configuration of Ming bureaucracy.

The Qing dynasty continued to follow the Ming model of examination system as the basis of its own personnel recruitment system. However, by the early nineteenth century, the system had become rigid and prone to corruption. It was finally discontinued in 1905.

[*See also* Censorate.]

Étienne Balazs, *Chinese Civilization and Bureaucracy: Variations on a Theme,* edited by Arthur Wright and translated by H. M. Wright (1964). Hans Bielenstein, *The Bureaucracy of Han Times* (1980). Ch'u Tung-tsu, *Local Government in China under the Ch'ing* (1969). John W. Dardess, *Confucianism and Autocracy: Professional Elites in the Founding of the Ming Dynasty* (1983). Charles O. Hucker, *The Traditional Chinese State in Ming Times* (1978). Edward A. Kracke, Jr., *Civil Service in Early Sung China, 960–1067* (1953). John D. Langlois, Jr., "Political Thought in Chin-hua under Mongol Rule," in *China under Mongol Rule,* edited by John D. Langlois, Jr. (1981), pp. 107–133. Brian McKnight, *Village and Bureaucracy in Southern Sung China* (1971).

Anita M. Andrew

BURGHERS, a small Sri Lankan community (1983 population about 40,000) descended from Dutch and Portuguese colonizers of the sixteenth to eighteenth century. The community is divided into Dutch and Portuguese Burghers, with little intermingling. Most Burghers live in towns. Dutch Burghers traditionally have been professionals or middle-class white-collar workers. Since 1950 many have migrated to Australia and Britain. Portuguese Burghers, traditionally craftsmen of a lower economic station, are concentrated on the East Coast of Sri Lanka. Burghers preserve residual elements of their ancestral culture, but are now primarily English-speaking. They are largely Christian (Dutch Protestants, Portuguese Catholics). Burghers have made a significant contribution to the cultural life of Sri Lanka; considerable recent assimilation has taken place with larger Sri Lankan ethnic groups.

[*See also* Portuguese: Portuguese in Sri Lanka; Dutch East India Company; *and* Sri Lanka.]

Journals of the Dutch Burgher Union of Sri Lanka (1925–1950). RALPH BUULTJENS

BURGOS, JOSE (1837–1872), friar who led the Philippine secular clergy in their petition that the Spanish friars allow them to administer the parishes. When he became leader of the movement, organized by Friar Pedro Pelaez (died 1863) and supported by university-educated priests who wanted to prove themselves the equals of the friars, Burgos subtly gave it a nationalist, secular orientation. By attacking Spanish racism, he aroused both the hostility of the friars and the suspicion of the governor. He was accused of organizing the Cavite Mutiny (1872) and executed with fathers Mariano Gomez and Jacinto Zamora. Burgos's ideas on national dignity would have a strong impact on the nationalist thinking of Jose Rizal in the next generation.

[*See also* Friars; Cavite Mutiny; and Rizal, Jose Mercado.]

John N. Schumacher, *Father Jose Burgos, Priest and Nationalist* (1972) and *The Revolutionary Clergy* (1981).

JOHN N. SCHUMACHER, S.J.

BURHANUDDIN HARAHAP (b. 1917), Indonesian politician. Trained as a lawyer, Burhanuddin represented the Masjumi, the political party uniting several Islamic organizations, in successive national parliaments from 1946. From August 1955 to March 1956 he headed a coalition of Islamic and socialist parties hostile to the Partai Nasional Indonesia (PNI). This government oversaw the general elections of September 1955 and dissolved the Netherlands-Indonesian Union in February 1956. In February 1958, alarmed by the growing power of Sukarno, the Partai Nasional Indonesia, and the Partai Komunis Indonesia (PKI), Burhanuddin joined the PRRI (Pemerintah Revolusioner Republik Indonesia, "Revolutionary Government of the Indonesian Republic") rebellion in Sumatra, for which he was jailed from 1962 to 1965.

[*See also* Masjumi; Partai Nasional Indonesia; Partai Komunis Indonesia; *and* Pemerintah Revolusioner Republik Indonesia/Perdjuangan Semesta.]

Herbert Feith, *The Decline of Constitutional Democracy in Indonesia* (1962). ROBERT B. CRIBB

BURMA. About the size of Texas, Burma occupies approximately 261,552 square miles, longer than it is wide. With its major mountain chains, the Arakan, the Pegu, and the Shan Hills, lying north to south, and its major rivers, the Irrawaddy and Salween, running parallel to these, Burma is divided into long, large plains, areas easily accessible in north–south movement but difficult when moving east–west. Burma's political and cultural history have been significantly determined by this geographical configuration.

The middle plain, the wide Irrawaddy River valley, has been Burma's political and cultural center: whatever group controlled that valley controlled Burma. Prior to drainage of the Burma delta in the twentieth century, the Irrawaddy Valley was Burma's most fertile area. Even though a large segment of it was extremely dry, receiving not much more than forty-five inches of rain a year, sophisticated irrigation works attracted much-needed labor to what would otherwise have been an arid environment. North and south of this dry belt, the conditions were not as harsh, and extensive irrigation was a luxury rather than a necessity.

Several groups dominated this nucleus. First, presumably, were the Pyu, whose civilization occupied and most likely controlled the country from the first millennium BCE until the ninth century CE. They were followed by the Burmans, who intermittently rose and declined in power and were challenged by two other major ethnic groups, the Mon and Shan. These three groups often changed positions throughout the precolonial period (until 1886), but it was the Burmans who dominated the country most often and the longest. Associated with these major ethnopolitical groups were the Chin, Kachin, and Karen, whose political role varied according to the times and to the structural relationships prevalent in the culture. The Siamese and Arakanese states, on either side of Burma, also periodically asserted their political power. [*See also* Pyu; Mon; Shan; Chin; Kachin; Karen; Thailand; *and* Arakan.]

Although very little archaeological work has been done in Burma, there is evidence of Paleolithic and early Neolithic (or Hoabinhian) cultures dating back to about 11,000 BCE; these were followed, around 200 BCE, by what may be termed an urbanized period of early city-states. This period sowed the seeds for the formation of a true state—what historians have labeled the "classical Burmese state"—which emerged in the city of Pagan in the mid-ninth century CE. [*See also* Pagan.] The traditions that Pagan established became the standard for Burmese society,

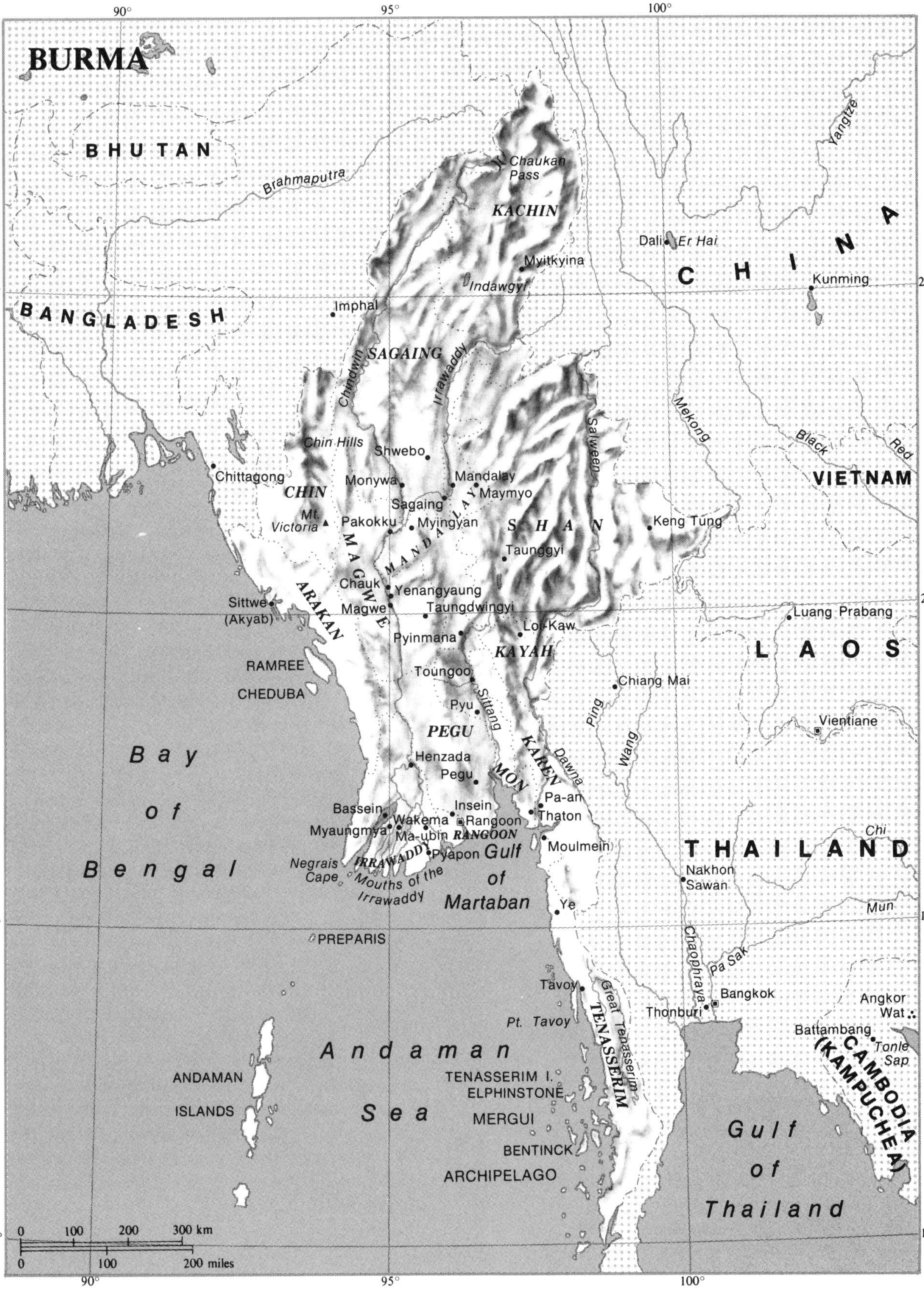
BURMA
BHUTAN
Brahmaputra
Chaukan Pass
KACHIN
Dali
Er Hai
CHINA
Myitkyina
Kunming
Indawgyi
Yangtze
BANGLADESH
Imphal
SAGAING
Chindwin
Irrawaddy
Mekong
Salween
Chin Hills
Shwebo
Black
Red
Chittagong
Monywa
Mandalay
VIETNAM
CHIN
Sagaing
Maymyo
Mt. Victoria
Pakokku
Myingyan
MANDALAY
SHAN
Keng Tung
MAGWE
Taunggyi
Chauk
Yenangyaung
ARAKAN
Sittwe (Akyab)
Magwe
Taungdwingyi
Luang Prabang
Loi-Kaw
Pyinmana
KAYAH
LAOS
RAMREE
Toungoo
Chiang Mai
CHEDUBA
Pyu
Sittang
Ping
Vientiane
PEGU
KAREN
Dawna
Wang
Bay of Bengal
Henzada
Pegu
MON
Bassein
Insein
Pa-an
Wakema
Rangoon
Thaton
Myaungmya
Ma-ubin
RANGOON
Moulmein
Chi
THAILAND
IRRAWADDY
Pyapon
Gulf of Martaban
Negrais Cape
Mouths of the Irrawaddy
Nakhon Sawan
Ye
Mun
PREPARIS
Chaophraya
Pa Sak
Tavoy
Great Tenasserim
Bangkok
Thonburi
Angkor Wat
Pt. Tavoy
TENASSERIM
Battambang
Tonle Sap
CAMBODIA (KAMPUCHEA)
Andaman Sea
ANDAMAN ISLANDS
TENASSERIM I.
ELPHINSTONE
MERGUI
BENTINCK
ARCHIPELAGO
Gulf of Thailand
0 100 200 300 km
0 100 200 miles
90°
95°
100°
25°
20°
15°
10°

1:10,000,000

and subsequent dynasties tried, particularly when their legitimacy was questionable, to link themselves with that earlier model. The end of the Pagan kingdom ushered in a period of decentralization, with different centers of power competing for paramountcy. Although this is known as the period of Shan domination, the significance of the Shan was political and historical, not ethnic. Nevertheless, by the second half of the fourteenth century, another dynasty, centered at Ava, had been established, ruled by people whose names were Shan. [*See also* Ava.]

Ava's domination, however, was short lived, for a competing power had emerged farther south at Toungoo, a provincial capital of earlier days. Toungoo's energetic leaders established their own dynasty, which recaptured the Irrawaddy River valley and opened their link to the outside world, the commercial ports of Lower Burma. By the first half of the seventeenth century, they had moved their capital back to agrarian and dry central Burma, the ancestral home of the Burmans. [*See also* Toungoo Dynasties *and* Pegu.] Ava was revived as a capital, and it remained one until 1752, when it was sacked by the Mon of Lower Burma, who had strengthened their power when the Toungoo leaders were resettling at Ava. The Mon's attempt to establish political dominance was also short-lived, for only a few months later they were expelled from Ava, and soon thereafter a new Burman dynasty, known as the Konbaung, was formed by the energetic monarch Alaunghpaya, who extended his hegemony over what was once the Pagan kingdom. [*See also* Konbaung Dynasty *and* Alaunghpaya.]

Alaunghpaya's Konbaung dynasty continued to rule the country until it collided with Britain, which, after fighting the Burmese in three different wars in 1824, 1852, and 1885, annexed Burma. [*See also* Anglo-Burmese Wars.] Burma was under Western colonial rule until the Japanese drove out the British in 1942. When they returned to Burma after the Second World War, the British faced a vastly different political situation. Armed, organized, more experienced both militarily and politically, and guided by strong and effective leaders, the Burmese (all those native to Burma, as opposed to the Burmans, the dominant ethnic group) now demanded independence. For a variety of complex reasons—ranging from the effects of World War II on both Southeast Asia and Europe to a change of government in Britain—these demands became a reality, and Burma was granted independence in 1948.

Since its independence Burma has experimented with parliamentary democracy, socialism, and a federalism of sorts. In 1962, however, with the partitioning of Burma into ethnopolitical spheres a real threat, General Ne Win reestablished the political paramountcy of what has always been the ruling institution in Burma: the military. [*See also* Ne Win *and* Burma, Socialist Republic of the Union of.] Socialism was kept but not parliamentary democracy—which in Burma, some felt, was rather more a cause of than a cure for anarchy. Based upon the Eastern European model of a tripod system comprising government, military, and party, Burma became a one-party socialist state, practicing what it calls "the Burmese way to socialism." Recently, Ne Win stepped down as official leader of the country, leaving power in the hands of the Burma Socialist Program Party (BSPP) and the military. [*See also* Burma Socialist Program Party.] Although in many ways Burma is a twentieth-century socialist state, certain deeply rooted institutions, such as Theravada Buddhism and the Buddhist monastic order, (*sangha*), remain important.

John F. Cady, *The United States and Burma* (1976). D. G. E. Hall, *Burma* (1960). G. E. Harvey, *A History of Burma from the Earliest Times* (1925; reprint, 1967). David I. Steinberg, *Burma: A Socialist Nation of Southeast Asia* (1982). MICHAEL AUNG-THWIN

BURMA, SOCIALIST REPUBLIC OF THE UNION OF, official name of the state of Burma following the inauguration of a new constitution on 2 March 1974. This constitution ended the twelve-year rule of the Revolutionary Council, formed by the army after the 2 March 1962 coup. The constitution formally established Burma as a one-party unitary socialist state under the control of the army-dominated Burma Socialist Program Party. The state is divided into seven subordinate states, each taking the name of an ethnic minority on the borders, and seven divisions within central Burma. Sovereignty formally lies with the people and is exercised by a unicameral legislature, the Pyithu Hluttaw (People's Assembly), elected every four years.

[*See also* Burma *and* Burma Socialist Program Party.]

Josef Silverstein, *Burma: Military Rule and the Politics of Stagnation* (1977). David I. Steinberg, *Burma's Road toward Development* (1981). ROBERT H. TAYLOR

BURMA, UNION OF, official name of independent Burma from 4 January 1948 until 2 March 1974. The constitution of the union provided for a two-house legislature, one representing all the people on an equal basis and one giving formal representation to ethnic minorities. The unique place of the minorities was further recognized through the provision of five subordinate states named after some of the major ethnic groups. The system was effectively unitary, however, as the central government maintained ultimate control over the budgets of the states. The union's constitution was superseded in 1962 by the military-led Revolutionary Council government.

[*See also* Burma.]

Maung Maung, *Burma's Constitution* (1961).

ROBERT H. TAYLOR

BURMA DEFENSE ARMY (BDA), originally named the Burma Independence Army (BIA); later known as the Burma National Army (BNA), the Burma People's Army, and the Patriotic Burmese Forces (PBF). The BIA was the forerunner of the armed forces of independent Burma. Formed under the auspices of the Japanese military, the BIA grew out of a nucleus of thirty young Burmese nationalists led by Thakin Aung San, who went to Hainan Island secretly in 1940 for military training. These "thirty comrades" then went to Bangkok with the Japanese army to prepare for its assault on British Burma in early 1942 and grew to a force of over 25,000 by the middle of 1942. Because of its undisciplined nature and competition with the Japanese for authority in Burma, the BIA was reduced in size by the Japanese and re-formed as the BDA.

When Japan granted Burma formal independence in 1943, the BDA was enlarged and became the BNA. During this period of consolidation and regularization, a military academy was opened and many officers were trained in Japanese military techniques. Becoming disillusioned with the nature of the Japanese fascist government, some officers of the BNA met in August 1944 with communist and noncommunist civilian politicians and formed the Anti-Fascist Organization, whose goals were to drive the Japanese out of Burma and to establish an independent state. On 27 March 1945 the BNA, under the leadership of Aung San, began a campaign against the Japanese in cooperation with Allied forces; in previous months, units in Arakan and Upper Burma had already attacked the Japanese. Following the defeat of Japan in August 1945 negotiations were concluded for the disbandment of the then-named PBF and for the incorporation of approximately 5,000 of its 15,000 men into the British Burma Army. Many of the remainder joined the paramilitary wing of the nationalist movement, the People's Volunteer Organization.

[*See also* Burma; Thirty Comrades; Aung San; *and* Anti-Fascist People's Freedom League.]

ROBERT H. TAYLOR

BURMA ROAD, the land line of communications between Burma and China in World War II. In 1937 and 1938, one hundred thousand Chinese laborers built an all-weather road from Kunming in Yunnan Province to Lashio in northern Burma. Supplies were docked in Rangoon and shipped up the Irrawaddy River to Lashio and thence to China, including US lend-lease aid from May 1941. The Japanese invasion of Burma in December 1941 closed the road. Until January 1945 the Chinese war effort and the US 14th Air Force in China were supplied entirely by the famous air route from bases in Assam "over the hump."

The road was a contentious issue in Allied strategy for the China-Burma-India theater. One view, supported by President Roosevelt and generals Arnold and Chennault, held that the road could not be reopened in time to move any quantity of supplies. An alternate view, supported by generals Marshall and Stilwell and ultimately accommodated to some extent, argued that the road had to be reopened with a land campaign in Burma. In January 1945 a road was opened from Ledo in Assam to Myitkina in northern Burma but was used only for local supply and one-way delivery of vehicles to China.

[*See also* World War II in China *and* Stilwell, Joseph W.]

William J. Koenig, *Over the Hump: Airlift to China* (1972). Charles F. Romanus and Riley Sunderland, *The United States Army in World War II: China-Burma-India Theater* (1952–1958).

WILLIAM J. KOENIG

BURMA SOCIALIST PROGRAM PARTY (BSPP), known in Burmese as the Myanma Hsoshelit Lanzin Pati, has been the only legal political party in Burma since 1964. It was formed on 4 July 1962 by the military-led Revolutionary Council, which was established by General Ne Win and other officers following the 2 March 1962 coup d'état.

The BSPP has slowly developed into a mass-based cadre-style party, similar to the ruling parties of Eastern Europe and the Soviet Union. Initially, party membership was restricted, and in 1966 there were only 20 full members and 185,000 candidate members. In 1971 the party was declared a mass party, and by 1981 membership was reported to stand at

1,500,902 full-time members. While the majority of members are civilians, the leadership and 9.6 percent of the membership are from the armed forces. A large proportion of civilian leaders are retired army officers, and former general Ne Win remains as chairman.

As "the party that guides the state," the BSPP provides the candidates who are elected every four years to the national legislature (Pyithu Hluttaw) and to the state or division, the township, and the village or ward People's Councils, which are the decision-making and administrative bodies of Burma. Other organizations within the party that function as instruments of mass mobilization are the Peasants' Asiayon, Workers' Asiayon, Veterans' Asiayon, Women's Asiayon, and the Lanzin Youth and other youth bodies. These encourage and guide public participation in developmental and political projects.

The ideology of the BSPP is an amalgam of Burmese Buddhist philosophy and Marxism. Critical of both capitalism and communism for their alleged neglect of human spiritual needs but recognizing the materialist basis of many aspects of social, economic, and political change, the party emphasizes the impermanence of matter and the ability of the people to reshape historical and material forces. The BSPP's political program not only stresses the importance of the state in controlling and guiding the national economy and the duties and responsibilities of the citizenry to support the state but also notes the rights of individuals to pursue religious and cultural practices of local traditions. In the minds of the founders of the BSPP, the relative stability that has marked Burma's political life since 1962 is due largely to their success in making the party the national political organization of Burma.

[*See also* Burma; Ne Win; *and* Burma, Socialist Republic of the Union of.]

Burma Socialist Programme Party, *The System of Correlation of Man and His Environment* (1963). Josef Silverstein, *Burma: Military Rule and the Politics of Stagnation* (1977). David I. Steinberg, *Burma's Road toward Development* (1981).

ROBERT H. TAYLOR

BURMA WORKERS AND PEASANTS PARTY, sometimes labeled the legal communist party, was formed in December 1950 by left-wing members of the Socialist Party within the Anti-Fascist People's Freedom League. The BWPP candidates who stood in the 1951 general election attacked the government's acceptance of US aid and its support for the initial activities of the United Nations in the Korean War. They achieved little success then, but in 1956 the BWPP was the major party of the National United Front coalition and gained 45 seats out of 248 in the legislature. When the army took over the government in a coup on 2 March 1962, the BWPP was the only party willing to cooperate with the military's plans, and many of its leaders became key government planning advisers.

[*See also* Burma; Anti-Fascist People's Freedom League; *and* Burma Socialist Program Party.]

Hugh Tinker, *The Union of Burma* (1967).

ROBERT H. TAYLOR

BURNEY, HENRY (1792–1845), British East India Company envoy to the court of Siam and British resident at the court of Ava (Burma). Born in India, Burney joined the company's army and served with the British forces in Java and then at Penang, where he was military secretary to the island's governor. Becoming fluent in Malay and then Thai, he undertook a series of diplomatic missions for the company, first to the Malay Peninsula and then to Bangkok (1825–1826), where he concluded the first Anglo-Siamese Treaty. As the first resident at Ava, he learned Burmese and for seven years worked to normalize relations with King Bagyidaw's court before withdrawing the residency in 1837. He was an important early amateur scholar, especially in Burmese subjects.

[*See also* Ava; Bagyidaw; Penang; *and* Phra Nang Klao.]

W. S. Desai, *The History of the British Residency in Burma, 1826–1840* (1939; reprint, 1972). Daniel George Edward Hall, *Henry Burney: A Political Biography* (1974).

DAVID K. WYATT

BURNING OF THE BOOKS, an infamous episode in 213 BCE in which the Chinese emperor Qin Shihuangdi ordered collected and burned all the records of the non-Qin states, copies of the *Shi* and *Shu* (Confucian classics of poetry and history), as well as the works of the philosophers. Exempted were copies of these texts held by official scholars and works on medicine and other practical subjects. As a byword in heinousness, this decree is often paired with an event of the following year, commonly known as the Burying of the Confucian Scholars, when more than 460 were buried alive. In the earliest record of these events, Sima Qian's *Shiji,* however, no connection is implied between them.

The extent of the destruction is not detailed in the *Shiji.* Its seeming thoroughness, however, has long been doubted: aside from the fact that official copies were preserved, the edict's effectiveness might have been limited by the emperor's death in 210 and the fall of Qin in 206. Another loss, however, was related: the concentration of permitted copies in official hands meant further destruction when the capital was burned upon the fall of Qin. Although neither unprecedented nor the last of its kind, the Burning of the Books achieved a unique reputation because the pre-Qin centuries produced the philosophical writings and texts that were later valued as central to Chinese culture, and because of the contrast with succeeding dynasties, which generally accepted responsibility for maintaining literary records.

[*See also* Qin Dynasty *and* Qin Shihuangdi.]

Derk Bodde, *China's First Unifier: A Study of the Ch'in Dynasty as Seen in the Life of Li Ssu (280?–208 B.C.)* (1938). John K. Shryock, *The Origin and Development of the State Cult of Confucius* (1932). Ssu-ma Ch'ien (Sima Qian), *Records of the Historian,* translated by Yang Hsien-yi and Gladys Yang (1974). SHAN CHOU

BUSHIDŌ. The Japanese term *bushidō* means "way of the warrior" and refers to a code that evolved in the seventeenth and eighteenth centuries to govern the behavior of the *bushi,* or samurai (warrior), class of Japan. The samurai emerged in the provinces of Japan in the tenth century. From the late twelfth century until the beginning of the modern period in the late nineteenth century, they were the ruling aristocracy of the country.

The history of the premodern samurai as a ruling elite can be divided into two stages: the medieval age, from 1185 to 1600, during which there was frequent civil warfare in Japan, and the early modern age, from 1600 to 1867, when the country, governed by the Tokugawa shogunate, was almost uninterruptedly at peace. During the medieval age the samurai were a true military class. They were organized into bands *(bushidan)* under feudal lords and functioned as professional soldiers. Their behavior was ruled by custom and they felt little need to speculate about or codify standards of conduct for their lives. The closest the medieval samurai came to a "code" or "way" was the vague concept of the "way of men" *(otoko no michi).*

During the Tokugawa period the samurai became a historical anomaly, inasmuch as fighting ceased and most samurai (with dependents they constituted about 7 or 8 percent of Japan's population) became idle stipendiaries. It was then that the samurai began to reflect on the principles of their class. No fixed definition of these principles as a "way of the warrior" was established, however. What we know as *bushidō* is an amalgam of ideas from many sources, two of which are generally regarded as particularly important.

The first of these is Confucianism, especially as found in the thought of Yamaga Sokō (1622–1685), who is often regarded as the formulator of *bushidō.* Yamaga regarded loyalty, in terms of absolute devotion to duty *(gi)* in the service of one's lord (and, at a higher level, of the emperor), as the basic ethic of the samurai. Yamaga further believed that the samurai should serve as a model to members of other classes of society by living a life of self-discipline and military preparedness and by developing his intellectual faculties.

The second major source of our knowledge of *bushidō* derives from the *Hagakure (In the Shadow of Leaves),* a collection of the sayings of Yamamoto Tsunetomo, a retainer of the domain of Saga, dating from 1716. Yamamoto called upon the samurai to be prepared at all times for death, indeed to think only of death. He was to regard victory and defeat as irrelevant. The way of the samurai was in resolution of action, in plunging forward recklessly with utter disregard for personal safety and self-interest.

In the Confucianism of Yamaga Sokō and the stern precepts of *Hagakure* the Japanese of the Tokugawa period found articulation of a code that was to remain an important guide to behavior even after formal dissolution of the samurai class between 1873 and 1876.

[*See also* Samurai; Seppuku; *and* Tokugawa Period.]

"Yamaga Sokō and the Origins of *Bushidō,*" in *Sources of Japanese Tradition,* edited by Ryusaku Tsunoda et al. (1958). Yamamoto Tsunetomo, *Hagakure,* translated by William Scott Wilson (1981). PAUL VARLEY

BUYID DYNASTY. The Buyid (also known as Buwaihid) dynasty was the most important political force in western Iran and Iraq from about 945 to 1055. In addition to their political accomplishments, the Buyids were responsible for a number of social, religious, and cultural innovations that left a lasting impression on the territories under their control.

The dynasty was the creation of three brothers

named Ali, Hasan, and Ahmad, sons of the actual eponym of the dynasty, a common fisherman (or woodcutter) named Buyeh or Buwaih. They left their home province of Dailam, a mountainous region near the southwestern shores of the Caspian, to pursue careers as military adventurers. After serving briefly in the forces of the Samanids they joined the forces of Mardavij ibn Ziyar, who had seized control of the Caspian provinces and central Iran. During the period of confusion immediately preceding and following the assassination of Mardavij in 935, Ali was able to take possession of the province of Fars; Hasan established himself in the Jibal (the mountains of west-central Iran); and Ahmad took provinces to the southeast (Kerman) and southwest (Khuzistan). The youngest brother, Ahmad, involved himself in the political intrigues surrounding the Abbasid court in Iraq and was "invited" to occupy Baghdad in 945. The Buyid dynasty thus came to include three essentially autonomous branches ruling three distinct geographical areas. Relations between the various branches were not always harmonious, but it was generally recognized that the eldest member of the family had the greatest authority. The closest approach to true unity under this cumbersome dynastic system was that imposed by the most vigorous and important of the Buyid commanders, Adud al-Daula Fana Khusrau, who governed Iraq, Fars, and Kerman from 978 to 983.

The Buyid state was from beginning to end a military enterprise held together and expanded by ties of blood kinship, tribal and ethnic solidarity, mercenary interests, and various religious and social loyalties. Aside from the family itself, one solid base of power for the dynasty consisted of the tribesmen from Dailam enrolled in the Buyid army. These Dailamites were famous as fierce fighters and were probably the best infantrymen of their time. Many had entered the service of the Abbasid caliphs; it is likely that Dailamites facilitated or encouraged the Buyid takeover of Iraq. The Buyid forces also came to include many Turkish "slave troops," primarily cavalrymen, and mercenaries of various ethnic backgrounds. The Buyid ruler was, in a real sense, simply the commander in chief of these military forces. To retain the loyalty of the military, the Buyids relied on two main devices: payment in cash to the lower ranks of troops and the award of *iqta* (i.e., fiscal control of landed estates) to the more important officers and officials of the government.

As a dynasty that owed its existence to simple military force, the Buyids were at pains to find ways to legitimize their rule in the eyes of their civilian subjects. This was done in part by extensive and judicious use of a traditional persianized bureaucracy, but it also required considerable innovation in political thinking, especially since the Abbasid caliph, nominal head of the Sunni Muslim world, was under Buyid domination. On one level, the Buyids appealed to anti-Arab and non-Islamic sentiments by posing as the true heirs of Sasanid Iran. Thus, some of the early Buyids minted coins bearing inscriptions in Pahlavi rather than Arabic; they depicted the ruler dressed as an Iranian king and using as his title *shahanshah* ("king of kings"). Adud al-Daula had a genealogy invented and imposed on the official historiography that portrayed the Buyids as actual descendants of the Sasanid shah Bahram Gur. The Buyids also tended to protect the remaining Zoroastrian population against Muslim harassment and appointed Zoroastrians to high office. Yet at the same time, they also attempted to legitimize their position in Islamic terms. They continued to support the existence of the Abbasid caliphate but openly promoted the concept that the caliphs had delegated legitimate political authority to the Buyid commanders. This process was symbolized by the caliph's bestowal of Arabo-Muslim honorific titles, such as Mu'izz al-Daula, "strengthener of the empire," on the Buyids, who then used them as regnal titles.

The Buyid effort to appeal to both Iranian and Islamic constituencies may explain another important aspect of their policy: the elevation of Imami, or Twelver, Shi'ism to the stature of an official state religion, or at least as an equal to the four Sunni schools of Islam. This religious policy can be explained in part by the fact that the Dailamite homeland of the Buyids had resisted Muslim colonization and had only recently begun to be converted by (mostly Zaidi) Shi'ite missionaries. Insofar as the Buyids had been exposed to Islam, it was probably in its Shi'ite manifestation. The policy was also politically expedient, however, in that it attracted the support of the Shi'ite population of Baghdad and Iraq and served to blunt the appeal of the Buyids' most immediate rivals—the Fatimids of Egypt, the Hamdanids of Syria, and the Qarmatis of Iraq—all of whom were Shi'ites. In any case, the Buyids were responsible for introducing the organization of descendants of the Prophet under the leadership of a chief *(naqib),* and they also promoted the feast of Ghadir Khumm, the Ashura commemoration of the martyrdom of Imam Husain, the rebuilding of Shi'ite shrines, the use of a Shi'ite call to prayer, public cursing of Mu'awiya, and the patronage of

Twelver religious scholars. They did not, however, contemplate replacing the Abbasids with an Alid caliphate. This has generally been explained as cynical political calculation on the part of the Buyids, but it may also have been based on the belief that the Abbasids, as relatives of the prophet Muhammad, were actually a Shi'ite dynasty, an idea that figured prominently in early Abbasid propaganda and that the Buyids clearly revived in their official historiography.

Culturally, the Buyid period was one of the most brilliant in Islamic history. The Buyids and their ministers, such as the great Sahib ibn al-Abbad, were famous patrons of the arts. They maintained libraries at Rayy, Shiraz, and Isfahan and sponsored works dealing with history, geography, poetry, calligraphy, medicine, astronomy, mathematics, and philosophy. Prominent cultural personalities in Buyid realms included, to mention only a few, the philosopher Ibn Sina (Avicenna), the poet Mutanabbi, the bibliographer Ibn al-Nadim, the historians Hilal al-Sabi and Miskawaih, and the anthologist Abu al-Faraj al-Isfahani.

The great failure of the Buyids was their inability to become anything more than a purely provincial dynasty. They were hemmed in on all sides by powerful adversaries—the Byzantines to the north, the Fatimids to the west, the Samanids and Ghaznavids to the east—and they were unable to break through on any front. As a consequence, they could not revive the trade that had been diverted from the Persian Gulf to Fatimid Egypt, and the progressive impoverishment of Iraq and western Iran continued. Thus weakened, the Buyids could not maintain the loyalty of their mercenary forces, control urban rioting, or prevent the disputes between the different branches of the family that plagued the dynasty during its final years. In 1029, the Ghaznavids took control of the Jibal from the Buyids, and by 1055 the staunchly Sunni Seljuk Turks had seized almost all their remaining territory, including Baghdad. The last branch of the Buyid dynasty, centered in the city of Fars, was destroyed by the Shabankara Kurds in 1062.

[*See also* Abbasid Dynasty *and the map accompanying* Samanid Dynasty.]

M. Kabir, *The Buwayhid Dynasty of Baghdad* (1964). D. S. Margoliouth and H. Amedroz, *The Eclipse of the Abbasid Caliphate* (1919–1921). Roy Mottahedeh, *Loyalty and Leadership in an Early Islamic Society* (1980).

E. L. DANIEL

C

CABINET MISSION. Following the nationwide elections of 1945–1946 in India, in which the Indian National Congress emerged as victor in the general constituencies and the Muslim League carried the majority of Muslim constituencies, the British government decided that the moment was ripe for significant constitutional progress. The secretary of state for India, Lord Pethick-Lawrence, with Stafford Cripps and A. V. Alexander, first lord of the admiralty, arrived in India on 23 March 1946. Initially they hoped that Indian political leaders would provide a plan, but the deadlock between the Congress and the Muslim League meant that the mission had to initiate proposals. Their plan, published 16 May 1946, was largely the work of Cripps. It envisaged an interim government, composed of Congress and league members, a constituent assembly, and a "three tier" form of government after independence. Power was to be distributed among the existing provinces, three regions or zones (comprised of northeast India, the northwest, and the rest of the subcontinent), and a central government that would be a loose confederation of all India. The plan was accepted and rejected with every kind of reservation by both the Congress and the Muslim League. The mission left India on 29 June with the two main parties locked in continuing conflict.

[*See also* Cripps Mission.]

Nicholas Mansergh, ed., *The Transfer of Power,* vol. 7, *The Cabinet Mission* (1977). R. J. Moore, *Escape from Empire: The Attlee Government and the Indian Problem* (1983). Hugh Tinker, *Experiment with Freedom: India and Pakistan, 1947* (1967).

HUGH TINKER

CACIQUE, Spanish term for a native chieftain with considerable local power and influence. It was applied, particularly in the nineteenth century, to wealthy members of the Philippine elite who wielded an all-pervasive influence over the people of a particular area (a landed estate, a village or municipality, and even an entire province). The term carried a definite pejorative sense, appearing most often in litigations filed by Spanish colonial officials. It was also widely used by early American colonial authorities, who frequently professed as one of their aims the eradication of "*cacique* rule." In the early 1900s it was used in a more purely political context, usually referring to local political bosses.

[*See also* Philippines *and* Spain and the Philippines.]

MICHAEL CULLINANE

CAITANYA. *See* Chaitanya.

CAI YUANPEI (1868–1940), Chinese educator who transformed himself from a traditional Hanlin scholar to an anti-Manchu revolutionary and later an official of the newly established Republic of China. Disappointed with China's ill-fated reforms and repeated defeats at the hands of foreigners, Cai helped organize the revolutionary Guangfuhui (Restoration Society) in 1904. In 1912 he became minister of education in the new government. From 1916 to 1926 he was the chancellor of China's prestigious Beijing University. Cai played a pivotal leadership role in the monumental May Fourth Movement, which stimulated nationalism and unprecedented cultural-intellectual ferment in China. As China's most influential educator, Cai recruited young talents to his university, advocated absolute academic freedom, and encouraged independent thinking and free discussion of divergent ideas.

[*See also* May Fourth Movement.]

Howard L. Boorman, ed., *Biographical Dictionary of Republican China* (1967–1971). William J. Duiker, *Ts'ai Yuan-p'ei: Educator of Modern China* (1977).

CHANG-TAI HUNG

CALCUTTA (Bengali, Kalikata), city in eastern India. It began as a trading settlement founded by Job Charnock in 1690. At that time the area consisted of three villages—Sutanuti, Gobindapur, and Kalikata. In 1698 the East India Company obtained the proprietary rights of three villages, thus becoming *zamindars* (landholders) under the Mughals. The early English traders often lived in improvised shelters amid jungles. The attraction of trade must have been great, for the English took great interest in the settlement despite high mortality with a life expectancy rhetorically described as "two monsoons." Some prominent Bengali merchant-weaver families as well as some members of the versatile Armenian merchant community had already been settled there. [*See also* Charnock, Job; East India Company; *and* Armenians in South Asia.]

In 1697 the nucleus of a fort, later called Old Fort William, was built. The English settlement, called White Town, began to grow up around the fort. The Indian settlement, then called Black Town, began to grow with Burrabazar ("great bazaar") as its nucleus. The Burrabazar supplied provisions to the European settlement. Its Indian merchants were involved in trade with the British in commodities such as cotton piece goods, which were the raison d'être for Calcutta's existence. Thus originated the basic framework of a dual city, which was to become a feature of colonial urban development. [*See* Fort William.]

The selection of the site of Calcutta was not accidental. It stood at the highest point at which the river was navigable for seagoing vessels. The Hughly River, a busy channel of commerce, protected the western flank of the town, while the eastern flank had the strategic advantage of vast salt marshes. The fine silks and muslins from Dhaka, cotton fabrics from different parts of Bengal, the saltpeter in Bihar (much in demand during the French wars), rice, sesame oil, sugar, lac, and other commodities had a ready export market for which Calcutta served as a natural outlet.

In 1700 Calcutta became the headquarters of a presidency described as Fort William in Bengal and took a significant step forward with the grant of a *farman* (order permitting them to trade) by the emperor following the success of Surman's embassy to Delhi. [*See* Surman's Embassy.] By 1727 the total shipping in Calcutta amounted to ten thousand tons and in 1735 the city population was estimated to be one hundred thousand—a sharp contrast to the meager population of twelve thousand in 1710.

Calcutta was sacked by Nawab Siraj ud-Daulah in 1756 but was quickly recovered by Robert Clive and Charles Watson. The famous battle, or skirmish, at Plassey on 23 June 1757 gave the East India Company effective control over Bengal, thus raising Calcutta to prominence and overshadowing Murshidabad, the earlier capital. The Regulating Act (1773) elevated the governor of Bengal, then Warren Hastings, to the position of governor-general of British-controlled India. Calcutta thus became the capital of the British empire in India, a position it retained until the transfer of capital to Delhi in 1912. [*See also* Siraj ud-Daulah; Clive, Sir Robert; Plassey, Battle of; *and* Hastings, Warren.]

The administrations of Warren Hastings (1773–1785) and Richard Colley Wellesley (1798–1805) saw the European enclave begin to take on a look of elegance with a distinct development of European architecture and general layout. Lord Wellesley, who had the Government House built on the design of Kedleston Hall in Derbyshire, was determined to see that India was "governed from a palace, not from a counting house." Public buildings tended to have a neoclassical facade, while private residences of well-to-do Europeans had large compounds and open porticos. [*See* Architecture: South Asian Architecture.] Between the Indian town and the European one were settlements of Armenians, Jews, Greeks, and Anglo-Indians. The first three were essentially business communities. [*See also* Anglo-Indians.]

The pattern of the Indian town was heavily influenced by bazaars and slums, representing a high degree of congestion that was occasionally relieved by spacious residences of opulent families, such as those built by Maharaja Nabakrishna (Nobkissen), who acted as a Persian secretary to Clive, and the Tagores, whose money came from business and real estate. [*See* Tagore, Dwarkanath.] The Indian town developed a complex pattern with neighborhoods representing the ethnic, linguistic, and religious distribution of population, which has made it a highly significant sociological phenomenon to this day.

The growth of a middle class began in the early nineteenth century. This class felt a keen desire for Western education through the medium of English, leading to the foundation of the Hindu College in 1817. The interaction of the East and the West caused a development often characterized as the Bengal Renaissance, represented by a number of personalities from Rammohan Roy (1772–1833) to Rabindranath Tagore (1861–1941). The city was the foremost center of India's cultural and social development until the beginning of the twentieth century. In the nineteenth century Calcutta saw the emergence of a young Bengal movement with an accent on intellectual freedom; a movement for the prohibition of the practice of *sati,* or "self-immolation" of widows, and for a general improvement in the status of women; the birth of the Brahmo Samaj, with a monotheistic version of Hinduism and a moral code suitable for an educated middle class; the introduction of a vernacular press; and new forms of literature. Notable among the leaders of these movements were Rammohan Roy, Henry Derozio, Isvarchandra Vidyasagar, Michael Madhusudan Dutt, and Bankim Chandra Chatterji. It was essentially a linguistic and literary renaissance that articulated a new consciousness within the constraints of colonial domination and a basically traditional social structure. [*See* Roy, Rammohan; Tagore, Rabindranath; Derozio, Henry Louis Vivian; Vidyasagar, Isvarchandra; Chatterji, Bankim Chandra; *and* Sati.]

A powerful spiritual movement led by Ramakrishna Paramahamsa and Swami Vivekananda in the late nineteenth century, followed by the *swadeshi* (nationalist) upsurge in the early twentieth century, gave the city a unique status in the political and cultural life of India during the period. [*See* Ramakrishna; Vivekananda; *and* Swadeshi.] Radicalism tended to become an established trend in the political culture of the city, later to merge with Marxism in the 1930s and Naxalism (a variant of Maoism) in the late 1960s. [*See* Communism: Communist Parties in South Asia *and* Naxalites.]

The late nineteenth and the early twentieth centuries also saw the appearance of a thriving commercial theater and a pioneering film industry. The emergence of a Bengal school in visual arts and significant activities in the field of scientific research and higher education revolved mainly around Calcutta University. The transfer of the capital to Delhi in 1912 did not dampen the ardor associated with these activities. Calcutta was still the foremost center of commerce and industry in India, and the elite and the middle class were still confident. Landed property in rural Bengal could be a source of security and, in some cases, of prosperity. One can even speak of the "golden thirties," with Calcutta's own classical vocalists and popular singers reflecting the leisurely mood of the well-to-do and even of the not so well-to-do.

All of this came to an abrupt halt in the 1940s. Human skeletons moved in the streets during the famine of 1943. War brought new anxieties, among them soaring prices. The communal riots of 1946 brought about a strange hysteria. Then came the partition of Bengal in 1947 followed by a massive migration of people from East Bengal, which practically changed the face of Calcutta and the moods of the people. [*See* Partition of India.]

The economy of Calcutta in the early twentieth century depended heavily on jute, tea, and Bengal coal. [*See* Jute *and* Tea in India and Sri Lanka.] It was the focus of trade of northeastern India as well as East Bengal and the Ganges valley. Although Calcutta still remained a commercial city with a large tertiary sector, an industrial belt tended to develop along the river, owing primarily to jute but also to paper and engineering industries. The city economy was under far greater European control than that of its counterpart, Bombay. The enterprising Marwari community was, however, entering such crucial fields as business, trade, and speculation. [*See* Marwaris.] Educated middle-class Bengali entrepreneurs were making significant experiments in small-scale and medium-scale industries such as pharmaceuticals.

Since the 1960s the city has been in a state of crisis. The port has been declining steadily and income tax receipts from the Calcutta region remain almost static. The general decline is sometimes attributed to the depressed state of Calcutta's hinterland and of eastern India. Although West Bengal has been moving toward a low-level equilibrium with declining industry, reflected in Calcutta with a depressed secondary sector and a disproportionate tertiary one, the tradition of cultural and educational life that is principally a residue of nineteenth-century developments occasionally reemerges through the medium of a great film or through resistance to the pressures of castism, communalism, and regionalism. While middle-class culture may appear beleaguered—and there might be reality behind appearance—the popular culture may represent an enjoyable urban experience denied to the middle class and the elite. Calcutta, once the "second city of the empire," perhaps remains a capital—the capital of poor, non-elitist, or even anti-elitist India.

Calcutta is now the largest urban agglomeration in India, with a population of 9.1 million. The total area of the Calcutta metropolitan district is 1,425 square kilometers. The Eastern Zone is the least urbanized of the five major census zones of India; according to urban planners, Calcutta's demographic influence on its hinterland is unduly heavy. Although crisis-ridden, Calcutta is still at the center of a system of interrelated cities in the eastern region, of a great area rich in natural resources with an infrastructure that although dated, can be utilized. With its past and present, its achievements and limitations, its political sophistication and naïveté, Calcutta poses a challenge to India's future.

[*See also* Bengal; Bangladesh; *and* Hughly River.]

Calcutta Metropolitan Statistics (1980, 1983). H. E. A. Cotton, *Calcutta Old and New* (1907; rev. ed., 1980). A. K. Ray, *A Short History of Calcutta* (1901). Pradip Sinha, *Calcutta in Urban History* (1978). C. R. Wilson, *Early Annals of the English in Bengal* (1895).

PRADIP SINHA

CALDERON, FELIPE (1868–1908), Philippine nationalist. Descended from a Spanish Creole from Mexico, Calderon grew up in Manila. He excelled as a student (LL.B., Santo Tomas, 1893), acquired wealth and landholdings through marriage, and practiced law and journalism in Manila. In mid-1898, he became affiliated with the revolutionary government and drafted the constitution of the first Philippine Republic. Shortly after the outbreak of hostilities with the Americans, Calderon abandoned the new government and rendered his services to the Americans. Although he was offered an official position with the American colonial government, he did not accept it. He devoted the rest of his life to law and the propagation of a Philippine nationalism rooted in his own interpretation of Philippine conditions.

[*See also* Philippines; Malolos Republic; *and* Philippine-American War.]

MICHAEL CULLINANE

CALENDARS AND ERAS

CHINESE CALENDARS AND ERAS

The oracle bones of the Shang dynasty (c. seventeenth to twelfth century BCE) reveal that the Chinese were concerned with the keeping of time. Although the Shang Chinese already knew that the solar year was approximately 365¼ days, the months were of twenty-nine or thirty days, in accordance with the lunar calendar. In order to make up the difference between the two systems and to ensure that the calendar would not deviate too much from the agricultural seasons, the Chinese practiced intercalation, in which an extra lunar month was added at appropriate points. Thus, about every third year the calendar would have thirteen months. This calendrical system is known as a luni-solar calendar.

According to Joseph Needham, the oldest known Chinese calendars are the *Xia xiao zheng (Lesser Annuary of the Xia Dynasty)*, which may date from about the fifth century BCE, and the *Yue ling*, later incorporated into the *Xiao Dai liji (Record of the Rites of Dai the Younger)* of the first century BCE; the calendar itself may date from between the fifth and third centuries BCE. The former, not actually related to the Xia dynasty at all, is arranged in a twelve-month lunar calendar. It was a farmer's calendar with comments on the weather, the stars, and animal life. The latter, much longer, gives astronomical characteristics of the lunar months, describes the imperial ceremonies to be performed, prohibits various activities, and provides warnings in regard to the consequences of not following the rites.

Named year periods began in 114 or 113 BCE. The custom was to name the emperor after his dynastic title, followed by his year of reign. (For example, the year 1894 would be denoted Guangxu 20, or the twentieth year of the Guangxu emperor's reign.) More characteristic, however, was the sexagenary cycle, in which the ten heavenly stems *(tiangan)* were combined with the twelve earthly branches *(dizhi)* to create a series of sixty (see figure 1). The cycle has existed as a day-count system since the Shang dynasty; the characters for the stems and branches are among the most common on the Shang oracle bones. Beginning in the first century BCE the system was used for years as well as days. The cycle ran continuously, regardless of dynastic fluctuations. Thus, the first year of a given reign period would be whatever year of the cycle it happened to fall on, just as the British would not start a new century with the crowning of a new king. The previous example of the twentieth year of the Guangxu reign (1894) was a *jiawu* year, the thirty-first year of the cycle. Another count system was duodecimal, borrowed from the Chaldeans, in which a group of twelve animals was named. Boodberg has concluded that this practice originated in the sixth century BCE. The twelve animals, corresponding in order to the twelve earthly branches, are rat, ox, tiger, hare, dragon, snake, horse, sheep, monkey, cock, dog, and pig.

Out of the day-count system developed a period of ten days *(xun)*, similar to the notion of a week. A full set of six ten-day periods was roughly equivalent to two months. In turn, six of these sixty-day periods was about a year. More important than the ten-day or monthly periods, however, were the twenty-four fortnightly periods. These are named for the equinoxes, the solstices, and the beginning

jiazi 1	yichou 2	bingyin 3	dingmao 4	wuchen 5	jisi 6	gengwu 7	xinwei 8	renshen 9	guiyou 10
jiaxu 11	yihai 12	bingzi 13	dingchou 14	wuyin 15	jimao 16	gengchen 17	xinsi 18	renwu 19	guiwei 20
jiashen 21	yiyou 22	bingxu 23	dinghai 24	wuzi 25	jichou 26	gengyin 27	xinmao 28	renchen 29	guisi 30
jiawu 31	yiwei 32	bingshen 33	dingyou 34	wuxu 35	jihai 36	gengzi 37	xinchou 38	renyin 39	guimao 40
jiachen 41	yisi 42	bingwu 43	dingwei 44	wushen 45	jiyou 46	gengxu 47	xinhai 48	renzi 49	guichou 50
jiayin 51	yimao 52	bingchen 53	dingsi 54	wuwu 55	jiwei 56	gengshen 57	xinyou 58	renxu 59	guihai 60

FIGURE 1. *The Sexagenary Cycle of the Ten Heavenly Stems and Twelve Earthly Branches.* The two series are combined in order, so that when the set of ten has completed six cycles, the set of twelve has completed five, yielding a set of sixty binomes ($6 \times 10 = 60$; $5 \times 12 = 60$). The most recent *jiazi* year, the first year of the cycle, was 1984.

of the seasons, and were thus solar rather than lunar terms. (The beginnings of the seasons are named separately from the equinoxes and solstices because in China they are arranged so that the equinox or solstice occurs at the season's midpoint; thus, the Spring Festival, the culmination of the Chinese New Year's celebrations, takes place forty-five days before the vernal equinox.) Other fortnightly periods have such names as "The Rains," "Lesser Heat," "Greater Heat," and "Descent of Hoar Frost."

The promulgation of the calendar was an imperial right; in fact, it was the duty of the ruler to issue the calendar so that the farmers would know when to plant, harvest, and so forth, since the lunar calendar was not in exact accord with the seasons. Insofar as the fixing of the calendar was associated with the power of the emperor, independent astronomers were viewed with suspicion; by proving the imperial calendar wrong, imperial authority would be weakened and the emperor's right to rule called into question. Rival astronomers could also be calculating new calendars for rebel dynasties. New dynasties overhauled the calendar and issued one with a new name; this could also be done with the establishment of the new reign period of a given emperor. More than one hundred new calendars were issued in China between the third century BCE and the nineteenth century. Although some involved only minor changes, some were foreign calendars, such as the Hindu, Muslim, and Gregorian calendars. The last was introduced by the Jesuit missionaries, notably Matteo Ricci, Johann Adam Schall von Bell, and Ferdinand Verbiest. Schall and Verbiest both held the position of director of the Bureau of Astronomy during the seventeenth century. [*See also* Schall von Bell, Johann Adam *and* Verbiest, Ferdinand.]

The Western calendar was not widely adopted until the establishment of the Republican government in 1912. Popular festivals, such as New Year's and the Mid-Autumn Festival, still follow the old lunar system.

Peter A. Boodberg, "Chinese Zoographic Names As Chronograms," *Harvard Journal of Asiatic Studies* 5 (1940): 128–136. Lionel Giles, *Six Centuries at Tunhuang*

(1944), plate 8. Joseph Needham, *Science and Civilisation in China,* vol. 3, *Mathematics and the Sciences of the Heavens and the Earth* (1959). Pan Ku (Ban Gu), *The History of the Former Han Dynasty,* translated by Homer H. Dubs, vol. 2 (1944), pp. 121–122. Jonathan Spence, *To Change China: Western Advisers in China, 1620–1960* (1969). Karl A. Wittfogel, "Meteorological Records from the Divination Inscriptions of Shang," *Geographical Review* (1940): 110–133.

L. CARRINGTON GOODRICH

INDIAN CALENDARS AND ERAS

Modern India, like the other countries of South Asia, uses the Western, or Gregorian, calendar, which was introduced into the area in the eighteenth century. There was, however, an interchange of calendrical information between India and the Western world from very early times. The days of the Indian week, for example, are named according to a system that corresponds to the Western astronomical system; thus Sunday is Ravivara, after Ravi, the sun god. After the Turkic conquests in the thirteenth century the Islamic system of dating began to be used for official purposes and in historiographical and other literary works. Older indigenous Indian systems of dating continued to be used by the bulk of the Hindu population, however, both for everyday life as well as for religious and literary purposes.

Texts dating from about 1000 BCE indicate that the basis of the Indian system was a solar year of 360 days divided into twelve lunar months. The lunar calendar underwent many complex refinements through the centuries and is still used for calculating religious festivals and rituals, including marriage ceremonies. The lunar month is divided into two equal parts *(paksha),* with the first half containing the new moon. Since the lunar days do not correspond with solar days, elaborate calculations are necessary to fix the beginning and end of the year. The difference between the solar year and the lunar calendar is adjusted by the assertion of an extra lunar month every thirty months. The lunar day is also subdivided into smaller units corresponding to hours, minutes, and seconds, with the smallest of these being equivalent to 0.4 seconds. The lunar year begins in the month known as Chaitra, which falls in March-April in the Western system. Two months make a season *(ritu),* with, for example, Varsha (July through September) being the rainy season and Vasanta (March through May) being spring. The seasons hold an important place in Indian culture and are celebrated in painting, poetry, and music.

While the lunar calendar is used for religious purposes, the solar calendar is also widely used in India for astrological calculations, which are of enormous importance to Indians of all classes for the casting of horoscopes to fix auspicious dates for important events and for foretelling the future. It has been suggested that some knowledge of solar astronomy came in ancient times from Babylon, but the evidence is fragmentary; much more certain is the diffusion of Greek and Hellenistic knowledge in the early centuries of the Christian era. Indian mathematicians refined some of this knowledge, and it passed back to the Western world through the Arabs. The Indian astronomical system assumed a geocentric universe, but in the fifth century the great mathematician and astronomer Aryabhata theorized that the earth revolved around the sun.

While the Indians had developed these exact lunar and solar calendars, they apparently did not devise a widely accepted system of eras to date events in relation to each other, as in the Christian and Islamic eras. The construction of a chronology for ancient Indian history has, therefore, been very difficult. [*See* India.] Furthermore, different regions of the subcontinent had their own eras, usually relating to some prominent ruler. The working out of a satisfactory chronology of history for India has depended upon the collation of various eras mentioned in inscriptions and texts. In the early nineteenth century the only certain dates that historians had to work with were those derived from the references of Greek writers to various rulers of the Maurya empire; this permitted the establishment of the chronology of the Maurya empire, and from this other dates were worked out. A number of eras did, however, come into use, and some of these are still used in religious writings or in self-consciously nationalistic ones that desire to stress the autonomy of the Indian tradition. Among the best known of these is the Vikrama era, dated from 58 BCE, which celebrates the beginning of the reign of King Vikramaditya of Ujjain in central India. Another commonly used era is that associated with the Saka kings of Ujjain, an era dated from 78 CE. In both cases the use of the era probably came into existence long after the date assigned to it; thus the Saka era may have been created by Kanishka, a great Saka ruler who came to the throne about 120 CE. Knowledge about the founding of the Gupta era is more certain; its beginning date, 320 CE, was probably the year in which Chandragupta I became ruler of the kingdom that formed the basis for the great Gupta empire. Following the decay of the Gupta empire, a powerful new conqueror, Harshavardhana of Kanyakubja, founded an empire, and the Harsha era, dating from 606 CE, was used in many inscriptions in North India.

In addition to these eras relating to actual Indian rulers there is a system of great cycles of time that are part of the cosmological and mythological thinking of India and are common, with some differences, to the Hindu, Buddhist, and Jain traditions. There is no beginning or end of time in these great cycles, but they recur endlessly in cycles of varying length. The primary cycle is 311,040,000 million years, which is itself repeated, but within it are other cycles, the smallest of which are the four *yugas* (ages), which are often referred to in the mythological accounts. Each *yuga* is characterized by physical and moral deterioration, until the *kaliyuga*—the most degenerate of all, and the one in which we are now living—finally comes to an end in utter chaos. This *yuga* is supposed to have begun in 3102 BCE and will last for 432,000 years.

[*See also* Astrology and Astronomy, Islamic.]

Alexander Cunningham, *A Book of Indian Eras* (1883). Government of India, *Calendar Reform Committee Report* (1955). L. D. Swamikannu Pillai, *Indian Chronology* (1911).
STUART W. SMITHERS

ISLAMIC CALENDARS AND ERAS

The most important calendar used by Muslims is certainly that of the Hijra, the flight of the prophet Muhammad from Mecca to Medina in the month of Rabi I (September/October 622 CE). Since that month was not the first month of the year, however, the epoch was calculated by astronomical reckoning to have occurred on 15 July 622, and by popular reckoning on 16 July. The reason for this double reckoning is that, unlike the astronomical day, the civil Muslim day begins after sunset.

The months of the Hijri calendar are strictly lunar, and thus the new year (1 Muharram) can fall on any day of the solar year. But because the lunar year itself is shorter than the solar year by about eleven days, the Muslim new year ultimately returns to the same solar date after some thirty years. The months themselves alternate between thirty and twenty-nine days, beginning with Muharram (thirty) and ending with Dhu al-Hijja (twenty-nine; thirty during leap years).

Although this calendar was widely used in the Muslim lands, its disadvantages in administrative matters were too obvious, for if one were to collect taxes on the produce of the land, one had to make sure that those taxes were collected during the harvest season, a strictly solar phenomenon. On account of these administrative exigencies, other calendars were used in conjunction with the Hijra calendar, and other techniques were also invented to circumvent the difficulties of paying taxes in kind at times other than the harvest season, or of paying yearly cash taxes every 354 days or so rather than every 365 days. In most of these cases the tax year was referred to as *hijri shamsi,* or Hijra solar year.

The second commonly used calendar was indeed solar, and was used for both scientific and civil purposes. Most astronomical texts date events in the Yazdigird calendar, of which the epoch was 16 June 632 CE, which was the date of the accession of Yazdigird III, the last Sasanid king. The months in this calendar were thirteen: twelve months of thirty days each, beginning with Farvardin, and one month of five intercalary days added at the end of the twelve months to bring the year to 365 days. Unlike the Julian calendar, in which one day is intercalated every four years, the Yazdigird calendar would in 1,460 years become one year out of step with a strictly solar year. For administrative purposes, however, that difference was too small to be adjusted. The constancy of the Yazdigird calendar made it one of the most favored of the Muslim astronomers, who took full advantage of the constant length of its year to facilitate their computations.

Other calendars that were strictly solar, with full intercalation schemes, were also known. The most famous of these is the one called the Alexander calendar (or that of Dhu al-Qarnain, as Alexander was known in Islamic sources), also known as the Rumi (Greek) calendar. Based on the Seleucid era, of which the epoch was 1 October 312 BCE, it was made up of the months now universally used in the Western world.

There are also detailed descriptions in the Persian sources of calendars of the post-Mongol era calendars using years close to 365¼ days; they were commonly known as the Khata'i and Uighur calendars. The Jalali, or Maliki, and other lesser-known calendars are mentioned in the works of Nasir al-Din Tusi, Ulug Beg, and Jamshid Ghiyath al-Din al-Kashi.

E. S. Kennedy, "The Chinese-Uighur Calendar as Described in the Islamic Sources," *Isis* 55 (1964): 435–443. S. H. Taqizadeh, "Various Eras and Calendars in the Countries of Islam," *Bulletin of the School of Oriental and African Studies* 9 (1937–1939): 903–922, and 10 (1940–1942): 107–132.
GEORGE SALIBA

CALICUT, port located on the northern Malabar coast of southwest India, which is today the state of Kerala in the Indian Union. In the mid-thirteenth century Muslim trade based on the Persian Gulf declined on account of the Mongol invasions. The Mamluk empire in Egypt became the great funnel for trade between the Indian Ocean and the Mediterranean, and Calicut, under a ruler titled the *zamorin*, thus rose to great prosperity because of its function as an entrepôt for trade within the Indian Ocean. Chinese and Southeast Asian goods, especially spices and local products, were obtained in Calicut by Red Sea Arab merchants.

The prosperity of the fourteenth and fifteenth centuries was rudely disrupted by the arrival of the Portuguese in 1498. They aimed to divert Calicut's trade to their ports of Cochin and Goa, and were fairly successful, although warfare between subjects of Calicut—especially the Mappilas—and Portugal was endemic in the sixteenth century. In the second half of the seventeenth century the Dutch replaced the Portuguese as the dominant power on the Malabar coast. Calicut then had to confront yet another monopolistic system. After a brief revival of prosperity in the early eighteenth century, Calicut returned to obscurity. It was acquired by the British in 1792.

[*See also* Mappilas; Portuguese: Portuguese in India; Dutch East India Company; *and* Kerala.]

K. V. K. Ayyar, *The Zamorin of Calicut* (1938). K. P. Padmanabha Menon, *A History of Kerala* (1924–1937).

MICHAEL N. PEARSON

CALIPHATE, term derived from the Arabic *khilafa,* commonly used to denote several groups of rulers regarded as the real or nominal leaders of the entire Muslim world and the legitimate representatives of the judicial, administrative, and military power of the Islamic state. The title of caliph, *khalifa* ("successor" or "deputy"), was actually only one of several applied to this office; in juridical theory, the institution is more correctly termed the imamate (Arabic, *imama*).

The office of caliph originated upon the death of the prophet Muhammad (632 CE) as a way of maintaining the spiritual and political unity of the Islamic community. It continued to develop on a more or less ad hoc basis under the pressure of specific problems and needs. The legal theory of the caliphate was not worked out until much later and in a way that accommodated and legitimized precedents set by early holders of the office. In Sunni Islam, a number of legal scholars dealt with the theory of the caliphate/imamate; the classic formulation was that of Abu al-Hasan al-Mawardi (974–1058).

The existence of the caliphate was considered an absolute necessity to prevent anarchy and preserve the religion. The Muslim community was responsible for seeing that the office was filled and obeyed. In accordance with the historical examples, a person could become caliph either through election by qualified electors ("people who loosen and bind") or upon designation by the preceding caliph. In practice, the office was often held by force of arms or dynastic succession. Some caliphs used the title *khalifat Allah* ("deputy of God") instead of *khalifat rasul Allah* ("successor of the prophet of God") to imply that their authority derived directly from God, but this was never widely accepted. According to the theory, qualifications for the office included moral and religious respectability, sound mental and physical capacities, courage and fortitude, and descent from the tribe of Quraish (again to accommodate the historical precedents). The caliph's primary duties were to preserve Islam as perfected by the early community, to suppress religious deviation, to execute the religious law, to lead the prayer services, to defend Muslim territories, to conduct the holy war, and to supervise taxation and administration.

Most sects of Shi'ite Islam used the title *imam* exclusively to denote the head of the Muslim community. Instead of belonging to Quraish, the imam had to be a member of the family of the prophet Muhammad and acquired the office only through the explicit designation of his predecessor (and under no circumstances by election). The true imam combined both absolute religious authority and legitimate political power. The Shi'ites generally regarded the Sunni caliphate as an essentially secular and illegitimate institution. As the power of the caliphate declined, many Sunni scholars also came to distinguish between the charismatic leadership of the first four Rightly Guided caliphs (Abu Bakr, Umar, Uthman, and Ali) and that of the merely "royal" Umayyad and Abbasid dynasties of caliphs (661–749 and 750–1258, respectively).

Aside from the Rightly Guided caliphs, the Umayyads, and the Abbasids, only a few other groups of rulers were regarded as caliphs, most notably the Spanish Umayyads of Cordova (755–1236) and the Shi'ite Fatimids (910–1171). The Mamluks of Egypt claimed to have maintained a shadow Abbasid caliphate after the Mongol sack of Baghdad, and the Ottoman sultans sometimes claimed to have inherited the caliphate from the

Abbasids. There is at present no recognized caliphate despite occasional calls by modern Muslim reformers to resurrect the office.

[*See also* Imam; Shi'a; *and* Sunni.]

Thomas W. Arnold, *The Caliphate* (1924).

E. L. DANIEL

CAMBODIA, Southeast Asian nation bordering Vietnam, Laos, and Thailand and opening onto the Gulf of Thailand in the south. Its area is about 67,000 square miles and its estimated population (1984) is 6,000,000. The dominant ethnic group is the Khmer; this is also the name of the national language. Cambodia (Kampuchea) has few mineral resources, but in prosperous times has produced sizable exports of rice, rubber, pepper, and other crops.

Archaeologists have shown that Cambodia has been inhabited by human beings for at least 40,000 years. It enters the historical record in the early years of the common era, when a kingdom known to the Chinese as Funan occupied part of the Mekong Delta. [*See* Funan.] Stone inscriptions begin to appear in the fifth and sixth centuries CE. By 802, a Cambodian monarch, Jayavarman II, had established the kingdom later known as Angkor in Cambodia's northwest. This kingdom lasted until the fifteenth century. Under several powerful monarchs, including Suryavarman II (1113–1150) and Jayavarman VII (1178–1220), Angkor expanded its control to include parts of present-day Laos, Thailand, and Malaysia. Monuments to its greatness include the Hindu temple of Angkor Wat, the Buddhist temple of the Bayon, and hundreds of others. The rulers of Angkor supervised a powerful bureaucracy, itself responsible for irrigation works and the collection of taxes. During its heyday, Angkor housed about a million people, most of them peasants laboring to provide surpluses to feed the small elite. [*See* Jayavarman II; Angkor; Suryavarman II; Jayavarman VII; *and* Angkor Wat.]

During the thirteenth and fourteenth centuries, the sovereignty of the Angkorean elite weakened appreciably. There were several reasons for this. One was the conversion of most of the population from Hinduism and Mahayana Buddhism to Theravada Buddhism, which stressed individual salvation rather than social obligations. Another was the rise of a powerful Thai kingdom to the west, which reduced the capacity of the regime to levy taxes and recruit soldiers and slaves. A third may have been that the irrigation works at Angkor were increasingly ineffective. Other, more speculative reasons include the appearance of malignant malaria in Southeast Asia at about this time and the pressures put on other parts of the region by China's Mongol (Yuan) dynasty.

In any case, by the end of the fourteenth century Cambodia had been invaded several times by Thai forces. Angkor was abandoned definitively in 1431. By that time, many of its learned men and artisans had sought refuge in the Thai capital of Ayudhya. Other members of the Cambodian elite, attracted by the possibility of becoming involved in international trade, moved to the vicinity of Phnom Penh, which soon became an important commercial center. Cambodian agriculture probably underwent a revolution at this time, reverting from the multicrop, irrigated system in effect at Angkor to single-crop, subsistence farming more appropriate to a relatively small and scattered population. At the same time, in the sixteenth century at least, Cambodia was able to regain some of its greatness at the expense of the Thai. Under King Ang Chan, Cambodian troops invaded Thailand on several occasions. In response, the Thai sacked the Cambodian capital of Lovek in 1594. [*See* Ang Chan *and* Lovek.] From then on, Cambodia never recovered its momentum, and the next three hundred years can best be understood as dark ages during which Cambodia was preyed on by foreign invaders from both Thailand and Vietnam and was subjected to murderous civil wars carried on at the behest of contending royal factions.

Although Western traders and missionaries had sought a foothold in Cambodia in the sixteenth and early seventeenth century, by 1700 the country was effectively isolated from the outside world. Its people were largely scattered into villages, growing rice for themselves. Links to the outside world were provided by immigrant Chinese merchants, by local Buddhist monks, and by government officials who made occasional forays to search for manpower and taxes. The Cambodian court, although isolated from most Cambodians, was located in a capital that was little more than a large village. Frequently, as during the Tay Son Rebellion in Vietnam in the late eighteenth century, foreign wars spilled into Cambodia, which was in no position, demographically at least, to offer much resistance. [*See* Tay Son Rebellion.]

The darkest point of these years occurred in the early nineteenth century, when Cambodia became the site of intensifying rivalry between newly installed dynasties in Bangkok and Vietnam. Thai patronage of the Cambodian court had been institutionalized in the 1790s, when the Cambodian king,

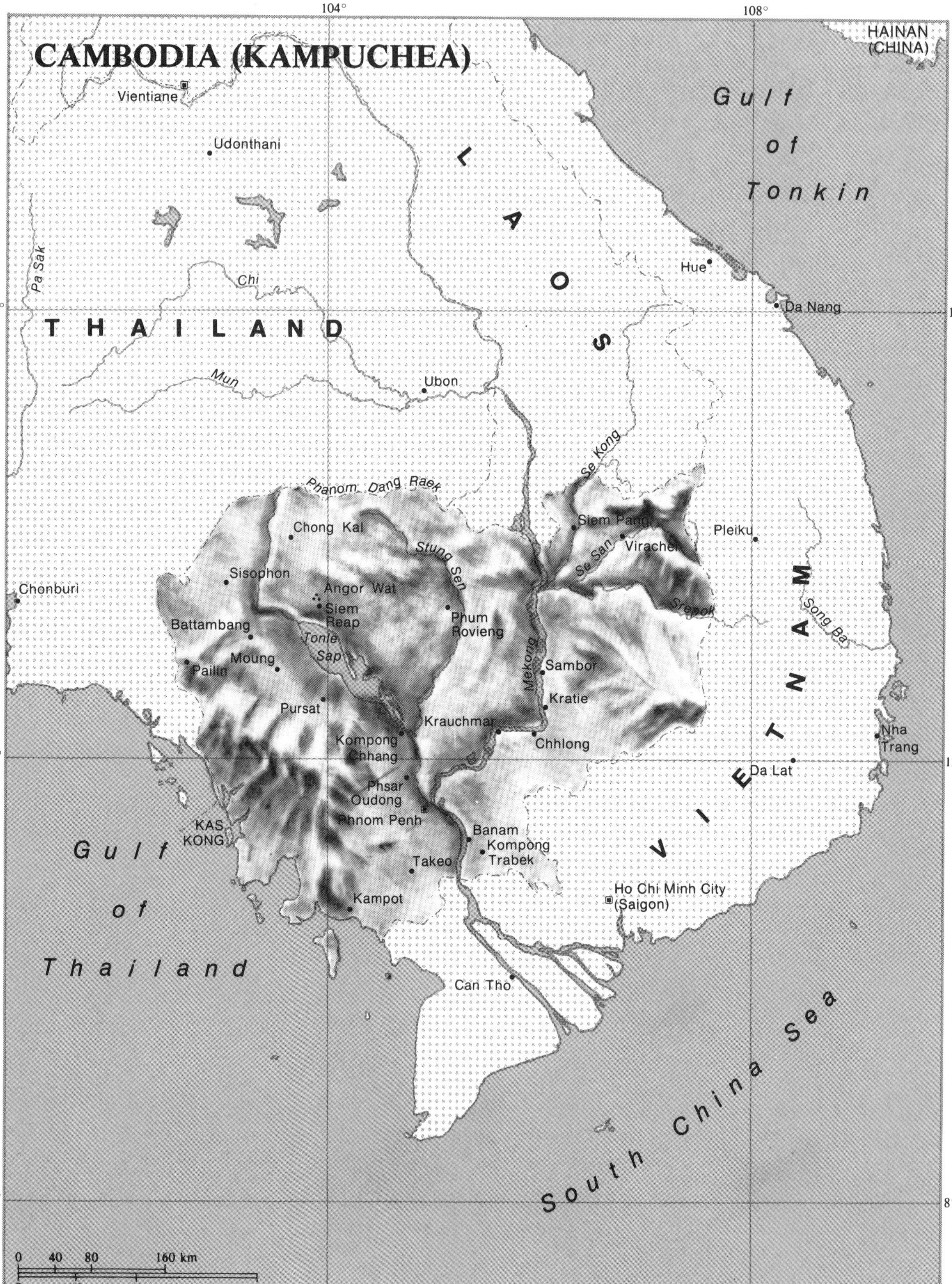
CAMBODIA (KAMPUCHEA)
104°
108°
HAINAN (CHINA)
Vientiane
Gulf of Tonkin
Udonthani
LAOS
Pa Sak
Chi
Hue
Da Nang
16°
THAILAND
Mun
Ubon
Se Kong
Phanom Dang Raek
Siem Pang
Pleiku
Chong Kal
Virachei
Stung Sen
Se San
Sisophon
Chonburi
Angor Wat
Siem Reap
Srepok
Song Ba
Phum Rovieng
Battambang
Tonle Sap
Mekong
Moung
Pailin
Sambor
Kratie
Pursat
Krauchmar
Nha Trang
Kompong Chhang
Chhlong
12°
Da Lat
Phsar Oudong
VIETNAM
Phnom Penh
KAS KONG
Banam
Gulf of Thailand
Kompong Trabek
Takeo
Ho Chi Minh City (Saigon)
Kampot
Can Tho
South China Sea
8°
0 40 80 160 km
0 40 80 160 miles

1:6,000,000

Ang Eng, had been anointed in Bangkok before being allowed to return to Cambodia. [*See also* Ang Eng.] He died after a very brief reign, and his heir, Ang Chan, was only seven years old. For the next ten years or so, Chan was forced to accept Thai control. He resented this, and when he reached his majority he tried to form an alliance with the Vietnamese court. His policy of playing larger powers off against each other foreshadowed the behavior of his descendant Norodom Sihanouk in the 1950s and 1960s. [*See* Norodom Sihanouk.] It was similarly doomed to failure, for from 1811 until Chan's death in 1835, the Vietnamese played an increasingly dominant role in Cambodian politics. When Chan died, the Vietnamese began to treat Cambodia more or less as a colony, working through a puppet monarch, Chan's daughter, Mei. An anti-Vietnamese rebellion, encouraged by the Thai, broke out in 1841 and was soon followed by a Thai invasion. When the Vietnamese finally withdrew from Cambodia in 1847, the Thai placed Chan's brother Duang on the throne and reestablished their protectorate over the kingdom. [*See* Ang Duang.]

Under Duang's son Norodom (r. 1860–1904) the French established a protectorate over Cambodia. Between 1863 and the 1880s, French officials worked through local officials, but after a royally sponsored rebellion in 1885–1886 they intensified their control. When Norodom died in 1904 the French placed his brother, Sisowath, on the throne. [*See* Norodom *and* Sisowath.] The first forty years of the twentieth century marked the heyday of French colonialism in Cambodia. Rice, rubber, corn, and pepper were grown for export; Phnom Penh, the capital, grew to a city of perhaps 300,000 people; thousands of miles of roads were built; and hundreds of thousands of Cambodians received rudimentary schooling. [*See* Phnom Penh.] During this period a small elite developed, primarily in the capital but also scattered throughout the provincial civil service. These men were largely pro-French or, at worst, indifferent to French rule, but by the late 1930s faint signs of nationalism were perceptible, particularly in the pages of a Cambodian-language newspaper, *Nagara Vatta (Angkor Wat),* which was published between 1936 and 1942.

World War II was a turning point in Cambodian history, as it was throughout Southeast Asia. Japanese forces occupied the kingdom from 1941 to 1945 but allowed the French to continue to administer it, working through a newly crowned king, the nineteen-year-old Norodom Sihanouk (r. 1941–1955). In the middle of 1945 the Japanese imprisoned the French throughout Indochina and encouraged Sihanouk, among others, to declare independence from France. For seven months Cambodia became a semiautonomous Japanese protectorate. For two months Son Ngoc Thanh, one of the editors of *Nagara Vatta,* acted as prime minister. Thanh was imprisoned by the French when they returned in force at the end of 1945. [*See* Son Ngoc Thanh.]

For the next nine years, the French fought a stubborn but losing battle to retain their grip on Indochina. In Cambodia, perhaps the most peaceable component of their Asian empire, they had to contend with guerrilla forces (the so-called Khmer Issarak, or "Free Khmers"), generally allied with their Communist-directed counterparts in Vietnam, and also with fierce but impotent opposition from Cambodia's newly installed National Assembly, dominated by the anti-French Democratic Party. [*See also* Khmer Issarak.] For a few years, the French could count on Sihanouk's cooperation; but as Sihanouk sensed, in the early 1950s, that France's days in the Far East were numbered, he launched his own Crusade for Independence, essentially a pressure campaign against the French, who finally granted Cambodia its freedom at the end of 1953.

Sihanouk moved swiftly to disband the Democratic Party, which had become increasingly antimonarchic. The Khmer Issarak, for the most part, laid down their arms, although about a thousand of them fled to political sanctuary in North Vietnam. In 1955 Sihanouk abdicated the throne and launched a national political movement, the Sangkum Reastr Niyum; for the next few years he walked a tightrope between conservative policies at home and an increasingly anti-Western foreign policy, benefiting from economic aid from the West as well as from the Communist bloc. [*See also* Sangkum Reastr Niyum.]

By the mid-1960s, the continuing war in Vietnam had begun to spill over into Cambodia. Pro-Vietnamese guerrilla bands took shape along Cambodia's borders, and the numerically insignificant Cambodian Communist Party began to capitalize on local discontent to launch a rebellion against Sihanouk's rule. By 1970, when he was overthrown by right-wing elements of his own government, Sihanouk's government controlled barely half of Cambodia's territory.

From 1970 to 1975 Cambodia was plunged into civil war, fought by the pro-American Khmer Republic on the one hand and Communist-led forces of Democratic Kampuchea on the other. American bombing, ostensibly to aid the republican forces, devastated the countryside in 1972 and 1973, but by 1974 the Khmer republican forces, led by President Lon Nol, controlled little more than the cities of Phnom Penh and Battambang. The end came in April 1975, when Democratic Kampuchean forces swept into the capital. [*See* Khmer Republic; Kampuchea, Democratic; *and* Lon Nol.]

From 1975 to early 1979, an indigenous communist regime, infused with Maoist ideology, sought to revolutionize Cambodia by destroying its somewhat rudimentary class structure and forcing the entire population either into the army or onto collective farms. An estimated one million people were assassinated or died of overwork, starvation, and disease. Although the murders were carried out under the aegis of Communist leader Pol Pot, tens of thousands of Khmer, drawn largely from the poorest rural strata of society, participated eagerly in an attempt to transform Cambodia by wiping out social forms, ideologies, and class divisions. As part of his policy of independence, and also to please his patrons in the People's Republic of China, Pol Pot initiated a full-scale war with Vietnam, beginning in 1977, at the same time purging the Communist Party of people suspected of pro-Vietnamese sympathies. [*See* Pol Pot.] The Vietnamese, in turn, welcomed refugees from Democratic Kampuchea and allowed some of them to form a government in exile. When Vietnam invaded Cambodia at the end of 1978, these people, under the leadership of Heng Samrin, were swept into power, and soon afterward they declared themselves as governing the Peoples' Republic of Kampuchea. [*See* Heng Samrin *and* Kampuchea, People's Republic of.]

The leaders of Democratic Kampuchea, in the meantime, accompanied by perhaps 30,000 armed followers, went into exile along the Thai-Cambodian border. Aided by China, Thailand, and indirectly by the United States, these forces preyed on the Vietnamese who occupied Cambodia and retained Cambodia's seat in the United Nations. In 1982 a coalition government in exile was formed, consisting of Democratic Kampuchea and Cambodians loyal to Prince Sihanouk, on the one hand, and to one of his former ministers, Son Sann, on the other. Despite international pressure from China and the ASEAN powers, Vietnam was reluctant to withdraw its forces from Cambodia or to allow the Cambodians to choose the form of government they preferred.

Throughout its recent history, then, Cambodia has had to come to terms with its location between two powerful and often antipathetic regimes, each seeking to turn it into a kind of buffer zone. Prince Sihanouk, Lon Nol, and Pol Pot sought to neutralize this situation by seeking protection from powers outside the region, particularly China and the United States. Other regimes have sought to escape the threats of one neighbor by becoming the client of the other.

TABLE 1. *Rulers of Cambodia, 1794–1984*

RULERS	DATES OF RULE
KINGS	
Ang Eng	1794–1797
Ang Chan	1797–1835
Ang Mei	1835–1848
Ang Duang	1848–1860
Norodom	1860–1904
Sisowath	1904–1927
Sisowath Monivong	1927–1941
Norodom Sihanouk	1941–1955
Norodom Suramarit	1955–1960
CIVIL HEADS OF STATE	
Norodom Sihanouk chief of state, Kingdom of Cambodia	1955–1970
Lon Nol president, Khmer Republic	1970–1975
Pol Pot president, Democratic Kampuchea	1975–1979
Heng Samrin president, People's Republic of Kampuchea	1979–

David P. Chandler, *A History of Cambodia* (1983). Michael Vickery, *Cambodia 1975–1982* (1984).

DAVID P. CHANDLER

CAMEL. The camel has served as a baggage and, to a lesser degree, riding and draft animal in several parts of Asia. The Silk Route across Central Asia depended upon camel transport, as many glazed pottery figurines of the Chinese Tang dynasty testify. More recently, camel hair has been an important export from Mongolia.

The one-humped and more heat-resistant species *(Camelus dromedarius)* is found primarily in Iran, Afghanistan, and northern India and the two-humped, cold-resistant species *(Camelus bactrianus)* in northern China and Central Asia. The hybrid of the two species, a large strong animal with greater resistance to cold than its one-humped parent, is valuable for caravan work and was once deliberately bred for this purpose.

Various pastoral peoples raise camels in arid

areas, the Baluch having the most one-humped animals and the Mongols the most two-humped. Two-humped camels, native to Iran and Central Asia and still found wild in Mongolia, once predominated as far west as the Zagros Mountains. The one-humped animal, native to Arabia, penetrated slowly eastward from Parthian times onward. In India and Pakistan it is used to draw carts, as two-humped camels do in Central Asia and China; camel-carts are unknown further west in Asia.

[*See also* Caravan *and* Silk Route.]

Richard W. Bulliet, *The Camel and the Wheel* (1975).

RICHARD W. BULLIET

CAN LAO. The Can Lao Nhan Vi Cach Mang Dang (Labor Personalist Revolutionary Party) was established during the 1950s in the early days of South Vietnam's Ngo Dinh Diem government. The personal creation and instrument of Diem's brother and adviser Ngo Dinh Nhu (1910–1963), the Can Lao movement infiltrated political, military, and trade union organizations to strengthen internal security. Through the Republican Youth Movement, which sprang from the Can Lao, the government developed the Strategic Hamlet program in an attempt to consolidate its hold over the villages. After the overthrow of the Ngo regime in November 1963, the Can Lao was disbanded and many of its leaders executed.

[*See also* Vietnam; Ngo Dinh Diem; *and* Ngo Dinh Nhu.]

Dennis Duncanson, *Government and Revolution in Vietnam* (1968). Denis Warner, *The Last Confucian* (1964).

BRUCE M. LOCKHART

CANNING, CHARLES JOHN (Lord Canning; 1812–1862), governor-general of India during the Mutiny of 1857 and first viceroy under the new Government of India Act of 1858. He was nicknamed "Clemency Canning" by a bitter European press in Bengal for his leniency during the suppression of the rebellion. As viceroy, Canning effected reforms in the army, civil administration, and finances, including a controversial income tax. Canning believed in racial tolerance and in extending the benefits of English government to Europeans and Indians alike.

[*See also* Mutiny, Indian.]

Michael Maclagan, *'Clemency' Canning* (1962).

LYNN ZASTOUPIL

CANTON (Guangzhou), foremost political and commercial center of South China for more than two thousand years. Its population in 1983 was estimated at more than three million. The city is located in the Pearl River delta of Guangdong Province. The delta, which covers about 3,000 square miles, is an intricate network of channels and streams created by the convergence of the West River with its two main tributaries, the North and East rivers, before flowing out to the South China Sea. Canton is situated on the banks of the Pearl River, a separate stream on the northern edge of the delta, about thirty miles northwest of its mouth at Humen (or the Bogue). Its accessibility by water has always been the key feature of Canton. Shallow-draft boats are able to go all the way up to the city proper, while oceangoing vessels can anchor twelve miles downstream at the suburban port of Huangpu (Whampoa).

The history of the city dates back to the Qin conquest of South China in the late third century BCE. When the Qin afterward organized the territory now called Guangdong into a commandery, its administrative center was established at or near present-day Canton. Ever since then Canton has usually, although not always, been the political capital of Guangdong. The city's Western name is derived from a corruption of the name of its province, Guangdong. Canton is known to the Chinese as Guangzhou.

Throughout its history Canton has been not only an administrative center but also a center of trade, particularly foreign trade. Its location on the extreme south coast made it the Chinese port most accessible to Southeast Asia and beyond. Foreign merchants, desiring Chinese silk, began calling at Canton as early as the Han period (202 BCE–220 CE). Arab traders, who were long dominant in Asian waters, lived there during the Tang period (618–907), when the city became the premier port of China. A mosque, said to have been built in 627 by an uncle of Muhammad, remains a prominent Canton institution to this day. The commercial fortunes of Canton, however, suffered a decline beginning in the late Tang period, when the city was sacked and its Arab residents scattered during the Huang Chao Rebellion (874–884), and continuing through the subsequent Song period (960–1279), when much of China's maritime trade moved up the coast to Quanzhou in Fujian Province.

Canton regained its commercial prominence in the sixteenth century with the arrival of the Europeans, particularly after 1557, when the Portuguese were allowed to establish a settlement 65 miles away at Macao. When the Kangxi emperor of the Qing dynasty revoked an earlier ban on foreign trade in 1684, Canton quickly came to dominate and eventually to monopolize China's trade with the maritime nations of Europe. This "Canton system" lasted until after China's defeat in the First Opium War (1839–1842). [*See* China Trade.]

Apart from its prominent role in China's international trade, Canton was also the center of a domestic regional marketing network that spread out over the entire West River basin and took in most of Guangdong as well as neighboring Guangxi Province. The core of this network was Canton and the Pearl River delta, which, with the population influx beginning in the Song period, became one of the most densely populated, most productive, and most commercialized areas in all China. Blessed with an abundant supply of water and a temperate climate, the delta regularly produced two crops of rice a year as well as a variety of cash crops, such as sugar. It was also a center of traditional handicrafts. The town of Foshan, for example, was noted for its metal casting and pottery; the county of Shunde, for its silk production.

The physical layout of the city, which reached its mature form in the Ming (1368–1644) and Qing (1644–1911) periods, expressed in spatial terms the dual nature of Canton as both a political and a commercial center. Like virtually all urban settlements in China, Canton was a walled city surrounded by a moat. All the governmental offices were housed within the city walls, while the commercial quarters generally lay outside, particularly in the Western Suburbs. The Thirteen Factories, where under the Canton system the European traders were confined when they came up from Macao for the winter trading season, were likewise outside the walls, not far from the Western Suburbs. The foreigners were specifically prohibited from entering the walled city.

According to a popular Chinese saying, "Everything new originates in Canton." Many of the critical events of modern Chinese history did indeed take place in Canton. In 1839 Commissioner Lin Zexu's confiscation and destruction of the British opium stock in Canton helped to precipitate the First Opium War. A few years later, the refusal of the Qing rulers to recognize the foreigners' new treaty right to enter the walled city of Canton similarly helped to precipitate the Second Opium War (Arrow War; 1856–1860). During this war, an Anglo-French military expedition invaded Canton and occupied the city for four years; during their occupation the British and French reclaimed a sandbar in the river off the Western Suburbs and created Shamian, which became an exclusive island settlement for foreigners. [*See* Arrow War.]

The "opening" of China as a result of the two Opium Wars was, economically, very costly to Canton. After it lost its monopoly on China's foreign trade it was quickly eclipsed as a foreign trade center both by Hong Kong, the nearby British colony, and by Shanghai, with its direct access to the vast and populous Yangtze River valley. Canton became simply one among many treaty ports. However, it retained its importance as a regional trade center. During the thirty-five years that followed the Second Opium War, Canton participated in but was not in the forefront of the limited modernization effort known as the Self-Strengthening Movement. In 1881, for example, a naval and military academy was established at Huangpu, but it closed down for lack of student interest in 1894, just as China was about to go to war with Japan.

To some Chinese, their country's defeat in the 1894–1895 Sino-Japanese War proved the bankruptcy not only of the Qing dynasty but of China's ancient monarchical system as well. Many leaders of the republican revolutionary movement, including Sun Yat-sen, were natives of the Pearl River delta, and they directed many of their activities at Canton. The single most dramatic moment of the movement was the Canton Uprising of 27 April 1911, which cost the lives of seventy-two martyrs. Although the revolt itself failed, it nevertheless paved the way for the ultimate success of the revolution only a few months later.

Canton welcomed the establishment of the republic, with its tinge of Western bourgeois liberalism. A portion of the ancient city walls, viewed now as an hindrance to the free flow of trade, was torn down immediately and replaced by broad avenues. Women won the right of representation in the provisional provincial assembly. But the triumph of the conservative president, Yuan Shikai, in Beijing in 1913 put an early end to the "liberal republic." The city then fell under the domination of a succession of warlords.

In the early 1920s, however, Canton once again became the center of revolutionary agitation. This time an alliance had been formed between the Nationalist Party of Sun Yat-sen and the fledgling Communist Party to combat the twin evils of warlordism and imperialism. In 1923 Sun gained a toehold for his movement in Canton, where for the next several years he and his collaborators were able to build up their military and political strength before confronting the rest of China. A military academy, headed by Sun's protégé Chiang Kai-shek, was once again set up at Huangpu to train officers for the new revolutionary army. Labor unions were formed to mobilize and politicize the urban masses. A peasant movement institute, led at one time by Mao Zedong, was created to teach organizers how to work in rural villages.

On 23 June 1925, while these preparatory activities were underway, the aroused masses of Canton staged a huge protest parade against the British for anti-Chinese atrocities committed a month earlier in Shanghai. As the chanting protesters marched by the Anglo-French concession on Shamian, they were fired upon by apprehensive European soldiers. More than fifty demonstraters were killed. These killings prompted a retaliatory year-long strike/boycott against the British in Canton and Hong Kong, which was a highpoint of Chinese anti-imperialism.

The alliance between the Nationalists and the Communists, which had not been without its strains while they were in Canton, broke down soon after their departure on the Northern Expedition in July 1926. When Chiang Kai-shek turned against his allies in 1927, the Communists fought back by launching a city-wide revolt in Canton. The "Canton Commune" uprising in December 1927, however, was crushed by forces loyal to Chiang. During the insurrection and in the reign of terror that followed, as many as five thousand Communists and suspected Communists lost their lives.

The victorious Nationalists moved their capital to Nanjing. Canton, while no longer the political vortex of China, nevertheless prospered during the relative peace of the Nanjing decade (1927–1937). In 1936, for example, the railroad between Canton and Wuhan was completed, thus offering for the first time a means of cheap and rapid communication with the rest of the country. But no sooner was the railroad finished than it was disrupted by the onset of the second war with Japan. The Japanese overran Canton in October 1938 and occupied it until the end of the war in August 1945, when Nationalist rule was restored. Canton was not much involved in the subsequent civil war between the Nationalists and the Communists, which took place far to the north. Soon triumphant in the struggle, the Communists rolled into Canton, virtually unopposed, in October 1949.

Under the Communists Canton has been transformed from essentially a commercial city into an industrial city as well. Its principal modern industries, most of them initiated since 1949, include sugar refining, newsprint manufacturing, cement, shipbuilding, and chemicals. Although still overshadowed by Hong Kong, it has recovered some of its importance as a center of foreign trade. Since 1957 it has been the site of the semiannual China trade fair, which, reminiscent of the days of the Canton system, attracts buyers and sellers from all over the world.

Canton, perhaps because of its long history of cultural intermingling with the various non-Han peoples along China's southern frontier, is almost a world apart from the rest of the country. It has, for example, its own dialect of spoken Chinese (Cantonese), which is unintelligible to the non-Cantonese. Its cuisine is famous throughout China; "to eat in Canton" has traditionally been regarded as one of the four great aspirations of life. Its people are reputed to be quick and calculating, adventurous and receptive to novelty. Canton is the ancestral home of many overseas Chinese who migrated abroad in great numbers in the nineteenth century. In part because of the continuing ties with those Overseas Chinese, but also because of the proximity of British Hong Kong, Canton is the most westernized of China's cities. It may still be true that "everything new originates in Canton."

Edward J. M. Rhoads, *China's Republican Revolution: The Case of Kwangtung, 1895–1913* (1975). Theodore Shabad, *China's Changing Map: National and Regional Development, 1949–1971* (rev. ed., 1972). Ezra F. Vogel, *Canton under Communism: Programs and Politics in a Provincial Capital, 1949–1968* (1696). Frederic Wakeman, Jr., *Strangers at the Gate: Social Disorder in South China, 1839–1861* (1966). EDWARD J. M. RHOADS

CAN VUONG. A response to the July 1885 edict of Vietmanese emperor Ham Nghi and his regent Ton That Thuyet, the Can Vuong ("loyalty to the king") movement was a series of local anti-French uprisings in Tonkin and Annam, particularly in the four provinces of Thanh Hoa, Nghe An, Ha Tinh, and Quang Binh. While most local movements were led by members of the scholar-gentry class, including Phan Dinh Phung, other figures, such as De Tham, emerged as well. The movements were suppressed by 1896, but according to David Marr, they "provided crucial moral and spiritual continuity to the long struggle against [the French]."

[*See also* Vietnam; Ham Nghi; Ton That Thuyet; Phan Dinh Phung; *and* De Tham.]

David Marr, *Vietnamese Anticolonialism 1885–1925* (1971). Nguyen Phut Tan, *A Modern History of Vietnam 1802–1954* (1964).

BRUCE M. LOCKHART

CAO BA QUAT (1808–1855), well-known poet who was involved in an abortive revolt against Vietnam's Nguyen dynasty. Although he was a brilliant scholar known for his satirical poetry, Cao Ba Quat was never able to pass the highest level of examinations. His skepticism and frustration led him to make criticisms of Vietnam's imperial institutions and values, a tendency that caused him to be frequently transferred from post to post. In 1854 he decided to support a Le claimant to the throne in the Locust Rebellion. The revolt was quickly suppressed, and Cao Ba Quat was executed.

[*See also* Le Dynasties *and* Locust Rebellion.]

Alexander Woodside, *Vietnam and the Chinese Model* (1971).

BRUCE M. LOCKHART

CAO CAO (150–220), renowned Chinese general and poet at the end of the Latter Han dynasty (25–220) and the beginning of the Three Kingdoms period (220–265). After helping to suppress the Yellow Turban revolts (184–215), Cao Cao became the military dictator of North China and started the process that was to culminate in the founding of the Wei dynasty (220–265) by his descendants. The many scholars he sponsored to legitimize his rule began the revival of Daoist and Legalist philosophy. After the fall of Wei, Cao Cao became a great villain in Chinese legend.

[*See also* Three Kingdoms.]

Étienne Balazs, *Chinese Civilization and Bureaucracy: Variations on a Theme,* translated by H. M. Wright, edited by Arthur F. Wright (1964).

JOHN A. RAPP

CAO DAI, sect founded in Saigon in 1925, combining elements of Daoism and Confucianism with veneration of Western religious figures such as Jesus and Muhammad. Essentially pro-Japanese during World War II, the Cao Dai joined the Viet Minh against the French in 1945. They were later coerced into cooperation with the French, however, and alternated between fighting the Communist-led forces and maintaining a more peaceful neutrality. The Cao Dai joined the Hoa Hao in opposing the Ngo Dinh Diem government but were defeated in early 1956. The sect continued to enjoy popular support, however, particularly in the Mekong Delta province of Tay Ninh, site of the Cao Dai Holy See.

[*See also* Viet Minh; Hoa Hao; *and* Ngo Dinh Diem.]

Victor Oliver, *Caodai Spiritism: A Study of Religion in Vietnamese Society* (1976). Jayne Werner, *Peasant Politics and Religious Sectarianism: Peasant and Priest in the Cao Dai in Vietnam* (1981).

BRUCE M. LOCKHART

CAO KUN (1862–1938), prominent militarist of the warlord era in China. A leading officer in Yuan Shikai's Beiyang Army, Cao became military governor of Zhili Province after Yuan died. At first he supported Duan Qirui's policy of unifying the country by force, but later came to oppose Duan and his Anhui clique. When Feng Guozhang died, Cao became the leader of the Zhili clique, although Cao's subordinate Wu Peifu was the effective military head of the group. In 1923, through massive bribery, Cao was elected president of China. When Feng Yuxiang seized Beijing in 1924, he forced Cao to resign the presidency. Cao was held under house arrest until 1926, after which he retired.

[*See also* Duan Qirui *and* Warlord Cliques.]

Andrew J. Nathan, *Peking Politics 1918–1923: Factionalism and the Failure of Constitutionalism* (1976).

JAMES E. SHERIDAN

CAO XUEQIN (1715?–1763?), author of the Chinese novel *Honglou meng* (*A Dream of Red Mansions;* often translated as *The Dream of the Red Chamber*), also known as *Shitou ji (The Story of the Stone).* Although born into a wealthy family, financial reverses caused Cao to be living in poverty when he wrote his famous novel. *Honglou meng* consists of 120 chapters, of which only chapters 1 through 80 are agreed to be Cao's. The novel is the richly detailed, psychologically vivid story of the large aristocratic Jia clan and centers on the loves and quarrels of its young scion, Jia Baoyu, and his two female cousins, Lin Daiyu and Xue Baochai. Otherwordly elements frame and recur in this earthly story. Considered the greatest of the traditional Chinese novels, *Honglou meng* has a following on all levels of society and has been retold often. Its literary quality and its textual and biographical problems have attracted much scholarship.

[*See also* Chinese Literature.]

Cao Xueqin, *The Story of the Stone,* translated by David Hawkes and John Minford (1973–1978). Na

Tsung Shun, *Studies on Dream of the Red Chamber: A Selected and Classified Bibliography* (1979; supplement, 1981).
SHAN CHOU

CARAVAN, the primary mode of commercial communication throughout Iran, Afghanistan, and Central Asia in premodern times, when sparse settlement, arid conditions, and the near absence of navigable rivers over most of this broad region forced merchants and travelers to travel overland in sizable groups. Carts were occasionally used in Central Asia and northern China, but pack animals were usually more economical as well as more flexible in the types of terrain and quality of roads they could traverse.

Camels were the dominant pack animal, carrying an average load of perhaps five hundred pounds, although estimates vary. A day's march for a camel train was about twenty miles. Overnight stops were made in or near villages, at walled caravansaries maintained by governments, or simply beside the track. Mules were often used in mountainous areas and yaks or dzos in the high mountains bordering Tibet.

Trans-Asian caravan trading along the Silk Route flourished, with intermittent political disruption, from the Parthian period (third century BCE to third century CE) to about 1600. Subsequently, European trading companies gained sufficient control of ocean trading to undermine the more expensive inland routes, and caravan trading greatly decreased in both volume and importance. This significantly altered the political and historical importance of the trading cities in and near Central Asia.

[*See also* Camel.]

Owen Lattimore, *The Desert Road to Turkestan* (1928). Edward H. Schafer, *The Golden Peaches of Samarkand* (1963).
RICHARD W. BULLIET

CAREY, WILLIAM (1761–1834), Baptist missionary to India, regarded as one of the founders of British and American Protestant missions in India. A shoemaker in Northamptonshire, England, he joined the Baptist church and became convinced that he should go to India as a missionary. Such activity was banned in territories controlled by the British, so after he arrived in 1793 he made his living as an indigo planter, and then in 1799 moved to Serampore, a small Dutch settlement outside Calcutta. There he established the first college in India with a Western-style curriculum, and began translating the Bible into many Indian languages and compiling dictionaries and grammars. In 1801 he became professor of Sanskrit at Fort William College, the institution established by the East India Company for the education of its young British officials.

AINSLIE T. EMBREE

CARPETS are knotted or pile fabrics made of wool, cotton, silk, goat hair, or camel hair that has been prepared, spun, and wound. The foundation of the carpet is the vertically strung warp, into which are woven horizontal wefts alternating with rows of knots, forming the pile. The asymmetrical Persian or Senneh knot (from what is now the town of Sanandaj) is considered typical of carpets woven in Persia, India, and Turkestan, but the symmetrical Turkish or Gordes knot, typical of carpets woven in Turkey, the Caucasus, and the Kurdish area of northwestern Iran, also occurs in Persian carpets. Correctly, *carpet* refers to larger pieces, while *rug* should be used for pieces measuring up to two hundred by three hundred centimeters, but in fact the terms are often used interchangeably.

Carpets have a long tradition in the Near East and Central Asia, for they play the role of furniture in a furnitureless society. The earliest known knotted carpet was discovered in the tomb of a local prince at Pazyryk in the Altai Mountains of Central Asia. On archaeological grounds the tomb is dated from the fourth century BCE, and on stylistic grounds the carpet is assigned to the Persian Achaemenid empire. Even at this early date, it exhibits remarkable proficiency in design and technique, with thirty-six hundred Turkish knots per square decimeter.

An enormous gap in evidence follows this unique specimen, for the oldest dated Persian carpets come from the first half of the sixteenth century. Their proficiency and expertise presuppose a long tradition, for which miniature painting gives us a general idea of the evolution from geometric patterns to arabesque and floral patterns during the fourteenth and fifteenth centuries. The successive Safavid capitals at Tabriz, Qazvin, and Isfahan had state manufactories, and other cities such as Kashan had important local industries, but the dearth of documented examples makes localization of pieces impossible. Instead, these carpets can be classified only by motif: hunting, vase, medallion, compartment, and garden carpets.

The economic importance of carpet manufacture to the Safavid state can be seen in the streamlining of the industry in the first half of the seventeenth

FIGURE 1. *Kazakh Carpet.* Nineteenth-century wool carpet with allover geometrical pattern of star-shaped polygons and compartments of irregular shapes adorned with latch-hooks. 188 cm. × 162.5 cm.

century. Carpets were produced in pairs, patterns limited to about a dozen basic systems, figures reduced, and lines coarsened. Nevertheless, this export ware could still achieve an astonishing level of technical sophistication, as seen in the group of about 230 "Polish" carpets that came into the possession of European courts or churches as ambassadorial gifts or on order. Two bear the arms of the Polish king Sigismund Vasa III, who is known to have commissioned silk carpets from Kashan. At this time Mughal rulers in India developed a taste for Persian art and recruited craftsmen to set up workshops producing carpets in Persian style, but with different motifs such as mythological beasts and naturalistic flowers.

The sixteenth and seventeenth centuries were the heyday for state production of carpets in Iran and India. Declining economic prosperity in Iran brought with it a simplification of patterns in the eighteenth century tempered by a revival of older traditions in the nineteenth.

Alongside these state-manufactured carpets, nomads also produced carpets, usually woven on smaller, portable looms. They served as tent furnishings, and because they were subjected to hard daily wear, very few pre-nineteenth-century specimens survive, except in the unpublished collection in the Ethnographic Museum in Leningrad. Ancient patterns probably persisted. In contrast to state-sponsored carpets woven with silk and metallic yarns, nomadic carpets are prized for their glossy wool and vegetable dyes.

[*See also* Weaving.]

Kurt Erdmann, *Oriental Carpets,* translated by C. G. Ellis (1962; reprint, 1976). S. I. Rudenko, *Frozen Tombs of Siberia,* translated by M. W. Thompson (1970). "Bisāṭ," in the supplement to *The Encyclopaedia of Islam* (new ed., 1960–).

SHEILA S. BLAIR

CASPIAN SEA, the largest inland sea in the world (143,500 square miles), located wholly within the USSR except for the southern coast, which borders Iran. The sea has been declining in level, particularly due to heavier usage of water from the Volga River, and the emerging shallows, spits, and sandbanks have become major obstacles to shipping, especially around the ports. Important for water transport and fish (including the sturgeon, the source of caviar), the Caspian plays a vital role in the economy of the USSR.

MICHAEL BONINE

CASTE. Portuguese seafarers traveling to India in the late fifteenth century first used the term *casta* ("genera, breed, race, lineage") to describe the society they found there. *Caste* is still used to designate the system of social stratification in South Asia. Commonly defined as corporate groups formed through descent and marriage, most castes are endogamous and are associated with hereditary "traditional" occupations. A caste is part of a system, ranked with respect to other castes in a hierarchy. Social relations among individuals are governed by the relative rankings of their castes.

The complexity and diversity of caste in South Asia is clear from the striking variation in scholarly models of the origin and evolution of the caste system. One or another explanatory factor can be emphasized: racial diversity; the interaction between invaders, settled agriculturalists, and tribal people; the development of complementary occupational specializations; the fission and fusion of diverse endogamous groups; and the elaboration of a Hindu theology based on relative degrees of purity and pollution.

There is little evidence regarding caste in South Asia's earliest civilization, which flourished in the Indus Valley from approximately 3000 to 1700 BCE. This urban, literate, and trading civilization left extensive archaeological remains, but its ideographic script still has not been deciphered definitively. Whether its language belonged to the Indo-Aryan, Dravidian, or yet another language family is unknown. Neither do we know whether the Indus Valley rulers were kings or priests, nor whether caste or class produced the stratification evident from the distinctive gradations of urban residences. The Indus Valley civilization declined shortly before the Aryans entered the subcontinent from the northwest, about 1500 BCE. The relationship between the Indus Valley and later Aryan civilizations remains conjectural. [*See* Indus Valley Civilization.]

At first Aryans were neither literate nor urban, but eventually they produced the Vedas, Sanskrit religious poems written down around 1200 to 1000 BCE. Vedic texts refer to two classes of people, the Aryans and the indigenous conquered people termed *dasa* (slaves, or inferiors). There is only one Vedic reference to the four *varnas* or caste categories, so prominent in the later Hindu model of caste. It tells of the sacrificial division of Purusha, the primeval man, into the four *varnas*: from his mouth came the brahmans (Sanskrit, *brahmanas*), or priests; from his arms the *kshatriyas*, or warrior rulers; from his thighs the *vaishyas*, or landowners and merchants; and from his feet the *shudras*, or artisans and servants. The so-called fifth *varna*, the Untouchables, those at the bottom of the hierarchy, was not mentioned, nor were the many thousands of named endogamous groups (*jatis*) evident in later times. A given *jati* (Hindi for "descent group, breed, lineage") sometimes cannot even be assigned to one of the four *varnas*, so far has empirical reality diverged from the classical model.

The early Sanskrit religious texts are biased sources for the evolution of the caste system. Their brahman authors were members of the conquering class, at the top of the ritual hierarchy they described. Initially limited to northern India, the texts cannot be checked against archaeological evidence until the Aryans began building cities of durable materials, some thousand years after their arrival. Thus, the numbers of indigenous people, their social structure and beliefs, and the nature of their interaction with the Aryans remain unknown.

From about the sixth century BCE, state building and settled agriculture produced a complex social structure in the North Indian heartland. Rising population density, coupled with the use of the plow and draft animals, led to male dominance of agricultural productivity and to stratification based on the use of hired or hereditary laborers. Among the higher castes women were relegated strictly to domestic production; control of women's marriages and procreation maintained caste boundaries and led to marriages at an early age. Elaborate kinship regulations developed, with some regional variations. In the North marriages between closely related persons and residents of the same village were prohibited, while in the South specified relatives were preferred partners and village endogamy was permitted. Such variations resulted in differences in the size and geographic range of kinship and caste groups in the subcontinent.

Economic interdependence at the village level was a basic characteristic of the social system. The concept of the dominant caste was developed to emphasize that those who control the land and its produce, whether or not they are brahmans, have political power in the local and regional context. Artisan and labor caste families worked for dominant caste families, often from generation to generation, but there were regional differences in the way occupational groups related to each other, were ranked with respect to one another, and were assigned to one of the all-India *varnas*. The normative and behavioral ranking systems, termed attributional and interactional, often produced different results when applied to the same set of local castes. There are also historical instances of a caste changing its local ranking over time.

The caste system has not prevented either individuals or groups from changing their status. Individuals within a caste can vary greatly in socioeconomic status. Hypergamous marriages, within and between castes, allow family rankings to rise and fall. Dowry and bride-price systems have changed over time, reflecting changes in occupational statuses and in the work done by women of various castes. In urban centers, linguistic and social heterogeneity have always made it difficult to identify people by caste or to establish any single ranking system; individual achievement has played a large role in urban stratification systems.

Corporate groups have also been able to change ranking. Through "sanskritization," or the emulation of Brahmanical practices, some castes have succeeded in attaining a higher rank in their locales. In other cases, upwardly mobile castes have emulated a regional dominant caste or worked through caste associations with modern organizational structures and goals. The marriage networks that link caste fellows as kinsmen provide horizontal alignments, spreading across many villages in North India. Such groups of kinsmen could build supralocal caste associations to carry out religious or social reform movements or to mobilize support for a political party.

In the countryside, where corporate group membership most strongly determined residential and occupational choices and regulated social intercourse, vertical alignments across caste boundaries provided the more significant economic and political linkages within villages. These vertical alignments structured politics, as rival dominant caste leaders mobilized their employees of diverse castes against each other. Political and economic pressures could change the supposedly hereditary ties between landholding families and artisan or labor families. A potter or washerman seeking better conditions might change employers, migrate to another village or town, or work as an agricultural laborer. The leatherworkers and sweepers or scavengers were poorest and most dependent. Considered "untouchable" because of their polluting traditional occupations, they were usually segregated in a separate quarter of the village; most worked as landless laborers. When someone violated the social norms, sanctions could be imposed by an employer or by one's own caste. Sanctions ranged from economic boycott to, in extreme cases, outcasting.

Recent scholarly debate has centered on the ideology of caste. A traditional perspective grounds the system in Hindu ideology, where members of different castes are unequal by birth and have differential capacities. Persons carry out the *dharma*, or duty, ascribed by caste, being reborn in successively higher ranks and finally attaining salvation, or freedom from the cycle of birth and rebirth. Men of the twice-born castes (the first three *varnas*) had privileges denied to those of lesser capacities (*shudras*, Untouchables, and women of all castes), such as studying the Vedas. It was a Hindu king's duty to maintain social order by enforcing legal rights and disabilities according to caste and gender. Louis Dumont's stimulating *Homo Hierarchicus* (1970) stresses the opposing principles of purity and pollution and the "encompassing" supremacy of the brahman ritual specialists over the *kshatriya* secular rulers in the hierarchy. From this perspective, caste cannot be fully present in non-Hindu groups and societies. Another perspective derives caste from the organization of royal rituals of kingship (Hocart, 1950), emphasizing the mediation of the ruler through court and temple institutions and through the castes controlling the rural economy.

An ethnosociological perspective postulates

widely shared South Asian cultural assumptions regarding the differentiation of all living beings into genera, or castes, each of which possesses a defining code of conduct carried in its bodily substance. Transmitted by descent within *jatis,* this coded substance is continually transformed by ritual performances and by everyday interaction with others. This understanding of caste applies across religions and helps explain the regional, religious, and historical variants in South Asian civilization.

Often viewed as uniformly rigid and inflexible, the local and decentralized nature of the caste system has allowed it to play a major adaptive and integrative function throughout South Asian history. Historical variations and discontinuities in caste ideology and behavior can be documented from the sixth century BCE, with the availability of both archaeological and written sources and their extension to regions beyond the northwestern Ganges Plain. Jainism and Buddhism, arising at that time, have often been interpreted as challenges to the caste system. Both new religions denied the authority of the Vedas, the caste system, and brahmans; both, however, retained some caste practices. Jainism's emphasis on nonviolence effectively restricted its followers to urban, mercantile occupations. Those Jains who migrated farthest from their western Indian homeland adapted their kinship and marriage regulations to approximate those of their new neighbors, and there are more than one hundred recognized endogamous groups, or castes, within Jainism.

Buddhism, perhaps originally a *kshatriya*-based revolt against corrupt Brahmanism, was not fundamentally opposed to a social system valuing status by birth; it only made that status irrelevant to the state and to the attainment of salvation. Long dominant in what are today Pakistan, Nepal, Bangladesh, and Sri Lanka, Buddhism remains important in Nepal and along the foothills of the Himalayas, and it is still dominant in Sri Lanka. With fewer castes, little elaboration of subcastes, and no indigenous brahmans, Sri Lanka's agrarian system was dominated by populous, high-ranking *shudra* castes. Caste in Sir Lanka is undeniably weaker than in India, but there are endogamous, communal groups marked by functional differentiation and restrictions on social intercourse. Buddhist sects in Sri Lanka frequently have been organized with reference to caste. Successive foreign and Christian rulers—Portuguese, Dutch, and British—over much of the island minimally affected and sometimes reinforced the caste system.

In South India, the Sangam poems in Tamil, oldest of the four Dravidian languages, date from the seventh to ninth centuries. They do not reveal an elaborate caste system, but they show a concern with pollution. Burton Stein's path-breaking delineation of the agrarian organization of the Tamil-speaking macroregion from the ninth to the twelfth century (1980) has pointed to the alliance between rural brahmans and powerful peasants of the *shudra varna* in villages. The narrower range of South Indian kinship systems reinforced the local, autonomous nature of these villages, where the Sanskritic, all-India learned tradition mingled with the regional vernacular tradition.

By the twelfth century, regional vernaculars reflected fully developed cultures throughout the South Asian subcontinent. Regional elite groups literate in both Sanskrit and the vernacular languages transmitted the Sanskritic culture and changed it in the process. New castes and classes developed and new institutions became important in some regions but not in others. In the Dravidian-speaking South, the concept of divine kingship led to the assumption of major roles by state and temple institutions in structuring relationships among castes, reinforcing the brahman–nonbrahman alliance. This model has been utilized to analyze historical alliances between high-ranking peasant castes in parts of Sri Lanka as well, where Tamils from South India settled from about 1200 CE.

Sectarian religious movements in the subcontinent also had a major impact on regional social structure. While the leaders of the Hindu sectarian movements always acknowledged the authority of the Vedas, they developed their own scriptures, systems of cosmological and philosophical thought, ways of representing the divine, and external signs for members. The Hindu devotional *bhakti* movements elevated the path of devotion as a way to salvation, even putting it above the earlier paths of knowledge and action (*jnana* and *karma*). While their sociohistorical context is seldom clear, early *bhakti* texts are commonly interpreted as products of lower-caste upward mobility movements, critical of brahman priests and caste-ascribed occupations and status. *Bhakti* movements helped incorporate lower-caste and tribal people into the Hindu social order. Non-Hindu sects also formed. Many of these explicitly opposed the Vedas, the brahmans, and the caste system, yet they retained significant elements of caste belief and behavior: the Lingayats in the Kannada-speaking area from the twelfth century and the Sikhs in the Punjab from the sixteenth century are good examples.

In the medieval period, Muslim invaders from the northwest took power in parts of the subcontinent. In medieval Bengal, the displacement of Hindu kings by Muslim conquerors seems to have produced more elaborate rankings through marriage among high-caste Hindus. But in Rajasthan in the west, Muslims and Rajputs shared a warrior culture, and their marriages, including some intermarriages, cemented political alliances. In many regions, the new rulers designated dominant caste lineages responsible for the collection of land revenue or the provision of military forces, thus linking village head men to the state bureaucracy through the landholding castes.

Urban clerical and trading castes also adapted themselves to the Muslim rulers. For example, the Kayasthas of North India learned Persian and Urdu and became closely associated with the Mughal emperors, who extended their rule from Delhi in the sixteenth and seventeenth centuries. Kayasthas who migrated to Hyderabad with the Mughals have been studied over a two-hundred-year period, and the changes in their occupations, strategies of marriage and inheritance, and self-concept show successive adaptations to retain control of economic resources.

Muslim rulers adopted existing social practices to reinforce their political control, entering into hypergamous marriages with the daughters of Rajput rulers and utilizing landholding and record-keeping castes to maintain territorial control. Earlier South Asian kings had established state patronage of learning, the arts, and religion, and the Muslim rulers continued to patronize scholars, artists, and religious specialists of diverse backgrounds. Muslim rulers (and after them the British to an even greater extent) also enforced Hindu law in particular contexts.

Islam provides no ideological or ritual basis for caste ranking, although castelike behaviors in commensal and marital relations exist among South Asian Muslims. Even among descendants of those Muslims who came from Arabia, Iran, Turkey, and Central Asia, marriage networks are based on national origin or class status. Most Muslims in the subcontinent converted from Hinduism, however, and family and caste customs have continued to determine many aspects of life among these Muslims. Converts to Islam frequently came from lower castes, and, like later converts to Christianity, they often proved unable to leave their traditional village occupations.

The British East India Company succeeded the Mughals as political rulers in most of the subcontinent from the mid-eighteenth century, and the effect of subsequent British colonial rule on the caste system was far-reaching. Individuals and groups aligned themselves with the company or its rivals throughout India, leading to changes in regional power structures and providing opportunities for social mobility. As a territorial ruler, the company administered the land revenue and judicial systems. British officials displaced or strengthened dominant castes in the countryside as they made revenue settlements and administered justice.

Scholarly employees of the company translated Sanskrit and Persian texts and wrote about the coherent Brahmanical model of the caste system. Missionaries, not so appreciative of the indigenous civilization, criticized what they perceived as brahman dominance and exploitation of other castes. The most important effect, however, came from the efforts of administrators to collect and publish information classifying groups for administrative purposes. Not only Hindu corporate groups but also Muslim, Sikh, Christian, and other groups were seen as autonomous and self-sufficient for certain purposes. As British judicial officials standardized and applied Brahmanical law, they substantially increased its influence, although they recognized regional and caste variations. Even the taking of the decennial censuses from 1871 strengthened the caste system, as the government of India initially described castes and then listed them in ranked order. This provoked controversy and protests from newly organized caste associations. While the system of Western education developed in the subcontinent from 1839 introduced a small indigenous elite to values antithetical to those of the caste system, the overall effect of British rule was to institutionalize rather than weaken the caste system.

After 1947 the independent governments of South Asia all made changes in the caste system by legislation. Pakistan, an Islamic theocracy, does not recognize caste. India, a parliamentary democracy with universal franchise, has a constitution that abolishes Untouchability and prohibits discrimination based on caste. India also has replaced particularistic caste codes by a uniform Hindu code and has constituted lists of disadvantaged castes and tribes (known as "scheduled castes") to whom economic and social resources are granted in compensation for past discrimination. Caste continues to play a role in the arrangement of marriages, but its influence in public life is diminishing throughout the subcontinent.

[*See also* Bhakti; Brahman; Buddhism: An Overview; Hinduism; Kayasth; Kshatriya; Shudra; Vaishya; *and* Untouchability.]

Imtiaz Ahmad, ed., *Caste and Social Stratification Among the Muslims* (1973). Louis Dumont, *Homo Hierarchicus* (1970). A. M. Hocart, *Caste: A Comparative Study* (1950). Iravati Karve, *Kinship Organization in India* (1965). Tom G. Kessinger, *Vilyatpur 1848–1968: Social and Economic Change in an Indian Village* (1974). Karen I. Leonard, *Social History of an Indian Caste: The Kayasths of Hyderabad* (1978). Owen Lynch, *The Politics of Untouchability* (1969). Dennis G. McGilvray, ed., *Caste Ideology and Interaction* (1982). McKim Marriott and Ronald Inden, "Caste Systems," in *The New Encyclopaedia Brittanica* (1985), vol. 27, pp. 982–991. Bryce Ryan, *Caste in Modern Ceylon: The Sinhalese System in Transition* (1953). Milton Singer and Bernard S. Cohn, eds., *Structure and Change in Indian Society* (1968). Burton Stein, *Peasant State and Society in Medieval South India* (1980). Romila Thapar, *Ancient Indian Social History* (1978). KAREN LEONARD

CASTIGLIONE, GIUSEPPE (known to the Chinese as Lang Shining; 1688–1766), famous Jesuit, unique for the use of his artistic talent in the service of the China Mission. He was born in Milan and entered the Society of Jesus, in which he was ordained as a brother. He arrived in China in 1715 and was almost immediately assigned to the court at Beijing, where he served continuously for more than fifty years until his death. Although an Italian, he was closely affiliated with the Portuguese Jesuits.

Most of Castiglione's service was under the Qianlong emperor, who took a liking to him and delighted in the many court scenes that he so realistically painted. Castiglione painted in a hybrid style that blended European naturalism with Chinese techniques. The range of his subject matter included horses, imperial concubines, and the Qianlong emperor himself. Nevertheless, his paintings remained largely curiosity pieces because of their negligible influence upon Chinese painters. Castiglione also had talents as an architect and designed as well as oversaw the construction of a pleasure house in the garden of the Summer Palace (Yuanmingyuan), located just outside of Beijing. Unfortunately, this palace was destroyed by British soldiers in 1860, although it was later rebuilt by Empress Dowager Cixi at the end of the nineteenth century. Although Castiglione had limited success in promoting Christianity in China, he did remain in imperial favor, and on his seventieth birthday the Qianlong emperor presented him with a number of gifts to mark the occasion.

[*See also* Jesuits: Jesuits in China; *and* Qianlong Emperor.]

George Robert Loehr, *Giuseppe Castiglione* (1940).

DAVID E. MUNGELLO

CATHAY, or Catai, is the medieval name of China and more particularly of northern China (the southern region being called "Mangi") used by the countries of Central and West Asia. Europe then adopted this name for the northeasternmost areas of Asia reached by land. *Catai* represents the name *Khitan*, an Altaic, seminomadic people of southern Manchuria who founded the Liao dynasty in 907 and were defeated by the Jurchen Jin in 1125. The name *Khitai (Khitan)* came into Russian and Greek through Turkish, and through a complicated linguistic transformation became *Catai* and *Cathay* in Western Europe.

It was as late as 1600 that China, reached from Europe by the sea route, and Cathay, reached by land, were discovered to be the same land. The early Jesuit missionary Matteo Ricci, who had sailed to China and lived there for years, had decided on the identity of the two. Yet there were those who still thought that the land of Cathay described by medieval European accounts was a Christian kingdom distinct from China. Ricci requested that someone be sent by land from India to Cathay. The Jesuit Bento de Goes, traveling eastward from the Near East (1605–1607), sent word from Suzhou in Gansu that he had looked for Cathay and found China. Goes died without meeting Ricci; however, his journey proved that China and Cathay were one.

[*See also* Khitan.]

Pasquale M. d'Elia, ed., *Fonti Ricciani,* vol. 2 (1942), pp. 391–445. Paul Pelliot, *Notes on Marco Polo,* vol. 1 (1959), pp. 216–229. THEODORE NICHOLAS FOSS

CATHOLICISM IN THE PHILIPPINES. The Roman Catholic church is the major institutional force shaping the Philippine nation. Even today, 84 percent of Filipinos consider themselves Catholics, although many are poorly instructed in their religion, particularly because of the lack of priests in the Philippines. Under the Spanish regime, church and state were closely united. All ecclesiastical personnel were appointed by the government, which paid for the transportation of missionaries and supported the missions. But the real power was with the church, for until the last half of the nineteenth century the missionaries were almost the only Spaniards outside Manila, and they became everything from teachers to architects to military leaders.

The early missionaries attempted to gather the scattered clans into towns in order to evangelize more efficiently, but since most Filipinos practiced subsistence agriculture, the plan was not a success. Eventually the priest resided in the town with the main church, periodically visiting the outlying villages. Conversion of the lowland Filipinos was accomplished within two generations, but the mountain peoples were reached only gradually, some only in this century. The disorganized traditional religions of all Filipinos but the Muslims of the south offered little overt resistance to Christianity. Converts were also persuaded by their perception of the missionaries as the defenders of the Filipinos against Spanish abuses and exactions and as leaders against the Muslim slaving raids.

The history of the church may be broken down into the following periods: (1) 1570–1650 (earlier in Luzon)—evangelization of lowlanders; (2) 1650–1770—established Catholicism, highly hispanized in Manila, with ordination of Filipino priests in modest numbers; village Catholicism strongly organized around the Spanish priest; (3) 1768–1830—expulsion of Jesuits; precipitous decrease in friars; massive and irresponsible ordination of Filipino priests; resultant collapse of church primary-school system and religious instruction; (4) 1830–1902—return of Spanish missionaries and subjection of Filipino priests; antifriar character of the nationalist movement and revolution, culminating in the schism led by Friar Gregorio Aglipay y Labayan in 1902; (5) 1898–1925—the church in chaos; departure of most Spaniards; massive lack of clergy; rejection by church of modernizing society; (6) 1925–1941—revitalization of church by new missionaries; growth of better-prepared but still Hispanic Filipino clergy and bishops; (7) 1945–1972—recovery from war; greatly expanded school system at upper levels; militant Catholic laity; involvement of priests, sisters, committed laymen in social action; political action of bishops; and growing filipinization.

During the early years of martial law, which President Ferdinand E. Marcos declared in 1972, the largely conservative episcopal hierarchy was opposed by a militant anti-Marcos minority among the bishops, most of the non-Hispanic religious orders of men and women, and by the militant Catholic laity. In the last years of the Marcos regime the different groups within the church united to form the main nucleus of opposition able to withstand the government. A small but significant minority, including priests and sisters, especially in depressed areas, allied themselves with the Communist-controlled National Democratic Front or even with the New People's Army, while a significant minority of bishops, though they were not pro-Marcos, remained passive or concerned about government retaliation against church institutions.

[*See also* Friars; Burgos, Jose; Cavite Mutiny; Aglipay y Labayan, Gregorio; *and* Philippine Independent Church.]

Gerald H. Anderson, ed., *Studies in Philippine Church History* (1969). H. de la Costa, *The Jesuits in the Philippines, 1581–1768* (1961). Felix Casalmo (pseud.), *The Vision of a New Society* (1980). Pablo Fernández, *History of the Church in the Philippines (1565–1898)* (1979). John L. Phelan, *The Hispanization of the Philippines* (1959). John N. Schumacher, *Readings in Philippine Church History* (1979) and *The Revolutionary Clergy* (1981).

JOHN N. SCHUMACHER, S.J.

CATTANEO, LAZZARO (known to the Chinese as Guo Zhujing; 1560–1640), one of the founders of the Jesuit mission in China. Cattaneo's remarkable talents were overshadowed by those of his near-contemporary, Matteo Ricci. Born in Sarzana, Tuscany (now part of Italy), Cattaneo was the son of an old and noble family. He entered the novitiate at Rome, served in Goa and on the Malabar Coast, and reached Macao in 1593. Cattaneo had remarkable linguistic talents, particularly an ear for tonal variations. Together with Ricci and Zhong Mingren, he produced a Chinese (Mandarin) vocabulary organized according to a European alphabet and the five Chinese tones. Cattaneo's greatest contribution to the China Mission was in the important role he played in the conversion to Christianity of two eminent scholar-officials, Xu Guangqi and Li Zhizao. He composed a number of works in both Chinese and European languages. He died in Hangzhou at the age of eighty.

[*See also* Xu Guangqi *and* Jesuits: Jesuits in China.]

L. Carrington Goodrich, "Lazzaro Cattaneo," in *Dictionary of Ming Biography*, edited by L. Carrington Goodrich and Chaoying Fang (1976), pp. 31–33.

DAVID E. MUNGELLO

CAVITE MUTINY (1872), a local revolt against Spanish rule in the arsenal across the bay from Manila, Philippines. Magnified into a national revolution by the Spanish governor, the Cavite Mutiny was a turning point in the evolution of Filipino national consciousness toward the goal of independence. During the short period of liberalism and reforms that occurred in Manila after the 1868 revolution in Spain, Filipino priests and lay liberals began to express their desire for independence in the open. On his arrival in 1871, Governor Rafael de Izquierdo put an end to liberalism in Manila and, antifriar though he was, gave full support to the friars, whom he considered the major backers of Spanish sovereignty. [*See* Friars.]

Izquierdo was immediately skeptical of the goals of the Filipino priests, led by Father Jose Burgos, and his suspicion was nurtured by various anonymous denunciations of conspiracy in the months before the revolt broke out on 20 January 1872. After the revolt Izquierdo immediately arrested a large number of Filipino priests, lawyers, and merchants. A summary court-martial condemned fathers Burgos, Gómez, and Zamora and a layman named Zaldua to death, while others were exiled to Guam or Africa. The records of the court-martial have never been found, but recently published documents show that the insurgents were in contact with only two men—Sergeant Lamadrid (killed in the fighting) and Zaldua. It seems certain that none of the priests were involved in the revolt, since they were actively lobbying, through agents in Madrid, for their rights and at that time had no motive to promote a revolt. The executions not only removed the priests whose influence Izquierdo feared but also eliminated Zaldua, the only witness to the falsehood of the accusation.

Izquierdo's measures resulted in the end of any hope for Filipino equality under Spanish rule. University students who had been influenced by Burgos, notably Jose Rizal and Marcelo del Pilar, concluded that Filipino national dignity could be obtained only by separation from Spain.

[*See also* Burgos, Jose; Rizal, Jose Mercado; Pilar, Marcelo H. del; *and* Propaganda Movement.]

John N. Schumacher, *The Revolutionary Clergy* (1982) and "The Cavite Mutiny: An Essay on the Published Sources," *Philippine Studies* 20 (1972): 603–632.

JOHN N. SCHUMACHER, S.J.

CAWNPORE. *See* Kanpur.

CEBU, important island, province, and city in the central part of the Philippine archipelago. Cebu province, which consists of the island of Cebu and its adjacent islands (Mactan, Bantayan, and the Camotes), has long supported a large population (1903: 653,727; 1970: 1,634,182) residing in fifty-three municipalities, all on or near the coast. The comparatively arid environment and rugged mountainous interior of Cebu Island have restricted wet-rice cultivation to a few places; corn has long been a more suitable crop and remains the main staple of Cebuanos. Cebu City (population, 1903: 31,079; 1970: 347,116), located midway along the east coast of Cebu Island (population, 1970: 569, 232), and its neighboring cities and municipalities make up the second largest urban and commercial complex in the Philippines. With its well-protected port area, Cebu City was an important pre-Spanish entrepôt, a large settlement that enjoyed considerable political organization.

In 1521 Ferdinand Magellan's efforts to secure the area for Spain failed when he was killed by forces of a local chieftain, Lapulapu. The more successful Miguel Lopez de Legazpi took control of the entrepôt of Cebu in 1565, establishing a permanent Spanish settlement and making it the first capital of the emerging Spanish colony. When the capital was moved to Manila, Cebu declined in commercial significance but became a major administrative and religious center under colonial rule. In the nineteenth century, the increased world demand for Philippine agricultural products led to the opening of Cebu's port (1860); since then Cebu has been the commercial center—the hub of interisland trade—for the southern Philippines. Cebu is also the homeland of the largest Philippine-language group, Cebuano-Visayan, spoken in the central Visayas (Cebu, Bohol, western Leyte, and eastern Negros). The gradual depletion of Cebu's soil has led large numbers of Cebuanos to migrate to Mindanao, where Cebuano-Visayan is the lingua franca in many communities. During the twentieth century, Cebu has been the political and cultural center for a large number of Filipinos.

Michael Cullinane, "The Changing Nature of the Cebu Urban Elite in the 19th Century," in *Philippine Social History*, edited by A. W. McCoy and E. C. de Jesus (1982). Canute Vendermeer, "Population Patterns on the Island of Cebu, the Philippines, 1500–1900," *Annals of the Association of American Geographers* 57 (1967): 315–337. Frederick Wernstedt, *The Role and Importance of Philippine Interisland Shipping and Trade* (1957).

MICHAEL CULLINANE

CELEBES. *See* Sulawesi.

CENSORATE. From the third century BCE the censorial system had a place in all Chinese imperial administrations. The term *censor* derives from a misleading analogy to the censors of republican Rome, who were responsible for supervising the census and collecting taxes. Chinese censors had much broader responsibilities: they were dispatched to investigate almost every aspect of imperial administration and to scrutinize the conduct of the bureaucracy.

The Chinese term for censor *(yushi)* literally means royal scribe or archivist. Prior to the Qin dynasty (221–207 BCE) such officials functioned primarily as recorders and secretaries of a king and were charged with overseeing the administration of his palace. It was from this close and intimate association with the ruler that the power of the office derived. During the Qin dynasty censors were raised in rank and made assistants to the prime minister, put in charge of judicial investigations, and sent out to inspect the various regional administrations of the empire.

Although the Qin dynasty was short-lived, its institutions endured. The succeeding Han dynasty (206 BCE–220 CE) kept the Qin administrative system almost intact. During the Han, censors were organized into offices that survived with continuous modifications until the end of the imperial period. The most significant administrative change in their organization occurred in 8 BCE, when the two highest ranked censors in the court were given discrete responsibilities. One remained in charge of the imperial palace while the other was put in charge of the imperial bureaucracy.

After this institutional change had been implemented, two distinct and independent groups of "speaking officials" (officials who spoke out on matters of policy or conduct) came into existence. One group was completely separate from the censorate. These officials, generally called "opinion officials," criticized imperial policy, judicial decisions, and even the emperor himself. The other group made up the censorate. Censorial officials were responsible primarily for investigating the bureaucracy.

By the end of the Han dynasty the censor in charge of the imperial bureaucracy had become in practice the head of all censorial officials and was considered one of the most powerful officials in the court. During the three centuries of disunity that followed the collapse of the Han dynasty, the powers and jurisdiction of censorial officials did not diminish; the chief censor was still considered second in influence only to the prime ministers.

During the Sui dynasty (581–618) two changes were implemented, both of which were designed to curb the power of censorial officials. First, the selection of censorial officials was entrusted to the Ministry of Personnel, whereas this process had previously been carried out by recommendations from censorial officials in office. Second, censorial officials were strictly excluded from any role in policy making: they were to investigate the bureaucracy, carry out special commissions, and inspect local administrations.

The succeeding Tang dynasty (618–907) followed this practice as well, but went far beyond the Sui in organizing and rationalizing the functions of censorial officials and in drafting rules and regulations that governed their procedures. Later imperial administrations by and large derived their censorial systems from this administrative model.

The Tang censorate was directly responsible to the throne and was not subordinate to any other civil or military authority. The censorate had three principal functions: it conducted judicial reviews at the highest level of appeal; it supervised the imperial palace; and it initiated investigations into the conduct of bureaucrats at all levels of administration.

The Tang censorate was made up of a relatively small group of officials. The institution operated under the general charge of a chief executive and was divided into three offices known as the three courts. One of these, the Court of Inquiries, was the seat of the censorate's real authority. Officials of this office, although they were as a rule young and of low rank, had the right to inspect and investigate officials of any rank both in the capital and in the provinces without first securing the approval of their superiors.

During the Tang dynasty officials holding the title of censor were also routinely dispatched to investigate fiscal and judicial affairs in local administrations; after 684 such investigations followed a detailed schedule that covered almost every aspect of administration. Censorial officials holding specific commissions came to constitute an informal administrative network with broad jurisdiction, and the provincial *(sheng)* administrations of later dynasties grew out of this Tang practice.

Under the aristocratic society of the Tang and earlier periods, when the emperor was considered a first among equals and when officials derived their power from family status as well as from public office, criticism was tolerated and censorial officials generally escaped punishment for their remarks, even when they concerned the emperor or his family. Under the Song (960–1279) and subsequent dynasties, when the power and authority of the emperor became in theory and to a lesser degree in practice absolute, there was less tolerance of criticism or any other kind of interference with imperial policy.

Southern Song (1127–1279) emperors often tried to hamstring their opinion officials and censors by playing them off against one another, by accepting advice but ignoring it, by reprimanding impeached officials but refusing to dismiss them, or by simply failing to acknowledge impeachments that displeased them. In effect, these emperors used various bureaucratic techniques to circumvent speaking officials when their remarks conflicted with imperial desires.

The censorates of the Jurchen Jin (1115–1234) and Mongolian Yuan (1271–1368) dynasties were organized on the Song model, but differed from it in that under both regimes the censorate remained structurally at least a strong and independent arm of the central government, although it served primarily as an instrument of control that foreign rulers used to watch their Chinese officials. Everything possible was done to ensure that Jin censors could exercise their powers of impeachment without interference or recrimination.

Such policies continued under the Yuan administration. The chief censor was raised to the first rank of the civil bureaucracy, whereas in Tang times he had been in the third rank and in Jin times in the second. This elevation in rank made the chief censor almost equal in rank to the prime ministers and once again one of the most influential officials at court. The function of the censorate was, however, limited to investigation and control.

The founding emperor of the succeeding Ming dynasty (1368–1644) at first simply took over the Yuan system of administration. However, in 1380 he abolished the censorate and the secretariat in an attempt to concentrate all executive and personnel decisions in his own hands. This institutional reorganization had two far-reaching consequences. First, there was no longer any balance of power in the civil administration between the censorate and the secretariat. Second, the "opinion officials," who had in Song times been under the control of the secretariat, also became independent and consequently more outspoken. The position of chief censor was later reinstituted, but was reduced to the third degree of rank, as had been the case in Tang times. Nonetheless, without a prime minister in the court, the chief censor remained a powerful official.

During the Ming dynasty the power and influence of the censorate reached its zenith. By the end of the sixteenth century the censorate had become the focal point of an adversarial relation between the emperor and the imperial bureaucracy. Speaking officials held that every aspect of the emperor's public and private behavior was subject to their scrutiny. However, most Ming emperors resisted such attempts to constrain their absolute authority, often by resorting to force. Although speaking officials had by tradition often been protected from punishment, Ming emperors routinely broke this tradition by beating, torturing, and sometimes putting to death officials whose remarks irritated or angered them. At the same time the censorate became the focus of partisan struggles in the bureaucracy; the power to demote and to dismiss officials through impeachments gave to whatever group controlled the censorate the power to influence affairs of state and to advance or destory careers.

Although censorial officials had been responsible for investigating local and regional administrations since the Tang dynasty, this was usually done on the basis of particular ad hoc commissions. Under the Song, local administrations were supervised by a number of intendants, who had no authority to control or to direct the officials whom they supervised, and this arrangement persisted into Ming times.

By the Ming period the fiscal, judicial, and administrative intendants in each new, enlarged provincial administration functioned independently of one another and of their counterparts in other provinces. When a coordinated effort of some sort had to be undertaken, a censorial official was given jurisdiction over all officials in one or more provinces and the authority to act as governor pro tempore. This procedure gradually became regularized, and by the early eighteenth century the succeeding Qing dynasty (1644–1911) had formally instituted the office of provincial governor and continued to fill this post with an official of the censorate. Because other officials in the imperial administration had very clearly delineated tasks and were not allowed to interfere with one another, the censorate became by default the only organ of government that could be used to coordinate the civil and military activities of various regional administrations.

Under the Qing administration the "opinion officials" were brought under the control of the censorate and for the most part carried out special censorial commissions. After 1723 the Qing emperors issued orders directly and dispensed with the practice of subjecting their edicts to review. Thus, by the eighteenth century the censorate had become an elaborate and highly refined instrument of surveillance designed to investigate every aspect of administration and every level of the bureaucracy, while its function as a check on imperial authority had virtually ceased to exist.

[*See also* Bureaucracy in China.]

Hans Bielenstein, *The Bureaucracy of Han Times* (1980). H. S. Brunnert and V. V. Hagelstrom, *Present*

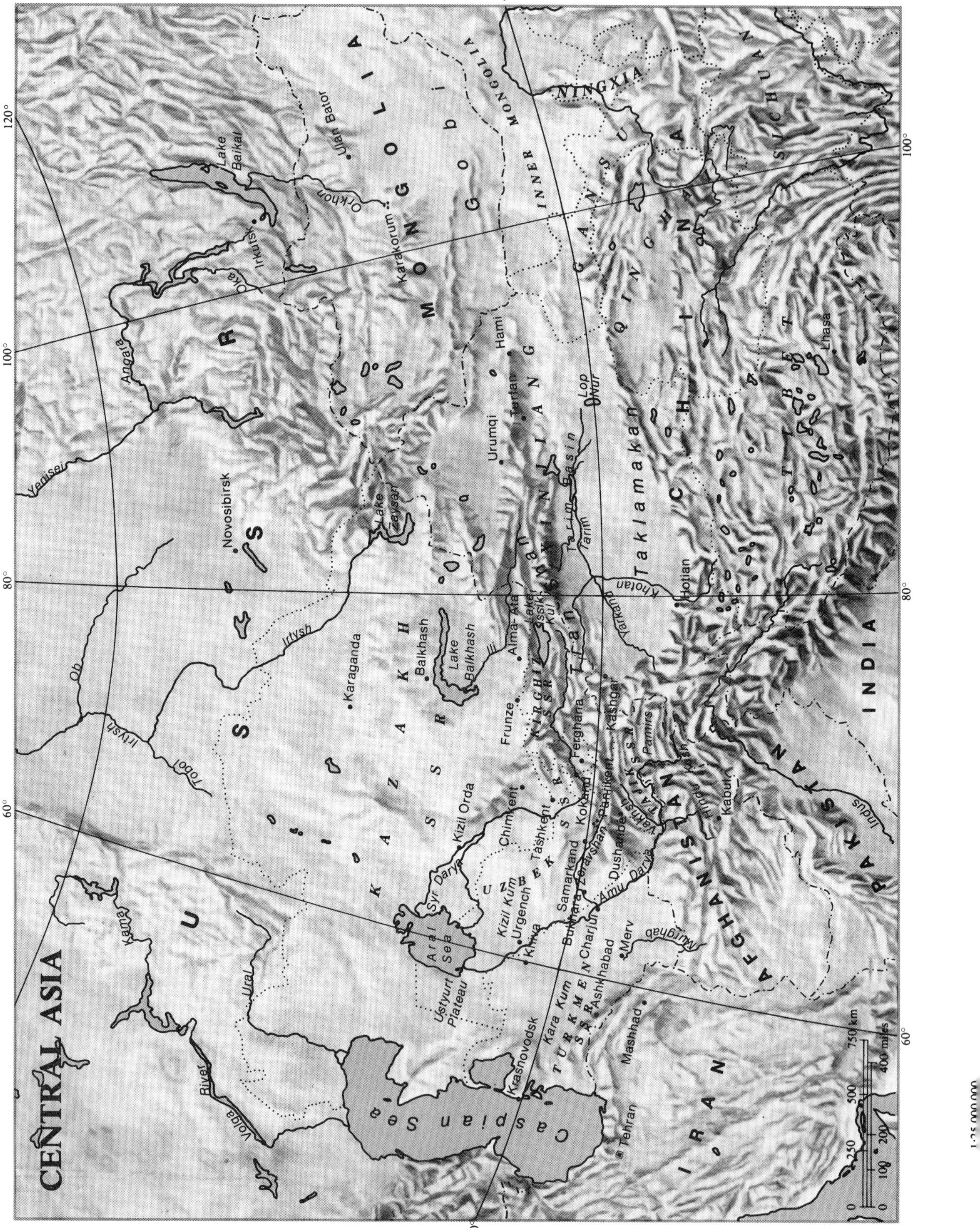
CENTRAL ASIA
U S S R
M O N G O L I A
Gobi
INNER MONGOLIA
NINGXIA
GANSU
QINGHAI
SICHUAN
TIBET
C H I N A
XINJIANG
Taklamakan
Tarim Basin
KAZAKH S S R
UZBEK S S R
TURKMEN S S R
KIRGHIZ S S R
TAJIK S S R
AFGHANISTAN
PAKISTAN
INDIA
IRAN
Caspian Sea
Aral Sea
Lake Balkhash
Lake Baikal
Lake Zaysan
Lake Issik Kul
Lop Nur
Volga River
Ural
Kama
Ob
Irtysh
Tobol
Yenisei
Angara
Oka
Orkhon
Syr Darya
Amu Darya
Zeravshan
Vakhsh
Murghab
Indus
Tarim
Khotan
Yarkand
Kizil Kum
Kara Kum
Ustyurt Plateau
Pamirs
Hindu Kush
Tian Shan
Kunlun
Novosibirsk
Irkutsk
Ulan Bator
Karakorum
Karaganda
Balkhash
Alma-Ata
Frunze
Chimkent
Tashkent
Kizil Orda
Kokand
Ferghana
Kashgar
Samarkand
Panjikent
Dushanbe
Bukhara
Charjui
Merv
Ashkhabad
Urgench
Khiva
Krasnovodsk
Mashhad
Tehran
Kabul
Hotian
Urumqi
Turfan
Hami
Lhasa
40°
60°
80°
100°
120°
0 250 500 750 km
0 100 200 400 miles
1:35,000,000

Day Political Organization of China (1911). Charles O. Hucker, *The Censorial System of Ming China* (1966). E. A. Kracke, Jr., *Civil Service in Early Sung China* (1953). Yü-ch'üan Wang, "An Outline of the Central Government of the Former Han Dynasty," *Harvard Journal of Asiatic Studies* 12 (1949): 134–187.

JAMES GEISS

CENTRAL ASIA is composed of the Xinjiang Uighur Autonomous Region (in China), the territory north of the Hindu Kush in Afghanistan, and the Uzbek, Kazakh, Kirghiz, Turkmen, and Tajik Soviet Socialist Republics (in the USSR). The region is landlocked and has little precipitation. Irrigation works are essential to the survival of the towns and oases scattered along the inhospitable terrain, which is composed principally of deserts, mountains, and steppelands. The Taklamakan Desert (in southern Xinjiang), the Tian Shan range between China and the USSR, and the Hindu Kush are only a few of the formidable barriers to human habitation.

Despite these obstacles, the fortuitous geographic location of Central Asia has enabled it to serve as a crossroads between China, Persia, Russia, and Europe. The principal trade routes linking the great civilizations of Europe and Asia passed through the Central Asian oases, and a variety of peoples, products, and ideas flowed in and out of the region. Its indigenous economy was composed of a mixture of nomadic pastoralism, subsistence agriculture, and trade. Most of the region's inhabitants converted to Islam about a century after the death of Muhammad (c. 570–632). The vast majority of the people in the area are Turkic-speaking.

Central Asia was traditionally a base for several nomadic empires. The Xiongnu, the Seljuk Turks, the Timurids (the descendants of Timur), and the Uzbeks constituted a few of these powerful military confederations. Their lack of both unity and an orderly system of succession to the throne hampered them and contributed to their decline and fall.

China and Russia, the great powers of the Eurasian land mass, have dominated Central Asia since the eighteenth century. In 1758 the Qing dynasty of China occupied the area now known as Xinjiang, and by 1873 the Russian tsarist government seized the western regions of Central Asia. Since then, both states have attempted to cajole or coerce the native inhabitants into assimilating with the Chinese and Russian peoples respectively. The predominantly Turkic peoples of Central Asia have generally resisted such efforts and have maintained a strong ethnic and religious consciousness. The economic attractiveness of modern Central Asia is undeniable. It has virtually untapped resources of coal, petroleum, uranium, and gold; it is relatively underpopulated; and the Soviet and Chinese governments have built roads and railroads to link their Central Asian territories with their other domains. Only time will tell whether they will gain the political allegiance of the peoples of Central Asia.

[*See also* Turkestan.]

Edward Allworth, ed., *Central Asia: A Century of Russian Rule* (1967). Joseph F. Fletcher, Jr., "Ch'ing Inner Asia c. 1800," in the *Cambridge History of China,* vol. 10, *Late Ch'ing 1800–1911, Part 1,* edited by John K. Fairbank (1978). Morris Rossabi, *China and Inner Asia from 1368 to the Present Day* (1975). Geoffrey Wheeler, *The Modern History of Soviet Central Asia* (1964).

MORRIS ROSSABI

CERAMICS

JAPANESE CERAMICS

The history of Japanese ceramics spans some twelve thousand years, beginning with earthenware made in Neolithic settlements of the Jōmon culture. Advanced techniques were introduced relatively late: high-fired wares in the fifth century CE, glazes by the seventh century, and porcelain in the seventeenth century. The coexistence of new technologies with older methods has resulted in a remarkable expansion of variety within the medium.

Throughout the Jōmon period (c. 10,000–200 BCE), only earthenware was produced. Hand built and fired in open bonfires, Jōmon pottery is technically simple, yet the sculptural forms and decoration are complex and distinctive. Ceramics of the subsequent Yayoi period (c. 200 BCE–300 CE) reflect shifts in settlement patterns. Finer, alluvial clay and improvements in technique, such as the potter's wheel, enabled Yayoi potters to produce smooth, symmetrical forms. [*See* Jōmon *and* Yayoi.]

The culture of the Kofun, or Tumuli, period (c. 300–710) reflects customs and technological advances brought to Japan from Korea and China. Tomb burials required grave goods made of pottery, and large quantities of earthenware figures and objects called *haniwa* were placed around the perimeter of tombs. High-fired ceramics of a type known as *sueki,* closely related to Korean gray stoneware, were first made in the Osaka region. The new technology, employing tunnel kilns (*anagama*) and improved techniques for building complex forms, spread to other parts of Japan. [*See* Tumuli.]

The prestige of imported Chinese glazed ceramics

FIGURE 1. *Ceramic Bowl.* By Ogata Kenzan (1663–1743). Kyoto ware, deep bowl with reticulated rim and decoration of mist and grasses. Buff stoneware with decoration in underglaze slips and overglaze polychrome enamels. Height 12.4 cm., diameter 19 cm.

led to the production of glazed ceramics in Japan from about the mid-seventh century. Lead glazes and ash glazes paralleled the color of Chinese celadon glazes and attracted the patronage of the Japanese aristocracy. Imported Chinese ceramics, scarce but more readily available in areas near trade routes, provided an important impetus to technical and formal changes in Japanese ceramics. The region around modern Nagoya, location of the Sanage and Seto kilns, became a leading producer of glazed ceramics. The Seto kilns continued to be a major source of glazed ceramics, which were widely distributed, especially in eastern Japan.

One of the characteristic products of the medieval period (twelfth through sixteenth century) was unglazed stoneware intended for agricultural use. More than thirty regional kilns active in the medieval period have been identified by archaeologists. Tokoname, a production center with access to sea routes, was a point of dispersal for an improved kiln design.

During the sixteenth century technological improvements expanded the production of glazed ceramics, and innovations in form and decoration were stimulated by the aesthetics of tea ceremony, which valued the individuality of each piece. The high status of ceramics in Japan from the sixteenth century onward reflects the appreciation of the objects in various media that were used for preparing and serving tea and the accompanying meal. [*See* Tea Ceremony.]

Glazed stonewares of a variety of types were produced at such sites as Mino near Seto and at various sites in Kyushu, where many Korean potters settled in the second half of the sixteenth century. New kiln designs, such as the *noborigama,* which had linked chambers that could be fired successively, permitted high-temperature firing of larger quantities of ceramics and prepared the way for a vast expansion of ceramic production in the Edo period.

Porcelain was first produced in Japan around the beginning of the seventeenth century at kilns in the Arita region in northwestern Kyushu. Both the quantity and quality of porcelain production improved rapidly, and porcelain decorated in underglaze cobalt blue and overglaze enamels introduced around the mid-seventeenth century became a major commercial product. The port of Imari gave its name to various porcelain wares exported from the kilns in Arita to Europe.

The diversity and quantity of ceramics production rapidly increased during the Edo period, with work coming from kilns ranging from highly productive commercial kilns with specialized divisions of labor to small kilns supervised by a single potter. Officially sponsored kilns were established by daimyo to produce luxurious wares for their private use. Kyoto, for centuries a center for fine Japanese crafts in media such as textiles and lacquer, nurtured individual artist potters such as Ogata Kenzan (1663–1743), who brought to ceramics his knowledge of calligraphy, literature, and painting.

Today, ceramic pieces of outstanding quality employing a broad range of techniques are being produced by Japanese potters, and their work continues to be admired by Japanese and international audiences. Research into modern applications of ceramic technology is actively pursued by Japanese scientists, while archaeologists and historians are rapidly extending our knowledge of the circumstances of production of Japanese ceramics in the past.

ANN YONEMURA

SOUTHEAST ASIAN CERAMICS TRADE

When the Portugese captured Melaka (Malacca) in 1511, they found an ancient and substantial network of maritime trade linking the coastal stations and upriver villages of Southeast Asia to the many trading ports of China, India, the Persian Gulf, and the East African coast. From as far back as the ninth or tenth century, a staple commodity in these exchanges, and the best preserved in the archaeological record, was China's glazed, high-fired ceramics. For many of the Southeast Asian villagers who collected aromatics, spices, and drugs (the principal exports of their region), the Chinese wares were objects of great potency, emblems of rank and status that played important roles in birth, marriage, and death rituals.

Chinese ceramics first appear at approximately 800 CE on the Persian Gulf. About this time, Arab shipping began to expand beyond Sri Lanka and directly into China. Chinese wares have been discovered in the ancient port of Siraf, a leading entrepôt in the ninth and tenth centuries, where, according to scholars David Whitehouse and Andrew Williamson, they were excavated below the platform of a mosque built in or shortly after 803/804. Reports by Arab travelers and geographers note that ships from Siraf had contact with Kalah, a center of trade and transshipment that many historical geographers believe was located on the Malay Peninsula. Moreover, distinctly Middle Eastern glass and blue-glazed earthenwares, as well as an assemblage of Chinese ceramics similar to those discovered at Siraf, have been excavated on the Bay of Bandon near Chaiya in southern Thailand.

FIGURE 1. *Covered Jar.* Thai, fourteenth to fifteenth century. Excavated at Sulawesi, Indonesia. Sawankhalok ware, light gray stoneware with incised decoration under celadon glaze. Height 15.2 cm., diameter 11.4 cm.

To meet the heavy demand of the Southeast Asian markets, production of ceramics in southern China intensified during the Southern Song (1127–1279) and Yuan (1279–1368) dynasties. For the first time, Chinese merchants sailed to Southeast Asia and established direct access to the rich market there. Trade routes and trading ports proliferated during this period. Among the best-documented ones are Kota Cina, near Medan in northeastern Sumatra; Pengkalan Bujang on the Merbok Estuary, western Malaysia; Santubong at the mouth of the Sarawak River in western Borneo; and Santa Ana in the Philippines.

Chinese trading patterns with Southeast Asia changed after the fall of the Yuan dynasty and the restoration of traditional tributary trade during the reign of the first Ming emperor Hongwu (1368–1398). By the last quarter of the fourteenth century, trade with China was at a low level, and this may have stimulated the rise in the number of ceramics produced for export in both Vietnam and Thailand. A substantial number of Thai wares and, to a lesser extent, Vietnamese wares have been recovered along with the larger concentration of Chinese ceramics in such fifteenth- and sixteenth-century sites as Kota Batu in Brunei, Calatagan in the Philippines, and Kampong Pareko in Sulawesi.

The Portuguese entered the flourishing ceramics trade during the early sixteenth century but were superseded by the Dutch and English in the next century. The traditional Chinese junk trade continued alongside European enterprise, and great quantities of porcelain and stoneware from southeastern China poured into Southeast Asia through the nineteenth century.

Roxanna Brown, *The Ceramics of South-East Asia* (1977). Margaret Medley, *The Chinese Potter* (1976). M. A. P. Meilink-Roelofsz, *Asian Trade and European Influence in the Indonesian Archipelago between 1500 and About 1630* (1962). O. W. Wolters, *The Fall of Srivijaya in Malay History* (1970). STANLEY J. O'CONNOR

CEYLON. *See* Sri Lanka.

CEYLON NATIONAL CONGRESS. The British stimulated political activity among low-country Sinhalese elites in 1915 by suppressing a temperance movement that had strong rural support. The Ceylon National Congress (CNC) was thus founded in

1919 and temporarily upstaged militant Sinhalese Buddhist activists. The CNC remained effective until 1942, but it never attained the significance of its Indian counterpart. In the 1920s the CNC lost Tamil and Kandyan Sinhalese support, and during the state council period (1931–1946) even low-country Sinhalese members were independent of CNC control.

[*See also* Sri Lanka *and* Indian National Congress.]

Michael Roberts, ed., *Documents of the Ceylon National Congress and National Politics in Ceylon, 1929–1950,* 4 vols. (1977). PATRICK PEEBLES

CHAGATAI, political and ethnic term derived from the name of Chagatai (d. 1242), Genghis Khan's second son by his chief wife, and designating the territory of the appanage *(ulus)* assigned to him by his father at the time of the division of the Mongol empire in 1224. The territory of the Ulus Chagatai consisted of Transoxiana (roughly the area between the Amu Darya and Syr Darya rivers in present-day Uzbek SSR), the Semirechie region of present-day Kazakh SSR, eastern Turkestan (present-day Xinjiang Uighur Autonomous Region of the People's Republic of China), and northern and eastern Afghanistan. Its capital was at Almaligh in the Ili Valley (near present-day Kuldja).

The Chagatai khanate was founded after Chagatai Khan's death by his grandson, Kara Hulegu (r. 1242–1246) on the territory of the Ulus Chagatai. The early khans preserved the nomadic Mongol traditions and avoided mixing with the sedentary population of Transoxiana. There was no centralized authority until the accession of Kebek Khan (r. 1318–1326), who attempted to consolidate his power in Transoxiana. In the second half of the fourteenth century, the khanate split into two sections: the western in Transoxiana, which retained the name *Chagatai* and favored assimilation with the sedentary Muslim population, and the eastern in Semirechie and eastern Turkestan, which did not want to break with the nomadic traditions. The latter became known as Mughalistan and its inhabitants as Mughals (i.e., Mongols). After the death of Kazan Khan in 1347, power in Transoxiana passed to various local Turkic emirs, and the Chagatai khans remained only nominal rulers until Timur (Tamerlane) established his supremacy in 1370.

The term *Chagatai* was also applied, by extension, to the nomadic Turkic and turkicized Mongol population (as distinct from the sedentary Iranian) that inhabited the territory of the Ulus Chagatai and constituted a privileged military caste. The term continued to be used in this sense in the fifteenth century under the rule of the Timurids and was used loosely to designate the entire Turkic population of the Timurid empire. After the collapse of the Timurids, the Chagatai became mixed with the nomadic Uzbeks, but the name was still used as a tribal designation. Moreover, the descendants of Timur who departed from Transoxiana under pressure from the Uzbeks at the beginning of the sixteenth century and founded an empire in India were also called Chagatai.

As an ethnic, tribal designation, *Chagatai* today is applied to a portion to the sedentary population of the Kashka-Darya and Surkhandarya regions of the Uzbek SSR, which is partly Uzbek- and partly Tajik-speaking. The term is also applied to the Eastern Turkic literary language that was formed in the fifteenth century on the territory of the former Ulus Chagatai.

[*See also* Mongol Empire.]

René Grousset, *The Empire of the Steppes,* translated by Naomi Walford (1970). Gavin Hambly, ed., *Central Asia* (1969). H. H. Howorth, *History of the Mongols* (1876). MARIA E. SUBTELNY

CHAGATAI LITERATURE, a medieval Islamic Central Asian literature written from the fifteenth to the twentieth century in Chagatai, an eastern Turkic literary language that developed from the Karakhanid and Khwarazmian Turkic literary languages. Chagatai literature assumed its classical form in the fifteenth century under the patronage of the princes of the Timurid dynasty (1405–1507), whose realm originally included most of the former Ulus Chagatai. Although the term *Chagatai* was rarely applied to this literature by fifteenth-century authors (who called the language Turki), it later gained currency among both Eastern and Western scholars, particularly in the nineteenth century. Chagatai literature is sometimes also referred to as Old Uzbek, since the modern language most closely related to Chagatai is Uzbek, although the term *pre-Uzbek* would be more accurate.

In its development, Chagatai literature was heavily influenced by Persian models, particularly in poetry. Persian verse forms, romantic themes, and poetical imagery and vocabulary were adopted wholesale. Certain native Turkic verse forms (e.g., *tuyug*) were also made to conform to the Arabo-Persian metrical system. Chagatai prose, on the other hand, remained relatively free of Persian influence.

The fifteenth century marked the golden age of Chagatai literature. In the first half of the century its main centers were the Timurid courts at Samarkand, Shiraz, and Herat, where poets such as Sakkaki, Lutfi, and Ata'i were active. It reached its apogee in the second half of the century in the poetical and prose works of Neva'i (1441–1501), who was attached to the court of Sultan Husain Baiqara in Herat. In the sixteenth century, Chagatai literature was patronized by the Shaibanid Uzbeks in Transoxiana, at whose courts Chagatai historiography developed, as well as by the Timurid dynasty established in India by Babur (1483–1530). Babur himself is regarded as the best Chagatai poet after Neva'i and the finest Chagatai prosaist.

Chagatai literature of the seventeenth and eighteenth centuries was characterized mainly by imitation of Neva'i's poetical works. It experienced a revival in the nineteenth century in the khanates of Khiva and Khokand before its demise after the delimitation of the Soviet Central Asian republics (1924) and the creation of national literary languages based on spoken dialects.

[*See also* Babur; Baiqara, Husain; Neva'i; Turkic Languages; *and* Persian Literature.]

E. Allworth, *Uzbek Literary Politics* (1964). E. G. Browne, *A Literary History of Persia* (1928). J. Eckmann, *Chagatay Manual* (1966).

MARIA E. SUBTELNY

CHAHAMANA DYNASTY. *See* Chauhan Dynasty.

CHAITANYA (c. 1485–1533), Hindu mystic whose disciples founded the religious movement known as the Chaitanya Sampradaya, which has been highly influential in Bengal, Orissa, and northern India. Born into a brahman family in Navadvipa, Bengal, Chaitanya received a traditional education in the Sanskrit scriptures. According to legends, while on a pilgrimage to a shrine at Gaya he had a religious experience that led him to become a devotee of the god Krishna. He gathered a group of followers who joined him in devotion that consisted of congregational singing known as *kirtan,* based on the repetition of the name Krishna, and ecstatic dancing. Chaitanya settled at Puri in Orissa, but he made a pilgrimage to Vrindavan, near Mathura, which was the center of the Krishna cult, especially as it related to Krishna's childhood and his love for Radha. Followers of Chaitanya believe that because of his intense devotion he became an incarnation of both Radha and Krishna in his own body. This identification of female and male in one person has great significance for believers, implying that the lover can become the beloved, that the male can become the female, and that Krishna, the great god, is at the same time the devotee of Radha, the object of his love.

Chaitanya returned to Puri, where he died, and although he did not leave a body of his own writings, his disciples through the years worked out a systematic statement of the beliefs and practices of the movement. They also built many temples at Vrindavan and restored some that had fallen into ruin, and identified many places around the area as the scenes of episodes in the Krishna stories. These became centers of pilgrimage, especially for Bengali followers of Chaitanya, but they are very popular with all Hindus who delight in the Krishna legends. The modern Western members of the International Society for Krishna Consciousness (ISKCON), known as the Hare Krishna movement, also claim to follow the teachings and practices of Chaitanya.

[*See also* Bhakti *and* Hinduism.]

John Stratton Hawley and Donna Marie Wulff, eds., *The Divine Consort* (1982). O. B. L. Kapoor, *The Philosophy and Religion of Sri Caitanya* (1976). M. T. Kennedy, *The Caitanya Movement* (1925). J. N. Sarkar, trans., *Chaitanya's Life and Teachings* (1922).

AINSLIE T. EMBREE

CHAIT SINGH, raja of Banaras (Varanasi) from 1700 to 1781. Following Mansa Ram (reigned c. 1732–1740) and Balwant Singh (reigned c. 1740–1770), who had established the family's power over Banaras, Jaunpur, and Mirzpur, and then over Ghazipur and Ballia—first as *amils* (tax officials), then as *zamindars* (land owners), and finally as rajas—Chait Singh's succession to these domains was recognized as such by the nawab of Awadh (Oudh), the emperor in Delhi, and the East India Company. When Asaf ud-Daula of Oudh ceded the territories of Banaras to the company in 1775, Chait Singh was allowed to continue ruling the province as his own kingdom in return for two million rupees and an agreement to provide troops. His rebellion against the company in 1781 provoked Warren Hastings, the governor-general, to remove him and to put a collateral relative, Mahip Narayan Singh, in his place. However, a charge of having caused the rebellion was later brought against Hastings as one of the articles of his impeachment. Indeed, whatever the facts of the matter, it is his appearance in the Articles of Charge of High Crimes and Misdemeanors against Hastings that, above all else, has made a place in history for Chait Singh.

[*See also* Varanasi *and* Hastings, Warren.]

P. J. Marshall, *The Impeachment of Warren Hastings* (1965), pp. 89–108. ROBERT E. FRYKENBERG

CHAKKRAPHAT (r. 1548–1569), king of Ayudhya prior to the first Burmese sack of Siam. The son of King Ramathibodi II, Chakkraphat followed several of his half-brothers as king and was enthroned by a palace coup that deposed a usurper. He assumed the Pali-derived title *chakkraphat,* designating the universal Buddhist monarch (Pali, *chakkavattin*) whose right is his might. From the beginning of his reign, Siam was subjected to almost constant invasions from Burma and Cambodia. He died in January 1569, with the capital under siege, and was succeeded by his son, Mahin, under whom the kingdom fell to the Burmese in August of that year.

[*See also* Ayudhya *and* Mahathammaracha.]

W. A. R. Wood, *A History of Siam* (1926). David K. Wyatt, *Thailand: A Short History* (1984).

DAVID K. WYATT

CHAKRAVARTIN, Sanskrit term of uncertain origin, literally, "wheel-turner." The term is used in classical Indian political literature (i.e., *Arthashastra, Nitishastra*) to refer to the ideal king as a "world conqueror." Every king was said to be *vijigishu,* "desirous, ready to conquer"; if he succeeded he became a *chakravartin*. The term (as *chakkavattin*) is also prominent in Pali Buddhist literature.

LUDO ROCHER

CHAKRI DYNASTY, ruling house of the kingdom of Thailand since 1782.

Building upon monarchical and administrative institutions inherited from the kingdom of Ayudhya and creatively refashioned by the founder of the line, Phraphutthayotfa Chulalok (Rama I, r. 1782–1809), the monarchs of the Chakri dynasty have ruled a prosperous and united kingdom for two centuries. Thai artistic culture blossomed and took form especially under Phraphutthaloetla Naphalai (Rama II, r. 1809–1824), while Phranangklao (Rama III, r. 1824–1851) expanded the kingdom far beyond even today's boundaries. King Mongkut (r. 1851–1868) opened the door to Western ideas and undertook the delicate task of accommodating the Western powers. To Mongkut and his son Chulalongkorn (r. 1868–1910) go the credit for a leadership in foreign policy and domestic reform that not only saved old Siam from the Western colonialism that subdued all Siam's neighbors but also laid the foundations for the modern state. King Vajiravudh (r. 1910–1925) began the process of turning the state into a nation, promoting both nationalism and modern ideas and values. He unwittingly sowed the seeds of the end of the absolute monarchy and the so-called Thai revolution of 1932. Although he was the revolution's immediate victim, King Prajadhipok (r. 1925–1935) eased the transition to a constitutional monarchy, and his abdication statement, which denounced military dictatorship, would prove a durable defense of democratic ideals upon which his nephews, Ananda Mahidol (r. 1935–1946) and Bhumibol Adulyadej who acceded to the throne in 1946, could build. The idea and institution of monarchy remain powerful in Thailand today, functioning as a focus for national loyalties and a source of benevolent leadership.

[*See also* Thailand; Bangkok; *and the biographies of the monarchs mentioned herein.*]

Prince Chula Chakrabongse, *Lords of Life: A History of the Kings of Thailand* (rev. ed., 1967). David K. Wyatt, *Thailand: A Short History* (1984). DAVID K. WYATT

CHALUKYA DYNASTIES, collective term for several dynasties in North and South India that claimed descent from the Early Chalukyas of Badami in South India. The most important were the Eastern Chalukyas of Vengi and the Late Chalukyas of Kalyani.

The Early Chalukyas took power in what had been the Kadamba region of northern Karnataka. Throughout their rule (sixth century–757 CE) their chief rivals were the Pallavas. Their principal cities were Aihole, Badami, and Pattadakal, where many early temples were constructed that are the precursors of both the northern and southern architectural styles. The Eastern Chalukyas were not nearly so important in the political history of South India. Owing to their position in central Andhra Pradesh, they were able to survive the fall of the parent dynasty. The Late Chalukyas of Kalyani (r. 973–1200) had much greater impact: taking power at the fall of the Rashtrakutas, they consolidated holdings in northern Karnataka and southern Maharashtra. Their chief adversaries in the South were the Cholas. Many dynasties of the period were their one-time feudatories, including the Hoysalas and the Kakatiyas. The Late Chalukyas suffered a defeat to the Kalachuris (r. 1156–1181), from which they never fully recovered.

[*See also* Pallava Dynasty; Chola Dynasty; Rashtrakuta Dynasty; *and* Kalachuri Dynasties.]

Krishna Murari, *The Calukyas of Kalyani* (1977). N. Ramesan, *The Eastern Chalukyas of Vengi* (1975). Ghulam Yazdani, ed., *The Early History of the Deccan* (1960), Part 4, pp. 201–246; Part 6, pp. 315–454.

ROBERT J. DEL BONTÀ

CHAM, a Malayo-Polynesian people who inhabit scattered areas along the coast of central Vietnam and the Vietnam-Cambodia border. Culturally and linguistically distinct from the ethnic Vietnamese, the Cham follow either Islam or a form of Brahmanism. Descendants of the people of the once-powerful kingdom of Champa, they were gradually absorbed by the Vietnamese over the course of Champa's expansion southward. Although the French allowed the Cham to remain relatively autonomous, the South Vietnamese government made efforts to integrate them. These had mixed results and led some Cham to participate with other minorities in opposition and separatist movements.

[*See also* Champa *and* Nam Tien.]

Gerald C. Hickey, *Free in the Forest: Ethnohistory of the Vietnamese Central Highlands, 1954–1976* (1982). Department of the Army, *Minority Groups in the Republic of Vietnam* (1966).

BRUCE M. LOCKHART

CHAMPA, hinduized kingdom, dating from between the second and seventeenth century, located on the eastern coast of the Indochinese peninsula. Cham archaeological remains have been found in Vietnam (between Hoanh Son and Bien Hoa) and as far inland as Kontum and Ban Me Thuot.

The Cham are an Indonesian people who began to move from the interior of the Indochinese peninsula to scattered coastal enclaves about the middle of the second century. There they practiced irrigated agriculture, but the principal economic basis of early Cham settlements was trade, especially in forest products, gold, and slaves. The Cham fleet influenced the South China Sea trade in spices and silk.

Although they were probably semi-independent, the early Cham settlements were known to the Chinese collectively as Linyi. The official history of China's Jin dynasty records that Linyi was established in the late second century, during the turmoil surrounding the collapse of the Han dynasty, in the area near the present-day city of Hue. Linyi sent its first embassy to China in 284 and in succeeding centuries alternated its diplomacy with attacks on Chinese territories south of the Red River delta of Vietnam. In 622 the new Tang dynasty (618–907) consolidated its authority over Tonkin and recognized the natural frontier of Hoanh Son as its border with Linyi.

The cultural heartland of Champa, known as Amaravati, was the region south of modern Da Nang. Amaravati contained the most important Cham religious sites (principally Shaivite, though there are Vaishnavite and Buddhist remains) and the political capitals of Tra Kieu (c. 370– c. 750) and Indrapura (c. 870–1000). The name Champa first appears here in an inscription of the seventh century.

In the eighth and early ninth centuries the southern Cham territories of Vijaya (near Qui Nhon),

FIGURE 1. *Head of a King or Deity.* Champa, Vietnam, tenth century CE. Bronze; height 40.2 cm.

Kauthara (Nha Trang), and Panduranga (Phan Rang) were politically predominant, but by 875 the capital was returned to the north. It was under the Indrapura rulers of the ninth and tenth centuries that Champa reached the height of its power.

The gradual encroachment of the expanding population of Dai Viet into Cham territory is the most likely cause of the conflict that dominated the next five centuries. Viet attacks on Indrapura caused the removal of the capital to Vijaya in 1000. Vijaya was sacked in 1044 and 1069, after which the area between Hoanh Son and Quang Tri was surrendered to Dai Viet. The cycle of Cham raids and Viet reprisals was interrupted by the Khmer occupation of Champa (1145–1149; 1203–1220), the Cham sack of Angkor (1177), and by the Mongol invasions of the late thirteenth century but resumed in the early fourteenth century following a brief marital alliance between the Cham and Viet ruling houses.

During the reign of Che Bong Nga (c. 1360–1390), the Cham enjoyed repeated military success against Dai Viet but were unable to impose their authority over the delta region. The Ming occupation of Dai Viet (1407–1427) relieved Viet pressure on Champa, allowing a brief political renaissance under Indravarman VI (r. 1400–1441). A series of civil wars ensued, during which the Viet renewed their attacks. In 1471 Vijaya was captured and Dai Viet annexed all Cham territory as far as Cape Varella. This was the effective end of Champa, although a Cham kingdom continued to exist in the Phan Rang-Phan Ri area until it was absorbed by the Nguyen lords of southern Dai Viet between 1692 and 1697. Many Cham then moved westward into Khmer-controlled territory.

Today the Cham, who have been Muslims since the fifteenth century, are one of the ethnic minorities of Democratic Kampuchea and the Socialist Republic of Vietnam.

[*See also* Cham; Indrapura; Vijaya; Dai Viet; Khmer; Angkor; Nguyen Lords; *and the map accompanying* Sukhothai.]

G. Coedès, *The Indianized States of Southeast Asia*, translated by Susan B. Cowing (1968).

JAMES M. COYLE

CHAMPASSAK, former principality in southern Laos. By the first half of the fifth century CE, the kingdom of Champassak (also known as Basak) was under the control of the kingdom of Champa, on the Vietnamese coast, and already its holy mountain, Vat Phu, was considered of sacral significance. In the second half of that century, Khmer from what is now Cambodia vanquished the Cham and took possession of Champassak; for some centuries thereafter Champassak and Vat Phu figured in the history of the Khmer and the kingdom of Angkor, falling into temporary oblivion after the decay of Angkor in the thirteenth century.

During the first few centuries of the kingdom of Lan Sang, but especially after the Lao capital was moved to Vientiane in 1569, the Lao population of the lower Mekong Valley grew, and by the seventeenth century there was a petty Lao principality in Champassak, ruled over by a queen. She urged a Buddhist monk from Vientiane, Phra Khru Phon Samek, to assume administrative power, and in 1713 he was enthroned as King Soisisamut (r. 1713–1737). He was allegedly a posthumous son of Surinyavongsa, the last king of Lan Sang, thus providing legitimacy to a true royal line and status as a kingdom for Champassak.

For the next half-century, Champassak's security was precarious: the kingdom survived because of the disinterest and disorganization of its neighbors. Following the great wars with Burma, a revived Siam invaded the Laos states and imposed its suzerainty over Champassak in 1778–1779, though King Sainyakuman (r. 1737–1791) remained on the throne. Following his death, Siam repeatedly intervened to manipulate the succession to the throne; Siam's appointment of the son of King Anuvong of Vientiane to the Champassak throne in 1819 contributed to Anu's Rebellion in 1827–1828 and to another Siamese invasion of the Mekong Lao states. After the rebellion, Siam reinstated Soisisamut's line but took away much territory from Champassak and kept it firmly under supervision. The east-bank territories were annexed by France in 1893 and the west bank in 1904. King Ratsadanay (r. 1900–1934) was treated as a petty *fonctionnaire* by the French, who retired him in 1934. His son and heir, Prince Boun Oum, served only symbolically as the king of the south, and the unification and independence of Laos ended his dreams of Champassak's revival.

[*See also* Champa; Angkor; Jayavarman II; Lan Sang; Soisisamut; *and* Boun Oum.]

C. Archaimbault, *The New Year Ceremony at Basak (South Laos)* (1971).

DAVID K. WYATT

CHAN BUDDHISM. *See* Buddhism: Buddhism in China *and* Zen.

CHANDELLA DYNASTY. Beginning in the early ninth century CE, the Chandella dynasty ruled the Bundelkhand Plateau of Madhya Pradesh from their capital, Khajuraho. Erecting at least thirty temples there, the Chandellas, particularly the monarch Dhanga (c. 950–1002), made their seat of secular power a seat of sacred power as well. In spite of attacks by Mahmud of Ghazna in 1019 and 1022, by Qutb ud-Din in 1202, and by a general of Iltutmish in 1233, the Chandellas maintained their territory at least until 1315, the date on the inscription made by the last known Chandella king.

[*See also* Madhya Pradesh; Mahmud of Ghazna; Qutb ud-Din Aibak; *and map 2 accompanying* India.]

R. K. Dikshit, *The Chandellas of Jejakabhukti* (1977). Eliky Zannas, *Khajuraho* (1960).

FREDERICK M. ASHER

FIGURE 1. *Chandella-period Relief.* Rajasthan, tenth century. *Surasundari* (celestial beauty), red sandstone. Height 49.5 cm.

CHANDIGARH, joint capital of the Indian states of Haryana and the Punjab. The construction of this modern city, planned by Le Corbusier, was begun in 1952 in order to provide a new capital for the Punjab. The partition of 1947 had divided the Punjab between Pakistan and India, placing the old capital, Lahore, within Pakistan. In 1956 Patiala and the other princely states in the area were incorporated into the Punjab, and Chandigarh became the capital of these combined territories. With the 1966 reorganization of the Punjab into three new states, Haryana and the Punjab began to share Chandigarh as their joint capital city, with Simla becoming the capital of the newly formed state of Himachal Pradesh. In an attempt to ease Sikh-Hindu conflicts, an accord was reached in the summer of 1985 that would give complete ownership of Chandigarh to the predominantly Sikh state of Punjab. The transfer of Chandigarh did not take place within the timetable established by the accord, however, because of an inability to establish new boundaries that would cede territory to Haryana in compensation for its loss of half of Chandigarh.

[*See also* Punjab *and* Patiala.]

BRUCE MCCOY OWENS

CHANDRABHANU, king of Tambralinga, was a thirteenth-century ruler from the Malay Peninsula who intruded in Sri Lanka's politics. His name first appears on a 1230 inscription from Chaiya as king of Tambralinga, an old polity centered on Nakhon Si Thammarat. In 1247 he sent a mission to Sri Lanka to request Buddhist relics but became involved in conflict and established a colony of his countrymen there. These people, called Javaka, remained a political force as late as 1270, when Chandrabhanu sent another expedition that was repulsed. Controlling the middle portion of the Malay Peninsula throughout much of the century, Chandrabhanu or his heirs must have been displaced later by Thai rulers.

[*See also* Tambralinga *and* Nakhon Si Thammarat.]

G. Coedès, *The Indianized States of Southeast Asia*, translated by Susan B. Cowing (1968). C. W. Nicholas and S. Paranavitana, *A Concise History of Ceylon* (1961).

DAVID K. WYATT

CHANDRAGUPTA MAURYA, first emperor of the Maurya empire. Known to classical historians in the west as Sandrocottus, Chandragupta conquered and ruled much of North India from about 324 to about 300 BCE. He rose to power under the influence of a minister named Chanakya, and with his assistance overthrew the last of the Nanda kings and captured their capital city of Pataliputra. He then turned his attention to northwestern India, where a power vacuum had been left by the departure of Alexander the Great. He conquered the lands east of the Indus and then, moving south, took over much of what is now central India. [*See also* Alexander III.]

The year 305 BCE saw him back in the Northwest, where Seleucus Nicator, the Macedonian satrap of Babylonia, was threatening fresh invasions. Chandragupta not only stopped his advance but pushed the frontier farther west into what is now Afghanistan. An apparently amicable settlement, however, was reached between the two monarchs. It included a matrimonial alliance of some kind between Chandragupta and Seleucus and the latter's dispatch of an ambassador, Megasthenes, to the Maury court at Pataliputra. [*See also* Seleucid Dynasty *and* Megasthenes.] Toward the end of his life, according to a Jain tradition, Chandragupta renounced his throne and became an ascetic under the Jain saint Bhadrabahu, ending his days in self-starvation.

[*See also* Maurya Empire.]

P. L. Bhargava, *Candragupta Maurya* (1936). Radhakumud Mookerji, *Chandragupta Maurya and His Times* (1943). Viśākhadatta, *The Minister's Seal (Mudrārākṣasa),* in *Two Plays of Ancient India,* translated by J. A. B. Van Buitenen (1969), pp. 181–271.

JOHN S. STRONG

CHANG'AN, ancient city located on the Wei River plain in the southern part of modern Shaanxi Province; served as the eastern terminus of the Silk Road and capital of some of China's most powerful dynasties, especially the Han and Tang. During the Tang (618–907), Chang'an was the veritable cultural capital of all of East Asia and the largest city by far in the world. So powerful was its influence that it served as the model for the capitals of other contemporary East Asian states, notably Parhae and Japan. The present city on the site is Xi'an, the provincial capital of Shaanxi, which, however, occupies less than one-seventh the area of the Tang capital. Although the Western Zhou (1122–771 BCE) and Qin (221–206 BCE) also built their capitals on the Wei River plain, the first time a city called Chang'an ("enduring peace") was designated a capital was around 200 BCE, at the beginning of the Han dynasty (206 BCE–220 CE). Han Chang'an was located about 10 kilometers to the northwest of Xi'an. It was irregular in shape, with an outer wall measuring 6.9 kilometers in length and containing twelve gates, each about 18 meters wide. In 2 CE it had a population of around 300,000.

After the fall of the Former Han, Chang'an's fortunes declined for several centuries until its adoption as the capital of the Western Wei (534–557) and Northern Zhou (557–581). In 582 the founder of the Sui dynasty (581–618), Wendi, decided to build a new capital, Daxingcheng ("great revival city"), southeast of the old city, into which he moved the following year. His chief architect was Yuwen Kai. Upon the founding of the Tang in 618 the new city was renamed Chang'an and expanded. At the height of the Tang in the eighth century, the population of Chang'an reached one million inside the walls and perhaps another million in the surrounding satellite towns. Late in the ninth century Chang'an fell victim to the ravages of the rebel Huang Chao, and in 904 many of its buildings were razed and transported to Luoyang by the founder of the Later Liang dynasty (907–923). Afterwards, while remaining a bustling trading center, its political importance declined.

Benefiting from recent innovations in city building on the North China Plain, especially those at the Northern Wei capital of Luoyang, Chang'an was the first totally planned Chinese city, constructed on the basis of the principles of axiality and symmetry. Its rectangular outer walls, made of pounded earth, measured 36.7 kilometers (9.7 kilometers east to west and 8.65 kilometers north to south). The city was divided into three major zones. To the extreme north was the Palace City *(gongcheng),* where the emperor resided with his harem, performed the rituals of office, and held court. At the beginning of the Tang, the emperor resided in the Taiji Palace, located on the central axis of the Palace City. Later, during the time of Gaozong (r. 650–683), the emperor's residence was moved to the Daming Palace, located to the northeast of the Palace City beyond the city walls. Under Xuanzong (r. 712–756) yet another imperial residence was built southeast of the Daming Palace, called the Xingqing Palace. Directly south of the Palace City was the Imperial City *(huangcheng),* which for the first time in Chinese history concentrated all the government offices in one district.

The remaining area, more than four-fifths of the total, was known as the Outer City *(waiguocheng).* It was comprised of 110 wards *(fang),* two of them marketplaces, the rest predominantly residential.

The wards were laid out on a grid pattern formed by the crisscrossing of fourteen north-south and eleven east-west avenues. Both sides of these avenues, most of which ranged from 55 to 150 meters in width, were lined with drainage ditches and planted with shade trees. Each of the wards was walled. The ward gates were opened at sunup and closed at dusk; it was a crime to be caught on the streets after the ward gates were closed. The marketplaces were also open from dawn to dusk. Although no stores were permitted in any other of the wards, literary evidence for these exist, especially late in the dynasty. The East Market connected with roads leading to the second Tang capital of Luoyang, the West Market with the Silk Road. Consequently, the West Market was the center of foreign trade and foreign residence. The mansions of aristocrats and officials were concentrated in wards near the Daming and Xingqing palaces and around the East Market, while those of commoners were likely to be found in the more densely populated area around the West Market.

There were a number of entertainment districts: the gay quarter and government-controlled pleasure district were situated southeast of the Imperial City, while the scenic Serpentine (Qujiang) and Fuyung Park, popular spots for excursions, were located at the extreme southeast corner of the Outer City. One remarkable feature of Tang Chang'an was an elevated covered roadway connecting these parks with the Daming and Xingqing palaces. By means of this road, the emperor could enjoy his scenic outings completely unseen by his subjects.

Because Chang'an was an international capital, people from all over the world congregated there, including diplomatic envoys, religious missionaries, merchants, and students. With them came foreign religions such as Zoroastrianism, Manichaeanism, and Nestorian Christianity and associated places of worship. But the most numerous and grandest religious edifices in Chang'an, which were located on almost every street, belonged to Buddhism and Daoism; some of them occupied entire wards.

Since the mid-1950s the Chinese have undertaken extensive archaeological investigations of Han and Tang sites in the Chang'an vicinity. Since modern Xi'an occupies the area above much of the Tang city, relatively little has been well preserved. Some nearby tombs of Han and Tang emperors have become popular tourist attractions, however, especially the joint tomb of Tang Gaozong and his wife, Empress Wu, with its spectacular "spirit road" of monumental sculptures and satellite tombs of royal family members, which contain extensive wall paintings depicting numerous aspects of aristocratic life.

FIGURE 1. *Little Goose Pagoda.* Built from 707 to 709, this pagoda, with fifteen tiers and a height of forty-three meters, was used to store Buddhist scriptures brought from India. The top of the pagoda was destroyed by an earthquake in the sixteenth century.

[*See also* Han Dynasty; Tang Dynasty; *and* Xi'an.]

Edward H. Schafer, "The Last Years of Ch'ang-an," *Oriens Extremus* 10 (1963): 133–179. Arthur F. Wright, "Symbolism and Function: Reflections of Changan and Other Great Cities," *Journal of Asian Studies* 24 (1965): 667–679 and "Changan," in *Cities of Destiny,* edited by Arnold Toynbee (1967), pp. 138–149.

HOWARD J. WECHSLER

CHANGCHUN, city located on the Yitong River, capital of Jilin Province in northeastern China, an area that was integrated into China under the Qing dynasty (1644–1911). Owing to its rich resource base and low population density, the Northeast (Manchuria) was developed by the Japanese in the late nineteenth and early twentieth centuries. Much of the city of Changchun was developed under the Japanese military occupation from 1933 to 1945, when the city was renamed Xinjing and was the capital of the Japanese puppet state, Manchukuo. Today Changchun is a major railway transshipment center and is noted for its motor vehicle plant that produces Liberator and Red Flag trucks and limousines.

Robert H. G. Lee, *The Manchurian Frontier in Ch'ing History* (1970). Sadako N. Ogata, *Defiance in Manchuria: The Making of Japanese Foreign Policy, 1931* (1964).

SALLY HART

CHANG MYŎN (John M. Chang; 1899–1966), president of the Republic of Korea in 1950, 1952, and again in 1960.

Chang was born in Inch'ŏn to a middle-class Catholic family of northwestern Korean origin that was engaged in customs administration. He graduated from the Suwon Agriculture and Forestry High School and the YMCA English course and studied for five years at Manhattan College, from which he later received a doctoral degree. Chang became principal of the Catholic Tongsung Commercial School in Seoul from 1931 until the liberation of Korea in 1945, leading a quiet, neutral life in the struggle against Japan. Entering conservative postwar political life, he became a member of both the Interim Legislative Assembly (1946) and the National Assembly (1948), serving in the latter year as Korean delegate to the third General Assembly of the United Nations. In 1949 he became Korea's first ambassador to the United States, representing Korea during the opening months of the Korean War. From 1951 until May 1952 he served as Syngman Rhee's prime minister. Although he filled these posts with a faultless conscientiousness and an amiable and trustworthy respectability, he was not noted for dynamism or courage.

In the middle of 1952 the rising repression of Rhee's leadership impelled Chang to join the opposition politics of the Democratic Party, whose supreme committee member he became in 1955. In 1956 he was elected vice president on the opposition ticket, defeating Rhee's candidate. Rhee reacted by ignoring and isolating him. As opposition leader, Chang was reelected to the Assembly in 1960 and, following Rhee's overthrow, was narrowly elected prime minister on 19 August 1960. As leader of the new cabinet-responsible system he had advocated, during the succeeding nine months Chang presided over Korea's only fully democratic government.

Chang assembled an able cabinet, but he then reshuffled their positions too frequently. He tried, with indecision and too much caution, to resolve the problems of clamorous new democratic and factional demands and threats of violence, inflation, and chaos. Chang's government was beginning to work more effectively, institute economic planning, and make progress when, for complex and enigmatic reasons, it failed to detect or defend itself from a military coup on 16 May 1961. Chang added to this failure by fleeing to a convent, where he could not be reached for two crucial days. The Chang government resigned on 18 May, ending for a generation Korea's democratic experiment. Thereafter, Chang Myŏn lived quietly in Seoul until his death.

[*See also* Rhee, Syngman; May Sixteenth Coup d'État; *and* Korea, Republic of.]

Sungjoo Han, *The Failure of Democracy in South Korea* (1974). John Kie-Chiang Oh, *Korea: Democracy on Trial* (1968).

GREGORY HENDERSON

CHANG PO-GO (d. 846), a man of obscure origins who became a major local leader and dominated the trade routes between southwestern Korea and China during the first half of the ninth century.

As a youth Chang Po-go traveled to China and through the force of his ambition and his intelligence became a powerful merchant in the Shandong area. Like many Koreans, Chang had gone to China for economic advancement, and once there he quickly emerged as leader of the overseas Korean community. From his secure economic position on the Chinese mainland, Chang returned to Korea to establish a base of power.

By the beginning of the ninth century Chang had emerged as the master of the sea routes between the Korean peninsula and China, and his influence extended to Japan as well. When the Japanese monk Ennin traveled to China in the middle of the ninth century, he came into contact with Chang Po-go's authority, and through his help Ennin was able to return safely to Japan. Chang Po-go is credited with policing the seas and eradicating piracy from the sea lanes around Korea. [*See also* Piracy: Japanese Piracy in Korea.]

From his headquarters at Ch'ŏnghae Garrison on modern Wando Island, Chang Po-go dominated the entire southwestern coastal area. He also quickly became a military leader on the peninsula and even became involved in court politics. To secure his power Chang amassed a force, described as numbering ten thousand soldiers, that he provisioned and trained himself. Because of the size of his army, some Silla aristocrats turned to him to support their causes. When Kim U-jing (King Sinmu) needed a military force to gain the throne in 839, he turned to Chang, who willingly helped and thus assured the success of the attempt. In short, Chang Po-go became a king-maker. To the status-conscious Silla aristocrats, Chang was a man to be closely watched, and when Chang next attempted to have the crown prince marry his daughter, the court aristocrats retaliated. Sending a man in disguise to Chang's castle, the aristocrats had Chang assassinated; they immediately dissolved his army.

The rise and fall of Chang Po-go has come to represent several trends that were emerging in Silla society. Because Silla was a closed aristocratic society, Chang had to leave Korea and go to China to improve his standard of life. From his position as a prosperous merchant he was able to secure power in Silla and quickly emerge as a regional strongman, part of a group that would soon dominate Korean politics. Silla still remained too closed, however, to allow even a merchant prince like Chang Po-go into the highest echelons of society.

[*See also* Silla.]

Edwin O. Reischauer, *Ennin's Travels in T'ang China* (1955). EDWARD J. SHULTZ

CHANGSHA, capital of Hunan Province, situated on the east bank of the Xiang River. The river, which empties into Lake Dongting and the Yangtze River, is divided into two parts at Changsha by a long, sandy island called Shuiluzhou. It is from this island that Changsha ("long sand") derives its name. Across the river is the gentle Yuelu Mountain, the site of one of the five famous academies of the Southern Song period (1127–1279).

Founded by Miao peoples in around 1100 BCE, Changsha is at the same latitude as Orlando, Florida—a few frosts occur in winter and clouds of mosquitos rise from numerous paddies and ponds to flourish in the blazing summer heat. Changsha remains Hunan's intellectual center, as it was when Mao Zedong was educated there from 1911 to 1922. In the mid-1980s the population was 750,000; most residences were in two- and three-story houses of dun-colored brick, with a sprinkling of taller buildings rising above the forested streets.

ANGUS W. MCDONALD, JR.

CHANG TSAI. *See* Zhang Zai.

CHARNOCK, JOB (d. 1693), the agent of the East India Company in Hooghly, the emporium of European trade in eastern India, when hostilities broke out between the Mughal governor and the (British) East India Company. Charnock decided to leave Hooghly for a safer place down the river at Sutanuti. The English finally landed in Sutanuti on 24 August 1690 and erected a few huts destined to grow into Calcutta, the "second city of the empire." Charnock was the first governor of the settlement and was said to have become increasingly tyrannical. He did, however, mix freely with Indians. His mausoleum still stands in the yard of Saint John's Church as the earliest architectural monument in Calcutta.

[*See also* Calcutta.]

P. T. Nair, *Job Charnock: The Founder of Calcutta: An Anthology* (1978). A. K. Roy, *A Short History of Calcutta* (1901; Reprint, 1982). PRADIP SINHA

CHARTER OATH. Issued in the name of Japan's Meiji emperor on 6 April 1868, this oath served as the initial policy declaration of the Meiji government. Designed to outline the political objectives of the imperial restoration and to secure internal unity, the oath included the following provisions: (1) deliberative assemblies shall be widely established and all matters decided by public discussion; (2) all classes, high and low, shall unite in vigorously carrying out the administration of affairs of state; (3) the common person, no less than the civil or military official, shall be allowed to pursue his own calling, so that there may be no discontent; (4) evil customs of the past shall be ended and everything based upon the just laws of nature; and (5) knowledge shall be sought throughout the world so as to strengthen the foundations of imperial rule. Originally written by Yuri Kimimasa, who incorporated many of the ideas of Yokoi Shōnan into the document, the oath was revised by Fukuoka Kōtei, a samurai from Tosa, and a final draft was prepared by Kido Takayoshi, a Chōshū samurai and central figure in the Restoration, who added the article on the evil customs of the past. [*See* Yokoi Shōnan *and* Kido Takayoshi.]

Portions of the Charter Oath were clear and straightforward. The emphasis in article 5, that knowledge should be sought from around the world, came to be implemented not only with the Iwakura Mission of 1871 to 1873, which took many of the government's leaders and a large number of students to the West, but also with the hiring of foreign experts who came to Japan to teach, innovate, and establish the basis for Japanese development and modernization. [*See* Iwakura Mission.]

In adding the clause on the need to rid Japan of

evil customs, Kido seems to have been concerned with eliminating the xenophobic antiforeignism and seclusionist sentiments that had troubled Japanese relations with the outside world during the last years of the Tokugawa shogunate. In appealing to the "just laws of nature," he appears to have alluded to international law as a new guideline for Japanese relations with the outside world.

The third clause, which called upon both civil and military officials to be allowed to pursue their own callings, indicated the strong antifeudal tone of the Restoration. Even before the official elimination of the domains and the abrogation of the samurai class, the Charter Oath made it plain that the new regime encouraged individuals to break from age-old restrictions and pursue their own interests and callings, thus recognizing one of the chief complaints against the old regime and the former feudal order.

Article 2 was basically a call for national unity at a time of great internal unrest. It also suggested the degree to which the creation of a modern state would have to cut across class lines and would have to involve the energies and commitment of the Japanese people as a whole.

Finally, article 1 was the most troubling and ambiguous. There were those who interpreted its statements that "assemblies shall be widely established" and that all matters should be decided by "public discussion" as suggesting a democratic course for modern Japan. This was certainly the view of many of Japan's liberals. And yet, as Fukuoka Kōtei explained, in revising the oath he was hardly concerned with the "masses," but envisioned "the administration of the government by the *kuge* [court nobles] and the daimyo." Still, as the government was soon to discover, there were also those who persisted in arguing for a more popular interpretation.

What the Charter Oath indicated was the early liberal tone of the Meiji Restoration. The need to rid the country of its feudal shackles, to allow talent to rise, to reject xenophobia for a willingness to learn from the outside world, and to involve the people in the quest to create a new nation and society—these were all serious considerations in the early Meiji years. That such goals were revised by changing domestic conditions and an altered international environment seems hardly surprising, and yet the very ambiguity of the Charter Oath allowed those outside the government's inner circle to argue for alternative visions and for a greater public role in determining modern Japan's future. It would be hard to deny that the great debates of Meiji political history had their roots in the policy parameters established by the Charter Oath.

[*See also* Meiji Restoration.]

F. G. NOTEHELFER

CHATTERJI, BANKIM CHANDRA (1838–1894), the first great modern novelist in the Bengali language. Educated at Presidency College, Calcutta, Chatterji worked in government service in Bengal from 1858 until he retired in 1891. Throughout the course of his life he wrote fifteen novels in Bengali, composed numerous sketches, essays, and book reviews, and founded the journal *Bangadarshan.* Among his novels were *Krishnakanter Will* (1878) and *Anandamath* (1882). Popular with Bengali readers, Chatterji's stories were romantic, often set in another historical period. Modern critics have credited him with the creation of the Bengali novel in its modern form. He is also remembered as the composer of "Bande Mataram," a famous patriotic song.

[*See also* Bande Mataram.]

S. K. Bose, *Bankim Chandra Chatterji* (1974). Bhabatosh Datta, "Bankim Chandra Chatterjee and Reform Movement in the Nineteenth Century Bengal," in *Social and Religious Reform Movements in the Ninteenth and Twentieth Centuries,* edited by S. P. Sen (1979). Sukumar Sen, *History of Bengali Literature* (1960).

JUDITH E. WALSH

CHAUHAN DYNASTY. The surname Chauhan (Sanskrit, Chahamana) is included in most medieval lists of the thirty-six Rajput families. The first reference to this family comes from an inscription in Gujarat dated 756 CE. It is clear that the Chauhans were feudatories of the Pratiharas of Kanauj during much of the eighth and ninth centuries, but they emerged as independent rulers of considerable importance in Rajasthan in the eleventh. Several different branches of the family ruled the Rajasthan towns of Jalor, Nadol, Ranthambhor, Sambhar, and Ajmer in the period from 1000 to 1300. Between 1153 and 1164 the Sambhar branch captured Delhi. It was these Chauhans, under the leadership of Prithviraj III (1177–1192), who met and defeated the Ghurids at the first battle of Tarain in 1191 and who, in 1192, were beaten decisively on that same battlefield with the resulting loss of Delhi to the Muslims. Branches of the Chauhan family retained power in Rajasthan until the end of the British period, however, and several Hada Chauhans from

Bundi and Kotah attained high rank in Mughal service.

[*See also* Prithviraj Chauhan; Rajput; Ajmer; *and* Rajasthan.]

D. Sharma, *Rajasthan through the Ages*, 2 vols. (1966); *Early Chauhan Dynasties* (2d ed., 1975).

RICHARD DAVIS SARAN

CHEDI DYNASTY. *See* Maha-Meghavahana Dynasty.

CHEFU. *See* Yantai.

CHEN BODA (b. 1904), also known as Chen Shangyu and Chen Zhimei; Chinese Communist leader. A native of Huian County, Fujian Province, Chen joined the Chinese Communist Party in 1927, was enrolled at Moscow's Sun Yat-sen University from 1927 to 1930, taught at China University in Beijing, and worked in the North China Communist underground in the 1930s.

Beginning in 1937 Chen was closely associated with Mao Zedong—Chen did ghostwriting for Mao, accompanied him to Russia in 1950 and 1957, and established himself as the Party's leading idealogue and an authoritative interpreter of Mao's thought. In 1966 Chen was appointed director of the Party's Cultural Revolution group to propel Mao's Great Proletarian Cultural Revolution. In 1969 Chen reached the pinnacle of power when he was elected one of the five members of the Politburo Standing Committee, but he was purged the following year. He was tried and received an eighteen-year sentence by a special court in 1980. Chen's prolific writings include *China's Four Big Families*, a book about the Chiangs, the Songs (Soongs), the Kungs, and the Chens.

PARRIS CHANG

CHEN DUXIU (1879–1942), leader of the New Culture Movement (1915–1932) and founder of the Chinese Communist Party. After Mao Zedong, Chen Duxiu was perhaps the most influential Chinese figure of this century.

Chen's father died when Chen was quite young, and he was raised by his uncle, an important official of the Qing dynasty (1644–1911). In 1896 Chen passed his *xiucai*, the first level of the Confucian civil service examination, at the precocious age of seventeen. A year later, however, he failed to pass his *juren*, the second level of the civil service exam. Within a few years he had become an important figure in the student revolutionary movement that opposed the Qing dynasty. Among the principal revolutionary organizations and periodicals in Tokyo and Shanghai with which Chen was involved were the Youth Society (Qingnianhui), the *Common Speech Journal (Su bao)*, the Restoration Society (Guangfuhui), and the *China National Gazette (Guomin riri bao)*. At the same time, he was the leading force in extending the revolutionary movement to his native Anhui Province. Between 1903 and 1907 Chen was responsible for a series of radical organizations in Anhui, the most important of which were the *Anhui Common Speech Journal (Anhui suhua bao)*, one of the first vernacular papers begun in China, and the Warrior Yue Society (Yuewanghui), a military organization dedicated to assassination and intrigue in the central Yangtze River valley. Unlike most other radical leaders of the time, however, Chen refused to join the Revolutionary Alliance (Tongmenghui), the revolutionary umbrella group begun by Sun Yat-sen in 1905.

Before 1911 Chen was also associated with the National Essence Movement. One of the motivations behind Chen's radical activities was the hope of restoring the great traditions of the Chinese past. Indeed, Chen was to continue his philological research into the origin of early Chinese characters throughout his life; his knowledge in this area made his later critiques of the traditional culture and language particularly incisive.

Following the successful Republican revolution of 1911, Chen served for a short time as a member of the new Anhui provincial government before resigning his post, complaining that under the influence of the new president, Yuan Shikai, "an old disease . . . bureaucratic government has resurfaced." In 1915, in opposition to Yuan Shikai's attempt to restore the monarchy, Chen began his highly influential journal *Youth*, later *New Youth (Xin qingnian)*, touching off what has come to be known as the New Culture Movement. Attempting to arouse a new generation of young people, Chen used Western ideas to attack the legitimacy of many of his former revolutionary comrades, whose continuing desires to restore the traditions of the past had led them to support a new autocratic government. Chen's influence expanded greatly after 1917 when he became dean of the College of Arts and Sciences at Beijing University and launched first the anti-Confucian movement and then the vernacular campaign in the pages of his journal, *New Youth*.

Both these campaigns seized the imagination of Chinese radical youth. The Confucian campaign attacked the authoritarian ideas and family structure that Chen felt was shackling Chinese society and helped to popularize democratic, egalitarian notions. The influence of the vernacular campaign was equally, if not more, profound. Chen had long been a pioneer in the use of the vernacular. It was Chen, in fact, in *New Youth,* who was to introduce the use of punctuation into Chinese writing. When Chen's younger colleague and fellow Anhui provincial Hu Shi published an essay for *New Youth* in January 1917 suggesting the reform of the Chinese writing style, Chen turned this into a call for a vernacular revolution and began the campaign to abolish the use of the thousand-year-old literary language and to undermine the influence of its conservative partisans.

Largely as a consequence of these two movements, Chen gained a considerable following among Chinese radical youth. Chen's radical influence on Chinese students alarmed the Beijing government, which in early 1919 forced him to resign from the university. This did not dampen Chen's activities, however, and following the May Fourth Incident later that year, when Chinese students took to the streets to protest the Versailles Peace Treaty granting the Japanese the rights to the former German concessions in China in Shandong Province, Chen joined his former students in the streets. For this he was imprisoned for eighty-three days. Released from jail in early September, he hurried to the relative safety of Shanghai, where he began to explore the possibilities of forming a new, independent party.

Chen had now become disillusioned by what he saw as the bankruptcy of Western democracy and was interested in socialism. After meeting with representatives of the Communist International in Shanghai in the spring of 1920, he began to form the Chinese Communist Party (CCP), establishing a small cell in Shanghai and encouraging former students and associates in other places to do the same. A year later, the Party had grown large enough to hold its first National Congress in Shanghai, electing Chen Duxiu in absentia as its first secretary-general.

Chen now returned to Shanghai from Guangzhou (Canton), where he had gone in October 1920 to serve as head of the educational committee of Guangdong Province for the warlord Chen Jiongming. Under Chen Duxiu's full-time control, the Party's organizational activities expanded greatly, but its base remained small. Thus, in June 1923, after the collapse of CCP efforts at an alliance with the Beijing warlord Wu Peifu, Chen acceded to Comintern demands for a United Front with the Guomindang (Kuomintang, KMT, or Nationalist Party) of Sun Yat-sen, whereby the Chinese Communists would as individuals join the Guomindang. Chen, who had been studying Marxist doctrine in the meantime, now wrote that the achievement of socialism, which he had previously hoped could be immediate, would have to wait until after the development of capitalism.

After the establishment of the United Front, the revolutionary movement began to expand rapidly. In March 1925 Sun Yat-sen died. A few months later, following the famous May Thirtieth Incident, Party membership increased explosively. The expanded left-wing influence within the Guomindang began to upset the more conservative members of that party, who agitated against the Communists. In response, Chen called for the Communists to withdraw from the United Front. He repeated this suggestion several times over the next few years, especially following the incident of 20 March 1926, when Chiang Kai-shek, then the head of the KMT military, launched a coup d'état to take over power in the Guomindang, ousting many Communists in the process. Each time, however, Chen failed to press his suggestions when they were opposed by Comintern representatives and the Comintern's powerful supporters within the CCP. In July 1926, when Chen called for the arming of the peasantry and workers so they could fight for themselves during Chiang Kai-shek's Northern Expedition to reunify China, the Comintern failed to provide the arms. Even after Stalin himself called for the arming of worker and peasant revolutionaries in May 1927, he still gave no arms. On 12 April 1927 Chiang Kai-shek turned on his erstwhile Communist allies in the so-called White Terror, a bloodbath that took the lives of Chen's two elder sons and many of his friends. Later that year, Chen, who had already resigned as secretary-general of the Party, was severely criticized by the Communists for his "opportunistic" policies.

For the next two years, Chen continued to work for the CCP, contributing articles to the party journal. By late 1928, however, Chen had become interested in the ideas of Trotsky, whose thought was introduced to him by students who had returned from Moscow. Between July and August of 1929 Chen wrote three famous letters to the Party in which he criticized the way in which it was supporting the Soviet Union in the Sino-Soviet clashes then occurring over the South Manchurian Railroad. Chen also lambasted the "adventurist" policies of the Party and suggested that only a "democratic revolution of the proletariat as well as the peasants" could help the working class achieve victory and create a socialist revolution. As a result of these Trotskyist criticisms of the Party, Chen and his supporters, who had already begun to organize a Trotskyist faction within the Party, were expelled. In May 1931 the four major Trotskyist factions united into a coherent organization under Chen's leadership. Before this new party could make much headway, however, its ranks were decimated by arrests. On 15 October 1932 Chen was also caught in the dragnet, and he spent the next five years in prison after a highly celebrated trial. Released on 8 August 1937 as a result of the new United Front between the Communists and the Guomindang, Chen attempted to forge an alliance of moderate Trotskyites and democratic elements. His efforts were unsuccessful, and in 1942 he died in Sichuan.

[*See also* Communism: Chinese Communist Party; Li Dazhao; Marxism and Socialism: Marxism in China; China, Republic Period; *and* May Fourth Movement.]

Lee Feigon, *Chen Duxiu: Founder of the Chinese Communist Party* (1983). Richard Kagan, trans., "Ch'en Tu-hsiu's Unfinished Autobiography," *China Quarterly* 50 (April–June 1972): 295–314. Benjamin Schwartz, "Ch'en Tu-hsiu and the Acceptance of the Modern West," *Journal of the History of Ideas* (January 1931). LEE FEIGON

CHEN DYNASTY. *See* Six Dynasties.

CHENG BROTHERS. Cheng Yi (1033–1107) and his brother Cheng Hao (1032–1085) were leading Northern Song literati thinkers. Their ideas helped redefine Confucianism and were fundamental to the philosophical synthesis of Zhu Xi (1130–1200), which provided the intellectual foundation for the Neo-Confucian movement in East Asia. Cheng Yi, the more influential of the two, held office only from 1086 to 1087 as a lecturer to the young emperor Zhezong, a post obtained for him by Sima Guang (1019–1086), after which he returned to Luoyang. Cheng Hao served as a local official in the 1060s and then briefly at court before being demoted for his opposition to Wang Anshi (1021–1086) and the New Policies. Most of his remaining years were spent with his brother in Luoyang, a center of the opposition.

For the Chengs learning to be a moral man was the true purpose of learning and the necessary basis for establishing an integrated human order. Their ideas gained a following among literati who, during a period of bitter political factionalism and increasing competition for government posts, had become disenchanted with official service or who had turned away from cultural studies and literary pursuits as a means of understanding universal values. In contrast to most other contemporary moralists, however, the Chengs sought a philosophical understanding of the foundations of morality. Their most important ideas concerned the concept of *li* (principle), which they presented as that which gave order and purpose to every thing and event. They claimed both that each and every thing had a specific principle that accounted for its particularity and that all specific principles were in fact one principle. Cheng Yi's preferred formulation was "Principle is one but its manifestations are many" (Chan, p. 544). To be moral was thus a matter of according with principle in all activities so that each action became an extension of unifying principle and furthered the creation of a coherent and harmonious human order.

The Chengs differed in their handling of the vital question of how individuals could gain insight into principle, which existed within men as human nature. Cheng Hao stressed the importance of cultivating an internal self. Cheng Yi, while recognizing the importance of "seriousness," also argued that knowledge of principle could be arrived at through the investigation of things external to the self, for "Things and events are governed by the same principle, if you understand one, you understand the other, for the truth within and the truth without are identical . . . every blade of grass and every tree possesses principle and should be examined" (Chan, p. 563).

Although the Chengs drew extensively on such classical Chinese sources as the *Lunyu (Analects)*, the *Mengzi (Mencius)*, the *Zhongyong (Doctrine of the Mean)*, the *Daxue (Great Learning)*, and the appendix to the *Yijing (Book of Changes)*, their understanding of principle bears some similarity to Huayan Buddhist ideas. They were also influenced by Zhang Zai's use of the concept of *qi* (material force) to establish a coherent philosophical system, although this concept lost some of its levels of significance in the Chengs' work. Like others who sought to persuasively define literati values in the late eleventh century, the Chengs claimed to have understood the true way of the sages of antiquity. They went beyond their contemporaries, however, by insisting that for nearly fifteen hundred years this way had remained lost until they had begun to propagate it. Their narrower definition of what it meant to be a *ru* (Confucian) and their adamant opposition to Buddhism and Daoism as sources of literati values also set them apart from many contemporary intellectuals. In spite of the existence of intellectual alternatives and official attempts to proscribe their works, their teaching gained extraordinary influence during the first half of the twelfth century. Their claim to knowledge of the true way, their rejection of Buddhism and Daoism, their success in formulating a doctrine that students could learn and practice, and their insistence on the universality and primary importance of moral principles may help explain why literati trying to cope with the collapse of the social and political order were eager to accept their ideas.

[*See also* Neo-Confucianism *and* Zhu Xi.]

Wing-tsit Chan, *A Source Book in Chinese Philosophy* (1963). A. C. Graham, *Two Chinese Philosophers: Ch'êng Ming-tao and Ch'êng Yi-ch'uan* (1958). PETER K. BOL

CHENGDU, capital of Sichuan Province. The city is located on the rich and densely populated Chengdu Plain, the only large level area in the province. One of the oldest cities in China, Chengdu was founded in the fourth century BCE; the Guanxian water conservatory works of the third century BCE are nearby. Chengdu was the capital of the state of Shu during the Three Kingdoms period (221–263), and the largest city in southwest China until overtaken by Chongqing in the twentieth century. Since World War II Chengdu has become a major industrial center. In the mid-1980s it had a population of approximately 2 million. ROBERT ENTENMANN

CHENG HAO. *See* Cheng Brothers.

CHEN GUOFU (1892–1951), nephew of Chen Qimei and early patron of Chiang Kai-shek in Guomindang (Kuomintang, KMT, or Nationalist Party) politics in China. Chen and Chiang became sworn brothers while both served the elder Chen in Shanghai after the 1911 Revolution. Chen thus became a Chiang loyalist and conservative anticommunist whose major responsibility was recruitment of personnel into the Guomindang. He headed the organization department of the KMT from 1926 to 1932, served as governor of Jiangsu from 1933 to 1937, and was head of the personnel department of the Chinese government during the anti-Japanese war. Followers of Chen and his brother Chen Lifu dominated the party and were identified by opponents as the "CC clique," one of several factions loyal to Chiang. After the Nationalist flight to Taiwan, Chen's career was curtailed by tuberculosis, which took his life in 1951.

[*See also* Chen Lifu; Chen Qimei; Chiang Kai-shek; *and* Guomindang.]

Lloyd E. Eastman, *The Abortive Revolution: China under Nationalist Rule, 1927–1937* (1974). Hung-mao Tien, *Government and Politics in Kuomintang China, 1927–1937* (1972). PARKS M. COBLE, JR.

CHENG YI. *See* Cheng Brothers.

CHEN JIONGMING (1878–1933), military and political leader in Guangdong Province during the early Chinese Republic. Chen supported Sun Yat-sen's secessionist government in Canton (Guangzhou), and in 1920 Sun named Chen governor of Guangdong Province. In this, as in earlier positions of regional authority, Chen launched a number of progressive social and educational reforms. Chen wanted to develop Guangdong, and therefore split with Sun, who wanted to use the province as a springboard for a northern military expedition to unite the country. From 1921 to 1925, Chen clashed several times with troops supporting Sun. After his defeat in 1925, Chen fled to Hong Kong, where he tried to continue his opposition to the Guomindang, but he had little influence.

Howard L. Boorman, ed., *Biographical Dictionary of Republican China*, vol. 1 (1967), pp. 173–180. Winston Hsieh, "The Ideas and Ideals of a Warlord: Ch'en Chiung-ming (1878–1933)," *Papers on China* 16 (December 1962): 198–252. JAMES E. SHERIDAN

CHEN-LA. *See* Zhenla.

CHEN LIFU (b. 1899), nephew of Chen Qimei and younger brother of Chen Guofu; major figure in Guomindang (Kuomintang, or Nationalist Party) politics. A Chiang Kai-shek loyalist, Chen and his brother controlled most personnel appointments within the party structure and created a large faction often called the "CC clique." Personally close to Chiang, Chen performed many political and diplomatic tasks not associated with any particular appointed office, such as traveling incognito to Berlin from 1935 to 1936. Chen developed a philosophical theory based on Chinese tradition called vitalism *(weisheng lun)* about which he wrote and spoke extensively. After the Communist victory in China, Chen moved to the United States in August 1950.

[*See also* Chen Guofu; Chen Qimei; Chiang Kai-shek; *and* Guomindang.]

Lloyd E. Eastman, *The Abortive Revolution: China under Nationalist Rule, 1927–1937* (1974). Hung-mao Tien, *Government and Politics in Kuomintang China, 1927–1937* (1972).

PARKS M. COBLE, JR.

CHEN QIMEI (1876–1916), a native of Zhejiang, China, studied in Tokyo, where in 1906 he became an ardent supporter of Sun Yat-sen's Tongmenghui (Revolutionary Alliance). In 1909 he returned to Shanghai to organize a secret revolutionary headquarters. In November 1911 he led revolutionary military forces to victory over Qing loyalists in Shanghai and Nanjing, thus allowing creation of the provisional government. Forces following Yuan Shikai defeated Chen in the second revolution, causing his flight to Tokyo to join Sun. Returning to Shanghai in early 1915 to lead anti-Yuan actions, Chen met death at the hands of a Yuan-sponsored assassin in May 1916. Chen is also remembered in Guomindang (Kuomintang, KMT, or Nationalist Party) history as an early patron of Chiang Kai-shek. He met Chiang while in Tokyo and sponsored his entry into KMT politics and his association with Chen's nephews, Chen Guofu and Chen Lifu.

[*See also* Chen Guofu; Chen Lifu; Chiang Kai-shek; Guomindang; Sun Yat-sen; Yuan Shikai; *and* China, Republic Period.]

Howard L. Boorman, ed., *Biographical Dictionary of Republican China* (1967–1971); Mary Backus Rankin, *Early Chinese Revolutionaries: Radical Intellectuals in Shanghai and Chekiang, 1902–1911* (1971).

PARKS M. COBLE, JR.

CHEN SHAOYU. *See* Wang Ming.

CHEN YOULIANG (1320–1363), Chinese rebel and warlord of the late Yuan period. Born in Hubei into a family of fishermen, Chen served for a time as a government clerk before joining the Red Turban rebellion of Xu Shouhui in 1351. Chen became a commander under the self-styled Tianwan emperor, but his own ambition led him to eliminate rivals blocking his own rise to the head of the movement. In 1360 he even disposed of Xu Shouhui and set himself up as emperor of the state of Han in Jiangxi.

Over the next three years, however, Chen was unable to expand his control over the middle Yangtze River region owing to the strength of another contender to the east, Zhu Yuanzhang. The inevitable showdown between the two regional hegemons came in a huge naval battle on Lake Poyang in 1363, during which Chen was killed by an arrow. Zhu's decisive victory instantly made him the strongest remaining contestant for power and prepared the way for elimination of his downriver rivals, Zhang Shicheng and Fang Guozhen, and his eventual establishment of the Ming dynasty (1368–1644).

[*See also* Zhu Yuanzhang.]

Edward L. Dreyer, *Early Ming China* (1982).

ROLAND L. HIGGINS

CHEN YUN (b. 1905), prominent Chinese Communist Party (CCP) leader known chiefly as a specialist in economic and commercial affairs since the Yan'an period, but also important in the Party rectification movements and labor union activity of the CCP. He joined the Party in 1924 and was elected to the Central Committee and the Politburo by the 1940s, afterwards serving in numerous high positions in the Party and state hierarchy. Since 1956 he has advocated balanced development of all sectors of the economy, utilizing material incentives and other market correctives to the command economy, while remaining a strong advocate of centralized planning to determine overall levels of allocation and production.

Although Chen's ideas are often contrasted with Maoist strategies of development, Mao seems to have relied on Chen for support during retrenchment phases of his radical mobilization campaigns in the mid- to late 1950s. Nevertheless, Chen retired from active politics during the radical heyday of the Great Leap Forward (1958–1960), returning in 1961 to play a key role in designing the policies that led to economic recovery from the Leap. Although he came back from his forced retirement in the Cultural Revolution (1966–1976) in the early 1970s, it was not until 1978 that he again played a dominant policy-making role. Still a member of the Standing Committee of the Politburo after Deng Xiaoping's September 1985 purge, Chen has emerged as the leading representative of conservatives in the ruling elite who resist many of Deng's economic reforms and who adamantly oppose political liberalization.

[*See also* Deng Xiaoping; Liu Shaoqi; *and* Marxism and Socialism: Marxism in China.]

Donald Klein and Anne Clark, *Biographical Dictionary of Chinese Communism 1921–1965* (1971). Nicholas Lardy and Kenneth Lieberthal, eds., *Chen Yun's Strategy for China's Development: A Non-Maoist Alternative* (1983). JOHN A. RAPP

CHETTIAR, endogamous subcaste *(jati)* of the *vaishya,* or merchant, caste, whose homeland was historically centered in the Ramnad and Pudokkottai areas of Tamil Nadu in South India. In the period of the ascendancy of the Chola dynasty (900–1250 CE), the Chettiars were primarily engaged in overseas trade, but from the sixteenth century onward they began to concentrate on banking and moneylending. As a major source of capital and of generous contributions to Hindu shrines or charities, the Chettiars came to play a significant role in the social and economic life of many areas of South India. Chettiar economic activities were organized on the basis of firms that usually involved financial and marital alliances between prominent Chettiar families. Intracaste links and sanctions, special training in financial affairs and in secret methods of accounting, and extensive networks of branch offices and outstations gave the Chettiars great advantages over less well-organized, smaller-scale rivals, allowing them to extend their banking networks widely across South India, Ceylon, and, in the period of British rule in India, to much of Southeast Asia, especially Burma and Malaya. Chettiar capital played a major role in the agricultural development of Burma and Malaya. The great wealth of the Chettiars, compounded by their prominent economic roles and alien dress, language, and religion, rendered them major targets of Burmese nationalist agitation in the 1920s and 1930s and in Malaya in the following decades. Chettiar activities continue in Malaya, but their enterprises have been forcibly driven out of Burma, Vietnam, and other overseas areas.

Michael Adas, "Immigrant Asians and the Economic Impact of European Imperialism: The Role of South Indian Chettiars in British Burma," *Journal of Asian Studies* 33 (1974). C. H. Rau, "The Banking Caste of Southern India," *Indian Review* 8 (1907). Edgar Thurston, *Castes and Tribes of Southern India* (1909). MICHAEL ADAS

CHIANG CHING-KUO (Jiang Jingguo, b. 1910), eldest son of Chiang Kai-shek; president of the Republic of China in Taiwan since 1978. Born of Chiang Kai-shek's first wife, Chiang Ching-kuo was reared in his father's hometown of Xikou in Zhejiang Province. In 1925, apparently with his father's blessing, he went to Russia and enrolled in Sun Yatsen University. After graduation in April 1927—the same month that his father broke with the Chinese Communists in Shanghai—Ching-kuo did not return to China (some accounts state that the Russians did not permit him to leave.) The ensuing nine years in Russia were difficult and tumultuous for the son of the leader of Nationalist China. He joined the Communist Youth League and may have become a member of the Russian Communist Party; he was assigned to take advanced study at the Central Tolmatchev Military and Political Institute in Leningrad, and served briefly in the Russian army. About 1930 he seems to have fallen into political disfavor, and in the following years he worked variously as an apprentice electrician, as a farmer in a village near Moscow, and in a gold mine in Siberia. In 1935 he married a Russian woman, and, while still in Russia, fathered two of his four children.

After the Xi'an Incident, during which the Russian authorities decided to support the leadership of Chiang Kai-shek in China, Ching-kuo was allowed to leave Russia, arriving in China in April 1937. His father apparently viewed him with some distrust—Ching-kuo while in Russia had publicly denounced his father, although this may have resulted from Russian coercion—and during the next ten years Ching-kuo gradually proved his ability and his loyalty to his father. From 1939 to 1943 he held the post of special administrative supervisor in Jiangxi Province. This was a decisive time for Ching-kuo, because he demonstrated that he was a highly capable, but authoritarian, administrator who was dedicated to economic and social reforms; at this time, too, he formed ties with such subordinates as Wang Sheng, who remained his intimate supporter throughout the remainder of his career, including the years in Taiwan. By 1945 he had clearly regained his father's trust, and he now received a series of highly responsible positions, such as special foreign affairs commissioner in Manchuria with the difficult task of negotiating the withdrawal of Russian forces there, a leading cadre in the Three-People's-Principles Youth Corps, and supervisor of economic control in the Shanghai area in 1948, when the Nationalist government made a last desperate effort to halt the inflationary spiral.

Ching-kuo's political star rose even more rapidly after Chiang Kai-shek and the Nationalist government retreated to Taiwan in 1949. A key to his growing influence and expanding coterie of followers was his effective control of the secret police organization, which became widely respected and feared for its stern treatment of enemies of his father's regime. In 1952 he became a member of the Standing Committee of the Central Committee of the Guomindang (Kuomintang). By this time it became evident that his father was grooming him as his successor. He was minister of defense (1965–1969), vice-premier (1969–1972), premier (1972–1978), and president (since 1978).

Chiang Ching-kuo was absolutely dedicated to the party and ideology of his father—his relations with his father acquired a rather maudlin, superfilial quality—but he also displayed a distinctive concern for the welfare of the common man that may have resulted from his education and experiences in Russia. As president, before his health declined, he often showed his common touch by chatting informally with peasants and children. Under his presidency, also, the number of Taiwanese joining the Guomindang and serving in administrative posts in the government has increased sharply.

[*See also* Chiang Kai-shek; Guomindang; China, Republic of; *and* Taiwan.]

LLOYD E. EASTMAN

CHIANG KAI-SHEK (Jiang Jieshi; 1887–1975), major political figure in twentieth-century China. Commander of the military forces of China's Nationalist government, he dominated the Guomindang (Kuomintang, KMT, or Nationalist Party) regime from 1928 until 1949, when he became president of the Taiwan-based Republic of China (ROC).

Chiang Kai-shek was born in Fenghua, Zhejiang Province, into the family of a salt merchant who died when Chiang was still a child. Chiang attended school in Ningbo and Fenghua and developed a strong interest in the military. After a brief trip to Japan from 1906 to 1907, he enrolled in the Chinese government's military academy at Baoding. From 1908 to 1911 Chiang studied at a military school in Tokyo.

Chiang began his political career during the Tokyo years. He became a protégé of Chen Qimei, who introduced Chiang to the revolutionary leader Sun Yat-sen. Chiang became a member of Sun's Tongmenghui in 1908. When the 1911 Revolution developed, Chiang left Japan for Shanghai to serve under Chen, who led revolutionary forces in Shanghai. Chen's military success permitted the establishment of the provisional government in Nanjing.

After Yuan Shikai defeated the revolutionaries in the "second revolution," Chiang followed Chen to Japan, where both men joined Sun Yat-sen's reorganized Gemingdang (Revolutionary Party). Chiang made return trips to Shanghai to assist in the anti-Yuan cause. Chen's assassination in May 1916 by Yuan's agents was a blow to Chiang, although he had already solidified a position in the revolutionary movement. Through his patron Chen he had formed ties with Sun Yat-sen and senior leader Zhang Renjie. Chen's two nephews Chen Guofu and Chen Lifu also became lifelong supporters and friends. [*See also* Chen Qimei; Chen Guofu; *and* Chen Lifu.]

Early Career. Chiang's activities during the next several years are somewhat obscure. He remained in Shanghai during much of the time, occasionally traveling south to assist Sun. He was sometimes assigned to the staff of Chen Jiongming, the principal military backer of Sun's Canton (Guangzhou) government until their break in 1922. Chiang accompanied Sun in June 1922, when Chen ejected the KMT leader from Canton. During his time in Shanghai, Chiang apparently became involved in stock market speculation. Zhang Renjie had important ties with leading Shanghai capitalists, giving Chiang access to the business world. Chiang also developed connections with the powerful Green Gang, an underworld organization.

Sun Yat-sen meanwhile began discussions with Comintern representatives to establish a KMT-Soviet tie, culminating in the Sun-Joffe declaration of January 1923. Sun then dispatched a study delegation to the Soviet Union in August 1923 headed by Chiang Kai-shek. After several weeks in Russia, Chiang returned to Canton just as the KMT was being reorganized under the tutelage of Comintern agent Michael Borodin. [*See also* Comintern *and* Borodin, Michael.]

A major attraction of the Soviet link was financial and military aid, as well as military advisers, to assist Sun in building a KMT army, a step that Sun felt necessary if the party were to unite China. In the spring of 1924 Sun created the Whampoa Military Academy near Canton to train officers. He appointed Chiang director. Liao Zhongkai, a KMT leftist, headed the political education program, and several members of the Chinese Communist Party (now also KMT members) served on the staff.

Chiang's appointment as commander of the academy was the turning point in his career. Over the next few months he produced several classes of military officers who became the leaders of the KMT army. Many became loyal followers of Chiang, forming the so-called "Whampoa clique." The army grew rapidly in size, aided by the influx of Soviet money, arms, and instructors. Chiang also directed military operations to secure the party's base in Canton between 1924 and 1925. Chiang thus became the dominant figure within the KMT military, a base from which he extended his political power. [*See also* Whampoa Military Academy.]

In March 1925 Sun Yat-sen died of cancer in Beijing, creating a political crisis within his Canton government. Despite Chiang's military power, his political standing within the KMT was relatively low; yet over the next few months he eliminated most of the obstacles to power. Many conservative stalwarts had objected to Sun Yet-sen's alliance with the Soviets. One such group formed the "Western Hills faction" and departed Canton for Shanghai. In August 1925 leftist Liao Zhongkai was assassinated and blame fell on the conservatives. Rightist Hu Hanmin, a major contender for party leader, left China under a cloud. [*See also* Sun Yat-sen *and* Hu Hanmin.]

Rise to Power. In the wake of these events the KMT was dominated by leftist Wang Jingwei, Borodin, and Chiang, considered pro-Soviet at the time. Actually, Chiang was unhappy with the leftist bent of the Canton regime but still required Soviet aid, precluding a total break with Moscow. Nonetheless, on 20 March 1926 Chiang precipitated a near coup, the Zhongshan Incident, in which he imposed martial law and arrested many leftists and communists. Although distraught at the turn of events, Borodin felt the KMT link was crucial and accepted Chiang's fait accompli. Wang Jingwei left China and activities of the Chinese Communist Party members were restricted. Chiang's patron, Zhang Renjie, became chairman of the Standing Committee of the Central Executive Committee of the KMT, and Chen Guofu took over the organizational department of the party. Chiang's star was in ascendancy.

In July 1926 Chiang Kai-shek served as commander in chief for the long-discussed Northern Expedition. Amid a military and political crusade, the party forces moved into Hunan and Hubei. The expedition exacerbated the struggle between left and right in the party. KMT-organized movements of peasants and urban workers mushroomed during the crusade and these were led primarily by leftists and Communists. When the civilian government moved from Canton to Wuhan in January 1927, Borodin and the leftists came to the fore, shortly to be joined by Wang Jingwei. After conquering Shanghai and Nanjing in March 1927, Chiang decided on a total break with the Wuhan group. Using his old connections in Shanghai, he obtained funds from banking and business leaders sufficient to finance his army without Soviet aid. Allied with his Green Gang cronies, Chiang launched a violent attack on the Communists and labor unions in Shanghai on 12 April 1927. Within a week Chiang created his own KMT regime in Nanjing, supported by many conservatives.

The Nanjing and Wuhan regimes attacked each other while both came unraveled. Wang Jingwei broke with Borodin and the Communists, while in Nanjing Chiang was beset with dissension and military defeats. He resigned in August and traveled to Japan, where he married Soong Mei-ling (Song Meiling). Chiang Kai-shek retained the loyalty of the core of the KMT's army and had thus become indispensable to a functioning party government. In January 1928 he resumed leadership in Nanjing as head of the party and military. In June 1928 KMT forces captured Beijing, completing the Northern Expedition. [*See also* Soong Mei-ling *and* Northern Expedition.]

The Nanjing Decade. The next decade, from 1928 to 1937, was the golden age of Chiang Kai-shek's rule in China. The Nanjing regime achieved international recognition. Problems, however, were severe. The civil war with the Communists continued. They established a base in Jiangxi in the early 1930s and later made their famous Long March to the northwest. Furthermore, Chiang had completed the Northern Expedition by allying with regional warlords such as Yan Xishan, Feng Yuxiang, and the Guangxi clique. In the early years of the Nanjing period, Chiang fought costly civil wars with all of these leaders. His superior financial base in Shanghai enabled him to keep his opponents divided, although residual regionalism only gradually diminished.

Chiang faced challenges within the party. His rise had been sudden, creating bitterness among many senior leaders. In the spring of 1931, when Chiang broke with Hu Hanmin, the old rightist with whom he had allied in 1928, his opponents bolted from the government and formed a rival KMT regime in Canton. Japan invaded Manchuria in September 1931, an incident that placed great pressure on both sides to resolve the crisis short of civil war. Chiang resigned briefly in late 1931 but returned to power in January 1932 after his opponents failed to create a viable government. This time Chiang allied with the old leftist Wang Jingwei. [*See also* Wang Jingwei.]

Despite these conflicts, Chiang dominated the Nanjing government. His titles occasionally changed but not his authority. A remote, almost regal figure, he cultivated the formation of various cliques such as the CC group, the Blue Shirt fascist group, the Political Study clique, and the Whampoa military group within the party. Chiang played one group off against another while holding ultimate power himself. He also relied on family members for many tasks, and placed great trust in his German military advisers.

Japan persisted in pressing Chiang Kai-shek. Following the attack on Manchuria in 1931, Japan pressured North China. Chiang tried to appease Japan and avoid war, a stand that was widely unpopular. In December 1936 Chiang was kidnapped at Xi'an by his commander Zhang Xueliang, who favored a policy of resistance. Chiang finally agreed to suspend the civil war and seek a united front with the Communist Party against the Japanese. [*See also* Zhang Xueliang; Xi'an Incident; *and* United Front.]

War with Japan. War erupted between China and Japan after 7 July 1937. Chiang's forces fought valiantly at Shanghai but were decimated. The Nanjing government retreated first to Wuhan and then to Chongqing, following a scorched-earth policy. After 1938 the war settled into a long and costly stalemate, the Japanese unable to secure victory, the Chinese unable to mount a meaningful offensive. Tokyo tried to undercut the Chongqing government by establishing a puppet KMT regime in Nanjing, and they attracted Wang Jingwei, who defected to the Japanese in December 1938. The puppet regime, however, acquired little support among Chinese.

Chiang's government was devastated by the war. Although his formal titles multiplied during these years, the base of his power—the army—had been mangled. The central forces were thus weaker compared to the regional militarists of the southwest. The retreat inland had also deprived Chiang's treasury of its economic base, the rich lower Yangtze River area. Chongqing responded by printing money and creating hyperinflation, which devastated morale in the government and army and stimulated corruption. Little outside aid was available. The German link was broken and only partially replaced by Soviet aid. After Pearl Harbor, American assistance was forthcoming but logistical difficulties were staggering. American aid also brought political difficulties; Chiang had strained relations with America's representative, General Joseph Stilwell. [*See also* Stilwell, Joseph W. *and* World War II in China.]

The morass in Chongqing contrasted vividly with the growing strength of the Communists, Chiang's nominal allies. A barter economy and guerrilla-style organization gave the Communist forces a decided advantage over the KMT in wartime conditions. By 1945 Mao's government in Yan'an had vastly increased its power and was ready to challenge the KMT.

Ironically, Chiang Kai-shek's international status reached its peak just as his domestic power sank. Franklin D. Roosevelt insisted that Chiang be elevated to "Big Four" status in the war, with Churchill, Stalin, and himself. At Cairo in late 1943 Chiang met with Churchill and Roosevelt. He obtained agreements ending extraterritoriality and most other provisions of the unequal treaties that dated back to the opium wars of a century earlier. China's "Big Four" status was belied by events on the battlefield, however, where China ceased to be a major factor. A Japanese offensive late in the war caused a near collapse of the KMT position, and the Allies placed little faith in China.

When Japan surrendered, Chiang's government was ill-equipped to reassert its authority in eastern China. Only with American assistance and sometimes that of puppet and Japanese troops could it reoccupy the coastal cities. The countryside in the North was largely under the control of the Communists, whose forces were better motivated and disciplined than those of the KMT. Although the United States tried to negotiate a settlement between the two parties, civil war was inevitable. After some early successes, the KMT position collapsed in late 1948 to early 1949. Chiang resigned in January 1949, avoiding the onus of presiding over the final collapse.

Chiang's career was not ended. In December of 1949 he established a government in exile in Taiwan, pledging to retake the mainland. After the outbreak of the Korean War the United States began to pour economic and military aid into Taiwan, which it recognized as the government of all of China. Following his death in 1975, Chiang's son Chiang Ching-kuo (Jiang Jingguo) succeeded him as leader of the Republic of China on Taiwan.

[*See also* China, Republic Period; China, Republic of; Guomindang; *and* Taiwan.]

Lloyd E. Eastman, *The Abortive Revolution: China under Nationalist Rule, 1927–1937* (1974) and *Seeds of Destruction: Nationalist China in War and Revolution,*

1937–1949 (1984). Pichon P. Y. Loh, *The Early Chiang Kai-shek: A Study of His Personality and Politics, 1887–1924* (1971). James T. Sheridan, *China in Disintegration: The Republican Era in Chinese History, 1912–1949* (1975). Hung-mao Tien, *Government and Politics in Kuomintang China, 1927–1937* (1972). Wu Tien-wei, *The Sian Incident: A Pivotal Point in Modern Chinese History* (1976). PARKS M. COBLE, JR.

CHIANG MAI, also known as Chiengmai, chief city of northern Thailand and capital of independent kingdoms until recent times.

The early inhabitants of the broad valley of the upper Ping River were probably Mon and Lawa and other non-Tai peoples who from the eighth century onward were integrated into the Buddhist kingdom of Haripunjaya, centered on nearby Lamphun. Increasing Tai movement into the area culminated in King Mangrai's foundation in 1296 of Chiang Mai ("new city") as the capital of the Tai kingdom of Lan Na.

For many centuries Chiang Mai was the center of religious and cultural life for the Tai peoples of the interior of the Indochinese peninsula. Two centuries (1558–1774) of almost continuous Burmese occupation contributed to the cultural distinctiveness that sets the north off from the rest of Thailand; northern speech, arts, handicrafts, and cultural and religious traditions reflect influences from Burma.

Chao ("ruler") Kavila (r. 1775–1813) moved to revive Lan Na in the chaotic period of the Burmese invasions, but he had to settle for the lesser status of vassal king of Chiang Mai with authority over the northern provinces, which were under the suzerainty of the Siamese kings at Bangkok. Pressure from the Burmese, and then from the British in Burma, worked to increase Chiang Mai's dependency on Siam. When the full force of Western imperialism reached the region in the last third of the nineteenth century, Chiang Mai soon found itself simply a Siamese province, a semiautonomous principality only in name.

Chiang Mai remains the chief city of the north and its economic, educational, religious, and cultural center. Its population has tripled in the past thirty years and now exceeds 100,000.

[*See also* Kavila; Intanon; Lamphun; *and* Lan Na.]

R. le May, *An Asian Arcady: The Land and Peoples of Northern Siam* (1926). David K. Wyatt, *Thailand: A Short History* (1984). DAVID K. WYATT

TABLE 1. Chao *(rulers) of Chiang Mai*

CHAO	REIGN YEARS
Kavila	1781–1813[1]
Thammalangka	1813–1821
Kham Fan	1821–1825
Phutthawong	1825–1846
Mahawong	1846–1854
Kavilorot	1856–1870
Intanon	1871–1897
Suriyawong	1901–1911
In Kaeo	1911–1939

1. Ruled in Lampang, 1775–1781.

CHIKAMATSU MONZAEMON (1653–1725), one of the great playwrights of Japan, wrote principally for the puppet theater *(bunraku* or *jōruri).* Chikamatsu Monzaemon was born in Fukui, Echizen Province (modern Fukui Prefecture), to a minor samurai family. When he was still in his teens the family moved to Kyoto, where the young man served as a page to a noble household. Chikamatsu may have had his first contact with the puppet theater during this time, since it often operated under the patronage of aristocrats. Uji Kaganojō (1635–1711), an innovative *jōruri* chanter who frequented aristocratic circles, is said to have persuaded Chikamatsu to write his first plays.

Chikamatsu's work revolutionized the puppet theater. *Yotsugi Soga* (*The Soga Heir,* 1683), probably his first play, challenged earlier dramatic conventions by taking a well-worn story and approaching it from fresh angles. Other plays from this period are even more experimental, abandoning the fantastic elements that had been *jōruri* staples for more realistic plots and characters. Chikamatsu's greatest contribution to world drama is the domestic drama, in which ordinary men and women—clerks, housewives, and prostitutes—are trapped by circumstances beyond their control. His love suicide plays, *Sonezaki shinjū* (*The Love Suicides at Sonezaki,* 1703) and *Shinjū ten no Amijima* (*The Love Suicides at Amijima,* 1721), are tragedies whose protagonists are socially inconsequential characters, rather than kings and generals. These plays strike us today as far more modern than works by Chikamatsu's Western contemporaries. *Kokusen'ya kassen* (*The Battles of Koxinga,* 1715), a historical drama set in China, was Chikamatsu's greatest popular success. Like many plays written for the puppet theater, *Koxinga* contains gory and supernatural scenes that could not be performed successfully by human actors.

Chikamatsu's plays are rarely presented in their original form. Ironically, the prosperity brought to the puppet theater by the great success of his plays resulted in technical improvements that necessitated altering Chikamatsu's texts. He had written for puppets operated by one man, but the development of the more complex, cumbersome three-man puppet in 1734 called for a more leisurely script. Modern *bunraku* generally presents only selections from a Chikamatsu play.

[*See also* Bunraku.]

Donald Keene, trans., *Major Plays of Chikamatsu* (1961). Donald Keene, *Bunraku: The Art of the Japanese Puppet Theatre* (1965, rev. ed. 1973) and *World within Walls* (1976).

AILEEN GATTEN

CHILD, SIR JOSIAH (1630–1699), a dominant administrator of the East India Company from 1677 to 1690. Child envied the success of the Dutch at Batavia and imitated it by establishing coastal forts in India capable of protecting company trade. Though unsuccessful in Bengal, Child's goal of a permanent British presence was realized at Madras and Bombay.

[*See also* East India Company.]

LYNN ZASTOUPIL

CHIN. The Chin and their close relatives inhabit the mountains and adjacent parts of the lowlands between Burma and the India-Bangladesh borderland. Their history can be reconstructed from ethnological and linguistic evidence as well as from documents from Burma and eighteenth- and nineteenth-century Europe (chiefly Britain). The first reference to the Chin occurs in an early twelfth-century Burmese inscription from the Chindwin River valley that states that a people named Chin will be left in possession of this region and its mountains as a buffer against the Sak to the west.

From about 1600 onward, wars between the Burmans and Shan and with Manipur, as well as Burmese expansion into the Chindwin, caused most Chin in the middle and upper Chindwin Valley to move into the mountains, pushing out their own relatives, who in turn took refuge in Manipur and Tripura and became the Kuki, client tribes of these states. The Kuki were chiefly members of the Lushai-Mizo branch of the Chin. Their development of supralocal chieftaincy and their aggressiveness toward plains peoples seem to have been largely a response to the unsettled conditions of the north and center. The southern Chin, who lived next to a much more stable area of Burma, remained more loosely organized than the Kuki and kept more to themselves.

In the 1880s Britain, which had by then acquired Upper Burma, made several expeditions into the mountain areas occupied by the Chin in an attempt to "pacify" them and to stop Chin and Lushai incursions into Burma, Manipur, Cachar, and Assam. By the end of the nineteenth century most, if not quite all, of the Chin region was under the frontier administration of Burma or India. Today the Chin form a constituent state within Burma, while Mizoram, inhabited by the Lushai, is a semiautonomous state in India.

F. K. Lehman, *The Structure of Chin Society* (1963).

F. K. LEHMAN

CHINA. Despite its extraordinarily long historical continuity, the definition of China has not been constant throughout history. At times China has been a culture zone analagous to Europe in scope and diversity, at other times it has been a unified empire, and in the twentieth century it has become a nation-state. Thus, China can variously be defined as a civilization, a territory, a series of political units, or a people with shared language and customs. Each of these definitions requires careful qualification.

In ancient times the Chinese viewed themselves as more culturally advanced than their neighbors, as an island of civilization in the midst of a sea of "barbarians," and so they coined the term *Zhongguo* ("central states" or "middle kingdom") to refer to their homeland. Another expression of ancient origin is *tianxia* ("under heaven"), which refers equally to the empire or the entire civilized world. A third name for China, *Hua* ("magnificent, flowery," or "elegant"), occurs in the names of both the People's Republic of China (PRC) and the Republic of China (ROC). All of these names imply the idea that China is an entity of advanced culture identified with an ongoing civilization.

China today consists of a socialist state, the People's Republic of China, which occupies most of Chinese territory and is governed by the Chinese Communist Party; the island of Taiwan, formerly known as the Republic of China, which is under the authority of the Chinese Nationalist Party, or Guomindang (Kuomintang); and the tiny colonies of Macao and Hong Kong, which are still subject to Portuguese and British control, respectively. There is general agreement among Chinese that all of these

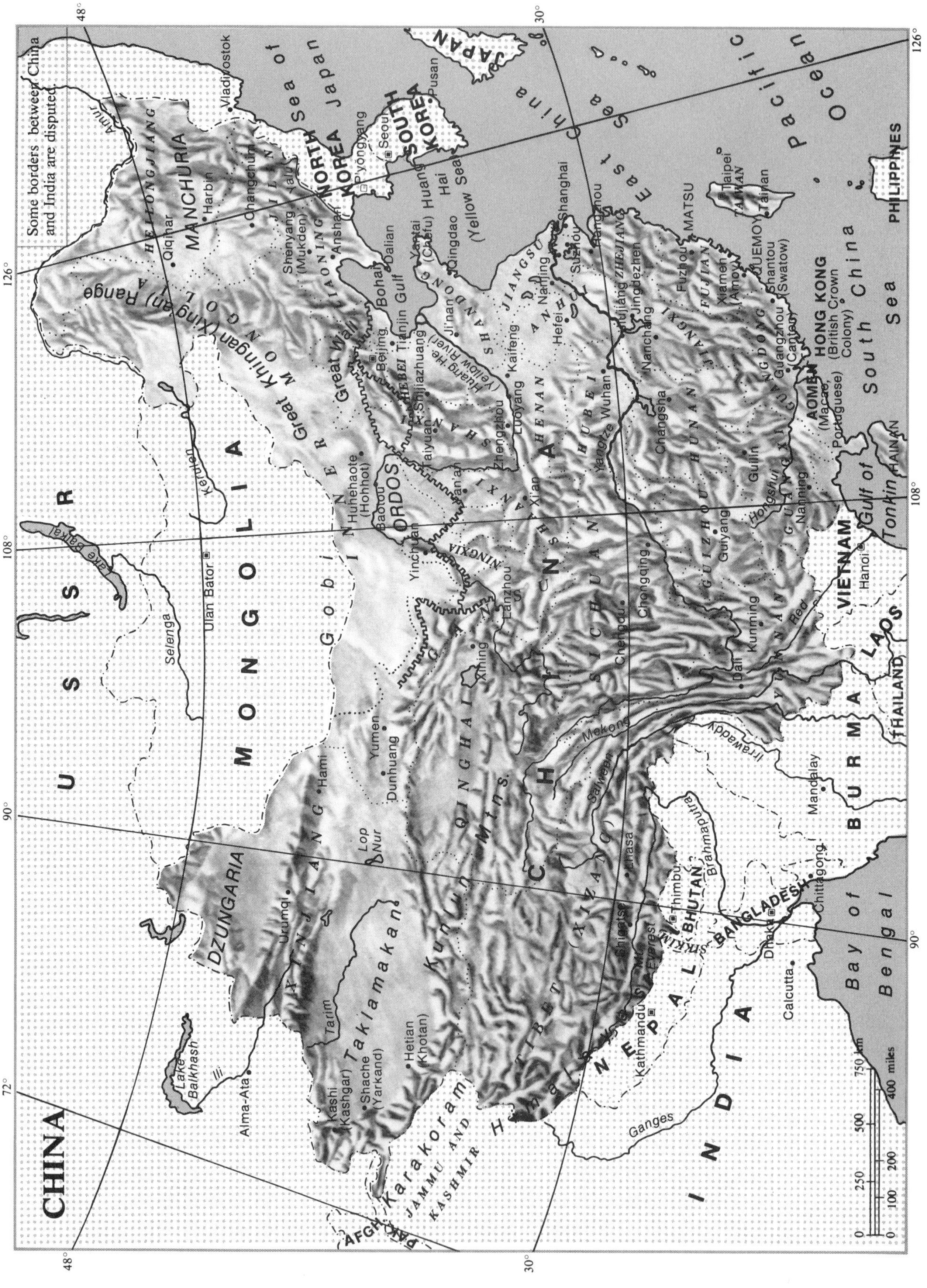
CHINA
Some borders between China and India are disputed.
U S S R
M O N G O L I A
MANCHURIA
HEILONGJIANG
JILIN
LIAONING
NORTH KOREA
SOUTH KOREA
JAPAN
Sea of Japan
Vladivostok
Harbin
Qiqihar
Changchun
Shenyang (Mukden)
Anshan
Dalian
Bohai
Bohai Gulf
Pyongyang
Seoul
Pusan
Yalu
Amur
Huang Hai (Yellow Sea)
East China Sea
Pacific Ocean
Great Khingan (Xingan) Range
NEI MONGOL
Great Wall
Gobi
Ulan Bator
Lake Baikal
Selenga
Kerulen
Beijing
Tianjin Gulf
HEBEI
Shijiazhuang
Taiyuan
SHANXI
SHANDONG
Yantai (Chefu)
Qingdao
Ji'nan
Huang He (Yellow River)
Huhehaote (Hohhot)
Baotou
ORDOS
Yinchuan
NINGXIA
Lanzhou
Xining
GANSU
QINGHAI
Yumen
Dunhuang
Hami
Lop Nur
XINJIANG
DZUNGARIA
Urumqi
Taklamakan
Tarim
Kashi (Kashgar)
Shache (Yarkand)
Hetian (Khotan)
Kunlun Mtns.
Karakoram
JAMMU AND KASHMIR
AFGH.
PAK.
Lake Balkhash
Ili
Alma-Ata
TIBET (XIZANG)
Himalayas
Lhasa
Shigatse
Mt. Everest
NEPAL
Kathmandu
SIKKIM
BHUTAN
Thimbu
BANGLADESH
Dhaka
Chittagong
Brahmaputra
Ganges
Calcutta
INDIA
Bay of Bengal
BURMA
Mandalay
Irrawaddy
Salween
Mekong
THAILAND
LAOS
VIETNAM
Hanoi
Red
Gulf of Tonkin
HAINAN
SHAANXI
Xi'an
Yan'an
HENAN
Zhengzhou
Luoyang
Kaifeng
JIANGSU
Nanjing
Suzhou
Shanghai
ANHUI
Hefei
Hangzhou
ZHEJIANG
HUBEI
Wuhan
Yangtze
SICHUAN
Chengdu
Chongqing
GUIZHOU
Guiyang
YUNNAN
Kunming
Dali
HUNAN
Changsha
JIANGXI
Nanchang
Jiujiang
Jingdezhen
FUJIAN
Fuzhou
Xiamen (Amoy)
MATSU
QUEMOY
TAIWAN
Taipei
Tainan
GUANGXI
Guilin
Nanning
Hongshui
GUANGDONG
Guangzhou (Canton)
Shantou (Swatow)
HONG KONG (British Crown Colony)
AOMEN (Macao) (Portuguese)
South China Sea
PHILIPPINES
126°
108°
90°
72°
48°
30°
0 250 500 750 km
0 100 200 400 miles

territories are, or ought to be, part of one Chinese nation despite the existence of temporary political divisions. The exact definition of what territory ought to belong to China has, however, been the subject of disagreements with other nations. Thus, there remain unsettled disputes over small islands and bits of territory along China's borders with the Soviet Union, India, and Vietnam. Furthermore, the extent of "Chinese" territory throughout China's long history has ranged widely from the great empires of the Han or Tang to prolonged periods of fragmentation when there was no unifying state authority.

It is customary to divide Chinese history according to the sequence of political units. Until the twentieth century it was Chinese practice to date the calendar according to the ruler's reign and to designate longer units of time by the name of the ruling house. Thus, there came into being a commonly recognized series of dynasties that account for all the years from the shadowy Xia at the dawn of historical memory, through the imperial unification of the Qin in 221 BCE, down to the end of the imperial era with the collapse of the Qing in 1911. A close scrutiny of this sequence of dynasties reveals that in some periods China was in fact divided among competing states, only some of which are fitted into the comfortable progression of "orthodox" dynasties to make up for an unbroken sequence. The term *Six Dynasties,* for example, lends the appearance of historical continuity to a time of profound disruption and fragmentation that lasted from the third to the sixth century. To speak of China at such a time in history is to speak of a whole greater than its parts, much as we might speak of Europe. Before the twentieth century, then, it is not very helpful to think of China as a nation. (The major divisions of Chinese history are outlined in table 1.)

Even today, the People's Republic is officially described as a multinational state. More than fifty nationalities are recognized, among whom the Han people make up 94 percent of the population. The remaining nationalities, although they constitute only about 6 percent of China's total population, nevertheless outnumber the Han people in some 60 percent of the land area of China. Large regions such as Tibet, Xinjiang, and Inner Mongolia are recognized as the homelands of non-Han peoples who are nonetheless Chinese. From this perspective the history of China is the history of multiple ethnic groups. Although the Han people were generally the

TABLE 1. *Major Periods of Chinese History*

PERIOD	YEARS	DEVELOPMENTS
Xia	2205–1766 BCE	Semilegendary dawn of Chinese history
Shang	1766–1122	Basic cultural forms evolve
Zhou	1122–256	Rise of Confucianism, Daoism, and Legalism
Qin	221–207	Unification of the empire
Han	206 BCE–220 CE	First empire; Confucianism becomes state ideology
Six Dynasties	222–589	Period of political division and foreign invasion; Buddhism flourishes
Sui	581–618	Reunification of the empire
Tang	618–907	Second empire
Five Dynasties	907–959	Political division
Northern Song	960–1126	Reunification; Khitan Liao control northeast Asia
Southern Song	1126–1279	Jurchen Jin control North China
Yuan	1279–1368	Mongol rule
Ming	1368–1644	Return to Han rule
Qing	1644–1911	Last era of imperial government; Manchu rule
Republic	1912–1927	Warlord division of China
ROC	1927–	Guomindang (Nationalist) rule
PRC	1949–	Communist rule

dominant group, there were substantial periods, notably the Yuan and Qing dynasties, when China was ruled by non-Han peoples, in these cases the Mongols and the Manchus. To recognize Manchus and Mongols as part of the Chinese people, however, could lead to some confusion. If, for example, one defines the Yuan dynasty as a period when China was under the rule of the Mongol nationality, what is to be said about the rest of the Mongol empire? Obviously the Mongols came into China from Central Asia and obviously the Yuan dynasty was only part of a greater Mongol empire that extended to Central Asia, Iran, and Russia. To recognize the Mongols as part of the Chinese people is to recognize a change in status of those Mongols who came to China and likewise a change in the composition of the Chinese people.

Language is another element in the identity of China and the Chinese. Because the form of the characters changed very little over a period of more than two thousand years, the Chinese written language made a great contribution to the continuity of Chinese culture. Indeed, all of East Asia gained definition from the Chinese written language, which was used extensively in Japan, Korea, and Vietnam. To call the classical written language "Chinese," however, is loose usage. In actuality it was the written form of the Han language. Strictly speaking there are dozens of Chinese languages, among which the most widely spoken is the Han language. The Han language, which takes its name from the Han dynasty of ancient times, also is divided into dialects. If China is defined in terms of all people who share the Han language, then many overseas Chinese in Asia or the Americas can be considered to be part of a greater China as well.

[*See also* Chinese Language. *The individual dynasties and divisions of Chinese history are the subject of independent entries.*]

EDWARD L. FARMER

CHINA, PEOPLE'S REPUBLIC OF. The founding of the People's Republic of China (PRC) in Beijing on 1 October 1949 marked the apparent consummation of the longest and most profound revolutionary upheaval in modern history ("apparent" because of the determination of the leadership to "continue the revolution"). Its development since that time may be divided chronologically into six periods: the period of socialist transformation (1949–1958); the Great Leap Forward (1958–1962); the period of recovery from the Leap and preparation for the Cultural Revolution (1962–1966); the Great Proletarian Cultural Revolution itself (1966–1976); the Hua Guofeng interregnum (1976–1978); and the period of reform and economic modernization (since 1978).

Socialist Transformation. During the period of socialist transformation, the PRC shifted from its early United Front stance to a basically Stalinist political-economic configuration in the interest of rapid industrialization. The theoretical underpinnings of the United Front were provided in Mao Zedong's concept of "new democracy," which arranged for representation of the petty and national bourgeoisie as well as the working classes in the national legislative forum, the Chinese People's Political Consultative Conference (CPPCC), foreseeing, however, that the nonproletarian classes would meanwhile be "reformed" to a socialist viewpoint. Although the United Front was never really laid to rest, and the CPPCC lingered on as its institutional symbol, New Democracy was officially superseded by "transition to socialism" in 1953. In 1954 a National People's Congress was established to exercise legislative power, based on indirect election of deputies from territorially defined constituencies. Beginning in the late 1950s the regime began to define itself as a "socialist state of the dictatorship of the proletariat," at which time the power of the government began to diminish (anticipating the "withering away of the state") and the power of the Party to increase concomitantly. [*See also* Chinese People's Political Consultative Conference.]

Although there has been a tendency among some post-Cultural Revolution commentators to look back on the period of socialist transformation as a golden age of stability and prosperity, it was actually a period of dynamic change in which "balance is relative, imbalance absolute," as Mao later put it. The regime's objectives were not merely to recover from the ravages of war, but to destroy the foundations of the old "half-feudal, half-bourgeois" system and establish a modernizing socialist regime. In retrospect, two aspects of this transformation were perhaps most telling: the "socialization of the means of production," involving the collectivization of agriculture and socialization of private industry, and the reshaping of the primary group, which entailed marriage reform.

The first phase of collectivization was land reform, which corresponded to liberal reform goals of "land to the tiller" and resulted in the redistribution of about 56 percent of China's farmland to between 60 and 70 percent of peasant households. Of the land that changed hands, two-thirds came from landlords and less than one-third from rich peasants; less than two-thirds of the land went to poor peasants, on the other hand, while more than one-third went to middle peasants. The notable effect, however, is that the power of the landlord class was broken and a basis laid for a postrevolutionary upending of the stratification pyramid based on the categorization of families into classes according to their occupations just before Liberation (as the establishment of the PRC was termed). In the cities, the "three-anti" and "five-anti" campaigns were mobilized to intimidate political opposition from the bourgeoisie and to rectify a bureaucracy that had been corrupted by sudden access to power and by the somewhat indiscriminate absorption of new cadres to run the country.

The new economic system was unstable: politically it threatened future progress toward socialism by providing small farmers with an interest in the status quo (as in the case of the kulaks who arose during the Soviet New Economic Policy), economically, it reduced the incentive for introducing machinery and other economies of scale. Thus, no sooner was land reform under way than the regime began to encourage farmers to place their individual plots under collective management. By 1954 some 58.3 percent of all peasant households had been incorporated into permanent mutual aid teams (in which peasants voluntarily pooled land, labor, and tools and received profits based on the amount of their investment as well as their labor contribution), and the first lower-level Agricultural Producers' Cooperative (APC) had been formed. By 1955, whereas 35 percent of all peasant households were still farming individually, 51 percent were members of mutual aid teams, and 14.2 percent had joined elementary APCs. In order to ensure that collectivization would not result in reduction of the commodity grain available to feed the cities and finance industrialization, "unified purchase" and sale of grain was also introduced by the government in 1955.

There seems to have been a disagreement among the elite over the pace of socialization, in which Mao outmaneuvered and overrode those who favored a slower pace. Following the public stimulus he gave to "socialist upsurge" in 1955, the pace quickened dramatically (and more coercion was exercised upon laggards). In July 1955 Mao proposed a doubling of the existing 650,000 cooperatives to be achieved by spring 1956, as opposed to the 55 percent planned by the Rural Work Department; but by the end of the year 70 to 80 percent of China's 110 million farm households had actually been collectivized. The policy of advance by stages was in effect abandoned, and many households joined advanced APCs without prior organization into mutual aid teams or lower-level APCs. By 1957 all but 2 percent of the farm population had been organized into advanced APCs, and socialist transformation of industry and commerce was speeded up in the cities, achieving basic completion by late 1957. By late 1956 a sufficient number of problems had surfaced to justify a temporary slowdown (to Mao's annoyance), but the overall impact of the process seems to have vindicated his somewhat impulsive leadership style and generated support for further advance. [*See also* Land Tenure and Reform: Land Reform in Modern China; Agriculture, Collectivization of; *and* Agricultural Producers' Cooperatives.]

The traditional family structure was likewise attacked headlong in the campaign following passage of the Marriage Law in May 1950. The initial consequences were mixed, resulting for example in a steep climb in divorce rates and in a rash of suicides among women apparently protesting male resistance of reform. The long-term consequences have also fallen somewhat short of original objectives, particularly in the countryside, which has seen the survival of bride price, arranged marriage, wedding banquets, and male chauvinism. Yet the clan was destroyed as a political force at the local level for the first time, to be replaced by the occupational "unit" *(danwei)*, which, with its corporate links to the state apparatus, has proved an effective means of control and mobilization. A modern "stem" family has emerged as the dominant pattern, and if complete female equality or courtship freedom has not yet emerged, this arrangement seems capable of accommodating such child-care and social security responsibilities that the state has not yet been prepared to assume. [*See also* Women: Women in China.]

Political arrangements during the period of socialist transformation showed a characteristic communist disjuncture between informal and formal institutional structures. Formally speaking, the PRC implemented "dual rule," with parallel hierarchies of Party and state pyramiding through indirect representation to national legislative assemblies. Informally speaking, the doctrines of the "leading role of the Party" and "democratic centralism" have ensured that government organs were subordinate to Party leadership at every level, and that legislative organs were subordinated to the executive organs they elected to function during the long intervals when they were not in session. In effect, this meant that the major national political decisions were made by the Politburo of the Party. Yet such characteristically Chinese notions as the "mass line" decreed a certain circularity in the policy-making process, adjuring cadre investigation of constituent problems and holding cadres responsible not only for implementation of policy but for the generation of mass consensus. This process entailed an emphasis on mass mobilization unique among communist regimes, in which every new leadership initiative was likely to be accompanied by a movement to generate popular enthusiasm. In the early years campaigns were launched to eliminate opponents, then to socialize the means of production. By the end of the 1950s, however, the attempt to turn mobilization to new objectives raised serious problems.

The first of these conflicts was the contradiction between elite leadership and the opportunity for mass spontaneity implicit in the notion of the mass line, which first became fully apparent in the so-called Hundred Flowers Campaign. In the spring of 1957 Mao issued an apparently open-ended invitation to China's intellectuals to speak out on various public issues of concern to them. After an initial period of hesitation, they did so, voicing trenchant criticisms of the regime that the leadership was not prepared to countenance. The license to "bloom and contend" was abruptly rescinded and those who had expressed criticisms were repressed in the ensuing Anti-Rightist Movement. The underlying tension between elite initiative and mass spontaneity, a symptom of growing mass political skill in the "steering" of movements toward the accomplishment of various popular objectives, would continue to plague attempts at mobilization throughout the Maoist era. [*See also* Hundred Flowers Campaign.]

The Great Leap Forward. The second dilemma was raised by the attempt to link central planning to the dynamics of mass mobilization, which was first done on mass scale in the Great Leap Forward of 1958 to 1960. Economically, the period of socialist transformation had been very successful, not only achieving rapid recovery from the war (although the artificially low level of wartime production also inflated the effect of the recovery), but also in stimulating extremely rapid industrial growth and a creditable agricultural performance. During the course of the First Five-Year Plan (1953–1957), the overall rate of growth probably averaged roughly 7 percent a year, with agricultural output increasing at an annual average of 3 percent and industrial growth averaging more than three times that rate. This was achieved primarily through regularized bureaucratic management of the economy by experts operating out of the ministries of the State Council on the basis of a central plan; mobilizational techniques were confined throughout most of this period to redistribution and began to affect production only in 1956. It had become apparent, however, that China's growth rate would almost certainly slow down if the policies of this period were continued in a second five-year plan. In 1957 the increase in grain output was only 1.3 percent according to official figures, and the industrial growth rate was the second lowest since 1949. Moreover, the annual rate of population growth had increased from 1 percent in the first half of the twentieth century to more than 2 percent in the 1950s, resulting in widespread underemployment. Finally, Mao and some others within the leadership had become increasingly disturbed by many of the political and social consequences of attempting to model China's developmental strategy on that of the Soviet Union.

All this provided an economic rationale for the so-called Three Red Banners, consisting of the Great Leap Forward, the Commune, and the General Line ("more, faster, better, and more economical"). This represented rejection of the Soviet model and improvization of a new and distinctive Chinese model, designed both to speed growth and to realize redistributive objectives, to absorb the surplus labor force in (rural) industrial projects while simultaneously improving farm production through the more extensive mobilization of unskilled labor. Many tasks were to be accomplished at once, enabling China to reach the economic levels of the advanced industrialized countries within fifteen years, and to introduce communist relations of production within perhaps three to five years: the commune was introduced in the countryside to facilitate this breakthrough, merging several APCs and thereby creating a larger labor pool for collective endeavors. The labor force was organized on semimilitary lines and mobilized to work for very long hours. The multiplication of objectives not only absorbed underemployed labor but actually created a labor shortage, diverting men from the fields for rural industry and inducing women to replace them; communal child-care and dining facilities were introduced to compensate for the absence of women from their homes. In order to give maximum ambit to mass initiative, power was decentralized and shifted from government professional cadres to the Party committees. Despite this decentralization, Mao's personal power was enhanced, as his vigorous personal advocacy of a populist high tide increased his public visibility. In an attempt to rationalize this bold initiative ideologically, he became more innovative in his construal of Marxism, arguing that changes in the ideological superstructure should sometimes precede changes in the economic base.

The results at the end of the first year were encouraging, their impact being magnified by the tendency to exaggerate reports implicit in the priority given to promoting morale. Agricultural output increased in 1958, even after discounting such inflation, and industrial output in 1959 increased by 36.1 percent over 1958, while that of 1960 showed an increase of 11.2 percent over 1959. Then a combination of disastrous weather conditions and political "errors" began to take its toll. Agricultural production, neglected or mismanaged in the turn to rural industrialization, declined consistently after 1958, falling 13.6 percent in 1959, 12.6 percent in 1960, and a further 2.4 percent in 1961, adding up to a total decrease of 26.3 percent in three years (according to recent PRC statistics). Industrial output declined by 38.2 percent from the 1960 level in 1961. During the period of the Second Five-Year Plan (1957–1962), industrial and agricultural production increased by an annual average of only 0.6 percent. The impact on living standards was severe, resulting in starvation in some parts of the country as a result of excessive procurement based on exaggerated local reports of increases in yield.

The failure of the Leap resulted in a general erosion of the prestige of the regime among the masses, in a decline of morale among cadres (as indicated, for example, by allegations of corruption), and by recrimination among the leadership. The latter first manifested itself in the case of Defense Minister Peng Dehuai, who criticized Mao for the excesses of the Leap in a series of high-level meetings in 1959. Although initial steps had already been taken to moderate the excesses about which Peng was complaining, Mao reacted defensively to the criticism, lashing back at Peng and forcing him to make a self-criticism and withdraw from the leadership. In the following months, radical policies such as the urban commune movement were pointlessly revived in order to vindicate Mao's position. Yet as the full magnitude of the disaster became apparent, Peng's critique acquired prophetic power. Mao's sensitivity precluded any recurrence of direct confrontation, but there seems to have been a progressive estrangement between Mao and those who took charge of salvaging the economy. [*See also* Great Leap Forward *and* Peng Dehuai.]

The Post-Leap Period. The aftermath of the Great Leap was thus a period of divided leadership and policy ambiguity, oriented backward to recovery from the Leap and forward toward the concerns of the Cultural Revolution. The leadership adopted a division between the "second front," consisting of Mao and an unspecified group of assistants, which became preoccupied with an investigation of the ideological reasons for the failure of the Leap and with foreign policy polemics; and a "first front," consisting of Liu Shaoqi, Deng Xiaoping, Peng Zhen, and others who were concerned with recovery from the worst depression since the birth of the PRC. Although there was ongoing cooperation between these two "fronts," and the first always acknowledged the ultimate superiority of the second, the preoccupation of the first with economic recovery induced a conciliatory posture toward the very spontaneous economic tendencies that Mao considered inimical to socialism and eventually stigmatized as the "capitalist road."

The second front was concerned first of all with elaborating a critique of such tendencies in China's intrabloc polemics with Yugoslavia and the Soviet Union, then with intervening in the domestic policy process to eliminate analogous tendencies and try to regenerate radical momentum. Mao's most sustained such domestic intervention was his four-year effort to promote the "Four Cleans," or "Socialist Education Movement," in the Chinese countryside. This movement may be seen as a preliminary attempt to realize the goals of what would subsequently emerge through bureaucratic channels as the Cultural Revolution. For Mao it was extremely frustrating, however, as he collaborated with first one set of first-front leaders, then with another set, resulting in the production of a series of campaign documents that he deemed either too harsh, too lenient, or otherwise misdirected. In his attempt to revolutionize the various components of the cultural superstructure he encountered similar frustrations. Eventually this ongoing friction culminated in a polarization between Mao and Peng Zhen, mayor of Beijing and leader of a group designated to rectify art, drama, and literature. Instead of allowing Peng to withdraw gracefully, Mao skilfully drew him deeper into the defense of his protégés, until Peng's position was so compromised that a sweeping purge was possible. This purge in May 1966 set off what became known as the Great Proletarian Cultural Revolution. [*See also* Peng Zhen.]

The Great Proletarian Cultural Revolution. The Cultural Revolution had the dual objective of (1) subjecting the "Party persons in authority [who were] taking the capitalist road" to mass criticism and eventual purge and (2) revitalizing the forces of radicalism and revolutionizing the cultural superstructure to be more compatible with the socialist economic base. Mao spurned attempts by the Party to lead the movement as heavy-handed and repressive, thereby granting unprecedented spontaneity to the "revolutionary masses" to organize their own "Red Guard" groups and select their own targets of criticism. The masses generated their own propaganda and circulated information through big-character posters, soon supplemented by a network of self-published polemical tabloids. Old restrictive definitions of class based on family origins were vigorously contested by those endorsing political performance criteria. This and other issues spawned violent factionalism among Red Guards even after most "authorities" had been toppled or intimidated.

The original plan seems to have been to coordinate the melee through the issuance of Chairman Mao's "instructions" and the channeling of mass criticism against centrally designated targets through the media, but mass spontaneity proved impossible to control through such means, and even personal visits by central leaders to local trouble spots sometimes failed to clear up the situation. Finally, the military had to be called in to restore order to China's chaotic urban centers, and in the fall of 1968 the Red Guard factions were forcibly disbanded and many of their members sent out to the countryside to learn from the peasants. [*See also* Red Guards.]

Because the Cultural Revolution resulted in the purge of the central and local leadership and in a generalized terrorization of the intellectual strata, it sometimes has been compared to Stalin's great purge. It is true that the Cultural Revolution occasioned widespread death and destruction, and although the level of economic damage remained well below that caused by the Leap, the humiliating mass-struggle tactics against elite errors and overall chaos seem to have given it even greater traumatic impact. This was a qualitatively different experience, however, stemming not from arrest, torture, or trial by a secret police or other organized state apparatus, but from spontaneous social groupings operating in the context of a framework of meaning in which they perceived their actions as contributing to the repression of evil and the onset of communist utopia.

The suppression of the Red Guards spelled the end of only the most dramatic phase of the Cultural Revolution, the phase of spontaneous mobilization. Although this implied an admission that the movement could not be permitted to continue along such lines, this was not a clear-cut defeat of the sort that marked the end of the Great Leap Forward, and the next eight years were to be devoted to an attempt to continue the movement in ways more compatible with rapid economic growth. By the end of 1968 the leadership had been thoroughly purged, the radical forces had "seized power," the hegemony of Mao Zedong Thought had been established, and circumstances seemed quite auspicious for the secure establishment of a truly radical regime. Yet this aspiration was not to be realized. Mao soon had a falling-out with Lin Biao, the heir apparent he had selected in 1966 to replace Liu Shaoqi, culminating in the violent death of Lin in an abortive flight to the Soviet Union. The sudden announcement that Mao's "closest comrade-in-arms" was a traitor did irreparable damage to Mao's credibility and left the regime without an assured future. Officials who had been disgraced soon had to be invited back to positions of authority, and although this was done under the premise that they had repented of their "errors," their policy preferences and factional alignment soon belied this notion. [*See also* Liu Shaoqi *and* Lin Biao.]

Those among the leadership who continued most zealously to support Mao's radical notions, including his wife, Jiang Qing, and her protégés Zhang Chunqiao, Yao Wenyuan, and Wang Hongwen, proved unable to ingratiate themselves with the career officials who resumed control of daily administration (indeed, according to later claims, with Mao himself), and equally unable to combine their radical ideological slogans with socioeconomic policies attractive to a broad-based mass constituency. In its obsession with egalitarianism and moral purity, late Maoist radicalism renounced opportunities to appeal to legitimate mass aspirations for material self-betterment, relinquishing power over the economic apparatus to the moderates and generally losing touch with the actual relations of production in pursuit of an increasingly rarified and ascetic vision. When Mao Zedong finally died in August 1976, he left Chinese radicalism in a weak and compromised position, as he was himself aware. The "Gang of Four" was deposed and arrested within a month of his death without any sign of popular resistance. [*See also* Great Proletarian Cultural Revolution *and* Gang of Four.]

The Hua Guofeng Years. The helm of leadership passed to Hua Guofeng, a second-ranking provincial official before the Cultural Revolution whose claim to Mao's legacy was based partly on his ability to outmaneuver the Gang of Four, but also on a credible claim to Mao's charismatic blessing. Under the circumstances Hua tried to "straddle two boats," reasserting the theory of "continuing the revolution under the dictatorship of the proletariat" while keeping the leading radicals under house arrest and suppressing their mass disciples, and launching another "leap forward" but doing so on the basis of the importation of foreign capital and technology without noticeable mass mobilization. Unable to disavow Maoist ideological commitments for fear of undermining his own legitimacy, he also shied away from radical policies for fear of alienating his moderate bureaucratic supporters.

Hua's economic initiatives in any case proved ill conceived, soon resulting in an imbalance of payments, fiscal deficit, and inflationary tendencies. Reluctantly acceding to the demands of his military backers to the third rehabilitation of Deng Xiaoping, he soon found himself unable to retain the initiative as Deng began to "float" policy and propaganda proposals diverging from his own that were quite embarrassing to him. The most renowned of these was the campaign launched in the spring of 1978 to popularize "practice as the sole criterion of truth," which shrewdly utilized a famous quotation from Mao himself to undermine Mao's continuing ideological hegemony (and, by implication, his choice of successor). Deng's appeal to pragmatism and common sense after a decade of apparently irrelevant cant struck a responsive chord among the populace, resulting in the mobilization of popular support for reform in the "Democracy Wall" movement and ultimately in Deng's victory at the Third Plenum of the Eleventh Party Congress in December 1978. Hua and his supporters were gradually eased out of their leadership positions to be replaced by Deng Xiaoping's "practice faction." [*See also* Democracy Wall.]

Reform and Economic Modernization. Under the leadership of Deng Xiaoping, the PRC has launched a series of bold departures from Maoist radical assumptions. In both economic and cultural realms the dominant trend has been toward liberalization, permitting substantially greater intellectual freedom to Chinese academics and literati (despite the recurrence of movements such as the criticism of "bourgeois liberalization" or "spiritual pollution," marking the limits of such freedom), and permitting the central planning mechanism to be abridged by growing private and collective economic activity. Economic changes have heretofore been most striking in the countryside, which has witnessed a de facto decollectivization of farmland and the transfer of accountability from local political authorities back to individual families. This change to the "responsibility system" has coincided with a striking increase in agricultural productivity, particularly in those cash crops whose prices were allowed to float on the free market but also in commodity grain—to be sure, these gains were achieved on the basis of previous collective investments, and there is some uncertainty about whether this rate of growth can be sustained. [*See also* Responsibility System.]

Industrial reforms have been less dramatic (most significant has been the introduction of enterprise profit retention), and industrial productivity seems to have declined by about one-third from the long-term growth trend (although gains have been made in light industry). China's economy as a whole has become more open to foreign trade, particularly to the free market economies, allowing for the first time for both joint ventures and direct capital investment by foreign firms, as well as loans and other forms of economic dependency. Class struggle and the mobilizational approach to policy implementation have been renounced, the dominant social cleavage now being the contradiction between advanced and backward economic sectors, to be resolved peaceably in the course of the "Four Modernizations" (of agriculture, industry, science and technology, and the military). This "contradiction" will take some time to resolve, however, and some will get rich sooner than others, implying an increased tolerance for inequality. [*See also* Four Modernizations.]

Although mass criticism of bureaucrats has been prohibited since the brief experiment with Democracy Wall, bureaucratism is still regarded pejoratively, and the apparent pervasiveness of bureaucratic corruption suggests that institutional remedies are not considered adequate. Although the political leadership is not yet contained by a fully institutionalized political framework—Deng Xiaoping's actual power, for example, greatly transcends his formal positions—any claims for charisma of the sort that once attached to Mao Zedong and his thought have been disavowed as feudal superstition, and a solid beginning has been made toward the functional division of authority in the attempt to separate Party, governmental, and military power. The Party and state constitutions adopted after an elaborate process of revision in 1982 bear cogent witness to an aspiration for rational-legal authority, as does the attempt, imperfect although it was, to submit the Gang of Four to a trial in which the defendents were accorded a right to reasoned self-defense.

The PRC's performance as a "developing country" over the thirty-five years since its founding has perhaps rested more on qualitative than on conventionally accepted quantitative indicators. It does seem to be true that the PRC has consistently achieved an unusual level of redistributive equality, even when measured against other socialist economies. Other aspects of political and social life have changed profoundly as a result of the revolution, despite evident backsliding. In terms of the growth of gross domestic product, China's performance has been impressive, although it does not rank among the leading success stories in the postwar Third World, averaging between 5 and 6 percent per annum from 1949 to the late 1970s. Although the more utopian aspects of the Maoist developmental mission have now been at least placed in abeyance, the attempt to "join the ranks of the foremost economic powers of the world" (implying a per capita gross national product of US $800) remains an ambitious one, and China's economic record suggests it should by no means be impossible to achieve. What that China will look like, assuming successful incorporation of a capitalist Hong Kong and continuing traffic with the "free world," is more difficult to predict.

[*See also* Marxism and Socialism: Marxism in China; Communism: Chinese Communist Party; Mao Zedong; Deng Xiaoping; *and the map accompanying* China.]

Hong Yung Lee, *The Politics of the Chinese Cultural Revolution* (1978). Roderick MacFarquhar, *The Origins of the Cultural Revolution,* vol. 1, *Contradictions Among the People, 1956–1957* (1974), vol. 2, *The Great Leap Forward, 1958–1960* (1983). William Parish and Martin King Whyte, *Village and Family in Contemporary China* (1978). Franz Schurmann, *Ideology and Organization in Communist China* (1968). John Bryan Starr, *Continuing the Revolution: The Political Thought of Mao* (1979). Frederick Teiwes, *Politics and Purges in China* (1979). Martin King Whyte, et al., *Urban Life in Contemporary China* (1984). LOWELL DITTMER

CHINA, REPUBLIC OF. The Republic of China (ROC), declared by Chiang Kai-shek in Nanjing on 10 October 1928, is heir to the first Chinese Republic, established in 1911. During 1929 the new government became the internationally recognized representative of China, replacing a series of warlord-backed regimes in Beijing that had filled that role since 1916.

The ROC, although it never ruled or controlled all of the eighteen home provinces of China, remained the recognized government until 1949, when the Communists, following great military victories in the Civil War, created their own state, the People's Republic of China (PRC), on 1 October 1949. Thereupon, the ROC retreated to the island province of Taiwan, where it remains today as a claimant to be the legitimate government of China. After 1950 the ROC retained a prominent role as an internationally recognized government of China through the backing of the United States. When a rapprochement between Washington and Beijing occurred between 1971 and 1972, the ROC's diplomatic position deteriorated rapidly. Nevertheless, the ROC continues to prosper as a separate regime on Taiwan.

Establishment of the ROC in 1928 fulfilled the plans made by Sun Yat-sen and his Guomindang (Kuomintang, KMT, or Nationalist Party). Sun began to create a new, politically loyal army in 1923 that was to undertake a Northern Expedition to defeat or absorb the great variety of warlords then blocking China's political unification. After Sun Yat-sen's death in October 1925, Chiang Kai-shek, a military officer who headed the party's Whampoa Military Academy at Canton (Guangzhou), emerged as an unexpected but powerful claimant for leadership. Between 1926 and 1928 Chiang Kai-shek carried out the Northern Expedition, while securing his own position within the party ranks from challenges of both the left and the right. He also deeply distrusted the Nationalists' chief foreign supporter, the Soviet Union, and China's own small Communist Party, which, under Comintern instructions, participated in the Nationalist Party and the Northern Expedition. [*See also* Sun Yat-sen; Northern Expedition; *and* Comintern.]

The decisive break came at Shanghai on 12 April 1927 when right-wing groups supporting Chiang Kai-shek turned on local Communists; Nationalist Army units joined in the suppression. From that time onward relations between the Nationalist and Communist parties have been marked by deep enmity. There were later instances of cooperation or compromise, but renewed struggle always broke out with compounded hatred on both sides.

From 1927 until his death in 1975 Chiang Kai-shek's leadership became a necessary element in both the Nationalist Party and the ROC. Chiang's power rested on his control over the Nationalist Army and came to include leadership in the ROC as well as domination of the Nationalist Party. He did not always need to hold formal leadership posts within all of these hierarchies. In the wake of certain crises, such as the years from 1931 to 1932 and

1949 to 1950, Chiang Kai-shek retired from direct leadership for brief periods, only to return to exercise even greater control. Upon his death, a son by his first marriage, Chiang Ching-kuo (Jiang Jingguo; b. 1910), succeeded to the presidency of the ROC.

Chiang Kai-shek wrapped himself in Sun Yatsen's mantle by claiming his leadership represented the intended succession for Sun's Three Principles of the People (Nationalism, Democracy, and Livelihood). Consequently, the form of the state and the official ideology in the ROC follow Sun's ideas closely. In actuality, however, Chiang Kai-shek introduced new elements to produce a somewhat different view of China as a modern nation.

According to Sun's *Fundamentals of National Reconstruction* (1924), the revolution would have three stages: a period of military rule in which the Nationalist Party's army swept away opposition and achieved unification; a period of tutelage in which the people would be prepared to govern themselves; and a third, final era of constitutional rule. In October 1928 an "Organic Law" was promulgated that established the state's organization for the period of tutelage. The structure embodied Sun Yatsen's conception of five branches, each called a *yuan*, which provided checks and balances. The familiar Western executive, legislative, and judicial functions were supplemented by an Examination Yuan for recruitment and advancement of officials and a Control Yuan to provide for independent review of official conduct. These last two branches drew on the model of traditional Chinese state organization.

The period of tutelage was extended under a Provisional Constitution adopted in 1931 and lasted until 1948. During these years the Nationalist Party controlled all five branches of the state. Chiang Kaishek was named president of the Republic and president of the Executive Yuan. The Nationalist Party, however, was not yet under his control; rivals such as Hu Hanmin on the right and Wang Jingwei on the left held positions of power in both the state and the party. The ROC's form still embodied the principle of unity among the state, the party, and the leadership. [*See also* Hu Hanmin *and* Wang Jingwei.]

Most interpretations of the ROC, both friendly and critical, have accepted that such a unity did exist among the Republican state, the Nationalist Party, and Chiang Kai-shek. In this dominant view the successes and shortcomings of the ROC are assigned to an interchangeable combination of these three factors. This view is found in the work of most ROC supporters. Chinese Communist historians also speak of this unity when criticizing the ROC, but add a factor that they term "bureaucratic capitalism," by which they mean the increasing domination of most modern portions of the Chinese economy by a small oligarchy of ROC political families. Four families, those of Chiang Kai-shek, his in-laws the Song (Soong) and Kong (Kung) families, and the Chen family (the descendants of Chiang Kai-shek's early benefactor Chen Qimei), are singled out. These charges, originally made in the prolonged struggle between the Communist and Nationalist parties, have been difficult to prove, but have focused attention on the question of the ROC's support from both the capitalist bourgeoisie and the rural landlords. [*See also* Soong Mei-ling; Soong, T. V.; *and* Chen Qimei.] Recent American research has emphasized how the ROC alienated much capitalist and bourgeois support in the 1930s through its insistence on control over commerce and industry coupled with its distrust of bourgeois liberalism. Although tension did exist between ROC aims and landlord interests, these were reconciled when the ROC increasingly dressed its version of China's modern future in conservative policies that did not threaten the landlords' role in rural China.

According to revisionist scholars Chiang Kai-shek used the ideas of Sun Yat-sen in order to secure an autocratic position within the new state and then proceeded to make himself the indispensable leader. By the mid-1930s he had reduced the Nationalist Party to a dogsbody. Subsequently, he ruled through a combination of charisma, military power, and factional elite politics similar to other military autocrats of the twentieth century. According to this view Chiang Kai-shek is shown to have favored a brand of political participation parallel to European fascism, in which conservative values are harnessed through strongly disciplined mass movements in order to support new national orders opposed to both Marxist socialism and bourgeois liberalism.

A somewhat different view emphasizes the ROC's militarism rather than its fascism. In this interpretation, the ROC's chief feature is its increasing militarization from 1928 through the early 1960s. This militarization is seen as a legacy of Chinese politics of the late nineteenth and early twentieth centuries that compelled all claimants for political power to emphasize military strength in order to achieve and maintain political control. In this view, Chiang Kaishek consistently pursued policies to increase ROC military power, but in 1945 found the ROC still lacked the military means to unite China.

The ROC's history usually is divided into four periods: (1) the Nanjing decade of 1928 to 1937, a period of nation building so named because the seat of national administration was moved from Beijing to Nanjing in the lower Yangtze River valley; (2) the Anti-Japanese War of 1937 to 1945, when the struggle against Japanese military occupation of China's coastal regions became the focus of a national resistance effort; (3) the Civil War of 1945 to 1949, when the ROC attempted for the first time to bring all of China under its rule, but became engaged in a losing war with the Chinese Communists; and (4) the Taiwan era of 1950 to the present, in which the ROC withdrew to Taiwan with the intent of someday returning to the mainland. By the 1960s the ROC had become absorbed increasingly with the economic development of Taiwan itself. Thus, attention shifted from the proclaimed goal of recovering the mainland to problems of economic development and political control in a single province.

The Nanjing Decade. In contrast to the great upheaval after 1937, the first years of ROC rule seem in retrospect to have been an oasis of progress and relative stability. The ROC did have considerable civil accomplishments, including the abolition of some forms of extraterritorial privilege, the establishment of a sound money and banking system, and increasing tariff autonomy, as well as marked improvements in the national communication system, some industrial development, and great success in the nationalization of education. The ROC did not, however, undertake a major commitment to rural social and economic reform. Its revenues, even in the best years during the 1930s, never matched its heavy expenditures, establishing a fatal fiscal weakness that later was to plague the ROC.

Chiang Kai-shek's own preferences, plus the considerable military challenges still facing the ROC, meant that building the army remained a top priority. The ROC stressed the expansion of the armed forces along modern lines with firm political loyalty. These armed forces were intended first to establish the ROC's authority against all domestic opposition and then to assist in asserting China's rights against the foreign powers. A modern, efficient bureaucracy was seen as a necessary adjunct, for it could help collect the required revenues, manage the civil administration, and deal with foreign states.

Internally, the ROC's authority was confined to the lower Yangtze region, while in the rest of China remnant warlords continued their largely independent rule. Chief warlords included the Guangxi clique, led by Li Zongren and operating in Guangxi, Guangdong, Hunan, and Hubei; Zhang Xueliang in the Northeast (Manchuria); Yan Xishan, solidly based in Shanxi; and Feng Yuxiang, less firmly placed in North China. Chiang Kai-shek directed efforts to bring these warlords to heel with considerable success. [*See also* Warlords *and* Warlord Cliques.]

Until 1935 the Nationalist Party remained beyond Chiang Kai-shek's domination, although he was not without influence. He worked through the so-called CC clique led by Chen Guofu and Chen Lifu, who controlled the Nationalist Party's Organizational Department. Chiang encouraged several similar groups: one was the Whampoa clique of officers trained in Canton; another was the Political Study clique of modern bureaucrats, joined by some generals and politicians. The CC clique gave him influence in the party, the Whampoa clique gave him influence among the military services, and the Political Study clique helped in managing the ROC bureaucracy.

Chiang Kai-shek never limited himself to these cliques, but showed a clear preference for personal politics within a small circle of advisers and confidants. He Yingqin was a key figure in the Whampoa group, while Zhang Chun, a former schoolmate and close adviser since 1926, became identified with the Political Study clique. Also important were relatives of his wife's family: T. V. Soong (Song Ziwen), his wife's brother, and H. H. Kung (Kong Xiangxi), his sister-in-law's husband. Following long-established patterns for factional politics in China, Chiang Kai-shek varied his support among members of these cliques and added new individuals who were loyal to him but not associated with any group. As a result, ROC politics in the 1930s developed a style that was both autocratic and uncertain, characteristics that seem to reflect both Chiang Kai-shek's own leadership and an inheritance from the nature of pre-1911 politics of the Qing court.

Thus, while liberal influences still were present in China during the 1930s, their role in the ROC became secondary. This shift represented a considerable change, for under Sun Yat-sen the Nationalist Party had been marked by an eclectic ideology and an extremely broad range of support. In the 1930s the ROC proclaimed a more narrow vision of the Chinese nation in which bourgeois laxity and Marxist socialism had no role, but instead a strong, conservative, and militaristic state was intended to dominate politics, the society, and the economy.

In the early 1930s Chiang Kai-shek became increasingly worried about the corrupting influences of capitalist materialism and bourgeois moral laxity. Hoping to save the ROC's new order, he turned to a program of mass participation strongly influenced by European fascist ideas. The duties of citizens, not their rights, were stressed. Citizens were expected to display martial virtues of discipline, obedience, and selfless sacrifice. These principles reflected Chiang Kai-shek's own beliefs about the proper political culture for China.

ROC fascism appealed to conservative ideologues such as Dai Jitao or Liu Jianchun. The Blue Shirts, a paramilitary organization modeled on the Italian and German fascist movements, started secretly in 1931. In 1934 a nationwide New Life Movement, opposed to unwanted influences—both Chinese and foreign—was launched as a moral campaign built around Confucian principles recast in terms compatible with modern nationalism. Neither was a success, but both revealed that conservatism, nationalism, and militarism were distinctive and lasting qualities of the ROC.

Nationalist armed forces sometimes fought against wayward warlords after 1928, but their primary target was the Chinese Communists. The Communists, under Mao Zedong's leadership, developed armed governments in the more inaccessible fringes of the central and lower Yangtze Valley regions. Chiang Kai-shek conducted five campaigns against the Communists from 1930 to 1934. The ROC forces, increasingly effective through a combination of Whampoa generals, German military advisers, and modern military equipment, threatened to destroy the rural Communist bases. In 1935 the Fifth Extermination Campaign against the main Communist base in Jiangxi was on the verge of success when the Communist forces broke out of their encirclement and started the Long March on 15 October. [*See also* Communist-Extermination Campaigns *and* Long March.]

Foreign states were hesitant to see a fully sovereign and independent government in China; such a state threatened their special privileges. The anti-imperialist policies of the ROC in diplomacy, foreign trade, taxation, and a host of other matters left many foreign governments unhappy with the ROC. Among the foreigners, Japan emerged as the chief opponent to the ROC. Serious problems began in 1928 during the Northern Expedition, when a clash occurred between Japanese and Nationalist forces at Ji'nan in Shandong. [*See also* Ji'nan Incident.] Chiang Kai-shek thereafter followed a policy of avoiding any provocation that Japan might use as an excuse for aggression. He feared Japanese military superiority and intended to consolidate internal power before attempting to check Japan.

Aggression was too powerful a force within Japanese society to be placated by the ROC's appeasement policy. The Japanese Kwantung Army created an incident at Shenyang (Mukden) on 18 September 1931. In the ensuing battles the Japanese pushed all Chinese administrative authority out of Manchuria. [*See also* Mukden Incident.] During the conflict the Japanese broadened their attack to include Shanghai in January 1932. After initial stiff resistance there, the Nationalist armies broke and the capital at Nanjing was threatened. A Sino-Japanese truce followed in May 1932, but not before the creation of a Japanese puppet state called Manchukuo in the Northeast.

The Japanese military continued a policy of continental expansion. They overran Rehe (Jehol) in 1933, and by 1935 were threatening China's home provinces south of the Great Wall. The ROC's tenuous control over much of North China led Chiang Kai-shek to accept the dilution of Chinese sovereignty in that region, and by 1936 Japanese engrossment appeared to be only a matter of time.

Resistance to Japan grew, especially in North China. Chinese armies led by generals such as Zhang Xueliang, who had been driven out of the Northeast by the Japanese, were located in North China and employed by the ROC against Chinese Communist base areas. Under Mao Zedong the Communists had ended their Long March in Yan'an, where they gave top priority to United Front resistance to the Japanese. Public opinion in China, mobilized by intellectuals and students in campaigns such as the December Ninth Movement of 1935, also called for more resistance.

A crisis in ROC policy occurred in December 1936 when Zhang Xueliang and Yang Hucheng took Chiang Kai-shek prisoner at Xi'an out of anger against his appeasement policy. Chiang eventually was freed and agreed to follow a more forward policy against Japan, based on a renewed Nationalist-Communist alliance and supported by all patriotic Chinese. Chiang Kai-shek emerged from the Xi'an Incident a hero with a strong mandate to lead the nation. [*See also* Xi'an Incident *and* United Front.]

The Anti-Japanese War. Inevitably, the Sino-Japanese War followed in the summer of 1937. Fighting began on 7 July after a clash between Chinese and Japanese units on the outskirts of Beijing at the Marco Polo Bridge (Lukouqiao). Following quick victories in North China, the Japanese attacked

Shanghai on 13 August. Chiang Kai-shek threw his best divisions into the fight, but their fierce resistance was overcome by strong Japanese armies. When the ROC capital of Nanjing fell on 12 December, the ROC had lost more than one-third of its modern, German-trained units. The orgy of looting, killing, and destruction by Japanese troops in the capital city became known as the "Rape of Nanjing," an event that swung foreign opinion, especially in the United States, in favor of the ROC.

The ROC withdrew to Wuhan, where in the summer of 1938 it reorganized on a wartime basis. A "Program of Armed Resistance and National Reconstruction" was established to bind the Nationalists and Communists into a common cause against Japan. Chiang's domination over the Nationalist Party and the ROC was strengthened by a new title of party director-general; his new military authority was represented by the title generalissimo.

On the battlefield the ROC adopted a policy of mobile offensive resistance to Japan. They won their most notable victory at Taierzhuang during March and April 1938. Still, the Japanese took both Wuhan and Canton by December 1938, driving the ROC out of its lower Yangtze River homeland and into Sichuan and the southwest, where its overseas supply lines became long and tenuous. In 1939 China's main source of outside support came from the Soviet Union, which supplied arms, advisers, and low-cost loans against a common enemy, Japan. Under Japanese aerial bombardment at Chongqing, the wartime capital, Chiang Kai-shek struggled to establish the ROC's control over these formerly independent regions and to relocate a portion of China's modern industry in this interior fastness.

ROC armies carried out a major offensive against the Japanese from November 1939 to April 1940. This winter offensive failed and caused further damage to the ROC's best fighting units. By the summer of 1940 the ROC's prewar military strength was largely destroyed and its continued existence as a state was in serious doubt. The Japanese established several puppet regimes claiming the banner of Sun Yat-sen's Nationalist Party. The most important of these was the Reformed Nationalist Government established in Nanjing in March 1940 under the senior Nationalist Party figure Wang Jingwei.

The noose around the ROC tightened further. The French administration in Indochina, at Japan's request, cut off rail traffic into southwest China in June 1940. The British in Burma agreed to close the Burma Road temporarily, but did reopen it in late 1940. In April 1941 Japan and the Soviet Union signed a Treaty of Neutrality and Friendship, ending the ROC's hope of further Soviet aid. American support, calculated not to provoke Japan into war, was insufficient to make up the ROC's losses from other sources.

The ROC passed through its decisive crisis before the outbreak of a wider Pacific War on 7 December 1941. Although the United States' entrance into the war gave the ROC reason to hope, the ROC itself had already lost its pre-1937 economic base. From the interior of China the ROC lacked the means to produce another modern army; it could not equip itself to fight in the European military style favored by Chiang Kai-shek and his generals. In addition, the ROC already was wracked by serious fiscal disorder, with war costs exceeding government revenues fivefold in 1941. Quarrels with the Chinese Communists reappeared, ending the effective wartime cooperation between the two old enemies. In this atmosphere reliance on Chiang Kai-shek further increased and his role became more dictatorial. Civilian political life withered and the ROC's existence increasingly depended upon military stability, backed with the vigilance of the secret police.

The United States proved a difficult ally for the ROC. Although the Americans could promise needed military supplies, the lack of ports or roads to reach the ROC and the higher strategic priority given other war theaters limited the real material aid the ROC received until after the Japanese surrender in August 1945. Still, the US gave the ROC $2 billion in aid and credits between 1942 and 1946.

The American price for this assistance was a coordinated strategy against the Japanese. Chiang Kai-shek opposed the plans of Joseph Stilwell, the American general appointed as the ROC's chief of staff. Stilwell's program intended to build up American-trained ROC divisions for use against Japan, first in Burma and then in China. Chiang feared Stilwell's new units would disrupt his carefully balanced control over the disparate elements in his armies, now a mixture of warlord forces, raw recruits, and the remnants of his pre-1937 German-trained elite units. Chiang realized any major campaigns would create losses and tensions within the armed services that might destroy both him and the ROC, so he resisted Stilwell's program. Chiang and his advisers also were dismayed by American willingness to accept Communist efforts against the Japanese, for the ROC leadership remained committed anticommunists. [*See also* Stilwell, Joseph W.]

Chiang Kai-shek, with the assistance of his wife, Soong Mei-ling (Song Meiling), developed an effective alternative to Stilwell's plan by encouraging American advocates of air power to stage a bombing campaign against Japan from ROC-built bases. Once the bases were built and the first attacks launched in the summer of 1944, the Japanese counterattacked and overran ROC armies and some air bases.

A crisis of policy and leadership followed in which Chiang won an apparent complete victory over Stilwell, who was replaced. The victory was pyrrhic, however, for it produced a lasting division in American opinion about Chiang Kai-shek and the ROC. One group saw the ROC as weak, ineffective, and increasingly corrupt; the other saw Chiang and the ROC as China's saviors and a force that must be backed against the Communists. Before 1950 American policymakers never decided between the two views, so the United States' policy varied from firm support to open criticism and finally, late in the Civil War, to disassociation from the ROC.

As Japan's war hopes dimmed in late 1944, the prospects for the ROC seemed to brighten. Differences with the Communists came to the fore again and civil war threatened. The United States tried to mediate, but to no avail, for Chiang remained adamant that the Communists could have no role in postwar China. [*See also* World War II in China.]

More dangerous than the Communists was the eight years of warfare that by the summer of 1945 had sapped the ROC's strength. Galloping wartime inflation had ruined the currency, destroyed the banking system, and forced many loyal supporters of the ROC to turn to corruption in order to survive. The ROC leadership saw Communist subversion as a major threat; secret police often killed or imprisoned anyone who did not unquestioningly accept ROC policy. Although some ROC army and air force units were excellent, many of the more than 3.7 million men in the armed services were poorly led, poorly trained, and not prepared to fight a tough civil war.

The Civil War. Chiang Kai-shek grasped Japan's defeat as an opportunity to extend ROC power throughout China. In addition to returning to its homeland in the central and lower Yangtze River valley, the ROC intended to rule North China, the Northeast (Manchuria), Mongolia, the Northwest, Xinjiang (Chinese Turkestan), and South China; all were areas beyond Nanjing's control in 1937. Chiang's plan had some basis for success, for all the ROC's rivals, except for the Communists, had been eliminated in the war. The United States willingly lent him assistance by ferrying military units and civil administrators to the far reaches of China. The Japanese helped by surrendering only to authorized ROC or Allied representatives.

The Chinese Communists also rushed to establish their territorial control, especially in North China and the Northeast. Soviet armed forces had occupied parts of the Northeast in the final weeks of the war and the Communists believed Soviet presence offered a special advantage to them in that region. The threat of open civil war between the ROC and the Communists increased and the United States renewed its mediation efforts. Talks between Mao Zedong and Chiang Kai-shek at Chongqing broke down in October 1945 as large amounts of American aid, both military and civil, flowed easily to the ROC across the Pacific and through the newly reopened coastal ports.

Still hoping to avoid a Chinese civil war, President Harry Truman sent George Marshall as a special ambassador to China in December 1945. Marshall worked hard for most of 1946, but his efforts were doomed from February on, when large-scale fighting between ROC and Communist forces erupted in the Northeast.

ROC armies, freshly supplied with American matériel, won a series of victories in 1946. By the end of the year Chiang Kai-shek proclaimed a hope to destroy the Communists militarily within the coming year. At the same time, he announced a new National Assembly that would shape a constitution to take the ROC beyond the period of tutelage and into the era of full representative democracy. Americans saw only a prolonged civil war that the ROC could not be certain of winning; Marshall returned to Washington and United States support for the ROC slackened. [*See also* Marshall, George C.]

Chiang Kai-shek's constitutional plans went as scheduled. The new constitution was adopted; national elections, with limited voting because of unsettled conditions, were held; the Nationalist Party won the great majority of seats in the elected bodies; and Chiang Kai-shek was elected president of the Republic. The rest of Chiang's hopes for China did not fare as well.

Domestically, postwar China continued to suffer from serious inflation. ROC authority controlled China's large cities and many towns, but often did not penetrate deep into the countryside. The loyalty of many who had remained under Japanese rule from 1937 to 1945 was considered doubtful. Politics were further poisoned by the fear of subversion and worsened by the frequent intervention of secret police. By mid-1947 the prospects for restoration of pre-1937 social and economic order, even in areas under clear ROC control, were not good.

By late 1947 Communist armies were winning important battles in North and Northeast China. These successes continued into 1948; by November the ROC had lost 500,000 troops, many of whom simply defected from the ROC cause, and large amounts of new American equipment from its best units.

The final, decisive battle was the Huaihai campaign fought in northern Jiangsu and southern Shandong from October 1948 to January 1949. Chiang Kai-shek personally insisted the ROC stand and fight. His armies lost and he was forced to resign as president of the Republic. The Communist armies crossed the Yangtze River and occupied Nanjing on 24 April 1949.

The ROC on Taiwan. The ROC first relocated itself in Canton and finally removed to Taiwan in December 1949. Chiang Kai-shek, supposedly in retirement at his family home in Ningbo, oversaw the withdrawal of considerable military, civilian, and financial resources to Taiwan. By early 1950 more than one million mainlanders had become refugees on China's island province. On 1 March 1950 Chiang Kai-shek resumed the presidency of the ROC. The interim president, Li Zongren, along with many former top leaders of the ROC, did not accompany Chiang Kai-shek to Taiwan, preferring exile in the United States or elsewhere.

Taiwan had become Japan's colony as a result of its victory in the Sino-Japanese War of 1894 to 1895. The island was returned to China in 1945; initially, the ROC sent the army of General Chen Yi to occupy it. Chen's men and their methods deeply antagonized the local Chinese population. A Taiwanese uprising began on 28 February 1947; General Chen put it down ruthlessly by killing thousands of Taiwanese youths and political leaders. Chiang Kai-shek, whose attention was centered on controlling the Chinese mainland, had paid little attention to the 6 million Chinese on Taiwan. After the February uprising, however, the ROC moved to remedy the situation. In January 1949 a more enlightened officer, Chen Cheng, took over. He was a loyal confidant of Chiang Kai-shek and together with an able civil official, Yan Jiagan (C. K. Yen), he put the island's administration on a sound footing. Since 1947, however, political and cultural animosity between the Taiwanese majority and the mainlander minority (meaning those Chinese who came to Taiwan with the ROC) has remained a serious problem.

In early 1950 it appeared Taiwan might quickly fall to the People's Republic of China (PRC) in spite of the formidable barrier presented by the 90 miles of water that separates Taiwan from the mainland. The ROC was without American support and its 800,000 soldiers were ill-prepared to repel any invasion. Following the outbreak of war in Korea on 25 June 1950, ties with the United States were quickly revived. When PRC volunteers entered Korea in October 1950, the ROC was again embraced by the United States as a close ally.

United States policy was to rearm the ROC, but to ensure that it would become a nonaggressive client. Through a Military Assistance Advisory Group the United States modernized the ROC's military equipment, improved its training, reduced its numbers, and monitored its plans to reconquer the mainland. From 1950 to 1970, the United States maintained a Taiwan Straits patrol, both to protect against PRC invasion and to restrain the ROC from undertaking major military adventures against the PRC. The Mutual Defense Treaty of 1954 settled the long-term arrangement in which the United States undertook a commitment to maintain the ROC's armed forces with up-to-date equipment and training, while the ROC agreed to use its military power for defensive purposes. In effect, the ROC was agreeing not to restart, on its own, the Chinese Civil War.

The Mutual Defense Treaty provided Chiang Kai-shek the means to re-create what he had always wanted most for the ROC: a large, powerful, and modern military establishment. At the same time, Chiang, as a proud, stubborn nationalist, resented the short tether of American policy. Probably believing that events would someday force a resumption of the Civil War, Chiang accepted the American insistence that the United States intended to avoid war with the PRC, either for itself or through its client, the ROC.

The ROC military has a strong tradition of loyalty to the state and its leaders. On Taiwan that characteristic has been strengthened. Intensive political indoctrination, skillful personnel management, including regular rotation of commands, and frugal but sound veterans' policies have improved the regime's control over the armed services. Still, the military's interests are a major, but often unseen, factor in shaping ROC policy on social, economic, and political issues, as well as on matters more directly concerning the armed services.

Beyond Taiwan, the ROC has controlled the Taiwan Straits through occupation of islands along the

Fujian and Zhejiang coast and the mid-channel Penghu archipelago. The PRC made efforts to dislodge the ROC from these islands in 1954, 1955, and 1958, thereby keeping the Civil War alive during the 1950s. The ROC withdrew from the Dachen islands off the Zhejiang coast in 1955, but has maintained control over the better-known Jinmen (Quemoy) and Mazu (Matsu), both adjacent to the Fujian coast. Defense of these outposts is expensive, but has the virtue of keeping the ROC's forces in a high state of combat readiness. About one-third of the ROC's military strength is committed to the defense of these islands. [*See also* Jinmen *and* Matsu.]

The possibility of PRC invasion, the fear of Communist subversion, and a large number of public security organizations have given Taiwan the character of a garrison state. Martial law was declared in Taiwan in 1949 and continued until 1987. Behind the continuing operation of constitutional representative government on Taiwan, a special Taiwan Garrison Command exists. This Garrison Command is a powerful but shadowy arbiter of life on Taiwan during what the ROC calls "the continuing Communist insurgency." The atmosphere of a garrison state remained strong into the 1960s, but ultimately has not throttled the forces of political and social change. The Garrison Command attempts to ensure that any changes will neither weaken the ROC nor open it to Communist subversion. The ROC on Taiwan has remained highly suspicious of even mild democratic criticism. A close watch is kept on intellectuals and students, who are believed particularly susceptible to Communist subversion.

The formal representative bodies called for by the 1948 constitution have remained in operation. A national government, with the apparatus for ruling the whole of China, exists in Taipei (Taibei), the island's largest city. The National Assembly and Legislative Yuan, with representatives from all of China, continues to sit. These bodies now contain around one-fifth of their authorized members, for death has reduced steadily the ranks of those elected in 1947. Only limited replacement is possible, for obviously elections in China are not feasible. A separate Taiwan provincial government exists in Taichung (Taizhong), with an elected legislature. Democratic elections for provincial and local government have been conducted on a fairly regular basis. Location of a national and a provincial government on a single island province creates some obvious questions of jurisdiction. In all major matters, Taiwan's affairs continue to be decided by national leaders in Taipei.

Although the concept of tutelage was abandoned in 1948, the ROC remains fundamentally a one-party state. Members of the national, provincial, and local government are drawn overwhelmingly from the Nationalist Party ranks. Authorities have never permitted a true opposition party to exist. Nevertheless, beginning in the 1970s a form of opposition has developed in the so-called *tang-wai (dangwai),* or "extra-party" movement. These politicians, usually of Taiwanese descent, have run as candidates for office without the endorsement or support of the Nationalist Party.

Given the garrison-state assumptions within the ROC and the residual animosity between the Taiwanese and mainlander communities, this independent political movement, although it never took on party form and was apparently not opposed to the ROC, inevitably became the source of political unrest. In the Kaohsiung (Gaoxiong) Incident of 10 December 1979 the ROC acted decisively to suppress what it saw as a Taiwanese effort to challenge the ROC's present form of rule in Taiwan. A small Taiwanese independence movement (often using the Portuguese name *Formosa* instead of Taiwan) does exist, primarily in exile, and calls for the establishment of a sovereign, independent Taiwanese nation, distinct from both the ROC and the PRC. Some ROC authorities have found evidence of similar ideas among the *tang-wai* adherents.

Still, the Nationalist Party has made a major and largely successful effort to recruit Taiwanese participation in its ranks. Today, Nationalist Party membership is 1.5 million, or about one-third of all adult males on Taiwan. Many Taiwanese have achieved positions of authority within the government, the party, and even the armed services. Cultural differences exist between the two communities, but common bonds as Chinese and as opponents of communism have been stressed. As a result, the ROC rule in Taiwan is marked by considerable cohesion, although somewhat short of Chiang Kai-shek's ideal of a disciplined, martial society with unquestioning loyalty.

After coming to Taiwan, the ROC reacted to criticism of its failure to achieve basic social reforms, especially in rural China, on the mainland. In 1949 the new governor, Chen Cheng, launched an important land reform. This moderate, legalistic reform took place gradually over eight years and was conducted by careful administrative law that included remuneration of landlords. The ROC's land reform makes an obvious contrast with the methods used by the PRC on the mainland. A great many

ROC policies since 1950 in such diverse areas as industrial development, political reform, education, and cultural affairs are often best understood as ROC efforts to show that their state can achieve national goals the PRC proclaims for China, but by more moderate means and with better results. [*See also* Land Tenure and Reform: Land Reform in Modern China.]

The United States has made considerable contributions to Taiwan's development. In the 1950s American aid intended for improvement of commerce, industry, and agriculture averaged more than $100 million a year. The Americans backed the ROC's moderate land reform and encouraged agricultural modernization through the Sino-American Joint Commission on Rural Reconstruction.

As American economic aid declined in the early 1960s, the ROC tried a new economic development strategy brought to the island largely by Chinese economists residing in the United States. These theories called for strong economic planning by the state, including strict management of money and banking, combined with tight control over luxury consumption and various inducements for savings and investment, while emphasizing industrial production for export. Foreign investors built new plants in return for tax advantages and the all-important promise of cheap, well-disciplined labor. The new strategy stresses export-oriented production, rather than the older strategy based on import substitution. This strategy has been used in Hong Kong, Korea, and Singapore, as well as in the ROC.

The ROC on Taiwan has developed a mixed capitalist-state economy in which the government owns certain monopolistic enterprises, such as public utilities and public transit. The state also owns other industries where the public interest is said to require government control, such as alcohol and tobacco manufacture and sales, and parts of the defense industry. Finally, some high-risk endeavors, especially when huge capital investments are necessary, such as in shipbuilding and automobile assembly, also are state-owned enterprises.

Beginning in the early 1960s the ROC's economic strategy has produced an impressive record of growth. From 1963 to 1973 the increase in gross national product averaged 9.7 percent annually; since then the results have fluctuated more broadly, but only during 1982, in a world recession, did this measure dip below a 5 percent increase. Taiwan has acquired modern industrial capacity, has created a highly skilled labor force well attuned to the needs of international trade, and has established close linkages with the Japanese and North American economies.

The result has been ready employment for most of Taiwan's growing population (18.7 million in 1983), and improved living conditions for most people. Average per capita income, in constant 1976 US dollars, grew from $48 in 1952 to $2,400 in 1983. Other standard measures of economic prosperity, including educational levels, caloric intake, life expectancy, distribution of consumer durables, levels of urbanization, and availability of housing, have all increased. Taiwan also shows the expected declines in death rates, infant mortality, the birth rate, and the role of agriculture in the economy.

While the ROC policies on the mainland did not always favor capitalism, on Taiwan the rapid expansion of the capitalist economy with encouragement of the government has transformed the nature of the ROC. The garrison-state dream of a return to the mainland has faded, but it continues to be invoked. Paradoxically, even the most revanchist elements in the ROC and its armed services have seen the increasing wealth of the Taiwanese economy produce greater military budgets, better-educated and healthier Taiwanese recruits for the military, as well as better living conditions and more opportunities for their own families.

In 1972 Chiang Ching-kuo became president of the Executive Yuan (or premier) and assumed real leadership within the ROC from his father, who was serving his fifth term as elected president. Under Chiang Ching-kuo the policy of economic development has been expanded and the reconciliation between mainlanders and Taiwanese given top priority. The ROC has undertaken major investments in education and in the economic infrastructure through the development of nuclear power, superhighways, electrified railways, modern ports, and steel mills. The ROC has left housing and medical care to private enterprise and done little to protect labor. A proud accomplishment is the relatively high ratio of income equality among wage earners: the top 20 percent of wage earners received only 4.18 times the average wage of the lowest 20 percent in 1978, a much smaller difference than prevails in most societies.

By the mid-1970s Taiwan's economic prosperity had become powerful enough to outshine other less favorable aspects of the ROC's situation. The loss of China's seat in the United Nations in 1971, President Nixon's visit to the PRC and the signing of the Shanghai Communiqué in 1972, and the oil shock of 1973 all were not sufficient to undermine the control of the ROC.

When Chiang Kai-shek died on 10 April 1975, his son was the only possible successor. Chiang Ching-kuo has proven less austere and less martial than his father. Chiang Ching-kuo's own age and health problems, including diabetes, have meant the ROC must prepare for another transition in leadership. Succession is unclear, and even the process of selecting the ROC's next leader remains uncertain.

The withdrawal of American diplomatic recognition from the ROC in January 1979 created the most serious problems since that government came to Taiwan in 1949. In that thirty-year period the ROC's armed forces, its economy, and its elite had become closely linked with the United States. The United States abrogated the 1954 Mutual Defense Treaty, but replaced it with the Taiwan Defense Act, which promises to continue supplies of essential items for defense. Because Taiwan's economy is so closely linked with the world economy, it suffered from the general world recession of 1980 to 1982, but it managed to weather economic storms through firm central government management and a willingness to see many small, private enterprises go bankrupt in bad times.

Tension between the ROC and the PRC has eased since Mao Zedong's death in 1976. The PRC has made several proposals for peaceful reunification of Taiwan and the rest of China, most dramatically in terms offered by Ye Jianying in October 1981. The ROC has rejected outright all these proposals and remains deeply suspicious of any dealings with the Chinese Communists. Still, some signs of a thaw in the glacial opposition is noticeable: PRC vessels began to sail through the Taiwan Straits for the first time in 1981, the volume of indirect trade between the two economies increased, and some residents of Taiwan have made visits to the PRC and returned to live under the ROC.

On Taiwan the ROC transformed itself from a weak but highly autocratic garrison state into a burgeoning example of capitalist economic success. In coping with diplomatic isolation and domestic opposition, the ROC has found the Nationalist Party and the leadership, as typified by Chiang Ching-kuo, willing to reconcile their differences in seemingly ad hoc but effective methods with the Taiwanese majority.

[*See also* China, Republic Period; Guomindang; Chiang Kai-shek; Chiang Ching-kuo; *and* Taiwan.]

Hsi-sheng Ch'i, *Nationalist China at War: Military Defeats and Political Collapse, 1937–1945* (1982). Joseph Fewsmith, *Party, State and Local Elites in Republican China* (1984). Samuel P. S. Ho, *Economic Development of Taiwan, 1870–1970* (1978). Pichon P. Y. Loh, *The Kuomintang Debacle of 1949: Conquest or Collapse?* (1965). Suzanne Pepper, *Civil War in China: The Political Struggle* (1978). James Sheridan, *China in Disintegration: The Republican Era in Chinese History, 1912–1949* (1975). Hung-mao Tien, *Government and Politics of Kuomintang China, 1927–1937* (1972). Dick Wilson, *When Tigers Fight: The Story of the Sino-Japanese War, 1937–1945* (1982).

DAVID D. BUCK

CHINA, REPUBLIC PERIOD. The political revolution that broke out in central China on 10 October 1911 was to mark the end of both the Qing dynasty and the two-thousand-year-old imperial system itself. Hope that the adoption of a republican form of government would be accompanied by new strength and respect in the world, however, was grievously disappointed. China would soon experience years of political disintegration and civil war as warlordism became pervasive. Even as the turmoil deepened, radical movements of cultural and social renovation emerged. By the mid-1920s these new movements had coalesced under a nationalist banner to offer a revolutionary vision of China's possibilities. Before national unity was achieved, however, the coalition split. Under Chiang Kai-shek, the consolidation of the nationalist movement in a new government for China in 1927 was given a conservative coloration.

The 1911 (Xinhai) Revolution quickly achieved the two fundamental goals prescribed by the revolutionary leadership: the overthrow of the Qing dynasty and its Manchu emperor and its replacement by a republic. The initial uprising in October was followed within two months by revolutionary seizures of power in a generous majority of provinces. The governments of the revolutionary provinces federated in a provisional government in Nanjing. Sun Yat-sen, veteran revolutionary, became its president on 1 January 1912. The remainder of the country, including the old imperial capital in Beijing, was won for the Republic, not by further battle but by negotiation and compromise. The Manchu Xuantong emperor, still a child, abdicated on 12 February 1912. [*See also* Xuantong Emperor *and* Xinhai Revolution.] As part of the deal, however, Sun Yat-sen also soon resigned. The presidency of the new, unified Republic of China was taken up in Beijing by a former official of the Qing, Yuan Shikai.

The republican era, then, began on an ambiguous note. How much change had been intended? It became apparent that there was no agreement on either the degree or the direction of change.

During the first year of the Republic, the institutions of a liberal republic were set in place. Representative assemblies, which had first emerged in the last years of the Qing, proliferated at all levels. Many provinces insisted on autonomy, including the local command of armed forces. The central government in Beijing was defined by a constitution that located sovereignty in the people and provided that power be shared by president and parliament. In the winter of 1912 to 1913 a restricted electorate chose a new national assembly, as well as new provincial assemblies, in the most open general election in China's history, before or since. The party that was identified with the revolution, the Guomindang (Kuomintang, KMT, or Nationalist Party), won.

The Yuan Presidency. President Yuan Shikai had never been happy with the political looseness of the liberal version of the Republic. He felt that his functions as chief executive were impaired and that the country needed strong leadership and centralized direction. He lashed out at the most formidable obstacle to his hegemony: the KMT. In March 1913 one of his aides arranged the assassination of the youthful Song Jiaoren, architect of the KMT's electoral triumph. He forced into rebellion KMT leaders in central and southern China, including Sun Yatsen. With the help of a large foreign loan, he defeated them decisively on the battlefield in the summer of 1913 (the most prominent managed to escape into exile). In the autumn, he outlawed the party altogether. In these measures, Yuan secured the support of others who were hostile to the KMT and shared Yuan's vision of a powerful central state.

Even his supporters hesitated as Yuan continued his campaign of establishing a bureaucratic system of national controls. He abolished all elected assemblies, subordinated the provinces to his administrative authority, instigated vast, bloody purges of the opposition, rescinded a number of reforms, and, in order to balance the budget, trimmed his military forces. This dictatorship was capped in late 1915 by his effort to revive the throne and make himself monarch. Disaffection was rampant by this time, and some of his erstwhile allies joined with his enemies in an armed revolt, starting in Yunnan Province, in December 1915. Yuan's power crumbled, even as he abandoned his monarchical pretensions. His death from illness in June 1916 saved him from a probable expulsion from Beijing. [*See also* Yuan Shikai.]

Republican institutions, just a few years after their adoption, seemed to have utterly failed. Yuan's dictatorship had forcibly obliterated the early growth of representative government. Neither the short-lived constitutional regime nor Yuan's authoritarian state had stemmed the steady encroachment of foreign power on Chinese sovereignty. President Yuan's submission to Japan's Twenty-one Demands in May 1915 was confirming evidence that the aftermath of the 1911 Revolution had left China even weaker than before. After Yuan's death China's polity, rather than recovering, fell even deeper into the abyss. [*See* Twenty-one Demands.]

Between 1916 and 1927 the country's political structure lacked any coherence, whether federal or centralized. Administrative authority devolved into the hands of military men, whose power rested on their control of troops and their ability to extract revenue from the region they dominated. Beijing retained a nominal role as national capital and was a special object of military rivalry for its prestige and its fiscal resources (some of which were guaranteed by foreign power). But Beijing's authority was soon not much greater than the influence of the particular military forces controlling the capital region. Unstable alliances or factions were formed among the generals, and the period is known as the time of administration by military cliques, often referred to as warlordism. No one general, or warlord, was able to prevail over the rest, despite sporadic warfare among them. The people's welfare and aspirations for national dignity were at stake.

Accompanying the collapse of China's political unity was widespread demoralization. Although some warlords proclaimed themselves reformers and nationalists, politics in practice was marked by blatant power plays, violence, and betrayal. Some of the leading players in the power game seemed vulnerable to foreign manipulation, even purchase. At a local level, social tensions were heightened under the impact of arbitrary financial exactions, the militarization of rural leadership, the growth of banditry, and the flight of the rich to the cities. The old order was in an advanced state of decay, but the new order had not taken root.

Intellectual and Political Radicalization. Out of the despair engendered by the feckless record of the early years of the Republic, startlingly radical currents emerged and set a new agenda for the country.

The New Culture Movement. The first was an intellectual current that sought to wash away the past. It began in 1915 with a journal, soon to be called *New Youth (Xin qingnian),* that for the next few years was the chief voice of an iconoclastic attack on China's tradition, especially its Confucian mainstream. Known as the New Culture Movement, this tendency bitterly assailed Chinese culture for its crippling effect on the development of the Chinese people. Cultural transformation was held to be a prerequisite to political progress. The standards of judgment were explicitly borrowed from the modern West, especially its liberalism and its reputedly scientific approach to problems. Rarely, if ever, have a country's intellectuals so harshly turned against their society's inherited moral system.

The New Culture Movement, as the title of its leading journal suggested, was especially directed at the country's youth, who were told to seek emancipation from the trammels of the old society. The Chinese family was pictured as a prison. Youth, it was urged, should seek its own fulfillment, not defer to age. Women should assert their equality with men. Beyond the family, Chinese should throw off the incubus, not just of the Confucian classics, but even of the classical language that monopolized learned writing. Democracy would be advanced by adoption of the written vernacular *(baihua)* for education and publication generally. These messages, detailed in the writings of Chen Duxiu and Hu Shi, among others, struck a responsive chord among the growing population of high school and university students. [*See also* Chen Duxiu *and* Hu Shi.]

The May Fourth Movement. The second radical current stressed politics rather than culture, and found its leadership not among university professors like Chen Duxiu and Hu Shi but in the students themselves. This current was a revived and intensified nationalism, focused on the injustice of continued foreign occupation of Chinese soil and on the treacherous collaboration of China's warlord governments in such arrangements. The occasion was the decision of the great powers after World War I to accept Japan's claim to Germany's former holdings in the Chinese province of Shandong, instead of their return to Chinese sovereignty. In response, on 4 May 1919 students in Beijing demonstrated against the decision and, more particularly, against the Chinese diplomats and politicians who during the war had secretly agreed to Japan's claims. The movement rapidly escalated as student demonstrators were jailed, and spread to other cities. Some of the New Culture Movement leaders, like Chen Duxiu, were drawn into the fracas on the student side. Other groups, such as merchants and, in Shanghai, industrial workers, joined forces with the students for several turbulent months, until the government conceded the main demands: release of the arrested demonstrators, refusal to sign the treaties embodying the Shandong decision, and dismissal of the most conspicuously pro-Japanese diplomats. [*See also* Versailles Treaty of 1918 *and* Shandong Question.]

This outburst in the spring and summer of 1919 is known as the May Fourth Movement. For many of China's subsequent leaders, it was a crucial experience of politicization and radicalization. Its importance has led to extending the application of the term *May Fourth Movement* to the general intellectual and political effervescence of the surrounding years, including the New Culture Movement.

Although the May Fourth Movement marched at first under the banner of liberalism, the intellectual climate became imbued with Marxism and the ideas of Lenin. The drama of the Russian Revolution made Marxism seem relevant to China's problems. The new Soviet government offered Chinese nationalism friendship and support. Furthermore, the confrontational politics of the May Fourth Movement had turned the attention of some Chinese to the latent possibilities in organizing the masses—workers, perhaps even peasants. Marxism-Leninism was primed to address such issues. Beginning in 1919, the flagship of the New Culture Movement, the journal *New Youth,* was increasingly Marxist. [*See also* May Fourth Movement.]

The Chinese Communist Party. In July 1921 the Chinese Communist Party (CCP) was formally founded in Shanghai by a small group of Chinese intellectuals. Most prominent among the first members were two leaders in the New Culture Movement, Chen Duxiu and Li Dazhao. Both had taken an interest in Marxism-Leninism during the May Fourth Movement and had nurtured study groups on the subject. The party's early emphasis was on organizing China's small industrial working class. [*See also* Li Dazhao.]

The fledgling Chinese Communist Party was not the chief recipient of Soviet assistance. In Lenin's analysis, bourgeois nationalists were the main revolutionary force in countries like China, where backwardness was the result of domination and exploitation by the great powers. Casting Sun Yat-sen in the role of leading bourgeois nationalist, the Soviet Union sent him matériel and advisers, beginning in 1923, so that he might reorganize and strengthen his party (the Guomindang) and free China from its imperialist subjugation. CCP members were required to enter the KMT and to work in its name, although the Communists maintained their own organization. This arrangement between the KMT and the CCP, with Soviet sponsorship, is often referred to as the First United Front.

The First United Front. Although short-lived, the First United Front enjoyed considerable success. Widespread support was found for the main aims of this new political movement: the defeat of warlordism, the reunification of the country, and the end of foreign encroachment on Chinese sovereignty. To achieve these goals, new methods were initiated. In 1924 the KMT, the movement's central organization, was reconstructed on the model of the Russian Bolshevik party, with the assistance of the Comintern representative, Michael Borodin. Military units were formed, ideologically and organizationally integrated with the KMT. Party headquarters and the new KMT army, including the Whampoa Academy for training officers, were located in Canton (Guangzhou) in southeast China, where Sun Yat-sen had recently established a tenuous foothold. Meanwhile, in several parts of China, activists worked at popular mobilization, especially labor unions, peasant leagues, and women's associations. [*See also* Comintern *and* Borodin, Michael.]

In 1925 demonstrations and strikes broke out all over the country in protest against the shooting of Chinese workers and students by foreign police in Shanghai and Canton. Known as the May Thirtieth Incident, the protests were touched off by a labor dispute in a foreign-owned factory in Shanghai and the violent repression by British-officered police of some Chinese demonstrators. The temperature of Chinese nationalism was high, and rising. [*See also* May Thirtieth Incident.]

The KMT, with its Chinese Communist allies and Soviet assistance, launched its major military campaign for national unification in 1926. Called the Northern Expedition, the campaign had as its first objective the elimination of warlord power in central China. Sun Yat-sen had died in March 1925, and KMT leadership was taken up by Chiang Kai-shek, who had played a large part in the formation of the KMT army. This army, the warlord forces that Chiang managed to ally to the KMT effort, the mass organizations that sometimes paved the way and lent support, and the nationalist fervor of the time—all contributed to the rapid elimination of the opposition. The KMT was dominant in southern and central China within a few months. [*See also* Northern Expedition *and* United Front.]

Fall of the First Republic. Success nourished suspicion and rivalry, however. Although the Northern Expedition would press on toward Beijing, it did so only after the First United Front had foundered—the Chinese Communists had been decimated and the Soviet advisers packed off for home. The mass movements of workers, peasants, and women had become socially threatening. The Chinese Communists had often taken the lead in this aspect of United Front work, and Chiang Kai-shek had reason to wonder how long his own position would survive the radicalization of the movement he led. From the beginning of the United Front, there had been opposition within the KMT to the alliance with the Communists, and by early 1927 Chiang was being pressed by conservative businessmen to take his party to the right. On 12 April 1927 Chiang attacked the Communists and their popular organizations in Shanghai. There ensued a concerted suppression of the left across the country, and after initial hesitation most KMT leaders rallied to Chiang. Surviving Communists dispersed or went underground. Chiang proclaimed a new national government the next year, but on the basis of a truncated movement, thus bringing to a close the first republican government in China.

[*See also* Warlords; Communism: Chinese Communist Party; Guomindang; China, Republic of; Sun Yat-sen; *and* Chiang Kai-shek.]

Jean Chesneaux, *The Chinese Labor Movement, 1919–1927* (1968). Hsi-sheng Ch'i, *Warlord Politics in China, 1916–1928* (1975). Tse-tsung Chow, *The May Fourth Movement: Intellectual Revolution in Modern China* (1960). Angus W. McDonald, Jr., *The Urban Origins of Rural Revolution: Elites and Masses in Hunan Province, China, 1919–1927* (1978). Maurice Meisner, *Li Ta-chao and the Origins of Chinese Marxism* (1976). Andrew J. Nathan, *Peking Politics, 1918–1923* (1976). Benjamin I. Schwartz, *Chinese Communism and the Rise of Mao* (1951). James E. Sheridan, *Chinese Warlord: The Career of Feng Yü-hsiang* (1966). C. Martin Wilbur, *Sun Yat-sen: Frustrated Patriot* (1976). Ernest P. Young, *The Presidency of Yuan Shih-k'ai: Liberalism and Dictatorship in Early Republican China* (1977). ERNEST P. YOUNG

CHINA INCIDENT. *See* World War II in China.

CHINA TRADE, the framework of commercial relations in the eighteenth and early nineteenth centuries between China and the maritime nations of the West, principally Britain. It is often referred to as the "old" China trade to distinguish it from the trade that was carried on under the very changed conditions that prevailed after the "opening" of China in 1842. It is sometimes also referred to as the "Canton system."

Although the Portuguese first established contact

with China in 1514, European trade with China did not become significant until the end of the seventeenth century. The Portuguese had pioneered the way from Europe to China by sailing first around Africa (1488), then across the Indian Ocean to India (1498), then beyond the Bay of Bengal to Melaka on the Malay Peninsula (1511), and finally up the South China Sea to Canton (Guangzhou). Four decades later, around 1557, they obtained permission from the local Chinese authorities to establish a settlement below Canton on the tiny peninsula of Macao at the mouth of the Pearl River. Portuguese Macao in time became the Europeans' main base of operations in the old China trade.

Early Contact and the Macao Settlement. For the first century and more, however, there was little direct trade between China and Europe. One reason was that the Europeans themselves were preoccupied with various other parts of Asia. The Portuguese, having ousted Muslim power from the East Indies, were content to capitalize on their newly won monopoly of the spice trade. So too were the Dutch when they, at the beginning of the seventeenth century, seized control of the "Spice Islands" from the Portuguese. The Spaniards were busy in the Philippines; the English, in India.

Another reason for the slow development of trade between China and Europe was the ethnocentric, isolationist attitude of China's rulers. They traditionally regarded foreign trade as unessential and often only grudgingly allowed foreign traders to come to China in the guise of subject peoples bearing tribute. The Portuguese had been permitted to reside at Macao only on the understanding that they would forbid vessels other than their own into port. When ships of other nationalities attempted, as they did sporadically, to approach the Chinese directly, they were usually driven off.

In 1684, however, after the new Qing dynasty consolidated its hold over South China, the Kangxi emperor (r. 1661–1722) issued an edict relaxing an earlier, temporary ban on foreign intercourse and permitting limited trade along the southeast coast. The first foreign ship to take advantage of this liberalized policy, an English vessel appropriately named *China Merchant,* arrived at Xiamen (Amoy) in 1685. Other nationalities soon followed, including the French in 1698, the Austrians in 1715, the Dutch in 1729, and the Americans in 1784, after the war of independence. These other Westerners were no match for the British, however, who quickly came to dominate the China trade. By the end of the century they were sending twice as many vessels as all the other nationalities combined; the Americans were a distant second. The Russians, it might be added, also traded directly with the Chinese, but their approach to China was overland across Siberia, not by sea. Their trade was funneled through the Mongolian border town of Kiakhta.

The maritime Westerners at first called at various ports along the South China coast, from Canton northward to Xiamen, Fuzhou, and Ningbo. Most of the trade, however, soon gravitated to Canton and eventually, as a result of a decision by the Qianlong emperor in 1760, it was restricted to that port alone. From then until the "opening" of China eighty years later, the European trade was, apart from the Russians at Kiakhta, confined to Canton.

The Canton System. The "Canton system," as set up by the Qing rulers and overseen by the superintendent of maritime customs (the "Hoppo"), was extremely restrictive. The foreigners were allowed in Canton only during the winter trading season; they had to spend the rest of the time in Macao. When at Canton they were confined to the Thirteen Factories, a small area along the waterfront that lay outside the southwest corner of the city walls, and were not permitted to venture into the walled city itself. They were also limited, in their commercial transactions, to dealing with a group of ten or so licensed merchants (the "Cohong," from the Chinese *gonghang,* "official companies"); they were not allowed to trade directly with any other Chinese merchants. Nor could the foreign traders have any direct dealings with the Chinese officials; they could make representations only through the Cohong, which, in return for its monopoly of the foreign trade, was held accountable by the officials for the behavior of the Europeans.

The old China trade, in the days of sail, depended upon the seasonal monsoons. The European ships, coming up the South China Sea, would arrive at Macao with the southwesterly winds of the summer monsoon. They then proceeded up the intricate Pearl River delta, pausing first at Humen (or the "Bogue") to pay a variety of fees. They finally anchored at Huangpu (Whampoa), beyond which the river was too shallow to go. Their cargoes were off-loaded into smaller crafts to be transported the last dozen or so miles to the Thirteen Factories. The return voyage, a few months later, made similar use of the winter monsoon. For those who had set out from Europe, the entire round trip took slightly more than a year.

The Westerners purchased from the Chinese a variety of goods, ranging from porcelains ("china") and lacquerware to rhubarb and fans, but the two products they most desired were silk and tea, especially tea. Tea, at this time, was grown only in China. As the vogue of tea drinking spread through the West in the eighteenth century to become the national drink of the English, the demand for Chinese tea soared. The British East India Company, which enjoyed a monopoly of the direct trade between China and England, profited enormously from this commerce in tea, as did the British government, whose tax on tea alone produced as much as one-tenth of its total revenue.

The main difficulty of the old China trade, from the perspective of the Westerners, was their inability to sell products of equivalent value to the Chinese, whose large, continental economy was nearly self-sufficient. The East India Company, with its monopoly of the British trade, exported English woolens, while private merchants ("country traders") in India, under license from the Company, exported raw cotton from Bombay. But such sales to China were not enough to balance the purchases of tea and silk by Britain. The British traders had to make up the difference by shipping silver bullion to the Chinese.

After close to a century of chafing under the restrictiveness of the Canton system, the British in 1793 tried to have the system changed. Lord Macartney was dispatched to China with requests that British ships be permitted to trade at other ports besides Canton and that the tariffs be regularized to eliminate the customary and capricious charges known collectively as "squeeze." He also brought with him some of the early products of the British Industrial Revolution to promote their sale. Macartney failed on both counts. The aged Qianlong emperor was not willing to alter the established framework of the China trade, nor was he impressed by the samples of British manufacture.

Opium and the Demise of the Canton System. After the Macartney mission the Canton system continued as before, but only for a few more years. Two developments in the early nineteenth century soon spelled its end. One was the rapid growth, beginning around the turn of the century, of opium imports from India to China, as more and more Chinese became addicted to the habit of opium smoking. Because opium at this time was not widely grown within China, the British at last had "solved" the problem of what to sell to the Chinese. By the 1830s opium from India was accounting for about two-thirds of the value of all British imports to China. With the Chinese now importing more than they were exporting, the balance of trade had turned and silver, which had been flowing into China, now began to flow out.

The Qing rulers tried to arrest the spread of the addiction and the outflow of silver along with it by prohibiting the importation of opium. But the British country traders were able, with the cooperation of venal local officials, to evade the ban and smuggle the drug into China at numerous points along the

FIGURE 1. *Porcelain Punch Bowl.* Decorated with a scene of European musicians, this eighteenth-century hard-paste porcelain bowl typifies the export china created for the China trade. Height 16.5 cm., diameter 41 cm.

south coast other than Canton. The result was an encroachment upon the city's monopoly of China's foreign trade which, if unchecked, would inevitably undermine the Canton system itself. In the late 1830s, therefore, the Chinese authorities decided to take firmer action against the opium problem.

The other development that hastened the end of the old China trade was the growing popularity in Britain of the doctrine of free trade. As industrialization proceeded so did the quest overseas for raw materials and for markets. That quest, the free traders argued, should be unhindered by any governmental restrictions. The private merchants engaged in the country trade, for example, argued thusly against the East India Company's long-standing legal monopoly of the trade between England and China and succeeded in 1834 in getting the monopoly abolished, thereby opening up the trade to all merchants. The country traders next brought pressure on the British government to renew and intensify its efforts to get the Chinese authorities to abandon the similarly restrictive Canton system.

The immediate result of these two developments in the late 1830s—as Chinese efforts to combat the opium menace collided against British insistence on free trade—was the Opium War of 1839–1842. As a consequence of Britain's victory in the war, the old China trade, conducted within the framework of the Canton system, came to an end. Canton's monopoly of the maritime trade was terminated, as was the Cohong's monopoly among Chinese merchants. Foreigners were now allowed to call at ports other than Canton and to trade freely with all Chinese merchants. The system of "squeeze" was replaced by the treaty tariff.

As the change in the tariff system suggests, however, the Chinese-imposed constraints of the Canton system had been abolished only to be replaced by a new set of Western-imposed restrictions. After 1842, the unequal treaty system became the framework within which the "new" China trade was to be conducted.

[*See also* Canton; Imperialism; Qing Dynasty; *and* Treaty Ports.]

John King Fairbank, *Trade and Diplomacy on the China Coast: The Opening of the Treaty Ports, 1842–1854* (1953). Peter Ward Fay, *The Opium War, 1840–1842* (1975). Holden Furber, *Rival Empires of Trade in the Orient, 1600–1800* (1976). Michael Greenberg, *British Trade and the Opening of China, 1800–42* (1951). Earl H. Pritchard, *Anglo-Chinese Relations during the Seventeenth and Eighteenth Centuries* (1929).

EDWARD J. M. RHOADS

CHINESE COMMUNIST PARTY. *See* Communism: Chinese Communist Party.

CHINESE LANGUAGE. Chinese (or the Han language as it is called in China) is known from written records from as early as the fourteenth century BCE. The earliest examples of Chinese writing are divinatory texts inscribed on bones and shells and inscriptions on bronze vessels. In addition, a large corpus of traditional literature beginning from the Western Zhou dynasty (eleventh century to 722 BCE) has been preserved. The classical form of Old Chinese took shape in the literary monuments of the Eastern Zhou period (770–256 BCE); among these works the *Lunyu, Mengzi,* and other Confucian classics were especially influential. On the basis of the classical language a literary written form of Chinese was created that has been in continuous use down to the present day.

The language of the early classical texts was probably relatively close to the contemporary spoken language, but in the course of succeeding centuries the written language became increasingly distant from contemporary vernacular forms, creating a situation of diglossia in which spoken and written forms of Chinese were sharply distinct. Vernacular elements can be found in texts of a popular nature throughout Chinese history, but it was not until the Tang dynasty (618–907) that texts of a more purely vernacular nature began to appear. By the Song (960–1279) and Yuan (1279–1368) dynasties a full-fledged vernacular literature written in a language easily identified as a form of early Mandarin made its appearance. By the Ming dynasty (1368–1644) there were two parallel forms of Chinese: the literary language based on pre-Han classical models and a vernacular written language based on northern Mandarin dialects. Serious writing, including most refined literature, continued to be written in the literary language while the vernacular was chiefly reserved for works of popular fiction, verse, and drama. It was not until the twentieth century that the traditional literary language was gradually abandoned in favor of a new form of written Chinese based on the vernacular of the national capital, Beijing.

Since Chinese is written in a logographic script, that is, a script in which each graph basically represents a word, the pronunciation of Chinese at different historical stages must be reconstructed on the basis of ancient rhyme dictionaries. By far the most important of these is the *Qieyun,* compiled by Lu

Fayan and completed in 601 CE. Each graph (character) in this dictionary is provided with a *fanqie* spelling consisting of two other characters, the first of which is used to represent the initial consonant and the second of which is used to represent the word's vowels, final consonants (if any), and its tone. For example the word *shŭi* is "spelled" with two characters pronounced *shì* and *gŭi.* One must remember, however, that *fanqie* spellings are based on early medieval pronunciation and that they do not necessarily work when one tries to interpret them in terms of modern Chinese. By comparing these early *fanqie* spellings with later dialect pronunciations, the pronunciation of Middle Chinese, the language of the sixth century, can be reconstructed in some detail. Attempts to reconstruct Old Chinese, the language of the pre-Han period, have been made based on the rhyme patterns of early verse (especially that found in the *Shijing*) and the structure of the so-called *xiesheng* characters, that is, those characters composed of two parts, one of which was used to indicate the pronunciation. Reconstructions of Old Chinese, while useful in the study of the philological problems of Han and pre-Han texts, are a great deal more speculative than Middle Chinese reconstructions and should be employed with some caution.

Middle Chinese was phonologically more complex than any modern dialect. It had thirty-six initial consonants; stops and affricatives occurred in three sets—voiceless unaspirated, voiceless aspirated, and voiced. At the end of the syllable only the consonants *m, n, ng, f, t,* and *k* were possible. The vocalic system of Middle Chinese was quite complex and remains the most controversial area in Middle Chinese reconstruction. The four tonal categories, *ping, shang, qu,* and *ru,* have been known since the Southern Dynasties period; the phonological properties of these Middle Chinese tones have been the subject of numerous studies, but no generally accepted theory has emerged.

A form of Old Mandarin can be reconstructed on the basis of a Yuan-dynasty rhyme book, the *Zhongyuan yinyun* of Zhou Deqing. The language of this book already resembles modern Beijing dialect more than it does the Middle Chinese reconstructed on the basis of the *Qieyun* dictionary.

Modern Chinese exhibits a remarkable degree of dialectal diversity. The term dialect may be a bit misleading to a speaker of English accustomed to only very minor regional linguistic variation. The Chinese dialects in some cases differ from one another as much as English does from German; not only are the dialects of the coastal region south of the Yangtze River totally unintelligible to a speaker of the Beijing dialect, they themselves constitute a network containing scores of mutually unintelligible forms of local speech.

The Chinese dialects are conventionally subdivided into seven groups. The largest of these groups is Mandarin, spoken everywhere north of the Yangtze (with the exception of some minority language regions) and in southwestern China. Mandarin represents a relatively homogeneous group of dialects that are for the most part mutually intelligible. Compared to other dialect groups Mandarin has a rather simple syllable structure, possessing generally four or five tones and retaining only two or three final consonants. A Mandarin dialect, that of Beijing, forms the basis of the national standard language, and its study is mandatory throughout the whole country.

Wu dialects are spoken south of the Yangtze in the provinces of Jiangsu and Zhejiang. These dialects are characterized phonologically by their retention of three distinct sets of stops and affricatives, one of which is voiced. They generally have seven or eight tones but have few diphthongs and final consonants. The most important dialect in the Wu group is that of Shanghai, China's largest city.

Min dialects are spoken south of Wu in Fujian Province as well as in the neighboring northeastern corner of Guangdong. In addition, Min dialects are the speech of the majority of people on both Taiwan and Hainan islands. The Min dialects are internally highly diversified and consequently difficult to characterize in a simple way. They commonly have seven or eight tones and show an apparently irregular development of the Middle Chinese voiced stops. Min vocabulary is very distinctive, utilizing a large number of words unknown in other dialects. Most linguists believe that Min split away from the main stock of Chinese linguistic development sometime before the compilation of the *Qieyun* dictionary and thus contains some elements inherited directly from Old Chinese.

Gan dialects are spoken in most of Jiangxi Province and some adjacent areas. In Gan speech the Middle Chinese voiced stops and affricatives have become voiceless aspirates in all tonal categories, a feature also found in Hakka; this has led some linguists to classify these two groups together. With the exception of this feature, however, they show few other common features that are limited to these two groups alone; in vocabulary, Gan dialects are closer to Wu and Xiang than to Hakka.

Xiang dialects are restricted to an area in central and southern Hunan. In Xiang dialects the Middle Chinese voiced stops have been retained in the more conservative dialects but have become voiceless non-aspirates in a number of more innovative areas. Xiang dialects have from four to six tones and have lost most of the Middle Chinese final consonants except for *n* and *ng*. Changsha is the largest city in the Xiang-speaking region.

Hakka dialects are found in northern Guangdong, southwestern Fujian, and southern Jiangxi. In Hakka, the Middle Chinese voiced stops and affricatives have become voiceless aspirates in all tonal categories. Hakka dialects generally have six or seven tones; the shift of a portion of the old lower rising tone *(yangshang)* to the upper level tone *(yinping)* category is probably the most distinctive feature of Hakka dialects. Lexically, Hakka is similar to Yue in many ways; it also has features linking it with Min, of which the retention of bilabials for the labiodentals of most other dialects is the most striking. Hakka is mainly a rural dialect; the standard form of the dialect is usually considered to be that of Meixian in northern Guangdong Province.

Yue (Cantonese) dialects are spoken in the Pearl River delta of Guangdong as well as in parts of Guanzxi Province. Yue dialects generally have eight or nine tones; the split of the entering tone category into three or four tones based partly on vowel length is a very typical Yue feature. Standard Yue is spoken in the two large cities of Canton (Guangzhou) and Hong Kong.

Although the phonological and lexical differences among the various historical stages and dialectal variants of Chinese are on the whole very great, the basic grammatical and typological structure have remained quite constant. Chinese is the classic example of an isolating language, that is, a language that lacks suffixes and prefixes and in which grammatical relationships are mostly shown by means of word order and independent particles. It is a monosyllabic language in the sense that virtually every syllable represents a meaningful unit; although there are disyllables that must be viewed as unanalyzable units (e.g., *zhīzhū*, "spider," and *púfú*, "to crawl"), such forms constitute only a very small part of the lexicon.

It was formerly assumed that tone was an inherent and very ancient feature of Chinese, and many scholars still adhere to this view. On the basis of ancient Chinese loan words in Vietnamese and other languages on the periphery of China as well as a number of ancient transcriptions of foreign words into Chinese, some scholars now believe that Old Chinese lacked tones and that the Middle Chinese tonal categories were formed as the result of the loss of consonants at the end of the syllable. The fact that both tonal and nontonal languages are found in the related Tibeto-Burman family and certain other nearby language families lends some support to this hypothesis.

It is very likely that in every period of Chinese history there has existed some form of administrative lingua franca based on the dialect of the capital in which the daily business of government was carried out. It was not until the twentieth century, however, that an attempt was made to establish a true national language with a standardized pronunciation and vocabulary that would be learned by people at all levels of society. This national standard, called *guoyu* ("national language") under the Nationalist government and *putonghua* ("common speech") in the People's Republic of China, is based on the dialect of Beijing. It is now an obligatory subject in all Chinese schools and its use is promoted in government and education. In most areas, local dialects maintain considerable vitality alongside the standard language, the dialect holding sway in the home and workplace with *putonghua* reserved for the school, official activities, and contacts with people from other regions.

Beginning in the 1920s the old written language based on the pre-Han classics has gradually come to be replaced by a new written standard called *baihua*. *Baihua* was initially based on the traditional vernacular found in such well-known novels as *Honglou meng (The Dream of the Red Chamber)*. It has increasingly been brought into conformity with the spoken standard so that at the present time the differences between the written and spoken languages are relatively small.

A major problem in popularizing the national standard has been the complicated Chinese script. In the early decades of this century there was strong sentiment in favor of abolishing Chinese characters and replacing them with some form of alphabetic writing. One of the major obstacles to doing this has always been the great degree of dialectal diversity in the country; to be effective in spreading literacy alphabetic writing would have to be introduced in many different dialectal varieties, thus strengthening the position of the local dialects vis-à-vis the standard spoken language. In the end romanization came to be viewed not as a viable alternative to writing in characters but as an auxiliary system of writing to be used for teaching the correct pronunciation of the national standard language.

Since the establishment of the People's Republic of China major attention has been given to script reform. In 1956 a list of 515 simplified characters was promulgated for official use; this list contained many so-called vulgar forms that had been in unofficial use for many centuries alongside a group of newly created forms; common to both types was an attempt to reduce the overall number of strokes required to represent the graph. In 1964 a further list of more than 2,000 was issued, including a number of simplified radicals and components that could be used in a wide range of characters. A further attempt to introduce a new list of simplified forms in 1977 was aborted after a few months. Prospects for further reform in this area are unclear at present.

[*See also* Sino-Tibetan Languages.]

Yuen Ren Chao, *Mandarin Primer* (1948) and *A Grammar of Spoken Chinese* (1968). R. A. D. Forrest, *The Chinese Language* (1984). JERRY NORMAN

CHINESE LITERATURE. An early reference to Chinese literature is found in the early document *Yaodian (Records of Yao)* of the *Shangshu* (the portion of the *Book of History* that predates the Zhou dynasty). Yao, the legendary monarch, appointed Kui to be Master Musician and gave him an epigrammatic statement of the functions of music and poetry. Yao's dictum, "Shi yan zhi" ("poetry expresses aspirations"), set down the first principle of Chinese literature and prescribed the dominance of the lyrical mode in it.

The Lyrical Mode. The earliest anthology of Chinese poetry is the *Shijing (The Book of Songs* or *Classic of Odes)*. The anthology includes folk songs, art songs, and liturgical chants, a total of 305 poems with their original composition dating back to the seventh or eighth century BCE. The philosopher Confucius is the acknowledged compiler and editor of this anthology. It was used as a primer in the canon of classical education. The importance given to the anthology in the Confucian curriculum generated schools of didactic commentaries on the love songs and instituted a long tradition of allegorical political satires. In the preface to the edition circulated during the first century BCE six artistic classificatory rules *(liuyi)* were given: *feng* (folk songs), *ya* (art songs), *song* (liturgical chants), *fu* (narration), *bi* (analogy, simile, metaphor), and *xing* (association, allegory, allusion). The first three classes represent functional parameters that identify the role of a poem; the other three are terms of elementary rhetorical devices interacting in a single poem. The classificatory rules indicate that the sophisticated artistry of the poems in the anthology was appreciated by the early scholars. As an anthology, the *Shijing* also represented the poetic creativity of various regions in the Yellow River area. Although the social condition and dialects of each area colored the theme and content of the poems, a common style unifies the volume: cogency in narration, clarity of imagery wherein complex human events or emotions are evoked, and frequent references to the reality of human existence.

Qu Yuan (340?–278 BCE), the statesman of the southern state of Chu, bequeathed his country an endowment of lyrical expressions of unsurpassed beauty. His anthology, the *Chuci (Songs of the South)*, contains not only the unique lyrical narrative *Li sao (Encountering Sorrow)*, the *apologia* of Qu Yuan, but also the *Jiu ge (Nine Songs)*, a lyrical suite with its origins in the shamanic chants of the folk tradition of the Chu region. In the same anthology is the *Tianwen (Heaven Questioned)*, a long tetrasyllabic poem that ponders the source and meaning of the accepted myths and legends of Qu's time, a poem in a form that suggests a possible influence of the ancient liturgical drum chants. [*See also* Qu Yuan.]

The southern lyrical tradition as found in the works of Qu Yuan and his followers differs from that of the *Shijing* not only in the verse forms but also in the texture of the imagery. The poems abound in names of plants and flora indigenous in the region. Gods and goddesses share the center of the stage with legendary sages and kings in the poet's lament of his fate or his questioning of the way of the universe.

Neither the date nor the authorship of the classic *Daodejing (Scripture of the Way and Its Power)* has been established. Nevertheless the mysticism expressed in the earthy imagery of this philosophical treatise has been a constant source of inspiration for Chinese writers throughout the centuries. The paradoxical metaphors include imagery drawn from the arts and crafts, elementary physics, and engineering, as well as familiar scenes in nature. The quietude and sense of peace evoked by these metaphors has challenged the doctrines of concord and harmony of the Confucian school through the centuries. [*See also* Laozi *and* Daoism.]

The *fu* (rhymed prose), which flourished especially during the first century BCE, demonstrates not only the thin line of demarcation between poetry and prose but also the coexistence of both the lyrical and the narrative modes in a single literary genre. The poet Sima Xiangru (179–117 BCE) inherited the form from Song Yu, a follower of Qu Yuan and the Confucian philosopher Xunzi, who wrote five expository pieces in the *fu* form. In the hands of Sima Xiangru, the parallel verse extended beyond stupendous landscape to debates on hunting and farming. The parallel or antithetic structure became a dominant form of composition in the ensuing years. The *pianwen* (antithetical prose), which evolved from the *fu*, was the main prose style until the *guwen* (ancient style) movement supplanted it.

Perhaps the best representation of the importance of the lyrical tradition is the anthology *Wenxuan (Literary Anthology)*, compiled by Prince Xiao Tong (501–531), the earliest extant anthology of Chinese literature. Other than the better known lyrical forms of *shi, ge, ci,* and *fu,* the anthology also includes selections from thirty-six categories of writing. The major categories in free verse include *songzan* (odes), *zhenming* (didactic epigraphs), *aiji* (elegy and grave-side oration), *beiming* (stela inscription). The anthology affirmed a distinction between literary writing and general writing. The parameter of the taxonomy was basically the presence or absence of a skillful control of the linguistic syntax, rhythm, and the use of reference in writing. The lyrical experience announced in this anthology is not restricted to the form of *shi* or *ci.*

The lyrical tradition, nevertheless, is best known through the works of the major poets of three periods: the *shi* (regulated verse) of the Tang dynasty; the *ci* (song verse) of the Song dynasty; and the *qu* (dramatic arias) of the Yuan. Among the great Tang poets, Li Bai (Li Bo; 701–762), Du Fu (712–770), and Bai Juyi (Bo Juyi; 772–846) experimented with new verse forms and gave the classical expressions, metaphors, and allusions a clarity in linguistic syntax and rhythmic cadence. The vision and sentiment of their poems inspired the poets of subsequent generations. [*See also* Li Bai; Du Fu; *and* Bai Juyi.] Of the masters of the *ci,* Li Yu (937–978), Ouyang Xiu (1007–1072), Su Dongpo (1021–1086), and Li Qingzhao (1084–1151?) created new worlds in the song verses that transcended the realm defined by the tune titles. [*See also* Ouyang Xiu *and* Su Dongpo.] In the *qu* form the poets had a stanzaic structure, which on the one hand was restricted by the demand of the melodies, but on the other hand had to accommodate added syllables, words, and phrases demanded by the function of the aria in the play. In the verses of the leading poets, Guan Hanqing (c. 1241–1320), Ma Zhiyuan (b. 1324?), Bo Pu (1226–1285), and Wang Shifu (b. 1324?), the imageries evoked by the multifarious allusions to the works of earlier poets are illuminated by the unadorned vernacular cohesive ties within the structure of the stanza.

In the history of Chinese literature there is still an unfinished chapter on the oral performing literature of ancient China. Recent articles on archaeology mention several excavations wherein murals and/or pottery figurines suggest a lively storytelling and performing tradition in ancient China. It is evident in these sources that music was an integral part of the form.

The earliest written record of the tradition of performing literature is the *Yuefu shi (Music Bureau Poems)*. The Music Bureau was established in 120 BCE and supervised the production of music and songs for ceremonies at court. Related to this canon, two folk ballads by anonymous authors, the *Mulan shi (Song of Mulan)* and *Kongque dongnan fei (The Peacock Flies Southeast),* written before the fifth or sixth century, provide textual evidence of the early lyrical narrative tradition. The better-known records of oral performances, popular during the golden age of Chinese literature, the Tang dynasty (618–907), are the manuscripts of the *bianwen* (transformation texts), found at one of the Caves of the Thousand Buddhas at Dunhuang in 1899. The subjects of these texts include narration of the miraculous birth of the Buddha, the popularization of the sutras, the life and deeds of kings and warriors, and humorous folktales and fables. The form of these texts is an amalgamation of rhymed verse and prose narrative. Some of the manuscripts also recorded different singing styles that might have been required in the performances.

The preeminent representative of oral performing literature is the previously mentioned *Yuanqu,* the dramatic arias in the theater of the thirteenth century, during the rule of the Mongols in China. This form of lyrical theatre continued in China to the present day in the theatrical forms of Beijing opera and other regional operas. A wealth of texts and textual criticism of *Yuanqu* has yet to undergo scholarly analysis.

The Narrative Mode. The beginning of expository writing in China, according to the sixth-century scholar Yan Zhitui (b. 531), was in the *Yijing (Book of Changes),* a divination text. Many epigrammatic explanations of the divinations narrate the life and manners of the early Chinese people, for example, fishing, hunting, husbandry, agriculture, battles, and rituals. Narration was an important mode of communication for the ancient philosophers. The *Lunyu (Analects)* of Confucius (Kongzi) was based on the notes of his disciples and it recorded the discourse between the master and his disciples. In the writings of the philosophers Mencius (Mengzi) and Zhuangzi, narration in the form of allegory and parable became the dominant vehicle for expressing ideas. [*See also* Confucius *and* Confucianism.]

The early chronicles, on the other hand, are not pure narrative writings. The *Shujing (Book of History)* is a collection of speeches, decrees, and documents of battles and explorations. The *Chunqiu (Spring and Autumn Annals)* is a brief year-by-year record of the events in the state of Lu between 722 and 481 BCE; the *Zuozhuan,* probably compiled in the third century BCE, is a commentary on the *Spring and Autumn Annals.* The events of the annals are transformed into anecdotes with characters playing their roles in the historical power struggles. The *Zuozhuan* introduced a narrative style that combined vivid characterizations in the record of the dialogue, a detached narrator who used the story to clarify a reference, and a storyteller who tolerated episodic arrangements of events within the larger framework of the annals.

The Grand Historian Sima Qian (c. 145–90 BCE) is considered to have written the first history of China in his work *Shiji (Records of the Historian).* In this masterpiece of historical writing, Sima Qian adopted the annal style of the earlier chronicles and broke new ground in the art of recording events of the past. His method allowed him to amend the written texts with material he collected from the oral tradition. He presented the records of ancient China in four different categories: (1) annals of the imperial reign; (2) tables of government organization, and so forth; (3) expositions of cosmology, the calendar, and the social sciences; (4) biographies of noteworthy individuals. It is in the writing of biographies that Sima Qian refined and enriched the art of narration of the earlier period. Although epigrams and anecdotes still abound in these full-length biographies, the unity in the story of the life of an individual provides internal evaluations of the narratives. [*See also* Sima Qian.]

A major narrative work outside the main stream of historical writing is *Shishuo xinyu (New Tales of the World)* by Liu Yiqing (403–444). The work is an anthology of brief sketches of unique persons and once more treads the thin line that separates the world of poetry from that of prose. These epigrammatic anecdotes are frequently imbued with a wistful tone, which gives them lyric unity.

The *guwen* (ancient style) movement in the eighth century produced a style for all types of prose and should be considered a hybrid of the lyrical and narrative modes. Many of the pieces in the tradition of the *Wenxuan* are narrative or expository in their objective, signified by the use of the word *ji* (record) or *lun* (dissertation) in the title, but the effects of the writings are often evocative or divinatory.

Between the seventh and ninth century the short story flourished. The art of recording became independent of the historical chronicles. The biographical form remained as a general structure, as many stories used the word *zhuan* (biography) in their titles, for example *Ying Ying zhuan (The Life of Ying Ying)* by Yuan Chen (779–831) and *Li Wa zhuan (The Life of Li Wa)* by Bo Xingjian (d. 826). Unlike the records of achievements and aspirations of noteworthy and unique people, the trials and tribulations of those heroes and heroines would have been lost to the world had they never been told. Once known and recited the stories continued to influence the writers of the subsequent periods.

Although stories abound in the early records of Chinese literature, the narrative art of storytelling before the tenth century remains undefined. The earliest classification of storytelling appears in the *Dongjing menghua lu,* published in 1147 by Meng Yuanlao (c. 1090–1150). Meng recorded the existence of five storytelling traditions: *jiangshi* (narration of history), *xiaoshuo* (anecdotes), *shuo hunhua* (telling jokes), *shuo sanfen* (narration of the three kingdoms), and *wudai shi* (history of the five dynasties). In the next century additional types of storytelling joined the ranks. In the *Ducheng jisheng* (1235) the four traditions are listed as the *yinzier* (a silver-lettered flute), *shuo tieqier* (narration of iron riders), *shuojing* (narration of the sutras), and *jiang shishu* (narration of history). The name *yinzier,* that of a musical instrument that must have accompanied the telling of the realistic stories of love or fantastic fables and adventure stories, is an indication of the role of music in the art of storytelling. Anthologies of these early stories, by Hong Pian (c. 1541) and by Feng Menglong, did not appear until a much later date.

Cycles of short stories gradually were linked with long novels of adventures and historical episodes. *The Journey to the West (Xiyouji)* by Wu Cheng'en (1500–1582) had its antecedents not only in the storytelling tradition but also in the earlier repertoire of the theater. The other novels, the *Romance of the Three Kingdoms (Sanguo yanyi)* by Luo Guanzhong, published in 1522, and the *Tale of the*

Marshes (Shuihu zhuan, often translated as *The Water Margin)* by Shi Naian, first printed in 1540, also evolved from the polymorphous oral tradition of the preceding centuries. The same episodic structure governs all three, although the worlds created by the three novels are quite different. Fantastic variations of the journey by the Buddhist pilgrim Xuanzang and his disciples from 629 to 644 provided matter for a humorous allegory in *The Journey to the West.* Various figures in history were transformed into unforgettable characters in the *Romance of the Three Kingdoms.* The exploits of the heroes in the *Tale of the Marshes* allowed the narrator to give fine delineation of the countryside where the actions took place.

A later novel, *The Golden Lotus (Jinpingmei),* depicts the corruption in urban life of sixteenth-century China; instead of heroic adventures the book presents webs of domestic intrigues. During the eighteenth century two important novels were published within a few years: *The Scholars (Rulin waishi)* by Wu Jingzi (1701–1754) and *The Dream of the Red Chamber (Honglou meng)* by Cao Zhan, also known as Cao Xueqin (1724–1764). Both novels are invaluable documents of the life and manners of eighteenth-century China. The setting of *The Scholars* is the towns and villages in the Yangtze delta. The locale of *The Dream of the Red Chamber* is the Grand View Garden of the patrician family of Jia Zheng in the imperial capital. *The Dream of the Red Chamber* may be the most studied novel in China. Volumes of articles and full-length monographs have appeared to decipher the textual and biographical information and the allegorical references in the puns, riddles, and events. The main fascination of the novel actually lies in the author's control of discourse. Works on Chinese grammar analyzing the syntax of vernacular Chinese have been based upon the dialogues in the work. More than four hundred characters populate the novel, and each person speaks in a distinctive voice. [*See also* Jinpingmei; Rulin Waishi; *and* Cao Xueqin.]

The last celebrated novel of the nineteenth century, *The Travels of Lao Can (Lao Can Youji)* by Liu E (1857–1908), actually first appeared in 1903 and was not published in full until 1906. The episodic structure persists in this novel. The protagonist Lao Can traveled along the Yellow River region and witnessed suffering humanity in an ailing country. In this novel, the lyrical element, which is never completely absent in Chinese narrative, is structurally integrated in the description of the scenes.

The Epistemic Mode. Although the aim of poetry, and literature in general, has been clearly stated in Yao's "Shi yan zhi," the boundary line between literary expression and philosophical exposition has never been clearly defined. The arcadian philosopher-poet Tan Qian (365–427), in the conclusion of the fifth of a suite of poems (on drinking wine) in which the serenity in nature is communicated through lucid images, wrote, "When I wish to make inquiry of the truth therein, all words fail me." His statement reflects the tenacious undercurrent of a didactic tradition in the epistemic mode of Chinese literature.

Ancient philosophers did not overlook the educational or pedagogical dimension of the use of poetry. Poetry as a creative act or as revelation of the mysteries in nature, however, appeared only in the *Wenfu (Fu* [rhymed prose] *on Literature)* by Lu Ji (261–303). Although he stressed the purity and integrity of the author and the importance of scholarship, Lu affirmed the primacy of the imagination and the observation of nature in the literary act. In the work of Cao Pei (187–226) an attempt to classify and evaluate the literary compositions can be found. The first systematic analysis of early Chinese literature was by Liu Xie (465–520), who, after having worked for Prince Xiao Tong, joined the Buddhist monkhood and produced *Wenxin diaolong (Carving the Dragon in the Literary Mind).* The work begins with an epistemic essay on truth and literature, then touches on such subjects as the nature of a classic, the essence of style, the distinction of forms, and the cultivation of a critical attitude.

The gem of the epistemic mode may be the *Shipin (Appreciation of Poetry)* of Sikong Tu (837–908). It is an elegant work in verse on the art of poetry, organized according to twenty-four ideal standards of poetic effects. These standards represent a fusion of the tradition of expressing aspiration in poetry with the metaphysical worldviews of Buddhism and Daoism. Such ideas as "naturalness," "harmony," "taste," and "vision" form a system of poetics that contributed to an article of faith that poets and critics of the later generations continued to refine. The long tradition of *shihua* (discourse on poetry) may be considered to have developed from those ideals. In the work of Yan Yu (fl. about 1200), *Canglang Shihua (Master Canglang's Discourse on Poetry),* and that of Wang Guowei (1877–1927), *Renjian cihua (Terrestrial Discourse on the Song Verses),* the belief in the validity of the worlds created and revealed by the poets is eloquently expressed.

The introduction of Western ideologies, art forms,

and literary genres since the nineteenth century precipitated the evolution in Chinese literature during the twentieth century. "A Modest Proposal for the Reform of Literature" (1917) by Hu Shi (1891–1962) and "On Literary Revolution" (1917) by Chen Duxiu (1879–1942) sounded the first clarion calls for a literature to lead China into the modern world. [*See also* Hu Shi *and* Chen Duxiu.]

The May Fourth Movement of 1919, a watershed in the history of modern Chinese literature, began as a political protest against the ineffectual foreign policies of the government. The outcome of the movement was more of a cultural change, especially in the areas of literary forms and values, than of politics. In literature, the target of a new generation of writers was to free the imagination from traditional metaphors and literary forms and sentiments, that is, the tyranny of the classical literary tradition, which separated writers from the life of the common man. The new writers advocated a style of *baihua* (plain discourse), based on the colloquial language of the early vernacular novels, for example, *The Tale of the Marshes* and *The Journey to the West.* [*See also* May Fourth Movement.]

The translation of Western writings into Chinese brought into focus the different taxonomy of Western literature. While drama and the novel were genres that had been considered to be on the fringes of Chinese literature, in the West these same literary genres constituted the mainstream. Mao Dun (Shen Yanbing; 1896–1981), one of the charter members of the Wenxue Yanjiuhui (Association for the Study of Literature) at its founding in 1920, gave the journal *Xiaoshuo yuebao (Short Stories Monthly)* a new editorial direction. Translations of works of leading European authors became models of new narrative forms.

Nevertheless, the lyrical mode and traditional literary considerations continued to exercise their influences on the major writers. From *The True Story of Ah Q* and other writings of Lu Xun (1881–1936), to the speech drama of Cao Yu and the novels of Lao She, Ba Jin, Mao Dun, and Ding Ling the tradition of the dictum of Yao, "Shi yan zhi," still reigns. [*See also* Lu Xun; Ba Jin; Mao Dun; *and* Ding Ling.] It is in the writing of poetry that the twentieth-century writers have taken a new epistemic direction. Here the rejection of traditional forms and themes is a determined will to lead the readers to discover the modern age. The experimental spirit that first guided Hu Shi and Guo Moruo (1892–1978) continues to exist today in the new poems of Zheng Min and the classical song verses of Zhao Puchu. Theirs are brave attempts to redefine "shi yan zhi." An important position paper on the function of literature for Chinese writers is the "Talk on Literature and Arts," given by Mao Zedong (1893–1976) at Yan'an in 1942. It may also be read as a chapter in the long didactic tradition in Chinese literature in its emphasis on the social function of the arts.

[*See also* Sanyan; Pu Songling; Guo Moruo; Lu Dingyi; *and* Hundred Flowers Campaign.]

John L. Bishop, ed., *Studies in Chinese Literature* (1965). Wm. Theodore de Bary, Wing-tsit Chan, and Burton Watson, comps., *Sources of Chinese Tradition* (1960). J. R. Hightower, *Topics in Chinese Literature* (2d ed., 1953). James J. Liu, *Chinese Theories of Literature* (2d ed., 1979). Wu-chi Liu, *An Introduction to Chinese Literature* (1970). Burton Watson, *Early Chinese Literature* (1962).

CHUN JO LIU

CHINESE PEOPLE'S LIBERATION ARMY.

Known in Chinese as the Zhongguo Jiefang Jun, the Chinese People's Liberation Army (PLA) officially dates from 1 August 1927, when the Communist Party, following a "left" line of triggering urban uprisings, invaded the Jiangxi provincial capital of Nanchang. The Nanchang Uprising lasted only five days but made a symbolic beginning: it was the Party's first major action undertaken independently of the Moscow-based Comintern, and it involved several future top Communist leaders, including Zhou Enlai. The Hunan Province Party Committee and Mao Zedong rejected similar orders to attack Changsha in September (as part of the so-called Autumn Harvest Uprisings). Mao retreated south to the Jinggang Mountains and there experimented with the organization of Party cells in army units. Mao's approach yielded enough success in the disorganized circumstances of the time to be adopted formally in December 1929 by an army conference meeting at Gutian. The seminal Gutian Resolution elaborated Mao's commitment to political education and to Party control of the army. [*See also* Jinggang Shan.]

As Mao's influence in the Party rose, a fundamental tension developed in the army between conventional military objectives and Mao's favored approach of combining military and political objectives. Frequent successes in battle (which sometimes meant simply avoiding defeat by superior forces) firmly embedded Mao's Party/Army and "people's war" in Chinese revolutionary legend and tradition. Most notable were the repeated defenses of the Jiangxi Soviet between 1930 and 1933 (the Nationalists finally uprooted the Communist base in 1934, prompting the legendary Long March) and guerrilla-style sabotage behind the lines of the occupation forces of Japan (especially after the Hundred Regiments campaign of late 1940 showed the futility of regular warfare against Japanese divisions). [*See also* Long March *and* World War II in China.]

Military professionalism reemerged during the final civil war years against Chiang Kai-shek's Nationalists (1946–1949). Relatively independently commanded PLA field armies operating simultaneously on five fronts engaged Chiang's larger and better-equipped forces with little resort to "people's war" tactics. The ultimate victory of the PLA led to the flight of the Nationalists to Taiwan and the proclamation of the People's Republic on 1 October 1949. Chinese entry into the Korean War a little more than a year later, seemingly intended as a massive preemptive strike at the United Nations Command before it could approach the Chinese border, also contained no element of the former "people's war" tactics. Pure professionalism was greatly advanced when Peng Dehuai replaced Lin Biao as commander of the "Chinese People's Volunteers" in February 1951. [*See also* Peng Dehuai.]

Peng went on to become China's first minister of defense in December 1954, and strove to build the PLA into a professional force along Soviet lines, following the example of Marshal Zhukov. A harsh critic of Mao's 1958 Great Leap Forward, including its emphasis on amateur militia training, Peng was purged in 1959 and replaced by Lin Biao. The new defense minister moved swiftly to revive Party organization and political study in the army in an effort to bolster sagging morale during a time of economic hardship. The principles of Mao's 1929 Gutian speech were reaffirmed. Among Lin's vehicles for ideological inculcation of his troops was the "little red book" of brief quotations of Mao Zedong that advanced the cultish worship of Mao as part of ideological study. By 1964 Lin's achievements were of such magnitude that a nationwide campaign was launched to "Learn from the PLA in Political Education and Ideological Work," and military organization was replicated in civilian bureaucracy.

Although occasionally becoming factional participants in the first phase of the Cultural Revolution (1966–1969), Lin and the major PLA commanders by and large remained aloof and emerged as winners by default, at least until Lin, sensing Mao's increasing opposition to his ambition to be the next Party chairman, attempted in September 1971 to assassinate Chairman Mao. This affair led to an immediate scaling down of military influence among the top leadership. [*See also* Great Proletarian Cultural Revolution *and* Lin Biao.]

With China's new commitment to comprehensive modernization, articulated in early 1975 and strongly reaffirmed by the post-Mao leadership, the highly politicized PLA found national defense in fourth place in the so-called Four Modernizations (behind science, industry, and agriculture). Although it used "human wave" tactics to its advantage against UN divisions in Korea, outmaneuvered India along the Tibetan border in 1962, successfully detonated an indigenous atomic bomb in 1964, and test-fired a land-based liquid-fueled ICBM in 1976, the PLA has not developed far beyond these showcase capabilities. Foreign observers invited to inspect the PLA of the 1970s found as much as thirty years' obsolescence. The PLA was unable to assist its ally Pakistan against India in 1965, unable to intervene effectively on behalf of its Vietnamese ally against the United States, unable to help its Kampuchean allies against Vietnamese forces, and unable to "teach Vietnam a lesson" in 1979. All indications are that the Soviet Union does not consider itself vulnerable to a military threat from China. Even the tiny island of Taiwan feels secure militarily for the near future.

Many improvements are planned, including reducing the unwieldy four-million-member PLA to three million and replacing the doctrine of "people's war" with a doctrine more relevant to the decades ahead. The traditions of a political army run deep in China, however, and the inevitable changes are expected to be gradual.

[*See also* China, People's Republic of; Communism: Chinese Communist Party; Mao Zedong; *and* Zhu De.]

John Gittings, *The Role of the Chinese Army* (1967). Harvey W. Nelsen, *The Chinese Military System: An Organizational Study of the Chinese People's Liberation Army* (2d ed., 1981). William W. Whitson and Chen-hsia Huang, *The Chinese High Command: A History of Communist Military Politics, 1927–71* (1973).

GORDON BENNETT

CHINESE PEOPLE'S POLITICAL CONSULTATIVE CONFERENCE. The Chinese People's Political Consultative Conference (Zhongguo Renmin Zhengzhi Xieshang Weiyuanhui), or CPPCC, headed since 1978 by China's leader, Deng Xiaoping, has risen and fallen in importance since its formation in 1949. At that time its purpose was to formally establish the People's Republic and to legislate a provisional constitution, the "Common Program." The CPPCC held no meetings from 1966 through 1977. Its ups and downs have left the impression that it fills a completely symbolic role—when the ruling Chinese Communist Party (CCP) has sought popular support, it has given well-publicized attention to the CPPCC. The potential support this body offers emanates from noncommunist elites: non-Han nationalities in China, compatriots from Hong Kong and Taiwan, Overseas Chinese holding foreign citizenship in Southeast Asia or North America (many of whom are prosperous local elites in their new country), members of so-called "democratic parties" (China's eight political parties besides the ruling Communist Party: Revolutionary Committee of the Guomindang, China Democratic League, China Democratic National Construction Association, China Association for Promoting Democracy, Chinese Peasants and Workers Party, China Zhigongdang, Jiusan Society, and Taiwan Democratic Self-Government League), and "intellectuals"—China's writers, artists, teachers, scientists, and professionals.

Lyman Van Slyke, *Enemies and Friends: The United Front in Chinese Communist History* (1967).

GORDON BENNETT

CHINESE RITUAL AND SACRIFICE. The Chinese term for ritual is *liyi. Li* denotes the total body of literature treating the theory and essence of ritual ceremonies, while *yi* refers primarily to their actual performance. Knowing the right ritual and performing it properly were considered to be prerequisite for any civilized person in traditional Chinese society. Ritual's significance can be seen from the curriculum of Zhou-dynasty China (eleventh to third century BCE). Ritual was the first of the six subjects required for study (the others being music, archery, charioteering, language, and mathematics). It was hoped that a harmonious social order could best be achieved by having everyone in the society adhere to a commonly accepted code of conduct. Ritual was utilized as an instrument to help fulfill this goal. The government devoted most of its attention to matters of ritual undertakings, while the educated, as the social leaders, established good ceremonial examples for others to emulate. High regard for ritual has been an indispensable element of the Chinese cultural legacy.

Sacrifice. Ritual originally was associated with the performance of religious sacrifices. The Chinese term consists of two characters: *si* (sacrifice to heavenly deities) and *ji* (sacrifice to earthly spirits). Originally a series of rudimentary rites in which oblations of wine and food were presented to the deities for various reasons and at different occasions, they were refined into elaborate ceremonies with strictly prescribed rules and procedures to become a state institution. A special office, known as the Ministry of Rites *(libu),* was established to organize and supervise their performance. Although their characteristic religiosity was never forgotten, they were to become more political and secular. As stated in the *Chunqiu (Spring and Autumn Annals),* a historical chronicle allegedly compiled by Confucius (c. 552–479 BCE), the chief responsibilities of the ruler were to control military affairs and sacrificial ceremonies. They remained royal prerogatives for all rulers of future Chinese dynasties.

The first recorded sacrifice in China can be traced back to inscriptions on oracle bones in the Shang dynasty (sixteenth to eleventh century BCE). Theocratic in nature, the Shang king was not only a supreme political leader but also the highest priest, commanding the religious power of all sacrifices and rituals. The two most frequently held sacrifices were those to ancestors and to Shangdi (High Lord). Ancestral names found on oracle bones, such as Zu Yi (Progenitor Yi), Zong Ding (Progenitor Ding), Di Yi (Emperor Yi), and Bi Jia (Progenitress Jia), provide evidence of the performance of these ceremonies by the royal house of the Shang dynasty.

Intrigued by the structure of the characters of Zu, Bi, and Di, Guo Moruo and other Chinese scholars suggest that these sacrifices might have been originally derived from a fertility cult. The graph of the name *Zu* resembles a pictographic symbol of a phallus, while the graph *Bi* is an ancient form that represents the female sexual organ. Since the Shang had already progressed from hunting and gathering to a food-producing agricultural economy, the worship of Di thus reflected this fundamental transition. The graph *Di* depicts the union between calyx and stem, a vegetative fertility symbol.

Sacrifices to ancestors and Shangdi in the Shang dynasty were integrated by the succeeding Zhou dynasty into the cult of Tian (Heaven). Although it continued the religious tradition of honoring the dynastic ancestors, sacrifice to Heaven came to acquire a nonreligious moral character. Heaven was considered to be the moral force and highest safeguard upholding the sacred but rational order of the whole universe. The secular ruler was its sole representative, who would administer the mundane world on its behalf. Adopted by the Zhou founder to justify his overthrow of the Shang dynasty, the concept of the "mandate of Heaven" *(tianming)* became a ritual legacy indispensable to future rulers in their legitimization of political authority. The sacrifice to Heaven held at a suburb of the royal capital *(jiaosi)* was a most solemn ceremony, in which the covenant between the leaders of the sacred and secular worlds was annually reiterated. Haotian Shangdi (High Lord of August Heaven) and his associate, the ancestor of the ruling dynasty, were the chief objects of worship in this oblational ceremony. By undertaking this suburban sacrifice, the ruler (*tianzi,* "son of Heaven") portrayed himself as both a successor of the royal lineage and the Heaven-mandated leader.

Following the rational order of the universe and reflecting the cosmological concern of Confucianism, the sacrificial ceremonies of imperial China were arranged in a hierarchical manner from the imperial capital to the prefectural, subprefectural, and county seats, finally reaching the level of the village centers, mirroring the pyramidal order of the human world. The government took special care to unify the local ceremonies so that they were in conformity with those performed at the capital. Observance of sacrifices not prescribed by the national registry of ceremonies was illegal, and the violator was subject to imprisonment; a serious offense such as the secret worship of Heaven was punishable by death. A handbook of sacrificial and ceremonial responsibility, compiled by the government, was given to new officials upon their appointment. Failure to follow instructions or deviation from the prescribed rules meant physical punishment or reduction of salary. Through personal participation in sacrificial ceremonies, the ruler, as the harmonizer of the natural and human worlds, had embedded his political legitimacy into the traditional ritual system to the extent that any opposition to him could be interpreted as a rejection of the will of Heaven.

Sacrifices were divided into three categories according to the objects of worship. The first group included the deities of Heaven *(tianshen),* with Heaven as the leader and the stars and constellations as associates. Those of the second group were the earth deities *(dizhi):* the deities of soil, grain, mountains, and rivers. The third group was that of human spirits *(rengui).* Sacrifices were also classified according to the degree of importance and location of their performance. In the capital there were three sacrifices: great sacrifices *(dasi),* superior sacrifices *(zhongsi),* and minor sacrifices *(xiaosi).*

Suburban sacrifice and ancestor worship required the emperor's personal participation. Influenced by the idea of harmony between the *yin* and *yang* elements, he offered oblations to Heaven on a round altar at the southern suburb of the imperial capital in the winter solstice; the earth received sacrifices on a square altar at the northern suburb in the summer solstice. Since the emperor was the head of the main lineage of the royal family, he also had the responsibility to worship the seven preceding generations of ancestors five times a year in the ancestral temple. These five occasions were the national memorial day (approximately the early part of April), midsummer, mid-autumn, the winter solstice, and the end of the year. To pray for rich soil and abundant food, the national leader also offered wine and food to the deities of soil and grain twice a year, in the second month of both spring and autumn.

The superior sacrifices were concerned with the worship of Xiannong (First Farmer), imperial mountains and rivers, founding emperors of preceding dynasties, and Confucius. The continuation of political legitimacy in the traditional dynastic line and the ideological orthodoxy of Confucianism were both reflected in the ceremonies. The minor sacrifices held at the imperial capital were performed by the imperial representatives. They consisted of a cluster of rites and were sometimes referred to as "collective sacrifices" *(qunsi).* Among them were those concerned with Xianyi (First Physician), Xiancan (First Sericulturalist), and the five sacrifices (hearth, portal, door, well, and impluvium). They were all designed to show that the government respected the patron spirit of all professions within the empire and was concerned with the basic livelihood of the people.

The sacrificial ceremonies held in the national capital provided the model for those performed by the officials at the local levels. Chief officials of the prefectural, subprefectural, and county governments offered sacrifices to local city gods, Confucius, local mountains and rivers, and those emperors of past dynasties whose tombs happened to be located within their jurisdiction. Finally, all local officials presented oblations to the local ghosts *(li).* These were the souls of the dead who had no living relatives or of people whose family background was unknown. At the bottom of the sacrificial ladder was the village. Two sacrifices were allowed according to the sacrificial registry. One was the worship of soil and grain and the other was the sacrifice to the village ghosts. Only ancestor worship was permitted to the common people.

Traditional China was steeped in sacrificial rituals. By taking the leading role in performing different kinds of religious sacrifices, the national leader assumed the role of the medium between the natural and mundane worlds. He carried on the tradition of primogeniture by continuing the worship of ancestors, retained the mandate of Heaven by performing suburban sacrifices to Heaven and earth, and portrayed himself as a guardian of Confucian ideology by personally offering oblations to Confucius. Sacrifices served to unite the people in support of the officially sanctioned value system and cemented different groups into a cohesive whole.

The Notion of Li. Sacrificing to natural deities and ancestors at the appropriate time and place with proper deportment and feeling of solemnity was understood as *li.* H. G. Creel has pointed out that the decorum observed in the religious ritual became the standard for conduct in other spheres. As time passed, *li* continued to denote religious observance, but at the same time it came to include the proper conduct in ritual of every sort. It meant the entire body of usages and customs, political and social institutions. In short, *li* constitutes both the concrete institutions and the accepted modes of behavior in a civilized state.

The application of the religious rituals to human affairs was well understood by early Chinese philosophers. The *Book of Rites (Zhouli),* an encyclopedic study of rituals and sacrifices, defines the function of *li* as teaching and instructing the people to understand the principle of propriety. It is hailed as the chief faculty that separates humans from beasts. It also establishes the orderly graded relationship among relatives, elucidates doubts and uncertainties, distinguishes agreement and discord, and reveals truth and fallacy. Confucius (552–479 BCE) was particularly interested in this functional aspect of *li.* He was convinced that it was by inculcating the value of *li* that society was able to shape individual members into socially acceptable human beings. Ritual was understood by him as a preventive device that helped people turn away from evil even before they had a chance of committing it. As he saw it, the force of coercion was crude and tangible, whereas the vast and sacred forces at work in ritual were invisible. Although both were designed to achieve the same purpose of controlling human conduct, ritual was far more efficient than punitive measures such as laws and punishments.

Xunzi (298–238 BCE), a Confucian scholar well known for his violent attack on the superstitious belief in magic, omens, and portents that dominated his age, nevertheless defended strongly the usefulness of ritual. To him, ritual was a restraining force that could be applied to tame the instinctive and bestial desires inherent in men. If unleashed, these desires could totally disrupt social harmony and stability. This regulatory and functional aspect of ritual became an important ingredient in the Confucian tradition. It was treated as such throughout Chinese history after Confucianism was adopted as the state ideology.

Since ritual was considered a social event, not a private personal matter, its performance was strictly regulated by the Ministry of Rites. A national registry listing those rituals that were permitted to be performed and the detailed description of their procedures was compiled as a guidebook. Violation and illegal ritual activities were punishable by jail sentence.

Classification of Rituals. The practice of classifying rituals according to their natures was begun in Zhou times. This precedent was followed by all succeeding dynasties. The categories were auspicious ritual *(qili),* festive ritual *(jiali),* ritual concerning guests *(binli),* military ritual *(junli),* and death, funeral, and mourning ceremonies *(xiongli).* The auspicious ritual included all ceremonies of worship and sacrifice. Arranged hierarchically, the national sacrifices ranged from the cult of Heaven performed by the emperor himself down to the ancestor worship practiced by everyone in the society. Since the objects in the sacrifices were sacred, all participants were required to maintain a vigil, abstain from offensive activities, and purify themselves prior to taking part in the ceremonies. No one was exempted from this requirement. Although social rank or political position might determine one's ritual responsibility, everyone within the nation had to fulfill his social obligation by performing the proper sacrificial ceremony in accordance with whatever position he happened to hold.

Nonreligious ceremonies and standards of daily behavior were organized in the festive ritual. Since the court was the focus of national attention, a majority of this ritual was devoted to official ceremonies such as court attendance, reception of foreign guests, enfeoffment of princes, and imperial weddings. In addition, the category of festive ritual also included sumptuary laws that were applied to everyone in the nation. These seemingly trivial requirements were designed to provide public recognition of one's designated place in the society so that no transgression could take place without being noticed.

Military rituals such as parades and the presentation of war prisoners to the emperor were held to show military strength. They created a feeling of national pride and heightened popular loyalty to the government. The last of the five types of ritual was concerned with the proper procedure for funeral service and observation of mourning, for it was believed that after having lived through a life full of rituals, one should be treated in the same manner after death.

For a Chinese person living in the traditional society, life was full of ritual obligations. From the moment of birth through the initiation into adulthood, receiving education, marriage, having children, assuming public office, and finally at death, one was constantly bound by ritual performances. A civilized life was a ritualized life; ritual was the basic fabric of civilized human society.

[*See also* Confucius; Confucianism; *and* Xunzi.]

Derk Bodde, *Festivals in Classical China: New Year and Other Annual Observances during the Han Dynasty, 206 B.C.–A.D. 220* (1975). Kwang-chih Chang, *The Archaeology of Ancient China* (1964). Herrlee G. Creel, *The Origins of Statecraft in China*, vol. 1, *The Western Chou Empire* (1970). J. J. M. De Groot, *The Religious System of China: Its Ancient Forms, Evolution, History and Present Aspect, Manners, Custom and Social Institutions Connected Therewith*, 6 vols. (1892–1910; reprint, 1964). Wolfram Eberhard, *Studies in Chinese Folklore and Related Essays* (1970). John C. Ferguson, *Chinese Mythology*, in *The Mythology of All Races*, vol. 8 (1928). Fung Yu-lan, *A History of Chinese Philosophy*, 2 vols., translated by Derk Bodde (1952–1953). Hsün-tzu, *The Works of Hsuntze*, translated by Homer H. Dubs (1928; reprint, 1966). James Legge, trans., *Li Chi: Book of Rites*, 2 vols. (1967). Ling Shun-sheng, "Ancestral Tablet and Genital Symbolism in Ancient China," *Bulletin of the Institute of Ethnology* 8 (Autumn 1959): 1–38 (English summary, 39–46). William F. Mayers, comp., *The Chinese Reader's Manual: A Handbook of Biographical, Historical, Mythological, and General Literary Reference* (reprint, 1968). Joseph Needham, *Science and Civilisation in China*, vol. 3, *Mathematics and the Sciences of the Heavens and the Earth* (1959). John Steele, trans., *The I-li or Book of Etiquette and Ceremonial*, 2 vols. (1917; reprint, 1966).

YUN-YI HO

CHINGGIS KHAN. *See* Genghis Khan.

CHIN PENG (b. 1922), Malayan Communist leader. Chin was born in Perak, learned English at a secondary school in Penang, and joined the Malayan Communist Party (MCP) in the late 1930s. During the Japanese occupation he fought with the Malayan People's Anti-Japanese Army and was described by Colonel Spencer Chapman as "Britain's most trusted guerrilla representative." In 1945 Chin was awarded the Order of the British Empire while in London for the Victory Parade. He became secretary general of the MCP in March 1947 and strongly supported a new strategy of armed struggle. When he went into the jungle in June 1948, he became Malaya's most hunted guerrilla leader. He surfaced in December 1955 at the Baling talks, where he failed to have the MCP recognized as a legal political party. Following the 1974 split in the MCP, Chin became secretary general of the "official" MCP-Central Committee faction. He is rumored to be in China.

[*See also* Malayan Communist Party *and* Malayan People's Anti-Japanese Army.]

F. Spencer Chapman, *The Jungle Is Neutral* (1951). Gene Z. Hanrahan, *The Communist Struggle in Malaya* (1954).

STANLEY BEDLINGTON

CHIONITES, the name of a tribe or people north of the Oxus River and in Bactria first mentioned by Ammianus Marcellinus (XVI.9) during the reigns of the emperor Constantius and Shapur II (c. 350). The Chionites are thought to be the first mention of Huns in the Near East, and Ammianus (XVIII.6) says that Grumbates, their king, became an ally of Shapur. The term *hyon* in Middle Persian and *hyaona* in the Avesta (perhaps a later emendation in the text) indicates the wide use of the name. The Sasanid king Bahram Gur (r. 420–438) defeated the Chionites, and by the end of the fifth century the Hephthalites replaced them.

[*See also* Shapur II; Bahram Gur; *and* Huns.]

H. W. Bailey, "Hārahūna," in *Asiatica* (1954), pp. 12–21.

RICHARD N. FRYE

CHISHTI TARIQA, a Sufi order of northern India. Its followers trace their spiritual genealogy back to Hasan al-Basra (d. 728), but the order's name derives from the natal village, near Herat, of another progenitor, Khwajah Abu Ishaq (d. 940). Nevertheless, the Chishti is the most uniquely Indian of the Sufi orders. Muinuddin, who eventually settled at Ajmer and died in 1236, brought it to the subcontinent. Saints of the Chishti order, including Baba Fariduddin Ganj-i Shakar (d. 1265), Nizam ud-Din Auliya (d. 1323), Muhammad Gisudaraz (d. 1422), and Shaikh Salim Sikri (d. 1571) were among the most famous in South and West Asia. Influenced by the teachings on the immanence of God, of the Islamic mystic philosopher Ibn al-Arabi (1165–1240), some Chishtis established close links with Hindu mystics of similar monist tendencies. That openness, however, made Chishtis most effective as Muslim missionaries. The order also accepted the use of music as an aid to mystical experience. When reformers such as Shah Walliullah (d. 1762) and his son Abd al-Aziz (d. 1824) began accepting membership in all major orders, the teachings and practices of the Chishtis came to resemble more closely those of other orders.

[*See also* Sufism; Ajmer; *and* Nizam ud-Din Auliya.]

A. Ahmad, *An Intellectual History of Islam in India* (1969). J. S. Trimingham, *The Sufi Orders in Islam* (1971).

GREGORY C. KOZLOWSKI

CHITOR, a heavily fortified town in Rajasthan, India, situated on the top of a rock outcrop five hundred feet high, up to one-half-mile wide, and three and one-half miles long. Founded during the eighth century CE, the town changed hands several times before becoming the capital of the Guhila Rajput dynasty of Mewar. The Guhilas were holding Chitor in 1303 when it was besieged by the Muslim armies of the Khilji dynasty. The siege ended in the mass immolation of the wives and daughters of the Hindu soldiers defending the town, followed by the death in battle of the soldiers themselves; this was but the first of three such episodes in the history of Chitor. After a short period of Muslim control Chitor was reoccupied by the Sisodiya branch of the Guhila family. In 1535 the sultan of Gujarat besieged Chitor with an enormous army, and once again the town was taken with terrible slaughter. The Sisodiyas were able to recover, but after 1568, when the Mughal emperor Akbar captured Chitor and executed 40,000 of its inhabitants, the town remained virtually deserted until modern times, as the Sisodiyas shifted their capital to Udaipur.

[*See also* Rajput; Rajasthan; *and* Mewar.]

RICHARD DAVIS SARAN

CHITPAVAN BRAHMANS. Chitpavan (or Konkanastha) brahmans are a caste numbering about 300,000, whose members figure among the educated elite of modern Maharashtra. The community emerged from obscure origins and a modest situation in the Konkan during the eighteenth century, when one member of the caste became the *peshwa* (chief minister) of the Marathas. Following the *peshwa*'s fall in 1818, British rule presented fresh opportunities for those with traditions of literacy and government service. Although some Chitpavans continued traditional cultural roles, many others took up Western education and, through capacity and connections, rose to prominence.

British colonial stereotypes portrayed India in terms of caste behavior generalized from individual characteristics of members. Chitpavans were thought a source of political discontent, owing to the examples of the Indian nationalists B. G. Tilak or V. D. Savarkar. However, other well-known Chitpavans included social reformers (M. G. Ranade, D. K. Karve, G. K. Gokhale), educators (G. G. Agarkar), and authors (H. N. Apte). The political prominence of Chitpavans in Congress was eroded after the death of Tilak (1920), and at the same time their social privileges were challenged by the militant Bahujan (anti-brahman) movement. In later years Chitpavans remained strongly represented in the Maharashtra middle class, while leaders contributed to Indian political life, espousing ideologies that cover the entire political spectrum from Marxism to militant Hinduism.

[*See also* Maharashtra.]

G. Johnson, "Chitpavan Brahmans and Politics in Western India in the Late 19th and Early 20th Centuries," in *Elites in South Asia*, edited by E. Leach and S. N. Mukherjee (1970), pp. 95–118. M. L. P. Patterson, "Changing Patterns of Occupation among Chitpavan Brahmans," *Indian Economic and Social History Review* 7 (1970): 375–396. FRANK F. CONLON

CHIT PHUMISAK (1930–1966), Thai intellectual, author, Marxist, and revolutionary. During his undergraduate years at Chulalongkorn University in Bangkok (1950–1953), Chit demonstrated both his brilliance as a historical and literary scholar and an intellectual and political originality that got him denounced as a Marxist and suspended from his studies. He returned to complete his degree a few years later and to publish *The Real Face of Thai Feudalism Today* (1957), a scathing critique of Thai society and government. Jailed (1958–1964) during the Sarit Thanarat regime, Chit continued to write, and on his release he joined the antigovernment insurgency in the northeast, where he was killed by government forces in 1966. In the 1970s his writings became a pervasive and powerful influence in Thai political and intellectual life. [*See also* Thailand *and* Sarit Thanarat.]

C. J. Reynolds and Lysa Hong, "Marxism in Thai Historical Studies," *Journal of Asian Studies* 43.1 (1983): 77–104. E. T. Flood, "The Thai Left Wing in Historical Context," *Bulletin of Concerned Asian Scholars* 7.2 (1975): 55–67.
DAVID K. WYATT

CHITRAL, a federated unit of Pakistan lying in that country's northwest corner. Mountainous and for centuries almost inaccessible, it borders Afghanistan, China, and the Soviet Union, with which it is connected by the Baroghil Pass. The population is largely Muslim, the majority of whom belong to a tribe known as Kho and speak Khowar, an Indo-Aryan language. Although there is some evidence of Chinese control in the first century CE, the ancient history of the region is largely unknown. In the tenth century it appears to have been ruled by Jayapala, the king of Kabul. Between the sixteenth and nineteenth centuries its history is one of internal conflict and constant feuding with local kingdoms. In the nineteenth century Chitral came into increasing conflict with the rulers of Jammu and Kashmir. In 1878 the *mehtar* (king) of Chitral recognized the supremacy of the maharaja of Kashmir. The British increased their influence in the area, finally taking military control in 1895. Chitral proved a useful ally to the British in the Afghan war of 1919. Mehtar Shudja al-Mulk began the modernization of the country and is remembered as the architect of modern Chitral. THEODORE RICCARDI, JR.

CHITRASENA, cousin and successor of Bhavavarman I as ruler of the Khmer kingdom known as Zhenla. During his cousin's reign Chitrasena commanded the army, then became king around 600, taking the regal name Mahendravarman. As ruler, he followed expansionist policies; sites of some of his inscriptions indicate the northward extension of his influence into what is now eastern Thailand, near the Mun River. He had *lingams* (pillar icons indicating Shaivite Hinduism) erected at sites along the Mekong River.

[*See also* Zhenla.]

Lawrence P. Briggs, *The Ancient Khmer Empire* (1951). G. Coedès, *The Indianized States of Southeast Asia*, translated by Susan B. Cowing (1968).
IAN W. MABBETT

CH'OE CH'I-WŎN (b. 857), scholar and official who worked to establish Confucian practices in the Korean state of Silla.

Not of the highest noble rank, Ch'oe Ch'i-wŏn was a member of Silla's second highest social class, the "head-rank six" aristocracy. Men of this status, as in the case of Ch'oe, were often learned scholars or famed monks. From his youth Ch'oe chose scholarship and traveled to Tang China to study. By the time he reached the age of eighteen he had passed the arduous Tang civil service examination and was well accepted within Chinese officialdom. Ch'oe Ch'i-wŏn was impressed by the relative lack of social restrictions in China and the potential for people to advance in society based on individual merit.

Returning to Silla when he was twenty-eight, Ch'oe immediately set out to introduce basic social and political reforms to his homeland. Power struggles among the ruling elite embroiled the Silla kingdom in warfare. Central aristocrats were losing their control to regional lords who built their power through military might. Social antagonisms were strong, as only the elite nobility could hold positions of power. Ch'oe Ch'i-wŏn offered many reform-minded proposals to resolve these tensions. In order to make Confucian ideology an instrument of reform, he seems to have advocated the introduction of a state civil service examination based on the Confucian classics, but his proposals were too radical to be accepted by the noble elite.

Frustrated by the central leadership, Ch'oe Ch'i-wŏn abandoned government service and retreated to rural temples. It was the loss of support from Ch'oe and other intellectuals that hastened the demise of the Silla kingdom. In retirement Ch'oe devoted himself to teaching and reading. A collection of his essays and poems, the *Kyewŏn p'ilgyŏngjip*, is the oldest extant Korean anthology. He is also credited with several other books of poetry and prose. Ch'oe's refined literary style won him acclaim in Tang China; he was also noted for his fine calligraphy.

[*See also* Silla.]

EDWARD J. SHULTZ

CH'OE CH'UNG (984–1068), one of the greatest Confucian scholars and educators in the Korean kingdom of Koryŏ. Ch'oe was a member of the Haeju Ch'oe lineage, a family that produced many of the important scholar-officials of Koryŏ. While still a youth he passed the state examination and became a public official. He served four Koryŏ monarchs and held many of the highest dynastic offices during the era in which Koryŏ institutions matured. Ch'oe also wrote the official dynastic records of several reigns, distinguishing himself as a historian.

Confucianism had played an important ideological role from the time of the founding of the Koryŏ kingdom. Ch'oe Ch'ung's studies marked a more profound use of Confucianism. Like his contemporaries in Song China, he studied Confucian thought, stressing the *Doctrine of the Mean,* which became an important Neo-Confucian text. His scholarship was prodigious, and his name was so closely associated with Confucianism that he was sometimes known as the Confucius of Korea.

Ch'oe also promoted education and founded his own private academy. Offering lectures in nine areas of Confucian study, his school was called the Nine Course Academy. Many of his students passed the state examination and reached the top ranks of Koryŏ officialdom. Many of his disciples followed his path and began similar academies throughout Koryŏ; these became known as the Twelve Assemblies *(sibi to)*. A network developed in which school ties influenced an individual's social and political success.

Among Ch'oe Ch'ung's significant contributions to Koryŏ life were his restructuring of the educational system, allowing greater access to learning. He changed the curriculum, infusing it with an even stronger Confucian content, and he became one of the nation's leading transmitters and promoters of Confucian scholarship. He wrote on many subjects; partly through his efforts, eleventh-century Koryŏ became a more highly literate society, one that produced some of Korea's greatest classics.

[*See also* Koryŏ.]

Edward J. Shultz

CH'OE CH'UNG-HŎN (1149–1219), general of the Korean state of Koryŏ who established a military rule that lasted sixty years.

The son of a general, Ch'oe entered the Koryŏ army through a protective *(ŭm)* appointment. Following the military coup of 1170, Ch'oe distinguished himself by subduing a revolt led by a disgruntled civilian leader. The period after 1170 was chaotic, however, and Ch'oe was an unhappy witness to many of the events that troubled the kingdom. One man in particular, Yi Ŭi-min, a man of slave ancestry, threatened the very life of the dynasty through his domination of the monarch and the kingdom.

In 1196 Ch'oe Ch'ung-hŏn, with support from his brother and several officials, led a successful coup, executed Yi Ŭi-min, and then took power themselves. Mindful of his own military lineage, Ch'oe Ch'ung-hŏn sought to rectify the ills of the reign and establish a more stable military authority. He immediately emphasized the employment of civilian officials and their professed Confucian ideology. Both the literati and their philosophy had been largely ignored since the 1170 military revolt. The Confucian elite possessed administrative skills that would help Ch'oe govern the country. They also were seen as the legitimate rulers of the dynasty and thereby potentially powerful allies to Ch'oe. One of Ch'oe's first acts was to stress the state examination; by supporting this venerated Confucian institution, he won many literati to his side.

There were challenges to the Ch'oe authority. Ch'ung-hŏn forced King Myŏngjong to abdicate in 1197. Fourteen years later he exiled King Hŭijong. He enthroned a total of four kings, turning the Koryŏ monarchs into his personal "puppets." The Buddhist establishment, another threat to Ch'oe power, was checked by forcing corrupt monks out of the capital and breaking the economic wealth of the richest temples. He confronted massive rebellions sparked by the leading temples of the kingdom. Ch'oe also had to subdue peasant and slave revolts, which spread as a result of the unrest engendered by the political confusion of the age.

Ch'oe Ch'ung-hŏn faced his challengers by force, but he also took charge and actively shaped the future. During his life he fashioned a number of new institutions to facilitate his control of the dynasty. As his power ultimately rested on his military might, he strengthened his own military force by building up his private army. He first institutionalized the private guard units called *tobang*. Ch'ung-hŏn's son Ch'oe U later expanded this private force, forming several other units. As the Ch'oe troops expanded, the dynastic army atrophied, assuring Ch'oe mastery of the kingdom. Retainers whose ultimate loyalty was to the Ch'oe leaders served as the backbone to these private military units and Ch'oe political institutions.

In a pattern similar to that of the Kamakura *bakufu* of Japan, Ch'oe Ch'ung-hŏn established a number of political organizations that evolved out of administrative necessity and operated alongside the court, rather than in direct competition with it. The Kyojŏng Togam ("directorate of decree enactment"), serving as the highest Ch'oe council, considered major policy under Ch'oe leadership. The Chŏngbang, a personnel authority, took charge of civil administrative matters and was later joined by a Sŏbang. These two agencies were not fully institutionalized until after Ch'oe's death.

Ch'oe was concerned with scholarship, the arts, and religion. He supported schools and scholars seeking to spread Confucian ideals. A number of Koryŏ's noted men of letters were recipients of his patronage. Ch'oe also fostered Sŏn (Zen) Buddhism, and through his generous donations, the Sŏn sect achieved a foothold in Koryŏ society that has remained to this day. Ch'oe's descendants, U, Hang, and Ŭi, in that order, inherited this structure and continued the Ch'oe regime until its collapse in 1258.

[*See also* Koryŏ.]

EDWARD J. SHULTZ

CH'OE IK-HYŎN (1833–1906), Korean Confucian scholar who led the movement to uphold Confucian orthodoxy and to reject Western ideas. Born in P'och'ŏn, Ch'oe studied under Yi Hang-no (1792–1868) and became a successful candidate in the civil service examination in 1855. He held government posts in the Office of the Inspector-General, the National Confucian Academy, and others.

In 1868 Ch'oe's strict views on Confucian orthodoxy prompted him to criticize the domestic policies, including excessive public works and heavy taxation, of the Taewŏn'gun, who was then wielding power as the father of King Kojong. Again in 1873, he wrote memorials bitterly denouncing the Taewŏn'gun for abolishing the Mandongmyo (the shrine for the last two Ming emperors of China, erected at the request of the eminent scholar Song Si-yŏl), for destroying a large number of private Confucian academies, and for other policies that, he claimed, led government, morality, and nature into disharmony. Although the young king tried to protect him by appointing him to the Royal Secretariat and as second minister of taxation, he was exiled to the island of Cheju. His criticism, however, was instrumental in forcing the Taewŏn'gun to surrender his power in 1873.

In 1876, one year after Ch'oe's release from exile, he led a band of scholars in a rally to protest the signing of the Kanghwa Treaty with Japan on grounds that signing a treaty out of weakness would invite foreign aggression and that any contact with the West and its surrogate, Japan, would undermine the Confucian order and moral fabric, reducing men, he argued, to animal status. He thus became Korea's most outspoken advocate of dogmatic Confucian conservatism. For this criticism, he was again exiled—this time, to the islands of Hŭksan. After his release in 1879, he remained a private scholar maintaining contact with the conservative Confucians throughout the country. Following the Reform of 1894, he was appointed to the Ministry of Public Works, the Council of State, and other high posts, but he rejected them all.

In 1905, upon hearing the news of the Protectorate Treaty with Japan, Ch'oe led a Righteous Army group to resist the Japanese penetration. He was captured by the Japanese in the following year, however, and was taken to Tsushima, where he refused to accept Japanese food or drink and died three months later. When his body was returned to Korea, he received a hero's welcome from the wailing crowd that lined the way to his burial.

[*See also* Taewŏn'gun *and* Kanghwa Treaty.]

Chai-sik Chung, "In Defense of Traditional Order: *Ch'ŏksa Wijŏng*," *Philosophy East and West* 30 (1980). Chong-sik Lee, *Politics of Korean Nationalism* (1963), chap. 5. James B. Palais, *Politics and Policy in Traditional Korea* (1975).

YŎNG-HO CH'OE

CH'OE NAM-SŎN (1890–1957), modern Korean writer, historian, and thinker. Ch'oe was born in Seoul, the second of six children. A child prodigy, he contributed articles to a newspaper at the age of eleven. He went to Japan twice during his youth (1904 and 1905), the first time on a government scholarship.

In 1904 Ch'oe bought a printing press, turned his residence into a publishing house, and began to issue journals and books, including the first literary monthly, *Children* (*Sonyŏn,* 1908–1911), *New Star* (*Saebyŏk,* 1913–1915), *Youth* (*Ch'ŏngnyŏn,* 1914–1918), and *Eastern Brightness* (*Tongmyŏng,* 1922–1923). His purposes were to encourage the correspondence of the spoken and written languages and to enlighten the reader in the new learning. In the first issue of *Children,* Ch'oe published "From the Sea to Children," the first new-style verse in the colloquial language. He also began to publish Korean classics and popular stories in paperback editions. In 1919 he drafted but did not sign the Declaration of Independence, for which he was jailed for two and a half years. In 1928 he became a member of the Japanese governor-general's Korean History Compilation Committee. On 20 September 1929 Ch'oe discovered the monument erected on Maun Pass to commemorate the tour of inspection of King Chinhŭng (r. 534–576). He also taught at a Buddhist college in Seoul (1932) and a university in Manchuria (1938). Because he gave a lecture at Meiji University urging Korean students to volunteer for the Japanese army (December 1943), he was jailed in 1949 but was later granted amnesty. In

November 1955 he was baptized Peter in the Catholic church.

One of Korea's most learned and influential historians and writers, his works include his own poetry, poems in the *sijo* form, and studies on Korean history, religions, and culture. He advocated the new literary movement and revived the *sijo,* the essay, and travel sketches. His editions of such classics as the *Memorabilia of the Three Kingdoms* (1285) by National Preceptor Iryŏn is exemplary. Through an account of his trips to Mount Paektu on the Korean-Manchurian border (1927) and the famous Diamond Mountains on the east coast (1928), he attempted to revive national consciousness. His 1943 lecture may have been the only blemish in his life.

Collected Works of Ch'oe Namsŏn, 15 vols. (1973–1975). Hong Ishik, *Studies in Ch'oe Namsŏn* (1959).

PETER H. LEE

CHOLA DYNASTY, a South Indian Tamil dynasty based in the valley and delta of the Kaveri River. Tamil literature of the first few centuries CE offers many descriptions of the society and kingship in the time of the early Cholas: Karikala is noted as being one of the greatest of the early Chola kings, and a fine warrior. The Chola coastal settlement of Kaveripattinam, or Puhar, appears to have attracted much seaborne trade. Uraiyur, in today's Tiruchchirappalli district, was the earliest Chola capital. Little is known about the Cholas during the dark, unexplored Kalabhra interregnum, but in the seventh century they reappeared as minor chieftains in the Kaveri valley and in the Telugu country.

The dynasty of the imperial Cholas of the line of Vijayalaya commenced by about the mid-ninth century, with Tanjavur (Tanjore) as its first capital. Under Vijayalaya's successors, Aditya I and Parantaka I, the Chola hold over the Kaveri valley and delta was consolidated, the Pallavas were overthrown, and the Kongu country recognized Chola supremacy. In the first quarter of the tenth century Parantaka defeated the armies of the Pandyans and the Sinhalese at Vellur. The Rastrakuta raid into Chola country in the mid-tenth century was a serious setback, but later the Cholas recovered under Rajaraja I (r. 985–1014) and Rajendra I (r. 1012–1044). Chola power expanded southward into

FIGURE 1. *Chola-period Somaskanda-murti.* Tamil Nadu, late eleventh century. Bronze statue depicting Shiva and Parvati, originally with a figure of their son, Skanda. Height 48.3 cm., width (at base) 60.3 cm.

northern Sri Lanka, northward into the kingdom of the Western Chalukyas, and, along the Coromandel plain, to include overlordship over the Eastern Chalukyan province of Vengi. Under Rajendra, the Tamils conducted a maritime raid on ports in the Thai-Malaysian peninsula and Sumatra in 1025. Rajendra claimed that in a northern expedition his armies reached the Ganges River, and he built a new capital there called Gangaikondacholapuram. Kulottunga I (r. 1070–1120) fought against the Western Chalukyas, the Pandyas, Kerala, and Kalinga. Toward the end of his reign, the Hoysalas conquered the Chola province of Gangavadi. However, Kulottunga maintained overseas contacts, in particular with Srivijaya, and perhaps also with the Khmers and China.

Kulottunga II became king around 1135 and is remembered for his interest in the city and temple of Chidambaram. Tamil culture flowered in his reign. The twelfth and thirteenth centuries were marked by such important social changes as the growth in the power of the landowning classes and the inclusion of nonbrahmans in temple ritual. In the same period we note the Pandyan resurgence. In the second half of the twelfth century the Pandyas, Sri Lanka, and the Cholas were involved in a three-cornered struggle. Kulottunga III, who ascended the throne in 1178, fought ably to maintain the Chola territories, defeating the Pandyas, Sri Lankans, and Cheras. He reestablished control over Kongu but by the end of his reign Maravarman Sundara Pandya retaliated with a crippling attack; Pandyan power was clearly in the ascendant. The Pandyan defeat of the Cholas and Hoysalas in 1279 marked the end of Chola rule.

[*Many of the dynasties mentioned in this article are the subject of independent entries. See especially* Pandya Dynasty, Hoysala Dynasty, *and map 2 accompanying* India.]

Noboru Karashima, *South Indian History and Society: Studies from Inscriptions A. D. 850–1800* (1984). K. A. Nilakanta Sastri, *The Colas*, 2 vols. (rev. ed., 1955). Burton Stein, *Peasant State and Society in Medieval South India* (1980). Y. Subbarayalu, *Political Geography of the Chola Country* (1973). MEERA ABRAHAM

CHOLA RAIDS. In 1024–1025 the South Indian Chola king Rajendra I (r. 1012–1044) sent a naval expedition against the ports of the Srivijaya maritime empire. What precipitated the conflict is unknown. Possibly Srivijaya had been restricting South Indian trade with the Southeast Asian archipelago and China, although it seems more likely that Srivijaya's prosperous ports, which are enumerated in a temple inscription at the Chola capital in Tanjavur (Tanjore), were attractive sources of plunder and personal glory for Rajendra, who was trying to outdo the accomplishments of his illustrious father, Rajaraja I (r. 985–1014). There is no evidence of subsequent Chola authority over the Srivijaya realm. Another Chola inscription claims that the Chola monarch Virarajendra (r. 1063–1069) conquered Srivijaya in about 1068 on behalf of a king who had sought his protection. These raids were most important because they destroyed Srivijaya's hegemony in the Straits of Malacca (Melaka) region. Various commercial centers on the mainland and in the Southeast Asian archipelago emerged to fill the vacuum that resulted, and international commerce, which had largely been confined to Srivijaya's ports, was subsequently diffused. By the late eleventh century the Srivijaya center had been shifted from Palembang to Jambi, and ports in northern Sumatra and Java were beginning to emerge as the new centers of the developing Southeast Asian export trade.

[*See also* Srivijaya *and* Chola Dynasty.]

George W. Spencer, *The Politics of Expansion: The Chola Conquest of Sri Lanka and Sri Vijaya* (1983).

KENNETH R. HALL

CH'ŎLLIMA MOVEMENT. In an effort to make rapid progress in economic reconstruction, the Ch'ŏllima movement was launched in North Korea to mobilize the people to maximize production with minimum costs. This campaign, inaugurated by Kim Il Sung (Kim Il-sŏng) at the December Plenum of the Third Central Committee of the Workers' Party of Korea in 1956, lasted for approximately ten years. It was most active during the First Five-Year Economic Plan (1957–1961) and was often cited as the reason for the early fulfillment of the goals of the Five-Year Plan in four years. The Ch'ŏllima movement also influenced the course of the subsequent Seven-Year Plan, but the campaign was not reemphasized when the Seven-Year Plan had to be extended three more years in 1966.

The literal meaning of *ch'ŏllima* is "horse of a thousand *ri*," signifying a horse that can trot a thousand *ri* (Chinese, *li;* roughly one-third of a mile) in a day, or figuratively, a flying horse. North Koreans credit the idea to their supreme leader Kim Il Sung, and the campaign is very similar in concept to the Great Leap Forward in China. The goal of the campaign was twofold: to build an independent and self-reliant economy by making rapid progress in socialist construction, and to create a new communist man in North Korea. The timing of this campaign was highly significant. The Ch'ŏllima movement was launched after Kim Il Sung successfully purged most of his political rivals after the end of the Korean War in 1953, and again in 1956 at the time of the de-Stalinization campaign in the Soviet Union. In December 1955 Kim made his first speech on the *chuch'e* idea, his effort to establish a self-reliant nation that was no longer dependent on the Soviet Union.

There are many unbelievable stories of increased production under this campaign. Kim Il Sung personally appeared in various factories to give "on-the-spot guidance," and the workers at the Kangsŏn Steel Mill were reported to have doubled their annual steel production from 60,000 to 120,000 tons at the urging of their supreme leader. Similarly Kim Ch'aek Steel Mill workers produced 270,000 tons of steel, surpassing the goal of 190,000 tons set by the party. There are many examples of this kind in light of industries, agriculture, and manufacturing.

At the height of the campaign in 1960, North Koreans erected a Ch'ŏllima statue 46 meters high in Mansudae, P'yŏngyang, signaling the coming of a new age in North Korea. The Party and the government began to recognize groups that surpassed their quota by awarding the titles of Ch'ŏllima factory, Ch'ŏllima collective farm, and even Ch'ŏllima school. Individual achievers were called the "riders of Ch'ŏllima."

The most significant development of this campaign was the creation of the Ch'ŏllima Workteam movement, initiated by Chin Ŭng-wŏn of the Kangsŏn Steel Mill in March 1959. Outstanding and industrious workteams were recognized two or three times, receiving the labels Double Ch'ŏllima Workteam or Triple Ch'ŏllima Workteam. Outstanding workers from these teams were singled out and heavily decorated to encourage others to emulate them.

Kim Il Sung said that the three most important tasks of the Ch'ŏllima Workteam are to work well with people, to work carefully with equipment and supplies, and to work on books. What Kim meant by these three tasks was ideological revolution among the people, technological revolution in equipment and supplies, and cultural revolution in learning. These three revolutions constituted the basic core of the Ch'ŏllima Workteam movement. There were only 928 Ch'ŏllima workteam units in 1960, with 21,102 workers involved, but by 1964 the Ch'ŏllima workteam units numbered more than 22,000 and involved more than three million workers.

In addition to the Ch'ŏllima workteam units, there were a number of other developments from the Ch'ŏllima movement, such as Ch'ŏllima workshop units in which every member of the unit became a decorated Ch'ŏllima rider. Such an honor was extremely difficult for any workplace to attain. Similarly, in agriculture there were Ch'ŏllima cooperatives. To encourage workers, a monthly magazine, *Ch'ŏllima,* was begun in 1959, honoring the diligent ones and prodding the uninitiated. The significance of the Ch'ŏllima movement was in the mobilization of the workers to bring about rapid progress in socialist construction and in the political training of the work force to forge a new and self-reliant socialist state in North Korea.

[*See also* Kim Il Sung *and* Korea, Democratic People's Republic of.]

Kim Il Sung, "Let Us Develop the Ch'ŏllima Workteam Movement in Depth, a Great Impetus to Socialist Construction," in *Selected Works,* vol. 5 (1972), pp. 44–73.

DAE SOOK SUH

CHO LON (Vietnamese, "big market"; Chinese, *ti'an,* "dike" or "levee") is the predominantly Chinese section of the municipality of Saigon (now Ho Chi Minh City). In the late seventeenth century, the Vietnamese sent large numbers of Chinese refugees to establish colonies in the Mekong Delta. As Tay Son forces approached in 1778, the two main Chinese villages of Thanh Ha and Minh Huong combined to form one city, called Ti'an. In 1782 the city was captured and thousands of Chinese were massacred. After the defeat of the Tay Son, Ti'an was named Cho Lon by the Nguyen. Since that time Cho Lon has been closely attached to Saigon, playing a key role in the city's economic and commercial affairs.

[*See also* Ho Chi Minh City *and* Tay Son Rebellion.]

BRUCE M. LOCKHART

CHO MAN-SIK (b. 1883), Korean nationalist leader, Christian layman, and founder (in 1945) of the Korean Democratic Party. Cho was born in P'yŏngyang (now capital of North Korea) and spent most of his life there. He disappeared while under Soviet detention in January 1946; his fate is unknown.

As a child of the gentry, Cho studied the Confucian classics, but then went into business. In 1904, during the Russo-Japanese War, he became a Christian; he then attended Sungsil Middle School (a leading Christian institution) and studied law at Meiji University in Japan, graduating in 1913, three years after Japan's annexation of Korea.

Returning to Korea, Cho became principal of the Osan Middle School in Chŏngju (another major Christian center). He resigned in 1919, the year of the March First Uprising for Korean independence, and was imprisoned by the Japanese for almost a year because of his nationalist activity. [*See also* March First Independence Movement.] Thereafter, he became a leading figure in the influential P'yŏngyang Christian community, as head of the YMCA (1923–1932); as principal of Sungin Middle School until forced by the Japanese to resign, then as chairman of its board; and as elder of the Sanjonghyon Church for more than twenty years (from 1925).

In addition to setting up several nationalist organizations himself (which the Japanese ordered him to disband in 1937), Cho was active in the Sin'ganhoe—an attempt at union among Korean nationalist groups—from its establishment in 1927, and resisted the left-wing pressure that dissolved it in 1931. After the "Tongjihoe Incident" Cho was included in widespread arrests of Korean nationalists. In 1944 he retired to farming.

Two days after the Japanese defeat in 1945, Cho returned to P'yŏngyang and headed a local preparatory committee for Korean independence, which became the nucleus—in coalition with the Communists—for the South P'yŏngan People's Political Committee, the provincial governing body under Soviet occupation, of which he was named chairman. At the same time, independent of the Communists, he set about organizing the Korean Democratic Party, which in only a few months had fifty thousand members.

Cho opposed the trusteeship plan announced at the Moscow foreign ministers' meeting in December 1945 and broke relations with Kim Il Sung's Communist Party. In consequence, Cho was put under house arrest by the Soviet Army. An unverified report stated that Cho was killed at a North Korean officer's order later in 1946. In November 1948 Cho's family fled to South Korea, where his fellow party members had moved the Korean Democratic Party headquarters. In June 1950 the North Koreans proposed an exchange of Cho for two men imprisoned by the South Korean government as part of the "peace offensive" preceding the Korean War.

DONALD S. MACDONALD

CHOMOLUNGMA. *See* Everest.

CHŎNDOGYO. *See* Tonghak.

CHŎNG MONG-JU (1337–1392), Confucian scholar and a leading official at the end of the Koryŏ kingdom of Korea. A man of virtue and talent, Chŏng Mong-ju was an accomplished student of Confucian thought. He passed the civil service examination, which led to a career of government service; because of his erudition he advanced rapidly. A witness to many of the ills of late Koryŏ society, he joined other reformers seeking to revitalize the dynasty. He became an early ally of Yi Sŏng-gye, the future founder of the Chosŏn Yi dynasty (1392–1910), and with Yi and others he sought to chart a realistic government policy in the 1380s.

A traveler to both Japan and China, Chŏng Mong-ju also served as a diplomat. He sailed to Japan to win the release of Koreans who had been captured by pirates and to end the piracy. Chŏng was even more active in trying to normalize relations with Ming China. He made seven journeys to China, met with the Ming emperor on several occasions, and was able to establish amicable ties.

When several powerful leaders attempted to change Koryŏ's foreign policy and attack the Ming, Chŏng joined Yi Sŏng-gye in resistance. From 1388 to 1392 Chŏng, Yi, and other reformers restructured the Koryŏ institutional order, focusing especially on the land system. Chŏng was a man of principle, however, very much influenced by the Confucian ideal of loyalty, and when Yi Sŏng-gye talked of deposing the last Koryŏ monarch, Chŏng refused to accept his plan. Realizing that Chŏng's prestige was significant enough to block a peaceful transfer of power from Koryŏ to Chosŏn, Yi Sŏng-gye's fifth son (the future King T'aejong) planned Chŏng's assassination. Chŏng was murdered in the Koryŏ capital of Kaesŏng; several months later Yi Sŏng-gye founded his new dynasty.

Because of his refusal to accept a new dynasty, Chŏng Mong-ju was labeled a traitor in early Chosŏn. Many of his writings were destroyed as the new government tried to obliterate his memory. A compilation of his prose and poetry, *P'oŭn-jip*, is all that remains of his writings. Despite early Chosŏn efforts, Chŏng Mong-ju was not forgotten. He emerged a hero among Confucian-conscious Chosŏn literati and was canonized in the national Confucian shrine in the sixteenth century.

Chŏng Mong-ju's legacy is immense. Not only did he serve the Koryŏ government in many capacities in its last years, he also fostered the advancement of Neo-Confucian learning in Korea. He helped apply Confucian practices more directly to daily life both by revitalizing the mourning system and by facilitating the creation of new schools. It was his resolute loyalty to Koryŏ, however, that captured the imagination of Confucian scholars and earned him their unending praise.

[*See also* Koryŏ *and* Yi Sŏng-gye.]

Edward W. Wagner, *The Literati Purges: Political Conflict in Early Yi Korea* (1974). Edward J. Shultz

CHONGQING, China's fifth-largest industrial center, is the most important city in Sichuan Province, and in west China more generally, much overshadowing the provincial capital, Chengdu. Chongqing, a "municipality" equal in status to a province, had a 1985 population of about 14 million, surpassing even that of Shanghai, 1,500 miles downstream.

Located at the confluence of the Jialing and the Yangtze rivers, Chongqing has a very ancient history. Its premodern importance as a transshipment point to and from central China was limited by the difficulty of navigating the awesome and dangerous gorges between Wanxian and Yichang. Chongqing became a treaty port in 1895 after the Sino-Japanese War, but only with effective steam navigation of the gorges after about 1910 did the city's modern history begin.

From early times until the twentieth century, the fertile, mountain-girded Sichuan basin has been an ideal haven for political refugees from the east. Chongqing served as Chiang Kai-shek's wartime capital from 1938 to 1945. Since 1949, the city has undergone rapid growth, with industry increasingly displacing commerce as Chongqing's main economic base. Lyman P. Van Slyke

CHŎNG TO-JŎN (1337?–1398), Korean scholar-official who played a key role in founding the Yi (Chosŏn) dynasty in 1392. After passing the civil service examination in 1362 he entered public life. An early follower of Zhu Xi Neo-Confucianism, Chŏng was frequently assigned duties with the National Confucian Academy, where he endeavored to have the Neo-Confucian teachings accepted by the young scholars. In 1375 he was dismissed from office when he vehemently opposed the policy of Koryŏ court, which favored the Mongol Yuan over the Ming in China.

In 1383 Chŏng visited General Yi Sŏng-gye at his military headquarters in the northeastern border and became his adviser. Thereafter, the two developed a special bond of friendship and cooperation. In 1384 Chŏng visited the Ming court at Nanjing as the secretary of the Korean embassy to China. After his return, he was appointed governor of Namyang and later director of the National Confucian Academy. In 1388, following the successful coup staged by Yi Sŏng-gye, Chŏng became Yi's closest adviser and played a key role in carrying out the drastic land reform that became the basis of the Yi-dynasty land system. In 1392 he helped Yi Sŏng-gye to overthrow the Koryŏ dynasty and inaugurate the new dynasty of Chosŏn, for which he was rewarded with the title "Dynastic Foundation Merit Subject."

Chŏng wrote a number of books that laid the institutional foundations of the new dynasty, including the *National Code* and the *Mirror for Managing the State,* which became the bases of the official Yi-dynasty statutes. His political goal was to make the Chosŏn dynasty a Neo-Confucian state, and he once boasted that it was he who used Yi Sŏng-gye to realize his (Chŏng's) political ideal. Later, he was closely involved in the feuds over the succession to the throne among Yi Sŏng-gye's sons and in 1398 he was executed by Prince Pang'wŏn, who two years later became the third Chosŏn king, T'aejong (r. 1400–1418).

[*See also* Yi Sŏng-gye *and* Neo-Confucianism in Korea.]

Han Yong-u, "Chŏng To-jŏn: His Political Reform Thought," *Korea Journal* 14.7 (1974): 46–51 and 14.8 (1974): 56–61. Yŏng-ho Ch'oe

CHŎNG YAG-YONG (Chŏng Tasan; 1762–1836), Confucian scholar recognized as the foremost representative of Korea's *sirhak* ("practical learning") movement. After twelve years as a government official, Chŏng was exiled in the persecution of 1801 for his connection with Korea's nascent Catholic community. During the next thirty-five years he devoted himself to study and writing, producing a body of works amounting to more than eighteen thousand pages. His works treating such practical matters as administrative and economic reform are especially valued by contemporary Koreans, who see him as the outstanding precursor of the modern era.

About half of Chŏng's writings are essays on the Confucian classics. Of particular interest, his early contact with the writings of the Jesuit Matteo Ricci had made him a theist, although not a Catholic. Instead he returned to the theism of the earliest Confucian classics and reviewed the entire heritage of Confucian scholarship in that light. With a surprisingly mature grasp of the philosophical implications of a theistic perspective he systematically established a Confucian theism. The potential of this unique achievement was not realized, however, for Korea was then on the eve of the tumultuous crisis and change that brought it into the modern world.

[*See also* Sirhak.]

Gregory Henderson, "Chŏng Tasan: A Study in Korea's Intellectual History," *Journal of Asian Studies* 16.3 (1957): 377–386. Michael C. Kalton, "Chŏng Tasan's Philosophy of Man: A Radical Critique of the Neo-Confucian World View," *Journal of Korean Studies* 3 (1981): 3–38. Ko Pyoung-ik, "Chong Yag-yong's View of Progress, as Expressed in his *Kiyeron*," *Bulletin of the Korean Research Center* 23 (1965): 29–36.

MICHAEL C. KALTON

CHŌNIN, Japanese urban merchants and artisans, particularly of the Tokugawa period (1600–1868). Literally, *chōnin* indicated the residents of the *chō* (also read *machi*), the administrative units into which the commoner districts of Japanese cities were typically divided.

In Kyoto of the Muromachi period (1338–1573), in which the prototypical *chōnin* emerged, the *chō* was typically an area encompassing both sides of a block-long street and was a source more of community identity than of administrative control. The term *chōnin* in sixteenth-century Kyoto accordingly was not limited to merchants and artisans, but also included aristocrats and samurai who resided in the *chō*. With the legal and residential separation of samurai and nonsamurai that was enforced under the new Tokugawa regime after 1603, however, *chōnin* came to refer exclusively to urban commoners, since the samurai (and, in Kyoto, aristocratic) communities were segregated into special districts within the cities.

In the broad sense of all residents of the *chō*, the *chōnin* of the Tokugawa period encompassed a wide socioeconomic spectrum, from wealthy merchant-financiers and privileged artisans at the top to street peddlers and day laborers at the bottom. In this sense, the majority of *chōnin* were poor and illiterate, living in cheap rental housing and surviving from hand to mouth.

A more narrow and legalistic definition of *chōnin*, however, referred in Tokugawa usage solely to the urban elite, the landowners who alone had the right to participate in the governance of the *chō*. The size of the group varied from widely from city to city, but tended to account for between one-fourth and one-half of all urban commoner households. Despite constant sumptuary edicts and official disparagement of commercial activity as immoral, the *chōnin* of the Tokugawa period grew in prosperity and prestige, largely at the expense of the samurai, and came to dominate much of urban cultural life.

It is primarily with reference to the elite segment of the *chōnin* estate that modern historians speak of a distinctive "*chōnin* culture," referring to the sophisticated and often ostentatious urban culture of the three great cities of Kyoto, Osaka, and Edo (modern Tokyo). This culture, which revolved around the puppet *(bunraku)* and *kabuki* theaters and the licensed pleasure quarters, was patronized primarily by literate and well-to-do *chōnin*, although samurai participation was not uncommon.

In the first half of the Tokugawa era, culminating in the Genroku period (1688–1704), the creative center of *chōnin* culture lay in west Japan, in the ancient imperial capital of Kyoto and the new merchant city of Osaka. Ihara Saikaku (1642–1693), a writer of popular fiction, and Chikamatsu Monzaemon (1653–1724), a playwright for the puppet theater, were central figures in this phase. In the course of the eighteenth century, the center of gravity of *chōnin* culture shifted to Edo, where it was exhibited mainly in *kabuki* theater, woodblock prints *(ukiyo-e)*, and popular fiction.

[*See also* Kabuki; Bunraku; Ukiyo-e; Genroku Culture; Ihara Saikaku; *and* Chikamatsu Monzaemon.]

Charles J. Dunn, *Everyday Life in Traditional Japan* (1969). Charles D. Sheldon, *The Rise of the Merchant Class in Tokugawa Japan, 1600–1868* (1958).

HENRY D. SMITH II

CHŎN TU-HWAN. *See* Chun Doo Hwan.

CHŌSHŪ, a feudal domain of Tokugawa-era Japan. Chōshū consisted of two provinces, Suō and Nagato, and had an official yield of 369,000 *koku* (a measure of rice equal to a little over five bushels).

Yamaguchi and Hagi served alternately as its capitals. The domain was founded during the Ashikaga era by the Ōuchi family but was taken over by Mōri Motonari in 1555. The loss of other Mōri holdings after the Battle of Sekigahara in 1600 left Chōshū with an unusually large number of samurai relative to its productive land. Although more rigorous land surveys and increases in productivity brought the actual yield of the *han* (domain) to more than 700,000 *koku,* this small domain of 600,000 persons was still hard-pressed to provide for its 11,000 families of samurai. The government therefore encouraged silk production, salt farming, and craft manufactures among peasants and then taxed these activities to increase revenue.

To cope with growing indebtedness Chōshū created an agency of debt management, the *buikikyoku,* whose strategy was to maximize fiscal leverage by saving and borrowing simultaneously. *Han* reforms in the Hōreki (1751–1764) and Tempō (1830–1844) periods helped curb spending. Chōshū was known for the high educational standards maintained at its academy, the Meirinkan. It was known as well for its flexible system of clique politics. Chōshū reformers such as Sufu Masanosuke, Kido Kōin, Yoshida Shōin, Itō Hirobumi, and Yamagata Aritomo were prominent in the political movements of the 1860s that led to the Meiji Restoration. Kido, Itō, and others assumed high posts in the Meiji government after 1868. They persuaded the daimyo Mōri Takachika to take the lead in returning domanial land registers to the emperor in 1869. Chōshū became Yamaguchi Prefecture in 1871.

[*See also* Mōri; Itō Hirobumi; Yamagata Aritomo; *and* Yoshida Shōin.]

Thomas M. Huber

CHOSŎN DYNASTY. *See* Yi Dynasty.

CHOU TUN-I. *See* Zhou Dunyi.

CHOWDHURY, ABU SAYEED (1921–1987), president of Bangladesh (January 1972–December 1973). Before becoming president, Chowdhury served as a justice of the East Pakistan High Court and vice chancellor of Dhaka University. In March 1971 he was attending a meeting of the United Nations Commission on Human Rights in Geneva when the Bangladesh civil war began; thereupon he began to serve as an unofficial roving ambassador of the Bangladesh government-in-exile. He served briefly as the foreign minister of Bangladesh in 1975.

[*See also* Bangladesh.]

Craig Baxter

CHRISTIAN GENERAL. *See* Feng Yuxiang.

CHRISTIANITY

AN OVERVIEW

Christianity began in Asia, but of all the great continents, Asia today is statistically the least Christian. In a world where one in every three people professes to be Christian, Asia's population of 2.75 billion (excluding the USSR) is only 5 percent Christian. Comparable estimates for other Asian religious groups are 23 percent Hindu, 18 percent Muslim, and 10 percent Buddhist; 20 percent claim to be nonreligious, principally in China. To understand the reasons for the numerical weakness of Christianity on its home continent one must turn first to history.

The Christian faith spread eastward across Asia as quickly as it moved west into Europe, but with one significant difference: in the West it converted and transformed the culture of a whole continent. In non-Roman Asia, not once in its first sixteen centuries did Christianity manage to achieve majority influence in any enduring national power center.

A history of Asian Christianity may be characterized in terms of alternating periods of expansion and decline: (1) early advance (50–650); (2) recession: the rise of Islam and the fall of the Tang dynasty in China (650–1000); (3) revival under the Mongols (1000–1370); (4) years of devastation (1370–1500); (5) the Catholic centuries (1500–1700); (6) controversy and decline (1700–1792); (7) Protestant beginnings and the rise of the Asian churches (1792–).

In its period of earliest expansion Asian Christianity was impressively successful in geographical extension, but less so in penetration of major cultures. Before the end of the first century, Thomas, "the apostle to Asia," had reached India, according to an ancient and fairly reliable tradition. [*See* Thomas.] About the same time the new faith broke across the Roman border into eastern Syria and Persian Mesopotamia. By the end of the second century the border principality of Edessa (Osrhoene) was largely Christian, and one of its kings, Abgar IX (r. 179–214), may well have been the world's first ruler of a Christian state. Around the year 300 Armenia officially adopted the Christian faith but ecclesiastically became more Western than Asian.

The church in Persia, however, was strong enough by the early fifth century to organize itself into a national church independent of the Western patriarchs. It called itself the Church of the East but is better known by its later name, the Nestorian church. In the remarkable missionary advance across Asia that followed, Nestorians carried the faith from the Red Sea to the heart of China. Three Arab Christian kingdoms emerged and some of the tribes of Central Asia began to convert to the Christian faith. Persian missionaries reached Chang'an, the Tang capital of China, as early as 635. But it was only in the fringe kingdoms at the edges of imperial power that decisive numbers became Christian. The key cultural and political centers, Persia, China, and India, were often hostile, at best tolerant. The first six centuries were thus years of steady but limited success.

By contrast, the next 350 years brought sharp setbacks. The first blow to the church was the rise of Islam. When the Arabs destroyed Persia and rolled Byzantine Rome back into Europe they quenched the flickering hope that the Nestorians might do for Asia what Catholic and Orthodox Christianity was accomplishing in the West: the conversion of a continent. Islam did not destroy Christianity, however, it simply encapsulated it, adapting from the defeated Persians a form of religious minority control called the *millet* (or *dhimmi*) system. Christians were offered no heroic choice of death or apostasy, only the eroding humiliations of isolation, second-class citizenship, double taxation, and harsh social discrimination. The best that can be said of the ghettos thus created is that they allowed the Nestorians to survive for centuries and to serve as conduits of Greek learning through the Arabs to Europe.

Beyond the limits of Arab conquest Christian growth was less restricted. The Nestorians were able to maintain intermittent contact with the Thomas Christians of South India, and the Persian mission to China flourished for two more centuries. Then suddenly it disappeared. The fall of the Tang dynasty in 907 was probably the major cause. The church had become too dependent upon imperial favor. But it had already been weakened by a spate of antireligious persecutions in the mid-ninth century, and more fundamentally by its failure to take root among the Chinese. In fact, Nestorianism in China seems to have remained a religion for Persian priests and tribal groups.

By the year 1000 Christianity appeared to be a receding wave in Asia. It persisted only in isolated pockets in the Arab caliphates, South India, and Central Asia. At this low point a Christian resurgence appeared in the wild heartlands of Asia among the Mongol and Turkic nomads. A chieftain of the Kereits was converted by Nestorian missionaries and was baptized with many of his people. When the Kereits were later drawn into the emerging Mongol confederation they became the unexpected avenue of Christian penetration into a new Asiatic center of power. Genghis Khan married his fourth son, Tolui, to a Nestorian Kereit princess. She became the mother of three sons, all of whom eventually ruled major divisions of the Mongol empire: Mongke, the third Great Khan (1251–1259); Hulegu, the *ilkhan* of Islamic Persia (1261–1265); and Kublai, most famous of all, who became Grand Khan (1260) and emperor of China (1280–1294). [*See* Hulegu *and* Kublai Khan.] None of the brothers became Christian, but their reigns marked the high point of the Nestorian church in Asia, and for a fleeting moment a Mongol monk, the Nestorian patriarch in Baghdad, Yaballaha III (1281–1317), ruled at least nominally a wider spiritual domain than did the pope in Rome. In 1287 Arghun, *ilkhan* of Persia, confirmed the prestige of the Nestorians by sending another Mongol monk as his ambassador to seek alliance with the Christian princes of Europe against the Muslims. [*See* Ilkhanid Dynasty.]

Once again, however, the Christian quest for political security in Asia proved illusory. The West, disillusioned with crusades, hesitated to be drawn into another. Arghun's son, the *ilkhan* Ghazan (1295–1304), repudiated his compatriot the patriarch and embraced Islam. Worse yet, before the century was out, Timur's (Tamerlane's) wars of annihilation (1363–1405) displaced the more tolerant Mongols with a Muslim Turkic fanaticism that devastated Central and Inner Asia as far south as Delhi. Few Christians were left alive and Nestorianism never recovered from the breakup of Mongol power. [*See also* Timur.]

It was also in the Mongol period that Roman Catholicism first reached Asia. Between 1245 and 1346 ten Catholic missions were sent to the Mongol khans. The most successful was that of the Franciscan Giovanni da Montecorvino, who reached Beijing in 1294, built two churches there, and was made archbishop with the authority of a patriarch. [*See* Giovanni da Montecorvino.] Like the Nestorians, however, China's first Catholics vanished with the collapse of the Mongols in 1368.

A third period of Christian advance in Asia opened with the dawn of the age of discovery. Da Gama's Portuguese fleet, anchoring off the coast of India in 1498, brought a host of Catholic missioners in its train. Goa became the center for ecclesiastical expansion, and the arrival of the first Jesuit, Francis Xavier, touched off ten of the most intensive years of Catholic missionary expansion in Asian history. Between 1542 and his death in 1552 Xavier laid foundations of mass evangelism in India that still endure; he strengthened mission outposts in Melaka (Malacca) and the Moluccas, and, as the first Christian missionary to Japan, so effectively pioneered the "Christian century" there (1549–1650) that Japan may well have had a higher percentage of Christians in 1600 than it has today. [*See* Xavier, Francis.] A tragic by-product of the coming of the West to India, however, was its effect on the ancient Thomas Christians. This Indian Syrian community had maintained tenuous connections with the Nestorians in Baghdad for centuries. Now it was first proselytized by the Portuguese and then fractured when large groups of Syrian Christians rebelled against the jurisdiction of Rome and reasserted their indigenous Christian loyalties. In Japan there was an even greater tragedy. The savage persecutions of the Tokugawa period (1600–1868) ended the Christian century, wiped out the church, and left only a shattered underground.

The Roman Catholics in China (1583–1774), as in Japan, enjoyed remarkable initial success. Matteo Ricci's strategy of accommodation to local customs and skillful use of Western science won the attention of the Confucian intelligentsia and gradually established Jesuit presence and influence at the court in Beijing. So strong was this influence that when the Ming emperors fell in 1644 the church in China for the first time was able to survive the fall of a friendly dynasty and make itself indispensable to the new Manchu rulers. [*See* Ricci, Matteo.] But an ecclesiastical catastrophe, the rites controversy, ended the Catholics' century-long rise to Chinese favor. At issue was the Jesuit policy of accommodation to such Confucian ceremonies as veneration of ancestors. In 1704 the pope ruled against the Jesuits. The result was an angry impasse between a Chinese emperor, Kangxi, resentful of foreign interference with his Jesuit advisers, and an inflexible pope.

The abolition of the Jesuit order in 1773 and the paralysis of France's great missionary societies by the French Revolution brought Catholic expansion throughout Asia almost to a standstill. Only in the Philippines did Roman Catholicism continue a phenomenal growth, one that by 1800 had made the islands the one land in Asia with a Christian majority.

Meanwhile, a fourth wave of Christian advance was moving into Asia, carrying Protestantism to the continent for the first time. As early as 1598 Dutch merchants began to send chaplains to their trading posts in the East Indies. Instructed to preach also to non-Christians, the chaplains baptized thousands throughout the islands of what is now Indonesia. The movement's weakness was its mixture of colonial, commercial, and religious motives, and it was only after a Danish mission of German Pietists to Tranquebar in 1706, and William Carey's still more significant mission to India in 1792, that Protestant missions picked up the momentum and clarity of focus that made them the dominant new factor in Christian advance in Asia in the nineteenth century. [*See* Carey, William.]

Among the pioneers after Carey were Robert Morrison in China (1807), Henry Martyn in Persia (1811), Adoniram Judson in Burma (1812), James Curtis Hepburn in Japan (1859), Ludwig Nommensen in Sumatra (1862), and Horace N. Allen in Korea (1884). [*See* Hepburn, James Curtis *and* Allen, Horace Newton.] Although Christianity and westernization often came hand in hand, evidence abounds of efforts by the missionaries to separate the advance of the faith from the spread of empire. Independent missionary societies multiplied. Emphasis on self-support, self-government, and self-propagation (the "three selfs") led toward church independence from foreign control and to interdenominational church unions. Especially noteworthy was Christian influence on Asian cultures in the fields of education, medicine, and the position of women.

The collapse of colonialism after World War II accelerated the rise of national Asian churches. Since 1900, despite countermovements like communism and revitalized Eastern religions, Asia's churches have multiplied the number of their adherents eight times, from only 19 million at the beginning of the century to an estimated 148 million in 1985, while continental population only tripled. Fervent evangelism, social compassion, and concern for justice in human affairs contributed to the growth of Christian influence. Theologians like P. D. Devanandan in India and K. Kitamori in Japan won new respect for the faith among intellectuals. Catholics in Asia outnumber Protestants by about five to three. Seventy percent of all Asia's Christians are concentrated in four countries: the Philippines (50 million), India

(27 million), Indonesia (17 million), and South Korea (12 million). It remains the case, however, that only one in about nineteen Asians is Christian.

[*See also* Nestorianism; Jesuits; Catholicism in the Philippines; *and* Philippine Independent Church.]

David B. Barrett, ed., *World Christian Encyclopedia* (1982). Charles Ralph Boxer, *The Christian Century in Japan: 1549–1650* (1951). Kenneth Scott Latourette, *The History of Christian Missions in China* (1929) and *The History of the Expansion of Christianity,* vols. 3, 5, 6, and 7 (1939–1945). Stephen Neil, *A History of Christianity in India,* vol. 1 (1984). P. Y. Saeki, *The Nestorian Documents and Relics in China* (1951).

SAMUEL HUGH MOFFETT

CHRISTIANITY IN JAPAN

Christianity developed in Japan in the aftermath of three major penetrations of foreign influence and missionary activity (after 1549, 1859, and 1945, respectively), each of which helped to shape Christianity's role in Japanese history.

Roman Catholic Christianity was introduced to Japan in 1549 by Francis Xavier (1506–1552), who with his Jesuit colleagues and successors laid the foundations of a flourishing mission. The country had been racked by internal political and religious conflicts and was receptive to new influences. The Jesuits sought contacts with Japanese feudal leaders and sought to impress on them the value of trading contacts with Western nations and the usefulness of Western advances in scientific fields. For their part, Japanese feudal lords were often eager to welcome the missionaries, whose services as interpreters, expediters of foreign trade, and workers among all classes of people were very useful. During his visitations to Japan as Jesuit vicar-general, Alessandro Valignano (1536–1606) stressed the need for the foreign missionaries to adapt to Japanese cultural norms and expectations, as well as the need to train Japanese priests and catechists to carry forward the missionary work. Under the patronage of Oda Nobunaga (1534–1582), who probably saw the new faith as a means of curbing the ambitions of rival Buddhist groups, Catholicism expanded, and by 1695 it may have counted 750,000 converts, or about 4 percent of the nation's population. [*See* Oda Nobunaga.]

Resistance to Christianity also grew apace. The regent Toyotomi Hideyoshi (1537–1598) became suspicious of the ways Portugal and Spain had used missions to expand their empires; he questioned also the willingness of the Jesuit missionaries to become involved in political and military affairs and their readiness to question his own moral and ideological authority. In 1587 Hideyoshi ordered the expulsion of all foreign missionaries, but prudential considerations led to the nonenforcement of this decree. [*See* Toyotomi Hideyoshi.] Despite traumatic setbacks, such as the crucifixion of twenty-six Christian martyrs in Nagasaki (1597), Christian mission work continued in numerous ways; Catholicism even greatly extended its territorial reach during this period, from the strongholds in Kyushu and Yamaguchi districts to central and northeast Japan.

Under the shogun Tokugawa Ieyasu (1542–1616) and his successors, the tide of persecution of Catholicism increased. When a group of Christian peasants took up arms against government forces in the Shimabara Rebellion (1637–1638), the shogunate completely crushed the rebels and then prohibited the Christian religion entirely, even setting up a surveillance system that was to be administered by local Buddhist temples. Despite such oppressive policies, groups of "hidden" Christians in Kyushu and elsewhere managed to maintain their faith in secret for over two centuries, cut off from all clergy and from all contact with foreigners.

After 1859, Japan was reopened to Western contacts with treaties that made it once again possible for foreigners to reside in Japan. Both Catholic and Protestant missionaries began to arrive at this time. French Catholic missionaries in Nagasaki opened the Ōura Church for foreign worshipers, and they were overjoyed to discover in 1865 that there were Hidden Christians in the area. Yet Christianity remained officially banned until 1873, when under foreign pressure the government finally removed the signboards prohibiting its practice.

Protestant missionaries from the United States, England, and Canada began their work in Japan with educational, medical, and linguistic efforts in port cities, and they came to find a response particularly among the former samurai who felt marginalized by the changes in Japanese society brought about by the Meiji Restoration (1867–1868). [*See* Meiji Restoration.] Japanese Protestants formed covenantal "bands," and Japanese Protestant leaders emerged, such as Niijima Jō (often known in the West as Joseph Hardy Neesima, 1843–1890), who helped found the Dōshisha in Kyoto (1871), one of the first Christian schools in Japan; Uemura Masahisa (1858–1925), who helped to establish the first Protestant congregation in Yokohama (1877); and the tenaciously independent Uchimura Kanzō (1861–1930), the founder of Non-Church Christianity (Mukyōkai).

Meanwhile, a vigorous Orthodox community was founded in Japan by a Russian Orthodox priest, Ivan Kasatkin (later known as Bishop Nikolai, 1836–1912), in one of the most remarkable chapters in the history of Orthodox mission work.

All Christian groups had their vicissitudes from the Meiji era through World War II. Protestants developed their mission schools and pioneered in education for women. Both Catholic and Protestant medical and social welfare institutions attracted widespread admiration among the Japanese public. Buddhist and Shinto groups felt the competition, and amid widespread talk that Japan might become a "Christian country," critics asserted that Christians were disloyal to the empire and its traditional values. Yet Christians' concern for the disadvantaged of Japanese society, as well as for its leaders, was manifest in the work of the Roman Catholic priest Iwashita Sōichi (1888–1940) and the Protestant pastor Kagawa Toyohiko (1888–1960).

In the 1930s, as Japan's foreign conquests moved the nation toward increasing tensions with the United States, Great Britain, and France—from which countries most Christian missionaries to Japan had come—the Japanese government took steps to keep Christian groups under surveillance and control. The Religious Bodies Law (1939) sought to eliminate foreign influence over Japanese religious groups. After the Allies entered the war against Japan (1941), Japanese Christians suffered alongside their compatriots through wartime privations and devastating bombing raids.

The American military occupation of Japan (1945–1952) unleashed a torrent of reforms on Japan, with substantial consequences for the country's slowly reviving Christian communities. Occupation measures to further freedom of religion became embodied in the nation's new constitution (1947); this led to a "religions boom" lasting several years, during which older Protestant, Catholic, and Orthodox groups increased their numbers, while newly introduced conservative Protestant groups thrived. The nation's educational system and social welfare practices were thoroughly revamped by the Occupation, and in the process Christian schools and social work agencies greatly expanded. Cooperative ties between Japanese and foreign mission agencies were reestablished, and joint programs for mass evangelism and for founding new churches were started.

By the time Japan's sovereignty was restored in the Peace Treaty of San Francisco (1951), the numerical gains of the Christian communities in Japan had become more modest, and altogether their total had not exceeded 1 percent of the population. Yet developments within the Christian groups were impressive. New translations of the Bible and creative theological works by Japanese Christians were highly successful. The Catholic novelist Endō Shūsaku (b. 1923) was widely read both at home and abroad. Ideological conflicts within Protestant groups sometimes led to polarization. The visit of Pope John Paul II to Japan (1981) brought encouragement to all Christians, who felt that their communities, despite difficulties and setbacks, would remain a significant influence on their nation's future.

[*See also* Kirishitan; Xavier, Francis; Valignano, Alessandro; Nikolai; Niijima Jō; Uemura Masahisa; *and* Uchimura Kanzō.]

C. R. Boxer, *The Christian Century in Japan* (1951). Richard H. Drummond, *A History of Christianity in Japan.* (1971). Joseph Jennes, *A History of the Catholic Church in Japan, 1549–1873* (1973). James M. Phillips, *From the Rising of the Sun: Christians and Society in Contemporary Japan* (1981). Stuart D. B. Picken, *Christianity and Japan: Meeting, Conflict, Hope* (1983). Joseph L. Van Hecken, *The Catholic Church in Japan Since 1859* (1963).

JAMES M. PHILLIPS

CHRISTIANITY IN KOREA

Christianity, which boasts a total community of about 10 million (25 percent of the population) and more than 25,700 churches, has become the strongest and most visible of all of South Korea's religions; in North Korea, however, it has been proscribed since the division of the peninsula in 1945. Although the practice of Christianity was legally forbidden throughout the nation until the 1890s, Catholics established a permanent presence in 1784, while significant Protestant activity began in 1883.

There is no verifiable evidence of Nestorians reaching Korea from China during the Tang (618–907) or Mongol Yuan (1279–1368) period. The first Christian on the peninsula was probably Gregorio de Cespedes, a Jesuit chaplain who arrived with invading Japanese troops (1592). [*See* Hideyoshi's Invasion of Korea.] In the early seventeenth century, writings of another Jesuit, Matteo Ricci, filtered across the border from China, but it was only when a Korean scholar, Yi Sŭng-hun, was converted in Beijing and returned in 1784 to organize a group of Catholics, that Christianity took permanent root. The first foreign missionary was a Chinese priest, James Chu, sent to legitimize the church in 1789; he was beheaded in 1801. With the arrival of the first European priests, beginning with Pierre Maubant in 1835, other persecutions followed, notably those of 1839 and 1846. Many were martyred, and in the final persecution (1866) more than two thousand Catholics were killed. Nevertheless, when Korea began to open to the West in 1882 there were still perhaps seventeen thousand Korean Catholics. A Catholic seminary was established in 1885.

Protestants entered as early as 1832, when Karl Gutzlaff, a German pietist, made an exploratory visit. An attempt in 1865 and 1866 by Welsh Congregationalist R. J. Thomas ended wtih his martyrdom. As with Catholicism, permanent Protestant work began with a Korean, Sŏ Sang-yun, who was converted by Scottish missionaries in Manchuria and returned to gather a group of believers in his home village in 1883, a year before the arrival of the first resident Protestant missionary, the American Presbyterian Horace N. Allen. In 1885 two clergymen joined him, Horace G. Underwood (Presbyterian), and Henry G. Appenzeller (Methodist). [*See also* Allen, Horace Newton.]

Although public evangelism was forbidden, when Allen's medical skill saved the life of a royal prince he was granted permission to open a hospital in 1885, the first legally permitted Christian institution in Korea. Appenzeller organized the first Christian academy, Paejae, in 1886. An even more dramatic breakthrough was the founding the next year of Korea's first school for girls, Ewha Academy. In 1887 Underwood organized the first Protestant church. All this activity, however, was in the capital, Seoul. Not until 1893 was the interior outside the treaty ports penetrated for open missionary residence by Samuel A. Moffett. Massive church growth began in the northeast, reaching a climax in the nationwide Korean Revival of 1907 to 1908. Protestant membership leaped from a few hundred in 1890 to fifty thousand in 1905, and to more than two hundred thousand in 1909.

The Japanese annexation (1910–1945) slowed but did not stop the growth of Christianity. A series of confrontations between Christians and the occupying authorities—the Conspiracy Trial (1912–1913), the defense of the right to teach religion in Christian schools (1915–1919), the 1919 Independence Movement, in which Christians played a leading role, and the bitter controversy over imperial shrine worship (1936–1945)—rather than diminishing Christian influence, increased its recognition nationally as a champion of Korean identity. At the same time Korea's traditional religions, Confucianism and Buddhism, were discredited by many as powerless in national crises. The nation's ancient shamanistic religious base, although still pervasive, saw its credibility eroded by Christian contributions to Korea's modernization, especially in education and medicine.

It was largely the ability of Christians to plant and organize their own institutions with effective Korean leadership in churches, schools, hospitals, and the YMCA and YWCA that kept Christianity from collapse in this troubled period. Protestants, especially Presbyterians, developed a successful mission strategy (the Nevius Plan) that stressed the autonomy of the church under self-governing, self-supporting, and self-propagating Korean direction. In 1901 they founded the first Korean Protestant theological seminary, in P'yŏngyang. In 1907 the Presbyterian Church in Korea was given its independence from the missions. Methodists followed suit in 1930, electing their first Korean bishop, Ryang Ju-sam. Roman Catholics convened their first national synod in 1931 and consecrated the first Korean Catholic bishop, Paul Ro, in 1942.

At the outbreak of World War II it was estimated that there were perhaps between 500,000 and 700,000 Protestant Christians and 150,000 Roman Catholics. During the war years, however, church membership fell sharply.

Postwar recovery brought another explosion of Christian expansion that was only temporarily broken off almost at the outset by the trauma of the division of the country and the Korean War (1950–1953). Before the war almost two-thirds of Korea's Christians had been in the north, but persecution soon wiped out organized Christianity in the Democratic People's Republic, and thousands fled south.

In South Korea Christianity has become the most active, effective, and perhaps largest organized religious force in the republic. Government satistics reported that in 1982 the size of the Christian community was about 25 percent of the population of 39 million (1981), or 10 million. The various churches claim a more modest membership, totaling 7.7 million Protestants and 1.6 million Catholics. The remaining half million probably have no direct church connection or belong to one of the many fringe cults such as the Unification Church of Sunmyong Moon. Growth has also been marred by sharp denominational divisions. The largest groupings are Presbyterian (more than 4 million in some thirty denominations), Roman Catholics (1.5 million), Methodists (885,000 in four denominations), Pentecostals (500,000 in seven denominations), and the Korean Evangelical Church, or OMS (470,000 in three denominations).

However uncertain the numbers may be, there is

no question of the strength and influence of Korean Christianity. It has become a force in Korean politics for democratic freedoms both within the government and in opposition parties. The first two presidents of the Republic were Christian, Syngman Rhee (Methodist) and Yun Po-sun (Presbyterian). Christians are increasingly middle class and well educated. Three of the five most prestigious universities are Christian. Christianity has helped to raise the status of women, to improve agricultural methods, and to introduce new standards of care for the poor and the sick. It is a significant presence in the arts and in the army. Most important for the future of Christianity in Korea, its membership has been growing at a rate of four times that of the population as a whole.

Allen D. Clark, *A History of the Church in Korea* (1971). J. Chang-mun Kim and J. Jae-sun Chung, *Catholic Korea Yesterday and Today* (1964).

SAMUEL HUGH MOFFETT

CHU, one of the Warring States of ancient China. Chu was the largest of the contending states that emerged in the seventh century BCE as the central authority of the Zhou dynasty disintegrated. Located in the central Yangtze region, Chu lay to the south of, and was culturally distinct from, the older states of the North China Plain. In the middle of the seventh century BCE the power of Chu inspired the other states to form a defensive league against the southern menace. In 334 BCE Chu absorbed the territory of Yue to the east and in 249 the tiny state of Lu. Chu expanded its territory until 223 BCE, when it succumbed to Qin in the first imperial unification of China. EDWARD L. FARMER

CHUANG-TZU. *See* Zhuangzi.

CHU HSI. *See* Zhu Xi.

CHULALONGKORN (Rama V), king of Siam (1868–1910), struggled to maintain Siam's independence in the face of Western colonialism and laid the foundations of modern Thailand.

Chulalongkorn was born 21 September 1853, the first son of King Mongkut by his half-sister and queen Thepsirin. He received the traditional princely education in the palace, to which was added some instruction by the Canadian governess Anna Leonowens. In his early teens he worked closely with his father and, because of both his birth status and experience, was an obvious choice to succeed to the throne on Mongkut's death on 1 October 1868. As the prince was only fifteen, he was placed under the regency of Somdet Chaophraya Sisuriyawong (Chuang), the most powerful official and leading member of the progressive Bunnag family.

During the regency period, Chulalongkorn continued his studies and traveled abroad to modern European colonies, visiting Singapore, Java, Burma, and India from 1871 to 1873. Approaching his majority and coronation as king in his own right in November 1873, Chulalongkorn felt politically vulnerable. Measuring his state by Western standards, he considered Siam corrupt, inefficient, and backward; practical power was in the hands of those either opposed to change or, like the Bunnags, with vested interests in the existing scheme of things. He looked to his younger brothers and the handful of Western-educated young men in the kingdom for support and began reforms. He announced the gradual abolition of slavery and moved to curb judicial and fiscal corruption. In 1874–1875 he provoked a confrontation with the old order that came close to costing him his throne and forced a slowing of the pace of reform for the next decade.

Only as the older generation of ministers died or retired in the mid-1880s could the king finally seize full power and implement the reforms that he considered vital for the kingdom to survive the threats and demands of France and Britain. He began the creation of a modern army, overhauled the revenue system, reorganized the provincial administration and extended the capital's control in outlying regions, began a modern education system, and reformed the bureaucracy. In most of these efforts he relied upon the best-educated young men he could find—men like the princes Damrong Rajanubhab and Devawongse Varopakar, who happened to be his brothers. Chulalongkorn's efforts could not forestall the loss of Laos and western Cambodia (now Kampuchea) to France or of Kelantan, Trengganu, Kedah, or Perlis to Britain. But with improving transportation facilities (e.g., modern railways) available to international trade, Western-style law codes and administration in place, and a growing reputation for progressive aspirations, Siam gained sufficient Western goodwill, or at least grudging acquiescence, to be allowed to retain its independence. Chulalongkorn himself assisted in the diplomatic effort, paying personal visits to Europe in 1897 and 1907, where he was greeted as an equal by monarchs and heads of state.

Chulalongkorn worked extremely hard during this critical period and took a keen interest in all the day-to-day aspects of government. He thought deeply and creatively about state policy and recognized the dangers of losing Thai identity in the process of modernization. Although he relied heavily upon the advice of his brothers, he was impatient with the less able among them and most readily listened to his three most competent brothers. He had seventy-seven children, not an uncommon number given the royal practice of polygamy, but indicated that succession to the throne should pass through the lines of his three queens, all of whom were his half-sisters. Crown Prince Vajiravudh succeeded to the throne on Chulalongkorn's death on 24 October 1910.

[*See also* Chakri Dynasty; Mongkut; Sisuriyawong; Bunnag Family; Damrong Rajanubhab; Devawongse Varopakar; Paknam Incident; *and* Wachirayan Warorot.]

Tej Bunnag, *The Provincial Administration of Siam 1892–1915* (1977). Chandran Jeshurun, *The Contest for Siam 1889–1902* (1977). Arnold Wright, ed., *Twentieth-Century Impressions of Siam* (1908). David K. Wyatt, *The Politics of Reform in Thailand* (1969) and *Thailand: A Short History* (1984). DAVID K. WYATT

CHUN DOO HWAN (Chŏn Tu-hwan; b. 1931), elected the first president of the Fifth Republic of Korea in 1981. Chun was born in Hapchonkun, South Kyŏngsang Province, Korea. His parents took the family to Manchuria when Chun was eight years old, but returned in 1943 to settle in Taegu. There Chun attended the Hido Elementary School, which had been founded by Christian missionaries.

In 1951 Chun graduated from Taegu Technical High School. He entered the Korean Military Academy, from which he graduated as a member of the first class to complete a four-year program. Following graduation, Chun was commissioned as a second lieutenant (1955) and joined the Special Forces Corps when it was created in 1958. Chun was among the first group of Korean officers to receive training at the US Special Forces and Psychological Warfare School in 1959 and the US Army Infantry School in 1960.

Before leaving for the United States, Chun married Lee Soon Ja (Yi Sun-ja) whom he first met when he was a sophomore at the Military Academy. Lee's father was the chief of staff at the Academy. They have three sons and a daughter.

When General Park Chung Hee (Pak Chŏng-hŭi) seized power in May 1961, Chun worked briefly as a secretary for domestic affairs at the Supreme Council for National Reconstruction, which was the highest organ of government at the time. He returned to active duty in 1963 as the Commander of the 30th Batallion of the Capital Garrison Command, and successfully led a defensive action against a North Korean commando raid on the presidential residence in 1968. In 1969 he became the first among his Korean Military Academy class to be promoted to the rank of captain.

Chun served for one year in Vietnam as commander of the 29th Regiment, 9th Army Infantry Division of the Republic of Korea. Upon his return from Vietnam, Chun was appointed commander of the 1st Airborne Special Forces Group and was promoted to lieutenant general in 1973. Five years later he was put in command of the Republic of Korea (ROK) 1st Army Infantry Division. It was as commanding general of this division that Chun helped discover an underground tunnel dug by the North Koreans, who apparently planned to use the tunnel to infiltrate behind South Korean defenses.

Chun Doo Hwan's last military assignment was as the commanding general of the Defense Security Command, to which he was appointed in March 1979. It was this assignment that led Chun to assume the responsibility of heading the military-civilian joint investigation team formed following President Park Chung Hee's assassination on 26 October 1979. As the chief investigating officer for the Park assassination, Chun had the Army chief of staff, General Chung Seong Hwa (Chŏng Sŏng-hwa), arrested on 12 December because of suspicions raised by his presence in the room adjoining the chamber where President Park had been assassinated. [*See also* Park Chung Hee.]

Meanwhile, Prime Minister Choi Kyu Ha (Ch'oe Kyu-ha), who was the next in line of succession, had been elected president of the republic by the nation's electoral college. He pledged to hold general elections to choose a new government at the end of one year, during which time a new constitution would also be adopted. Choi's vision was that the nation should transform its constitutional system into a more liberal one in an orderly fashion without disrupting its fundamental stability.

Events, however, did not follow this orderly sequence. The Korean economy had its worst record in more than a decade, inflation mounted, strikes broke out, and student demonstrations, described by many as riots, grew in number and size. In May riot police moved against the students. They required particular force to regain command of the city of Kwangju, where civil disobedience had assumed major proportions. Those arrested included the opposition leaders Kim Jong Pil (Kim Chong-p'il) and Kim Dae Jung (Kim Tae-jung). Choi's government extended martial law to the entire nation, suspended the National Assembly, created a special committee for national security measures, and appointed Chun as the chairman of its standing committee. The imposition of martial law, believed by many to have been initiated by Chun, ended any progress toward achieving President Choi's democratic reforms.

Under Chun's leadership the Committee for National Security, which was now effectively running the government, gave its highest priority to carrying out reform measures intended to win public approval, such as initiating radical measures against bribery and corruption. Chun's aim apparently was to win the confidence of the majority of people in the government's ability to rule. He adopted measures intended to put an end to chaos and instability as seen at Kwangju as well as populist reform measures such as the campaign for clean government. Chun has been criticized, however, for closing down publishing houses and periodicals and sending more than thirty thousand people to jail or reeducation camps.

On 16 August 1980 Choi Kyu Ha publicly announced his decision to retire from the presidency. The same electoral college that had elected President Park and President Choi chose Chun Doo Hwan, the sole candidate, as successor, and he was duly sworn in on 27 August 1980. Immediately following his accession to the presidency, Chun lifted martial law and promulgated a new constitution prohibiting all future presidents from seeking a second term beyond the seven-year first term of office. Chun was elected as the first president under the new constitution of the Fifth Republic of Korea on 25 February 1981. Despite the government's civilian appearance, however, it is with the military that ultimate power still rests.

With the return of domestic stability, Korea under Chun regained the momentum of its economic growth. A negative growth rate of 5.6 percent in 1980 became a positive increase of 6.2 percent in 1981. Price inflation, which was more than 20 percent in 1980, was reduced to 3.7 percent in 1981.

Chun Doo Hwan also took foreign policy initiatives, beginning with a visit to Washington to meet with President Reagan in 1981. That summer he became the first Korean President to visit all five ASEAN (Association of Southeast Asian Nations) capitals and, a year later, the first to visit African nations (Kenya, Nigeria, Gabon, and Senegal).

In October 1983 Chun was on a goodwill visit to Burma when a bomb placed by North Korean agents killed seventeen South Korean officials, including four cabinet ministers. Despite this incident he traveled abroad again in 1983 to become the first Korean head of state ever to make a state visit to Japan.

In an attempt to reduce tension on the Korean peninsula and create the basis for eventual reunification of Korea, Chun Doo Hwan proposed a face-to-face meeting with North Korea's top leader in a speech on 12 January 1981 and repeated the offer several times. North Korea had not yet responded affirmatively to the proposal in 1986, and negotiations on two-way trade and exchange of families separated by war showed no real progress.

The International Olympic Committee's decision to hold the 1988 Olympic Games in Seoul, Korea, also may be seen as one of Chun's important foreign policy initiatives. Because of this decision and Korea's economic growth, South Korea began to have a higher profile in the international community. Chun's government remained troubled, however, by the absence of reforms that would allow direct democratic elections. In the face of mass demonstrations in 1987, the Chun government agreed to significant concessions to the opposition, making fully democratic elections a real possibility.

[*See also* Korea, Republic of.]

KYUNG-WON KIM

CHUNGKING. *See* Chongqing.

CHU NOM, a script using both standard Chinese and uniquely Vietnamese characters to write the Vietnamese language. Although the script is believed to have been in use as early as the eighth century, the earliest extant texts using *chu nom* date from the thirteenth century. While most traditional Confucian scholars scorned *nom* script, writers such as Nguyen Trai (1380–1442) and Nguyen Du (1765–1820) favored it over classical Chinese as a literary medium. Certain rulers, including Ho Quy Ly (r. 1400–1407) and Nguyen Hue (r. 1788–1792), promoted *chu nom* as an official script. During the colonial period, however, it was gradually replaced by *quoc ngu*.

[*See also* Quoc Ngu.]

John De Francis, *Colonialism and Language Policy in Viet Nam* (1977). Nguyen Khac Vien, *Glimpses of Vietnamese Literature* (1977). BRUCE M. LOCKHART

CHUNQIU PERIOD. *See* Spring and Autumn Period.

CHŪSHINGURA *(The Treasury of Loyal Retainers)*, a Japanese play in eleven acts, written in 1748 for the puppet theater by Takeda Izumo II (1691–1756), Miyoshi Shōraku (1696–1772), and Namiki Senryū (1695–1751). The plot of *Chūshingura* is based on an actual event that occurred in early 1703. Forty-six *rōnin* (masterless samurai), formerly retainers of Lord Asano Naganori, took vengeance on their dead master's enemy, Lord Kira Yoshinaka, by attacking his mansion in Edo and beheading him. Lord Kira had provoked Lord Asano into wounding him in the shogun's palace, a breach of decorum so grave that Lord Asano was ordered by the government to commit suicide. His lands were confiscated and his retainers became *rōnin*. The *rōnin* planned their attack carefully; having executed Lord Kira, they presented his head before Lord Asano's tomb at the Sengakuji temple in Edo. Two months later the forty-six *rōnin*, led by Ōishi Kuranosuke, received a government order to commit suicide by *seppuku*. They were buried at Sengakuji with their former lord.

The vendetta captured the imagination of the Japanese, who were hungry for stories of martial valor after a century of peace under the Tokugawa shoguns. Within two weeks of the burial of the *rōnin*, a *kabuki* play based on the incident appeared in Edo. It was quickly closed down by government censors. In 1706 the great dramatist Chikamatsu Monzaemon (1653–1725) wrote a one-act puppet play, *Goban taiheiki*, which formed the basis for *Chūshingura*. Both it and *Chūshingura* follow the convention of setting the events in the Middle Ages and changing the names of the characters to avoid censorship. Lord Asano and Lord Kira are represented by two characters from the fourteenth-century classic *Taiheiki*, En'ya Hangan and Kō no Moronao, respectively. Ōishi Kuranosuke, Lord Asano's chief retainer, appears in the play as Ōboshi Yuranosuke.

Chūshingura was an immediate success at its 1748 debut in Osaka and was soon performed as a *kabuki* play as well. It remains a staple of the *kabuki* and *bunraku* repertoires and often appears in television and film versions. Since a full performance takes about eleven hours, *Chūshingura* is usually performed in excerpts.

[*See also* Bunraku; Chikamatsu Monzaemon; Akō Gishi; *and* Kabuki.]

James R. Brandon, ed., *Chushingura: Studies in Kabuki and the Puppet Theater* (1982). Donald Keene, trans., *Chushingura* (1971). Donald Keene, *World within Walls* (1976). AILEEN GATTEN

CHU VAN AN (d. 1370), Vietnamese poet and scholar during the Tran dynasty (1225–1400). A village schoolteacher, he went on to receive higher degrees and became vice-rector of the Royal College (Quoc Tu Giam) under emperors Minh Tong (1314–1329) and Hien Tong (1329–1341), the latter his former pupil. He later petitioned Emperor Du Tong (1341–1369) for the execution of seven corrupt mandarins and upon the emperor's refusal retired from official service. Chu Van An is known to have written poetry in both Vietnamese *chu nom* script and classical Chinese, although only the poems in Chinese have been preserved.

[*See also* Chu Nom *and* Tran Dynasty.]

BRUCE M. LOCKHART

CIREBON, principality on Java's north coast founded in the sixteenth century. The earliest references to Cirebon emphasize the intimate connection between its history and that of its founder, Sunan Gunung Jati (d. 1570), one of the nine *wali*, or Moslem saints, to whom tradition ascribes the conversion of Java to Islam. By 1640 the principality had become a vassal of the kingdom of Mataram, then under Sultan Agung, from which it was freed only by the outbreak of the Trunajaya revolt of 1677. In 1681 Cirebon submitted to the authority of the Dutch East India Company and for the remainder of the company era was the center of the Priangan Regencies' administration and the collection point for its deliveries of tropical produce. Today the principality is characterized by its almost equal number of Javanese and Sundanese speakers and by the relatively high position of its Chinese, or Peranakan, minority.

[*See also* Java; Mataram; Agung; Trunajaya; *and* Dutch East India Company.]

M. C. HOADLEY

CIS-SUTLEJ STATES. Located in the doab between the Sutlej and Yamuna rivers in India, the Cis-Sutlej states were independent principalities until the early ninteenth century. Under pressure from Ranjit Singh (d. 1839) and the British, they came under British "protection" in 1809. In 1948 they were amalgamated into the administrative unit of PEPSU (Patiala and East Punjab States Union). The region now belongs to the states of Punjab and Haryana.[*See also* Singh, Ranjit; Punjab; *and* Haryana.]

USHA SANYAL

CITIES. Until recent times the great cities of world history—from Constantinople to Beijing—were predominantly in Asia. The title of the world's largest city shifted progressively eastward, from Chang'an (now Xi'an) between the seventh and ninth century, to Kaifeng in the tenth and eleventh, to Lin'an (Hangzhou) in the twelfth and thirteenth, and then, after a northern detour to Nanjing and Beijing between the fourteenth and seventeenth century, to Edo (now Tokyo) in the eighteenth. Most of these cities are credited with populations of approximately one million at their peak. High population densities, large-scale political units, flourishing trade routes, and venerable traditions of city building contributed to this continent's rich and variegated urban history.

The many functions and images of urban life were well represented across traditional Asia. Here could be found (1) the "cradles of civilization" in Mesopotamia and the Yellow River valley of Shang-dynasty China; (2) the holy and ancient places of the world's most prominent religions, in Jerusalem, northern India, northern China, and elsewhere; (3) the caravan stops that dotted early trade routes such as the Silk Route, which wound through the mountains and deserts of Central Asia, and the treaty ports that developed along the sea lanes charted by the profit-seeking and empire-building European trade companies beginning in the sixteenth century; (4) the almost uniformly distributed district, prefectural, and provincial administrative centers, each functioning as part of a regional and national urban network centered on one of Asia's great state capitals; (5) the capitals themselves, the grand scale of which projected a majestic imperial presence; and (6) the nearly ubiquitous market towns, post stations, and local ports that diffused elements of the urban presence deep into rural hinterlands.

China stands out under each of these categories. Its 1,600 administrative centers, 30,000 additional market towns, and an estimated seven cities in excess of 300,000 inhabitants in the early nineteenth century offer impressive numerical evidence of a grand urban tradition. Possessing close to half of Asia's total population and one-quarter to one-third of the world's population, China enjoyed a long and continuous history of large-scale urban development.

During the Mughal period (1526–1857) India also counted thousands of marketplaces and small cities. Agra, the capital of the empire, and provincial capitals such as Ahmadabad, Delhi, Hyderabad, and Lahore each combined the many functions expected of great cities to register sizable populations. Although city records are not as plentiful as for China and Japan, we can surmise that India's urban population around 1800 totaled less than half of the Chinese figure (over twenty million) but more than Japan's five million.

In modern times, new urban images and experiments distinguish the Asian continent. Asia, especially South and Southeast Asia, is now known for huge cities such as Calcutta. Selected parts of Asia have also become noted for tightly restricted urban life under communist leadership, made possible (as in China during the 1960s and 1970s) by strictly controlling residential movement and sending millions of youths to the countryside or (as in the extreme case of Kampuchea in the 1970s) by forced and often fatal mass depopulation of cities. Modern urban planning has taken on novel forms, beginning with the new socialist city found in the Soviet Union's fully planned mining and industrial centers of the Urals and Siberia, whose urban designs became a model for other socialist countries, and including the futuristic underground shopping plazas in such Japanese cities as Tokyo and Osaka. In the postwar period a new factor emerged. A rapid influx of wealth into export-oriented cities such as Singapore, Hong Kong, and Seoul accelerated city growth on the basis of labor-intensive industries and eventually high technology.

Whereas in premodern times city building was largely inland and was enmeshed in large urban networks established by great states and empires, from the time of the treaty ports most development has occurred close to the sea and has been linked recently to international Arab oil wealth in the west and a trading edge based on skilled labor in the east. These foreign trade successes have brought rapid urbanization to the edges of the continent. Yet the three largest Asian countries, China, India, and the Soviet Union, trade a relatively small portion of their domestic production with the outside world. Before the end of the 1970s, when China's Special Economic Zones were approved to stimulate foreign trade, the two socialist countries gave high priority to inland city development. [*See* Special Economic Zones.] Except for sparsely populated Siberia, inland Asia is now among the least urbanized regions of the world.

Empires arose early in Asia and their leaders engaged in city building on a large scale. Frontier outposts were transformed into district capitals. New walls and buildings appeared on the ruins of old cities. Once established, thousands of cities, especially those in China, continued for a millennium or even two as urban centers. Nevertheless, some areas remained sparsely settled into modern times. It was not until the late nineteenth century that Hokkaido in Japan and Manchuria in northeast China were urbanized.

Elsewhere, the inspiration of great empires had led to the diffusion of urban plans to previously nonurbanized territories. New cities had been modeled on existing examples. For example, Japan's early capitals of Heijō (now Nara) and Heian (now Kyoto) were close copies of great Chinese capitals including Chang'an.

Walls were visible features in the historic cities of Asia. They enclosed residential units, many of which had their own courtyards. In some periods, for example in China before the Song dynasty (960–1279), they separated one residential ward from another. Locked gates at night helped to maintain urban order. Prominent marketing areas or building complexes were often enclosed by walls. In Japan during the three centuries that preceded the Meiji Restoration of 1868 the most prominent wall in each castle city was encircled by a moat and enclosed the centrally located castle complex of the local lord. For more than two millennia, high, thick, well-constructed walls, often several kilometers in perimeter, enclosed most or all of the area of Chinese administrative cities. Throughout the continent walls retained some protective significance in separating ethnic, kin, or occupational groups and in symbolizing governmental authority.

Spontaneous urban communities formed around periodic markets, transshipment points, and a small number of religious centers. Rarely were these walled communities. The state's role was more limited here than in administrative centers, but many Asian governments found ways to regulate city development. Along major roads they designated some places as post stations. They also granted permission for markets and fairs to be held at specified times. Sometimes they reserved monopolies over certain crafts or trade routes for artisans and merchants from particular cities, usually administrative centers rather than rival cities. Despite these monopolies, the privileged big city merchants often were less flexible owing to state and guild regulations and higher costs. In some periods, as in eighteenth- and nineteenth-century Japan, the urban population shifted toward smaller, local communities. In China, the nonadministrative cities could grow to a great size; the most striking example is Jingdezhen, the great porcelain center of the Ming and Qing dynasties (seventeenth to early twentieth century), with a few hundred thousand residents.

Particular cities were often designated as gateways for foreigners, while all other centers were closed to them. Before the mid-nineteenth century Canton (Guangzhou) was the only entry point by sea for China and Nagasaki was the lone city where the Dutch and Chinese were allowed to maintain a foreign presence in Japan. The tradition of restrictive entry persists in the socialist countries—in North Korea, Vietnam, Outer Mongolia, and Afghanistan there are cities inaccessible to most foreigners.

Restrictions have also taken the form of denying residents of one city the right to move to another city in the same country. Tight controls on household registration to prevent movement into the most desirable cities were difficult to enforce in premodern times, but contemporary socialist countries have been more successful.

In the literature on cities one often encounters the negative judgment that city life in Asia was not "free" in comparison to that of Western Europe. Apart from certain sixteenth-century Japanese ports, there were few cities in which merchant associations wielded great power; nor was there a tradition of royal charters that limited the rights of national rulers to interfere in city life. Some writers have construed this legal difference as the basis for a fundamentally different urban environment in Asia, one in which officials dominated and merchants were secondary. In fact, merchant prosperity could be considerable. City commerce—both local and long-distance—over many centuries was probably at least as lively, and the populations engaged in it at least as sizable, as in great European cities. Domestic merchants, who were often identified by their city or area of origin, established groups in their host cities and came to dominate particular trades. Dependent on the commercial prosperity of their cities, Asian officials were usually reluctant to interfere with the business community.

The most spectacular urbanization in both premodern and modern times seems to have occurred in Japan. In the late sixteenth and seventeenth centuries Japan's city population may have quadrupled, placing the country in the forefront of world urbanization at that time. Roughly 17 percent of the population lived in cities, including more than one million in Edo and more than 300,000 in both Osaka and Kyoto; close to 100 cities had a minimum of 10,000 residents. From the late nineteenth century, under the influence of modernization, Japanese cities resumed their rapid growth. It required fewer decades than elsewhere for Japan to join the ranks of the highly urbanized modern countries in which 70 percent or more of the people live in cities. Very high population densities without many high-rise buildings typified large cities of both premodern and modern Japan as well as in other Asian countries.

Although the overall urbanization of Asia is relatively low, many cities have grown rapidly. In the early part of the twentieth century Calcutta and Bombay, Shanghai and Tianjin, Bangkok and Jakarta were gaining population rapidly. Hong Kong, Singapore, Tehran, Kaohsiung (Gaoxiong), Seoul, Manila, and the great bureaucratic centers of Beijing and Delhi were later growth centers. Some of the newly growing cities were great cities of old, and one can still find there vestiges of a bygone era. The many wars that have racked Asia in this century have taken their toll in urban sites, as did China's Cultural Revolution, especially in minority areas such as Tibet's Lhasa. Built with ephemeral materials, mainly wood, the structures of Asian cities have required repair and replacement that has often not been forthcoming. Even so, there are cities such as Kyoto where much historic beauty remains. While less is preserved than in Europe, it is not just in the historical records that one learns of the tapestry of urban images that made this continent the dominant area of world urban history.

[*The cities mentioned above are the subject of independent entries.*]

Ronald P. Dore, *City Life in Japan: A Study of a Tokyo Ward* (1958). Mark Elvin and G. William Skinner, *The Chinese City between Two Worlds* (1974). T. G. McGee, *The Southeast Asian City* (1967). Gilbert Rozman, *Urban Networks in Ch'ing China and Tokugawa Japan* (1973). G. William Skinner, ed., *The City in Late Imperial China* (1977).

GILBERT ROZMAN

CIXI TAIHOU. *See* Empress Dowager.

CLEMENTI, SIR CECIL (1875–1947), British governor of Malaya and Hong Kong. After a distinguished career at Oxford, he followed his uncle, Sir Cecil Clementi Smith, into an Eastern cadetship. While serving in Hong Kong (1899–1913) he traveled widely in China. He then served as colonial secretary in British Guiana (1913–1921) and Sri Lanka (1922–1925). His experience with the Guomindang (Kuomintang) in Hong Kong, where he was governor (1925–1930), influenced his approach to dealing with the Chinese of Malaya when he was governor and high commissioner there (1930–1934). His design to decentralize the Federated Malay States in order to unite all nine states and, perhaps, the Straits Settlements and British Borneo encountered difficulties, leading Sir Cecil to retire prematurely.

A. J. STOCKWELL

CLIFFORD, SIR HUGH (1866–1941), British colonial officer who played an important role in establishing Britain's control of Malaya, known for his affinity with the Malays. Scion of a Catholic aristocratic family, Clifford arrived in Malaya in 1883. A man of immense enthusiasm and vigor, he played a critical part in the negotiations and counterinsurgency that established British domination of Pahang (1887–1895). Having been resident of Pahang and governor of North Borneo, Clifford left Malaya in 1903 to pursue a distinguished career in the colonial service. After holding governorships in the Gold Coast, Nigeria, and Sri Lanka, he returned to Malaya in 1927. Malaya was his greatest love and inspired his literary writings, which are not only imaginative but also contain much of ethnographic interest. His governorship, however, was ended prematurely by mental illness.

H. A. Gailey, *Clifford: Imperial Proconsul* (1982). W. R. Roff, ed., *Stories by Sir Hugh Clifford* (1966).

A. C. MILNER

CLIVE, SIR ROBERT (1725–1774). Governor of Bengal (1758–1760; 1765–1767) under the East India Company, Clive was also made a *mansabdar*, a high-ranking official of the Mughal empire, and held such Mughal titles as *sabut jang, zabat ul-mulk,* and *nazir ud-daula,* together with a *jagir* (estate) worth some 300,000 rupees (£30,000) a year. His career began as a writer, or clerk, in 1744. When Madras fell to the French two years later, he escaped and became a military officer of the East India Company. As such he showed natural aptitude and was extraordinarily successful. He seized the princely capital of Arcot in 1751, so as to divert the besiegers of Nawab Muhammad Ali at Trichinopoly, and was himself besieged for fifty days by Chanda Sahib's vastly larger forces. His defense, a brilliant feat, not only established the company's reputation for valor but also set Clive onto his path as a "heaven-born general." Company officials, who previously had dealt mainly in textiles, went increasingly into an "arms trade," with their newly modeled regiments of "sepoys-for-hire" as their main commodity. After many further victories, interrupted by a stay in England (1753–1756), Clive took an army of sepoys to Bengal to recapture Calcutta from the forces of Nawab Siraj ud-Daulah. This being done, after some murky maneuvering and negotiating Clive won his greatest victory at Plassey on 23 June 1757. The nawab, who fled and was killed, was replaced by Mir Jafar. Huge gratuities and reparations were exacted.

On his return to England as a nouveau riche "nabob," Clive obtained an estate, an Irish peerage, and much power within the company. But unable to stem the corruption of its servants in India, the company sent him back. In 1765 he obtained from the emperor Shah Alam the *diwani,* or imperial authority over civil government (revenue administration), for Bengal on behalf of the company. When attacked and subjected to Parliamentary enquiry into his vast wealth upon his return, he replied: "I walked through vaults . . . piled on either hand with gold and jewels! Mr. Chairman, at this moment, I stand astonished at my own moderation!" Exhausted and suffering from recurring bouts of depression, he finally took his own life.

[*See also* East India Company; Plassey, Battle of; *and* Nabob.]

Nirad K. Chaudhuri, *Clive of India* (1975). A. M. Davies, *Clive of Plassey* (1939). Percival Spear, *Master of Bengal: Clive and His India* (1975).

ROBERT E. FRYKENBERG

COCHIN, important port on the Arabian Sea in Kerala state, India, and the name of the former princely state in which it is situated. The region was once part of the kingdom of the great Chera dynasty, but by the middle of the ninth century a separate principality had been formed under the raja of Cochin, from whom the later rajas claimed descent. By the eighth century Arab traders had established themselves along the coast and introduced Islam. The history of the area is obscure, however, until the arrival of the Portuguese, who had first landed in Calicut, to the south, in 1498. The Portuguese viceroy, Affonso de Albuquerque, was given permission by the raja to build a fort in Cochin in 1503, and this, the first European fortification in India, became the base from which the Portuguese extended their control over trade with India. The Portuguese also sought to bring the Christians of the region, who traced their origins back to the apostle Thomas, and who were in communion with the ancient church of Syria, not of Rome, under the control of the Roman Catholic hierarchy. [*See* Thomas.] The Portuguese were driven out of Cochin in 1663 by the Dutch, who used the port as a center for their Eastern trade. In 1776 the raja of Cochin was defeated by Haidar Ali, the Muslim chieftain who had gained control of the state of Mysore, and was forced to pay tribute to him. In 1791, after the defeat of Haidar Ali's successor by the British, the raja entered into an alliance with them, becoming, in effect, their subsidiary or vassal. Cochin was thus one of the earliest of the Indian states to become part of the system of alliances that the British formed with Indian rulers to create "princely India." With an area of 1,300 square miles and a population at the beginning of the twentieth century of about 800,000, it was one of the smaller of the princely states.

The town of Cochin, which had been the capital of the raja's territory, was taken over by the British, who began its development as a modern port early in the twentieth century. It is one of the few ports on the west coast of India that is well protected from the monsoon winds, and after India became independent in 1947 it was developed as the chief training center for the Indian navy. Cochin had been the home of a small but ancient Jewish community with a beautiful synagogue, but most of the Jews have now migrated. The population of the municipal area in 1981 was estimated at 513,249.

[*See also* Albuquerque, Affonso de; Jews; Kerala; Princely States; *and* Dutch East India Company.]

L. K. Anantha Krishna Iyer, *The Cochin Tribes and Castes,* 2 vols. (1909–1912). A. Sreedhara Menon, *A Survey of Kerala History* (1967). AINSLIE T. EMBREE

COCHINCHINA, a term that appeared in the sixteenth century and was derived from *Kōshi,* the Japanese pronunciation of *Jiaozhi* (Vietnamese, *Giao Chỉ*), an ancient Chinese name for Vietnam. The Portuguese rendered it Cochinchina to distinguish it from Cochin in India. Europeans applied it to the realm of Nguyen lords, who resided at Hue from 1558 to 1775 and controlled the expanding frontier from Dong Hoi southward. From 1859 to 1954, the term was used by the French to designate the plain surrounding Saigon and the estuaries of the Mekong. It was the only formal colony among the five

nch Indochina; Tonkin, Annam,
a were protectorates.
Lords.]

KEITH W. TAYLOR

OEDÈS, GEORGE (1887–1969), French historian who specialized in early Southeast Asia. Born in Paris, Coedès was for many years associated with the École Française d'Extrême-Orient in Hanoi; from 1928 to 1947 he served as its director. His publications, appearing steadily for over sixty years, provided a chronological framework for the history of mainland Southeast Asia. Almost single-handedly, Coedès reconstructed the history of Angkor from over one thousand undeciphered stone inscriptions. His eight-volume edition of these inscriptions was completed in 1966; in 1964 he published an important historical synthesis, *Les états hindouisés d'Indochine et d'Indonésie.*

G. Coedès, *The Indianized States of Southeast Asia,* translated by Susan B. Cowing (1968).

DAVID P. CHANDLER

COEN, JAN PIETERSZOON (1587–1629), twice appointed governor-general (1619–1623, 1627–1629) by the Dutch East India Company to preside over its affairs in Asia. Coen acted with enterprise and ruthlessness to establish Holland's commercial preeminence in the Indonesian archipelago. He founded Batavia as a military, administrative, and commercial capital in 1619; drove the English and other competitors out of effective commercial competition; and reduced several eastern Indonesian spice islands to subject status through a process of deportation, massacre, and crop destruction. Coen is commonly considered the founder of Netherlands India, although he did not foresee the vast territorial empire that evolved in his wake but envisioned instead a far-flung network of fortified Dutch trading posts and a few island possessions, all linked by sea and colonized by immigrants from Holland.

[*See also* Dutch East India Company *and* Jakarta.]

JAMES R. RUSH

COHONG, the association of Chinese merchants holding the officially authorized monopoly over foreign trade at Canton (Guangzhou) between 1760 and 1842. The term *Cohong* is a Western corruption of *gonghang,* "official firms." The origins of the Cohong can be traced to 1720, when about thirteen Hong *(hang)* merchants (owners of private commercial firms specializing in foreign trade) formed a guild to protect their economic interests. Through payments to the throne and to the Hoppo, the imperially designated superintendent of trade at Canton, the Cohong eventually obtained exclusive monopoly privileges over conduct of trade.

Cohong members also carried out a number of important governmental duties, such as collecting tariffs, supervising commercial transactions, and enforcing restrictions on foreigners' movements and conduct. In addition, they were made responsible, as "security merchants," for guaranteeing the behavior of foreigners and for serving as formal intermediaries between the traders and the Hoppo. From the Chinese government's point of view, the Cohong acted as a convenient buffer between Chinese officialdom and foreigners.

While it is true that some Hong merchants became fabulously rich in their potentially lucrative positions, many fell into bankruptcy. Actually, their financial security was by no means assured, since they were often obliged to maintain their status by paying "squeeze," or bribes and kickbacks, to the Hoppo and other Chinese officials, and forced to make contributions to the court in support of military campaigns and the like.

The Cohong soon became a target of the foreigners' hostility as a result of frustration over the Canton system's restrictions. In the late eighteenth century, when Westerners began to demand more free trade, they called for an end to the Cohong's monopoly. In 1816 the Amherst Mission to Beijing made this one of its specific objectives, but was unsuccessful in having the monopoly lifted. Finally, at the conclusion of the Opium War, the 1842 Treaty of Nanjing abolished the Cohong and removed the barriers to private trade.

[*See also* Canton; China Trade; Compradors; *and* Qing Dynasty.]

William C. Hunter, *The 'Fan Kwae' at Canton before Treaty Days, 1825–1844* (1911).

ROLAND L. HIGGINS

COINAGE. *See* Money.

COLEBROOKE-CAMERON REFORMS. The Colebrooke-Cameron reforms created the legislative and administrative framework for the government of the British colonial government of Ceylon that united the territory of the old kingdom of Kandy, which included the interior of the island, with the coastal districts. The Dutch, who had controlled the coastal areas in the last half of the eighteenth century, ceded them to the British in 1802 at the Treaty of Ameins, and then in 1815 Kandy was conquered by the British. At first, little attention was paid by the British government to the new colony, which had current deficits that had to be met from London, but in 1829 a royal commission of inquiry consisting of William Macbean Colebrooke and Charles Hay Cameron began to investigate the island's economic and political situation. In his portion of the report that was presented to the Colonial Office in London, Colebrooke proposed to create a laissez-faire economy by encouraging foreign investment, abolishing compulsory labor services (known as *rajakariya*), doing away with government trade monopolies, and reducing government expenditure. Cameron proposed reforms that simplified judicial procedures and placed more power in the hands of judges. While these proposals were not accepted in their entirety by the Colonial Office, except for the cuts in government spending, after 1833 the bureaucracy was reformed along the lines that Colebrooke had proposed, which gave most of the power to the British officials, who occupied almost all the higher posts, and took it away from the local officials.

[*See also* Sri Lanka *and* Pilima Talauve.]

Garrett Champness Mendis, ed., *The Colebrooke-Cameron Papers. Documents in British Colonial Policy in Ceylon, 1796–1833*, 2 vols. (1956).

PATRICK PEEBLES

CO LOA ("old snail"), capital of the Viet kingdom of Au Lac, an important archaeological site located about 20 kilometers north of Hanoi. Supposedly built at the order of An Duong Vuong, Co Loa derives its name from the shape of its ramparts, a series of concentric circles surrounding a rectangular citadel. The large scale of the fortifications (the outer rampart is approximately 7.6 kilometers in circumference) suggests that Au Lac had both a substantial population and a high degree of social organization.

When China's Latter Han dynasty began its direct administration of Viet territory during the first century CE, Co Loa declined in importance because the Chinese governors established their headquarters farther south in the more commercially active centers of the Red River delta. Nonetheless, Co Loa retained its symbolic significance as the authentic, pre-Chinese Viet capital, as may be seen in its subsequent designation as capital by the Former Ly rulers of the sixth century and the Ngo rulers of the tenth century.

[*See also* Au Lac; An Duong Vuong; Former Ly Dynasty; *and* Ngo Quyen.]

Thomas Hodgkin, *Vietnam: The Revolutionary Path* (1981). Keith W. Taylor, *The Birth of Vietnam* (1983).

JAMES M. COYLE

COLOMBO, the capital of the Republic of Sri Lanka and its largest port of overseas trade. The city had its beginnings in the eighth century as a trading settlement of primarily Arab traders participating in trade throughout the Indian Ocean. This early settlement and port was probably situated at the entrance of the Kolon Ganga, a tributary of the Kelani Ganga, the wide river that flowed a few miles to the north. The port developed as a major center of Indian Ocean trade, an outlet for its chief exports of cinnamon and precious stones, and an entry point for the import of consumer goods. When the Arab traveler Ibn Battuta visited Colombo around 1330 he described it as "one of the finest and largest cities of the island of Serendib [Sri Lanka]."

When the Portuguese landed in Colombo in 1505 the port was the major outlet for the Sinhalese kingdom of Kotte, whose rulers had come to a working arrangement with Arab and Indian traders, who had settled in self-contained communities within Colombo and managed the trade of the kingdom. The Portuguese built a fort in Colombo, expelled the Muslims, and launched their penetration of the interior and the coast. Under the Portuguese (1517–1658), and later under the Dutch (1658–1796), Colombo became tied to the Europe-Asia trade as well as a part of the trade within Asia. The construction and enlargement of port facilities and the increased trading and administrative activity brought a large settler population from the interior and the coast, and Colombo grew as an urban port-settlement.

This growth accelerated rapidly under the British (who ruled the island as a colony from 1833 until 1948) with the increasing tempo of Sri Lanka's foreign trade. The expansion of cash crop cultivation for export necessitated better facilities in the port. A breakwater was completed in 1884 for the safe anchorage of a number of vessels, and land was reclaimed in the foreshore for the construction of jetties and coal bunkers. The completion of facilities for the repair of ships and steamers made the port the most useful place in the Indian Ocean for such activity.

Parallel to the growth of the port in the twentieth century was the growth of the city as an industrial, administrative, and cultural center. The expansion of colonial administrative departments in Colombo led to the growth of a large English-educated middle class earning a steady income. A number of educational institutions sprang up with state initiative and under the sponsorship of Christian, Buddhist, and Hindu missionary bodies. The facilities of the port and the increasing population attracted investment in industry which, combined with the commercial and service sectors, made the city the major economic center of the island.

[*See also* Kotte; Portugese: Portuguese in Sri Lanka; *and* Sri Lanka.]

B. L. Panditharatna, "Colombo City: Its Population Growth and Increase from 1824–1954," *Ceylon Geographer* 14 (1960):1–16. B. L. Panditharatna, "The Harbour and Port of Colombo: A Geographical Appraisal of Its Historical and Functional Aspects," *Ceylon Journal of Historical and Social Studies* 3.2 (1960):128–143.

S. Arasaratnam

COLOMBO PLAN. The purpose of the Colombo Plan for Co-operative Economic and Social Development in Asia and the Pacific is to improve the standard of living of the peoples residing in South and Southeast Asia. Begun on 1 July 1951 in Colombo, Ceylon (now Sri Lanka), the plan was originally meant to run for three to six years, but its success brought about repeated extensions and there now is no definite date for the Colombo Plan's dissolution. The Colombo Plan does not operate through a formal organization, nor is there one master plan for regional development. Rather, it is an aggregate of bilateral agreements in which donor states are committed to providing capital aid and technical assistance to developing Asian nations.

When the Colombo Plan was first considered in 1950, China had just become a communist state. Concerned noncommunist leaders believed that economic growth was the best defense against future communist insurrections. This concern about the spread of communism in addition to the prospect of increased world trade made the Colombo Plan's goal of economic development attractive to the donor nations as well as to the developing states, and made the plan's creation possible.

L. P. Goonetilleke, *The Colombo Plan 1951–1971: Two Decades of Constructive Effort* (1971). L. P. Singh, *The Colombo Plan: Some Political Aspects* (1963).

William A. Kinsel

COMINTERN, an abbreviation for the Third Communist International, an organization for the coordination of communist parties around the world. Founded in the Soviet Union in 1919, the Comintern was intended to promote an expected world revolution. After Lenin's death in 1924, Stalin transformed the Comintern into an instrument for promoting Soviet interests around the world. Many Asian revolutionaries were trained and directed by the Comintern. In China, Comintern agents organized the Chinese Communist Party in 1921 and reorganized the Guomindang after 1923, both on the pattern of the Communist Party of the Soviet Union. The Comintern was officially dissolved in 1943 when the USSR was allied to capitalist countries during World War II.

[*See also* Borodin, Michael; Communism; Guomindang; Ho Chi Minh; *and* Sneevliet, Hendricus J. F. M.]

Edward L. Farmer

COMMANDERIES IN KOREA, CHINESE. In 109 BCE Chinese armies dispatched by Emperor Wu of the Han dynasty invaded Korea and, after a campaign that lasted into the following year, the Chosŏn kingdom ruled by the descendants of Wei Man (Korean, Wiman) was annexed to the Han empire. Four administrative districts or commanderies were set up to control the newly conquered people: Lelang (Korean, Nangnang), with its headquarters in Wanggŏm, the old Chosŏn capital; Lintun (Korean, Imdun), in eastern Korea; Zhenfan (Korean, Chinbŏn), farther south; and Xuantu (Korean, Hyŏnt'o), in the angle inhabited by the Okchŏ tribes of northeastern Korea.

After Emperor Wu died in 87 BCE his successors realized that the resources of the empire had been overextended in the numerous foreign campaigns, and began a process of withdrawal. Zhenfan was abandoned in 82 BCE and much of Lintun soon after, while the headquarters of Xuantu were shifted to the upper Yalu River to facilitate contact with China and keep control over one of the empire's dependencies in this area, the Koguryŏ tribes. Lelang remained the hub of the Chinese administration in Korea, and continued to attract Chinese settlers. The tombs of a number of petty officials in the Lelang administration have been excavated, principally by Japanese archaeologists working between 1910 and 1945; the tombs have revealed the existence of a wealthy colonial elite importing luxury items from China and evidently exploiting the labor of the local population. The wealth can be partly explained by the fact that "tribute missions" from the Japanese archipelago and the Han tribes inhabiting southern Korea (not to be confused with the Han Chinese) were obliged to use Lelang as a key staging post.

The fortunes of Lelang tended to reflect major political changes in China. Thus, during the usurpation of Wang Mang (9–23 CE) conditions in Korea deteriorated to the point where the Han tribes were raiding the commanderies and carrying off Chinese settlers as slaves. After the collapse of Wang Mang's regime, one of the settlers in Lelang, a certain Wang Tiao, seized control of the commandery and ruled for five years. His murder in 30 CE coincided with the reestablishment of stable government in China and the recovery of Chinese control in Korea. But the Latter Han dynasty in China (25–220) never succeeded in holding much more than half of Emperor Wu's original conquests in the peninsula, for eastern Korea had passed entirely out of Chinese hands and was falling increasingly under the control of the now hostile Koguryŏ tribes, who had set up a kingdom on the frontiers of Xuantu. By the end of the second century CE, when the Latter Han government was beginning to collapse, the Korean commanderies were again threatened by the incursions of Koguryŏ and of the Han tribes farther south.

In 189 the warlord Dong Zhuo seized power in the Chinese imperial capital, Luoyang, and appointed a certain Gongsun Du governor of Liaodong. Unlike Dong Zhuo, Gongsun Du was able to establish his power on a firm basis and found a warlord dynasty that lasted for three generations. Soon after his death in 204 his son and successor, Gongsun Kang, dispatched armies into Korea to reassert Chinese rule there. In order to give greater stability to the Korean administration the southernmost prefectures of Lelang were detached to form a separate commandery named Daifang (Korean, Taebang).

In China itself three competing states had arisen on the ruins of the Latter Han empire, and of these by far the strongest was the Wei dynasty, which ruled North China. In the autumn of 238 Wei armies under the great general Sima Yi overthrew the warlord state of Liaodong and executed Gongsun Yuan, its ruler at that time; a separate expedition was dispatched to take over the Korean commanderies. These victories represented the strongest reassertion of Chinese control over the area since the original conquest in 108 BCE and led to an immediate series of tribute missions to the Wei court from southern Korea and Japan. In 245 another Wei expedition under Guanqiu Jian sacked Hwando, the capital of Koguryŏ, and ravaged that kingdom so thoroughly that it disappeared from history until the next century.

The period from the Wei reconquest to the beginning of the fourth century is really the final flourishing of the commanderies, which now contained a smaller but still considerable number of Chinese settlers, approximately thirty thousand in all. During this period the commanderies also served as a place of exile for members of the imperial house who had fallen from favor. Beginning in 301 the "Wars of the Eight Princes" brought any semblance of orderly administration in North China to an end and the Korean commanderies were isolated for the last time. Lelang now came under increasing pressure from the revived power of Koguryŏ, while Daifang succumbed to the kingdom of Paekche, newly founded by immigrants from the central Manchurian state of Puyŏ. To the north of Liaodong the Murong Xianbei tribes had set up a kingdom that showed a great readiness to adopt Chinese culture and in many respects succeeded to the role of the old Gongsun lordship. In 313 many of the Chinese settlers in Lelang emigrated to the Murong kingdom, and in the winter of 342 to 343 Murong armies sacked the Koguryŏ capital. The commandery of Lelang still led a shadowy existence at this time, as can be seen from the magnificent tomb of Dong Shou, a Liaodong Chinese who may have been its last governor. Soon after his death in 357 Koguryŏ finally swallowed up Lelang.

It is difficult to estimate the effect of four centuries of Chinese rule upon Korean culture. It seems likely that the greatest impact took place after the fall of the commanderies themselves, when their dispossessed ruling elite became advisers and officials in the various Korean kingdoms.

[*See also* Puyŏ; Xianbei; *and* Koguryŏ.]

KENNETH H. J. GARDINER

COMMUNES, CHINESE. *See* People's Communes.

COMMUNISM

CHINESE COMMUNIST PARTY

The founders of the Chinese Communist Party (CCP) sought at first to give intellectual form to an emergent historical situation brimming, they believed, with revolutionary potential. Almost no political experience had been accumulated among the fourteen delegates, representing six Communist cells in Chinese cities, a cell in Japan, and the Communist International in Moscow, who met clandestinely in July 1921 in Shanghai to formally establish a Communist Party. Maring (Hendricus Sneevliet), a Comintern delegate, predicted the group would never be very effective. This "First Congress," as later designated, was dominated by heated arguments about the correct approach to existing political forces, including Sun Yat-sen's National People's Party (Guomindang, Kuomintang, often simply Nationalists). Even though the first meeting ended divisively, labor organization and Party recruitment did continue and the Second Party Congress (July 1922) moved closer to Leninist principles. It adopted a set of organizational principles modeled on the Russian Communist Party's 1919 rules. It also joined the Third International, which involved subjugating itself to the Executive Committee of the Comintern in Moscow, completely centralizing along Leninist lines, and committing itself to multiple underground activities. Membership grew slowly (surpassing one thousand only in 1925), but new recruits were dedicated to effective action and willingly traded their individualism for Party discipline.

The Second Congress, responding to Comintern demands, and against the better judgment of most Chinese delegates, gave tentative approval to explicit collaboration with Sun's Guomindang. Moscow, desiring to ally with Sun for reasons of foreign policy, pressed the CCP to cooperate. The so-called "bloc within" strategy—whereby Communists retained their CCP membership while seeking to push the larger, more powerful Guomindang toward creation of a popular mass base—dominated CCP policy until early 1927. [*See also* Comintern.]

Budding nationalism, fanned by a wave of antiforeign protests and strikes in 1925 (the May Thirtieth Movement), fueled a sharp growth in both labor union and Party membership (almost sixty thousand by April 1927). This Communist drive, by itself enough to unsettle the Nationalists, coincided with the two years following the March 1925 death of Sun, the single leader able to command the respect of all factions. Sun's nominal successor, Chiang Kaishek, subsequently suppressed the Communists and other Guomindang leftists, and in 1927 effectively terminated the first United Front.

Party membership plummeted under Chiang's pressure to ten thousand in just a few months. Mao Zedong, known until then mainly for his contributions to peasant work, emerged along with Zhu De, Peng Dehuai, and others as an advocate of building rural base areas straddling remote provincial borders, defended by units of an independent Red Army. The CCP Central Committee, as it was called after the Sixth Party Congress (18 June to 11 July 1928, held in Moscow by Comintern order), resisted this deviant strategy.

The urban Central Committee in Shanghai met with repeated failure while the rural "soviets" (*suweiai,* borrowing the Russian term for local self-rule along Communist lines) survived and expanded despite material hardship and Nationalist attack. After 1930 the urban strategy collapsed. The Central Committee gradually moved to Ruijin in the "Central Soviet" straddling southern Jiangxi and western Fujian provinces, defended by the Red Army forces of Mao and Zhu. By 1933 the various Red Army units had attained a strength of 200,000 or more, and Party membership had grown to more than 300,000, now mostly peasants instead of classical "proletarians." Moreover, the Party's five years of experience in southern China with soviets, which necessitated close cooperation with local populations, contributed heavily to the "fish in water" military tactics and "mass line" political style characteristic of Mao's later writings and leadership. The altered membership, coupled with long years of revolutionary civil war mounted from rural base areas, caused the Chinese Party to evolve much differently than did its more urban Russian prototype.

Nationalist armies finally drove the CCP from its border-region soviets in mid-1934. As a result, in October of that year the Communists embarked on the year-long, six-thousand-mile Long March, a symbolically heroic epic of incredible endurance and few survivors. Along the way, at an enlarged Party Politburo meeting at Zunyi in Guizhou Province, Mao was named chairman of the Party's influential Military Affairs Committee and was also elected to the Standing Committee of the Politburo, positions that represented a major advance in Mao's status. With only about 10 percent of those who retreated from the South China soviets surviving, the Long March ended in a Communist base area in northern Shaanxi and eastern Ningxia provinces, with the Party leadership headquartered at Yan'an. [*See also* Long March.]

Temporary respite from continuing Nationalist attack was afforded by Japan, whose military pressure on northern China erupted into full-scale invasion in 1937, exciting ever stronger sentiments of Chinese patriotism. Problems of factionalism among the Yan'an leadership were subsumed by the popularity of the spirited CCP resistance against the Japanese invaders. Patriotic youths flocked to Yan'an, and Party membership catapulted from perhaps twenty thousand in 1936 to more than 1.2 million by the time of the Seventh Party Congress in 1945.

Northern Shaanxi, like southern Jiangxi before it, generated strong and symbolic traditions. The Yan'an base was relatively desolate and isolated from almost all outside contact and trade. The Party's socioeconomic programs in "red" base areas under its control were both helped and hurt by its concurrent guerrilla activities in Japanese-occupied "white" areas. The anti-Japanese resistance helped by linking the CCP with a current of intense nationalism. It hurt by forcing several compromises with the more thoroughgoing revolutionary program favored by some Party leaders. Nevertheless the "spirit of Yan'an" would later come to imply stubborn self-reliance in the face of adversity, belief in human will as a real economic and military force, a people's army that refused to burden civilians, and the mass campaign style of political leadership. The well-known two-year Party Rectification Campaign launched in 1942 was only one of several campaigns to follow. Increasingly, both political organization and military strategy reflected the ideas of Mao Zedong, who flowered as a major Marxist theorist during the Yan'an period, writing several treatises on broad problems facing the revolution.

The Seventh Party Congress (23 April to 11 June 1945) confirmed Mao's political rise. Liu Shaoqi praised Mao lavishly, anticipating the leadership cult to follow: "The principal task at present is to mobilize the entire Party to study the Thought of Mao Zedong." [*See also* Liu Shaoqi.] The Seventh Central Committee elected Mao to its newly created post of chairman in June. Chairman Mao went on to dominate Party leadership for thirty-one years until his death in 1976.

During the final four years of civil war against the Nationalists, CCP membership climbed to 4.5 million (late 1949), still mostly peasants. Predictable problems of bureaucracy arose. Nonetheless, despite several leadership disputes over military strategy, united front policy, land reform, and how to treat elites from the old regime, the Party managed to operate effectively with impressive unity. Almost no meetings of central leaders were held during the final years of the civil war. For one and one-half years after the Nationalists invaded Yan'an (March 1947) the Central Committee was split into two groups, one under Mao and one under Liu Shaoqi; each maneuvered separately in combat.

As the Republic of China collapsed and was replaced with a People's Republic (1 October 1949), the CCP was faced with the ultimate problem of revolutionary success: first, building Party organizations in vast new territories, including the big cities, which in the Chinese case fell last; and second, using its leading position to map out and manage the implementation of revolutionary programs. By the time of the Eighth Party Congress (15 to 27 September 1956), membership had grown to more than 10.5 million. Conflict between charismatic leader and Party organization became visible. Mao had engineered both the disbanding of the Party's six powerful regional bureaus during 1954 and 1955 as well as the purging of regional leaders he accused of acting too independently—Gao Gang in the Northeast (Manchuria), and Rao Shushi in east China. [*See also* Gao Gang.] In 1955 Mao had forced a faster pace of agricultural collectivization on reluctant Party bodies responsible for rural affairs. At the Eighth Congress itself, references to Mao personally and to "Mao's Thought" as a guide for all Party activity were conspicuously fewer than they had been eleven years before at the Seventh Congress. The Party organization was developing consensual norms of collective rule and intra-Party democracy. The Party leader was developing his suspicions that such ideals could be corrupted into "independent kingdoms" of self-serving influence. Thus, Mao's call for "people outside the Party to help the Party rectify itself" during the Hundred Flowers period (1956–1957) presaged more dramatic measures to prevent the giant Party bureaucracy from alienating its grass roots. About one million Party members were criticized, placed on probation, or purged as "rightists" during 1957 and 1958. [*See also* Hundred Flowers Campaign.]

The aftermath of the Great Leap Forward and formation of rural people's communes (1958), both Mao's initiatives, led directly to the fateful 1959 Peng Dehuai affair. Marshall Peng, minister of defense and veteran revolutionary from the very first days of the Red Army in Jiangxi, staying well within bounds by existing norms of intra-Party debate, read a "letter of opinion" to the Central Committee in July criticizing the Great Leap. In a surprise reaction, Mao moved vengefully, causing Peng and some of his followers to be removed from all responsible positions. It is possible to date the decline in Party norms, the greater personalization of Mao's leadership, and the origins of the legitimacy crisis that followed Mao's death to this attack on Peng, who appears to have acted loyally. [*See also* Great Leap Forward *and* Peng Dehuai.]

One year later Mao led the CCP to break with Krushchev and the Communist Party of the Soviet

Union over a series of disputes, centering about a Chinese charge that Krushchev was timid in exploiting Soviet nuclear and rocketry capabilities in relations with the United States, and to begin challenging Soviet leadership of international communism. Parties throughout the world developed pro-Soviet and pro-Chinese factions; some (like the Communist Party of Japan) even ended with more nativist parties loyal to neither Moscow nor Beijing. According to one unsubstantiated theory, Mao's attack on Peng can be explained by Mao's belief that Peng was giving voice in Chinese debates to positions favored by Khrushchev.

In the decade after the Eighth Congress, membership doubled to an estimated twenty million (1965). At leading levels almost no changes occurred by purge, retirement, or death. The influx of a new generation of Party members grown up after the revolution, coupled with the absence of opportunities for promotion, added generational cleavage and "stickiness at the top" to universal problems of bureaucracy. Mao supported several intra-Party efforts in the early 1960s to improve Party work style. Notable among them were campaigns to emulate model Party leaders; campaigns to criticize corrupt Party officials; emulation of the political style of the army (where Peng Dehuai's successor, Lin Biao, had initiated study of "the little red book" of quotations from Mao's writings in 1961); creation of army-style "political work departments" in civilian bureaucracies in 1964; a Socialist Education Campaign to clean up lax local organization in the countryside; and a proposal (never implemented) to review every Party member's performance and hence suitability to remain a member.

By early 1966, however, Mao, now sixty-two years old, decided the organization was entrenched enough to resist such a reformist approach. The charismatic leader's answer, which addressed other concerns as well, was to call "the people" one more time and direct a mass campaign against established Party authorities on a scale never before imagined, the Great Proletarian Cultural Revolution of 1966 to 1969. As elite resistance grew, Mao proved willing boldly to lend his authority to an ad hoc "Small Group in Charge of the Cultural Revolution" presided over by his wife, Jiang Qing. The Small Group encouraged mass factions of student "Red Guards" and workers to arrest and persecute Party leaders, and to completely suspend Party meetings and operations for nearly two years. Lin Biao kept the army on the sidelines for the most part, which allowed the People's Liberation Army (PLA) to be held up as a political model for a reorganized Party; participants in the Cultural Revolution waved Lin's little red book of Mao quotations ritualistically.

When the tumult was brought under control in late 1968 with the help of PLA commanders, and a Ninth Party Congress finally held (1–24 April 1969), the reconstituted CCP displayed factional victory for supporters of the Cultural Revolution. Of the twenty-one members of the new governing Politburo, only nine were veterans of the old one: six new Politburo members were part of Lin Biao's faction; another six were part of Jiang Qing's faction. A precise measure is not available, but at least several hundred thousand Party members at all levels were replaced with Cultural Revolution activists. [*See also* Great Proletarian Cultural Revolution.]

Lin's advance proved very temporary. Mao resisted Lin's drive for succession to Party leadership; Lin, increasingly desperate, plotted to assassinate the chairman. Apparently he was betrayed by his daughter and died trying to escape (September 1971). Reaction to the Lin Biao affair caused military influence in Party leadership to decline again quickly. The Tenth Party Congress, convened only four years later (24–28 August 1973), was an arena for conflict between those who defended and opposed the Cultural Revolution. Jiang's "Gang of Four," as her faction was labeled after it was toppled in 1976, defended the Cultural Revolution's radical policies and personnel changes. Their adversaries, rallying about Premier Zhou Enlai and former Party General Secretary Deng Xiaoping, favored scuttling "ultraleft" policies and rehabilitating Party members who had been criticized or purged in the late 1960s. Time was on the side of Zhou and Deng, but Mao's enormous authority remained a trump card for the Jiang group until the chairman died in September 1976. [*See also* Lin Biao; Jiang Qing; Gang of Four; *and* Zhou Enlai.]

Party membership continued to rise in the post-Mao era, surpassing 40 million by 1984. More than 5 million new members had joined since Mao's death, 800,000 of them in 1983 alone. New recruits' "history and behavior during the Cultural Revolution" is now being examined carefully to screen out former supporters of Jiang Qing who might oppose Deng Xiaoping's modernization policies. At the same time, a special effort is being made to overcome the Party's "traditional bias" against intellectuals and to recruit more students and more workers in industry, communications, finance, commerce, and agriculture. The 1960s problem of "stickiness at the top" is being replaced with a fundamental cleavage dividing Cultural Revolution activists loyal to the ideological style of Mao and supporters of modernization policies more favorable to the professional style of Deng.

The Eleventh Party Congress (12–18 August 1977) confirmed Hua Guofeng as chairman, succeeding Mao Zedong; Deng delivered a key speech. The path-breaking Third Plenum of the Eleventh Central Committee (December 1978) reflected Deng's growing influence and set in place important economic policies that widened the scope of individual incentives. The Fifth Plenum (February 1980) removed Hua's allies from the Politburo and added two Deng allies—Zhao Ziyang and Hu Yaobang—to the Politburo's Standing Committee. It restored the Central Secretariat, which Mao had abolished in his Cultural Revolution, and elected Hu Yaobang as general secretary. It also approved "Guiding Principles for Inner-Party Political Life," reviving Party norms in operation in the 1950s before Mao started to discard them beginning with his purge of Peng Dehuai. The CCP of Deng Xiaoping, it was decided, would be controlled from within the organization, not from without by Mao's "mass line" techniques. Finally, the Twelfth Party Congress (1–11 September 1982) demoted Chairman Hua Guofeng to simple Central Committee member status; eliminated Hua's post of chairman, thereby raising General Secretary Hu to the equivalent of Party leader; created a new "Central Advisory Commission" to which most aging senior leaders were to be gracefully retired; and approved a three-year "rectification" designed to retire Party members who would not support Deng's reforms. In a Party shake-up that followed massive student protests in December 1986, however, Hu was dismissed as Party secretary and was temporarily replaced by Zhao Ziyang; this shift was an apparent victory for those opposed to the changes imposed by Deng. [*See also* Hu Yaobang and Zhao Ziyang.]

Flowing beneath the surface of more visible political currents in the 1980s, at unsounded depth, is a legitimacy crisis, described in official statements as a "crisis of confidence," betraying dangerous popular fascination with materialist, capitalist, and foreign values. Deng's response, a comprehensive effort to build "socialist spiritual civilization," pinpoints the CCP's next major task—recapturing the belief of the Chinese people that the Communist Party deserves to rule.

[*See also* Marxism and Socialism: Marxism in China; Chen Duxiu; Li Dazhao; Zhu De; Mao Zedong; *and* Deng Xiaoping.]

Lowell Dittmer, "The 12th Congress of the Communist Party of China," *China Quarterly* 93 (March 1983): 108–124. James Pinckney Harrison, *The Long March to Power: A History of the Chinese Communist Party, 1921–1972* (1972). Hu Ch'iao-mu, *Thirty Years of the CCP* (1952). Warren Kuo, *Analytical History of the CCP*, 4 vols. (1968–1971). John Wilson Lewis, ed., *Party Leadership and Revolutionary Power in China* (1963; reprint, 1978). Stuart R. Schram, "To Utopia and Back: A Cycle in the History of the Chinese Communist Party," *China Quarterly* 87 (September 1981): 407–439. Franz Schurmann, *Ideology and Organization in Communist China* (1968). Frederick C. Teiwes, *Politics and Purges in China* (1979).

GORDON BENNETT

COMMUNIST PARTIES IN SOUTH ASIA

Although there had been some influence of Marxism on early South Asian nationalists, the 1917 Russian Revolution gave great impetus to the formation of communist parties in the region.With the help and direction of the Comintern, Indian leaders both inside and outside India tried to organize communist groups and a communist party in India from about 1919. Some contacts were made in Tashkent by M. N. Roy, who had joined the Comintern in 1919. He became a conduit for funds and sent agents to Bombay and Calcutta, where Communists tried to shape the labor movement, influence the Congress, and recruit intellectuals. [*See* Roy, Manabendra Nath.]

The Communist Party of India (CPI) was secretly formed in the early 1920s, while workers' and peasants' parties helped to bridge the illegal activities of the Communists with their open efforts at mass organizing. The British government of India combatted this activity through the Cawnpore and Meerut conspiracy cases (1924 and 1929), in which key Communist organizers were tried and imprisoned. Communist leaders were also bedeviled by their wavering approach to noncommunist nationalists. They alternately praised and attacked Mohandas Gandhi and even the more left-wing nationalists Jawaharlal Nehru and Subhas Chandra Bose.

From the mid-1930s, when the Comintern shifted to a United Front line in its efforts to oppose fascism, the Communists worked within the Congress Socialist Party and the Indian National Congress.The Communists were pushed out of the Congress Socialist Party at the beginning of World War II, but they had already built strong cadres in Bengal and Kerala, which have been maintained.

The CPI at first stood on the side of other nationalists in opposing the forced entry of India into the war by fiat of the government of India. But all changed with the Nazi invasion of the Soviet Union, and within a short time CPI policy shifted in favor of the war effort. An imperialist war had now become a people's war and in 1942 the CPI was declared legal. The support for the government's position at this crucial time when most noncommunist nationalists were imprisoned, underground, or outside India was not forgotten, and did the CPI no good.

At the end of the war Gandhi moved to eliminate the Communists from the Congress, for he and the High Command believed that the Communists were more concerned with orders from Moscow than with the fate of India. The Communists were not in tune with the Congress on another vital concern: the Pakistan issue. In the early 1940s, following what they believed to be Stalin's view of the nationality question, the CPI supported the movement for a separate Muslim state in India as a legitimate nationalism.

In the period just after independence and partition, the Communists shifted to the ultra-left line under pressure from the international Communist movement. During the years 1948 to 1951, many Communists encouraged violent uprisings, and, consequently, they were imprisoned or had to go underground. In 1948 the CPI guided the formation of the Communist Party of Pakistan (CPP), which has remained numerically very small. General Secretary Sajjad Zaheer led some two hundred Communists in West Pakistan; the party has not been able to gain much ground and was declared illegal for much of the 1950s and 1960s. Some of the Communists entered other parties sympathetic to leftist ideas, such as Mian Ifikarudin's Azad Pakistan Party and the left wing of the National Awami Party. Radical ideas spread more through leftist newspapers such as the *Pakistan Times* (up to 1959, when the government of Pakistan took it over) than through an explicitly communist movement.

Within India, the CPI moved away from violent uprisings (such as the Telengana Movement) in 1951 and entered legal and parliamentary politics. The movement has remained strong in West Bengal and Kerala and has shown some strength in Andhra Pradesh, Bihar, and the Punjab. [*See* Telengana Movement.] The CPI formed a state government in Kerala in 1957 with E. M. S. Namboodripad as chief minister, but the central government toppled this government in 1959. The CPI continued to manifest support in Kerala and West Bengal and was an important opposition group in the Lok Sabha while the party was united. [*See also* Namboodripad, E. M. S.]

In 1964 the CPI split just after India's border war with China. The party still called CPI was more closely tied to Moscow, and the new Communist Party of India (Marxist), or CPM, initially said to be more pro-Chinese, was generally less beholden to foreign sources. The CPM and the CPI have participated in state governments in Kerala and the CPM has dominated coalition state governments in West Bengal in the periods from 1967 to 1971 and from 1977 to the present. The CPM has also organized the state government in Tripura. Both in Kerala and West Bengal the successful Communists have had considerable support in the countryside, particularly among lower ranks of the peasantry, as well as some urban middle-class and worker support. They have tried to pass legislation favoring the lower peasantry and the workers. What neither the CPI nor the CPM has been able to do is to build a national party, with strength in many regions, that could serve as a potential national governing party.

In the mid-1960s another split in the movement occurred with the development of the Naxalites, who decried the parliamentary approach of the CPI and CPM and wanted an immediate communist revolution. Much to their chagrin, the more parliamentary Communists often had to watch and participate in the ruthless crushing of the Naxalite efforts by the Indian government and the forces of law and order. [*See* Naxalites.]

In East Pakistan, Moni Singh helped to establish the Communist Party of East Pakistan (CPEP), which was pro-Moscow, as was the CPI. Communists in East Pakistan entered other parties, including the Ganatantri Dal, the Awami League, and especially the National Awami Party of Maulana Bhasani. The East Pakistani Communists also split in the mid-1960s into more pro-Moscow and more pro-Beijing factions, and then the factions split into factions with different views of the sociopolitical situation, different strategies, and little doctrinal unity. In independent Bangladesh several parties of Communists continue despite rule by military governments. [*See* Awami League.]

The Marxist parties of Sri Lanka had their origins in the Lanka Sama Samaja Party (LSSP), founded in 1935. In 1940 supporters of Stalin and the Comintern left to form the Ceylon Communist Party, leaving the LSSP to Trotskyites. Both the LSSP and the CP flourished in the Western Province of the island and split in the 1960s, but the major parties remaining from these divisions joined with the Sri Lanka Freedom Party in a United Front that was victorious in the 1970 elections. They participated in the new government, which was shortly hampered by an uprising of young revolutionary Communists in 1971. Since 1977 the communist parties in Sri Lanka have opposed the government. [*See* Lanka Sama Samaja Party *and* Sri Lanka Freedom Party.]

Communist parties in South Asia have been riven by factionalism and doctrinal disputes but nevertheless have had an influence on the political culture of their nations far beyond their party membership. They have had success in only a few regions of the area, particularly in Kerala and West Bengal in India and the Western Province of Sri Lanka. There has been a tension in all of these parties between those wishing to adopt more revolutionary means to the eventual triumph of the working masses of the population and those desiring more constitutional means. Marxists in an ethnically plural area of the world have had to tussle again and again with different forms of the national question, and neither they nor their respective nations have yet resolved the bitter choices involved.

[*See also* Kerala; Bengal; Sri Lanka; *and* Tripura.]

G. Adhikari, ed., *Documents of the History of the Communist Party of India* (1971–1979). Paul B. Brass and Marcus F. Franda, eds., *Radical Politics in South Asia* (1973). Bipan Chandra, ed., *The Indian Left* (1983). Marcus F. Franda, *Radical Politics in West Bengal* (1971). T. J. Nossiter, *Communism in Kerala: A Study in Political Adaptation* (1982). Gene D. Overstreet and Marshall Windmiller, *Communism in India* (1959). Bhabani Sen Gupta, *Communism in Indian Politics* (1972).

LEONARD A. GORDON

COMMUNISM IN JAPAN

The writings of Karl Marx were first introduced into Japan in the 1880s, but serious interest in socialist doctrines developed only with the industrial expansion that followed the Sino-Japanese War in 1895. Intellectuals, many of them Christians, formed study groups and fledgling political parties that were quickly banned by the authorities, who bracketed socialism with anarchism. Patterns of radical activity sometimes seemed to confirm such fears; Kōtoku Shūsui, who published a translation of the *Communist Manfesto* in the *Commoners' Daily (Heimin shimbun)* in 1904, went on to become a pioneer anarchist and was ultimately executed for alleged complicity in the Great Treason Plot of 1910.

The years after World War I produced a new wave of interest in reformist thought, and the Bolshevik Revolution made Marxism seem more applicable. In July 1922 the Japan Communist Party (JCP) was founded as a branch of the Comintern by a group of socialists. Younger members included Nosaka Sanzō, Tokuda Kyūichi, and Shiga Yoshio. Until 1945 the Party remained a small group, vigorously pursued by government legislation against dangerous thought. The Peace Preservation Act of 1925 established Special Higher (thought control) Police to guard against criticism of the "national polity," and in 1928 sanctions were increased to include the death penalty. In 1928 and 1929 sweeping roundups of Communists were followed by sensational and public trials that ended in 1932 with convictions for all those accused.

Some recanted under the emotional pressure of the wave of nationalism that followed the Manchurian Incident of 1931; others (Nosaka) managed to make their way to China and the headquarters of the Chinese Communist Party after serving their terms, while others (Tokuda) were in prison until 1945. [*See* Nosaka Sanzō *and* Tokuda Kyūichi.] While politically ineffective, Marxist thought nevertheless became powerful in social science analyses of modern Japanese society and the nature of Japanese capitalism. Communist Party theses prescribed from Moscow took confusing turns, as a result of political and ideolical struggles there, but also contributed powerful slogans (e.g., the "emperor system" as a construct for capitalist and landlord oppression) for postwar debate.

When veteran Communist leaders were released from prison on orders of the American Occupation forces in 1945, the JCP was reformed in October 1945. The Party prospered in the confusion of postsurrender days, but after the Office of the Supreme Commander of the Allied Powers ruled against a general strike in 1947, a first wave of activism receded. Even so, the JCP rose to claim approximately 10 percent of the votes and 35 seats in the lower house of the Diet in 1949. The Korean War, however, brought a "red purge" of JCP leaders, and when the party responded with violence and terrorism it rapidly lost public support.

The JCP learned from this to refrain from slavish subordination to the Russian and Chinese parties. Instead, it developed tactics calling for a peaceful transition to socialism, stressing that postwar modernization in Japan had removed the need for extremist measures or for dictatorship. The Party formally broke with the Russian Communist Party in 1963/1964 and with the Chinese Communist Party in 1966/1967 and thereafter showed a more independent and nationalist disposition. In parliamentary elections the JCP has drawn approximately 10 percent of the votes, but seldom more than 6 or 7 percent of the seats.

George M. Beckman and Okubo Genji, *The Japanese Communist Party, 1922–1945* (1969). Robert A. Scalapino, *The Japanese Communist Movement, 1920–1966* (1967). Rodger Swearingen and Paul Langer, *Red Flag in Japan* (1952).

MARIUS B. JANSEN

COMMUNISM IN KOREA

The first Korean communist organization was created in Khabarovsk, Siberia, in June 1918, under the name Korean People's Socialist Party (Hanin Sahoedang) by exiled nationalists struggling for the liberation of Korea from Japanese rule. It had the encouragement and blessing of the Bolsheviks who were fighting against the White Russians and the Allied Expeditionary Forces in Siberia. The Koreans believed that the Bolsheviks could be induced to fight against Japanese imperialism, or at least to give active assistance to the nationalist cause, if the Koreans supported them in their early struggles. In April 1919 the Korean socialists took the name Korean Communist Party (Koryŏ Kongsandang) and moved their headquarters to Vladivostok. Soon afterward the headquarters was moved to Shanghai, where the nationalist Korean provisional government had been established.

While Lenin's government provided some financial assistance, the Bolsheviks failed to move against the Japanese after consolidating their power, and the Korean Communists fell into dissension. The Comintern instructed them to concentrate on forming a party based in Korea itself. Agents from Vladivostok and young Korean intellectuals recently converted to Marxism in Japanese universities became the nucleus of the new Korean Communist Party (KCP, or Chosŏn Kongsandang), founded on 25 April 1925 in Seoul.

Soon after its founding the underground party ran into a formidable obstacle—the Japanese police. Mass arrests in December 1925, June 1926, and February and July 1928 virtually wiped out the small number of converts. Serious internal dissension also developed, and in December 1928 the Comintern rescinded its recognition of the KCP as a section and ordered the Korean Communists to build a strong base among workers and peasants.

Various communist groups inside and outside Korea did make serious efforts. The Chinese Communist Party, which absorbed the Korean Communists in Manchuria in 1930, sent agents into Korea through its branches in Manchuria and Shanghai. The Comintern and Profintern dispatched a score of Moscow-trained agents between 1930 and 1935. Most of those sent, however, were intercepted by the Japanese police, and although some did succeed at various times in organizing farmers in the northwestern parts of Korea, these movements, each involving a few hundred persons, were suppressed. By the early 1940s the Japanese had imposed totalitarian control over Korea, and the Communist efforts could not be continued.

The Japanese surrender in August 1945 dramatically altered that situation. Particularly in Soviet-occupied North Korea, the building of the Communist Party became a priority task. Even in American-occupied South Korea the Communists enjoyed considerable freedom during at least the first two postwar years. These efforts were accompanied by an intense power struggle among the Communists—Pak Hŏn-yŏng and his comrades of the "domestic faction," who had weathered the storms of Japanese persecution in Korea during the previous two decades, Kim Il Sung (Kim Il-sŏng) and his followers, who had been a part of the Chinese Communist-controlled Northeastern Anti-Japanese Allied Army in Manchuria and engaged in guerrilla warfare against the Japanese there between 1934 and 1941; and the "Yan'an returnees" from China, who had collaborated with the Chinese Communists in northwest China in the anti-Japanese struggle. The guerrillas under Kim Il Sung's personal command had once numbered between two and three hundred men but had been reduced to a much smaller contingent after their retreat to Siberia in 1941. Kim's group returned to Korea with the Soviet army, which also brought in a number of Koreans born and raised in Siberia who were subsequently identified as the "Soviet faction." The Yan'an returnees were also few in number, although the group had built up a sizable army in Manchuria after the Japanese surrender by enlisting young Korean men who had previously been conscripted into the Japanese army.

In September 1945 the domestic-faction Communists began the task of rebuilding the KCP and established a party headquarters in Seoul. Kim Il Sung, however, established the North Korean branch of the KCP in P'yŏngyang in October 1945, taking office as first secretary. Recruitment was emphasized and in December the North Korean group was reorganized as the North Korean Communist Party (NKCP, or Puk Chosŏn Kongsandang). In August 1946 the NKCP merged with the New Democratic Party (NDP, or Shinmindang), which had been organized since March by the Yan'an returnees and was rapidly expanding its membership, particularly among the middle class. The NKCP, in contrast, had emphasized its efforts among the workers and peasants. The merged party was named the North Korean Workers' Party (NKWP, or Puk Chosŏn Nodongdang).

Within a few days—on 4 September—the KCP in South Korea took part in a similar merger with a radical segment of the People's Party (Inmindang) and the NDP, which had only nominal existence in South Korea, and established the South Korean Workers' Party (SKWP). The timing and manner of the merger suggest that the developments in South Korea were not totally voluntary.

The Communist movement in South Korea suffered from the unfavorable attitude taken by the United States occupation authorities after 1946, but food shortages, political confusion, and the delay in implementing reform measures created opportunities for the Communists. They staged numerous strikes and riots, including armed riots on Cheju Island, extending from April 1948 into the following year. A regiment of the South Korean army rebelled under Communist leadership in the port city of Yŏsu, precipitating a major crisis for the new regime in Seoul and providing the basic forces for guerrilla operations in the mountains. There is no doubt that the Communists had a large following in South Korea. At its peak, the SKWP is said to have had 370,000 members.

The Republic of Korea government, formed in South Korea in August 1948, suppressed all manifestations of the radical left, and many of the principal Communist leaders went North. Finally, in June 1949, the SKWP and the NKWP united officially as a single party, the Korean Workers' Party (KWP), signaling the final capitulation of the domestic-faction leaders to Kim Il Sung. Kim became the chairman of the united party, and Pak Hŏn-yŏng the vice-chairman.

It was under these conditions that the Communist regime in the North launched the Korean War in June 1950. Although the North Korean army occupied most of South Korea by August, the unexpected US intervention, particularly General MacArthur's Inch'ŏn landing in September 1950, frustrated the original aim of a Communist unification of the country. The disastrous outcome of the attempted Communist takeover affected Party politics. Soon after the 1953 truce, leaders of the domestic faction who had held important cabinet and Party positions in North Korea were tried and convicted as American spies. The Soviet and Yan'an faction objected to Kim Il Sung's concentration of power, and there were differences of opinion regarding the pace of agricultural collectivization and industrial construction. The Kim Il Sung group, however, outmaneuvered and outnumbered the opposition in a 1956 purge and another purge of the same nature in 1958, effectively eliminating all opposition.

Even before opposition leaders were eliminated, Kim Il Sung had begun the task of rebuilding the Party, which had suffered a severe loss in membership during the war. Not only was the quality of the membership extremely low, but the new recruits suffered from severe deficiencies as well. The task of remodeling and strengthening the Party organization received special attention in 1955. Kim stressed the need to domesticate or "koreanize" communism. He emphasized the need to establish *chuch'e,* or "the foundation of self-determinant action." In order to accomplish this goal, Kim proceeded to exalt the experiences of the anti-Japanese guerrillas in Manchuria. A massive campaign to "learn from the guerrillas" was to follow. The Party stressed ideological fortification, dedication to nationalism, and loyalty to the leader.

The newly fostered revolutionary tradition thus served as a background for building a heightened cult of personality centered on Kim Il Sung. The cult subsequently extended to his family. Since 1968 numerous books and articles have been published extolling the "revolutionary family" that produced the great leader. The unprecedented building of the cult around the leader's family was to assume significance in the selection of the leader's son, Kim Jong Il (Kim Chong-il), as his successor at the Sixth Congress of the Korean Workers' Party held in November 1980. He was reportedly groomed for leadership as early as the mid-1960s.

The KWP's estimated membership in the late 1970s was 2.5 million out of a total population of approximately 17 million. The Party is governed by the top elite of the Political Bureau, or Politburo, (formerly the Political Committee) and the second echelon leaders of the Central Committee. The Party has provincial, country, and other local branches and party cells. As in other Communist countries, party members are selected carefully on the basis of their family background, ideological dedication, and competence, although not necessarily in that order.

Few parties in the world stressed the importance of ideological education more strenuously than the KWP. All undesirable elements were purged from the Party at all levels. The society itself was carefully insulated from all possible "corrupting" influences from abroad. Accordingly it was reasonable to presume that every aspect of the Party had been remolded to the satisfaction of the leader.

Despite this, indications were that the leader did not find the performance of the top-level cadres and membership fully satisfactory, as indicated by the high rate of turnover in top-level Party organizations, including the Politburo and the Central Committee. The Party's top elite also has undergone a rapid generational change as most of Kim Il Sung's cohorts have died of old age.

The launching in 1973 of the Three Revolution Team Movement was an indication that, at least from Kim Il Sung's perspective, problems existed among lower- as well as higher-level cadres. The movement was aimed at speeding up the pace of economic development by doing away with outdated ideas and methods. Leadership was to be provided by teams of young intellectuals, who between 1973 and 1975 were dispatched in groups of about thirty or forty to factories and other enterprises to provide guidance to local cadres in carrying out ideological, technical, and cultural revolutions.

In a number of major speeches in 1976 Kim Il Sung identified the source of the problem as "old cadres," ill-equipped by education and experience to work in the area of modern science and technology, as was required in all domains of economic construction. Although the basic problem was that of lagging behind in scientific and technological studies, the Party leadership also found defects in the old cadres' ideology, viewing them as being imbued with "conservatism, empiricism, bureaucratism, and other outdated ideas." By "empiricism" was meant the tendency to exaggerate the significance of old experience, trying to fit the knowledge gained from it into new realities through stale formulas. A cadre exhibiting "empiricism," might, for example, cling to the announced capacity of a machine, not trusting the creativity of the masses and the might of their reform movement to increase it.

Kim's observations in 1976 left the impression that residual "decadent" thought and behavioral patterns remained and that the work of the Three Revolution Teams would be continued. Like China's Mao Zedong, Kim has affirmed the need for protracted or permanent revolution. In this context his remark that ideological activities carried out by the Three Revolution Teams were analogous to a first weeding on the farms revealed ongoing leadership concerns. Some of the Party branches were dormant or inactive; some young people and some Party cadres were accused of behaving in high-handed ways. "Bureaucratism," even after two decades of intensive campaigning, had not been eradicated and public property was not always properly maintained. The Three Revolution Teams had modified some anti-Party behavior, but as Kim admitted, its roots remained deeply imbedded despite the repeated weeding. The Sixth Party Congress installed Kim Jong Il in the fourth position in the Politburo, the second position in the Secretariat (after General Secretary Kim Il Sung), and the third position in the Military Commission. The younger leader reportedly spearheaded the Three Revolution Team Movement, and will undoubtedly affect the future course of the KWP.

[*See also* Korea, Democratic People's Republic of; Korean War; Kim Il Sung; *and* Kim Jong Il.]

Chong-sik Lee and Robert A. Scalapino, *Communism in Korea* (1974). CHONG-SIK LEE

COMMUNISM IN SOUTHEAST ASIA

Communism is firmly established in three Southeast Asian states—those constituting former French Indochina—but the rigors of this consolidation have effectively reduced prospects of communist expansion elsewhere in the region. The falling dominoes apparently ended with Cambodia (Kampuchea).

Communism first appeared in Southeast Asia after the Bolshevik Revolution in 1917. In 1920 Dutch and native revolutionaries in Java launched the Partai Komunis Indonesia (PKI), the first communist party in Asia. A decade later communist parties were established in Indochina, Malaya, and the Philippines and at the end of the 1930s in Burma. During World War II a clandestine party was formed in Thailand, the only independent Southeast Asian state at the time.

Moscow considered communist activity appropriate in these predominantly agrarian areas since Lenin had argued in 1920 that colonies represented the "weakest link of imperialism" and that national liberation in peripheral areas might trigger proletarian revolution in metropolitan ones. But while the Comintern observed communist activity in Southeast Asia, it made little effort to direct or coordinate strategies. Native revolutionaries, such as Nguyen Ai Quoc (Ho Chi Minh) of Vietnam, played the leading roles in fashioning most Southeast Asian parties; however, in colonies with active overseer Chinese communities, such as Malaya and Thailand, Chinese communist influence was dominant. Even without explicit guidance from Moscow, the Southeast Asian parties followed the international communist line on such issues as the united front against fascism and, later, Japanese militarism.

The outbreak of World War II in Southeast Asia

prompted new roles for local communists, profoundly affecting the region's politics after the war. During 1941 and 1942, communist-led military coalitions formed against the Japanese and their local allies in Indochina, Malaya, and the Philippines (the Viet Minh, the Malayan People's Anti-Japanese Army, and the Hukbalahap). In Indonesia and Burma, underground communist guerrillas, in an effort to ensure independence after the war, coordinated strategies with local nationalists collaborating with the Japanese occupation.

Communist prospects in Southeast Asia after the war, considered daunting by noncommunist observers and promising by the communists themselves, were frustrated by the course of events. Moscow, preoccupied with the consolidation of wartime gains both in Eastern Europe and northeast Asia, did not encourage Southeast Asian communists to use their current advantage to seek power through insurrection before the colonial armies returned. Although Chinese communist victories in 1948–1949 stimulated a round of communist rebellions—successively in Burma, Malaya, Indonesia, and the Philippines—these risings were poorly coordinated, and none succeeded.

Only in Indochina, where civil war broke out between the Viet Minh and returning French colonists in 1946, did communism become established. The Geneva Agreement of 1954 assured the Viet Minh sovereignty in North Vietnam, but it was not until the mid-1970s that bitter war between the North Vietnamese and Viet Cong, on one side, and the South Vietnamese and Americans, on the other, guaranteed Hanoi control over all of Vietnam. Vietnamese communists quickly extended their influence over Laos, and in 1978 they invaded Kampuchea to complete hegemony in former French Indochina.

This was the high point of communist expansion in Southeast Asia. Vietnam's armed hegemony since 1976 has resulted in a clear division of Southeast Asia into two irreconcilable camps. Six states outside the Vietnamese orbit—Indonesia, Thailand, Malaysia, Singapore, the Philippines, and now Brunei—are joined in the Association of Southeast Asian Nations (ASEAN), initially an economic union but one with increasing overtones of a defensive barrier against communist expansion; Burma, though neutral, also opposes Vietnamese expansion. Meanwhile, the lure of communism as a social and economic order has dimmed as a result of intractable problems in Vietnam. The Soviet Union has assisted the Vietnamese, both in domestic reconstruction and in regional ventures, but has failed to add luster to either Hanoi or to the communist experience. The most influential state in the area, potentially China, has become so estranged from the Vietnamese communists that Beijing may be more likely to block communist expansion in Southeast Asia than to promote it.

[*See also* Partai Komunis Indonesia; Ho Chi Minh; Malayan People's Anti-Japanese Army; Huk; Viet Minh; New People's Army; Pathet Lao; Malayan Communist Party; Geneva Conference of 1954; Indochina War; *and* Association of Southeast Asian Nations. *For further information on communism in Southeast Asia, see articles on the individual countries.*]

Charles B. McLane, *Soviet Strategies in Southeast Asia: An Exploration of Eastern Policy under Lenin and Stalin* (1966). Ruth T. McVey, *The Rise of Indonesian Communism* (1965). Robert A. Scalapino, ed., *The Communist Revolution in Asia: Tactics, Goals and Achievements* (2d ed., 1969). Anthony Short, *The Communist Insurrection in Malaya, 1948–1960* (1975). Justus Maria Van der Kroef, *Communism in Southeast Asia* (1980).

CHARLES B. MCLANE

COMMUNIST-EXTERMINATION CAMPAIGNS (1930–1934), attempt by Chiang Kai-shek to completely destroy the Communists in China. Following the breakdown of the first United Front between the Guomindang (Kuomintang, or Nationalist Party) and the Chinese Communists, Mao Zedong and Zhu De established a revolutionary base in the remote and mountainous area of southeastern Jiangxi Province. In 1930 the Central Committee of the Communist Party, headed by Li Lisan in Shanghai, ordered the Communist army to seize the perceived opportunity of a "rising revolutionary tide," unite with the urban proletariat, and occupy such urban centers as Wuhan and Changsha. This attempt at armed revolution failed miserably, but it alerted Chiang Kai-shek to the threat that the Communists still posed to national stability and unity. He therefore determined to launch a "bandit-suppression" campaign to wipe out the last traces of communism in China.

Since breaking with Soviet Russia in 1927, Chiang Kai-shek had turned to the Germans for assistance in training and equipping the Nationalist army. Convinced that his well-trained army could easily defeat the ill-equipped guerrilla forces of the Communists, Chiang launched his first "Communist-Extermination" campaign in December 1930, announcing that the Communists would be eliminated "within three months, or six months at most." However, the political leadership and socioeconomic reforms of the Communists had made the army of Mao and Zhu a spirited fighting force. By employing guerrilla tactics and emphasizing effective intelligence and rapid mobility, they repulsed the attacking Nationalist forces. Between 1931 and 1933 Chiang launched three more unsuccessful bandit campaigns, each time with larger concentrations of troops.

Chiang's fifth campaign, from April 1933 to October 1934, was more successful. With the advice of the famed German strategist General Hans von Seeckt, Chiang adopted a plan of blockading the Communist area, impeding all ingoing and outgoing traffic, and progressively drawing tighter the string of fortifications surrounding the area. These measures blunted the effectiveness of the Communists' guerrilla tactics, and the Communist leadership subsequently admitted that their own commanders had committed the error of resorting to positional warfare. Outnumbered 700,000 to 150,000 men, the Communists faced certain defeat. In October 1934, therefore, they broke out of the blockaded area with a remnant force of 90,000 troops and set off on the fabled Long March, which ended one year and six thousand miles later in the arid hills of Shaanxi Province.

[*See also* Chiang Kai-shek; Communism: Chinese Communist Party; Guomindang; Long March; Mao Zedong; Northern Expedition; *and* Zhu De.]

LLOYD E. EASTMAN

COMPRADORS (Chinese, *maiban;* "purchasers"), the "Chinese managers" of foreign business firms in modern China. The compradors were regarded by many as tools of Western economic imperialism; others considered them promoters of China's modernization and middlemen who bridged the economic and cultural gap between East and West. With the rise of nationalism and Marxism, China's economic relations with the West during the mid-nineteenth to mid-twentieth century came to be regarded by many Chinese as detrimental to its national economy. Because they worked professionally for the foreign merchants, the compradors were often viewed as spearheads of foreign colonialism and economic imperialism. In many respects, however, the compradors played a significant role in modern China's economic development, for the foreign trade they promoted provided a tremendous impetus for economic change. Wealthy (with a total income of around 530 million taels in the 1842–1894 period), willing to take risks, and possessing business and financial experience, the nouveau riches compradors (such as Tong King-sing and Zheng Guanying) became investors, managers, and entrepreneurs in China's leading modern enterprises, such as the China Merchants' Steam Navigation Company (1872), the Kaiping Mines (1878), the Yuanchang Machinery Company (1883), and the Shanghai Cotton Cloth Mill (1890).

The compradors' sociopolitical role was that of a commercial gentry, serving as social leaders in the treaty ports. Inasmuch as new ideas and attitudes underlay the modern enterprises, they became promoters of new ideas (e.g., limited liability) and, consequently, challengers of some of China's traditional values (such as civil service examinations). Because the compradors' activities involved interaction between two cultures at a variety of levels, the compradors serve as examples of the "marginal man"—influenced by, and in turn exerting influences on, different cultures, while belonging to neither.

[*See also* Canton; China Trade; *and* Qing Dynasty.]

Yen-p'ing Hao, *The Comprador in Nineteenth Century China: Bridge between East and West* (1970).

YEN-P'ING HAO

CONFRONTATION (Indonesian, Konfrontasi), Indonesia's sustained campaign of opposition to the formation of Malaysia from 1963 to 1965, based on a widely held belief that Britain's Malaysia proposal, which retained the significant authority of Malay sultans and allowed the British to maintain their military bases, would create a neocolony on Indonesia's borders. Indonesia's claims to a regional sphere of influence were also aroused by Britain's failure to consult Indonesia over the proposal, and the abortive Brunei revolt of December 1962 appeared to many Indonesians to indicate that the scheme was being imposed against the will of local inhabitants.

Confrontation also served specific political interests within Indonesia. It gave Sukarno an external focus for antagonism that could diffuse the growing political and social tension within Indonesia and distract public attention from the perilous state of the economy. It enabled the Indonesian Communist Party (the Partai Komunis Indonesia, or PKI) to campaign on an issue that was both nationalist and leftist and to argue that workers and peasants be armed for the struggle. It also kept Indonesia antagonistic to Western powers and removed important anti-Communist army units from the centers of political power in Java. Although it strengthened the army's claim to a larger share of the budget and to political influence, some army leaders were unhappy with the political consequences of Confrontation and maintained clandestine contact with British and Malaysian authorities to ensure that the conflict did not escalate into war.

Hostilities were limited to the sacking of the British embassy in Jakarta in September 1963, a protracted but small-scale war along the land border in Kalimantan, and a number of Indonesian commando raids in peninsular Malaysia in August and September 1964. In late 1965 the Suharto government gradually relaxed Confrontation, and in August 1966 relations between Indonesia and Malaysia were normalized.

[*See also* Malaysia; Sukarno; *and* Partai Komunis Indonesia.]

Michael Leifer, *Indonesian Foreign Policy* (1983). Franklin B. Weinstein, *Indonesia Abandons Confrontation* (1969). ROBERT B. CRIBB

CONFUCIANISM. A modern term for which there was no exact equivalent in premodern East Asia, *Confucianism* refers to a social and political philosophy and to a political ideology derived from that philosophy. In both senses, Confucianism was profoundly influential in China and in surrounding countries where the Chinese cultural influence was strong, especially Korea, Japan, and Annam (Vietnam).

The founders of the Confucian school were Confucius (latinized form of the name Kong Fuzi; 551–479 BCE) and his most important followers, Mencius (Mengzi; late fourth century BCE) and Xunzi (third century BCE). Confucius's sayings, collected in the *Analects* (*Lunyu*), along with the *Mencius* and two short sections of the *Book of Rites*, "The Great Learning" and "The Doctrine of the Mean," were later collected as the Four Books, which from the Song dynasty to the twentieth century were the core texts of Confucian teachings. These, plus the Five Classics (*Book of Changes, Book of History, Book of Odes, Spring and Autumn Annals,* and *Book of Rites*) and several other works, such as the *Book of Filial Piety,* made up the basic Confucian canon. The thought of later Confucians in China and elsewhere was often expressed in the form of commentaries on these texts.

Philosophy. As a social and political philosophy, Confucianism was humanistic, rational, and moralistic. In general, it was secular, although some scholars have seen religious elements in it, such as the devout sense of mission exhibited by Confucius and many later Confucians, the notion that morality linked the individual with a higher, cosmic order, and the seemingly religious solemnity of the ceremonies conducted in Confucian temples. Yet few would call Confucianism a religion in any usual sense of the term, and Confucius was honored far more often as a sage than as a deity. His few elliptical remarks on religious matters have been variously interpreted as indicating he was (1) religious, but thought religion too recondite to discuss with his students; (2) not religious and deliberately evasive to avoid controversy; or (3) agnostic.

Followers of Confucianism were principally concerned with understanding and improving human life in this world. Such improvement was possible because there is a right "Way" (Dao), which can be known by the human mind and practiced through human effort. Indeed, the Dao has effect only through human action, hence living according to the Dao is the highest of human responsibilities as well as the most lofty of human goals. In this and other ways, duties, rather than rights, are natural to human beings; indeed, the latter are not part of the Confucian philosophical vocabulary.

The two basic themes of Confucianism are the good life and good government, which are intertwined because both are ethical questions and the same morality pertains to each. Man is by nature a social being, and morality is social: essentially, proper behavior in social relationships, of which family relations are paradigmatic. Of the Three Bonds (ruler-subject, father-son, and husband-wife) and the Five Cardinal Relations (the Three Bonds plus elder brother–younger brother and friend-friend), all but the relationship between friends are hierarchical and thus typical. Hierarchical relations are characterized by reciprocal, but not identical, obligations, each party being responsible for maintaining a harmonious relationship by fulfilling the duties of his or her role. Most Confucians saw social roles as naturally moral because the proper behavior associated with each reflected natural human feelings, such as the filial piety of a son for his father or the love of a mother for her children. Some, however, saw norms more as social conventions created by human reason arising from the realization that they were necessary for social order. In either case, according to the doctrine of the "rectification of names," if each person abided by the principles of his or her social roles, the ideal society would prevail.

Morality was thus good both in itself and as the means to political stability because individual moral behavior produced harmonious relationships, resulting in social cohesion and an orderly state. Even in war right made might, for the same process that produced cohesion would create high morale in an army defending its own land, whereas invading forces would eventually be sapped of their will to fight by the knowledge that their expedition was wrong, demonstrated by the very act of aggression. Offensive campaigns could be justified only if the object was to relieve people suffering under unjust rule.

In contrast to the effects of morality, the pursuit of individual self-interest produced or intensified conflicts of interest, resulting in a divisiveness that could lead to instability or disorder. Confucians disagreed over the source of selfishness. Idealistic Confucians followed Mencius in believing human nature was good, in the sense that everyone possesses an innate potential for altruistic behavior, and attributing selfish actions to bad influences from an aberrant social environment. Realistic Confucians were more inclined toward Xunzi's view that human nature was evil, in the sense that spontaneous desires tended to be self-centered and antisocial. Yet even Xunzi did not conceive of evil as capricious or ineluctable malevolence; he believed that selfish impulses could be tempered or even overcome. Confucians were therefore able to agree on the solution: education to train men who could, as government officials, create a social environment conducive to good behavior.

Education. Both Confucius and Mencius spent many years as teachers, and Confucius remained the model teacher into modern times. With the exception of dullards, everyone was deemed educable; neither low social status nor poverty were disqualifications, although by implication (confirmed in practice) most students were males from families that could afford to do without their labor. Confucian education combined the acquisition of skills, such as literacy, with ethical training. It was a blend of study and thought, with emphasis given to mastery of the wisdom of the ancients embodied in canonical texts. The teacher was both instructor and exemplar of Confucian principles, while the student was expected to be diligent and alert to what was implied as well as what was said. The goal was a self-conscious, self-disciplined, morally motivated individual, the Confucian gentleman.

The Gentleman. The Confucian gentleman (*junzi,* also translated "superior man") had the wisdom to distinguish right from wrong and the courage to act accordingly, in spite of threats or blandishments. He was well-rounded and moderate, upright yet sympathetic and unpretentious, conscientious yet relaxed. He had high moral standards but was not rigid; a favorite symbol of artists and writers was the humble bamboo, extremely flexible but firmly rooted in fundamental principles, and hence able to weather any storm.

The supreme Confucian virtue was *ren* (variously translated as "humaneness, humanheartedness, benevolence, goodness"), which Confucius said means "love human beings" and entails "subduing the self and returning to the rituals." Other important virtues were *yi* ("righteousness, rightness, duty, justice"), which meant fulfilling one's obligations out of a sense that they were inherently right; wisdom; courage; trustworthiness; sincerity; conscientiousness; loyalty; propriety; harmony; filial piety; brotherly love; and reciprocity, the key to harmonious relationships, which Confucius said is not doing to others what you would not want them to do to you. In all these, the gentleman was contrasted with the small man (*xiaoren,* also translated as "inferior or petty man"), who, because he was inclined to disregard morality and pursue his personal advantage, was cowardly, untrustworthy, insincere, and so forth.

Government. Although he could live an ethical life in his own community, it was in government that the gentleman could best fulfill his duties as a human being. He, not the small man, was best qualified for office because the state existed for its most important element, the people, not for the rulers, and hence officials should be motivated by concern for the common good, not personal ambition. Officials should thus be appointed on the basis of virtue and ability, not birth, although it was assumed that the ruler himself would be a hereditary monarch. Confucius ascribed almost mystical efficaciousness to good character: "If the ruler is upright, people will behave properly without orders; but if he is not upright, even though he gives orders they will not be obeyed" (*Analects* 13.6). He also stressed ritual (*li,* a broad term, also translated "rites," covering everything from solemn ceremonies to everyday etiquette) as providing guidelines that the people would follow because of the example set by their superiors and because of a sense of shame. Mencius added that government should be mindful of the material well-being of the people and provide them with enough land to enable them to feed and clothe themselves.

In Confucianism the basic economic issue was not production but distribution. Inequalities of wealth were justifiable but gross disparities were wrong and potentially dangerous. The common people could tolerate the inevitable hard times of an agrarian economy subject to the vagaries of the weather if they knew the rulers shared adversity with them, but uncaring extravagance by the ruling elite while the people were starving would create discontent and even rebellion. Contrary to Confucius and Mencius, Xunzi stressed the need for laws, enforced by punishments. On this issue most later Confucians thought government by men of virtue was superior to government by fixed, impersonal laws, although many, especially those with experience as officials, recognized the practical necessity of laws and punishments.

Failure by the government to fulfill its responsibilities nullified its subjects' obligation of allegiance. Following the logic of the Rectification of Names, Mencius argued that an immoral ruler no longer deserved the title or position of ruler, and hence killing him was not regicide. This is the famous theory of the mandate of Heaven, whereby the ruler's mandate to rule is not absolute, but contingent upon his performance. Thus, although Confucian theory contained no formal institutional checks to prevent rulers from abusing their power, that power was seen as ultimately resting upon the consent of the governed. This idea furnished a theoretical justification for the transfer of authority and allegiance from a fallen dynasty to its successor, and has been called a right of revolution; although this view is consistent with Confucian principles, Mencius expressed it as a dereliction of duty on the ruler's part, not as a right of the people to rebel.

Ideology. Beginning with the appointment of specialists in the Confucian classics by Emperor Wu of the Han dynasty (r. 141–87 BCE), Confucianism was institutionally linked to the Chinese state, a relation that was intensified with the establishment of the civil service examinations, which were based on Confucian texts. In Japan, the influence of Confucianism can be seen from the time of Shōtoku Taishi (574–622), and became pervasive in the Tokugawa era (1603–1868). In Korea as well, Confucianism was introduced fairly early, and was later officially espoused by the Yi dynasty (1392–1910), while its introduction to Vietnam dated from the time of the Han dynasty in China. [*See also* Confucianism in Vietnam *and* Neo-Confucianism in Korea.]

Official sponsorship of Confucianism has raised the issue of the functions it performed and the interests it served. Confucianism has been viewed as an ideology in the sense that it functioned as a belief system that guided social behavior and government policies in ways that were widely beneficial. Its ideological character is also manifest as a set of principles publicly espoused, but rarely followed, by the ruling elite, principles that served to mask the self-interested motives of the elite by justifying their power, wealth, and privileges. In this case, however, the benefits of the ideology redounded more closely to the interests of only a small part of society.

Supporters of the former view have argued that Confucianism gave a meaningful sense to life and cohesion to society through the family and other local associations, encouraged meritocracy in government, inspired the lofty sense of responsibility for the welfare of the people, and inhibited arbitrary rule. Confucianism has also been credited with providing the sense of continuity and the social discipline and respect for authority that made modernization a relatively smooth process in Japan and Taiwan.

In contrast, modern critics of Confucianism, especially prominent in China since the May Fourth Movement of 1919, have attributed the stagnation and injustices of traditional society to Confucianism. They note in this respect the way in which it encouraged blind adherence to the status quo and provided the theoretical justification both for inequalities between the sexes and age groups—especially through the Confucian family system—and for the authoritarian political system that obstructed equality, freedom, democracy, and individualism. As evidence of Confucianism's general conservativism and support of the status quo, they quote a famous passage from the *Analects:* "There have been few who were filial and loved their elder brothers who have been fond of offending their superiors; no one who disliked offending his superiors has been fond of disrupting social order" (1.2). As proof that Confucianism was antidemocratic, they cite Mencius's distinction between those who work with their minds and those who work with their hands, and his identification of the former as rulers and the latter as the ruled. Any attempt to resolve these differences would entail a comprehensive interpretation of government and society in premodern East Asia, a good indication of the historical importance of Confucianism.

[*See also* Confucius; Mencius; Xunzi; Zhu Xi; *and* Neo-Confucianism.]

Wing-tsit Chan, *A Source Book in Chinese Philosophy* (1963). Wm. Theodore de Bary, Wing-tsit Chan, and Burton Watson, comps., *Sources of Chinese Tradition* (1960). Herbert Fingarette, *Confucianism—The Secular as Sacred* (1972). Kung-chuan Hsiao, *A History of Chinese Political*

Thought, vol. 1, *From the Beginnings to the Sixth Century A.D.*, translated by F. W. Mote (1979). Charles E. Moore, ed., *The Chinese Mind: Essentials of Chinese Philosophy and Culture* (1967). John K. Shryock, *The Origin and Development of the State Cult of Confucius* (1932). Sybille van der Sprenkel, *Legal Institutions in Manchu China* (1962). Ryusaku Tsunoda, Wm. Theodore de Bary, and Donald Keene, comps., *Sources of Japanese Tradition* (1958).

J. Mason Gentzler

CONFUCIANISM IN VIETNAM. The Chinese occupation between the third century BCE and the tenth century CE of what would later become Vietnam left a considerable cultural and intellectual legacy in the form of Confucian thought. Vietnam has therefore traditionally been viewed as confucianized in the same way that the other classical polities of Southeast Asia were hinduized. As recent scholarship has increasingly emphasized, however, the Confucian influence in Vietnam was far from being uniform; indeed, it varied considerably according to the historical period, geographical region, and social class one chooses to examine.

With its emphasis on a strong state based on morality and propriety, Confucian ideology had its greatest appeal among Vietnam's ruling elite. It was the establishment of a regular, Chinese-style examination system under the Tran (1226–1400) that marked an important step in the institutionalization of Confucianism. During the fifteenth century, the Confucian scholarly elite gained power, particularly after their "victory" over the predominantly military supporters of Le Loi (r. 1428–1433). The next three centuries saw alternating periods of decline and strength for Confucian institutions, the first caused in part by the political chaos of the sixteenth century and the second attributable to the patronage of several Trinh lords in the north. The Tay Son Rebellion of the late eighteenth century again disrupted the existing political and social order; it was followed by a return to Confucian orthodoxy under Nguyen emperors Minh Mang (r. 1820–1840) and Thieu Tri (r. 1841–1847). Within several decades, however, Vietnamese Confucianism was to face the political challenge of colonialism and the intellectual challenge of Western thought, both of which considerably weakened Confucianism's hold over the Vietnamese.

Even in its more popularized forms, Confucianism was forced to compete with other belief systems, both foreign and indigenous. During the Ly (1010–1225) and Tran dynasties, Mahayana Buddhism enjoyed considerable royal patronage, and periods of Buddhist revival continued to occur through the eighteenth century. Popular Buddhism, including Theravada elements in the south, has remained strong to this day. At the same time, Confucianist practices have never successfully stifled the indigenous spiritual and religious traditions that Vietnam shares with other Southeast Asian cultures. Such beliefs frequently posed a subtle threat to the intellectual and moral orthodoxy of Confucian philosophy, which for the ruler and scholarly elite represented the basis of the political and social status quo. (Indeed, the honoring of "national" spirits such as that of Tan Vien Mountain and the granting of recognition to important local deities constituted an important part of the legitimation of imperial rule in Vietnam.) In any case, no Vietnamese emperor or scholar, however deeply steeped in Chinese tradition and Confucian thought, would have attempted to deny Vietnam's own cultural heritage and independence from the Middle Kingdom.

[*See also* Tran Dynasty; Le Loi; Trinh Lords; Minh Mang; Thieu Tri; *and* Ly Dynasty.]

R. B. Smith, "The Cycle of Confucianism in Vietnam," in *Aspects of Vietnamese History*, edited by Walter F. Vella (1973). John K. Whitmore, "Social Organization and Confucian Thought in Vietnam," *Journal of Southeast Asian Studies* (1964). A. B. Woodside, *Vietnam and the Chinese Model* (1971).

James M. Coyle and Bruce M. Lockhart

CONFUCIUS (551–479 BCE), China's most famous philosopher, founder of the philosophical school known as Confucianism. Named Kong Qiu, with the formal name Kong Zhongni, he was called Kong Fuzi, Master Kong, which Jesuit fathers in the sixteenth century latinized as Confucius. Confucius was born in the state of Lu on the Shandong Peninsula into a family that had fallen from the aristocracy. A second son, Confucius was orphaned at an early age and grew up with little money. Despite the fact that he had no regular teacher Confucius managed to educate himself and become a private tutor, training the sons of gentlemen.

During the time when Confucius lived the Zhou dynasty had declined as China became divided into competing states. Confucius was concerned, as were other thinkers of his time, with saving the world from disorder. At the age of fifty-six Confucius began to travel about the area of modern Henan and Shandong to the courts of the contending rulers, offering his services as an adviser. Confucius was unsuccessful in his search; he never won major office or had a chance to put his ideas into practice. Instead, he attracted a group of students or disciples who sought his instruction and kept his ideas alive after his death. Long after Confucius died his ideas were recorded in the *Analects (Lunyu),* fragmentary reconstructions of exchanges with his disciples. It is from this source that the best picture of Confucius's life and ideas can be gleaned.

Confucius addressed himself to the problem of social order. The central value in his teaching was benevolence or goodness *(ren).* The man who practiced goodness was the gentleman, or man of virtue *(junzi),* a man distinguished not by hereditary standing but by moral worth. The ruler who wanted to order the world could do so by instituting good government. To do this the ruler needed to hire a virtuous minister who could manage the affairs of state. Confucius emphasized education, moral suasion, virtuous example, and ritual correctness. He wanted to return the world to an ordered hierarchy that had supposedly existed in the past in the time of the ancient culture heroes such as Yao, Shun, and the Duke of Zhou. Confucius claimed that he was a transmitter, not an originator, yet his ideal of a moral meritocracy, as opposed to an aristocracy, was a major innovation.

The layers of lore and myth surrounding Confucius grew greatly after his death. His ideas were developed and elaborated by later thinkers, particularly Mencius (latinized form of Mengzi; 371–289 BCE?) and Xunzi (fl. 298–238 BCE). Under the Han dynasty (206 BCE–220 CE), when his teachings received state patronage, he was already portrayed as a sage. His biography in the *Shiji (Records of the Historian)* by the Han historian Sima Qian is full of fanciful anecdotes and questionable characterizations. During imperial times he was revered in Confucian temples and hailed as the First Teacher or the Uncrowned King. He was also given credit for having written or edited many texts in the classical canon. Kong family ancestral shrines were maintained at Qufu in Shandong and Confucius's descendants were honored by the state.

In the twentieth century Confucianism was condemned as the ideological source of much of the repressive character of the old society. Confucian thought was vigorously attacked in the May Fourth Movement around 1919. Confucius and his teachings were restored to a place of honor by the Nationalist government in the 1930s. In the 1950s and 1960s Confucius was evaluated from a Marxist point of view. He was alternatively found to have been progressive or reactionary, either a spokesman for the progressive landowning class of late Zhou times or a mouthpiece of surviving slave-owning elements. The most sharply focused attack was that of the Gang of Four, who conducted a campaign from 1973 to 1975 to "criticize Confucius and Lin Biao." The connection between Confucius and Lin Biao, who had recently died attempting to assassinate Mao Zedong, is far from obvious. There is some reason to believe that Confucius was used as a token to represent an unnamed target, most probably Premier Zhou Enlai. In the 1980s a more moderate line has been taken toward Confucius by the Chinese authorities. His great impact on Chinese history over a period of twenty-five hundred years assures Confucius's continued influence on Chinese thought and culture.

[*See also* Confucianism; Guwen; Jinwen; Mencius; Neo-Confucianism; Warring States Period; *and* Zhou Period.]

Wing-tsit Chan, *A Source Book in Chinese Philosophy* (1963). H. G. Creel, *Confucius and the Chinese Way* (1949). Kung-chuan Hsiao, *A History of Chinese Political Thought,* translated by F. W. Mote, vol. 1 (1979); Kam Louie, *Critiques of Confucius in Contemporary China* (1980). Ssu-ma Chien (Sima Qian), *Records of the Historian,* translated by Yang Hsien-yi and Gladys Yang (1974). EDWARD L. FARMER

CONJEEVARAM. *See* Kanchipuram.

CON SON ISLANDS, often referred to as the Con Dao islands or as Poulo Condore, lie some fifty miles off Vietnam's southern coast near the mouth of the Mekong River. Mentioned by Marco Polo, they later fell prey to Vietnamese southward expansion. The islands were coveted by the French and English alike, and a short-lived British settlement was established in 1702. The 1787 Treaty of Versailles ceded Con Son to France but was never carried out. During the French colonial period, the islands were a major penal colony, and they continued to serve as a prison under the South Vietnamese government.

[*See also* Versailles Treaty of 1787.]

BRUCE M. LOCKHART

CONSTITUTIONAL REVOLUTION. The revolution of 1905 to 1911 expressed the widespread discontent of many urban Iranians, especially the bazaar classes, intellectuals, and some *ulamas* (religious scholars), with the autocratic and inefficient rule of the Qajar shahs and with the increasing power of foreigners, especially the Russians and the British. The revolution succeeded in bringing many Iranians into national politics and mass struggles and, despite its ultimate defeat, left Iran with a constitution that endured until 1979.

The revolution was preceded by a large growth in oppositional newspapers from abroad, a flowering of progressive literature, secret societies, and an influence of Iranians abroad (including hundreds of thousands, mainly workers, who migrated temporarily or permanently to Russian Transcaucasia). Sparks came from the Russo-Japanese War of 1904 to 1905, which saw Asia's only constitutional power defeating Europe's only major nonconstitutional one. Constitutions were seen as a secret of strength, and the Russian Revolution of 1905 temporarily removed the threat of Russian intervention in an Iranian revolt.

The revolution began in December 1905, when the governor of Tehran beat some sugar merchants by the feet for not lowering prices. A group of bazaar-merchants and mullas then took sanctuary *(bast)* in Tehran's royal mosque, whence they were dispersed by government agents. A crowd of *ulamas,* led by the liberal *mujtahid* Sayyid Muhammad Tabataba'i, took sanctuary at a shrine near Tehran and formulated demands to Shah Muzaffar al-Din, including a representative "House of Justice." The shah agreed and the *ulamas* returned. The shah did nothing, however, and when a crowd tried to prevent a popular preacher from being expelled from Tehran, an army group killed a sayyid. Then many mullas and others took *bast* in the holy city of Qom, in July 1906, while a crowd of between twelve and fourteen thousand merchants and tradesmen took *bast* in the British legation and halted business in Tehran.

Intellectuals and merchants now demanded a representative assembly *(majles),* which was elected by a six-class division that gave heavy representation to Tehran's guilds. The Majles opened in October 1906 and assigned a committee to write a constitution, which the dying shah signed in December; a supplementary law was drafted in 1907 and was signed by the new shah, Muhammad Ali. These laws, based largely on the Belgian constitution, were the core of Iran's constitution until 1979. The intent was to create a true constitutional monarchy, with Majles approval needed in all important matters. Equality before the law and personal rights were guaranteed, with a few limits insisted upon by the clerics, who also added a provision that all laws must be passed as compatible with Islamic law by a committee of *ulamas.* No law was ever so rejected, however.

Newspapers and popular organizations flourished. Muhammad Ali Shah, however, who acceded in January 1907, wanted to kill the constitution, and invited as prime minister a conservative ex-prime minister, the Atabak. Although the Majles could have rejected him, conservative clerics favored cooperation with the shah, and democrats led by men like Taqizadeh from Tabriz lost out. The Atabak tried to create an alliance between the shah and the conservatives, but he displeased royalists and radicals, both of whom plotted his assassination in August 1907. On the same day the Anglo-Russian Entente divided Iran into Russian, British, and neutral spheres, with the result that Iranians could no longer get British aid against Russia.

The shah led a successful coup against the Majles in June 1908, helped by the Russian-led Cossack Brigade. Many democrats were arrested and executed, and most of Iran was brought under royal control. Under the leadership of two guerrilla leaders of popular origin, Sattar Khan and Baqir Khan, Tabriz held out against the royalists. When Russian troops entered Tabriz many of the resisters (called *mujahidin* or *fida'iyan*) joined the resistance in neighboring Gilan and were aided in retaking Tehran in July 1909 by the Bakhtiari tribe from Isfahan. Muhammad Ali Shah took refuge with the Russians, and his minor son Ahmad became shah under a regent.

The second Majles, with a one-class electoral system, was marked by strong differences between the clerically led Moderates and the progressive Democrats. Facing a financial crisis brought about by internal disorder, the Iranians brought in a young American expert, William Morgan Shuster, to control their finances. Shuster planned a tax gendarmerie headed by a major with the British legation, who would resign his post. The Russians said any such appointment was against the 1907 Entente; in November 1911 they sent an ultimatum demanding Shuster's dismissal and Iran's agreement not to engage foreigners without Anglo-Russian consent. The Majles refused, but the Moderate Bakhtiari-led cabinet accepted, dissolved the Majles, and dismissed Shuster in December 1911.

The revolution left important legacies in the constitution, financial and judicial reforms, a new public role for some women and minorities, and the continuation of the institution of the Majles, although it was often controlled from above. It also led to Iran's first political parties, with the Democrats remaining important for years. The entry of many Iranians into the political arena was an important legacy of this period.

[*See also* Bihbahani, Abd Allah; Persian Cossack Brigade; Qajar, Muhammad Ali; Shuster, William Morgan; *and* Tabataba'i, Muhammad.]

E. G. Browne, *The Persian Revolution of 1905–1909* (1910). Nikki Keddie, *Roots of Revolution* (1981). R. A. McDaniel, *The Shuster Mission and the Persian Constitutional Revolution* (1974). NIKKI KEDDIE

COOLIE TRADE. *Coolie* is the term Europeans in India and China gave to native, hired laborers. Its derivation may be Indian or African, but it mainly was used to describe peasant workers who were Chinese. The coolie trade was part of a vast migration that carried hundreds of thousands of people from South China to Southeast Asia and the New World between the fifteenth and the nineteenth century.

Most Chinese emigrants, including nearly all who went to North America, paid their own passage or borrowed money from friends and relatives; on arrival at their destinations, they were free people. In the nineteenth century, however, one-fourth of those who went to Southeast Asia and nearly all who went to Peru, Cuba, and Hawaii went as contract laborers under the "credit-ticket" system, or coolie trade. Labor brokers, usually Chinese themselves, worked in Macao and other cities in Guangdong and Fujian provinces. There they made contact with young men, luring them with tales of riches and easy living abroad. If that ploy failed, kidnapping was the recruitment device of choice.

In theory, these men were voluntary emigrants, indentured for a period of service in return for passage. In fact, they lived in conditions little better than slavery. They often were kept in large cages while ashore. Sometimes they were taken to ports other than the ones for which they had contracted. They were passed from broker to broker; with each transaction their debt increased and the term of their service lengthened. Whether they tapped rubber trees in Malaysia, harvested sugar cane in Cuba, or worked the mines of Peru, they were driven to back-breaking work without much hope of release.

Although the center of the coolie trade was Portuguese Macao, much of the traffic was carried in British ships. After about 1850, the British government began to take steps to curb the trade. Officials inspected ships and interviewed coolies to make sure they were not being held against their will. Such steps met with only limited success. In the 1870s the Portuguese also started to back away from the trade, closing their export facilities for human cargoes. The Chinese government belatedly awakened to the nature of the trade in the 1880s. Thereafter, the Chinese and British cooperated in trying to bring an end to the practice. Few workers left China under oppressive contracts after the turn of the century, but thousands continued to go as free, not indentured, emigrants. The coolie trade had ended, but the Chinese diaspora continued.

[*See also* China Trade; Imperialism; Overseas Chinese; *and* Emigration: Chinese Emigration.]

Persia Crawford Campbell, *Chinese Coolie Emigration to Countries within the British Empire* (1923; reprint, 1969). Ta Chen, *Chinese Migrations, With Special Reference to Labor Conditions* (1923). Watt Stewart, *Chinese Bondage in Peru, 1849–1874* (1951).

PAUL R. SPICKARD

COOMARASWAMY, ANANDA KENTISH (1877–1947), Indian scholar famous for his multifaceted approach toward the understanding of Indian art and culture. His *History of Indian and Indonesian Art* and his *Rajput Painting* laid the foundation for art history as an independent discipline in India. His later and perhaps better-known works explore the symbolical and metaphysical content of Indian art. His works are of significance to this day, containing intuitive insights that have been most fully recognized only in the past few decades. His two hundred titles speak of his vision, imagination, and genius.

[*See also* Painting: South Asian Painting *and* Architecture: South Asian Architecture.]

Roger Lipsey, *Selected Papers,* 3 vols. (1977).

VIDYA DEHEJIA

COORG, now an administrative district in the state of Karnataka, in India, is situated on a rugged plateau that permitted the chieftains who ruled there to maintain considerable independence through the centuries from the great neighboring kingdoms that surrounded it, such as Vijayanagar. The people of the region are quite distinct in culture, with two classes predominating; the Kodagas, or Coorgs, who were the ruling group, are tall and fair-skinned, and the Eravas, their hereditary servants or slaves, are short and dark. Coorg was annexed by the British in 1834, and was administered as a separate province until its incorporation, after India's independence, into the state of Mysore, which later became Karnataka. Tea and coffee plantations, which were established in the nineteenth century, are an important feature of the economy.

M. N. Srinivas, *Religion and Society among the Coorgs of South India* (1952).

Carol Appadurai Breckenridge

CORNWALLIS, CHARLES (Lord Cornwallis; 1738–1805), governor-general of India (1786–1793, 1805). With the strong support of the British government, Cornwallis's task was to bring reform to East India Company affairs. Such was the trust he inspired that, although he had surrendered to American colonials at Yorktown, he was sent to restore confidence in Calcutta.

The East India Company was searching for a leader whose position and wealth put him above temptation in order to attain its goals of ending corruption among the company's European servants, reorganizing the company's Indian government, clearly separating governing and trading functions, and establishing fairer sets of rules for governing the peoples of India without altering their ways of life. If Cornwallis's predecessor Warren Hastings was considered too "Indian" in his ways, however, Cornwallis was, if anything, too English. His honesty and integrity were beyond question. While victorious in war, his main legacy was constitutional. He ensured the separation of power between the executive, judicial, and revenue branches of government; created an elite imperial bureaucracy, known as the Indian Civil Service, a "steel frame" that became famous for high standards, dedication, and integrity; and established codes of regulations to guarantee rule of law, especially on judicial and revenue issues. The most notable of these was perhaps the 1793 Permanent (or Zamindari) Settlement of Bengal. This was essentially an agreement by which enormous grants of governing power over localities ("estates" often consisting of hundreds of villages) were delegated. Great *zamindars* ("landholders") ruled the agrarian countryside in perpetuity, in return for a regular payment of revenue or tribute *(beriz)* to Calcutta. By such means Cornwallis sought to make sure that a handful of Europeans could govern in such a way as to remain untainted by corruption and thereby maintain their favored position as rulers. As the Great Lawgiver of the Raj, it is not surprising that, in statues erected in Calcutta and Madras, he wears a Roman toga and carries symbols of justice.

[*See also* Governor-General of India; Hastings, Warren; *and* Indian Administrative Service.]

Arthur Aspinal, *Cornwallis in Bengal* (1931). W. S. Seton-Karr, *The Marquess Cornwallis and the Consolidation of British Rule* (1890). Franklin Wickwire and Mary Wickwire, *Cornwallis: The Imperial Years* (1980).

Robert E. Frykenberg

COUNTRY TRADE, the short-haul trade within Asian waters, as opposed to the direct trade between Asia and Europe (the "European trade"), particularly as carried on by the Europeans from the sixteenth to the nineteenth century.

The country trade did not originate with nor was it confined to the Europeans. From the east coast of Africa across the Indian Ocean and the China seas all the way to Japan, Asian merchants of different nationalities had long been engaged in transporting and exchanging local goods between nearby ports. Even after the Europeans came to dominate much of maritime Asia, local Asian traders continued to participate, although on a diminished scale, in this intra-Asian regional trade.

Nevertheless, the term *country trade* is generally associated with the Europeans in order to distinguish it from their "European trade." Beginning with the Portuguese in the sixteenth century and continuing with the Dutch in the seventeenth and the British in the eighteenth century, the European merchants, particularly if they were organized (as the Dutch and the British were) into East India companies, were primarily concerned with the long-haul trade in exotic commodities that fetched high prices in Europe, notably spices from the East Indies and tea from China. As the number of European traders increased in eastern waters, however, some of them began to intrude on the Asians' well-established country trade. They might, as an example, carry piece goods and sugar from Bengal to Arabian Sea ports and return with cotton from Surat, pepper from Malabar, and silver bullion from Arabia and Persia. Despite the prosaic quality of their cargoes, the Europeans' country trade, in time, came to rival the glamorous European trade in value.

The British East India Company, for instance, enjoyed, by royal charter, a legal monopoly of British trade with all Asia. In practice, however, it devoted most of its resources to the lucrative tea trade from China to England. It therefore delegated the trade within Asian waters (i.e., the country trade) to private merchants in India, whom it licensed. By the end of the eighteenth century the British country traders had developed a thriving trade of their own between India and China, involving the export to China of raw cotton from Bombay and, most profitably, opium from Bengal. It was these exports from British India, carried to China by the country traders, that provided the silver that financed the company's voracious tea purchases at Canton (Guangzhou). The country traders, in return, received from the company bills of exchange payable in London. The apparently straightforward tea trade from China to England was thus, in reality, a vast, complex, triangular relationship in which India and the country trade played an indispensable part.

[*See also* Canton; East India Company; *and* Dutch East India Company.]

Holden Furber, *Rival Empires of Trade in the Orient, 1600–1800* (1976). Michael Greenberg, *British Trade and the Opening of China, 1800–1842* (1951).

EDWARD J. M. RHOADS

COW. The Indian cow *(Bos indicus)* occupies a special place in the cultural history, agricultural economy, and political life of the Indian subcontinent. Along with another bovine, the water buffalo, the cow provides milk and meat, dung for fuel, leather for footwear, and male offspring that are the mainstay of traction in Indian agriculture. Male cattle play a critical role in agricultural operations, but cows have a place in Hindu thought and sentiment that is neither reducible to, nor deducible from, their practical uses. The Hindu prohibition against the eating of beef, the traditional attribution of powerful ritual and therapeutic powers to the five products of the cow (*panchagavya:* milk, curd, clarified butter, urine, and dung), and the sentimental view of the cow as the pinnacle of purity, nurturance, and innocence, are parts of a single ideological system. These beliefs have their historical roots in the political conflicts, religious controversies, and socioeconomic transformations that took place in North India between the fifth century BCE and the fourth century CE; they were not factors in the earlier, Vedic period.

The economic implications of the special status of the cow in contemporary India are matters of considerable controversy among economists, anthropologists, geographers, and veterinarians. Social scientists question whether Hindu beliefs about the cow have adversely affected the Indian agricultural economy, and whether such effects can be detected in the numbers, distribution, composition of the herds, and sex-ratios of cattle in various parts of India. Is the best determinant for understanding the Indian reverence for the cow the factor of microecology or macroeconomics, or is it one of religion? Although these are issues of general significance for social science, most of the views held by participants in these debates share certain utilitarian assumptions that are fundamentally alien to the indigenous Hindu perspective.

Debates about the status, meaning, and role of the cow in India are not only matters of religious sentiment or economic progress. The cow has been a potent symbol of ethnic, communal, regional, and national ideologies and movements—in earliest Hindu history, in the more recent periods of Islamic and British rule, and in Indian nationalist politics both before and after independence. The confrontation of these ideologies finds its cultural roots in the special Hindu reverence for the cow. But it takes its practical force from the profound relevance of the cow to everyday life.

W. N. Brown, "The Sanctity of the Cow in Hinduism," *Economic Weekly* 16 (1964): 245–255. V. M. Dandekar, *The Cattle Economy of India* (1980). F. J. Simoons, "Questions in the Sacred-Cow Controversy," *Current Anthropology* 20.3 (1979): 467–476. A. Vaidyanathan, K. N. Nair, and M. Harris, "Bovine Sex and Species Ratios in India," *Current Anthropology* 23.4 (1982): 365–373.

ARJUN APPADURAI

COX, HIRAM, British East India Company resident in Burma (1796–1798). After the favorable report of the 1795 mission of Michael Symes, Governor-General Sir John Shore sent Captain Hiram Cox to be resident in Rangoon in late 1796 to improve relations and trade and particularly to monitor the activities of French merchants and privateers. Cox's tenure was characterized by conflicts over protocol and his pretensions to ambassadorial status. After a period of conflict with the local officials in Rangoon, Cox of his own accord journeyed to court to seek redress. After nine months of self-perceived humiliation there, he chose to return to India in early 1798 with a report critical of Symes and hostile to the Burmese. Although the British authorities sent an apology of sorts to Burma, Cox's ill-tempered report biased Western historians against Symes and his Burmese hosts until it was placed in proper perspective by D. G. E. Hall over 150 years later.

[*See also* East India Company; Burma; Symes, Michael; *and* Hall, D. G. E.]

Hiram Cox, *Journal of a Residence in the Burmhan Empire . . .* (1821). D. G. E. Hall, ed., *Michael Symes' Journal of His Second Embassy to the Court of Ava in 1802* (1955). William J. Koenig

CRAWFURD, JOHN (1783–1868), Orientalist, second British resident of Singapore, and envoy to Thailand and Burma. He studied medicine at Edinburgh University and in 1803 was appointed assistant surgeon in the medical service of the British East India Company. He served in the North-West Provinces of India and between 1808 and 1811 in Pinang, Malaysia, where he became acquainted with Malay culture. He joined the British expedition against Java in 1811 and after the conquest of the island held a number of senior appointments, including that of resident of Yogyakarta. He learned Javanese and drew on his experience in Indonesia for his three-volume *History of the Indian Archipelago* (1820), a useful if uninspiring work. He was employed by the governor-general of India on an embassy to Thailand during 1821–1822, and after his period as resident of Singapore (1823–1826) he was appointed British envoy to the court of Ava. He published excellent accounts of both missions in 1828 and 1829, as well as *A Grammar and Dictionary of the Malay Language* (1852), *A Descriptive Dictionary of the Indian Islands and Adjacent Countries* (1856), and papers on the Malay Archipelago. He was a fellow of the Royal Society and of the Royal Geographical Society, and during the last part of his life was regarded in Great Britain as the leading authority on Malaysia and Indonesia.

Dictionary of National Biography (London, 1888), vol. 13, pp. 60–61. J. S. Bastin, "Malayan Portraits: John Crawfurd," *Malaya* 3 (1954): 697–698.

John S. Bastin

CRIPPS MISSION, largely the initiative of Clement Attlee, an attempt to counter Japanese military successes in Southeast Asia in 1941 and 1942 by associating Indian political leaders with the Allied war effort. Sir (Richard) Stafford Cripps (1889–1952) arrived in India on 22 March 1942 with proposals designed to bring Indian politicians into the Government of India in return for a promise of immediate independence at the end of the war. Despite early optimism, and some encouragement from Nehru, the plan ran into difficulties. Cripps left India on 12 April, announcing that he had failed. All plans for further political advance were put in cold storage. Both privately and publicly Cripps blamed Gandhi for the breakdown of the talks, referring to Gandhi's apocryphal statement that the mission's declaration was "a postdated cheque on a crashing bank." Some historians have suggested that both Prime Minister Churchill and Viceroy Linlithgow deliberately sabotaged Cripps's efforts. By contrast, Nicholas Mansergh considers that the mission never had any hope of success.

Nicholas Mansergh, ed., *The Transfer of Power,* vol. 1, *The Cripps Mission* (1970). R. J. Moore, *Churchill, Cripps, and India, 1939–1945* (1979). Hugh Tinker

CTESIPHON, an ancient Parthian and Sasanid city on the left bank of the Tigris River in Iraq, about forty kilometers southeast of Baghdad. The meaning of the name (Greek, Ktesiphon; Middle Persian, Tyspwn; Arabic, Tays[a]fun) is unknown.

Not long after the Parthians defeated the last of the Seleucids and conquered Babylonia in the second century BCE, they selected the village of Ctesiphon, opposite the Hellenistic city of Seleuceia, as their main administrative center and western capital; the earlier capitals in the Parthian homeland to the northeast had become too distant from the focus of the empire. The choice of the Ctesiphon area was undoubtedly because of its location on the Tigris near the Euphrates, where the two rivers were connected by canals, so that the area was at the crossroads of several important trade routes. Ctesiphon also served as capital under the Sasanid kings, from Ardashir I's defeat of the last Parthian ruler and capture of the city in 226 CE until the demise of the Sasanid empire in the seventh century. During that period, if not earlier, Ctesiphon came to comprise a group of towns and suburbs, as is indicated by its name, "The Cities," in both Aramaic (Mahoze) and Arabic (al-Mada'in).

During the Parthian and Sasanid periods, Ctesiphon was frequently captured and sacked by Roman and, later, Byzantine armies, but it was never held for long. The Arabs' capture and looting of the city in 637 presaged the end of the Sasanid empire fourteen years later. With the founding of the Abbasid capital at Baghdad in 762, Ctesiphon was abandoned.

The major ruin at Ctesiphon is the Taq Kisra ("Kisra's arch"), an immense vaulted hall (more than thirty-five meters high) and facade of brickwork that is the vestige of the Sasanid royal palace (see figure 1). The traditional name suggests that the builder was Khusrau I (531–579), but it was probably erected earlier, perhaps by Shapur I (241–272).

[*See also* Parthians *and* Sasanid Dynasty.]

JOHN HUEHNERGARD

CULTIVATION SYSTEM. *See* Kultuurstelsel.

CULTURAL REVOLUTION. *See* Great Proletarian Cultural Revolution.

CUNEIFORM, a system of writing devised about 3100 BCE by the Sumerians in Mesopotamia. The signs were at first simple pictures of objects; they evolved into sets of wedges (Latin, *cuneus*) impressed into moist clay with a triangle-headed stylus (see figure 1). Another early development was the use of some signs to express syllables phonetically. By 2500 BCE this mixed logosyllabic system had been borrowed by the Semitic Akkadians and Eblaites.

FIGURE 1 (CTESIPHON). *House Tile.* Umm ez-Zatir. Sasanid period (third to seventh century). Stucco, molded in relief, and depicting a boar in a swamp. Height 29.2 cm., width 37.5 cm.

FIGURE 1 (CUNEIFORM). *Inscription.* Brick, Susa(?), c. fifth century BCE, 36.8 cm. × 17 cm.

Later, Mesopotamian cuneiform was also adopted by the Elamites, the Hurrians, and the Hittites. Under the Achaemenids a much reduced cuneiform system (forty-one signs), semialphabetic in nature, was devised to write Old Persian.

[*See also* Old Persian.]

I. J. Gelb, *A Study of Writing* (1963). R. G. Kent, *Old Persian* (1953). JOHN HUEHNERGARD

CUONG DE (1882–1951), Nguyen prince who collaborated with Boi Chau, a leading patriotic and revolutionary figure in colonial Vietnam. Involved with the Duy Tan Hoi (Vietnam Modernization Association), an organization formed by Phan in 1904 to end French rule and set up a constitutional monarchy under the prince, Chong De was smuggled from Vietnam to Japan in 1909. There he attended the Shimbu Military Academy and became active in the Dong Du Movement, which exhorted Vietnamese to study in Japan. When Phan's party was expelled from Japan in 1909, Cuong De worked with Phan's movement in Canton. After Phan's conversion to the Chinese republican cause and the establishment of the Viet Nam Quang Phuc Hoi (Vietnam Restoration Society), Cuong De was briefly active in Cochinchina but then returned to Japan, remaining there until his death.

[*See also* Phan Boi Chau; Vietnam Modernization Association; *and* Vietnam Restoration Association.]

William J. Duiker, *The Rise of Nationalism in Vietnam, 1900–1941* (1976). David Marr, *Vietnamese Anticolonialism, 1885–1925* (1971). BRUCE M. LOCKHART

CURZON, GEORGE NATHANIEL (Lord Curzon; 1859–1925), one of the leading figures of British foreign policy in the late nineteenth and early twentieth centuries. His rise to political preeminence was so dramatic that at age thirty-nine he succeeded Lord Elgin as governor-general and viceroy of India.

Curzon's viceroyalty (1898–1905) marked the apogee of British imperialist rule in India. Curzon was imperious and autocratic, overbearing and contemptuous. He once likened the Indian princes to unruly schoolboys and often spoke of the Indian people as if they were so many children or pets. He sincerely believed, however, that it was Britain's responsibility to rule India benevolently.

Curzon exhibited an extraordinary capacity for work and an intense dedication to making British administration in India more efficient and effective. To combat famine Curzon undertook the extension of irrigation projects, the rapid development of the railway network, and the establishment of the Institute of Agricultural Research. Curzon improved the selection and training of Indian police officers and established the first national police force. In addition, a separate government department was established to spur India's industrial and commercial growth, and government assistance was provided to mutual loan societies.

Curzon's greatest weakness, however, was the willful disdain that accompanied his drive for efficiency. The 1904 Universities Act, for example, aroused widespread opposition because it centralized the control of admissions and examinations at local private colleges. More important, the partition of Bengal (1905), another administrative measure, sparked a nationwide protest.

Curzon was forced to resign as viceroy over an administrative dispute with Lord Kitchener, commander-in-chief of the army in India. Still, Curzon went on to become foreign secretary in successive interwar governments in Britain, although his dream of becoming prime minister was never realized.

David Dilks, *Curzon in India,* 2 vols. (1969). S. Gopal, *British Policy in India, 1858–1905* (1965).

JAMES A. JAFFE

CYRUS II (Persian, Kurush; 599–529 BCE), known as "Cyrus the Great," founder of the Persian empire, son of Cambyses I, dynast of Persis, and Mandane, daughter of the Median great king, Astyages. Cyrus succeeded his father when he was forty years old. He united the Persian tribes, won over Median aristocracy displeased with Astyages' lack of military ambition, and rose in rebellion against his own grandfather, whom he defeated and captured (550) but treated honorably.

The rapid rise of Cyrus provoked Croesus of Lydia, who concluded a military alliance with Egypt, Sparta, and Babylon and attacked Cyrus. Swiftly marching through Anatolia, Cyrus met Croesus in battle, pursued him to Sardis, and captured the town after a short siege (547). Croesus was taken prisoner but treated well (the reference to the death of a king in the Nabonidus Chronicle is not, contrary to the usual interpretation, related to Croesus). Leaving his Median generals to subdue the rest of Anatolia, Cyrus went eastward, consolidated his power, and built Pasargadae. He then embarked on an eastern campaign that brought under his sway the regions of Parthia, Drangiana, Sattagydia, Margiana, Sogdiana, Bactria, Chorasmia, Gandhara, Aria, the Saka lands north of the Oxus, and the eastern edge of the Indus. He built a fortified town, Cyropolis, south of the Jaxartes' great bend to ward against nomadic threats. Greatly strengthened, he marched on Babylonia, defeated Nabonidus's army, and received the surrender of the ancient city, which he entered in peace, as the rightful sovereign chosen by Marduk, patron deity of Babylon (539). From this event to the Seleucid era, which was known as "Alexander's era," 228 years elapse; this period was later borrowed by Zoroastrian scholar-priests to invent a date for the prophet Zoroaster, whose call at thirty they dated to 228 years before Alexander's era, and hence his birth at "258 years before Alexander." The date of Cyrus's Babylonian conquest was thus identified with the coming of God's message to Zoroaster.

In Babylon Cyrus ordered the rebuilding of the Temple of Esagila, and his charter for this occasion survives in his famous "Cyrus Cylinder." His religious policy of tolerance benefited other nations, including the exiled Jews, whom he returned home with honor and restored property, earning for himself the rank of Lord's Messiah and Shepherd in the Bible, through which his name still has currency in the Western world. The ever-present threat of an onslaught of Central Asian nomads induced Cyrus to lead a preventive expedition against them, but his Saka cousins ambushed and killed him. Mummified, he was brought to Pasargadae and placed in a tomb, which was guarded as a shrine by priests until Alexander's conquest in 330 BCE. Local tradition preserves its sanctity still.

Cyrus married only once, and left two sons, Cambyses and Bardya/Smerdis, and three daughters, the oldest of whom, Atossa, married Darius I and was Xerxes' mother. He was remembered as "father" by Persians, as a liberator by his subjects, and as a wise, gentle, and honored sovereign dear to the gods by his Greek adversaries. Shrewd, farsighted, brave, resolute, ambitious, and forgiving, Cyrus was a great king and conqueror, but whomever he conquered was left the freedom of language, religion, and institutions. His empire was in reality a confederation of autonomous states. His legacy has been maintained through the Bible, the vivid and romantic account of Herodotus in the *Histories*, and in the romance of *Cyropaedia* by Xenophon, who chose him as the ideal king.

[*See also* Pasargadae.]

J. Cargill, "The Nabonidos Chronicle and the Fall of Lydia," *American Journal of Ancient History* 2 (1978): 97–116. C. Hignett, *Xerxes' Invasion of Greece* (1963), pp. 78ff. G. Rawlinson, *The Five Great Monarchies of the Ancient Eastern World* (1871), pp. 361–390. A. S. Shahbazi, "The 'Traditional Date of Zoroaster' Explained," *Bulletin of the School of Oriental and African Studies* 40 (1977): 25–35. A. Shahpur Shahbazi

D

DACCA. *See* Dhaka.

DAENDELS, HERMAN WILLEM, Napoleonic governor-general of Indonesia. Born in Harderwijk, the Netherlands, on 21 October 1762, Daendels died in the Gold Coast on 2 May 1818. Trained as a lawyer, he participated in the Patriot Revolt against the Dutch *stadhouder,* or governor, and was forced to flee Holland in 1787. Between 1787 and 1795 he played an active role in French revolutionary politics and served in the Batavian legion (recruited from Dutch republican exiles), eventually returning to Holland with the victorious French armies in January 1795. Forced to resign his commission in 1800 after bungling the defense of north Holland against the British and Russians the previous year, he went into retirement but was recalled in 1806 and appointed as marshal of Holland and governor-general designate of Indonesia by Napoleon. He served in the last capacity from January 1808 to May 1811. His administration is characterized by its ruthless reform of the old Dutch East India (VOC) system of government and a harsher policy toward the independent Indonesian rulers. Despite his so-called revolutionary principles, Daendels used corvée (unpaid labor) from the local population on a vast scale to enhance the military defensibility of Java against the British. Recalled by Napoleon in 1811 because of complaints of peculation against him by ex-VOC officials, he took part in the ill-fated Russian campaign (1811–1812). After the establishment of the kingdom of the Netherlands in 1813, he returned to Dutch service and died in office as governor-general of the Gold Coast.

[*See also* Java, British Occupation of.]

Peter Carey

DAENG PARANI (d. 1724), a Bugis prince from Bone, Sulawesi, was the eldest of a group of five brothers who in the early eighteenth century sailed west with their followers to make their fortunes. Daringly seizing opportunities offered by the fluid political situations in the Malay states, they all attained high rank. His brothers were Daeng Marewa, the first Bugis *raja muda* of Johor; Daeng Cellak, who succeeded the latter in 1728; Daeng Menambom, who became *pangeran mas seri negara* of Mempawah; and Daeng Kumasi, who became *pangeran mankubumi* of Sambas. Daeng Parani, after helping to establish Bugis settlements in Selangor and Riau, was killed in Kedah, where the Bugis intervened in a civil war. The story of the brothers is told in the Bugis chronicle *Tuhfat al Nafis.*

[*See also* Bugis; Johor; *and* Raja Muda.]

Barbara W. Andaya and Leonard Y. Andaya, *A History of Malaysia* (1982). Virginia Matheson and Barbara Watson Andaya, trans., *The Precious Gift (Tuhfat al-Nafis)* (1982).

Dianne Lewis

DAGON. *See* Rangoon.

DAGU FORTS, a series of defensive fortifications and gun emplacements located at the mouth of the Beihe (Northern River), near Tianjin, China. The forts were the scene of numerous engagements between Qing forces and the imperialist powers during the nineteenth century.

Consisting of four main forts, two on each side of the river, the Dagu earthworks presented a formidable obstacle for any expedition seeking to reach Beijing. During the Arrow War the forts were attacked three times, once unsuccessfully. After first falling to a joint Anglo-French force in May 1858, the defenses were much improved by the Mongol general Senggerinchin, who then routed a second Anglo-French flotilla in June 1859. Nevertheless, in August 1860 the Europeans outmaneuvered the defenders and captured the forts from the rear, thus opening the way to Beijing.

Subsequently, the forts were restored and upgraded with modern weapons, but fell once again to the Allies during the Boxer Uprising in June 1900. Finally, by the provisions of the Boxer Protocol of 1901, all the forts between Beijing and the sea, including Dagu, were ordered destroyed.

[*See also* Arrow War; Senggerinchin; *and* Yihetuan.]

Jack Beeching, *The Chinese Opium Wars* (1975).

ROLAND L. HIGGINS

DAI CO VIET ("great Viet"), name given to the Viet state by Dinh Bo Linh in 966 and maintained by subsequent Viet rulers until 1054. The term *Dai Co* probably is a compound of the Sino-Viet and Viet words for "great" and is regarded by some scholars as an early example of *chu nom* (Viet characters).

[*See also* Dinh Bo Linh.]

Keith W. Taylor, *The Birth of Vietnam* (1983).

JAMES M. COYLE

DAI LA THANH ("great rampart"), capital of the Viet territories during the last years of Chinese rule and the period of autonomy preceding Viet independence of China (767–939). It is located within the confines of the present-day city of Hanoi. After the former capital had been devastated in the Indonesian raids of 767, the Tang governor of Annam had a new capital built slightly to the east of the ruins. Dai La Thanh, the third capital to be built on this site since 767, was erected by the Tang military governor Kao Pian in 866, after he had driven the armies of Nanzhao out of the delta. The name of the capital derives from the extensive fortifications surrounding it.

[*See also* Hanoi *and* Annam.]

Keith W. Taylor, *The Birth of Vietnam* (1983).

JAMES M. COYLE

DAIMYO, principal landholding vassals of the premodern Japanese shogunate with incomes in excess of ten thousand *koku* (a measure of value in terms of rice equivalence). The term *daimyo* is a combination of *dai* ("large") and *myō* ("name"; from *myōden,* "name land," which referred to privately owned land). The first appearance of the term is in eleventh-century documents.

As sworn vassals of the shogun, Tokugawa daimyo received fief lands rated at least ten thousand *koku* in productivity, which were utilized not only to support the daimyo and his family but also to underwrite military or other service to the shogun. The band of daimyo retainers were called the *kashindan.* Endowed with autocratic power, each daimyo administered his domains from a central headquarters in conjunction with a retainer-staffed bureaucracy. This did not, however, extend to the basic units of governance for most premodern Japanese, that is, the village and the urban ward, which were largely autonomous under regional retainer supervision. Daimyo seldom saw direct shogunal interference in their affairs unless there was evidence of corruption or maladministration. In 1871 the daimyo domains were abolished by the new Meiji (1868–1912) regime and replaced by the modern prefectural system, and the daimyo became a pensioned nobility residing in Tokyo.

Postwar scholarship has identified a process of daimyo evolution commencing with the constable *(shugo)* daimyo of the Muromachi period (1333–1573) and culminating in the early modern *(kinsei)* daimyo of the Tokugawa period (1600–1868). This evolution saw the increasing institutionalization of daimyo subordination to shogunal overlords.

During the Muromachi period, the Ashikaga shoguns enlisted the support of powerful provincial warrior houses by appointing them as constables *(shugo)* with administrative and fiscal powers in the provinces. As the reality of a weakening central government became increasingly evident, the *shugo* expanded their provincial power bases and subinfeudated other warriors as their vassals, thus becoming *shugo* daimyo. The Hosokawa, Takeda, Hatakeyama, Uesugi, Ouchi, and Shimazu *shugo* daimyo came to control extensive lands (frequently scattered over several provinces) that were administered by their principal vassals, for the *shugo* daimyo preferred residence in the shogunal capital of Kyoto and involvement in intrigues at the center. Their absentee status, together with involvement in successional disputes, resulted in conflicts and reduction in the *shugo* daimyo ranks in the period of the Ōnin War (1467–1477), as their retainers took advantage of their absence to seize control at the local level and thus initiated the second stage of daimyo evolution, the Sengoku ("warring states") daimyo of the late medieval period.

Famous Sengoku daimyo houses like the Chōsokabe, Mori, Ukita, and Ryūzōji controlled domains that were much smaller and more integrated than those of the *shugo* daimyo. Two other important differences were the building of castles and the establishment of castle towns to serve as both military and administrative centers (thus providing the Sengoku daimyo with a physical presence in their domains) and the weakening of central government. It is because these daimyo were ruthless and resorted to force that the preimperial Chinese term *zhanguo* (Japanese, *sengoku;* "warring states") is used. As a result of the complete breakdown of central authority, the Sengoku era is considered the period of high feudalism in Japanese history.

Into this chaos came the late-sixteenth-century unifiers Oda Nobunaga (1534–1582) and Toyotomi Hideyoshi (1536–1598), who began the process of eliminating daimyo autonomy and welding the daimyo once again into a group of loyal vassals much more responsive to the demands of their overlords while at the same time extending their own control over core sections of Japan. The new daimyo are referred to by historians as *shokuhō* daimyo (*shoku* and *hō* being alternative readings for the first characters of the surnames of Oda and Toyotomi). [*See* Oda Nobunaga *and* Toyotomi Hideyoshi.]

The establishment of the Tokugawa *bakufu* (1600–1868) produced the final stage in the long process of daimyo evolution. The Tokugawa shogunate exercised a greater degree of control over its daimyo than had its predecessors, developing a system of controls that included constraints on new castle construction and castle repairs; forbidding intermarriage among daimyo houses without shogunal consent; inspection trips by shogunal officials to daimyo domains; status distinctions between related *(shinpan),* inner *(fudai),* and outer *(tozama)* lords; and the *sankin kōtai* ("alternate attendance") system.

[*See also* Shugo; Sengoku Period; Bakufu; Tozama Daimyo; *and* Sankin Kōtai.]

Peter Arnesen, *The Medieval Japanese Diamyo: The Ouchi Family's Rule of Suo and Nagato* (1979). Harold Bolitho, *Treasures among Men: The Fudai Daimyo in Tokugawa Japan* (1974). John Hall, *Government and Local Power in Japan, 500–1700: A Study Based on Bizen Province* (1966). John Hall and Marius B. Jansen, eds., *Studies in the Institutional History of Early Modern Japan* (1968). John Hall, K. Nagahara, and K. Yamamura, eds., *Japan Before Tokugawa: Political and Economic Growth, 1500–1650* (1981). Jeffrey Mass, *Warrior Government in Early Medieval Japan* (1974). H. Paul Varley, *The Ōnin War* (1967). RONALD J. DICENZO

DAI NAM ("great south"), official name of Vietnam under the Nguyen dynasty from 1838 to 1945. The name was adopted by the Minh Mang emperor in celebration of his achievements. The Chinese were not informed and continued to refer to Vietnam as Annam in official documents. The name was used by the Nguyen court even after the division of Vietnam by France.

[*See also* Nguyen Dynasty *and* Minh Mang.]

A. B. Woodside, *Vietnam and the Chinese Model* (1971). JAMES M. COYLE

DAI NGU ("great Yu"), name of the Viet state under the short-lived Ho dynasty (1400–1407). Ho Quy Ly, founder of that dynasty, claimed descent from the legendary Chinese sage-king Shun.

[*See also* Ho Dynasty.]

E. Gaspardone, "Le Qui Ly," in *Dictionary of Ming Biography*, edited by L. Carrington Goodrich (1976).

JAMES M. COYLE

DAI VIET ("great Viet"), name of the Viet state from 1054 to 1802, except during the period of the Ho dynasty and Ming occupation (1407–1427). Emperor Ly Thanh Tong changed the name of the country from Dai Co Viet to Dai Viet.

[*See also* Ho Dynasty.]

Thomas Hodgkin, *Vietnam: The Revolutionary Path* (1981). JAMES M. COYLE

DAI VIET PARTY. Organized in 1939 by nationalist intellectuals, the Dai Viet (Greater Viet) Party collaborated with Japanese occupation authorities in the hope of obtaining Vietnamese independence from the French. After the war, it competed for power in the new Democratic Republic of Vietnam but was outmaneuvered by the Communists.

In 1949 some party leaders joined the French-sponsored Bao Dai government but later left in disillusionment. After 1954 the party was active in South Vietnamese politics, opposing the Ngo Dinh Diem regime and playing a role in the governments formed after its overthrow. The party lacked a solid popular base, however, and its influence declined under the presidency of Nguyen Van Thieu.

[*See also* Vietnam *and* Bao Dai.]

Allan E. Goodman, *Politics in War* (1973). Archimedes Patti, *Why Viet Nam? Prelude to America's Albatross* (1980). WILLIAM J. DUIKER

DAI ZHEN (1723–1777), also known as Dai Dongyuan, outstanding Chinese thinker of the mid-

Qing dynasty, editor or author of some fifty works. Born in Anhui, the son of a merchant, Dai became a scholar in the Hanlin Academy. Dai was a leading figure in the Han Learning movement, in which early Qing scholars turned away from the orthodox Neo-Confucianism of Zhu Xi (1130–1200) and sought concrete knowledge in subjects such as phonology, history, astronomy, mathematics, geography, and textual analysis. Dai went beyond others to develop the moral side of the new philosophy, stressing the material ether *(qi)* at the expense of principle *(li)* and embracing instincts and emotions.

Wing-tsit Chan, *A Source Book in Chinese Philosophy* (1963). Arthur W. Hummel, ed., *Eminent Chinese of the Ch'ing Period* (1943–1944). EDWARD L. FARMER

DAJŌKAN (Council of State), the supreme policy-making and administrative office in Japan in the Nara and Heian periods. As established in the Taihō Codes of 702, the Dajōkan was essentially a body of aristocrats who advised the emperor. The Dajōkan was divided into three parts. First, high-ranking aristocrats *(kugyō)* held the offices of minister of the left, minister of the right, grand councillor *(dainagon),* and adviser *(sangi).* The *kugyō* discussed national issues and advised the emperor. Second, a group of lesser aristocrats served as minor councillors *(shonagon)* and secretaries *(geki).* This second rank of councillors advised the emperor on lesser matters and conveyed his edicts to other officials. The third and largest component of the Council of State consisted of controllers *(benkan)* and lesser functionaries, who oversaw the implementation of policy at one of the eight major ministries (for example, the Ministry of War or the Ministry of Population) and in the provinces.

Advisory bodies like the Council of State had assisted the Yamato king during the sixth and early seventh centuries, yet the true creator of the Nara Council of State was Emperor Temmu. He borrowed heavily from Sui and Tang Chinese governmental models, copying the Six Ministries (Chinese, *liubu*), and establishing the office of controller *(daibenkan)* to manage the implementation of laws in the provinces. Unlike later emperors, however, Temmu retained the right to bypass all aristocratic councils and give orders directly. After Temmu's death, the imperial line lost power, and the aristocratic Council of State became all-important.

With the rise of the Fujiwara and the creation of the offices of regent and civil dictator, the power of the Dajōkan waned. It continued, in name only, through the Heian, the medieval, and even the Edo period and was later revived in a different form by the Meiji leaders after the Meiji Restoration.

[*See also* Temmu.]

James Crump, Jr., " 'Borrowed' T'ang Titles and Offices in the Yoro Code," *Occasional Papers of the University of Michigan Center for Japanese Studies* 2 (1952): 35–58. George Sansom, "Early Japanese Law and Administration." *Transactions of the Asiatic Society of Japan,* series 2, 9 (1932): 67–109, and 11 (1934): 117–149; and *A History of Japan to 1334* (1958).

WAYNE FARRIS

DALAI LAMA. Tibetan Buddhists believe that the Dalai Lama is the incarnation of the Buddhist angelic bodhisattva Avalokiteshvara, reborn on earth especially to help the Tibetan people. The Dalai Lamas served as spiritual and secular rulers of Tibet from 1642 until 1959. The present Dalai Lama, Tenzin Gyatso, the fourteenth of the line of incarnations, fled the Chinese Communist invasion of Tibet in 1959 along with about 100,000 Tibetans. He heads the Tibetan government in exile in Dharamsala, India, and travels widely around the world, teaching Buddhism and representing his nation's plight to the international community.

The line of incarnations is believed to have begun in previous aeons, but the first Dalai Lama is usually considered to be Gendun Druba (1391–1474), a nephew and disciple of Tsong Khapa (1357–1419), the founder, in 1400, of the modern Gelugpa monastic order. Gendun Druba was a leader in the new order, writing important works and founding many new monasteries. [*See also* Gelugpa.] His successor Gendun Gyatso (1475–1542) served as charismatic leader of the order, clearly remembering his former life while still a child. Sonam Gyatso (1543–1588) followed as leader during a time of difficulties for the order, as the older Tibetan Buddhist orders were staging a militant "counterreformation" in alliance with the reigning Tsangpa kings. In 1578 he visited Altan Khan of the Tumet Mongols, converting him and his entire nation from the indigenous shamanistic religion to Buddhism. Sonam Gyatso first received the title Dalai Lama ("oceanic teacher") from Altan Khan. Yonden Gyatso (1589–1617), born a Mongol, a grandson of Altan Khan, was the fourth Dalai Lama. [*See also* Altan Khan.]

It was the "Great Fifth" Dalai Lama, Losang Gyatso (1617–1682), who accepted the help of the Mongols to defend the Gelugpa order against various enemies, unify the country, and initiate Tibet's unique system of monastic, bureaucratic government. He built the monumental Potala in Lhasa to celebrate the modern synthesis of church and state that completed Tibetan Buddhist culture. Tsangyang Gyatso (1683–1706), the sixth Dalai Lama, refused ordination as a Buddhist monk, wrote love poems, and, although beloved by the people, could not hold the system together. [*See also* Tsangyang Gyatso.] Kalsang Gyatso (1708–1757) and Jambel Gyatso (1758–1804), the seventh and eighth Dalai Lamas, restored the government and presided over a very creative century for Tibet. None of the ninth through twelfth Dalai Lamas reached majority and was able to assume the reigns of power; the result was a period of instability in Tibet. Thupten Gyatso (1876–1933), the thirteenth Dalai Lama, evaded the same fate and lived to reign significantly. He made considerable efforts to bring Tibet into the modern world, at first largely frustrated by a declining Manchu empire and later by a declining British empire.

The fourteenth Dalai Lama, Tenzin Gyatso (b. 1935), assumed the throne at the moment of the 1950 invasion of the Chinese People's Liberation Army. He has spent more than half of his life in exile, successfully preserving the culture of his land and working toward the day he foresees when he and the more modernized Tibetans educated in India and the West will return to Tibet to reconstruct a nation.

[*See also* Buddhism; Lamaism; Panchen Lama; *and* Tibet.]

John F. Avedon, *In Exile from the Land of Snows* (1984). Charles Bell, *Portrait of the Thirteenth Dalai Lama* (1946). Tenzin Gyatso (Dalai Lama), *My Land and My People* (reprint, 1983). ROBERT A. F. THURMAN

DALHOUSIE, MARQUIS OF. *See* Ramsay, James Andrew Broun.

DALI, small city on the western shore of Erhai in Yunnan Province, China. Traditionally the center of northwestern Yunnan, in the eighth century it was the capital of the Nanzhao state, which controlled parts of Burma, Thailand, and Vietnam, as well as southwestern China. From the early tenth century to the Mongol conquest in the thirteenth century it was the center of the kingdom of Dali. Since the construction of the Burma Road at the end of World War II, Dali has been replaced by Xiaguan as the main commercial and industrial city of the region.

JOHN A. RAPP

DAMBADENIYA, Sinhalese kingdom in Sri Lanka that lasted for just over a century, from the beginning of the reign of Vijayabahu III (r. 1232–1236). It was a period of decline in the political power of the Sinhalese on the retreat to the hills under pressure from South Indian invaders. The capital of the kingdom, also called Dambadeniya, was a rock fortress located in the northwest of the island. Despite its political weakness, if not instability, the period of the Dambadeniya kings, especially its first ruler and his successor, Parakramabahu II (r. 1236–1270), was remarkable for its vigorous and renewed creativity in literature and the revival of Buddhism.

[*See also* Parakramabahu II *and* Sri Lanka.]

K. M. de Silva, *A History of Sri Lanka* (1981). A. Liyanagamage, *The Decline of Polonnaruva and the Rise of Dambadeniya* (1968). K. M. DE SILVA

DAMRONG RAJANUBHAB (1862–1943), major reformer of Thailand's education and provincial administration, historian, and leading intellectual.

Prince Damrong was a son of King Mongkut by a lesser wife and was but a child when his older half-brother Chulalongkorn came to the throne in 1868. He attended the special school the king founded for his younger half-brothers in the early 1870s, worked in various palace offices, and entered the Royal Pages' Bodyguard Regiment in 1877, becoming its commander three years later when only eighteen. In the early 1880s he took on the administration of a succession of new government and military schools in addition to helping organize the modern army. He became deputy commander-in-chief of the army in 1887 and, at the same time, director and minister-designate of the Department of Education. In 1891 he represented the king on a tour of Europe and South Asia and returned to Siam expecting to be appointed the new minister of education in the government reorganization of April 1892. To the surprise of all, including the prince, he was named minister of interior, charged with supervising the complete overhaul of provincial administration in the face of dangerous Western (especially French) expansionism.

Within a few years, Damrong completely changed the methods by which the provinces were governed. He created a completely new central bureaucracy staffed with the graduates of modern educational institutions, consolidated provinces into eighteen administrative "circles," instituted tight budgeting and fiscal controls, introduced modern laws, and promoted public works and social services. He drastically reduced provincial autonomy—which often had amounted to anarchy—and instituted the rule of law. More than any other figure in the government, he worked for social change, opening public office to men of talent irrespective of their social origin. When other organs of government proved unable to work effectively in the provinces to reorganize the Buddhist monkhood and introduce mass primary education, Damrong's Ministry of Education took on the tasks. Throughout the rest of the reign, to 1910, Damrong was, with his half-brothers princes Wachirayan and Devawongse, one of the king's most valued advisers and servants, as well as the most powerful man in the kingdom next to the king.

Damrong found working under his nephew King Vajiravudh difficult and resigned his ministry in 1915. Thereafter he threw himself fully into work as director of what ultimately were to become the National Library and National Museum. He wrote extensively on every aspect of Thai history, literature, culture, customs, and arts and promoted the practice by which books were distributed at funeral ceremonies in honor of the deceased—a practice that brought most of Thailand's literary heritage into print for the first time. He usually wrote a biography of the deceased for the book. He is revered as the father of history in Thailand, but he is also the father of modern administration, modern medicine and hospitals, and schools.

Prince Damrong fled to exile in Penang (Malaya) after the 1932 coup that ended the absolute monarchy; he died there in 1943.

[*See also* Chulalongkorn; Devawongse Varopakar; and Wachirayan Warorot.]

Tej Bunnag, *The Provincial Administration of Siam 1892–1915* (1977). David K. Wyatt, *The Politics of Reform in Thailand* (1969) and *Thailand: A Short History* (1984).

DAVID K. WYATT

DANCE. Like the musical and dramatic traditions of various Asian cultures, the major traditions of Asian dance reflect the interplay of both local and regional influences. Principal among these latter are the cultures of India and China, which have loaned their distinctive cast to a wide spectrum of social institutions throughout Asia.

South Asian Dance Traditions. India is a complex world of performing arts. Over a period of two thousand years, India was a significant crossroads of East and West, a major cultural source for the Himalayan region as well as for Inner and East Asia, and the most potent contributor to the development of the arts of literature and theater in Southeast Asia. At various points in history, beginning as early as the first century of the common era, India's commercial, religious, literary, and artistic patterns and models penetrated much of Asia. During the first millennium of the common era Hinduism was transmitted from India to Southeast Asia, and Buddhism to Southeast, Central, and East Asia. This penetration had significant results, including the stimulation of new developments that changed the face of dance and theater in Burma, Malaysia, Java, Bali, Cambodia, Thailand, and, to perhaps a lesser degree, Tibet, China, and Japan. By the fourteenth and fifteenth centuries elements of Muslim culture originating from sources in Turkestan, Persia, and Arabia and synthesized in India were already spreading by sea routes to the island and coastal kingdoms of Southeast Asia as far as the Philippines. Thus, India's legacy to other areas of Asia is not confined to the arts, crafts, and aesthetic literature that accompanied Buddhism and Hinduism. It also includes the genius for abstraction and rich ornamentation of Islamic culture that was later applied to music and dance as well as to art and architecture.

Dance in India is such an important part of drama that traditional Indian theater can scarcely exist without the presence of dance. Pure dance, as differentiated from dance within drama, has also existed from a very early period; this is evident from the figures of dancers sculpted as early as the first century at Bharhut. Although the roots of dance in India are very ancient, the dance forms themselves have undergone many transformations over the course of the centuries. For example, the solo dance form known as *bharatanatyam,* an art of the temples and of the royal courts of South India, was recodified and reformed in the late eighteenth or early nineteenth century. The musical compositions that are the basis for some of the items in the *bharatanatyam* repertoire date from the sixteenth century, but the roots of the tradition are undoubtedly much older than that. *Kathak,* the major classical dance form of North India, is a product of a synthesis of Hindu and Muslim culture made primarily between the sixteenth and eighteenth century. It is likely, however, that *kathak* has its roots in the art of storytellers who practiced their art in the temples, gradually adding dramatization and dance to their recounting of myth and legend. The solo female dance forms of India, which included such forms as *mohiniyattam* of Kerala and the dances of the Maharis of Orissa, suffered a decline in the nineteenth and early twentieth centuries because of the social stigma that came to be attached to the dancers' profession (some dancers were also courtesans). The dance traditions survived this misfortune, and today dance has become an accepted social accomplishment as well as a worthy profession. Outstanding dance artists are honored by the central government, and grants are awarded to support schools of classical dance.

A major form of dance from the courts of Java is the *bedhaya,* a graceful swaying dance for women. The origins of the *bedhaya* are shrouded in myth. It is said that the god Brahma created a series of beautiful women. To please the deity they began to dance, whereupon he created three more faces for himself so that he could see all of the dancers at once. There are also many forms of solo dance for women in Java, such as the *serimpi* and the *golek.* Although the court was the principal center of dance and music in the past, these arts are gradually becoming more accessible to dancers outside the court. In Bali, the trance dances of young girls, called *sang hyang dedari,* have origins in antiquity. In the eighteenth century, *sang hyang dedari* developed into *sang hyang legong,* a sacred masked dance, which is now rarely performed. This form eventually became the *legong* that we know today. Classical *legong* was originally a palace art, but it is now performed throughout Bali in connection with many kinds of ceremonies and as an entertainment for tourists. The *baris* dance for men is derived principally from the martial arts. Another, more recent, solo dance for men is the *kebyar,* which was influenced ultimately by the *legong* and which dates only from the early twentieth century.

The classical dance form of Cambodia is believed to have existed at the time of the Khmer empire (804–1431). If so, it has undergone many transformations since that period. In the fifteenth century, the Thai conquered the land and carried off, among their spoils, the court dance troupe. The Khmer dance form continued its development in Thailand, and about the nineteenth century was reintroduced into Cambodia. The result was the formal Royal Cambodian Ballet. *Lakhon nai* is the principal type of female classical dance in Thailand; about the eighteenth century it developed essentially into a dance-drama form rather than a form of pure dance. The Burmese dance form *pwe* reveals clear historic and choreographic relationships with Thai dance and theater as well as much older connections with the dance and theater of eastern India and Sri Lanka.

East Asian Dance Traditions. Although the influence of India seems prevalent in much of Southeast Asia, it is the influence of Chinese culture that has most strongly affected dance in Japan and Korea. Some insights into the role of dance in the Zhou dynasty of China (c. 1111–222 BCE) can be gleaned from such early texts as the *Shijing (Book of Songs).* Dance was important in ancestor worship and in the worship of nature spirits; it was important also as a social accomplishment and in preparation for the hunt and for battle. Dance was performed by the common folk and by nobility; the dances of shamans, especially those invoking the spirits of rain to insure a good harvest, were perhaps the most important of all.

Dance also played a prominent role at the Chinese imperial court. In the seventh century the music and dance of many countries found their way to the Chinese court. Their influence greatly changed the nature of these arts in China. After the fall of the Tang dynasty in the early tenth century, there was a decline of court music and dance, and their importance was correspondingly greatly diminished.

In Korea, the formal dances of the ladies of the court owed much to Chinese influence. Other dance forms in Korea range from the sacred trance dances of shamans to *salp'uri,* performed by *kisaeng,* or courtesan-entertainers.

In Japan, the mythological origins of dance involve the well known myth of the sun goddess, Amaterasu Ōmikami, who was enticed out of the cave where she had hidden herself by the lewd dancing of a lesser goddess, Ame no Uzume no Mikoto, stamping on a drum and evoking the laughter and applause of other assembled deities. The association of dance with religion has persisted in Japan. *Bugaku,* an art form of the imperial courts, believed to be one of the oldest living dance traditions in the world, is performed also at Shinto shrines and is involved with rituals of purification. Some of the *bugaku* dances were derived from music and dance that came originally from India, Vietnam, China, and Korea, although other *bugaku* dances had their origins in sacred dance and music indigenous to Japan. *Bugaku* reached its zenith near the end of the Heian period (794–1185).

A major category of religious dance in premodern Japan was the *kaguramai,* still performed today at a few Shintō shrines. Also common were communal dances performed as recreation, and religious dance meant to supplicate the deities or to gain some special favor. An example of a group dance performed for pleasure was *furyū odori* of the late sixteenth and early seventeenth centuries; this dance developed gradually into a presentational art form, a pattern of development that is not uncommon in the history of dance in Japan.

Dance as a part of the dramatic form *kabuki* is another major facet of dance in Japan. In the early twentieth century dances from *kabuki* dramas, including what is essentially a new dance genre in that style, began to emerge as an independent art form. This new genre was called *Nihon buyō*. In the recent past, trends in Japanese dance that are closely related to contemporary dance in the West have also made their appearance and are continuing to develop. [*See also* Kabuki.]

The transition from sacred to secular is a familiar theme in the history of Asian dance forms. Another common aspect is the role of the martial arts as inspiration for the development of dances for men. A number of the dances mentioned above have close connections with religion and ritual. Folk dances of great variety, beauty, and vitality are found in each of these areas. Perhaps the most salient characteristic of Asia's myriad dance forms is the intricate interrelationship between the dances of one cultural/linguistic area and another, which has shaped the patterns and theories of these ephemeral forms of art.

[*See also* Drama *and* Music.]

Reynaldo Alejandro, *Philippine Dance* (1978). Miguel Covarrubias, *Island of Bali* (1938). Earle Ernst, *The Kabuki Theatre* (1974). Masakatsu Gunji, *Buyō: The Classical Dance* (1970). Betty True Jones, ed., *Dance As Cultural Heritage* (2 vols., 1983, 1985). Kapila Vatsyayan, *Classical Indian Dance in Literature and the Arts* (1968) and *Indian Classical Dance* (1974). Beryl de Zoete and Walter Spies, *Dance and Drama in Bali* (1939).

CLIFFORD REIS JONES

DANISH EAST INDIA COMPANY. Founded in 1616, the company established its first Indian settlement at Tranquebar, on the Coromandel coast, in 1620, and its second in Serampore, near Calcutta, in 1755. Never numerous in India and politically unambitious as to empire, the Danes sold their factories to the British in 1845.

[*See also* Imperialism.]

USHA SANYAL

DANJŪRŌ, the most celebrated name in the history of Japanese *kabuki* drama. The first actor to bear the name was Ichikawa Danjūrō (1660–1704), the pioneer Edo actor who originated the *aragoto* ("rough stuff") style of portraying superhuman heroes with exaggerated postures and bravura language. He made his debut at the age of eleven under the name Ebizō in the role of the strong boy Kintoki, for which he wore red body paint and red and black facial makeup in bold lines. Later his acting was influenced by the movements of the *kimpira*-style puppets that were popular in Edo at the time. He played in *aragoto* style the principal roles in the dramas *Narukami, Shibaraku,* and *Kanjinchō*. He was stabbed to death on stage by a fellow actor, Ikushima Hanroku. His son, Danjūrō II (1688–1758), was also the leading Edo actor of his day. He played the romantic lover in *Sukeroku* as well as the *aragoto* parts of Soga Gorō and Watōnai (in *Kokusen'ya kassen*). He furthered the success of the Ichikawa lineage as the leading stage family and added luster to the name Danjūrō. Danjūrō VII (1791–1859) compiled a list of eighteen pieces to be considered the vested property of the Ichikawa family *(kabuki jūhachiban)*. The six selections still in the current repertoire are all one-act works and include the perennial favorites *Kanjinchō, Shibaraku, Sukeroku,* and *Narukami.*

The name Danjūrō has come to be reserved for actors born or adopted into the Ichikawa lineage who have achieved the highest level of proficiency. The conferral of the name *(shūmei)* on Danjūrō XI (1909–1965) took place only three years before his death. His son, who like his father bore the name Ebizō, succeeded to the name of Danjūrō XII at an announcement ceremony *(kōjō)* performed on the stage at the Kabuki-za in Tokyo during April and May of 1985.

[*See also* Kabuki.]

DONALD H. SHIVELY

DAN NO URA, bay on which sits the port city of Shimonoseki, on the western tip of Honshu, Japan. Dan no Ura was the site of the final naval battle in the war between the Taira and the Minamoto clans in 1185. The battle marked the final destruction of the Taira clan and the ascendance of the Minamoto as the greatest military house in Japan.

The Taira clan was driven from Kyoto along with the imperial family in the summer of 1183 but remained in control of western Japan. According to the *Azuma kagami,* Minamoto no Yoshitsune prepared more than eight hundred ships for the battle, while the Taira leader Munemori gathered a flotilla of over five hundred ships. As the two navies drew up battle lines, Munemori divided his force into three parts and opened the attack. At first the Taira strategy seemed to succeed. However, the Taira suffered casualties when their ships came within range of Minamoto archers on shore, and they also suffered several desertions, such as that of Tauchi Shigetoshi of Awa. As the battle turned against the Taira, Taira no Tomomori advised his most prominent passengers, including the consort Kenreimon'in and the infant emperor Antoku, to drown themselves in the sea. A certain Lady Azechi also leaped into the sea clutching the sacred sword of the imperial family. While the consort and Lady Azechi were saved, the emperor and the sacred sword were both lost. The Taira leader Munemori and his son Kiyomune were captured and taken by Minamoto no Yoshitsune to Kamakura for their executions. Only twenty-eight members of the Taira clan survived, none of them generals.

Minoru Shinoda, *The Founding of the Kamakura Shogunate* (1960). Bruce Tsuchida, trans., *The Tale of the Heike* (1960).

WAYNE FARRIS

DAO DUY TU (1572–1634), military adviser to the Nguyen lord Sai Vuong (Nguyen Phuc Nguyen, r. 1613–1635) of Vietnam. Rejected from the imperial examinations because of his family background, Dao Duy Tu was living as a herdsman when he composed a plaintive poem about his situation. Sai Vuong heard of this work and called him into his service. Dao proposed and supervised the construction of walls at Dong Hoi and Truong Duc (Quang Binh Province), which served as defense fortifications against the northern Trinh. He also guided the Nguyen lord's dealings with the Trinh, counseling him first to acknowledge their position and later to reject it.

[*See also* Nguyen Lords *and* Trinh-Nguyen Wars.]

BRUCE M. LOCKHART

DAOISM. An indigenous Chinese religion, Daoism originally was a school of thought associated with several texts dating from the late Zhou dynasty (1122?–256 BCE). In subsequent centuries, the name *Daoist* came to denote a variety of religious groups, each claiming the authority of Laozi, the alleged author of one of these texts, the *Daode jing.* It has been common for scholars to treat this religious tendency separately from the more abstract school of Daoist philosophy.

Daoist Religion. Elements of the Daoist belief system (known in Chinese as *daojiao,*) such as the Daoist pantheon, shamanism, divination, and the attempt to prolong life through systems of hygiene, ingestion of herbal concoctions, and alchemical elixirs all had their origins in late Zhou dynasty times or earlier. Its long institutional history, however, did not begin until the Latter Han period (25–220 CE).

Early Movements. Two great popular religious movements, each a "state within a state," nearly toppled the Han dynasty in its declining years. Both were organized in self-governing parishes of the faithful who joined in search of personal salvation, social justice, and security within their new communities. One of these movements, the Taipingdao, Way of Great Equilibrium, or (as they were called from their distinguishing headdress) Yellow Turbans, won a vast following in the modern province of Shandong. The other group, originally called the Five Pecks (or Bushels) of Rice Sect because of the annual dues paid by members, later would become the Tianshidao, or Way of the Celestial Master, based in modern Sichuan Province. The movements were nearly identical in their beliefs, practices, and organization.

The organization of the Daoist parish communities was roughly modeled on the subbureaucratic administrative units called *ting* ("communes") of the Han government. Thus, each parish had its own priest-officials who were responsible for all aspects of the material and spiritual well-being of the community. Some of the parish officials used titles that were borrowed directly from the lexicon of the imperial bureaucracy. The supreme leadership of both movements was hereditary in families surnamed Zhang. The chief of all the Five Pecks parishes was titled the *tianshi* ("celestial master"). With longer or shorter lapses, this office has been held for some two thousand years by Daoist priests claiming descent from the founder, Zhang Daoling (fl. 142 CE). The present incumbent still lives in Taiwan.

The main source of information about the principles of these early Daoist movements is a book entitled *Taiping jing (Classic of the Way of Great Equilibrium).* The surviving version of this work is attributed in part to the first *tianshi.* The *taiping* ("great equilibrium" or "great peace") of the title refers to the utopian society that the parish members sought to realize. The society of the Great Equilibrium was a "golden age" concept widely shared in one form or another among late Zhou schools of thought. A sage ruler presided effortlessly over a perfectly harmonious society that was itself perfectly attuned to a harmonious cosmic order. This society was hierarchical, rather than egalitarian, but in perfect justice everyone occupied his proper place and was justly rewarded, and no one was in want.

This imagined golden age had long ago given way to a world made unhappy by strife, illness, untimely death, and natural disasters. But the cyclical theories of cosmology and history that were popular in late Zhou and Han times encouraged the hope that the conditions of the golden age could be restored. According to the Confucians, this could be achieved by reestablishing and revitalizing the "rites and music," that is, the cultural, social, and governmental patterns of the Zhou founders. The people of the Five Pecks and the Yellow Turbans adopted a different course, however, which gave each movement its distinctive Daoist stamp.

For the faithful of the new religion, the way to the society of the Great Equilibrium led through spiritual purification. For the individual, organic diseases were attributed to moral faults and could therefore be cured by public confessional, repentance, and punishment. A common sentence was a term of work on the roads *(dao),* by which the Way *(dao)* of the Great Equilibrium would be advanced. Violations of the ban on drinking wine in the spring or summer were punished by service in building earthen walls because in the cosmologists' cycle of the five material forces, "earth" absorbed "water," or in this case, wine. Good physical and spiritual health and long life were also maintained by positive measures such as meditation upon the Dao as the principle of unity, and by various exercises in dietary and sexual hygiene. Extraordinary individuals might even escape the finality of death and the dispersal of their vital essence by becoming *xian,* "immortals."

At the level of community, failure to attain the Great Equilibrium was caused by the imposition of obstacles to the circulation of "essences" *(qi).* For example, in relations between the sexes, sexual abstinence was condemned because it upset the interaction of *yin* (female) and *yang* (male) essences, and the killing of infant girls was severely condemned because the practice caused an imbalance in the strength of *yin* and *yang.* In a similar kind of reasoning, since all material goods were bestowed upon mankind collectively by heaven and earth, hoarding them was forbidden because it blocked their circulation through the community.

For these early Daoists as for other people of that time, heaven and earth were inhabited by largely the same assortment of benign and malignant spirits and, like others, they believed that certain celestial and terrestrial spirits recorded the deeds and misdeeds of the living and punished them according to their deserts. But as Daoists, they attached particular importance to the spirit of Laozi, the late Zhou philosopher, whom they adopted as their divine patron, and the work attributed to him, *Daode jing (The Way and Its Power),* was held to be a sacred text.

Although the Yellow Turbans were suppressed in a bloody war beginning in 184 CE, the Five Pecks were more fortunate. They were able to negotiate a surrender, and so preserved their local organization, even though they lost their political independence. From the defeat of these two early Daoist movements, the Daoist religion emerged with parishes presided over by a largely hereditary priesthood; the core of what was to become an immense canonical literature; a pantheon with its associated cults and temples; and a repertoire of practices aimed at the prolongation of life or physical immortality. [*See also* Yellow Turbans *and* Five Bushels of Rice Sect.]

The later history of Daoism was shaped in part by the further development of its own principles. Daoist priests presided over communal rites, officiated at temple sacrifices, said masses for the dead, exorcised demons, cured illnesses, used their skill in geomancy *(fengshui)* in the siting of buildings and tombs, and advanced the arcane arts of prolonging life by their systems of "interior and exterior hygiene." Daoist experiments with herbal elixirs led to the compilation of immense pharmacological encyclopedias that are a valuable medical source today, and their experiments with mineral elixirs constituted the basis of traditional Chinese chemical science. One consequence of this continuing research was that Daoist sectarianism proliferated as fresh revelations from the world of spirits were secretly handed down to generations of disciples.

Competition with Buddhism. The Daoist religion was no sooner well established, however, than its priests found themselves faced with powerful competition. Mahayana Buddhism, introduced into China from India, was rapidly popularized during the fourth, fifth, and sixth centuries. Buddhist missionaries arrived with promises of individual salvation through divine grace; a splendid pantheon and vividly represented heavens and hells; monastic orders with a long tradition behind them; a ready-made art and iconography; and a rich and varied religious literature that ranged from subtle metaphysical speculation to cosmology, ethics, and mythology, plus stories that entertained as well as instructed. The also arrived with supernatural arts that rivaled those of the Daoists.

Without abandoning their roots in the indigenous religion, the Daoist clergy successfully adapted certain Buddhist ideas and practices to their own purposes. During the sixth century, most of the Daoist resident temples *(guan)* became monastic institutions for celibate monks or nuns governed by a strict code of behavior *(qinggui)* like the Buddhist monastery temples with their Vinaya rules. Married priests thereafter usually lived at home. At about the same time, the Daoists began to organize their scriptures in what they called the *Daozang (Daoist Treasury)* in obvious emulation of the (Buddhist) Tripitaka, or *Sanzang*. Moreover, the Daoist pantheon was changed in response to the popularity of Mahayana Buddhism's bodhisattva ideal: devotional worship of compassionate gods dedicated to universal salvation. The *san qing* ("three pure ones") now made their appearance. These were Yuanshi Tianzun ("Celestial Honored Being of the Original Beginning") and his deputies Yu Huang ("Jade Emperor") and Jinque Yuchen Tianzu ("Celestial Honored One of the Golden Gate and the Jade Dawn"). The many halls of the Three Pure Ones still to be seen in Daoist temples testify to the popularity of this triad.

During the period of division between the end of the Han and the beginning of the Tang period, Daoism and Buddhism both enjoyed the patronage of a powerful and self-confident aristocratic class. There were imperial patrons as well. On two occasions, in the fifth and ninth centuries, Daoists had a hand in imperial persecutions of Buddhism. They often enjoyed the favor of the Tang emperors, who were persuaded that they were lineal descendants of Laozi since they shared his surname of Li. But the decline of the aristocracy during late Tang and the Five Dynasties periods deprived both Buddhism and Daoism of their wealthiest patrons.

Late Imperial Developments. Both religions lost ground with the new office-holding class, which depended upon the Confucian-based civil service examination system to establish their elite social status. On the other hand, emperors of the Song (960–1279) and Ming (1368–1644) dynasties were often drawn to Daoism for various reasons. Some, hoping for immortality, lavishly patronized alchemists, while others felt more secure on their thrones when they were in communication with gods of the Daoist pantheon. Indeed, throughout the Ming dynasty, the great imperial sacrifices to Heaven and Earth were carried out with the aid of Daoist dancers and musicians because of their presumed special relation with the cosmic powers, and a Daoist monastery was maintained next to the Altar of Heaven to house them. Under these circumstances, Daoists often found themselves allied with emperors and the common people against hostile Confucian bureaucrats.

During this late imperial period of Daoist history, from Song through Qing (1644–1911), most of the ordained Daoist clergy were distributed between two great sects. One of these was the Way of the Celestial Masters, which gained imperial recognition in the eleventh century. The Celestial Masters resided on Dragon-Tiger Mountain (Longhu Shan) in Jiangxi Province until 1949. The priests of this sect are not celibate, live at home, and pass down their calling within their families. The other principal sect is the Quanzhen ("Perfect Realization") sect. This is a monastic sect that maintains its national seat in the Baiyunguan (White Cloud Monastery) in Beijing. This monastery, recently reopened to the public, now serves as a Daoist seminary.

Despite the evident importance of Buddhist-Daoist interaction, the strongest affiliations of Daoist religion throughout its history were with popular religion on the one hand and the state religion on the other. As late as the Song dynasty, after the wide dissemination of the more accessible doctrines of Buddhism in China, popular religion assumed its modern form. The popular religion, for all its diversity and variability in its details, is fairly consistent in its principles, which include hierarchy, retributive justice, and the origin of most of the pantheon in the spirits of historical or legendary persons.

In the popular religion, hierarchy is implicit in the notion that the spirits are unequally endowed with effective power *(ling);* the greater the *ling,* the higher the rank. The principle is often expressed in the representation of the pantheon as a spiritual empire of bureaucrats in service to the court of a celestial sovereign, usually the Jade Emperor. Retributive justice is expressed, for example, in the pervasive notion that everyone's behavior is observed by the Stove (or Kitchen) God (Zaojun), whose picture is pasted up near the stove, and reported by him monthly to the local City God and annually to the Jade Emperor. This belief in retribution was also reflected in popular books that spelled out the rewards and punishments in great detail. The spirits are understood to behave much like ordinary people, however, and can be swayed by generous offerings. As a consequence of the third principle, the spirits of extraordinary people are presumed to survive as divinities of some importance and are therefore to be housed in new or existing temples, where they may be approached by worshipers seeking their help. Thus, as old spirits may sometimes pass into oblivion because their worshipers have forgotten them, new ones are always being added to the popular pantheon.

Daoism and the popular religion deeply interpenetrated. On the one hand, it was the Daoist clergy, far more than the Buddhist monks, who served and managed the popular temples and shrines that housed the mountain spirits, dragon kings, military heroes, immortals, good officials, and, perhaps most important, communal protectors such as the city gods and neighborhood gods (*chenghuang* and *tudi*). The popular religion, therefore, gave them an important role as community leaders. This role, more than anything else, may account for the religion's long survival. On the other hand, many of the cults continually being added to the Daoist pantheon must have originated in the domain of the popular religion. The Daoist clergy therefore found it necessary continually to redefine the boundary that divided their orthodox pantheon from those popular cults they considered to be unorthodox and unacceptable.

Daoism also interpenetrated with the official religion of the empire. Daoism, like Buddhism, was given an officially recognized place in the empire's universal order. Parallel hierarchical offices were set up in the Ministry of Rites and in local government to enforce rules regarding the construction and size of monasteries and the ordination and discipline of the clergy of both religions. In this sense, the entire religious establishment was subsumed directly under the imperial regime.

It was also the case, however, that Daoist priests enjoyed an important role in the official religion itself. The official religion comprised an annual schedule of tens of thousands of sacrifices to the spirits of the official pantheon, which were to be offered at all levels of government from the emperor himself down to the district magistrate. And even below the level of the district magistrate, the sacrifices in township, village, and home were also prescribed by law. Among the cults of the official religion, some of the most important served the spirits of nature. Daoists not only performed in the sacrifices to Heaven previously mentioned, but Daoist priests were also regularly in charge of the official temples of the sacred mountains and rivers, and of the city gods, even though the local civil officials were required to preside over the statutory sacrifices that were offered there.

The Daoist School. The term *daojia* ("Daoist school") denotes an ill-defined tendency within the history of Chinese thought that can reasonably be associated with the late Zhou dynasty books of Laozi and Zhuangzi as among its most important texts. Common to both these works is the rejection of the arbitrary and the calculated in favor of the spontaneous *(ziran)* in action, or *wuwei* ("non-[purposive] action"); and the rejection of perceptions of multifarious phenomena as the access to truth in favor of the intuitive grasp of the Dao as the indescribable and inexhaustible source of all being.

The Han historian Sima Qian asserted in his *Historical Records* that leading thinkers of the Legalist school of politics, Shen Buhai and Han Fei, were inspired by the "Huang-Lao" doctrines. [*See also* Legalism; Shen Buhai; *and* Han Feizi.] On other good evidence, it has long been known that the Huang-Lao school was the dominant ideology of the Han dynasty for some seventy years until Emperor Wu assumed the throne in 141 BCE and established a Confucian-based syncretism. It was assumed that the name *Huang-Lao* concerned the mythical emperor Huangdi and the philosopher Laozi, but the recent archaeological discovery of lost texts of the school now makes it possible to begin to describe its doctrines as an accommodation of Daoist ideas to the requirements of rulership. The Legalist description of the ruler as detached and remote, yet acutely aware and perfectly responsive, appears to owe something to Huang-Lao inspiration, and the early Han style of rulership was consistent with Huang-Lao doctrines. Simplicity and frugality at court and minimal government activity were joined to the ruler's *wuwei* practice of simply weighing ministerial proposals instead of initiating policies. On a deeper level, Daoist principles encouraged the expectation that if the world of men could be harmonized with the Dao, the empire would run itself.

Largely eclipsed in the late second century BCE by the eclectic mélange of imperial Confucianism, Daoism became the subject of renewed interest at the end of the Latter Han. The *xuanxue*, or Dark Learning, school of the third and fourth centuries is sometimes described as "neo-Daoist" for its addressing of metaphysical problems posed by Laozi and Zhuangzi, but because its followers were committed disciples of Confucius, one effect of the school's speculations was to provide a metaphysical foundation for Confucian ethics. The world was in flux and spontaneously self-generated, and in the absence of arbitrary human interference, the spontaneously generated institutions and ethics of each age were valid for that age.

Commonly grouped with *xuanxue* under the head of neo-Daoism were the philosophical movements *qingtan* ("pure conversation") and *fengliu* ("wind and stream"), the latter of which was roughly equivalent to our "romanticism." These circles among the aristocracy of Nanjing in the third and fourth centuries adopted the Daoist notion of spontaneity in justification of their unconventional and sometimes outrageous behavior. [*See also* Qingtan.] Daoist tendencies may also be seen in the formation of subitist Chan Buddhism in the seventh and eighth centuries, with its use of baffling paradoxes to break down conventional patterns of thought and to facilitate the direct apprehension of the Dao.

The tendency toward syncretism in philosophy that characterized the development of a Daoist-inspired five-forces *(wuxing)* cosmology and a possibly Buddhist-influenced concept of enlightenment in the Neo-Confucianism of the Song dynasty, and the appearance of eclectic *sanjiao* ("three teachings," i.e., Buddhism, Confucianism, and Daoism) systems of the Ming period, testify to the pervasiveness of Daoist thought in later times.

[*See also* Laozi *and* Zhuangzi.]

Judith A. Berling, *The Syncretic Religion of Lin Chao-en* (1980). Fung Yu-lan, *A Short History of Chinese Philosophy,* translated by Derk Bodde (1960). Max Kaltenmark, *Lao Tzu and Taoism,* translated by Roger Greaves (1969). Henri Maspero, *Taoism and Chinese Religion,* translated by Frank A. Kierman (1980). Tu Wei-ming, "The 'Thought of Huang-Lao': A Reflection on the Lao Tzu and Huang Ti Texts in the Silk Manuscripts of Ma Wang-Tui," *Journal of Asian Studies* 39.1 (1979). Holmes Welch, *Taoism: The Parting of the Way* (1957). Holmes Welch and Anna Seidel, eds., *Facets of Taoism* (1979).

ROMEYN TAYLOR

DAR AL-FONUN, the Polytechnic School, was established in Tehran in 1851 as part of a series of modernist reforms promulgated by the Iranian reformist Mirza Taqi Khan Amir Kabir, the prime minister of Nasir al-Din Shah Qajar. The Dar al-Fonun pioneered modern, secular education in Iran and was created to provide officers for the newly established army. French was the language of instruction. The curriculum consisted of military subjects such as ballistics and military engineering, as well as medicine, science, and mathematics. Under its auspices, many Western books were translated into Persian, the first Persian textbooks were published, and some of the next generation of Iranian government officials received their education. The Dar al-Fonun, having produced some eleven hundred graduates, was changed into a high school at the end of the nineteenth century, mainly as an attempt by the shah to curb reformist activities and student protests.

[*See also* Amir Kabir *and* Education: Education in Iran and Central Asia.]

Hamid Algar, *Mirza Malkum Khan* (1973). J. Szyliowicz, *Education and Modernization in the Middle East* (1973).

NEGUIN YAVARI

DARA SHIKOH (1615–1659), eldest of the four sons of Mughal emperor Shah Jahan and his favorite. Dara was inclined toward religious eclecticism in the tradition of Akbar: he held discussions with exponents of Islam and Hinduism, studied deeply, and wrote on problems of mysticism. He remained mostly in the capital while his brothers governed provinces; this allowed him a wide-ranging experience of administration but denied him familiarity with details that provincial administration provided. He had very little combat experience, which proved to be a setback during the War of Succession among the four brothers, from which Aurangzeb emerged victorious.

The War of Succession in the last years of Shah Jahan's reign (1627–1658) was long portrayed as an ideological conflict between religious liberalism represented by Dara and fanaticism personified in Aurangzeb. Marked differences in their religious attitudes notwithstanding, a recent analysis of the alignment of their support has shown that it was evenly distributed across religious and sectarian divides. Dara's failure was indeed a personal one arising from his inexperience of battle and inability to assess human character: some of his most trusted men were Aurangzeb's sympathizers. Yet admiration for Dara at all levels was immense and his cruel execution greatly enhanced his popular image.

[*See also* Shah Jahan; Aurangzeb; Akbar; *and* Mughal Empire.]

M. Athar Ali, *Mughal Nobility under Aurangzeb* (1966). K. R. Qanungo, *Dara Shukoh* (1952).

HARBANS MUKHIA

DARBAR. *See* Durbar.

DARD, SAYYID KHVAJA MIR (1720–1785). Along with Sauda and Mir, Dard (whose pen name means "pain") was part of the first generation of great Urdu poets of Delhi. Born into a well-known

Sufi family, he studied theology, literature, and music; at the age of thirty-nine he succeeded his father as head of a small Sufi order. His poetry, written in Urdu and Persian, is markedly intellectual as well as passionately mystical.

[*See also* Sufism *and* Indo-Aryan Languages and Literatures.]

Annemarie Schimmel, *Pain and Grace: A Study of Two Mystical Writers of Eighteenth-Century Muslim India* (1976). FRANCES W. PRITCHETT

D'ARGENLIEU, GEORGES-THIERRY (1889–1964), first high commissioner of Indochina (1945–1947). A priest and former naval officer, Admiral d'Argenlieu bitterly denounced the March 1946 agreement recognizing Vietnam as a "free state" within the French Union. Determined to oppose Ho Chi Minh's government, he sponsored a Republic of Cochinchina under the leadership of Vietnamese collaborators, as well as a Montagnard "state." When the Democratic Republic of Vietnam represented Vietnam at the Fontainebleau Conference, d'Argenlieu organized the August 1946 Second Dalat Conference, claiming to support representation of all Indochinese peoples. After his role in the November 1946 French attack on Haiphong, he came under increasingly strong criticism and was replaced in March 1947.

[*See also* Vietnam; Vietnam, Democratic Republic of; *and* Fontainebleau Conference.]

Joseph Buttinger, *Vietnam: A Dragon Embattled* (1967). Ellen Hammer, *The Struggle for Indochina, 1940–1955* (1966). BRUCE M. LOCKHART

DARI. The term *Dari,* which literally means "courtly," has at least three different usages. Early Islamic writers used it to refer to the spoken vernacular language of the Sasanid court and, by extension, of the upper classes in Sasanid and early Islamic Iran (third to eleventh century), in contrast to Pahlavi, the Sasanid literary language. This spoken language formed the basis of the earliest Persian written in the Arabic script. *Dari* has also come to refer to the modern spoken language of Zoroastrian communities in Iran (a language called Gabri by the Muslim population). Finally, it refers to the variety of New Persian used officially in modern Afghanistan, in contrast to Farsi, the official New Persian of modern Iran.

[*See also* Farsi; Pahlavi; *and* Persian Literature.]

Mary Boyce, *A Persian Stronghold of Zoroastrianism* (1977), p. 13. Richard N. Frye, *The Golden Age of Persia: The Arabs in the East* (1975). DAVID A. UTZ

DARIUS I, often known as Darius the Great, organizer of the Persian empire, son of a cousin of Cyrus the Great, Prince Hystaspes. Born in 550 BCE, Darius was educated at Cyrus's court and served as an officer of the guard under Cambyses in Egypt. In September 522 his high birth and leadership qualities won over six senior Persian nobles; with their support he acted resolutely against the False Smerdis, a Median magus who had usurped the throne in Cambyses' absence by pretending to be Bardya/Smerdis, the younger son of Cyrus whom Cambyses had secretly put to death. The "Seven Persians" killed the pretender, restored Achaemenid kingship, and strove, under Darius's leadership and with small forces, to ward off the dangers of various rebellions in Armenia, Media, Babylon, Arachosia, Elam, and even in Persis. They fought nineteen battles in one year, capturing and executing rebel leaders, before the unity of the empire could be restored.

The events from Cambyses' accession to Darius's final victory are documented in the record-relief of Behistun carved in 519 on a cliff between Kermanshah and Hamadan and published in copies throughout the empire. The relief depicted Darius and two of his helpers triumphant over the False Smerdis and other pretenders, all labeled originally in Elamite. Afterward, when he had had the Old Persian syllabary invented, three texts (in Old Persian, Babylonian, and Elamite) were carved next to the relief. These were deciphered and published in the middle of the last century by H. Rawlinson. The texts constitute the longest surviving Persian historical record and give Darius's personal account in an honest, straightforward, and moving style. Some modern scholars, wishing to vilify Darius, have misinterpreted the texts and resorted to fancy, but ancient writers support Darius's veracity.

After defeating the False Smerdis, Darius embarked on a fourfold plan. Militarily, he established the "Immortals," a standing army of ten thousand men; extended Persia's borders to the Indus Valley; subjugated the Central Asian Sakas again; pacified Egypt; conquered Thrace and Macedonia; and led a preventive expedition against the European Sakas in 513 by crossing the Danube and subduing the northern shore of the Black Sea. Politically, he organized the empire into regions (satrapies), dividing the authority in each region among a satrap, a general, and a tax official, thereby safeguarding against rebellions; he also invited noble and experienced men of nations related to him, such as Greeks, Bactrians, and Sakas, to join in the administration and rewards of the empire. Economically, he coined the first Persian money (the gold coin, *daric,* was named after him), established fixed tribute to be paid by each subject nation (the rate remained unchanged for two centuries), built roads, bridges, and waterways (one was his "Suez Canal" linking the Red Sea to the Mediterranean via the Nile), and constructed forts and extensive palaces at Persepolis, Susa, Ecbatana, and Egypt. By these measures he provided employment for a large number of people. Religiously, he reestablished rites and temples that the False Smerdis had deprived of support, and he codified local laws (in Egypt he was counted as a lawgiver), and continued Cyrus's policy of religious tolerance and protection of local faiths. Culturally, he brought together artists, doctors, astronomers, and many other learned men from various parts of his empire at his capitals and camps, thereby stimulating exchanges of ideas and knowledge.

Darius's one major setback was in Greece: the Greeks, especially the Athenians, induced the Ionians to rebel, and, sending troops into Asia Minor, burned Sardis; the insurrection was put down, and a lightly armed Iranian force under Datis landed at Marathon but was checked by Athenian hoplites in 490, a battle that the Greeks celebrated out of all proportion. Darius prepared to lead a second expedition in person, but he took ill and died in 486, leaving Xerxes as a successor inheriting a major war.

The character and importance of Darius are sufficiently clear from his achievements: his organizations lasted for two centuries and served as foundations for many succeeding empires, earning for him fame as one of the most judicious statesmen in history.

[*See also* Achaemenid Dynasty; Behistun; *and* Cyrus II.]

J. M. Cook, *Persian Empire* (1983), pp. 46ff. C. Hignett, *Xerxes' Invasion of Greece* (1962), pp. 55ff., 82ff. R. G. Kent, *Old Persian* (2d ed., 1953), pp. 116–147 (inscriptions). G. Rawlinson, *The Five Great Monarchies of the Ancient Eastern World* (1871), vol. 3, pp. 404–445. A. SHAHPUR SHAHBAZI

DARIUS III, great-grandson of Darius II in a cadet line, last legitimate Achaemenid king. Darius (personal name Artashata), served as royal courier under Artaxerxes III, then as satrap of Armenia. Distinguished for bravery, he was raised to the throne by the vizier Bagoas (spring 336 BCE), who had killed Artaxerxes and his successor; Darius soon secured his power by executing Bagoas.

An invasion of Asia Minor by Philip II of Macedon was aborted by Philip's assassination, but Alexander the Great's invasion (334) found the army ill prepared and Darius's control over his satraps inadequate. After a defeat at the Granicus and the failure of a counteroffensive, Darius felt obliged, as king, to confront Alexander in person. Meeting him on ill-chosen terrain at Issus (333), he was defeated and lost his harem and his western provinces. Alexander completed their conquest and, unwilling to negotiate, advanced across the Euphrates and Tigris. Darius waited for him on carefully prepared terrain at Gaugamela but was defeated through tactical errors and, abandoning all his other capitals, fled to Ecbatana (October 331). Failing to mobilize forces over the winter, he fled on Alexander's approach (May 330) and, closely pursued by Alexander, was put in chains. Two of his nobles killed him, presumably to prevent him from coming to terms with Alexander. One of the assassins proclaimed himself king and continued the war but was later caught by Alexander and executed for regicide. Darius received royal burial, and his relatives were treated with special favor. Ill-fated and personally brave, as we see Darius in the "Alexander Mosaic" (the only portrait of an Achaemenid king), he had little experience of command and succumbed to the duties imposed by his station.

[*See also* Alexander III.]

J. M. Cook, *Persian Empire* (1983). Arthur T. Olmstead, *History of the Persian Empire* (1959). W. W. Tarn, *Alexander the Great* (1948). ERNST BADIAN

DARJEELING, a popular Indian tourist resort in the hills of West Bengal, 400 miles north of Calcutta. Originally a dominion of Sikkim, Darjeeling was ceded by the Bhutanese in 1770 and later overrun by the army of the raja of Gorkha. Following the Anglo-Nepal War, the British restored Darjeeling to the Sikkim raja but pressed their interest in developing the site, with its cool climate and commanding view of the Himalayas, as a sanatorium for soldiers. In 1835 Sikkim presented Darjeeling as a gift to the governor-general of India and it eventually became the summer capital of the Bengal government.

Under the British, Darjeeling was developed as a center for tea production. The first plantation in the district was opened in 1856 and within twenty years

113 estates were in operation producing nearly four million pounds of tea annually. After World War I Darjeeling became a major staging ground for expeditions to Mount Everest through Tibet.

[*See also* Sikkim *and* Tea in India and Sri Lanka.]

A. J. Dash, *Darjeeling* (1947). RICHARD ENGLISH

DARUL ISLAM, popular name for a rebellion whose aim was the establishment of an Islamic state in Indonesia. Its principal leader was Sekarmadji Maridjan Kartosuwirjo (1905–1962), who, on 7 August 1949, after dissociating himself from the Indonesian Republic, proclaimed the Islamic State of Indonesia. The Negara Islam Indonesia had its own army (the Tentara Islam Indonesia), police force, government, and constitution. Its main area of operation was the Priangan in West Java. In the course of time, rebellions with a similar aim broke out in Pekalongan in Central Java, led by Amir Fatah; in South Sulawesi, headed by Kahar Muzakkar; in South Kalimantan, under Ibnu Hadjar; and in Aceh, where its main leader was Tunku Daud Beureu'eh. There was not much cooperation between these movements, although theoretically they all formed part of the Islamic State of Indonesia. All these rebellions were, moreover, inspired by religious motives, regional sentiments combined with a fear for Javanese domination, and opposition to the demobilization and promotion policy of the Republican army. Consequently, part of the movement troops consisted of members of former irregular guerilla units who had fought alongside the Republican army against the Dutch between 1945 and 1950.

For years the rebels succeeded in holding their ground against Republican army operations and in occupying large parts of the aforementioned regions. The turning point came in the second half of the 1950s when the rebels in Pekalongan had already been defeated. Still, final defeat came only with the arrest, execution, or killing of the main leaders: in West Java in 1962, in South Kalimantan in 1965, and South Sulawesi in 1965. Only in Aceh, in 1959, was a peaceful compromise reached. Daud Beureu'eh, however, did not surrender until 1962.

[*See also* Indonesia, Republic of *and* Daud Beureu'eh, Muhammad.]

C. van Dijk, *Rebellion under the Banner of Islam: The Darul Islam in Indonesia* (1981). C. VAN DIJK

DAS, CHITTARANJAN (1870–1925), called Deshbandhu ("friend of the country"), important Bengali leader and a key figure in all-India politics in the post–World War I period. Trained as a barrister, Das returned to India and was particularly skillful in courtroom defenses of nationalists. A member of the extremist wing of the Indian National Congress, he became the leader of the Bengal Congress about the time that Mohandas Gandhi took control nationally. Das worked under Gandhi in the Noncooperation movement and was imprisoned. When Gandhi halted this movement, Das, along with Motilal Nehru, formed the Swaraj Party. The goal of this new group was to disrupt the legislative councils from within. With the solid backing of most Hindu and many Muslim elected members, Das effectively challenged the Raj within the Bengal Legislative Council in 1924 and 1925. He was the first mayor of Calcutta under the Calcutta Municipal Act of 1923 and president of the Bengal Provincial Congress and the All-India Swaraj Party. He gained the trust of some Muslim leaders with the forging of the Bengal Pact of 1924 and challenged Gandhi in the Congress. His adept political work was cut off by his untimely death.

[*See also* Indian National Congress *and* Nehru, Motilal.]

Subhas Chandra Bose, *The Indian Struggle 1920–1942* (1964). J. H. Broomfield, *Elite Conflict in a Plural Society* (1968). Hemendranath Das Gupta, *Deshbandhu Chittaranjan Das* (1960). LEONARD A. GORDON

DASHT-I KAVIR, more correctly called Kavir-i Bozorg ("great *kavir*"), is a desert basin of interior drainage in north-central Iran. This *kavir,* 230 miles long and 40 to 150 miles wide, is a salt-encrusted surface underlain by hidden channels of slimy mud. Devoid of human habitation, it is very treacherous to cross, with humans and animals breaking through the crust and disappearing in the slime. Caravan routes connecting the major oasis settlements west and north of the *kavir* had to avoid the region, which is ringed by smaller *kavirs.* MICHAEL BONINE

DASHT-I LUT, also called the Southern Lut, is the major basin of interior drainage of southeastern Iran. A long, narrow sump of salt water, the *namaksar,* occurs in the west, while the largest complex of mobile dunes in Iran forms the eastern border. In the center is the Lut City (Shahr-i Lut), a region of wind-blown structures resembling ruined buildings. Oasis settlements occur around the basin, particularly to the west in the vicinity of Kerman, but the Lut itself is totally devoid of human habitation or use. MICHAEL BONINE

DATONG, city in northern Shanxi Province, 180 miles west of Beijing, China, today an industrial center with a population of about 926,000 (1982). With easy access to the Mongolian steppe to the north, the Ordos to the west, and the area of modern Beijing to the east, through most of its history Datong has been important chiefly for its strategic location and as a place where nomadic and settled realms came together. The Northern Wei state (386–535), which included both cultures, placed its capital Pingcheng near the present city. In 1044 the Liao, another such mixed polity, made it their western capital and gave it the modern name. In Ming times Datong was the most important of the border garrisons. The famous Buddhist cave-temples of Yungang, dating from Northern Wei times, are nearby.

ARTHUR N. WALDRON

DAUD BEUREU'EH, MOHAMMED (1909–1978), prime minister of Afghanistan from 1953 to 1963. Born in Kabul, Daud was the cousin and brother-in-law of Afghanistan's last king, Zahir Shah. He studied in France from 1921 to 1930 and in 1953 was appointed the country's prime minister. He ruled the country until 1963, dominating the king in the process. Daud pushed for rapid modernization of Afghanistan and pursued irredentist claims against Pakistan, supporting ethnic Pakhtuns against Islamabad. Zahir Shah dismissed Daud in 1963 because of differences over policy toward Pakistan.

Daud remained bitter and waited for an opportunity to remove the king. With support from several young officers he overthrew the monarchy on 17 July 1973. He ruled the country until April 1978, when he was overthrown and killed in a communist coup.

ZALMAY KHALILZAD

DAUD BEUREU'EH, MUHAMMAD (b. 1899), Islamic leader of Aceh (northern Sumatra). Educated at traditional Islamic schools in his native Pidie region of Aceh, Tunku Daud Beureu'eh nevertheless championed more modern methods of teaching and organization, notably as president of the All-Aceh Association of Ulama (PUSA) in 1939–1942. PUSA became a vehicle for Acehnese protest against the ruling class, the *uleebalang,* and aided an anti-Dutch revolt on the eve of the Japanese occupation. Daud remained the most influential Acehnese *ulama* during the revolutionary destruction of *uleebalang* authority (December 1945), and in 1947 he was named military governor of Aceh by the republic. He did not accept the merger of Aceh into a North Sumatra province (1950), and in September 1953 he led a rebellion against Jakarta, proclaiming Aceh part of Kartosuwirjo's Negara Islam Indonesia. He surrendered in 1962, after Aceh was recognized as an autonomous region.

[*See also* Darul Islam *and* Aceh.]

ANTHONY REID

DAULATABAD, a South Indian hill-fort so named by Muhammad bin Tughluq (r. 1325–1351). The fortress is built upon a conical rock, scarped from a height of 150 feet from the base. Originally it was named Devagiri and was ruled by the Yadavas, who made it the center of a great power in the Deccan. Ala ud-Din Khalji attacked Devagiri in 1296 and acquired enormous wealth from Ram Chandra, the ruler, who also promised to pay yearly tribute. In 1318 Qutb ud-Din Mubarak Khalji marched against its raja, who had defaulted in the payment of tribute, and annexed it. The fort was then named Qutbabad, after Qutb ud-Din Mubarak. Muhammad bin Tughluq made it the second administrative city of the Tughluq empire and forced the Muslim elite of Delhi to migrate there. He provided facilities for them and marked out different quarters of the city for different groups of migrants. Daulatabad remained in the possession of the Bahmani dynasty until 1526, when it was taken by the Nizam Shahis; Akbar wrested it from the Nizam Shahis.

Amir Khusrau praised the climate and geographic location of Daulatabad in his poem *Sahifat-ul-Ausaf.* Its chief buildings are the Chand Minar, erected by Ala ud-Din Bahmani, and the Chini Mahal.

[*See also* Deccan Sultanates; Bahmani Dynasty; Tughluq Dynasty; *and* Yadavas.]

T. W. Haig, *Historical Landmarks of the Deccan* (reprint, 1919). *Imperial Gazetteer of India, New Edition* (1908–1909), vol. 11.

KHALIQ AHMAD NIZAMI

DAVAO, the Philippines' fourth largest city, is located on the northwest coast of Davao Gulf in the province of Davao del Sur on the island of Mindanao. During the American colonial era prior to World War II, Davao and its environs became the center of highly productive and very prosperous abaca (Manila hemp) cultivation. Most of this remarkable economic development was the result of the investment of Japanese capital and of the infusion of Japanese immigrant labor, which reached about eighteen thousand by 1941. Despite certain fears of a potential Japanese enclave in the southern Philippines, both the American and Philippine governing authorities welcomed the economic benefits that the Japanese presence generated.

[*See also* Philippines.]

Grant K. Goodman, *Davao: A Case Study in Japanese-Philippine Relations* (1967).

GRANT K. GOODMAN

DAYAK, a general, ethnographically imprecise term long applied by Westerners to the non-Muslim indigenous peoples of Sarawak and Indonesian Kalimantan (but seldom Brunei or Sabah). Hence it refers to a wide variety of peoples (including 45 percent of Sarawak's population) who differentiate themselves from the mostly coastal-dwelling Malayo-Muslims and Chinese. Certain common patterns do link the diverse Dayak ethnic groups. Traditionally, most employed shifting cultivation of dry rice, spoke related languages, practiced some degree of headhunting, and dwelled in longhouses along riverbanks in the hilly interior. Most possessed animistic religious traditions, but in recent years some have adopted Islam or Christianity. Many now find their livelihood, customs, and autonomy altered by economic development, political change, and sociocultural influences emanating from outside.

[*See also* Sarawak; Kalimantan; *and* Iban.]

Tom Harrison, ed., *The Peoples of Sarawak* (1959). Victor T. King, ed., *Essays on Borneo Societies* (1978).

CRAIG A. LOCKARD

DAYAL, HAR (1884–1939), intellectual anarchist, Indian revolutionary, and founder of the Ghadr ("mutiny") movement, a loosely knit coalition of expatriate Indian nationalists. Dayal devoted himself to journalism and anti-British propaganda, publishing from California such journals as *Ghadr* during 1913 and 1914. After living in Germany during World War I he became an advocate of home rule for India within the British empire. [*See also* Ghadr.] USHA SANYAL

DAYANANDA SARASWATI (1824–1883), founder of the Arya Samaj, a Hindu reform movement. Dayananda was born in Tankara, Gujarat, with the name Mul Shankara, and was raised an orthodox Shaivite brahman. He left home in 1846 and after taking *sannyas* (monk's vows) he adopted the name Dayananda Saraswati. In 1860 he became the disciple of Swami Virajananda of Mathura, and left in 1863 to begin preaching his restructured Hinduism. Dayananda held his first religious debate with Christian missionaries at Ajmer in 1866. In 1867 he attended the Kumbha Mela at Hardwar, where he proclaimed his Vedic faith while denouncing popular Hinduism. He toured Uttar Pradesh and in 1872 reached Calcutta, where he met Brahmo Samaj leaders Keshub Chandra Sen and Debendranath Tagore. Dayananda founded the first successful Arya Samaj in Bombay on 10 April 1875 and published the *Satyarth Prakash* in Banaras that same year. In 1877 he visited Delhi and was invited to Lahore; he toured the Punjab and Uttar Pradesh, establishing branches of the Arya Samaj. Dayananda published the *Sanskar Vidhi* in 1877 and the *Rigveda Bhashya Bhumika* in 1878. He met the leaders of the Theosophical Society at Saharanpur in May 1879 and was allied with them until May 1882. In 1881 he published the *Gokarunanidhi* and began a campaign of cow protection. Dayananda reached Rajasthan in June 1882 and toured there until his death.

[*See also* Arya Samaj; Brahmo Samaj; Besant, Annie; Sen, Keshub Chandra; *and* Tagore, Debendranath.]

J. T. F. Jordens, *Dayananda Sarasvati, His Life and Ideas* (1978). Har Bilas Sarda, *Life of Dayanand Saraswati, World Teacher* (2d ed., 1968).

KENNETH W. JONES

DAYAN KHAN, "khan of the great Yuan," title of Batu Mongke (c. 1464–1532), famous as unifier of the Eastern Mongols. The death of the previous khan left the Mongols divided between Isma'il, leader of the Western Mongols and Oirats, and Batu Mongke. After defeating Isma'il in about 1488, Batu quickly became paramount leader and eventually extended his control to all of Inner Mongolia and part of the eastern border of Outer Mongolia. Probably ambitious to reestablish Mongol rule in China, he led repeated raids on the Ming and built a series of forts along the northern Chinese border from which attacks could be mounted. Batu's attempt to place one of his sons in charge of portions of Mongol territory stirred up dissension in the steppe, and during the sixteenth century he had to devote much attention to internal conflict.

Roy Andrew Miller, "Batu Möngke," *Dictionary of Ming Biography, 1368–1644,* edited by L. Carrington Goodrich and Chaoying Fang (1976), pp. 17–20.

ARTHUR N. WALDRON

DAZAIFU, a major Japanese military base, administrative center, and foreign port during the Nara and Heian periods (from the eighth to the twelfth century). Located in northern Kyushu across the Tsushima Straits from Korea and the Asian mainland, Dazaifu was designed to protect Japan from invasions, oversee governmental matters for all of Kyushu, and greet foreign dignitaries on their way to the capital. Archaeologists have uncovered the remains of several temples, a school, office buildings, two mountain fortresses (Ōno and Ki) and a giant barrier *(mizuki),* although they have yet to confirm the existence of a Chinese-style grid plan like that of Nara.

Dazaifu was founded in 664 CE, just after Japan's disastrous defeat at the hands of Tang and Silla forces in Korea. The names and duties of more than twenty-five major and minor officials were spelled out in the Taihō Code of 702. Dazaifu was active throughout the eighth century and was the scene of a major rebellion led by Fujiwara no Hirotsugu in 740. During the ninth century the center entered a period of decline, as the Heian court abolished offices, cut salaries, withdrew troops, and curtailed the lavish welcome given foreigners. The offspring of former officials settled in the area and were responsible for defending Dazaifu against both the rapacity of Fujiwara no Sumitomo in the 940s and the incursion of the Toi people from the continent in 1019. Although politically less important, Dazaifu became the focus of booming trade in the eleventh and twelfth centuries. In the early Kamakura era, Minamoto no Yoritomo bypassed Dazaifu and established a new chief office *(chinzei bugyō)*. However, it was later moved to the location where Dazaifu had been, a testimony to the strategic importance of the region.

J. E. Kidder, *Early Buddhist Japan* (1972).

WAYNE FARRIS

DEB, RADHAKANTA (1783–1867), important figure in the modernization of the Indian educational system. A member of the wealthy landowning family of Sobhabazar, Bengal, Deb advocated English education as necessary for the advancement of India, but he opposed such social reforms as the abolition of *sati* (the burning of widows) and polygamy, while supporting the education of women. He also encouraged the introduction of Western medicine, including dissection of corpses. He regarded English rule as beneficial for India, but argued that qualified Indians should be given a role in the administration. He sponsored the publication of an eight-volume Sanskrit encyclopedia. His wide-ranging activities included the improvement of agriculture and schemes to export Indian tea.

[*See also* Education: Education in South Asia; Women: Women in South and Southeast Asia; *and* Sati.]

AINSLIE T. EMBREE

DECCAN. Literally meaning "south," the term *Deccan* (Hindi, *dakhin;* Sanskrit, *dakshina*) has a diversity of connotations but is perhaps most widely understood in contradistinction to the term *Hindustan,* which refers to northern India. [*See* Hindustan.] The boundary between the two is normally taken to be the Narmada River or the Vindhya Escarpment, slightly to its north. The Puranas and other sacred texts refer to the southern country by the names Dakshinapatha and Dakshinatya, from which is derived the Greek Dachinabades, noted in the *Periplus of the Erythraean Sea* (first century CE). In physical geography the Deccan often refers to the tableland between the Western and Eastern Ghats. Within Maharashtra state and, previously, the Bombay Presidency, Deccan connotes the interior region, in opposition to coastal Konkan. Politically, *Deccan* has, at times, been used to designate specific states. The Portuguese referred thus to the sultanate of Bijapur in the sixteenth century and the British subsequently to the domains of the *nizam* of Hyderabad.

[*See also* Deccan Sultanates *and* Maharashtra.]

Imperial Gazetteer of India, New Edition (1908–1909), vol. 11, pp. 205–208. Henry Yule and A. C. Burnell, *Hobson-Jobson* (1903), pp. 301–302.

JOSEPH E. SCHWARTZBERG

DECCAN RIOTS. During what are known as the Deccan Riots of 1875, peasants in the Poona and Ahmadnagar districts of India rose up against village moneylenders to destroy written documentation of their indebtedness to them. A recent fall in cotton prices, government enhancement of the land-revenue demand, and disturbance of long-standing credit relations between cultivators and moneylenders were the underlying factors in the peasants' discontent. [*See also* Land Tenure and Reform: Land Tenure, Revenue, and Reform in South Asia.]

USHA SANYAL

DECCAN SULTANATES. Between the mid-fourteenth and late seventeenth century six Indo-Muslim sultanates ranged over the Deccan plateau of India, each evolving distinctive cultures that absorbed and modified cultural elements deriving from both Indian and Middle Eastern traditions.

History. The Deccan plateau comprises the upper portion of peninsular India, stretching from the range of mountains just inland from the west coast to the Bay of Bengal in the east, and from the Vindhya Mountains in the north to the Tungabhadra River in the south. This area had already been substantially hinduized before the arrival of Muslim influence, with three vernacular language regions—Marathi, Telugu, and Kannada—clearly emerging from about the twelfth century. Islamic influence in the plateau proper commenced in 1296 when Ala ud-Din Khalji, a Turkish officer serving the Delhi sultanate, raided and sacked the Yadava capital of Devagiri in the Marathi country. [*See* Khalji Dynasty.] This was followed by a series of military incursions in the early fourteenth century, culminating in the Delhi sultanate's formal annexation of the Marathi-speaking northern Deccan in 1318. The whole period from 1296 to 1347 was thus one in which Turkish or Indo-Turkish settlers, adventurers, soldiers, saints, and scholars migrated into the Deccan, forming as it were the cutting edge of the Delhi sultanate's expanding military and cultural frontier. [*See also* Delhi Sultanate.]

By the middle of the fourteenth century, however, the Delhi sultanate ceased to exercise its authority over the class of transplanted northerners in the Deccan who, settled in a region far from their homelands, began to feel a sense of their own cultural and political autonomy. Led by one Isma'il Mukh, these settlers declared their independence from the Delhi sultanate in 1345, and two years later they established the first independent sultanate in the Deccan. This was the Bahmani kingdom, named after its first sultan, Ala ud-Din Bahman Shah. Lasting from 1347 to 1526, this dynasty of kings managed to establish its hegemony over the entire Deccan plateau, at its height extending its domain from the Arabian Sea to the Bay of Bengal. This was accomplished in part from an efficient administrative system that used the same basic formula of success that was found in most Indo-Muslim sultanates: on the civil side, the Bahmani rulers managed to appropriate the services of the existing class of Hindu land revenue collectors, while on the military side, it combined a central body of crack troops personally loyal to the sultan with a decentralized network of officer-nobles who were assigned territorial administration in return for maintaining irregular troops.

This combination of military systems, especially when backed up by infusions of cavalry horses from Central Asia or through the port of Goa, proved extremely effective in dislodging local Hindu princes from power. But the system also contained the seeds of its own demise, as local commanders possessing local bases of power could, like Isma'il Mukh, entertain the possibility of rebelling against the center and establishing new, independent sultanates. In time, in fact, the governors of the more important Bahmani provinces did just that, and by the late fifteenth century five independent sultanates had broken off from the disintegrating parent Bahmani sultanate. These were the Imad Shahi kingdom of Berar (1460–1574) in the northern part of the former Bahmani domain, the Barid Shahi kingdom of Bidar (1487–1619) in the central Deccan, the Nizam Shahi kingdom of Ahmadnagar (1490–1633) in the northwest, the Adil Shahi kingdom of Bijapur (1490–1686) in the southwest, and the Qutb Shahi kingdom of Golconda (1496–1687) in the eastern Deccan. The first two, smaller and weaker, were absorbed by their neighbors, whereas the last three were more powerful and were each in turn eventually absorbed by the supreme power of seventeenth-century India, the Mughal empire.

One of the central social problems of the Bahmani sultans, inherited too by each of the successor kingdoms, stemmed from administrative necessity. Reluctant to entrust their upper civil and military bureaucracies to Hindus, most sultanates sought Muslim immigrants from either North India or the Middle East to meet their staffing needs. But once recruited, these fresh immigrants tended not to assimilate easily with older classes descended from earlier migrants, and in fact often affected a sense of superiority over the latter. Thus, in the course of the fifteenth century two rival social groups emerged within the ranks of the ruling class: the "foreigners" (called *afaqi*) and the Deccanis. Whereas the former were often Iranian, spoke Persian, and were Shi'a Muslims, the latter considered themselves natives of the Deccan, spoke a proto-Urdu language called Dakhni, and were usually Sunni Muslims. The poisonous animosity that existed between these two classes of ruling Muslims occasionally erupted in armed conflict and formed another cause of the political decline of the Deccan sultanates. Moreover, the Shi'a orientation of the foreigners was ultimately to provide the Mughal emperor Aurangzeb, a devout Sunni, with a pretext for waging disastrous wars against the last surviving sultanates, Bijapur and Golconda, in the late seventeenth century. [*See* Aurangzeb.]

The contemporary Persian chronicles that form our primary sources for the history of these sultanates are replete with narratives of their various military affairs and political intrigues. First, there were the wars waged by two sultanates, Bijapur and Ahmadnagar, against the Portuguese in the early sixteenth century. Vastly superior Portuguese naval power decided most conflicts in the Europeans' favor, resulting in the establishment of Portuguese coastal enclaves such as in Goa, which was seized from Bijapur in 1511. More typical were the civil wars that plagued all five successor sultanates throughout their history. Rulers owed their political existence to their sheer military capacity to wrest independence from former overlords and to maintain that independence against the encroachments of their neighbors. Consequently, the sultanates were always jockeying for position, with challenges to the control of key hill-forts typically touching off costly wars between them. The most disastrous wars for those sultanates that survived into the seventeenth century, however, were those waged against the Mughal empire. After absorbing Malwa and Gujarat into the Mughal empire, the emperor Akbar began putting pressure on the Nizam Shahi kingdom of Ahmadnagar in the 1590s, and, though heroically defended first by the queen Chand Bibi and later by the Abyssinian *vazir* Malik Ambar, the kingdom eventually fell to Mughal arms in 1633. The same fate was to befall Bijapur and Golconda later in that century.

Finally, there were the wars waged by the Deccan sultanates against the powerful Hindu state to the south, Vijayanagara. Ever since 1296 Indo-Turkish pressure from North India had forced Telugu- and Marathi-speaking Hindu warrior groups from the northern Deccan to migrate to the south, where they reestablished themselves as warrior states armed with an explicitly Hindu ideological orientation. The most important of these, Vijayanagara, was founded in 1336 and established an immense capital city of the same name along the banks of the Tungabhadra River, which formed a bulwark against the further southward expansion of Indo-Turkish power. [*See* Vijayanagara.] Eight major wars were fought between Bahmani and Vijayanagara armies between 1349 and 1481; after the fall of the Bahmani dynasty, its successor states continued this tradition of hostility until 1565, when Sultan Ali Adil Shah I of Bijapur forged an alliance of Deccan sultanates that managed to defeat the Hindu state and sack its great capital city in the Battle of Talikota.

Culture. The cultural traditions of the Deccan sultanates were shaped by two factors: their desire to recruit Muslim administrators, soldiers, Sufis, and scholars from Iran and the Arab Middle East, to which they looked for cultural inspiration, and their tendency over time to adopt local Marathi, Telugu, or Kannada customs in the area of speech, dress, diet, art, and architecture. Thus, for example, in the reigns of Sultan Firuz Bahmani (r. 1397–1422) and especially his son Ahmad Bahmani (r. 1422–1436), foreigners, mainly Iranians, were actively recruited and rapidly filled ranking social and political positions. By the sixteenth and especially the seventeenth century, however, when European naval power and Mughal land power had cut off the Deccan's access to the Middle East, the Deccan sultanates were forced to rely upon local Muslims (Deccanis) and Hindus to run their kingdoms. In fact, from the mid-1500s Bijapur had turned over the major part of its revenue bureaucracy to local Marathi-speaking Hindu classes, and the other sultanates were to follow suit. At the same time, the defeat of Vijayanagara in 1565 prompted the exodus of thousands of artists, masons, artisans, singers, and dancers formerly dependent upon Vijayanagara patronage to move northward and seek such patronage in the "Muslim" courts of Bijapur and Golconda.

The net result was the gradual indianization of the Deccan sultanates, a process most vividly seen in the court patronage of Dakhni, the local lingua franca that borrowed freely from the indigenous languages of the Deccan, and in the miniature painting and architectural projects sponsored by these same courts. The two richest Deccan sultanates, Bijapur and Golconda, carried these artistic traditions the furthest, with Golconda's Charminar gate in modern Hyderabad and Bijapur's Ibrahim Rauza and Mihtar Mahal being perhaps the most outstanding architectural manifestations of a composite cultural tradition beautifully combining elements from the Middle East and the Deccan plateau.

[*See also* Deccan; Bijapur; Golconda; Ahmadnagar; Mughal Empire; *and* Bahmani Dynasty.]

Richard M. Eaton, *Sufis of Bijapur, 1370–1700* (1978). Hermann Goetz, "The Fall of Vijayanagar and the Nationalization of Muslim Art in the Dakhan," *Journal of Indian History* 19 (1940): 249–255. J. F. Richards, *Mughal Administration in Golconda* (1975). Annemarie Schimmel, *Islamic Literatures of India* (1973). H. K. Sherwani, *The Bahmanis of the Deccan* (1953) and *History of the Qutb Shahi Dynasty* (1974). H. K. Sherwani and

P. M. Joshi, eds., *History of Medieval Deccan (1295–1724)*, 2 vols. (1973). Radhey Shyam, *The Kingdom of Ahmadnagar* (1966).
RICHARD M. EATON

DECOUX, JEAN (1887–1963), French admiral who served as governor-general of French Indochina from 1940 to 1945. In 1940 the Vichy regime authorized him to allow Japanese troops to be stationed in Indochina in exchange for Japanese guarantees of French sovereignty there. Decoux worked hard to foster sentiments of solidarity among the Indochinese people while maintaining cordial relations with Japan. In March 1945 he was imprisoned by the Japanese along with all other French authorities. When the war ended, he was flown to France and forced to retire, narrowly escaping trial on charges of treason to General de Gaulle.

DAVID P. CHANDLER

DELHI. For over ten centuries the capital of varying regimes, this Indian city has enjoyed a charisma comparable to that of Rome or Isfahan. At the intersection of the route from the Khyber Pass to the Ganges-Yamuna valley, the Aravalli Hills, and the south-flowing Yamuna River, it was the central place for regimes aspiring to hold the Panjab, Afghanistan, Rajasthan, and the plains east of the Yamuna. In the eighteenth century the Marathas from the southwest and the British from the east saw in Delhi a springboard for territorial expansion to the northwest.

The term *Delhi* is used more for the region than for specific urban settlements. In the triangle of 180 square kilometers bounded by the Ridge on the west and south and the Yamuna on the east, there have been at least eight townships. Two variables explain the shifting pattern—changes in political authority, and the changing course of the river. The Yamuna has been moving steadily eastward with the silting of its bed. Many rulers deliberately built completely new towns here, for practical, political, or personal reasons. These were usually named after the sovereign, the British "New Delhi" being an exception; a new city to be called Victoria had been proposed in 1858, but the name was not used.

The earliest settlement, located on the river, is supposed to have been that of Indraprastha, the town of the Pandavas, dating to about 1400 BCE. Little is known about the next two-and-a-half millennia. Architectural remains from the twelfth to the fourteenth century CE indicate that the royal enclaves were located 15 kilometers west of the river. Obtaining and storing water therefore became of vital importance. Deep walls and large rainwater tanks were supplemented, from the thirteenth century, by an elaborate network of canals linked to the river at Karnal, 120 kilometers to the north. From the end of the fourteenth century, settlements were once again near the river, but by the twentieth century New Delhi had come to lie further west, not touching the river at all.

Even as late as the nineteenth century walled cities were considered more secure than open ones. The town walls of Delhi were made of random rubble, while red sandstone and black and white marble were used for town gateways and for palace walls. Recycling material from older buildings was a common feature of construction. The architecture is a harmonious combination of indigenous craftsmanship with West Asian, particularly Persian, styles. An excellent example is the Qutb Minar, the 72-meter-high watchtower begun by Qutb ud-Din, governor of Delhi after the Ghurid Turks defeated the local Rajput ruler Prithviraj Chauhan in 1192. [*See*

FIGURE 1. *Qutb Minar.* A victory tower begun by Qutb ud-Din at the beginning of the thirteenth century.

also Prithviraj Chauhan.] The Il-baris (1206–1290) occupied the fort of Prithviraj on the hills in Mehrauli (the southernmost tip of present-day urban Delhi). Ala al-Din, of the shortlived Khalji dynasty (1290–1320), built a round fort, Siri, northeast of Mehrauli, and planned the canal system. The Tughluqs(1320–1412) were a family of prolific builders. Ghiyas al-Din's reign saw the construction of the massive fort of Tughluqabad, 11 kilometers east of Mehrauli. His son, Muhammad, began a gigantic wall to enclose the four Delhis—Old Delhi (Mehrauli), Siri, Tughluqabad, and his own Jahanpanah. His impulsive decision in 1326 to move the capital to Devgiri (Daulatabad) in central India caused considerable upheaval in Delhi. But the city's natural advantages led to its reaching the optimum spatial and perhaps demographic extent for the pre-railway era within a few decades, when Firuz Tughluq built yet another citadel on the river, 23 kilometers north of Mehrauli. He took active interest in conserving older public works; his prime minister, an Andhra Muslim, constructed eight large mosques.

Timur of Samarkand invaded Delhi in 1398; this was the first of many such devastations. [*See* Timur.] In the following century the territorial domains of the regimes that ruled from Delhi were considerably smaller than before. Delhi now alternated with Agra, 200 kilometers further south on the Yamuna, as capital. The Sayyids and the Lodi dynasty(1414–1526) built no citadel, but their mosques and mausoleums are of outstanding architectural merit. Timur's descendants, the Mughals, occupied Delhi after 1533. For Humayun, the second Mughal emperor, planning a new city on the river was a form of relaxation. His plans were to be completed by his rival, Sher Shah Sur. Akbar and Jahangir (1556–1627) preferred Agra, but the fifth Mughal, Shah Jahan (1627–1657), indulged his passion for building in both towns. By 1648 the city of Shahjahanabad was built, north of Firuz Tughluq's capital. The opulence of its red sandstone palace and the grandeur of its main boulevard, the Chandni Chowk, became widely known through travelers' accounts. When Mughal rule weakened in the eighteenth century, the city became prey to raids from local rural dacoits and to invasion by the Persians under Nadir Shah, in 1739. From 1771 the Mughal rulers were controlled by the Maratha chieftains, who in turn were defeated by the British in 1803.

The name of the Mughal emperor was a rallying cry for the rebels from a Meerut regiment who captured Delhi on 11 May 1857. The British reconquered the city, imprisoned the eighty-two-year-old emperor, Bahadur Shah, and stationed their army in the palace. The British civilians moved to the northern Ridge, which became the "Civil Lines," that stereotype of town planning created by racial insecurity. The city was made part of the province of the Punjab. In the next fifty years it became the major railway junction of North India. In 1911 volatile nationalist agitation made the officials decide to move the winter capital from Calcutta to Delhi; during the summer the Himalayan resort of Simla continued to serve as the capital. Ecological and political arguments were adduced by Patrick Geddes and Viceroy Hardinge to suggest that the new city be integrated with Shahjahanabad. The chief architect, Edwin Lutyens, disagreed, and he shifted New Delhi southward and separate from the older city. [*See also* Lutyens, Sir Edwin.]

The twin cities of Delhi were hit by the partition of the subcontinent in August 1947. Many Muslims left the city for Pakistan, and many Hindus flocked to Delhi from the western Punjab. They were allotted the area west of the Ridge, which became a third town. From the 1960s, the proliferation of the bureaucracy led to the filling in of the area between Mehrauli and Lutyens's New Delhi. Yet another addition to the urban area was one east of the river, resulting from the expansion of commercial and smallscale industrial activity. The urban population, 214,115 in 1901, doubled after partition (695,686 in 1941 to 1,437,134 in 1951) and in 1981 stood at 5,713,581. Today Delhi is India's third largest city, ranking after Calcutta and greater Bombay. Shahjahanabad, like the older Delhis, has lost much of its city wall. It is recognizable in its wide main avenues and its lanes curving cleverly to minimize the sun's heat, but its water channels are dry and its fabric made ragged by overcrowding and by modern traffic. New Delhi is very distinctive with its wide tree-lined avenues and its architectural mix of the formal Romanesque and the "bungalow" pattern; the threat to this "garden city" is from highrise buildings. Older Delhis survive in monuments and in the names of areas in the city: Kotla Mubarakpur (the fort of the city of Mubarak), Hauz Rani (the Queen's Baths), Roshan Chiragh Delhi ("The light of Delhi," a title given to a famous saint).

Its long life as capital helped develop in Delhi an urban culture, distinguishing it from its rural hinterland. After the sack of Baghdad in 1258, Delhi's court and *madrasas* made it the most important cultural center of the Muslim east. Urdu, which began as the pidgin phrases of the early Turkish soldiers at Delhi, developed into an elegant language that linked Sanskrit and North Indian vernaculars with Arabic and Persian. The writings of Delhi's Persian and Urdu poets from the fourteenth to the nineteenth century—Amir Khusrau, Mir, Ghalib—were widely known. Before 1947 the city had roughly equal numbers of Hindus and Muslims, who shared many secular festivals and a love of Urdu poetry. [*See also* Amir Khusrau; Mir, Muhammed Taqi; *and* Ghalib, Mirza Asadullah Khan.] This sense of community has become eroded by the city's urban sprawl and the linguistic heterogeneity of its population.

[*See also* Mughal Empire; Lodi Dynasty; *and* Yamuna River.]

Narayani Gupta, *Delhi between Two Empires 1803–1931: Society, Government and Urban Growth* (1981). Gavin Hambly, *Cities of Mughal India: Delhi, Agra and Fatehpur Sikri* (1968). R. G. Irving, *Indian Summer: Lutyens, Baker and Imperial Delhi* (1981). H. K. Kaul, *Historic Delhi: An Anthology* (1983). M. M. Kaye, ed. *The Golden Calm: An English Lady's Life in Moghal Delhi* (1980). A. D. King, *Colonial Urban Development: Culture, Social Power and Environment* (1976). Ralph Russell, ed. *Ghalib: The Poet and his Age* (1972). T. G. P. Spear, *Twilight of the Mughals* (1951).

NARAYANI GUPTA

DELHI SULTANATE, name given to the governments of dynasties that ruled India from 1210 to 1526. Iltutmish established the Delhi sultanate in 1210; it was replaced by the Mughal empire in 1526, when Babur defeated Sultan Ibrahim Lodi at the battlefield of Panipat. Five dynasties of Delhi sultans ruled during this period: the Early Turks (also called the Ilbaris; 1206–1290), the Khaljis (1290–1320), the Tughluqs (1320–1414), the Sayyids (1414–1451), and the Lodis (1451–1526).

History. The establishment of the Delhi sultanate, which followed the overthrow of the Rajput kingdoms of northern India, led to vital changes in the political, social, and economic life of the country. It liquidated the multistate system and the feudal polity of the Rajputs and paved the way for a centralized monarchy with a pan-Indian administrative service. The land grants given by the sultans were essentially bureaucratic assignments and proved an effective local apparatus for the integration of the country part by part. The Rajput cities, as described by al-Biruni in his *Kitab al-Hind,* were planned on the basis of caste. The Early Turkish sultans initiated an urban revolution by throwing open these cities to all types of people and converting them from "caste cities" into "cosmopolitan cities." These new cities led to readjustment in social relationship and changed the entire milieu. The Turkish power was sustained and stabilized by these cities. The sultans restored India's broken contact with the outside world and gave a new fillip to commercial activity. In place of a limited market, conditioned by caste and feudal situation, there appeared an international market stretching from Baghdad to Lakhnauti. One other important impact of the establishment of the sultanate was that throughout the entire territory Persian became the language of administration, replacing the innumerable languages and dialects that were spoken from one part of the country to another.

The rise of the Delhi sultanate was synchronous with the rise of Genghis Khan in Central Asia. Iltutmish tactfully avoided confrontation with the Mongols. His successors, until the time of Nasir ud-Din Mahmud (1246–1266), followed a policy of appeasement and aloofness, so much so that in 1260, barely two years after the sack of Baghdad by Hulegu and the murder of the legal sovereign of the Delhi sultanate (the *khalifa* of Baghdad), the Delhi court received the Mongol emissaries with great enthusiasm. Balban (1266–1287) changed the Mongol policy of the sultanate and garrisoned the frontier region to meet the Mongol challenge. But this affected his expansionist ambitions and he could only maintain a status quo so far as territorial growth was concerned. He succeeded in his objective to a large extent but the assassination of his eldest son, Prince Muhammad, at the hands of the Mongols shattered his position.

Ala ud-Din Khalji (1296–1316) followed a policy of firm resistance toward the Mongols but he also initiated an era of imperialism and forced the rajas of the Deccan to accept his overlordship. Mubarak Khalji (1316–1320) appointed a viceroy in the Deccan and attempted annexation of the region. Muhammad bin Tughluq (1325–1351) completed the process of integration of the South with the North, and created a second administrative city in the Deccan, renaming it Daulatabad. [*See* Daulatabad.] Under Muhammad bin Tughluq the frontiers of the Delhi sultanate reached their greatest extent, as the sultan vigorously pursued his policy of completing the political and administrative unification of the country. When the Delhi sultanate began to disintegrate under Firuz and his successors, provincial kingdoms rose up at Jaunpur, Malwa, Gujarat, and other places. In 1526, when Babur defeated the last sultan of Delhi, the empire was confined to some parts of the Punjab and the Ganges valley (see map 1).

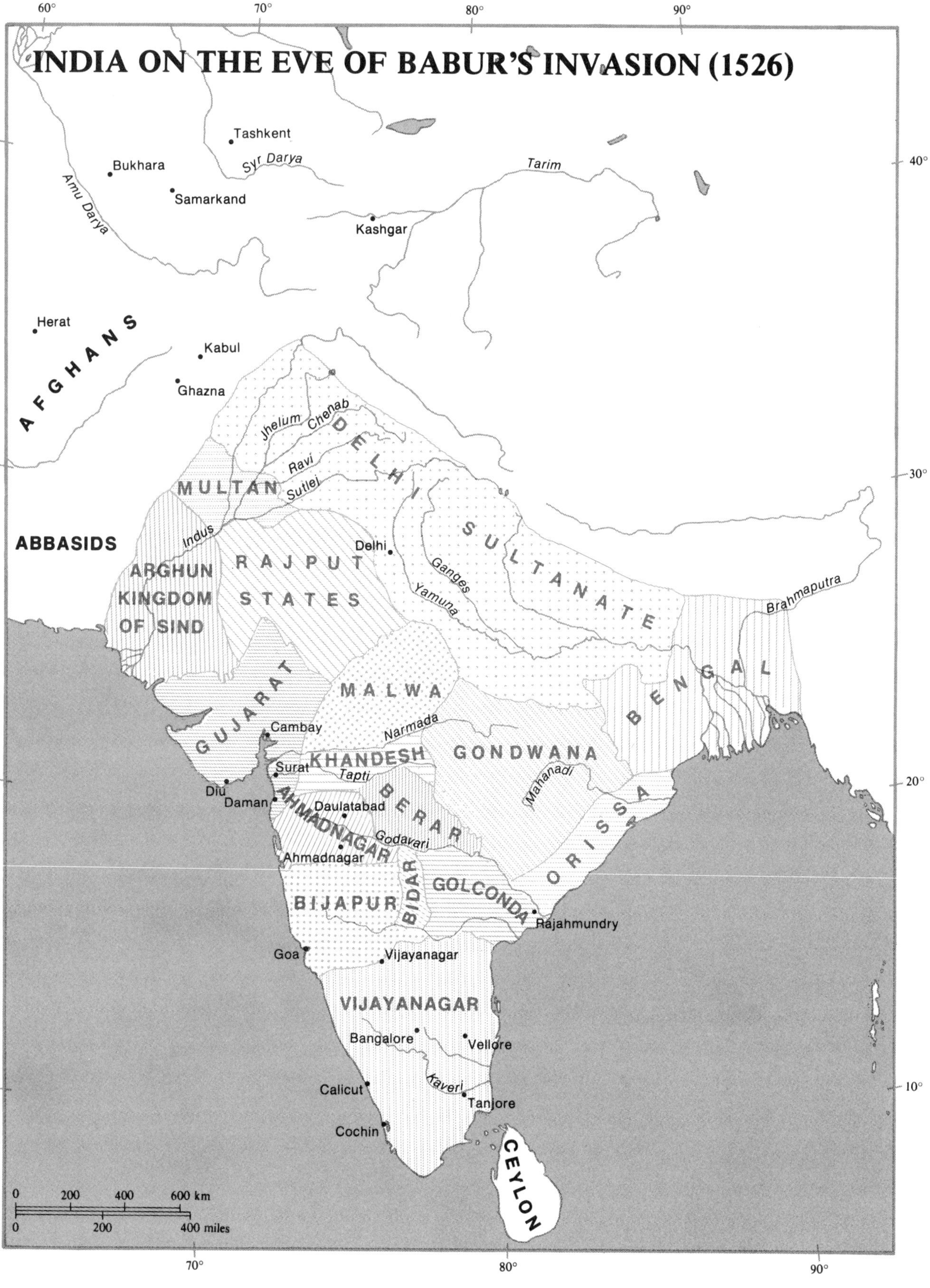
INDIA ON THE EVE OF BABUR'S INVASION (1526)
60°
70°
80°
90°
40°
30°
20°
10°
Tashkent
Bukhara
Samarkand
Syr Darya
Amu Darya
Tarim
Kashgar
Herat
Kabul
Ghazna
AFGHANS
Jhelum
Chenab
Ravi
Sutlej
Indus
MULTAN
DELHI SULTANATE
ABBASIDS
ARGHUN KINGDOM OF SIND
RAJPUT STATES
Delhi
Ganges
Yamuna
Brahmaputra
GUJARAT
MALWA
BENGAL
Cambay
Narmada
KHANDESH
GONDWANA
Surat
Tapti
Mahanadi
Diu
Daman
Daulatabad
BERAR
AHMADNAGAR
Godavari
ORISSA
Ahmadnagar
BIDAR
GOLCONDA
BIJAPUR
Rajahmundry
Goa
Vijayanagar
VIJAYANAGAR
Bangalore
Vellore
Kaveri
Calicut
Tanjore
Cochin
CEYLON
0 200 400 600 km
0 200 400 miles

Legally, the Delhi sultanate was a part of the Abbasid caliphate and the rulers did not claim for themselves a position higher than that of "lieutenant of the *khalifa*." Iltutmish was the first to obtain an investiture from the caliph at Baghdad. Even after the fall of the caliphate (1258), the sultans of Delhi continued to pronounce their affiliation with the *khilafat*. Muhammad bin Tughluq received recognition from the caliph in Cairo. In 1517 when Ibrahim Lodi ascended to the throne, the Abbasid caliphate had long been overthrown by the Ottomans.

The early sultans of Delhi believed in the Iranian theory of kingship and attributed divine source to their authority. Ala ud-Din Khalji introduced the element of force and claimed obedience on the basis of his power to rule. The Tughluqs, the Sayyids, and the Lodis made lofty claims about their genealogy, but after the Ilbaris the principle of legitimacy could never effectively be applied. Under the influence of the renowned fundamentalist scholar of Damascus, Ibn Taimiya, Muhammad bin Tughluq propounded the theory that "state and religion are twins." The position of the monarchy received a serious setback under the Lodi Afghans, who considered their sultan as *primus inter pares* within the Afghan elite.

Polity. The polity of the Delhi sultanate passed through different phases. The Early Turkish sultans created Turkish nobility as the main prop of their power and the sultanate became a Turkish state; the Khaljis broadened the base and converted it into an Indo-Muslim state; under Muhammad bin Tughluq an effort was made to make it an Indian state, coterminous with all Indian people, in which the nobility came to be recruited from all sections of the population. This policy no doubt broadened the base of the state but destroyed its compactness and homogeneity, making the governing class a promiscuous mass of people without any common ideal or loyalty. Tribal traditions of the Lodi nobility further weakened the position of monarchy.

The administrative structure of the Delhi sultanate was an amalgam of four traditions: (1) Islamic traditions as evolved during the Abbasid period and transmitted to the Delhi sultans through the Samanids and the Ghaznavids, (2) Iranian traditions as imbibed and articulated by the Minor Dynasties, (3) Indian traditions as continued from generation to generation throughout the ages, and (4) Mongol traditions as adopted by the sultans on the basis of expediency or experience. In nomenclature, many of the institutions showed either Abbasid or Iranian influence. The taxation system had all the terms of the classical period—*kharaj* (land tax), *ushr* (a one-tenth land tax from Muslims), *zakat* (payment by Muslims on a year's accumulated income), *jizya* (tax from non-Muslims), *khams* (war booty), and so forth—but their connotations had undergone great change. The term *jizya,* for example, came to be used for *kharaj* in general, and the distinction between Muslim and non-Muslim holders of land ceased to operate in the taxation system. The army of the sultans was organized on the decimal system and was directly recruited and paid by the center. From the footman and the bowman of the Rajput period the emphasis now shifted to the mounted horseman. The Turks are therefore referred to in Indian literature as "lords of the horse."

The sultan was assisted by ministers in carrying on the administration of the empire. The *vazir* was the chief minister, whose powers and functions varied with the attitude of the sultans. Other important ministries were *diwan-i risalat* (which dealt with religious matters, trusts, stipends, etc.), *diwan-i arz* (army department), and *diwan-i insha* (royal correspondence). The provinces were administered and looked after by the governors. In the rural areas the *khuts, muqaddams,* and *chaudhris* constituted the local administrative apparatus. Many of the officers of the Hindu period were allowed to continue, although their duties and functions underwent some change with the policies of the sultans. The land tax varied from time to time, with the maximum realized during the reign of Ala ud-Din Khalji being 50 percent of the produce.

The Tughluq sultans initiated an elaborate agrarian policy. Muhammad bin Tughluq adopted different methods to encourage agriculture, such as collective farming and farming by contract. A department called the *diwan-i amir kohi* looked after the promotion of agriculture. The power of the state to control essential commodities and fix prices was accepted. Ala ud-Din Khalji successfully implemented his policy of market control. [*See also* Land Tenure and Reform: Land Tenure, Revenue, and Reform in South Asia.] The state undertook many welfare activities: it founded colleges and hospitals, dug canals, provided assistance for the elderly, and laid out gardens and orchards.

Judicial administration of the sultanate was run by the *qazis,* Islamic legal officers. In rural areas the Hindu inhabitants enjoyed a kind of autonomy under the Hindu local officers. The *muhtasib* (censor of public morals) was responsible for suppressing immoral activities.

The secular nature of the institutions of the Delhi sultanate has been well brought out by the historian

Zia ud-Din Barani (1285–1357). He reports that the sultanate had to frame laws that had no sanction in Islamic law *(shari'a),* but without which no government could be run. Religious attitudes of the individual rulers did in certain measure influence the general spirit of the government but the general policies of the sultanate were not decided on the basis of religion. Ala ud-Din is reported to have said, "I do not know what is lawful or unlawful; whatever I consider in the interest of the state, that I decree."

A principle of religious coexistence evolved in the Delhi sultanate. Hindus were not obstructed in the performance of their religious duties and temples were not destroyed in times of peace. Iltutmish and Ala ud-Din Khalji brushed aside the suggestions of orthodox theologians to deal strictly with the Hindus and stop their religious practices. Some rulers took interest in Hindu festivals. Muhammad bin Tughluq celebrated Holi and made huge endowments to Hindu *gao maths* (cow centers).

The sultanate encouraged trade, and while large numbers of foreign traders visited India, many Indian merchants went to Central Asia, Iran, and West Asian countries. Writers of the period refer to the affluent condition of Khurasani merchants in India. Muhammad bin Tughluq abolished import duty in order to encourage trade with foreign lands, and during his time gold could be taken out of India in any quantity. It is said that the Delhi sultanate was the root, and the Mughal empire, the fruit, of Muslim statesmanship in India.

[*See also* Barani, Zia ud-Din; Khalji Dynasty; Tughluq Dynasty; Lodi Dynasty; Mughal Empire; Iltutmish; *and* Babur.]

M. Habib and K. A. Nizami, *A Comprehensive History of India,* vol. 5, *The Delhi Sultanate* (1970). Wolseley Haig, ed., *The Cambridge History of India,* vol. 3, *Turks and Afghans* (1928). R. C. Majumdar, ed., *The Delhi Sultanate* (1960). Ishwari Prasad, *History of Medieval India* (1928). I. H. Qureshi, *Administration of the Sultanate of Delhi* (1942). R. P. Tripathi, *Some Aspects of Muslim Administration in India* (1936).

KHALIQ AHMAD NIZAMI

DEMAK, the first Muslim kingdom of Java. According to Central Javanese legend, its first ruler was Raden Patah, a prince of Majapahit who was mysteriously exiled to Palembang and defeated the great Hindu empire in the Javanese year 1400 (1478 CE). The true founder of the Demak dynasty appears to have been a Muslim Chinese trader who settled there in the last decade of the fifteenth century. It was his powerful grandson, Sultan Tranggana of Demak (c. 1504–1546), who finally conquered the Majapahit capital about 1527. He dominated Central Java and influenced Palembang and Benjarmasin. Demak became the center for Muslim expansion, and its wooden-pillared mosque remains the oldest and most sacred one in Java. Tranggana died while besieging Panarukan, and hegemony passed to Pajang and then Mataram, farther inland.

[*See also* Java *and* Majapahit.]

ANTHONY REID

DEMOCRACY WALL refers to a brick wall near Xidan Street in downtown Beijing, China, where wall posters first appeared in the so-called 'Beijing Spring, or Democracy Movement, of 1978 to 1979.

The first phase of the movement began in March 1978 when posters appeared at the site celebrating the Tiananmen demonstration of 1976 and criticizing the official primarily responsible for its suppression, Wu De. After Wu De was dismissed from his posts and the verdict on the Tiananmen incident was officially reversed in October 1978, the more famous second phase of the movement began. At this time posters voicing three categories of dissent appeared: continued criticism of remaining Maoist policies and their supporters, individual complaints of persecution and injustice, and calls for democratic reforms and human rights. Crowds gathered around the wall, debating with each other and even with foreigners present the issues raised in the posters. Numerous self-mimeographed journals calling for changes ranging from reform to abolition of the socialist system were distributed at the foot of the wall.

Most observers now believe that Democracy Wall was initially tolerated by Deng Xiaoping and his supporters as a way to demonstrate widespread support for their reform policies at the time of their successful confrontation with the "Whateverist" faction (remaining leaders committed to upholding Maoist ideology) at the Third Plenum of the Eleventh Central Committee in November and December 1978. After Deng's victory, and after February 1979 when the posters shifted from criticizing Deng's opponents and calling for reforms to criticizing the socialist system itself, the suppression of the movement began. Some scholars believe that the crackdown was accelerated particularly after mass rallies occurred that began to link the young, mostly working-class poster writers with peasants coming into the cities to air their grievances. While in November 1978 Deng had expressed his support for the movement, in March 1979 he warned that the movement had "gone too far" and might not be in the interest of "stability, unity, and the Four Modernizations." In the future, debate was to be within the framework of Marxism-Leninism–Mao Zedong Thought and support for the socialist system under the leadership of the Chinese Communist Party.

In late March 1979 the human rights activist Wei Jingsheng was arrested, soon joined by other leaders of the Democracy Movement. In October he was tried and convicted for his activities and sentenced to fifteen years in prison. In December 1979 Democracy Wall was moved by the authorities to a site in the far western suburbs of Beijing, where would-be poster writers were required to register with the authorities before they were allowed, at specified times, to post their opinions. Coupled with the announcement that poster writers would be held accountable for any opinions going beyond those officially tolerated, this action ensured the effective abolition of Democracy Wall and the Democracy Movement.

[*See also* April Fifth Movement; Deng Xiaoping; Gang of Four; Marxism and Socialism: Marxism in China; *and* Zhou Enlai.]

Kjeld Erik Brodsgaard, "The Democracy Movement in China, 1978–1979: Opposition Movements, Wall Poster Campaigns, and Underground Journals," *Asian Survey* 21.7 (July 1981): 747–774. Chen Ruoxi, *Democracy Wall and the Unofficial Journals* (1982). Roger Garside, *Coming Alive: China after Mao* (1981). David S. G. Goodman, *Beijing Street Voices: China's Democracy Movement* (1981). James D. Seymour, *The Fifth Modernization: China's Human Rights Movement, 1978–1979* (1980).

John A. Rapp

DEMOGRAPHY. *See* Population.

DENG TUO, journalist and member of the Chinese Communist Party (CCP). Born in 1911 in Shandong Province, Deng joined the CCP in 1935 while attending college. After having played an active role in the December Twenty-ninth Movement, which demanded that the Guomindang (Kuomintang, Nationalist Party) stop civil war and form a united front with the Communists against the Japanese, he became editor in chief of *Xinhua ribao (New China Daily)* in Chongqing. Thereafter he stayed in the field of journalism; his positions included editor in chief of the *People's Daily* until his purge in 1966. As the editor in chief of *Frontline,* the official magazine of Beijing Municipal Party Committee, he coauthored with Wu Han and Liao Mosha a column entitled "The Notes of the Three-Family Village." The official criticism that he had used the column to ridicule Mao's Great Leap Forward signaled the beginning of the Cultural Revolution (1966–1976). He died during the Cultural Revolution and was posthumously rehabilitated.

[*See also* Great Proletarian Cultural Revolution; Liao Mosha; *and* Wu Han.]

Hong Yung Lee

DENG XIAOPING (b. 1904), leader of the People's Republic of China since the late 1970s. Besides being a member of the Politburo Standing Committee of the Chinese Communist Party (CCP), Deng became in 1981 the Chairman of the Party's Military Commission—a body that controls and directs the most important source of power in the PRC, the People's Liberation Army (PLA). A pragmatic leader and experienced administrator, Deng is the chief architect of China's modernization program today.

Deng was born in Guang'an, Sichuan Province, and joined the CCP in 1924 while on a work-study program in France. Before returning to China in 1926, he studied in Moscow for several months. Back in China, he was assigned to be a political officer in the army of the northern warlord Feng Yuxiang, who in 1926 was in a temporary alliance with the Guomindang (Kuomintang, KMT, or Nationalist Party) and was receiving Soviet assistance. After the CCP-KMT United Front collapsed in April 1927, Feng also turned against the Communists, and Deng fled to Shanghai, where he worked for two years as the CCP secretary-general in the underground movement. In mid-1929 Deng was assigned the task of building rural guerrilla bases; he launched a series of unsuccessful revolts and in 1931 led his forces to Jiangxi, where the Communists had established their headquarters. In 1933, when Mao Zedong was defeated in a leadership squabble and censured, Deng and those who sided with Mao were dismissed from their leadership positions, but when Mao regained the upper hand, Deng was reinstated.

During the fabled Long March, Deng served as director of the political department of the First Army Corps and then as its political commissar. After the war with Japan began in 1937 Deng was appointed political commissar of the 129th Division, one of the three divisions in the reorganized Communist

Eighth Route Army, which was commanded by Liu Bocheng, also a native of Sichuan. The forces under the two Sichuanese grew into a large military machine and became one of the four largest Communist army units during the war. Renamed the Second Field Army when the Civil War with the KMT began in 1946, these troops fought and won a number of major battles. In the critical Huaihai battles in east China of November 1948 to January 1949, the CCP military high command set up a special five-man General Front Committee to coordinate the strategy of participating Communist troops; Deng had the distinction of serving as secretary of the committee and directing the military actions of the army. In 1949 and 1950 the Second Field Army took southwest China, where Deng was the ranking Party leader in the early 1950s. While such a power base enabled Deng to propel himself into the national political limelight in the 1950s, the personal ties he established with numerous Communist cadres during wartime proved highly valuable to him many decades later.

Deng rose quickly in the leadership hierarchy after his transfer to Beijing in 1952. He became a vice-premier under Premier Zhou Enlai in 1952, concurrently serving as minister of finance from 1953 to 1954. He became secretary-general of the CCP in 1954 and a member of the Politburo the following year, apparently a major political beneficiary of the purge of Gao Gang and Rao Xishi, the recalcitrant regional leaders of Manchuria (northeast China) and east China, respectively. During the Eighth CCP Congress in 1956, Deng was elevated to the six-man Politburo Standing Committee (together with Mao, Liu Shaoqi, Zhou Enlai, Zhu De, and Chen Yun) and appointed general secretary heading the Party Secretariat. Since the Secretariat was in charge of daily administration, the appointment to this post made him one of the most powerful men in China.

By many accounts, Deng is able, talented, and knowledgeable. He was nicknamed "a living encyclopedia" by his colleagues. If Khrushchev's account is to be trusted, Mao allegedly pointed Deng out to Khrushchev and said, "See that little man there? He is highly intelligent and has a great future ahead of him." Deng visited the Soviet Union several times in the 1950s and 1960s, since he was closely involved in Sino-Soviet relations and the international Communist movement.

Mao and Deng parted ways in the 1960s, disagreeing over the strategy of development and other policies. Deng's pragmatism, embodied in his well-known remark, "It does not matter whether they are black cats or white cats; so long as they catch mice, they are good cats," was heresy to Mao's ears. Mao also resented Deng for making decisions without consulting him—he scolded Deng in a 1961 Party meeting, saying, "Which emperor did this?" In 1966 Mao launched the Great Proletarian Cultural Revolution and mobilized the youthful Red Guards to purge the "capitalist power holders" in the Party. Liu Shaoqi was labeled "number one capitalist power holder"; Deng was named number two, accused of following Liu's "revisionist line," and dismissed from office and publicly humiliated. From 1969 to 1973 Deng and his family were exiled to a "May Seventh cadre school" in rural Jiangxi, where he underwent reeducation, performed manual labor, and studied the writings of Mao and Marx. Deng's elder son, Deng Pufang, was permanantly crippled in an assault by Red Guards. [*See also* Great Proletarian Cultural Revolution; May Seventh Cadre Schools; *and* Liu Shaoqi.]

In the spring of 1973 Deng was brought back to Beijing and reinstated as a vice-premier in the wake of the major realignment of political forces that followed the demise of Defense Minister Lin Biao and the purge of Lin's followers. Deng's ability and experience were highly valued in the Chinese leadership, and he quickly assumed important roles. In late 1973 he carried out a major reorganization of regional military leaders and was elevated to the Politburo. In April 1974 he journeyed to New York to address a special United Nations session, in which he expounded Mao's theory of the "three worlds."

When Premier Zhou Enlai, suffering from cancer, was hospitalized in May 1974, the burden of political leadership and administration increasingly fell on Deng's shoulders. Clearly, Deng was the choice of Zhou and other veteran Party and military leaders to be the future premier and Party chairman. In January 1975 Deng was elevated to the positions of Party vice-chairman, senior vice-premier, and PLA chief of staff. However, Deng's eagerness to carry out the Four Modernizations—a policy, announced by Premier Zhou and endorsed by the National People's Congress in early 1975, that was designed to make China an advanced country by the year 2000—and the political and other reforms he sought to institute alienated Mao and other radicals led by Mao's wife, Jiang Qing.

Thus, soon after Premier Zhou died on 8 January 1976 Deng disappeared from public view and became the target of an attack in the Chinese media, which vilified Deng as "an unrepentant capitalist roader." On 5 April, when demonstrations in memory of Premier Zhou turned into a massive riot, Deng was accused of instigating the incident; two days later the Party Politburo, at Mao's urging, passed a resolution to oust Deng from all leadership posts. Vice-Premier Hua Guofeng, largely unknown outside China at that time, benefited greatly from Deng's downfall. In February 1976 Hua was made acting premier by Mao; two months later Hua was appointed premier and first Party vice-chairman, putting him in a favorable position to contend for Mao's mantle. [*See also* April Fifth Movement.]

Barely a month after Mao died on 9 September 1976 Hua teamed up with Marshal Ye Jianying and Mao's former bodyguard Wang Dongxing to stage a coup and put Jiang Qing and three other top radicals, since labeled the "Gang of Four," under arrest. Hua was named chairman of the CCP and its Military Commission. Hua and other Maoists tried to block Deng's political comeback, but Deng's allies eventually prevailed, and Deng was reinstated in July 1977.

Following his return to a leadership position in the summer of 1977 and his struggle for ascendancy thereafter, Deng's first and foremost task was to destroy the cult of Mao and to downgrade Mao's ideological authority. The reasons for de-Maoization were twofold: (1) to remove ideological constraints on a series of pragmatic (or revisionist) modernization programs that Deng sought to institute and (2) to undercut Deng's chief rival, Hua Guofeng, and other leaders who derived their political influence from association with Mao or invocation of the late chairman.

In pursuing the goal of de-Maoization, Deng and his associates took several well-concerted steps. First, they worked through the press and publications under their control to discredit Mao's revolutionary precepts. In 1977 and 1978 numerous articles attacked and repudiated the regime's excessive emphasis on politics, revolution, class struggle, egalitarianism, subjective human factors, the principle of self-reliance, and "mass democracy"—Maoist values that were closely identified with the Cultural Revolution. Instead, these articles propagated the need for political stability, discipline, and economic growth; supported material incentives and expertise; and stressed an "open door" to foreign technology and capital.

Beginning in May 1978 Deng and his associates mounted a campaign to establish a new ideological line in order to further dilute the aura of Maoist authority and simultaneously legitimate their reform programs. The line first surfaced in an article entitled "Practice Is the Sole Criterion of Truth," by the "Special Commentator" in Beijing's *Guangming ribao*. The article, among other things, pointed out that any theory or policy line's correctness or accordance with reality must be tested by practice and that Marxism-Leninism–Mao Zedong Thought is not the measure of truth because it also has to undergo the test by practice.

These were not idle theoretical statements. Simply put, Deng's view is that no policy, including those put forth or favored by Mao, should be venerated as truth if it does not work or fails to produce positive results. In a system in which the Party and state constitutions have sanctified Marxism-Leninism–Mao Zedong Thought as the guiding principle, the tenet "Practice is the sole criterion of truth" is highly iconoclastic.

At the same time, Deng sought the political rehabilitation of virtually every official of consequence, living or dead, who was a victim of Mao's purge. Memorial services were held for the dead to restore their honor and position within the Party history; among those honored were Liu Shaoqi, marshals Peng Dehuai and He Long, and Tao Zhu, all of them once members of the Politburo. For those still living, rehabilitation usually meant a return to a position of power: Chen Yun and Peng Zhen, who were elected to the Politburo in 1978 and 1979, respectively (in Chen's case he is also a CCP vice-chairman), and have had important roles in Chinese politics in recent years (particularly since the fall from power of Hu Yaobang in December 1986), are only two outstanding examples.

The restoration of these former alleged "capitalist roaders" to office had serious political implications. Their political comeback called into question the very legitimacy of the Cultural Revolution and challenged the infallibility of Mao's leadership. The reinstatement of these veteran CCP leaders also weakened the power of Chairman Hua Guofeng and others who had benefited from the events of the Cultural Revolution. The policy effect of their restoration was also highly evident—indeed, there has been a discernible "thermidorian reaction" to the Cultural Revolution in every area of Chinese life.

Another Deng de-Maoization measure was to put the Gang of Four on public trial, a trial that began in Beijing on 20 November 1980 and lasted several weeks. These four radical leaders, including Mao's widow, Jiang Qing, were the late chairman's most ardent supporters and the prime movers behind the Cultural Revolution, on which they rode to power. The trial symbolizes the triumph of veteran officials, led by Deng, who fell victims to the radical crusade from 1966 to 1976. [*See also* Gang of Four.]

Moreover, Deng also used the trial as the *coup de grâce* against Hua Guofeng. Although Hua was not a defendant and had been credited with ousting the radicals from power and putting them under arrest in October 1976, he did not have an unblemished record. Since Hua had collaborated with the radicals before Mao's death and, as minister of public security, had an inglorious part in suppressing the Tiananmen Square demonstration of April 1976, Deng believed that the trial would probably produce evidence exposing Hua's duplicity. Understanding the trial's implications for his career, Hua made a deal and consented to step down as CCP chairman soon after the Gang of Four went on trial. In a central committee plenum in June 1981, Hu Yaobang, Deng's protégé, replaced Hua as the Party chairman. The same Party gathering also approved a thirty-five-thousand-word decision, entitled "Resolution on Certain Questions in the History of Our Party," which critically evaluated Mao's career and sharply rebuked the mistakes he made in the last two decades of his life, thereby further demythologizing the late chairman.

Deng has sought to ensure the continuation of the "open door" policy and the modernization programs that he has fashioned in recent years. In this, he has support from the Party's moderates, many of the intellectuals, the technocrats, and certain key military leaders at the central and provincial levels. Since his return to power in 1977, Deng has consolidated his control in the CCP, the government, and the military by rehabilitating experienced leaders who were dismissed by the radicals, placing many in influential positions. He has named experienced colleagues as well as younger protégés to the ruling Politburo. As former chief of staff and current chairman of the Party's Military Commission, Deng has control of the military establishment and has removed many of those who collaborated with the radicals or who are lukewarm to policies of moderation and modernization.

Deng's visits to Japan in 1978 and the United States in 1979 suggest that he has been the prime mover toward close relations with these two former adversaries. He also sets policy for China's overall foreign relations. China's policies for welcoming foreign investment and joint ventures have been formulated at Deng's urging and with his blessing. From time to time, Deng has had to compromise with other leaders, slow down the pace of reform, or shift priorities to placate his critics, but this has not seriously affected his control of the regime's direction.

Currently, Deng has staked his reputation on the government and Party bureaucratic reform movement and on the attainability of the current Five-Year Plan targets. Apparently Deng believes that economic modernization depends on eliminating obstructionist bureaucrats, replacing the old and untrained, and renewing the prestige of the Party. If bureaucratic reform and economic readjustment proceed without major disruption, Deng's followers should have enough control of the government, CCP, and army to enable Deng to serve only as an adviser to his younger colleagues.

[*See also* Communism: Chinese Communist Party; Marxism and Socialism: Marxism in China; *and* Mao Zedong.]

David Chang, *Zhou Enlai and Deng Xiaoping in the Chinese Leadership Crisis* (1984). David Klein and Anne B. Clark, *Biographical Dictionary of Chinese Communism, 1921–1965,* vol. 2 (1971). Andrew J. Nathan, *Chinese Democracy* (1985).

PARRIS CHANG

DENGYŌ DAISHI. *See* Saichō.

DENKARD *(Acts of the Religion),* a ninth-century compendium of the teachings of Zoroastrianism in nine parts, of which books three through nine survive. The text was published with an obsolete English translation by P. B. Sanjana in nineteen volumes (Bombay, 1928). D. M. Madan published the standard Pahlavi text in two volumes (Bombay, 1911), and M. J. Dresden published a facsimile and concordance of editions (Wiesbaden, 1966). J. de Menasce gives an indication of the thematic discontinuity of much of the work. The sixth book is a collection of moral and theological maxims. The eighth and ninth books provide summaries of the twenty-one *Nasks* of the Avesta, most of which are now lost. Parts of the other surviving books have also been edited and translated.

[*See also* Avesta *and* Zoroastrianism.]

Mary Boyce, "Middle Persian Literature," in Bertold Spuler, ed., *Handbuch der Orientalistik,* pt. 1, vol. 4, sec. 2, chap. 1 (1968), pp. 43–45. S. Shaked, ed. and trans., *Wisdom of the Sasanian Sages: Denkard VI* (1979). E. W. West, trans., *Pahlavi Texts* (1974), vol. 4.

JAMES R. RUSSELL

DE NOBILI, ROBERTO (1577–1656), Jesuit missionary to India. An Italian nobleman, deeply influenced by the Counter-Reformation and by Jesuit chronicles, de Nobili entered the Society of Jesus in 1596 and arrived at Goa on 20 May 1606. He is regarded as the founder and organizer of the Jesuit Madura Mission, moving the focus of Jesuit missionary endeavor from the coast to the interior. De Nobili adopted as his missionary strategy the "principle of accommodation," whereby he made himself an "Indian in matters of dress and diet in order to save the Indians."

[*See also* Jesuits: Jesuits in India.]

Vincent Cronin, *A Pearl to India: The Life of Roberto De Nobili* (1959). PATRICK ROCHE

DEOBAND, country town located some ninety miles northeast of Delhi, known for its Dar ul-Ulum, or Muslim seminary, founded by a group of religious scholars in 1867. The school trained students in *hadith,* the words and deeds of the Prophet, and in the Hanafi legal tradition in order to preserve the teachings of the faith in a period of non-Muslim rule and considerable social change. Students typically sought the personal transformation of sober Sufism at the hand of a spiritual guide; many also studied the Muslim medical science of *yunani tibb*. Graduates often served as prayer leaders; advisers in legal and spiritual matters; guardians and custodians of property; and teachers, writers, and publishers in the Urdu language. Many participated in the endemic public debates carried out in this period of self-conscious cultural redefinitions. In these debates the Deobandis represented a reformed position, concerned with eliminating what were seen as customary accretions stemming from the influence of false Sufism, Shi'a error, and Hindu custom. By emphasizing individual responsibility for correct belief and practice, they provided an alternative to an intercessory religion focused on the Sufi shrines and elaborate customary celebrations. The school, supported by popular subscriptions and organized in a modern bureaucratic style, set a pattern of religious education that was increasingly common. Deoband has been a metropolitan center for students from India and beyond. Schools sharing its orientation are now spread throughout the subcontinent. Originally quiescent politically, its leaders largely opposed the movement for Pakistan and supported Congress in the hope of having a larger arena in which their teaching, unhampered by colonial restrictions, would thrive.

[*See also* Sufism; Islam; *and* Pakistan.]

Ziya-ul-Hasan Faruqi, *The Deoband School and the Demand for Pakistan* (1963). Yohanan Friedmann, "The Attitude of the Jami'yyat-i 'Ulama'-i Hind to the Indian National Movement and the Establishment of Pakistan," in *The 'Ulama' in Modern History,* edited by Gabriel Baer (1971). Barbara Daly Metcalf, *Islamic Revival in British India: Deoband, 1860–1900* (1982).

BARBARA D. METCALF

DEROZIO, HENRY LOUIS VIVIAN (1809–1831), Indian poet and brilliant intellectual. Born in Calcutta to a family of mixed descent—his mother English, his father part Indian and part Portuguese—Derozio wrote in English, in strict metrical form. His poems are among the earliest expressions of nationalist sentiment in India. His teaching at Hindu College, as well as his discussion group (the Academic Association), flourished on skepticism and modes of argument inspired by the Western discursive tradition but drew sharp criticism from the religious orthodoxy. He was an inspiration for a whole generation of young Bengalis.

[*See also* Bengal.]

F. Bradley-Birt, *Poems of Henry Louis Vivian Derozio* (1923). MEENA ALEXANDER

DERVISH. *See* Sufism.

DESAI, MORARJI (b. 1896), prime minister of India from 1977 to 1979. The eldest of six children, Desai was married at the age of fifteen (to a bride of eleven) three days after his schoolmaster father committed suicide. Gaining confidence from his studies of science and mathematics at Wilson College, and from his association with Mohandas K. Gandhi's political and social movements, Desai left the civil service in 1930 to take part in nationalist civil disobedience campaigns. A teetotaler who abstains also from coffee and tea, refuses inoculations, and publicly lauds "urine therapy" (drinking one's own urine), Desai has five times defeated opponents on political issues by threatening to fast to death unless the opponent gave in.

After India's independence, Desai first established himself as an able administrator of Bombay Province, then as minister of commerce and finance in the cabinets of Jawaharlal Nehru. Having contested and lost Congress Party leadership to Indira Gandhi after Nehru's death, Desai was summarily dropped from Mrs. Gandhi's cabinet in 1969, at which point he joined a rival Congress Party and eventually became prime minister himself. Desai's cabinets were marked by factionalism and ineffectiveness, in large part because of his unwillingness to pursue or countenance compromise with his personal or political principles.

[*See also* Indian National Congress.]

Morarji Desai, *The Story of My Life,* 3 vols. (1974). Ved Mehta, "Letter from New Delhi," *The New Yorker* 53 (17 October 1977). MARCUS FRANDA

DESHIMA, or Dejima, a small, man-made island in Nagasaki harbor, Japan. Deshima was built by the Tokugawa *bakufu* to house the Portuguese traders in Japan, thus to inhibit contact with Japanese society; after the expulsion of the Portuguese in 1639 the island was used to house the Dutch operation in Japan.

Deshima was the only legal site for European residence and trade in Japan from 1641 until ratification of the Treaty of Kanagawa in 1855, and through it came Japan's only regular access to information from the West. The fan-shaped island was separated from the mainland by a guarded, gated bridge, Deshima Bridge, meant to confine the European residents and to restrict both their access to the town and the access of Japanese to the foreigners, their ideas, and their material culture, as well as to facilitate *bakufu* supervision of trade. The establishment of Deshima for the Portuguese and the later confinement of the Dutch there were part of a range of policies instituted in the 1630s in order to place all foreign contact completely under *bakufu* control or supervision, policies usually, if somewhat misleadingly, called the "policy of national seclusion."

Deshima contained a wharf for ships of the Dutch East India Company; warehouses; residences for the *opperhoofd* (chief of the Dutch Trading Factory), his merchants, seamen, and his physician; and offices for both the company and the Office of Interpreters of Dutch (Oranda Tsūji), who were employed by the Nagasaki magistrate. The island was surrounded by a palisade in the water some yards offshore, and the bridge was guarded and the gates shut at night so that unauthorized persons could not enter. Only specially licensed merchants could enter to trade, while the Dutch bought their provisions through agents, who provided them even with prostitutes. The Dutch also used part of the island to raise vegetables and pasture a small herd of livestock, as well as for an exercise ground. Indeed, the Dutch saw Deshima as the Dutch prison in Japan, "for so I may deservedly call their habitation and factory at Nagasaki," wrote Engelbert Kaempfer, their resident physician from 1690 to 1692. [*See* Kaempfer, Engelbert.]

Deshima's importance was more than economic. The island became Japan's best source of information about the West, which came in the form of the military and political intelligence reports that the *opperhoofd* was required to submit on the arrival of each ship (and about which he was questioned closely on his annual journey to the shogun's court at Edo) and in the form of information more informally acquired about developments in European medicine, science, and technology. With regard to the latter, as the Dutch regularly employed a physician on Deshima the island became a major stimulus to Japanese interest in "Dutch" (i.e., European) medicine and the Dutch language, especially after the eighth shogun, Yoshimune, relaxed the ban on importing Western books in 1720. This sparked widespread interest among Japanese physicians and intellectuals in what was called "Dutch studies" *(rangaku)* from the mid-eighteenth century on. *Rangaku* and the attendant "Japanese discovery of Europe" in the last century of Tokugawa rule transformed not only Japanese medicine and science but also art, military technology and science, and political and philosophical debate.

Deshima was engulfed by landfill in the Meiji period and is now part of the Nagasaki mainland, well in from the waterfront. In 1957 the site was restored as a historical museum.

[*See also* Nagasaki; Seclusion; *and* Rangaku.]

C. R. Boxer, *Jan Compagnie in Japan, 1600–1817* (2d rev. ed., 1950). Grant Kohn Goodman, *The Dutch Impact on Japan, 1650–1853* (1967). Engelbert Kaempfer, *The History of Japan, Together with a Description of the Kingdom of Siam, 1690–1692,* 3 vols. (1906). Donald Keene, *The Japanese Discovery of Europe, 1720–1830* (rev. ed., 1969). RONALD P. TOBY

DE THAM (1862–1913), leader of a resistance group in the Yen The region of Tonkin, Vietnam. Although he had contacts with the Can Vuong movement and with Phan Boi Chau, De Tham remained an essentially independent figure, engaging in guerrilla activities for over twenty years. His base of support was sufficiently strong to permit negotiated agreements with the French, although neither side entirely ceased harassing the other. De Tham's participation in the abortive June 1908 coup in Hanoi brought renewed efforts to capture him, as well as a price on his head, and he was assassinated in March 1913.

[*See also* Can Vuong *and* Phan Boi Chau.]

David Marr, *Vietnamese Anticolonialism, 1885–1925* (1971). Nguyen Phut Tan, *Modern History of Vietnam 1802–1954* (1964). BRUCE M. LOCKHART

DEVANAMPIYA TISSA (250–210 BCE), Sinhalese king. According to the chronicle *Mahavamsa,* the entry of Buddhism into Sri Lanka occurred during the reign of Devanampiya Tissa. He was a contemporary of the great Maurya emperor Ashoka, whose emissary Mahinda (Ashoka's son, according to some authorities, or his brother, as suggested by others) converted Devanampiya Tissa to the new faith. It is very probable that Buddhists and Buddhism came to the island much earlier than this, but it was from the time of Devanampiya Tissa that Buddhism became the bedrock of the culture and civilization of the island and of the town of Anuradhapura, itself a great center of Buddhist civilization.

At this time the Anuradhapura kingdom was merely the strongest, if that, of several others in the island. Devanampiya Tissa made a purposeful bid to convert the prestige attached to his links with Ashoka and the Maurya empire into the hard reality of overlordship over the whole island. But other rulers in the island, most notably those in Rohana, did not readily concede him this position.

[*See also* Buddhism: An Overview; Mahinda; Ashoka; Anuradhapura; Rohana; *and* Sri Lanka.]

K. M. de Silva, *A History of Sri Lanka* (1981).

K. M. DE SILVA

DEVARAJA, name of a cult, ritual, or cult icon instituted on the order of Jayavarman II, the founder of the Cambodian monarchy of Angkor. *Deva* is Sanskrit for "god," *raja* for "king"; thus the term may mean "god-king" or "king of the gods." Where the cult is mentioned in bilingual or Old Khmer inscriptions, the Old Khmer is *Kamraten jagat ta raja,* which may have much the same meaning.

According to the eleventh-century Sdok Kak Thom stele inscription, the purpose of the cult was to commemorate the new unity of the Khmer people under Jayavarman and their independence from the Javanese: "Then a brahman called Hiranyadama, expert in magic science, came from Janapada, because His Majesty . . . had invited him to perform a ceremony such as to make it impossible for this land of the Kambujas to offer any allegiance to Java, and such as to make possible the existence of a lord over the earth who was absolutely unique." Thereafter, as the inscription tells us, the descendants of the court chaplain Shivakaivalya officiated at the *devaraja* under successive rulers to protect their royal power.

Apart from the Sdok Kak Thom stele, only a few inscriptions mention the *devaraja,* sometimes only incidentally among a number of institutions, and they leave in doubt whether the *devaraja* was a major focus of ritual legitimacy after the first few reigns. G. Coedès thought that the *devaraja* cult was identical with those of the great pyramidal temple-tomb shrines built by so many rulers. H. Kulke has argued that it was a separate cult, centered on a portable bronze icon. Because *devaraja* can mean "god-king," the term has passed into general currency, perhaps illegitimately, to denote the claims to god-like despotic power sometimes thought to have been made by rulers like those of Angkor.

[*See also* Jayavarman II *and* Angkor.]

A. K. Chakravarti, *The Sdok Kak Thom Inscription, Part I: A Study in Indo-Khmer Civilization* (1978). G. Coedès, *Angkor, An Introduction* (1962). H. Kulke, *The Devarāja Cult* (1978). IAN W. MABBETT

DEVAWONGSE VAROPAKAR (1858–1923), prince and first modern foreign minister of Siam and architect of its independence. Devawongse was born on 27 November 1858 to his consort Piyamawadi. His younger sisters Sunantha, Sawangwatthana, and Saowapha all became queens of his half-brother, King Chulalongkorn (r. 1868–1910). Following the traditional palace education and a brief stint with an English tutor, Devawongse began his public career in the Royal Secretariat, the Royal Audit Office, and the Royal Pages' Bodyguard Regiment in the 1870s; all of these were modern undertakings through which the young king was attempting to reform an antiquated and corrupt old administration. Devawongse worked very closely with his brother and by his energy and intelligence earned ever-greater responsibilities, becoming personal secretary to the king in 1878, with special responsibility for foreign affairs, while continuing his audit functions in the Treasury. On the resignation of Chaophraya Phanuwong (Thuam Bunnag), the surviving leader of the powerful Bunnag family, from the Ministry of Foreign Affairs in 1885, Devawongse—who quite apart from being a loyal and experienced brother of the monarch was also the most knowledgeable in foreign affairs of his generation—was appointed to succeed Bunnag. Devawongse rapidly modernized the ministry, enforcing regular office hours in new government quarters rather than carrying on business from his home, as was the traditional practice, and adopting all the niceties and formalities of Western diplomatic practice.

As foreign minister at a time when Western imperialism was at its peak and Siam's neighbors were coming under colonial control, Devawongse abided by a few simple general principles that worked in the end to maintain Siam's independence: to persuade the powers that Siam was, or soon would be, a modern, civilized nation; to gain Siam's rulers a status equal to that of other world monarchs; to play strictly by the rules of international law and diplomacy; and, in the dangerous world of Great Power politics, to court Britain's goodwill and benevolent protection but at the same time to evenly balance French and British interests. He weathered the dangerous Franco-Siamese Paknam Incident of 1893 and carried through to successful completion negotiations with the French and British that ended territorial and security threats to the kingdom by 1909. His final years in office were devoted to attempts to end foreign extraterritoriality and the unequal treaties that continued to infringe upon Siam's sovereignty, but he died in 1923, shortly before the culmination of these efforts in 1925.

[*See also* Mongkut; Chulalongkorn; Bunnag Family; Phrakhlang; Paknam Incident; *and* Vajiravudh.]

Chandran Jeshurun, *The Contest for Siam, 1889–1902* (1977). David K. Wyatt, *The Politics of Reform in Thailand* (1969) and *Thailand: A Short History* (1984).

DAVID K. WYATT

DEVKOTA, LAXMIPRASAD (1909–1959), Nepali poet and essayist who initiated his country's twentieth-century literary renascence. His major works, based on both mythology and contemporary life and often focusing attention on Nepal's social and political problems, include the epic *Nepali shakuntala,* the present-day romance *Sulochana,* and many collections of short lyrics.

David Rubin, *Nepali Visions, Nepali Dreams: The Poetry of Laxmiprasad Devkota* (1980).

DAVID RUBIN

DEWANTARA, KI HADJAR (1889–1959), also known as Soewardi Soeryaningrat, was the grandson of Paku Alam III of Yogyakarta. In his youth Dewantara was a radical journalist for *De Express* and *Persatoen Hindia* and active in the Budi Utomo, Sarekat Islam, and Indische Partij. In 1913 he became secretary of the Komite Bumi Putra, calling for a boycott of the centennial celebrations of the liberation of Holland from France. After being exiled he went to Holland (1913–1919), where he edited *Hindia Poetra.* On his return he became chairman of the Nationaal Indische Partij. In 1922 he founded the first Taman Siswa school in Yogyakarta. He was the first Indonesian minister of education (1945). [*See also* Taman Siswa.]

S. P. Scherer, *Harmony and Dissonance: Early Nationalist Thought in Java* (1975).

C. VAN DIJK

DHAKA (Dacca), capital of Bangladesh, is centrally located in the Ganges-Brahmaputra delta region. Founded as a Mughal garrison town in 1610, Dhaka became a provincial capital and an active river port. Trade in fine muslins and silks attracted both Indian and European merchants to the city. Dhaka's rulers adorned the city with buildings and gardens, and their courts were centers of learning and art. By the end of the seventeenth century the city's size had increased greatly. Estimates of the population at that time vary between four hundred thousand and one million.

In 1702 the Mughal governor transferred his court to Murshidabad. [*See* Murshidabad.] This event, followed by a steady decline in the Indian textile trade and a series of famines, reduced Dhaka's population to a few thousand by the mid-1800s. Under the (British) East India Company (1765–1858) and British imperial rule (1858–1947), Dhaka was extended and improved. From 1905 to 1912, during the temporary partition of Bengal, Dhaka was the capital of the newly created Province of Eastern Bengal and Assam. From 1947 to 1971 Dhaka was the capital of the eastern wing of Pakistan. The city expanded, with new districts for business, housing, and administration, and with a variety of educational and artistic institutions. Meanwhile, East Pakistani discontent with the dominance of West Pakistan had found its strongest expression in Dhaka. After the resulting struggle for independence in 1971, Dhaka became the capital of the new nation of Bangladesh. An active administrative, commercial, and cultural center, Dhaka today supports a population of more than three million.

[*See also* Bangladesh; Pakistan; Assam; *and* Bengal.]

Francis Bradley Bradley-Birt, *The Romance of an Eastern Capital* (1906). Ahmad Hasan Dani, *Dacca: A Record of Its Changing Fortunes* (rev. ed., 1962). Azimusshan Haider, ed., *A City and Its Civic Body* (1966). Abdul Karim, *Dacca, the Mughal Capital* (1964).

MARY FRANCES DUNHAM

DHAMMAPALA was reputedly a fifteenth-century Mon monk assigned at the Burmese capital of Ava to tutor a captive Mon queen, Lady Shin Saw Bu. According to Upper Burmese tales, Dhammapala and his monk friend Dhammazeti (Dhammacedi) helped the captive queen escape to Pegu, where eventually Dhammazeti became king and married Queen Shin Saw Bu. Each night Dhammapala, skilled in the use of magic powers, won the queen from Dhammazeti, but eventually Dhammapala lost to the superior arts of his old rival. When Dhammapala died, the king refused to eat the body to acquire its *weikza* (wizard) powers, and through such forbearance he honored his former friend. The story is a popular subject for traditional Burmese *pwes* (dance dramas).

[*See also* Dhammazedi.]

JOHN P. FERGUSON

DHAMMAZEDI, king of the Burmese kingdom of Pegu (1472–1492), ruled at a time when there was no power strong enough to unify all of Burma, and Pegu was only one of several centers. Yet the heritage of the Kingdom of Pagan continued to be compelling, and all the Burmese centers, including Pegu, attempted to establish kingdoms in its image. Dhammazedi (Pali, Dhammaceti) continued the tradition of strong kings by purifying the *sangha* (the Buddhist monastic order) and maintaining influence and perhaps control over the clergy. He sent monks to Sri Lanka, where they were reordained in the "pure" tradition, then returned to reordain Burma's monks. Dhammazedi's purification of the *sangha* rearranged its hierarchy to favor his chosen primate. All of this was inscribed on at least ten stones known as the Kalyani inscriptions, which have become the text par excellence concerning religious purification.

[*See also* Pegu.]

Michael Aung-Thwin, "The Role of *Sasana* Reform in Burmese History: Economic Dimensions of a Religious Purification," *Journal of Southeast Asian Studies* 38.4 (1979): 671–688. D. G. E. Hall, *Burma* (3d ed., 1960). G. E. Harvey, *A History of Burma from the Earliest Times* (1925; reprint, 1967).

MICHAEL AUNG-THWIN

DHARMAPALA, DOM JOÃO (r. 1551–1597), the last Sinhalese king of Kotte, Sri Lanka. Throughout his reign he was overshadowed by the rulers of Sitavaka (his uncle and cousin), who laid claim to Kotte and were only thwarted in their ambitions to rule over it by Dharmapala's Portuguese mentors. His succession to Kotte had been effected under Portuguese auspices and his dependence on them kept increasing. He converted to Roman Catholicism in 1557 and thereby alienated the affections of his subjects. After 1565, when the Sitavaka rulers compelled him to abandon Kotte and seek the security of the fort of Colombo under Portuguese control, he became a *roi faineant*. Dharmapala bequeathed his rights to Kotte to the Portuguese, who took control in Kotte as his heirs after his death.

[*See also* Kotte; Sinhala; Colombo; Portuguese: Portuguese in Sri Lanka; *and* Sri Lanka.]

K. M. de Silva, *A History of Sri Lanka* (1981).

K. M. DE SILVA

DHIMMI, a member of a non-Muslim community to which the Muslims accorded protection of its rights and property in return for acknowledgement of the political superiority of Islam. The non-Muslims retained autonomy in their own laws and customs, and their affairs were regulated by their respective religious leaders. Their separate status was expressed by payment of a special tax, the *jizya*. The term *dhimmi* at first applied to Jews and Christians, but soon the Zoroastrians and many smaller religious communities, especially in Central Asia, were assimilated to these. Other religious groups under Muslim rule received the same status in practice.

[*See also* Jizya.]

Claude Cahen, "Dhimma," in *The Encyclopaedia of Islam* (new ed., 1960–), pp. 227–231.

JEANETTE A. WAKIN

DHONDU PANT. *See* Nana Sahib.

DIAOYUTAI ISLANDS, located off the northwest coast of Taiwan; regarded by both the Nationalist regime on Taiwan and the government of the People's Republic as Chinese territory. These small, uninhabited rocky islets, reportedly containing petroleum deposits, were the subject of an international dispute in the early 1970s. After Japan activated its claim to the islands (known in Japanese as the Senkaku) as part of the Ryūkyū chain, which was soon to revert from US administration to Japanese control, Chinese students all over the world, but primarily in US cities, carried out patriotic demonstrations. The protesters accused Japan and the United States of conspiring to include the islands in the Ryukyus and chastised Taiwan for failing to protect Chinese territory. Students in Taiwan were also part of this movement, which was quashed by Taiwanese authorities after it escalated into calls for social reform and increased political and academic freedom. The dispute was reactivated following the appearance of a fleet of armed Chinese fishing boats off the islands in 1978, leading to the construction of a heliport there by Japan in 1979.

Ralph N. Clough, *Island China* (1978).

JOHN A. RAPP

DIEN BIEN PHU, or Muong Thanh, district capital in Lai Chau Province, northwestern Vietnam; site of the climactic battle of the French Indochina War (1945–1954).

Dien Bien Phu lies about ten miles from the border of Laos, in a broad valley surrounded by steep hills. It was occupied by the Viet Minh during the offensive of autumn 1952. In 1953 the new commander of the French Expeditionary Corps in Indochina, General Henri Navarre, conceived the idea of using Dien Bien Phu as a forward base, to be supplied by air, from which Viet Minh movement into Laos could be interdicted and Viet Minh base areas disrupted. French paratroopers reoccupied Dien Bien Phu on 20 November 1953, and in early December the French high command decided to hold it. Thereafter the camp was reinforced until it contained nearly 11,000 troops—3,600 of whom were Vietnamese or Tai.

Vo Nguyen Giap, commander of the Vietnam People's Army, saw the presence of this strong but exposed base as an opportunity to strike a heavy blow at the expeditionary force. He therefore decided to give battle at Dien Bien Phu and surrounded the base with four divisions and over 200 heavy guns.

The Viet Minh assault began on 13 March 1954. Strongly entrenched in the hills, Viet Minh artillery soon closed the airstrip and overwhelmed French counterbattery fire. Poor weather and heavy antiaircraft fire reduced the ability of the French to provide aerial support, reinforcement, and resupply. One by one, the camp's strongpoints were overrun by Viet Minh infantry. On 7 May the French headquarters was captured and resistance ceased. Over 10,000 prisoners were taken by the Viet Minh.

This decisive Viet Minh victory ended French attempts to maintain control of Indochina.

[*See also* French Indochina War *and* Vo Nguyen Giap.]

Bernard Fall, *Hell in a Very Small Place* (1966). Jules Roy, *The Battle of Dien Bien Phu* (1965). Vo Nguyen Giap, *Dien Bien Phu* (1964). JAMES M. COYLE

DIHQAN, a term applied primarily to proprietors of small landholdings in Sasanid and early Islamic Iran. Muslim lexicographers understood it to denote "chiefs, proprietors of land and villages" or more precisely, owners of large estates (sg., *day'a*) or "enclosed gardens" *(kurum)*. Some were only village headmen or peasant district representatives; others lived on relatively large estates; still others were quite wealthy, lived in the cities, and were often associated with the merchants. This is reflected by Mas'udi, who reported that the *dihqans* were divided into five subclasses, each distinguished by a particular form of dress.

The *dihqans* first appeared as a distinct social group during the Sasanid period (226–641 CE). They were not members of the privileged aristocracy *(shahrdaran, vaspuhran)* but rather the *azadhan,* free functionaries responsible for some military service, assisting in the assessment and collection of taxes, and mediating between the peasantry and the central government. Some high officials such as the *shahrigh* (representative of the king in a district) were also chosen from among the *dihqans.* The *dihqans* provided the Sasanid monarchs with a useful counterbalance to the power of the provincial nobility. Thus, Khusrau Anushirvan praised the *dihqans* and used the myth that all the *dihqans* were descended from Vehghard, brother of the legendary King Hoshang, to emphasize that the *dihqans* and the monarchs were "brothers."

The Arab-Muslim conquest of the Sasanid empire actually enhanced the position of the *dihqans* in eastern Iran. When some of the Umayyad governors of Khurasan allied themselves with the provincial aristocracy and attempted to humiliate and degrade the *dihqans,* the latter threw their support to anti-

Umayyad movements in the region and were instrumental in winning rural support for the Abbasid revolutionary coalition (c. 747–750 CE). The *dihqans* remained politically important until the eleventh century and also helped achieve the synthesis of Islamic and Iranian cultural traditions represented by Firdausi's *Shahnama.* They were gradually supplanted by the class of holders of *iqta* ("fief"). Today the term is often used for a common peasant or rustic character.

[*See also* Khusrau Anushirvan.]

E. L. DANIEL

DINAR, an Arabic word that formerly meant both a gold coin and a unit of money payable in gold currency (see figure 1). It is derived from the Latin *denarius,* the name of a Roman coin. The word *dinar* was used in its original sense only from the seventh to the fourteenth century, but it is still the name of a monetary unit in several Muslim countries.

[*See also* Dirham *and* Money: Money in the Islamic World.]

MICHAEL L. BATES

DING LING (b. 1907), pseudonym of Jiang Bingzhi, twentiety-century Chinese short story writer and literary figure. Ding won early celebrity with "Mengke" and "Diary of Miss Sophie" (1927), short stories capturing the inarticulate dissatisfactions of youth that are still among her best-known pieces. She moved to Shanghai in 1930, where she joined both the League of Left-Wing Writers and the Communist Party. Three years later Ding was put under house arrest, but she was able to slip away to Yan'an, which had become the Communist base after the Long March. Ding Ling was among the intellectuals whose criticism of certain policies triggered the disciplinary Yan'an Forum on Literature and Art of 1942. Sent away, she drew on her experiences in land reform for her only novel, *Sanggan River* (1948). The chief target of the 1957 antirightist drive, she was vilified in twenty-seven public meetings. Ding was rehabilitated in 1979.

[*See also* Hundred Flowers Campaign.]

Chang Jun-mei, *Ting Ling: Her Life and Her Work* (1978). Yi-tsi Mei Feuerwerker, *Ding Ling's Fiction: Ideology and Narrative in Modern Chinese Literature* (1982). Ting Ling (Ding Ling), *The Sun Shines over the Sangkan River,* translated by Yang Hsien-yi and Gladys Yang (1954).

SHAN CHOU

FIGURE 1. *Gold Dinar.* Damascus, dated AH 77 (697 CE).

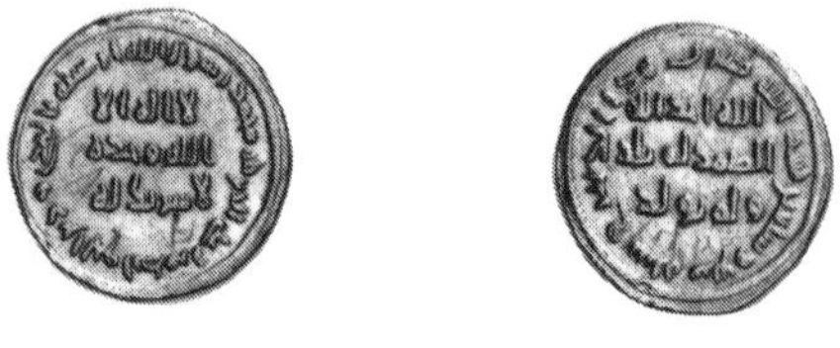

DING WENJIANG (1887–1936), internationally known geologist; noted in China for his participation in intellectual and political controversies. Ding received his scientific training in Britain, mostly at the University of Glasgow, from which he graduated in 1911. He became the first director of the China Geological Survey in 1916 and served in that position until 1921. In 1923 his friend Zhang Junmai (Carsun Chang) published an article asserting that science could not solve the most important problems in human life, which he claimed were spiritual in nature, and that science had caused the moral degeneration of Western civilization. Ding wrote an angry reply defending science and asserting its potential power to solve all of life's problems. This article established Ding's reputation as China's most outspoken proponent of scientific positivism. Although a close friend of many of China's leading liberals, such as Hu Shi, Ding abandoned that ideology in 1934, when, in his political writings, he argued that an enlightened dictatorship and state planning of the economy were essential for China to modernize and become strong.

[*See also* May Fourth Movement.]

LLOYD E. EASTMAN

DINH BO LINH was born in 923 at Hoa Lu, Vietnam. In 965, with the help of alliances and warfare, he gained control of all Vietnam and proclaimed himself king. In 966 he named himself emperor, thereby earning himself a respected place in traditional Vietnamese historiography as the "first emperor," within the "southern," or Vietnamese, imperial tradition, separate from the "northern," or Chinese, imperial tradition. He called his realm Dai

Co Viet ("great Viet") and ruled from Hoa Lu. Dinh Bo Linh unified the Vietnamese lands, established a diplomatic relationship with Song-dynasty China, and organized a peasant militia. He was assassinated in 979 by a low-ranking member of his entourage.

[*See also* Hoa Lu *and* Dai Co Viet.]

Keith W. Taylor, *The Birth of Vietnam* (1983).

KEITH W. TAYLOR

DINI-I ILAHI. The concept of a religion of harmony, initiated by the Indian Mughal emperor Akbar as *tauhid-i Ilahi* ("unity of God"), later came to be known as *din-i Ilahi* ("religion of God"). It interpreted monotheism as the single object of diverse paths to spiritual attainment, and thus sought to harmonize different religions. Akbar visualized in it a bond that would tie its adherents directly to him. He personally conducted their initiations; they were to carry his miniature portrait in their turban and be prepared to sacrifice their life, property, honor, and religion for him. Akbar used neither temptation nor coercion to attract individuals into this religion, and very few of his nobles actually joined it.

[*See also* Akbar.]

Sri Ram Sharma, *The Religious Policy of the Mughal Emperors* (1972). Vincent A. Smith, *Akbar, the Great Mogul, 1542–1605* (1919; 2d ed., 1966).

HARBANS MUKHIA

DIPANAGARA (1785–1855), Javanese prince. The eldest son of Sultan Hamengkubuwana III (r. 1812–1814) by an unofficial wife, Dipanagara was brought up by his great-grandmother, Ratu Ageng, on her estate at Tegalreja near Yogyakarta. From his youth, he evinced an interest in Javanese-Islamic mysticism and undertook long periods of retreat *(tirakat)* and meditation. Between 1809 and 1812, he witnessed the humiliation of the sultanate at the hands of Herman Daendels (who was in office from 1808 to 1811) and Thomas Stamford Raffles (in office from 1811 to 1816) and became a political adviser to his father during his brief reign. After the latter's death in November 1814, Dipanagara found himself increasingly isolated at court because of his opposition to the aggressive land-lease policies pursued by the pro-European clique around the queen mother. During the "fasting months" *(puwasa)* of 1824 and 1825, he experienced a series of visions, among them that of the Javanese "just king" *(ratu adil)*, indicating that he would shortly be required to lead the *ratu adil*'s armies in a war of moral purification in Java. After the outbreak of the Java War (1825–1830) in July 1825, he took the title *Sultan Ngabdulkamid Erucakra Kabirul Mukminin Sayidin Panatagama Jawa Kalifat Rasulullah* (Sultan Ngabdulkamid, the Just King, First among the Believers, Lord of the Faith, Regulator of the [Islamic] Religion in Java, Caliph of the Prophet of God). His leadership transformed what would have been an inchoate agrarian uprising into a major challenge to Dutch authority in Java. Summoned to a "peace conference" at Magelang in March 1830, he was treacherously captured by the Dutch and sent into exile in Sulawesi, where he died in his seventieth year.

[*See also* Java; Daendels, Herman Willem; Raffles, Sir Thomas Stamford; Ratu Adil; *and* Java War.]

Peter Carey, *Babad Dipanagara: An Account of the Outbreak of the Java War (1825–30)* (1981) and *Pangéran Dipanagara and the Making of the Java War (1825–30): The End of an Old Order in Java* (1986).

PETER CAREY

DIRHAM, an Arabic word designating a silver coin or a unit of money payable in silver currency. It is derived from *drachma,* the term for a Greek coin. Over the centuries, *dirhams* in the Muslim world varied greatly in weight, purity, and appearance. *Dirham* is also the name of a small weight unit, about three grams.

[*See also* Dinar *and* Money: Money in the Islamic World.]

MICHAEL L. BATES

FIGURE 1. *Silver Dirham.* With name of Ayyubid sultan Salah al-Din, Damascus mint, dated AH 573 (1177/1178 CE).

DIWANI. Derived from *diwan,* the chief financial officer and civil administrator in Mughal practice, the term *diwani* was used in India in the seventeenth and eighteenth centuries to describe revenue administration; it contrasted with *nizamat,* executive functions that included law and order. In 1761 the East India Company made Shah Alam emperor, and on 12 August 1765 Robert Clive extracted from him the company's appointment as *diwan* of the Province of Bengal. In theory, the company thus became the emperor's tax collector while general administration remained the duty of the governor, or nawab; in fact, however, the nawab was a British puppet. *Diwani* thus practiced gave the company power without responsibility.

[*See also* East India Company *and* Clive, Sir Robert.]

Nandalal Chatterji, *Bengal under the Diwani Administration* (1956). Upendra Nath Day, *The Mughal Government A. D. 1556–1707* (1970). FRITZ LEHMANN

DJAKARTA. *See* Jakarta.

DJAMBI. *See* Jambi.

DOBAMA ASIAYON (We Burmans Association), also referred to as the Thakin movement, was a popular Burmese nationalist organization during the 1930s, founded by Thakin Ba Thaung in 1930. Asiayon members took the title *thakin* (master) to indicate that they, rather than the British, were the rightful masters of Burma. The Dobama song, written in 1933, formed the basis of the national anthem of independent Burma.

The movement grew slowly during its initial years, concerning itself primarily with the publication of nationalist tracts that argued for the rights of the indigenous population against others, such as the British and Indians in Burma. Its narrow nationalist ideology was broadened in the late 1930s by the addition of Marxist-Leninist ideas and organization forms. At that time many student nationalists from Rangoon University joined, and their advocacy of socialism and nonracial ideals was one of the reasons the organization split in 1937. Among the prominent former student leaders of the Asiayon at this time were Thakin Nu and Aung San. The Thakin movement played a key role in the organization of the political agitation of 1938–1939 known as the 1300 Revolution, which brought down the government of Dr. Ba Maw. As war approached in Asia, another split developed between those who felt that an alliance with Japan to gain Burma's independence was ideologically acceptable and those who did not. The movement merged organizationally with Ba Maw's Sinyetha Party in 1942, and though an attempt to revive it by one faction was made in 1945, its political importance came to an end. Dobama Asiayon's major lasting impact on Burma's politics was its introduction of Marxist ideas through the publications of its affiliated Nagani (Red Dragon) Bookshop.

[*See also* Burma; Aung San; Ba Maw; *and* Sinyetha Party.]

Maung Maung, *From Sangha to Laity* (1980).

ROBERT H. TAYLOR

DŌGEN KIGEN (1200–1253), founder of the Sōtō school of Zen Buddhism in Japan. Sōtō teaching stresses the crucial importance of seated meditation, *zazen,* and the identity of spiritual practice with enlightenment. As the leader of the monastic community at Eiheiji, Dōgen spoke and wrote prolifically on all aspects of Zen thought and training. Many of his teachings were gathered in his great work, the *Shōbōgenzō (Eye Storehouse of the True Law),* one of the most original and powerful works in the history of Japanese Buddhist thought.

Dōgen was born into an aristocratic family in Kyoto in 1200. He was a gifted child, but his childhood was not a happy one. His father died when Dōgen was two, and at seven he lost his mother. He later stated that this double loss so impressed upon him the transience of human life that he determined to enter the religious life and seek to understand the true meaning of life and death. At the age of thirteen Dōgen took the vows of a Buddhist monk on Mount Hiei, the center of Tendai Buddhism in Japan. There he threw himself into the study of both Mahayana and Hinayana Buddhism. Soon, however, he encountered what he called a "great doubt" about the very core of Buddhist teaching: "If, as the sutras say, all human beings are originally endowed with Buddha nature, why do they still have to train themselves so strenuously to realize that Buddha nature; that is, to attain enlightenment?"

Unable to resolve his "great doubt" in Japan, Dōgen in 1223 set out for China in quest of an "authentic teacher." There, after meeting many monks and studying in numerous monasteries, he encountered the Chan (Zen) master Rujing (1163–1228), abbot of Tiantong monastery and a master belonging to the Caotong (Sōtō) line of Chan. Rujing was a severe teacher who demanded an unremitting practice rooted in *zazen*. Spurred on by Rujing, Dōgen attained a deep spiritual insight in which he resolved his doubt by "dropping away body and mind." Rujing acknowledged that Dōgen had transcended his discriminating mind and attained enlightenment. He accepted him as his Dharma heir and urged him to spread the true Buddhist Dharma *(shōbō)* in Japan.

In 1227 Dōgen returned to Japan. His first treatise on Zen Buddhism, *Fukan zazengi (A Universal Recommendation for Zazen),* written shortly after his return, expressed the great importance he attached to *zazen* as the core of Zen practice. After a brief and disappointing stay in the monastery of Kenninji in Kyoto, Dōgen established his own small community at Kōshōji to the south of the city. Here he built a Zen meditation hall, instituted the rules of Zen monastic practice, devoted himself to the training of those monks and laymen who came to him for guidance, and began to write the discourses on Zen Buddhist thought and practice that were to make up the *Shōbōgenzō.*

Dōgen's growing popularity attracted the enmity of followers of the older Buddhist schools, especially the monks of Enryakuji. They regarded his exclusive emphasis on *zazen* as a perversion of traditional Tendai teaching, branded him a heretic, and put pressure on the court to have him driven from Kōshōji. In 1243 Dōgen and a small band of disciples moved to a remote part of the province of Echizen (modern Fukui Prefecture), where, under the patronage of a local warrior leader, Hatano Yoshishige, Dōgen established the monastery of Eiheiji ("temple of eternal peace"). Here, in a remote mountain valley, he enforced a strict Zen monastic practice centering on *zazen,* prayer, and study. In Echizen, Dōgen added some thirty more chapters to the *Shōbōgenzō* and compiled detailed rules of monastic life in the *Eihei shingi.* He left Eiheiji only twice, once in 1247 when he journeyed to Kamakura to instruct the regent Hōjō Tokiyori in Zen and again in 1253 to seek treatment for a severe illness in Kyoto. The treatment was to no avail and he died shortly after his arrival in the capital.

Dōgen's Zen teachings quickly took hold in Japan. Eiheiji grew into one of Japan's great monastic centers, and Sōtō Zen attracted monks and laypeople from throughout the country. The school, tracing its descent from Dōgen, is now the largest branch of Japanese Zen. Dōgen, for his part, has become one of the most widely studied and influential Japanese religious thinkers.

Hee Jin Kim, *Dōgen Kigen: Mystical Realist* (1975).

MARTIN COLLCUTT

DOKMAISOT (1905–1963), nom de plume of Mom Luang Bubpha Kunchon. Daughter of Chaophraya Thewetwongwiwat, she was educated according to the French curriculum at Saint Joseph's Convent School in Bangkok. She began writing novels in 1929 and was not only the first woman novelist in her country but also one of the pioneers of modern Thai literature. Her contemporaries were Prince Akatdamkoeng Raphiphat, Humorist, Yakhob, and Siburapha. A meticulous writer, Dokmaisot wrote thirteen novels in which she presented an idealized picture of Thai society, tradition, culture, and values. Dokmaisot died in New Delhi, where her husband, Professor Sukit Nimmanhaemin, was ambassador.

THAK CHALOEMTIARANA

DONG DU MOVEMENT, an anticolonial movement organized by patriotic Vietnamese scholars in the early twentieth century. Its prime organizer was the Vietnam Modernization Association, which hoped to create an anti-French revolutionary organization by encouraging educated young Vietnamese to go to Japan (*Dong Du* literally means "go to the east") to study Western culture and institutions. They would then return to Vietnam and help the association provoke an uprising against colonial rule. The movement came to an end when Japan signed a treaty with France and expelled the Vietnamese exile movement in 1908.

[*See also* Vietnam Modernization Association.]

David G. Marr, *Vietnamese Anticolonialism, 1885–1925* (1971).

WILLIAM J. DUIKER

DONG KHANH (c. 1862–1888), eighth Nguyen emperor (r. 1885–1888) of Vietnam. Enthroned in September 1885 to combat the influence of Ham Nghi, Dong Khanh was portrayed as restoring the continuity of Vietnam's monarchical tradition. In actuality, however, his reign saw the tightening of French control following the 1884 Patenotre Treaty, which established a protectorate over Tonkin and Annam. The parallel decline in royal power and authority, to the benefit of colonial officials such as Paul Bert and General DeCourcy, brought considerable derision from supporters of the Can Vuong movement. Upon his death in 1888, Dong Khanh was succeeded by Thanh Thai.

[*See also* Ham Nghi; Patenotre Treaty; *and* Can Vuong.]

Nguyen The Anh, *The Withering Days of the Nguyen Dynasty* (1978). BRUCE M. LOCKHART

DONG KINH NGHIA THUC (Hanoi Free School) was founded by patriotic scholars in French-ruled Vietnam in 1907. The founders of the school, such as the scholar-patriot Phan Chu Trinh, hoped to introduce young Vietnamese to Western knowledge and to encourage the use of *quoc ngu* (the romanized transliteration of written Vietnamese) as a means of promoting reforms in colonial society in Vietnam. At first the French administration reluctantly permitted the school to operate, but it soon began to suspect the political motives of the organizers and in December 1907 ordered the school to close down.

[*See also* Phan Chu Trinh.]

Vu Duc Bang, "The Dong Kinh Free School Movement, 1907–1908," in *Aspects of Vietnamese History,* edited by Walter F. Vella (1973). David Marr, *Vietnamese Anticolonialism, 1885–1925* (1971). WILLIAM J. DUIKER

DONGLIN ACADEMY, private institution of Confucian education first established in the Song dynasty (960–1279). Located in Wuxi, Jiangsu Province, the Donglin (Eastern Grove) Academy was named for a nearby grove of willow trees. In 1604 Donglin again became an important center of intellectual life when it was reconstructed by a group of scholar-officials who had been removed from government service as a result of political intrigues at the court of the Wanli emperor (r. 1573–1619).

The leaders of this group, Gu Xiancheng (1550–1612) and Gao Panlong (1562–1626), embarked upon a crusade that sought to instill morality in politics. The academy quickly attracted many scholars and officials who shared the belief that a moral revival in politics must be shaped by the proper philosophical foundation. By 1620 the Donglin movement had so grown in influence that it constituted a faction at court and its partisans dominated key government posts during the period from 1620 to 1623. The notorious eunuch Wei Zhongxian launched a bloody purge of the Donglin partisans from 1625 to 1627, but the Donglin Academy again enjoyed prominence after Wei was removed from power in 1629, receiving government sponsorship until the end of the Ming dynasty in 1644.

[*See also* Ming Dynasty; Neo-Confucianism; *and* Wei Zhongxian.]

Henrich Busch, "The Tung-lin Shu-yuan and Its Political and Philosophical Significance," *Monumenta Serica* 14 (1949–1955): 1–163. Charles O. Hucker, "The Tung-lin Movement of the Late Ming Period," in *Chinese Thought and Institutions,* edited by John K. Fairbank (1957), pp. 132–163. John Meskill, "Academies and Politics in the Ming Dynasty," in *Chinese Government in Ming Times—Seven Studies,* edited by Charles O. Hucker (1969), pp. 149–174. ANITA M. ANDREW

DONG SON, civilization from the late Bronze or early Iron Age that flourished in northern Vietnam from the middle of the first millennium BCE and was brought to an end by the Han Chinese conquest of 43 CE. Dong Son developed from a series of consecutively related culture complexes that began at the end of the third millennium BCE with Phung Nguyen, a settlement in the valley and plain of the Hong River, northwest of Hanoi (Vinh Phu). Phung Nguyen, a late Neolithic and early Bronze Age culture, developed into Dong Dau about the middle of the second millennium BCE; Dong Dau developed into Go Mun around the end of the second millennium BCE; and Go Mun, in turn, evolved directly into Dong Son. Dong Dau and Go Mun represent, respectively, the growth and highest achievement of a Bronze Age culture in northern Vietnam. Related but technically inferior cultures developed in the valleys and plains of the Ma River (Thanh Hoa) and the Ca River (Nghe Tinh) and along the northern coast (Quang Ninh); these were all culturally united under the influence of Dong Son.

Phung Nguyen's Stone Age background can be traced back to the Paleolithic culture of Son Vi, which is dated between the twentieth and tenth millennium BCE. Son Vi developed into the Mesolithic culture of Hoa Binh, which developed into the Neolithic culture of Bac Son around the fourth or fifth millennium BCE.

Dong Son shared certain characteristics with contemporary civilizations in Yunnan (e.g., the Dian culture, as revealed in the excavations at Shizhaishan) and southeastern China (the Yue culture), in particular the use of bronze drums and amphibious art motifs. Dong Son also exemplified the legacy of prior Bronze Age development in northern Vietnam, beginning with Phung Nguyen.

Single Phung Nguyen sites covered tens of thousands of square meters and accommodated thousands of inhabitants. This is usually interpreted as evidence of a primitive communalism, built up from aggregations of clans and tribes. As the use of bronze developed, reaching the level found at Dong Son, this primitive communalism broke up into a more hierarchical society, characterized by smaller, more scattered habitation sites and the burial of ruling-class people in richly endowed graves.

The most characteristic artifact of Dong Son, the bronze drum, is thought to have evolved from the rice mortar; the scenes on the drums of boats bearing warriors point to maritime contacts. The bronze pediform ax is the most distinctive of a large arsenal of Dong Son weaponry, suggesting the early strategic significance of northern Vietnam as the only lowland corridor between the Tibetan highlands and the South China Sea. Bronze plowshares, fishhooks, and butchering implements reveal a well-developed economy. Evidence suggests that the bronze technology of northern Vietnam may have developed independently from Chinese influence, perhaps through contacts with northern Thailand.

Vietnamese scholars associate the legendary traditions about the Hung kings and the kingdom of Van Lang with the Dong Son civilization.

[*See also* Hung Vuong *and* Van Lang.]

R. B. Smith and W. Watson, eds., *Early South East Asia* (1976). KEITH W. TAYLOR

DONG ZHONGSHU (179–104 BCE), Chinese philosopher, founder of Han-dynasty Confucian orthodoxy. Dong also held administrative offices under Emperor Wu of the Former Han dynasty. A proponent of the Jinwen (New Text) School, he used his systematic exposition of the *Spring and Autumn Annals,* the *Chunqiu fanlu (Luxuriant Dew from the Spring and Autumn Annals),* as a vehicle for a new syncretic philosophy. In essence, Dong Zhongshu combined the ethics, propriety, ritual, hierarchy, and emphasis on virtue of Confucianism with the statist administrative techniques and Yin-yang/Five Phase *(wuxing)* cosmology of the Huang-Lao school. The resulting doctrine emphasized the unity of the realms of heaven, earth, and man; hierarchy and mutual obligation in human society; the primacy of virtue in government; and the role of the emperor in taking warning from portents and in maintaining the stability of the natural cycles of the cosmos. He rejected the Legalism of the Qin dynasty (221–207 BCE), but his interpretation of Confucianism was itself adapted to the needs of a central, imperial state and was perpetuated through the use of examinations on the Confucian classics for the recruitment of civil servants.

[*See also* Jinwen.]

Feng Yu-lan, *A History of Chinese Philosophy,* vol. 2, translated by Derk Bodde (1953). JOHN S. MAJOR

DONOUGHMORE CONSTITUTION, constitutional reforms for the British colony of Ceylon, proposed by a commission led by the earl of Donoughmore from 1927 to 1929. The constitution advocated a state council, which was in effect from 1931 to 1947, that included universal adult franchise, a committee system, and dyarchy. Its fifty members were divided into seven powerful committees (Home Affairs; Health; Education; Agriculture and Lands; Local Administration; Communication and Works; and Labor, Industry and Commerce) that initiated postindependence welfare policies. The British reserved control over the rights of public servants, administration of justice, defense, foreign trade and shipping, and "financial stability."

[*See also* Sri Lanka.]

PATRICK PEEBLES

DORGON (1612–1650), fourteenth son of the Manchu leader Nurhaci; de facto ruler of the newly established Qing dynasty in China from 1644 to 1650. A favorite prince of the throne, he received a banner in his early teens. During Huang Taiji's reign Dorgon took part in many campaigns and demonstrated both valor and wisdom. In 1628 he was awarded the title *mergen daicing* ("wise warrior"); eight years later he was made a first-degree prince with the designation *rui* ("sagacious prince").

Dorgon was essential to the success of the early Qing dynasty. Princes struggled for succession after the death of Huang Taiji in 1643. Despite the possibility of himself taking the throne, Dorgon supported Fulin, a five-year-old son of Huang Taiji. Dorgon and another prince, Jirgalang, served as regents. Thus, he saved the court from divisiveness. With the collaboration of Wu Sangui, the Ming general guarding Shanhaiguan, he defeated the rebel leader Li Zicheng and took Beijing in June 1644. From there he took various measures to consolidate the Qing regime. [*See also* Wu Sangui *and* Li Zicheng.]

Dorgon laid down the grand design of Qing administration. The Chinese were administered by the bureaucratic machinery adopted from the Ming dynasty and operated by Chinese officials under Manchu direction. Together with their Chinese and Mongol comrades in arms, the Manchus were under the banner system, separate from the Chinese institutions. The low land-tax rate Dorgon set for the farmers was largely observed throughout the dynasty. For the Manchus he appropriated the banner lands in the metropolitan area of the capital and prohibited Chinese slaves or servants from deserting their Manchu masters. For their oppressiveness these two laws were finally revoked.

Dorgon had many designations, the highest of which was Imperial Father Regent. He was posthumously honored as an emperor. After his death some princes avenged the humiliation that Dorgon had inflicted upon them; they denounced him as corrupt and abusive of power and deprived him of all honors and his princedom. He was subsequently rehabilitated in 1778.

[*See also* Manchus; Qing Dynasty; Huang Taiji; *and* Nurhaci.]

Arthur W. Hummel, ed., *Eminent Chinese of the Ch'ing Period (1644–1912),* vol. 1 (1943), pp. 215–219.

PEI HUANG

DOUMER, PAUL (1857–1932), French politician, governor-general of Indochina (1897–1902), and later president of France.

A lawyer and journalist, Paul Doumer was first elected to the Chamber of Deputies in 1888, becoming minister of finance in the Leon Bourgeois cabinet (1895–1896). His ability, frequently expressed interest in colonial affairs, and abrasive personality caused him to be chosen to replace the late Paul-Armand Rousseau as governor-general of the deficit-ridden Indochinese Union.

Doumer's policies as governor-general had a twofold objective: to make Indochina fiscally independent of France and to promote its economic development. To achieve these goals it was necessary to establish the fiscal and administrative supremacy of the union over its constituent states. Doumer thus suppressed the remnants of Vietnamese imperial autonomy in Annam and Tonkin, created a Superior Council of Indochina with authority over state councils, and established a general budget for the union. The budget was supported by customs revenues and by newly extended monopolies *(regies)* on alcohol, opium, and salt. The administrations of the states were funded by dramatic increases in personal and land taxes.

Within a year, Doumer had succeeded in balancing the budget. Having obtained a 200-million-franc loan from France on the strength of the fiscal reforms, he embarked on a vast program of public works, especially railroads. At the completion of his term, Doumer returned to French political life, twice becoming minister of finance (1921, 1925) and eventually president of the republic. He was assassinated on 6 May 1932.

Doumer's impact on Indochina was enormous. His fiscal and administrative structure was retained until the end of French rule. The cost of this structure, coupled with the expenses of the public works program, led to the increasing impoverishment of the peasantry of Indochina, especially of Vietnam.

[*See also* Indochinese Union.]

Joseph Buttinger, *Vietnam: A Dragon Embattled* (1967). JAMES M. COYLE

DOUWES DEKKER, EDUARD (1820–1887) was taken to Java in 1839 by his father, an Amsterdam shipper, and obtained a post in the East Indies civil administration the next year. He served in minor posts until January 1856, when he was appointed assistant resident in Lebak, Bantam, West Java. Within a month he levied charges of corruption and extortion against the Sundanese *bupati* (regent), but his own unofficial behavior led to his dismissal in March 1856. Feeling misunderstood and unjustly treated, Douwes Dekker wrote a tract novel about this situation under the nom de plume Multatuli. The book, *Max Havelaar* (1860), made him famous immediately, for it had not only a dramatic story of maladministration in Java but also a style that makes it perhaps the greatest piece of nineteenth-century Dutch literature. Widely and frequently translated, it was made into a motion picture in 1976. ROBERT VAN NIEL

D'OYLY, SIR JOHN (1774–1824). As chief translator for the Ceylon civil service, D'Oyly recommended the British invasion of the Kandyan kingdom in 1815. He drafted the Kandyan Convention and was appointed British resident at Kandy. He tried to win the support of Kandyan chiefs and Buddhist monks and used his influence to end the 1817–1818 Rebellion. He administered the Kandyan provinces until his death in 1824.

John D'Oyly, *A Sketch of the Constitution of the Kandyan Kingdom* (1832). PATRICK PEEBLES

DRAMA. There are few cultures in Asia in which the concept of drama may be considered to be separate from dance and music. Although there may be polarities of emphasis, degrees of abstraction and stylization and of formalism or realism, or an emphasis on verbal over vocal and instrumental elements, theater in Asia is essentially a combination of the performing arts. All genres of Asian theater are primarily entertainment; their function in a ritual, symbolic, or religious context on the one hand, and in social, political, or commercial contexts on the other may vary widely in the thousands of performance genres throughout Asia that may be identified as theater.

The two major cultural traditions that seem to have had the most far-reaching influence in all of Asia are those of India and China. The effects of these two great Asian traditions upon each other and upon other centers of culture in Asia have involved a process of adaptation, transformation, and synthesis over almost two millennia. The other principal element in Asian theater is the influence of indigenous cultures. The complex interaction of these three traditions constitutes the history of the performing arts in Asia.

India and Its Sphere of Influence. The earliest references to dramatic elements in the Indian tradition are found in Vedic literature; the existence of drama, dance, and music is mentioned in more substantial terms, however, in Panini's time (c. fourth century BCE). The principal theoretical and descriptive work on theater of the early period in India is the *Natyashastra* of Bharata, an encyclopedic text composed over a period between the fourth century BCE and the fourth century CE. Theoretical and technical literature on drama also appeared throughout history in such works as the *Vishnudharmottara Purana* (third to fifth century), the *Dasharupaka* (tenth century), the *Abhinayadarpana* (fifth to thirteenth century), the *Sangitaratnakara* (thirteenth century), and the *Hastalakshanadipika* (fourteenth century). In addition to theoretical and technical literature concerning the concepts, technique, training, and production of drama and its related arts, there are a great many plays in Sanskrit and Prakrit that have survived from an early period. Among the earliest extant works are those plays alleged to be the work of Bhasa (c. fourth century BCE). A traditional form of Sanskrit drama, known as *kutiyattam,* survives today in South India. Popular regional forms of theater, such as *kathakali* in Kerala, *yakshagana* in Karnataka, *terukkuttu* in Tamil Nadu, and *bhagavata mela natakam* in Tamil Nadu and Andhra Pradesh, were much influenced in their development by the classical Sanskrit drama tradition that at one time was prevalent throughout India.

By about the tenth century the two great Indian epics, the *Ramayana* and the *Mahabharata,* were widely dispersed throughout Southeast Asia, a continuing process that had begun as early as the second and third centuries. [*See also* Ramayana *and* Mahabharata.] The epic themes that are so important as thematic material for theater in India have also survived in the classical theater traditions of Cambodia, Thailand, Malaysia, and Indonesia. Trade relations were the vehicle for the spread of Indian art and culture. In the twelfth century India's contact with Asia through the southeastern sea routes was at its apogee.

Perhaps the most eloquent example of the persistence of the effects of this early Indian contact with Indonesia is the Hindu culture of the people of Bali, one of the richest areas of Asia in its scope of artistic expression. The *gambuh,* a classical dance-drama of a highly refined type, is associated with the Hindu-Javanese culture that was strengthened in Bali by the presence of aristocratic Javanese who fled Java after the fall of the Majapahit empire in 1520. Two masked forms of theater, *topeng* and *wayang wong,* are the products of the Hindu-Balinese courts of the seventeenth and eighteenth centuries; the theme of the *wayang wong* performance is the *Ramayana.* The early nineteenth century saw the development of *arja;* the *parwa,* based on themes from the *Mahabharata,* is believed to have had its origins in the late nineteenth century. A more modern form of dance-drama in Bali, dating from the 1960s, is called *sendratari.*

In Java, the great importance given to the *wayang kulit,* the shadow puppet theater that takes its themes principally from the *Mahabharata,* tends to overshadow other dramatic forms, which include *wayang topeng,* a form of masked theater; *wayang wong;* and *ketoprak,* a product of the twentieth century.

Although the *Ramayana* theme in theater is widespread in Southeast Asia, the Cambodian tradition of the *Ramayana* play is alleged to be the oldest and is said to be a direct descendant from the traditions of the ancient Hindu kingdom of Champa in Vietnam. The Khmer imperial schools (tenth to fourteenth century) provided the immediate source of the later Thai tradition that was in turn adopted by the Burmese directly from Thailand in about the sixteenth century.

Cultural relationships between Cambodia and Thailand were of vital importance to the development of the arts in both countries. Cambodia has a shadow puppet theater called *nang sebek* based on the *Ramayana.* So does Thailand, whose principal shadow puppet tradition is known as *nang yai. Lakhon kawl* is a Cambodian dance-drama that, like the Thai *khon,* is performed in mask by men and with the *Ramayana* as the theme. The oldest form of theater in Thailand is said to be the *lakhon chatri.* Until recently, the only play performed by *lakhon chatri* troupes was *Manora,* based on a Buddhist story. About the fourteenth or fifteenth century *lakhon chatri* developed into the *lakhon nok,* and its repertoire of plays expanded greatly. *Lakhon nok* flourished for a time but has essentially disappeared today. The government-supported National Theater in Thailand and the associated schools for actors, dancers, and musicians have done much to foster Thailand's traditional performing arts in this era of rapid change and diminished patronage.

Theater in Malaysia includes shadow puppet plays similar to the Javanese *wayang kulit,* and it was in fact the Javanese domination of the region in the thirteenth and fourteenth centuries that led to the existence of this form of theater in Malaysia. The *bangsawan,* a form that developed recently, is an indigenous form of theater that takes its themes principally from Islamic literature. In the Philippines, a type of play called *moro-moro* is said to date from about the seventeenth century; the stories of *moro-moro* are always based on the defeat of the Moors by the Christian Filipinos. The *zarzuela* of Spain was also popular for a time but is now performed only as a kind of folk drama.

China and Its Sphere of Influence. China has a long history of performing arts; many of the early ritual ceremonies of state incorporated diverse elements of a theater constantly transforming itself. In the *Tongdian,* an encyclopedia compiled in the Tang period (618–907), there are references to the earlier Han period (206 BCE–220 CE) in which dance, juggling, acrobatics, and mime were among the "hundred amusements." The use of acrobatics, juggling, and legerdemain in a form of variety theater persists in traditional Chinese popular dramatic performance. A number of forms of theater have flourished and declined in China over the centuries. Today the form of the magnificent Chinese opera most familiar in the West is the Beijing (Peking) Opera, a genre that includes many lesser popular forms as well. The less-well-known Cantonese Opera is found at various levels of excellence in South China and even in Thailand, Malaysia, and Singapore. A vast literature of plays from antiquity is drawn upon for production. There is also a modern Chinese theater form, a legacy of the influence of the Soviet Union.

One of China's significant cultural roles has been the transmission of literature, philosophy, religion, and the arts to Korea and ultimately to Japan. In fact, many aspects of music, drama, and dance that have clear historical associations with imported models from ancient imperial China are preserved in Japan. A description of a *sarugaku* performance in the *Shin sarugaku ki,* written by Fujiwara Akihira (991–1066), describes this kind of Japanese variety theater and mentions its Chinese sources. *Sarugaku* was closely associated with temples and shrines but was also performed at the residences of members of the nobility. It was refined and developed into a more elegant form by Kan'ami (1333–1384) and his son Zeami (1363–1443); at a later date it became known as *nō.*

The popular theater form *kabuki* originated in the performances of Okuni, a famous dancer and actress of the late sixteenth century. *Kyōgen,* another traditional form of theater in Japan, is related to *nō* but deals with stories of everyday life and ordinary people rather than with plots about the aristocratic elite or tales of otherworldly beauty and solemnity. All of these forms of Japanese theater are combined performances, utilizing the arts of dance and music as integral parts of the performance. The elements carefully preserved from the Chinese tradition have been of course subtly transformed over the centuries by Japanese aesthetic taste and creative sensibility. The Japanese genius for adaptation, invention, and transformation in dramatic art is perhaps best seen in the popular *kabuki* drama, which is eclectic in its source material and theatrically creative in a number of differing manners ranging from romantic realism to the highest degrees of abstract stylization. [*See also* Nō; Kabuki; *and* Kyōgen.]

Western Influence. The advent of Western models of drama into Asia since the nineteenth century has produced a variety of hybrid theater forms. One characteristic development of the nineteenth and twentieth centuries was the rewriting of English dramas in a local indigenous cultural setting. For decades Shakespeare's plays have been performed in a number of ways in India, Sri Lanka, and Malaysia. The naturalistic, realistic modes of production of modern Western theater, as opposed to the highly stylized ones of traditional Asian theater, have been adapted in all genres of Asian contemporary theater. Particularly suited to the social drama form, Western production has also been adapted for traditional drama on mythological and historical themes. The mythological plays make appropriate use of the latest developments in cinema technology to create magical and supernatural effects, which are sometimes more creative and inventive than the effects suggested in the original myths. The media of radio and television, as well as cinema, in South and Southeast Asia, China, and Japan have put these regions in close touch with the latest developments in contemporary theater. The technological advances in communications media and recording techniques have greatly reinforced the popularity of contemporary theater in Asia. It may be many years before it will be possible to judge whether this emphasis on contemporary theater will hasten the disappearance of the thousands of forms of traditional performing arts that have developed over the centuries in the Asian world.

[*See also* Dance *and* Music.]

James T. Araki, *The Ballad-Drama of Medieval Japan* (1978). James R. Brandon, *Theatre in Southeast Asia* (1967). Balwant Gargi, *Theatre in India* (1962). Norvin Hein, *The Miracle Plays of Mathurā* (1972). Claire Holt, *Art in Indonesia, Continuities and Change* (1967). Colin P. Mackerras, *The Rise of the Peking Opera; 1770–1870: Social Aspects of the Theatre in Manchu China* (1972). P. G. O'Neill, *Early No Drama: Its Background, Character and Development, 1300–1450* (1959). Adolphe Clarence Scott, *The Classical Theatre of China* (1957).

CLIFFORD REIS JONES

DRAVIDIAN LANGUAGES AND LITERATURES.

The word *Dravidian* has been used with varying degrees of precision to describe a family of languages spoken in South Asia, the literatures in these languages, an ethnic type, and a cluster of cultural beliefs and practices, including a distinctive kinship system. With the exception of the application in the areas of linguistics and kinship, the provenance of the term is tenuous at best. The great diversity in lifestyles, cultural forms, and racial types found among the peoples of the Indian subcontinent strongly suggests a complex history of contact, borrowing, and partial assimilation by people of diverse origins. Even the earliest inscriptions and literary artifacts from South Asia reflect a culture created by such processes. Indologists have relied primarily upon the methods of historical linguistics to unravel and identify the several strands that together constitute South Asian culture.

Language. The vast majority of languages spoken in South Asia can be grouped, in accord with historical linguistic principles, in four originally independent language families—Indo-Aryan, Dravidian, Tibeto-Burman, and Munda. The Dravidian languages are predominant south of the Vindhya Mountains but are also found in pockets elsewhere. Very broad correlations have been noted between various cultural traits, ethnic characteristics, and the speakers of languages belonging to the Dravidian family, and this naturally has led to speculation on the original "Dravidian" provenance of various cultural forms and ethnic characteristics.

Among the languages spoken in South Asia today, twenty-three have been identified as belonging to the Dravidian family. (The number may vary slightly depending upon the criteria used to distinguish a language from a dialect.) The vast majority of Dravidian speakers (over 95 percent) speak one of the four "literary" languages—Telugu, Tamil, Malayalam, and Kannada, respectively the predominant languages in the four South Indian states of Andhra Pradesh, Tamil Nadu, Kerala, and Karnataka. Many of the nonliterary languages are spoken by tribal peoples in South and Central India, some by only several thousand people, or even several hundred in the cases of Kota and Toda, two languages spoken in the Nilgiri Mountains. One of the most important of the "nonliterary" languages is Tulu, a language spoken by over one million people in southwestern Karnataka. [*See also* Adivasis.] Geographically most isolated from other Dravidian languages is Brahui, which is spoken in a region of present-day Pakistan by about 300,000 people. In the 1971 Indian census the number of speakers of the four major Dravidian languages of South India was given as follows (figures are rounded off to the nearest thousand): Telugu, 44,708,000; Tamil, 37,593,000; Malayalam, 21,917,000; and Kannada, 21,575,000. There is also a significant number of speakers of these languages outside of India, especially in the case of Tamil, which is spoken in Sri Lanka by about 2.5 million people and by descendants of migrants to Southeast Asia and other locations. [*See also* Andhra Pradesh; Tamil Nadu; Kerala; Karnataka; *and* Sri Lanka.]

By isolating linguistic features at various levels (e.g., phonological, morphophonemic, etc.) linguists have identified three subfamilies within the Dravidian family of languages. The three subfamilies are called South Dravidian, Central Dravidian, and North Dravidian and are named in accordance with geographic distribution. Among the four literary languages, Tamil, Malayalam, and Kannada care assigned to the South Dravidian subfamily, and Telugu, while it is considered to be a Central Dravidian language, exhibits evidence of prolonged contact with South Dravidian languages. Scholars have conjectured that the breakdown of the proto-Dravidian parent language began as early as the fourth millennium BCE with the separation of Brahui. At the other end of the historical spectrum, Malayalam, originally a regional dialect of Tamil, became established as a full-fledged literary language, distinct from Tamil, only in the thirteenth and fourteenth centuries CE; the earliest Malayalam inscriptions are assigned to the tenth century CE.

The issue of the relation of Dravidian languages to other languages spoken outside India is a topic of considerable interest. This issue is, of course, directly tied to the question, Who were the ancestors of the Dravidian speakers and where did they originally come from? The existence of a Dravidian language family was first recognized in the West by Francis W. Ellis in his "Note to the Introduction" of A. D. Campbell's *Grammar of the Telugu Language* (1816). But the recognized father of comparative Dravidian linguistics was Robert Caldwell, author of *A Comparative Grammar of the Dravidian or South Indian Family of Languages* (1856). In his *Grammar,* Caldwell hypothesized that the Dravidian family is a branch of a Scythian language family that includes the Uralic and Altaic languages, which are spoken in Eastern Europe and in Central and northeastern Asia. Caldwell believed that Central Asia, the "seed-plot of nations," was the ancestral home of the early Scythian speakers. Caldwell's hypothesis that Dravidian, Uralic, and Altaic languages are related is considered to be viable by some linguists today, though many details are yet to be worked out. Another line of investigation proposes a relationship between Dravidian and the language of the inhabitants of the ancient Indus Valley cities, and yet another with Elamite, a language of ancient Mesopotamia. In direct contradiction to the now widely accepted theory that Dravidian speakers migrated to India, probably from the northwest, sometime before the Indo-Aryans reached the subcontinent, some Tamil pandits hold that the earliest Dravidian (or Tamil) speakers inhabited a landmass now submerged in the Indian Ocean, a lost continent of Lemuria.

Literature. The most straightforward way to understand the term *Dravidian literature* is simply as all literature, written or oral, for which the linguistic medium is a Dravidian language. But while this definition may appear to be unproblematic, even self-evident, in purely literary terms it offers little. The question remains, Is it possible to speak of a Dravidian literature in the sense of a body of literary works that share clusters of literary features in contradistinction to non-Dravidian literatures? This does not mean, however, that language is irrelevant to a literary definition. For instance, it is possible that similar sound-patterning in Dravidian languages provides a foundation for a distinctive "Dravidian" metrical system.

Comparative study of South Asian literatures has not advanced to the point where it is possible to pass judgment one way or the other on the question of the distinctiveness of Dravidian literature, but a few observations and generalizations are in order. First, the major Dravidian languages, especially Tamil, exhibit a pattern linguists call diglossia—a formal differentiation between the language of colloquial speech and the language of formal pronouncements. By and large, learned literature adheres to formal "literary" language, although other, more informal genres freely incorporate colloquial forms. To take just one example, present-day Tamil novelists generally employ colloquial forms in dialogue and the literary language in narrative passages.

From the perspective of the language of literature, genres in all four major Dravidian languages can be plotted along a continuum with genres favoring a highly ornate, formal literary style at one end and genres employing a freer, more colloquial style at the other. These two poles can be thought of loosely as "classical" and "popular," or "folk," but it is important to keep in mind that two largely independent classical traditions are involved here. Throughout India, genres and themes from Sanskrit literature have contributed a great deal to the development of the vernacular literatures (with Persian and Arabic playing an equivalent role in the case of Urdu), and this is true in varying degrees of the languages of South India. Sanskrit influence is clearly evident in the earliest Kannada and Telugu literary works. Early authors working in both languages favored an ornate genre called *champu,* also popular with medieval Sanskrit authors, which mixes passages of verse and prose. The period of true momentum for Kannada literature was the tenth century CE, a period dominated by the poets Pampa, Ponna, and Ranna, "the three gems," all of whom composed works in *champu* style. Many early Kannada authors, including "the three gems," were Jains, and thus many early works deal with Jain legends and heroes. The Hindu epics *Mahabharata* and *Ramayana,* however, were also important sources of subject matter. The *adikavi* ("first of poets") in Telugu literary history is Nannaya Bhatta (1100–1160), who composed a Telugu version of the *Mahabharata.* The Sanskrit epics and Puranas (mythological texts) continued to be a major reference point for Telugu authors for several centuries. [*See also* Mahabharata *and* Ramayana.]

High literary style in Kannada and Telugu has generally been associated with sanskritized diction and a predilection for Sanskritic literary conventions. In the case of Tamil, however, the situation is very different. The earliest extant Tamil poems are thought to have been composed around the second century CE, and the prestigious grammar *Tolkappiyam* is probably even older. *Tolkappiyam* and the earliest Tamil poems set the standard for a classical literary tradition in Tamil that is largely independent of Sanskrit prototypes.

The poetic universe of classical Tamil is divided into two realms, called *akam* ("the interior") and *puram* ("the exterior"). *Akam* poems deal with the phases of erotic love between man and woman, and *puram* poems, with the public life of kings and warriors. Both varieties of poetry are closely controlled by convention, suggesting that there was a tightly knit community of poets and patrons in ancient Tamil Nadu. The language of the early Tamil poems is the least sanskritized among the literatures of South India; the most polished literary style in Tamil is modeled after the language of the classical poems and avoids Sanskrit loanwords. (An important exception is the highly sanskritized Tamil in the theological works of the Shri Vaishnava sect.)

The early Tamil poems are as much a part of the literary prehistory for Malayalam as they are for modern Tamil, because the distinct identity of Malayalam as a language separate from Tamil was not established until several centuries after the composition of these poems. In fact, ancient Tamil literature speaks of three Tamil kingdoms: the Chera, the Chola, and the Pantiya, the first being located in present-day Kerala, where Malayalam is spoken today. The connotations of "classical" in Malayali literary tradition pull in two directions. Both tamilizing and sanskritizing trends are present in Malayali literary history, some genres favoring the first and others the latter. This pattern begins quite early. Among the earliest Malayali works found are sanskritized *champus* as well as poems belonging to a genre called *pattu* ("song"), which adheres closely to Tamil models.

The literatures of all four major Dravidian languages encompass a wide spectrum of genres and styles. Rather than attempting to survey the history of each, only a few major trends will be mentioned here. In all four literatures the impetus toward erudition and classicism plays off a contrary impetus toward more immediately accessible, popular forms, although it should be remembered that in different times and places the specific meaning of "classical" may vary. Some genres lean very heavily in one particular direction. For instance, in Tamil, many of the medieval genres (beginning c. eighth century CE) known collectively as *prabandha* are very closely related to the poems of the classical anthologies. In the literatures of Telugu, Kannada, and Malayalam, the *champu* comes to mind as a genre with a decided orientation toward Sanskrit classicism.

Popular themes and diction are evident in the literature of *bhakti* (devotional Hinduism). The earliest vernacular *bhakti* poems in India were composed by the Tamil saints who lived during the period from the sixth to the ninth century, known as Alvars in the Vaishnavite tradition and Nayanars in the Shaivite tradition. The language of these poems is close to the speech of the day, in marked contrast to that of the learned *prabandhas*. Also, the saints' poems elicit a sense of being in direct contact with the thoughts and emotions of their authors, unlike more formal genres that are tightly controlled by convention. Informal devotional poetry also occupies an important place in Kannada and Telugu literary history. The *vacanas* ("sayings") of the Virashaiva saints (twelfth to thirteenth century) are the earliest *bhakti* poems in Kannada. They are closer in spirit to the poems of the iconoclastic Tamil *cittars* (Sanskrit, *siddhas,* "perfected ones"), who are also Shaivites, than they are to canonical devotional poetry in Tamil, whether Vaishnavite or Shaivite. Vaishnavite devotional poetry appears later in Kannada, with the songs called *padas,* composed by the *dasas* ("servants [of God]"). One such poet, Purandaradasa (sixteenth century), is revered for his contribution to the development of Karnatic (South Indian classical) music. The mainstay of the Karnatic musician's repertoire, however, is a large corpus of Telugu songs, especially the songs of Tyagaraja, a devotee of Rama. The influence of Tyagaraja, actually a native of Tiruvaiyaru in Tamil Nadu, and other Telugu poets of his day was felt throughout the sphere of influence of the former Vijayanagar empire, thus including much of Karnataka and Tamil Nadu.

There are also works that show a responsiveness to both classical and popular influences. The Tamil version of the *Ramayana* by Kampan (twelfth century), for instance, blends elements found in classical Tamil poetry, in Sanskrit epic and *kavya* (refined poetry), and in the devotional poems of the Tamil saints. Poets in Kerala composed dance-dramas called *kudiyattam,* using the Sanskrit for characters of high status and Malayalam for characters of lesser status. There are also purely vernacular dramatic traditions, such as *kathakali* (Malayalam), *yakshagana* (Kannada), and *terukkuttu* (Tamil). These forms vary in regard to their status as classical or popular. *Kathakali* is a "high" art form in Kerala, and its status is reflected in the training of its performers and in the kind of audience it attracts. In contrast, *terukkuttu* in Tamil Nadu is much more a "village art."

There are many more traditional genres besides these, not to speak of the poems, short stories, novels, and plays written during the past century. A major preoccupation of many modern writers has been to maintain a distinctive Indian identity while accepting and making full use of genres introduced from the West. In this respect, writers working in Dravidian languages are no different from writers working in Hindi, Marathi, and other North Indian languages. Therefore it is probably not very meaningful to speak of "Dravidian literature" as a self-contained literary field. The body of literature with the strongest claim to a unique classical status among the literatures in Dravidian languages is the earliest Tamil poetry and later works in Tamil that develop out of the same framework of conventions. The influence of Sanskrit is strong in the literatures of Telugu, Malayalam, and Kannada, and it is present, though not nearly as decisive, in Tamil. Literature is a reflection of history and culture as well as of personal insights. For most Indians and foreign travelers, *South India* is more than a geographic designation, but at the same time the exact boundaries of the extended cultural and historical implications of this term are elusive. It is no easier to pin down the extended meaning of *Dravidian literature*, which is, after all, a reflection of the experiences of people with diverse but interrelated cultural experience.

[*See also* Indo-Aryan Languages and Literatures.]

Robert Caldwell, *A Comparative Grammar of the Dravidian or South Indian Family of Languages* (3d ed., 1913). Madhav M. Deshpande and Peter Edwin Hook, eds., *Aryan and Non-Aryan in India* (1979). R. C. Nigam, *Language Handbook on Mother Tongues in Census* (1972). Andree F. Sjoberg, ed., *Symposium on Dravidian Civilization* (1971). Kamil V. Zvelebil, "Dravidian Languages," in *Encyclopaedia Britannica* (1985), vol. 22, pp. 715–718. NORMAN CUTLER

DRAVIDIAN MOVEMENT, attempt by South Indians to foster a sense of political and cultural identity in the twentieth century. The Justice Party, Self-Respect League, Dravida Kazhagam (Dravidian Association), Dravida Munnetra Kazhagam (Dravidian Progressive Association), and its offshoots are all linked by common ideological themes and form the most significant organizational components of the Dravidian Movement.

Prior to the twentieth century South Indians thought of themselves as members of specific castes but rarely, if ever, as part of a Dravidian "nation." An initial step in the creation of Dravidian identity was the articulation of a distinction between brahmans and all others, viewed together as "nonbrahmans." In the early twentieth century the nonbrahman nomenclature gained political currency as a result of conflict between brahmans and nonbrahmans over allocation of university seats and government jobs. Because of theories that hypothesized that twentieth-century brahmans were the descendants of ancient Aryan invaders of Dravidian South India, the brahman-nonbrahman separation was thought to be racial, historically documented, and in some intrinsic sense fundamental.

E. V. Ramaswami Naicker's founding in 1925 of the Self-Respect League, which rejected Hinduism and supported a casteless society, reinforced the emerging idea of a Dravidian identity. In the 1930s and 1940s, faced with the prospect of eventual Indian independence from England, Dravidian Movement leaders from the Justice Party, Self-Respect League, and Dravida Kazhagam demanded a separate Dravidian nation composed of the area then constituting Madras Presidency.

More successful in the Tamil-speaking areas of Madras Presidency, the Dravidian Movement soon began to focus on Tamil language and culture as an expression of Dravidian identity. By the early 1960s the Dravida Munnetra Kazhagam was instrumental in modifying the ideological tenets of the Dravidian Movement to reflect its base of support and the need to contest elections. Tamil cultural nationalism became the focus. Demands for a separate state were abandoned, radical social reform was reduced to calls for uplift of "backward" castes, and emphasis was placed on a Tamil renaissance and opposition to Hindi as the official language of India.

When the Dravida Munnetra Kazhagam became the governing party in Tamil Nadu in 1967, the exigencies of governance created pressure for further modification. All but the most general symbols of the early Dravidian Movement ideology were transformed beyond recognition by the mid-1970s. Remaining, however, was Tamil nationalism and the pervasive idea of the Tamils as a single "people" sharing a common Dravidian past.

Marguerite Ross Barnett, *The Politics of Cultural Nationalism in South India* (1976). Robert L. Hardgrave, Jr., *The Dravidian Movement* (1965). Eugene F. Irschick, *Politics and Social Conflict in South India: The Non-Brahman Movement and Tamil Separatism, 1916–1929* (1969). Lloyd I. Rudolph and Susanne H. Rudolph, *The Modernity of Tradition: Political Development in India* (1967).

MARGUERITE ROSS BARNETT

DRUKPA, subsect of the Kagyapa school of Tibetan Buddhism founded in the twelfth century. In the seventeenth century the sect extended its influence into Bhutan and eventually became the most important sect in that country. The leading figure in its growth was Ngawang Namgyal, who arrived in Bhutan from Tibet in 1616 and became the country's first *shabdung*. By the time of his death in 1652 the sect had established its authority through most of western Bhutan, eventually spreading throughout the entire country. [*See also* Bhutan.]

THEODORE RICCARDI, JR.

DUAN QIRUI (1865–1936), one of Yuan Shikai's chief subordinates in the Beiyang Army; held high government positions during Yuan's presidency of China. Duan was also premier in several governments after Yuan's death, concluding his fourth term in that office in 1918. In 1917 and 1918, Duan's government concluded the Nishihara Loans, by which Japan provided large sums of money in return for substantial economic concessions in China. Duan also headed the Anhui faction of warlords in rivalry with the Zhili clique under Feng Guozhang. That rivalry led to the Anhui-Zhili War in 1920. The defeat of Anhui forced Duan into retirement until 1924, when Feng Yuxiang and Zhang Zuolin summoned him to head a compromise government in North China. That government fell in the war between Feng and Zhang between 1925 and 1926, and Duan retired permanently.

[*See also* China, Republic Period; Warlords; Warlord Cliques; *and* Yuan Shikai.]

Howard J. Boorman, ed., *Biographical Dictionary of Republican China,* vol. 3 (1970), pp. 330–335. Andrew J. Nathan, *Peking Politics, 1918–1923: Factionalism and the Failure of Constitutionalism* (1976).

JAMES E. SHERIDAN

DU FU (712–770), Chinese poet, almost universally acknowledged as the supreme poet of the Tang dynasty, an age that was itself the apogee of poetry writing in China. Du was born to a distinguished family of Henan Province with strong connections to the capital region around Chang'an. Although he achieved fame as a poet at an early age, he failed the civil service examinations several times and never rose very far in the official ranks. Du's poetic output consisted of almost fifteen hundred poems on every conceivable subject and in every verse form. He is perhaps most celebrated as a poet of conscience, opposing social injustices and holding up a mirror to the hardships of everyday existence, particularly during and after the greatest social upheaval of the age, the An Lushan Rebellion.

William Hung, *Tu Fu: China's Greatest Poet* (1952).

HOWARD J. WECHSLER

DULLES, JOHN FOSTER (1888–1959), American lawyer, diplomat, and secretary of state who played an important role in American relations with Asia. Dulles was born in Washington, D.C.; his father was a Presbyterian minister and his mother was the daughter of a former secretary of state. Early in his law career he revealed an interest in and talent for international affairs. By World War II he had emerged as a prominent spokesman of the Republican Party on foreign affairs. In 1945 he was a principal United States delegate to the San Francisco conference that established the United Nations and was responsible for a number of provisions in the UN charter.

In 1950 Dulles became consultant to Secretary of State Dean Acheson in working out the treaty of peace with Japan. Both he and his government were convinced that a lenient treaty was necessary if Japan were to become a member of the Western alliance and a stabilizing factor contributing to Asian peace and security. This stance involved him in negotiations with Great Britain, the Philippines, Australia, and New Zealand, all of which favored a stern treaty because they feared a revival of Japanese power. Dulles succeeded in winning their acceptance of a treaty that was more in accordance with US wishes.

In 1953 Dulles was appointed secretary of state by President Eisenhower and served until he died of cancer in 1959. In matters relating to Asia, his tenure as secretary was marked by a China policy that was strongly in favor of Nationalist China and firmly opposed to the People's Republic; the espousal of a domino theory, which held that if one country became communist others would; the ending of the Korean War; and the completion of a network of bilateral and multilateral security arrangements designed to limit communist or Soviet influence.

John Robinson Beal, *John Foster Dulles: 1888–1959* (1959). Louis L. Gerson, *John Foster Dulles* (1967).

JOHN M. MAKI

DUNHUANG, oasis town on the extreme western edge of Gansu Province that for millennia served as a major entrepôt on the famed Silk Road, the main caravan route connecting China with Central and Western Asia and the Mediterranean world beyond. The road was actually composed of two routes, skirting the northern and southern edges of the Taklamakan Desert of modern Xinjiang Province, that joined east of the desert at Dunhuang. Because of its strategic location, Dunhuang was continually an object of contention between China and her neighbors, first the nomadic Xiongnu and Turks, later the Tibetans and the kingdom of Turfan. It was first brought under Chinese domination by the expansionist emperor Han Wudi at the end of the second century BCE and was intermittently controlled by China for the next two thousand years. It is now administered as a *xian* of Gansu Province.

FIGURE 1. *Buddhist Hanging Scroll.* Eleven-headed Guanyin surrounded by quotations and illustrations from chapter 25 of the *Lotus Sutra,* dated 986. One of the many examples of the artwork and texts preserved in the caves of Dunhuang for nearly one thousand years. Ink on hemp; height 96.5 cm., width 61 cm.

As Dunhuang was the first port of entry into China for Buddhist missionaries traveling on the overland route from Central Asia and India, the town developed into a major Buddhist center from the fourth century onward. About nineteen kilometers south of the town, hundreds of cave temples, known as the Caves of the Thousand Buddhas, were dug out and decorated with wall paintings, many of them scenes of various Buddhist paradises. The caves were commissioned and paid for over the centuries by pious donors, whose portraits and names were often painted on the walls. About 1900 a sideroom of one small cave temple was discovered filled with about twenty thousand old Chinese manuscripts, largely in scroll form, dating from the fifth to the eleventh century. Although most of the scrolls were Buddhist, there were also Daoist, Confucian, Nestorian, and Zoroastrian scriptures, as well as subjects of a more secular nature. The latter manuscripts especially have revolutionized our understanding of medieval Chinese society and the development of vernacular literature in China.

[*See also* Buddhism: Buddhism in China; Confucianism; Daoism; Nestorianism; Silk Route; *and* Tang Dynasty.]

Victor H. Mair, *Tun-huang Popular Narratives* (1983). Aural Stein, *On Ancient Central-Asian Tracks* (1933). Irene Vongehr Vincent, *The Sacred Oasis* (1953). Arthur Waley, *Ballads and Stories from Tun-huang* (1960).

HOWARD J. WECHSLER

DUPLEIX, JOSEPH FRANÇOIS (1697–1763), governor of Pondicherry (1741–1754), director-general of all stations in India belonging to the French East India Company. He took Madras from the British in 1746 and, refusing to give it up when ordered to do so by Nawab Anwar ud-Din, defeated the Mughal army at Saint Thomé with a tiny force of sepoys (Indian infantry) and artillery. Therewith the myth of European valor was born.

As the father of the lucrative arms trade that followed, Marquis Dupleix showed how Indian princes would vie with one another for these new-model

Indian regiments of European-trained "sepoys-for-sale," heedless that, by competing in the purchase of these "Trojan horses," they were nourishing the growth of European power. Yet while showing how India could be conquered with Indian manpower and Indian money—schemes that the British learned and used to their great advantage—Dupleix was recalled and died impoverished and unrecognized.

[*See also* French East India Company.]

H. H. Dodwell, *Dupleix and Clive: The Beginning of Empire* (1920; reprint, 1967). G. Malleson, *Dupleix* (1899).

ROBERT E. FRYKENBERG

DUPRÉ, JULES-MARIE (1813–1881), French admiral and governor of Cochinchina (1871–1874). A firm advocate of French expansion in Indochina, he supported Jean Dupuis's efforts to occupy Hanoi in 1873. Convinced of Tu Duc's weakening hold over Tonkin, Dupré took the initiative of summoning Francis Garnier and sending him to assist Dupuis. Upon the failure of this campaign, Dupré turned his attention to forcing Vietnamese recognition of France's territorial gains. This came with a March 1874 treaty, but Dupré's hopes of a continued French presence in Tonkin were smashed for the time being, particularly after a cable from France forbid such a policy.

[*See also* Dupuis, Jean; Tu Duc; *and* Garnier, Francis.]

Joseph Buttinger, *The Smaller Dragon: A Political History of Vietnam* (1958). John Cady, *The Roots of French Imperialism in Eastern Asia* (1954).

BRUCE M. LOCKHART

DUPUIS, JEAN (1828–1912), French adventurer who worked to open the Red River to French vessels. Having found the river to be navigable between Hanoi and Yunnan, Dupuis made one successful voyage but was prevented by the Vietnamese from making a second. Occupying part of Hanoi in May 1873, he called upon Admiral Dupré in Saigon for help, whereupon the latter sent Francis Garnier to aid Dupuis. Although his initial attack on Hanoi was successful, Garnier was killed in December 1873. Following the signing of the March 1874 treaty in Hue, which annulled Garnier's gains in Tonkin, Dupuis was expelled from the region.

[*See also* Dupré, Jules-Marie *and* Garnier, Francis.]

Joseph Buttinger, *The Smaller Dragon: A Political History of Vietnam* (1958). John Cady, *The Roots of French Imperialism in Eastern Asia* (1954).

BRUCE M. LOCKHART

DURAND LINE, the name assigned in 1893 to the erstwhile Indo-Afghan frontier from the eastern extremity of the Wakhan strip in the northeast to the Persian (now Iranian) border in the southwest. Agreed to in principle in negotiations held in Kabul by the Indian foreign secretary, Mortimer Durand, and the Afghan amir, Abdul Rahman, the border was demarcated in the next two decades, but only along the short strategic stretches (e.g., at the Khyber Pass) from the Safed Koh Range northeastward to Wakhan. Subsequently, the whole line has sometimes been interpreted as an impermanent division of areas of control over the tribes on either side, and at others, as a permanent boundary. As legatee of the British in the region, Pakistan insists on the legality of the border, whereas Afghanistan, in effect, repudiated it in 1947, declaring that the Pakhtun tribesmen within Pakistan's Northwest Frontier Province should have had the option of joining Pakistan, joining their fellow Pakhtun in Afghanistan, or choosing independence within a state of "Pakhtunistan."

[*See also* Khyber Pass.]

Thomas Hungerford Holdich, *The Gates of India: Being an Historical Narrative* (1910). James William Spain, *The Pathan Borderland.*

JOSEPH E. SCHWARTZBERG

DURBAR, anglicized form of the Persian word *darbar,* a royal court or center of authority in an Indian state, or the hall of audience where justice was administered and the monarch received his nobles and visitors. The central ritual of a durbar involved a carefully ordered reciprocal exchange of honors between ruler and subject, in which the latter offered gold coins as a sign of loyalty while the ruler distributed jeweled robes to signify the bonding of his subjects to himself. Following the award of the title "Empress of India" to Queen Victoria in 1876, the British made successive coronation durbars—in 1877, 1903, and 1911 (although the monarch was personally present only at the last)—an occasion to elaborate a symbolic focus for their rule. Held in the Mughal capital of Delhi, these durbars provided an opportunity to define India's princes as a privileged "feudal" aristocracy.

Bernard Cohn, "Representing Authority in Victorian India," in *The Invention of Tradition,* edited by E. Hobsbawm and T. Ranger (1983). Narayani Gupta, *Delhi Between Two Empires* (1981). THOMAS R. METCALF

DURRANIS. Ahmad Shah, founder of the Afghan state (r. 1747–1773), decreed that *Durrani* would be the new name of the Abdalis. The change from *Abdali,* a term for a category in the Sufi hierarchy, to *Durrani,* derived from a word meaning "pearl," was symbolically significant. The change also allowed for modifications in the genealogical charter: some Abdali clans were not recognized as Durrani, and some subclans in the Peshawar valley were renamed Bar ("upper") Durrani.

During the imperial period (1747–1818), Durrani clans were the military backbone of the state. They consolidated their hold on southwestern Afghanistan and acquired property in eastern Afghanistan and northern India. Several previously nomadic clans became settled.

In the postimperial period, the institutionalization of a standing army gradually weakened the privileged position of the Durranis. Nevertheless, as members of the Durrani Muhammadzai lineage held state power from 1880 to 1978, Durrani clans were able to claim a symbolically superior social status. This was especially important in northern Afghanistan, to which Durrani nomadic clans moved from 1880 on. Some Durrani clans have played an active role against Soviet occupation in their localities, but no Durrani leader of national significance has yet emerged.

[*See also* Abdalis.]

H. Rawlinson, "Report on the Durranis," in *Kandahar,* vol. 5 of *Historical and Political Gazetteer of Afghanistan,* edited by L. Adamec (1980), pp. 509–577.

ASHRAF GHANI

DUTCH EAST INDIA COMPANY (Vereenigde Oost-Indische Compagnie, or VOC), Dutch trading corporation in Asia in the seventeenth and eighteenth centuries. The VOC was formed in March 1602 by the merger of a number of separate companies founded in the late 1590s to conduct trade to the Indian Ocean. It was a joint-stock company, with a governing body (the *Heeren XVII,* or the "Seventeen Gentlemen") that met in turn at the different provincial capitals of the Netherlands. The charter of the VOC, granted by the States-General, gave the company a monopoly for all Dutch commerce in Asia as well as the right to exercise sovereignty in Asia on behalf of the Dutch state.

In its first century the VOC pursued three principal objectives in the Indian Ocean. First, it sought to establish a restrictive monopoly of the supply of spices, notably in the Moluccas (Maluku), comparable to the monopoly that it had been granted in the Netherlands. This frequently involved the company in major military expeditions in the eastern Indonesian Archipelago. In the early 1620s, for example, the Dutch conquered the Banda Islands in a particularly ruthless and brutal manner, in an attempt to secure for the VOC the monopoly supply of nutmeg and mace. In addition, periodic raids were undertaken into areas beyond Dutch authority in order to destroy spice-bearing trees. Finally, the VOC sought to curb, if not destroy, all trade in the spices of the Indonesian Archipelago that lay beyond their authority; thus the Dutch conquered Makassar between 1666 and 1669, thereby severely curtailing the local smuggling trade, and established their authority over Banten (Bantam) in 1682, which denied that port to other European merchants.

Second, the Dutch East India Company sought to bring under its control a major part of the intra-Asian trade that flowed into the archipelago, particularly the long-distance trade with the Indian subcontinent, for the company was aware that its ability to extract spices from the eastern islands would depend greatly on its capacity to supply Indian cotton textiles in exchange. In 1617 the Dutch established a permanent factory in Surat, primarily to secure Gujarat cloth: by the mid-1630s the VOC had firmly organized its trade with the Coromandel coast and had begun to establish factories in Bengal, whose products came to occupy a crucial importance in the company's European and Asian trade. In 1656 the Dutch seized Colombo from the Portuguese in order to capture the supply of cinnamon in Ceylon, while Cochin, an important source of black pepper, fell to the company in 1663. [*See* Surat *and* Cochin.] During the seventeenth and early eighteenth centuries the VOC also extended its trade into East Asia. A military outpost was established in Formosa in 1624 and a commercial presence at Canton in 1727, while trade was conducted with Japan from the early seventeenth century, although under very restrictive conditions. Third, the Dutch East India Company sought to expel the Portuguese from the archipelago (the latter were forced out of the Moluccas in 1605 when the Ambonese accepted Dutch suzerainty, while Melaka [Malacca] fell to superior Dutch arms in 1641), and then to exclude English merchants from the region.

The expansion of the commerce of the Dutch East India Company in the archipelago was secured by the founding of a number of heavily fortified settlements (including, most notably, Batavia in 1619 as the territorial headquarters of the VOC commercial organization in Asia) and the extension of Dutch political authority through major parts of the islands, a process frequently achieved through the exploitation of succession disputes that weakened indigenous polities. Most importantly, the Central Javanese sultanate of Mataram came under the authority of the company toward the end of the 1670s, while Banten was conquered by the company's forces in the early 1680s. [*See* Mataram.] Thus, underlying the commercial activities of the VOC was a readiness to use armed force and territorial acquisition to secure trading advantages. It is in this respect, as well as in its considerably greater strength and size, that the Dutch East India Company is mainly distinguished from the English East India Company of the same period. [*See* East India Company].

Throughout the eighteenth century the commercial strength of the VOC was in decline. The diminishing importance of the spice trade coupled with the company's failure to secure the development of alternative crops of comparable commercial potential, the increasing burden of administering the eastern possessions with a bureaucracy weakened by widespread financial corruption, and the territorial losses inflicted on the Dutch during European wars at the end of the eighteenth century brought the VOC to the edge of bankruptcy. Its charter was allowed to lapse on 31 December 1799, and from that date the Dutch state assumed responsibility for all the debts and possessions of the Vereenigde Oost-Indische Compagnie.

[*See also* Indian Ocean; Sri Lanka; India; Melaka; Spice Trade; Maluku; Banten; Mataram; *and* Portuguese: Portuguese in Southeast Asia. *For European contact with Asia to 1700, see the map accompanying* Imperialism.]

C. R. Boxer, *The Dutch Seaborne Empire 1600–1800* (1965) K. N. Chaudhuri, *Trade and Civilisation in the Indian Ocean: An Economic History from the Rise of Islam to 1750* (1985). Kristof Glamann, *Dutch-Asiatic Trade, 1620–1740* (1958). M. A. P. Meilink-Roelofsz, *Asian Trade and European Influence in the Indonesian Archipelago between 1500 and about 1630* (1962). Niels Steensgaard, *The Asian Trade Revolution of the Seventeenth Century: The East India Companies and the Decline of the Caravan Trade* (1974).

Ian Brown

DUTT, MICHAEL MADHUSUDAN (1824–1873), early nineteenth-century Indian poet. A convert to Christianity in 1843, Dutt became known as the "Milton of India" for his introduction of the English poetic forms of blank verse and the sonnet into Bengal. His early poetry was in English, but his later work, such as his most famous poem *Meghanadvadh* (1861), was written in Bengali.

Amit Sen, *Notes on the Bengal Renaissance* (1946). Sukumar Sen, *History of Bengali Literature* (1960).

Judith E. Walsh

DUTT, ROMESH CHUNDER (1848–1909), member of the Indian civil service, novelist, historian, and public figure. In 1871 he passed the Indian Civil Service examinations in London and became one of only five Indian members of that service. For the next twenty-six years Dutt complemented a distinguished civil service career with a literary output so varied that it included works on history, economics, and travel; translations; historical novels in Bengali; and school textbooks. In 1897 Dutt retired to England, but he returned to India in 1899 to preside over the Indian National Congress meetings at Lucknow. Dutt's best-known work is the two-volume *Economic History of India* (1902–1904), a critical assessment of a century and a half of British rule in India.

[*See also* Indian National Congress.]

R. C. Datta, *Romesh Chunder Dutt* (1968). Leonard Gordon, *Bengal: The Nationalist Movement 1846–1940* (1974).

Judith E. Walsh

DUTTHAGAMANI (r. 161–137 BCE), Sinhalese king and unifier of Sri Lanka. Dutthagamani's fifteen-year campaign against the Tamil ruler Elara, which culminated in the latter's defeat and death, is dramatized as the central theme of the later chapters of the *Mahavamsa,* the great chronicle of Sri Lanka, as an epoch-making encounter between the Sinhalese and the Tamils, and is extolled as a holy war fought in the interests of Buddhism. What was epochal in all this was Dutthagamani's success in the face of substantial opposition from Sinhalese rivals and from Elara, who had considerable Sinhalese support, in bringing the whole island under a single ruler for the first time in its history.

The *Mahavamsa* portrays Dutthagamani as the model ruler, and the attributes of monarchical virtue assigned to him—patriotism, munificence to the *sangha* and Buddhism, and a concern for the public welfare—have had a powerful influence on Sinhalese attitudes to monarchs in later eras.

[*See also* Mahavamsa; Elara; *and* Anuradhapura.]

K. M. de Silva, *A History of Sri Lanka* (1981), pp. 15–54.

K. M. de Silva

DUY TAN (1900–1945), tenth Nguyen emperor (r. 1907–1916) of Vietnam. Placed on the throne after the exile of his father, Thanh Thai, Duy Tan proved to be independent and uncooperative with the French, even accusing them of failing to adhere to the Patenotre Treaty (1884). In 1916 he became involved in a plot, led by Tran Cao Van and Thai Phien, to stage an uprising among native troops in Hue, Quang Nam, and Quang Ngai. The mutiny took place on the night of 2 May 1916 but was betrayed. Its leaders were executed, and Duy Tan joined his father in exile on Réunion.

[*See also* Patenotre Treaty.]

William J. Duiker, *The Rise of Nationalism in Vietnam, 1900–1941* (1976). Nguyen The Anh, *The Withering Days of the Nguyen Dynasty* (1978).

Bruce M. Lockhart

DVARAVATI, Buddhist civilization in Siam between the sixth and ninth century. Although scattered earlier sites are known, it was only around the sixth century CE that large numbers of cities and towns arose, primarily around the lower basin of the Chaophraya River, attesting to the existence of a consistent and distinctive regional culture in what is now Thailand. The most extensive sites were at Nakhon Pathom, U Thong (near Suphanburi), and Lopburi in the central region, with related offshoots at Haripunjaya (Lamphun) in the north and near Nakhon Ratchasima in the northeast, later extending even into the Vientiane region of Laos. All these sites have in common inscriptions in the Mon language, circular or oval-shaped town plans, and abundant Buddhist art objects—often including images of the Buddha seated in European fashion—of a distinctive style and workmanship. There is little evidence to support the contention that all these sites were included within a single political entity, save a single coin from Nakhon Pathom bearing the inscription "lord of Dvaravati." The inscriptions attest to the presence of Mon, but many Khmer (and possibly some Thai) also lived within the region.

Dvaravati played an important role in popularizing Buddhism at a time when brahmanic religion was promoted by eastern neighbors, and its Buddhist connections with India and perhaps Sri Lanka promoted both cultural and commercial interchange. Although the region was incorporated into the Angkorean empire in the tenth century, elements of Dvaravati's Buddhism and distinctive culture persisted, and the name of Dvaravati was perpetuated as part of the names of Ayudhya and Bangkok.

[*See also* Phra Pathom Chedi; Lopburi; Lamphun; *and* Mon.]

H. G. Quaritch Wales, *Dvaravati* (1969). David K. Wyatt, *Thailand: A Short History* (1984).

David K. Wyatt

DZUNGARIA, primarily the steppe regions in northern Xinjiang, formerly inhabited by the Dzungar Mongols. Lying north of the Tian Shan range, Dzungaria's climate and environment are more similar to those of Soviet Central Asia and the Siberian steppes to the north than to the arid region of southern Xinjiang. To the east of Dzungaria are the Altai Mountains of Mongolia; to the west lie the Tarbagatai and the Ala-Tau mountains. Adjacent to the bases of these mountains are a number of oases and towns, including Urumqi, the provincial capital. Unlike southern Xinjiang, Dzungaria is exposed to the cold and moist Siberian air. The resulting precipitation provides the water in the grasslands.

Although Dzungaria has traditionally been the domain of herdsmen, important economic changes have occurred since 1949. The largely Muslim and Turkic-speaking Kazakhs are now the principal pastoralists, although some Mongols also inhabit the region. The shepherds still lead their flocks to the mountains in summer and to the plains in winter. The People's Republic of China has, however, encouraged the development of agriculture through the promotion of irrigation. Wheat and sugar beets are the two most important new crops grown in the region. Another emphasis of the People's Republic has been the exploration and exploitation of Xinjiang's mineral resources. Petroleum has been discovered adjacent to the town of Karamai, and coal mines have been established near Urumqi. These agricultural and industrial developments have attracted numerous Chinese colonists into Dzungaria. This large influx of Chinese, together with the government's policy of collectivization, has created tensions and conflicts, leading about 60,000 Kazakhs to flee to the USSR in 1962 and precipitating pitched battles between the Chinese and the non-Chinese inhabitants during the Cultural Revolution (1966–1976). Since the Cultural Revolution, the Chinese government has become more sensitive to the economic, ethnic, religious, and linguistic concerns of the non-Chinese peoples of Dzungaria.

Lawrence Krader, *Peoples of Central Asia* (1973). Morris Rossabi, *China and Inner Asia from 1368 to the Present Day* (1975). Theodore Shabad, *China's Changing Map: National and Regional Development, 1949–1971* (1972).

MORRIS ROSSABI

E

EAST ASIA. Including China, Japan, Korea, and Vietnam, East Asia is a region historically defined by a common civilization characterized by such traits as the use of the Chinese written language and the ideological and cultural preeminence of Confucianism and Mahayana Buddhism. Since World War II the term *East Asia* has gradually replaced *Far East* as the preferred term because the latter is vague and Europocentric. *Western Pacific* is another term sometimes used to refer to the same region.

EDWARD L. FARMER

EASTERN JIN DYNASTY. *See* Jin Dynasty.

EAST INDIA COMPANY. One of the greatest business organizations of its time, the British East India Company was at once a manifestation and a propelling force of Western capitalism and overseas expansion. The company received its foundation charter from Elizabeth I in 1600 and was dissolved by Queen Victoria in 1858 when the British Parliament made the political administration of India a responsibility of the government. During the long period of its history, the character, aims, and functions of the company changed profoundly. At the turn of the seventeenth century, a group of London merchants had founded the company in order to extend English seaborne trade to the Indian Ocean. Halfway through the eighteenth century, the East India Company, now grown to immense wealth and naval power, overthrew the semi-independent Mughal viceroy of Bengal and was on the point of assuming the functions of a great territorial and military power in India. The Battle of Plassey (1757), which was in reality a political revolution, not only changed the status of the company in the Indian subcontinent but also gave rise to a curious constitutional situation in England. As a business organization mainly involved in transcontinental trade (although it possessed semisovereign territorial enclaves as well), the company was allowed by Parliament and crown alike to become a state within a state. It was gradually brought under the control of the government and became accountable to Parliament for its day-to-day administration of the Indian empire. The Court of Directors retained its executive role in that process, however, subject to the formal approval of the president of the Board of Control, as the minister in charge of the India Department was named. Had it not been for the terrible events of the Indian Mutiny (1857), this constitutional anachronism might well have continued.

The early history of the East India Company up to the period of the Stuart Restoration (1660) was marked by successes as well as failures. The record of success was to be seen in the company's ability to create a commercial organization in the Indian Ocean, together with a bureaucratic structure for economic decisions and operations in Europe. On the other hand, the financial rewards to the merchants and general investors were meager, even when the company was not actually taking losses. Its business managers proved relatively inexperienced in their handling of joint-stock capital, and the Dutch East India Company (founded in 1602 and known by its initials, VOC), with its greater financial strength and a stronger determination to dominate the trade between Europe and Asia, overshadowed the English organization. For the greater part of the seventeenth century the London merchants followed the lead taken by the VOC.

The early aim of the East India Company was to supply England with pepper and spices purchased directly in the Indonesian Archipelago. The foundation of the company can be traced to the revolt of the Netherlands against Spanish rule, which led

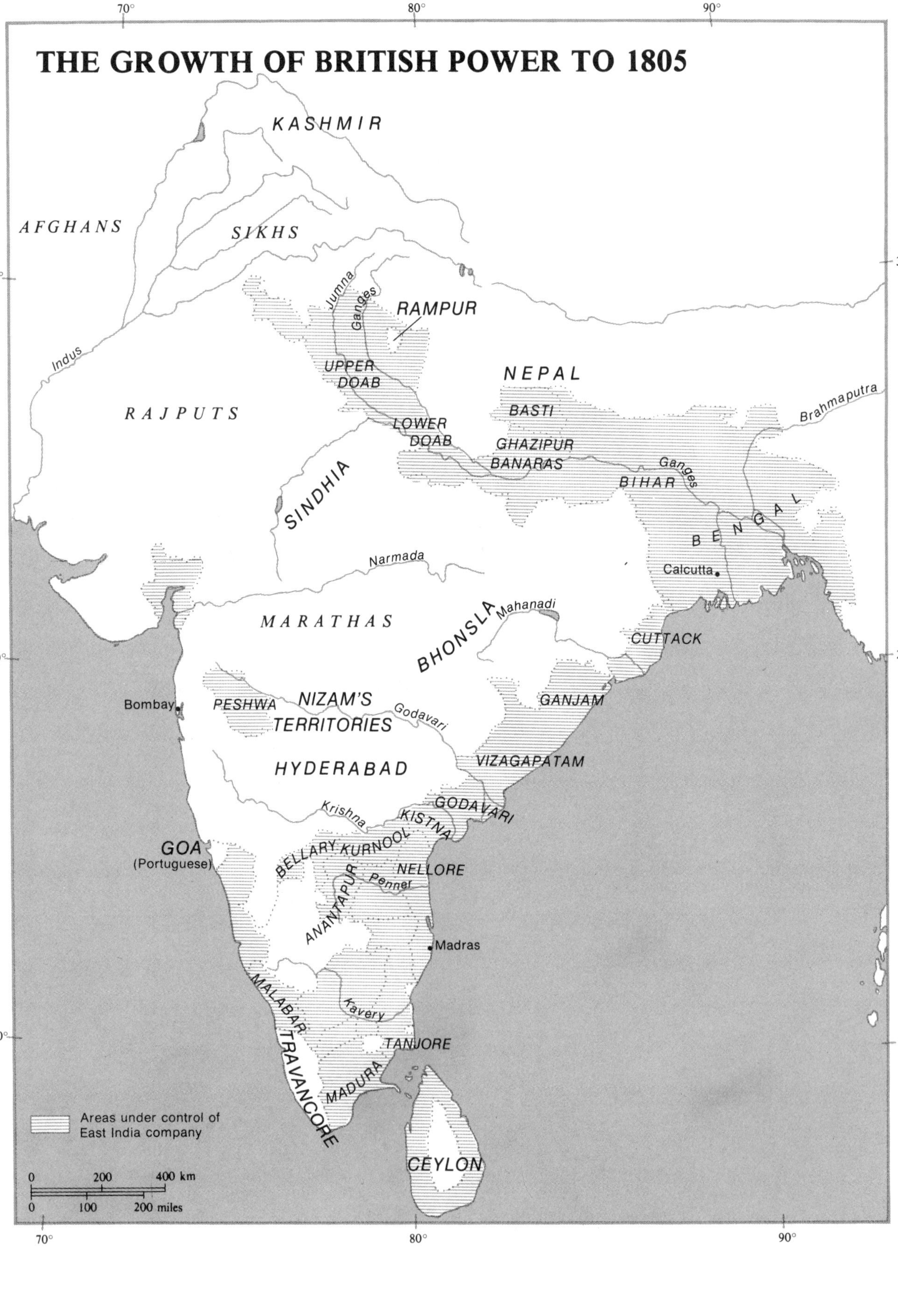
THE GROWTH OF BRITISH POWER TO 1805
KASHMIR
AFGHANS
SIKHS
Jumna
Ganges
RAMPUR
Indus
UPPER DOAB
NEPAL
RAJPUTS
BASTI
Brahmaputra
LOWER DOAB
GHAZIPUR
BANARAS
Ganges
BIHAR
SINDHIA
BENGAL
Narmada
Calcutta
Mahanadi
MARATHAS
BHONSLA
CUTTACK
Bombay
PESHWA
NIZAM'S TERRITORIES
Godavari
GANJAM
HYDERABAD
VIZAGAPATAM
GODAVARI
Krishna
KISTNA
GOA (Portuguese)
BELLARY
KURNOOL
NELLORE
Penner
ANANTAPUR
Madras
MALABAR
Kavery
TANJORE
TRAVANCORE
MADURA
CEYLON
Areas under control of East India company
0 200 400 km
0 100 200 miles
70°
80°
90°
30°
20°
10°

to the decline of Antwerp in the 1570s and 1580s. This great European commercial city had previously distributed the Portuguese imports of Asian goods. The commercial success of the English Levant Company, founded in 1581, encouraged its members to look for economic opportunities farther east in the Indian Ocean itself, particularly in the late 1590s, when the Dutch merchants of Amsterdam began to send direct voyages to the Indonesian Archipelago.

The constitution of the new company was modeled on the pattern of the regulating companies that had begun to appear in England in the sixteenth century. But there were many novel features in the organization of the East India Company. The national monopoly granted by the state was stringently enforced; only the members of the company could engage in trade with the East Indies. The principle of trading with joint-stock capital received justification from the argument that such a distant trade could not be managed by members acting individually. The use of heavily armed ships and the readiness to go into instant naval action were prompted by fear of Portuguese sea power and uncertainty of the company's reception by Asian political rulers.

The corporate organization of trade and the formulation of policies called for a central management committee. The investing members of the East India Company constituted a body known as the General Court, which exercised overall control through the individual vote. But the actual management of the company and all the detailed functions of decision making were assigned to a smaller committee of twenty-four directors elected from the General Court. At first known as the Court of Committees, it was changed after 1709 to the Court of Directors. There were also other subcommittees that handled different aspects of the East India Company's business. The most important ones dealt with correspondence, shipping, the provision of treasure for shipment to Asia, the purchase of export goods, and the auction sales of the company's Asian imports. The administration and the implementation of the commercial or political decisions devolved on professional salaried officials, the secretary, the treasurer, the accountant, warehouse keepers, and so on. The whole organization of the company as a corporate institution developed rapidly, and by 1621 it had taken on a form that was to last, with only small modifications, to the end of its existence.

The great achievement of the London merchants who ran the East India Company was to devise a bureaucratic method of long-distance trade that was independent of individual judgment, although of course the quality of the company's management was closely dependent on the caliber of its personnel. The financial and commercial success of the company from the 1670s onward can be ascribed to a systematic application of organizational logic to contemporary business problems. The company set up a very comprehensive system of information and records, both in London and in Asia. Its accounting system was based on double-entry bookkeeping, and after 1709 the account books were organized in such a way that the policymakers had quick access to the company's overall financial position. Through constant interaction between recorded internal information and external factors (such as the movements of prices, expanding consumer demand, and wars and famines), the managers of the East India Company were able to reduce the effects of uncertainty in markets separated by many thousands of miles.

The East India Company organized its first voyage to the East Indies in 1601, and the ships were sent to Java mainly to buy black pepper and the finer spices of the Moluccas (Maluku). The large quantities of pepper brought back produced a serious oversupply in the domestic markets in England and convinced the company that it was essential both to diversify the range of Asian products and to expand the reexport trade to Europe and elsewhere. Beginning in 1607 the company's ships carried instructions to go to the Red Sea and India and to explore the possibility of establishing commercial relations in the western Indian Ocean. The company was well aware by now that the seasonal movements of its European ships and the structure of interport trade in the Indian Ocean required permanent commercial quarters in the most important centers of Asian trade. It was especially important for the company to gain access to the sources of Indian cotton textiles, which were widely marketed in South Asia and the Indonesian islands by Indian and Portuguese merchants. The sales proceeds of the piece goods provided a most profitable means of buying pepper and spices.

The officials of the East India Company founded "factories" (named after factors or agents) in Banten (Bantam), in the Spice Islands, and in Masulipatam in southern India during the first two decades of trade. In 1612 they also gained entry to the great Mughal port of Surat, which dominated the seaborne trade of the western Indian Ocean. This was a period of active exploration in many directions. Voyages were dispatched to Japan, to the Persian Gulf, and to the Red Sea. The most notable naval success of the company came in 1622 when a combined Anglo-Persian force captured Hormuz from the Portuguese and freed the trade of the Persian Gulf from the latter's control. The new port of Gombroon became the center of the company's activities in the Middle East. The company suffered a severe setback, however, at the hands of the Dutch in 1623 when ten members of the Amboina Factory in the Spice Islands were executed by the local Dutch governor of the VOC on a suspicion of conspiracy. The incident left a bitter legacy in Anglo-Dutch relations and effectively excluded the East India Company from a share in the trade of nutmeg, mace, and cloves. The Banten Factory in Java, together with those in Sumatra, continued to buy and export black pepper.

The strong Dutch policy in Southeast Asia forced the British East India Company to look for greater opportunities in the Indian subcontinent. In the long run the trade in new Asian commodities proved more profitable than that in pepper and spices. Indian export goods, such as coarse and luxury cotton textiles, indigo, saltpeter, and raw silk, found a ready and expanding market in Europe, the Levant, and the New World. The demand for Indian cotton goods particularly increased in the second half of the seventeenth century and posed a serious threat to the European domestic textile industries. From the end of the century, the Indian exports were joined by coffee from the Arabian port of Mocha and tea from China. The import of Asian goods was paid for by the export of woolen textiles and metals such as iron, tin, and copper, but the bulk of the company's purchasing power came from the export of American silver and small quantities of gold. The higher proportion of treasure in the company's exports was mainly owing to the high cost of industrial production in Europe.

The East India Company's commercial organization in India steadily advanced throughout the seventeenth century. The Surat and Masulipatam factories at first supplied most of the export goods. When a devastating famine destroyed the economy of Gujarat in the 1630s, the company's activities gradually shifted to southern India and then to Bengal. The township of Madras was acquired by charter from a local ruler in 1639, and in 1665 the Portugese crown handed over Bombay to the company as part of its marriage agreement with Charles II. The company's commercial enclaves in the main areas of Indian trade were completed with the foundation of Calcutta in about 1690. Although Bombay was never able to supplant Surat as a commercial metropolis, both Madras and Calcutta enjoyed a considerable volume of Asian seaborne trade in their own right and became the headquarters of the company's organization in South India and Bengal.

The 1680s, however, were a disturbing period for the East India Company in Asia and Europe. In 1682 the VOC at last succeeded in gaining political control of the sultanate of Banten and expelled the English from the port. The East India Company thereafter removed its pepper trade to the Sumatran settlement of Bencoolen. The fall of Banten, a severe shock for the company, was followed by an even greater blow. [*See also* Banten.] Under the belligerent policy of Sir Josiah Child, it was decided to wage a naval war on the Mughal empire and seize an important port or territory in India. The war went badly against the company, and the English were forced to accept hard terms from the Mughal emperor for a restoration of their trade. At home in England, the defeat of the company in India was used by its many opponents to bring about an expansion in its membership and even to challenge its legal monopoly by means of unauthorized, noncompany voyages to the Indian Ocean. The English revolution of 1688 placed the company in a difficult situation, as it had been associated closely with James II. In 1698 Parliament and government served notice of termination to the company and authorized the foundation of a new company trading with the East Indies. But in 1702 the two rival East India Companies agreed on a merger, and the United Company of Merchants, trading to the East Indies, finally emerged in 1709.

The first half of the eighteenth century brought great prosperity and political strength to the East India Company, which was part of the new economic strength of the city of London and of the nation in general. The scale of the company's operations can be gathered from the size of its permanent subscribed capital, which was £3.5 million. The close relationship between the company and the British government manifested itself not only in the delegation of sovereign powers to the company's settlements in Asia but also in the loan to the Exchequer of its entire trading capital. In return the company received the right to raise an equivalent amount of capital in the London money market through fixed-interest bonds. In the eighteenth century the East India Company took on a triple role: that of trader, banker, and political administrator. The company's naval fleets in the Indian Ocean created a strong political presence and began to eclipse the operations of the VOC. In 1717 the company secured exceptional fiscal treatment in the Mughal empire from the reigning emperor and became as privileged in India as it was in England. The industrial prosperity of large areas of the subcontinent was enhanced by the financial liquidity injected by the East India Company in its purchase of Indian goods.

Beginning in 1740 the British East India Company found itself strongly challenged by the rival French organization, the Compagnie des Indes Orientales, and became involved in local dynastic wars in southern India. In Bengal the attack on Calcutta (1756) by the Maratha nawab Siraj ud-Daulah led to the dispatch of a military expedition under Robert Clive (who had defeated the French at Arcot in 1751) and the revolution of Plassey (1757). In 1765 the East India Company assumed the revenue administration of Bengal in its own name and was able to use public funds to finance its export trade from India. [*See also* Siraj ud-Daulah; Clive, Sir Robert; *and* Plassey, Battle of.]

The company's constitutional position in England was defined by Lord North's Regulating Act (1773) and Pitt's India Act (1784). The Charter Acts of 1813 and 1833 abolished the company's commercial monopoly and its exclusive right to trade. By the beginning of the nineteenth century, the commercial role of the company was far surpassed by its administrative functions. The Revolution of Plassey opened the door to a rapid expansion of the company's military power in India, and through a series of probing expeditions and brief wars the East India Company extended its political frontiers to Delhi by 1804. The downfall of the Maratha empire in 1818 and the annexation of the Punjab in 1849 completed the final shape of the British empire in India.

The real task and the achievement of the East India Company in the last period of its history, however, lay in introducing European civil administration and reorganizing the Indian land system and land taxation on which the government depended for the bulk of its income. In the second half of the eighteenth century, the quality of the company's rule was badly tarnished by the corruption and financial excesses of its servants. The reforms of Lord Cornwallis (1786–1793) in civil administration, in the judiciary, and in the collection of land revenue were the first real initiatives toward a systematic and responsible form of government under the East India Company. The process of modernization continued for the next half century and reached its definitive stage only after the abolition of the company in 1858.

[*See also* India; Dutch East India Company; French East India Company; Governor-General of India; Government of India; Indian Administrative Service; Portuguese: Portuguese in India; *and* Imperialism.]

Kirti N. Chaudhuri, *The English East India Company: The Study of an Early Joint-Stock Company 1600–1640* (1965) and *The Trading World of Asia and the English East India Company 1660–1760* (1978). Kirti N. Chaudhuri, ed., *The Economic Development of India under the East India Company 1814–1858* (1971). Holden Furber, *Rival Empires of Trade in the Orient 1600–1800* (1976). P. J. Marshall, *East Indian Fortunes: The British in Bengal in the Eighteenth Century* (1976). Cyril Henry Philips, *The East India Company 1784–1834* (2d ed., 1961). Lucy S. Sutherland, *The East India Company in Eighteenth-Century Politics* (2d ed., 1962).

K. N. Chaudhuri

EBINA DANJŌ (Kisaburō; 1856–1937), leading Japanese Congregationalist minister and president of Dōshisha University. Ebina was born into a samurai family in Yanagawa on the island of Kyushu. In 1872 he enrolled in the Kumamoto School for Western Learning, where he studied English, mathematics, and science with Captain L. L. Janes. Janes converted him to Christianity, and Ebina was one of thirty-five students who signed the Hanaoka Oath (1876), which constituted modern Japan's first Christian declaration and established the Kumamoto Band.

From 1876 to 1879 Ebina studied in Kyoto at the American Board of Commissioners for Foreign Missions' Kyoto Training School (later Dōshisha University). Here he worked with Niijima Jō, studied in the seminary, and after graduation took a series of local pastorates. In the late 1890s he moved to Tokyo as pastor of the Hongō church and over the next two decades turned this church into one of the leading intellectual centers in the nation's capital. A powerful preacher and compelling thinker, Ebina attracted to his church many of Japan's bright young minds, particularly the younger generation of writers.

Liberal in his Christian theology, Ebina attempted to form a creative mix between Japanese tradition and Christian values. An energetic publicist, writer, and educator, he wrote numerous books, edited and founded the magazine *Shinjin (New Man)*, and from 1920 to 1928 served as president of Dōshisha University.

[*See also* Niijima Jō *and* Christianity: Christianity in Japan.]

F. G. Notehelfer

ECHIGO, premodern Japanese province (modern Sea of Japan coast of Niigata Prefecture) on the northern Honshu. Enchigo was one of the sixty-six provinces created by the Taika Reform of 645. The mountainous region, famed for its heavy snowfalls and remoteness, remained isolated well into the medieval period. During the late Muromachi period (1334–1573), it was the power base of Uesugi Terutora (Kenshin; 1530–1578), one of the most powerful Warring States (Sengoku) daimyo, whose battles with Takeda Shingen (1521–1573) are legendary. During the Tokugawa period (1600–1868) the province was divided among several daimyo, including the Makino *(fudai)* at Nagaoka (with an assessed productivity of 74,000 *koku*, a *koku* being a measure of rice) and the Sakakibara *(fudai)* at Takata (150,000 *koku*). The latter daimyo house was established by Yasumasa (1548–1606), who was in the service of Tokugawa Ieyasu (1542–1616) and whose heirs received the Takata fief in 1741. In the late sixteenth century, the Takata domain, which was then governed by Matsudaira Mitsunaga (1615–1707), a *shinpan* daimyo of some fame and ability, was the scene of a major scandal (the Echigo *sōdō* of 1679–1681) that resulted in the exile of Mitsunaga and the confiscation of his fief because of maladministration and corruption on the part of his advisers.

RONALD J. DICENZO

ECHIZEN, premodern Japanese province (modern Fukui Prefecture) along the Sea of Japan coast of central Honshu. Archaeological evidence indicates early settlement of Echizen. During the late medieval period, Echizen was controlled by Asakura Toshikage (1428–1481), whose castle town at Ichijodani was a cultural center rivaling Kyoto. The Seventeen Article Code attributed to Toshikage is a famous example of the administrative laws promulgated by the Warring States (Sengoku) daimyo. The daimyo Shibata Katsuie (1522?–1583) developed the castle town of Fukui. During the Tokugawa period (1600–1868), Echizen was governed by the *shinpan* (collateral) Matsudaira family; their troubled relations with Edo earned them the name "black sheep of the family." The most famous Matsudaira daimyo was Yoshinaga (Keiei; 1829–1890), who played an important national role during the late Tokugawa period.

Echizen's history is closely connected with Buddhism. Dōgen (1200–1253) founded the great Zen temple of Eiheiji there in 1243. In the fifteenth century, Rennyo (1415–1499) of the True Pure Land Sect (Jōdo Shinshū) established a strong Buddhist religious-political presence in Echizen, which played a part in the Ikkō uprisings *(ikkō-ikki)* that swept the Hokuriku region during the medieval period.

Ceramics distinctive to Echizen have been produced ever since late in the Heian period (794–1185).

[*See also* Ikki *and* Sengoku Period.]

RONALD J. DICENZO

ECONOMIC DEVELOPMENT. Asia encompasses twenty-four autonomous lands where more than 55 percent of the world's people live on less than 17 percent of the world's land area. Together the 2.46 billion people of Asia generated gross national product (GNP) averaging US $840 per capita. The comparable magnitude for the 1.96 billion people outside of Asia is close to $5,600, more than 6.5 times Asia's level. (Data, all for 1980, are based on the World Bank's *World Development Report, 1982*, pp. 110–111.)

There is, of course, great diversity among nations in each of these averages. Thus, Bangladesh and Japan are at opposite ends of the world range of national per capita income levels. A comparable spread exists in the non-Asian world between Zaire, for example, and the United States. But the people of Bangladesh are among the 82 percent of all Asians in the World Bank's low-income category of nations: their average per capita GNP is $260 and their adult literacy rate is 50 percent; Zaire's population is part of but 13 percent of all non-Asian people in this category. The people of Japan alone exhaust Asia's 5 percent in the World Bank's high-income nations: Japan's average per capita GNP is $8,500 and its literacy rate is 99 percent; the US, on the other hand, contributes less than one-fifth of the 62 percent of the non-Asian world in that top category. The World Bank's middle group encompasses the residual 13 percent of Asia's people, predominantly in the lower range of this medium group, and the remaining 25 percent of those outside Asia, mostly Latin American and some African lands higher in the middle-income range. Clearly the wide disparity between the average levels of Asian and non-Asian per capita product in 1980 reflects primarily these marked differences in the distribution of national incomes in the two regions of the world.

Are these disparate records for the two regions in process of change? What does past experience promise for the decades ahead? Comprehensive international data became available around the middle of the twentieth century; the World Bank reported in 1982 that average annual growth rates of per capita GNP were three times as high over the period from 1960 to 1980 in the richer lands than in the low-income nations where most Asians live and work. The development levels in Asia and the rest of the world were thus becoming increasingly disparate in the years until 1980. Modern development doctrine puts increasing emphasis on the role of quality of inputs relative to quantity of inputs in generating growth of economic output per head of population. Expanded quantity of capital inputs relative to expanded levels of the labor force can assure persistent growth of GNP per capita only as administrative, entrepreneurial, and technological skills provide conditions for effective use of capital and labor. Over decades these quality attributes make their key contributions through changes in rates of growth in both population and GNP.

Such persistent expansion involves major shifts over time in the structure of GNP as the relative importance of key sector output changes with national growth. From theory and measurement, a condition for persistent development is that the spread in the relative levels of average product per worker must narrow, especially among such major sectors as agriculture, industry, and services (Kuznets, 1966, pp. 86–126). The process of growth thus poses continuing tasks of adjustment upon labor, capital, and effective public and private leadership; again this is a capability associated with an expanding role of quality inputs in the nation's economy.

Appropriate skills, attitudes, and aspirations of people and of their social, political, and economic organizations are today less prevalent in low-income lands. Meeting human (quality) needs in addition to material (quantity) needs poses a more difficult and more lengthy growth process than obtains in nations with past decades of high and persistent rates of expansion in per capita output. The relevance of a hypothesis of relatively slow economic progress for Asia as a whole is a major theme of this article.

Other Views on the Asian Development Prospect. The majority of United Nations members supports a New International Economic Order (NIEO) to enhance the relative development opportunities of poor lands. Discussions initiated in the United Nations in the early 1970s (*Yearbook of the United Nations, 1974,* vol. 38, pp. 325–332) have yet to generate an accepted NIEO. Relevant international conferences (the Williamsburg Virginia Summit of seven major world industrial powers, May 1983; the Belgrade Yugoslavia UN Conference on Trade and Development, June 1983) may have served to formalize contrasting poor nation/rich nation views on growth programs in the world's poor lands. NIEO advocates tend to focus principally on the role of expanded material inputs for more rapid economic growth; such a view counters the hypothesis posed above.

Some academic reports and ongoing economic programs do visualize relatively favorable Asian development prospects over future decades and a next century that is Asian in contrast to past centuries, when nations of Europe and the West were the economic and political world leaders. An "East Asia Edge" speared by Japan is in operation today. The enduring "newly industrializing countries" (the so-called NICs of today's less-developed lands) are Asian—Hong Kong, Korea, Singapore, and Taiwan—in contrast to important non-Asian NICs (Brazil, Mexico), where economic progress now seems much less assured. In the early 1980s economic experts outside China shared the view of top government officials of the People's Republic that China can expect to emerge as one of the world's top five industrial superpowers by the year 2000. Indeed both China and India are widely acclaimed for the high priority they give their development programs. Both identify with the NIEO effort. Together the two nations contain more than 75 percent of the people in the World Bank's low-income category and close to 70 percent of the total population of Asia. Impressive developmental achievement in China or India (and more so in both) could thus significantly increase Asia's overall rate of economic growth in future decades.

Judgments on Asia's economic development record and potential must mesh with the comprehensive detail available on the world's economies for the decades since 1950. But they must also mesh with modern interpretations of the longer-period growth experiences of the world's regions and nations. Given the multidisciplinary dimension in the economic development process, what guides emerge for Asia in historical analysis of man's advancement in the world from ancient times?

Ancient Roots. In the ten thousand years since man began to adapt the environment to serve his evolving sense of personal, familial, and societal well-being, there has been, as Douglas North put it, "an endless parade of kingdoms, empires and whole civilizations appearing and then disappearing." The emergence of an Egyptian empire with a centralized government by the start of the second millennium

BCE offers some insights into man's progress in life expectancy, in economic activity, and in the diversity of output and trade up to that time. A millennium later the Persian empire emerged preeminent among the powers of the classical world. It was centered in western Asia and comprised a diverse and decentralized collection of twenty satrapies stretching from the Aegean Sea to beyond the Indus River, where sophisticated urban societies such as Mohenjo-Daro were flourishing in 2500 BCE. Persian power retained control over these reasonably autonomous units, providing military and other public services and collecting taxes and tribute appropriate to each region's wealth and importance—in large flows of gold dust from India, for example. [*See also* Achaemenid Dynasty.]

Persia's dominance of the ancient world passed to Greece in 331 BCE through achievement in Athens of political discipline and organization (and the military effectiveness of Alexander the Great). Gradually, Greek rule merged with ascendant Roman power. In its long history the Roman empire appears to have achieved unique efficiencies in forms of government and of productive organizations, military and civilian. Roman citizens may have attained new world heights of average product per person, and the disintegration of that empire in the fifth and sixth centuries of the common era created, according to North, "perhaps the most striking watershed that exists in economic history." Not until about 1500 did man's understanding of technical, societal, and institutional relationships again permit the emergence of nations capable of long-term growth in political and economic power. It was an understanding acquired slowly and painfully over some five centuries of social and economic reorganizations, as varied forms of feudalism flourished and faded in regions of western Europe.

Medieval Roots. Political and economic ties between West and East were established in ancient times: Rome's ships sailed the Red Sea to India; its merchants reached China by sea in 166 CE. In the centuries after the fall of Rome, exchanges began to flow from the East. The mechanics of predominantly overland routes served integration of cultural, religious, and political forces, as well as the exchange of economic goods and services. Such is the legacy of the art produced from the seventh through the seventeenth century in the Buddhist monasteries of the trans-Himalayan regions of North India and along trade routes into Central Asia. Merchants in caravans plying this luxury trade on a complex of routes between China, India, and the Mediterranean world (collectively known as the Silk Route) found rest and relaxation in the monasteries. They helped finance the spread of monastery construction along the trade routes as well as supporting those with artistic talent in the monastic orders. As meeting points for travelers from diverse parts of the world, the monasteries became centers of political and cultural force as well as economic and religious force. They spread religion, material goods, and political power. [*See also* Roman Empire *and* Silk Route.]

The medieval period shows "asianization" effects in Europe, noteworthy not only in expensive fabrics and exotic spices for luxury consumption but also in the transfers of inventions and technological achievements from East Asia—paper, printing, the wheelbarrow, the crossbow, canal lock-gates, gunpowder, the compass, and more (to say nothing of the effects of the Mongol invasions of eastern Europe in the thirteenth century). Scholars have judged these westward movements more important than the reverse eastward flows of that time. Thus, "China under the Sung (10th–14th century) was a far greater civilization, in both size and accomplishment, than its contemporary, medieval Europe." In the sixteenth century payments from the West may have reflected the booty of Europe's adventures in America more than its crafts and skills. If such Asian predominance emerged, however, it was short-lived. By the eighteenth century the Industrial Revolution provided Europe with technical and scientific bases for exploration and exploitation in Europe and abroad, for trade and settlement in the Americas as well as in Asia. Primarily, however, European lands entered the modern era with new expectations and rules of human interrelations, with new attitudes of mind—self-confidence, independence, spiritual vigor, quality—prerequisite to the realization by any nation of its technical and material potential.

Western pressures on Asia in the sixteenth and seventeenth centuries had economic, political, cultural, and religious frontiers. The military and industrial eminence of the West was overwhelming; Asia had to cope at least by adopting technically superior goods from abroad. But the dynamics of change also required organizational and attitudinal adaptations. Here the civilizations of Asia coped in differing ways and less well on the whole.

Modern Growth. Opportunities for Asian contact with the West did expand rapidly beginning about 1500. Trade and proselytism from the West found root in both China and Japan. The power of Ming China's rulers was in decline during the sixteenth century, however, and Japan experienced prolonged civil strife. The pressures from the West accentuated Asia's relative weakness. Eventually the emergence of Tokugawa power in Japan and Manchu control in China brought dramatic change; Western economic involvement became quiescent for some two hundred years, until the middle of the nineteenth century.

This long isolation confined direct European participation in East and Southeast Asian economies to Indonesia (Dutch), the Philippines (Spanish), Macao (Portuguese), and Canton (British). It left Japan and China far behind Europe in the technology of industry, to say nothing of the motivational drive for modern economic progress. Rather, both Asian nations tended to rest at ease with relative self-sufficiency in production and with strong and traditional social and family order. It was an environment in dramatic contrast to the aggressive drives of European nations and the United States, riding high in their expanding economic and political potential elsewhere in the world. With changed regimes in China and Japan the door sprung open in the nineteenth century to new opportunities for Western establishment and trade in these major lands of Asia.

The Meiji Restoration in 1868 laid foundations for Japan's entrance into the modern growth patterns of Western countries. The shift from very low levels of well-being per person to its high status today—the only success story of the modern growth epoch—took about a century of time, several important changes in government leadership, plus a major period of foreign occupation. It also involved a program of development priorities relatively unique in modern poor-land growth efforts. It emphasized increases in productivity of rural labor and marked domestic consumption gains before its modernizing industry became an important exporter. The key government objective in the process, according to Japanese scholars, was to "move the population out of feudalism" and to "marry Confucian doctrine to the ethos of a capitalist society." Such institutional and attitudinal goals were facilitated by Japan's common language and an educational heritage that emphasized the philosophical and social dimensions of Confucianism rather than its religious appeal. By 1930 Japan's national product was growing at world-record levels—some sixty years after the Restoration began.

The industrial push of the 1950s associated with the creation of modern Japan was preconditioned by the economic, social, and psychological ingredients of Japan's development programs of the nineteenth century. Japan certainly provides a showpiece of Western-type growth in Asia, but it scarcely offers a readily duplicable or easy model.

China's development experience from a comparable economic status about a century ago was extremely different. In the nineteenth century it experienced neither the dynamic force of a progress-oriented central authority nor cumulative benefits from active participation by foreign economic and governmental interests. Included here are the direct occupation of Manchuria and Taiwan by Japan with positive consequences—true also in Korea—for later economic growth in these areas. A turbulent century without economic progress in China ended with revolution and the establishment in 1949 of the People's Republic of China. The official and broadly accepted expert view is that the Communist regime mastered the tools for economic expansion, albeit in a non-Western tradition. Available data showed that for the period 1950 to 1980, China's economic development, measured in the growth rate either of per capita GNP or of modern industrialization, was without any near competitors among poor lands.

India, the second most populous world nation, progressed in reasonable parallel with China from the fourteenth to the mid-twentieth century. Like China and Japan, India was a magnet for commercial interests of the West in the early part of this long period; by 1950, however, India joined China among the world's lowest per capita income lands, despite the early economic, cultural, and intellectual eminence of both nations. Through long periods India's most powerful rulers were not native to the subcontinent: Turkic rulers became important after the twelfth century; Britain's influence took prime place in the nineteenth century, eventually reducing India to colonial status for almost one hundred years, until 1947. This situation is in sharp contrast with China's independent status, but this did not dictate a contrast in economic progress. It is true that the two lands were reasonably comparable in material endowments relative to large populations. What is more important is that neither nation could long muster enough of the human quality input that was essential for effective use of its rich material endowments in a continuing development process.

As in China after its internal revolution, independent India mounted a major economic development effort in the 1950s with tasks and goals parallel to China's, but with very different tools of implementation. In India parliamentary processes and private market decisions persisted; China's economy was conducted through the decrees and controls of its new Communist bureaucracy. Official, broadly accepted records from India show less than one-third the annual rate of growth of GNP per capita revealed in data for China over the decades to 1980.

For both nations, with more than two-thirds of Asia's people, and for the remaining twenty-two nations in Asia, there does exist from official sources and academic research a considerable volume of relevant economic measures for parts of the period 1800 to 1950. No major regional component of Asia other than Japan has yet amassed the economic advantages of even a half-century of persistent economic output expansion relative to population growth. For the almost two hundred years since the mid-eighteenth century, therefore, the broad trend of modern development shows an Asia (excluding Japan) that grew less affluent relative to the trend of per capita real product elsewhere, particularly relative to economic development in Europe and the areas of European settlement in America and Oceania.

The Prospect. This summary account of relative progress in Asia and in the rest of the world from ancient to modern times is broadly supportive of a multidisciplinary theoretical framework of growth of economic power: quality inputs are prerequisite to effective use of expanding quantity of inputs. Reasonable facts from the late 1700s to the mid-1900s support the relative gains in average per capita product in the non-Asian lands; a similar conclusion was drawn on the basis of the comprehensive real measures available in the decades since 1950. Thus, theory, history, and reality prompt little expectation of significant realignment in the relative position of Asia over the decades ahead.

The modern development experiences of India and China and their growth expectations might seem to indicate a more optimistic view of Asia's prospects. Given their preponderance in Asian population, the growth record reported for China alone might itself alter Asia's relative position for the next decades, as for the next century. It is important to note, however, that the recent China-India contrasts cited above are today in the process of reappraisal. Thus, the World Bank's initial *Development Reports,* until the 1979 issue, did portray striking specific differences in relative achievement over decades: GNP annual growth rates of 7.1 percent for China and 3.5 percent for India, and comparable per capita GNP levels in China in 1976 and 1977 that were more than 2.5 times India's level (from the essential equality of the two in 1950). Since 1979 the World Bank's annual reports have continuously narrowed this real comparison. By the end of 1983 India's per capita GNP was listed at 87 percent of the comparable measure for China; this is against the 38 percent ratio in the 1979 report. Moreover, the altered relationship in this four-year interval must be attributed to changes in the Chinese experience; the average per capita growth rate of India's GNP has remained essentially unchanged in these years. Indeed, persisting relative levels of real GNP per capita in the two lands to date (1987) makes clear that annual growth rates are not appreciably different in India and China.

Recent research, which focused on comparative structural change in the total growth experience of China and India, also suggests parallels rather than contrasts in overall growth in recent decades, and perhaps also greater future growth potential in India than in China. In both lands the per capita product of some 80 percent of the population has since 1950 become more separated from the much higher per capita product of the remaining 20 percent. As argued earlier, persistent long-term economic advance has been associated with structural readjustments that serve to narrow the gaps in levels of output per worker between major sectors of an economy. Such adjustments are associated with the process of relative expansion in human quality inputs in the development effort.

This process began to be manifest in western Europe before the Industrial Revolution as feudal societies were displaced over centuries. In Japan the critical changes were initiated by the Meiji rulers and furthered during the Allied Occupation after World War II. In Korea, Taiwan, and perhaps other NICs of Asia, these narrowing ratios of sectoral per capita GNP may be the result of Japan's influence early in the present century. The present contrasting position in both China and India suggests that persistent growth in both lands still remains in an early stage.

In a world now struggling to emerge from severe and regionally imbalanced stagnation, the Japanese economy seems assured of continued progress. Japan's prospect is apt not to differ much from the favorable outlook now visualized for the major industrial powers in the world. Such recovery must gradually benefit the less-developed lands. But neither trade and aid gains nor, indeed, any specific programs of NIEO can assure the major structural changes required for any continuous path of economic expansion in the poor nations of the world. The essential tasks involve the capacity to organize a scale of quality inputs that will assure the continuing structural shifts of an economy in progress.

In sum, then, the outlook remains the persistence,

if not accentuation, of the wide average difference between the economic state of Asia and the rest of the world as regions. The heterogeneity of each permits scope for progress in Japan and perhaps in other Asian lands already well along in their structural readjustment. While it also permits short-term gains for individual Third World lands for special resource and skill reasons, even nations that have shown some evidence of modernization over past decades, such as Indonesia, Iran, Pakistan, the Philippines, and Sri Lanka, are at best beginning to establish the conditions for persistent growth.

John K. Fairbank, Edwin O. Reischauer, and Albert M. Craig, *East Asia: The Modern Transformation,* vol. 2 (1965). Dharma Kumar and Meghnad Desai, eds., *The Cambridge Economic History of India,* vol. 2 (1983), chap. 4. Simon Kuznets, *Modern Economic Growth* (1966). Wilfred Malenbaum, "Modern Economic Growth in India and China: The Comparison Revisited," *Economic Development and Cultural Change* 31.1 (October 1982): 45–84, 34.1 (October 1985): 163–166. Douglas C. North, *Structure and Change in Economic History* (1981). Edwin O. Reischauer and John K. Fairbank, *East Asia: The Great Civilization,* 2 vols. (1958–1960). World Bank, *World Bank Development Report, 1982* (1982), and *World Bank Development Report, 1986* (1986).

WILFRED MALENBAUM

EDEN MISSION, a mission led by Ashley Eden to Bhutan in 1863. After a series of border raids by the Bhutanese, the government of India sent Eden to Bhutan to negotiate an agreement. Eden arrived in Punakha on 18 March 1864 and was immediately made captive, subjected to personal insults, and forced to sign a treaty. He escaped through the town of Paro, and in his report of 1864 gave a full account of his mission. The Bhutanese version of these events is still to be researched. In 1865 hostilities broke out between the British and the Bhutanese, and in January 1866 the Bhutanese signed a treaty, ceding the eleven *duars,* or passes, leading into Bengal and surrendering the document that Eden had been forced to sign.

THEODORE RICCARDI, JR.

EDO, seat of the Tokugawa *bakufu* from 1603, political capital of early modern Japan, and predecessor of modern Tokyo, as the city was renamed in 1868. For much of its history, Edo was the world's largest city, and it served as a powerful engine of economic and cultural change during the Tokugawa era (1600–1868), commonly known as the "Edo period."

The site of Edo lies at a strategic point in the Kantō Plain, on the east side of the Sumida River as it flows into Edo (today Tokyo) Bay. The word *Edo* probably means "head of the inlet," referring to the shallow Hibiya inlet, which extended about a mile inland just west of the mouth of the Sumida. The inlet was later filled in to provide the land that today underlies the Marunouchi business distict and the Imperial Palace plaza.

This site at a strategic transport node explains the choice of Edo as a military fortification in the early twelfth century by Edo Shigenaga, leader of a military clan of Minamoto descent that took its name from the place. The Edo clan established itself as a powerful local family in medieval times, but the immediate area appears to have been little more than a fortified outpost.

Edo became more widely known in the Muromachi period, following the building of a substantial castle in 1456–1457 by Ōta Dōkan (1432–1486), a famous military lord of the times who as a vassal of the Uesugi clan came to control much of the Kantō region. After Dōkan's death, however, the castle fell into disrepair and the settlement waned.

Following the defeat in 1590 of the Hōjō clan at its castle in Odawara, control of the Kantō Plain was given by the victorious Hideyoshi to his vassal Tokugawa Ieyasu in exchange for the former domain of Suruga. Ieyasu promptly chose Edo rather than Odawara as the capital of his new domain, and he entered the castle on the auspicious day of the autumn harvest, the first day of the eighth month.

Ieyasu immediately undertook the repair and expansion of Edo Castle, which by this time was little more than some earthen walls surrounding a handful of thatched buildings. A new city was sited according to the principles of Chinese geomancy, and a commoners' settlement was laid out below the castle to the west in regular blocks of 121 meters (398 feet) square with a large open space in the middle (in time to be built over). In its first decade, however, Edo was less a city than a large military camp in the midst of a cluster of peasant villages. It was only with Ieyasu's victory at the Battle of Sekigahara in 1600 and his subsequent assumption of the title of shogun in 1603 that Edo began its rapid evolution into a huge national capital.

From as early as 1602, when two of the great daimyo paid formal visits to the Tokugawa castle, a pattern was set whereby the lords (daimyo) not only visited Edo regularly but also maintained large mansions in the city as the permanent residences of members of their families, whose presence in the city served to guarantee the loyalty of the daimyo. Although not to be formalized for over three decades, this pattern of daimyo presence in Edo was essential to the city's growth.

The daimyo presence was also demanded by the vast and ambitious program of building that Ieyasu initiated after assuming the title of shogun. From 1603 until 1640, under the first three shoguns, the city was constantly under construction, much of it achieved with labor and material requisitioned from the great daimyo. One of the first steps was to level Kanda Mountain to the north, which provided the earth with which to fill in the Hibiya inlet. This enabled a far larger commoners' district, which would come to be known as the Shitamachi, or the "city below [the castle]." Its center was Nihonbashi, a bridge from which the major highways extended north and south. Near Nihonbashi lay the Edo fish market and the establishments of many of the wealthiest merchants and financiers.

Subsequent construction created a large and elaborate system of moats lined with stone walls, which came to establish a rough spiral shape for the city, moving counterclockwise from the Shitamachi around in two diminishing loops into the center of the castle itself. The huge stones needed for the building of the castle walls were taken from quarries on the Izu Peninsula and were transported in boats provided by the daimyo.

Construction continued after Ieyasu's death in 1616 under his son Hidetada and his grandson Iemitsu. The crowning achievement was the construction of the great donjon *(tenshukaku)* of Edo Castle, which at 59 meters (192 feet) was the tallest ever built in Japan. This imposing five-story tower, with its elaborate gilded trim, was a fitting symbol of the power of the shogun.

By the time of the completion of the castle in 1640, the earlier pattern of periodic voluntary visits to Edo by the daimyo had been formalized into the compulsory system of *sankin kōtai,* whereby almost all of the two-hundred-odd feudal lords were required to keep their families in Edo as hostages, and themselves to spend every other year in the city in attendance on the shogun. The system was in effective operation by the time of Ieyasu's death in 1616, although it was not formalized, with prescribed one-year stays, until 1635.

The *sankin kōtai* was critical in determining the size and character of Edo. Without the daimyo presence Edo would probably have been less than half its actual size, although, as capital of the shogunal realm, it would still have been the largest city in Tokugawa Japan. Each daimyo maintained at least two mansions in the city, one the permanent residence of the consort and heir and the other for the semiannual visits of the daimyo himself. Following the Meireki Fire of 1657, a third mansion, normally in a suburban location, was required as a place of refuge in case of fire. The daimyo properties thus covered over one-half of the total area of the city, and the consumption demands of their population constituted a critical factor in the economic well-being of Edo.

Edo for its first half-century was a characteristic boomtown: rough and rowdy, with a heavily male population, as was well reflected in the flourishing Yoshiwara prostitution quarter. Many of the merchants and artisans were immigrants from eastern Japan, particularly Kyoto, and what higher culture there was in early Edo was largely transplanted from elsewhere. Economically, as well, Edo's own Kantō hinterland was relatively backward, and the city relied heavily on supplies from western Japan via Osaka, the "pantry of Japan."

A major turning point in Edo's history came with the Meireki Fire of 1657, which destroyed over two-thirds of the city, including most of Edo Castle and hundreds of temples, shrines, and daimyo mansions. The *bakufu* perceived that overcrowding had encouraged the rapid spread of the fire and in its aftermath carried out a wide variety of reforms to relieve the congestion. Daimyo mansions were excluded from the inner area of Edo castle, temples were relocated from the center to the edge of town, and commoners' residences were demolished to provide firebreaks. [*See* Meireki Fire.]

Edo after the Meireki Fire was more spacious but in certain ways less impressive. The great donjon of Edo Castle was not rebuilt, and the daimyo were prohibited from rebuilding in the ornate Momoyama style, with heavy use of gilt and carved ornament, which had typified their mansions before the fire. Display turned indoors, into the theater district and the Yoshiwara pleasure quarters that formed the center of Edo culture in the Genroku era (1688–1704). [*See* Genroku Culture.]

The fire seems to have scarcely slowed the growth of the city's population, which continued to swell in the prosperous period of rebuilding that followed. Unfortunately, no reliable evidence survives for Edo's population before 1721, when the first official enumeration revealed a population of 501,394 commoners (of whom 64 percent were male). Regular counts thereafter showed a slight decline in the course of the eighteenth century and a slight rise again in the early nineteenth, but the overall pattern was one of stability. The most significant change in the population of Edo commoners occurred rather in the sex ratio, which had reached equality by the 1860s.

These figures exclude, however, large segments of the population, so that it is impossible to know the total population of Edo with any accuracy. To the above numbers must be added, for example, some 50,000 priests, outcastes, and members of other nonenumerated categories. The biggest imponderable, however, is the samurai population, which for reasons of both status and security was kept secret. Scattered evidence suggests that the direct retainers of the shogun numbered between 200,000 and 300,000 (including servants and dependents, the most difficult segment to estimate), while the population of the daimyo establishments was between 400,000 and 500,000, for a total population of Edo of 1.1 to 1.3 million. This figure is considered to have changed little after the 1720s and is the basis for considering Edo the world's largest city in the eighteenth century: Beijing was then about 800,000, while London's population, the highest in Europe, did not pass one million until after 1800.

The government of Edo was complex and divided into a number of independent jurisdictions. The land inhabited by the samurai, which accounted for close to 70 percent of the area of the city, was officially under the control of *bakufu* inspectors *(metsuke)*, although in practice the daimyo mansions enjoyed a kind of extraterritorial immunity. Temple and shrine lands, covering 16 percent of the city, were under the shrine and temple magistrates *(jisha bugyō)*, while the remaining 16 percent, occupied by the commoners, was under the authority of the town magistrates *(machi bugyō)*.

It was the administration of the commoners' land that constituted the major task of governance in Edo, and in this area there evolved the most complex institutions. The town magistrates were generally two in number and were shogunal retainers of *fudai* daimyo rank, serving in monthly rotation from separate offices ("north" and "south"). The town magistrates were responsible for public order and for the administration of justice among the commoners, and they maintained a modest police force also drawn from the ranks of shogunal retainers.

Below the town magistrates were a hierarchy of commoner officials, who constituted a narrowly circumscribed system of autonomous internal governance. At the top were three hereditary "town elders" *(machi toshiyori)*, and below them some 250 "headmen" (*machi nanushi,* a post which by the late Edo period could be purchased), each of whom was responsible for a number of *chō*, the "wards" that were the basic units of local autonomy in Edo. The *chō* numbered some 1,700 throughout the latter part of the Tokugawa period, with an average population of eighty households each.

Within the *chō*, only those owning land had the rights—and the obligations—of involvement in urban governance. This landlord class constituted 14 percent of all household heads in the commoner population of Edo, although its authority extended in practice to the *yamori* ("housewatchers"), a peculiar class, about equal in number to the landlords, who superintended the landlords' rental properties. These superintendents, popularly known as *ōya*, were organized into five-man groups *(goningumi)* that were held mutually responsible for any infractions of the law committed by their tenants.

During the second half of the Tokugawa period, Edo became less and less dependent on western Japan, although contact among the three great cities of Kyoto, Osaka, and Edo, if anything, increased, thanks to increased travel by all classes. Economically, Edo's huge population was a constant stimulus to the rapid agricultural and commercial growth of its Kantō hinterland, which came to supply more and more of the city's needs.

Culturally, as well, Edo began in the eighteenth century to evolve a distinctive culture of its own, wholly separate from developments in Kyoto or Osaka, and in time this became the dominant cultural force within the nation as a whole. From the 1760s onward, Edo's influence was spread through literature, particularly popular fiction and comic verse, and through the multicolored woodblock prints *(ukiyo-e)* that were made in growing numbers in Edo after 1764. From the late eighteenth century there emerged the image of the "Edokko" ("child of Edo"), the fast-talking, easy-spending, stylish figure who was Edo's counterpart to London's cockney.

Edo popular culture reached its peak in the early nineteenth century, particularly in the prosperous and peaceful years of the Bunka-Bunsei eras (1804–1830). Publishing of all types flourished with the growth of literacy, and popular pastimes of all sorts, from the tea ceremony and incense sniffing to samisen performance and the cultivation of exotic plants, spread rapidly to the middle classes of both samurai and commoner society. These influences spread in turn, by way of travel, commerce, and *sankin kōtai* processions, throughout the country, so that it seems possible to speak of the "edoization" of Japanese culture at large.

Edo had a good share of physical and social problems. Fire continued to be a constant threat, with major conflagrations striking the city about a dozen times in the course of its history. Although none of the later fires exacted as high a toll in lives and property as the Meireki Fire of 1657, the cumulative price was very high. In time, however, the population seems to have become resigned to the frequency of fires, which were even greeted with a certain festive sense of renewal. Rebuilding in the wake of fire was remarkably fast and efficient and brought prosperity to those in the building trades.

Edo was also faced with a variety of social problems, particularly that of urban poverty. The stereotype of the carefree Edokko artisan, happy to "spend all his wages in a single night," belied the reality of a large and persistent underclass in Edo. The suffering was most acute in times of famine, when the numbers of the poor were swelled by rural refugees. The great Temmei famine led to serious riots in Edo in 1787, protests against high prices, and hoarding of rice by merchants. Similar disturbances were avoided in the Tempō famine of the 1830s, thanks in part to relief anxiously provided by the government and by wealthy merchants and landlords.

The coming of Commodore Matthew C. Perry in 1853 and the subsequent opening of the country to international trade marked the start of a period of rapid change for Edo. The opening in 1859 of the port of Yokohama severely disrupted traditional patterns of commerce in Edo and its hinterland and triggered an inflationary spiral that was further aggravated by the tumultuous political events of the 1860s, leading finally to widespread rioting in the late summer of 1867. [*See* Perry, Matthew C.]

The event that most profoundly changed Edo, however, was the relaxation of the *sankin kōtai* regulations in 1862, creating an exodus of as many as 200,000 domain samurai and depriving the city of an important source of income. The commoner population nevertheless appears to have remained stable until the eve of the Meiji Restoration. In the course of 1868, however, with the collapse of the *bakufu,* there followed a far larger drop in population as many of the shogunal retainers fled and substantial numbers of commoners evacuated the city for fear of civil war. The designation of Edo as the new imperial capital in September 1868 opened a new chapter in the city's history.

[*See also* Tokugawa Period *and* Tokyo.]

William Coaldrake, "Edo Architecture and Tokugawa Law," *Monumenta Nipponica,* 36.3 (1981): 235–284. Gilbert Rozman, "Edo's Importance in the Changing Japanese Society," *Journal of Japanese Studies* 1.1 (1974): 91–112. Takeo Yazaki, *Social Change and the City in Japan* (1968).

HENRY D. SMITH II

EDUCATION

EDUCATION IN IMPERIAL CHINA

In traditional China, the condition of education—the nature of curricula, the organization of institutions of learning, and the proper pursuits of students—was regarded as a correct and important concern of the state, just as the condition of the state was a proper and important concern of the educator. Both the institutions and the content of education in China must be evaluated in terms of this symbiosis.

Educational Institutions. Although there were, no doubt, institutions of primary education in imperial China, for the most part the tasks of learning to write the first several thousand characters and to read classical literature for the first time were carried out in the home, under the guidance of family members or hired tutors. While the arrangements for such education were obviously varied, a common curriculum, at least in the later imperial period, would have included the *Three Character Classic,* the *Hundred Names,* and the *Thousand Character Classic.* As Evelyn S. Rawski has noted, the main purpose of these three texts was to introduce students to characters: "Emphasis was put on the recognition of characters rather than complete understanding, and interest was a secondary consideration." The *Hundred Names* was simply a list of surnames found in China, most of which were characters in fairly common use. Still, even texts of primary education could subtly convey political and social messages. The *Three Character Classic* was organized in short, easily memorizable three-character sentences, and its text was divided into subsections entitled "Man's Original Nature," "Duty to Parents," and "Advice as to Learning and Diligence." At least some versions of the *Three Character Classic* contained a summary of Chinese history, from which one might draw correct lessons about political conduct and attitudes. Attitudes toward authority in general, as well as conceptions of specific figures of authority, were reinforced by sacrifices to clan ancestors or to Chinese political sages that often opened the day at clan and village schools.

The finer honing of expository and analytical skills was likely to have taken place, at least after the Song dynasty (960–1279), in an academy *(shuyuan).* These institutions, inspired perhaps by the model of the Buddhist monastery but Confucian in tone and often the recipients of official patronage, were founded as early as the late Tang dynasty but reached their apogee in the Southern Song and Ming dynasties. While much of the training they provided focused on preparing students for the official examinations, the academies were one of the few institutions in Chinese society in which the importance of education in the spiritual life of the individual, as well as its role in the political life of the state, was recognized. Zhu Xi, whose "Articles of Instruction at Bailudong Academy" formed the basis for the regulations of most academies in later imperial China, saw academies both as places for the inculcation of proper values and as institutional vehicles for the advancement of his own Neo-Confucian conception of Chinese learning.

The use of academies as centers for the development of independent intellectual visions became particularly pronounced in the Ming dynasty (1368–1644), when the practice of education came under the influence of the thought of Wang Yangming. Wang wrote that students were like plants beginning to sprout: "If they are allowed to grow freely, they will develop smoothly. If twisted and interfered with, they will wither and decline." Of course, as John Meskill has pointed out, for Wang Yangming students were like "plants in a garden, not in the wild," and even at the most liberal of Ming academies, education would strike the modern observer as heavily structured and examination-oriented. Still, there existed within Wang Yangming's educational framework a potential for intellectual development outside the political order. Partly because of this orientation, but also because Ming academies became associated with political factionalism, they fell into disfavor in the late Ming dynasty.

Early rulers of the Qing dynasty (1644–1911) viewed academies with extreme suspicion, even refusing in some cases to sanction the appointment of directors for major academies. As the Qing became more secure both politically and socially, new regulations for academies were promulgated (1733) in which students were given official stipends in return for strict conformance with government regulations. With this financial support, and with increasing subventions from China's growing commercial elite, academies began to function again in the late eighteenth and early nineteenth centuries, although they never again attained the political importance they had had in the sixteenth century.

The highest center of learning in the empire was a national university, known by various names but established as early as the second century BCE in the capital. During Han times (206 BCE–220 CE) the Taixue, as it was then called, was quite a lively center of intellectual life with professors or "erudites" *(boshi)* established for each of the Confucian classics. As the interpretation of the Confucian texts and their role in the education process became more established, the national university became more of a finishing school where would-be bureaucrats developed the skills of factional maneuver and ideological debate so necessary to service in government. In Ming and Qing times, the Guozijian took on some of the work of editing imperial publications and advising the emperor on matters of text.

The Examination System. The traditional Chinese educational system culminated in the civil service examination system. Although the idea of testing literary ability as a means of determining fitness for political office was a very old one in China, the actual arrangements for testing underwent many changes as the Chinese conception of political power and its relation to social structure has evolved. The Tang dynasty (618–907) combined a system of recommendations with recognition of hereditary status and examinations to select its bureaucracy. Moreover, the Tang examination system recognized a variety of skills with separate tests in law, history, classics, and even mathematics, although they did not lead to high office. Alternative methods for recruitment continued during the Song dynasty, but gradually, through the active encouragement of the central government, the taking of civil service degrees and particularly the doctorate in letters became the favored route to office of successful bureaucrats. The Yuan dynasty saw the classical commentaries of the Neo-Confucian school enthroned as the basic texts for the examination system.

The examination system of the Ming and Qing dynasties is most often taken as the prototypical Chinese civil service testing system. The examinations in the Ming and Qing dynasties were of one type, all examinations other than those leading to the doctorate in letters having atrophied. There were, however, many more examinations in Ming and Qing times than in earlier dynasties; the successful Qing candidate had to undergo some fourteen tests that, if taken consecutively, would have required over three months to complete. The process is usually represented as having three stages. In the first, involving at least three examinations usually held in district or prefectural capitals, the candidate received his *xiucai* degree and status as a *shengyuan,* or district student. The second stage also involved three tests, these held in provincial capitals.

Success on the provincial examinations, by all accounts the hardest to pass, theoretically entitled the candidate to hold office, although few who held only the second degree were actually appointed to office. The third level of examinations was held in the national capital and ultimately culminated in the Palace Examinations held within the Forbidden City. Passing this examination was tantamount to being admitted to the bureaucratic elite. According to one poet, the four greatest moments in a man's life were sweet rain after a long drought, meeting a friend after a long separation, one's wedding night, and seeing one's name on the golden placard that listed the successful candidates on the capital examination.

Perhaps better than any other institution of Chinese education, the examination system embodied the symbiosis between education and politics in China, for as each stage in the process tested more rigorously the candidate's knowledge of the complex and allusive language of the Chinese classics, it testified to his eminence over a wider geographical area and qualified him for a higher political office. The actual moment of the examinations was one of great political and psychological gravity; students were ushered into the examination hall with pomp and ceremony, and sacrifices were offered to the gods of war and of literature. Any breach of examination decorum could have serious consequences for student and examiner alike, and boycotts of the examinations by members of the local elite were an important mode of political protest throughout the imperial period. Not surprisingly, in view of the pressure almost everyone felt about the examination process, the examination compound was the scene of many outbursts of "madness," and the testing process has produced a lively tradition of ghost literature.

The questions on the imperial examinations were not meant to test general knowledge; in fact, only a small proportion of the corpus of knowledge made its way onto the tests. An enormous catalog of books extant in China, issued under imperial patronage in 1782, divided the world of Chinese learning into four categories: classics, history, philosophy, and belles lettres. In most general terms, the classics division included the works of those regarded as sages in the Chinese tradition, and the exegetical and interpretive traditions that had grown up around them—statements, couched in highly metaphorical form, of the ideals of Chinese society. The history section was composed of discussions of the Chinese past often implicitly addressed to the question of how well a given era or person had lived up to the ideals of the classics. Under philosophy were classified works of what might be called general knowledge, books on agriculture, medicine, and the like. Belles lettres contained works of China's literary tradition.

The questions of the examination system tested primarily the candidates' knowledge of the classics: by far the majority of questions on the tests required the candidate to reproduce or explicate classical passages. Historical knowledge was tested as well, although not as thoroughly, in the required essays on law and current affairs. A solid grounding in literature was necessary to write the poetry that the examinations demanded. In contrast, the category of philosophy hardly appeared on the tests at all. Many have argued that the examination system therefore represented a brake on China's intellectual development, turning the most creative Chinese minds away from the future toward the past and the ideals it was said to embody. This argument is not supported by the evidence provided by the 1782 catalog, however, in which the philosophy section was the largest; philosophy also represented the fastest-growing area of knowledge at the time. But the content of the imperial examinations probably was a fair indication of the amount of time and energy Chinese devoted to their political order and the sacrifices they were willing to make to maintain and participate in it.

[*See also* Confucianism *and* Neo-Confucianism.]

John Meskill, *Academies in Ming China: A Historical Essay* (1982). Ichisada Miyazaki, *China's Examination Hell,* translated by Conrad Schirokauer (1976). Evelyn S. Rawski, *Education and Popular Literacy in Ch'ing China* (1978).

R. KENT GUY

EDUCATION IN TWENTIETH-CENTURY CHINA

Education in China at the turn of the twentieth century was in a state of flux. The old civil service examination system, which for centuries had determined the content of learning and provided impetus for tens of thousands of scholars, was still in effect. In addition, modern educational institutions, teaching foreign languages and science, had been established as early as 1860 in response to the Western imperialist challenge to the old Confucian order.

In 1901 the emperor issued a proclamation establishing a Western-style imperial university in Beijing and ordering all provinces to convert their *shuyuan* (provincial colleges) into modern institutions modeled after the one in the capital. In 1903 a special commission on education drew up a detailed plan for a modern school system from kindergarten through graduate school. The central government would take the lead by establishing model schools for the provinces and localities to emulate. The curriculum at every level, as in the traditional education system, was designed on the premise that inculcation of moral values is the principal objective of education, but the inclusion of such values as patriotism and physical culture was new.

By 1905 the acute contradictions between the old system of learning and the new would no longer permit compromise and accommodation. The civil service examination system, a cornerstone of cultural continuity and political stability for a thousand years, was removed. Six years later, the imperial edifice that it supported collapsed. A new Ministry of Education was created in 1905 to implement the 1903 plan replacing the old Board of Rites *(libu)*, which was formerly responsible for scholarship. By 1910 there were 52,650 modern schools with 1,625,534 students, according to government records. Geographical distribution was very uneven, and only a small percentage of school-age children attended in any location, but a start had been made. One of the most radical departures from the old system was the provision of education for girls. Special elementary schools, separate from boys' schools, were established; these emphasized homely arts in addition to moral studies and literacy. The first was created in 1898. By 1907 there were 391 such schools, and the government recognized them as a regular part of the system.

Another new trend in education, which was to accelerate in succeeding years, was study abroad. From the time of its victory over China in 1895 until the end of World War I, Japan was the principal recipient of Chinese students. Thousands went to learn the secrets of Japan's transformation from an isolated feudal state to a powerful modern empire. The student flow increased following Japan's defeat of Russia in 1905. European countries and America were also receiving Chinese students and would continue to do so for many decades. Schooling for many of them was supported by Boxer Rebellion indemnity funds, which, following the lead of the United States in 1907, many European countries designated for educational purposes, both in China and abroad.

Schools established by Christian missionaries played an important role in the early modernization of education in China, especially at the university level. In 1879 Saint John's University was founded in Shanghai. By 1922 there were sixteen missionary colleges and universities and dozens of schools, both Protestant and Catholic, at lower levels. From the beginning, Chinese students were attracted to them more for their dissemination of science than for theology. They had important seminal influence, but after the first decade of the twentieth century they were outstripped by Chinese government universities in both quantity and quality.

With the establishment of the Republic of China in 1912, there was a dramatic shift in educational objectives. European-educated Cai Yuanpei, the first minister of education under the Republic, declared that ethical education would remain foremost in the curriculum, but that its purpose would be to instill "the right knowledge of liberty, equality, and fraternity." For the first time, the old Chinese classics were entirely eliminated from the curriculum, females were declared equal to males in the education system, and the first four years of elementary school were made compulsory.

During Yuan Shikai's brief tenure as president of China (1912–1915), Cai Yuanpei's liberal idealism was discarded in favor of an emphasis on military education and rigid surveillance of potentially subversive curricular materials. Only in universities, such as Beijing University, where Cai became president, did intellectual pursuits briefly triumph over political controls.

The disintegration of the political structure after Yuan's death allowed, by default, a rare period of academic freedom for Chinese intellectuals. A heady period of iconoclasm for traditional learning and the absorption of new ideas from the West culminated in the "intellectual renaissance" of the May Fourth period, so called because of a student demonstration on that date in 1919 that both symbolized and reinvigorated a national reform movement. Two significant and related trends began in the May Fourth era that later would have a profound impact. One was the plain speech *(baihua)* movement, which for the first time unified the Chinese written and spoken languages; the other was the rural education movement led by American-trained Tao Xingzhi and James Y. C. Yen. The latter movement was an attempt to make education in rural areas conform to the interests of the peasants and the needs of daily life. Tao and Yen's work in mass literacy provided a model for others, particularly the Communists, when political stability was restored. [*See* May Fourth Movement.]

When a new national government, led by the Guomindang (Kuomintang, or Nationalist Party), was established in Nanjing in 1928, it greatly reduced the warlord anarchy of the previous decade and gave rise to optimism among educators. In May the First National Education Conference set the agenda for the new era of national unity. A centralized education administration based on the French model was created to implement throughout the country an educational structure similar to that of the United States (six years of elementary education, six of secondary education, and a four-year university). As always, moral training remained at the core of the curriculum; the content now emphasized Sun Yat-sen's "Three Principles of the People" as well as nationalism, anticommunism, and the principles of Neo-Confucianism.

Unfortunately, the ambitious plans of the new government remained largely on paper as the demands of the military for funds rendered detailed education regulations meaningless. Teachers' salaries were not paid for months, and students' discontent with their schools and with Chiang Kai-shek's national policy of civil war in the early 1930s threatened the whole system with collapse. Neglect owing to lack of funds and interest was particularly apparent in the countryside. A League of Nations Mission of Educational Experts invited to China by the government in 1931 concluded that there was an overemphasis on higher education resulting in a growing separation between an ignorant and illiterate general populace and an "intelligentsia educated in luxurious schools and indifferent to the wants of the masses."

When parts of China were under Japanese occupation for eight years (1937–1945), the faculty and students of most of the major universities followed the Nationalist government beyond the Yangtze gorges to the relative safety of Sichuan and Yunnan provinces, carrying with them what books and equipment could be transported. Combining into conglomerates, such as Southwest United University, they made a valiant effort to carry on as before. Despite government surveillance and thought control, which increasingly alienated intellectuals from Guomindang leadership, they remained a bastion of liberalism in a hostile environment.

In Communist-controlled areas of the northwest the situation was very different. All secondary schools and institutions of higher education were concerned exclusively with training cadres to address the pressing needs of war and revolution. Elementary schools also concentrated on teaching practical skills that could be immediately applied. Popular management *(minban)* schools, relying on local sources of funding and instruction, spread rudimentary education into rural areas never before touched, and mass-literacy campaigns somewhat increased adult ability to read. The whole education system was overtly political, serving to propagate the ideology of the Communist leadership.

Communist triumph over the Guomindang government in the civil war that followed the defeat of Japan set the stage for a new era in education, with the implementation of a new system modeled after that of the Soviet Union. It is estimated that thirty-six thousand Chinese students and six hundred scientists and engineers went to the Soviet Union to study in the decade following the establishment of the People's Republic. Hundreds of Soviet teachers and approximately eleven thousand Soviet technical experts came to China. Over fourteen hundred Soviet textbooks and more than twice as many Soviet literary works were translated into Chinese and provided the schools with much of their curricular material.

The structure of the school system remained basically the same as before at the elementary and secondary levels, but the system grew rapidly. The state statistical bureau claimed that between 1949 and 1959 enrollment in elementary schools had grown from 23,680,000 to 86,400,000, and in secondary schools from 1,496,000 to 8,520,000, with an additional 383,000 in technical middle schools and hundreds of thousands more in spare-time schools of all sorts in both city and countryside.

The structure of the university system changed considerably to conform with the Soviet model. It included comprehensive, polytechnic, and specialized universities, and academies for engineering, agriculture, medicine, teacher training, economics, politics, physical education, fine arts, and foreign languages. Enrollment in the first decade was reported to have grown from 155,000 to 660,000.

Political content informed the curriculum at every level. In secondary- and tertiary-level schools, math and science courses predominated. History, humanities, and literature were severely circumscribed by a narrow definition of ideological orthodoxy. Intellectuals, particularly those trained in the West, were brought into line or silenced by a campaign to "reform their thoughts," reinforced in 1957 by an "anti-rightist" campaign that subjected intellectuals as a group to abuse and, save a number of the most prominent of them, sent them to remote rural areas to undergo "reform through labor."

During the Great Leap Forward of 1958 to 1960,

the system of education during the first decade of the People's Republic came under attack as being too foreign-oriented and too elitist. Mao Zedong himself took the initiative in setting the guidelines. Political content, with particular emphasis on the "thought of Chairman Mao," was greatly increased, as was manual labor for both faculty and students to help them become "proletarian intellectuals."

For the next two decades the policy struggle among leaders in the Party was reflected in the theory and practice of education. At the simplest level of abstraction, the debate was between those who favored an education system adapted above all to the needs of economic growth versus those who favored a system designed primarily to foster socialist goals of equality. The former advocated concentrating scarce resources in a relatively few elite schools, mostly in urban areas, staffed by the most qualified teachers and populated by the ablest students, selected by competitive examinations. The curriculum would include politics but be largely academic, drawing heavily on the advanced experience of foreign countries. Students not privileged to enter those schools would attend less prestigious regular schools or work-study schools. The latter, run largely with local resources, were all that were available in most rural areas.

The contrary policy of social egalitarianism criticized this two-track system as a bourgeois perversion of the ideals of socialism. It advocated instead that all schools be work-study schools; that scarce resources go to build education in areas furthest behind, particularly in rural areas; that the children of workers and peasants receive admissions priority to higher education; and that schools be opened to society, particularly by forming links with production units. Teachers and students were to engage in manual labor, and the curriculum was to be heavily politicized with the "thought of Chairman Mao."

The debate came to a head with the Great Proletarian Cultural Revolution. Encouraged to take an active role in pursuing Mao's vision of equality through class struggle, student Red Guards closed the schools for several years and proceeded to attack "those in authority taking the bourgeois road." The result was a disaster for education. For ten years (1966–1976), very little academic work was done in Chinese schools; intellectuals were beaten and terrified into inactivity, and urban students were sent by the millions to the countryside after the first heady years of destructive rebellion. Only with the death of Mao Zedong and the arrest of the Gang of Four in 1976 did the struggle that had paralyzed education for a decade come to an end. Under the new leadership of Deng Xiaoping and his allies, the slogan "Four Modernizations" came to symbolize national aspirations. The academic educational model was reinstated and strengthened, and China once again began to look abroad for inspiration and advanced training. The emphasis has been on slow, steady growth of quality education in a diversified school system, with "key" schools receiving priority in the allocation of resources.

Statistics published by the Chinese government comparing school enrollment for 1983 with that for 1949 indicate impressive growth: from 24.39 million to 135.78 million in elementary schools, 1.04 million to 43.98 million in regular secondary schools, 0.23 million to 1.14 million in secondary technical schools, and 0.12 million to 1.21 million in universities and colleges (*Beijing Review*, 27 September 1984). On the other hand there is still great disparity between city and countryside. In the latter many students drop out of school after three years or so. The secondary school statistics mask the fact that most of the enrollment is in junior secondary schools, and that most senior secondary school students live in urban areas. University students overwhelmingly come from the cities and constitute only about 0.1 percent of the total population. The achievements have been great, but so are the remaining problems.

C. H. Becker et al., *The Reorganization of Education in China* (1932). Theodore H. E. Chen, *Chinese Education since 1949: Academic and Revolutionary Models* (1981). Shi Ming Hu and Eli Seifman, eds., *Toward a New World Outlook: A Documentary History of Education in the People's Republic of China, 1949–1976* (1976). P. W. Kuo, *The Chinese System of Public Education* (1915). R. F. Price, *Education in Communist China* (1970). Victor Purcell, *Problems of Chinese Education* (1936). Peter J. Seybolt, *Revolutionary Education in China* (1973).

PETER J. SEYBOLT

EDUCATION IN SOUTH ASIA

Despite foreign conquests, Indian education has demonstrated a surprising consistency of character over its long history. This is partly due to the fact that initially new ruling groups rarely took an active interest in educational change and were content to continue with the system they found. This indifference also served the political goal of securing the goodwill of the people; no ruling group set out from the start to overturn the existing educational system completely, but rather sought to adapt its own to the indigenous. Another reason for the continuity of Indian education is the Indian tendency toward syncretism, by which aspects of a new system found their way into the old, and vice versa, through the incorporative action of historical change. This has given Indian education a layered quality that is reflected in the diversity of its institutions and philosophies.

Little is known about the precise beginnings of educational activity in ancient India. Some historians go as far back as the Indus Valley civilization. Evidence of a highly organized society strongly suggests that there must have been a formal educational system of note to transmit the knowledge and skills required for such a society to function. But for more reliable evidence of educational development, one must look to the period when the Vedas were composed (c. 1500 BCE). Whether the educational system evolved from the need to preserve and transmit the hymns or whether the religious function was adapted to an already existing system is difficult to determine. What is known is that the duty of preserving the Vedas and handing them down from generation to generation devolved upon the priestly family, which functioned as the smallest unit of instruction in early Vedic society. [*See* Vedas.]

Some of the more rigorous practices associated with the learning of the Vedas—memorization, recitation, meditation—became part of the formal pattern of Brahmanic education. The pupil-master relationship complemented and in time superseded the father-son pedagogical arrangement. The Upanayana, the initiation ceremony into the world of learning, was an adolescent male's most important rite of passage. In time, the individual relationship enjoyed by the pupil with his master was enlarged to include other pupils, and the first *gurukulas,* or schools of Vedic learning, were established. The goals of Brahmanic education and religious devotion were identical: both aimed at the union of the individual with the Absolute. Accordingly, the pursuit of objective knowledge had little place here, as it assumed a mind-matter dualism that led to individuation and separation from the Absolute. The Brahmanic theory of knowledge directly influenced the method and content of education. Attention to sound rather than meaning was seen to induce the desired reflexiveness, and it took the form of mass recitation of texts (compared in the literature with the croaking of frogs during the monsoon).

By at least the seventh century BCE Brahmanic education was highly elitist; whole classes of people, particularly women and the lower castes, were excluded from formal instruction. The increased numbers of pupils entering these institutions created a demand for more teachers, and there soon developed a division of labor in the teaching of different subjects. The trend toward specialization was further augmented by the *brahmana sangham,* an annual conference held by brahmans to debate issues of theology and philosophy. [*See also* Brahman.]

The elitism of Brahmanic education became the focal point of attack by reformist groups. The most important of these was Buddhism. Buddhist education was open to all castes, and especially to women and the poor. It centered on *viharas,* or monasteries, and was conducted entirely by monks. Despite its reaction against the caste basis of Brahmanic education, Buddhist education preserved a number of elements of the system it opposed. Among these were its emphasis on meditation and the formation of right habits of mind; on the methods of debating, questioning, and discussion; on ceremony and ritual; and on the individual relationship between pupil and master. Buddhist education gave India several great centers of learning, such as Odantapuri and Vikramasila, but none was more illustrious than Nalanda, which flourished from 450 to 850 CE and attracted some of the greatest scholars of the age. [*See* Nalanda.] Not all students underwent training for the purpose of entering the Buddhist order. Those who showed remarkable progress often obtained appointments in practical government. Nor was Buddhist education solely for the poor and the outcasts; it was patronized by wealthy merchants as well.

Muslim conquests in India, beginning in the eighth century, did not result in any immediate changes in the pattern of Indian education. *Maktabs,* or primary schools, and *madrasas,* or centers of higher learning, were established for the education of the Muslim ruling classes. While there was initially little exchange between Hindu and Muslim culture, the later practice of appointing Hindus to public office encouraged the study of each other's languages. It was with Akbar's reign (1556–1605) that Muslim education became more integrated with indigenous forms. A patron of both Muslim and Hindu learning, Akbar established schools and colleges, founded numerous libraries, and authorized the translation of Sanskrit books into Persian. He continued the Brahmanic and Buddhist practice of holding conferences and initiated the *ibadat khana,* the holding of discussions in his presence on topics ranging from religion and philosophy to science and history. With Akbar the curriculum became more secularized, and less emphasis was placed on book learning in favor of practical knowledge for preparing the individual to find a place in the public world. [*See* Akbar *and* Madrasa.]

In the meantime the Hindu system of learning continued to exist side by side with the Muslim. But its heyday was long gone, and the spirit of intellectual vigor that had marked its early forms gave way to a dull, outmoded system of teaching that stressed memorization and rote learning above understanding and critical thinking. Muslim education, on the other hand, had not integrated with the existing system to create a truly indigenous form of learning. The result was that the Hindu and Muslim systems functioned apart from each other, each catering to a different clientele and representing in the main a fractured Indian identity.

Such was the state of affairs when the East India Company began its commercial operations in India. Although missionaries had been active in educational work as early as the seventeenth century, the company officially refrained from interfering in the education of Indians. Mounting pressure from the English Parliament to discharge its responsibilities to the Indians forced the company in 1813 to allot some portion of its revenues to education. It took ten years, however, for the proposal to be implemented, and it became further embroiled in controversy over which form of learning was to be promoted. The conflict was effectively silenced in 1835 with Lord Macaulay's *Minute on Education,* which was both a stinging critique of Orientalist policy and a passionate plea for making Western literature and languages the medium of Indian higher education. [*See* Macaulay, Thomas Babington.] The English Education Act of 1835, which followed the *Minute,* made English the medium of higher learning and henceforth set the tone for Indian education for the duration of British rule in India. Unlike the French in their colonies, the English did not give very high priority to the learning of English. The demand for English education came from the Indian elites themselves, who saw it as the means of social and political influence.

In 1854 a proposal was made to set up universities modeled on the University of London in the three presidency towns of Calcutta, Madras, and Bombay. These were primarily examining, not teaching, bodies and were responsible for setting up curricula and examinations and for awarding degrees. The new university system was marked by a strong tendency toward centralization. This education was also clearly elitist: while a small group of Indians sought English education, others continued to receive education in the vernaculars. The "filtration theory," as this policy came to be known, was based on the premise that through a class of English-educated Indians, Western ideas would percolate down to the masses. In reality, however, this scheme of education kept the top layers of Indian society isolated from the masses.

The opportunities offered by English education led to growing discontent among the English-educated population. The discontent took the shape of a strong nationalist movement; at its vanguard were men educated in the best tradition of Western thought, among them Gandhi, Tilak, Gokhale, and Nehru. A movement for national education, to be controlled by Indians and devoted to Indian ideals and culture, gathered strength. The offshoot of the movement was the Wardha Scheme of 1937, which proposed free compulsory education in the mother tongue and a curriculum organized around manual and socially productive work. Basic Education, as this craft-oriented training was called, was Gandhi's concept; although it was less than heartily embraced in the years after independence, when science and technology received top priority, it remains one of the most interesting educational philosophies to come out of modern India. [*See also* Gandhi, Mohandas Karamchand; Tilak, Bal Gangadhar; Gokhale, Gopal Krishna; Nehru, Jawaharlal; *and* Besant, Annie.]

With independence the urgency of formulating a national educational policy was obvious. But several issues had to be settled first; their irresolution has made the pace of educational reconstruction painfully slow. First, the relationship between the central government and the states on matters of education has yet to be clearly defined. This ambiguity has led to tension in recent years, with several states accusing the center of foisting unwanted policies on them and withholding funds if they resist. Second, despite some attempts to harness education to personnel requirements, the nation has not been able to prevent wastage and stagnation. The "brain drain" (the emigration of Indian professionals) is one example of the failure to educate for local and national needs; the educated unemployed is another. Recently there has been much discussion about separating degrees from jobs so that students with limited resources would not be compelled to go through a college route to secure jobs that do not in fact require an academic degree. Another proposal has been to provide two distinct streams, the academic and the vocational, to broaden the range of skills and abilities required for a diversified economy. Both measures are designed to relieve higher education of the pressures of coping with large numbers of often poorly qualified candidates, but the prestige value attached to degrees and to the traditional academic course is still so great as to render the proposals ineffective. Casteism, a restricted job market, and an increasingly irrelevant educational system have all contributed to student unrest, which has reached epidemic proportions. [*See also* Untouchability.]

The thorniest issue of all, however, is undoubtedly the language problem. The Indian constitution declared that Hindi would be the official language of the union. In order to make this transition gradual and acceptable, it was agreed that English would continue to be used indefinitely for official purposes. Pressures from regional language groups resulted in a three-language formula for schools, with the mother tongue (or regional language) being the medium of instruction in the primary grades and Hindi and English introduced at the secondary level. Vernacular-medium schools, however, have yet to be a potent force in Indian education in light of the enormous prestige enjoyed by English education. The view that democracy must accept multilingualism has been strongly counteracted by considerations of the marketplace, social prestige, and international opportunity. [*See also* Indo-Aryan Languages and Literatures *and* Uttar Pradesh.]

This is not to say that Indian education has made no gains. Although universal education still remains an unrealized dream, educational opportunities have been greatly widened through a system of quotas and scholarships to include larger sections of the rural poor and the urban depressed. There has been a steady streamlining of university education in an effort to maintain standards. The University Grants Commission was established in 1953 to define qualifications of university faculty members, inspect universities, make grants, and provide faculty with opportunities for advanced study. The UGC has also granted institutional autonomy to selected colleges to enable them to offer enriched curricula to qualified students. More gains, however, have been registered by professional and technical education. By 1966 there were six agricultural universities of the land-grant pattern and five institutes of technology, and together with the rapid expansion of research programs they have set the trend for the concerted development of a technological and scientific base in Indian education.

[*See also* India.]

B. K. Boman-Behram, *Educational Controversies in India* (1943). Humayun Kabir, *Education in New India* (1959). F. A. Keay, *Indian Education in Ancient and Later Times* (1938). N. N. Law, *Promotion of Learning in India under Mohammedan Rule* (1916). Bruce McCully, *English Education and the Origins of Indian Nationalism* (1940). R. K. Mookerji, *Ancient Indian Education: Brahmanical and Buddhist* (1969). J. P. Naik and Syed Nurullah, *A Students' History of Education in India, 1800–1965* (1964). Amrik Singh and Philip G. Altbach, eds., *The Higher Learning in India* (1974).

GAURI VISWANATHAN

EDUCATION IN JAPAN

Credited with the high motivation for learning and the high level of skills among the Japanese people but criticized for an emphasis on certification, based on school entrance examinations, that has stricken the country with a "diploma disease," Japanese education remains one of the most contested issues in modern Japanese society. The issues that surround demands for educational reform provide a constant measure of the values that the Japanese have sought to maintain and of the process by which foreign ideas and institutions have been accommodated to Japanese needs.

The Japanese owe much of their early educational tradition to China. Formal education was made possible by the introduction of writing from China in the early fifth century, and in the eighth century Tang China provided the model for Japan's first school system. As described in the Taihō Codes of 701, a Confucian college, the Daigakuryō, provided training in the Chinese classics to the court nobility in Kyoto, and branch schools *(kokugaku)* educated the provincial aristocracy. The meritocractic principles of the Chinese examination system were never fully implemented in this early system because they conflicted with a Japanese preference for inherited privilege. During the ninth century, aristocratic families set up private schools for their members, and at least one school, that of the Shingon monk Kūkai (Kōbō Daishi; 774–835), was open to commoners. By the tenth century, Confucian scholarship was in decline, and court culture centered on a more Japanese form of aesthetic refinement. The development of a phonetic syllabary *(kana)* made possible a vernacular literature and the spread of literacy in the native language.

During the medieval age (twelfth to sixteenth century), Zen Buddhism became part of the training of the samurai along with the practical techniques of warfare. Scholarship was sheltered in Buddhist monasteries, and priests taught young acolytes and other children in their temples, but there were few schools. Not until the prolonged era of stability and peace of the Tokugawa period (1600–1868) did the systematic education of the samurai and the extension of popular literacy become possible.

By 1853, when Commodore Matthew Perry intruded on Japan's 250 years of isolation from the West, the samurai were not only fully literate but also had been largely transformed into urban bureaucrats, wielders of the pen rather than the sword. The Neo-Confucian curriculum at official schools trained leaders in the ethical responsibilities of good government through the Chinese classics. The Neo-Confucian insistence on "the investigation of things" stimulated an intellectual flowering. Private academies *(shijuku)* sprang up by the thousands to satisfy interests of students in Western science, military technology, foreign language, national studies, and the traditional arts—adding considerably to the complexity and diversity of Tokugawa schooling.

Another important aspect of the Tokugawa legacy was the spread of learning beyond the samurai classes. Tens of thousands of local *terakoya* (temple schools) were established, without official support, by public-spirited citizens to train commoners in the rudiments of reading, writing, and calculation. It is believed that 40 percent of boys and 15 percent of girls were receiving such training by the middle of the nineteenth century. This meant that before the modern period Japan had a highly skilled leadership group, and wide segments of the population were prepared to take advantage of the opportunities that modern education would offer.

Following the Meiji Restoration of 1868, education became the foundation for a strong, unified state. Borrowing freely from European and American models, the Meiji leaders planned a national system that would provide training in basic skills and create a citizenry responsive to state goals. In 1872 the Fundamental Code of Education called for a nationally organized system of schools administered by a central Ministry of Education. By 1886 a comprehensive system was implemented by Mori Arinori, the first minister of education, that provided the framework for Japanese education until 1945. Elementary schools were redesigned to inculcate patriotic loyalty, a new Imperial University provided free access to Western higher learning, and middle schools acted as sorting mechanisms, steering an elite through the narrow channels to higher education. The central mission of the schools, to provide service to the state, was set forth in the Imperial Rescript on Education of 1890. [*See* Imperial Rescript on Education.]

Although liberalism and innovation in educaton gained currency in the 1920s, by the 1930s, with the outbreak of war on the Asian mainland, an extreme form of nationalism and patriotism was inculcated in the morals courses *(shūshin)* in Japanese schools. The appointment of General Araki Sadao as minister of education in 1938 signaled the complete military takeover of the school system. Elementary schools were reorganized as people's schools *(kokumin gakkō);* military drill and evacuations to the countryside became ordinary parts of student life.

Following defeat in World War II, Japan was occupied by the Allied Forces, and education was singled out for special attention by Occupation reformers. Under American guidance the goals of postwar education became the development of individual personality and the nurturing of an independent spirit. The School Education Law of 1947 codified an extensive reorganization. The elitist multitrack system of the prewar period was replaced with a single track in a 6–3–3–4 structure (six years of elementary school through secondary schools to four years of undergraduate education). Technical colleges, normal schools, and higher schools were upgraded and absorbed into new four-year colleges on the American model; a single comprehensive high school replaced the specialized schools of the old system. Compulsory education was extended from six years to nine years, and the principle of coeducation was established for all schools.

While the expansion of opportunity provided by the Occupation reforms has been welcomed, not all the effects have been positive. Competition for university entrance has, in fact, been intensified by greater numbers of students and the Japanese preference for ranking schools. Because the graduate of a highly rated school has a far better chance of securing a more desirable job than the graduate of a lesser school, the pressure to enter one of the very few prestigious national schools has created an "examination hell."

In the mid-1980s statistics show the Japanese educational system to be among the most successful in the world in providing broad access to higher levels of schooling. In 1984 virtually 100 percent of the age-group eligible for high school had completed the nine years of compulsory schooling. Almost 94 percent went on to high schools, which are noncompulsory, and all but 2.2 percent graduated. In 1984, 35.5 percent of the age-group went on to universities or junior colleges—a figure that is second only to America but represents a slight falling off from previous years.

Despite the impressive numbers, many Japanese are concerned that the social cost may be too high. Among the many ills blamed on school entrance pressures are a rise in school violence and a profusion of costly "cram" schools *(juku),* which give wealthy families advantages and undermine the egalitarian thrust of the entire educational system. Against a backdrop of complaints from business leaders, educational authorities, and the public, a Provisional Council on Educational Reform was established by Prime Minister Nakasone Yasuhiro in September 1984 to make recommendations to guide Japanese education into the twenty-first century. The extent to which the Japanese will be able to ease pressures and provide greater flexibility in the school system without undermining quality remains to be seen.

William K. Cummings, *Education and Equality in Japan* (1980). Ronald P. Dore, *Education in Tokugawa Japan* (1984). Herbert Passin, *Society and Education in Japan* (1984). Thomas Rohlen, *Japan's High Schools* (1983).

RICHARD RUBINGER

EDUCATION IN SOUTHEAST ASIA

The history of education in Southeast Asia may be divided into three broad phases, corresponding to the precolonial, colonial, and postcolonial periods.

Well before the nineteenth century, indigenous institutions had produced a high level of male literacy in most of the major cultures of Southeast Asia, largely because of the teaching missions assumed by the world religions established in the area. Most Buddhist boys and young men spent some time in monasteries, learning to read and write; such institutions had thrived as early as the seventh century. Similar schools were run for Muslim youth in the Malay world and by missionary friars in the Philippines from the seventeenth century onward. Some observers remarked that in the late nineteenth century Burmese and Thai men were more literate than their English counterparts.

Colonial regimes for the most part neglected mass education and concentrated their efforts on developing modern education for a small segment of the indigenous elite. Secondary and higher schools were almost unknown, for example, in Cambodia, Laos, and British Malaya; prior to World War II only a small handful of Southeast Asians had attained professional and university degrees. The only exceptions to this pattern were in Siam (Thailand) and the American-run Philippines, where mass, compulsory primary education, a healthy secondary school system, and a few universities were flourishing before the war.

In the postwar period, newly independent governments made a high priority of instituting mass, compulsory primary education using the indigenous languages, and by the 1960s the systems had grown to the university level. The main obstacle to continuing educational development is the shortage of resources in relatively underdeveloped economies where close to half the population is under the age of twenty.

J. S. Furnivall, *Educational Progress in Southeast Asia* (1943).

DAVID K. WYATT

EDUCATION IN IRAN AND CENTRAL ASIA

Until the introduction of modern Western school systems during the late nineteenth century and their rapid spread in the twentieth, the educational system in Iran and Central Asia was based on the Islamic *madrasa* (Islamic religious college), with only minor competition from private tutorials or similar minority schools for Christians and Jews. The *madrasa* is not merely a place of preparation for a ritual leader; it is also a kind of legislature and judiciary. To varying extents, depending on the polity within which the *madrasa* operates, the opinions of its scholars have the force of legal and judicial decisions. In contrast with modern mass education, which is concerned with training a labor force, institutionalizing scientific innovation, social mobility, and citizenship training, the *madrasa,* although concerned with justice and welfare, lays primary stress on the relation between the individual and God or the social collectivity and God.

***Madrasa* Education.** The conventional date for the beginning of the *madrasa* as a system, not merely as individual schools or scholarly circles, is 1066, when the vizier Nizam al-Mulk opened the first of a series of Nizamiyya schools across the Seljuk empire that were publicly endowed with stipends for students and salaries for teachers. [*See* Nizam al-Mulk.] In the sixteenth century, with the establishment of the Safavid and Ottoman religious ideologies, political conditions reduced tolerance for diversity of opinion. *Madrasas* continued to be built by the rulers. Most of the older *madrasas* of contemporary Qom were initially constructed and endowed by the sixteenth-century Safavids, who invited Shi'ite scholar-clerics from Lebanon and Bahrain to Iran to transform their empire into a Shi'ite one. At the same time, religious leaders successfully separated the actual administration of the *madrasas* from state interference, using the *sahm-i imam* (half of the *khoms* tax) to create financial independence.

The Shi'ite *madrasa* system developed a standard curriculum; certification was by *ijazas,* letters of permission by recognized scholars stating that one was qualified to teach specified items. Students started learning the alphabet in the local *maktab* (elementary school), often run by women. Boys would then proceed to provincial towns for the lower levels of education, then to larger cities for the upper levels, ultimately trying to go where the most renowned scholars lectured. In the nineteenth century this meant Isfahan and then Najaf; in the twentieth century it has meant Qom and Najaf. There are three levels in the curriculum: *muqaddamat,* or preliminaries, which includes etymology, syntax, and rhetoric; *dhat,* or the subject proper, including logic, *usul-i fiqh* ("principles of jurisprudence"), and *fiqh* ("law"); and *dars-i kharij,* external studies, assuming mastery of the books in the curriculum and ability to refine the skills of disputation. Through this last stage one compiles a *taqrirat* ("setting down") of the principles of jurisprudence, which makes one eligible for an *ijaza-i ijtihad,* the permission and obligation to follow one's own reasoning skills, to be a *mujtahid. Ayatollahs,* in prerevolutionary Iran, were those *mujtahids* who performed the dual functions of administering *madrasa* systems, religious taxes, endowments, and contributions and serving laymen as *marja taqlid,* guides in religious matters; since the 1979 Revolution the title *ayatollah* has been used somewhat more loosely. [*See* Ayatollah.]

In the 1970s there were attempts in Qom to introduce a wider range of topics of study into the *madrasa* system, including English, spoken Arabic, mathematics, the natural sciences, Persian and Arabic literature, and, more hesitantly, the social sciences. In 1975 there were more than 6,500 *madrasa* students in Qom, 1,800 in Mashhad, 1,000 in Isfahan, 500 in Tabriz, 250 in Shiraz, and 300 in Yazd. A large proportion of these came from peasant or clerical families. The clerical leadership itself tended to ensure that its sons received modern university education, and not merely traditional religious education. [*See* Madrasa.]

Modern Education. Modern schools on the secular European pattern were introduced into Iran sporadically during the second half of the nineteenth century. The government's Dar al-Fonun, or Polytechnic Institute, opened in 1851 and was followed, by the end of the century, by the School of Political Science in the Ministry of Foreign Affairs and two military schools. [*See* Dar al-Fonun.] In provincial cities, schools were introduced more widely through Zoroastrian, Baha'i, Christian, and Jewish organizations headquartered in India, Palestine, England, France, and the United States; these schools were intended to provide services to their coreligionists in Iran but also were open to others. Muslims also began introducing such schools at the turn of the century, beginning with Hasan Roshtiyya in the late 1890s (Tabriz, 1897; Qom, 1898). Government secular elementary schools were introduced in the first decades of the twentieth century: in 1906 Tehran had fourteen such elementary schools; by 1911 there were 123. By 1965 Iran had 2,181,600 students in primary schools, 493,700 in secondary schools, and 28,900 in higher education. There followed both major literacy campaigns and rapid expansion of higher education. By 1975 there were 135,300 higher education students in domestic institutions, some 30,000 in the United States and Great Britain, and others in India, Germany, and elsewhere. Three years later there were some 40,000 Iranian students at universities in the United States alone. Pressure for places at the universities, as well as for jobs commensurate with them, contributed to chronic dissatisfaction.

Syntheses between traditional Shi'ism and modern technological society may be seen as the central dynamic of the decade or two leading to the 1979 Revolution. The Madrasa Alavi was one of a series of semireligious schools (i.e., schools with secular curriculums approved by the government but also with considerable religious curriculum) started by Shaikh Abbas-Ali Islami, under the name Jama'i-yi Talimat-i Islami, including schools for girls where they would not have to confront male teachers. The most important institution for synthesizing educational trends was the Husainiyya Irshad, a mosque and modern teaching facility established in northeastern Tehran, where Ali Shari'ati conducted discussions and lectures on the topic of creating an Islamic sociology. [*See* Shari'ati, Ali.]

Soviet Central Asia. The development of education in Central Asia from a *madrasa* system to a secular system is similar but distinct. The Soviets closed all theological seminary *madrasas* between 1917 and 1941. Two have been allowed to reopen: the Madrasa Mir-i Arab (founded in 1535) was reopened in Bukhara in 1952, and the Madrasa Barak Khan was reopened in Tashkent in 1958. Bukhara maintained a vigorous tradition as a center of theological education into the nineteenth century; the first half of that century saw the building of new *madrasas* in Samarkand, Kokand, and Andizhan, as well as an expansion of *maktabs*. In the early-nineteenth-century penetration of Kazakhstan, the Russians supported Tatar *mullahs*, who set up modified Muslim schools; in the 1850s Kazakh was transcribed into Cyrillic in an attempt to introduce Russian culture gradually. In Turkestan there were efforts to open Russian schools to local children after 1875, but because of the Christian slant of the curriculum, these efforts met with little success. Russo-native schools (using local languages to introduce Russian culture, as well as some Russian-language instruction) were introduced after 1884; by 1911 there were 89 such schools in Turkestan, and they were also introduced into Kazakhstan. Even more successful were the New Method *(usul-i jadid)* schools founded by Tatars associated with the modernist Jadid movement; for example, in 1910 in Tashkent there were eight Russo-native schools but sixteen New Method ones.

The effort after the Bolshevik Revolution to eliminate the teaching of religious doctrines could not be enforced immediately. Despite purges of the Muslim modernists (Jadidi) between 1917 and 1920, Muslim schools continued at least until the introduction of universal compulsory primary education in 1930. Literacy expanded rapidly, with the medium of instruction the local languages, first written in the Latin alphabet (adopted in 1928) and then in Cyrillic (after 1940), thereby enforcing a break with premodern literature as well as with the non-Soviet Islamic world. Russian-language instruction is of course encouraged and is a *sine qua non* for advancement.

Richard W. Bulliet, *The Patricians of Nishapur* (1972). Michael Fischer, *Iran: From Religious Dispute to Revolution* (1980). Roy Mottahedeh, *The Mantle of the Prophet* (1985). MICHAEL FISCHER

1884 COUP D'ÉTAT, climax of a struggle over the course of Korea's modernization between the reformists, led by Kim Ok-kyun, and the Min, the royal in-law clan. After the disruption of the self-strengthening program in 1882, reform-minded young Koreans, among them Kim Ok-kyun (1851–1894) and Pak Yŏng-hyo (1861–1939), were fascinated by Meiji Japan's experimentation with Western ideas and institutions. Their ideas and postulates covered a wide spectrum: national defense and independence, economy, education, government, hygiene, and so forth. Collectively known as the Enlightenment Party (Kaehwadang), these young men initially worked within the framework of the self-strengthening movement controlled by the Min. Soon, however, a rift opened between the reformers' idealistic approach to modernization and the Min's more pragmatic, Chinese-backed program. While King Kojong was sympathetic with the reformers, the Min reached the zenith of their power in the summer of 1884, and the reformers came to realize that they would not reach their goal under Min tutelage.

During the fall of 1884 the reformers, with Japanese support, began to make concrete plans for violent action because they had become convinced that the seizure of power had to precede the pursuit of modernization. The occasion chosen for the coup was the inauguration party for the new Post Office on the evening of 4 December. Several members of the Min clan were killed and the royal palace was placed under Japanese protection. On 5 December Kim Ok-kyun and Pak Yŏng-hyo proclaimed a newly constituted government and drafted a fourteen-point program of reform. Meanwhile, Chinese troops, called in by a former high official, moved against the royal palace, and the reformers had to abandon their position under Japanese guard. Excited mobs in the streets attacked Japanese and burned their property, and the Japanese minister, joined by the defeated reformers, had to retreat to Inch'ŏn. With the Chinese in control in Seoul, the old government was reconstituted. The coup d'état had failed, and while its impact on the domestic scene was slight, its international repurcussions were disastrous.

War between China and Japan over Korea seemed imminent, but both sides signaled peaceful intentions. Negotiations started on two levels. On 9 January 1885 Japan and Korea signed the Treaty of Seoul, according to which the Koreans were to apologize to Japan, had to pay an indemnity, and were obliged to provide a site and funds for the reconstruction of the Japanese legation. The actual settlement of the crisis, however, was reached when, after tough bargaining, Itō Hirobumi of Japan and Li Hongzhang of China signed the Convention of Tianjin on 18 April 1885. It stipulated the bilateral withdrawal of troops from Korea, the encouragement of the Korean king to hire foreign military instructors, and mutual notification in case either side wanted to send troops back to Korea. This convention, concluded without consulting the Koreans, was a face-saving device for China as well as for Japan, but it did not bring peace to Korea.

[*See also* Yi Dynasty; Kojong; Kim Ok-kyun; *and* Pak Yŏng-hyo.]

Harold F. Cook, *Korea's 1884 Incident* (1972). Martina Deuchler, *Confucian Gentlemen and Barbarian Envoys: The Opening of Korea, 1875–1885* (1977).

MARTINA DEUCHLER

1882 UPRISING, military revolt in Korea that was both antigovernment and antiforeign. In the early 1880s the Korean government's modernization program, the increased Japanese presence in Korea, and Western encroachment were interpreted by the people as a betrayal of the traditional order and stirred widespread unrest. In mid-July 1882 a small riot of an army regiment over rice distribution escalated into a popular uprising under the lead of the Taewŏn'gun, who had been forced to retire from his position of authority in 1873. The Japanese legation was attacked and burned, and Japanese personnel fled in panic to Inch'ŏn. Several Japanese and high Korean officials were killed, and finally even the royal palace came under attack. King Kojong (r. 1864–1907) had no other choice but to hand all government affairs back to his father, the Taewŏn'gun, who immediately abolished the Foreign Office and the new army unit.

Both China and Japan took advantage of the disturbances. In August, China, on the pretext of protecting her tributary, dispatched troops whose first objective was the abduction of the Taewŏn'gun to China. The operations against the rebels were commanded by Yuan Shikai and terminated in early September. King Kojong was restored to power, but no one had the illusion that the previous order had been reestablished.

Japanese demands were presented to the Korean government on 20 August. After negotiations initially broke down, they were continued under Chinese sponsorship and ended on 30 August with the signing of the Treaty of Chemulp'o and the Additional Convention. The principal points of the treaty were the punishment of the culprits, proper funerals for the Japanese killed during the disturbances, payments to the wounded and to the families of the dead, indemnity to the Japanese nation, the building and maintenance of quarters for the Japanese soldiers stationed in Korea, and the dispatch of a mission of apology to Japan. The Additional Convention concerned the extension of treaty limits in the treaty ports and inland travel of Japanese diplomats. In July 1883 trade regulations were added.

The Chinese further strengthened their presence in the peninsula by forcing the Koreans to conclude the Regulations for Maritime and Overland Trade between Chinese and Korean Subjects on 4 October 1882. This document, the first written understanding between China and one of her vassals, granted China special trade privileges and opened Korea's market to Chinese traders. On Li Hongzhang's initiative, a Chinese high commissioner of trade was sent to Seoul.

[*See also* Yi Dynasty; Kojong; *and* Taewŏn'gun.]

Martina Deuchler, *Confucian Gentlemen and Barbarian Envoys: The Opening of Korea, 1875–1885* (1977).

MARTINA DEUCHLER

1857 REVOLT. *See* Mutiny, Indian.

EIGHTH ROUTE ARMY, the principal military force under Chinese command during the war of resistance against Japan (1937–1945). It was created in August 1937 from units of the Red Army following United Front agreements between the Communists and Nationalists (Guomindang). Ostensibly directed by the National Government of Chiang Kai-shek (who preferred to call it the Eighteenth Group Army), in fact it operated under the general command of a Communist, General Zhu De, with divisions led by Lin Biao, He Long, and Liu Bocheng. Noted for its political as much as for its military effectiveness, the Eighth Route Army contributed significantly to the expansion and consolidation of Communist-controlled areas during the war. In 1946, together with other military units, it was redesignated the People's Liberation Army.

[*See also* Chinese People's Liberation Army; He Long; Lin Biao; World War II in China; *and* Zhu De.]

Samuel P. Griffiths, *The Chinese People's Liberation Army* (1967). James P. Harrison, *The Long March to Power: A History of the Chinese Communist Party, 1921–1972* (1972).

PETER J. SEYBOLT

EISAI (1141–1215), Japanese Zen monk, revered as the founder of the Rinzai school of Zen Buddhism in Japan. Eisai's full name was Myōan Eisai; he is also sometimes referred to as Yōsai. Having begun the study of Buddhism in the great Tendai monastery of Enryakuji while still a child, Eisai became convinced of the need to reform Japanese Buddhism. He made the first of two visits to China in 1168. During a six-month pilgrimage he collected Tendai texts and visited Chinese monastic centers. For the twenty years after his return to Japan, Eisai devoted himself to the revival of Tendai monastic practice and to the recovery of the ideals of Saichō (766–822), the founder of Japanese Tendai Buddhism.

In 1187, Eisai made a second, longer pilgrimage to China. This time he studied under the Chan (Zen) master Xu'an Huaichang, who recognized his enlightenment and accepted him as a disciple. Eisai returned to Japan in 1191 determined to propagate Zen. Meeting opposition from Tendai supporters in the capital, Eisai wrote the *Kōzen gokokuron (Promotion of Zen in Defense of the Nation)* to defend the new Zen teachings. Frustrated in Kyoto, he went to Kamakura, where he secured the patronage of the Minamoto shoguns and the Hōjō regents who dominated the Kamakura *bakufu.* They built for him the monastery of Jufukuji in Kamakura and later the Kenninji in Kyoto, where he practiced an eclectic mix of Zen, Tendai, and Shingon Buddhism.

Eisai is also credited with the popularization of tea drinking. In 1214 he compiled a treatise on tea, the *Kissa yōjōki,* which he presented to the shogun Minamoto Sanetomo. In this Eisai advocated the medicinal value of tea. The book was later incorporated into the aesthetic literature of the tea ceremony as one of the early classics on the art of tea.

[*See also* Zen.]

Martin Collcutt, *Five Mountains* (1981). Heinrich Dumoulin, *A History of Zen Buddhism* (1960).

MARTIN COLLCUTT

EKATHOTSAROT, king of Ayudhya (r. 1605–1610 or 1611), comrade-in-arms and successor to Naresuan the Great of Siam. The son of Mahathammaracha, Ekathotsarot was constantly at his elder brother Naresuan's side throughout the wars with Burma and Cambodia in the 1580s and 1590s; when Naresuan became king in 1590, Ekathotsarot may have been named, at least formally, his coruler. As king, he was preoccupied with rebuilding the kingdom after decades of warfare, in part through promoting foreign trade. The date of his death is uncertain, but it likely occurred between October 1610 and November 1611.

[*See also* Ayudhya *and* Naresuan.]

W. A. R. Wood, *A History of Siam* (1926). David K. Wyatt, *Thailand: A Short History* (1984).

DAVID K. WYATT

ELAMITES, an ancient people of southwestern Iran. The Elamite language, still imperfectly understood, is not demonstrably related to any other.

The kingdom of Elam (roughly the province of Khuzistan in modern Iran) existed from about 2500 to 640 BCE; Susa was its capital. Constant contact with Mesopotamia led to both trade and military encounters, recorded from around 2700, and at times the Elamites fell under Mesopotamian suzerainty. About 2000, they delivered the final blow to the Sumerian Ur III dynasty; as a major power in

FIGURE 1. *Elamite-period Statuette of a Woman.* Probably from the temple of Shoushinak, Susa, c. thirteenth century BCE, bronze. Height 11.4 cm.

the twelfth century, Elam also ended the four-hundred-year Kassite rule of Babylonia. The history of the Elamites went unrecorded from the twelfth to the eighth century, but Elam probably remained an independent state until the Assyrians sacked Susa about 640. As a satrapy under the Achaemenids and under later dynasties, Elam was incorporated into the Persian empire.

Elamite royal succession was fratriarchal, and in the royal family both sister-brother marriage and levirate were practiced; these customs suggest that succession was also matrilineal. Elamite religion was polytheistic; the pantheon comprised both ill-defined national deities and local gods, one of whom, In-Shushinak, "the lord of Susa," achieved preeminence. Artistically the Elamites are best known for their superb metalwork and especially their bronze statuary; the serpent was a dominant religious motif in Elamite art.

Two distinct writing systems were used by the Elamites. One, an indigenous pictographic script called Proto-Elamite, appears on clay tablets from about 3000; it has not been fully deciphered. The other, the cuneiform script, was borrowed from Mesopotamia around 2300. Most Elamite texts date from the thirteenth to the twelfth century, the seventh century, and the Achaemenid period, when Elamite continued as an official language alongside Old Persian and Babylonian.

[*See also* Cuneiform *and* Metalwork.]

G. G. Cameron, *History of Early Iran* (1936). W. Hinz, *The Lost World of Elam,* translated by Jennifer Barnes (1972).

JOHN HUEHNERGARD

ELARA (c. 205–161 BCE), ruler of ancient Sri Lanka. Elara was the third such ruler among a group of Cholas and Dravidians who, in 237 BCE, usurped the throne at Anuradhapura. The attitude taken by the *Mahavamsa* (*Great Chronicle,* a history of Sri Lanka) toward Elara is somewhat ambivalent. On the one hand, the *Mahavamsa* is lavish in its praise of Elara's statesmanship and his sense of justice and fair play; on the other hand, it describes him as a man of false beliefs and as the champion of the Tamils who eventually falls in combat at the hands of the great Sinhalese hero Dutthagamani, who was destined to unite the island under a single ruler.

[*See also* Dutthagamani.]

K. M. de Silva, *A History of Sri Lanka* (1981).

K. M. DE SILVA

ELBURZ MOUNTAINS, located along the southern shore of the Caspian Sea, are high, steep mountains forming a major climatic and cultural barrier within Iran. Abundant rainfall and moderate temperatures on the northern slopes create the Hyrcanian forest, a unique jungle vegetation of deciduous trees and thick underbrush. In contrast, the southern slopes are arid, with semidesert scrub and oasis settlements. Several intrusive volcanic cones penetrate the crystalline core and younger limestones and sandstones, including the highest peak in Iran, the 18,955-foot Mount Demavand.

MICHAEL BONINE

ELLENBOROUGH, EARL OF. *See* Law, Edward.

ELLORA, in Maharashtra, India, site of thirty-four Hindu, Buddhist, and Jain rock-cut cave temples of the mid-sixth to tenth centuries CE. Ellora's earliest temples were dedicated to the worship of the god Shiva; they feature elaborate pillared halls that lead to rear-wall shrines housing *lingams* (stylized phallic symbols of Shiva's procreative energies). By 600 the caves became centers of Buddhist worship, with Buddha images carved both in shrines of pillared halls and in the apsidal *caitya* (worship hall), where the Buddha is carved on the front of a monolithic stupa. Later (c. 675–720), three-storied Buddhist caves focused worship on multiple Buddhas and other deities. A second Shaivite phase, sponsored by the Rashtrakutas, included one cave, called the Kailasa, that is carved to resemble a freestanding temple complex behind a high screen wall. Other caves are elaborate Jain temples of the ninth and tenth centuries; there and in the Kailasa important fragments of early medieval-style paintings are preserved.

[*See also* Ajanta *and the figure on the following page.*]

J. Burgess, *Report on the Elura Cave Temples* (1882). J. Burgess and J. Fergusson, *Cave Temples of India* (1880).

GERI HOCKFIELD MALANDRA

ELPHINSTONE, MOUNTSTUART (1779–1859) served as political agent in Nagpur and Poona before becoming governor of Bombay (1818–1827). After the defeat of the Marathas in 1818, Lord Elphinstone pursued a policy of moderation, keeping as much as possible of the Maratha system, including the use of Indian officers in the administration of conquered areas. He tried to balance the preservation of existing customs and governmental machinery with a concern for social reform, including Western education and the abolition of *sati*. Before retiring he revised the legal code for the Bombay presidency. Appreciative Indians established a college in his name that still exists in Bombay.

Kenneth Ballhatchet, *Social Policy and Social Change in Western India, 1817–1830* (1957).

LYNN ZASTOUPIL

EMERALD BUDDHA, Buddha image, palladium of the kingdom of Thailand. Fashioned of green malachite and thus of an emerald color, the statue betrays a style of craftsmanship not nearly as old as the legends that recount its history would suggest; it is believed to date from the first century BCE. It was uncovered at Chiang Rai in the far north, in a monument struck by lightning in 1436, and in 1470 was enshrined in Chiang Mai by King Tilokaracha. King Setthathirat of Lan Sang removed it to Vientiane, in Laos, in 1548, and the future King Rama I of Siam brought it to Bangkok in 1779, where it was enshrined as the kingdom's palladium in a temple within the Grand Palace compound.

[*See also* Tilokaracha; Setthathirat; *and* Bangkok.]

C. Notton, trans., *The Chronicle of the Emerald Buddha* (1932).

DAVID K. WYATT

EMERGENCY IN INDIA, THE. On 26 June 1975 the president of India promulgated an order under article 352 of the constitution declaring that a grave emergency existed whereby the security of India was threatened by internal disturbance. Civil liberties were suspended and press censorship was imposed.

The disturbance that allegedly threatened the security of India grew out of the series of economic and political developments of the previous four years. Following the 1971 elections, India experienced an acute economic crisis. The mass discontent that followed was translated into a political response by the emergence of a popular protest movement led by J. P. Narayan.

The crisis deepened on 12 June 1975, when the Allahabad High Court found Prime Minister Indira Gandhi guilty of violating India's electoral laws in her 1971 election to the Lok Sabha. The court declared her election void and disqualified her from office for six years. The implementation of the order, however, was stayed for twenty days pending appeal. On 24 June 1975 the Supreme Court extended the stay order until Mrs. Gandhi's appeal could be heard by the full court, but it attached a series of conditions. Without consulting her cabinet, Mrs. Gandhi recommended to the president that he proclaim a state of emergency.

After the president's proclamation that an emergency existed that threatened the security of the na-

FIGURE 1. *Kailasa Temple, Ellora.*

tion, Mrs. Gandhi's administration used a number of legislative acts that had already been passed to curb opposition. These included a Press Act against the publication of "objectionable matter," which made it possible to impose press censorship in a legal fashion; an act that could declare a strike illegal on the grounds that it posed a threat to essential services; and, most important, the Defence of India Act of 1962 and the Maintenance of Internal Security Act of 1971, which made it possible to imprison citizens without trial. Because of this legislation, the administration could claim that the imprisonment of over 100,000 people, including many of its political opponents, was legal. There were widespread rumors of torture and mistreatment of prisoners, and there were reports of a campaign of forced sterilization of males to control the growth of the population. Mrs. Gandhi's son Sanjay was widely believed to be the dominant force in these and other coercive measures.

Apparently convinced by her intelligence services that the majority of the people approved of what she regarded as needed steps to bring order and discipline to India, Mrs. Gandhi decided to hold an election in March 1977. Her opponents from both the right and left formed a coalition, the Janata Party, to defeat her, and the new administration, with Morarji Desai as prime minister, restored democratic freedoms.

[*See also* Gandhi, Indira; Narayan, Jayaprakash; Gandhi, Sanjay; *and* Desai, Morarji.]

Government of India, Shah Commission of Inquiry, *Interim Report*, 3 vols. (1978). Michael Henderson, *Experiment with Untruth* (1977). Kuldip Nayar, *The Judgement* (1977).

STANLEY A. KOCHANEK

EMERGENCY IN MALAYSIA, THE, name given to a communist insurrection in Malaysia from 1948 to 1960 that directly cost eleven thousand lives. The communist-led Malayan People's Anti-Japanese Army (MPAJA) was active against the Japanese during Japan's occupation of Malaysia and was disbanded only with some difficulty by the British in 1945. In 1948 the communists took direct action, partly because they were threatened by legislation to limit their power in the trade unions. The MPAJA provided a core of fighters that reached about ten thousand at the peak of the Emergency. By about 1955 it was clear that the rebels could not win, although the Emergency was not declared over until 1960.

Even in 1984 there were about two thousand guerrillas on the Thai border and a few hundred in Sarawak. The rebels benefited from mobility, and it took the efforts of Malayan, British, Australian, New Zealand, and Fiji troops to defeat them. But they also had handicaps. Malaya had no border with a communist state that could channel help to the rebels, and their terrorism alienated some possible sympathizers. Because they were overwhelmingly Chinese, they won virtually no support from the Malays. Moreover, in order to prevent the Chinese from aiding the rebels with food or medical supplies, the Malaysian government concentrated one-fifth of the Chinese population in about five hundred new villages. This measure was quite effective, although predictably unpopular. Additionally, British cooperation in promoting independence (1957) strengthened the government's legitimacy.

[*See also* Malaysia; Malayan People's Anti-Japanese Army; *and* Communism: Communism in Southeast Asia.]

Gene Z. Hanrahan, *The Communist Struggle in Malaya* (1954). Anthony Short, *The Communist Insurrection in Malaya, 1948–1960* (1975). Michael R. Stenson, *Repression and Revolt: The Origins of the 1948 Communist Insurrection in Malaysia and Singapore* (1969).

R. S. MILNE

EMIGRATION

CHINESE EMIGRATION

[*This article primarily discusses Chinese emigration to the United States. For discussion of Chinese emigration to other parts of the world, see* Overseas Chinese.]

Chinese people are found not only in China but all over the world. More than 800,000 (1980 est.) live in the United States. About half are emigrants from China; the others are the children and grandchildren of emigrants. For more than a century, Chinese Americans have endured hardships and discrimination to build a lasting place for themselves in American society.

There is a legend that a fifth-century Buddhist priest, Huishen, rode the Japanese current east to North America, although historical records are scanty. A few Chinese sailors traveled to North America on European and American ships in the seventeenth and eighteenth centuries, and a small number of merchants and students came to America's East Coast in the first half of the nineteenth century. Large-scale immigration, however, did not start until gold was discovered in California in 1848. By 1850, 4,000 Chinese lived in the United States. The number jumped to nearly 35,000 in the next decade and continued upward until 1890, when the census recorded 107,488 Chinese Americans.

The Chinese who came to America were part of a vast diaspora. In the fifteenth century, large numbers of South Chinese made their way to Southeast Asia to seek their fortunes. Some were assimilated into their host countries, but others maintained their separate identities and kept contact with family members in China. Emigration was reinvigorated in the nineteenth century, when conditions in South China drove natives of Guangdong and Fujian provinces overseas to Singapore, Siam, the Philippines, the Dutch East Indies, Peru, Cuba, Hawaii, the British Caribbean colonies, and the United States. Population pressures, concentration of land in the hands of the wealthy few, tax abuse, insurrection, secret society activity, and ethnic warfare between Hakka (Kejia) and Punti (Bendi) made life intolerable for many South Chinese peasants. Simultaneously, foreign ships at Guangzhou (Canton) and Xiamen (Amoy) provided vehicles for escape. Chinese middlemen, often working for Western businessmen, provided the money for passage in exchange for repayment of a term of service in the foreign land. Emigrants to Peru, Hawaii, and Cuba usually went out as contract laborers, often under slavelike conditions. Those who went to Southeast Asia and North America more often went as free laborers.

Occupations. Several thousand Chinese miners worked the California goldfields in the 1850s. Often, they would take over worn-out claims that other miners had abandoned and glean a living from them by dint of hard work. In the next three decades adventurous Chinese made their way to gold strikes in Nevada, Colorado, British Columbia, and other parts of the North American West. Periodically, white miners would attack their Chinese neighbors. One such incident occurred in Idaho in 1875 at a camp near the Snake River: sixty-two Chinese miners were murdered by whites dressed as Indians.

As the mines played out, Chinese moved into other lines of work. Between twelve and fourteen thousand Chinese laborers built the western portion of the Central Pacific, America's first transcontinental railroad, although none was recorded present at Promontory, Utah, when the golden spike was driven in 1869. Other emigrants helped build a series of other western railroad lines in the succeeding decades. Thousands worked in agriculture, converting swampland around San Francisco Bay into farmland and cultivating vegetables and fruits. In San Francisco, Chinese factory workers dominated the manufacture of cigars, shoes, garments, and woolen textiles. Chinese laborers found work in the West Coast and Gulf Coast fishing industries and in Alaskan canneries. They dug coal, copper, and other minerals out of the Rocky Mountains. Some entered service industries, operating laundries and restaurants and working as domestic servants, while others ventured farther east, replacing newly freed slaves in Mississippi and Louisiana or taking factory jobs in eastern cities.

Anti-Chinese Backlash. Not all American natives appreciated the contributions of the Chinese. The 1870s and 1880s saw a steady stream of anti-Chinese violence. In 1871 a mob of Los Angeles whites, inflamed by the murder of a white man in Chinatown, killed twenty-one Chinese at random, beat scores of others, and burned and looted throughout the Chinese district. In 1885 white miners at Rock Springs, Wyoming, attacked Chinese laborers in a union dispute. Twenty-six Chinese were killed and five hundred were forced to flee. Scores of other, similar incidents took place.

In some cases, such as the 1870 dispute over strikebreaking in North Adams, Massachusetts, the anti-Chinese activity focused on economic issues. With periodic downturns in the business cycle, native laborers thrown out of work vented their frustration on the Chinese. In California in the late 1860s and 1870s, an anti-Chinese movement grew out of a dispute between captains of industry, large landowners, and their Chinese workers, on one side, and labor unions, small-business men, and small farmers on the other. Demagogues such as Denis Kearney shouted that "the Chinese must go!" They held anti-Chinese conventions that called for exclusion of Chinese immigrants and applauded when Chinese were killed or made to flee their homes.

Kearney and other agitators played on a rising tide of racism in white America. The ideals of imperial conquest in Europe and Manifest Destiny in America were based in part on an assumption of racial superiority on the part of Caucasians. Anti-Chinese activists decried the "heathen Chinee" as filthy, immoral, antifamily, slavelike, unassimilable, and degrading to society. Those charges were drawn not so much from white Californians' actual experiences with Chinese expatriates as from the images of Chinese in China circulated throughout the United States a generation earlier by returned traders, diplomats, and missionaries. These negative predispositions toward the Chinese created a national constituency for anti-Chinese activity.

Politicians picked up the cry for exclusion. For years, California Chinese had been subject to discriminatory laws that taxed them more heavily than others and restricted their occupations and places of residence. In 1877 California legislators asked Congress to restrict Chinese immigration. Two years later they wrote a new constitution that contained several anti-Chinese passages. By 1882 they and other white Americans had succeeded in persuading Congress to exclude the Chinese, in violation of the Burlingame Treaty of 1868. The 1882 law, designed to last ten years, denied Chinese laboring people access to the United States but allowed government officers, merchants, tourists, and students to continue to come. Laws passed in 1884 and 1888 broadened the definition of laborer and denied reentry to any Chinese laborer already here who might go home for a visit. The exclusion law of 1882 was renewed in 1892 and again in 1902, and finally made permanent in 1904.

Community Associations. White opposition and the desire to keep alive memories of home drew Chinese Americans together. In mining camps, cities, and farming areas Chinese emigrants formed communities of their own. These were bachelor societies. Like earlier generations of Chinese emigrants to Southeast Asia, Chinese men—and nearly all were men—who went to America saw themselves not as permanent dwellers but as sojourners: birds of passage who would go to the new land to make some money but who always intended to return to their home villages once their fortunes were made. Many did return, especially after the exclusion law was passed, to buy land and claim places of modest honor in rural Guangdong. Others stayed on in America, hoping to make enough money to return home in triumph. In the meantime they lived as frugally as they could, sending remittances to their home villages to help support relatives and maintain clan temples. Many had wives and children they hardly knew back home. They might make a brief trip home to visit their ancestors and sire children, but usually Gumshan (Jinshan)—America, the Golden Mountain—called them back. Some men rejoined their families only at their funerals; others, not at all.

Discrimination and the sojourner mentality meant that Chinese emigrants remained apart from other Americans. An entire set of Chinese American social institutions sprang up wherever Chinese congregated. At first this might simply be a Chinese store, where one could find Chinese faces and conversation, home-cooked meals, perhaps help finding a job and a place to sleep. The men tended to congregate according to the region from which they came. They formed *huiguan,* or district associations, led by merchants, for purposes of fraternity, mutual aid, and protection. Most Chinese Americans came from one of three areas in Guangdong: the Sam Yap ("three districts") near Guangzhou; the Sze Yap ("four districts"), a rural area just to the southwest; or Zhongshan, a district in the Pearl River delta near Macao. In San Francisco, where the largest number of Chinese gathered, several *huiguan* came together into an umbrella organization known as the Chinese Six Companies, a consolidated benevolent association. This became the dominant voice in the affairs of San Francisco Chinese and formed the pattern for community organizations in other cities. Sojourners also formed family or clan associations, made up of people who bore the same surname. Tongs, or secret societies, in particular the Triads, found their way into Chinese American society as well. They provided an antiestablishment force in the early years, trafficking in opium, prostitution, and gambling, although eventually they lost their radical flavor and became part of the accepted power structure of most Chinese communities.

Chinatown Society. As anti-Chinese hysteria died down after 1885, and as the numbers of Chinese men in America dwindled, white Americans by and large left them alone. Chinese suffered segregation and discrimination, but the forces of white authority seldom ventured into Chinatown. Under the supervision of the merchant elite who ran the district and family associations, the increasingly urban Chinese settled down to a proletarian existence. Some went back to China, sending their sons to the Golden Mountain to take their places.

A brisk trade in immigration papers developed during the late nineteenth and early twentieth centuries. The 1906 San Francisco earthquake and fire destroyed many immigration and birth records. That allowed hundreds, perhaps thousands of Chinese emigrant men to claim birth on American soil and, therefore, United States citizenship without fear of contradiction. Each time such a citizen returned to China he would register the birth of a child, usually a son, who was then qualified for American citizenship and entry to the United States. He might then sell that real or imagined child's papers to someone else, who would, on reaching adolescence, change his name and go to America as the "paper son" of his benefactor. American immigration authorities caught on to this practice and detained incoming Chinese at a prison on Angel Island in San Francisco Bay. There they made each entering Chinese repeat his story over and over, in an attempt to catch him in a slip and send him back to China. The anguished poems on Angel Island cell walls testify to the hardship and frustration endured by twentieth-century emigrants to Chinese America. Despite such official harassment, Chinese sons, real or fictive, continued to arrive in America. By the 1930s the emigrant bachelor society was entering its fourth generation.

The economies of most Chinatowns were largely enclosed and self-sustaining. In the 1910s and 1920s Chinese entrepreneurs founded a few banks and a short-lived steamship company. Lack of capital, however, kept most Chinese businesses small and labor-intensive. Restaurants, laundries, groceries, and sewing factories were most common. The restaurants served the largest number of non-Chinese and generated the most capital. Their owners became leaders of Chinatown's polity and speakers for Chinese Americans to the larger society. Members of the merchant class were the only Chinese allowed to bring in wives and start American families. Their children provided Chinese American communities with a small second generation, more americanized than their parents and largely bent on achieving middle-class status.

Chinese Americans remained intensely interested in Chinese politics. They provided a large portion of the financial support for Kang Youwei's attempts to reform China in the first years of the twentieth century, Sun Yat-sen's revolutionary efforts, and the Guomindang (Kuomintang) of Chiang Kai-shek. Chinese American popular opinion was divided over the 1946 to 1949 civil war. The power of the pro-Guomindang merchant elite and the influence of American anticommunism, however, kept pro-Beijing sentiment underground until the late 1960s.

Postwar Trends. World War II and the decades that followed changed the demography of Chinese America: the bachelor society became a family society. The alliance between the United States and China against Japan made Chinese exclusion embarrassing to the American government, so the ban on immigration was replaced in 1943 by a token quota of 105 per year. Resident Chinese were allowed to become citizens, however, and after the war several thousand Chinese women were admitted as war brides. The Communist victory in 1949 spurred emigration to America by new classes of Chinese: students, professionals, and people from northern and central China. Gradually, overt discrimination was discontinued, although subtler forms of prejudice remained. Finally, in 1965 the Johnson administration ended the immigration quota system. That meant that an average of more than twenty thousand Chinese—most of them from Hong Kong—would come to the United States each year for the next decade and a half.

A new emigrant generation formed in American Chinatowns, but this one was female as well as male, and largely urban in origin. The majority was still Cantonese, but Taiwan and other regions sent significant minorities. The new, greatly expanded emigration meant that families long separated were reunited. Chinese neighborhoods and businesses boomed. Many of the new emigrants, in addition to those Chinese who grew up in America, worked their way into colleges and universities and ultimately into secure professions. They assimilated American culture to a greater degree than earlier Chinese Americans, and most left Chinatown for comfortable suburbs.

Others, mainly unskilled emigrants, found themselves trapped in low-paying jobs in Chinatown restaurants and shops. Health, housing, crime, and other problems plagued them. In the late 1960s and 1970s young, middle-class university students began to look for their ethnic roots in Chinatowns and discovered some of those problems. Modeling themselves on black community activists, they tried to alleviate the distress. They rallied, lobbied, organized, and allied themselves with older Chinese Americans to fight for health care, housing, bilingual education, and other reforms. In the liberal climate of the 1970s they were in large part successful. With large numbers of emigrants continuing to arrive, however, overcrowding, youth gangs, and other problems were not completely conquered.

In the 1970s, as the United States restored relations with the People's Republic of China, both the mainland and Taiwan governments sought to gain the favor of overseas Chinese. Chinese Americans were offered trips to the old country at attractive prices. Many visited, seeing family and friends for the first time in decades, or showed other signs of renewed interest in China. Very few were inclined to abandon America for the land of their ancestors, however; after generations of discrimination and hard work, Chinese emigrants had become Chinese Americans.

[*See also* Coolie Trade.]

Jack Chen, *The Chinese of America* (1981). Mary Roberts Coolidge, *Chinese Immigration* (1909; reprint, 1968). Maxine Hong Kingston, *China Men* (1980). H. Mark Lai and Philip P. Choy, *Outlines: History of the Chinese in America* (1971). Diane Mark and Ginger Chih, *A Place Called Chinese America* (1982). Stuart Creighton Miller,

The Unwelcome Immigrant: American Images of the Chinese, 1785–1882 (1969). Victor G. Nee and Brett de Bary Nee, *Longtime Californ': A Documentary Study of an American Chinatown* (1973). Alexander Saxton, *The Indispensible Enemy: Labor and the Anti-Chinese Movement in California* (1971).

PAUL R. SPICKARD

SOUTH ASIAN EMIGRATION

Along with China and Africa, the Indian subcontinent has provided the main recruitment area of Third World emigration. Yet, just as certain provinces of South China have provided a constant flow of emigrants while other areas have contributed little to the process, there is a strong regional identification in Indian emigration. Punjab with its "frontier" character has been a zone of movement throughout history; Gujarat, looking west over the Arabian Sea, has long had external links; parts of South India such as Kerala and Tamil Nadu have tried to ameliorate population pressures by sending forth the most enterprising. Elsewhere, migration has only been a marginal phenomenon.

Throughout ancient and medieval times most of the emigrants retained links with their home village or town: indeed, it was common for a man to make protracted working visits to a far country while his dependents remained at home with the extended family. While most went overseas—to Southeast Asia or the western littoral of the Indian Ocean—for trade, some were drawn abroad by religion or priestcraft. Hinduism and Buddhism were taken to Sri Lanka (Ceylon) and Southeast Asia centuries before the common era, and these religions became vehicles for social and political control. The caste system was exported, although in simplified form. The brahman priest or minister was important in legitimizing the indigenous rulers. The regimes they helped to establish were "Indian" in terms of culture rather than in their personnel. The actual volume of Indian emigration was less important than its influence, which was pervasive.

The formation of communities of overseas Indians—as compared with the evolution of hinduized or Buddhistic societies in Southeast Asia and elsewhere on the fringes of the Indian Ocean—was largely the consequence of Western colonial expansion. British penetration of Southeast Asia, the Far East and East Africa developed from India. Many of these peripheral areas of British activity were only lightly populated by peoples for whom wage labor was not part of their economy or culture. It became necessary to import workers from India, where, by the eighteenth century, there were already sources of industrial labor. During this phase, considerable use was made of convicts serving long sentences who were transported overseas (as were contemporary British convicts). Indian convicts built many of Singapore's public buildings, including its cathedral.

An even greater demand for Indian labor came when slavery was abolished throughout the British Empire in 1833. When former African slaves left the hated plantations on their emancipation, the planters turned to India. It soon became evident that in the new labor system there were abuses: irregular methods of recruiting, inadequate care on the ocean voyage, and above all harsh treatment on the colonial plantation. The Government of India stepped in with a code of regulations, stipulating a period of five years indenture, after which the migrant worker was entitled to a passage home. Government "protectors" were appointed at the ports of embarkation and in the receiving colonies. Despite these and other precautions the exploitation of the "coolies" continued largely unchecked. One feature of the system was the small proportion of females—less than one-fifth of the emigrants. Hence it was necessary to keep numbers up by continued recruitment.

The earliest and largest emigration was to Mauritius; British Guiana also recruited sizable numbers. A large proportion of emigrants were Bhojpuris from Bihar and eastern Uttar Pradesh. The rise of the tea industry in Sri Lanka stimulated a massive movement from the southern Tamil districts, although for many decades this was mainly a seasonal or annual migration. Other colonies joined in the demand, notably Trinidad, Natal in South Africa, and later Fiji. In East Africa the railroad was built by indentured labor. Jamaica and other West Indian islands recruited on a small scale, while Malaya was to become a major importer of Indian labor when rubber became its chief industry, although, as in Sri Lanka (and also in Burma, another field for Indian labor) the migration was largely outside the indenture system. Indentured emigration was also permitted by the Government of India to places outside the British Empire—to the French colonies of Réunion, Martinique, Guadeloupe and Cayenne, and to Dutch Surinam.

Periodically, scandals on the plantations were exposed and official inquiries were held, as in British Guiana in 1871 and in Mauritius in 1875. Both the British government and the Government of India remained unmoved. Public opinion in India was aroused by Mohandas Gandhi's campaign in South

Africa for civil rights, in which laborers (many still in indenture) played an outstanding part. Indentured migration to South Africa was abolished, but it continued to other sugar colonies into the first years of the 1914–1918 war, when a sensation was created by C. F. Andrews's inquiry uncovering a story of iniquity and injustice in Fiji. The viceroy, Lord Hardinge, was moved to condemn the system and halt all further recruitment. Indenture was finally abolished in 1920.

As a consequence of eighty years of indentured emigration, today in the independent states of Mauritius, Guyana, Surinam, and Fiji a majority of the population is of Indian origin, while in Trinidad Indians form 45 percent of the total population. In Sri Lanka and West Malaysia about 10 percent of the population are descendants of former Indian laborers.

However, from the mid-nineteenth century onward there was also a migration of traders, craftsmen, clerks, mechanics, and professional people, sometimes called "passenger Indians." Many came from Gujarat, some from Punjab. In Southeast Asia the Chettiars of Madras were prominent. [*See* Chettiar.] They settled in all the colonies where there were immigrant Indian laborers. Gujarati traders and manufacturers were especially important in East Africa. Because of their remarkable enterprise and performance, the Indian business community found themselves at odds with those who coveted their position after independence.

Most recently, the impulse to emigrate has been strong in communities disturbed by the partition of 1947: notably the Sikhs, but also others such as the Mirpuris. Britain, with its open door to Commonwealth citizens, and its aging industries requiring labor, provided the main opening in the 1950s and 1960s. When severe immigration restrictions came into effect, the "Asian" (South Asian) community was well established in Britain and, by natural increase, passed the one million figure in the 1970s. An important component were the business and professional people who arrived via East Africa, including the 80,000 expelled from Uganda by Idi Amin.

The principal outlet for emigrants from the subcontinent in the 1980s is found in the oil states of the Arabian Gulf. They can absorb every kind of incomer, from the highly qualified economist or accountant to the unskilled laborer of traditional migration. These immigrants are overwhelmingly male, and their terms of employment are for limited periods only. Yet, as in the past, this temporary movement is gradually assuming an aspect of permanence. For India, and even more so Pakistan, the emigrants provide the greatest source of foreign exchange. The impact upon certain limited areas—notably in the Punjab, on both sides of the partition line—appears enormous.

Meanwhile, small numbers of highly skilled people, such as doctors, go elsewhere, particularly to North America. The Indian subcontinent is left to calculate how far this vast emigration represents profit or loss.

[*See also* Mauritius.]

A. W. Helweg, *Sikhs in England* (1979). C. Kondapi, *Indians Overseas* (1951). Ursula Sharma, *Rampal and His Family* (1971). D. P. Singhal, *India and World Civilization*, 2 vols. (1969). Hugh Tinker, *A New System of Slavery: The Export of Indian Labour Overseas* (1974); *Separate and Unequal: India and the Indians in the British Commonwealth* (1976); and *The Banyan Tree: Overseas Emigrants from India, Pakistan and Bangladesh* (1977).

HUGH TINKER

JAPANESE EMIGRATION

Although Japanese moved overseas in modest numbers relative to the population flows from most European and Pacific countries, the matter of Japanese settlement in the United States was seized upon by opportunistic American politicians, who made it a major irritant in Japanese-American relations in the early decades of the twentieth century.

Japanese colonies of traders dotted Southeast Asia in the late fifteenth and early sixteenth centuries, but with the implementation of the "seclusion" (*sakoku*) policy by the Tokugawa shogunate in the 1630s it became impossible for Japanese to emigrate or even travel. The abandonment of seclusion in the 1860s reversed such policies, but it was not until the 1880s that the Japanese government negotiated an immigration treaty with the kindom of Hawaii. Chinese immigration to the United States had been cut by the Federal Exclusion Act of 1882. Japanese laborers who went to the US soon inherited the fears, although little of the violence, that had greeted the Chinese. They were welcomed as employees but not as competitors. In 1900 more than twelve thousand Japanese entered the US; additional transfers from Hawaii were more difficult to count.

After the Japanese victory over Russia in 1905 Japanese settlers in the US inherited the discrimination that had earlier been directed toward Chinese. Labor organizers warned that Japanese laborers would lower the wage rate, and within a few years, once Japanese farmers proved their ability on rented and purchased land, there were charges that

Japanese would come to dominate the California countryside. In 1906 the San Francisco Board of Education required all Asian pupils to attend a special public school, a measure that inflamed Japanese public opinion because it was discriminatory. President Theodore Roosevelt, after denouncing this ruling, quietly arranged with the Meiji government to stop further immigration of laborers under the so-called Gentleman's Agreement. In 1913 the California legislature denied aliens ineligible for citizenship the right to own land or to lease agricultural land for more than three years, thus reopening the immigration question, and in 1924 Congressional immigration legislation that barred "aliens ineligible to citizenship" effectively closed the door to further Japanese entry. These developments did serious harm to American-Japanese relations and greatly weakened the position of pro-American Japanese.

The United States was not alone in fearing and restricting Japanese entry. Australia ruled against Japanese immigrants in 1898, and Canada in 1908. In that same year Japanese emigration to Brazil began, and by 1940 Japanese-born immigrants in South America approximately equaled the 250,000 resident in Canada and the United States.

A larger community of more than one million, the majority in trade, were living in Asian countries at the time of World War II. With the Japanese defeat these people were repatriated to Japan. Emigration resumed after the conclusion of the Allied Occupation in 1952, but Japan's rapid economic growth after that decade ended made overseas emigration less attractive to Japanese.

During World War II Japanese communities in the United States (although not in Hawaii) and Canada received harsh treatment through expropriation and internment, but the performance of Japanese special forces recruited for military service in the European theater of war, combined with the discovery that there had been no authenticated instances of "subversion," made for radically different circumstances. Wartime dispersion of previously close communities served to accelerate the assimilation of second-generation Japanese into the mainstream of North American and Brazilian life.

Roger Daniels, *The Politics of Prejudice* (1962). T. Suzuki, *The Japanese Immigrant in Brazil* (1969). D. Eleanor Westney, "Emigration," in *The Encyclopedia of Japan* (1983), vol. 2, pp. 200–201.

MARIUS B. JANSEN

EMPRESS DOWAGER (Cixi; 1835–1908), conservative, ambitious, and manipulative force behind the imperial throne of the late Qing dynasty (1644–1911) in China. Née Yehonala of the Manchu Blue Banner, she became known as Empress Xiaoqin to the Chinese and as the "Empress Dowager" or "the Old Buddha" to the West.

In 1851, Cixi became a low-ranking concubine to the Qing emperor Xianfeng (r. 1850–1861). Her status rose considerably when she gave birth to a son, Caichun, in April 1856. Her son became her "ticket" to absolute power when he was designated as the heir apparent. In 1861 he became emperor at the age of five. Since he was too young to rule alone, both his mother and another empress, Consort Cian, were named as empresses dowager or imperial mothers and established themselves as the regents for the emperor. His reign was named Tongzhi ("coeval rule"; 1862–1874); it represented a time of restoration of traditional values and did little to alleviate the political, social, and economic problems that were plaguing the late Qing empire.

In 1865 Cixi displaced her fellow regent and took sole possession of power as regent for her son. When the Tongzhi emperor died in 1875 the empress dowager moved quickly to consolidate her supreme authority. She managed to put her three-year-old nephew on the throne, thereby violating the established rules for succession. The child became the Guangxu ("glorious succession") emperor (r. 1875–1908), but the real power rested with the empress dowager, who ruled from "behind the screen" and allied herself with the conservative antiforeign cliques at court.

The Guangxu emperor enjoyed a brief period of independent action in implementing a program of reform during the One Hundred Days period of 1898. However, the empress dowager returned with a vengeance in September of that year and did not relinquish her absolute power until her death on 14 November 1908. Her reign was indicative of an empire in decline with no hope of recovery.

[*See also* Qing Dynasty.]

Jean Chesneaux et al., *China from the Opium Wars to the 1911 Revolution* (1976). Arthur W. Hummel, ed., *Eminent Chinese of the Ch'ing Period* (1943–1944). Mary C. Wright, *The Last Stand of Chinese Conservatism: The T'ung-chih Restoration (1862–1872)* (1957).

ANITA M. ANDREW

ENNIN (794–864), a monk of the Tendai school of Japanese Buddhism. Ennin is chiefly remembered for his travel diary, a long account of a pilgrimage he made to Buddhist sites in China between 835 and 847. He has, however, other claims to fame. As one of Saichō's students, he was a pioneer in the early doctrinal and institutional development of Tendai Buddhism in Japan. He taught monks and members of the imperial court and served as the third chief priest, or *zasu,* of Enryakuji.

Ennin was born in 793 or 794 into a provincial family, the Mibu, in eastern Japan. He lost his father while still an infant and from the age of nine began to study Buddhism with a local priest. At the age of fifteen or so Saichō appeared to him in a dream. Taking this as an omen Ennin enrolled as a novice in Enryakuji, where he began to study the *Lotus Sutra* and Tendai meditation, *shikan,* with Saichō himself, becoming a favored disciple. After Saichō's death in 822, Ennin traveled for more than ten years as an itinerant preacher spreading Tendai teachings. He lectured on the *Lotus Sutra* at Hōryūji, Shitennōji, and other monasteries.

In 835 Ennin was honored by being appointed one of several scholar-monks joining an embassy to China. Ennin was thus continuing the work of Saichō in transmitting the latest and fullest expression of Chinese Tiantai Buddhism to Japan. After several abortive attempts Ennin reached China in 838. He spent nine years in China. Although the Chinese authorities would not allow him to realize his most cherished dream of retracing Saichō's footsteps and visiting Mount Tiantai in the South, he was able to visit the sacred Buddhist sites on Mount Wutai in the northeast, a center of devotion to the bodhisattva Manjusri. His diary, the *Nittō guhō junrei gyōki (The Record of a Pilgrimage to China in Search of the Law),* provides a full and fascinating picture of Buddhism and Chinese society in the Tang dynasty. It includes accounts of his many encounters with Chinese monks, descriptions of his Buddhist studies in Chang'an, and observations on the great persecution of Buddhism between 842 and 845.

In 847, loaded with sutras, paintings, mandalas, ritual implements, and much new knowledge, Ennin arrived back in Japan. He was immediately lionized by the imperial court and heaped with clerical honors. Even before Saichō was accorded the honor, Ennin was named National Master. In 854 he was appointed head of the Tendai school by Emperor Montoku. He spent the closing years of his life lecturing on the *Lotus Sutra* and Esoteric Buddhism and administering the precepts to emperors and courtiers as well as monks.

Edwin O. Reischauer, *Ennin's Diary* (1955) and *Ennin's Travels in T'ang China* (1955).

Martin Collcutt

ENOMOTO TAKEAKI (1836–1908), Japanese sailor, rebel, and statesman. Born into a family of *bakufu* retainers, Enomoto was sent to Nagasaki in 1853 for training in Western seamanship at the newly established naval academy. In 1862 he was selected for further training in the Netherlands, where he studied chemistry, engineering, and international law. On his return to Japan in 1867, he passed through a series of official posts, winning an appointment as second in command of the *bakufu's* navy just before the government's collapse.

Left in charge of six ships, Enomoto could have attempted either to buy favors from the new Meiji government or to help abort it by joining the resistance in the northeast. He did neither for some months, but, finally, in the autumn of 1868 he sailed north. In 1869, at Hakodate, he joined forces with what remained of the resistance in an attempt to set up an independent state in Hokkaido. It was far too late for such an effort, and he surrendered later that year. His experience and qualities, however, were such that in 1872, after three years in confinement, he was pardoned and then given highly responsible positions for the rest of his life. As a diplomat he was called upon to negotiate the Treaty of Saint Petersburg, under which Japan acquired the Kurile Islands, and to play a leading role in concluding the Treaty of Tianjin. As an administrator, he was entrusted by the government with such portfolios as education, commerce, and foreign affairs.

[*See also* Meiji Restoration *and* Russo-Japanese War.]

Harold Bolitho

ENRYAKUJI, the principal monastery of the Tendai school of Japanese Buddhism. Situated on the summit of Mount Hiei to the northeast of Kyoto, the monastery was founded by the Japanese monk Saichō (766–822) in 788 and given the name Enryakuji by imperial decree in 823. It flourished under the patronage of Emperor Kammu (737–805), who moved the capital from Heijō to Heian (Kyoto), and succeeding emperors.

For over one thousand years Enryakuji has been one of the great centers of Japanese Buddhism. In addition to the study of the *Lotus Sutra* and other Mahayana Buddhist texts, Enryakuji monks were students and practitioners of Tantric Buddhism, of meditation *(shikan),* and of Pure Land devotion. Among the more famous monks trained in Enryakuji were Ennin (794–864), who made a long pilgrimage to China; Enchin (814–891), the founder of the rival

Tendai monastery of Onjōji; Genshin (942–1017), the author of an important treatise on the Pure Land, *The Essentials of Salvation;* the poet and historian Jien (1155–1225); Hōnen (1133–1222), the founder of the Pure Land school of Buddhism; Shinran (1173–1262), the founder of the True Pure Land school; Eisai (1141–1215) and Dōgen (1200–1253), who introduced Rinzai and Sōtō Zen, respectively, from China; and Nichiren (1222–1282), who advocated a radical revival of devotion to the *Lotus Sutra*.

The monastery wielded great economic, political, and even military power. Between the ninth and the thirteenth centuries Enryakuji and its subtemples amassed hundreds of landholdings *(shōen)* scattered over most of the provinces of Japan. To protect these holdings and advance the interests of their monastery the chief monks of Enryakuji, the *zasu,* used their political and social connections. When these failed, Enryakuji, like other monastic centers, frequently resorted to force. It had at its disposal an army of monk-soldiers *(sōhei),* several thousand strong. The military and secular power of great monasteries like Enryakuji was finally broken by Oda Nobunaga and Toyotomi Hideyoshi in the sixteenth century. Nobunaga razed Enryakuji in 1571. Hideyoshi and Tokugawa Ieyasu partially restored it but never permitted it to regain its former power or wealth. The monastery survived several severe fires in the Edo period (1600–1868) and an outburst of anti-Buddhist sentiment during the separation of Buddhism and Shinto early in the Meiji period (1868–1912). Although none of the early buildings has survived, monks are still in residence at the monastery, and visitors to Kyoto can still climb Mount Hiei to see the Great Central Hall, or Konpon Chūdō, and other monastic buildings.

[*See also* Ennin *and* Tendai.]

MARTIN COLLCUTT

ETHICAL COLONIAL POLICY. In 1901 the Netherlands' crown formally announced a policy of "ethical obligation and moral responsibility to the people of the East Indies." This was to replace the policy of exploitation that had prevailed in the previous century. These noble and humanitarian words came to mean many things to many people. The policy has been summarized as "education, irrigation, and emigration." Schooling for Indonesians was improved and extended, giving rise to a Western-educated elite, and many villagers were exposed to a minimal and rather useless instruction. Agricultural extension not only opened new areas to

FIGURE 1. *Enryakuji.* Part of the central monastic compound.

cultivation but also introduced improved crops and livestock in a ceaseless but never totally successful effort to achieve self-sufficiency in food. Families from overcrowded Java were resettled in more thinly populated areas after parts of Sumatra were colonized in 1905, but the exodus remained a trickle and did not ease Java's population pressure.

The ethical policy also implied the extension of rational and efficient government throughout the archipelago, the development of infrastructure facilities to encourage economic growth and development, and the opening of the archipelago to Christian missionary activity. All these areas saw growth and development in the early years of the twentieth century. Local persons were trained and educated for administrative posts and for positions in various sorts of enterprises. Exports climbed, especially from the islands outside Java, which by 1930 accounted for 55 percent of total exports. Educated Indonesians became self-consciously interested in political advancement. Christian missions led to the formation of similar groups by Muslims. The years up to about 1920 were the real heyday of modernization and development; thereafter enthusiasm waned and only limited growth occurred.

[*See also* Indonesia, Republic of.]

Robert Van Niel, *The Emergence of the Modern Indonesian Elite* (1960).

ROBERT VAN NIEL

ETŌ SHIMPEI (1834–1874), activist in the movement that brought down the Tokugawa shogunate of Japan in 1868. Etō became a key member of the new Meiji government in its early stage. A self-taught legal specialist, Etō's contributions to Japan's first modern government lay in his numerous legal reforms.

Born into a samurai family of low rank in Saga on the island of Kyushu, Etō spent much of his time under house arrest in his own domain during the final years of Tokugawa rule for his participation in antishogunal activities. During the civil war that followed the imperial restoration, Etō was a military and legal adviser. From then on, he served the new government in various capacities, including vice-minister of education and minister of justice. In 1873 Etō aligned himself with a group in the government, including Saigō Takamori and Itagaki Taisuke, that advocated sending a military mission to Korea. Once the policy was defeated by the other members of the government, Etō sought various means of making the government respond to this demand, as well as to those of disgruntled former samurai. This eventually led him to lead an unsuccessful antigovernment uprising with some three thousand followers in Saga in 1874. He was captured and executed in that year.

[*See also* Saga Rebellion.]

MICHIO UMEGAKI

EURASIANS. *See* Anglo-Indians.

EVANGELISTA, CRISANTO (1888–1942), Filipino political activist. Evangelista was the son of tenant farmers in the village of Meycanayan Bulacan. After finishing his primary education he moved to Manila, where he found a menial job at the Bureau of Printing and learned his trade as a printer. He continued his studies by reading and attending Manila labor union activities, which were closely watched and occasionally repressed by the American authorities.

The liberation of the poor and exploited soon became Evangelista's major concern, and he wrote essays on this topic for the *Tambuli, Ang Manggagawa,* and May 1 souvenir programs. From 1906 to 1941, he joined or spearheaded mutual aid societies, the Union of Printers in the Philippines, the Philippine Labor Congress, and the Proletarian Labor Congress. The latter, founded in May 1929, reflected Evangelista's adoption of Marxism. In November 1930 he helped launch the first communist party of the Philippines.

Evangelista's career was interrupted by government prosecutions and the Japanese invasion of the Philippines. On 2 June 1942 the Japanese had Evangelista executed at Fort Santiago, Manila.

MELINDA TRIA KERKVLIET

EVEREST, the world's tallest mountain, located on the border between Nepal and Tibet in the eastern Himalayas. Known as Sagarmatha ("peak of the heavens") to the Nepalese and Chomolungma ("mother goddess of the land") to Tibetans, the peak (29,028 feet, or 8,848 meters, tall) was named for George Everest, surveyor-general of India from 1830 to 1843. Beginning in 1921, ten successive attempts were made by British and Swiss teams to establish a route to the summit, but each was thwarted by extreme cold and brutal winds. Not until 1953 did a British expedition under the leadership of John Hunt open the way for a successful assault along the mountain's southeast ridge. The New Zealander Edmund Hillary and Sherpa Tenzing Norgay reached the summit on 29 May 1953. The Japanese team that scaled the peak in 1970 was the first to include a woman.

[*See also* Norgay, Tenzing.]

Toni Hagen, *Mount Everest* (1963). Edmund Hillary, *High Adventure* (1955). RICHARD ENGLISH

EVIDENTIAL RESEARCH, SCHOOL OF. *See* Kaozheng Xue.

EXAMINATION SYSTEM. *See* Bureaucracy in China *and* Korean State Examination System.

EXPORT PROCESSING ZONES. *See* Special Economic Zones.

F

FA-HSIEN. *See* Faxian.

FAJIA. *See* Legalism.

FAMILY AND MARRIAGE. With rare exceptions—few, if any, in Asia—the cultures on this planet have recently undergone extensive alterations in their marital forms and family structures. Cultures that once stressed unilineally extended kin groups, especially clans and lineages, now find that nuclear families are overwhelmingly the structural norm. Kinship extensions with strong functional associations are rare or extinct, as are several forms of marriage such as polyandry, the condition in which one woman simultaneously has two or more husbands (who are usually siblings, in which case the marital form is known as fraternal polyandry). This article deals primarily with contemporary usage but locates the present against an earlier ethnographic background.

The various geographic and cultural areas of Asia show significant differences from each other, but convergences are quite obvious. To some extent these convergences are in large measure the result of substantial political pressures emanating from obvious centers. Other changes are less dependent on political factors and seem more influenced by changing conditions of technology and economy. These latter causes of social change have been active for a century, but the rate of change has been tremendously accelerated all over Asia (and the rest of the world) since World War II.

East Asia. Marriage patterns in nineteenth-century China, Japan, and Korea were structurally quite similar. In all three cultures, the selection of a spouse was usually carried out with only minor input from the man and woman who were to be mates. The most important voices in the transaction were those of the couple's fathers and mothers and possibly the paternal grandparents, if they were still alive. Actually, grandparents would often be alive, since the couples tended to be married quite young, females often not having reached seventeen and males being under twenty. (There is a preference for brides younger than their husbands, a trait Asia shares with most of the world.) Throughout China the selection of mates involved use of different systems of divination that now seem discarded, vitiated by a variety of other social alterations, most conspicuously that which now permits a much more extensive personal choice of mates by the bride and groom themselves.

Particularly in China, the services of a professional go-between were often used. Although they were mainly women, go-betweens might also be male. In any case, the matchmaker would give little attention to pleasing either intended bride or groom, emphasizing instead the desires expressed by the family heads. This system still continues, even in the People's Republic of China (PRC), although it is more common in rural areas. It is rare for a couple to wed if they have not met before, perhaps under circumstances arranged by the go-between.

Throughout East Asia, the nineteenth century was a period in which small families were typical. Extended families, those that would see married brothers and their children living in one house and taking their meals together from a single kitchen, usually were to be found among those who had achieved some degree of economic success, although there could be exceptions, such as the typical family unit of southeast China, where fortlike houses developed. These had hundreds of rooms, inhabited by closely knit families that formed lineages made up of rich and poor branches. In such villages a large number of men could be quickly summoned, and records of the nineteenth century and earlier show that such defense (or raiding) was not uncommon. (The town of Kamting in the center of the New Territories in Hong Kong was exactly such a place, although its population is now rather heterogeneous.)

Finally, in the early 1980s, as the population of the PRC approached one billion, the size of the population was recognized as one of China's most serious problems. Nuclear families in urban areas were strictly limited to one child, regardless of the child's gender; families in rural areas were to have no more than two children. Taken to its logical conclusion, this policy would lead to an extraordinary social pattern, one in which there will be no collateral relatives, no aunts, uncles, brothers, sisters, or cousins. Under the current rules, however, a married couple who are themselves both only children may have more than one child, thus precluding this development.

Although different from China, particularly in their nobilities and aristocracies, Korea and Japan manifested a very similar pattern of patrilineal joint families. A notable difference involved the Japanese treatment of inheritance. The classical Japanese system was more similar to that of Europe than it was to that of China, featuring strong emphasis on primogeniture. While the Japanese left the bulk of an estate to the eldest son, the Chinese practice was generally to split the estate among all male heirs. Two major exceptions in the Chinese case must be noted. The inheritance was rarely divided absolutely equally; one son often would take over the support of an aged surviving parent and would usually get a larger share (or two shares) to cover the expense. Another common exception applied in families with limited resources whose total productive capacity was adequate for only one nuclear family. Often in such families the number of children would have been limited through infanticide, or by giving up additional children for adoption. Usually two sons would be kept since child mortality was high; to face old age without a son to support and care for one was a miserable fate.

Southeast Asia. The situation was quite different in Southeast Asia. This extensive region, much of which is insular, shows a number of highly distinct patterns of marriage and social organization. To begin with, unlike China, Japan, and Korea, patrilineality is not virtually universal. (We must say "virtually universal," because China includes several non-Han cultures, such as part of the Li population living on Hainan Island, who do not trace descent patrilineally. Indeed, linguistically and in other aspects of culture, the Li are often classified with populations of northern Southeast Asia.)

In Southeast Asia, except where Chinese influence was very strong, as in Vietnam, there were few formally structured patrilineally extended families. It was more common for villages to be made up of nuclear families, although these were often components of tightly structured lineages that collectively carried out most functions of daily life. In this context, the disastrous consequences of the Indochina War have virtually eliminated most of the Montagnard societies that maintained their distinctive basic cultures for centuries.

Southeast Asia was long the site of cultures with extremely sophisticated matrilineal organization, a matriliny that survived political changes that elsewhere in the world saw a turn to patriliny or bilaterality. This must not be taken to indicate that invariably, or even usually, matriliny precedes patriliny. Such a view, commonly held in the nineteenth century and often found in current Chinese theory, is incorrect. A clearly matrilineal system operated, for example, in Minangkabau, a populous society found in northern Sumatra. That society, however, did not become directly involved in its own state structure until Dutch conquest. An offshoot of Minangkabau, however, was the former Malayan state of Negri Sembilan, which achieved its state organization in the late eighteenth century while retaining its matrilineal organization. Despite matriliny, the political leaders of Negri Sembilan were invariably male. Another society that displayed matriliny was the Cham, which existed in mainland Southeast Asia centuries ago, occupying a coastal area in what is now Vietnam and extending into what is now Cambodia. [*See* Minangkabau; Negri Sembilan; *and* Cham.]

South Asia. The area occupied by the island of Sri Lanka and the Indian subcontinent also shows a wide range of family types, which included one of the most unusual in all of ethnography. This group's home was the Malabar coast of southwest India, and the people in question are the Nairs (Nayars). Nair weddings had an unusual feature—the groom was a transient who soon disappeared, often at the very end of the ceremony or within a day or two. He would probably never see his wife again. She, in turn, continued to live with her mother and mother's sisters and with their children, as well as with her own. Her children, of course, could not be the issue of the man to whom she was married. Instead, they would be the biological sons of various lovers, usually other Nair men. Those biological fathers would be considered sociologically childless; the socially recognized father of a child was its mother's husband, who might never have had sexual intercourse with her and who may have died years before his "child" was born. [*See* Nairs.]

A variety of conditions of modern life have swept away such unusual postmarital structures, but the patrilineal family continues to be common throughout South Asia. Perhaps the broadest alteration of domestic patterns has been that involving concepts of ideal family size. A variety of fertility-limiting processes are in common use. Very successful but quite controversial is one method that once done requires no further action: sterilization of men by simple surgery. A man is encouraged to be sterilized after two children, at least one a son, are born to his wife. The operation is free, and those who get it receive a cash reward. Still, only a relative few volunteer for it. Population control in India, as in China, is far from assured.

Islamic Asia. Proceeding to the west, we come into the center of Islamic culture: Pakistan, Afghanistan, Iran, the Gulf States, Arabia, and so forth. Actually, Islamic culture, especially the religion itself, is important not only in western Asia but also in China, where sections of the country have a predominantly Muslim population; in the Philippines, where the southern islands are heavily Muslim; and in Indonesia and Malaysia, where Islam is the dominant religion. Given this sweeping geographical presence, many variations occur; nonetheless, a certain general Muslim regularity of marriage and family structure can be described. Indeed, more important than geographical variation is the change brought by modern life. To a considerable degree, the important variable seems to be the political handling of the modern multinational economy. Yet there are at least two radical movements in western Asia. The older one went from being heavily influenced by Western liberalism to a much more militant socialism, extensively influenced by the Soviet Union. The newer one is a remarkable revitalization of a much more traditional view, one that sees itself as supremely Muslim and therefore meaningful beyond such common sectarian credos as Sunni and Shi'ite Islam.

Historically, fundamental Muslim practice, in a religious sense, is closest to Arabian usage of the early seventh century as modified by the Prophet and by subsequent generations of practice. One of the most interesting differences has to do with polygyny (polyandry is not known ever to have existed in this region). Muhammad made it clear that the number of legal wives a man might have at any one time was four (although he, himself, by special dispensation, had nine). This limitation applies only to wives; a married man may also have an unlimited number of female slaves. Despite these provisions, most Muslims are monogamists; it takes a rich man to support more than one wife, and Muhammad made it clear that all wives had to be treated equally or divorce, otherwise mainly open to men, could easily be obtained by a wife.

As in China, parents often engaged infants; some actually pledged unborn children to future marriage, this being a method of solidifying friendships and alliances. It applied only to the first marriage; subsequent marriages were very much the business of the principal parties.

Modern marriage occurs at age twenty or later for a woman and perhaps five years later for a man. In places remote from urban centers, the first marriage tends to occur at younger ages. In former times girls might be married at twelve or thirteen, boys by fifteen.

Once married, the bride and groom usually live virilocally, at least for the first few years. Thereafter, they may live neolocally, in their own house, but that depends on a variety of circumstances, such as the wealth and occupation of the husband. At present, there is exceptionally heavy migration of young men from non-oil-producing regions to oil-producing regions of western Asia. Although some, particularly higher-placed workers, bring their wives and families, most do not, or are yet unmarried. In all cases, the common practice of sending much of their pay back to their parental families is sparking a revival of the extended family in the home districts, especially in Pakistan.

Particularly since the nineteenth century, and perhaps because of the popularity of such works as Burton's translation of *The Arabian Nights,* people in Europe and America have entertained a fantastic image of western Asian patterns of marriage and family. Central to their erroneous view was their belief in a high frequency of polygyny, sanctioned by the Islamic acceptance of as many as four simultaneous wives. As previously noted, economic considerations have often precluded the practice, and most Muslims are monogamists. There is evidence that this has been true for a long time. Although variations in the frequency of polygyny are evident, the evidence shows that monogamy was by far the major form of marriage in the nineteenth century and perhaps prior to that time.

Until the latter half of the twentieth century, the

social status of women in Islam ensured that most women did not circulate in the society of men to whom they were not related. Purdah, the absolute restriction of women to their dwellings, was common, as was veiling on rare exposures to the outside world (although the etiquette of the veil shows considerable subcultural variation). Whereas the third quarter of the twentieth century saw significant change in the sociopolitical treatment of women in Islam, including the movement of numbers of women into the labor force and into higher education, this movement has been substantially reversed in recent years. Although this reversal has been seen most conspicuously in Iran under Ayatollah Khomeini, other countries have also made attempts to return to earlier conditions. Once again, variability must be noted. This variability correlates with local politics. In general, the further left the society is politically, the greater the favor with which it regards female involvement in tasks previously considered male.

Central Asia. Proceeding from western Asia, we traverse Afghanistan and enter Central Asia. This region extends through the "Inner Asian frontiers" of China, as Owen Lattimore put it, and mainly includes several Soviet republics, such as Uzbekistan and Kazakhistan, the nominally independent state of the Mongolian Peoples Republic, and certain Chinese provinces, including Gansu, as well as a number of areas in China that are called "autonomous regions": Inner Mongolia, Xinjiang, and Ningxia, home of the Mongols, Uighurs, and Hui (Chinese Muslims), respectively.

Populations in this part of the world show a fair degree of stability over recent millennia despite the association of these peoples with various mobile conquests both in Europe and Asia. Composed most extensively of speakers of Altaic (Turkic, Mongol, and Tunguz) languages, they now emphasize nuclear families, which have apparently always been important, but which were earlier dominated by clan and lineage structures. Thus, in previous centuries, common clanship serves as the basis for military position in the field. Meanwhile, lineages were securely based on patrilineal kinship, generally through nine generations.

Nuclear families were primary units in control of herds of domesticated animals. Usually several individual families would group their animals together, the composite herd being better controlled by the larger number of herdsmen. In earlier times, especially in the twelfth to fourteenth century and occasionally later on, especially among the Mongols, the independence of the nuclear family correlated with the major means of transportation utilized by women, children, and the aged. The usual Mongol habitation, the tent like yurt, was pitched upon a two-wheeled cart drawn by a horse or by cattle; the Mongol cavalry was never very far from its families. [*See* Nomadism; Tribes; *and* Yurt.]

Mongol life has changed. Extended kinship units have lost most or all of their function, not merely in the USSR and the PRC, but in the Mongolian People's Republic as well. Islam is the predominant religion in Altaic-speaking, or formerly Altaic-speaking, areas except in the east, where forms of Buddhism predominate. Shifts in culture, particularly shifts in religion, are important, for usually changes in this cultural realm precede changes in other aspects of culture. Thus, under Muslim influence, Central Asian populations began to see a preference for marriage between patrilateral cousins, although old customs that prohibited marriage with patrilateral cousins within seven degrees of shared kinship still operate for two or three degrees of consanguinity.

The extended family has become a rarity, while large nuclear families are generally desired. This is true in both the USSR and PRC. In the former, continued plurality of offspring is involved in the tipping of the population in the USSR from Russian numerical dominance to the numerical superiority of Asians, a shift viewed with anxiety by the power structure. Meanwhile, in China, the Mongols and other non-Han populations have received special dispensations from Beijing relieving them of limiting nuclear family fertility to one child, an effort to increase the proportions of the non-Han population.

Tibet. No ethnic population of China has suffered more under the PRC than the Tibetans. Part of the Tibetan population, including the Dalai Lama and many monks, have fled to India; many of those remaining died while in prison or were executed. Over the past several centuries, the importance of lamaseries has reinforced a special kind of marriage pattern that has only a few other exemplars, mainly in India. This practice is polyandry, referred to above. In the Tibetan form one husband would be a farmer or pastoralist while the other husbands of the same woman were likely to be the first husband's brothers, monks who spent most of their time in a distant lamasery. Given the dislocation of lamas and other recent contingencies, the contemporary frequency of fraternal polyandry is probably nil, but detailed ethnography has not been carried out under the new regime.

Siberia and Northeast Asia. The last area comprises the extreme northern and eastern regions of Siberia. Until the 1930s, the populations here comprised pastoralists, fishermen, and hunters who, for the most part, could be identified with their ethnic ancestors. In the 1930s, however, a system that gave priority to local ethnic identity was replaced by one that emphasized acculturation. Family structure and marriage saw little change. The nuclear family was already frequent, and individuals were mainly responsible for their mating choices. Once again we confront a paucity of ethnographic work, particularly by foreigners.

Not merely Siberia but all of Asia has undergone change. Changes in family form and marriage seem to have been effected, not primarily by the diffusion of new forms, but through indigenous adjustment to new technological, economic, and social conditions.

[*See also* Women *and* Population.]

Imtiaz Ahmed, ed., *Family, Kinship and Marriage in India* (1976). Elizabeth E. Bacon, *Obok: A Study of Social Structure in Eurasia* (1958). Hugh D. Baker, *Chinese Family and Kinship* (1979). Reuben Hill and Rene Konig, eds., *Families in East and West* (1970). Indian Social Institute, *The Indian Family in the Change and Challenge of the Seventies* (1972). International Conference on the Family, *Changing Family Patterns in Asia* (1966). William L. Parish and Martin K. Whyte, *Village and Family in Contemporary China* (1978). Polycarpio Mendez Paz, *The Filipino Family in its Rural and Urban Orientation* (1974). Edwin Perry Prothro and Lufty Najib, *Changing Family Patterns in the Arab East* (1974). Jacob S. Quambao, *The Asian Family in a Changing Society* (1965). Margery Wolf, *Women and the Family in Modern Taiwan* (1972).

MORTON H. FRIED

FAMINE. Popularly, and often in scholarship, China and India are referred to as "lands of famine," although famine was probably no more characteristic of these societies than of Europe before modern times. Classical European authors assumed Asia to be full of grain, and subsequent travelers like Marco Polo confirmed an Eastern abundance. Only when the West solved its own chronic food problems did Asian subsistence come to be regarded in a new light. Famines gradually disappeared from Europe after 1750, except in time of war, but the great agrarian societies of Asia continued to exhibit—as they occasionally do today—instabilities in food production and uncertainties in food distribution. In the nineteenth and early twentieth centuries, famines were particularly numerous in China and India, but wherever industrial economies came to dominate in Asia, famines ceased.

Natural disasters have always been the leading cause of Asian famines, but the fact of regional grain markets in China from at least the eighteenth century, and in India from the nineteenth, means that market disturbances such as sudden price shifts, large-scale exports, or the collapse of consumer income must be added to droughts, floods, blights, and insects as characteristic famine triggers. The presence of specialized grain traders and transporters and of the infrastructure for distribution and exchange—roads, ports, storage, credit, and so forth—also affect the onset and outcome of famine episodes. In some cases the absolute size of the available food stock may be less important in understanding famine processes than the distribution of rights over this supply; indeed, there have been Asian famines where the food supply was normal but consumers' "exchange entitlements" in the market shifted suddenly.

Famine is not the same as hunger and poverty, but the latter are predisposing factors. Famines most often occur when the hungry and poor are denied their usual subsistence, leading to social disruption, marked starvation, epidemics, and eventually to heightened mortality. Distress begins at different consumption levels for different individuals, and there is no universal caloric minimum that represents a famine threshold. Even in the worst of famines entire populations do not starve, and the social profile of famine distress is closely related to existing patterns of patronage, enfranchisement, and wealth. On the whole, urban populations fare better than rural. Distress is modified by access to private and official relief, and the development of international relief organizations since World War I has lowered famine mortality in Asia on many occasions. Since the 1960s international relief has concentrated on small children and pregnant and lactating women—groups particularly susceptible to starvation. Despite the effectiveness of relief, a full understanding of the causes, effects, and historical significance of famines has been slow to develop.

The bold hypothesis of Thomas R. Malthus (1766–1834), who held that famines are natural "checks" that keep rapidly growing populations below their more slowly growing food supplies, continues to be applied to the study of Asian history. Malthus's logic stimulated historical demography in its relation to the history of agriculture, but the results have confounded his hypothesis. For example, the population of China in the eighteenth century is now believed to have doubled despite occasional famines, and this experience was repeated between 1953 and 1982, when the Chinese population increased by nearly 90 percent despite a major famine between 1958 and 1960. While the food supply obviously increased in these periods, in both cases scholars have identified governmental activism rather than production of food grains as a key variable. That is, the commitment and capacity of the Chinese state to assume responsibility for popular subsistence was the prerequisite to a range of activities—extension of cultivation, introduction of new food crops, surveillance of market conditions, provision of relief supplies—that prevented famine by increasing the food supply and by relieving critical points of scarcity as they occurred. The Malthusian hypothesis, rooted in a laissez-faire institutional environment, emphasizes the futility of official action in preventing famine, but centuries of Chinese experience point to the opposite conclusion.

All governments of present-day Asia actively guard popular well-being, but few possess the political and administrative traditions of China. In South and Southeast Asia, where vigorous official involvement in subsistence was uncommon before the end of the colonial period, scholars have described widespread, nonofficial, and presumably traditional peasant practices that are intended to stabilize consumption. These elements of culture—technical, social, and moral—are often so deeply embedded in the fabric of rural life as to seem unrelated to the threat of famine. For example, in arid zones of India the reluctance of peasants to adopt new crops and technologies was long attributed to a deplorable "irrationality." This reluctance is now thought prudent, because only a safety-first approach to subsistence—planting drought-resistant crops, storing rather than marketing grain surpluses, hoarding a portfolio of ornaments and animals for crisis divestiture, and so forth—ensures long-term survival. Communal granaries, religiously sanctioned almsgiving, ceremonial feasting, distant refuges for cattle, and far-flung networks of social support further serve to cushion the impact of crop failure. All these devices are within the control of cultivators themselves. Of course, peasants also maintain links to officials and wealthy landlords, and major debate has developed over the so-called moral economy of traditional Asia, that is, the duty of Asian elites to help their peasant clients in times of scarcity.

In short, famines are not inevitable, and some combination of peasant practice and government activism usually serves to blunt the "positive check." It is when these defenses fail that famines occur. Since a sufficient body of historical literature has not yet accumulated on West and Southeast Asia, this article shall concentrate on South and East Asia.

Famine in South Asia. One compilation reports at least 126 major famines in South Asia between 298 BCE and 1944 CE, but record keeping is deficient and hundreds of other local episodes undoubtedly occurred. Major famines were most common in the monsoon-dependent, wheat- and millet-growing regions of the upper Ganges valley and northern Deccan, where drought was the usual trigger of crop failure; famines were least common in the river-irrigated, paddy-growing regions of the lower Ganges valley, where flooding was a hazard. We have only a vague picture of famines in ancient India, but it is evident that wholesale migration and mass mortality occurred. The *Mahabharata,* an epic text, portrays famine as a time of anarchy, when norms of morality *(dharma)* collapse and exceptional rules of conduct *(apaddharma)* become necessary. The policy-oriented *Arthashastra* speaks of famines as "great calamities of divine origin," that is, natural disasters for which rulers have no responsibility. During the Mughal period (c. 1550–1750) there was a limited official response to famine; Akbar's fiscal policy, for example, authorized remissions of land revenue and even cash advances to cultivators. The distribution by nobles of free cooked food in the larger cities was common, but this food was given as personal charity and not as part of a relief program. Mughal officials sometimes forced merchants to transport grain into provincial capitals, but rarely were efforts made to organize the transport of grain between provinces. As in the past, migration of peasants and herds out of famine zones was a common defense, and the depopulation for decades of whole districts resulted.

The British inherited Mughal famine policy, and famine relief did not become a regular part of Indian administration until 1880. An ideological aversion to giving food to starving people led to indirect practices; railway lines were built to link surplus with deficit regions, transport subsidies were offered to grain importers in famine tracts, public works projects were spread through rural areas to generate wage income, and famine insurance funds were founded to meet extraordinary costs. By 1900 every Indian province had its "famine code," a manual that indicated steps to be taken at each phase of an impending crisis. Despite these innovations, famines claimed an estimated 25 million lives between 1860 and 1920. British India's last major famine occurred in 1943 and 1944, when between 2 and 4 million people died in Bengal. Historians take sharply differing positions about British success in coping with famines, reflecting larger disagreements about the impact of British rule on Indian economic development. Since independence in 1947, two fairly serious famines have occurred, in India's Bihar state in 1967 and in Bangladesh in 1974 and 1975, along with a dozen lesser episodes of high prices and popular distress.

Famine in East Asia. There are references to at least 1,800 famines in China, but, as noted above, premodern Chinese governments often showed great skill in ensuring food security, even when the population was increasing rapidly. There is no contradiction here, for meticulous record keeping reflects the seriousness with which officials regarded subsistence problems, and most of the 1,800 famines were localized episodes. Chinese political theory distinguished between natural disasters *(tianzai)* and famines *(zaihuang),* the latter being recognized as interactions between human and natural forces. As a consequence, the Chinese state, unlike the Indian state, was thought to risk its legitimacy if it failed to protect the people from starvation.

The success of the Chinese in averting famine reached a high point in the eighteenth century, when Qing officials mastered techniques for stabilizing subsistence. Because flooding was a constant danger, a vigilant eye was kept on the complex dike system. Officials understood the dynamic relationship among crop failure, high food prices, and famine, and they systematically collected weather and market data while monitoring the popular mood. When necessary, they moved large quantities of grain from one region to another, then gave it away or sold it at a low rate to nervous consumers. State granaries, which had always been a feature of Chinese rule, were built on a large scale in the Qing period and served three functions—price stabilization, short-term loans to peasants, and famine relief. The state also required wealthy nonofficials to maintain a complementary system of private granaries. As a consequence of these measures, the Chinese people came to expect a rapid, effective response to their subsistence problems. Throughout the Qing there were widespread food riots that kept officials on their toes. Crowds gathered at markets, at the homes of rich persons, and before government offices and granaries to demand food or lowered prices, and in some cases they forcibly resisted exports from food-growing regions. The ability of officials to manage the food economy declined dramatically with the decline of the Qing state during the nineteenth century, and a devastating series of famines occurred in the 1850s, from 1876 to 1879, in 1920 and 1921, from 1928 to 1931, and again in 1943. In 1984 the Chinese government admitted that as many as 10 million Chinese died from starvation and related effects during the Great Leap Forward period (1958–1960).

Famines were less frequent in premodern Japan than in China or India, although they were by no means rare. Japanese scholars agree, for example, that there was no major famine in the seventeenth century. Subsequently there were three—the Kyōhō famine of the 1730s, the Temmei famine in the 1780s, and the Tempō famine in the mid-1830s—during the course of which between 10 and 20 percent of the population in some areas died. Marxist historians argue that Tokugawa exploitation precipitated these rural famines, which halted population growth. Non-Marxist demographers, however, hold that these famines had no impact on the population growth rate, which was already declining after 1700, because peasants were raising smaller families as a trade-off for rising living standards. The industrialization of Japan during the Meiji period (1868–1912) generated resources that made the country nearly invulnerable to famine except during the Great Depression and the Pacific War.

Arjun Appadurai, "How Moral Is South Asia's Economy," *Journal of Asian Studies* 43.3 (May 1984): 481–497. B. M. Bhatia, *Famines in India: A Study in Some Aspects of the Economic History of India (1860–1965)* (2d ed., 1967). Bruce Currey, Ali Mehtabunisa, and Nitaya Khoman, comps., *Famine: A First Bibliography* (1981). Robert Dirks, "Social Responses during Severe Food Shortages and Famine," *Current Anthropology* 21.1 (February 1980): 21–44. Paul R. Greenough, *Prosperity and Misery in Modern Bengal: The Famine of 1943–44* (1982). Mikiso Hane, *Peasants, Rebels, and Outcasts: The Underside of Modern Japan* (1982). Susan B. Hanley and Kozo Yamamura, *Economic and Demographic Change in Preindustrial Japan, 1600–1868* (1977). Charles F. Keyes et al., "Peasant Strategies in Asian Societies: Moral and Rational Approaches—A Symposium," *Journal of Asian Studies* 42.4 (August 1983): 851–868. James Lee, Pierre-Etienne Will, and R. Bin Wong, eds., *State Granaries and Food Redistribution in Qing China* (1987). Lillian M. Li et al., "Food, Famine, and the Chinese State—A Symposium," *Journal of Asian Studies* 41.4 (August 1982): 685–797. Michelle B. McAlpin, *Subject to Famine: Food Crisis and Economic Change in Western India, 1860–1920* (1983). Amartya Sen, *Poverty and Famines: An Essay on Entitlement and Deprivation* (1982).

PAUL R. GREENOUGH

FANG GUOZHEN (1319–1374), Chinese pirate-rebel of the late Yuan period. Born into a family of Zhejiang salt traders and fishermen, Fang ran afoul of the law in 1348 for engaging in smuggling. Then, wanted for murder, Fang and his brothers fled to Zhoushan Island, where they rapidly gathered followers and assembled a pirate fleet that eventually numbered a thousand ships. Preying on the government's coastal grain-transport ships, Fang threatened the dynasty's lifeline.

Unable to suppress Fang, Yuan authorities repeatedly cajoled him into "surrendering" with offers of official rank and title, but each time, flaunting his independence, the wily rebel reverted to marauding. By 1356, after he controlled the cities of Ningbo, Taizhou, and Wenzhou, the Yuan reluctantly acknowledged Fang's de facto power as governor of the coast. Next, Fang extended his control as far as Shaoxing but quickly confronted the growing power of Zhu Yuanzhang. After fending Zhu off for several years, Fang finally surrendered in December 1367, but only when faced with annihilation. Treated leniently, he died in Nanjing in 1374. Although dominating the coast for twenty years, Fang flourished because of central government weakness; he never became a serious contender in the power struggle for the throne that resulted in Zhu Yuanzhang's establishment of the Ming dynasty in 1368.

[*See also* Zhu Yuanzhang.]

ROLAND L. HIGGINS

FANG LA (d. 1121), born in Qingxi, Zhejiang Province, rebelled against the Northern Song government in 1120 to protest exorbitant taxes and rapacious officials. Calling himself the Sage Duke and adopting the reign title Yongle (Everlasting Happiness), Fang fought a fierce guerrilla war against government forces. His uprising engulfed much of Zhejiang, touching off numerous local revolts by religious heretics such as the Manichaeans. Fang himself had traditionally been identified as a Manichaean, but recent revisionist studies dispute that point. Although lasting less than a year, his movement has been immortalized by the popular novel *Shuihu zhuan (The Water Margin)*, which describes the exploits of another rebel, Song Jiang.

Kao Yu-kung, "A Study of the Fang La Rebellion," *Harvard Journal of Asiatic Studies* 24 (1962–1963): 17–63; 26 (1966): 211–240. Vincent Shih, "Some Chinese Rebel Ideologies," *T'oung pao* 44 (1956): 151–226.

RICHARD SHEK

FA NGUM, king of Lan Sang (r. 1353–1373) and founder of the first major kingdom of Laos at Luang Prabang. Born in 1316, the son of Suvannakhamphong, chief of the old principality of Luang Prabang, Fa Ngum was exiled to Cambodia for having seduced one of his father's concubines. In 1351, with the aid of an army lent him by the Khmer ruler, he began the conquest of all of Laos, capturing Khammouane, Kham Keut, and Siang Khwang before taking Luang Prabang and his father's throne in 1353. Over the next twenty years he campaigned far afield to expand his kingdom: northwest almost to Chiang Hung, northeast to the Black River and Dien Bien Phu, and through much of the central Mekong region from Vientiane south to Nakhon Phanom. Fa Ngum was the first to unite the Lao principalities of the Mekong region, perhaps preempting future expansion into that area by Ayudhya or Lan Na. However, his warfare, taxation, and continued fondness for beautiful women alienated his ministers, who deposed him and placed his son Un Huan (Sam Saen Thai, r. 1373–1416) on the throne. He went into exile in Nan and died in 1394.

[*See also* Lan Sang.]

DAVID K. WYATT

FAN ZHONGYAN (989–1052), leading Northern Song literatus. Fan served in a variety of local and central government posts, dealing with both civil and military affairs before becoming a chief minister in the reform administration of 1043 to 1044. He became prominent early in his career as spokesman for a new generation of literati officials but was repeatedly demoted for his outspoken criticism of the court. Fan's demand that the court accept advice from and give greater authority to literati committed to realizing ideal interests, and his proposals for administrative and educational reform are generally seen as key precedents for the New Policies of Wang Anshi (1021–1086) in the 1070s.

[*See also* Song Dynasty *and* Wang Anshi.]

James T. C. Liu, "An Early Sung Reformer: Fan Chung-yen," in *Chinese Thought and Institutions*, edited by John K. Fairbank (1957), pp. 105–131.

PETER K. BOL

FARABI, AL- (d. 950), more fully Abu Nasr ibn Muhammad ibn Tarkhan ibn Auzlagh al-Farabi, perhaps the greatest of all the Muslim philosophers, of Turkish descent. He was active primarily in Baghdad and later in Aleppo. He died in Damascus. Farabi was widely appreciated among almost all subsequent generations of philosophers, both in the Islamic world, where he was referred to as the "Second Master" (after Aristotle, the "First Master"), and in the Latin West, where he was known as Alfarabius. He was largely responsible for cementing the position of Peripatetic philosophy at the core of nearly all philosophic thought in the Islamic world through such an extensive series of written commentaries on Aristotle's works that philosophical studies were henceforth dominated by them. Farabi's other major achievement was the creation of a cogent theory of an Islamic political philosophy based on Plato's notions of supreme ruler-philosopher. This theory allowed a rational explanation of prophecy and the relatively unique role of prophetic revelation in a particular time and place. It also provided a universal definition of the purpose and goal of human society and government in general.

PAUL E. WALKER

FARANGI MAHAL. In 1694 the emperor Aurangzeb provided a grant for the family of a deceased scholar named Qutb ud-Din. They took up residence in Lucknow in a household *(mahal)* formerly occupied by a Frenchman (*farangi* means "foreigner"), hence the name. Not a school in the Western sense, the Mahal served as a place of residence for Qutb ud-Din's descendants. The family has continued to produce noted religious scholars and Sufis until the present day.

Qutb ud-Din's son, Nizam ud-Din, developed the *Dars-i Nizamia,* a syllabus of Islamic learning used by many religious scholars. Abd al-Hai (1848–1886) was one of the most famous authorities of his day, and his opinions *(Fatawa)* were collected and widely circulated. Abd al-Bari was a very powerful figure in the 1910s and 1920s. After studies in Mecca and Constantinople, he founded his own branch of the school and counted many aristocrats and politicians (e.g., the Ali brothers) among his spiritual disciples. Possessed of a violent temper, he was prone to extremist political views. Other members of the family in his generation were more moderate; indeed, Abd al-Bari's activities caused a lasting personal and political split in the Farangi Mahal group.

[*See also* Ali Brothers *and* Khilafat Movement.]

A. Ahmad, *An Intellectual History of Islam in India* (1969). F. Robinson, *Separatism among Indian Muslims* (1974).

GREGORY C. KOZLOWSKI

FARA'ZI MOVEMENT. Founded in what is today Bangladesh in 1818 by Haji Shari'at Allah (1781–1840), the Fara'zi movement rallied rural Muslim peasants and artisans to observe the obligatory practice *(fara'zi)* of Sunni Islam and to reject the syncretism associated with Hindu and Shi'ite elites. Unlike other reformist movements of the period such as the Ahl-i Hadith, the Fara'zis affirmed their devotion to established legal and mystical traditions. They were, however, unique in forbidding congregational prayers under British rule. From 1838 to 1857, under the leadership of the founder's son Dudu Miyan (1819–1862), the Fara'zis developed into a violent resistance against Hindu landholders and British indigo planters. The movement continues into the present but has long lacked its revolutionary fervor.

[*See also* Bengal; Bangladesh; *and* Blue Mutiny.]

Muin-ud-din Ahmad Khan, *History of the Fara'di Movement in Bengal (1818–1906)* (1965).

DAVID LELYVELD

FAR EAST. As a geographical designation, *Far East* refers to East Asia (usually including China, Japan, Korea, and Mongolia) and sometimes Siberia in the north and parts of Southeast Asia (especially Vietnam) in the south. Because it is Europocentric, implying that the user is located in Europe, and because its limits are vague, the term *Far East* has fallen into disfavor. *East Asia* and, less frequently, *Western Pacific* are now preferred.

EDWARD L. FARMER

FARQUHAR, WILLIAM (1770–1839), British colonel and first British resident of Singapore. He was appointed ensign in the Madras Engineers in 1791 and after service in India was placed in charge of the engineers on the British expedition that captured Melaka (Malacca) from the Netherlands in 1795. He was appointed chief of staff to the British military government of Melaka in 1798 and in 1803 became resident and commandant. After the restoration of the settlement to the Netherlands in 1818, he joined Sir Thomas Stamford Raffles on his mission to establish a British base at Singapore and served as resident and commandant of the new settlement from February 1819 until May 1823.

[*See also* Singapore *and* Raffles, Sir Thomas Stamford.]

JOHN S. BASTIN

FARSI. Farsi is that variety of New Persian used officially in modern Iran, in contrast to Dari, used officially in Afghanistan, and Tajik, used officially in Soviet Central Asia. The term is also applied to all of premodern New Persian written in the Arabic script (ninth to nineteenth century). Farsi developed during the early Islamic period with efforts in Transoxiana and elsewhere in the eastern Iranian lands to write Dari, the Sasanid vernacular court language, in Arabic script. The earliest extant examples of Farsi are lyric verses dating from the ninth century. In time, this literary language developed a number of standard prose and verse genres that evolved continuously until almost the end of the nineteenth century, when different genres and forms of expression began to develop under European influence.

As a direct result of the growing and all-pervasive influence of Islam upon Iranian life, the language gradually acquired an extensive Arabic element, principally in vocabulary, but also in rhetorical features such as Arabic phrases and passages from an Islamic context, especially from the Qur'an. As time passed, this element became a permanent feature of not only elite literature but also the vernacular speech of ordinary people. During the Pahlavi period (1925–1979), concerted efforts were made by the Persian Academy (Farhangistan-i Iran) and other agencies of the imperial government to replace this Arabic element, especially the innumerable Arabic words used in spoken Farsi, with a Persian counterpart. However, these efforts met with little success beyond the self-conscious usage of some educated persons.

The history of Farsi literature can be divided into three general periods: the "Khurasani style" (*sabk-i Khurasani,* ninth to thirteenth century); the "Indian style" (*sabk-i Hindi,* thirteenth to nineteenth century); and the modern period (nineteenth and twentieth centuries). The literature of the Khurasani style, so called because so many of its exponents were natives of Khurasan, is noteworthy for its relative lack of rhetorical conceits and relatively greater range and variety of literary motifs. During the period of the Indian style, so called because of its popularity at the courts of Indo-Muslim rulers, verse genres exhibit an increasingly narrower range and variety of motifs, and both prose and verse genres become increasingly more preoccupied with rhetoric instead of content. The modern period is particularly characterized by a complete rejection of the rhetorical Indian style and a reliance upon very colloquial idiomatic language as well as an interest in completely new themes, taken particularly from folklore and contemporary urban culture. During the later part of its history, especially from the sixteenth to the nineteenth century, Farsi exerted a profound influence, both linguistic and literary, in Turkey, Central Asia, and India.

[*See also* Dari; Pahlavi; *and* Persian Literature.]

E. G. Browne, *A Literary History of Persia,* 4 vols. (1928). H. Kamshad, *Modern Persian Prose Literature* (1966).
DAVID A. UTZ

FATAWA-I ALAMGIRI, a compendium of Islamic law compiled in Arabic by a committee of Indian theological doctors appointed by the Mughal emperor Aurangzeb (1658–1707). Shaikh Nizam was the chairman of the committee, and among its members was Shah Abdur Rahim, father of the renowned Shah Waliullah of Delhi. Aurangzeb commissioned the project because he wanted his people to follow the *shari'a* closely, but ironically the *Fatawa* did not address itself to the specifics of the Indian situation. Its uniqueness lies in the fact that it is not the result of an individual's juristic activity but is based on the collective wisdom of a board of scholars. Perhaps it was also the first venture of the Mughal empire in which both the esoteric and the orthodox religious authorities cooperated. The *Fatawa* follows the arrangement of the *Hidaya* and avoids lengthy discussions. On controversial issues it favors one opinion and adds further arguments to reinforce it. Known outside India as *Fatawa-i Hindiyyah,* it is considered to be one of the best works on Hanafi law.

[*See also* Mughal Empire.]

M. G. Zubaid Ahmad, *The Contribution of India to Arabic Literature* (1946).
FARHAN AHMAD NIZAMI

FATEHPUR SIKRI. Commissioned in 1569 by Akbar (1542–1605) but abandoned in 1586 owing to severe water shortage, Fatehpur Sikri is the best intact example of a Mughal walled city and palace. Akbar shifted his capital from Agra, 37 kilometers to the west, to this site in order to be closer to the Chishti saint Shaikh Salim, his spiritual adviser and the man who predicted the birth of his son and successor, Jahangir. Among the extant buildings are monumental entrances, public and private audience halls, office buildings, an extensive harem, a mosque, and Chishti shrines. Except for the mosque and large entrances, post and lintel construction predominates. The post and lintel form appears to have been

FIGURE 1. *Buland Darwaza, Fatepur Sikri.*

used in domestic architecture by all sectarian groups in North India; its use at Fatehpur Sikri was possibly motivated by Akbar's policy of *sulh-i kull,* or universal tolerance. Fatehpur Sikri's red sandstone structures are thought to have been modeled on tent types that previously formed the transportable cities of the militarily oriented Mughals.

[*See also* Architecture: South Asian Architecture; Agra; *and* Akbar.]

Saiyid Athar Abbas Rizvi and Vincent John Adams Flynn, *Fathpur-Sikri* (1975). Edmund W. Smith, *The Moghul Architecture of Fathpur-Sikri,* 4 vols. (1894–1898).

CATHERINE B. ASHER

FAXIAN (d. about 418–423), Chinese Buddhist monk renowned for being the first pilgrim to cross the wastes of Central Asia, penetrate India proper, and successfully return to China to record his experiences.

Motivated by the desire to locate (and translate) a complete copy of the Buddhist Vinaya, or codes of monastic discipline, in 399 Faxian (together with four other Chinese monks) set out from Chang'an. He traveled northwest to Karashahr, then turning to the south he passed through Khotan and crossed the Pamirs into Kashmir. From Kashmir he entered northwest India. After visiting various sites there he followed the Yamuna and Ganges rivers to the Ganges Plain. He remained there for several years in order to learn Sanskrit and study Buddhist scriptures. From Tamralipti, Faxian sailed to Sri Lanka, where he settled for two years. Finally, boarding a merchant vessel, he sailed for home. After being waylaid temporarily in Java, in 413 he landed on the Shandong Peninsula and in 414 arrived in the Eastern Jin capital in modern Nanjing. His journey lasted nearly fifteen years and took him through more than thirty countries.

What Faxian saw and heard was set down in writing in the *Chronicle of the Eminent Monk Faxian,* known alternately as *Records of Buddhist Lands.* Although the work mainly discusses items of Buddhist interest, it nevertheless offers valuable information concerning Central Asia, Sri Lanka, and Gupta-period India and stands with the seventh-century monk Xuanzang's *Records of Western Regions* as one of the great Chinese sources for the history and geography of these regions.

[*See also* Buddhism: Buddhism in China.]

Herbert A. Giles, *The Travels of Fa-hsien, 399–414, or Record of the Buddhist Kingdoms* (1956).

DAN STEVENSON

FAZLI HUSSAIN, SIR MIAN (1877–1936), Punjabi statesman. After the Montagu-Chelmsford reforms of 1921, Indian politicians began to acquire substantial power in provincial governments. Operating as minister of education in the Punjab, Fazli

Hussain was one of those who used his office most effectively. He generally displayed a preference for rural over urban interests in his province. For example, he used his department's grants-in-aid to establish primary schools in the countryside, rather than sustaining secondary schools for the elite in cities.

When Mohammed Ali Jinnah returned to India in 1935 and set about reviving the Muslim League, Fazli Hussain ignored his efforts; shortly before his death, Hussain resurrected the Punjab Unionist Party, which brought together Muslim, Sikh, and Hindu leaders. The elections of 1937 kept the Unionists in power with the League winning only two seats in the Punjab. Sir Sikandar Hayat Khan (d. 1942), Hussain's successor, worked out a loose alliance with the Muslim League in 1937, but the Unionists retained power until 1947.

[*See also* Muslim League *and* Montagu-Chelmsford Reforms.]

A. Husain, *Fazl-i-Hussain, A Political Biography* (1946). P. Hardy, *Muslims of British India* (1972).

GREGORY C. KOZLOWSKI

FAZLUL HUQ, ABUL KASEM (1873–1962), Indian political leader for nearly half a century. Abul Kasem Fazlul Huq was mercurial, talented, and enormously popular among the Muslims of Bengal. From Bakarganj District, now in Bangladesh, he was trained as a lawyer at Calcutta University and first entered politics as a protégé of Nawab Salimullah of Dhaka. Once in politics, Huq made his own way and just after World War I was a member of the Muslim League and the Indian National Congress. Entering the Bengal Legislative Council in 1913, he gained a considerable following and could be elected from almost any Muslim seat; he served in the Legislative Council until 1936, briefly as a minister in 1924.

One of the founders of the All-Bengal Praja Samiti (a peasant organization), Huq became the foremost leader of the Krishak Praja Party, which won one-third of the Muslim seats in the 1936–1937 elections for the Bengal Legislative Assembly. Rebuffed by the Congress, Huq formed an alliance with the Muslim League, joined the League, and became chief minister of Bengal from 1937 to 1943. He was also the proposer of the famous Lahore, or Pakistan, Resolution in 1940 calling for separate Muslim states in South Asia.

In 1941, however, Huq broke with the Muslim League, formed an alliance with the dissident wing of the Congress in Bengal called the Progressive Coalition, and formed a new government without the League. This lasted until 1943, when Huq fell before the machinations of the Raj and the rise of the Muslim League, which formed two cabinets without him.

Huq remained in East Pakistan after independence and eventually re-formed his party as the Krishak Sramik (Peasants and Workers) Party. This party joined the United Front, which won the 1954 elections, and Huq formed the ministry, but this was shortly dismissed. He served briefly as a central government minister and then as governor of East Pakistan from 1956 to 1958. A renowned speaker in Bengali and English, Huq was affectionally known as Sher-e-Bangla ("tiger of Bengal") by his followers.

[*See also* Indian National Congress; All-India Muslim League; and Bangladesh.]

John Broomfield, *Mostly about Bengal* (1982). Gautam Chattopadhyay, *Bengal Electoral Politics and Freedom Struggle, 1862–1947* (1984). Leonard A. Gordon, "Divided Bengal: Problems of Nationalism and Identity in the 1947 Partition," *The Journal of Commonwealth and Comparative Politics* 16.2 (July 1978): 136–168. Shila Sen, *Muslim Politics in Bengal, 1937–1947* (1976).

LEONARD A. GORDON

FEBRUARY TWENTY-SIXTH INCIDENT, the greatest internal upheaval experienced by Japan between the world wars, in which a group of young army officers, leading about 1,800 troops, seized the center of Tokyo on 26 February 1936 and assassinated several prominent statesmen and military leaders. The young officers who carried out the uprising had been alarmed by the economic distress of the farmers and by the growth of Soviet power in East Asia. They advocated a national reform (Shōwa Restoration) to strengthen the state and wanted to eliminate the power of party politicians and financial magnates. By killing the "traitors around the throne," they hoped to bring about the establishment of a new government, headed by General Mazaki Jinzaburō of the Kōdōha faction, which they supported.

In the early hours of 26 February they attacked and murdered Lord Privy Seal Saitō Makoto, Finance Minister Takahashi Korekiyo, and Inspector General of Military Education General Watanabe Jōtarō. Grand Chamberlain Suzuki Kantarō was seriously wounded, and Prime Minister Okada Keisuke barely escaped death when his brother-in-law was mistakenly killed.

For four days the rebels occupied the center of Tokyo, demanding a change of government, but Emperor Hirohito, enraged by the murder of his closest advisers, refused to heed the rebels' demands and ordered the army to suppress them immediately. Thus, sympathetic army officers were prevented from intervening on the rebels' behalf.

After martial law was declared and reinforcements were called in, the authorities embarked on a course of "psychological warfare" aimed at the soldiers under the rebels' command. Through leaflets and radio broadcasts, the soldiers were asked to lay down their arms and return to the barracks. This strategy worked, and on 29 February the soldiers capitulated. Two of the rebel officers committed suicide and the rest surrendered. They were brought before a secret court martial and nineteen, including their civilian accomplices, were sentenced to death and executed.

The army took advantage of the incident to obtain increased budgets and greater leverage in the affairs of state. After World War II the rebels were romanticized in movies and novels as opponents of the regime that dragged Japan into war.

Masao Maruyama, *Thought and Behavior in Modern Japanese Politics* (1963). Mark R. Peattie, *Ishiwara Kanji* (1975). Ben-Ami Shillony, *Revolt in Japan* (1973). Richard Storry, *The Double Patriots* (1957).

BEN-AMI SHILLONY

FEDERATED MALAY STATES (FMS), formed in 1895, comprise Perak, Selangor, Pahang, and Negri Sembilan. After the British established the Straits Settlements (Penang, Melaka, and Singapore) they wished to ensure that trade through them, particularly in tin, should not be hindered by local quarrels. They therefore pressed rulers of the states to accept residents (British advisers) whose advice would be accepted except on questions of Malay religion and custom. The states agreed, but in Perak the first British resident was killed and the British had to reassert their authority by force.

The 1895 Malay "federation" was different from federations today. A British resident-general, to whom the four residents were responsible, was appointed, and he himself was responsible to the governor of the Straits Settlements (now also to be the high commissioner of the FMS). Thus began a system of indirect rule, similar to that set up by the British in some parts of Africa. British control of the "unfederated" states was even looser. Indirect rule had the advantage of cheapness but tended to overprotect local peoples from Western influences, thus making it more difficult for them to adjust to "modern" ways when they later acquired independence.

C. D. Cowan, *Nineteenth-Century Malaya: The Origins of British Political Control* (1961). Rupert Emerson, *Malaysia, A Study in Direct Rule* (1937). C. Northcote Parkinson, *British Intervention in Malaya, 1867–1877* (1960). Francis Swettenham, *British Malaya* (rev. ed., 1948).

R. S. MILNE

FEI RIVER, BATTLE OF. The Fei River was the site of a battle in 383 between Fu Jian (r. 357–385), emperor of the Northern Qin, one of the so-called Sixteen Kingdoms in North China during the period of the Southern and Northern Dynasties, and Xie Xuan, a general of the Eastern Jin (317–420) at Nanjing. Allegedly, the total defeat of Fu Jian's huge army (variously given as between 600,000 and 1,000,000 men) meant the end of non-Chinese attempts to conquer the South, thus ensuring the survival of Chinese culture. In fact the great battle is largely a myth, originally fabricated to aid the Xie in rivalry with another clan and expanded by Tang-dynasty scholar-officials to deter Emperor Taizong (r. 626–649) from his planned invasions of Korea.

[*See also* Jin Dynasty *and* Southern and Northern Dynasties.]

Michael Rogers, *The Chronicle of Fu Chien* (1968).

EDWARD L. DREYER

FELT is a nonwoven fabric made by matting together fibrous materials such as wool, fur, and hair and packing them by pressure, moisture, and heat to obtain a strong, firm fabric. Predating spinning, it is the characteristic indigenous fabric of Inner Asia for clothing and covering.

Some of the earliest and most extraordinary examples of felt produced in Inner Asia were discovered preserved in the Scythian tombs at Pazyryk in the Altai Mountains. The standard Scythian horse trapping consisted of a felt square on the horse's back covered by pillows of tanned leather and felt stuffed with reindeer hair; on top of these lay the saddle cover, secured by chest, belly, and tail straps. One complete saddle cover, made of felt, leather, fur, hair, and gold and found in a grave dated to the fifth century BCE, is decorated with vivacious griffins attacking mountain goats in felt appliqué outlined by cords. Yurts, felt-covered tents, are ideal for resisting steppe winds, and Turkman nomads used them in Central Asia and Iran as far west as Anatolia.

[*See also* Yurt.]

"Khaima," *The Encyclopaedia of Islam* (new ed., 1960–). Metropolitan Museum of Art and the Los Angeles County Museum of Art, *From the Lands of the Scythians: Ancient Treasures from the Museums of the U.S.S.R. 3000 B.C.–100 B.C.* S. I. Rudenko, *Frozen Tombs of Siberia,* translated by M. W. Thompson (1970).

SHEILA S. BLAIR

FENG GUIFEN (1809–1874), Chinese scholar and official. A native of Wuxian (Suzhou), Jiangsu Province, Feng was recommended by his teacher, Li Zhaoluo (1769–1841), to serve on the staff of the governor of Jiangsu, Lin Zexu. In 1840 Feng received his metropolitan degree with highest honors and entered the prestigious Hanlin Academy. During the Taiping Rebellion and postwar reconstruction, Feng distinguished himself as a military leader, a strategist, and a proponent of comprehensive local reform. Best known for his persuasive writings on statecraft, which drew upon those of Gu Yanwu, Feng proposed instituting new subcounty infrastructure and utilizing bursaries and rent bureaus.

Frederic Wakeman, Jr., and Carolyn Grant, eds., *Conflict and Control in Late Imperial China* (1975), pp. 213–270 and passim.

JUDITH A. WHITBECK

FENG GUOZHANG (1859–1919), one of Yuan Shikai's chief military subordinates in the Beiyang Army, vice-president of China (1916–1917) after Yuan's death, and acting president (1917–1918). Feng also headed the Zhili clique of warlords, in competition with the Anhui clique of Duan Qirui. Feng was more or less forced into retirement in 1918 and died the following year.

[*See also* China, Republic Period; Warlord Cliques; *and* Yuan Shikai.]

Howard L. Boorman, ed., *Biographical Dictionary of Republican China,* vol. 2 (1968), pp. 24–28. Andrew J. Nathan, *Peking Politics, 1918–1923: Factionalism and the Failure of Constitutionalism* (1976).

JAMES E. SHERIDAN

FENGTIAN CLIQUE. *See* Warlord Cliques.

FENG YUXIANG (1882–1948), prominent Chinese warlord of the 1920s, often called the Christian General. A self-educated man, Feng rose from the ranks to head a powerful army allied with the Zhili clique. Feng became widely known for the discipline of his troops and his attempts at social reform in the provinces he ruled.

In 1924, during the second war between the Zhili and Fengtian cliques, Feng turned against his superior, Wu Peifu, seized Beijing, forced Cao Kun to resign the presidency, and ousted Puyi, the last Manchu emperor, from the Forbidden City. This coup left Feng sharing power in North China with Zhang Zuolin. In late 1925 Feng and Zhang began a war that swiftly went badly for Feng. Early in 1926 his army retreated westward and Feng, who had been receiving help from the Russians, went on a lengthy visit to the Soviet Union. When he returned, he joined the Guomindang (Kuomintang, or Nationalist Party), reorganized his forces, and took part in the Northern Expedition against Zhang Zuolin.

After the establishment of the Nationalist government at Nanjing in 1928, relations between Feng and Chiang Kai-shek became increasingly strained as Chiang sought to undermine the power of regional militarists. In 1929 war between the two began, and in 1930 Yan Xishan came to Feng's support. The Nationalist armies defeated the Feng-Yan coalition in late 1931, however, and Feng lost command of his troops. From that time until his death in 1948, he occupied various posts in the Nationalist government and the Guomindang but held no real power.

[*See also* Cao Kun; Guomindang; Northern Expedition; Warlord Cliques; Warlords; Wu Peifu; Yan Xishan; *and* Zhang Zuolin.]

James E. Sheridan, *Chinese Warlord: The Career of Feng Yu-hsiang* (1966).

JAMES E. SHERIDAN

FERGHANA, a valley on the upper course of the Syr Darya (Jaxartes), about three hundred by seventy kilometers, now divided between the Uzbek, Tadzhik, and Kirghiz republics of the Soviet Union. The valley is largely surrounded by loops of the Tian Shan range but is open to the west through the Syr Darya valley. The chief towns are Namangan, Khokand, Andizan, Margilan, and Ferghana, with many smaller settlements interspersed among these.

Ferghana is first mentioned in Chinese sources of the second century BCE, when it appears to have had a dense population. Turks from the areas surrounding Ferghana continually fought for control over the valley and were periodically successful but never displaced or outnumbered the indigenous population. The first recorded Turkish success, in 649 CE, was supplanted by a similarly short-lived Chinese rule from 657 to about 680 as part of the Tang dynasty's imperial expansion; in 719 the valley was overrun by the Arab conquest. The Iranian Samanids ruled the area for most of the ninth and tenth centuries until 992, when control passed to the Karakhanids. The Mongols conquered the valley in their sweep through Central Asia in 1220, and Timur incorporated it in his empire in the late 1300s; Timurid rule ended only with the retreat of Babur, the great-grandson of Timur, from Ferghana in 1504. The Uzbeks then took control of the area; their rule was uneasy and chronically contested by both their Turkic brethren of the steppe and the well-organized armies of the vigorous new Safavid state in Iran. In 1876, the khanate of Ferghana was annexed by the Russians, who made the town of Ferghana the administrative center, although Khokand and Namagan were larger.

Wilhelm Barthold, "A Short History of Turkistan," in *Four Studies on the History of Central Asia,* translated by V. and T. Minorsky (1956–1962), vol. 1, pp. 1–68.

RHOADS MURPHEY, JR.

FERISHTA, MUHAMMAD QASIM (c. 1560–c. 1620), Indian historian of the seventeenth century whose *Tarikh-i Ferishta* is considered to be the best general history of India from the early Hindu rajas to his own day. Ferishta supplies detailed information about the Ghaznavids, the sultans of Delhi, the Deccan states, and the regional kingdoms of Kashmir, Gujarat, Malwa, Bengal, and Sind. The last chapter of the work deals with the Sufi saints of India. Ferishta was in the service of the ruler of Bijapur, Ibrahim Adil Shah II, and dedicated the work to him. In July 1604 Ferishta accompanied Ibrahim Adil Shah's daughter, Begum Sultan, to Paithan, where she was married to the emperor Akbar's son Daniyal. In 1605 Adil Shah sent Ferishta to Lahore. Ferishta is known for his meticulous collection of data, chronological arrangement, and simple but effective presentation. He also wrote a book on the indigenous system of medicine entitled *Dastur ul-Atibba.*

Henry Miers Elliot and John Dowson, *History of India,* vol. 6 (1867–1877; 2d ed., 1963–1964), pp. 207–236. C. A. Storey, *Persian Literature* (1935), pp. 442–450.

KHALIQ AHMAD NIZAMI

FIRDAUSI (940/941–1020/1025), Hakim Abu al-Qasim, the author of the Persian epic *Shahnama* and one of the greatest epic poets of the world. Very little is known about his personal life, as the data found in biographical dictionaries and other sources are often mixed with obviously unfounded materials. He was born to the family of a petty landlord *(dihqan)* in the village of Bazh near Tus in Khurasan. It is clear from his own poetry that he had received a sound education and was well versed in the legends and traditional history of pre-Islamic Iran. As a youth he was a man of adequate means, which enabled him to devote thirty years of his life to composing the *Shahnama* without the support of a royal court.

Firdausi undertook the composition of his monumental work around the year 980, shortly after the death of Abu Mansur Daqiqi, another poet from Tus, who had been composing a national epic of his own (most probably under the patronage of the Samanid *amir* Nun ibn Mansur) when his sudden death left the work unfinished. The Samanids had fostered a keen interest in the history of pre-Islamic Iran, and already more than one prose *Shahnama,* based mainly on the Pahlavi *Kvadai-namag* (translated into Arabic in the eighth century), had appeared; the most important version was the Abu Mansuri *Shahnama,* produced in Tus in 957. Firdausi had also versified isolated episodes before he obtained Daqiqi's work, which he incorporated into the *Shahnama.* At the beginning of his career he had the support of some local dignitaries in Tus, but, living mainly on the income of his family estate, he experienced dire poverty at advanced age. His main source was the Abu Mansuri *Shahnama* (now lost except for the introduction), but he also used other materials, including oral traditions. The first version of Firdausi's *Shahnama* was finished in 994 and the revised version in 1010.

Firdausi's epic would have probably been received with honors at the court of the Samanids, but by the time it was finished Sultan Mahmud of Ghazna was the master of eastern Iran. Although a Turk by birth, Sultan Mahmud had gathered a large number of Persian poets at his court and was served by the vizier Isfarayini, whose patronage of Persian letters was well known. It is possible that Firdausi, as an old man badly in need, had been sending portions of his work to the court at Ghazna (probably to Isfarayini) in the hope of securing royal support. Finally he decided to present his epic personally. But the *Shahnama* was not received well by the king, who, being attuned to hearing only panegyric poetry and not familiar with the Iranian lore, could not really appreciate the value of the *Shahnama.* The fact that Mahmud was a fanatical Sunni and Firdausi a Shi'ite must have laid the groundwork for the hard feelings that the poet refers to. Besides, Isfarayini, his main supporter at the court, had fallen from favor. According to an early source, an unhappy encounter with the king resulted in Firdausi's writing a satire published only after the poet's death. Firdausi spent the rest of his life running from the reach of Mahmud, who had threatened him with death. Finally, pardoned by the sultan, he came back to his native town, where he died a poor man.

Firdausi's *Shahnama* is the versified history of Iran, in about fifty thousand distichs, from the most ancient times to the conquest of the country by the Arabs. It includes the mythical, heroic (by far its best part), and historical periods and is divided into the reigns of fifty kings. The Medes and the Achaemenids are not mentioned, and the Parthians are remembered only in about one hundred lines.

[*See also* Mahmud of Ghazna; Persian Literature; *and* Shahnama.]

E. G. Browne, *A Literary History of Persia* (1928), vol. 2, pp. 129–148. "Firdawsi," in *The Encyclopaedia of Islam* (new ed., 1960–). R. Levy, trans., *The Epic of the Kings: Shah-nama* (1967). R. Levy, *An Introduction to Persian Literature* (1969). J. Rypka, *History of Iranian Literature* (1968).

MANOUCHEHR KASHEFF

FIRE TEMPLE, a Zoroastrian place of worship enshrining a permanently burning sacred fire. Zoroastrians require for high rituals only a ritually pure hearth fire; a cult of fire was probably instituted by the priesthood only in the Achaemenid period, in opposition to image-shrines (Old Iranian, **bagina-;* Armenian, *bagin,* "place of the gods") introduced from Mesopotamia. These early fire "sanctuaries" were probably called simply "[place of] burning fire" (cf. the Parthian *ataroshan* and the Armenian loanword *atrushan*), but certain fires, such as Adar Burzen Mihr in Khurasan, were accorded particular reverence in Parthian times, and under the Sasanids there were three grades of consecrated temple fires: the *atashi-i Bahram,* the "victorious fire," or "fire of Varathraghna," the highest grade, followed by the *adaran* and the *dadgah.*

In Sasanid times, the fire was enthroned in a bowl of ash on a stone altar in a square, windowless cell topped by a two-layered dome and surrounded by a corridor; it was thus protected from contamination and shielded from the greater light of the sun. A priest offered aromatic woods and incense to the flame in each of the five watches of the day; a mask over the lower part of his face prevented pollution of the fire by his breath. Sasanid law treats in detail the foundation and maintenance of fire temples, which formed the focus of religious life in every Iranian village. As the living icon of Zoroastrianism, fire is still venerated in temples by the Parsis of India, who founded the *atash-i Bahram* called Iranshah shortly after their arrival from Muslim Iran (Khurasan) in the tenth century; it has burned continuously since then and is now enthroned at Udwada in Gujarat. Bombay, the center of the Parsi community, has forty-four fire temples. Adar Farnbag, the sacred fire of Sasanid Fars, still burns in the little Zoroastrian village of Sharifabad, Iran.

[*See also* Parsis *and* Zoroastrianism.]

Mary Boyce, "On the Zoroastrian Temple Cult of Fire," *Journal of the American Oriental Society* 95 (1975).

JAMES R. RUSSELL

FIRISHTA, MUHAMMAD QASIM. *See* Ferishta, Muhammad Qasim.

FITCH, RALPH (c. 1550–1611), one of the first Englishmen to visit India. He left London in 1583 with other merchants with the intention of exploring the possibilities for trade among England, India, and China. He and two companions were seized by the Portuguese at Hormuz and taken to Goa, but they escaped into the territories of the ruler of Bijapur. They made their way to the court of the Emperor Akbar at Fatehpur Sikri, but it is not known if they were able to give him the letter they had brought for him from Queen Elizabeth. On his own, Fitch sailed down the Yamuna and Ganges rivers to Bengal, and then went on by ship to Pegu and Melaka in Southeast Asia. He made his way back to India and finally reached England in 1591. Because of his unique knowledge of India, he was consulted in 1600 by the London merchants who were given a charter in that year for the East India Company. Fitch's account of his travels was published by Richard Hakluyt in his famous collection of early voyages, *Principall Navigations* (1598–1600).

[*See also* East India Company.]

William Foster, ed., *Early Travels in India, 1583–1619* (1968).

USHA SANYAL

FIVE BUSHELS OF RICE SECT, name adopted by a Daoist cult founded in Sichuan, China, in the middle of the second century by Zhang Ling (fl. 157–178), who healed the sick in return for payment of five pecks of rice a year. The head of the third generation of the family, Zhang Lu (fl. 188–220), led an army that conquered a border region between Sichuan and southwest Shanxi. According to Holmes Welch, Zhang Lu was allied with Zhang Xiu (d. about 190), who in 184 had led a similar healing sect of his own in rebellion in southern Sichuan at the same time as the Yellow Turban Uprising in east China. Other scholars, however, believe that Zhang Xiu may in fact have been Zhang Lu's father, Zhang Heng, thus making the two movements in Sichuan identical. Soon after the conquest of the border region, Zhang Lu amalgamated the two cults, executed Zhang Xiu, and began teaching new ascetic doctrines (suggesting to some scholars possible early Buddhist influence). Zhang ruled an independent theocracy that survived until the year 215, when he surrendered peacefully to the warlord Cao Cao.

Although the sect had certain egalitarian practices such as lenient punishment of criminals and free wayside inns, the potentially anarchic ideas of philosophical Daoism were not utilized; instead an elaborate hierarchy of priests and soldiers was established under the "celestial master," as Zhang and his descendants were called. After Zhang's surrender, the sect continued to flourish as a religion. Indeed, modern religious Daoism is the direct descendant of both the Yellow Turbans and the Five Bushels of Rice sect.

[*See also* Han Dynasty; Cao Cao; Daoism; *and* Yellow Turbans.]

Howard Levy, "Yellow Turban Religion and Rebellion at the End of the Han," *Journal of the American Oriental Society* 76.4 (1976): 214–227. Anna Seidel, "The Image of the Perfect Ruler in Early Taoist Messianism: Lao-tzu and Li Hung," *History of Religions* 9.2–3 (1969–1970): 216–247. Vincent Y. C. Shih, "Some Chinese Rebel Ideologies," *T'oung pao* 44.1–3 (1956): 150–226. Holmes Welch, *Taoism: The Parting of the Way* (rev. ed., 1957).

JOHN A. RAPP

FIVE DYNASTIES. The period of the Five Dynasties (907–959) in China has been considered by some to be an extension of the Tang era (618–907) and by others to constitute the beginnings of the Song era (960–1279). Broadly speaking, the orthodox view, which stresses dynastic succession and political control, or the manifestations of such control, would see the Five Dynasties as part of a glorious era that ended in great disorder. A modern socioeconomic approach would tend to favor the depiction of the period as a messy struggle among new forces that eventually gave birth to a different era.

The period is commonly examined in two parts: the Five Dynasties in the North and the Ten Kingdoms that, with one exception, were in South and central China. This article concerns the five dynastic houses in the North: the Liang (907–923), the Later Tang (923–936), the Later Jin (936–946), the Later Han (947–950), and the Later Zhou (951–959).

The Liang dynasty has been unjustly neglected. Its founder, Zhu Wen, began his career in the ranks of one of the great rebellions of Chinese history, that of Huang Chao (875–883). Zhu was one of the senior rebel officers, but he betrayed his leader and surrendered to the Tang. The emperor was grateful and rewarded him with the name Totally Loyal and the governorship of a province in the north central plains, at a key point of the Grand Canal. There he consolidated his power and, twenty years later, betrayed the Tang and prepared to usurp the throne. He remained a plebeian leader and hated the snobbish aristocratic and eunuch courtiers who dominated the Tang court. When he established the new dynasty, the Liang, in 907, he rejected most aspects of Tang government and introduced a system of administration mainly modeled on the provincial government that had been his power base.

Had Zhu been successful in unifying China, he might have been forgiven his treachery and even credited with the contributions he made toward the new power structure that eventually emerged at the end of the Five Dynasties period. However, there were simply too many military satraps, he had too many enemies, and, what was more, he was unable to control rebellious members of his own family. One of his sons murdered him, and this son in turn was overthrown by a younger half-brother. After that, reunification of the whole of China was out of the question, and the Liang struggled to survive for an additional ten years. Despite its pathetic end, the dynasty had introduced reforms that proved to be timely; many reappeared a decade later under different names. Most of them confirmed the need to use the military, financial, and administrative instruments developed in the late Tang provinces as the basis of a centralized imperial government.

A more profound change that occurred during the Liang must be traced back to the peasant rebellions and mutinies of the last three decades of the Tang. These attacks on the court eventually destroyed the economic foundations of a decaying aristocratic society and forced some of the older elite families of North China to disperse and flee south or to abandon their estates and privileged local positions to make their peace with new plebeian military leaders. It took several decades before a new structure of power emerged, one based largely on soldiers, merchants, and the lesser intelligentsia. Most of them had become officials and had acquired lands for their families, and their descendants were to provide the nucleus of the new class of gentry-literati prominent during the Song dynasty.

It is in this context that the four decades from 880 to 923 may be said to mark the end of aristocratic society and politics while the next three were to lead to the rise of the new literati. This explains why the Five Dynasties period, obviously one of transition, has been seen as an end by some and as a beginning by others.

An additional reason for uncertainty was the nominal restoration of the Later Tang in 923. Its founder, Zhuangzong (Li Cunxu), a Shato Turk whose father and grandfather had helped the Tang crush mutinies and peasant rebellions, considered himself a Tang loyalist who would restore Tang institutions and revive Tang glory. His brief reign of three years was too short to save the Tang heritage. His successor, Mingzong (Li Siyuan), one of his father's barely literate retainers, was less concerned with the Tang past and established a structure based on the provincial military government with which he and his supporters were much more familiar. Nevertheless, the fact that the dynasty was called Tang and that the successive brief dynasties after 936 were founded by men from the same Turkic-Han alliance tended to obscure the fact of Mingzong's break with the Tang political structure. As a result, the Liang dynasty came to be seen as an aberration that was irrelevant to later periods of history instead of being recognized as the precursor of the system that was to develop and provide the political and military foundations of the Song.

The Later Tang victory in 923 should have provided enough momentum to reunify China. At the time, none of the seven territories (not all called themselves kingdoms) in the South was strong; nor were any of the foreign kingdoms, whether Khitan, Tibetan, or Uighur Turk, stronger than Tang. Zhuangzong did pursue his advantage and conquered one of the richest of the southern kingdoms, that of Shu (in Sichuan), but that momentum was lost when he was killed in 926. By the time Mingzong died in 933, the Tang center had become too weak to control even its own provinces in North China. Two very brief reigns followed, both showing the dismal failure of the Tang "restoration."

The final end of the Tang produced no fresh start. Its successor, the Later Jin dynasty, was founded by another Central Asian follower of Zhuangzong and his father. This founder, Shi Jingtang (r. 936–942), came to power by bribing the Khitan with sixteen Chinese prefectures south of the Great Wall. It was a disastrous start that doomed the new dynasty to extreme weakness. Not surprisingly, peace could not be maintained between the two states for long. When war came during the reign of Shi Jingtang's successor, the Khitan armies marched in and destroyed the dynasty ten years after it was founded.

Ironically, by appealing to the Khitan to help him seize the throne, Shi Jingtang had contributed to another kind of turning point in China's frontier history. The deterioration of order in North China coincided with the consolidation of Khitan power under the second ruler of the Khitan Liao empire, Taizong (r. 926–947). This new strength made it possible for the Khitan to interfere directly in Chinese politics. The sixteen prefectures in modern Hebei and Shanxi seemed not too high a price to pay for Shi Jingtang if that gave him supreme power in China. With that power, he might have hoped to regain the prefectures sooner or later. No one at the time could have expected this relatively minor event during a period of considerable anarchy to have long-term consequences for Chinese history. But the Khitan invasions launched from within the Great Wall for the rest of the tenth century were to result in a series of failures for the Song dynasty that left that dynasty permanently weakened in its northern frontiers. That was to have great psychological as well as strategic effect on all Song emperors and officials for the next three hundred years. China's weakness led to a defensive mentality that contributed to the formation of a narrower view of Chinese nationhood than had hitherto prevailed.

Shi Jingtang did not rule long enough to test his power against the Khitan. He died at the age of fifty after reigning for only five and one-half years. His nephew, who succeeded him, was persuaded that the position of a Chinese emperor who was subordinate to a foreign ruler was intolerable and sought to get the sixteen prefectures back. He did not make adequate preparations, however; his armies were of poor quality, loyalties were uncertain, and the Khitan had a clear strategic advantage. The

Jin forces were easily defeated, and North China was saved only by the sudden death of the Khitan emeror in early 947 while still fighting in China. This gave an opportunity for the remaining generals of the Jin who had not surrendered to rally around the strongest among them to proclaim a new dynasty. The general chosen was Liu Zhiyuan and his dynasty was the Later Han.

Like the Jin before it, this dynasty had no claim to legitimacy and represented nothing more than the common military takeover that characterized the succession among provincial governors during a period of confusion. This new Han dynasty controlled the large and strategic province of central Shanxi. It became credible only because the death of the Khitan emperor led to the complete withdrawal of Khitan armies from the central plains. That withdrawal enabled Liu Zhiyuan to assert some authority over a large part of the Jin territories.

To call the Han an empire is totally misleading. Its three predecessors had some claim to legitimacy: the Liang had destroyed a great empire and sought to replace it; the Tang had tried to restore what had been a great empire; and even the very weak Jin had some claim, if only because it finally brought an end to the glorious name of Tang. The Han's only justification, however, was to have given the demoralized forces of North China a name to rally around, thus making it possible for more determined new leaders to emerge and bring about the eventual reunification of China. It was primarily a central Shanxi "kingdom," and as such was to survive for another twenty-nine years, mainly with support from the Liao dynasty, after having given up any pretense of being an empire. The Later Han did not become part of Song China until 979.

The last of the Five Dynasties, the Later Zhou, did not start with any better claim than the Han. Guo Wei, its founder, was chosen leader through a military coup, the classic way to power of provincial governors. What distinguished him was that he was a Han Chinese whose success finally brought a generation of Turkic-Han military alliance to an end. However, he inherited a corrupt and inefficient army, a devastated economy, and a feeble authority that did not extend much beyond Henan Province and parts of neighboring Shandong, Hebei, and Shaanxi. Furthermore, he was relatively old for a dynastic founder, and there was simply too much to be done. He died at the age of fifty, after having ruled for only just over three years.

Guo Wei had no surviving sons but was most fortunate in his heir, an adopted son who was also his wife's nephew. This new leader was Chai Rong, then only thirty-two, who turned out to be one of the ablest men of the tenth century. He listened to good advice about military and economic reforms and adopted a successful strategy of attacking southward into the rich agricultural lands of Nan Tang (one of the Ten Kingdoms). His success in Huainan (all the Nan Tang lands north of the Yangtze River) not only immediately helped the economic recovery of North China but also was the single most important factor in providing the succeeding Song dynasty with sound economic foundations for the eventual reunification of China. Indeed, had Chai Rong not died at the early age of thirty-eight, the whole course of Chinese history might have been changed. The period might then be marked by a great Zhou dynasty that followed the "Four Dynasties."

Unfortunately, Chai Rong died during one of his campaigns against the Liao and left a six-year-old son as heir. Like so many of the military contenders for the throne during this period, Guo Wei's and Chai Rong's children had been left as hostages at court to ensure their loyalty; they were brutally murdered when that loyalty was in question. Chai Rong's eldest surviving son, therefore, was one born only after the dynasty was founded. Thus, there was very little to prevent the Song founder, Zhao Kuangyin, from doing what had become normal at the time: he seized the throne from the boy in the name of the empire's safety.

The Five Dynasties period contributed, however erratically, toward the making of the Song state and society. Although none of the dynasties individually established anything permanent, the decades of disorder cleared the way for (1) a new military system; (2) new ideas of centralization; and (3) new social and economic classes in place of the old great aristocratic families. In addition, they were also years when west, central, and South China were largely independent and new creative forces there were released to reshape their economies. These in turn were to contribute enormously to the prosperity of the Song empire after reunification.

[*See also* Ten Kingdoms *and* Liao Dynasty.]

Wang Gungwu, *The Structure of Power in North China during the Five Dynasties* (1963). WANG GUNGWU

FIVE-YEAR PLANS. [*This article discusses five-year plans in India. For treatment of five-year plans elsewhere in Asia, see* China, People's Republic of *and* Korea, People's Democratic Republic of.]

Five-year plans are social blueprints reflecting the development goals of India's central leadership and are central documents of Indian economic policy. Responsibility for drawing up and monitoring these plans rests with the Planning Commission, an expert body established in 1950, but planning is in fact a political process involving the wider public. Political parties, the press, and other groups scrutinize the commission's preliminary drafts and "approach papers," and final plans reflect compromise between interests and ideologies. Planning is further complicated by the federal constitution, which places considerable power in the states, and by unanticipated events such as war, monsoon failure, election results, and energy crises. Since 1950 planning strategies have slowly changed along with public perceptions of India's problems and needs.

The First Plan (1951–1956), announced after several years of debate over the idea of planning itself, put priority on agriculture, especially irrigation, fertilizers, and other technical needs. The plan also stressed institutional reform, such as land ceilings, community development, rural cooperatives, and local governance *(panchayats)*. Actual outlay was relatively modest at Rs. 2,069 crores.

In the Second Plan (1956–1961) the financial outlay doubled, establishing clearly that the state was to be the major factor directing the economy. The plan emphasized rapid industrialization and, in the public sector, large basic enterprises such as iron and steel and machine tools. Consumer goods were to be promoted, on the other hand, by smaller, labor-intensive village industries. Relative expenditure for agriculture and irrigation was sharply reduced, dropping from 34.6 percent in the First Plan to 17.5 percent.

The Third Plan (1961–1966) was developed amid controversy over basic approach: whether priority should be placed on agriculture or industry, on the public or private sector, on rapid economic growth or social and institutional change. The plan's goal of a self-sustained economy was undercut by drought and poor agricultural production, necessitating large grain imports, as well as by the 1962 war with China, which wrought havoc with plan targets and led to heavy deficit financing, foreign aid, and, eventually, rupee devaluation.

By the mid-1960s, when the draft of the Fourth Plan was prepared, the economy was stagnating. Recovery was hampered by two consecutive monsoon failures (1965–1967), the Indo-Pakistan War (1965), two changes in the prime ministership, and reduced financial resources available for the plan. The Fourth Plan was therefore postponed and replaced by a series of Annual Plans (1966–1969). Finalized in 1969, the Fourth Plan attempted to reduce deficit financing and foreign aid. The aim was rapid economic growth with stable prices and improved conditions for the poor. Increasing agricultural production was an urgent necessity. Greater scope was given to private investment, although the public sector was still dominant in heavy industry.

The Fifth Plan (projected for 1974–1979) was finalized after Prime Minister Indira Gandhi's strong victory in the March 1971 elections. Put into effect only in 1976, however, the plan reemphasized self-reliance and the public sector. Projected outlays doubled over the Fourth Plan and focused on agriculture, energy, employment, and science and technology.

After its 1977 election victory, the Janata Party government terminated the Fifth Plan and set up a system of Rolling Annual Plans. The new economic policy, influenced by Mohandas K. Gandhi's philosophy, envisioned a more decentralized, village-based approach. With the return to power of Indira Gandhi's Congress Party in January 1980, however, five-year planning was revived. The Sixth Plan (1980–1985) projected a public sector outlay of Rs. 97,500 crores, more than the total of all preceding plans. Top emphasis was given, for the first time, to energy development (27.3 percent), followed closely by programs in agriculture, irrigation, flood control, and rural development (23.7 percent).

The final arrangements for the Seventh Plan (projected for 1985–1990) were made after Mrs. Gandhi's death in October 1984 and the Congress Party's strong election victories under the new prime minister, Rajiv Gandhi. The impact, if any, of the new government's economic policies on the plan was not immediately apparent.

[*See also* Land Tenure and Reform: Land Tenure, Revenue, and Reform in South Asia; Nehru, Jawaharlal; *and* Gandhi, Indira.]

F. R. Frankel, *India's Political Economy 1947–1977: The Gradual Revolution* (1980). A. H. Hanson, *The Process of Planning: A Study of India's Five Year Plans 1950–1964* (1966). L. K. Jha, *Economic Strategy for the 80s: Priorities for the Seventh Plan* (2d ed., 1985).

FRANKLIN A. PRESLER

FLYING TIGERS. Formally the "American Volunteer Group," the Flying Tigers were part of an effort to aid China in its war against Japan while the United States was still technically neutral. The unit, commanded by Claire L. Chennault (1890–1958), was formed in early 1941, commissioned as part of the Chinese air force in August, and went into operation in November. A few months after Pearl Harbor it was disbanded and merged into the US Tenth Air Force. At its peak it numbered about one hundred pilots—army and navy officers on "inactive status"—and an equal number of Curtiss-Wright P-40 fighter planes. This colorful group, operating from Burma and Yunnan Province, had an outstanding combat record but had no significant impact on the course of the war.

[*See also* World War II in China.]

LYMAN P. VAN SLYKE

FONTAINEBLEAU CONFERENCE. The Fontainebleau Conference, which opened on 6 July 1946, focused on four problems: the status of the Indochinese Federation, Vietnam's position vis-à-vis France in the French Union, the inclusion of Cochinchina in a Vietnamese state, and the military, economic, and diplomatic powers of such a state. Negotiations faltered when Georges-Thierry D'Argenlieu organized the "rival" Dalat Conference of puppet Vietnamese "states." The conference finally ended on 10 September 1946 after weeks of French intransigence had produced no significant concessions. The only tangible result of the negotiations was a *modus vivendi,* signed by Ho Chi Minh, giving France a greater role in Vietnamese economic and cultural affairs.

[*See also* D'Argenlieu, Georges-Thierry; Vietnam, Democratic Republic of; *and* Ho Chi Minh.]

Ellen Hammer, *The Struggle for Indochina, 1940–1955* (1966).

BRUCE M. LOCKHART

FORBES, WILLIAM CAMERON (1870–1959), governor-general of the Philippines from 1909 to 1913 and United States ambassador to Japan from 1930 to 1932. Forbes began his Philippine career as secretary of commerce and police in 1904. He led the American program to modernize economic infrastructure and promote foreign investment, hoping that economic growth would neutralize Philippine nationalism. Forbes shrewdly identified and patronized rising nationalist leaders such as Sergio Osmeña and Manuel Quezon but could not fully win them over. Recalled to public life by Herbert Hoover, he was ambassador in Tokyo when fighting broke out between Japan and China in Manchuria in 1931. Convinced that American pressure upon Japan would backfire, Forbes lost the confidence of Secretary of State Henry L. Stimson and resigned.

Peter W. Stanley, *A Nation in the Making: The Philippines and the United States, 1899–1921* (1974).

PETER W. STANLEY

FORMER LY DYNASTY, a Sino-Viet clan that exercised authority over the Viet lands from 542 to 602 CE. Ly Bi (or Ly Bon), an officer in the service of the Liang-dynasty governor of Jiao Province, rebelled against Chinese rule, drove out the governor (542), and proclaimed himself king of Nam Viet (544). The country was officially named Van Xuan. In 546 Liang forces drove Ly Bi into the mountains, where he either died of disease or was killed by the Lao. Disturbances elsewhere caused the removal of the Liang army (548), after which Ly Bi's subordinates and kinsmen regained control of the delta. Ly Phat Tu, a relative of Ly Bi, reunified the delta under Ly power (591) and ruled it until his surrender to the armies of the Sui dynasty in 602. Thien (Zen) Buddhism became established among the Viet at this time.

[*See also* Ly Bon *and* Van Xuan.]

Thomas Hodgkin, *Vietnam: The Revolutionary Path* (1981). Keith W. Taylor, *The Birth of Vietnam* (1983).

JAMES M. COYLE

FORMOSA. *See* Taiwan.

FORSTER, EDWARD MORGAN (1879–1970), noted English writer whose novel *A Passage to India* (1924) eloquently expressed the doubts about empire felt by many English people after World War I. For many, the novel was a startling and effective indictment of British rule in India, shattering traditional nineteenth-century fictional stereotypes—wicked Hindu priests, heroic district officers, tragic interracial liaisons. Forster felt that the Raj was a failure because the British had isolated themselves from India and its people, and the clear-headed realism of the book's final scene declares that the two protagonists, one Indian and one English, can meet again in the future only as equals in a free India.

Forster visited India twice before the publication of *A Passage to India*—once in 1912–1913 and again in 1921–1922, when he served briefly as the private secretary to the maharaja of Dewas Senior, a tiny state in central India. His experience of India during these two trips gave *A Passage to India* its shape and tone. Forster's other Indian work, *The Hill of Devi* (1954), is an assemblage of letters, diary entries, and essays from the second visit.

G. K. Das, *E. M. Forster's India* (1977). P. N. Furbank, *E. M. Forster: A Life* (1977–1978). Robin Jared Lewis, *E. M. Forster's Passages to India* (1979).

ROBIN JARED LEWIS

FORT WILLIAM, constructed by the British East India Company between 1696 and 1715 in what is now Calcutta, India. The original site was near the present Dalhousie Square. The pond in its front was called Lal Dighi by the Indians, and Green or Park by the Europeans, who used it as a promenade. Mughal authorities encouraged the establishment of such fortified European commercial settlements in the late eighteenth century. Later, however, the nawabs of Bengal opposed construction of strong fortifications, and the fort was heavily damaged during Siraj ud-Daulah's attack on Calcutta. After 1757 the English started building a new fort farther to the south, and the old fort was finally demolished in 1819 to make way for a new administrative and commercial complex for the capital of Britain's Indian empire.

[*See also* Calcutta; Black Hole; *and* Siraj ud-Daulah.]

Alexander Hamilton, *A New Account of the East Indies,* 2 vols. (3d ed., 1930). C. R. Willson, *Old Fort William in Bengal,* 2 vols. (1906).

PRADIP SINHA

FOTUDENG (232–348), early promulgator of Buddhism in China. A native of Central Asia (probably Kucha), Fotudeng became a Buddhist monk at an early age and studied under various Buddhist teachers in Kashmir. In 310 he traveled east to China. With the destruction of the Eastern Jin dynasty in 316, North China was thrown into chaos. Through various feats of thaumaturgy, such as producing rain or foreseeing the outcome of military exploits, Fotudeng gained the confidence of the powerful Xiongnu chieftain Shi Le. When Shi Le established the state of Later Zhao in 330, Fotudeng's influence reached its peak. Through his capacity as both a religious and political adviser Fotudeng secured official support for the Buddhist teachings and was able, through court patronage, to disseminate the religion through all segments of the populace. Fotudeng's importance to the history of Buddhism in China is twofold. First, his approach of seeking esteem through displays of shamanic prowess and promoting Buddhism as a religion in support of the state came to be a characteristic mark of medieval Chinese Buddhism as it developed under the non-Han dynasties of North China. Second, through such illustrious disciples as Daoan, Falang, Zhu Fatai, and Zhu Faya, Fotudeng sowed the seeds for the first real growth of Buddhism on Chinese soil.

[*See also* Buddhism: Buddhism in China.]

Arthur F. Wright, "Fo-t'u-têng: A Biography," *Harvard Journal of Asiatic Studies* 11 (1948): 321–371.

DAN STEVENSON

FOUR MODERNIZATIONS. The Four Modernizations include the modernization of Chinese agriculture, industry, national defense, and science and technology (counted as one). The notion of a comprehensive development program was first advanced by Zhou Enlai but had to await the death of Mao Zedong in 1976 before it could be fully implemented. Deng Xiaoping, in his dramatic rise to leadership in 1978, advocated the Four Modernizations as a positive program around which all Chinese could unite and as an alternative to the ideological struggles that had divided the Chinese leadership for more than two decades. An essential element in the modernization program was the opening of China to increased trade with the nonsocialist world. Human rights advocates such as Wei Jingsheng called for a "fifth modernization," by which they meant democracy.

[*See also* China, People's Republic of; Deng Xiaoping; *and* Wei Jingsheng.]

EDWARD L. FARMER

FRANCO-SIAMESE WAR (1940–1941). Under the first Luang Phibunsongkhram regime (1938–1944), Thailand emulated Japan's assertive nationalistic policy by demanding the return of territories lost to France and Great Britain in the early colonial period. With France weakened by defeat to the Germans in June 1940, Phibun stepped up his pan-Thai claims, which were advocated by Luang Wichitwathakan. The ensuing Franco-Siamese War was settled in 1941 through Japanese mediation. France agreed to cede four western Cambodian provinces and contiguous Laotian territories. However, at the end of World War II, Thailand gave back those territories to France in return for French support of Thailand's application for membership in the United Nations.

[*See also* Phibunsongkhram, Luang *and* Wichitwathakan, Luang.]

Direk Jayanam, *Siam and World War II,* translated by Jane Keyes (1978).

THAK CHALOEMTIARANA

FREE THAI, resistance movement organized to counter Japanese influence upon official Thai policy during World War II. On 8 December 1941 Japanese troops landed on Thai soil, demanding that Thailand grant Japan free passage to Burma and Malaya. They encountered resistance from the Thai armed forces, but eventually the government, then led by Luang Phibunsongkhram, capitulated and signed a treaty of friendship and cooperation with Japan. Soon afterward, Thailand declared war on the Allies.

Finance minister Pridi Phanomyong, however, opposed the government's pro-Japanese policy, and as a result he was removed from the cabinet and given the prestigious but powerless position of regent. Combining the Seri Thai and Thai Issara organizations, which had started in Thailand, the United States, and Great Britain, Pridi organized the Free Thai movement to resist the Japanese. The movement's major tasks were intelligence and communications work for the Allies. Among its prominent members were Pridi, Seni Pramoj, Luang Aduldetcharat, Direk Chaiyanam, Puey Ungphakorn, Net Kemayothin, Thanat Khoman, Thawi Bunyaket, and Admiral Sangwon Suwannachip.

Eleven Free Thai units were trained in Great Britain, thirteen in the United States, and eight local chapters outside of Bangkok. As a result of the movement's close association with the American Office of Strategic Services and British intelligence during the war, the Allies treated Thailand leniently at the end of the war. Pridi later used the Seri Thai as a political base in his struggle with Phibunsongkhram for leadership of the country. But both his influence and that of the Seri Thai declined after the army's coup d'état in 1947 and the unsuccessful Seri Thai countercoup of 1949.

[*See also* Phibunsongkhram, Luang; Pridi Phanomyong; *and* Seni Pramoj.]

David Wilson, *Politics in Thailand* (1962).

THAK CHALOEMTIARANA

FRENCH EAST INDIA COMPANY, founded in 1662 and inspired and guided by Jean-Baptiste Colbert from 1664 until his death in 1683. The company established settlements at Pondicherry (1674), Chandernagore (1690), and Mahé (acquired 1721), supplemented by factories at important trading centers; considerable trade was channeled through Mauritius and Réunion. Weakened by shortage of finance and close government control that led to lack of public interest, the company was reorganized in 1723. Anglo-French hostilities in Europe in the 1740s and 1750s, however, drew the respective companies into political entanglements in India, further undermining the French company. Disbanded in 1769, it was revived for the last time between 1785 and 1795.

S. P. Sen, *The French in India 1763–1816* (1958).

USHA SANYAL

FRENCH INDOCHINA WAR (1945–1954), the political and military conflict between France and the Vietnam Independence League (Viet Minh) that came about as a result of French attempts to reimpose political control over Indochina at the end of World War II.

Following the surrender of Japan on 10 August 1945 and the Viet Minh August Revolution, Vietnam established a provisional government with Ho Chi Minh as president. The Potsdam Declaration of the Allies (26 July 1945) stated that the surrender of the Japanese army in Indochina would be taken by Chinese forces north of the sixteenth parallel and by British troops to the south.

The British helped the French reassert their authority in the south. Hostilities first erupted when French troops, newly released from captivity and armed by the British, forcibly evicted Viet Minh representatives from Saigon government offices on 23 September 1945. The Viet Minh resisted, but they were driven out of the city. Between October 1945 and January 1946 the French garrison, reinforced by the rapidly growing French Expeditionary Corps, gained control of most of Cochinchina and southern Annam.

In the north, the entry of French troops was delayed by the Chinese, who sought to extract maximum concessions from France. No French troops were allowed back into Tonkin until March 1946. On 6 March, Ho Chi Minh and Jean Sainteny, French chief of mission in Hanoi, reached a provisional agreement calling for French recognition of Viet independence "within the French Union" and

Viet agreement to the temporary presence of French troops. Negotiations between Ho Chi Minh and French representatives held at Fontainebleau from 6 July to 14 September ended without agreement, and the 6 March accords broke down shortly thereafter. A dispute between French customs officials and Vietnamese in Haiphong led to the shelling of the Vietnamese sector of the city by the French cruiser *Suffren,* causing about six thousand civilian deaths. On 19 December—the date that is often taken to be the start of the war—Ho Chi Minh authorized an attack against the French in Hanoi. The Viet Minh were driven from Hanoi and gradually withdrew to their base areas in the Viet Bac. By late March 1947 French forces controlled most of the major cities and towns of Vietnam.

From 1947 to 1950 the Vietnam People's Army conducted low-level guerrilla warfare against the French Expeditionary Corps, but most Vietnamese efforts were concentrated on enlarging, training, and equipping their forces. The French launched major attacks against Vietnamese base areas in November 1947 (Operation Lea) and autumn 1948, but they achieved only limited gains before they were bogged down by the difficult terrain.

Having failed both to negotiate a political settlement with the Viet Minh and to defeat them on the battlefield, the French now sought to establish a noncommunist Vietnamese government that would accept the limited form of independence offered by France. A tentative agreement was reached with the former emperor Bao Dai at Ha Long Bay on 5 June 1948 and formalized in the Elysee Agreement of 8 March 1949. The State of Vietnam was proclaimed in July 1949 as "an independent state within the French Union." Bao Dai became head of state. Defense and foreign relations remained the responsibility of France.

In January 1950, Communist Chinese forces reached the Vietnamese border. Thereafter, for the duration of the war, the Viet Minh enjoyed rest and training areas and a steady source of supplies across the frontier. The French war effort was strongly supported by the United States, particularly after the outbreak of the Korean War in June 1950. By the end of the war the United States had paid more than half of French war expenses.

Early in October 1950 the Vietnam People's Army launched a series of attacks against French positions along Colonial Route 4, near the Chinese border. The garrison of Cao Bang was overwhelmed as it attempted to evacuate, and Lang Son and Lao Cai were abandoned. These events left the whole of the Chinese border region in Viet Minh hands.

In January 1951 General Vo Nguyen Giap, commander of the Viet Minh forces, sought to exploit these successes by attacking the Red River delta, strongly defended by the French. In the battles of Vinh Yen (13–17 January), Mao Khe (23–28 March), and the Day River (29 May–18 June), the Viet Minh suffered heavy losses and withdrew. Although costly to the Viet Minh, these battles demonstrated that the French Expeditionary Corps no longer held the strategic initiative.

Between early October and early December 1952 the Viet Minh conducted an offensive in the mountainous northwestern region of Tonkin, threatening Luang Prabang in Laos and reducing French control in the area to a series of increasingly isolated outposts. To diminish the threat to Laos and draw Viet Minh away from the Red River delta into a set-piece battle, General Henri Navarre, the new commander of the French Expeditionary Corps, decided in 1953 to establish a fortified camp at Dien Bien Phu in the northwest. By January 1954 the camp, containing eleven thousand of the best troops of the corps, was surrounded by fifty thousand regulars of the Vietnam People's Army. On 7 May, after a fifty-four day battle, the camp was surrendered to the Viet Minh. This was the most important Viet Minh victory of the war.

The increasing domestic unpopularity of the war convinced the French government to reopen negotiations with the Viet Minh. In March 1954 France agreed to allow the question of Indochina to be discussed at the forthcoming Geneva Conference, and on 20 July a cease-fire agreement was reached between French and Viet Minh representatives at the conference. Some scattered fighting took place thereafter.

The French Indochina War left Vietnam independent but divided into communist and noncommunist zones. The failure of attempts at peaceful reunification, called for by the Geneva accords, led to a renewal of warfare on an even larger scale several years later.

[*See also* D'Argenlieu, Georges-Thierry; Lattre de Tassigny, Jean de; Fontainebleau Conference; Geneva Conference of 1954; Ho Chi Minh; Indochinese Communist Party; Viet Minh; Bao Dai; Dien Bien Phu; and Vo Nguyen Giap.]

Joseph Buttinger, *Vietnam: A Dragon Embattled* (1967). William J. Duiker, *The Communist Road to Power in Vietnam* (1981). Bernard Fall, *Street Without Joy* (1957). Ellen Hammer, *The Struggle for Indochina* (1954). Donald Lancaster, *The Emancipation of French Indochina* (1961). Edgar O'Ballance, *The Indochina War 1945–1954* (1964).

James M. Coyle

FRIARS, a technical term for religious orders of monastic origin. In the Philippines it is often applied incorrectly to all clergy and carries a derogatory connotation. Except for the Jesuits, all the missionaries who came to the Philippines until the mid-nineteenth century were friars. The principal differences between the friars and Jesuits were that the latter were organized precisely for active mission work and were highly centralized and international because of their special vow to the pope. In the early centuries, however, the differences were not of great significance.

In the eighteenth century, the Spanish crown expelled the Jesuits from all Spanish dominions. At the same time, the friars were put under government control and practically severed from the papacy. The result was a decline in discipline among the clergy, as well as bitter antagonism between the friars and the Filipino secular clergy, who had been hurriedly ordained to replace them but had received negligible training. When the secular clergy proved incompetent, the government reversed its policy, influenced perhaps by the revolutionary leadership roles that had been assumed by native priests in Mexico. Taking advantage of the influence of the friars on the ordinary Filipino, who associated Catholicism with Spanish rule, even anticlerical governments made wide civil as well as ecclesiastical use of friar parish priests and reduced the Filipino priests to the role of coadjutor.

Their influence made the friars the prime target of all nationalist Filipinos. The Propaganda Movement accused them of violations of celibacy, of avarice and great wealth, and of political interference. Although these accusations were exaggerated, and more true during the early part of the century, there was some truth to them. The real issue, however, was who should control the Philippines. The Malolos Republic took friars prisoner. The American government, which wanted to conciliate the Filipino elite, bought the friar haciendas, and the great majority voluntarily left the country. The net result was an enormous lack of priests, while the haciendas passed into the hands of the Filipino elite and big American firms.

[*See also* Catholicism in the Philippines; Cavite Mutiny; Propaganda Movement; Pilar, Marcelo H. del; *and* Rizal, Jose Mercado.]

Marcelo H. del Pilar, *Monastic Supremacy in the Philippines*, translated by Encarnacion Alzona (1958). John S. Schumacher, *The Propaganda Movement* (1979) and *Readings in Philippine Church History* (1979).

John N. Schumacher, s.j.

FUBING SYSTEM. Best translated as militia, the *fubing*, a corps of mainly self-supporting farmer-soldiers performing periodic tours of duty, was an important Chinese military institution from the sixth through the eighth century. Its origins are traceable to the non-Chinese Northern Wei dynasty (386–535). At first the *fubing* was a privileged and prestigious force made up of Xianbei tribal nobles who performed hereditary military service. They owed no tax or labor service obligations but were required to supply their own weapons, animals, and food rations. In the sixth century the *fubing* gradually became sinicized with the addition of troops recruited locally from among Chinese militarized families. During the Sui (581–618) and early Tang (618–907) dynasties Chinese military needs were largely served by the *fubing* system, in which military power was divided into small, centrally controlled but locally recruited and administered units *(fu)*, none of which was powerful enough to challenge the government's supremacy.

The high point of *fubing* development came in 636 under Emperor Taizong, who established about 630 units, each consisting of between 800 and 1,200 men, who were heavily concentrated in and around the capital region of Chang'an. *Fubing* troops were active between the ages of about twenty and sixty and were expected to serve short periodic tours of duty in Chang'an, the frequency of which depended on their geographical proximity to the capital. They were also assigned to take part in special military campaigns or to serve for up to three years on the frontiers. Since they were allocated land under the equal field (juntian) system, when not on duty they probably devoted themselves to agricultural labor. As threats along China's borders became more serious, the *fubing* were gradually replaced by professional long-service troops, leading to the formal abolition of the system in 749. Between the tenth and fourteenth century, the *fubing* system was employed by the Korean kingdom of Koryŏ.

[*See also* Northern Wei Dynasty *and* Tang Dynasty.]

Denis C. Twitchett, "Lands under State Cultivation during the T'ang Dynasty," *Journal of the Economic and Social History of the Orient* 2.2 (1959): 162–203, 2.3 (1959): 335–336.

Howard J. Wechsler

FUJIAN, coastal province in southeast China; capital, Fuzhou. Facing the island of Taiwan (across the strait to the east), Fujian lies between Zhejiang Province to the north and Guangdong to the southwest. Its area is 123,100 square kilometers and its population in 1980 was estimated at 25,180,000, of which 12 percent is urban. More than 100,000 of its inhabitants belong to the She minority.

One of the most rugged of China's provinces, with about 90 percent of the terrain taken up by hills and mountains, Fujian has a history of comparative isolation, remaining a frontier area later than most other provinces. Since arable land is limited to riverbottoms and a narrow strip along the coast, the population has turned repeatedly to the sea to make a living from fishing or maritime trade. The long rocky coastline provided many deep natural harbors for ports while scores of offshore islands provided staging areas and dens for smugglers and pirates. In the interior, dense forests supplied timber and masts for shipbuilding and wood products for export. In addition, lively trade in local handicrafts, lacquerware, porcelains, silks, and agricultural products such as tea, sugar, exotic fruits, and later tobacco, all contributed to making Quanzhou, Fuzhou, Xiamen (Amoy), and Zhangzhou world-famous entrepôts.

In ancient times, Fujian was called Min and was inhabited by an aboriginal people known as the Yue. In 110 BCE invading Han armies destroyed the independent Yue kingdom. After the sixth century, Chinese settlement in the frontier area became significant, and as prosperity grew from domestic and maritime trade, more settlers were attracted to the area. Fujian became independent again for a brief time in the early tenth century as the kingdom of Min but was rejoined to the empire under the Song. By the twelfth century, the port of Quanzhou had become a great center of foreign trade (the fabulous "Zayton" described by Marco Polo) and drew Arab merchants from western Asia.

Owing to the restrictive foreign trade policies of Ming and Qing rulers, however, Fujian's fortunes declined in subsequent years. The province suffered also from the Wokou pirate depredations of the 1550s and, a century later, from Manchu suppression of both Ming loyalist resistance and the rebel Koxinga (Zheng Chenggong). (After 1684, the Manchus governed Taiwan as part of Fujian Province.) As population density grew in the latter half of the Qing period, and as agricultural land became scarce, thousands of Fujianese emigrated to Taiwan, the Philippines, Southeast Asia, the Americas, and Europe. They remain the second largest component (next to those from Guangdong) of the Overseas Chinese.

In 1842 two treaty ports, Xiamen and Fuzhou, were opened to foreign trade, but foreign competition hurt tea and sugar exports, preventing economic expansion. The Nationalist blockade of the province after 1949 and continued occupation of offshore islands have also limited foreign trade.

Since 1949, however, agricultural production has increased and new rail links to the interior have stimulated light industry. More recently, in 1979, Fujian was designated a "special economic zone" by the government in an effort to encourage foreign economic activity and investment.

ROLAND L. HIGGINS

FUJITA YŪKOKU (1774–1826), a Japanese Confucian scholar and reformer from the Mito domain. Fujita Yūkoku was born to a merchant family; his father was a dealer in used clothing. Early in life he demonstrated his scholastic abilities, and in 1789 he entered the Mito Historiographical Institute, where he earned full, if low, samurai status for his descendants. Thus it would seem that the Mito domain permitted a degree of upward social mobility through scholarly distinction.

Yūkoku was made head of the institute in 1807, became a district intendant responsible for agricultural administration, and remained an energetic domain reformer until his death. His thought was characterized by a desire to return the Tokugawa polity and economy to seventeenth-century conditions of agricultural self-sufficiency and—his own family background notwithstanding—to uphold strictly the system of hereditary social status. He also stressed the responsibility of the ruling samurai class to minister to the needs of commoners and thus keep the realm well ordered.

His son, Fujita Tōko (1806–1855), while carrying on most of the elder Fujita's political ideas, was willing to accommodate commerce and handicraft industries and to tap these as a source of domain revenue. He tried to implement these policies in the Mito reforms of the 1830s, reforms that attracted national attention. Tōko became head of the Historiographical Institute in 1827. From the 1830s to his death in 1855 he served as a district intendant in the domain and as chief aide to Tokugawa Nariaki, lord of Mito and *bakufu* adviser on national defense and foreign affairs. Tōko is best known, however, as a hero to young samurai activists in the "honor the emperor, expel the barbarians" movement in the 1850s and 1860s. He died, fittingly for a model Confucianist, while rescuing his mother during an earthquake.

H. D. Harootunian, *Toward Restoration* (1970).

BOB TADASHI WAKABAYASHI

FUJIWARA LINEAGE, an aristocratic lineage that has been active in Japanese political and cultural life since the seventh century and that dominated the court government from 858 until 1086. The Fujiwara were descended from the Nakatomi, a clan of Shinto ritualists. In 669 Nakatomi Kamatari (614–669) was granted the surname Fujiwara in recognition of his contributions to the Taika Reforms, which introduced to Japan bureaucratic institutions of government based on Chinese models. [*See* Taika Reforms.] Subsequently, the Fujiwara lineage divided into four "houses," each of which produced important statesmen during the Nara period (710–794). In the subsequent Heian period (794–1185), however, the "Northern House" (Hokke) alone flourished. Its leaders succeeded in marrying their daughters to emperors and then serving as regents to their imperial relatives. This practice began in 858, and eventually representatives of the Fujiwara lineage came to hold the title of regent (or its equivalent) continuously until modern times. The most powerful of these regents was Fujiwara Michinaga (966–1028), who dominated the government from 995 until his death. Ironically, as the Fujiwara came to monopolize political power, they undermined the Chinese-style system of bureaucratic government that their ancestors had helped to create. [*See* Fujiwara Michinaga.]

The actual political power of these regents effectively came to an end in 1086, when Shirakawa (1053–1129, r. 1072–1086), an emperor not closely related to the Fujiwara, abdicated and took control of the government as a retired emperor. Although politically weakened, Michinaga's descendants continued to hold the title of regent. By the early Kamakura period (1185–1333), they had divided themselves into sublineages known as the Five Regental Houses (Gosekke), each of which adopted the name of an ancestor's residence as a new surname. The new branches of the Fujiwara were, in order of seniority, the Konoe, Kujō, Nijō, Ichijō, and Takatsukasa. All subsequent regents were selected from among the heads of these families. Other key posts just below the regents came to be monopolized by a group of nine families known as the Seika, of which seven were branches of the Fujiwara. In addition, there were many branches with lesser status at court. At the time of the Meiji Restoration, fully 96 of the 137 court families were of the Fujiwara lineage. Although the descendants of the ancient Fujiwara no longer use that surname, a few have maintained their family's tradition of political leadership, the most famous being Iwakura Tomomi (1825–1883), an activist at the time of the Restoration; Saionji Kimmochi (1849–1940), a statesman with liberal beliefs; and Konoe Fumimaro (1891–1945), a prime minister during the 1930s.

In addition to political leaders, the Fujiwara lineage produced major cultural figures, including some of Japan's greatest classical writers, for example Murasaki Shikibu (978–1016), the author of the *Tale of Genji,* and the poet Saigyō (1118–1190). The role of the Fujiwara as arbiters of conservative cultural tastes helped preserve the family in medieval times when their political and economic power declined, for even as the ancient institutions of government had become hollow shells, forms of traditional culture preserved by the Fujiwara continued to enjoy prestige. Even warriors came to patronize the Fujiwara poets and calligraphers who maintained classical traditions. Today, many priceless literary manuscripts and examples of calligraphy are preserved in the private collections of descendants of some of the original writers.

[*See also* Kujō; Iwakura Tomomi; Saionji Kimmochi; Konoe Fumimaro; Murasaki Shikibu; Saigyō; *and* Fujiwara Period..]

Ivan Morris, *The World of the Shining Prince* (1969). George B. Sansom, *Japan: A Short Cultural History* (1952) and *A History of Japan to 1333* (1958).

ROBERT BORGEN

FUJIWARA MICHINAGA (966–1027), Japanese court noble. The most powerful of Fujiwara leaders, Michinaga dominated the Japanese court for thirty years and is sometimes thought to be the model for the hero of the *Tale of Genji.* [*See* Genji Monogatari.] His career exemplified the techniques by which the Fujiwara controlled the court government. Two of his elder brothers preceded him in the office of regent, but in 995 they both died. The first brother had hoped his own son would follow him as regent, but Michinaga's sister, the emperor's mother, blocked that appointment and persuaded the emperor to give the powers of regent to Michinaga. A year later, Michinaga had his rival nephew banished. He consolidated his power by means of strategic marriages: four of his daughters married emperors, and subsequently three of his grandsons became emperors. When the first of these grandsons became emperor in 1016, Michinaga was duly named regent, but a year later he turned that office over to his eldest son, thereby insuring that it would continue to be held by his descendants. Although Michinaga chose not to retain the title of regent, his power was undiminished.

In 1019 he fell seriously ill, and in his remaining years he increasingly sought comfort in Buddhism. He formally took the tonsure, established his residence in a temple, and devoted himself to pious works—all the while remaining involved in court politics. Michinaga is said to have died praying for his own salvation in 1028. As he had hoped, his descendants continued to serve as regents until modern times, but their power was greatly reduced after 1068 with the succession of an emperor who was not closely related to them.

[*See also* Fujiwara Lineage.]

G. Cameron Hurst, "Michinaga's Maladies," *Monumenta Nipponica* 34.1 (1979): 101–122. Helen Craig McCullough, *Okagami: The Great Mirror, Fujiwara no Michinaga (966–1027) and His Times* (1980). Mildred Tahara, "Fujiwara Michinaga," in *Great Historical Figures of Japan,* edited by Hyoe Nakamura and Thomas Harper (1978), pp. 48–59.

ROBERT BORGEN

FUJIWARA PERIOD, the age when the Fujiwara family dominated Japanese political and cultural life (roughly the years from 858 to 1086, although scholars differ in dating the period). The ascendancy of the Fujiwara family coincided with the appearance of distinctively Japanese forms of political organization and cultural expression that evolved out of the Chinese modes adopted earlier. The Fujiwara, a noble family that had long been active in court government, became preeminent largely through their successful manipulation of strategic marriages with reigning emperors. As a result of these family ties, the head of the Fujiwara lineage assumed the powerful office of regent. Japanese society was polygamous, however, and emperors might have numerous Fujiwara relatives all seeking the title of regent. The rewards at stake were great, for the Fujiwara had come to own extensive landed estates *(shōen)* and the regents controlled the income from them. As a result, although the Fujiwara period was an aristocratic age famous for its courtly culture, behind the elegant facade unseemly political feuds were common. The Fujiwara monopoly on political power also led to a weakening of the regular organs of government, and the growth of privately held landed estates interfered with provincial administration and the collection of taxes.

Culturally, the Fujiwara period is regarded as Japan's classical age. The Japanese had created a convenient phonetic script and used it to produce some of their greatest literary monuments, including the *Tale of Genji* by Murasaki Shikubu, the *Pillow Book* by Sei Shōnagon, and numerous anthologies of poetry. Distinctively Japanese styles of art and architecture evolved out of the styles based on Chinese models that had been fashionable in the preceding age. Within the established Buddhist sects, new beliefs appeared offering the promise of salvation based on pure faith. Although these cultural forms originated in the capital among aristocrats, some of them spread to the provinces, and the new Buddhism was propagated among the common people.

[*See also* Fujiwara Lineage *and* Genji Monogatari.]

Ivan Morris, *The World of the Shining Prince* (1969). George B. Sansom, *Japan: A Short Cultural History* (1952) and *A History of Japan to 1334* (1958).

ROBERT BORGEN

FUKUDA TAKEO (b. 1905), prime minister of Japan from 1976 to 1978. Fukuda was born in Ashikado, Gumma Prefecture, the son of a wealthy farmer. After graduating from Tokyo Imperial University he entered the Ministry of Finance, where he became director of the powerful budget bureau. He resigned this post after being implicated (although later acquitted) in one of the major postwar scandals in 1947.

In 1952 Fukuda ran for the Diet as an independent and served continuously until 1978. Owing to his long career in the Ministry of Finance, Fukuda was considered an expert in economics, and he became identified with conservative elements in the Liberal-Democratic Party, serving as its secretary general and later as its president. He was suspicious of the "growth first" policy of the principal followers of Yoshida Shigeru and instead forged close ties with Kishi Nobusuke (under whom he served as minister of agriculture) and Satō Eisaku (who appointed him minister of finance and foreign minister). In the cabinet of Miki Takeo (1974) he was deputy prime minister and director of the Economic Planning Agency.

In 1976 Fukuda became Miki's successor as prime minister, but despite Fukuda's long wait for the post his tenure proved to be short. Economic problems that followed the oil crises and debilitating factional strife led to reforms in the manner of selection of party chief, and when the new "primary" system was implemented, Fukuda was unseated by Ōhira Masayoshi in December 1978. As leader of a large party faction, however, Fukuda continued to be a powerful figure.

MICHIO UMEGAKI

FUKUZAWA YUKICHI (1835–1901), modern Japanese educator and advocate of "civilization and enlightenment." The son of a middle-ranking samurai of Nakatsu *han,* Kyushu, Fukuzawa later became a severe critic of feudal relations and customs. His reputation as a student of Dutch studies *(rangaku)* led an elder statesman of his *han* to bring him to Edo to teach at the Edo office of his lord. After the opening of Japan, Fukuzawa learned that the first language for Western learning was English and set out to master it. Even during the struggle for control of Edo at the time of the Meiji Restoration in 1868, he was reading an English economics book with his students at Keiō Gijuku, a private school of Western learning that he had founded several years earlier.

Fukuzawa traveled to the West three times before the end of the Tokugawa *bakufu.* His book *Seiyō jijō* (*Conditions of the West,* 1866–1870) was drawn from his experiences in the United States and other industrializing countries of the West. As a record-setting best-seller of modern Japan, this work, along with his *Gakumon no susume* (*Invitation to Learning,* 1872–1876), profoundly influenced those Japanese who were working toward "civilization and enlightenment," the goal he and his colleagues of the Meirokusha, founded in 1873, were trying to achieve for the Japanese. The most representative of all his publications, however, was perhaps *Bummeiron no gairyaku* (*A Survey of Theories of Civilization,* 1875). It was a determined call for Japan's modernization along Western lines.

Fukuzawa had always supported people's rights. He advocated the monarchy as a means toward building a unified nation as the feudal age of Japan was drawing closer to its conclusion. He initially believed that such a monarchy could be built around the Tokugawa, but later he was able to support the Meiji Restoration because he saw it as a vehicle for the unified nation-state he had envisioned.

Fukuzawa next found that on the one hand his modern ideas were used to justify oligarchic control of government and, on the other, the radicalism of the Popular Rights (Jiyū Minken) movement, while he himself sought a middle course. Within the government, Ōkuma Shigenobu, a parliamentarian and gradualist, shared Fukuzawa's concern. Ōkuma introduced Fukuzawa to Itō Hirobumi and Inoue Kowashi. They agreed that Fukuzawa should publish a daily newspaper to guide public opinion in what they considered constructive views. After Itō betrayed both Ōkuma and Fukuzawa by his political coup known as the political change of 1881, however, Fukuzawa preferred to "diagnose," rather than practice, politics.

Fukuzawa is also known for "Datsu-A ron" ("Departure from Asia"), an essay he published in Tokyo (1885) in his own daily, *Jiji shimpō (News of Current Affairs).* It is often held that he was the first political theorist of modern Japan who revealed an attitude of imperialism toward Japan's Asian neighbors, and in particular toward the Koreans. Yet the main thrust of Fukuzawa's essay was more a concern for modernization than an advocacy of aggression. From the outset Fukuzawa urged the building of a modern nation-state. For a while he worked with a sense of urgency, and then he had moments of doubt about what he had been advocating. Writings that reflected such doubts, as revealed in his self-criticism and criticism of those in power, were often withheld from immediate publication. Some, such as "Yase gaman no setsu" ("On Perseverance"), dealt with themes of localism as opposed to centralization and on the need to keep alive some feudalistic virtues. Keiō Gijuku, the private school Fukuzawa founded in late Tokugawa days, became one of Japan's great universities, sharing repute with Waseda (founded by Ōkuma Shigenobu in 1881) as a large preeminent private universitiy.

[*See also* Keiō Gijuku; Jiyū Minken; Ōkuma Shigenobu; *and* Meiji Period.]

Carmen Blacker, *The Japanese Enlightenment: A Study of the Writings of Fukuzawa Yukichi* (1964). David Dilworth and G. Cameron Hurst, trans., *Fukuzawa Yukichi's An Outline Theory of Civilization* (1973). Fukuzawa Yukichi, *The Autobiography of Fukuzawa Yukichi,* translated by Eiichi Kiyooka (1934), and *An Encouragement of Learning,* translated by David Dilworth and Umeyo Hirano (1969). KIMITADA MIWA

FUNAN, Chinese name for an Indochinese kingdom that lasted from the second to sixth century and was strongly influenced by Indian court culture. Much of our knowledge of this kingdom comes from Chinese sources, such as the account of the envoy Kang Tai, and the reality behind such indirect information is difficult to measure.

It was long thought that Funan was a major imperial power, one of the first indianized states. Its capital, Vyadhapura, was near Ba Phnom (in modern Prei Veng Province, Cambodia), and Oc Eo, its great seaport in the Mekong Delta, was a flourishing commercial city whose trade links extended to the Mediterranean. It was surrounded by a system of drainage canals and is now an important archaeological site. A myth paralleled in other countries attributed the foundation of Funan to Kaundinya, an Indian brahman. Chinese accounts refer to Funan's conquests, which extended imperial control around the coast of the Gulf of Siam and down the Malay Peninsula.

It has more recently been accepted, however, that the Chinese picture of Funan might be misleading and that Funan may have been one of a number of small decentralized indianized kingdoms in the area.

Claude Jacques, " 'Funan,' 'Zhenla.' The Reality Concealed by These Chinese Views of Indochina," in *Early South East Asia,* edited by R. B. Smith and W. Watson (1979). IAN W. MABBETT

FUTABATEI SHIMEI (1864–1909), Japanese novelist, translator, and student of Russian language and literature. After studying at the Tokyo School of Foreign Languages, Futabatei followed a literary career, which eventually led him to the production of what has been called Japan's first modern novel, *Floating Clouds* (*Ukigumo,* 1887–1889). It was influenced, in roughly equal measures, by the author's knowledge of Russian literature and the tradition of late Tokugawa fiction. He was the first Japanese writer to succeed in developing a psychologically convincing portrayal of a modern figure and one of the first to create a modern literary language closer to everyday speech than to received literary styles.

Prophetically, this first modern hero is a disaffected intellectual trapped within his own outworn norms of behavior and unable to adapt to the brash new Meiji spirit. The novel begins as social parody, but its modernism lies in its gradual concentration on the mind of the central figure, Bunzō; the effect is claustrophobic.

Discouraged by what he saw as failure, Futabatei gave up writing novels and took on work first as a staff writer for a government gazette and later as a Russian language specialist. A variety of jobs followed, including teaching, work in a government agency in Manchuria and Beijing, and journalism. Although reluctant, he was persuaded to produce two more novels for the *Asahi shimbun* (an Osaka newspaper), one of which, *Mediocrity* (*Heibon,* 1907), is an important precursor of Japanese naturalism.

Futabatei traveled to Russia as a special correspondent but fell ill in Saint Petersburg in 1908 and died on board ship in the Bay of Bengal. He is buried in Singapore. Unflinching in his self-criticism, he is seen by many as one of the most attractive of those who sacrificed themselves for the creation of modern literature.

Masao Miyoshi, *Accomplices of Silence: The Modern Japanese Novel* (1974). Marleigh Grazer Ryan, *Japan's First Modern Novel, "Ukigumo" of Futabatei Shimei* (1967). RICHARD BOWRING

FUZHOU, capital and largest city of Fujian Province; population, 1.05 million (1980 est.). Fuzhou has traditionally functioned as the administrative center of the province and twice served as capital of independent states: the ancient state of Min Yue and the early tenth-century kingdom of Min. Situated near the sea on the north bank of the Min River, Fuzhou's proximity to the mouth of the province's principal waterway has long made it a natural center of domestic and international commerce.

At its apogee, the twelfth-century port hosted a large cosmopolitan community of merchants and craftsmen, including many West Asian Muslims and Manichaeans. Late in the Ming period (1368–1644), European Jesuits established a Christian mission there. Coastal trade, mostly clandestine, continued through Ming and Qing times until 1842, when Fuzhou became an open treaty port. In the 1860s Europeans residing there helped build a modern Western-style arsenal and shipyard. Today, with rail links to the interior, Fuzhou prospers from the fishing industry and production of sugar, tea, paper, chemicals, and umbrellas. ROLAND L. HIGGINS

G

GAGAKU, the music performed at Japanese court ceremonies. *Gagaku* is a general term meaning "court music," as opposed to *zokugaku,* or "popular music." This music was originally imported from China and the Korean kingdoms, and it encompasses a variety of forms. The *Nihon shoki (Chronicles of Japan)* mentions Korean teachers who instructed the Japanese court in music and dance during the reign of Empress Suiko (592–628). An Office of Court Music (Gagakuryō) was established in the imperial bureaucracy, and performances of *gagaku* are still held on important court occasions today. The two major genres of court music are known as *Tōgaku* ("Tang music") and *Kōraigaku* ("Koryŏ music"). *Gagaku* included a large repertoire, of which 110 *Tōgaku* scores and 35 *Kōraigaku* scores are extant.

FIGURE 1. *Gagaku Drum.* A member of the Osaka Garyōkai troupe seated before a highly decorated drum during a performance.

The dance performances often staged during *gagaku* concerts are known as *bugaku. Bugaku* is performed on a raised platform covered with brocade. The orchestra is seated right and left, with the dancers in the center. The *gagaku* orchestra includes flutes, flageolets, and various drums. *Koto* and *biwa,* usually included in a *gagaku* ensemble, are not used during *bugaku.*

IAN HIDEO LEVY

GAHADAVALAS. A warrior dynasty of India, the Gahadavalas (1089–1198) seized the imperial city of Kanyakubja (modern Kanauj) and thereby ended the recurrent invasions of the Ganges Plain by the Muslims of the Punjab and the Northwest. Dominating what is modern Uttar Pradesh, they then conquered parts of Bihar and Madhya Pradesh and attained the height of their power under King Govindrachandra (r. 1114–1154), who established diplomatic relations with the powers of Tamil Nadu, Gujarat, and Kashmir. The Gahadavalas competed with the Chauhan king Prithviraja III for the parmountcy of northern India. This self-destructive struggle ended with their defeat by Muhammad Ghuri, who conquered both powers in 1192 and 1194 in campaigns that laid the foundation of the Delhi sultanate.

[*See also* Kanyakubja *and* Chauhan Dynasty.]

R. Niyogi, *History of the Gāhadavāla Dynasty* (1959).

SHIVA BAJPAI

GAJAH MADA, chief minister of the Javanese kingdom of Majapahit between 1330 and 1364. Seemingly of modest origins, Gajah Mada demonstrated his political sagacity and loyalty to the realm as early as 1319, when through a daring stratagem he regained control of the capital from the hands of rebels. For this feat he was rewarded with the appointment of *patih,* or "minister." In 1330 he was raised to *mapatih,* or "chief minister," and until his death in 1364 he was in essence ruler of Majapahit, being largely responsible for the resumption of Kertanagara's imperialistic foreign policy. A measure of the chief minister's unprecedented power and influence is provided by the decision of the Majapahit council of state not to appoint a successor; instead, Gajah Mada's functions were to be distributed between four separate ministers.

[*See also* Majapahit; Java; *and* Indonesia, Republic of.]

M. C. HOADLEY

GAJAPATI DYNASTY. From about 1434 to 1541 kings of the Gajapati dynasty ruled Orissa, India, and under the dynasty's founder, Kapilendra (ruled c. 1434–1467), the Gajapati domain extended south to Tamil Nadu, including Kanchi. The dynasty's history and relations with its neighbors are commonly seen in Hindu-Muslim terms, although it is doubtful that the faith of adversaries was of particular concern to the Gajapatis. Their rule in South India proved a threat to the powerful Vijayanagar dynasty, and during the rule of Prataparudra (ruled c. 1497–1540), the Vijayanagar king Krishnadevaraya drove the Gajapatis back to Orissa, where the house continued to rule only about a year after Prataparudra's death.

[*See also* Orissa *and* Vijayanagara.]

R. D. Banerji, *History of Orissa,* vol. 1 (1970). K. C. Panigrahi, *History of Orissa: Hindu Period* (1981).

FREDERICK M. ASHER

GALDAN (d. 1697), leader of the Dzungar Mongols, who challenged Chinese authority along its borders in Mongolia and Central Asia. His grandfather Kharakhula had attempted to unify the Dzungars and the other Western Mongols and to transform them from a nomadic to a more settled society. Kharakhula's policies promoted agriculture, encouraged the development of crafts and manufacturing, and stimulated changes in social patterns. He tried, in short, to create a unified state out of the tribes under his jurisdiction.

Kharakhula's grandson Galdan eventually continued his efforts. Originally dispatched to Tibet to study in a lamasery, he abandoned the religious life when his brother, who had been the ruler of the Dzungars, was assassinated. Seeking to avenge his brother's death, he became the undisputed leader of the Dzungars by 1677. Like his grandfather, he now promoted the economic development of the Dzungars. He persuaded or compelled his nomadic subjects to farm the land and to produce their own manufactured articles.

Capitalizing on this more productive economy, Galdan began to enlarge the Dzungars' territory. By 1679 he had moved south and occupied such oases as Hami and Turfan. Shortly thereafter he received the support of the Dalai Lama of Tibet. He then turned his attention to the Khalkha Mongols of Eastern Mongolia, but here he faced opposition from both their khans and their religious leader, the Jebtsundamba Khutughtu. The Manchu rulers of the Qing dynasty also became concerned about the threat posed by Galdan. They assisted the Khalkha against Galdan and signed the Treaty of Nerchinsk (1689), which resolved their economic and frontier difficulties with Russia, so that their Dzungar enemy could not seek the support of the tsarist court.

Without the aid of his fellow Mongols and the Russians, Galdan could not match the power of the Qing forces. Their first military encounter in 1690 at the Battle of Ulan Butung ended inconclusively, but only a year later the rulers of the Eastern Mongols met at Dolon Nor to pledge their loyalty to the Qing and to renounce any alliance with Galdan. This lack of support clearly placed Galdan on the defensive, and it was only a matter of time before the Qing crushed him. In 1695 he made a fatal misstep, invading the lands of the Khalkha, who immediately called upon the Qing for help. The Kangxi emperor of the Qing raised an army of eighty thousand troops, which pursued Galdan and finally defeated him at Jao Modo (in central Mongolia) in June 1696. His own followers now turned against him, and in May 1697 he apparently committed suicide, concluding the threat to China's borders.

[*See also* Kangxi Emperor *and* Qing Dynasty.]

Arthur Hummel, ed., *Eminent Chinese of the Ch'ing Period* (1943–1944). Mark Mancall, *Russia and China: Their Diplomatic Relations to 1728* (1971). Jonathan D. Spence, *Emperor of China: Self-Portrait of K'ang-hsi* (1974).

MORRIS ROSSABI

GALLEON TRADE. *See* Manila Galleon.

GAMA, VASCO DA (c. 1460–1524), the first European navigator to reach India, paving the way for Portuguese and other European trade and conquest in Asia. After his two voyages in 1497–1498 and 1502–1503 to the Malabar coast, he returned in 1524 as viceroy of Portuguese India. He died at Cochin in the same year.

[*See also* Portuguese: Portuguese in India.]

USHA SANYAL

GAMBIER, important Southeast Asian export crop in the nineteenth century. The leaves of the gambier bush were used as a medical astringent, a tanning agent in production of leather, and in betel chewing. A traditional crop in Sumatra and Malaya, gambier first became commercialized for export production in Riau in the 1730s. In the nineteenth century it spread to Singapore, Johor, and Sarawak and was produced on plantations for export to Java, Siam, China, and later Britain, where leather had important industrial functions. Chinese planters and laborers dominated the gambier industry, which often functioned in conjunction with pepper production. Hence the gambier boom provided a major impetus for heavy Chinese immigration. By 1900 gambier was replaced by rubber as a plantation crop and for industrial purposes in Europe.

Poh Ping Lee, *Chinese Society in Nineteenth-Century Singapore* (1978). Carl A. Trocki, *Prince of Pirates: The Temenggongs and the Development of Johor and Singapore, 1784–1885* (1979).

CRAIG A. LOCKARD

GANDHARA, an Indo-Hellenistic school of art that flourished between the first and fifth century CE in the area of ancient Gandhara, which includes northwestern India, Pakistan, and Afghanistan. The art was devoted to the Buddhist religion, and it produced freestanding images of the Buddha modeled on a Hellenistic Apollo type and clad in a togalike robe with classical folds. Bas-relief slabs were carved in large numbers to illustrate the legend of the Buddha.

The story of Gandharan art revolves around the Kushan dynasty and its occupation of the ancient Greek kingdom of Bactria. When the Kushans reached India they were confronted with Buddhism and the need to express its legends in art. Drawing upon the Hellenistic traditions of Bactria, the Kushans possibly also recruited craftsmen from Persian territories and from the Roman provinces of western Asia. The mingling of East and West in Gandhara resulted in a composite art that can rarely be mistaken for a Western product but that always includes recognizable Hellenistic elements.

FIGURE 1. *Buddha.* Dating from the Kushan period (second to third century), this statue, in its stylized drapery, modeling of the features, and classical proportions, reflects the influence of Greek art on the Gandhara style. The face has been recut in recent times; height 183 cm.

Gandharan art appeared at a stage of great importance in the history of the Buddhist art of India when a demand had arisen for a human image to replace a symbol in the worship of the Buddha. While it may have had only a marginal impact on the mainstream of Indian artistic development, Gandharan art exercised considerable influence along the entire Silk Route of Central Asia. Certainly the depiction of the legend of the Buddha in an eclectic Indo-Hellenistic style is in itself of intrinsic interest.

[*See also* Buddhism: An Overview; Bactria; Kushan Dynasty; *and* Silk Route.]

Madeleine Hallade, *Grandharan Art of North India and the Graeco-Buddhist Traditions in India, Persia and Central Asia* (1968). VIDYA DEHEJIA

GANDHI, INDIRA (1917–1984), prime minister of India from 1966 to 1977 and 1979 to 1984. The only child of Jawaharlal Nehru, she was raised in a home that was at the center of India's nationalist movement during its most tumultuous period. Her grandfather Motilal Nehru was a major financial supporter of Mohandas Gandhi and the Congress movement; her father occupied center stage within the Congress Party for two decades before independence in 1947; and her mother, although less involved politically, was subject to political arrest by the British. Mrs. Gandhi has described her childhood as lonely, with some of her most vivid remembrances being the entry into her home of British policemen. Because her parents did not want to send her to any of the British schools in India, her education took place at a series of Indian schools and at non-British schools in Europe, with a number of private tutorials interspersed between periods at school. [*See* Nehru, Motilal *and* Nehru, Jawaharlal.]

As a child Mrs. Gandhi was torn between an orthodox mother (Kamala Nehru, who died of tuberculosis in 1936) and a modern, English-speaking aunt (Vijaya Lakshmi Pandit, who later served as India's high commissioner in London and as the first president of the United Nations General Assembly). [*See* Pandit, Vijaya Lakshmi.] Indira's marriage to Feroze Gandhi (not related to the Mahatma) in 1942 was almost universally denigrated by orthodox Hindus, primarily because it was an intercommunal "love marriage," not arranged by her parents. Her father, Jawaharlal, opposed the marriage on grounds that the couple were somewhat incompatible because both possessed fiery tempers. Publicly, however, both her father and Mohandas Gandhi strenuously defended the marriage, with the Mahatma writing in the journal *Harijan* that "his [Feroze Gandhi's] only crime in their [orthodox Hindus'] estimation is that he happens to be a Parsi."

Arrested and jailed for nationalist activities shortly after their marriage, Mrs. Gandhi was imprisoned for eight months and Feroze for a full year. Feroze then became editor of *The National Herald*, a newspaper founded by his father-in-law, and Mrs. Gandhi became the principal confidant and hostess of her father during the period of Nehru's prime ministership (1947–1965). The couple separated for a number of years during the 1950s as Feroze Gandhi launched his own political career in Parliament and was often at odds with Nehru's policies and style. The death of Feroze (from a heart attack) in 1960, and the subsequent death of her father in 1964, caused Mrs. Gandhi to become increasingly withdrawn into herself and her immediate family until she was chosen as party leader and prime minister in January 1966.

Selected as prime minister by party bosses ("the Syndicate") within the Congress Party, Mrs. Gandhi was at first quite pliable and compromising. However, after the Congress suffered unprecedented defeats in the 1967 national elections, hard on the heels of a devaluation of the rupee that adversely affected the poorer segments of the Indian population, she became dramatically assertive and opted for a series of choices that pitted her directly against the Congress Party high command, which had previously been built up by her father. As a consequence of her backing V. V. Giri for the presidency of India in 1969 and her activities in subsequent election campaigns, Mrs. Gandhi caused a major split in the Congress Party, resulting in the eventual acceptance by the Election Commission of the official name Congress Party-Indira (or Congress-I) to describe the party led by Mrs. Gandhi. [*See* Giri, Varahagiri Venkata.]

Although Indira's New Congress, or Congress-I, was dependent on the pro-Moscow Communist Party of India immediately after the 1969 split, it gained an unprecedented two-thirds majority in both houses of Parliament in the early 1970s. The initial thrust for such dominance came from an overwhelming victory in the 1971 elections, fought around the slogan *garibi hatao* (abolish poverty). Claiming that she had "a time-bound scientific program for abolishing poverty," Mrs. Gandhi secured substantial support in 1971 from India's lower castes, minority groups, and the urban poor. When, in 1971, her New Congress government waged a successful war against Pakistan in support of the Bangladesh liberation movement—in the face of diplomatic opposition from both China and the United States and a lack of international support from almost every other nation except the Soviet

Union and the Eastern Bloc countries—Mrs. Gandhi was often likened to a goddess by ordinary Indians, and her popularity within India reached a crest never equaled before or thereafter.

Expectations raised by the *garibi hatao* campaign and India's victory over Pakistan in 1971 led to great disappointment and political difficulties in the mid-1970s, owing in part to the severe economic problems associated with a sixteenfold increase in world oil prices between 1973 and 1975 but also to the inclination of Mrs. Gandhi to become more and more defensive and insecure in the face of mounting political and economic problems and her open attempts to thrust her sons, Sanjay and Rajiv, forward as successors to her leadership. [*See* Gandhi, Sanjay *and* Gandhi, Rajiv.]

In June 1975 Mrs. Gandhi took the unprecedented but constitutional step of jailing her opponents under emergency provisions of the constitution after she had been convicted in the Allahabad High Court of two charges of electoral impropriety. The so-called Emergency lasted until March 1977, when lower castes and minorities deserted the New Congress in a national election and it was defeated by a coalition of parties known as the Janata Morcha. [*See* Emergency in India, The.] Factionalism among the Janata partners and their inability to succeed in bringing Mrs. Gandhi to trial (despite her arrest and several Janata attempts to build a legal case against her) resulted in the defeat of the Janata government in 1979 elections and the return of Mrs. Gandhi's Congress-I to a dominant position in Indian politics.

After Mrs. Gandhi returned to power, her government was confronted with serious challenges to its ability to maintain law and order as conflicts between religious and ethnic groups broke out in different parts of the country. In Assam, long-standing hostility between local political parties and the Congress-I Party merged with the antagonism the Assamese felt toward illegal immigrants from Bangladesh and settlers who had come from West Bengal. [*See* Assam.] When Mrs. Gandhi insisted that the Bengalis be allowed to vote in elections, there was widespread violence, culminating in a massacre in which hundreds were killed. An even more severe threat to national unity came from the violent protests of members of the Sikh community in the Punjab against Mrs. Gandhi and her government. After the army had invaded the Golden Temple in Amritsar, the chief shrine of the Sikhs, which had been held as an armed camp by a group of militant Sikhs, she became the target for Sikh anger, and on 31 October 1984 she was assassinated by Sikh members of her own bodyguard. Her son Rajiv was chosen by her party to succeed her.

Mrs. Ghandi is said to have been shy and diffident as a young woman, and people who knew her well have stressed that despite her domineering public personality in later life, she retained her strong sense of privacy, along with a concern for a few close personal friends. Her elegant, aristocratic manner was often in striking contrast to that of the politicians who surrounded her.

It is difficult to give a summary evaluation of Mrs. Gandhi's role in modern India. While it is generally agreed that she was a very skillful politician and that she was enormously popular with the masses, many thoughtful people believed that her drive for personal power, symbolized in the long domination of Indian politics by the Nehru family, had weakened democratic development.

Mary C. Carras, *Indira Gandhi in the Crucible of Leadership: A Political Biography* (1979). Zareer Masani, *Indira Gandhi: A Biography* (1975). Nayantara Sahgal, *Indira Gandhi: Her Road to Power* (1982). Uma Vasudev, *Indira Gandhi: Revolution in Restraint* (1974).

MARCUS FRANDA

GANDHI, KASTURBAI (1869–1944), wife of Mohandas Gandhi, was associated with him both in campaigns for India's freedom and in creating a utopian village community. Like Gandhi, she was born in Porbandar, Gujarat, and was a member of the merchant caste; they were married at the age of thirteen. Her father, Gokaldas Makanji, was a shopkeeper. She accompanied Gandhi to South Africa but appears not to have been in full sympathy with his ideas. After returning to India with Gandhi in 1915, however, she began to play a more active role in the nationalist campaigns and in organizing the households at the Satyagraha, Sabarmati, and Sevagram ashrams that she and Gandhi developed. At these ashrams she came to be known as Ba ("Mother"). During the Quit India movement she was arrested along with Gandhi, and died on 22 February 1944, while they were in detention at the Aga Khan Palace. [See also Gandhi, Mohandas Karamchand.]

MARK JUERGENSMEYER

GANDHI, MOHANDAS KARAMCHAND (1869–1948), India's major nationalist leader, often known by the Hindu title *mahatma* ("great soul"). Gandhi was assassinated in New Delhi on 30 January 1948, six months after India's independence, by a Hindu who blamed him for the subcontinent's partition into India and Muslim Pakistan when the British left. [*See* Godse, Nathuram.]

Gandhi's family came from a trader caste in Gujarat, western India. [*See also* Kathiawar.] Several relatives had served in the administration of a minor princely state, but the family had no connections with developing continental politics in British India, which was largely dominated by the Indian National Congress. Gandhi's emergence as a major figure in the Congress after World War I was even more unlikely because he was diffident as a young man. Despite reading for the bar in London in 1888–1889, he had no university degree and had failed in legal practice in Bombay; from 1893 he spent two decades in South Africa, then returned permanently to India in 1915, a middle-aged stranger to public life.

South Africa, however, had proved a crucial experience. As a lawyer, gradually drawn in to lead the diverse Indian community in its struggle against white discrimination, he taught himself the political skills of organization, publicity, negotiation, and agitation; gained public repute in Britain and in India; and learned to work with Indians from different religious and regional backgrounds and to involve women in political action. Furthermore, his personal life and values underwent a radical change, symbolized by his vow of celibacy and his experiments with a simple community life, in the manner of a Hindu ashram, for his relatives and close associates.

Drawing on experience, on his reading of Christian and Western religion and philosophy, and on his Hindu inheritance, Gandhi became convinced that all persons have an innate spark of truth or ultimate reality deep within them; to strive for perfection, each must learn to respond to inward truth by listening to what Gandhi called the "inner voice" and disciplining himself by simplicity and self-denial in preparation for such spiritual receptivity. In later life Gandhi would say not "God is Truth" but "Truth is God." He believed that none of the world's religions had completely discovered such truth, although all gave sincere believers a path toward it and a partial vision of it. Consequently, in his view there were as many religions as there were individuals. From Gandhi's belief in the spiritual nature and destiny of man, a nature and destiny imperfectly realized by reason of man's faulty apprehension of truth, flowed a passionate dedication to religious tolerance, to nonviolence *(ahimsa)* in all conflicts as the safeguard of the integrity of all involved, and to a way of life markedly contrasting with Western, industrial civilization, which in his eyes corrupted humanity with false ideals of wealth and competitiveness. He castigated British rule in India and Indians who absorbed or aped Western culture, claiming that they destroyed India spiritually, and believed that India's mission in the world was to be true to itself by basing national life on sufficiency and not on endless accumulation, on interdependence and not on competition and exploitation—a way of life possible only in a village setting.

Gandhi's ideas about India's present and future became more definite after 1915. When people accused him of inconsistency, he argued that courage to modify opinions was a hallmark of the truth seeker. He increasingly concentrated on softening communal hostilities; on changing Hindu attitudes that oppressed those at the base of caste society, particularly the Untouchables; and on reviving spinning, by hand, along with other village industries, as part of a total plan of village uplift. [*See* Khadi *and* Untouchability.] Politically, he began to work for the demolition of the British Raj, but for him *swaraj* ("self-rule") was never just political independence: it meant reconstructing an Indian nation from its spiritual and social roots. His ashrams strove to build this new identity in microcosm and to train people to be spiritually aware and dedicated to the service of mankind.

Gandhi's participation in Indian politics before 1920 was limited to occasions in which he perceived a wrong or grievance that could be righted by the method of nonviolent protest that he had begun to forge in Africa. He called his method *satyagraha* ("truth-force") and believed it was far more than the passive resistance of the weak known in the West, for it demanded courage of mind and body, and it also purified and turned to a fuller vision of truth those who practiced it and those against whom it was deployed. It could take various forms, from mass nonviolent noncooperation with the government or the breaking of unjust laws to individual demonstrations and fasts. After 1920 Gandhi assumed that full participation in the anti-British struggle was not only his rightful role but also an integral part of his wider-ranging work for true *swaraj*. He began to make more than brief appearances at Congress sessions, and, in fact, his dramatic rise to leadership in the Indian National Congress began at this time. He called for noncooperation and nonviolence, which, he predicted, would result in *swaraj* in one year. Gandhi's rise in power rested not on large-scale conversion to his views but on politicians' calculations—in terms of all-India and provincial politics—that alliance with Gandhi and a temporary strategy of noncooperation with the government might prove productive, since cooperation and violent resistance offered equally little prospect of political achievement.

Thereafter, Gandhi's career was one of political peaks and troughs: times of apparent retirement, in which he concentrated on the reconstruction of villages and the amelioration of conditions for Untouchables, and phases in which he led all-India *satyagrahas,* as in 1920–1922, 1930–1934, and 1940–1942 (the last, the Quit India movement, quickly slipped from direction either by Gandhi or the Congress leadership). Recurring characteristics of these agitations included very loose central control and a tendency to degenerate into violence as they became the focus and channel of myriad local grievances and aspirations. Gandhi and other major leaders were regularly jailed. Congressmen followed Gandhi, not blindly or constantly, but only when his particular technique suited their needs and interests or seemed the only basis for much-needed unity. This support was equally true both of provincial Congressional groups or Congress as an all-India vehicle of nationalism. Even in his apparently fallow phases Gandhi remained a seminal figure in Congressional deliberations, revered and often deferred to, even by those whose views differed from his.

Once World War II had ended and it was clear that the British were intent on departure, the Mahatma played a less significant role in the intricate negotiations for independence. A tired old man, deeply hurt and even demoralized by the horrific evidence of communal violence that he had tried to stem in strife-torn areas, Gandhi called himself "a back number." In many ways partition and the nature of government and politics after independence made him realize that Indians had neither achieved nor desired the true *swaraj* of his vision.

Understandably, Gandhi was and is a controversial figure. Despite the awe and devotion that surrounded him, in his lifetime British and Indians alike questioned his priorities, particularly his concentration on social work and his attempt to swing India from the path of industrialization. Many found his religious vision inexplicable or doubted his integrity, judging him a charlatan who manipulated religion for political ends. Muslims increasingly perceived him as the symbol of a future Hindu-dominated India despite his work for communal harmony, a misconception explicable, however, in light of the Hindu style of his leadership and appeal and the growing adherence of the Hindu majority to Congress, of which he was the figurehead. Since his death he has become a living myth and is often called the "father of the Indian nation." Yet his priorities and prescriptions for India are ignored and variants of *satyagraha* are used in the most un-Gandhian ways.

Later commentators from many disciplines have been similarly intrigued and perplexed by Gandhi's role and significance. Some have delved into the early emotional experiences that produced a man so dedicated to public action yet overscrupulous about his motivation and most private life, a man so highly driven yet so full of self-doubt, a man of immense moral and physical courage who delighted in a maternal role. Others, who have examined the origins and internal coherence of his beliefs, recognize that he was neither trained philosopher nor founder of a philosophical school but a pragmatic seeker after truth who was guided by a few fundamental principles. Among historians, interest has focused on his political role. Earlier, hagiographical studies have given place to more realistic assessments, based on his copious writings and a weight of other primary evidence generated by the political interplay of British and Indian leaders and Indians with one another. Simple assertions about his charismatic appeal and ability to generate and lead mass political campaigns now tend to be replaced by more detailed investigations of precisely who followed him and why, the evidence being illuminated by a deeper awareness of the differing characteristics of politics in the diverse regions of so vast a land.

As an all-India leader with a flexible method and a flair for conciliation, Gandhi was often highly attractive for limited periods in specific political circumstances; his personality undoubtedly brought thousands onto the streets in political demonstrations. Yet this support could ebb as quickly as it had flowed, both among permanently committed political activists and those who were temporarily motivated into agitational campaigns. Furthermore, investigations of the weakness and internal contradictions of the British Raj, and of the declining worth of India to Britain from the 1920s, have lessened the long-term historical significance of Gandhian *satyagraha* in undermining the imperial edifice.

It is clear nonetheless that Gandhi's campaigns had great importance in educating Indians in political awareness and action and in bonding them across old barriers of region and caste—key factors in India's subsequent stability as a democratic nation. As an inspirer and educator who changed the nation's sense of identity, Gandhi played a highly creative public role. He underlined and confronted some of the critical problems facing the new nation and illuminated the lives of the countless individuals to whom he gave time, affection, and advice, tempering discipline with tenderness and humor. He remains an enigmatic, powerful figure who demands attention and whose life and death ask uncomfortable yet abiding questions about the nature of the self and its relationship to the environment and to all humanity.

[*See also* Indian National Congress *and* Satyagraha.]

Judith M. Brown, *Gandhi's Rise to Power: Indian Politics 1915–1922* (1972) and *Gandhi and Civil Disobedience: The Mahatma in Indian Politics 1928–1934* (1977). Mohandas Karamchand Gandhi, *An Autobiography,* 2 vols. (1927, 1929). R. A. Huttenback, *Gandhi in South Africa: British Imperialism and the Indian Question 1860–1914* (1971). Raghavan Iyer, *The Moral and Political Thought of Mohandas Gandhi* (1973). D. Anthony Low, ed., "Introduction: The Climactic Years 1917–47," in *Congress and the Raj: Facets of the Indian Struggle 1917–47* (1977). Bal Ram Nanda, *Mahatma Gandhi: A Biography* (1959). JUDITH M. BROWN

GANDHI, RAJIV (b. 1944), prime minister of India since 1984. He was born in Bombay, the son of Feroze and Indira Gandhi, who was the daughter of Jawaharlal Nehru. Educated in India at the Doon School, he also took courses in the Imperial College, London, and in Trinity College, Cambridge, in mechanical engineering. On returning to India he became a pilot for Indian Airlines. He took no part in politics, despite being a member of India's most famous political family, until the death in 1980 of his brother, Sanjay, who had been groomed by his mother, Prime Minister Indira Gandhi, to succeed her. Rajiv then quickly assumed a leading role in politics, as a secretary-general and president of the Indian National Congress, the ruling party. He was elected to Parliament from Amethi constituency in a by-election in 1981. When his mother was assassinated on 31 October 1984, he was immediately selected to succeed her as prime minister. His first task was to end the wave of violence against the Sikh community, members of which had been responsible for the assassination. In assuming office he indicated his intention of continuing the foreign and domestic policies of his mother and grandfather, but he moved quickly to dismantle many of the controls that had regulated trade and manufacturing, suggesting that he favored free enterprise rather than state regulation.

Gandhi married Sonia Maino, an Italian, in 1968. They have two children, Rahul and Priyanka.

[*See also* Gandhi, Indira *and* Nehru, Jawaharlal.]

B. K. Ahluwalia and Shashi Ahluwalia, *Rajiv Gandhi* (1985). Rai Singh, *Resurgence of Rajiv Gandhi* (1985).

AINSLIE T. EMBREE

GANDHI, SANJAY (1946–1980). The youngest son of Indira Gandhi, Sanjay rose to prominence in the 1970s by obtaining a license to manufacture a small car (the Maruti)—the first such license granted in India in two decades. Openly grooming himself to succeed his mother as prime minister, Sanjay was embroiled in controversy as a result of his leadership of a forced-sterilization campaign (1975–1977). In February 1979 he was sentenced to two years in prison for criminally destroying all copies of a film critical of the prime minister, but the conviction was overturned when Mrs. Gandhi returned to power. Sanjay was killed when his private plane crashed in June 1980.

[*See also* Gandhi, Indira.]

Jyotirindra Das Gupta, "India in 1980: Strong Center, Weak Authority," *Asian Survey* 21.2 (1981): 147–161. "Sanjay Gandhi, The Last Interview," *Surya* 4 (July 1980): 25–32. MARCUS FRANDA

GANGA DYNASTIES. Several Indian dynasties used the family name Ganga. The original family ruled the southern part of Karnataka from the second half of the fourth century until the medieval period. After the collapse of the dynasty the name reappeared in many of the later dynasties of the area, particularly the Hoysalas, who claimed Ganga descent on a number of occasions. Many of the Jain edifices whose remains are found throughout the state were erected by the Gangas, and the Hoysala general Gangaraja, probably a descendant of the family, was one of the most important patrons of the religious site at Sravana Belgola.

[*See also* Hoysala Dynasty.]

M. V. Krishna Rao, *The Gangas of Talakad* (1936). R. C. Majumdar, ed., *The History and Culture of the Indian People,* vols. 3, 4, 5 (1954–1957).

ROBERT J. DEL BONTÀ

GANGES RIVER. The Ganges (Sanskrit, Ganga) River is held sacred by devout Hindus and is worshiped as the form of a goddess. The river flows 1,557 miles (2,506 kilometers) from its Himalayan source through the North Indian states of Uttar Pradesh, Bihar, and West Bengal; a mostly wide and languid river, the Ganges is essential to one of the most intensely cultivated and densely populated regions of the world.

Although the Hindu tendency of attributing great sanctity to rivers can be traced from the earliest Vedic periods, the Ganges did not begin to enjoy its supreme status among holy rivers until the Indo-Aryan culture expanded eastward near the end of the Vedic age (c. ninth century BCE). The Greek ambassador to the Maurya court, Megasthenes (c. 350–290 BCE), mentions the river in his writings, but it is not until Strabo (c. 64 BCE–23 CE) that we find reports that the river was worshiped as a deity. Strabo further asserts that the Ganges is the greatest river of the "three continents," followed by the Indus, Danube, and Nile.

According to legend (cf. *Mahabharata* 3.104–108), the Ganges was originally a heavenly river whose holy waters were needed by King Bhagiratha so that he might raise his dead ancestors up and restore them to the Pitriloka, the heavenly World of the Fathers. Granted the boon of the river's descent, Bhagiratha then sought the intercession of the god Shiva, who, by catching it on his head, broke the force of its descent and saved the earth from certain destruction. In later times the Ganges came to be indentified with Shiva's consort, Parvati, as well as other forms of the so-called Mother Goddess.

Several purification rites are associated with the waters of the Ganges. The Chinese Buddhist pilgrim Xuanzang (seventh century CE) reported the already common practice of ritual bathing in the river in order to purify the soul from sin; Ganges water is carried to all parts of India as it is believed to possess extraordinary healing powers; and it is the wish of all devout Hindus to have their ashes thrown into the river after cremation.

Today the great river is seriously polluted by industrial seepage and raw sewage. The Indian government is attempting to check the problem through the offices of the Central Ganga Authority.

[*See also* Hinduism *and* Varanasi.]

Diana Eck, *Banaras: City of Light* (1982).

STUART W. SMITHERS

GANG OF FOUR, derogatory term applied to Jiang Qing, Zhang Chunqiao, Yao Wenyuan, and Wang Hongwen, leaders of the ultraleftist faction of the Chinese Communist Party during and immediately following the Cultural Revolution. Jiang, Zhang, and Yao became nationally prominent when they were made members of the Cultural Revolution Small Group in May 1966. In that capacity, they led the Cultural Revolution in a radical direction, supporting the radical mass organizations and instigating them to revolt against the Party leaders. Personally close to Mao Zedong (Jiang was his wife), they further radicalized Mao's theory of "permanent revolution," justifying their purge of the top Party leaders and their bid to power with the theory of "the new stage." According to this theory, each stage of the Chinese revolution required a new type of leadership, and the old Party leaders were no longer suitable to lead the Chinese revolution.

As the national leaders of the rebel factions and all other political groups that benefited from the chaos of the Cultural Revolution, the Gang of Four eagerly promoted the Cultural Revolution activists to leadership positions, while endeavoring to purge all the old Party leaders, including Zhou Enlai. Despite their vigorous and often ruthless effort to build up their own power base, their attempts to seize the control of China's huge bureaucracy produced only limited results; they managed to dominate the propaganda and educational fields, but utterly failed to develop any influence over the military. This lack of support from the military leaders, plus their total alienation from the old cadres and lack of legitimacy in the eyes of the Chinese people, explains the ease with which Hua Guofeng and some senior military leaders purged them soon after Mao's death.

After the return of Deng Xiaoping, whom the Gang of Four had purged twice, they were put on public trial from 1980 to 1981. The charges brought against them include conspiring to seize power illegally, persecuting the old cadres by falsifying evidence, attempting to assassinate Mao, and organizing an abortive coup d'état by mobilizing the Shanghai militia right after Mao's death. Jiang Qing and Zhang Chunqiao received death sentences with two years of suspension of execution, later commuted to life imprisonments; Wang Hongwen received a life imprisonment; and Yao Wenyuan got a term of twenty years of imprisonment.

[*See also* Great Proletarian Cultural Revolution; Jiang Qing; Wang Hongwen; Yao Wenyuan; *and* Zhang Chunqiao.]

HONG YUNG LEE

GANSU, province of north-central China, between the Ningxia Hui Autonomous Region to the north and Qinghai Province to the south. Made a province only in 1911, Gansu until recent times was chiefly important for the trade routes that passed through it. The Gansu corridor, the narrow pathway dotted with oases that lies in the western part of the province between the impassable Alashan Desert to the north and the Qilian Mountains to the south, was in traditional times followed by the Silk Road and is today traversed by the railroad that terminates at Urumqi.

The coming of the railroad in the 1950s has led to industrial development in the area: at Yumen lies a major oilfield, first developed in the 1930s and today linked to petrochemical industries at Lanzhou, the provincial capital; while Jiuquan is the site of an iron and steel mill. Nearby is Jiayuguan, famous as the westernmost fortress of the Ming dynasty Great Wall. Shuangchengzi, in the valley of the Ruo River to the northeast, is China's missile launching and space center. East of the corridor and west of the Liuban Mountains lies the Longxi Basin, the relatively fertile area around Lanzhou and Tianshui, that is drained by the Yellow River. Gansu's population of more than 21 million includes many Muslims; the area was racked by a great Muslim rebellion from 1862 to 1878, the suppression of which cost millions of lives. Marginal agriculturally, with low rainfall and harsh climate, Gansu remains one of China's poorest provinces. It is, however, rich in ancient sites, perhaps the most famous of which is the great Buddhist cave temple complex at Dunhuang.

ARTHUR N. WALDRON

GAO GANG (c. 1902–1954), early Chinese Communist leader. Although important as a guerrilla leader in Shanxi Province in the early 1930s before the arrival of the armies of the Long March, Gao Gang, a key figure in the national hierarchy from the founding of the People's Republic of China (PRC) until 1954, is known chiefly for his still-mysterious fall as the PRC's top party, state, and military leader of northeastern China (Manchuria). In trouble by late 1953, it was not until March 1955 that Gao was openly denounced along with Rao Shushi, as leader of the "Gao-Rao alliance" and accused of plotting to seize supreme power based mostly on his "independent kingdom" in Manchuria. Gao was removed from all posts and expelled from the Communist Party, posthumously as it turned out, since it was also announced that he had committed suicide sometime in the same year.

Franz Schurmann links Gao's fall to his stress on the Stalinist technique of one-man management in industry, as opposed to the Party's stress on collective leadership. While other scholars suggest ties between Gao and the Soviets, Frederick Teiwes finds neither argument to be totally accurate or persuasive. Instead, Teiwes finds the purge more likely to have been the result of a classic factional power struggle in which Gao led a "weak, pitiful" attempt to step in the line of succession in a period when Mao's health may have been in question.

Donald W. Klein and Anne B. Clark, *Biographic Dictionary of Chinese Communism, 1921–1965* (1971). Franz Schurmann, *Ideology and Organization in Communist China* (2d enl. ed., 1968). Frederick Teiwes, *Politics and Purges in Contemporary China* (1978).

JOHN A. RAPP

GARCIA, CARLOS P. (1896–1971), Visayan poet-statesman and fourth president of the Philippines (1957–1961). Garcia began his public career as a schoolteacher and entered politics after graduating from the Philippine Law School in 1923. He served as a congressman from 1925 to 1931, as governor of Bohol from 1931 to 1940, and as senator from 1941 to 1953. During the war he was hunted by the Japanese for his refusal to cooperate with them and was consistently voted by the press as one of the nation's outstanding senators.

An old-guard *nacionalista* from the south, Garcia was tapped as running mate of Ramon Magsaysay in 1953. In Magsaysay's cabinet, Garcia served concurrently as secretary of foreign affairs and was involved in negotiations for Japanese reparations and US bases agreements. Upon Magsaysay's death in 1957, Garcia succeeded to the presidency and was elected on his own in November 1957. The elections of 1957 were unprecedented in Philippine political history, for Garcia was elected with a vice-president from the rival Liberal Party. In 1961 he lost out to that vice-president, Diosdado Macapagal.

The main challenge to the Garcia administration was economic. Garcia immediately moved toward the adoption of an austerity program and an economic development program anchored on the Filipino First policy, which was intended to give Filipinos every preference in matters pertaining to the economic development of their country. In the field of foreign policy, the Garcia administration marked the beginning of a discernible shift away from almost total dependence of the Philippines on the United States (especially in matters of economic and strategic security) and a new orientation toward

Asia. (In his role as secretary of foreign affairs, Garcia had strongly advocated a policy of "Asia for the Asians.")

Garcia's last public office was chairman of the 1971 Constitutional Convention. He died of heart failure in June 1971.

[*See also* Philippines; Nacionalista Party; Magsaysay, Ramon; *and* Macapagal, Diosdado P.]

BERNARDITA REYES CHURCHILL

GARDENS. Iran's ecological environment—an arid and relatively treeless landscape, blazing sun, and water from mountain runoff brought through underground canals *(qanats)*—was a natural incentive to the cultivation of gardens. The royal hunting park outside a town was a common type of Iranian garden. Wall reliefs at Taq-i Bustan near Kermanshah illustrate a Sasanid king hunting amid a fenced enclosure stocked with game.

More common was the formal garden with pool or canal, meant to be viewed from a palace or pavilion. Archaeological investigations show that this type of garden already existed at Pasargadae in the sixth century BCE. Medieval texts describe Islamic palaces that include orchards, groves, and streams overlooked by pavilions and belvederes, and Timurid miniatures depict splendid fifteenth-century tent-palaces in the midst of watercourses, pools, and avenues of shade trees. Garden carpets—of which the most spectacular example now in the Jaipur Museum was probably woven at Isfahan in the early seventeenth century—show a rectangular field divided by fish-inhabited water channels into compartments crowded with all kinds of flowers and trees. These may represent the idealized *chahar bagh* ("four gardens") so often extolled in Persian poetry and imagery. One of the words Iranians use for "garden," *firdaus,* also means "paradise," and the image of Paradise as the ideal garden still exists today.

[*See also* Isfahan *and* Pasargadae.]

Elisabeth B. Macdougall and Richard Ettinghausen, eds., *The Islamic Garden* (1976). G. Marçais, "Bustān," *The Encyclopaedia of Islam* (new ed., 1960–). Donald Wilber, *Persian Gardens and Garden Pavilions* (2d ed., 1979).

SHEILA S. BLAIR

GARHWAL, a mountainous region of India's Uttar Pradesh state comprising the modern administrative districts of Garhwal, Tehri Garhwal, and parts of Dehra Dun. Two of the rivers considered sacred in India, the Ganges and Yamuna, have their source in Garhwal, which is known in Hindu scripture as Kedarkhand, or "Land of Shiva." In 1805 the Gurkhas overran Garhwal, but the region came under British control after the Anglo-Nepali War in 1815. Tehri Garhwal remained a semi-independent princely state within British India until 1947.

RICHARD ENGLISH

GARNIER, FRANCIS (1839–1873), French naval officer and member of the official French expedition (1866–1868) that mapped the upper reaches of the Mekong River. After the expedition, Garnier returned to France, published a two-volume report, and participated in the Franco-Prussian War. In 1873 he was back in Indochina and without authorization almost single-handedly captured the Vietnamese citadel of Hanoi, only to be killed soon afterward by local troops. His report on the exploration of the Mekong is a fascinating primary source. To many French authors his gallant, tempestuous life epitomized the heroic age of French colonialism.

[*See also* Mekong Expedition.]

Milton Osborne, *River Road to China* (1975).

DAVID P. CHANDLER

GARO, a Bodo-speaking tribe concentrated in Meghalaya state in eastern India. The Garo are matrilineal and matrilocal, with exogamous clans and a pattern of daughters marrying the mother's brother. Traditionally the fundamental political and economic unit was lineage, and villages were loosely ruled by councils of the various lineage elders. Internal warfare and headhunting were endemic. British intervention stopped warfare and made the system more hierarchical, and large-scale Christian conversion eroded local beliefs. Resistance to assimilation into Assam state led to an alliance between the Garo and the neighboring Khasi tribes in 1960. After a largely peaceful struggle, the movement succeeded in 1970 in gaining relative independence for the new state of Meghalaya.

[*See also* Meghalaya *and* Assam.]

Robbins Burling, *Rengsanggri* (1963). D. M. Majumdar, "The Garo National Council," in *Tribal Movements in India,* edited by K. S. Singh, vol. 1 (1982).

CHARLES LINDHOLM

GASPRINSKII, ISMAIL (1851–1914), Crimean Tatar educator, journalist, and reformer; leading advocate of socioeconomic change and cultural transformation designed to restore the competitive ability of Muslim communities, especially in Russia, vis-à-vis the West in particular. Through the vehicles of education, for which he pursued substantial reforms of the traditional curriculum and pedagogy, and publishing—his newspaper *Tercuman (The Interpreter)* appeared from 1883 until 1918—Gasprinskii sought to alter the consciousness of his coreligionists and to inform them of both the roots of and the remedies for their current social malaise. Drawing upon a syncretic view of human culture, he strove to combine the best of Islamic and Western achievements to create the possibility of *Dar ul-Islam* ("the world of Islam") once again playing a major role in human social development.

Gasprinskii's thought and activity were central to the emergence of a broad movement of change among Russian Muslims called Jedidism, from *usul-i jedid* ("the new method"), originally applied to the phonetic approach to language instruction that Ismail supported but gradually extended to a wide range of issues touching upon most significant aspects of Muslim life. Axiomatic to Jedidism, as propounded by Gasprinskii, were attitudes typical of the spirit of the European Enlightenment: unbounded faith in progress and its beneficial social effects; belief in the value of science; commitment to secularization; and, above all, dedication to the rational ordering of society. From this intellectual base, Gasprinskii moved beyond educational reform to propose creation of a common Turkic language to enhance communications and unity among most Muslims within Russia (and Turkey); emancipation of women, so as to involve the "other half" of Muslims in socially productive activities outside familial life; and economic development, in order to ensure a prosperous and independent society.

[*See also* Tatars.]

Thomas Kuttner, "Russian *Jadidism* and the Islamic World: Ismail Gasprinskii in Cairo, 1908," *Cahiers du monde russe et soviétique* 16.3–4 (July–December 1975): 383–424. Edward Lazzerini, "*Ǧadidism* at the Turn of the Twentieth Century: A View from Within," *Cahiers du monde russe et soviétique* 16.2 (April–June 1975): 245–277.

EDWARD J. LAZZERINI

GELUGPA, dominant sect of Tibetan Buddhism under the supreme authority of the Dalai Lama; it is also known as the Yellow Hat sect. The Gelugpa monastic order was founded in the fourteenth century by the reformer Tsong Khapa (1357–1410), who established Ganden Monastery as one of the major centers of this school. The current tradition of succession to spiritual leadership of the Gelugpa order through reincarnation was firmly established by the middle of the sixteenth century, and a century later this position came to entail supreme temporal authority in Tibet. [*See also* Tibet *and* Lamaism.]

BRUCE MCCOY OWENS

GENERAL COUNCIL OF BURMESE ASSOCIATIONS (GCBA), the major political organization in Burma between 1920 and 1936, also known by its Burmese name, Myanma Athinchokkyi. The GCBA was formed from the nationalist-minded sections of the Young Men's Buddhist Association to press for the development of self-government. Its first leader, U Chit Hlaing, toured the country in 1921, organizing *wunthanu athin* (village nationalist associations) that coordinated boycotts of the government. The *wunthanu athin* became the rural basis of the nationalist movement.

The popular strength of the GCBA was subsequently squandered during the 1920s and early 1930s because of quarrels among the council's leaders. Whereas some leaders advocated cooperation with British schemes to introduce limited forms of self-rule, others demanded complete home rule. Some encouraged peasants to boycott elections and not to pay taxes; others urged cooperation with the colonial state. The leaders were also divided on the question of whether Burma should remain a province of British India. As the GCBA split over these issues, some factions took new names, although may retained GCBA in their titles. The GCBA collapsed before the 1936 elections since most of its leaders had entered into electoral politics, but the spirit of the original village boycott movement lived on.

[*See also* Young Men's Buddhist Association.]

John F. Cady, *A History of Modern Burma* (1958). Maung Maung, *From Sangha to Laity* (1980).

ROBERT H. TAYLOR

GENERAL SHERMAN INCIDENT, sinking of an American ship in Korea that led to an unsuccessful attempt by the United States to force Korea to open its ports to foreign trade.

After an American trading ship received kind treatment from the Korean authorities in the vicinity of Pusan in March 1866, an American merchant, W. B. Preston, decided to send his schooner to Korea with a cargo of cotton goods, tin sheets, glass, and other items that were to be exchanged for Korean paper, rice, gold, ginseng, and leopard skins. In mid-August 1866 the *General Sherman* reached the mouth of the Taedong River and, despite repeated warnings from local Korean officials, appeared off P'yŏngyang on 27 August. A clash between some crew members and Koreans forced the ship to leave. When it ran aground, its sailors killed some Koreans, and on 2 September the schooner was burned.

This incident had serious international repercussions. After China declined any responsibility for Korea, the Americans decided to investigate the *General Sherman*'s fate themselves. This initiated the American expedition to Korea in 1871, but the Americans were repulsed by the Taewŏn'gun's forces at Kanghwa.

[*See also* Taewŏn'gun *and* Yi Dynasty.]

Ching Young Choe, *The Rule of the Taewŏn'gun, 1864–1873: Restoration in Yi Korea* (1972).

MARTINA DEUCHLER

GENEVA CONFERENCE OF 1954, attended by representatives of Cambodia, the People's Republic of China, France, Laos, the United Kingdom, the United States, the USSR, the Viet Minh (that is, the North Vietnamese), and the state of Vietnam (the South Vietnamese), produced the Geneva Accords, ten documents relating to Indochina.

The conference began with negotiations on Korea, which lasted from 26 April to 15 June but produced no result. Separate negotiations on Indochina began on 8 May—a day after the fall of French headquarters at Dien Bien Phu. The accords reached on 20–21 July 1954 included peace agreements for Laos, Cambodia, and Vietnam (signed by French, Viet Minh, and Cambodian officers) and a final unsigned declaration of the conference. None were treaties binding the participants.

The Laotian and Cambodian governments, which had sided with the French during the recent war, were left in control of their respective countries, except for two provinces of northeast Laos where the Pathet Lao (Laotian communists) were to concentrate their forces pending a political settlement.

Vietnam was temporarily split approximately in half, the north to be governed by the Viet Minh and the south by the French Union until 1956; this gave the Viet Minh less territory and population than they had controlled in July 1954. Civilians could move from one zone to the other if they chose. (Many northerners, especially Catholics, moved south.) The two zones were to be reunified following internationally supervised elections in 1956; most participants at the conference assumed the Viet Minh would win such elections.

China and the Soviet Union urged the Viet Minh to accept the accords. The Viet Minh, not sure that reunification of the north and south would actually occur as promised (and by some accounts, they were sure it would *not* occur), submitted reluctantly to this pressure.

The United States hoped to prevent reunification but was not sure of its ability to do so. The widespread belief that the United States pledged not to violate the accords arises from misreading of a US declaration presented in Geneva on 21 July.

[*See also* Cambodia; Laos; Viet Minh; Vietnam; Vietnam, Democratic Republic of; French Indochina War; Dien Bien Phu; Pathet Lao; *and* Indochina War.]

The Geneva Accords and the US declaration of 21 July are in US Department of State Publication 9167, *Foreign Relations of the United States, 1952–1954,* vol. 16, *The Geneva Conference* (1981), pp. 1500–1501, 1505–1546.

EDWIN E. MOISE

GENEVA CONFERENCE ON THE LAOTIAN QUESTION. In May 1961 fourteen nations (United Kingdom, Soviet Union, United States, People's Republic of China, France, India, Thailand, Cambodia, Canada, Poland, Burma, Democratic Republic of Vietnam, Republic of Vietnam, Laos) convened in conference at Geneva to find a settlement for the factional conflict in Laos, onto which had been grafted the confrontation between the "big powers" of the East and West. On 3–4 June, before the conference came to grips with its problem, President Kennedy and Premier Khruschev held a summit in Vienna at which they agreed to support a "neutral and independent Laos under a government chosen by the Lao themselves." At a meeting in Zurich on 22 June 1961 three princes representing the three disputing Lao factions—Prince Souvannaphouma for the Neutralists, Prince Souphanouvong for the left, and Prince Boun Oum for the right—agreed to a set of principles for the formation of a government of national union that would represent the three parties, pursue a foreign policy of "peace and neutrality in conformity with the Geneva Agreements of 1954," and reinstitute the electoral law and democratic liberties of 1957. Despite the agreement in principle, the deadlock within Laos was not broken until the Pathet Lao forces scored a convincing military victory against the Royal Lao Army.

On 23 June 1962 the king of Laos formally approved a new government, led by Prince Souvannaphouma as prime minister, with Prince Souphanouvong serving as deputy prime minister and minister of economic planning, and rightist leader Phoumi Nosavan as another deputy prime minister and minister of finance. The new government dispatched its representative to the Geneva Conference. On 23 July 1962 the conference participants signed the Declaration on the Neutralization of Laos and a related protocol outlining the provisions for the neutralization. Although this was to have been the first step toward a complete withdrawal of foreign forces from Laos and the beginning of an era of national reconciliation, it served only as a brief pause in the continuing revolutionary struggle.

[*See also* Souvannaphouma; Souphanouvong; Boun Oum; Geneva Conference of 1954; *and* Phoumi Nosavan.]

JOSEPH J. ZASLOFF

GENGHIS KHAN (1162?–1227), Mongol ruler and military genius who led his people in the conquest of one of the greatest empires in world history. Our knowledge of his early life is limited to a fragmentary account found in the *Secret History of the Mongols*. Since the *Secret History* is a mixture of historical truths and self-serving legendary incidents that are difficult to disentangle, it is almost impossible to obtain a clear view of Genghis's youth. However, his later life and career are better documented.

Genghis was born into the family of Yesugei, a chieftain of a minor Mongol noble clan. His father was murdered by a rival tribe when Genghis was only eight years old. His mother thus assumed the principal responsibility of teaching Genghis the skills he needed to be a Mongol chief. He owed some of his proficiency in hunting and warfare to her. The most important principle she taught him was that he needed to create a network of loyal friends and allies in order to increase his power and to do battle against his enemies. Early in his career, he began to develop such a coterie of associates; one explanation for his ultimate success in unifying the Mongols is that he was adept at forging alliances with influential leaders. He cooperated with his allies in campaigning against other tribes, yet his standard practice was to turn against his allies when he no longer needed them. He wanted to be *the* ruler and *the* unifier of the Mongols, not simply one member of a coalition. During his rise to power, he attacked, captured, and executed his "sworn brother" Jamukha and his first patron, the Ong Khan. Throughout the 1180s and 1190s, he assembled a trustworthy private army *(nokod),* which he rewarded by dividing among them the spoils that accrued from their campaigns.

By the beginning of the thirteenth century Genghis was ready to challenge the more important Mongol tribes. He first crushed the Tatars who had murdered his father. Then he defeated, in rapid succession, the Kereit, the Naiman, and the Merkid. By 1206 the chieftains of the leading tribes in Mongolia gathered together at an assembly (known as a *khuriltai*) to endorse Genghis as the ruler of all the Mongols. Kocochu, the leading shaman among the Mongols, challenged Genghis's supremacy, but Genghis won the battle and ordered his loyal aides to execute the shaman by breaking his back.

Much of Genghis's success lay in his military organization and tactics. His army was divided into groups of one thousand, each of which constituted a chiliarchy and was headed by a nobleman known as a *noyan*. This new organization was designed to undermine the authority of the old clan and tribal leaders, who would be superseded by the *noyan*. The *noyan* levied taxes, raised the military forces, and, most important, obeyed Genghis's dictates. Genghis also selected an imperial guard *(keshigden)* from the aristocratic families of Mongolia and assigned them responsible positions in civil and especially military affairs. He thus created a new nobility that was loyal to him. The campaigns that he and his *noyan* initiated were meticulously planned. Tactics and strategy were carefully worked out to capitalize on the information about the enemy obtained from spies and allies. His troops consisted primarily of cavalry, who had the advantage of mobility. He sought an edge over his enemies through the use of psychological terror; his deliberate massacres so frightened his opponents that they often surrendered without putting up a fight. The actual massacres he condoned have led later historians to exaggerate his ruthlessness and savagery. There is no proof that Genghis planned to conquer the world; one military campaign simply led to another.

There is no single satisfactory explanation for the sudden eruption of the Mongols. The gradual desiccation of Mongolia; the decline in the mean annual temperature, which led to a shorter growing season and thus less grass; the reluctance of the dynasty in

China to trade and thus to provide essential goods to the Mongols; and Genghis's own ambitions have all been suggested as possible reasons for the Mongol conquests. Whatever the explanation, Genghis first attacked the Tanguts, who had established a Chinese-style dynasty, the Xixia, and who controlled northwest China. Commercial disputes and Genghis's desire to dominate the trade routes to the West inevitably led to war. By 1209 the Tanguts submitted and pledged to offer tribute to the Mongols, but they were not completely subdued. Conflicts over trade gave rise also to a war with the Jurchen, who ruled North China as the Jin dynasty. In 1215, Genghis achieved his greatest success to date. He captured the Jin capital of Yanjing (modern Beijing), indicating that his troops had learned to besiege and occupy towns.

His next military engagement is often portrayed as a reaction to the provocation of his opponent. In 1216 he had sent an embassy and a trading caravan to the Khwarazmian shah Ala al-Din Muhammad, who governed much of Central Asia. One of the shah's officials killed the merchants. When Genghis learned of the fate of his men, he sent a second embassy demanding that the shah hand over his official for punishment. Instead, the shah executed the unfortunate envoys, and Genghis was handed an excellent pretext for the declaration of war. To all outward appearances, the shah had provoked the conflict that was about to erupt. Genghis made elaborate and detailed preparations before embarking on the campaign. In 1219, leading about 200,000 troops, many of whom were non-Mongols who had decided to ally themselves with Genghis, he set forth for Central Asia. By this time his soldiers had become adept at besieging towns. Employing catapults, which could hurl enormous rocks at the enemy, they devastated one town after another. In February of 1220 they entered and sacked the town of Bukhara, and within a year they occupied Balkh, Merv, and Nishapur. The destruction and the loss of life were, according to the Persian chroniclers, staggering. Genghis inflicted a stiff penalty for the murder of his envoys. The shah died in 1221, and his son Jalal al-Din fled to North India accompanied by a small detachment.

Genghis remained in Central Asia from 1222 to 1225, but his underlings conducted campaigns in other areas. Jebe and Subotei briefly occupied Tiflis (in Georgia) and reached all the way to the Crimean Sea before rejoining Genghis. Mukhali persisted in attacking the tottering Jin dynasty. Another of Genghis's armies coerced the Korean king into submitting tribute. From the time of his investiture as khan of the Mongols in 1206, Genghis had expanded the territory under Mongol control enormously.

Yet the Tanguts, the first group Genghis had subjugated, were now uncooperative. They refused to accede to Genghis's demands that they send troops for his forays into Central Asia. Their ruler also refused to send his son as a hostage to the Mongols. Genghis was determined to punish them for their insolence. In 1226 he headed for Ningxia, the Tangut capital. This campaign turned out to be his last, for he died in August 1227 without having pacified the Tanguts. The body of the dead khan was transported to Burkhan Khaldun ("Buddha Cliff"), a mountain range in northeast Mongolia. He was buried there in 1229 with forty young women; forty horses were sacrificed at his tomb. The Mongols deliberately concealed the precise location of his burial site to stymie grave robbers.

Genghis bequeathed not only a vast territory to his descendants but also policies that were to prove invaluable in ruling the diverse ethnic, religious, and national groups in the domains he had conquered. One of his most important legacies was his policy of religious toleration. He recognized that good relations with the religious potentates in a region facilitated Mongol control over its inhabitants. His principal interest was to use religion to help him govern. Yet he was also eager to meet with learned men and talk about different religions with them. Having heard that the Daoists had developed an elixir of immortality, he invited Changchun, one of their leaders, to his camp in Central Asia. Changchun disabused him of that view, responding, "I have means of protecting life, but no elixir that will prolong it." Despite this disappointment, Genghis did not withdraw his invitation. In fact, he was so delighted with his guest that he exempted Changchun's pupils and Daoist monks in general from taxation. Similarly, Genghis was generous to Islam, Nestorian Christianity, and the other foreign religions he encountered.

Genghis's toleration extended not only to different religions but also to different ethnic groups and nationalities. He placed quite a few foreigners in influential positions in government because he realized that the Mongols lacked the administrative skills to rule a great empire. He recruited a sinicized Khitan official named Yelü Chucai to devise plans for an administrative structure. He ordered a Turk named Ta-ta Tong-a to adapt the Uighur Turkic script to provide a written language for the Mongols. He employed Uighurs as tutors for his sons, advisers, secretaries, and interpreters. During his own lifetime, Genghis did not truly develop a sophisticated administration, but he laid the foundations for his descendants to do so. He also promoted commerce, from which his descendants also profited handsomely.

One of Genghis's most enduring legacies to his successors was the *Jasagh,* a series of rules that is often cited as the first Mongol law code. His descendants added to and emended the *Jasagh,* but most of the laws refer to early Mongol society and appear to mirror Genghis's own views. They reflect the mores and customs of a nomadic society. There are no provisions concerning ownership of land, the rights and duties of tenants, or the inheritance of property; the specifics of the tax structure are not described; and commerce is not mentioned. Instead, the edicts emphasize the concerns of a pastoral society. They provide for capital punishment for horse thieves, inflict severe punishments on soldiers who did not perform their duties properly, and prohibit the washing of clothes.

On the other hand, a few of the pronouncements in the *Jasagh* reflect the new responsibilities and concerns imposed upon the Mongols by their conquests. It officially prohibits religious discrimination and forbids favoritism toward any specific foreign sect. It exhibits a desire for a more centralized military and political organization that was essential in ruling the new domains. Genghis, through these orders, mandated the decimal system of organizing the army. Mongol troops were divided into units of tens, thousands, and ten thousands, each with its own commander. The commanders, in turn, were obliged to carry out the orders of the khan. Even the most important commanders were to follow his dictates.

The lack of a precise and orderly means of succession proved to be the Mongols' undoing. An assemblage of the leading Mongol nobles convened to elect the new khan. In theory, the most talented or oldest chieftain was selected as the khan. Genghis himself had four sons from his principal wife, Borte. Jochi, the oldest (c. 1184–1227), may not have been Genghis's son, since Borte had been kidnapped and raped by Genghis's enemies and Jochi was born just a few months after Genghis had rescued Borte. Genghis accepted Jochi as his son, but their relationship was fraught with tension; therefore, Jochi was not considered as a candidate for the succession. Chagatai, the second son (c. 1185–1242), was a fierce warrior and a stern upholder of Mongol traditions. His repressive acts earned him the wrath of Persian historians. They characterized him as "a tyrannical man, cruel, sanguinary, and an evil-doer." His lack of toleration and his severity ruled him out as the sovereign of a great empire that governed a diversity of peoples and tribes.

Genghis's youngest son, Tolui (c. 1190–1231/1232), might have seemed the logical choice to succeed his father as the khan. He was probably the most accomplished of Genghis's sons in warfare, but he was a rough-and-tumble military man who did not have the administrative skills to govern a great empire. Tolui's son Kublai (1215–1294) later became great khan and established Mongol rule in China. The third son, Ogedei (1186–1241), was flexible, tolerant, and conciliatory, and recognized that a civilian government was needed to rule the Mongol empire. Ogedei was clearly the optimal choice for the khanate, and sources written much later indicate that Genghis chose him as the successor. Even with such an anointment, two years elapsed before Ogedei was selected as the khan, as it appears that Tolui challenged him. Genghis's choice seems to have tipped the balance in Ogedei's favor, but the lack of an orderly system of succession inevitably provoked conflicts later and finally led to the destruction of Genghis's empire.

[*See also* Central Asia; Mongol Empire: An Overview; Kublai Khan; Chagatai; Hulegu; *and* Ogedei.]

John Andrew Boyle, trans., *The History of the World-Conqueror,* 2 vols. (1958). Francis Woodman Cleaves, trans., *The Secret History of the Mongols* (1982). René Grousset, *Conqueror of the World: The Life of Chingis-khan,* translated by Marian McKellar and Denis Sinor (1966). H. Desmond Martin, *The Rise of Chingis Khan and His Conquest of North China* (1950). H. G. Raverty, trans., *Tabakat-i-Nasiri: A General History of the Muhammadan Dynasties of Asia,* 2 vols. (1881). Boris Vladimirtsov, *The Life of Chingis-Khan,* translated by D. S. Mirsky (1930). Arthur Waley, *The Travels of an Alchemist* (1931).

MORRIS ROSSABI

GENJI CLAN. *See* Minamoto.

GENJI MONOGATARI (the *Tale of Genji*), a long work of Japanese prose fiction written in the early eleventh century by Murasaki Shikibu (978?–1031?), a lady-in-waiting at the court of Emperor Ichijō (r. 986–1011). Often called the world's first novel, the *Tale of Genji* was an immediate and lasting success, revolutionizing the art of prose fiction in Japan. Nothing comparable had been written before, and many believe it remains superior to every work of Japanese literature written since, be it prose, poetry, or drama. Certainly the *Genji* greatly influenced Japanese culture from the eleventh century on. Its themes and motifs constantly recur in Japanese fiction. Both the content and the romantic mood of the *Genji* inspired generations of poets, whether writing in the thirty-one-syllable *waka* form, in linked verse *(renga),* or in the seventeen-syllable *haikai* form. Well-known themes and episodes from the *Genji* also appear in Japanese drama, from the *nō* plays of the fourteenth century through the Edo-period puppet theater and *kabuki* and on into modern plays and cinema. Over the centuries, chapter titles and memorable episodes from the *Genji* became popularized as the subjects of parlor games, and noteworthy scenes from the novel were depicted on innumerable folding screens, in illustrated scrolls and books, and in woodblock prints. It would be difficult to find another work of literature that has so dominated Japanese cultural life for so long a period.

The *Tale of Genji* survives in fifty-four chapters, although it may once have contained others now lost. Analysis of clothing fashions, music, furnishings, and other cultural elements in the novel suggests that Murasaki Shikibu intended to write a historical narrative that begins about a century before the time in which she wrote. The story covers about seventy-five years, beginning with the birth of the hero, Genji, and concluding after his death, when his acknowledged son, Kaoru, is in his late twenties. The principal setting for the novel is Kyoto, at that time the capital of Japan, and much of the action occurs in the urban mansions and great gardens of the aristocracy and royal family. However, the author also uses areas outside the city effectively: the young Genji's exile to the seacoast of Suma and the pious Eighth Prince's retreat at Uji are impressive examples of realistic natural description and evocative imagery.

Despite the title of her novel and the central position of her hero, Murasaki Shikibu seems to have taken particular interest in exploring the lives and character of her fellow noblewomen. The *Tale of Genji* is filled with memorable women. Some, like Yūgao (the "lady of the evening faces"), appear only briefly, but they are so intensely portrayed that readers recollect them vividly. Others, like Genji's great love Murasaki, are introduced early in the novel as children or young women, and the reader follows them as they mature, grow old, and die. Few female characters in the *Genji* enjoy thoroughly happy lives. One of the principal themes of the *Genji* is the precarious nature of human life, even the lives of those who seem most secure. This point is made time and again with the heroines of the novel, who live in a polygamous society governed by delicate distinctions of status. Murasaki is beautiful, talented, and witty, perceived by her world and readers alike as the focus of Genji's life; yet she is constantly afraid of losing his affection. She must also suffer two very real humiliations: unable to provide Genji with a

FIGURE 1. *Section of a Genji Scroll.* Scene illustrating the *Genji monogatari,* with an example of the "blown-off roof" style.

child, Murasaki is charged with rearing his daughter by another woman; and her relatively low status and lack of powerful relatives disqualify her to be Genji's principal wife, an honor given instead to a vapid, childish princess.

Another major theme is closely linked to Buddhist concepts current in Japan in the eleventh century. The *Tale of Genji* rests on the Buddhist idea that all acts have consequences: good works will be rewarded by good fortune, sins will bring calamity, and such retribution for past deeds may even be exacted in an individual's future lives. The evil or tragic consequences of sins committed by Genji haunt him and his descendants throughout the narrative. Genji falls in love with Fujitsubo, the beloved consort of his father the emperor; she bears Genji a son who in time becomes emperor. Fujitsubo, tormented by guilt, becomes a nun to expiate her sin, while Genji is punished in middle age when his own young wife is seduced and bears a son whom Genji must acknowledge as his own. Expert characterization and plot development combine with the themes of evanescence and retribution to produce a masterful work of literature.

[*See also* Murasaki Shikibu.]

Jin'ichi Konishi, *A History of Japanese Literature,* vol. 2, *The Early Middle Ages* (1986). Ivan Morris, *The World of the Shining Prince: Court Life in Ancient Japan* (1964). Andrew Pekarik, ed., *Ukifune: Love in the Tale of Genji* (1982). Edward Seidensticker, trans., *The Tale of Genji,* 2 vols., (1976. Arthur Waley, trans., *The Tale of Genji* (1925–1933; reprint, 1960). AILEEN GATTEN

GENOUILLY, CHARLES RIGAULT DE (1807–1873), key figure in early French military action against Vietnam. As commander-in-chief of France's Far Eastern forces, he commanded the successful attack on Tourane in September 1858. Disappointed by the lack of popular support from native Christians that had been promised him by French missionaries, he set out for Saigon, which was captured in February 1859. Resistance and disease took their toll in both cities, however, and de Genouilly relinquished his command in October 1859. In 1867, having now been appointed Minister of the Marine and of Colonies, he actively supported Admiral de la Grandière's occupation of the last three Mekong Delta provinces.

[*See also* La Grandière, Pierre-Paul-Marie de.]

Joseph Buttinger, *The Smaller Dragon: A Political History of Vietnam* (1958). John Cady, *The Roots of French Imperialism in Eastern Asia* (1954).

BRUCE M. LOCKHART

GENROKU CULTURE. Originally used more restrictively to designate the period of Japanese history from 1688 to 1703, the term *Genroku* is now used more broadly as a cultural designation for the period from 1680 to between 1710 and 1740. The term conjures up an image of the golden age of Tokugawa culture, when the fruits of a long peace were at their ripest and the economic dislocation that was to follow had yet to materialize. It was during this period that the culture of the merchant class finally asserted itself over the preceding culture, one defined by a combination of aristocratic and military (samurai) elements. This shift was an economic consequence of the lasting Tokugawa peace, during which the long-held ideal of a society divided hierarchically into samurai, farmer, artisan, and merchant classes proved impossible to maintain. The merchant, economically, was climbing to the top of the social ladder. Indeed, the continuing tension between supposition and reality, ideal and practice, was the major dynamic for conflict and change throughout the whole Tokugawa period. The culmination that was Genroku culture was the result of the spread of literacy, the redistribution of wealth and resources that came in the wake of merchant domination of the economy, the willingness of a section of samurai society to participate in a culture that was evolving in new directions quite outside its control, and the development of block printing on a large scale. It was not so much cultural revolution as a slow cultural adaptation to a different social and economic environment, and thus the classical tradition, as it became increasingly more available to a wider audience, retained much of its ubiquitous influence. Parody, the style that characterizes the early seventeenth century, played on a tradition still in the common memory.

Genroku made permanent shifts in cultural attitudes and focus. The term *ukiyo,* which previously had meant "sad world" and carried Buddhist connotations of impermanence, came to mean "floating world," a semantic shift documented in the introduction to Asai Ryōi's *Tales of the Floating World* (c. 1661). Here we have a psychological move from a world of medieval secrecy and religious pessimism to one of delight in the present and conspicuous consumption. Fortunes made on the Osaka rice exchange were spent on material pleasures. In literature there was a totally new arena in which the heroic was portrayed: the city, the merchant class, and the pleasure quarters. Ihara Saikaku's first prose work, *The Life of an Amorous Man (Kōshoku ichidai otoko,* 1682), had as its hero a merchant's son rather than a member of the samurai or court.

The government rightly feared these general trends, for they struck at the philosophical and psychological underpinnings of the status quo in a manner that was difficult to combat. Genroku culture existed in an atmosphere of political repression characteristic of the Tokugawa period. Criticism of the nature and form of government, or of the social structure as it had been idealized, invited disaster. Such impulses, therefore, tended to be channeled into artistic expression, in the invention of a world where heroic action was still possible. The world of the military romance had lost immediacy; the world of the *Genji monogatari* was too distant. The one area of license that was allowed was the pleasure quarters, and for this reason much of subsequent Tokugawa culture seems to be obsessed with this last refuge; only here could men or women flout the rules, break the codes, or sacrifice themselves for greater ideals (and in the process perhaps indulge in sex to the point of self-destructiveness). Thus, an essentially sordid world was elevated to a cultural ideal, its heroes endowed with the samurai virtue of self-sacrifice. No wonder that the government looked upon this development with dismay; slowly but surely the power to appear heroic was wrested from the samurai and given into the hands of the ordinary man. Given that the Confucian bias of political thought presented great barriers to the development of sound economic policy, it is hardly surprising that the main object of concern was this apparently frivolous but in reality deeply destructive shift in cultural values. The number of decrees against "improper" behavior and lax morals and the amount of largely futile sumptuary legislation provide eloquent testimony to the obsessions of the period.

Another aspect of Genroku culture was the way in which supposedly rigid class distinctions began to give way under economic pressure. Those samurai who had no place in government, who were little more than parasites living off increasingly debased stipends, tended to become part of the new culture and hence to undermine the privilege of their own class. One area where this tendency was prominent was in poetry, where the new practice of *haikai,* or comic linked-verse, brought samurai and merchant into close contact. Linked-verse was a communal art demanding not only a knowledge of conventions but also an ability to empathize with colleagues; it produced a kind of camaraderie that transcended social barriers. The comic aspect of this kind of poetry consisted of a breaking of old restrictions on themes, vocabulary, and subject matter, a break that reflects the iconoclastic nature of Genroku culture in general. In its early days *haikai,* particularly as exemplified by the poets of the Danrin school, which was founded by Nishiyama Sōin (1605–1682) and of which Ihara Saikaku (1642–1693) was an important member, went to extremes of linguistic experimentation, seeking to shock with dislocated syntax and scabrous themes. It is in this sense that the term "carnival" is appropriate: the given order was reversed, the tradition subject to merciless parody.

This "rebellion in language" was symptomatic of the disorder just below the surface that reemerged in the late Tokugawa period in the form of popular literature known as *gesaku.* In due course, however, *haikai* was itself tamed and became high art. The man who achieved this was Matsuo Bashō (1644–1694), who transformed an essentially comic form into something transcendental. Bashō moved away from language as play toward a serious attempt to create an autonomous world in seventeen syllables—a world called into being by the act of juxtaposing disparate images. In Bashō's case restlessness took the form of constant travel, and his poetic travel diaries are among the best of his works.

The Genroku period also saw the emergence of two forms of dramatic entertainment that have survived to the present day, *kabuki* and the puppet theater *(jōruri). Kabuki,* which originated as entertainment for the lowest strata of society, had become more sophisticated by 1700 but never entirely lived down its origins and was subject to government repression on numerous occasions. It was theater in which the actor had full control over staging and dialogue and in which the playwright was of little consequence. Partly for this reason good playwrights were more attracted to the puppet theater, which relied on the language of the text and the verve of its chanters to achieve many of its effects. Unlike *kabuki, jōruri* (or *bunraku*) was not automatically equated with life in the pleasure quarters, and it was in general considered to be more respectable. Both kinds of theater borrowed heavily from the other, and they were constant rivals. In the beginning both were characterized by the fantastic exploits of unreal heroes, but what marks Genroku drama, and *jōruri* in particular, is the emergence of a major playwright, Chikamatsu Monzaemon (1653–1725), whose play *The Love Suicides at Sonezaki (Sonezaki shinjū,* 1703) brought a new contemporary realism to the theater. The series of successful domestic dramas *(sewamono)* that ensued developed in parallel with Ihara Saikaku's works, which explored the behavior of men and women who break rules and risk all for forbidden love. In theater then, also, we see the creation of a world in which the ordinary man could reach out toward heroism. The atmosphere of the time made risk-taking an inevitable gamble with death, and so great was the desire for larger-than-life heroes that these plays bear witness to an extraordinary degree of single-mindedness, as the central figures, types though they be, reach out for self-fulfillment in self-destruction.

Chikamatsu's *The Love Suicides at Sonezaki* was based on a real occurrence, and the theater in turn had its effect on life. Indeed, the government became disturbed at the number of double suicides in the early 1700s and in 1722 banned stories and plays romanticizing lovers' suicides.

The Genroku era is also noted for considerable achievements in the fields of art and philosophy. The theater helped spawn the industry of *ukiyo-e* prints, which successfully combined a high level of artistic technique with a commercial intent to satisfy the public's thirst for information about contemporary fads and theater idols. On another level, and in a different world, one that looked askance at the theater as disruptive and at fiction as decadent, were those samurai who concentrated on history, philosophy, and the composition of Chinese, on what contemporary opinion would have recognized as true "high culture." Among these samurai are some of the most famous thinkers of the Tokugawa period: Kumazawa Banzan (1619–1691) and Arai Hakuseki (1657–1725), who struggled to naturalize Confucianism and face up to the implicit Sinocentricism of the creed they wished to adopt; and Itō Jinsai (1627–1705) and Ogyū Sorai (1666–1728), who stressed the importance of returning to the ancient Chinese texts and of disregarding the "mistakes" of later commentators. Although later periods in Tokugawa history are equally interesting, Genroku culture is important as the source of much that was to follow. It has the added attraction of engendering a *joie de vivre* in art and literature that later ages regarded with affection and took as a source of inspiration.

[*See also* Ukiyo-e; Woodblock Prints, Japanese; Haikai; Kabuki; Bunraku; Matsuo Bashō; Ihara Saikaku; Chikamatsu Monzaemon; Kumazawa Banzan; Itō Jinsai; Ogyū Sorai; *and* Tokugawa Period.]

Joyce Ackroyd, trans., *Told round a Brushwood Fire: The Autobiography of Arai Hakuseki* (1979). James R. Brandon, William P. Malm, and Donald H. Shively, eds., *Studies in Kabuki* (1978). John W. Hall and Marius B. Jansen, *Studies in the Institutional History of Early Modern Japan* (1968). Howard Hibbett, *The Floating World in Japanese Fiction* (1959). Donald Keene, trans., *Major Plays of Chikamatsu* (1961). Donald Keene, *World within Walls* (1976). Maruyama Masao, *Studies in the Intellectual History of Tokugawa Japan,* translated by Mikiso Hane (1974). Ryusaku Tsunoda, Wm. Theodore de Bary, and Donald Keene, comps., *Sources of Japanese Tradition*, vol. 1 (1958), pp. 384–433. George B. Sansom, *A History of Japan, 1615–1867* (1963). Makato Ueda, *Matsuo Bashō* (1970).

RICHARD BOWRING

GERINDO (Gerakan Rakyat Indonesia, or Indonesian People's Movement), Indonesia's principal leftist nationalist party from 1937 to 1941. Gerindo was formed in May 1937 to fill the gap left by the dissolution of the Sukarnoist Partindo in 1936. Gerindo believed the new "common front against fascism" justified limited cooperation with Dutch-created organs, in contrast to the noncooperation stance of its predecessors. Its leading founders, the young Sumatran intellectuals Amir Sjarifuddin, Muhammad Yamin, and Dr. A. K. Gani, all went in different directions after 1942. The most important elements within Gerindo, however, were made up of those who followed Amir Sjarifuddin, the charismatic left-wing Christian lawyer, in an increasingly Marxist direction.

[*See also* Indonesia, Republic of *and* Amir Sjarifuddin.]

ANTHONY REID

GESTAPU, a pejorative Indonesian acronym for the 30th September Movement. On 1 October 1965 this movement, ostensibly led by Lieutenant Colonel Untung, killed six senior generals and seized the state radio and telecommunications center in Jakarta. A supportive action was launched in Central Java by elements of the Diponegoro division. This coup attempt was quickly crushed by forces loyal to Major General Suharto.

Responsibility for the affair has been hotly debated outside Indonesia. At least five alternatives have been proposed: (1) the Indonesian Communist Party (PKI), (2) a group of middle-ranking "progressive" officers from the Diponegoro division; (3) the air force, (4) Sukarno, and (5) Suharto. Within Indonesia, the army's view that the PKI was the sole mastermind has been little challenged publicly. Although some of the evidence on which its case was originally based has been discredited (e.g., a "confession" by Dipa Nusantara Aidit) or might be explained in other ways (e.g., the presence of Aidit at Halim Airbase), other evidence now available, such as statements by PKI emigré groups and admissions in trials by some PKI leaders, makes it difficult to maintain that the PKI was uninvolved. But the army's attempt to establish that the PKI was solely responsible depends largely on the evidence of Sjam, head of the PKI's secret Special Bureau. Many foreign observers remain unconvinced that middle-ranking officers who participated in the coup attempt were PKI puppets.

The leaders of the movement initially claimed it was purely an internal army affair. This was echoed by the PKI itself and by some foreign observers. Although this position seems untenable in the light of later evidence, there are grounds (particularly the extent and coordination of the involvement of Diponegoro division officers, and the slightness of the evidence that they were controlled by the PKI) for believing that progressive officers played an independent role.

The air force was implicated in the movement in several ways: (1) the bodies of the generals were found at Halim Airbase, which was the headquarters of the movement; (2) the air force commander, Omar Dhani, had foreknowledge of the movement against the generals and publicly supported it; and (3) one of the key actors, Major Sujono, was an air force officer.

The cases against Sukarno and Suharto are mainly speculative. The alleged involvement of Sukarno rests on his presence at Halim throughout the day and on largely uncorroborated testimony given long after the event. The alleged involvement of Suharto rests heavily on his known connections with the main army officers involved in the 30th September movement, his unsatisfactorily explained meeting on the night of 30 September with one of them, and the fact that he turned out to be a principal beneficiary of the affair.

The full story may never be known, but the affair marks a major turning point in Indonesian political history, as it led to a massacre of PKI members and supporters, large-scale detention of political prisoners, a purge of the bureaucracy, and the reversal of many government policies.

[*See also* Indonesia, Republic of; Suharto; Partai Komunis Indonesia; Sukarno; *and* Aidit, Dipa Nusantara.]

Benedict R. Anderson and Ruth T. McVey, *A Preliminary Analysis of the October 1, 1965, Coup in Indonesia* (1971). Harold Crouch, *The Army and Politics in Indonesia* (1978). Nugroho Notosusanto and Ismail Saleh, *The Coup Attempt of "The September 30 Movement" in Indonesia* (1968).

CHARLES A. COPPEL

GHADR. The Ghadr party was a loosely knit organization of expatriate Indian nationalists centered in the United States in the early decades of the twentieth century. It printed revolutionary literature against the British and made an abortive attempt in 1915 to send guns and guerrilla soldiers to India for an armed uprising.

The movement was founded in 1913 by Har Dayal, a visiting professor of philosophy at Stanford University. Most of the support for the movement came from immigrant Sikh farmers in California's upper San Joaquin Valley, and many of the active members of the movement were Indian students attending the University of California at Berkeley. An office was established at 5 Wood Street, San Francisco, which served as the headquarters for an international network that included cadres in Shanghai and Kabul. The office published a variety of nationalist pamphlets and a newspaper, which was also called *Ghadr* (sometimes spelled *Ghadar* or *Gadar*), an Urdu word that means "mutiny" or "revolution." The growth of the movement was spurred by the negative publicity of an incident in Vancouver, Canada, in 1914, when British immigration officials prohibited Punjabis on board the ship *Komagata Maru* from landing, an act that many Indian immigrants regarded as an ethnic insult.

The five boats that the Ghadarites launched from various ports in California in 1915 were supposed to spark an uprising on their arrival in India. The British had infiltrated the movement, however, and the revolution foundered. Financial support for the quixotic venture had come from the German government, a fact that prompted the American government to bring leaders of the Ghadr movement to trial in 1918 for violating America's neutrality during the early years of World War I. In a dramatic moment during the trial, the Hindu editor of the Ghadr newspaper, Ram Chandra, was shot and killed by a leader of the Sikh faction. After the trial many Ghadarites were deported, others left voluntarily, and the movement never regained its former momentum. Efforts were made in the 1920s to revive the movement, and new plans for invading India were drawn up, including a route by airplane from China over the Himalayas. In the 1970s the Ghadr name was utilized by a radical political movement in the Indian immigrant community in Canada.

The Ghadr movement is remembered in Indian history as an attempt at a military overthrow of British power. In the Punjab it is also remembered as having played a role in the formation of the communist parties of that region, since many of the Ghadarites who returned to India from California did so by way of Moscow, where they became schooled in Marxism. The movement was also a training ground for leaders of Sikh and Untouchable political movements. In the United States, the Ghadr movement has become a symbol of nationalist pride for the Indian immigrant community, and a memorial hall has been built on the site of the former headquarters in San Francisco. Former Ghadarites in the US include Dilip Singh Saund, the first politician of Asian descent to be elected to the US House of Representatives; Gobind Bihari Lal, a journalist who received a Pulitzer Prize for science reporting; and Taraknath Das, a professor at Columbia University and one of its benefactors.

[*See also* Dayal, Har.]

Emily Brown, *Har Dayal: Hindu Revolutionary and Rationalist* (1975). G. S. Deol, *The Role of the Ghadar Party in the Nationalist Movement* (1969). Mark Juergensmeyer, "The Ghadar Syndrome: Immigrant Sikhs and Nationalist Pride," in *Sikh Studies: Comparative Perspectives on a Changing Tradition,* edited by Mark Juergensmeyer and N. G. Barrier (1979). Harish Puri, *The Ghadr Party: A Study in Militant Nationalism* (1982).

MARK JUERGENSMEYER

GHALIB, MIRZA ASADULLAH KHAN (1797–1869) one of the two greatest poets—along with Mir Taqi Mir—in the classical Urdu genre of *ghazal,* a form of tightly structured lyric poem derived from Arabic and Persian models that tends toward romantic or mystical reflection.

Proud of his Turkish ancestry and perfect command of Persian, Ghalib strove to live the life of a Mughal aristocrat in Delhi, even though his only income came from a patchwork of small pensions. For a time (1854–1857) he was court poet to Bahadur Shah Zafar. In Persian Ghalib wrote brilliantly in the *qasida* (eulogy), *ghazal,* and other classical genres. In Urdu he left a number of irresistibly readable letters, as well as the *ghazals* that assure his immortality. He was a passionately intellectual poet, at times multifaceted and paradoxical, at others deceptively simple, but always ironic, humorous, and proud. Ghalib gave the Urdu *ghazal* a markedly cerebral turn, together with a sort of baroque verbal complexity; he alone among Urdu poets has inspired a whole tradition of explication and commentary. He has had no successful imitators, but no later poet has entirely escaped his influence. His *ghazals* are sung, read, and discussed throughout the Urdu-speaking world.

[*See also* Mir, Muhammad Taqi.]

Aijaz Ahmad, ed., *Ghazals of Ghalib* (1969). R. Russell and K. Islam, trans. and eds., *Ghalib: Life and Letters* (1969).

FRANCES W. PRITCHETT

GHAZALI, AL- (1058–1111), more fully Abu Hamid Muhammad ibn Muhammad al-Ghazali, one of the most influential minds in Islamic philosophical theology *(kalam),* jurisprudence *(fiqh),* and mysticism (*tassawwuf,* or Sufism).

Al-Ghazali was born at Tus, near the present-day Iranian city of Mashhad. His studies at Nishapur were guided by al-Juwaini, the Imam al-Haramain, until the latter's death in 1085. After joining the camp/court of the Seljuks, al-Ghazali was appointed professor in 1091 at the Nizamiyya in Baghdad by the vizier Nizam al-Mulk, his ardent admirer.

In 1094/1095, al-Ghazali suffered a spiritual crisis that had serious psychological consequences. He was no longer able to teach and abandoned his academic career in order to dedicate himself to the mystical quest, Sufism. Some scholars attribute his departure from Baghdad not only to personal motives but also to politics: his patron Nizam al-Mulk had been murdered in 1092 by Batinites (Isma'ilis) who were terrorizing the eastern empire, supported by the Fatimid authorities in Egypt.

In the eleven years following his resignation al-Ghazali traveled widely and eventually retired to Baghdad and Tus, where he composed his most influential work, the massive *Ihya ulum al-din (The Revivification of the Religious Sciences).* The work contains four volumes of ten books each. The first volume opens with two books that discuss knowledge and the foundations of religious orthodoxy. It then proceeds to a discussion of *ibadat,* that is, ritual purity, worship, the pillars of Islam, and other religious practices.

The second volume focuses on *adat,* the conduct of daily life, and the third and fourth volumes analyze the interior life. The third addresses *muhlikat,* those practices that lead to damnation. This is not a dry catalog of vices but an often subtle and astute inquiry into psychological and ascetic theory. Volume four explores those actions that lead to salvation *(munjiyat)* in terms that resonate strongly with the stages and states of the Sufi mystical path of repentance, patience, gratitude, fear, and hope.

In 1106 the vizier Fakhr al-Mulk, son of al-Ghazali's former patron Nizam al-Mulk, convinced him to return to public life as professor at the Nizamiyya in Nishapur. Soon after, he wrote his autobiography *Al-munqidh min al-dalal (Deliverance from Error)*, which encapsulates his own personal religious crisis as well as his intellectual stance vis-à-vis Islamic philosophy and sectarian movements like that of the Batinites. Al-Ghazali's own training in philosophy had begun under al-Juwaini, but while teaching at Baghdad he had pursued privately a thorough study of Arab Neoplatonism exemplified in the works of al-Farabi and Ibn Sina. Before his crisis he published a stinging refutation of their work in *Tahafut al-falasifa (The Incoherence of the Philosophers)*.

In his autobiography, al-Ghazali does not reject philosophy outright. Logic and philosophical methodology are acceptable as long as they do not contradict the truth of God's word, which is ultimately inaccessible to the fallible human intellect. Al-Ghazali's personal crisis convinced him that philosophical theology and law were by themselves inadequate means to knowledge of God. It is mysticism that affords the seeker a true personal taste *(dhauq)* of the divine. Both mysticism and the religious sciences must be pursued if one is fully to experience Islamic life.

A short time before his death, al-Ghazali retired to Tus, where he established a Sufi convent *(khanqah)*. There he taught his disciples and directed their spiritual progress. He died on 18 December 1111. Al-Ghazali is revered by Muslims and non-Muslims alike as an intellectual giant who wedded philosophical method to theology and established mysticism on a firm intellectual base within the mainstream Muslim community.

[*See also* Farabi, al-; Ibn Sina; Nizam al-Mulk; *and* Sufism.]

Majid Fakhry, *A History of Islamic Philosophy* (1970). Richard J. McCarthy, *Freedom and Fulfillment* (1980), a translation of al-Ghazali's *Al-munqidh min al-dalal.* Simon van den Bergh, trans., *Averroes' Tahafut Al-Tahafut* (1969). William Montgomery Watt, *The Faith and Practice of Al-Ghazali* (1953) and *Muslim Intellectual: A Study of Al-Ghazali* (1963).

PETER J. AWN

GHAZAN (1271–1304) ruled Iran from 1295 to 1304 and is considered the greatest of the Mongol Ilkhans. Although he had an active military career, he is remembered primarily for his administrative achievements. He became a Muslim shortly before his accession and set out to reimpose Islam as the official religion of the realm. His first decree ordered the destruction of the churches, synagogues, and Buddhist temples built by earlier, non-Muslim Ilkhans. Ghazan also instituted reforms systematizing the chaotic administration of the Ilkhanid realm. He reorganized taxation, currency, weights and measures, and the system of military support. These reforms did much to improve the Ilkhanid economy and administration.

Ghazan was a patron of culture, both Islamic and foreign. He valued his Mongolian heritage highly and was expert in its traditions. The history of the world that he commissioned from his vizier, Rashid al-Din, includes the history of the Turks, the Mongols, Europe, India, and China. Ghazan died on 11 May 1304 at the age of thirty-two.

[*See also* Ilkhanid Dynasty.]

J. A. Boyle, ed., *The Saljuq and Mongol Periods* (1968), vol. 5 of *The Cambridge History of Iran,* edited by Ehsan Yarshater, pp. 379–397. René Grousset, *The Empire of the Steppes,* translated by Naomi Walford (1970), pp. 378–383.

BEATRICE FORBES MANZ

GHAZNAVID DYNASTY. The house of the Ghaznavids (977–1187), the first independent line of Turkic origin in Islam, was founded by Subuktigin (r. 977–997), a commander in the service of the Samanids, who followed another Turkic officer, Alptigin, in the command of Ghazna, an outpost in mountainous east-central Afghanistan. From this base, Subuktigin's son Mahmud (r. 998–1030) established the Ghaznavid empire by taking the Buyid territories in eastern Iran as well as by conducting almost yearly campaigns to the Punjab.

Mahmud's son Mas'ud (r. 1030–1040) was unable to control the Seljuks then entering Khurasan from Transoxiana. Defeated at Dandanqan on 23 May 1040, the Ghaznavids lost eastern Iran, but under Maudud (r. 1041–1048), the murdered Mas'ud's successor, the dynasty was able to hold its central Afghanistan homeland as well as its possessions in the Punjab. Ibrahim (r. 1059–1099), another of Mas'ud's sons, came to power after a decade of internecine strife following Maudud's death; by making peace with the Seljuks he was able partially to reconsolidate the family's position. Ibrahim's son, Mas'ud III (r. 1099–1115), continued his father's policies.

None of their successors was able to maintain successfully the territorial claims of the Ghaznavids against the aspirations of the Seljuks, the Ghuzz (Oghuz) Turks, and the newly powerful Ghurid sultans. Ghazna was devastated by the Ghurid Ala al-

Din Husain in 1150, and the last Ghaznavid ruler was captured at Lahore by the Ghurid Shihab al-Din in 1187.

The Ghaznavids introduce several themes of subsequent Islamic history: the concept of a "slave" dynasty attaining independence; the interaction of Turkish, Persian, nomadic, and sedentary traditions and systems; and the attractiveness of India for income, refuge, "holy war," and empire.

Hundreds of scholars, including the poet Firdausi and the scientist Biruni, were in residence at Mahmud's court. Baihaqi's history of Mas'ud's reign is exemplary of a new Persian prose style; the architect of the Seljuk state, the vizier Nizam al-Mulk, began his career in the Ghaznavid chancellery. Although the minarets of Ghazna are the better known architectural remains of this dynasty, the ruins of the palaces at Bust, comprising residences, mosques, baths, and so on, are more spectacular.

[*See also* Biruni, al-; Firdausi; Mahmud of Ghazna; *and* Samanid Dynasty.]

C. E. Bosworth, *The Ghaznavids* (1963) and "The Political and Dynastic History of the Iranian World (A.D. 1000–1217)," in *The Cambridge History of Iran,* vol. 5, *The Saljuq and Mongol Periods,* edited by J. A. Boyle (1968). Bertold Spuler, "Ghaznawids," in *The Encyclopaedia of Islam* (new ed., 1960–).

RUSSELL G. KEMPINERS, JR.

GHI HIN, also spelled Ghee Hin, generally thought to be the earliest Chinese secret society in the Malay world. In the 1840s, it was also identified as the Tian Ti Hue (Chinese, Tiandihui), or Heaven and Earth Society, in Singapore, where it apparently was the largest secret society during the first half of the nineteenth century. It was initially dominated by Teochin pepper and gambier planters, whose crops were major export items.

In 1846–1847, 1854–1855, and 1862, serious disturbances broke out between the Singapore Ghi Hin and the Ghi Hock, a Hokkien society. In the 1860s and 1870s, Ghi lodges in Perak and Selangor came into conflict with the Hakka-dominated Hai San over control of the tin fields. In Johor, the Ngee Heng was recognized as the only legal Chinese trade group until 1912, when the installation of a British adviser brought about its abolition.

[*See also* Hai San Society; Singapore; Pepper; *and* Gambier.]

Carl A. Trocki, *Prince of Pirates: The Temenggongs and the Development of Johor and Singapore, 1784–1885* (1979).

CARL A. TROCKI

GHILZAIS, a group of Pakhtun clans, have traditionally inhabited the southern and eastern regions of Afghanistan. Around the 1880s Ghilzai nomads established summer pastures in Hazarajat. At about the same time, large numbers of both nomadic and settled Ghilzais were forcibly relocated in the northern regions by Abd al-Rahman. As a result of Soviet repression since December 1979, most Ghilzais have sought refuge in the North-West Frontier Province of Pakistan, a Pakhtun area and their traditional winter pasture and trading market. The origin of the term *Ghilzai* is uncertain; it may derive from Khalaj, the name of a medieval Hephthalite or Turkish clan whose members established Muslim dynasties in India.

Ghilzai political history has been turbulent. The Lodi (1451–1526) and Sur (1539–1555) established short-lived dynasties in India, and the Hotak (1707–1738) conquered the Safavid capital of Isfahan in 1722. They were, however, compelled to leave Iran in 1730, and their capital of Kandahar fell to Nadir Shah Afshar in 1738, who settled Durrani Pakhtuns on their lands.

From 1747 to 1978, despite several attempts to break the Durrani hold on state power, the Ghilzais have remained subordinated. Between April 1978 and December 1979, the two leaders of the ruling Khalq party, Noor Mohammed Taraki and Hafizollah Amin, were Ghilzais. They failed, however, to win over their fellow Ghilzais, who, for the most part, took to armed resistance to their rule and that of their Soviet allies.

[*See also* Amin, Hafizollah; Durranis; Pakhtun; *and* Taraki, Noor Mohammed.]

Monstuart Elphinstone, *An Account of the Kingdom of Caubul* (1839). J. A. Robinson, *Notes on the Nomad Tribes of Eastern Afghanistan* (1935; reprint, 1978).

ASHRAF GHANI

GHOSE, AUROBINDO (1872–1950). Having followed the strange but possibly consistent path from classical scholarship to revolutionary plotting to seclusion in an ashram, Aurobindo Ghose is revered by many as an extraordinary religious teacher and philosopher; he is best known as Sri Aurobindo. Born in Bengal, he spent many of his formative years in England, where he eventually won prizes in classics. Returning to India in the 1890s, he worked for the Gaekwar of Baroda and began writing political articles. In 1906 he came to Calcutta, entered the Swadeshi ("own country") movement, and became a leader of the Extremist group in the Congress, a powerful political journalist, a participant in the national education movement, and a secret revolutionary plotter. After a year in prison, with incarceration threatened again, he allegedly heard God's call and left for Pondicherry in 1910. He founded the Sri Aurobindo Ashram, wrote prolifically (notably *The Life Divine* and *Essays on the Gita*), and did not venture into politics again during the remaining forty years of his life. He was assisted by Mira Richard, a Frenchwoman whom he called "the Mother" and who ran the ashram.

[*See also* Swadeshi *and* Indian National Congress.]

Sri Aurobindo, *The Complete Works,* 30 vols. (1970–1975). Leonard A. Gordon, *Bengal: The Nationalist Movement 1876–1940* (1974). A. B. Purani, *The Life of Sri Aurobindo (1872–1926)* (2d ed., 1960).

LEONARD A. GORDON

GHUZZ (Oghuz), a political confederation of nomadic tribes that played an important role in the history of the Eurasian steppe and the Middle East. Its influence was particularly important in the Middle East, as it gave rise to the dynasties of the Seljuks, Akkoyunlu, and Ottomans.

The name appears as early as the seventh century in the Orkhon Inscriptions in the form Tokuz Oghuz ("nine clans"), which refers to a confederation that belonged to the Turkut empire. During the eighth century the Ghuzz, as they are referred to in Arabic sources, began to move westward toward the Aral Sea, where they entered into the Islamic world around 775. This early invasion was the main factor in the ninth-century migration of the Magyars and Pechenegs across the Black Sea steppe.

By the tenth century a major Ghuzz state, Oghuz Yabgu, had arisen on the north coast of the Aral Sea; its center was the city of Yanikent. This state was important not for its existence but for its fall, which was tied in with two major events: the rise of the Seljuks and the appearance of the Cuman (Kipchak, Polovtsi) in western Asia and eastern Europe. This came about as a result of nomadic migrations from eastern Asia in the middle of the eleventh century set in motion by the Khitai, who caused a chain reaction ending with the Cuman, who expelled the Ghuzz from the Aral Sea. At this time the Oghuz steppe became the Kipchak steppe. The Ghuzz then split into a northern group called the Torki, who migrated with the Cuman, disappearing around 1171, and a southern group that became the Seljuks. From this point on the name *Ghuzz* merges with the name *Turkmen,* which designated those nomadic groups outside the control of the Seljuks: the Akkoyunlu, and later the Ottomans.

[*See also* Akkoyunlu; Orkhon Inscriptions; Pechenegs; Seljuk Dynasty; *and the map accompanying* Samanid Dynasty.]

P. B. Golden, "The Migrations of the Oğuz," *Archiv Orientální* 4 (1972): 45–84. Omelian Pritsak, "The Decline of the Empire of the Oghuz Yabghu," *The Annals of the Ukrainian Academy of Arts and Sciences in the United States* 2 (1952): 279–292.

JAMES M. KELLY

GIA LONG, or Nguyen Phuoc Anh (1762/3–1820), last of the Nguyen lords *(chua)* of Dai Viet and founder of the Nguyen dynasty.

Although a grandson of Nguyen Khoat (Vo Vuong), the future Gia Long emperor was not in the direct line of Nguyen succession. He became head of the clan following the deaths of Dinh Vuong and the heir presumptive at the hands of the Tay Son forces (19 October 1777).

After three unsuccessful attempts to regain control of the Mekong Delta (1778–1782, 1783, 1785), followed by exile in Siam, Nguyen Anh took advantage of dissension among the Tay Son brothers to establish a permanent foothold in Gia Dinh (September 1788). Thereafter he conducted a series of seasonal campaigns (1790–1802) that brought about the gradual expansion and consolidation of the territory under Nguyen rule. In these campaigns he was aided by a corps of mercenaries, some of the most valuable of whom had been recruited from among the unemployed military forces of French India by the French missionary Bishop Pierre Pigneau de Béhaine, a friend and ally of Nguyen Anh. The last major battle against the Tay Son was won at the Son Gianh on 3/4 February 1802. Nguyen Anh proclaimed the opening of the Gia Long reign period on 1 June and entered Thang Long on 20 July.

As emperor, Gia Long's principal concern was the preservation of the hard-won hegemony of the Nguyen family. He made the former Nguyen capital of Hue (Phu Xuan), which was then the capital of Vietnam, the center of a highly centralized administration and began a massive program of construction. His policies, best exemplified by the promulgation of a new law code based on that of Qing China (1815) and the selection of his classically educated fourth son, Prince Dam, as heir (1816), set the Nguyen dynasty on a course leading in later reigns to a degree of centralization and absolutism unprecedented in Viet history.

[*See also* Dai Viet; Nguyen Lords; Nguyen Dynasty; Pigneau de Béhaine, Pierre; Tay Son Rebellion; *and* Gia Long Code.] JAMES M. COYLE

GIA LONG CODE, promulgated in 1815 by the Vietnamese emperor Gia Long (r. 1802–1820), consisted of 398 articles in twenty-two books. Although Gia Long declared that the code was based on Vietnam's fifteenth-century Hong Duc legal code, most of the laws were culled from those of the Qing dynasty in China. Consequently, the code tended to strengthen the position of the ruler and ruling class while weakening that of women, whose status had been somewhat improved under the Hong Duc laws. Although officially in effect until 1884, the Gia Long Code was often bypassed or ignored when it conflicted with Vietnamese custom.

[*See also* Gia Long *and* Hong Duc Code.]

Nguyen Phut Tan, *Modern History of Vietnam (1802–1954)* (1964). BRUCE M. LOCKHART

GIAO CHAU. *See* Jiaozhou.

GIAO CHI. *See* Jiaozhi.

GILAKI, an Indo-European language of the West Iranian branch spoken in Gilan. The language is closely related to Persian and bears the marks of its long and profound influence.

On the Caspian lowlands dialects of Bia Pas and Bia Pish are spoken on the west and east sides, respectively, of the Safid Rud River, which divides the province roughly into two halves. In the mountains of Dailam to the south of the province, the dialects of Fumani and Galishi, as well as several other minor dialects of Gilaki, are spoken. Past migrations of Gilanis have resulted in many influences of Gilaki on other languages. The Zaza dialect of Kurdish seems to have been heavily influenced in the early stages of its development by Gilaki.

Some 1 to 1.5 million people (provincial census of 1975) speak Gilaki. The language has not cus-

FIGURE 1. *Gia Long Code.* Chinese, dated 1806. Engraving on gold in the form of a book with four leaves. Height 25.4 cm., width 14 cm.

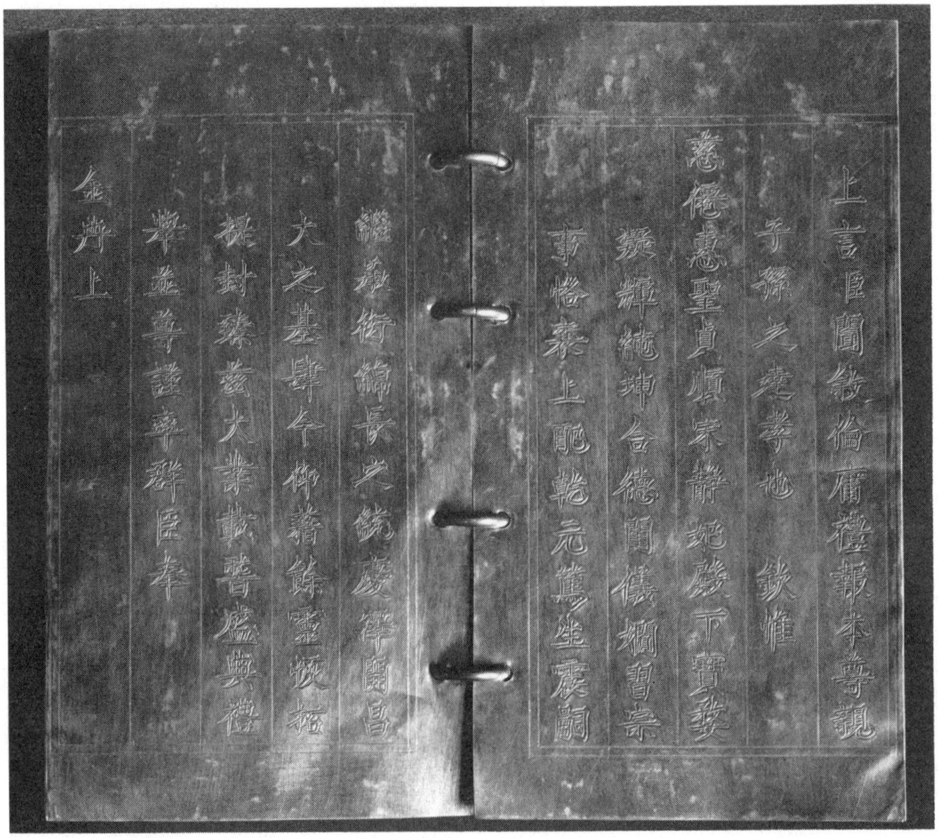

tomarily been committed to writing, except for poetry, and for that purpose the Persian alphabet has been used. Educated Gilanis use the Persian language and script for correspondence and sundry other needs.

[*See also* Gilan *and* Kurdish.]

MEHRDAD IZADY

GILAN, Jil or Jilan to the medieval historians, is a northern province of Iran bordering the Caspian Sea. Its major city is Rasht. Gilan has a subtropical climate supporting a rich agriculture and dense forests and is one of the richest and most densely populated regions of Iran.

Gilan, site of some of the earliest Neolithic civilizations in the Middle East, was overrun by Aryan immigrants in the second millennium BCE. In the early Islamic period Gilan was a place of refuge for the Zaidi Muslims. By the ninth and tenth centuries an increasing number of Gilanis, more specifically those of the Dailam district, entered the Muslim military forces. They set up dynasties of their own, the Ziyarids and Buyids among them. From the eleventh to the thirteenth century Gilan witnessed an emigration that resulted in the colonization of Shirvan, Arran, and parts of eastern Anatolia.

In the Safavid period (1501 – 1722) Gilan was the center of a lucrative silk industry, that enriched the imperial coffers with European gold. In the early twentieth century Gilan became a hotbed of antigovernment movements, including the Jangal movement headed by Mirza Kuchik Khan. A Soviet Republic of Gilan was declared in 1920, only to be overrun by Iranian government forces a year later.

[*See also* Buyid Dynasty; Gilaki; *and* Ziyarid Dynasty.]

Vladimir Minorsky, *A History of Sharvan and Darband in the Tenth–Eleventh Centuries* (1958), chap. 1.

MEHRDAD IZADY

GILGIT, town and district in the far northeastern corner of Pakistan. Gilgit has had close historical ties to the Jammu-Kashmir region but was ceded to Pakistan in 1947. The British looked upon Gilgit as vital to the defense of India and had therefore declared the territory a protectorate. In recent times it has once again assumed strategic importance. Because it borders China it has become the point of contact between China and Pakistan. Despite the protests of the Indian government, China drove a road through to this area in the late 1970s.

R. F. Nyrop, *Area Handbook of Pakistan* (1975). V. Smith, ed., *Oxford History of India* (1967).

GREGORY C. KOZLOWSKI

GIOVANNI DA MONTECORVINO (c. 1247–1328), Franciscan missionary to Asia and first Catholic archbishop of Khanbaliq (Beijing), capital of the Mongol empire in China. Giovanni's mission to China was prompted by the 1287–1288 visit to Europe of the Nestorian prelate Rabban Sauma, who had been born in Khanbaliq. The new pope, Nicholas IV, who had earlier been general of the Franciscan order, encouraged his confreres to take on the mission in farthest Asia. Giovanni da Montecorvino's work is known through the existence of two letters delivered to Rome after his death.

Rather than taking the usual land route to Asia, Giovanni, together with four Franciscan companions, sailed from Italy to Persia. From there in 1291 they journeyed to India, where they spent a little more than a year in evangelical work. (The Polos were in Malabar at about the same time, but there is no evidence that they met.) The Franciscans proceeded to North China, then known to Westerners as Cathay, where they arrived in 1294, shortly after the death of Kublai Khan.

In 1295, in the region of Tenduc (Chinese, Tiande) in what is now Inner Mongolia, Giovanni converted a Nestorian Ongut prince known by the name George to Catholicism. The latter would prove to be the first and last Catholic ruler in East Asia. Giovanni moved on to the Great Khan Temur, successor to Kublai, but with no success. In 1298 Prince George died and his people returned to Nestorian practice.

Giovanni da Montecorvino translated the Gospel and the Psalms into either Mongolian or Turkish, but his version has been lost. He built two Catholic churches in Khanbaliq, but found that Nestorian Christian opposition was fierce. Almost all of his pastoral success was in the foreign community in Khanbaliq, but by the time of his death he had extended Catholic missionary activity to the southern provinces of China.

I. de Rachewiltz, *Papal Envoys to the Great Khans* (1971). Henry Yule, ed. and trans., *Cathay and the Way Thither,* vol. 3, newly edited by Henri Cordier in *Works Issued by the Hakluyt Society,* ser. 2, vol. 37 (1914).

THEODORE NICHOLAS FOSS

GIRI, TULSI (b. 1926), cabinet member of Nepal's first popularly elected government and later prime minister of Nepal. A political protégé of the Nepali National Congress (NNC) party leader, B. P. Koirala, Giri publicly broke with the NNC leadership and resigned from the Koirala government in 1960 to protest what he claimed was its failure to fulfill election pledges for social and economic reform. Shortly thereafter, King Mahendra dismantled the Koirala government and appointed Giri to his own Council of Ministers for the new National Panchayat. As foreign minister, Giri drafted an agreement with the Chinese fixing the Sino-Nepal border and became an advocate of closer economic and political ties with the Chinese government. Giri served as prime minister under Mahendra from 1962 to 1965 and under King Birendra from 1975 to 1977.

[*See also* Nepal; Koirala, Bishweshwor Prasad; Mahendra; *and* Birendra.]

B. L. Joshi and L. Rose, *Democratic Innovations in Nepal* (1966).

RICHARD ENGLISH

GIRI, VARAHAGIRI VENKATA (1894–1980), president of India from 1969 to 1974. As a law student at Dublin from 1913 to 1916, he was profoundly influenced by Irish nationalism and trade unionism. In India he helped found the All-India Railwaymen's Federation (1923), was president of the Trade Union Congress (1926 and 1942), and, in 1969, precipitated a split in the Indian National Congress by his election as president of India.

[*See also* Indian National Congress.]

USHA SANYAL

GIYANTI, TREATY OF, signed in February 1755 in the village of Giyanti, southeast of Surakarta in Central Java, ended the Third Javanese War of Succession, which had begun in 1746 with the rebellion of Prince Mangkubumi against Susuhunan Pakubuwana II (d. 1749). Having fought the Dutch East India (VOC) forces supporting the incumbent monarch to a stalemate, Mangkubumi agreed with the VOC to a partition of the kingdom between himself and the new Surakarta king, Pakubuwana III. The Treaty of Giyanti established this partition as well as a general peace and decided other detailed arrangements. In addition the VOC recognized Mangkubumi as the sultan of half the kingdom. Pakubuwana III was not a signatory but was obliged to accept the partition.

[*See also* Javanese Wars of Succession; Mangkubumi; *and* Pakubuwana.]

M. C. Ricklefs, *Jogjakarta under Sultan Mangkubumi, 1749–1792* (1974).

M. C. RICKLEFS

GLASS PALACE CHRONICLE, Burmese dynastic history composed between 1829 and 1832 by a committee of learned monks and ministers at the request of King Bagyidaw (1819–1837). Beginning with early Buddhist history, the chronicle covers Burmese history to 1821 and takes its name from the Hmannan, or Glass Palace, in which the committee worked. The two stated purposes were to correct the errors of earlier chronicles and provide a standard for kings in their conduct of affairs of state and religion. In 1867 King Mindon (1853–1878) ordered a second committee to cover the period from 1821 to 1854 in the *Second Glass Palace Chronicle.* In 1905 U Tin of Mandalay published a chronicle for the years 1752 to 1854, together with his own account of the reigns of Mindon and Thibaw (1878–1885), as the *Konbaungzet (History of the Konbaung Dynasty).*

[*See also* Bagyidaw; Mindon; Thibaw; *and* Konbaung Dynasty.]

D. G. E. Hall, *Historians of Southeast Asia* (1961). Pe Maung Tin and G. H. Luce, *The Glass Palace Chronicle of the Kings of Burma* (1923; reprint, 1961).

WILLIAM J. KOENIG

GOA, area located on the western Indian coast 250 miles south of Bombay, ruled by the Portuguese from 1510 to 1961. Prior to the Portuguese conquest Goa had been part of several inland states, and ports on the area's two main rivers, the Mandovi and the Zuari, had been important in local trade for many centuries. In the late fifteenth century the area was ruled by the Muslim state of Bijapur and was the center for the importation of horses to central and southern India.

Portuguese strategists realized the advantages of Goa's location for their thalassocratic aims. Governor Affonso de Albuquerque conquered the capital city and the island on which it was located in 1510. In 1543 the districts to the north and south were also acquired from Bijapur, the three areas making up the "Old Conquests." In the eighteenth century seven more inland districts (the "New Conquests") were acquired.

The city of Goa (now known as "Old Goa") was

a lavish and profligate town in the sixteenth century. It was the seat from which the Portuguese governor directed Portuguese activities from East Africa to East Asia. The city had a population of approximately 75,000 in 1600, quite large by contemporary European standards, although several other Indian cities were much larger. Profits from Portuguese activities in Asia poured into Goa to finance lavish public buildings and churches, including a huge cathedral and Bom Jesus, where the body of the great Jesuit missionary Francis Xavier (1506–1552; canonized 1622) is still preserved (see figure 1). He and other Jesuits provided much of the impetus for the conversion of the Old Conquests to Christianity, and the Inquisition, established in Goa in 1560, discouraged backsliding.

As Portuguese power waned in the seventeenth century, Goa's trade, and so her prosperity, declined. In the late eighteenth and early nineteenth centuries health problems dictated the removal of most public offices to the present capital, Panjim (Panaji, Pangim). The area slumbered on through the nineteenth century, with its main export now people: Goans in British India acquired a reputation as cooks, waiters, and musicians. Goans also settled, and served on ships, all around the Arabian Sea. After World War II iron ore mining for export to Japan was developed, and there was some improvement in education. The area was conquered by India in 1961 and incorporated as a union territory. Iron ore exports have increased dramatically, and during the last fifteen years Goa has been developed, or overdeveloped, as a center for Indian and foreign tourism. In 1980 Goa had a population of about 850,000 and an area of approximately 1,350 square miles.

FIGURE 1. *Catholic Cathedral, Goa.* Founded in the early sixteenth century, the cathedral is a legacy of Portuguese rule.

[*See also* Portuguese: Portuguese in India; Bijapur; Albuquerque, Affonso de; *and* Xavier, Francis.]

Michael Naylor Pearson, *Coastal Western India* (1981). James Maude Richards, *Goa* (1982). T. R. de Souza, *Medieval Goa* (1979). Bento Graciano d'Souza, *Goan Society in Transition* (1975).

MICHAEL N. PEARSON

GOA, KINGDOM OF, the leading Makassarese dynasty in Sulawesi. Goa (Gowa) traditions become historically firm during the reign of its ninth king, Tumapa'risi Kallonna (c. 1512–1548), who conquered the region south of present-day Ujung Pandang but forged a durable alliance with the neighboring maritime dynasty of Tallo'. This dual kingdom, better known as Makassar, accepted Islam in 1605, imposed it on the Bugis states from 1608 to 1611, and proceeded to dominate south and central Sulawesi, Sumbawa, Buton, and eastern Borneo. After a series of defeats by the Dutch and Bugis (1666–1669), Goa was reduced to a small state in the hinterland of Dutch-occupied Makassar. Frequently in rebellion (1739, 1745, 1778, 1828, 1859), Goa was only subjugated by the Dutch in 1905–1906. The throne remained empty until 1936 and was abolished by the Indonesian Republic in the 1950s.

[*See also* Makassar.]

ANTHONY REID

GOBI, the Mongolian term for desert, now applied almost exclusively to the generally arid southern region of the Mongolian People's Republic. The Gobi stretches from the Greater Khingan Range in Manchuria to Xinjiang Province in China, a distance of some 1,300 miles. Its vast expanse of 500,000 square miles, with its sandy and gravelly land, is characterized by bitterly cold winters and brief but blisteringly hot summers. Powerful winds blow the topsoil to North China, where it serves as the fertile loess in the original Chinese heartland. The vegetation is sparse, although it provides much-needed relief and color to the drab, monotonous land. Beautiful, multicolored wildflowers occasionally sprout after a heavy rain, but the downpours do not come often enough. The land, with two exceptions, is parched. Along the northern boundary of the Gobi the Kerulen River valley provides some pasture land. The southeast corner receives sufficient rain to sustain a simple agrarian economy.

Most of the Gobi is, however, unsuitable for human habitation except for nomadic pastoralists. Only the sturdiest of men and animals could survive in this bleak and hostile environment. The camel was most valuable because it could carry more weight than other pack animals and could be employed in the trade caravans that crossed the desert from Mongolia to Central Asia. In prehistoric times the Gobi was not as inhospitable. It had more rainfall and more animal life. At the site of an ancient lake near the so-called Flaming Cliffs, the explorer Roy Chapman Andrews (1884–1960), who was associated with the American Museum of Natural History, found dinosaur eggs and the skeletons of prehistoric animals. The gradual desiccation of this terrain has prevented its use for productive purposes, and it is uncertain whether more advanced technology will permit China and the Mongolian People's Republic to integrate it into their economies.

Sechin Jagchid and Paul Hyer, *Mongolia's Culture and Society* (1979). A. M. Pazdneyev, *Mongolia and the Mongols,* translated by John Roger Shaw and Dale Plank (1971). Roy Chapman Andrews, *On the Trail of Ancient Man* (1935).

MORRIS ROSSABI

GO-DAIGO (1288–1339), Japanese emperor *(tennō)* from 1318 to 1339; his historical prominence rests with his unsuccessful attempt to restore imperial rule that came to be known as the Kemmu Restoration *(Kemmu no chūkō*; 1333–1336*)*.

The second son of Emperor Go-Uda, Go-Daigo was an emperor of the Daikakuji-tō, the southern or junior line of the Japanese imperial house. He was appointed emperor as a temporary measure in 1318 but resented the fact that the Kamakura *bakufu,* dominated by the Hōjō regents, regulated the imperial succession and the alternation of sovereigns from the Jimyōin and Daikakuji lines. From 1321 he began to challenge the authority of the Hōjō regents by reestablishing the court Records Office, Kirokujo, as an agency for direct imperial rule.

Go-Daigo was implicated in plots against the Kamakura shogunate in 1324 and again in 1331. After the 1331 revolt he was arrested and exiled to the island of Oki. In 1333 he escaped and, with the help of his son Prince Morinaga and the warrior Kusunoki Masashige, rallied loyalists, disaffected warriors, and monk-soldiers from Enryakuji to overthrow the *bakufu*. Having recovered his throne (the Kemmu Restoration), Go-Daigo sought to reinstitute direct imperial rule. Because of his determination to restore the fortunes of the imperial house and the nobility and his attempts to reassert imperial control over lands held by warriors, tensions quickly developed between Go-Daigo and both the nobility and erstwhile warrior supporters like Ashikaga Takauji. The division between Go-Daigo and Takauji led to the collapse of the Kemmu regime in 1336. Takauji gave his support to a rival northern-line emperor, Kōmyō. Go-Daigo fled the capital and established a southern court in Yoshino. This ushered in half a century of sporadic civil war known as the era of the Northern and Southern Courts, the Nambokuchō. A reconciliation between the courts was achieved by the shogun Ashikaga Yoshimitsu in 1392.

[*See also* Kemmu Restoration; Ashikaga Takauji; Nambokuchō; *and* Yoshino Line.]

H. Paul Varley, *Imperial Restoration in Medieval Japan* (1971).

MARTIN COLLCUTT

GODSE, NATHURAM, Indian journalist from Pune and a member of the RSS (Rashtriya Swayamsevak Sangh). Godse was part of an assassination squad that was displeased with what they felt to be Mohandas Gandhi's pandering to Muslim interests and neglect of Hindus. A fellow conspirator, Madan Lal, had made an attempt on Gandhi's life with a bomb explosion on 29 January 1948; the next day Godse, pretending to be an admirer bowing before Gandhi as he walked through the garden at the Birla House in Delhi on his way to afternoon prayers, fired three shots from a pistol in quick succession and accomplished his mission. Godse was tried, sentenced to life imprisonment, and eventually died in prison.

[*See also* Rashtriya Swayamsevak Sangh.]

MARK JUERGENSMEYER

GOKHALE, GOPAL KRISHNA (1866–1915), a leading Indian nationalist who advocated constitutional advance to dominion status. A Chitpavan brahman, Gokhale studied at the Deccan College, Pune, and Elphinstone College, Bombay, for a bachelor's degree.

In Pune he taught at the New English School before joining the Deccan Education Society and its Fergusson College (1886–1904). Influenced by the social reformer and nationalist M. G. Ranade, he joined Pune's political association, the Sarvajanik Sabha, edited its *Journal,* and was its secretary (1890–1895). He was joint secretary for the 1895 Indian National Congress Pune session. After disputes with B. G. Tilak, he and Ranade formed the Deccan Sabha (1896). In 1905 he founded the Servants of India Society to train young men in national service. He served as Congress president in 1905 and he supported the moderates when Congress split in 1907. [*See* Ranade, Mahadev Govind *and* Tilak, Bal Gangadhar.]

A member of the Bombay Legislative Council (1899–1901) and the Imperial Legislative Council (1901–1915), he gave evidence to the Welby (1897) and Decentralization (1908) commissions, and served on the Public Service Commission (1912). He visited England to influence the 1905 elections. He campaigned for the Morley-Minto Reforms (1909) for economic change and primary education. During a campaign in South Africa in 1912 he met Mohandas Gandhi, who called him his "political guru."

[*See also* Indian National Congress.]

B. R. Nanda, *Gokhale, the Indian Moderates and the British Raj* (1977). S. A. Wolpert, *Tilak and Gokhale: Revolution and Reform in the Making of Modern India* (1962).

JIM MASSELOS

GOLCONDA, a hill fort in the central Deccan plateau in peninsular India, located six miles from the modern city of Hyderabad. Occupying the last prominent spurs of the Deccan tableland before the low-lying plains of the eastern Deccan begin, Golconda figured prominently from the eleventh century on as a key military and administrative center under the Kakatiya dynasty of Hindu kings. In 1363 the fort was ceded to the Indo-Turkish Bahmani dynasty, and in the late fifteenth century a Bahmani governor of Golconda, Quli Qutb al-Mulk, carved the sultanate of Golconda out of part of the disintegrating Bahmani kingdom. This dynasty of kings, known as the Qutb Shahi kings after its founder, ruled the eastern Deccan until 1687, when it was annexed by the Mughal empire. Golconda's name is associated with fabulous wealth because of its successful exploitation of diamond mines in the Krishna River valley. Its most lasting legacy is the city of Hyderabad, planned in 1590 by Muhammad Quli Qutb Shah as a suburb of Golconda fort.

[*See also* Bahmani Dynasty *and* Hyderabad.]

W. H. Moreland, ed., *The Relations of Golconda in the Early Seventeenth Century* (1931). H. K. Sherwani, *History of the Qutb Shahi Dynasty* (1974).

RICHARD M. EATON

GOLDEN KHERSONESE, name assigned in Greek and Roman accounts, beginning in the first centuries of the common era, initially to Southeast Asia in general and subsequently to Lower Burma and the Malay Peninsula in particular. During this period the maritime route through Southeast Asia became an important source of commercial contact between China and the West. The toponym *Golden Khersonese* is based on Indian references, especially those in Buddhist literature, to Southeast Asia as "the Gold Land" *(suvarnabhumi)* and "the Gold Islands" *(suvarnadvipa).* These may have been merely colorful expressions describing Southeast Asia's mythical wealth, although references in third-century Chinese records to the gold-producing areas of Southeast Asia indicate that the region had a genuine reputation as an important source of gold. A number of scholars have suggested that the search for gold was an important motive for the original Western interest in Southeast Asia; later, during the first century, the temporary closure of the Central Asian caravan routes between China and the West necessitated a maritime contact. Such literary references imply that few Western sailors voyaged to Southeast Asia in that age but instead depended on India- or Southeast Asia–based seamen to provide them with products that traveled to the West by way of the Land of Gold.

Paul Wheatley, *The Golden Khersonese* (1961).

KENNETH R. HALL

GOND. *See* Gondwana.

GONDOPHERNES was the most powerful of the Pahlava kings ruling over the Punjab, northwest India, and parts of southern Afghanistan in the first half of the first century CE. Saint Thomas is believed to have visited India during his reign. Gondophernes issued a large number of coins, many of which show Hellenic influence in style. His successors quickly succumbed to the Kushans.

[*See also* Kushan Dynasty *and* Thomas.]

Percy Gardner, *The Coins of the Greek and Scythic Kings of Bactria and India* (1966). R. C. Majumdar, ed., *The Age of Imperial Unity* (1968).

A. K. NARAIN

GONDWANA, the "land of Gond," the largest tribal group in India. Gondwana is first mentioned in medieval chronicles. The Gond rose to be a dominant power with their four states at Garha, Deogarh, Kherla, and Sirpur-Chanda, which flourished from the fourteenth to the eighteenth century. They opened up their country for colonization by peasantry, constructed tanks (manmade lakes), improved agriculture, and enjoyed a measure of affluence. The approximately one hundred years of Maratha rule that followed left local Gond domains intact. In the ten districts of Madhya Pradesh that roughly constitute Gondwana today the Gond are still the dominant peasant community. The hypothetical paleozonic continent, Gondwanaland, derives its name from this country of the Gond.

[*See also* Adivasis *and* Madhya Pradesh.]

Indrajit Singh, *The Gondwana and Gonds* (1944).

K. S. SINGH

GONGSI (Chinese, "company, firm"), term used widely among the overseas Chinese in Southeast Asia to describe diverse organizations and undertakings. These included secret societies and their branches; syndicates formed to exploit colonial revenue farms in opium, gambling, and prostitution or to engage in other kinds of contracting; mining, farming, and import-export companies; and other Chinese commercial enterprises. In West Borneo a federation of autonomous Hakka gold-mining communities *(gongsis)* founded in the late eighteenth century was called the Lanfang Gongsi. *Gongsi* often implied a corporate identity recognized in colonial and postcolonial law but was also used informally to designate a constellation of individuals associated with one or another powerful figure.

Mary F. Somers Heidhues, *Southeast Asia's Chinese Minorities* (1974). G. William Skinner, *Chinese Society in Thailand: An Analytical History* (1957).

JAMES R. RUSH

GONGSUN LONG, Chinese philosopher of the Warring States period who lived during the first half of the third century BCE. Along with the philosopher Hui Shi he was one of the major proponents of the School of Names (Mingjia), also known as the School of Forms and Names (Xingmingjia). He expounded a collection of paradoxes intended as logical exercises, the most famous of which is "The white horse is not the same as a horse." Gongsun raised issues of logic, semantics, and epistemology also treated by other Warring States philosophers contemporaneous with him. The later Mohists and the Daoist Zhuangzi also expounded paradoxes or disputed epistemological issues. Thus, members of the School of Names are variously termed dialecticians, logicians, or sophists. Gongsun Long's work, called the *Gongsun Longzi,* is listed in the catalog of the great Han Imperial Library and is still extant.

John Cikoski, "Standards of Analogic Reasoning in Late Chou China," *Philosophy East and West* 2 (1975): 325–327. A. C. Graham, "The Logic of the Mohist Hsiao-chu," *T'oung pao* 51 (1964): 1–54; and "The Place of Reason in Ancient Chinese Philosophic Tradition," in *The Legacy of China,* edited by Raymond S. Dawson (1964), pp. 29–49. Y. P. Mei, *"The Kongsun Lung Tzu,* with a Translation into English," *Harvard Journal of Asiatic Studies* 16 (1953). Frederick Mote, *The Intellectual Foundations of China* (1971), pp. 93–109.

VICTORIA B. CASS

GONG YIXIN (1833–1898), signer of the Unequal Treaties of 1860, head of the Grand Council and Zongli Yamen, and a leading spirit of the Self-Strengthening Movement in nineteenth-century China. After negotiating a peaceful settlement with Britain and France in 1860 and following a coup d'état in late 1861, Prince Gong was a powerful man, with the titles of prince regent, grand councillor, chief minister of the imperial household, and head of the newly established Zongli Yamen (Foreign Office).

Prince Gong had been vehemently antiforeign, but the experience of peace negotiation with Britain and France in 1860 changed his perspective. He developed a new policy for China: peace through diplomacy and making China strong by learning from the West. This policy served the Self-Strengthening Movement, in which he played a crucial role. The power of Prince Gong, however, became too great for the comfort of Empress Dowager Cixi, who chastised him in 1865 and 1869. Following this reprimand he lost heart for state affairs and in 1884 went into political eclipse after being deprived of all his offices.

[*See also* Empress Dowager; Grand Council; Qing Dynasty; *and* Zongli Yamen.]

YEN-P'ING HAO

GONG ZIZHEN (1792–1841), Chinese poet, essayist, and minor official. Gong was descended from an upper gentry family in Hangzhou; his life and writing exemplified the redirection of literati within the community of *kaozheng* (evidential research) scholars to a greater involvement in matters of statecraft reform. Gong was best known for his outspoken criticism of abuses of imperial power and his formulation of a rationale for basic institutional change to deal with the manifest problems of population pressure, chronic flooding, fiscal instability, widespread drug addiction, and frontier insecurity.

[*See also* Kaozheng Xue; Neo-Confucianism; *and* Qing Dynasty.]

Judith Whitbeck, "Kung Tzu-chen and the Redirection of Literati Commitment in Early Nineteenth Century China," *Ch'ing-shih wen-t'i* 4.10 (December 1983): 1–32. Shirleen Wong, *Kung Tzu-chen* (1975).

JUDITH A. WHITBECK

GOONETILLEKE, SIR OLIVER ERNEST (1892–1978), a civil servant who became auditor-general and civil defense commissioner of Ceylon. During World War II Goonetilleke negotiated the terms of independence with Britain. He was minister for home affairs in the first United National Party government. As governor-general, he asserted extraconstitutional powers in the ethnic riots of 1958 and after the assassination of S. W. R. D. Bandaranaike. As a Christian, he was forced out of office after the coup attempt of 1962 and replaced by a Buddhist.

[*See also* Sri Lanka *and* Bandaranaike, Solomon West Ridgeway Dias.]

Charles Jeffries, *O.E.G.: A Biography of Sir Oliver Ernest Goonetilleke* (1969).

PATRICK PEEBLES

GOVERNMENT OF INDIA. Following the demise of the East India Company in 1858, Britain's Indian empire was placed under the direct authority of the secretary of state for India. He was advised by a Council of India, but this did not function as a corporate body. The secretary of state was, constitutionally, the arbiter of Indian policy, but only a few holders of the office made a significant impact. Among these were John Morley (1905–1910), Edwin Montagu (1917–1922), and Samuel Hoare (1931–1935). Several viceroys were effectively the initiators of policy, notably Lord Curzon (1899–1905), Lord Irwin (Edward Wood; 1926–1931), and Lord Mountbatten (1947). The final solution adopted for the Indian tangle owed little to the secretaries of state responsible, L. S. Amery (1940–1945), and Pethick-Lawrence (1945–1947).

The viceroy (the title assumed under the crown) was chosen for long experience in public life, although only a few were in the political front rank, such as Ripon, Curzon, Reading, and Irwin. The viceroy governed with and through a council of executive members numbering four in 1858. In addition, the commander in chief sat on the council. A finance member was added in 1861 and a member for public works in 1874: all were British, drawn mainly from the public services in India. The first Indian member was S. P. Sinha, appointed law member in 1909. Thereafter, the membership was increased (twelve members in 1942) and in September 1946 the council became the "Interim Government," with its twelve members all Indian political leaders.

In addition, the viceroy headed a Legislative Council, which included all the members of his own (executive) council with others to represent Indian opinion. The Indian Councils Act of 1861 provided for six to twelve additional members, all appointed. British India was made up of a number of provinces. The original structure of the three presidencies (Bengal, Bombay, and Madras) was already inadequate before 1858 and the swollen Bengal Presidency lost territory to new units: the North-Western Provinces (later United Provinces), Punjab, the Central Provinces, and Assam. Bombay and Madras each had a governor, drawn from British public life. The new provinces had at their head a lieutenant-governor or chief commissioner. Following the Montagu-Chelmsford Reforms the head of each province was designated governor. Apart from Bombay and Madras, all these heads of provinces were drawn from the Indian Civil Service.

The principal unit of administration within the province was the district, of which there were about three hundred throughout India. The head of the district was known either as the collector or the deputy commissioner. The distinction dated from the time when the outlying provinces were "nonregulation provinces," but in the late nineteenth century this had ceased to be important. The district officer was the acknowledged chief of all public services in his district, including the police. He was almost invariably a member of the Indian Civil Service.

Districts were divided into subdivisions and into tahsils, revenue areas derived from the Mughal administration. As communications improved in the nineteenth century, however, these smaller units were brought increasingly under the control of the district officer. Whatever innovations might have been taking place centrally or at the provincial level, district administration remained intact. Even the growth of local self-government did not affect the authority of the district officer.

Bombay and Madras had their own legislative councils from 1861, with local legislatures for Bengal (1862), the North-Western Provinces (1886), Punjab, and Burma (1897). However, these early legislatures were more akin to the durbar of an Indian prince than to a parliament. [*See* Durbar.] The first minor change came in 1892, when an elective element was introduced into the central legislature and some provincial legislatures. The mode of election was indirect, the members being chosen by municipal and district councils.

The port cities—Calcutta, Bombay, and Madras—were given municipal government in the eighteenth century, and self-government was cautiously extended to other towns in the mid-nineteenth century. Local self-government as a school of political education for Indian leaders owed its real foundation to Lord Ripon (George Frederick Robinson), however, who promoted legislation (1883–1884) to set up municipal councils with an elected majority and rural district boards with a small elective element. These bodies became the main sphere of action of the new "political India" and it was from this group, in which lawyers predominated, that the elected members of the 1892 legislatures were drawn.

These marginal changes in the manner in which India was governed were of little importance compared to the continuing grip of the higher bureaucracy on Indian administration. The "Covenanted Service," the Indian Civil Service, was drawn from the elite of the British university students. Beginning in 1853, entry was based upon a competitive examination. Although Indians were eligible to compete, and the first Indian joined the service in 1864, by the start of World War I there were only sixty Indians in a total of eleven hundred civil servants. What Prime Minister Lloyd George was to call the "steel frame" of Indian administration remained effectively British.

Meanwhile, Indian Muslim political leaders argued that elections to the legislatures only exposed their weakness within the system. They demanded separate representation, and in 1909 the Morley-Minto Reforms met this demand. Seats were specially reserved for Muslims at the center and in the provincial legislatures, now considerably expanded. The Morley-Minto Reforms gave Indians a greater voice, but no greater share in government. This was achieved a decade later with the Montagu-Chelmsford Reforms, which came into effect in 1920. The main innovation of dyarchy, as it was known, was the transfer of the so-called "nation-building" functions of the provincial governments to elected ministers. The provincial legislatures were now three-quarters elected by direct vote. The franchise was given to about 5.5 million voters out of a total population of 247 million. The separate electorates for Muslims were preserved, and other minorities were also separately represented. [*See* Morley-Minto Reforms *and* Montagu-Chelmsford Reforms.]

All municipal and district boards became entirely elective and official supervision ended, the boards being responsible to an Indian minister. The new system was a major advance in the direction of political education, but Congress now rejected this gradualist approach and demanded full self-government without delay.

The next set of reforms came into effect in 1937. Under the 1935 Government of India Act, government at provincial level was transferred entirely to elected ministries. The creation of new provinces from existing ones, which in the twentieth century began with the North-West Frontier Province (1905) and Bihar (1912), was taken further: Orissa and Sind became separate entities under the 1935 Act. At the same time Burma became a separate country altogether. Elections took place in the winter of 1936–1937, with about 30 million voters out of a total population of 256 million in British India. Congress won this election, and after internal debates took office in eight of the eleven provinces.

The second part of the 1935 Act provided for an all-India federation with a federal legislature. This was designed to bring princely India into the political process: it could become operative only after half the princes had accepted the scheme. By the outbreak of war in 1939 insufficient numbers had acceded, and the federal scheme was suspended. In addition, in October 1939 all the Congress provincial governments resigned and in all those provinces administration reverted to the governors and their officials. An elected ministry continued to function in Punjab, formed by the Unionist Party, while ministries also functioned sporadically in Bengal and Assam. New elections took place in 1945–1946, and the new legislators provided the basis for the Constituent Assembly of 1946. A year later India and Pakistan became independent nations.

[*See also* East India Company; Government of India Acts; Indian Administrative Service; Governor-General of India; Curzon, George Nathaniel;

Robinson, George Frederick; Mountbatten, Louis; *and* Wood, Edward Frederick Lindley. *For the geopolitical situation circa 1931, see the map accompanying* Princely States.]

S. V. Desika Char, ed., *Readings in the Constitutional History of India, 1757–1947* (1983). Courtenay Ilbert, *The Government of India* (1898; rev. ed., 1907). A. B. Keith, *A Constitutional History of India, 1600–1935* (1936). V. P. Menon, *The Transfer of Power in India* (1957). C. H. Philips, ed., *The Evolution of India and Pakistan, 1858–1947* (1962). Hugh Tinker, *The Foundations of Local Self-Government in India, Pakistan and Burma* (1954).

HUGH TINKER

GOVERNMENT OF INDIA ACTS. In its preamble, the Government of India Act of 1919 stated that British policy was intended to promote "the gradual development of self-governing institutions with a view to the progressive realisation of responsible government." This led to the introduction of dyarchy in the provinces, whereby so-called nation-building departments were placed under ministers, members of provincial legislatures. This was the "transferred" side; the "reserved" side—finance and law and order—remained under official control.

Under pressure for change, dyarchy was replaced by a wider measure of devolution under the Government of India Act of 1935. It is claimed that this is the longest measure ever enacted by the British Parliament and it was passed only after two years of bitter opposition by Winston Churchill and right-wing conservatives. The 1935 Act completed the transfer of power at the provincial level to ministerial government. Also, the provincial franchise was extended, giving the vote to about 20 percent of the adult population. The new feature was the creation of a federal structure for the central government. The provinces of British India and the princely states were to combine to form a federal legislature. The new federation could only become operative when the rulers of states representing one-half of the population of princely India acceded to the federation. The required number did not accede before September 1939 and this part of the act remained a dead letter.

The 1935 act was condemned by Mohandas Gandhi and the Indian National Congress as a "slave constitution" and "a new charter of bondage." Nevertheless, congress governments were formed in 1937, resigning in 1939 on the instructions of their leaders. When the two new dominions came into being in 1947, both continued to function under the 1935 Act, suitably amended; India was governed under the act until 1950, and Pakistan until 1956.

[*See also* Princely States; Indian National Congress; India; *and* Pakistan.]

Samuel Hoare, *Nine Troubled Years* (1954). A. B. Keith, *Constitutional History of India, 1600–1935* (1936). V. P. Menon, *The Transfer of Power in India* (1957).

HUGH TINKER

GOVERNOR-GENERAL OF INDIA, the title used, with various modifications, for the head of the government of the British possessions in India from 1773 to 1947, and then for the head of the interim government in independent India until 1950. After 1858 the holder of the office was often referred to by the courtesy title "viceroy." The office was established by the Regulating Act of 1773 to give the British Parliament more control over the activities of the East India Company. The act required the directors of the East India Company in London to appoint as their chief official in India a governor-general with a council of four members; his official designation was "Governor-General of Fort William in Bengal." He was given limited control over the governors of the company's possessions in Madras and Bombay.

The first holder of the office was Warren Hastings (1774–1785). The system worked badly as a result of the divided authority between the governor-general and his councillors, and in 1784 Parliament passed a new act (known as Pitt's India Act), which, while modified in details by subsequent acts, essentially defined the government of the British possessions in India down to 1858. The governor-general was given power, in the words of the act, "to superintend, direct and control" all British territory in India. The number of councillors was reduced to three, so the governor-general could use his casting vote to overrule them providing he had one supporter. The first governor-general under the new act was Lord Cornwallis (1785–1793), and henceforth all appointees (except for temporary replacements) were noblemen, without previous Indian experience, who had the backing of the political party in power in England, even though their appointment was nominally made by the directors of the East India Company. In 1833 the title of the office was changed to "Governor-General of India," indicating both a new sense of permanence of British rule in the whole of the subcontinent and the importance of the office.

As the East India Company's government in India came increasingly under the control of the British

TABLE 1. *The Governors-General of India**

GOVERNOR-GENERAL	ACCESSION
GOVERNORS-GENERAL OF FORT WILLIAM IN BENGAL	
Warren Hastings	1774
Lord Cornwallis (Charles)	1786
Sir John Shore	1793
Lord Wellesley (Richard; Lord Mornington)	1798
Lord Cornwallis (second tenure)	1805
Sir George Barlow (temporary)	1805
Lord Minto I (Gilbert Elliot-Murray Kynynmond)	1807
Lord Hastings (Francis Rawdon-Hastings; Lord Moira)	1813
Lord Amherst (William)	1823
Lord William Bentinck	1828
GOVERNORS-GENERAL OF INDIA	
Lord William Bentinck	1834
Sir Charles Metcalfe	1835
Lord Auckland (George Eden)	1836
Lord Ellenborough (Edward Law)	1842
Sir Henry Hardinge	1844
Lord Dalhousie (James Andrew Broun Ramsay)	1848
Lord Canning (Charles)	1856
GOVERNORS-GENERAL AND VICEROYS	
Lord Canning	1858
Lord Elgin I (James Bruce)	1862
GOVERNORS-GENERAL AND VICEROYS (cont.)	
Lord Lawrence (John)	1864
Lord Mayo (Richard Southwell Burke)	1869
Lord Northbrook (Thomas George Baring)	1872
Lord Lytton (Edward Robert Bulwer-Lytton)	1876
Lord Ripon (George Frederick Robinson)	1880
Lord Dufferin (Frederick Hamilton-Temple-Blackwood)	1884
Lord Lansdowne (Henry Petty-Fitzmaurice)	1888
Lord Elgin II (Victor Alexander Bruce)	1894
Lord Curzon (George)	1899
Lord Minto II (Gilbert John Elliot-Murray-Kynynmond)	1905
Lord Hardinge (Charles)	1910
Lord Chelmsford (Frederick John Napier Thesiger)	1916
Lord Reading (Rufus Isaacs)	1921
Lord Irwin (Edward Frederick Lindley Wood)	1926
Lord Goschen (temporary)	1929
Lord Willingdon (Freeman Freeman-Thomas)	1931
Sir George Stanley (temporary)	1934
Lord Willingdon	1936
Lord Wavell (Archibald)	1943
Lord Mountbatten (Louis)	1947
C. R. Rajagopalachari	1948

*Names of those who had temporary appointments for less than a year are omitted. The titles are those by which the holders were generally known in India; nontitled and given names are shown in parentheses.

Parliament, strong governors-general, such as lords Wellesley (1798–1805), Bentinck (1828–1835), and Dalhousie (James Andrew Broun Ramsay; 1848–1856), were the effective rulers of British territories in India, providing they were supported by the government in power in England. There were, however, built-in limitations on their power, since the members of the Indian Civil Service, who occupied all the executive positions in British India, were appointed in England and had the daily administration in their hands. The governor-general was also subject, until 1858, to the advice and authority of the president of Board of Control in London, the arm of the British government that shared in the political management of the East India Company, and then after 1858 to the secretary of state for India, who was a member of the cabinet.

After the suppression of the uprisings in North India in 1857 to 1858 against British authority, the East India Company's control of India, long only nominal, came to formal end, and in 1858 all its territories were transferred to the British crown, that is, to parliamentary control. Queen Victoria's proclamation in 1858 appointed Lord Canning as governor-general under the new arrangements, although in fact he had held the office since 1856. The proclamation referred to him "as our first Viceroy," indicating that the governor-general would be the personal representative of the British monarch in India. This was a courtesy title, not an official designation, but it was the way the office was usually referred to in India. This became of even more symbolic significance after 1877, when Queen Victoria assumed the title of empress of India, indicating a relationship between the British crown and India that did not exist anywhere else in the British empire. Lord Curzon (1899–1905) was perhaps the most influential of the holders of the office after 1858, although Lord Mountbatten (1947–1948) had a central role in the transfer of power. The last person with the title was an Indian, C. R. Rajagopalachari, who succeeded Mountbatten in 1948 and held office until the new constitution, adopted in January 1950, abolished the postition.

[*See also* East India Company; Government of India; India; *and* Mutiny, Indian. *Many of the figures mentioned in this article are the subject of independent entries.*]

A. C. Banerji, *The Constitutional History of India,* 3 vols. (1977). C. H. Philips, *The East India Company, 1784–1834* (1940; reprint, 1961). Philip Woodruff, *The Men Who Ruled India,* 2 vols. (1964).

AINSLIE T. EMBREE

GRAND COUNCIL *(junjichu),* ruling instrument of the Qing dynasty in China. Strictly speaking, the council was formalized when the Yongzheng emperor (r. 1722–1735) was preparing a war against the Dzungars, a Mongol tribe, in 1726. More generally, however, the inspiration for the council derived from the perennial desire of autocratic rulers of the traditional Chinese state for unlimited imperial power. Like the rulers before them in Chinese history, the early Qing emperors appreciated the services of a compact, informal, efficient, and controllable group of officials. They were also interested in keeping direct communication with provincial and local officials. When combined, these two motives gave birth to the Grand Council.

Yongzheng's predecessor, the Kangxi emperor (r. 1661–1722), had allowed some officials outside Beijing to send directly to him palace memorials containing their reports, requests, or suggestions. After writing comments on these memorials, the emperor returned them to the memorialists. Some imperial orders were also sent in the form of court letters. Upon receiving court letters or imperial comments, the officials submitted additional palace memorials, to which the throne responded further. These exchanges created a channel of direct communication between ruler and officials.

During the early Yongzheng reign period the imperial confidants who transmitted the court letters and the palace memorials formed a small and informal group. The emperor selected from this group a few well-qualified individuals as his personal aides to provide both transmitting and advising service and, for efficiency, put them in the same office. Because of its informal and confidential nature, this office had neither an exact beginning date nor a definite name in its early stage. Not until 1732 was it officially named *junjichu.* The imperial personal assistants became the grand councillors, the earliest staff of the office. Later, they were assisted by secretaries known as *junji zhangjing.* Competent, secret, and independent of all bureaucratic procedure or institutional checks, the Grand Council was the most powerful autocratic tool ever founded in traditional China.

[*See also* Grand Secretariat.]

Alfred Kuo-liang Ho, "The Grand Council in the Qing Dynasty," *Far Eastern Quarterly* 11.2 (1952): 167–182. Pei Huang, *Autocracy at Work: A Study of the Yung-cheng Period, 1723–1735* (1974).

PEI HUANG

GRAND SECRETARIAT *(neige),* a small and prestigious office in the central government of the Ming and Qing periods in China. It sprang chiefly from the emperor's struggle for personal rule at the expense of the premiership, a struggle that had existed since the Former Han dynasty (206 BCE–9 CE). After abolishing the premiership in 1380, Zhu Yuanzhang, founder of the Ming dynasty (1368–1644), abolished the office of prime minister and put the Six Boards directly under the emperor. For clerical and consulting needs, he selected four literary men as secretaries *(sifu guan).* These were replaced in 1382 by grand secretaries *(da xueshi).* During the Yongle period (1403–1424) their office became known as the Grand Secretariat.

From a humble beginning, the Grand Secretariat grew to be the highest office in Ming times. It accumulated power through its expanding function. Toward the end of the Yongle reign it increasingly functioned as a consulting office. Among its duties after 1425 was rescript-drafting *(piaoni),* a procedure in which the opinions of drafters played an important part.

The Grand Secretariat also derived its strength from the individual grand secretaries, who became influential because of their easy access to the throne. Several grand secretaries of the Hongxi period (1424–1425) had tutored the emperor when he was the crown prince, a relationship that further enhanced the influence of their office. After about 1500, when some Ming rulers were indifferent to administrative work, the grand secretaries became the actual operators of the state machinery. Their official rank, however, always remained low.

At its inception, the grand secretaries were the only staff of the Grand Secretariat. In later years some clerks were added, and a senior grand secretary emerged as the leader of the group. Despite its importance in the early Qing dynasty, the Grand Secretariat took charge of merely routine affairs after the rise of the Grand Council in the 1720s.

On occasion the Grand Secretariat is referred to in Western literature as "inner cabinet." This rendering is incorrect because the office was basically an autocratic tool, never functioning as a "cabinet."

[*See also* Ming Dynasty; Bureaucracy in China; *and* Grand Council.]

Tilemann Grimm, "Das Neiko der Ming-Zeit von den Anfängen bis 1506," *Oriens Extremus* 1.2 (1954): 139–177.
PEI HUANG

GRAND TRUNK ROAD, the largest and most famous highway in South Asia, running some fifteen hundred miles from Peshawar (in Pakistan) to Calcutta (in eastern India). Its origins date to Maurya times (c. third century BCE), when it was the "royal road" connecting the Northwest with the Maurya capital at Pataliputra (modern-day Patna) and the ports at the mouth of the Ganges. It was improved in the sixteenth century by Sher Shah, but it was not until the 1830s, when the British graded and metaled it from Lahore to Calcutta, that it gained its popular designation. The Grand Trunk Road was extended from Lahore to Peshawar in the 1850s, and it later took hold of the popular imagination through Rudyard Kipling's novel *Kim* (1901), where its sights and sounds are described in loving detail by the author, who calls it "India's backbone."

John Wiles, *The Grand Trunk Road, Khyber to Calcutta* (1972).
ROBIN JARED LEWIS

GRANT, CHARLES (1746–1823), director and chairman of the East India Company and a key figure in the establishment of British rule in India. He went out to India in 1767 and became secretary of the Board of Trade and commercial resident at Malda. He was a supporter of the reforms carried out by Lord Charles Cornwallis in the company's management of Bengal. After making a large fortune in trade he returned to England in 1790 and soon became known as an advocate of sending Christian missionaries to India. His views were elaborated in a remarkable book on the need for Great Britain to support religious and social change in India. He was an enthusiastic member of the Clapham Sect, the evangelical group of which William Wilberforce was the leader. Grant was a bitter opponent of the expansionist policies of Lord Wellesley, arguing that British territorial control should be confined to Bengal. He was a member of Parliament for Inverness from 1802 to 1808 and was one of the chief founders of Haileybury, the school for training the East India Company's officials. One of his sons, Lord Glenelg, became the colonial secretary from 1835 to 1839, and another, Robert, was governor of Bombay from 1834 to 1838. [*See also* East India Company *and* Haileybury College.]
AINSLIE T. EMBREE

GREAT LEAP FORWARD. Stretching from late 1957 to mid-1960, the Great Leap Forward was one of the most tumultuous periods in the history of the People's Republic of China. During the Great Leap Forward, communes were established in the Chinese countryside, China proclaimed that it would overtake England in the production of major products in fifteen years, and Chinese leaders thought that the nation was on the verge of the transition to communism. In this period, China and the United States almost went to war over Jinmen (Quemoy) Island off the coast of China, Sino-Soviet differences grew into a major schism, and the worst case of intra-Party conflict since the regime came to power in 1949 erupted. The Great Leap created an economic disaster: millions died in a severe famine and a deep depression in industry occurred.

The Great Leap was the outcome of two strands of policy development in 1957, those in the political and economic realms. Mao Zedong was most responsible for the political developments. In early 1957 he encouraged a more open political system and called on intellectuals and others to criticize the Communist Party in a campaign known as the Hundred Flowers Movement. Mao and the Party were not prepared for the outpouring of censure that ensued. They responded angrily to these remarks, and instead of a more open political system, a more politically charged atmosphere appeared by the summer of 1957. Mao and other leaders who had come to rely on China's intellectuals as the major force in modernizing China's backward economy now had to discard this approach in light of the extensive criticism by intellectuals; they were uncertain of where another model of development would be found.

Part of the resolution of this problem came from developments in the economic realm. China's top economic official in the 1950s, Chen Yun, launched a minor readjustment of the Chinese economy in late 1956 and 1957 with the backing of Premier Zhou Enlai. Chen's program, which included the use of the market as a supplement to the planned economy and less emphasis on the development of heavy industry, provoked opposition from top planning and heavy-industry officials. As a counter to Chen and in response to the relatively poor economic conditions of 1956 to 1957, these officials offered an alternative program that emphasized industry aiding agriculture, self-reliance, decentralization, and a greater stress on medium-sized and small industry (as opposed to large factories). These policies not only met pressing economic needs, but also protected the institutional interests of this group. [*See also* Chen Yun.]

In October 1957, Mao essentially co-opted the program of the planners and merged it with a series of mass campaigns that were the Communist Party's response to the criticism of the intellectuals, thus launching the Great Leap Forward. Peasants were galvanized to build large-scale water conservancy projects and participate in a "socialist education campaign." An "anti-rightist campaign" aimed at all those who had spoken out against the Party was also launched. This campaign stifled all debate on Party policies. A major decentralization of power occurred, giving a much larger role to the provinces and the Party in economic affairs. Mao summed up the emerging Great Leap with the slogans "More, faster, better, and more economical" (referring to production) and "Politics in command." Consequently, expertise was unimportant to those leading the Great Leap Forward.

To mobilize support for the Great Leap Forward, Mao toured many of China's provinces in early 1958, persuading other leaders of the wisdom of his program. Mao and Liu Shaoqi, the second-highest leader of the Party, codified a set of work methods that included a system in which the central government formulated a minimum and a maximum production plan. The maximum plan was then broken down for each province, and became the province's minimum plan. Each province then set its own maximum plan, which in turn was passed down as the minimum plan for the next lower administrative unit, and so on. As a result of this method, planners lost control over economic activity and targets escalated to absurd levels. Counties claimed 1,000 and even 10,000 percent increases in agricultural production. In order to quell doubters of this and other aspects of the Great Leap Forward, Mao also tongue-lashed potential opponents. However, there was surprisingly little dissent within the Communist Party on the Great Leap Forward until mid-1959.

By the middle of 1958 a number of collective farms had experimentally banded together to carry out water conservancy projects. Mao became convinced that this new type of organization, the rural people's commune, which combined industry, agriculture, trade, education, and military affairs, was the key to the rapid development of the Chinese countryside. In late August 1958 Mao gained the support of his colleagues for the establishment of communes throughout the Chinese countryside. In the space of six weeks almost all Chinese peasants were nominally organized into communes.

Between August and November 1958, utopianism gripped the Chinese leadership, which encouraged the formation of "backyard steel furnaces" in the communes in an effort to double the amount of steel produced in 1957. In this way, small, native, and mass techniques were to be combined with large, foreign, and specialized ones. This stage was called "walking on two legs." In addition, mess halls and dormitories were established in some communes. Commentators hailed this as a major step in the transition to a communist (as opposed to a socialist) society, and in the destruction of the family. The frenzy and spirit that gripped China during the summer of 1958 are indescribable.

By November 1958, however, the Chinese leadership began to reconsider some of the more fanciful claims made during the summer of 1958. Very slowly, a more realistic spirit began to circulate in inner Party discussions. Mao himself was one of the leaders of this shift. In late February 1959 he made several hardheaded speeches calling for the consolidation of the communes and a more realistic attitude in all activities. Mao and his colleagues were not abandoning the Great Leap and the communes; rather, they were calling for a measured and less frenetic style of leadership and administration.

This gradual retreat continued until July 1959. At a series of Party meetings in July and August 1959, however, the Great Leap Forward was reintensified. In the first of these meetings, the minister of national defense, Peng Dehuai, criticized many aspects of the Leap, apparently unconvinced that the retreat of the first half of 1959 was sufficient. Mao took Peng's criticisms as a personal affront. The chairman vehemently countered Peng's charges and forced the Party to choose between Peng and him. Peng was subsequently removed from all positions of authority. After Peng's removal, no one had the temerity to question any of the policies of the Leap. Problems with the Leap were now blamed on Peng and all those like him who questioned its premises. Mao now believed that the way to make the Great Leap Forward proceed more smoothly was no longer to rectify policies, but to attack those who doubted the Leap. In a pyrrhic victory for the chairman, utopianism was revived. The retreat of early 1959 was forgotten.

Urban communes were established and many wild claims were made for the new upsurge. Although the Leap continued until mid-1960, the problems could not be denied forever. The weather in 1958 had been remarkably good, and a bumper harvest was achieved, although this was greatly exaggerated by the Party. In 1959, however, the weather worsened. Coupled with the lack of incentives, poor leadership in the communes, and irrational policies coming from upper levels, disaster struck the Chinese countryside in the winter of 1959 to 1960. According to one prominent Chinese economist, between 1957 and 1960 the death rate more than doubled. In the years 1960 to 1962, known to the Chinese as the Three Hard Years, untold millions died of starvation and diseases affecting the malnourished. The collapse of agricultural production had a similar effect on industry. Between 1960 and 1962 the gross value of industrial output fell by almost 50 percent.

During the Great Leap Forward, Chinese foreign policy was also characterized by a radical position. In mid-1958 the Chinese started to interdict supplies to the island of Jinmen, occupied by the Nationalist forces of Chiang Kai-shek, in an effort to force its surrender. Chinese artillery barrages were extremely effective, and the United States, then Chiang's ally, considered the use of nuclear weapons in an effort to lift the blockade. Fortunately, a settlement was negotiated to break the blockade. This incident hardly served to improve the state of Sino-American relations. [*See also* Jinmen.]

The Jinmen incident also further strained Sino-Soviet relations. The Russians had looked askance at a number of Chinese ideological pronouncements beginning in 1957. With the Great Leap Forward, they began to question many Chinese policies, and the communes in particular. The Soviet experience with communes in the 1920s had been one of total failure. Soviet leaders were also appalled by Mao's downplaying of the threat posed by nuclear weapons. They were afraid that through confrontations like that over Jinmen, the Chinese would drag the Russians into war with the United States. The Chinese, especially Mao, felt that the Soviet leader, Nikita Khrushchev, was unqualified to lead the Soviet bloc. The Chinese also believed that since the Russians had been the first to develop an intercontinental ballistic missile and launch satellites, the Soviets should not be afraid to challenge the US. Sino-Soviet relations became more acrimonious by the month. Finally, in the summer of 1960, the Soviet Union ordered all of its technical advisers to leave China. The Sino-Soviet split was visible for all to see.

The significance of the Great Leap Forward was varied. First, the Leap and the catastrophe that followed marked the failure of one of the Maoist models of development. Never again would Chinese leaders, including Mao, consent to the intense mobilization of the populace, especially the peasants, to bring about rapid economic development. Labor could not be turned into capital very efficiently. The failure of the Great Leap Forward, however, did not dampen Mao's belief in the efficacy of mass mobilization for political purposes.

Second, during the Leap, Mao began to withdraw from the "first line" of decision-making. As some of the blame for the failure of the Leap was pinned on him, the chairman either chose to remain in the background in the early 1960s, or was forced to stay there. His colleagues, especially Liu Shaoqi and Deng Xiaoping, took over many of the decision-making responsibilities Mao had held. Mao found their policies increasingly distasteful, and began to question their political loyalty. Ultimately, the chairman felt he had to purge Liu and Deng. Thus, some of the seeds of the Cultural Revolution were sown by the Great Leap.

Finally, the policies of the early 1960s, designed to bring China out of the economic crisis caused by the Leap, remain significant to this day. Liu, Deng, Chen Yun, and Zhou Enlai called for the readjustment of heavy industry, with agriculture (nominally) as the most important sector. Again, the market was used as a supplement to the plan. Quality was more valued than quantity. With the passing of the Maoist era, these policies have been revived and inform many of the economic policies of China in the mid-1980s.

[*See also* China, People's Republic of; Communism: Chinese Communist Party; Hundred Flowers Campaign; Liu Shaoqi; Mao Zedong; Marxism and Socialism: Marxism in China; Peng Dehuai; *and* Zhou Enlai.]

David Bachman, *Chen Yun and the Chinese Political System* (1985). Thomas P. Bernstein, "Stalinism, Famine, and Chinese Peasants," *Theory and Society* 13.3 (May 1984): 339–377. Parris Chang, *Power and Policy in China* (1975). Harry Harding, *Organizing China* (1981). Roderick MacFarquhar, *The Origins of the Cultural Revolution, 1: Contradictions among the People, 1956–1957* (1974) and *The Origins of the Cultural Revolution, 2: The Great Leap Forward, 1958–1960* (1983). Frederick C. Teiwes, *Politics and Purges in China* (1979). Ezra Vogel, *Canton under Communism* (1969).

DAVID BACHMAN

GREAT PROLETARIAN CULTURAL REVOLUTION. Officially lasting for the ten-year period 1966 to 1976, China's Great Proletarian Cultural Revolution was undertaken by Mao Zedong and his supporters as an absolutely necessary measure to preserve revolutionary puritanism. Although the Cultural Revolution (CR) involved all political groups in China—the Communist Party, government, military, students, intellectuals, workers, and, to a lesser extent, peasants—Mao undoubtedly played the most crucial role. Since his death, the official view of the CR has changed; present leaders totally repudiate it for having thrown China into "ten years of calamity and chaos."

Mao initiated the CR partially for political and partially for ideological reasons. Politically he wanted to regain the power that he had been losing since the failure of his Great Leap Forward. His ideological motive was to cleanse the nation of what he regarded as pernicious bourgeois influence. Mao was concerned about remnants of bourgeois attitudes in the superstructure, but what alarmed Mao most was the emergence of new inequalities and the privileged social groups around the Chinese Communist Party, the supposed vanguard party of China's working class. Mao learned that the inevitable process of bureaucratization of the ruling party would distance it from the majority of the Chinese masses and make its members more concerned with maintaining their own privileged positions than with revolutionary changes of the entire society.

Thus, claiming that his opponents had formed a bourgeois dictatorship within the Party—in effect, a new ruling class—Mao called on the masses to rise up and purge the "capitalist roaders" and bourgeois thinkers, even if they existed at the highest levels of the Party bureaucracy. The Chinese Communist Party, which had hitherto been the agent of revolution, was to be the object of revolution. In its place, Mao designated the young as a new vanguard and mobilized the students.

The result was a disappointment not only to Mao but also to the Chinese young people. When Mao removed or weakened the control exercised by the Party organization, all the latent tensions and contradictions in the society surfaced. The Chinese masses quickly polarized into two factions: one interested in the radical restructuring of the Chinese political system, and the other in maintaining the political status quo. As the CR unfolded along its unexpected course, the Chinese elite was further divided over the constantly arising political and socioeconomic issues. As a result, the CR underwent many twists and turns, making all participants at the end feel that they suffered from the movement.

Initial Outbreak. The CR started with a very insignificant incident. In October 1965 Mao asked Peng Zhen, the mayor of Beijing, to criticize Wu Han's play *Hai Rui's Dismissal from Office.* Instead of complying with Mao's wish, a Party meeting chaired by him concluded that thorough historical research was needed to render a final judgment on Wu Han's play. Dissatisfied with the attitude of the Party establishment, Mao turned to the People's Liberation Army (PLA), which, under the leadership of Minister of Defense Lin Biao, was willing to politically condemn Wu Han and uphold Mao's view of "politics in command." Once the support of the military was secured, Mao convened a meeting in May 1966 of top-level Party members, who adopted the May Sixteenth Circular, established the Cultural Revolution Small Group with his wife, Jiang Qing, as a key member, and purged Peng Zhen. [*See also* Peng Zhen; Wu Han; *and* May Sixteenth Circular.]

About the same time, six graduate students in Beijing University put up a big-character poster accusing the University Party Committee of having opposed Mao's ideas; the school leadership responded by suppressing the challengers. Mao intervened on behalf of the rebelling students by instructing radio broadcast and publication of the big-character poster. Soon students of other campuses started to challenge their own school administrators.

As the school Party authorities collapsed, the top Party apparatus led by Liu Shaoqi and Deng Xiaoping decided to dispatch work teams to lead the student movement in campus. The decision became controversial, however, since some students rejected the authority of the work teams and others defended them. While the students were debating whether or not the work teams were carrying out the Maoist line, Mao intervened again, ordering the withdrawal of the work teams and forcing the Party to adopt the "Sixteen Articles," which included provisions that demoted Liu Shaoqi, promoted Lin Biao, and promised a free mobilization of the students without being controlled from the Party organization. [*See also* Liu Shaoqi.]

Soon after, the Chinese students organized themselves into the Red Guards, filling the power vacuum on the campuses and taking the Maoist message to the society at large. The initial membership of the Red Guards was limited to those with "good class backgrounds"—the children of peasants, workers, cadres, military men, and revolutionary martyrs. Encouraged by the existing Party organization and led by the children of high-ranking cadres and military officers, the early Red Guards advocated a simple class line; while boasting themselves to be "natural reds," they considered as the main target of the movement the former exploiting classes, which, having been subjected to the fifteen years of "proletarian dictatorship," did not have any political influence. The Red Guards were particularly active in criticizing the existing educational system for its failure to give enough consideration to such political criteria as class status and political performance, holding their teachers rather than the Party leaders responsible for the allegedly mistaken educational policy. They treated their fellow students from ordinary or bad class backgrounds with contempt at best or made them the object of the class struggle at worst. At the same time, they completely avoided the questions of new privileged groups in socialist China.

The students from ordinary or bad class backgrounds experienced great difficulties. Largely because of their less desirable class status, many of them were viewed as the target of the movement first by the work teams, and then by their fellow students now organized into the Red Guards. Nonetheless, they gradually formed their own organizations, calling themselves rebels in order to distinguish their group from the initial conservative Red Guards. Criticizing the initial Red Guards for advocating a "feudalistic blood theory"—which assumed a deterministic link between class background and political attitude—they emphasized one's loyalty to Mao Zedong Thought as a true criterion for defining a revolutionary. In other words, the rebel faction stressed political behavior over class status, influences of the society over those of the family, and political performance during the Cultural Revolution over that of the past. [*See also* Red Guards.]

While the two factions were debating among themselves, the Maoist leaders convened a top-level Party meeting in October 1966. The meeting compelled Liu Shaoqi and Deng Xiaoping to make self-criticisms, made Lin Biao Mao's successor, and rendered judgment against the initial Red Guards. Encouraged by the official decision, the rebel groups seized the leadership of the student movement from the initial conservative Red Guards. With the students lacking any close ties to the Party leaders in charge of the student movement, the thrust of the CR was turned against the Party leaders themselves.

By November, another group was mobilized to participate in the Cultural Revolution: the workers. Initially the regime intended to limit the political mobilization to the students. With the rise of the radical Red Guards to the predominant position, however, the mass movement expanded to the factories; the rebel students went to the factories in order to instigate workers against the Party leaders, justifying their action in terms of learning from the workers. The discontented workers (those who felt discriminated against by the existing system) organized themselves and revolted against the Party leaders, largely because of their economic grievances, but justifying their actions in terms of Mao's radical ideology. Local and factory Party leaders responded by relinquishing responsibility to control the economy; they freely raised the wages, handed out bonuses, offered travel allowances, and sometimes even allowed collective welfare funds to be distributed among the workers. The result of the "economism" was economic chaos.

Mao responded to the economism in January 1967 by instructing the students and workers to seize power from those whom he considered corrupt revisionist Party leaders. The power seizure started in Shanghai, the most industrialized city of China, where the radical workers already were well organized. When power seizure became the official policy and other areas that lacked the necessary conditions of power seizure tried to imitate the events in Shanghai, however, it created confusion and chaos because there were no specific guidelines as to who would take over which powers. Consequently, many people wanted to seize power, claiming to be "revolutionary," and the power seizure proceeded at all levels and in all areas simultaneously: the students and workers seized power in their own schools and factories, and took part in the power seizure in the various governmental organs as well. The net result was the intensification of conflict. A mass organization would initiate power seizure and another would challenge it as "sham power seizure," and attempt "counter–power seizure."

Military Involvement. After the collapse of the Party and the government apparatus, the only organization capable of restoring any semblance of order was the People's Liberation Army (PLA), whose involvement in the CR until that time had been very limited. As the chaos spread, Mao had to turn to the PLA to prevent China from completely disintegrating. The PLA was thus given various conflicting tasks: (1) to help the leftists with the seizure of power, while instilling them with a sense of discipline by providing military training; (2) to exercise military control over some localities and some Party organs; and (3) to ensure production at the basic level of industry and agriculture. The contradictory nature of these assignments allowed the PLA to pursue its own interests by supporting conservative mass organizations while suppressing and quite often disbanding the rebel organizations as "counterrevolutionary."

As a result the mass movement entered a moderate phase in February 1967—the period that the Maoist radicals called the "February Adverse Current." By April Maoist leaders initiated a counterattack by criticizing the PLA for supporting the wrong side and reducing their authority. This encouraged the radical mass organizations to intensify their efforts to seize power. The conservative mass organizations were not willing to yield to the pressure of the Maoists this time, and put up strong resistance. Thus, both sides began to use weapons that they seized from the PLA to settle their differences. Having been criticized for having supported the wrong side, the PLA contentedly watched the deteriorating social order.

In July 1967 the conservative organization of Wuhan kidnapped two Beijing emissaries at the encouragement of—or at least with the acquiescence of—local military leaders. The Cultural Revolution Small Group responded to this open insubordination by calling on the masses to arm themselves for defensive purposes and to seize military power from the "handful of power holders within the Army." Thus, the CR entered its most violent stage, during which the radical and conservative mass organizations engaged in a deadly freewheeling armed struggle, even threatening the organizational integrity of the PLA. Meanwhile, the social order was completeley collapsing. Communication and transportation systems came to a standstill and consumer goods became scarce in urban areas.

The Revolutionary Committees. Faced with this deteriorating situation, Mao had no alternative but to moderate the whole movement in order to prevent it from degenerating into a civil war. Thus, Mao intervened again by signaling the end of the mass mobilization phase of the Cultural Revolution.

Thereafter Mao and the Party leaders concentrated their efforts on bringing the warring factions of the mass organizations into a great alliance and setting up revolutionary committees as a new power structure in the place of the now defunct Party committees. The organizing principle of the revolutionary committee was the three-in-one combination of the representatives of mass organizations, the revolutionary cadres, and the PLA, who would share seats in each revolutionary committee. The central leadership helped set up the provincial revolutionary committees, which in turn would supervise the establishment of revolutionary committees at the municipal level. Since the factional conflict between the radical and mass organizations continued even after the establishment of revolutionary committees, the PLA emerged as the dominant force in every revolutionary committee. Now appropriating the authority of the revolutionary committee, the military continued to discriminate against the radical mass organizations, almost forcing them to challenge the revolutionary committees themselves. [*See also* Revolutionary Committees.]

After establishing the revolutionary committees, the regime moved to reorganize the Party organizations at the various levels. Since the revolutionary committees that the PLA controlled were to supervise the reorganization of the Party committees, it is not an exaggeration to say that the PLA reorganized the Party organizations. When the Ninth Party Congress was convened in 1969, the military obtained approximately one-third of the Central Committee membership, and helped the congress to name Lin Biao as Mao's successor in the Party constitution. With the Ninth Party Congress the CR as a mass movement virtually ended; however, since the vicious power struggle and extreme radical ideology continued, the present official line holds that the CR ended only after Mao's death.

The Final Phase. After Lin Biao's attempted assassination of Mao and subsequent purge in 1971, many military leaders were removed from politically powerful positions, creating a power vacuum. [*See also* Lin Biao.] The radical Jiang Qing group hoped to promote the former Red Guards to the vacated positions, while the moderate faction led by Zhou Enlai wanted to bring back the experienced cadres purged in the preceding stage of the CR. By 1973 many of the victims of the CR—including Deng Xiaoping—were reinstated to important political positions, thus threatening the radical faction largely composed of the beneficiaries of the CR. In January

1976 Zhou Enlai died. When the Beijing citizens spontaneously gathered on 5 April to pay respects to the late premier at Tiananmen Square, the radical faction condemned it as "counterrevolutionary" and purged Deng Xiaoping, holding him personally responsible for the incident. Before his death in October 1976, Mao appointed Hua Guofeng, the compromise candidate of the two factions, as his successor. After Mao's death Hua Guofeng purged the Gang of Four with the support of other senior Party leaders and military. [*See also* Zhou Enlai; April Fifth Movement; *and* Jiang Qing.]

The most difficult question facing Hua was what to do with Deng Xiaoping, whom the now discredited radicals had purged several months before. Even though Hua did not want to, he had no choice but to rehabilitate Deng Xiaoping a second time because of his popularity. Once returned to active political life, Deng maneuvered skillfully by bringing back all the victims of the CR—all together 2.9 million—and with their political support he managed to ease out Hua Guofeng. When the victims of the CR returned, the official view of the CR also changed.

[*See also* China, People's Republic of; Communism: Chinese Communist Party; Gang of Four; Mao Zedong; *and* Deng Xiaoping.]

Byung-joon Ahn, *Chinese Politics and the Cultural Revolution: Dynamics of Policy Processes* (1976). Jack Chen, *A Year in Upper Felicity: Life in a Chinese Village during the Cultural Revolution* (1973). Lowell Dittmer, *Liu Shao-ch'i and the Chinese Cultural Revolution: The Politics of Mass Criticism* (1974). Hong Yung Lee, *The Politics of the Chinese Cultural Revolution* (1978). Simon Leys, *The Chairman's New Clothes: Mao and the Cultural Revolution* (1977) and *Chinese Shadows* (1977). Thomas W. Robinson, ed., *The Cultural Revolution in China* (1978). Stanley Rosen, *Red Guard Factionalism and the Cultural Revolution in Guangzhou* (1982). Roxane Witke, *Comrade Chiang Ch'ing* (1977). Tien-wei Wu, *Lin Piao and the Gang of Four: Contra-Confucianism in Historical and Intellectual Perspective* (1983).

HONG YUNG LEE

GREAT WALL. The name *Great Wall* is commonly applied to a variety of Chinese border fortifications, usually taken as referring to a single

FIGURE 1. *The Great Wall.* Restored section at Badaling, north of Beijing.

structure, thought to have been created by Qin Shihuangdi and subsequently maintained and enlarged. A Great Wall of China, so understood, has never existed, although it is firmly entrenched in both Chinese and Western cultural mythology.

Chinese states have built "long walls" (the literal meaning of the Chinese *changcheng*) since the fourth century BCE; among the important wall-building dynasties were the Qin, Han, Northern Wei, Northern Qi, Sui, and Jin. Of simple tamped-earth construction, their works have left few traces. The Ming border defense line, whose ruins at such sites as Juyongguan, Shanhaiguan, and Jiayuguan define the concept and constitute the "Great Wall" visited today, follows a route south of most of these earlier lines.

The Ming walls were begun in the late fifteenth century with a line across the southern margin of the Ordos Desert, followed in the next century by construction in the area west of Beijing, and in the latter part of the sixteenth century in the eastern sector between the capital and the sea. Made of earth at first, portions of these walls were faced with or reconstructed in stone beginning in the mid-sixteenth century. Sense can best be made of the Ming building program by considering the strategic problem posed by a strong nomadic enemy, the Mongols; the various options, offensive and defensive, available; and the political process of choice among them at the faction-ridden Ming court.

Unaware of the recent origins of these walls, early Western visitors associated them with Qin Shihuangdi's long-vanished work, well known from historical texts and popular tradition, and transmitted to Europe an account of an ancient yet still-extant Great Wall that quickly captured the Western imagination. Although its error has been repeatedly pointed out by both Chinese and Western scholars, this account remains widely accepted.

[*See also* Jiayuguan; Juyongguan; *and* Shanhaiguan.]

Arthur N. Waldron, "The Problem of the Great Wall of China," *Harvard Journal of Asiatic Studies* 43 (1983): 643–663.

ARTHUR N. WALDRON

GREEKS. The Greeks had already settled in Asia Minor early in the first millennium BCE. By the sixth century BCE, most of their Asian cities and islands formed part of the Persian empire. The Greeks were known as *Yawan* in Hebrew, *Yauna* in Old Persian, and *Yavana* in the Indian languages.

Some Greeks were sent as punitive exiles to Bactria and the Indo-Afghan borderlands, where they founded settlements. Alexander, who added there another layer of Greco-Macedonian habitation in the fourth century BCE, fought the most difficult and dangerous battles of his career in the East. He encouraged the mixing of ideas, peoples, and cultures and thus ushered in what is known as the Hellenistic phase of ancient Eurasian history. Seleucus Nicator, Alexander's general and the founder of the Seleucid dynasty, succeeded the conqueror in western Asia, but elements of resistance already evident in the East before Alexander's death finally led the Greeks to surrender territories to Chandragupta Maurya and to establish friendly relations with him and his successors; Ashoka (third centry BCE) sent Buddhist missionaries and medicinal plants to Greeks of western Asia and issued copies of his edicts in the Greek language and script.

The Seleucid kings were forced also to accept the independence of Bactria under the local Greeks led by Diodotus I and his son, Diodotus II, in the third century BCE. Forty or more kings and subkings and two queens, known as Indo-Greeks or Bactrian Greeks, ruled from 256 to about 50 BCE. At the height of their rule their power extended from beyond the Oxus to the Beas. Their attempts to extend Bactrian rule farther east into the center of the Ganges Valley were unsuccessful.

The Bactrian Greeks belonged to various lineages and often fought among themselves, dividing territories with overlapping jurisdiction. The better known among the kings are Euthydemus I, Antimachus I, Demetrius I and II, Eukratides I, Agathokles, Menander, Heliokles, Apollodotus, Antialkidas, Amyntas, and Hermaeus, and among queens, Agathokleia. Their history is known primarily from their abundant coinage, mostly silver and copper, some in gold, bearing their names and titles in Greek and Indian languages and scripts. These coins were generally struck with a portrait head on the obverse and a deity, or its symbol, on the reverse, in both Attic and Indian weight standards. Some of the best-known portraits of kings of antiquity are found on their coins.

Menander, the most famous among the Indo-Greeks, is remembered in the Buddhist tradition (where he is known as Milinda) for his catechetical dialogue with the Buddhist monk Nagasena. Although he and others might well have become Buddhists, Heliodorus, an ambassador sent by Antialkidas to the court of the Central Indian king Bhagabhadra, called himself a Bhagavat, a follower of the *bhakti* cult dedicated to Vishnu. Several of the Indo-Greeks were, like Agathokles, eclectic in their religious policy; this eclecticism contributed in turn to a syncretism in cult, myth, and iconography that was reflected in their coin motifs and art productions. Heliodorus erected a pillar at Besnagar in dedication to Vasudeva. Agathokles depicted Vasudeva and Samkorshana on his coins. Menander used the Buddhist *dharmachakra*, or "wheel of the Dharma," as one of his coin types, and others made attempts to define anthropomorphic representations of Brahmanic gods and goddesses. A long period of fruitful interaction merged the Indo-Greeks into the Indian population and culture, upon which they left indelible imprints, particularly in such fields as astronomy and the monetary system. Although Bactra (Balkh), their capital city, still eludes archaeologists, the recent discovery of Ai Khanoum, a city with Greek features such as an acropolis, gymnasium, and a theater, but with Iranian and Central Asian elements in the palace, temple, and cult objects, confirms the character and content of their role; so do the material remains from the early excavations at Taxila.

[*See also* Bactria; Balkh; Taxila; Alexander III; *and* Seleucus I.]

John Marshall, *Taxila* (1951). A. K. Narain, *The Coin-Types of the Indo-Greek Kings* (1967) and *The Indo-Greeks* (1980). W. W. Tarn, *The Greeks in Bactria and India* (1951).

A. K. Narain